Copyright
in a
Global Information
Economy

ASPEN PUBLISHERS

Copyright in a Global Information Economy

Third Edition

Julie E. Cohen

Professor of Law
Georgetown University Law Center

Lydia Pallas Loren

Jeffrey Bain Faculty Scholar and Professor of Law
Lewis and Clark Law School

Ruth L. Okediji

William L. Prosser Professor of Law
University of Minnesota Law School

Maureen A. O'Rourke

Dean, Michaels Faculty Research Scholar,
and Professor of Law
Boston University School of Law

Wolters Kluwer
Law & Business

AUSTIN   BOSTON   CHICAGO   NEW YORK   THE NETHERLANDS

Aspen Publishers
Attn: Permissions Department
76 Ninth Avenue, 7th Floor
New York, NY 10011-5201

To contact Customer Care, e-mail customer.service@aspenpublishers.com, call 1-800-234-1660, fax 1-800-901-9075, or mail correspondence to:

Aspen Publishers
Attn: Order Department
PO Box 990
Frederick, MD 21705

Printed in the United States of America.

1 2 3 4 5 6 7 8 9 0

ISBN 978-0-7355-9196-7

Library of Congress Cataloging-in-Publication Data

Copyright in a global information economy / Julie E. Cohen . . . [et al.]. — 3rd ed.
   p. cm.
   Includes index.
   ISBN 978-0-7355-9196-7 (hardcover : alk. paper) 1. Copyright — United States. 2. Copyright, International. 3. International and municipal law — United States. I. Cohen, Julie E.

   KF2996.C67 2010
   346.7304'82 — dc22   2010015756

About Wolters Kluwer Law & Business

Wolters Kluwer Law & Business is a leading provider of research information and workflow solutions in key specialty areas. The strengths of the individual brands of Aspen Publishers, CCH, Kluwer Law International and Loislaw are aligned within Wolters Kluwer Law & Business to provide comprehensive, in-depth solutions and expert-authored content for the legal, professional and education markets.

CCH was founded in 1913 and has served more than four generations of business professionals and their clients. The CCH products in the Wolters Kluwer Law & Business group are highly regarded electronic and print resources for legal, securities, antitrust and trade regulation, government contracting, banking, pension, payroll, employment and labor, and healthcare reimbursement and compliance professionals.

Aspen Publishers is a leading information provider for attorneys, business professionals and law students. Written by preeminent authorities, Aspen products offer analytical and practical information in a range of specialty practice areas from securities law and intellectual property to mergers and acquisitions and pension/benefits. Aspen's trusted legal education resources provide professors and students with high-quality, up-to-date and effective resources for successful instruction and study in all areas of the law.

Kluwer Law International supplies the global business community with comprehensive English-language international legal information. Legal practitioners, corporate counsel and business executives around the world rely on the Kluwer Law International journals, loose-leafs, books and electronic products for authoritative information in many areas of international legal practice.

Loislaw is a premier provider of digitized legal content to small law firm practitioners of various specializations. Loislaw provides attorneys with the ability to quickly and efficiently find the necessary legal information they need, when and where they need it, by facilitating access to primary law as well as state-specific law, records, forms and treatises.

Wolters Kluwer Law & Business, a unit of Wolters Kluwer, is headquartered in New York and Riverwoods, Illinois. Wolters Kluwer is a leading multinational publisher and information services company.

For Andrew and Eli.
                    —J.E.C.

For Kurt, in spite of ourselves.
                    —L.P.L.

For Tade, and in honor of Mom and Dad.
                    —R.L.O.

For the faculty, students, and staff of Boston University School of Law.
                    —M.A.O.

Summary of Contents

Contents

PART II
The Subject Matter of Copyright Law

2 *Authors, Writings, and Progress*   45

3   *Acquiring and Maintaining Copyright*   *145*

4   *Protected Works and Boundary Problems*   *191*

PART III
Copyright Scope and Enforcement

5 *The Statutory Rights of Copyright Owners*   *289*

6 *The Different Faces of Infringement*   469

🎵 The Copyright Infringement Lawsuit   763

Preface

In the eight years since the first edition of this text was published the one constant has been change. The relentless pace of technological innovation, particularly with respect to digital communication technologies, continues to challenge well-settled copyright doctrines, creating new opportunities to contest the nature and scope of the various interests implicated by copyright. This third edition therefore continues to emphasize the evolving nature of copyright law, and the copyright system more generally, in response to technological change and the pressures of globalization. We provide students with not only a firm foundation in the traditional precepts of copyright law, but also a strong theoretical background with which to evaluate the public policy implications of the ongoing changes. We begin each chapter with an overview of the classical principles of the particular topic or subject matter, followed with material carefully selected and arranged to help students appreciate how the law has evolved over time and the complexities introduced by new technologies and/or new theoretical approaches.

As is expected of a new edition, we have updated all the materials to reflect new legislation and case law, including legislation and cases reflecting international trends. We also have updated our website at www.coolcopyright.com, which contains background materials (including pictures) for the cases in the book, as well as some alternative cases. We trust that students and teachers will find these materials useful to augment the text or to provide resources for deeper study of a particular topic.

The third edition maintains much of the structure, style, and approach of the first edition, and therefore still differs in important ways from the traditional copyright text.

First, we continue to hold to the belief that understanding the role of copyright law in the information economy requires more than a study of the Copyright Act and copyright case law. To understand why copyright law is the way it is, and to develop an appreciation for what it might become, one must consider the history and evolution of technologies for creating and distributing copyrighted works; the structure and political influence of the major copyright industries; and the availability of other legal regimes (such as contract law) to supplement or even supplant copyright protection. We include introductory materials on these topics and then give substantial consideration throughout the book to the historical, technological, political, and legal contexts within which copyright law operates.

Second, we have retained the use of secondary source materials by legal academics and other commentators seeking to understand and shape the evolution of copyright and information policy. To better aid students in comprehending the wealth of academic opinion and the importance of economic analysis which has become prevalent in judicial opinions, we have streamlined the use of secondary materials and asked questions designed to facilitate a firmer understanding of how theory and practice converge in assessing copyright claims and defenses.

Finally, we continue to emphasize the importance of international developments and to show how international events influence U.S. copyright law and policy. We integrate both international and comparative materials throughout the text, rather than leaving these materials until the end of the book as is usual in many introductory copyright texts. For each chapter and topic, we consider relevant treaty provisions and, in many instances, we ask students to compare specific domestic copyright rules with the corresponding rules of other countries.

The third edition differs from the second edition in several important respects. Most important, we have added a new chapter. That chapter, Chapter 8, explores the legal problems that arise at the intersection of contract and copyright. We have also restructured the material in Chapter 5 that explores the reproduction right, to provide students with a clearer understanding of the two leading approaches to evaluating substantial similarity. Finally, we have revised the coverage of remedies in Chapter 11 to reflect the post-*eBay Inc. v. MercExchange, L.L.C.* landscape, and also to provide increased attention to issues related to statutory damages.

Our hope is that students who use this book and our supporting website will come to understand and appreciate the copyright system as a work-in-progress, and recognize that copyright is not simply a regime of private law, but rather one that implicates both private and public interests. We believe that we offer students a unique text that will help them develop the skills necessary to identify and think critically about both contested issues in particular cases and larger patterns of change within the copyright system as a whole. Our expectation is that students will emerge from this process of exploration well-informed and better equipped to practice copyright law in a world in which continual change is the norm.

Julie E. Cohen
Lydia P. Loren
Ruth L. Okediji
Maureen A. O'Rourke

May 2010

Acknowledgments

We gratefully acknowledge the assistance of many people who have helped us since we began work on this book. The first edition benefited greatly from the many helpful and generous suggestions offered by Richard Chused, Shubha Ghosh, Paul Goldstein, Dennis Karjala, David Lange, Mark Lemley, Jessica Litman, Michael Meurer, Harvey Perlman, Pamela Samuelson, and a number of anonymous colleagues. In addition, we acknowledge the research assistance of Teeshna Bahadur, Stacy Blasberg, Casey Caldwell, Mitzi Chang, Cyrus Christenson, Olivia Farrar-Wellman, Sally Garrison, Stephen Goldberg, Michael Green, Scott Katz, Anne Koch, Charles McLawhorn, Ilana Safer, Julie Short, Stephanie Smith, and Victor Wandres, and the secretarial and administrative assistance of Melissa Adamson, Suzan Benet, Sue Morrison, and Irene Welch. We would also like to thank John Showalter for his expert assistance in obtaining permission to reproduce excerpts from the various books, law review articles, and other secondary sources quoted in the text of the first edition; Andy Marion for word processing wizardry; and Lisa Bowles, Tracey Bridgman, Stephanie Burke, Raquel Ortiz, Russ Sweet, and Joel Wegemer for library services.

For their assistance with our preparation of the second edition, we would like to thank Robert Brauneis, Richard Chused, Wendy Gordon, Jessica Litman, Peter Maggs, James Speta, Rebecca Tushnet, Philip Weiser, and a number of anonymous colleagues who generously provided Aspen with detailed reviews based on their experiences teaching from the first edition. We also gratefully acknowledge the research assistance of Andrew Crouse, Robert Dowers, Tomas Felcman, Laura Hayes, David Hesford, Jon Putman, Duke Tufty, Kathryn Ward, Marci Windsheimer, and Matthew Windsor; the secretarial and administrative assistance of Melissa Adamson, Suzan Benet, Liz Cerrato, Tiowa Collier, Daphne Edwards, and Michael Mercurio; and the library assistance of Steve Donweber, Terri Gallego O'Rourke, Mary Rumsey, and David Zopfi-Jordan. In addition, we would like to extend special thanks to Matthew Windsor for the comprehensive redesign of the book's companion website, www.coolcopyright.com.

The third edition has benefited considerably from the detailed, insightful feedback offered by Margreth Barrett, Mark Bartholomew, Annemarie Bridy, Wendy Gordon, James

Grimmelmann, Rita Heimes, Jessica Litman, Michael Madison, Kenneth L. Port, Pam Samuelson, and John G. Sprankling. In addition, we acknowledge the research assistance of Emily Adams, Theresa Coughlin, Ryan Houck, Robert Insley, Andrew Jacobs, Christopher Klimmek, Jack Mellyn, John Rankin, and Dan Roberts; the secretarial and administrative assistance of Margaret Flynn, Julie F. Hunt, and Pamela Malone; and the library assistance of David Bachman, Raquel Ortiz, Mary Rumsey, and Stefanie Weigmann.

In keeping with Aspen style guidelines, omissions of citations and footnotes are not noted with ellipses, while omission of text is appropriately indicated. Omission of entire paragraphs is indicated with ellipses at the end of the preceeding paragraph or text. Finally, we acknowledge the authors and/or copyright owners of the following excerpts and images, used in this book with their permission.

Books and Articles

Cohen, Julie E., *The Place of the User in Copyright Law*, 74 Fordham Law Review 347 (2005). Reprinted courtesy of Julie Cohen.

Ginsburg, Jane C., *No "Sweat"? Copyright and Other Protection of Works of Information After Feist v. Rural Telephone*, 92 Columbia Law Review 338 (1992). Reprinted courtesy of Jane Ginsburg and the Columbia Law Review.

Goldstein, Paul, *Derivative Rights and Derivative Works in Copyright*, 30 Journal of the Copyright Society 209 (1983). Reprinted courtesy of Paul Goldstein.

Gordon, Wendy J., *Fair Use as Market Failure: A Structural and Economic Analysis of the Betamax Case and Its Predecessors*, 82 Columbia Law Review 1600 (1982). Reprinted courtesy of Wendy Gordon.

Hardy, Trotter, *Property (and Copyright) in Cyberspace*, 1996 University of Chicago Legal Forum 217 (1996). Reprinted courtesy of the University of Chicago Legal Forum.

Lee, Edward, *Warming Up to User-Generated Content*, 2008 University of Illinois Law Review 1459. Reproduced by permission of the publisher from 2008 *University of Illinois Law Review* 1459. Copyright 2008 by The Board of Trustees of the University of Illinois.

Lemley, Mark A. & Eugene Volokh, *Freedom of Speech and Injunctions in Intellectual Property Cases*, 48 Duke Law Journal 147 (1998). Reprinted courtesy of Mark Lemley.

Litman, Jessica, *The Public Domain*, 39 Emory Law Journal 965 (1990). Reprinted courtesy of Jessica Litman.

Netanel, Neil Weinstock, *Copyright and a Democratic Civil Society*, 106 Yale Law Journal 283 (1996). Reprinted courtesy of Neil Netanel and by permission of The Yale Law Journal Company and William S. Hein Company.

Reichman, J.H. & Pamela Samuelson, *Intellectual Property Rights in Data?*, 50 Vanderbilt Law Review 51 (1997). Reprinted courtesy of J.H. Reichman and Pamela Samuelson.

Samuelson, Pamela, et al., *A Manifesto Concerning the Legal Protection of Computer Programs*, 94 Columbia Law Review 2308 (1994). Reprinted courtesy of Pamela Samuelson and the Columbia Law Review.

Yen, Alfred C., *Copyright Opinions and Aesthetic Theory*, 71 Southern California Law Review 247 (1998). Reprinted courtesy of Alfred C. Yen.

Illustrations

Air Pirates cover illustration. Mickey Mouse © Disney Enterprises, Inc. Reprinted courtesy of Disney Enterprises, Inc.

Bolling, Ruben, editorial cartoon, "Library System Terrorizes Publishing Industry." © 2000 Ruben Bolling. Reprinted courtesy of Ruben Bolling.

Borgman, Jim, editorial cartoon, "No More Packing in the Middle of the Night!" © 1984 King Features. Reprinted with special permission of King Features Syndicate.

Gere, Joanne, photograph of "RIBBON Rack in Shadow." Reprinted courtesy of Brandir International, Inc.

Kieselstein-Cord, Barry, "Winchester" and "Vaquero" belt buckles. © 1976 (Winchester) and 1978 (Vaquero) Kieselstein-Cord. Reprinted courtesy of Barry Kieselstein-Cord.

IBM Corporation, screen shot of Lotus 1-2-3 release 2.01. Reprint Courtesy of International Business Machines Corporation, © 1987 International Business Machines Corporation.

Mannion, Jonathan, photographs of Kevin Garnett, "Iced Out Comp Board" and infringing detail from Coors Billboard. Original photograph of Kevin Garnett © Jonathan Mannion. Photographs reprinted courtesy of Jonathan Mannion.

Martin, Jan, "Symphony #1." © 1987 Jan Martin. Photograph reprinted courtesy of Jan Martin.

Nelson-Salabes, Inc. Architects/Planners, photographs of Satyr Hill assisted living facility as proposed by Nelson-Salabes, Inc. and as built by Morningside Holdings. Photographs reprinted courtesy of Nelson-Salabes, Inc. Architects/Planners.

Reid, James Earl, "Third World America: A Contemporary Nativity." © 1985 James Earl Reid. Photograph reprinted courtesy of James Earl Reid, Sculptor.

Steinberg, Saul, "View of the World from 9th Avenue," cover image from the March 29, 1976 issue of *The New Yorker*. Original Artwork by Saul Steinberg. © 1976 The Saul Steinberg Foundation/Artists Rights Society (ARS), New York. Cover reprinted with permission of *The New Yorker* magazine. All rights reserved.

Ty, Inc., "Squealer" beanbag toy. © 1993 Ty, Inc. Reprinted courtesy of Ty, Inc. Photograph of "Squealer" and "Preston" beanbag toys reprinted courtesy of Banner & Witcoff, Ltd.

Copyright
in a
Global Information
Economy

I

INTRODUCTION TO COPYRIGHT LAW

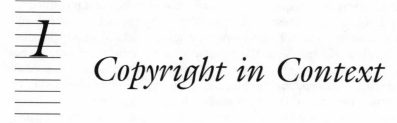

Copyright in Context

Copyright law is a pervasive feature of our information society, and its role and effect on the ordinary lives of citizens are often the subjects of heated debate. Our present law is derived from a set of rules first adopted in the eighteenth century, when no one could foresee either the extent to which information technologies would evolve or the role that information industries would eventually play in the national and global economies. Today, copyright law confronts the realities of the continuously evolving modern networked world. Satellites beam broadcasts around the globe in seconds, and the Internet provides individuals the potential to reach an audience of millions. As new technologies challenge the traditional copyright framework, it is essential that those who study, practice, and make copyright law understand the fundamental policies underlying the copyright system. Additionally, in an era of globalization, it is imperative to situate U.S. copyright law within the larger context of international copyright law.

This chapter places the issues surrounding copyright law in historical, theoretical, and international context. First, however, we provide a brief summary of the major principles of U.S. copyright law and their organization within this book.

Copyright law in the U.S. is a federal statute, codified in Title 17 of the U.S. Code. The authority for Congress to enact the copyright law derives from an express grant of power in Article I of the Constitution:

> The Congress shall have Power . . . To promote the Progress of Science and the useful Arts, by securing for limited Times to Authors and Inventors the exclusive Right to their respective Writings and Discoveries.

U.S. Const., Art. I, §8, cl. 8. Throughout this book, we refer to this clause as the "Intellectual Property Clause."[1] To get a feel for the current Copyright Act (the "Act"), adopted in

---

1. For many years, the clause was known as the Patent and Copyright Clause. The term *Intellectual Property* came into vogue only during the last several decades of the twentieth century. More recently, some commentators have begun calling Art. I, §8, cl. 8, the "Exclusive Rights Clause" or the "Progress Clause" because these labels are more faithful to the literal constitutional text.

1976 and amended many times since then, spend a few minutes examining its table of contents.

The Act imposes certain threshold requirements a work must meet before it is entitled to protection. In Chapter 2, we consider these requirements and why the Act imposes them. Generally, the Act grants a limited statutory monopoly in original works of authorship that are fixed in a tangible medium of expression. We examine what it means for a work to be *original* and *fixed*. In addition, Chapter 2 introduces the principle known as the *idea/expression distinction*, which limits the scope of copyright protection to the expression of ideas and facts and excludes from protection the ideas or facts themselves. The latter items are part of what is called the *public domain*, a concept we discuss in more detail later in this chapter. Finally, Chapter 2 examines who is an *author* entitled to claim rights under the Act.

Many people believe that one must register a work to "have" a copyright or that, at a minimum, there must be a symbol, "©", appearing on the work for it to be copyrighted. However, the Copyright Act does not require *registration* as a condition of copyright protection and, since 1989, it has not required that any *notice* of copyright be placed on the work itself. Once an original work of authorship is fixed in a tangible medium of expression, that work is protected by federal copyright law. There are, however, good reasons for both registering copyright and using a copyright notice, and we discuss them in Chapter 3.

Importantly, the Act limits copyright's *duration*. For works created today, the Copyright Act provides protection that lasts for the life of the author plus 70 years. If the author is not a real person, but instead a corporation, the Act provides copyright protection lasting for 95 years from publication or 120 years from creation, whichever term is shorter. Chapter 3 explains the complicated rules governing copyright duration and considers why those rules are in the Act.

Chapter 4 explores the *categories of works* that are eligible for protection under the Act and the limits on those categories. Copyrightable works run the gamut from traditional art (books, poems, musical works, drawings, paintings, and sculptures) to popular entertainment products (sound recordings, movies, and video games) to computer software, databases, and architectural works. Some of these works test the outer boundaries of copyright protection. Chapter 4 considers these works and the roles played by copyright and other intellectual property laws in protecting them.

The limited statutory monopoly granted by the Copyright Act takes the form of a grant of specific *exclusive rights*. In the language of property law, these exclusive rights make up the "sticks" in the copyright owner's bundle of rights. For all categories of works, the Act grants copyright owners the rights to (1) reproduce the work, (2) prepare derivative works based on the work, and (3) publicly distribute copies of the work. The Act also grants copyright owners of certain categories of works the right(s) to publicly display the work and/or to publicly perform it. For one category of works, sound recordings, the Act limits the right of public performance to performance by digital transmission. We explore all these rights, including their justifications and limits, in Chapter 5. Chapter 5 also discusses how a copyright owner proves infringement of one or more of the exclusive rights. Chapter 6 discusses who may be held liable for *civil and/or criminal copyright infringement*.

Many people misunderstand the scope of copyright protection based on information gathered from the popular press, word of mouth, or the Internet. Some think that it is always permissible to copy copyrighted works as long as they do not sell the copies they have made. Others think that *any* such copying is unlawful. Indeed, members of the copyright industries frequently state as much. For example, many books contain a statement under the copyright notice that asserts "no portion of this book may be reproduced for any purpose without the written consent of the copyright owner." Neither of these understandings of copyright law is entirely accurate. While the Act does grant copyright owners certain rights, including the right to control reproduction of the work, it expressly provides that those rights are not absolute. Many *limiting doctrines* have been codified in the Act or incorporated into copyright law through judicial decisions. These doctrines authorize users of copyrighted works to copy, distribute, or publicly display or perform portions of works and sometimes even entire works without incurring liability for infringing the copyright owner's exclusive rights. We discuss these limiting doctrines, including the essential doctrine of *fair use*, in Chapters 5, 6, and 7.

Understanding the relationship between contract and copyright is critically important to any study of copyright law today. In Chapter 8, we tackle issues related to the use of *contracts* and *licenses* in the context of copyrighted works. We explore the rules that govern transfer of ownership of a copyright, the nuances of arrangements that give rise to implied licenses, and the copyright issues triggered by the ubiquitous use of shrinkwrap licenses. Chapter 8 also addresses new forms of licenses, including open source and Creative Commons licenses, that seek to change the default rules to make more user activities permissible.

Faced with the advent of digital technologies, which enable instantaneous, mass distribution of perfect copies, the copyright industries have sought additional protection for their works both through *technological protection measures*, such as encryption, and expanded legal rights. Chapter 9 addresses those efforts and the legal battles that have ensued as a result.

Some copyright industries also have explored the use of contract and other state laws to augment the protection available under copyright law. Understanding the interplay between copyright law and state law requires mastery of federal *preemption* principles. Chapter 10 explores these principles and their application in the specific context of the federal intellectual property system.

The final chapter, Chapter 11, provides a study of the *copyright infringement lawsuit*. Litigating (or settling) a copyright dispute requires understanding a variety of procedural matters ranging from exclusive federal court jurisdiction to issues of standing. Chapter 11 also discusses the panoply of remedies available in a civil infringement action under the Copyright Act.

Before delving into the details of the Act in Chapters 2 through 11, we turn in the remainder of this chapter to the theoretical justifications for copyright law, the history of U.S. copyright law, and an overview of how U.S. copyright law fits within the international copyright system.

A. THE THEORETICAL UNDERPINNINGS OF COPYRIGHT LAW

Many people believe that the reason copyright exists is to protect those who create works from those who would pilfer their works. While this is, in many ways, the effect of copyright law, and indeed it is copyright law's intended effect, it is not exactly the reason that copyright law exists. As stated in the Constitution's Intellectual Property Clause, the fundamental purpose of the U.S. copyright system is to "promote . . . Progress." Simply pointing to the constitutional language, however, masks the complexity of why copyright exists. What did the Framers mean by "Progress"? Why do other countries, not guided by the U.S. Constitution, grant copyright protection?

1. Incentives for Authors and Publishers

To understand why copyright might be necessary, consider a world in which no copyright protection exists. An author may spend months or even years writing a novel that, once completed, she hopes will earn her a comfortable income as recompense for her efforts. The author's publisher decides to sell copies of her novel for a modest $20. This price will allow the publisher to recover the costs of reproduction, distribution, and marketing, and, of course, provide the author's compensation. In a world without copyright, once the novel is publicly available, no legal rule would prevent others from freely copying it. In fact, another publisher could take our hypothetical author's novel, reproduce copies of it, and sell them for less than $20, say $16. Sales at $16 would still be profitable because this publisher need not pay the author. Who would buy the $20 copies from the author's publisher when the exact same novel is available elsewhere for $16? In fact, another company could begin making copies for even less than $16, and so on, until the price approached the cost of the cheapest way to make and distribute the copies. While these copyists might be able to recover their full cost of production, in this hypothetical world, the author does not receive anywhere near the same level of compensation for her efforts. She will receive payments from her publisher, but the amount will decrease toward zero over time as the copyists make cheaper versions of her work available. The total she receives may no longer provide her with sufficient compensation to write the novel in the first place! Thus, while at first glance the public might seem to benefit from lower prices in a world without copyright, in fact it might be harmed if, on the whole, fewer works were produced.

This example illustrates what economists call the public goods problem in intangibles. The cost of creating new works is often high, but the cost of reproducing them is low and, once the work is created, reproducing it in no way depletes the original. This latter characteristic is referred to as "nonrivalrous" consumption: One party's use of the good does not interfere with another party's use. Intangible goods, including copyrighted works, are not like tangible goods with rivalrous consumption characteristics. For example, if one person eats an apple it interferes with another person's ability to eat the same apple. In contrast, if one person sings a song it does not interfere with another person's ability to sing the same song. Similarly, one person reading a novel does not interfere with another person's ability to read the same novel. The second person may not be able to use the same *copy* of the book at the same time, but once the work has been released to the public, an unlimited number of people may "consume" the work without depleting it.

Importantly, public goods also have the characteristic of nonexcludability. Once the good is produced, there is no way to exclude others from enjoying its benefits. The classic example of national defense best illustrates the nonexcludability principle. When a country's citizens' tax dollars pay for the national defense, there is no way to exclude non-taxpaying citizens from the benefits of that defense system. Similarly, once a copyrightable song is released to the public, it is impossible to exclude non-paying members of the public from hearing and enjoying it. And unless the manuscript of a novel is kept under lock and key, it will be impossible to restrict appreciation of its plot, characters, and wording only to those who have paid for a copy.

One explanation for copyright protection is that it is necessary to solve the public goods problem. By granting the bundle of rights enumerated above, copyright law gives the copyright owner a legal entitlement to exclude others from enjoying certain benefits of the work. This enables an author to recoup her investment in the creation of the work. Legal protection will also encourage disclosure and dissemination of the work because the author no longer needs to fear the copyist; the law will provide a remedy to stop unauthorized copying and to compensate for the harm caused by it. By solving the public goods problem, copyright law furnishes appropriate incentives to creators and publishers and thereby prevents underproduction of creative works.

This is not to suggest that the only (or primary) reason authors create is the promise of monetary reward. To the contrary, ego, passion, or dedication to an endeavor may motivate many creative works. However, the promise of a reward is another factor motivating many others; without it, some works would not be produced, and some authors might not create at all. There are economic costs associated with creative activity (e.g., the purchase of materials and dissemination costs that include advertising, marketing, and sales) as well as opportunity costs when authors choose to invest full time in their creative endeavors rather than pursue other, more immediately lucrative, vocations. By establishing a baseline set of rights, copyright yields a mutually beneficial outcome: Those who are economically motivated may choose to exercise their rights, and those who produce works for other reasons may choose not to do so.

As thus described, copyright's purpose is purely utilitarian. Copyright law exists to provide a marketable right for the creators and distributors of copyrighted works, which in turn creates an incentive for production and dissemination of new works. As we discuss in Section B.2 *infra*, the Framers of the U.S. Constitution embraced this utilitarian rationale for copyright protection in granting Congress the power to enact the copyright laws. Granting a limited monopoly to the authors of creative works provided a means for the fledgling country to supply incentives to encourage progress in knowledge and learning.

As you will learn, however, the question of how to define the scope of the exclusive rights of copyright owners has been controversial throughout history. Granting property rights may solve the public goods problem, but if the rights are too extensive in scope, they may introduce costs of their own. Keep in mind that no work is truly original. Rather, all works build to some extent on earlier creations: Would the Coen brothers have filmed *O Brother, Where Art Thou?* or James Joyce have written *Ulysses* if not for Homer's *Odyssey?* Property rights in the original creation have implications for follow-on creative efforts. Property rights that are too strong may result in overproduction of works initially, followed by less-than-optimal production of second-generation works.

The state of technology for copying and distributing works also affects the optimal scope of copyright protection because technology determines the ease with which a copyright may be enforced or infringed. Recent developments in digital technology have threatened the efficacy of the exclusive rights. Paradoxically, at the same time such technology has caused some to question the assumptions that lead to the conclusion that copyright protection is necessary for progress. Consider the following excerpt.

Trotter Hardy, Property (and Copyright) in Cyberspace
1996 U. Chi. Legal F. 217, 220-28

Conventional wisdom argues that informational works, because they exhibit such a low ratio of copying-to-creating costs, must be protected by copyright, or else no one will take the time or trouble to produce them in the first place. . . . At best, however, this conclusion is a half truth. It is more accurate to say that information works — and for that matter, any nontrivial creative efforts — require the existence of an incentive for their creation. Whether the incentive necessarily must be copyright is a different matter. To make that determination, we must look at other types of incentives. . . .

We can find the typical incentives that face most information producers by asking what information producers need to overcome their fears of cheap copying. The general answer is not "copyright law," because that reflects too narrow a conception. The better answer is that would-be producers of information need *some assurance that copying will be limited*. The notion of "some assurance" rather than "complete assurance" reflects the fact that 100 percent assurance of anything — or zero risk — has never been a requirement of any business. Similarly, I use the deliberately vague notion of "limited" copying rather than "no copying" because the exact amount of copying that an information producer will tolerate will vary widely depending on the type of information being produced, the goals of the producer, and so on.

For example, some products, such as commercial business software, apparently can be profitable even with a fairly large amount of illegal copying, as long as "most" or "many" copies are lawfully purchased. Prices would be lower in the absence of copying, of course, and we accordingly would be better off if all copying could cheaply be prevented. But business software sellers in fact enter software markets that exhibit some amount of copying — hence they must expect the existence of "limited copying," not "zero copying." . . .

Given, then, that producers of information products need some assurance that copying will be limited, the next question is how producers obtain that assurance. In other words, how do they "limit" copying? This question is best answered by looking at the aggregate combination of four factors: 1) entitlement-like protection; 2) contract-like protection; 3) state-of-the-art limitations; and 4) special-purpose technical limitations. Other factors also could be listed; I do not mean that these four are exclusive, but rather that they seem intuitively important enough to merit particular attention. In any event, nothing will be lost by a simplified analysis because my essential points do not depend on the exact number of factors.

. . . The first factor is "entitlement-like protection." By this I mean the wide recognition that informational products have an "owner" and that this owner has some "rights" that would be violated by unauthorized copying of the product. Such rights inhere in the product or the owner and are binding on the world in general; they are not a matter of contract. . . .

The second limitation on copying arises from contract. In contrast to the entitlement regime, a contract regime protects information only because two or more parties have agreed to treat the product as protected. Those who are not a party to any such contract are not bound by its terms. . . .

. . . This happens, for example, when users of an information service such as Lexis or Westlaw sign an access agreement. Much of the information on these services consists of public-domain material: cases and statutes. Without a contract limiting the practice, the user of such a service could copy and resell the material. Contracts with the services provide otherwise, of course, and these contracts are based not on any entitlement to the public-domain information, but rather on the consideration of allowing access to the service. . . .

After entitlements and contracts comes a third form of limitation on copying — the state-of-the-copying art. For any medium of expression, making a copy entails costs, yet obviously different media entail very different copying costs. Technological changes affect this cost. For example, if a manuscript must be written out by hand to make a copy, the cost of doing so — in time, money, and "trouble" — imposes a natural limit on how many copies one will make of the manuscript. Similarly, a glossy magazine like the *National Geographic* can be photocopied on a photocopier, but this fact seems almost irrelevant to the *National Geographic*'s plans for distribution. Readily accessible, inexpensive copy machines only produce black and white copies on poor quality paper. Photographs reproduce especially poorly. . . .

Finally, special-purpose technological restrictions can limit copying. A typical example of such self-help measures is the use by cable companies of signal "scrambling." For a home viewer to have access to certain channels, the viewer must pay the cable company for a piece of electronic equipment that will "descramble" the signal and render it viewable. This has nothing to do with the state-of-the-cable art: cable companies are able with present technology to send a signal down the cable wire for viewing. Rather, it is the result of individual effort by the information owner (or transmitter) to overcome what otherwise might be too little limitation from entitlement-like rules, unenforceable contracts, or a state-of-the-art that permits ready copying. . . .

It is helpful to think of this four-part "aggregate assurance" of limited copying in the form of a pie chart. One slice of the "pie" represents the limitations inhering in the "state-of-the-copying art," another represents "entitlement-like" protection, and so on. The overall size of the pie — the sum of all four factors — is what matters to information producers, because the overall size determines how limited the unauthorized copying of their product will be.

. . . The taxonomy implies that if one of the "slices" of the pie grows or shrinks, other slices must shrink or grow proportionally if the producer is to preserve the same overall assurance of limited copying. . . .

NOTES AND QUESTIONS

1. Professor Hardy's "slices of the pie" metaphor is one way to understand recent movements in copyright law. Another way to conceptualize these issues is to consider the slices of the pie as different kinds of "fences." As you learned in property law, a legal system for delineating and protecting property rights can be efficient. Without legal entitlements, individuals would spend considerable resources fencing in "their" property. Legal entitlements provide a certain level of protection, thereby reducing the need to build the most secure fence possible. Legal entitlements, however, are not perfect. People do disobey laws for a variety of reasons. Consider the kinds of copying that occur via the Internet. When copying becomes prevalent enough, a copyright owner may feel that she cannot rely solely on legal entitlements as her only fence and that other fences, such as technological and/or contractual restrictions that make copying more difficult, are needed. Are there "informal" fences that can also serve to delineate property rights? Consider, for example, ethics that define appropriate behavior in a particular community (e.g., academic norms regarding plagiarism and citations). Do such social norms merely reinforce existing fences or constitute a separate fence altogether?

2. The "pie" to which Professor Hardy refers effectively provides authors with property rights to avoid the underproduction problem associated with public goods. Could Professor Hardy's pie ever result in creators receiving too many property rights? What would be the costs associated with such rights? According to Professor Julie Cohen, "Hardy's 'pie' is incomplete, in that it omits the slice consisting of 'no-protection,' or entitlements belonging to the public — a slice not currently conceived as 'property' in the same sense as the interest belonging to the copyright owner." Julie E. Cohen, Lochner *in Cyberspace: The New Economic Orthodoxy of "Rights Management,"* 97 Mich. L. Rev. 462, 510 (1998). Professor Cohen argues that the public's "slice" of the pie is essential to achieving copyright's goal of promoting "progress":

> . . . [T]he current market for creative and informational works generates at least two different kinds of ancillary social benefit. First, society . . . realizes benefits from the content of certain works. Creative and informational works educate and inform the public, shape individual and community perceptions of the world, and set the parameters of public debate. . . . Second, social benefit accrues from the rights to access and use unprotected, public domain elements of existing works, and to re-use and transform existing works in certain settings and circumstances. These rights and practices lead to the development of creative and scholarly talents and, ultimately, to the creation of new works. . . .

... [B]oth types of uncompensated positive externality are woven into the fabric of the existing market for creative and informational works; they are the background conditions against which the market operates.

... Th[is] analysis suggests ... that public access and use privileges do not in fact represent a tax on copyright owners to subsidize the reading public, as some copyright owners have claimed. If anything, they represent a tax on the reading public to subsidize the creative public, both present and future.

Id. at 547-49. Can you reconcile Professor Hardy's and Professor Cohen's views? Within Professor Hardy's model, is it possible to take into account the public's interests to which Professor Cohen refers? Would Professor Hardy object if a copyright owner could employ technological measures to make copying impossible? Would Professor Cohen?

3. Commentators have struggled to define the level of copyright protection that is necessary to supply the socially optimal level of production of creative works. As noted above, too little protection may result in underproduction, while too much may result in initial overproduction followed by fewer second-generation creations. Recall that the Constitution authorizes Congress to grant exclusive rights to "promote ... Progress." How should the law define "Progress"? Do the excerpts above give you any clues? For other attempts to give meaning to the term, see Margaret Chon, *Postmodern "Progress": Reconsidering the Copyright and Patent Power*, 43 DePaul L. Rev. 97 (1992) (arguing that the notion of progress as an unbroken linear forward motion is too limiting); Glynn S. Lunney, Jr., *Reexamining Copyright's Incentives-Access Paradigm*, 49 Vand. L. Rev. 483, 487-88, 589-99 (1996) (arguing that in evaluating the success of a copyright regime, society must also consider the opportunity costs, measured by other, non-creative activities forgone, that might produce greater social welfare).

4. It is important to view copyright as one of many options for providing incentives for creation and dissemination of new works. Can you think of other government incentives that could cause individuals to create new works? Think, for example, about how the government often uses tax breaks and/or direct subsidies to encourage investment in activities it views as desirable. If the purpose behind copyright law is to promote progress in knowledge and learning, would tax breaks, subsidies, or other non-copyright incentives likely be sufficient to achieve that goal? As you go through this course, consider as well whether such incentives might be more efficient than copyright.

2. Authors' Rights

The utilitarian justification for copyright protection is not the only possible rationale for granting a marketable right to authors of creative works. Certainly one could argue that such a right is morally required. The countries of Continental Europe generally subscribe to the notion that an author's natural right in her creation forms the principal justification for copyright protection.

As Professor Jane Ginsburg explains:

... [P]ost-revolutionary French laws and theorists portray the existence of an intimate and almost sacred bond between authors and their works as the source of a strong literary and artistic property right. Thus, France's leading modern exponent of copyright theory, the late Henri Desbois, grandly proclaimed: "The author is protected as an author, in his status as a creator, because a bond unites him to the object of his creation. In the French tradition, Parliament has repudiated the utilitarian concept of protecting works of authorship in order to stimulate literary and artistic activity."

Jane C. Ginsburg, *A Tale of Two Copyrights: Literary Property in Revolutionary France and America*, 64 Tul. L. Rev. 991, 992 (1990).

Most European countries also recognize a concept called *moral rights* that protects certain non-economic interests of authors. Authors have rights to prevent distortion, destruction, or even misattribution of a work. As we discuss later (in Chapter 5), despite global harmonization efforts, U.S. copyright law with its utilitarian underpinnings does not fully embrace protection for moral rights.

Even in the U.S., one can detect in copyright law at least strands of the idea that authors have certain natural rights in their works. Unlike Continental Europe's conception of an almost sacred bond of personality between an author and her work, however, to the extent that American law incorporates a natural rights theory, it relies in large measure on premises derived from the writings of John Locke, particularly his *Two Treatises on Government*.

John Locke, Two Treatises on Government
Book II, ch. V (1690)

God, who hath given the World to Men in common, hath also given them reason to make use of it to the best advantage of Life, and convenience. . . . [Y]et being given for the use of Men, there must of necessity be a means *to appropriate* [the earth and its contents] some way or other before they can be of any use. . . .

Though the Earth, and all inferior Creatures be common to all Men, yet every Man has a *Property* in his own *Person*. This no Body has any Right to but himself. The *Labour* of his Body, and the *Work* of his Hands, we may say, are properly his. Whatsover he then removes out of the State that Nature hath provided, and left it in, he hath mixed his *Labour* with, and joyned to it something that is his own, and thereby makes it his *Property*. . . . [I]t hath by this *labour* something annexed to it, that excludes the common right of other Men. For this *Labour* being the unquestionable Property of the Labourer, no Man but he can have a right to what that is once joyned to, at least where there is enough, and as good left in common for others.

He that is nourished by the Acorns he pickt up under an Oak, or the Apples he gathered from the Trees in the Wood, has certainly appropriated them to himself. . . . I ask then, When did they begin to be his? . . . And 'tis plain, if the first gathering made them not his, nothing else could. That *labour* put a distinction between them and common. . . . And will any one say he had no right to those Acorns or Apples he thus appropriated, because he had not the consent of all Mankind to make them his? Was it a Robbery thus to assume to himself what belonged to all in Common? If such a consent as that was necessary, Man had starved, notwithstanding the Plenty God had given him. . . .

It will perhaps be objected to this, That if gathering the Acorns, or other Fruits of the Earth, &c. makes a right to them, then any one may *ingross* as much as he will. To which I Answer, Not so. The same Law of Nature, that does by this means give us Property, does also *bound* that *Property* too. . . . As much as any one can make use of to any advantage of life before it spoils; so much he may by his labour fix a Property in. Whatever is beyond this, is more than his share, and belongs to others. Nothing was made by God for Man to spoil or destroy. . . .

NOTES AND QUESTIONS

1. Locke argued that labor gives rise to ownership of tangible property. Applying this principle to intangible property may be difficult, however. For example, in general, copyright law does not ask how hard someone worked in creating a particular work and then assign rights commensurate with that effort. In fact, some creative works that are afforded copyright protection are the result of mere fortuity. *See, e.g., Time, Inc. v. Bernard Geis Assocs.*, 293 F. Supp. 130 (S.D.N.Y. 1968) (acknowledging copyright protection for a home movie of the presidential motorcade during which JFK was shot). Other works are not granted protection despite painstaking effort exerted in their creation. *See, e.g., Hearn v. Meyer*, 664 F. Supp. 832 (S.D.N.Y. 1987) (refusing to recognize copyright protection in reproduction of public domain art prints completed through an exacting and time-consuming process). Is this consistent with Lockean labor theory? With the utilitarian justification for copyright?

2. Consider this contemporary explanation of how Locke's arguments translate into our time and, specifically, into the intellectual property context:

> Locke's property theory has many strands, some of which are overtly utilitarian and others of which draw on varying notions of desert. To the extent that his theory purports to state a nonconsequentialist natural right in property, it is most firmly based on the most fundamental law of nature, the "no-harm principle." The essential logic is simple: Labor is mine and when I appropriate objects from the common I join my labor to them. If you take the objects I have gathered you have also taken my labor, since I have attached my labor to the objects in question. This harms me, and you should not harm me. You therefore have a duty to leave these objects alone. Therefore I have property in the objects.
>
> Similarly, if I use the public domain to create a new intangible work of authorship or invention, you should not harm me by copying it and interfering with my plans for it. I therefore have property in the intangible as well. . . .

Wendy J. Gordon, *A Property Right in Self-Expression: Equality and Individualism in the Natural Law of Intellectual Property*, 102 Yale L.J. 1533, 1544-45 (1993). How might the difference between tangible objects and intangible "labors of the mind" affect the types of rights that society should grant to a "laborer"? How should Locke's view of labor apply to production of a database comprising digitally scanned works of art from the public domain? Does the use of digital technology diminish the nature and quality of the "labor" used in such an enterprise?

3. As noted above, in the U.S., the utilitarian justification for copyright protection predominates, as evidenced by the constitutional grant of authority. There are, however, pronounced strains of Lockean labor theory in U.S. copyright law. For a thorough discussion of the role of natural rights in U.S. copyright law, see Alfred Yen, *Restoring the Natural Law: Copyright as Labor and Possession*, 51 Ohio St. L.J. 517 (1990). Similarly, although Continental European copyright systems emphasize the primacy of author's rights, those systems also have some utilitarian aspects. *See* Jane C. Ginsburg, *A Tale of Two Copyrights: Literary Property in Revolutionary France and America*, 64 Tul. L. Rev. 991 (1990).

4. How do Locke's labor theory and the French natural rights theory differ? In the context of tangible property, some scholars have developed an alternate theory of property rights based on the writings of German philosopher G.W.F. Hegel. Hegel reasoned that property is an extension of human autonomy. As Professor Margaret Jane Radin explains: "Hegel concludes that the person becomes a real self only by engaging in a property relationship with something external." Margaret Jane Radin, *Property and Personhood*, 34 Stan. L. Rev. 957, 972 (1982). Professor Radin concludes that this view of the origin of property rights justifies

stronger property rights in objects that are most closely bound up with one's personhood, such as a wedding ring or one's home:

> A person cannot be fully a person without a sense of continuity of self over time. To maintain that sense of continuity over time and to exercise one's liberty or autonomy, one must have an ongoing relationship with the external environment, consisting of both "things" and other people. . . . One's expectations crystallize around certain "things," the loss of which causes more disruption and disorientation than does a simple decrease in aggregate wealth. For example, if someone returns home to find her sofa has disappeared, that is more disorienting than to discover that her house has decreased in market value by 5%.

Id. at 1004.

Under this "personhood" theory of property, property exists not because of the labor that has gone into producing or maintaining it (as it does under Locke's theory), but because an object or piece of land has become invested with human will. Does the personhood theory of property supply a plausible justification for copyright in works of authorship? How does the personhood theory compare to the French natural rights theory?

5. As you read the material in this book, consider how differences in theoretical justifications might influence the design of the legal rules of copyright law. How much do the underlying justifications inform the scope of rights to be granted or the duration of those rights?

3.   A Robust Public Domain

The existence of the public domain is a foundational principle of the U.S. copyright system. Unfortunately, the term "public domain" is not amenable to a simple definition. Certainly, it includes works for which copyright protection has expired. Recall that the Intellectual Property Clause expressly states that rights may be granted to authors only for "limited Times." Passage into the public domain is thus mandated by the Constitution itself. But what else does the public domain include, and what purposes does it serve?

Jessica Litman, The Public Domain
39 Emory L.J. 965, 965-67, 975-77 (1990)

Our copyright law is based on the charming notion that authors create something from nothing, that works owe their origin to the authors who produce them. Arguments for strengthening copyright protection, whether predicated on a theory of moral deserts or expressed in terms of economic incentives, often begin with the premise that copyright should adjust the balance between the creative individuals who bring new works into being and the greedy public who would steal the fruits of their genius.

The process of authorship, however, is more equivocal than that romantic model admits. To say that every new work is in some sense based on the works that preceded it is such a truism that it has long been a cliché, invoked but not examined. But the very act of authorship in *any* medium is more akin to translation and recombination than it is to creating Aphrodite from the foam of the sea. Composers recombine sounds they have heard before; playwrights base their characters on bits and pieces drawn from real human beings and other playwrights' characters; novelists draw their plots from lives and other plots within their experience; software writers use the logic they find in other software; lawyers transform old arguments to fit new facts;

cinematographers, actors, choreographers, architects, and sculptors all engage in the process of adapting, transforming, and recombining what is already "out there" in some other form. This is not parasitism: it is the essence of authorship. . . .

The lay understanding of the public domain in the copyright context is that it contains works free from copyright. Works created before the enactment of copyright statutes, such as Shakespeare's *Macbeth* or Pach[el]bel's *Canon*, are available for fourth grade classes across the nation to use for school assemblies without permission from any publisher or payment of any royalties. Another class of old works in the public domain are works once subject to copyright, but created so long ago that the copyright has since expired, such as Mark Twain's *Huckleberry Finn*. . . .

But the class of works not subject to copyright is, in some senses, the least significant portion of the public domain. The most important part of the public domain is a part we usually speak of only obliquely: the realm comprising aspects of copyrighted works that copyright does not protect. Judge Learned Hand discussed this facet of the public domain in connection with an infringement suit involving a play entitled *Abie's Irish Rose*:

> We assume that the plaintiff's play is altogether original, even to an extent that in fact it is hard to believe. We assume further that, so far as it has been anticipated by earlier plays of which she knew nothing, that fact is immaterial. Still, as we have already said, her copyright did not cover everything that might be drawn from her play; its content went to some extent into the public domain.

The concept that portions of works protected by copyright are owned by no one and are available for any member of the public to use is such a fundamental one that it receives attention only when something seems to have gone awry. Although the public domain is implicit in all commentary on intellectual property, it rarely takes center stage. Most of the writing on the public domain focuses on other issues: Should the duration of copyright be extended? Should we recognize new species of intellectual property rights? Should federal intellectual property law cut a broad preemptive swathe or a narrow one? Copyright commentary emphasizes that which is protected more than it discusses that which is not. But a vigorous public domain is a crucial buttress to the copyright system; without the public domain, it might be impossible to tolerate copyright at all. . . .

NOTES AND QUESTIONS

1. What do you think Professor Litman means by "aspects of copyrighted works that copyright does not protect"? Remember the idea/expression distinction that we mentioned at the outset of this chapter. The ideas contained in a work are not protected by copyright, but their expression is. Ideas, then, are among the "aspects of copyrighted works that copyright does not protect." Why shouldn't copyright law protect ideas? We return to this question, and also consider other unprotected aspects of copyrighted works, in Chapter 2.

2. Is Professor Litman's account of the public domain consistent with the utilitarian theory of protection as articulated by Professor Hardy? By Professor Cohen?

3. In what ways is the importance of a rich public domain consistent with Lockean labor theory justifications for copyright law? According to Professor Gordon:

> [R]ecall how the laborer's claim to deserve property is itself justified. . . . [T]he same no-harm principle dictates that the laborer should not do harm to other peoples' claim to the common. When the two conflict, the common must prevail. . . .

Thus no natural right to property could exist where a laborer's claims would conflict with the public's claim in the common. . . . Locke's own resolution is to declare the conditions under which a natural right to property *is* justified: if there is "enough, and as good left in common for others" after the appropriator has taken up his share, then no one has grounds for complaint. . . .

Wendy J. Gordon, *A Property Right in Self-Expression: Equality and Individualism in the Natural Law of Intellectual Property*, 102 Yale L.J. 1533, 1561-62 (1993). In this excerpt Professor Gordon highlights what is sometimes referred to as Locke's proviso: Property rights are only appropriate when there is enough left in common for others. Does the authors' rights theory discussed by Professor Ginsburg yield a similar conclusion?

4. An Uncensored Marketplace of Ideas

Those who emphasize the importance of the public domain in copyright law seek to understand copyright in the context of the creative practices that occur within society. A different approach to the social context of copyright law views copyright as effectuating purposes more commonly associated with the modern First Amendment. This approach draws on the fact that the constitutional grant of authority to enact copyright protection is the only part of the original Constitution to address the issue of freedom of expression. Remember, the Bill of Rights, including the First Amendment, came later.

Professor Neil Netanel argues that copyright is best understood as a system intended to support our democratic civil society. *See* Neil Weinstock Netanel, *Copyright and a Democratic Civil Society*, 106 Yale L.J. 283 (1996).[1] He argues that copyright fulfills both a "production function" and a "structural function" that together create a marketplace characterized by a diversity of expression. Such diversity supports, and is a necessary condition of, a democratic regime.

According to Professor Netanel, copyright law's production function "encourages creative expression on a wide array of political, social, and aesthetic issues. The activity of creating and communicating such expression and the expression itself constitute vital components of a democratic civil society." *Id.* at 347. He stresses that by encouraging production and dissemination of works, copyright law helps to ensure that the body politic has the information it needs to participate in democratic processes. His reasoning applies not only to factual works but also to creative ones, on the ground that "[m]any creative works have broad political and social implications even if they do not appear or even seek to convey an explicit ideological message." *Id.* at 350.

In Professor Netanel's model, copyright law also performs a structural function by encouraging the creation of copyright industries that are independent of government control:

Prior to the first modern copyright statutes in the eighteenth century, writers and artists were heavily dependent on royal, feudal, and church patronage for their livelihoods. This dependency undermined expressive autonomy and thwarted the development of a vital, freethinking intelligentsia. . . .

When the Framers drafted the Copyright Clause and the Copyright Act of 1790, they took as self-evident that the diffusion of knowledge and exchange of view through a market for printed matter was a pillar of public liberty. . . .

---

1. Excerpts reprinted by permission of the author and of The Yale Law Journal and William S. Hein Company from The Yale Law Journal, Vol. 106, pages 347, 350, 353, 356-58, 360-61.

> Part and parcel of this vision was an understanding that democratic governance requires not simply the diffusion of knowledge per se, but also an autonomous sphere of print-mediated citizen deliberation and public education. . . . It was only by maintaining their fiscal independence that authors and publishers could continue to guard public liberty. . . .

Id. at 353, 356-58.

NOTES AND QUESTIONS

1. Do you read Professor Netanel to be arguing that the Framers originally conceived copyright as a means for social engineering or that the modern state should use copyright this way to effectuate the Framers' more general purpose? Do you agree with either argument?

2. Do modern government grant programs that subsidize the production of creative works pose structural risks to freedom of expression similar to those identified by Professor Netanel? Does public university funding of various creative endeavors pose such risks?

Some countries have dedicated tax revenue to supporting their film industries. For example, Canada has the Canada Feature Film Fund, administered by Telefilm Canada, which provides assistance for screenwriting, production, marketing, and promotion of feature films. Do national film industry subsidies threaten expressive freedoms?

3. Professor Netanel makes the following observations regarding the private-sector copyright industries:

> Our public discourse is far more dissonant and eclectic than that envisioned by the Framers. The political elite of the early Republic abhorred expressions of ideological faction and generally disdained fiction and "light" entertainment. Such works, however, form a major part of our copyright-supported discursive universe. From our perspective, the Framers' watchdog view of literature and the press also seems somewhat simplistic. Today's media conglomerates have attained an agenda-setting power that rivals that of state officials and, in the view of some commentators, undermines the democratic character of public discourse by skewing it towards those with the financial wherewithal to obtain access or buy advertised products.

Netanel, *supra* at 358. He concludes that, on balance, the copyright market continues to function as the Framers envisioned:

> But the copyright market also contains room for highly innovative and provocative expression, as well as that targeted for specialized or minority audiences. Significantly, copyright's fundamental capacity to support expressive diversity will likely grow dramatically in the digital age. The ease and low cost of digital production and dissemination has the potential of enabling authors, for the first time, to communicate directly with audiences throughout the world. As a result, many authors will be able to bypass media conglomerates, creating a copyright market characterized by an even greater multiplicity of view.

Id. at 360-61. As you continue through the book, consider whether you agree. Consider also what effects different copyright doctrines have on expressive freedoms.

5. A Theory of Users' Rights?

The world to which Professor Netanel alludes is literally at our fingertips. It is characterized by ubiquitous creative expressions from individuals disparately situated culturally, geographically, economically, and technologically. Within the traditional copyright framework, copyright law is addressed either to authors on whom the law confers protection or to users whose activities the law purports to constrain. The rise of "Web 2.0" communications platforms — technologies that facilitate sharing and creative collaboration involving all types of content via the World Wide Web — has challenged long-held assumptions about both groups.

The central role of users in the production and exchange of creative materials has given rise to a nascent theory of users' rights as an important justification for copyright law. Professor Jessica Litman observes:

> We sometimes talk and write about copyright law as if encouraging the creation and dissemination of works of authorship were the ultimate goal, with nothing further required to "promote the Progress of Science." We have focused so narrowly on the production half of the copyright equation that we have seemed to think that the Progress of Science is nothing more than a giant warehouse filled with works of authorship. When we do this, we miss, or forget, an essential step. In order for the creation and dissemination of a work of authorship to mean anything at all, someone needs to read the book, view the art, hear the music, watch the film, listen to the CD, run the computer program, and build and inhabit the architecture. . . .
>
> Copyright law is intended to create a legal ecology that encourages the creation and dissemination of works of authorship, and thereby "promote the Progress of Science." . . . [L]aws that discourage book reading end up being bad for book authors. Thus, it isn't difficult to frame an argument that copyright law cannot properly encourage authors to create new works if it imposes undue burdens on readers. . . . [C]opyright law encourages authorship at least as much for the benefit of the people who will read, view, listen to, and experience the works that authors create, as for the advantage of those authors and their distributors.

Jessica Litman, *Lawful Personal Use*, 85 Tex. L. Rev. 1871, 1879-82 (2007).

Other scholars have argued for a more accurate representation of users and their interests in copyright law. According to Professor Julie Cohen, "users play two important roles within the copyright system: Users receive copyrighted works, and (some) users become authors. Both roles further the copyright system's larger project to promote the progress of knowledge." Julie E. Cohen, *The Place of the User in Copyright Law*, 74 Fordham L. Rev. 347, 348 (2005). Professor Cohen identifies three models of the user in copyright jurisprudence and in the academic literature:

> [T]he economic user, who enters the market with a given set of tastes in search of the best deal; the "postmodern" user, who exercises limited and vaguely oppositional agency in a world in which all meaning is uncertain and all knowledge relative; and the romantic user, whose life is an endless cycle of sophisticated debates about current events, discerning quests for the most freedom-enhancing media technologies, and home production of high-quality music, movies, and open-source software.

Id.

Characterizing these models of the user as artificial, she advances a fourth model, the "situated user," who "deserves copyright law's solicitude precisely because neither her tastes nor her talents are . . . well formed." *Id.* at 349. According to Professor Cohen:

> [T]his imperfect being requires our attention because she must nevertheless become the vehicle by and through which copyright's collective project is advanced. The situated user engages cultural goods and artifacts found within the context of her culture through a variety of activities, ranging from consumption to creative play. The cumulative effect of these activities, and the

unexpected cultural juxtapositions and interconnections that they both exploit and produce, yield what the copyright system names, and prizes, as "progress." This model of the situated user suggests that the success of a system of copyright depends on both the extent to which its rules permit individuals to engage in creative play and the extent to which they enable contextual play, or degrees of freedom, within the system of culture more generally. . . . [For the situated user, b]oth her patterns of consumption and the extent and direction of her own authorship will be shaped and continually reshaped by the artifacts, conventions and institutions that make up her cultural environment. . . .

Id. Cohen argues that "[s]cholars and policymakers should ask how much latitude the situated user needs to perform her functions most effectively, and how the current entitlement structure of copyright law might change to accommodate that need." *Id.* at 374.

Other scholars, however, assert that users exert powerful influence on accepted practice with respect to copyrighted works. According to Professor Edward Lee:

> The most significant copyright development of the twenty-first century has not arisen through any law enacted by Congress or opinion rendered by the Supreme Court. Nor has it come from an organized group, movement, or industry seeking to effectuate a change to the copyright system. Instead, it has come from the unorganized, informal practices of various, unrelated users of copyrighted works, many of whom probably know next to nothing about copyright law. . . .
> . . . Whether in blogs, fan fiction, videos, music, or other mashups, many users freely use the copyrighted works of others without prior permission and even beyond our conventional understandings of fair use. Yet, often, as in the case of noncommercial uses of copyrighted works on blogs or in fan fiction, the copyright holders do not seem to care, and, in some cases, publicly condone the general practice. Moreover, the mass practices of many users of popular Web 2.0 sites, like YouTube, of ignoring the need to obtain permission before using someone else's copyrighted work have even prompted the securing of commercial licenses between Web 2.0 sites and the copyright holders in order to ratify the mass practices of users. Thus, instead of being condemned as infringement, the unauthorized mass practices of users may have, in some instances, turned out to be the catalyst for subsequent ratification of those practices, albeit in some bargained-for exchange not even involving the users themselves.
> Put simply, copyright law as we know it "on the books" is not exactly how copyright law operates in practice. Instead of being defined a priori by statute or at a single snapshot in time, the contours of an author's exclusive rights in the Web 2.0 world are being defined by a much messier and more complex process involving a loose, unorganized "give and take" of sorts among users, copyright holders, and intermediaries. . . .

Edward Lee, *Warming Up to User-Generated Content*, 2008 U. Ill. L. Rev. 1459, 1460-62.[3]

NOTES AND QUESTIONS

1. As you know, the Intellectual Property Clause makes no mention of users at all. Is developing a theory of users' rights a credible constitutional exercise?

2. Can users' rights be conceptualized using other theories of copyright discussed in this section? Can you articulate a theory of users' rights using the tools of economic analysis? To what extent does Professor Gordon's account of the Lockean proviso support an argument for users' rights? In what ways does a users' rights theory align with Professor Netanel's argument

---

3. Reproduced by permission of the publisher from 2008 *University of Illinois Law Review* 1459. Copyright 2008 by The Board of Trustees of the University of Illinois.

that the Framers intended copyright to function as a means to preserve a democratic civil society?

3. What do you make of the four models of the copyright user outlined by Professor Cohen? Into which model do you fit?

4. Is the difference between Professor Lee and Professor Cohen simply one of form? If users have as much freedom within the interstices of copyright law as Professor Lee argues, is a doctrine of users' rights needed?

5. Should a theory of the user inform the rights that copyright confers on authors, or should it merely inform defenses to claims of copyright infringement?

6. What Progress, and Whose Welfare?

Although the authors quoted above might disagree about exactly how copyright law should be structured, all would agree that copyright law is intended to promote the general public welfare. But is copyright law *necessary* to promote general welfare? "Public welfare" is a slippery concept, and particularly so when one adopts a global perspective. As the following excerpt explores, western-style copyright systems do not fully account for some other cultures' understandings of what "progress" and "welfare" mean.

≡ *William P. Alford, To Steal a Book Is an Elegant Offense*
≡ *28-29 (1995)*

[Professor Alford describes the cultural acceptance of copying in China before the imposition of western notions of intellectual property protection in the late nineteenth and early twentieth centuries. Chinese culture develops with significant reference to the past. The importance of this interaction with the past for further cultural development makes copying of earlier works a culturally valuable activity.]

. . . Nor, as was often the case in the West, was such use accepted grudgingly and then only because it served as a vehicle through which apprentices and students developed their technical expertise, demonstrated erudition, or even endorsed particular values, although each of these phenomena also existed in imperial China. On the contrary, in the Chinese context, such use was at once both more affirmative and more essential. It evidenced the user's comprehension of and devotion to the core of civilization itself, while offering individuals the possibility of demonstrating originality within the context of those forms and so distinguishing their present from the past.

In view of the foregoing, there was what Wen Fong has termed a "general attitude of tolerance, or indeed receptivity, shown on the part of the great Chinese painters towards the forging of their own works." Such copying, in effect, bore witness to the quality of the work copied and to its creator's degree of understanding and civility. Thus Shen Zhou (1427-1509) is reported to have responded to the suggestions that he put a stop to the forging of his work by remarking, in comments that were not considered exceptional, "if my poems and painting, which are only small efforts to me, should prove to be of some aid to the forgers, what is there for me to grudge about?" Much the same might be said of literature, where the Confucian disdain for commerce fostered an ideal, even if not always realized in practice, that true scholars wrote for edification and moral renewal rather than profit. Or, as it was expressed so compactly in a famed Chinese aphorism, "Genuine scholars let the later world discover their work [rather than promulgate and profit from it themselves]."

NOTES AND QUESTIONS

1. As the excerpt from Professor Alford's book demonstrates, perspectives on the legitimacy and social value of copying others' creations can vary significantly. During the many centuries in which China fully ascribed to the views described by Professor Alford, Chinese civilization produced a rich bounty of scientific, technical, and artistic creations. Can that reality be squared with the utilitarian justification for copyright protection? Can it be squared with justifications for copyright protection based on authors' rights? What does this suggest about the adequacy of those justifications? As you continue through this book, consider whether copyright functions primarily as a tool for stimulating creativity or primarily as a tool for commercializing it.

2. Article 27(2) of the Universal Declaration of Human Rights (UDHR) (1948) recognizes the right of authors to the "protection of the moral and material interests resulting from any scientific, literary or artistic production of which he is the author." Article 27(1), however, provides that "[e]veryone has the right freely to participate in the cultural life of the community, to enjoy the arts and to share in scientific advancement and its benefits." UDHR art. 27, G.A. Res. 217A(III), U.N. GAOR, 3d Sess., 1st plen. mtg., U.N. Doc. A/810 (Dec. 10, 1948). If copyright protection and cultural participation are considered human rights, how should copyright law respond? To what extent should copyright law reflect or accommodate different cultural conceptions regarding the value of creativity and copying? Should differences in cultures or changes in technology affect the scope of protection afforded authors? Is a human rights perspective consistent with the utilitarian justification for copyright? For analysis of the implications flowing from a human rights conception of intellectual property, see Laurence R. Helfer, *Towards a Human Rights Framework for Intellectual Property*, 40 U.C. Davis L. Rev. 971 (2007). For an argument that human rights norms are implicit in the design of intellectual property laws, see Ruth L. Okediji, *Securing Intellectual Property Objectives: New Approaches to Human Rights Considerations, in* Casting the Net Wider: Human Rights, Development and New Duty-Bearers (Margot E. Salomon, Arne Tostensen & Wouter Vandenhole eds., 2007).

In light of the different justifications for copyright protection, consider how you believe copyright law should resolve the following hypotheticals. How much does the underlying policy rationale that you emphasize influence your desired outcome?

a. A company partners with a number of leading libraries to create a fully searchable database of all the books in their collections. Entire books are scanned into the database, and the search engine allows full-text searches and full-text search returns. Publishers that do not want their books included can opt out. The company informs users of where they may purchase or borrow the books.

b. An author writes a book, *The Wind Done Gone*, that retells the story of Margaret Mitchell's classic novel, *Gone With the Wind*, from the perspective of Scarlett O'Hara's black half-sister, who is a slave on the family plantation. Mitchell's estate sues to block publication of the book.

c. A researcher combs through libraries and archives, conducts a number of interviews, and develops a new theory about the death of the infamous criminal John Dillinger. In a series of books, he contends that the FBI did not kill Dillinger in 1934. Instead, Dillinger escaped and retired to the West Coast where he lived until at least 1979. A network television station produces an episode of a popular detective series set in

California, in which the protagonists investigate the possibility that Dillinger is still alive. The TV show cites some of the evidence the researcher used to support his theory. The researcher sues for copyright infringement.

d. A carpet manufacturer reproduces traditional designs originating from an indigenous people. The carpet manufacturer copied the designs directly from paintings created by living artists of native descent without permission from anyone. The designs in the paintings are sacred images that date back many centuries. In the culture of these indigenous people, only certain individuals who know and adhere to traditional laws and rituals are permitted to reproduce ancestral images. The carpets are mass produced and sold in the country now encompassing the lands of the indigenous people as well as in other countries.

e. A teenager lip-synchs to a video of Michael Jackson performing the hit song "Beat It." He posts the video on YouTube.

f. An individual digitally manipulates several press clips of President George Bush and Prime Minister Tony Blair, synchronizing their lip movements to the recording of "Endless Love" performed by Lionel Ritchie and Diana Ross, to reflect the close political alliance of the U.S. and the U.K. during the Iraqi war. She posts the video on YouTube.

B. THE HISTORY OF U.S. COPYRIGHT LAW

The basic copyright framework devised over 200 years ago has weathered dramatic changes in the means of producing and distributing creative works. This section reviews the history of copyright law in the context of these changes and sketches the new challenges that lie ahead.

1. From Censorship to Markets

The history of copyright law in the U.S. begins, not surprisingly, in England. What *is* surprising to many students of copyright law is that the first real copyright statutes were tools for government censorship and press control. Copyright did not become a tool for promoting knowledge and learning until later.

In the years before the printing press, reproducing a work involved the laborious task of hand copying. This fact, along with an extremely low literacy rate, made legal regulation of unauthorized copying practically unnecessary. When William Caxton introduced the printing press in England in 1476, the economics of copying changed drastically. Booksellers felt this advance to be a mixed blessing. The printing press reduced both the time it took to bring a book to market and the cost to print copies. However, other printers could wait to see if a book would be a "bestseller." If it were, they could use the press to produce their own copies of it quickly enough to take advantage of the market for the work. Such printers could then make a handsome profit, unencumbered by any requirement to pay some of their income to either the author or the original publisher.

The English printers and booksellers had been organized as a guild for nearly 100 years before the introduction of the printing press. Rules governing the members of the guild, however, were nothing more than a "gentlemen's agreement" that could be enforced only among the guild's own membership. Because of this "private law" characteristic, there existed the threat that a printer who was not a member of the guild would copy a work previously published by a member. The aggrieved member would have no recourse against the nonmember not bound by the terms of the membership agreement.

The threat of encroachment by outsiders caused the guild to seek ways of making its private law enforceable against nonmembers as well. Printing patents, granted by the sovereign at his royal prerogative, offered one such method of enforcement by giving the holder of the patent a state-sanctioned monopoly over the printing of the work specified. The printing patent, however, was limited to a favored few, so the printers turned to a second method of enforcement beyond the members of the guild: the creation of the royally chartered Stationers' Company.

During the mid-sixteenth century, the desires of the booksellers for greater enforcement ability coincided with the desires of the Crown to gain control over the dangerous possibilities of the printed word and to prevent the publication of "seditious and heretical material." Lyman Ray Patterson, *Copyright in Historical Perspective* 20-29 (1968). The result was the grant of a royal charter in 1557 that reserved the printing of most works to members of the Stationers' Company and granted the company the right to search out and destroy unlawfully printed books. The stationers' right served the booksellers well by providing them with a monopoly on registered titles. It served the Crown's ends by providing it with the ability to destroy books it viewed as heretical.

In the seventeenth century, several Star Chamber decrees and the Licensing Act of 1662 continued the regime of press control using the members of the Stationers' Company as enforcers. By agreeing to assist in the censorship desired by the Crown, the members of the Stationers' Company obtained a mechanism for preventing nonmembers from publishing works "owned" by the members.

This system of copyright protection was designed to benefit the publishers and the Crown, not authors, and became widely criticized. In a now-famous passage, author John Milton wrote in protest that ideas were not "a staple commodity . . . to [be] mark[ed] and license[d] like our broadcloth and our woolpacks." John Milton, *Areopagitica: A Speech for the Liberty of Unlicensed Printing* 29 (1644) (H.B. Cotterill ed. 1959). After the Glorious Revolution of 1688, the royal licensing laws were allowed to lapse. In 1694, the last of the legally sanctioned censorship acts ended and the stationers were unsuccessful in convincing Parliament to reinstate their control.

After their defeat in Parliament, the publishers changed their tactics and sought to obtain legal protection for writings on behalf of authors who, of course, would have to assign their rights to the publishers in order to be paid. In 1710, Parliament enacted the Statute of Anne, which granted an assignable right to authors to control the publication of their writings. This new copyright act was fundamentally different from the previous proclamations and licensing laws in two important ways. Instead of a tool of censorship, the Statute of Anne was expressly meant to be, as its title stated, "[a]n act for the encouragement of learning."[1] Additionally, the Statute of Anne granted rights of limited duration (two 14-year terms), whereas previously the stationers' right had endured in perpetuity. This limited duration created, for the first time, a

---

1. The statute's preamble stated:

WHEREAS Printers, Booksellers, and other Persons have of late frequently taken the Liberty of printing, reprinting and publishing, or causing to be printed, reprinted and published, Books and other Writings, without the Consent of the Authors or Proprietors of such Books and Writings, to their very great Detriment, and too often to the Ruin of them and their Families: For preventing therefore such Practices for the future, and for the Encouragement of learned Men to compose and write useful Books [this statute is therefore enacted].

Statute of Anne, 8 Anne, c. 19 (1710).

legally recognized public domain consisting of works in which copyright protection could no longer be claimed.

Of course, a copyright of limited duration does not hold the same profit potential for authors and publishers as one that extends in perpetuity. Before the English courts, the publishers sought ways to obtain a copyright of longer duration than the statute provided. For a number of years, they were successful in persuading the courts that they also had a common law copyright, separate from the statutory copyright, that lasted forever. However, in the case of *Donaldson v. Beckett*, 1 Eng. Rep. 837 (H.L. 1774), the House of Lords rejected this claim. In accord with the custom of the day, each judge stated his opinion separately. Addressing the issue of common law copyright and exposing the self-interested nature of the publishers' arguments, Lord Chief Justice De Grey stated:

> The truth is, the idea of a common-law right in perpetuity was not taken up till after that failure (of the booksellers) in procuring a new statute for an enlargement of the term. If (say the parties concerned) the legislature will not do it for us, we will do it without their assistance; and then we begin to hear of this new doctrine, the common-law right, which, upon the whole, I am of opinion, cannot be supported upon any rules or principles of the common law of this kingdom.

17 Cobbett's Parl. Hist. 953 at 992. *Donaldson* established beyond a doubt that the Statute of Anne defined the only copyright to which authors or their assignees, the publishers, were entitled.

For a detailed account of the historical development of copyright law, see Patterson, *supra*. *See also* Ronan Deazley, *On the Origin of the Right to Copy* 194-210 (2004) (discussing the controversy surrounding the reporting of the judges' opinions and the ultimate outcome in *Donaldson*).

2. "Progress," Incentives, and Access

England had taken centuries to arrive at a copyright law that embodied a public purpose and reduced the threat that copyright could be used as a tool for government censorship. This history was not lost on the Framers of the Constitution, who expressly incorporated the requirement that copyright must serve a public purpose in the wording of the Intellectual Property Clause: "The Congress shall have Power . . . *To promote the Progress of Science and useful Arts*, by securing for limited Times to Authors and Inventors the exclusive Right to their respective Writings and Discoveries." U.S. Const., Art. I, §8, cl. 8 (emphasis added).[2] Note that under principles of parallel construction, the exclusive rights granted to "Authors" in their "Writings" are to "promote the Progress of Science." At the time of the Constitution's adoption, the word "Science" had a different meaning than it does today. Today, "Science" conjures up images of laboratories, test tubes, and microscopes. Then, "Science" broadly connoted knowledge and learning. The Constitution, like the Statute of Anne, also makes explicit the guarantee of a public domain; the "exclusive Right" granted to authors may only be for "limited Times."

In 1790, the first Congress embraced the idea of copyright's having an educational purpose, titling the first copyright law "An act for the encouragement of learning" and

---

2. Before the adoption of the Constitution, each of the original 13 states except Delaware enacted its own copyright statute. Many followed the example of the Statute of Anne, and many began with a preamble that stated the public purposes that the grant of copyright was intended to serve.

providing for two 14-year terms of protection. Act of 1790, 1st Cong., 2d Sess., ch. 15, 1 Stat. 124 (1790). To receive this Act's protection, an author had to comply with various formalities, including registration of title, publication of the registration in a local newspaper, and deposit of a copy of the work with the Secretary of State within six months of publication.

The deposit requirement effectively meant that the federal government came into possession of a great store of knowledge. In 1800, Congress passed legislation authorizing the establishment of a library for its own use. This institution evolved into the Library of Congress, which today is the de facto national library of the U.S. Beginning in 1846, the Library became the repository for copies of works deposited under the Copyright Act. The Copyright Act of 1870 centralized all registration and deposit activities in the Library of Congress. Finally, in 1897, Congress established the Copyright Office as a department of the Library of Congress and created the position of Register of Copyrights to oversee the administration of the copyright system.

In the U.S., as in England's *Donaldson* case, litigants presented arguments to courts claiming the existence of a perpetual, common law copyright. In the famous case of *Wheaton v. Peters*, 33 U.S. (8 Pet.) 591 (1834), the Supreme Court addressed the question of copyright protection for reports of the Court's opinions. The Court recognized that the opinions themselves could not be copyrighted, but other material added by the Court's reporter, such as summaries of the arguments of the parties, was eligible for protection. However, the reporter had failed to comply with the statutory formalities required for protection. Thus, if there were to be any copyright protection for the reporter's material, it would have to arise outside the bounds of the federal statute. As in *Donaldson v. Beckett*, the plaintiff asserted common law copyright protection; as in *Donaldson*, the high court rejected it:

> That an author, at common law, has a property in his manuscript, and may obtain redress against any one who deprives him of it, or by improperly obtaining a copy endeavours to realise a profit by its publication, cannot be doubted; but this is a very different right from that which asserts a perpetual and exclusive property in the future publication of the work, after the author shall have published it to the world.
>
> The argument that a literary man is as much entitled to the product of his labour as any other member of society, cannot be controverted. And the answer is, that he realises this product by the transfer of his manuscripts, or in the sale of his works, when first published.
>
> A book is valuable on account of the matter it contains, the ideas it communicates, the instruction or entertainment it affords. Does the author hold a perpetual property in these? Is there an implied contract by every purchaser of his book, that he may realise whatever instruction or entertainment which the reading of it shall give, but shall not write out or print its contents.
>
> In what respect does the right of an author differ from that of an individual who has invented a most useful and valuable machine? In the production of this, his mind has been as intensely engaged, as long; and, perhaps, as usefully to the public, as any distinguished author in the composition of his book.
>
> The result of their labours may be equally beneficial to society, and in their respective spheres they may be alike distinguished for mental vigour. Does the common law give a perpetual right to the author, and withhold it from the inventor? And yet it has never been pretended that the latter could hold, by the common law, any property in his invention, after he shall have sold it publicly.
>
> It would seem, therefore, that the existence of a principle may well be doubted, which operates so unequally. This is not a characteristic of the common law. It is said to be founded on principles of justice, and that all its rules must conform to sound reason. . . .

> That every man is entitled to the fruits of his own labour must be admitted; but he can enjoy them only, except by statutory provision, under the rules of property, which regulate society, and which define the rights of things in general.

Id. at 657-58.

The Court's rejection of any kind of common law copyright in published works effectively meant that copyright in such works would be governed exclusively by the federal statute adopted by Congress. This is the rule today. As you will see later, Congress has extended the exclusive scheme of federal protection to unpublished works as well.

Court opinions from the nineteenth century also recognized that not every piece of written expression is subject to copyright protection. As already noted, the *Wheaton* Court observed that the opinions of the Court could not be copyrighted but were part of the public domain — free for anyone to copy. Several years later, in *Emerson v. Davies*, 8 F. Cas. 615 (1845), Justice Story reasoned that the nature of authorship requires some freedom to build on certain aspects of past works:

> In truth, in literature, in science and in art, there are, and can be, few, if any, things, which, in an abstract sense, are strictly new and original throughout. Every book in literature, science and art, borrows, and must necessarily borrow, and use much which was well known and used before. No man creates a new language for himself, at least if he be a wise man, in writing a book. He contents himself with the use of language already known and used and understood by others. No man writes exclusively from his own thoughts, unaided and uninstructed by the thoughts of others. The thoughts of every man are, more or less, a combination of what other men have thought and expressed, although they may be modified, exalted, or improved by his own genius or reflection. If no book could be the subject of copy-right which was not new and original in the elements of which it is composed, there could be no ground for any copy-right in modern times, and we should be obliged to ascend very high, even in antiquity, to find a work entitled to such eminence. Virgil borrowed much from Homer; Bacon drew from earlier as well as contemporary minds; Coke exhausted all the known learning of his profession; and even Shakespeare and Milton, so justly and proudly our boast as the brightest originals would be found to have gathered much from the abundant stores of current knowledge and classical studies in their days.

Id. at 619.

Courts further reasoned that the same policies required some leeway to use copyrighted material produced by others. Four years before his opinion in *Emerson*, in the case of *Folsom v. Marsh*, 9 F. Cas. 342 (1841), Justice Story expressly recognized that using selections from a preexisting work "fairly" did not constitute an infringement of copyright. This recognition marked the beginning of the venerable fair use doctrine in U.S. copyright law.

By the end of the nineteenth century, copyright protection was firmly established in U.S. law as a means of encouraging progress in knowledge and learning. The protection afforded by copyright law was subject to important limits, and those limits were also seen as necessary for encouraging the creation of new works. The rapid technological changes that began at the start of the twentieth century, however, posed difficult challenges for this basic copyright framework.

3. Copyright Law and Technological Change

The copyright system established by the first Congress has expanded considerably beyond its original bounds. As new forms of creative expression have developed, Congress has extended copyright protection accordingly. The current Copyright Act thus covers a much greater variety of creative output than the original Act of 1790. And as new technologies have emerged for disseminating creative products, Congress has revised the protections afforded by copyright law to reach these new distribution and communication media.

a. New Methods of Creating New Works

The first Copyright Act, enacted in 1790, extended copyright protection to authors of maps, charts, and books. Over the next century, Congress gradually expanded the list to include engravings, etchings, and prints (1802); musical compositions (1831); dramatic compositions (1856); photographs and negatives (1865); and paintings, drawings, chromolithographs, statuary, and "models or designs intended to be perfected as works of the fine arts" (1870).

As this brief history illustrates, continuing change in the prevailing methods of producing creative works required numerous amendments to keep the list of protected works current. This legislative practice continued in the 1909 overhaul of the Copyright Act, which stated that copyrightable works included "all the writings of an author," but then proceeded to list the following as classes of works protected by copyright:

(a) Books, including composite and cyclopaedic works, directories, gazetteers, and other compilations;
(b) Periodicals, including newspapers;
(c) Lectures, sermons, addresses, prepared for oral delivery;
(d) Dramatic or dramatico-musical compositions;
(e) Musical compositions;
(f) Maps;
(g) Works of art; models or designs for works of art;
(h) Reproductions of a work of art;
(i) Drawings or plastic works of a scientific or technical character;
(j) Photographs;
(k) Prints and pictorial illustrations.

Almost immediately, Congress amended this list to include "motion-picture photoplays" and "motion pictures other than photoplays" (1912). Still later, Congress added "prints or labels used for articles of merchandise" (1939) and, finally, sound recordings (1971).

In the 1976 Act, Congress chose a new approach to enumerating the works protected by copyright. This approach was intended "to free the courts from rigid or outmoded concepts of the scope of particular categories." H.R. Rep. No. 94-1476, 94th Cong., 2d Sess. at 53 (1976), *reprinted in* 1976 U.S.C.C.A.N. 5659, 5666. Rather than listing works according to the particular form or medium in which they were expressed (e.g., "books" and "periodicals"), the Act set forth broad categories of content that the law protects. Section 102(a) of the 1976 Act listed seven such nonexclusive categories: "(1) literary works; (2) musical works, including any accompanying words; (3) dramatic works, including any accompanying music; (4) pantomimes and choreographic works; (5) pictorial, graphic, and sculptural works; (6) motion pictures and other audiovisual works; and (7) sound recordings." These categories subsume many of the kinds of works that were listed separately in the 1909 Act and have proved more adaptable to change. Congress did not, for example, need to amend the Act when digital audio recordings and later DVD movies became available, because the statutory definitions of "sound recordings" and "audiovisual works" were already worded broadly enough to encompass these new media. Since 1976, Congress has added only one more category to the list in §102(a) — architectural works (1990).

b. New Technologies for Distributing and Copying Works

In addition to enabling new forms of creative expression, technological changes have transformed the ways in which creative works are produced, distributed, and accessed by members of the public. These changes have greatly complicated the task of defining a copyright owner's rights.

For hundreds of years, the only viable means of making copies of creative works for mass distribution was the printing press, and proximity to a physical copy was required to read or view a work. Musical compositions were distributed in the form of sheet music, which musically inclined customers could play on instruments of their own.

Near the start of the twentieth century, however, the print-based copyright landscape began to change rapidly. First came methods for distributing and playing recorded sounds and displaying moving images. The late 1800s and early 1900s witnessed the commercial marketing of both the mechanical player piano and motorized players for phonograph records. In 1894, the motion picture was invented and the first films were exhibited to the public. Shortly thereafter, in the 1920s and 1930s, first radio and then television provided means for transmitting sounds and images over great distances. Both radio and television penetration increased sharply after World War II. By 1950, radio ownership averaged 2.3 sets per household, and more than 50 percent of U.S. households owned a television.

Next, in the mid-twentieth century came inexpensive, readily available methods of reproducing texts, images, and sounds that did not require the assistance of the customary publishing intermediaries. In 1948, Bing Crosby produced the first professional sound recordings on magnetic audiotape; by the late 1970s, analog audiotape equipment capable of recording as well as playing pre-recorded tapes was widely available in consumer markets. A U.S. government study conducted in 1989 found that 41 percent of respondents had engaged in home audiotaping during the previous year. U.S. Congress, Office of Technology Assessment (OTA), Copyright and Home Copying: Technology Challenges the Law 151 (1989). The automatic plain-paper photocopier, first marketed by the Xerox Corporation in 1959, was in widespread use in offices by the 1960s. By 1966, 14 billion photocopies were made each year; by 1985, the annual total exceeded 700 billion. The first videocassette recorders were marketed in the U.S. in the early 1960s; by 1987, VCRs were in use in 50 percent of U.S. homes.

The digital technologies that emerged in the late twentieth century accelerated these trends. The introduction of the personal computer (PC) in the late 1970s and early 1980s was followed in rapid succession in the late 1980s and 1990s by pre-recorded compact discs; digital audio recording media; digital multimedia technology; sophisticated desktop publishing software; pre-recorded and recordable DVDs; the Internet; the World Wide Web; digital compression formats for storing and transmitting high-fidelity audio and video files; and software-based audio and video players, "rippers," and recording tools. These technologies provide enormous versatility. Once a work consisting of text, sounds, and/or images has been rendered in digital form, it can be reproduced instantaneously without the degradation in quality that characterizes analog reproduction technologies such as traditional tape recorders. Anyone with access to the Internet can transmit such works instantaneously, with a few taps on a keyboard, to anywhere else in the country or the world, and anyone with access to a Web server can display the works for others to see, modify, and forward to others with access to the Internet.

More recently, the emergence of densely networked communication platforms, including so-called Web 2.0 platforms that facililtate the sharing and tagging of media files, has introduced additional change to the digital technology scene. Web 2.0 technologies empower users to engage in a variety of activities that utilize creative works available in digital formats. The well-known social networking site, Facebook, has over 300 million users, and in 2009 was adding an average of at least 450,000 users per day. In 2006, Google purchased the video-sharing platform YouTube for $1.65 billion; as of June 2009, YouTube hosted approximately 7 billion video streams.

c. Legal Responses to New Technologies

As you will see, copyright law has attempted to respond to all these changes. Nineteenth-century copyright law generally granted copyright owners the rights to control printing and publication of their works. The law additionally granted the right to control public performances to the owners of copyright in dramatic compositions. As public performances of first live, and then recorded, music grew in popularity and sales of sheet music declined, however, the owners of copyrights in musical compositions demanded broader protection.

In 1909, Congress enacted a comprehensive revision of the copyright law. The Copyright Act of 1909 extended rights of public performance to musical compositions and granted owners of musical composition copyrights a limited right to compensation, via a compulsory license, from those who prepared "mechanical" sound recordings of their works. (At the time, this meant phonograph records and player piano rolls.) The 1909 Act also extended the term of copyright protection, which had evolved over time from a maximum of 28 years in 1790 to a maximum of 42 years in 1908, to a new maximum of 56 years.

The new media of the twentieth century rapidly tested the limits of the new statute. Public performance rights had to be extended to other works enabled by new technologies, such as motion pictures and television broadcasts. Owners of copyright in pictorial works such as drawings and photographs argued that they deserved analogous rights to control the broadcasting of these works. Meanwhile, the existing formal requirements for copyright protection, which were based on concepts like publication of copies with notice of copyright, could not easily be applied to the new broadcast technologies.

These and other perceived inadequacies ultimately led to enactment of the 1976 Copyright Act, which took effect on January 1, 1978. The 1976 Act defined five exclusive rights of copyright owners. Those rights included not only the traditional rights of reproduction and distribution, but also broadened rights of public performance and display and a newly defined right to create derivative works based on the copyrighted work. In addition, it abandoned the 1909 Act's focus on publication as triggering federal copyright protection and provided that protection would attach from the moment that a work was fixed in a tangible medium of expression — which, for broadcast works, could be the making of a contemporaneous recording. Finally, the 1976 Act substantially lengthened the copyright term once again. Although, as you will soon see, the 1976 Act has undergone numerous changes in recent years, it provides the basic structure for U.S. copyright law today. Note, though, that many works under copyright today were created before 1978, so it will be necessary for you to study certain provisions of the 1909 Act as well.

4. The Copyright Legislative Process

The 1976 Act is a curious amalgam of broad, general rights; vague exceptions like the fair use doctrine; and complex, technical licensing provisions. In part, this facially odd mesh of different types of provisions reflects the continuing challenges posed by new technologies; for example, past practice did not offer any obvious, principled way to deal with rebroadcast of network television programming over cable systems. In part, however, it reflects an unusual degree of involvement by affected constituencies in the drafting process.

The process of copyright revision that culminated in the 1976 Act witnessed the full-fledged emergence of a novel interest-group model for drafting copyright legislation. As Professor Jessica Litman describes:

> A review of the 1976 Copyright Act's legislative history demonstrates that Congress and the Registers of Copyrights actively sought compromises negotiated among those with economic interests in copyright and purposefully incorporated those compromises into the copyright revision bill, even when they disagreed with their substance. Moreover, both the Copyright Office and Congress intended from the beginning to take such an approach, and designed a legislative process to facilitate it.
>
> One might argue that this was an improper way to create a statute, on the ground that it involved an egregious delegation of legislative authority to the very interests the statute purports to regulate. Alternatively, one might argue that the process constituted an ingenious solution to the problem of drafting a statute for an area so complicated that no member of Congress could acquire meaningful expertise.

Jessica Litman, *Copyright, Compromise, and Legislative History*, 72 Cornell L. Rev. 857, 879 (1987).

Participants in the drafting process hoped that the eventual result would be a statute both sufficiently flexible and sufficiently enduring for the modern era. Technologies, however, have continued to change, putting pressure on copyright law, and the demands of globalization have increased, adding to that pressure. In the 34 years since the 1976 Act was enacted, it has been amended over 25 times. Today, the Copyright Act is a complex and ungainly document. The Copyright Act of 1909 was 14 pages long. The Copyright Act of 1976 was 62 pages long when enacted; after all the intervening amendments, the current Act is closer to 300 pages.

5. The Copyright Industries

As information and entertainment goods have assumed increasing importance within the U.S. and global economies, the industries that produce and disseminate these goods have grown correspondingly. It should come as no surprise, then, that these industries wield considerable political power, both domestically and in international trade matters. No study of modern copyright law would be complete without consideration of the economic and political roles of the copyright industries and the resulting effects on copyright law and policy.

In 2007, the "core" copyright industries (motion pictures, sound recordings, music publishing, print publishing, computer software, theater, advertising, radio, television, and cable broadcasting) contributed approximately $889.13 billion to the U.S. economy, or 6.44 percent of the gross domestic product (GDP). Stephen E. Siwek, *Copyright Industries in the U.S. Economy: The 2003-2007 Report*, at 3 (2009). In 1977, the last year before the 1976 Copyright Act took effect, these industries contributed approximately $43 billion, or about 2.2 percent of GDP. From 1977 to 2001, the core copyright industries' contribution to GDP grew at an average annual rate of 7 percent per year — a rate more than twice that of the GDP overall. Stephen E. Siwek, *Copyright Industries in the U.S. Economy: The 2002 Report*, at 11-13 (2002). The rate of growth has slowed in more recent years but still exceeds the annual growth rate of the GDP overall. Siwek, *2003-2007 Report, supra*, at 4. For 2006-2007, the core copyright industries accounted for 22.74 percent of all U.S. GDP growth. Siwek, *2003-2007 Report, supra*, at 3.

The numbers for some industries are particularly striking. U.S. consumer spending on pre-recorded music totaled approximately $10.3 billion in 2007. Standard & Poor's (S&P), *Movies & Home Entertainment Industry Survey*, Mar. 2009, at 9. Motion picture industry revenues within the U.S., including revenues from rentals and purchases of pre-recorded movies, exceeded $50 billion in 2008. *Id.* at 8. Cable television, which reached only 12 percent of U.S. households in the early 1970s, had achieved approximately 87 percent penetration (including satellite penetration) in 2007 and $86.2 billion in total revenue for 2008, with 26.6 billion coming from advertising revenue. S&P, *Movies and Home Entertainment Survey*, July 2008, at 10; National Cable & Telecommunications Association, *available at* http://www.ncta.com/Stats/CustomerRevenue.aspx.

The most striking growth, however, has occurred in the software industry, which was in its infancy in 1976 and certainly would not have been considered a core copyright industry then. The first PCs were marketed to the public in the 1970s. Sales grew slowly until the early 1980s, when IBM entered the market and selected Microsoft's DOS as its operating system, and other manufacturers began producing compatible equipment. This standardization, followed in the mid-1980s by the deployment of user-friendly graphical interfaces, stimulated rapid growth in the market for both stand-alone operating systems and applications software and networking software. 2 *Encyclopedia of American Industries* 1140-42 (2d ed. 1998). By the mid-1990s, the worldwide market for prepackaged software alone exceeded $100 billion. *Id.* at 1139. This rapid growth has continued in the past decade, fueled by the increasingly widespread use of the Internet as a mass medium for communications and commerce and the consequent need for new kinds of software to manage online activities.

As one might expect from these numbers, U.S.-produced entertainment and information goods also represent a large and growing component of foreign trade. In 2007, the core U.S. copyright industries generated approximately $125.6 billion in foreign sales and exports. Siwek, *2003-2007 Report, supra*, at 11. Of that amount, computer software, including business and entertainment software, accounted for nearly $92 billion. *Id.* at 24. The U.S. is home to 22 of the world's top 30 software suppliers. S&P, *Computers: Software Industry Survey*, Oct. 2008, at 7. The U.S. motion picture and recorded music industries, meanwhile, generated approximately $28 billion in foreign sales and exports in 2007. Siwek, *2003-2007 Report, supra*, at 24.

As the economic power of the core copyright industries has grown, so has their political power. Each of these industries is represented on Capitol Hill by at least one, and often more than one, major trade association. These associations have large budgets and considerable clout. The model described by Professor Litman, *supra* page 29, remains in effect today. New copyright legislation typically is initiated at the copyright industries' request, and the relevant legislative committees routinely invite representatives of the copyright industries to submit proposed statutory language. Trade associations representing the major copyright industries also play a significant role in both international trade negotiations and unilateral trade proceedings. We discuss international trends in more detail in Section C *infra*.

Particularly in recent years, a number of other organizations have become involved in copyright lawmaking and policy. Some of these organizations, such as the American Library Association and the Association of American Universities, represent constituencies that, like the core copyright industries, play central roles in the production and distribution of creative works. Others, such as the Home Recording Rights Coalition, represent electronics companies that are concerned about proposals to regulate equipment that might be used to infringe copyrights. Still other organizations, such as Public Knowledge, were formed expressly to engage in copyright-related lobbying and public relations. Quite often, some or all of these groups have opposed legislative proposals sponsored by the copyright industries. We consider these proposals and the shape of the eventual legislation, in Chapters 3, 4, 6, and 9.

In addition, in response to the reports regarding the value of copyright protection to U.S. industries, the Computer & Communications Industry Association (CCIA) published a competing report that highlighted the economic importance of the "fair use" industries, i.e., industries that benefit from and/or rely on limits to copyright. *See* Thomas Rogers & Andrew Szamosszegi, *Fair Use in the U.S. Economy: Economic Contribution of Industries Relying on Fair Use*, CCIA, Sept. 2007. According to the authors, these industries include manufacturers of consumer devices that allow individual copying of copyrighted programming, educational institutions, software developers, and Internet search and Web hosting providers. *Id*. at 6. So defined, the fair use economy in 2006 accounted for $4.5 trillion in revenues, representing a 31 percent increase over the 2002 figure of $3.5 trillion. *Id*. at 44. According to the report, the fair use industries produced about one-sixth of the total U.S. GDP. *Id*. at 45.

NOTES AND QUESTIONS

1. What do you think of the method of legislative drafting described by Professor Litman? Professor Litman identified several drawbacks:

[O]f course, it wasn't possible to invite every affected interest. Some interests lacked organization and had no identifiable representatives. . . . In the conferences convened in the 1960s, painters and sculptors did not attend and the Copyright Office's efforts to seek them out proved unavailing. Choreographers, theatrical directors, and computer programmers sent no representatives because they had no representatives to send. Other interests that would have profound effect on copyright did not yet exist at the time of the conferences. . . . [T]here were no video cassette manufacturers, direct satellite broadcasters, digital audio technicians, motion picture colorizers, or on-line database users to invite in 1960.

Nor could the rest of us be there. . . . Many of us are consumers of copyrighted songs and also consumers of parodies of copyrighted songs, watchers of broadcast television and subscribers to cable television, patrons of motion picture theatres and owners of videotape recorders, purchasers and renters and tapers of copyrighted sound recordings. Although a few organizations showed up at the conferences purporting to represent the "public" with respect to narrow issues, the citizenry's interest in copyright and copyrighted works was too varied and complex to be amenable to interest group championship. Moreover, the public's interests were not somehow approximated by the push and shove among opposing industry representatives.

Jessica Litman, *Copyright Legislation and Technological Change*, 68 Or. L. Rev. 275, 311-12 (1989). What is your response to these criticisms? Is it practical to expect all relevant constituencies to be represented whenever new legislation is drafted? Who is "the public," and who should represent its interests?

2. Why wouldn't industries that both produce and use creative works be adequate proxies for consumer interests and have the incentive to strike an appropriate balance between the rights of creators, publishers, and users of copyrighted works? The branch of economic analysis known as public choice theory would predict that legislation on copyright issues would be shaped by the parties who have the greatest interest in, and set the highest monetary value on, the outcome. *See, e.g.*, Daniel A. Farber & Philip P. Frickey, *Law and Public Choice: A Critical Introduction* (1991). If this prediction is accurate, is there any reason why we should be concerned?

3. Examine some of the Web sites maintained by copyright industry associations and other interested groups. You can find links to these sites at *http://www.coolcopyright.com/*.

6. New Challenges

Ensuring that copyright law can respond effectively to continuing changes in the nature, distribution, and consumption of creative works, while preserving its original mandate to foster "Progress," is a demanding task. In particular, copyright law must confront new challenges posed by digital technologies, computer networks, and the new types of information goods that comprise the "information economy." Consider these issues that policymakers must confront today:

- Digital technology coupled with a global computer network facilitates rapid dissemination of not just text, but sound files and video as well. Will the ease of copying in a digital environment result in a loss of control? Or will information providers use technology to exert enhanced control over access to and use of information? In either case, how should copyright law respond? When should third-party providers of devices and services that facilitate the use of digital content be liable for copyright infringement committed by their users? We consider these issues in Chapters 5, 6, 7, and 9.
- The interplay of copyright law with contracts is taking on increased significance. On the one hand, movements that seek to use the combination of copyright and contract to force a culture of sharing, such as the open source movement and the Creative Commons movement, challenge assumptions about how best to promote progress. On the other hand, increased use of clickwrap and shrinkwrap agreements to specify permitted and prohibited acts threatens to redefine the scope of rights that copyright owners possess. Should copyright law interfere with the enforceability of these contracts? If so, on what grounds and in what ways? We consider these issues in Chapters 3 and 8.
- Copyright protects original expression, while patents protect new, useful, and nonobvious inventions. Neither regime protects facts, ideas, or abstract functional principles, all of which are considered part of the public domain and essential building blocks for future innovation. The development of new sorts of economically valuable information products poses novel problems. What sort of protection, if any, is appropriate for computer software, or for a useful compilation of factual data? Copyright protects expression, but the valuable aspects of software or a database tend to be its functional features; patents protect functionality, but most software and nearly all databases have difficulty meeting the rigorous nonobviousness standard necessary to qualify for a patent. Should Congress create new kinds of intellectual property rights in these information goods? We consider these issues in Chapters 4 and 10.
- The global nature of the Internet, and globalization more generally, present particular enforcement and regulatory challenges for domestic copyright law. As consistent, predictable copyright protection has become more important to the content industries, nation-states and international institutions have responded in a number of ways. For better or worse, copyright policy is increasingly made at the global level by trade negotiators who draft treaties on a wide range of subjects. The interplay between domestic and international law and lawmaking processes is addressed throughout the book, beginning with the next section of this chapter.

C. THE ROLE OF INTERNATIONAL TREATIES AND INSTITUTIONS

Many of the changes to the Copyright Act described in Section B.4, *supra*, are the product of domestic implementation of international treaties. Indeed, Congress has made some of the most significant changes to U.S. copyright law in the last two decades in response to international treaties or legislative developments in other countries. The U.S. has also initiated several multilateral and regional treaties, all intended to raise international standards for the protection of copyright.

There is considerable irony in the U.S. role at the forefront of advocating enhanced global copyright protection and enforcement. As the following materials reveal, the U.S. has evolved from a copyright isolationist to a leader in setting and enforcing global copyright policy. Below, we trace that evolution as well as that of the international system of copyright law generally.

1. From Pirate to Holdout to Enforcer: International Copyright and the United States

Following passage of the Statute of Anne in England in 1710, other European countries began to enact legislation to protect the rights of authors in their creative works. The internecine European wars that accompanied empire building and the resulting conquests of other nation-states helped expose new countries to the emerging system of copyright protection. In more peaceful times, trade relations with countries that lacked domestic copyright protection typically led to recognition of such protection on a *reciprocal* basis: Two countries would agree that each would protect copyrighted works of the others' citizens, but each would remain free to provide that protection under its own substantive law. Finally, countries such as England, Germany, and France, that had significant colonial territories in Africa, Asia, and the Americas, typically extended domestic copyright legislation to these overseas territories. These developments signaled the beginnings of an international system of copyright protection.

To say that some form of copyright protection existed in many parts of the world from the eighteenth century onward, however, is not to say that authors could obtain protection for their works in any part of the world. Instead, the copyright laws of most countries explicitly excluded foreign authors and their works from protection.

The U.S. was no different. For more than a century after independence, foreign works could be freely copied and sold. This rule allowed U.S. publishers to pirate popular works of foreign authors such as Charles Dickens, Sir Walter Scott, William Makepeace Thackeray, and William Wordsworth. Indeed, much of Dickens's tour of the U.S. in the 1840s was devoted to arguing for protection for his works.

Discrimination against the works of foreign, non–U.S.-domiciled authors continued to be the rule until 1891. The Copyright Act of 1891 extended copyright protection to works of non–U.S.-domiciled, foreign authors if their home countries accorded comparable protection to works of U.S. authors. With this change, the U.S. took an important first step toward the national treatment principle that is the cornerstone of modern trade agreements, including international copyright agreements. Under a national treatment principle, member countries cannot discriminate against foreign authors and instead must accord the same protection to foreign authors as to their own authors. The 1891 Act also extended protection to works of foreign authors if the U.S. joined an international agreement that required reciprocal protection of the works of citizens of other countries that were parties to the agreement.

The 1891 Act, however, conditioned protection for foreign authors (and for U.S. authors) on *production* of their works within the U.S. The statute required that deposited copies "be printed from type set within the United States, or from plates made therefrom, or from negatives, or drawings on stone made within the limits of the United States, or from transfers made therefrom," and prohibited importation of copies made outside the country for the duration of the copyright. Act of Mar. 3, 1891, §3, 26 Stat. 1106, 1107 (1891). This provision became known as the "Manufacturing Clause." Although amendments over the years narrowed its scope, it remained in force until July 1, 1986.

The 1909 and 1976 revisions to the copyright law retained the then-existing three categories of foreign authors whose works the copyright law would protect: (1) foreign authors domiciled in the U.S. at the time of first publication of their works in the U.S., (2) foreign authors whose countries afforded comparable protection to the works of U.S. authors, and (3) foreign authors from countries that were parties to an international agreement ratified by the U.S. The 1976 Copyright Act also extended copyright protection to unpublished works regardless of the author's nationality or domicile.

Although the 1891, 1909, and 1976 Acts provided for reciprocal copyright protection under an international agreement, for most of the twentieth century the U.S. declined to join the preeminent international copyright treaty, the Berne Convention for the Protection of Literary and Artistic Works (1886), for reasons discussed below. Instead, in 1954, the U.S. joined the Universal Copyright Convention (UCC), a less rigorous agreement developed by the United Nations Educational, Scientific, and Cultural Organization (UNESCO) whose members primarily included developing countries. Consistent with the provisions of the 1909 Act, the U.S. then extended protection to works of citizens of UCC member states.

As international trade flows became more and more important to the U.S. economy, and particularly as intellectual goods became major export commodities, Congress gradually grew more interested in international enforcement of intellectual property rights. First, it entered into several bilateral trade agreements that included provisions for protection of intellectual property rights. In the 1980s, reliance on this strategy increased dramatically. The Omnibus Trade and Competitiveness Act of 1988 amended §301 of the Trade Act of 1974 to authorize the U.S. Trade Representative (USTR) to identify nations that have violated a trade agreement with the U.S. or whose policies unjustifiably burden or restrict U.S. commerce. A derivation of this provision, known as "special 301," authorizes the USTR to target violations of U.S. intellectual property rights in foreign countries by publicly listing such countries and using the listings to press for strengthened intellectual property protection and enforcement. Finally, the U.S. embarked on a process to accede to the Berne Convention.

2. The Berne Convention

Before the mid-nineteenth century, bilateral trade agreements were the most common and effective method for a country to ensure protection of its citizens' creative works outside its own boundaries. The proliferation of such agreements, and the uncertainty and confusion they generated, ultimately led European states to form a multilateral agreement regarding copyright protection. In 1886, ten countries signed this agreement, known as the Berne Convention.[1]

---

1. These countries were Belgium, France, Germany, Haiti, Italy, Liberia, Spain, Switzerland, the United Kingdom, and Tunisia. The U.S. and Japan attended the final drafting conference as observers only.

The signatory countries included the greatest colonial powers, so the Berne Convention encompassed a significant part of the world.

For a number of reasons, however, the U.S. did not join the Berne Convention for over 100 years. First, the Berne Convention imposed certain minimum substantive standards that its members had to meet. While both the UCC and Berne Convention called for national treatment, the U.S. did not wish to be obligated to provide all foreign works with a uniformly high substantive standard of protection on a national treatment basis. Second, the Berne Convention provided that the enjoyment of copyright "shall not be subject to any formality," Berne Conv., art. 5(2), and the U.S. did not want to abandon the formalities, such as publication with notice of copyright, that it had chosen to impose on authors who wished to gain federal copyright protection. Third, the Berne Convention required protection for some works, such as architectural works, that were not currently protected under U.S. copyright law. Finally, it required protection for non-economic or "moral" rights of authors, which the U.S., with its emphasis on economic rights, had never explicitly protected in its copyright law.

In the 1980s, as international protection of intellectual property rights became a high priority for the U.S., and as the U.S. copyright industries agitated for U.S. adherence to the Berne Convention, Congress reconsidered its resistance to ratification. The legislative history of the Berne Convention Implementation Act (BCIA), which took effect on March 1, 1989, observed: "Adherence to the [Berne] Convention . . . will ensure a strong, credible U.S. presence in the global marketplace" and "is also necessary to ensure effective U.S. participation in the formulation and management of international copyright policy." S. Rep. No. 100-352, 100th Cong., 2d Sess. 2-5 (1988), *reprinted in* 1988 U.S.C.C.A.N. 3706, 3707-10.

However, Congress also sought to respond to the concerns of groups that opposed ratification of the Berne Convention. Some copyright industry groups feared that ratification would require recognizing distinctly European copyright concepts, including moral rights, that they viewed as inimical to the purposes of U.S. copyright law. Furthermore, library associations and other "public interest" groups expressed concern about the impact of higher levels of protection on public access to copyrighted works. Specifically, these organizations pointed to the absence of a limitation similar to the U.S. fair use doctrine in the Berne Convention.

These objections ultimately did not derail the accession process, but they did affect how the U.S. achieved ratification. Generally, a treaty may or may not be *self-executing*. A self-executing treaty is one whose terms have the force of law domestically once the U.S. agrees to be bound by it. A non-self-executing treaty is one for which Congress must enact implementing legislation. A U.S. litigant, therefore, can only sue to enforce rights arising from such a treaty that have been incorporated into federal law through the implementing legislation passed by Congress.

Most treaties in the U.S. are non-self-executing, and the Berne Convention was no exception: merely signing the treaty would not effect any change in U.S. law. Rather, Congress had to enact implementing legislation to bring the U.S. into compliance with the new treaty obligations. In the Berne Convention Implementation Act of 1988, Congress adopted a "minimalist" approach to ratification, making only those changes to copyright law that were absolutely necessary to qualify it for membership. This minimalist approach has left some international copyright scholars questioning whether the U.S. is in full compliance with the Berne Convention in key areas such as formalities, protection of moral rights, and the fair use doctrine. We consider these questions in Chapters 3, 5, and 7.

Once the U.S. ratified the Berne Convention, it turned its attention to one of its principal motivations for joining: proposing an intellectual property agreement to be adopted within the context of the multilateral trade system of the General Agreement on Tariffs and Trade (GATT).

3. The TRIPS Agreement

The Agreement on Trade Related Aspects of Intellectual Property Rights (TRIPS Agreement, or TRIPS) is one of a number of Agreements that comprise the Final Act of the 1994 Uruguay Round of multilateral trade negotiations under the auspices of the GATT. This celebrated round of negotiations, which involved the majority of the trading nations of the world, commenced in 1986 and concluded in 1994. The Final Act created a new institution, the World Trade Organization (WTO), to provide a forum for ongoing trade negotiations and to oversee the administration and implementation of the various agreements that constitute the Final Act. As of October 2009, 153 countries are members of the WTO.

The TRIPS Agreement is premised on the position, advanced primarily by the U.S., that intellectual property protection is a trade issue. According to this view, in a global economy increasingly characterized by trade in information goods, failure to protect intellectual property rights distorts the flow of trade and undermines the welfare benefits flowing from the GATT system. Thus, the TRIPS Agreement's preamble states that an overall concern is "to reduce distortions and impediments to international trade . . . taking into account the need to promote effective and adequate protection of intellectual property rights, and to ensure that measures and procedures to enforce intellectual property rights do not themselves become barriers to legitimate trade. . . ."

To this end, the TRIPS Agreement establishes minimum universal substantive standards for the protection of intellectual property. It covers all of the major categories of intellectual property — copyrights, patents, and trademarks — as well as ancillary categories such as geographical indications, industrial designs, layout designs of integrated circuits, and trade secrets. Member countries may choose to enact protection that exceeds the level specified by the TRIPS Agreement's provisions and may also adopt enforcement measures more stringent than TRIPS requires.

Part I of the TRIPS Agreement sets forth the basic rules that apply to all categories of intellectual property protection. These include the classic international trade standard requiring national treatment (art. 3) and the related concept of most-favored-nation (MFN) treatment (art. 4). Like the national treatment principle, the MFN principle is one of nondiscrimination; it requires each member nation to accord other members the same level of treatment that it currently extends to the nation with which it has the best relations (in other words, its most favored nation). Finally, and importantly, Article 8 of the TRIPS Agreement sets forth the agreement's goal:

> The protection and enforcement of intellectual property rights should contribute to the promotion of technological innovation and to the transfer and dissemination of technology, to the mutual advantage of producers and users of technological knowledge and in a manner conducive to social and economic welfare, and to a balance of rights and obligations.

Part II of the TRIPS Agreement outlines the substantive requirements for copyright protection. Article 9 requires members to comply with the substantive provisions of the Berne Convention, thus explicitly incorporating the Berne Convention standards into the TRIPS Agreement. Article 9, however, does not require recognition of moral rights; consequently, countries that have not ratified the Berne Convention can join the WTO without having to provide protection for moral rights. In addition, the TRIPS Agreement mandates protection for some subject matter not covered by the Berne Convention, such as computer programs and compilations of data, and requires recognition of some additional rights not mentioned in the Berne Convention, such as rental rights for cinematographic works. Article 12 sets the minimum duration of copyright protection at life of the author plus 50 years. Finally, Article 13 of the TRIPS Agreement provides that members should, in their domestic laws, confine limitations or exceptions to owners' rights to "certain special cases which do not conflict with a normal exploitation of the work and do not unreasonably prejudice the legitimate interests of the right holder." As you will see, this latter provision is proving particularly important in defining the scope of copyright law in the post-WTO era.

The TRIPS Agreement represents an important departure from the Berne Convention framework, however, in its standards for both domestic enforcement of the substantive requirements within member countries and international enforcement of treaty obligations among member countries. The Berne Convention prescribes neither type of standard. Indeed, members often criticized the Berne Convention's failure to provide an enforcement mechanism. The U.S. and other nations that pushed for adoption of a trade agreement on intellectual property rights argued that both types of enforcement are necessary for effective protection on a global basis. Under the TRIPS Agreement, member nations are obligated to provide procedures for copyright owners to secure enforcement of both the rights enumerated in the Berne Convention and those added by the TRIPS Agreement within their domestic legal systems. Disputes between member nations about compliance with the TRIPS standards are subject to the dispute settlement system of the WTO, which we discuss in Section C.4.a *infra*.

NOTES AND QUESTIONS

1. Why do you think Congress was reluctant to extend reciprocal copyright protection to works by European nationals for so long?

2. What was the purpose of the Manufacturing Clause? Did it protect authors?

3. Like the Berne Convention, the TRIPS Agreement also is not self-executing: its provisions are enforceable only through implementing legislation that makes the Agreement a part of domestic law. Thus, while the TRIPS Agreement is a source of U.S. copyright law, it is only an indirect source of rights for individual copyright owners. The only direct (and actionable) source of rights is the implementing legislation, which amended the Copyright Act.

4. Note the practical effect of the international agreements. Works by U.S. authors that are protected by copyright in the U.S. are protected by copyright in Berne Convention and TRIPS countries without the authors having to take any additional steps. Whether a work by a U.S. author would be protected in a non-Berne, non-TRIPS country would depend on whether the U.S. has an agreement with that country. If not, the U.S. author would have to comply with the individual country's copyright law. Foreign authors from Berne or TRIPS countries, meanwhile, are protected under U.S. law without registering their copyrights here. For reasons we discuss in Chapters 3 and 11, however, such authors should consider registering in the U.S. even though they are not required to do so to obtain protection.

4. Copyright Lawmaking and Enforcement Under the Berne Convention and the TRIPS Agreement

As described above, the Berne Convention offered important substantive protections, but these protections were not effective because the Convention lacked a mechanism to ensure the compliance of member countries. The TRIPS Agreement supplies such a mechanism, and the dispute settlement system of the WTO has influenced the relationship between international and domestic copyright law in important ways. In addition, the advent of the Internet spurred a new round of treaty-making and domestic implementing legislation outside of the WTO framework.

a. The World Trade Organization

Established in 1995, the WTO is the international organization responsible for administering the multilateral trade agreements concluded in the Uruguay Round, including the TRIPS Agreement. The functions of the WTO also include providing a forum for negotiations for member states and administering the Dispute Settlement Understanding (DSU). Commentators regard the DSU as one of the most important accomplishments of the Uruguay Round, particularly because of its implications for intellectual property enforcement. In essence, all WTO member countries have agreed to limit their sovereignty by submitting to a binding international process for the settlement of disputes, including those relating to TRIPS obligations. As you have learned in other law school courses, the power to settle disputes is rooted in the authority to interpret rules. The WTO, through its dispute settlement process, is responsible for interpreting the TRIPS Agreement, and thus, as a practical matter, for setting the level of international protection for copyright owners.

The DSU establishes a Dispute Settlement Body (DSB) charged with administering the rules and procedures of the DSU. The DSB establishes panels to hear disputes, adopts the reports of the panels, and oversees the disputing parties' implementation of panel rulings and recommendations. In many ways, the DSU hearing process resembles a typical lawsuit in an American court, except that the parties are countries. Parties have strict time limits for all submissions, and ex parte communication with the panel members is forbidden. Citizens of countries that are parties to a dispute are disqualified from serving on the panel. Panels may seek information, technical advice, and expert counsel on aspects of the dispute. In addition, the DSU provides for third-party submissions from countries that have interests in a disputed issue. Finally, and importantly, there is appellate review. Both panels and the DSU's appellate body are charged with resolving disputes promptly.

The DSB will adopt the panel's report or, if applicable, the appellate body's report unless it decides by consensus not to do so. Afterward, the member nation whose laws or measures were ruled inconsistent with the TRIPS Agreement must inform the DSB of its intentions. If a member asserts that it cannot comply immediately with the ruling, the member is required to state a reasonable time period in which it will do so. Failure to comply with the DSB's ruling may lead to the suspension of concessions or other trade privileges by the aggrieved member until the offending country corrects the problem or the parties reach a mutually satisfactory agreement. A panel may also award the aggrieved party compensation for the value of lost benefits under the TRIPS Agreement.

Several copyright-related disputes have been submitted to the WTO to date, including two that involve the U.S. as the defendant. The first, which involves public performance rights in musical compositions, is discussed in Chapter 5.G *infra*. In the second, the EU filed a complaint against the U.S., alleging that §301 of the 1974 Trade Act and the "special 301" proceedings it authorizes are inconsistent with the WTO dispute settlement process. The WTO panel ruled in favor of the U.S. but noted that its decision was based "in full or in part" on undertakings by the U.S. executive branch that the U.S. would not use §301 to violate international obligations. The panel noted that "should [these undertakings] be repudiated or in any other way removed by the U.S. Administration or another branch of the

U.S. Government, the findings of conformity contained in these conclusions would no longer be warranted." Panel Report, *United States — Section 301-310 of the Trade Act of 1974*, WT/DS152/R, at 351 (Dec. 22, 1999).

On January 26, 2009, a WTO Panel issued a report on a third copyright-related TRIPS dispute. In Panel Report, *China — Measures Affecting the Protection and Enforcement of Intellectual Property Rights*, WT/DS362/R (Jan. 26, 2009), the U.S. filed a complaint at the WTO against China, alleging a number of ways in which China's laws fall short of the protection and enforcement provisions required by the TRIPS Agreement. Pertinent aspects of this case are discussed in Chapters 3.A, 6.E, and 11.G *infra*.

b. The World Intellectual Property Organization (WIPO) and the 1996 WIPO Treaties

The World Intellectual Property Organization (WIPO) is the oldest and most well known of the international intellectual property institutions. WIPO's origins date back to 1883, when European nations adopted the major international patent treaty, the Paris Convention for the Protection of Industrial Property. Both the Paris Convention and the Berne Convention provided for international secretariats. These secretariats were placed under the supervision of the Swiss government and located in Berne, Switzerland. In 1893, the two organizations were integrated; over the next several years, the new organization went through several name changes. The Convention Establishing the World Intellectual Property Organization was signed in 1967 and entered into force in 1970. Today, WIPO is located in Geneva, Switzerland, and is one of the specialized agencies of the United Nations. It operates autonomously, with its own membership, budget, staff, programs, and governing bodies.

In the 1980s, WIPO attempted unsuccessfully to sponsor new treaties on patents, semiconductors, and trademarks. In 1996, however, it did succeed in sponsoring two important treaties designed to address copyright protection and related rights in the digital age. These are the WIPO Copyright Treaty, which we discuss in Chapter 9, and the WIPO Performances and Phonograms Treaty. The U.S. ratified both treaties and passed implementing legislation in 1998. A third proposed treaty addressing rights in databases failed to secure adoption. We consider the question of legal protection for databases in Chapters 4 and 10.

An obvious question is how a post-1994 WIPO treaty fits within the framework of the TRIPS Agreement. As we discussed earlier, the TRIPS Agreement explicitly incorporates the Berne Convention's standards (except those relating to moral rights). Under Article 20 of the Berne Convention, member countries may enter into "special agreements among themselves, in so far as such agreements grant to authors more extensive rights than those granted by the Convention." Thus, TRIPS members may agree to other intellectual property treaties that implement higher standards of protection than what TRIPS requires. Additionally, countries that are not members of TRIPS may sign WIPO treaties on particular topics. WIPO has become a forum for ongoing discussion of the substantive policy questions concerning the optimal scope of intellectual property rights. WIPO regularly convenes expert panels on a range of intellectual property–related topics within the context of its mandate "to promote the protection of intellectual property throughout the world through cooperation among States and, where appropriate, in collaboration with any other international organization." Convention Establishing the World Intellectual Property Organization, art. 3.

NOTES AND QUESTIONS

1. A copyright owner may not directly invoke the WTO's DSU to challenge a country's domestic implementing legislation as inconsistent with TRIPS, but must pursue such a grievance through its own country's representatives to the WTO. Another alternative for a copyright owner is to sue a private party in the other country's courts under its TRIPS-implementing legislation and raise the issue of TRIPS compliance during the litigation. As we shall see, however, such arguments have rarely been successful in U.S. courts.

2. Should other countries be in a position to influence the content of U.S. copyright law? Why, or why not? Some scholars, concerned about the use of international agreements and enforcement proceedings to expand the scope of copyright protection, have suggested that the Constitution may limit Congress's ability to implement continued expansion. Certainly, both history and theory suggest that the Framers, who adopted a utilitarian rationale for intellectual property rights and expressed distaste for perpetual protection, would wish to see some limits on copyright. It is difficult, however, to determine exactly what those limits should be. As a political matter, do you think that Congress is likely to recognize constitutional limits on its authority to implement international copyright treaties? Are courts? We return to these questions in Chapters 3, 5, 7, and 10.

The negotiations that led to the Final Act of the Uruguay Round often pitted developing countries against developed ones. The TRIPS Agreement, in particular, posed difficulties for developing countries. Like the U.S. in its first century of independence, developing countries today are interested in inexpensive access to copyrighted works; developed countries generally are not. States that wished to accede to the Final Act of the Uruguay Round by joining the WTO, however, had to accept all of the Agreements included therein. This "single package" rule corrected what was perceived as a major deficiency in the previous GATT system whereby member states could join the system à la carte, choosing which rules they would accept and which ones they would reject. Ultimately, developing countries accepted the TRIPS Agreement in exchange for liberalized trade rules regarding agricultural goods and textiles. Developing countries continue to argue, however, that the high standards in the TRIPS Agreement do not promote their domestic welfare and raise the costs of access to protected works necessary for economic development.

Ruth Gana Okediji, Copyright and Public Welfare in Global Perspective
7 Ind. J. Global Legal Stud. 117, 147-50 (1999)

The divergent philosophies of Europe and the United States in the protection of intellectual property did not weaken initial attempts to extend the system beyond their national boundaries. Instead, these philosophies successfully legitimized the argument that the international protection of intellectual property is an indispensable requirement of international, and ultimately national, economic well-being. . . . To this end, the utilitarian justification of intellectual property had its earliest triumph over competing philosophical perspectives. International institutions, influenced by success stories of technological innovation in England and the United States, adopted the philosophy that national protection of intellectual property was key to *every* country's industrialization, growth, and development. . . .

Notwithstanding intellectual property laws, developing countries remained marginalized in the global economy. . . . Overall, the experiment with intellectual property laws in developing countries was broadly regarded as a failure in terms of accomplishing economic development goals. The persistent economic malaise in many developing countries, despite elaborate technology transfer regimes, gradually diminished the legitimacy of national intellectual property laws and, ultimately, of the international system. Dominant issues of concern included the prohibitive costs of licenses for copyrighted works, the strict terms of use imposed by licensing agreements over patented products, and the disparate levels of bargaining power between users of protected goods and intellectual property owners. Countries at the margins experienced the social and economic costs associated with intellectual property rights, but none of the perceived systemic benefits — in particular, the stimulation of local inventiveness.

NOTES AND QUESTIONS

1. Are copyright systems transplantable? Developing countries were given a five-year grace period to implement the TRIPS requirements. TRIPS, art. 65(1)(2). Certain "least-developed countries" were given a grace period of ten years. *Id.* art. 66(1). In November 2005, WTO member countries agreed to extend the deadline for compliance for least-developed countries until 2013. The original deadline was January 1, 2006. Do you think that developing countries made a good bargain?

2. Since the conclusion of the TRIPS Agreement, the U.S. and the European Union have embarked on an aggressive program of bilateral and regional trade agreements with developing and least-developed countries. These bilateral and regional free trade agreements characteristically feature provisions requiring the developing countries to implement substantive and procedural standards that are more stringent than those imposed by the TRIPS Agreement. These so-called "TRIPS-plus" provisions also include requirements that the countries ratify the WIPO Copyright Treaty (WCT) and WIPO Performances and Phonograms Treaty (WPPT), both concluded within a few years of the TRIPS Agreement. Why do you think the U.S. has pursued these bilateral/regional agreements? Can you think of any benefits of incorporating intellectual property protection in regional agreements that would not be available through the TRIPS Agreement? What factors might contribute to the willingness of developing and least-developed countries to agree to TRIPS-plus provisions?

3. Would you expect a bilateral trade agreement requiring copyright protection for U.S. works to have the effect of encouraging an optimal level of intellectual property protection in Zimbabwe? Brazil? China?

4. In 2007, the WIPO General Assembly adopted the "Development Agenda" in response to concerns expressed by developing countries about, among other things, the need for a more balanced approach to WIPO's fundamental mission of promoting the harmonization of international intellectual property rights. It consists of 45 recommendations divided into 6 clusters, many directed at re-orienting WIPO's operational philosophy and its technical assistance programs. *See* http://www.wipo.int/ip-development/en/agenda/recommendations.html.

The Development Agenda is viewed by scholars, commentators, and many international consumer advocacy groups as an important response to longstanding complaints by developing and least-developed countries about WIPO's singular dedication to achieving stronger levels of protection globally without consideration of the public policy objectives that inform the regulation of intellectual property rights in most industrially advanced countries. Although the Development Agenda has been widely regarded as a victory for the developing and least-developed countries, it remains unclear how its adoption will transform the substantive obligations of prevailing intellectual property treaties such as the TRIPS Agreement and bilateral/regional agreements that embody high standards for global intellectual property protection. There are also questions about the extent to which WIPO's core mission to strengthen and promote intellectual property protection can be realistically altered to accommodate norms that promote access to, and dissemination of, knowledge-based goods.

5. In addition to adopting the WIPO Development Agenda, WIPO member states also established a Committee on Development and Intellectual Property (CDIP). The CDIP is charged with the task of developing a framework for implementation of the recommendations. Do you think developing and least-developed countries will be the sole beneficiaries? For example, under the Cluster B recommendations (dealing with norm-setting, flexibilities, public policy, and the public domain), WIPO is required to "consider the preservation of the public domain . . . and deepen [its] analysis of the implications and benefits of a rich and accessible public domain" in carrying out its norm-setting activities. Is the preservation of a strong public domain an issue of significance solely to developing and least-developed countries?

THE SUBJECT MATTER
OF COPYRIGHT LAW

2

Authors, Writings, and Progress

Chapter 1 introduced some of the reasons that society might find it desirable to implement a legal rule that grants creators certain exclusive rights in their works. Translating this theory into practice, however, raises a number of important questions: What works should be protected? Who should be entitled to claim copyright in those works? What should the scope of the exclusive rights be? This chapter addresses the first two of these questions, discussing the basic requirements that a work must meet to qualify for copyright protection and the rules that determine who is eligible to claim authorship.

A. THE ELEMENTS OF COPYRIGHTABLE SUBJECT MATTER

Chapter 1 revealed that over time Congress has changed its answer to the question of what works should be protected by copyright. Its starting point is, of course, the Constitution:

> The Congress shall have Power . . . To promote the Progress of Science and the useful Arts, by securing for limited Times to Authors and Inventors the exclusive Right to their respective Writings and Discoveries.

U.S. Const., Art. I, §8, cl. 8. Does this clause appear to place any limits on congressional power to grant exclusive rights in creative works? As we will see, Congress has broad (although not infinite) leeway in defining what the terms in the clause mean. Thus, the congressional decision about which "writings" should be eligible for copyright protection is primarily one of policy.

From an economic perspective, the grant of exclusive rights entails a variety of costs. First, any system of rights entails costs of administration and enforcement. In the particular case of copyright, there also will be "deadweight losses" that result because copyright enables creators to price above the marginal cost of their works.[1] Indeed, for the rights to achieve the goal of correcting the public goods problem discussed in Chapter 1, they must allow such pricing. However, the higher price means that some consumers will not be able to purchase copies of the protected work. This limits dissemination of the knowledge contained within the work — knowledge that might provide the basis for further progress. This is a second cost of a copyright system, albeit one that is hard to quantify.

Simple economic theory would hold that a system of exclusive rights should not incur these costs unless the benefits it produces exceed them. Granting exclusive rights in a work that would have been created in their absence imposes a loss on society; granting stronger exclusive rights than necessary to induce creation of a work also imposes a loss. Further, different types of works and different industries have widely varying incentive structures. Is the incentive required to encourage the efficient level of software production the same as that required for novels? Should policymakers conduct a cost-benefit analysis for each individual work, for each type of work, or in the aggregate?

In reality, of course, the decision to grant exclusive rights in particular works does not depend entirely on cost-benefit analysis. Other, non-economic considerations also will militate for (or against) grants of copyright protection. Is the work of a sort that appears to require creativity to produce? Does copyright protection for that work therefore seem theoretically justified? Would extending protection to a particular kind of subject matter jeopardize Locke's proviso (*see* Question 3, pp. 14-15, *supra*) that "enough, and as good" remain for others?

Finally, once the initial cost-benefit decision to create a copyright system has been made, decisions about which works should benefit may simply reflect considerations of equity and consistency. Once some works are designated to receive copyright protection, it may seem only fair that other, similar works also receive it. Are grants of copyright protection for these reasons appropriate?

Section 102 of the Copyright Act represents the congressional judgment as to what works merit the grant of the exclusive copyright rights and provides, in part:

§102. Subject matter of copyright: In general

(a) Copyright protection subsists, in accordance with this title, in original works of authorship fixed in any tangible medium of expression, now known or later developed, from which they can be perceived, reproduced or otherwise communicated, either directly or with the aid of a machine or device. . . .

(b) In no case does copyright protection for an original work of authorship extend to any idea, procedure, process, system, method of operation, concept, principle, or discovery, regardless of the form in which it is described, explained, illustrated, or embodied in such work.

---

1. Marginal cost is the additional cost to produce one more unit of output. Standard economic theory holds that in a competitive market, sellers will price their products at marginal cost. Deadweight loss is the loss associated with noncompetitive pricing (i.e., non-marginal cost pricing) or other factors that move the market away from the competitive output.

In the case of copyrighted works, the marginal cost is the expense to produce and distribute one more unit of the medium embodying the work. Pricing at marginal cost, however, does not permit the creator of the work to recoup the fixed costs incurred in creating the work initially. Copyright gives the rightholder some market power to enable pricing above marginal cost. Copyright thus produces some amount of deadweight loss. Note that the grant of copyright protection will not necessarily result in the rightholder's obtaining an economic monopoly, because market substitutes for the work may exist. The deadweight losses associated with above marginal cost pricing will increase as the rightholder's market power increases.

Thus, §102 establishes three requirements for copyrightable subject matter. First, the work for which protection is sought must be "fixed" in a tangible medium of expression. Second, it must be an "original work of authorship." The third and final requirement is a negative one: Copyright protection for a work that is both fixed and original will not extend to elements of the work that constitute ideas, procedures, and the like. In other words, copyright protection does not attach to every element of a work.

We begin with fixation.

1. Fixation

Section 102(a) states that a work must be "fixed in a tangible medium of expression" to be protected by copyright. Many, if not most, countries' laws do not contain a comparable provision. The Berne Convention leaves the decision about whether to require fixation to each of the member countries (*see* Berne Conv., art. 2(2)), and neither the WIPO Copyright Treaty nor the TRIPS Agreement mentions fixation. As you read the following, consider why the U.S. requires fixation as a condition of copyright protection. What is the purpose of this requirement? Is there any constitutional basis for it? Assuming that a fixation requirement is desirable (or constitutionally required), how should "fixed" be defined?

a. A Functional Approach

We start with the first sentence of the definition of "fixed" in §101: "A work is 'fixed' in a tangible medium of expression when its embodiment in a copy or phonorecord, by or under the authority of the author, is sufficiently permanent or stable to permit it to be perceived, reproduced, or otherwise communicated for a period of more than transitory duration." This sentence is framed in purely functional terms. The particular *means* used to fix the work are irrelevant; one must focus, instead, on the *effect* produced. How did Congress arrive at this definition, and what does it mean?

According to the legislative history, Congress chose this approach because of cases such as *White-Smith Publishing Co. v. Apollo Co.*, 209 U.S. 1 (1908). There, the Supreme Court held that a player-piano roll was not a "copy" of the musical composition it represented, and that owners of the copyrights in musical compositions therefore could not prohibit (or require payment for) this type of reproduction. The Court interpreted the existing copyright statute to require that a "copy" of a musical composition be "a written or printed record of it in intelligible notation"—i.e., intelligible to a human reader, not simply to a machine such as a player piano. *Id.* at 17. The Court acknowledged the free-riding problem that its ruling might create: "It may be true that the use of these perforated [player piano] rolls, in the absence of statutory protection, enables the manufacturers thereof to enjoy the use of musical compositions for which they pay no value. But such considerations properly address themselves to the legislative, and not to the judicial, branch of the government." *Id.* at 18.

In the 1909 Act, Congress responded to *White-Smith* by creating a special statutory provision that subjected so-called 'mechanical' reproductions of musical works to a compulsory license. Under this provision, the copyright owner could not prohibit someone from preparing a mechanical reproduction so long as that person paid the copyright owner a small, statutorily determined fee. This solution, however, left intact the existing, medium-specific approach to determining when a "copy" had been created. As the technologies of reproduction began to evolve more and more rapidly (see Chapter 1.B.3, *supra*), this approach began to seem increasingly inadequate.

In the 1976 Act, Congress chose a more global approach to the problem of identifying when a copy of a work could be said to exist: the concept of fixation in a tangible medium of expression. Because the 1976 Act also extended federal copyright protection to unpublished works (previously, most works had to be published to be eligible for federal copyright protection), fixation in a tangible medium of expression also became the standard for determining when the work itself could be said to exist for purposes of federal copyright law. As Congress explained, it drafted the new statutory definition to provide flexibility as new technologies developed:

> [The] broad language is intended to avoid the artificial and largely unjustifiable distinctions, derived from such cases as *White-Smith* . . . under which statutory copyrightability has been made to depend upon the form or medium in which the work is fixed. Under the bill it makes no difference what the form, manner, or medium of fixation may be — whether it is in words, numbers, notes, sounds, pictures, or any other graphic or symbolic indicia, whether embodied in a physical object in written, printed, photographic, sculptural, punched, magnetic, or any other stable form, and whether it is capable of perception directly or by means of any machine or device "now known or later developed."

H.R. Rep. No. 94-1476, 94th Cong., 2d Sess. 52 (1976), *reprinted in* 1976 U.S.C.C.A.N. 5659, 5665. Note, however, that in §101, Congress preserved the distinction between media embodying sounds and other fixed embodiments of copyrighted works. Only the latter are technically "copies"; the former are called "phonorecords."

The broad, technology-neutral language of the first sentence of the statutory definition of "fixed" has produced unforeseen difficulties, however. The meaning of this provision seemed obvious enough in the case of the phonorecords with which members of Congress in 1976 were familiar — clearly, under the new statutory language, mechanical reproductions of a preexisting musical composition qualify as fixed. As a test for initial creation of a copyrightable work, the meaning of the provision was also fairly obvious — e.g., a traditional literary work such as a novel exists, for purposes of federal copyright protection, from the moment that the author causes it to be fixed on paper or in a word processing file. But how should courts interpret the statutory language in the case of digital images that seem to have an ephemeral existence?

Williams Electronics, Inc. v. Artic International, Inc.
685 F.2d 870 (3d Cir. 1982)

SLOVITER, J.: . . . Plaintiff-appellee Williams Electronics, Inc. manufactures and sells coin-operated electronic video games. A video game machine consists of a cabinet containing, *inter alia*, a cathode ray tube (CRT), a sound system, hand controls for the player, and electronic circuit boards. The electronic circuitry includes a microprocessor and memory devices, called ROMs (*Read Only Memory*), which are tiny computer "chips" containing thousands of data locations which store the instructions and data of a computer program. The microprocessor executes the computer program to cause the game to operate. . . .

In approximately October 1979 Williams began to design a new video game, ultimately called DEFENDER, which incorporated various original and unique audiovisual features. The DEFENDER game was introduced to the industry at a trade show in 1980 and has since achieved great success in the marketplace. One of the attractions of video games contributing to their phenomenal popularity is apparently ~~their use of unrealistic fantasy crea-~~ ~~tures,~~ a fad also observed in the popularity of certain current films. In the DEFENDER game, there are symbols of a spaceship and aliens who do battle with symbols of human figures. The player operates the flight of and weapons on the spaceship, and has the mission of pre- venting invading aliens from kidnapping the humans from a ground plane.

Williams obtained ~~three copyright registrations relating to its DEFENDER~~ game: one covering the computer program . . . the second covering the ~~audiovisual effects~~ displayed dur- ing the game's "attract mode"[2] . . . and the third covering the ~~audiovisual effects~~ displayed during the game's "play mode"[3] . . .

Defendant-appellant Artic International, Inc. is a seller of electronic components for video games in competition with Williams. The district court made the following relevant findings which are not disputed on this appeal. Artic has sold circuit boards, manufactured by others, which contain electronic circuits including a microprocessor and memory devices (ROMs). These ~~memory devices incorporate a computer program which is virtually identical to Williams'~~ ~~program for its DEFENDER game.~~ The result is a circuit board "kit" which is sold by Artic to others and which, when connected to a cathode ray tube, produces audiovisual effects and a game almost identical to the Williams DEFENDER game including both the attract mode and the play mode. The play mode and actual play of Artic's game, entitled "DEFENSE COMMAND," is virtually identical to that of the Williams game, i.e., the characters displayed on the cathode ray tube including the player's spaceship are identical in shape, size, color, manner of movement and interaction with other symbols. Also, the attract mode of the Artic game is substantially identical to that of Williams' game, with minor exceptions such as the absence of the Williams name and the substitution of the terms "DEFENSE" and/or "DEFENSE COMMAND" for the term "DEFENDER" in its display. App. at 204a-206a. Based on the evidence before it, the district court found that the defendant Artic had infringed the plaintiff's computer program copyright for the DEFENDER game by selling kits which contain a computer program which is a copy of plaintiff's computer program, and that the defendant had infringed both of the plaintiff's audiovisual copyrights for the DEFENDER game by selling copies of those audiovisual works. App. at 207a-209a.

In the appeal before us, defendant does not dispute the findings with respect to copying but instead challenges the conclusions of the district court with respect to copyright infringe- ment and the validity and scope of plaintiff's copyrights. . . .

With respect to the plaintiff's two audiovisual copyrights, ~~defendant contends that there~~ ~~can be no copyright protection for the DEFENDER game's attract mode and play mode~~ ~~because these works fail to meet the statutory requirement of "fixation."~~ . . . Defendant claims that the images in the plaintiff's audiovisual game are transient, and cannot be "fixed." Specifically, it contends that there is a lack of "fixation" because the video game generates or creates "new" images each time the attract mode or play mode is displayed, notwithstanding the fact that the new images are identical or substantially identical to the earlier ones.

We reject this contention. The fixation requirement is met whenever the work is "suffi- ciently permanent or stable to permit it to be . . . reproduced, or otherwise communicated" for more than a transitory period. Here the original audiovisual features of the DEFENDER game repeat themselves over and over. The identical contention was previously made by this

___

2. The "attract mode" refers to the audiovisual effects displayed before a coin is inserted into the game. It repeatedly shows the name of the game, the game symbols in typical motion and interaction patterns, and the initials of previous players who have achieved high scores.

3. The "play mode" refers to the audiovisual effects displayed during the actual play of the game, when the game symbols move and interact on the screen, and the player controls the movement of one of the symbols (e.g., a spaceship).

defendant and rejected by the court in *Midway Manufacturing Co. v. Artic International, Inc.*, *supra*, slip op. at 16-18. Moreover, the rejection of a similar contention by the Second Circuit is also applicable here. The court stated:

> The [video game's] display satisfies the statutory definition of an original "audiovisual work," and the *memory devices of the game satisfy the statutory requirement of a "copy" in which the work is "fixed."* The Act defines "copies" as "material objects . . . in which a work is fixed by any method now known or later developed, and from which the work can be perceived, reproduced, or otherwise communicated, either directly or with the aid of a machine or device" and specifies that a work is "fixed" when "its embodiment in a copy . . . is sufficiently permanent or stable to permit it to be perceived, reproduced, or otherwise communicated for a period of more than transitory duration." 17 U.S.C. App. §101 (1976). *The audiovisual work is permanently embodied in a material object, the memory devices,* from which it can be perceived with the aid of the other components of the game.

Stern Electronics, Inc. v. Kaufman, 669 F.2d at 855-56 (footnote omitted; emphasis added).

Defendant also apparently contends that the player's participation withdraws the game's audiovisual work from copyright eligibility because there is no set or fixed performance and the player becomes a co-author of what appears on the screen. Although there is player interaction with the machine during the play mode which causes the audiovisual presentation to change in some respects from one game to the next in response to the player's varying participation, there is always a repetitive sequence of a substantial portion of the sights and sounds of the game, and many aspects of the display remain constant from game to game regardless of how the player operates the controls. *See Stern Electronics, Inc. v. Kaufman,* 669 F.2d at 855-56. Furthermore, there is no player participation in the attract mode which is displayed repetitively without change. . . .

As noted above, the statutory definition of "fixed" determines both when a work is considered eligible for federal copyright protection (e.g., the first time it is committed to paper or to a ROM device) and what constitutes a "copy" of the protected work. Review the definitions of "copies" and "phonorecords" in §101 now. Both of these provisions incorporate the basic definition of fixation and rely on it to establish the point at which copies/phonorecords come into existence. As we explore in detail in Chapter 5, this process in turn helps to define who is an infringer. But, as the next case explains, digital technology operates by repeated, automatic copying of the files being used. Does this process, an artifact of the technology, constitute fixation? Is everyone who uses digital works therefore an infringer?

MAI Systems Corp. v. Peak Computer, Inc.
991 F.2d 511 (9th Cir. 1993), cert. dismissed, 510 U.S. 1033 (1994)

BRUNETTI, J.: . . . MAI Systems Corp., until recently, manufactured computers and designed software to run those computers. The company continues to service its computers and the software necessary to operate the computers. MAI software includes operating system software, which is necessary to run any other program on the computer.

Peak Computer, Inc. is a company organized in 1990 that maintains computer systems for its clients. Peak maintains MAI computers for more than one hundred clients in Southern California. This accounts for between fifty and seventy percent of Peak's business.

Peak's service of MAI computers includes routine maintenance and emergency repairs. Malfunctions often are related to the failure of circuit boards inside the computers, and it may be necessary for a Peak technician to operate the computer and its operating system software in order to service the machine.

In August, 1991, Eric Francis left his job as customer service manager at MAI and joined Peak. Three other MAI employees joined Peak a short time later. Some businesses that had been using MAI to service their computers switched to Peak after learning of Francis's move. . . .

IV.   Copyright Infringement

The district court granted summary judgment in favor of MAI on its claims of copyright infringement and issued a permanent injunction against Peak on these claims. The alleged copyright violations include: (1) Peak's running of MAI software licensed to Peak customers. . . .

A.   Peak's Running of MAI Software Licenced to Peak Customers

To prevail on a claim of copyright infringement, a plaintiff must prove ownership of a copyright and a " 'copying' of protectable expression" beyond the scope of a license. *S.O.S., Inc. v. Payday, Inc.*, 886 F.2d 1081, 1085 (9th Cir. 1989).

MAI software licenses allow MAI customers to use the software for their own internal information processing. This allowed use necessarily includes the loading of the software into the computer's random access memory ("RAM") by a MAI customer. However, MAI software licenses do not allow for the use or copying of MAI software by third parties such as Peak. Therefore, any "copying" done by Peak is "beyond the scope" of the license.

It is not disputed that MAI owns the copyright to the software at issue here, however, Peak vigorously disputes the district court's conclusion that a "copying" occurred under the Copyright Act.

The Copyright Act defines "copies" as:

material objects, other than phonorecords, in which a work is fixed by any method now known or later developed, and from which the work can be perceived, reproduced, or otherwise communicated, either directly or with the aid of a machine or device.

17 U.S.C. §101. . . .

The district court's grant of summary judgment on MAI's claims of copyright infringement reflects its conclusion that a "copying" for purposes of copyright law occurs when a computer program is transferred from a permanent storage device to a computer's RAM. This conclusion is consistent with its finding, in granting the preliminary injunction, that: "the loading of copyrighted computer software from a storage medium (hard disk, floppy disk, or read only memory) into the memory of a central processing unit ("CPU") causes a copy to be made. In the absence of ownership of the copyright or express permission by license, such acts constitute copyright infringement." We find that this conclusion is supported by the record and by the law.

Peak concedes that in maintaining its customer's computers, it uses MAI operating software "to the extent that the repair and maintenance process necessarily involves turning on the computer to make sure it is functional and thereby running the operating system." It is also uncontroverted that when the computer is turned on the operating system is loaded into the computer's RAM. As part of diagnosing a computer problem at the customer site, the Peak technician runs the computer's operating system software, allowing the technician to view the systems error log, which is part of the operating system, thereby enabling the technician to diagnose the problem.[4]

Peak argues that this loading of copyrighted software does not constitute a copyright violation because the "copy" created in RAM is not "fixed." However, by showing that Peak loads the software into the RAM and is then able to view the system error log and diagnose the problem with the computer, MAI has adequately shown that the representation created in the RAM is "sufficiently permanent or stable to permit it to be perceived, reproduced, or otherwise communicated for a period of more than transitory duration."

After reviewing the record, we find no specific facts (and Peak points to none) which indicate that the copy created in the RAM is not fixed. . . .

The law also supports the conclusion that Peak's loading of copyrighted software into RAM creates a "copy" of that software in violation of the Copyright Act. In *Apple Computer, Inc. v. Formula Int'l, Inc.*, 594 F. Supp. 617, 621 (C.D. Cal. 1984), the district court held that the copying of copyrighted software onto silicon chips and subsequent sale of those chips is not protected by §117 of the Copyright Act. Section 117 allows "the 'owner'[5] of a copy of a computer program to make or authorize the making of another copy" without infringing copyright law, if it "is an essential step in the utilization of the computer program" or if the new copy is "for archival purposes only." 17 U.S.C. §117 (Supp. 1988). One of the grounds for finding that §117 did not apply was the court's conclusion that the permanent copying of the software onto the silicon chips was not an "essential step" in the utilization of the software because the software could be used through RAM without making a permanent copy. The court stated:

> RAM can be simply defined as a computer component in which data and computer programs can be temporarily recorded. Thus, the purchaser of [software] desiring to utilize all of the programs on the diskette could arrange to copy [the software] into RAM. This would only be a temporary fixation. It is a property of RAM that when the computer is turned off, the copy of the program recorded in RAM is lost.

Apple Computer at 622.

While we recognize that this language is not dispositive, it supports the view that the copy made in RAM is "fixed" and qualifies as a copy under the Copyright Act.

We have found no case which specifically holds that the copying of software into RAM creates a "copy" under the Copyright Act. However, it is generally accepted that the loading of software into a computer constitutes the creation of a copy under the Copyright Act. *See, e.g., Vault Corp. v. Quaid Software Ltd.*, 847 F.2d 255, 260 (5th Cir. 1988) ("the act of loading a program from a medium of storage into a computer's memory creates a copy of the program"); 2 *Nimmer on Copyright*, §8.08 at 8-105 (1983) ("Inputting a computer program entails the preparation of a copy."); *Final Report of the National Commission on the New Technological Uses*

---

4. MAI also alleges that Peak runs its diagnostic software in servicing MAI computers. Since Peak's running of the operating software constitutes copyright violation, it is not necessary for us to directly reach the issue of whether Peak also runs MAI's diagnostic software. However, we must note that Peak's field service manager, Charles Weiner, admits that MAI diagnostic software is built into the MAI MPx system and, further, that if Peak loads the MAI diagnostic software from whatever source into the computer's RAM, that such loading will produce the same copyright violation as loading the operating software.

5. Since MAI licensed its software, the Peak customers do not qualify as "owners" of the software and are not eligible for protection under §117.

of Copyrighted Works, at 13 (1978) ("the placement of a work into a computer is the preparation of a copy"). We recognize that these authorities are somewhat troubling since they do not specify that a copy is created regardless of whether the software is loaded into the RAM, the hard disk or the read only memory ("ROM"). However, since we find that the copy created in the RAM can be "perceived, reproduced, or otherwise communicated," we hold that the loading of software into the RAM creates a copy under the Copyright Act. 17 U.S.C. §101. We affirm the district court's grant of summary judgment as well as the permanent injunction as it relates to this issue. . . .

NOTES AND QUESTIONS

1. Many countries, including Belgium, France, Brazil, Italy, and Germany, accord a work copyright protection as soon as it is in a form from which others can perceive it, regardless of whether it is also fixed in a tangible medium. Such works might include, for example, improvisational performances and off-the-cuff lectures. Why do you think the U.S. has elected to retain a fixation requirement? The Constitution provides that Congress may grant exclusive rights in "writings." Do works that are not fixed qualify as writings? If not, why not? Are there policy reasons that might militate in favor of requiring fixation as a condition of copyright protection? In particular, might fixation serve important evidentiary purposes?

2. *Williams* says that player participation that changes the screen display does not make the audiovisual work "unfixed" for copyright purposes. Do you agree with the court's reasoning? What about newer generations of games in which artificial intelligence and virtual reality techniques increasingly allow the player to "create" the game as he or she plays? If the display may never be repeated (because the same interaction may never occur), is it copyrightable?

3. If your copyright professor gives an off-the-cuff lecture and you make an audiotape of it, is the work thereby "fixed in a tangible medium of expression" for purposes of copyright protection? Review the first sentence of the statutory definition carefully. It appears that no copyrightable work has been created! Why do you think Congress included the phrase "by or under the authority of the author" in the definition? Now review the definitions of "copies" and "phonorecords" again. Note that neither of these definitions includes the phrase "by or under the authority of the author." Why the omission?

4. The House Report accompanying the 1976 Act states that "the definition of fixation would exclude from the concept purely evanescent or transient reproductions such as those projected briefly on a screen, shown electronically on a television or other cathode ray tube, or captured momentarily in the memory of a computer." H.R. Rep. No. 94-1476, 94th Cong., 2d Sess. 53 (1976), *reprinted in* 1976 U.S.C.C.A.N. 5659, 5666. Is *MAI* consistent with this history?

5. How would the *MAI* reasoning apply to streamed video content stored in buffer memory in increments of 1.2 seconds, and continually overwritten? Cablevision used such an arrangement to enable a "remote DVR" system. First, Cablevision split its programming data stream into two identical streams. One stream was transmitted to Cablevision's customers, and the other was routed through a buffering device called the Broadband Media Router (BMR) (in 1.2-second increments) and then through the "primary ingest buffer" in Cablevision's remote DVR data center (in 0.1-second increments). If a customer wished to record a particular program to watch later, a dedicated copy for that customer would be created and stored in server space allocated to that customer. Otherwise, the programming data continued to pass through buffer memory, continually overwritten by new programming data. In *Cartoon*

Network LP v. CSC Holdings, Inc., 536 F.3d 121 (2d Cir. 2008), *cert. denied*, 129 S. Ct. 2890 (2009), the court held that the programming data stored in Cablevision's buffers were not fixed. The court observed:

> . . . The Act . . . provides that a work is "'fixed' in a tangible medium of expression when its embodiment . . . is sufficiently permanent or stable to permit it to be . . . reproduced . . . *for a period of more than transitory duration.*" *Id.* (emphasis added). We believe that this language plainly imposes two distinct but related requirements: the work must be embodied in a medium, i.e., placed in a medium such that it can be perceived, reproduced, etc., from that medium (the "embodiment requirement"), and it must remain thus embodied "for a period of more than transitory duration" (the "duration requirement"). . . . Unless both requirements are met, the work is not "fixed" in the buffer, and, as a result, the buffer data is not a "copy" of the original work whose data is buffered. . . .
>
> The district court's reliance on cases like *MAI Systems* is misplaced. In general, those cases conclude that an alleged copy is fixed without addressing the duration requirement; it does not follow, however, that those cases assume, much less establish, that such a requirement does not exist. Indeed, the duration requirement, by itself, was not at issue in *MAI Systems* and its progeny. . . .
>
> The *MAI Systems* court referenced the "transitory duration" language but did not discuss or analyze it. . . . This omission suggests that the parties did not litigate the significance of the "transitory duration" language, and the court therefore had no occasion to address it. This is unsurprising, because it seems fair to assume that . . . the program was embodied in the RAM for at least several minutes.
>
> Accordingly, we construe *MAI Systems* and its progeny as holding that loading a program into a computer's RAM *can* result in copying that program. We do not read *MAI Systems* as holding that, as a matter of law, loading a program into a form of RAM *always* results in copying. Such a holding would read the "transitory duration" language out of the definition, and we do not believe our sister circuit would dismiss this statutory language without even discussing it. It appears the parties in *MAI Systems* simply did not dispute that the duration requirement was satisfied; this line of cases simply concludes that when a program is loaded into RAM, the embodiment requirement is satisfied. . . .
>
> Cablevision does not seriously dispute that copyrighted works are "embodied" in the buffer. Data in the BMR buffer can be reformatted and transmitted to the other components of the RS-DVR system. Data in the primary ingest buffer can be copied onto the Arroyo hard disks if a user has requested a recording of that data. Thus, a work's "embodiment" in either buffer "is sufficiently permanent or stable to permit it to be perceived, reproduced," (as in the case of the ingest buffer) "or otherwise communicated" (as in the BMR buffer). 17 U.S.C. §101. The result might be different if only a single second of a much longer work was placed in the buffer in isolation. In such a situation, it might be reasonable to conclude that only a minuscule portion of a work, rather than "a work" was embodied in the buffer. Here, however, where every second of an entire work is placed, one second at a time, in the buffer, we conclude that the work is embodied in the buffer.
>
> Does any such embodiment last "for a period of more than transitory duration"? *Id.* No bit of data remains in any buffer for more than a fleeting 1.2 seconds. And unlike the data in cases like *MAI Systems*, which remained embodied in the computer's RAM memory until the user turned the computer off, each bit of data here is rapidly and automatically overwritten as soon as it is processed. While our inquiry is necessarily fact-specific, and other factors not present here may alter the duration analysis significantly, these facts strongly suggest that the works in this case are embodied in the buffer for only a "transitory" period, thus failing the duration requirement.

Id. at 127-30 (emphasis in original). Do you agree with the court's reading of the statute? Is the court correct in concluding that its interpretation of the statutory definition is consistent with the *MAI* court's interpretation? If not, which interpretation is preferable as a policy matter?

6. Based on the reasoning in *MAI*, are the following "fixed" (or "copies") under §101? Does the reasoning in *Cartoon Network* cause any of your answers to change?

a. images retrieved from web sites by your browser when you are surfing the web;
b. cache (temporary storage that allows fast retrieval. For example, when you load a web page, a copy often resides in cache on your computer. Cache allows retrieval to occur more quickly than it would if your computer queried the server on which the page resides. The contents in cache generally remain for the period defined by your browser software);
c. e-mail;
d. online chat;
e. a YouTube video that you are watching as it is streamed to your computer.

7. Congress amended §117 of the Act in the wake of *MAI*. Read §117(c)-(d). We return to §117 in Chapter 5.

b. A Technology-Specific Approach: Transmission and Contemporaneous Fixation, and the Problem of Bootleg Recordings

The first sentence of the definition of "fixed" creates a problem for live transmissions: Is a song or television program that is performed over the airwaves embodied in a copy that is sufficiently stable for it to be perceived for "a period of more than transitory duration" as required for protection under U.S. copyright law? Broadcasts are clearly able to be perceived by their intended audiences. Failure to protect broadcasts would produce the paradoxical result that no one could claim a copyright right to control dissemination of a work via a medium capable of reaching thousands or even millions of listeners or viewers simultaneously. This problem also illustrates the difference between U.S. copyright law and that of other countries that accord protection to perceptible works regardless of fixation.

To solve this problem while still retaining a fixation requirement in U.S. copyright law, Congress chose a narrow, situation-specific solution, which contrasts sharply with the broad, technology-neutral approach adopted in the first sentence of the statutory definition of "fixed." The second sentence of that definition states: "A work consisting of sounds, images, or both, that are being transmitted, is 'fixed' for purposes of this title if a fixation of the work is being made simultaneously with its transmission." 17 U.S.C. §101. According to the legislative history, this sentence resolved

the status of live broadcasts — sports, news coverage, live performances of music, etc. — that are reaching the public in unfixed form but that are simultaneously being recorded. When a football game is being covered by four television cameras, with a director guiding the activities of the four cameramen and choosing which of their electronic images are sent out to the public and in what order, there is little doubt that what the cameramen and the director are doing constitutes "authorship." The further question to be considered is whether there has been a fixation. If the images and sounds to be broadcast are first recorded (on a video tape, film, etc.) and then transmitted, the recorded work would be considered a "motion picture" subject to statutory protection against unauthorized reproduction or retransmission of the broadcast. If the program content is transmitted live to the public while being recorded at the same time, the case would be treated the same; the copyright owner would not be forced to rely on common law rather than statutory rights in proceeding against an infringing user of the live broadcast.

Thus, assuming it is copyrightable—as a "motion picture" or "sound recording," for example—the content of a live transmission should be regarded as fixed and should be accorded statutory protection if it is being recorded simultaneously with its transmission.

H.R. Rep. No. 94-1476, 94th Cong., 2d Sess. 52-53 (1976), *reprinted in* 1976 U.S.C.C.A.N. 5659, 5665-66.

Strict construction of the statutory provision for fixation of broadcast transmissions can lead to an anomalous result: When a live performance of a work is given to an audience present at the location of the performance, a contemporaneous recording technically does not qualify as "fixed" under the second sentence of the statutory definition, which covers only works "that are being transmitted." Only if that live performance is also simultaneously transmitted, for example by either radio or television, will the contemporaneous recording satisfy the second sentence of the definition. Arguably, a contemporaneous recording of a live performance that is not being transmitted could still qualify as a fixation *of the work being performed* under the first sentence of the statutory definition as long as it is prepared by or under the authority of the author. However, the leading treatise on copyright law takes the opposite view. *See* Melville B. Nimmer & David Nimmer, 1 *Nimmer on Copyright* §1.08[C][2], at 1-115 (concluding that the second sentence of the definition sets forth the only circumstances in which "the simultaneous recordation concept" can effect a fixation).

Almost as soon as the 1976 Act took effect, it became apparent that this statutory construction debate had important real-world ramifications. In the mid-1970s, consumer electronics companies began widely marketing good-quality audiotape recording equipment at prices that ordinary individuals could afford. As a result, the practice of making and distributing audience-prepared recordings of live performances—known as "bootleg" recordings—became more common. Absent copyright protection for the live performance, this conduct would not violate any copyright rights belonging to the performer.[1] As discussed above, it was unclear that the performer could cause copyright to subsist in the performance by making a simultaneous recording. Some performers—most notably the Grateful Dead—encouraged bootleg recordings, but many others objected. Why might a performing artist encourage the creation and distribution of bootleg recordings? What laws might artists use to seek protection against such conduct in the absence of copyright?

In 1994, Congress enacted an amendment to the Copyright Act to implement the TRIPS Agreement, which requires protection for live musical performances. Section 1101(a) prohibits the fixation or transmission of a live musical performance without the consent of the performers, and also prohibits the reproduction or distribution of copies or phonorecords of an unauthorized fixation of a live musical performance. Does this legislation protect "unfixed" works? May it constitutionally do so? How can Congress consider live performances to be "writings"? If the legislation is not authorized under the Intellectual Property Clause, might it pass constitutional muster under the Commerce Clause?

In *United States v. Moghadam*, 175 F.3d 1269 (11th Cir. 1999), the Eleventh Circuit rejected a constitutional challenge to the criminal version of the anti-bootlegging legislation, 18 U.S.C. §2319A, based on the "Writings" requirement of the Intellectual Property Clause. The court concluded that the extension of legal protection to unfixed performances was a valid exercise of Congress' commerce power because it also served to promote creativity, and therefore was not "fundamentally inconsistent" with the Intellectual Property Clause. *Id.* at 1282.

---

1. If the *work* being performed—e.g., a musical composition or dramatic monologue—were protected by copyright, the bootlegger would need permission from the copyright owner of that work to make copies of the tape and distribute them. You will learn about the complicated field of music copyrights in Chapter 5.G.

It reserved judgment on whether §2319A, which specifies no time limits, was fundamentally inconsistent with the Intellectual Property Clause's reference to "limited Times" because the defendant had not raised that challenge in the district court proceedings. Considering the "limited Times" question, the Second Circuit opined that a legislative enactment implicates the Intellectual Property Clause only when it creates or bestows property rights in expression. Because the criminal anti-bootlegging legislation simply "creates a power in the government to protect the interests of performers from commercial predations," it was not an exercise of the Intellectual Property power and the limitations on that power therefore did not apply. *United States v. Martignon*, 492 F.3d 140, 151 (2d Cir. 2007). The court reserved judgment on the constitutionality of the *civil* anti-bootlegging provision, which was not at issue in the case before it. If the civil provision were to be challenged as violating the "limited Times" requirement, how should a court rule? *See KISS Catalog v. Passport International Prods.*, 405 F. Supp. 2d 1169, 1175 (C.D. Cal. 2005) (declining to evaluate §1101(a) for fundamental inconsistency with the Intellectual Property Clause as long as "an alternative source of constitutional authority" existed). We will return to questions about constitutional limits, in Chapter 10.

Regardless of constitutional questions, do §§1101 and 2319A represent good policy? Why provide special protection for musical performers but not for the comedian doing a stand-up act at a comedy club? Is there some economic or other policy reason to treat musical performers differently?

Both the second sentence of the §101 definition of "fixed" and the special protection granted to live musical performances under §1101 are narrow, medium-specific solutions to known problems. Such a legislative approach is not necessarily undesirable simply because the statutory language will not stretch to cover new problems. As the discussion of fixation and digital works above illustrates, broad legislative drafting has its own perils. Where eligibility for copyright protection is concerned, is it better to err on the side of underinclusiveness or over-inclusiveness? You will see many more examples of both types of drafting in the Copyright Act. Learn to recognize these styles of drafting, and to evaluate their advantages and disadvantages.

2. Originality

The second requirement for copyrightability is that a work be an "original work[] of authorship." 17 U.S.C. §102(a). Once again, neither the Berne Convention nor the TRIPS Agreement expressly imposes any requirement of originality or creativity, although both agreements assume an authorial presence. Nonetheless, nearly all countries require some level of creativity as a prerequisite for copyright protection. To see why, consider whether it would make sense to grant exclusive rights to someone who merely copies a preexisting work. There is general agreement that it would not. From an economic perspective, the mere copyist has supplied nothing to justify the cost of a grant of copyright; from a non-economic perspective, the copyist has supplied nothing of his or her "own." But what level of originality is most likely to accomplish copyright law's goals? Should the law award exclusive rights to anyone who can show simply that he or she has not copied a preexisting work? Or should the law require more? In a sense, isn't every author a secondcomer because he or she builds on prior works? How much should a secondcomer have to add to the store of knowledge to merit the grant of a copyright? Can economic arguments help to answer this question? What about non-economic arguments? As you will see, it is possible to define the term *originality* in different ways.

Although U.S. copyright law has always required originality as a condition of copyright protection, it has not always done so expressly. Instead, courts found an originality requirement implicit in the statutes, and in the underlying language of the constitutional grant of authority to enact copyright laws. Perhaps for this reason, the first time that Congress attempted a comprehensive statement of the sorts of works entitled to copyright protection, it chose language that mirrored that of the constitutional grant. Section 4 of the 1909 Act provided that "[t]he works for which copyright may be secured under this title shall include all the writings of the author."

In the 1976 Act, however, Congress deliberately chose different language — "original works of authorship." As the legislative history of the Act explains:

> [A] recurring question [under the 1909 Act] has been whether the statutory and the constitutional provisions are coextensive. If so, the courts would be faced with the alternative of holding copyrightable something that Congress clearly did not intend to protect, or of holding constitutionally incapable of copyright something that Congress might one day want to protect. To avoid these equally undesirable results, the courts have indicated that "all the writings of an author" under the [1909 Act] is narrower in scope than the "writings" of "authors" referred to in the Constitution. The bill avoids this dilemma by using a different phrase — "original works of authorship" — in characterizing the general subject matter of statutory copyright protection.

H.R. Rep. No. 94-1476, 94th Cong., 2d Sess. 51 (1976), *reprinted in* 1976 U.S.C.C.A.N. 5659, 5664. In other words, the intent of the 1976 Act was to "avoid exhausting the constitutional power of Congress to legislate in [the] field" of copyrightable subject matter. *Id.* But the 1976 Act does not indicate exactly what Congress meant by "original works of authorship." According to the legislative history, "[t]he phrase 'original works of authorship,' which is purposely left undefined, was intended to incorporate without change the standard of originality established by the courts under the [1909 Act]. This standard does not include requirements of novelty, ingenuity, or esthetic merit, and there is no intention to enlarge the standard of copyright protection to require them." *Id.* The task of interpreting the scope of the statutory grant of copyright protection was thus left, once again, to the courts.

As you will see, the courts have progressively lowered both statutory and constitutional standards for originality. In the U.S., both as a statutory matter and as a constitutional matter, the modern definition of "originality" requires more than mere independent creation, but not much more. In *Feist Publications, Inc. v. Rural Telephone Service Co.*, 499 U.S. 340 (1991), the Supreme Court articulated the modern definition of originality:

Feist Publications, Inc. v. Rural Telephone Service Co.
499 U.S. 340 (1991)

O'CONNOR, J.: This case requires us to clarify the extent of copyright protection available to telephone directory white pages.

I

Rural Telephone Service Company, Inc., is a certified public utility that provides telephone service to several communities in northwest Kansas. It is subject to a state regulation that requires all telephone companies operating in Kansas to issue annually an updated telephone directory. Accordingly, as a condition of its monopoly franchise, Rural publishes a typical telephone directory, consisting of white pages and yellow pages. The white pages list in alphabetical order the names of Rural's subscribers, together with their towns and telephone numbers. The yellow pages list Rural's business subscribers alphabetically by category and feature classified advertisements of various sizes. Rural distributes its directory free of charge to its subscribers, but earns revenue by selling yellow pages advertisements.

Feist Publications, Inc., is a publishing company that specializes in area-wide telephone directories. Unlike a typical directory, which covers only a particular calling area, Feist's area-wide directories cover a much larger geographic range, reducing the need to call directory assistance or to consult multiple directories. The Feist directory that is the subject of this litigation covers 11 different telephone service areas in 15 counties and contains 46,878 white pages listings — compared to Rural's approximately 7,700 listings. Like Rural's directory, Feist's is distributed free of charge and includes both white pages and yellow pages. Feist and Rural compete vigorously for yellow pages advertising. . . .

Of the 11 telephone companies, only Rural refused to license its listings to Feist. Rural's refusal created a problem for Feist, as omitting these listings would have left a gaping hole in its area-wide directory, rendering it less attractive to potential yellow pages advertisers. . . .

Unable to license Rural's white pages listings, Feist used them without Rural's consent. Feist began by removing several thousand listings that fell outside the geographic range of its area-wide directory, then hired personnel to investigate the 4,935 that remained. These employees verified the data reported by Rural and sought to obtain additional information. As a result, a typical Feist listing includes the individual's street address; most of Rural's listings do not. Notwithstanding these additions, however, 1,309 of the 46,878 listings in Feist's 1983 directory were identical to listings in Rural's 1982-1983 white pages. Four of these were fictitious listings that Rural had inserted into its directory to detect copying. . . .

II

A

This case concerns the interaction of two well-established propositions. The first is that facts are not copyrightable; the other, that compilations of facts generally are. Each of these propositions possesses an impeccable pedigree. . . .

There is an undeniable tension between these two propositions. Many compilations consist of nothing but raw data — *i.e.*, wholly factual information not accompanied by any original written expression. On what basis may one claim a copyright in such a work? Common sense tells us that 100 uncopyrightable facts do not magically change their status when gathered together in one place. . . .

The key to resolving the tension lies in understanding why facts are not copyrightable. The *sine qua non* of copyright is originality. To qualify for copyright protection, a work must be original to the author. Original, as the term is used in copyright, means only that the work was independently created by the author (as opposed to copied from other works), and that it possesses at least some minimal degree of creativity. 1 M. Nimmer & D. Nimmer, Copyright §§2.01[A], [B] (1990) (hereinafter Nimmer). To be sure, the requisite level of creativity is extremely low; even a slight amount will suffice. The vast majority of works make the grade quite easily, as they possess some creative spark, "no matter how crude, humble or obvious" it might be. *Id.*, §1.08[C][1]. . . .

Originality is a constitutional requirement. The source of Congress' power to enact copyright laws is Article I, §8, cl. 8, of the Constitution, which authorizes Congress to "secur[e] for limited Times to Authors . . . the exclusive Right to their respective Writings." . . . [T]hese terms presuppose a degree of originality. . . .

It is this bedrock principle of copyright that mandates the law's seemingly disparate treatment of facts and compilations. "No one may claim originality as to facts." *Id.* [Nimmer], §2.11[A], p. 2-157. This is because facts do not owe their origin to an act of authorship. The distinction is one between creation and discovery: The first person to find and report a particular fact has not created the fact; he or she has merely discovered its existence. . . .

Factual compilations, on the other hand, may possess the requisite originality. The compilation author typically chooses which facts to include, in what order to place them, and how to arrange the collected data so that they may be used effectively by readers. These choices as to selection and arrangement, so long as they are made independently by the compiler and entail a minimal degree of creativity, are sufficiently original that Congress may protect such compilations through the copyright laws. . . .

C . . .

Not every selection, coordination, or arrangement will pass muster. This is plain from the statute. It states that, to merit protection, the facts must be selected, coordinated, or arranged "in such a way" as to render the work as a whole original. This implies that some "ways" will trigger copyright, but that others will not. . . .

As discussed earlier, however, the originality requirement is not particularly stringent. A compiler may settle upon a selection or arrangement that others have used; novelty is not required. Originality requires only that the author make the selection or arrangement independently (*i.e.*, without copying that selection or arrangement from another work), and that it display some minimal level of creativity. Presumably, the vast majority of compilations will pass this test, but not all will. There remains a narrow category of works in which the creative spark is utterly lacking or so trivial as to be virtually nonexistent. Such works are incapable of sustaining a valid copyright. Nimmer §2.01[B]. . . .

NOTES AND QUESTIONS

1. The Court went on to hold that Rural's white pages directory did not meet the minimum standard of originality required for copyrightability. We will return to the *Feist* opinion in Section A.4.b, *infra*, which addresses the copyrightability of compilations.

2. As described by the Court, the originality threshold is very low. Consider whether the following items would qualify:

   a. Text that you have posted on your Facebook page (or the equivalent page on the social networking service of your choice) describing what activities you enjoy;
   b. A comment that you have posted on a travel website reviewing a hotel at which you recently stayed;
   c. A paragraph of text on the back of a shampoo bottle that extols the shampoo's cleansing properties;
   d. A digital photograph of a dining room table taken for the purpose of offering the table for sale on craigslist.org;
   e. A child's drawing of his or her family standing in front of the family home.

3. Should the items listed in Question 2 qualify for copyright protection? Does extending copyright to these items serve any of the goals identified in Chapter 1? Why, or why not? If you think not, what else might justify setting the bar so low? The remainder of this section explores

the evolution of and justifications for the originality standard, and then considers some problems that have resulted as courts have attempted to apply the *Feist* standard to different kinds of works.

a. The Road to Feist

Judicial exposition of the concept of originality did not begin with the generous formulation set forth in *Feist*. As you read the next two cases, identify and evaluate the definition of originality that each chooses.

Burrow-Giles Lithographic Co. v. Sarony
111 U.S. 53 (1884)

MILLER, J.: . . . The suit was commenced by an action at law in which Sarony was plaintiff and the lithographic company was defendant, the plaintiff charging the defendant with violating his copyright in regard to a photograph, the title of which is "Oscar Wilde No. 18." . . . [The defendant assigns as error the finding of] the court below . . . that Congress had and has the constitutional right to protect photographs and negatives thereof by copyright. . . .

The constitutional question is not free from difficulty. . . .

The argument here is, that a photograph is not a writing nor the production of an author. Under the acts of Congress designed to give effect to this section, the persons who are to be benefited are divided into two classes, authors and inventors. The monopoly which is granted to the former is called a copyright, that given to the latter, letters patent. . . .

It is insisted in argument, that a photograph being a reproduction on paper of the exact features of some natural object or of some person, is not a writing of which the producer is the author.

Section 4952 of the Revised Statutes places photographs in the same class as things which may be copyrighted with "books, maps, charts, dramatic or musical compositions, engravings, cuts, prints, paintings, drawings, statues, statuary, and models or designs intended to be perfected as works of the fine arts." "According to the practice of legislation in England and America," says Judge Bouvier, 2 Law Dictionary, 363, "the copyright is confined to the exclusive right secured to the author or proprietor of a writing or drawing which may be multiplied by the arts of printing in any of its branches."

The first Congress of the United States, sitting immediately after the formation of the Constitution, enacted that the "author or authors of any map, chart, book, or books, being a citizen or resident of the United States, shall have the sole right and liberty of printing, reprinting, publishing, and vending the same for the period of fourteen years from the recording of the title thereof in the clerk's office, as afterwards directed." 1 Stat. 124, 1.

This statute not only makes maps and charts subjects of copyright, but mentions them before books in the order of designation. The second section of an act to amend this act, approved April 29, 1802, 2 Stat. 171, enacts that from the first day of January thereafter, he who shall invent and design, engrave, etch, or work, or from his own works shall cause to be designed and engraved, etched or worked, any historical or other print or prints shall have the same exclusive right for the term of fourteen years from recording the title thereof as prescribed by law. . . .

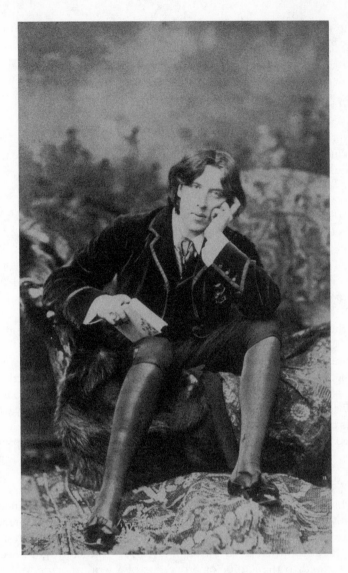

Oscar Wilde No. 18

The construction placed upon the Constitution by the first act of 1790, and the act of 1802, by the men who were contemporary with its formation, many of whom were members of the convention which framed it, is of itself entitled to very great weight, and when it is remembered that the rights thus established have not been disputed during a period of nearly a century, it is almost conclusive.

Unless, therefore, photographs can be distinguished in the classification on this point from the maps, charts, designs, engravings, etchings, cuts, and other prints, it is difficult to see why Congress cannot make them the subject of copyright as well as the others.

These statutes certainly answer the objection that books only, or writing in the limited sense of a book and its author, are within the constitutional provision. Both these words are susceptible of a more enlarged definition than this. An author in that sense is "he to whom anything owes its origin; originator; maker; one who completes a work of science or literature." Worcester. So, also, no one would now claim that the word writing in this clause of the Constitution, though the only word used as to subjects in regard to which authors are to be secured, is limited to the actual script of the author, and excludes books and all other printed matter. By writings in that clause is meant the literary productions of those authors, and Congress very properly has declared these to include all forms of writing, printing, engraving, etching, &c., by which the ideas in the mind of the author are given visible expression. The only reason why photographs were not included in the extended list in the act of 1802 is probably that they did not exist, as photography as an art was then unknown, and the scientific principle on which it rests, and the chemicals and machinery by which it is operated, have all been discovered long since that statute was enacted. . . .

We entertain no doubt that the Constitution is broad enough to cover an act authorizing copyright of photographs, so far as they are representatives of original intellectual conceptions of the author.

But it is said that an engraving, a painting, a print, does embody the intellectual conception of its author, in which there is novelty, invention, originality, and therefore comes within the purpose of the Constitution in securing its exclusive use or sale to its author, while the photograph is the mere mechanical reproduction of the physical features or outlines of some object, animate or inanimate, and involves no originality of thought or any novelty in the intellectual operation connected with its visible reproduction in shape of a picture. That while the effect of light on the prepared plate may have been a discovery in the production of these pictures, and patents could properly be obtained for the combination of the chemicals, for their application to the paper or other surface, for all the machinery by which the light reflected from the object was thrown on the prepared plate, and for all the improvements in this machinery, and in the materials, the remainder of the process is merely mechanical, with no place for novelty, invention or originality. It is simply the manual operation, by the use of these instruments and preparations, of transferring to the plate the visible representation of some existing object, the accuracy of this representation being its highest merit.

This may be true in regard to the ordinary production of a photograph, and, further, that in such case a copyright is no protection. On the question as thus stated we decide nothing. . . .

The third finding of facts says, in regard to the photograph in question, that it is a "useful, new, harmonious, characteristic, and graceful picture, and that plaintiff made the same . . . entirely from his own original mental conception, to which he gave visible form by posing the said Oscar Wilde in front of the camera, selecting and arranging the costume, draperies, and other various accessories in said photograph, arranging the subject so as to present graceful outlines, arranging and disposing the light and shade, suggesting and evoking the desired expression, and from such disposition, arrangement, or representation, made entirely by plaintiff, he produced the picture in suit."

These findings, we think, show this photograph to be an original work of art, the product of plaintiff's intellectual invention, of which plaintiff is the author, and of a class of inventions for which the Constitution intended that Congress should secure to him the exclusive right to use, publish and sell, as it has done by section 4952 of the Revised Statutes. . . .

Does the standard of originality identified by the *Burrow-Giles* Court suggest that copyright protects unposed photographs? How about representational art intended for use in advertising? Consider the Supreme Court's next pronouncement on originality:

Bleistein v. Donaldson Lithographing Co.
188 U.S. 239 (1903)

HOLMES, J.: This case comes here from the United States Circuit Court of Appeals for the Sixth Circuit by writ of error. It is an action brought by the plaintiffs in error to recover the penalties prescribed for infringements of copyrights. The alleged infringements consisted in the copying in reduced form of three chromolithographs prepared by employees of the plaintiffs for advertisements of a circus owned by one Wallace. Each of the three contained a portrait of Wallace in the corner and lettering bearing some slight relation to the scheme of decoration, indicating the subject of the design and the fact that the reality was to be seen at the circus. One of the designs was of an ordinary ballet, one of a number of men and women, described as the Stirk family, performing on bicycles, and one of groups of men and women whitened to represent statues. The Circuit Court directed a verdict for the defendant on the ground that the chromolithographs were not within the protection of the copyright law, and this ruling was sustained by the Circuit Court of Appeals. *Courier Lithographing Co. v. Donaldson Lithographing Co.*, 104 Fed. Rep. 993. . . .

We shall do no more than mention the suggestion that painting and engraving unless for a mechanical end are not among the useful arts, the progress of which Congress is empowered by the Constitution to promote. The Constitution does not limit the useful to that which satisfies immediate bodily needs. *Burrow-Giles Lithographing Co. v. Sarony*, 111 U.S. 53. It is obvious also that the plaintiffs' case is not affected by the fact, if it be one, that the pictures represent actual groups — visible things. They seem from the testimony to have been composed from hints or description, not from sight of a performance. But even if they had been drawn from the life, that fact would not deprive them of protection. The opposite proposition would mean that a portrait by Velasquez or Whistler was common property because others might try their hand on the same face. Others are free to copy the original. They are not free to copy the copy. . . . The copy is the personal reaction of an individual upon nature. Personality always contains something unique. It expresses its singularity even in handwriting, and a very modest grade of art has in it something irreducible, which is one man's alone. That something he may copyright unless there is a restriction in the words of the act. . . .

We assume that the construction of Rev. Stat. §4952, allowing a copyright to the "author, inventor, designer, or proprietor . . . of any engraving, cut, print . . . [or] chromo" is affected by the act of 1874, c. 301, §3, 18 Stat. at L. 78, 79. That section provides that, "in the construction of this act the words 'engraving,' 'cut' and 'print' shall be applied only to pictorial illustrations or works connected with the fine arts." We see no reason for taking the words "connected with the fine arts" as qualifying anything except the word "works," but it would not change our decision if we should assume further that they also qualified "pictorial illustrations," as the defendant contends.

These chromolithographs are "pictorial illustrations." The word "illustrations" does not mean that they must illustrate the text of a book, and that the etchings of Rembrandt or Steinla's engraving of the Madonna di San Sisto could not be protected today if any man were able to produce them. Again, the act however construed, does not mean that ordinary posters are not good enough to be considered within its scope. The antithesis to "illustrations or works connected with the fine arts" is not works of little merit or of humble degree, or illustrations addressed to the less educated classes; it is "prints or labels designed to be used for any other articles of manufacture." Certainly works are not the less connected with the fine arts because their pictorial quality attracts the crowd and therefore gives them a real use — if use means to increase trade and to help to make money. A picture is none the less a picture and none

Circus Poster

the less a subject of copyright that it is used for an advertisement. And if pictures may be used to advertise soap, or the theatre, or monthly magazines, as they are, they may be used to advertise a circus. Of course, the ballet is as legitimate a subject for illustration as any other. A rule cannot be laid down that would excommunicate the paintings of Degas.

Finally, the special adaptation of these pictures to the advertisement of the Wallace shows does not prevent a copyright. That may be a circumstance for the jury to consider in determining the extent of Mr. Wallace's rights, but it is not a bar. Moreover, on the evidence, such prints are used by less pretentious exhibitions when those for whom they were prepared have given them up.

It would be a dangerous undertaking for persons trained only to the law to constitute themselves final judges of the worth of pictorial illustrations, outside of the narrowest and most obvious limits. At the one extreme, some works of genius would be sure to miss appreciation. Their very novelty would make them repulsive until the public had learned the new language in which their author spoke. It may be more than doubted, for instance, whether the etchings of Goya or the paintings of Manet would have been sure of protection when seen for the first time. At the other end, copyright would be denied to pictures which appealed to a public less educated than the judge. Yet if they command the interest of any public, they have a commercial value — it would be bold to say that they have not an aesthetic and educational value — and the taste of any public is not to be treated with contempt. It is an ultimate fact for the moment, whatever may be our hopes for a change. That these pictures had their worth and their success is sufficiently shown by the desire to reproduce them without regard to the plaintiffs' rights. We are of opinion that there was evidence that the plaintiffs have rights entitled to the protection of the law. . . .

NOTES AND QUESTIONS

1. Identify and compare the originality standards that *Burrow-Giles* and *Bleistein* employ. Which makes more sense in light of copyright law's goals? How does each compare to the standard of originality described in the excerpt from *Feist, supra* pp. 58-60.

In Europe, prior to recent EU directives, the requirements for originality varied a great deal, but can be classed into three categories. Countries like the UK and Ireland require only that "the work originate[ ] from the maker and . . . not be[ ] copied from another source." Herman Cohen Jehoram, *The EC Copyright Directives, Economics and Authors' Rights*, 25 Int'l Rev. Indus. Prop. & Copyright L. 821, 828 (1994). Italy, France, and most other nations set the bar a bit higher, requiring that the work be an author's personal expression. *See id.* at 828-29. Finally, Germany even requires works to pass additional "qualitative or aesthetic tests." *See id.* at 829. Similarly, Japan typically requires a relatively high level of originality in which "thoughts or sentiments are expressed in a creative way" and "fall within the literary, scientific, artistic, or musical domain." Michael J. Bastian, *Protection of "Noncreative" Databases: Harmonization of United States, Foreign and International Law*, 22 B.C. Int'l & Comp. L. Rev. 425, 433 (1999). Into which category do the rules announced in *Burrow-Giles* and *Bleistein* fall? What about the rule announced in *Feist*?

2. The *Burrow-Giles* Court notes that the Framers could not have considered photographs because the technology did not exist at the time. Should courts extend protection to new technologies or items produced by them in the absence of congressional action? After all, Congress can conduct studies to determine if the grant of exclusive rights is required for new subject matter. What are the pros and cons of waiting for congressional action?

3. Focus on the statement in *Bleistein*: "Others are free to copy the original. They are not free to copy the copy." Why not? Suppose, for example, that an artist travels to Colorado and paints a landscape of the Rocky Mountains. A company based in New York wishes to use the landscape to advertise its product. Can it copy the painting without the author's permission or must it send someone to Colorado to paint the same landscape? Isn't it wasteful for the law to require the firm to send someone else to Colorado?

4. In *Bleistein*, the court states, "That these pictures had their worth and their success is sufficiently shown by the desire to reproduce them without regard to the plaintiffs' rights. We are of the opinion that there was evidence that the plaintiffs have rights entitled to the protection of the law." Is the court saying that if a work has value its creator should be given legal rights? Does this reasoning risk being circular?

5. Perhaps the most famous part of the *Bleistein* opinion is Justice Holmes' discussion of the dangers of requiring judges to evaluate aesthetic merit. His conclusion that judges should not do so has become known as the *Bleistein* nondiscrimination principle. But is this principle really justified for all types of works? In particular, why should the artwork in advertisements be protected by copyright? Is the incentive afforded by copyright protection required for the creation of advertisements?

6. Consider whether copyright law should protect the following:

   a. a photograph generated by a professional photographer whose goal is not to produce a "staged" photo like that in the *Burrow-Giles* case, but rather to reproduce reality in every detail;

   b. a photograph taken by a parent whose goal is to produce a likeness of her child as a keepsake;

   c. a snapshot taken by a tourist whose goal is to produce a vacation memento;

d. a photograph taken by a camera that has been set up to produce a likeness of whatever appears in front of it at a particular time of day.

Consider these questions again after reading the *Alfred Bell* case, *infra*.

7. Finally, recall Chapter 1's discussion of the prevailing construction of Art. I, §8, cl. 8. Copyright refers to advancing "Science" by granting "Authors" exclusive rights in their "Writings." Patent corresponds to furthering progress in the "useful Arts" by granting "Inventors" exclusive rights in their "Discoveries." Is that what *Bleistein* says? If Justice Holmes had read the constitutional grant of authority this way, do you think he would have reached the same conclusion about the copyrightability of the circus posters?

Alfred Bell & Co. v. Cataldo Fine Arts, Inc.
191 F.2d 99 (2d Cir. 1951)

[The plaintiff asserted copyrights in eight mezzotint engravings of paintings from the late eighteenth and early nineteenth centuries. The mezzotint process involved drawing a hand tool across a copper plate, tracing a photograph of the original work, pressing the tracing on the copper plate, and hand-scraping the picture on the plate to produce images of light and shadow. The plate was then covered with steel. Color would be applied by hand before the production of each print. The artist's goal was to reproduce the paintings as accurately as possible in the mezzotints. The paintings on which the mezzotints were based were no longer protected by copyright. The defendants produced and sold color lithographs of the mezzotints.

The district court found that

> [i]t is possible by this [mezzotint] process to make quite a satisfactory reproduction of the original painting in whatever size desired . . . preserving the softness of line which is characteristic of the oil painting. It is not, however, possible to make a photographic copy of the painting by this method exact in all its details. The work of the engraver upon the plate requires the individual conception, judgment and execution by the engraver on the depth and shape of the depressions in the plate to be made by the scraping process in order to produce in this other medium the engraver's concept of the effect of the oil painting. No two engravers can produce identical interpretations of the same oil painting.

74 F. Supp. 973, 975 (S.D.N.Y. 1947). The district court found the plaintiff's copyright valid and infringed. Defendant appealed.]

FRANK, J.: . . . Congressional power to authorize both patents and copyrights is contained in Article 1, §8 of the Constitution. In passing on the validity of patents, the Supreme Court recurrently insists that this constitutional provision governs. On this basis, pointing to the Supreme Court's consequent requirement that, to be valid, a patent must disclose a high degree of uniqueness, ingenuity and inventiveness, the defendants assert that the same requirement constitutionally governs copyrights. As several sections of the Copyright Act — *e.g.*, those authorizing copyrights of "reproductions of works of art," maps, and compilations — plainly dispense with any such high standard, defendants are, in effect, attacking the constitutionality of those sections. But the very language of the Constitution differentiates (a) "authors" and their "writings" from (b) "inventors" and their "discoveries." Those who penned the Constitution,[2] of course, knew the difference. The pre-revolutionary English statutes had made the

_____

2. Many of them were themselves authors.

distinction. In 1783, the Continental Congress had passed a resolution recommending that the several states enact legislation to "secure" to authors the "copyright" of their books. Twelve of the thirteen states (in 1783-1786) enacted such statutes. Those of Connecticut and North Carolina covered books, pamphlets, maps, and charts.

Moreover, in 1790, in the year after the adoption of the Constitution, the first Congress enacted two statutes, separately dealing with patents and copyrights. The patent statute, enacted April 10, 1790, 1 Stat. 109, provided that patents should issue only if the Secretary of State, Secretary of War and the Attorney General, or any two of them "shall deem the invention or discovery sufficiently useful and important"; the applicant for a patent was obliged to file a specification "so particular" as "to distinguish the invention or discovery from other things before known and used . . ."; the patent was to constitute *prima facie* evidence that the patentee was "the first and true inventor or . . . discoverer . . . of the thing so specified." The Copyright Act, enacted May 31, 1790, 1 Stat. 124, covered "maps, charts, and books." A printed copy of the title of any map, chart or book was to be recorded in the Clerk's office of the District Court, and a copy of the map, chart or book was to be delivered to the Secretary of State within six months after publication. Twelve years later, Congress in 1802, 2 Stat. 171, added, to matters that might be copyrighted, engravings, etchings and prints.

Thus legislators peculiarly familiar with the purpose of the Constitutional grant, by statute, imposed far less exacting standards in the case of copyrights. They authorized the copyrighting of a mere map which, patently, calls for no considerable uniqueness. They exacted far more from an inventor. And, while they demanded that an official should be satisfied as to the character of an invention before a patent issued, they made no such demand in respect of a copyright. . . . [T]he Constitution, as so interpreted, recognizes that the standards for patents and copyrights are basically different.

The defendants' contention apparently results from the ambiguity of the word "original." It may mean startling, novel or unusual, a marked departure from the past. Obviously this is not what is meant when one speaks of "the original package," or the "original bill," or (in connection with the "best evidence" rule) an "original" document; none of those things is highly unusual in creativeness. "Original" in reference to a copyrighted work means that the particular work "owes its origin" to the "author."[8] No large measure of novelty is necessary. . . .

[N]othing in the Constitution commands that copyrighted matter be strikingly unique or novel. Accordingly, we were not ignoring the Constitution when we stated that a "copy of something in the public domain" will support a copyright if it is a "distinguishable variation"; or when we rejected the contention that "like a patent, a copyrighted work must be not only original, but new," adding, "That is not . . . the law as is obvious in the case of maps or compendia, where later works will necessarily be anticipated." All that is needed to satisfy both the Constitution and the statute is that the "author" contributed something more than a "merely trivial" variation, something recognizably "his own." Originality in this context "means little more than a prohibition of actual copying." No matter how poor artistically the "author's" addition, it is enough if it be his own. *Bleistein v. Donaldson Lithographing Co.*, 188 U.S. 239. . . .

. . . We consider untenable defendants' suggestion that plaintiff's mezzotints could not validly be copyrighted because they are reproductions of works in the public domain. Not only does the Act include "Reproductions of a work of art," but — while prohibiting a copyright of "the original text of any work . . . in the public domain" — it explicitly provides for the copyrighting of "translations, or other versions of works in the public domain." The mezzotints were such "versions." They "originated" with those who made them, and — on the trial judge's

8. *Burrow-Giles Lithographic Co. v. Sarony*, 111 U.S. 53, 57-58. . . .

findings well supported by the evidence — amply met the standards imposed by the Constitution and the statute.[22] There is evidence that they were not intended to, and did not, imitate the paintings they reproduced. But even if their substantial departures from the paintings were inadvertent, the copyrights would be valid.[23] A copyist's bad eyesight or defective musculature, or a shock caused by a clap of thunder, may yield sufficiently distinguishable variations. Having hit upon such a variation unintentionally, the "author" may adopt it as his and copyright it.

Accordingly, defendants' arguments about the public domain become irrelevant. They could be relevant only in their bearing on the issue of infringement, *i.e.*, whether the defendants copied the mezzotints. But on the findings, again well grounded in the evidence, we see no possible doubt that defendants, who did deliberately copy the mezzotints, are infringers. For a copyright confers the exclusive right to copy the copyrighted work — a right not to have others copy it. Nor were the copyrights lost because of the reproduction of the mezzotints in catalogues. . . .

NOTES AND QUESTIONS

1. Should copyright protect the result of "[a] copyist's bad eyesight or defective musculature, or a shock caused by a clap of thunder"? After *Feist* (decided in 1991), does it? Are the *Feist* and *Alfred Bell* standards of originality equivalent?

2. If "minimal creativity" means something more than "independently created," how much more is required? Consider whether, after *Feist*, copyright would (or should) protect the following:

   a. digital photographs of public domain paintings;
   b. digital photographs of public domain sculptures;
   c. an Andy Warhol painting of a Campbell's soup can;
   d. a design for a calendar using particular petroglyph symbols as the middle two zeros in depiction of the year "2000."

In *Bridgeman Art Library, Ltd. v. Corel Corp.*, 36 F. Supp. 2d 191 (S.D.N.Y. 1999), Bridgeman had been authorized to prepare and sell color reproductions of public domain paintings residing in museum and private collections. Corel allegedly copied Bridgeman's color transparencies to produce its own CD-ROM product. The court dismissed Bridgeman's copyright infringement claim, ruling that the transparencies did not contain the required "distinguishable variation," but reflected only "slavish copying." Do you agree with the court's conclusion? If so, are the works in hypothetical b, above, distinguishable?

22. See Copinger, The Law of Copyrights (7th ed. 1936) 46: "Again, an engraver is almost invariably a copyist, but although his work may infringe copyright in the original painting if made without the consent of the owner of the copyright therein, his work may still be original in the sense that he has employed skill and judgment in its production. He produces the resemblance he is desirous of obtaining by means very different from those employed by the painter or draughtsman from whom he copies: means which require great labour and talent. The engraver produces his effects by the management of light and shade, or, as the term of his art expresses it, the *chiaroscuro*. The due degrees of light and shade are produced by different lines and dots; he who is the engraver must decide on the choice of the different lines or dots for himself, and on his choice depends the success of his print."

23. See *Kallen*, Art and Freedom (1942) 977 to the effect that "the beauty of the human singing voice, as the western convention of music hears it, depends upon a physiological dysfunction of the vocal cords. . . ."

Plutarch tells this story: A painter, enraged because he could not depict the foam that filled a horse's mouth from champing at the bit, threw a sponge at his painting; the sponge splashed against the wall — and achieved the desired result.

3. Both *Alfred Bell* and *Bridgeman* involved the preparation of "derivative works" — works based on preexisting works. The 1976 Act makes separate provision for the copyright-ability of derivative works; the preceding 1909 Act did not use that terminology, but allowed copyright protection for "reproductions of a work of art." As discussed in Section A.4.a, *infra,* there is a debate about whether the threshold originality requirement should be determined differently for such works. For now, note that the *Bridgeman* decision effectively permitted the copying of images of underlying works that are in the public domain, while the *Alfred Bell* decision had the opposite effect. Which outcome is more likely to promote progress?

4. Many photographs, including a large number in the public domain, are held in private collections and made available to the public only as digital replicas. For example, Corbis, a company founded by Bill Gates, acquired the Bettman Archive's collection of 16.5 million photographs, including 30 years' worth of United Press International photographs. To preserve the original photographs, Corbis has buried them in an underground, climate-controlled storage facility. Digital reproductions are available via license. Can Corbis copyright the digital images? Would it make any difference to your answer if Corbis digitally watermarks each image? If Corbis cannot copyright the images under the Copyright Act, should it be able to place contractual restrictions on access to and use of them?

Note on Nonobviousness and Originality

The Court's opinion in *Burrow-Giles* hinted at some of the differences between copyright law and patent law, which offers protection to certain technological innovations. Copyright law requires that a work of expression be "original" to be protected. Patent law, in contrast, requires that an invention be new, useful, and nonobvious to qualify for protection. Section 103 of the Patent Act, which defines nonobviousness, specifies that a patent may not issue "if the differences between the subject matter sought to be patented and the prior art are such that the subject matter as a whole would have been obvious at the time the invention was made to a person having ordinary skill in the art to which said subject matter pertains." 35 U.S.C. §103(a). Under the 1976 Copyright Act, no prior assessment of the work's level of originality is required; instead, copyright automatically subsists in an original work of authorship at the time the work is fixed in a tangible medium of expression. In contrast, to obtain a patent, the inventor must file an application with the Patent and Trademark Office (PTO). An examiner will assess whether the application meets the statutory requirements. Often, the examiner will determine that the application as written does not meet the nonobviousness standard, and the inventor will need to narrow the claims to avoid rejection.

As both the Patent Act and the patent practice of examination make clear, the requirement of nonobviousness is significantly more stringent than the copyright requirement of originality. In *Graham v. John Deere Co.,* 383 U.S. 1 (1966), the Supreme Court indicated that the nonobviousness threshold for patentability is constitutionally mandated:

> The [Intellectual Property] clause is both a grant of power and a limitation. This qualified authority, unlike the power often exercised in the sixteenth and seventeenth centuries by the English Crown, is limited to the promotion of advances in the "useful arts." It was written against the backdrop of the practices — eventually curtailed by the Statute of Monopolies — of the Crown in granting monop-olies to court favorites in goods or businesses which had long before been enjoyed by the public. See Meinhardt, Inventions, Patents and Monopoly, pp. 30-35 (London, 1946). The Congress in the exercise of the patent power may not overreach the restraints imposed by the stated constitutional purpose. Nor may it enlarge the patent monopoly without regard to the innovation, advancement or social benefit gained thereby. Moreover, Congress may not authorize the issuance of patents whose

effects are to remove existent knowledge from the public domain, or to restrict free access to materials already available. Innovation, advancement, and things which add to the sum of useful knowledge are inherent requisites in a patent system which by constitutional command must "promote the Progress of . . . useful Arts." This is the *standard* expressed in the Constitution and it may not be ignored. And it is in this light that patent validity "requires reference to a standard written into the Constitution." *A. & P. Tea Co. v. Supermarket Corp., supra,* at 154 (concurring opinion).

383 U.S. at 5-6.

One consequence of this difference in threshold standards for protectibility is that the copyright and patent systems have very different rules about the treatment of independently created works and inventions, respectively. Recall again Justices Holmes' statement in *Bleistein* that "[o]thers are free to copy the original. They are not free to copy the copy." Because copyright law requires simply that a work not have been copied, a copyright owner cannot obtain relief against another author who independently generates expression that replicates the copyrighted work. Instead, a secondcomer who is an independent creator may receive her own copyright. Because patent law requires that a patentable invention represent a nonobvious advance over all existing prior art, a secondcomer who independently generates an already-patented invention may not receive a patent. Further, a patent confers the exclusive right to make, use, or sell the invention; thus, the secondcomer who independently generates a patented invention may not make, use, or sell it without infringing the patent.

Laureyssens v. Idea Group, Inc., 1991 WL 190539 (S.D.N.Y. Sept. 13, 1991), illustrates these differences between the copyright and patent standards. The plaintiff, Dirk Laureyssens, had designed a series of foam rubber puzzles, each consisting of six flat pieces that could be assembled to form a three-dimensional hollow cube. After its efforts to enter into a marketing agreement with Laureyssens broke down, defendant IGI designed its own six-piece "flat-to-cube" puzzles. When Laureyssens sued IGI for copyright infringement, IGI argued that Laureyssens' puzzles were insufficiently original to merit copyright protection. In support of this argument, IGI introduced a series of expired patents relating to toy cube puzzles. The court rejected IGI's argument:

> IGI does not seriously contend that Laureyssens did not in fact design his puzzles and select the particular individual puzzle piece shapes himself. As the Supreme Court has recently made clear, "[o]riginal, as the term is used in copyright, means only that the work was independently created by the author (as opposed to copied from another work), and that it possesses at least some minimal degree of creativity." *Feist Publications.* . . . The Laureyssens Puzzles clearly meet this standard of originality, and are therefore deserving of protection as original works.

1991 WL 190539, *16. That Laureyssens' puzzles were actually quite similar to the patented inventions, and so would not have met patent law's stringent nonobviousness standard, was irrelevant. The court subsequently concluded that IGI's puzzles—which were also similar to the patented puzzles—differed sufficiently from Laureyssens' puzzles and therefore did not infringe Laureyssens' copyright.

NOTES AND QUESTIONS

1. Why do you think patent law and copyright law have such different threshold standards for protectability, and such different rules about independent creation? If patented works are more expensive to develop than copyrighted works, might that explain the differences? *See* Dan L. Burk, *Patenting Speech,* 79 Tex. L. Rev. 99, 153 (2000). Or do the threshold requirements reflect

a trade-off between quality (patent) and quantity (copyright)? *See* Paul Goldstein, *Infringement of Copyright in Computer Programs*, 47 U. Pitt. L. Rev. 1119, 1121 (1986). If so, why choose this trade-off? Does copyright law's threshold standard differ from that of patent law because copyright protects aesthetic works rather than useful ones? *See* Douglas Y'Barbo, *The Heart of the Matter: The Property Right Conferred by Copyright*, 49 Mercer L. Rev. 643, 665-66 (1998).

   2. Consider, again, whether a higher standard of originality would be appropriate. Should the copyright originality standard perform the sort of gatekeeping function that the patent nonobviousness standard performs? For discussion of this question, see Joseph Scott Miller, *Hoisting Originality*, 31 Cardozo L. Rev. 451 (2009) (arguing that the social cost of copyright protection has grown as copyright's reach has expanded, and that such cost can be mitigated by recalibrating originality to reward the production of unconventional expression).

b. Some Contemporary Originality Problems

   After *Feist*, just how minimal can an author's creative contribution be and still qualify as copyrightable? Are there any other tools that courts can use to identify original contributions in cases involving works that raise originality problems? The next two cases address these questions.

Meshwerks, Inc. v. Toyota Motor Sales U.S.A., Inc.
528 F.3d 1258 (10th Cir. 2008)

GORSUCH, J.: . . . [Toyota and its advertising agency, Saatchi & Saatchi, hired Grace & Wild, Inc., to supply digital models of Toyota's vehicles for its model-year 2004 advertising campaign.] . . . G&W subcontracted with Meshwerks to assist with two initial aspects of the project — digitization and modeling. Digitizing involves collecting physical data points from the object to be portrayed. In the case of Toyota's vehicles, Meshwerks took copious measurements of Toyota's vehicles by covering each car, truck, and van with a grid of tape and running an articulated arm tethered to a computer over the vehicle to measure all points of intersection in the grid. Based on these measurements, modeling software then generated a digital image resembling a wire-frame model. . . .

   At this point, however, the on-screen image remained far from perfect and manual "modeling" was necessary. Meshwerks personnel fine-tuned or, as the company prefers it, "sculpted," the lines on screen to resemble each vehicle as closely as possible. Approximately 90 percent of the data points contained in each final model, Meshwerks represents, were the result not of the first-step measurement process, but of the skill and effort its digital sculptors manually expended at the second step. For example, some areas of detail, such as wheels, headlights, door handles, and the Toyota emblem, could not be accurately measured using current technology; those features had to be added at the second "sculpting" stage, and Meshwerks had to recreate those features as realistically as possible by hand, based on photographs. Even for areas that were measured, Meshwerks faced the challenge of converting measurements taken of a three-dimensional car into a two-dimensional computer representation; to achieve this, its modelers had to sculpt, or move, data points to achieve a visually convincing result. The purpose and product of these processes, after nearly 80 to 100 hours of effort per vehicle, were two-dimensional wire-frame depictions of Toyota's vehicles that appeared three-dimensional on screen, but were utterly unadorned — lacking color, shading, and other details. Attached to this opinion as Appendix A are sample screen-prints of one of Meshwerks' digital wire-frame models.

With Meshwerks' wire-frame products in hand, G&W then manipulated the computerized models by, first, adding detail, the result of which appeared on screen as a "tightening" of the wire frames, as though significantly more wires had been added to the frames, or as though they were made of a finer mesh. Next, G&W digitally applied color, texture, lighting, and animation for use in Toyota's advertisements. An example of G&W's work product is attached as Appendix B to this opinion. . . .

[Meshwerks sued Toyota, Saatchi & Saatchi, and G&W, asserting that it had contracted for only a one-time use of its models and that subsequent, unauthorized uses infringed its copyrights in the models. The district court granted defendants' motion for summary judgment, and Meshwerks appealed.]

II . . .

A . . .

What exactly does it mean for a work to qualify as "original"? In *Feist [Publications, Inc. v. Rural Telephone Service Co.*, 499 U.S. 340 (1991)], the Supreme Court clarified that the work must be "independently created by the author (as opposed to copied from other works)." *Id.* at 345 . . . ; see also *Burrow-Giles Lithographic Co. v. Sarony*, 111 U.S. 53, 58 . . . (1884) (the work for which copyright protection is sought must "owe[ ] its origin" to the putative copyright holder) (internal quotation omitted). In addition, the work must "possess[ ] at least some minimal degree of creativity," *Feist*, 499 U.S. at 345. . . . [5]

The parties focus most of their energy in this case on the question whether Meshwerks' models qualify as independent creations, as opposed to copies of Toyota's handiwork. But what can be said, at least based on received copyright doctrine, to distinguish an independent creation from a copy? And how might that doctrine apply in an age of virtual worlds and digital media that seek to mimic the "real" world, but often do so in ways that undoubtedly qualify as (highly) original? . . .

[P]hotography was initially met by critics with a degree of skepticism: a photograph, some said, "copies everything and explains nothing," and it was debated whether a camera could do anything more than merely record the physical world. . . . [In *Burrow-Giles*], the Court indicated [that] photographs are copyrightable, if only to the extent of their original depiction of the subject. Wilde's image [was] not copyrightable; but to the extent a photograph reflects the photographer's decisions regarding pose, positioning, background, lighting, shading, and the like, those elements can be said to "owe their origins" to the photographer, making the photograph copyrightable, at least to that extent.

As the Court more recently explained in *Feist*, the operative distinction is between, on the one hand, ideas or facts in the world, items that cannot be copyrighted, and a particular expression of that idea or fact, that can be. . . . So, in the case of photographs, for which Meshwerks' digital models were designed to serve as practically advantageous substitutes, authors are entitled to copyright protection only for the "incremental contribution," *SHL Imaging, Inc. [v. Artisan House, Inc.]*, 117 F. Supp. 2d at 311 [(S.D.N.Y. 2000)] (internal quotation omitted), represented by their interpretation or expression of the objects of their attention.

---

5. The two pertinent concepts — independent creation and minimal creativity — are intertwined and overlap, at least to some degree: After all, if something qualifies as an independent creation (that is, it is more than a copy) won't it also usually betray some minimal degree of creativity? Still, though the independent test imputed by the creativity requirement is low, it does exist. *Feist*, 499 U.S. at 345, 362. . . .

B

Applying these principles, evolved in the realm of photography, to the new medium that has come to supplement and even in some ways to supplant it, we think Meshwerks' models are not so much independent creations as (very good) copies of Toyota's vehicles. . . .

1

Key to our evaluation of this case is the fact that Meshwerks' digital wire-frame computer models depict Toyota's vehicles without any individualizing features: they are untouched by a digital paintbrush; they are not depicted in front of a palm tree, whizzing down the open road, or climbing up a mountainside. Put another way, Meshwerks' models depict nothing more than un-adorned Toyota vehicles — the car *as* car. *See* Appendix A. . . . [I]n short, its models reflect none of the decisions that can make depictions of things or facts in the world, whether Oscar Wilde or a Toyota Camry, new expressions subject to copyright protection.

The primary case on which Meshwerks asks us to rely actually reinforces this conclusion. In *Ets-Hokin v. Skyy Spirits, Inc.*, 225 F.3d 1068 (9th Cir.2000) (*Skyy I*), the Ninth Circuit was faced with a suit brought by a plaintiff photographer who alleged that the defendant had infringed on his commercial photographs of a Skyy-brand vodka bottle. The court held that the vodka bottle, as a "utilitarian object," a fact in the world, was not itself (at least usually) copyrightable. *Id.* at 1080 (citing 17 U.S.C. §101). At the same time, the court recognized that plaintiff's photos reflected decisions regarding "lighting, shading, angle, background, and so forth," *id.* at 1078, and to the extent plaintiff's photographs reflected such original contributions the court held they could be copyrighted. In so holding, the Ninth Circuit reversed a district court's dismissal of the case and remanded the matter for further proceedings, and Meshwerks argues this analysis controls the outcome of its case.

But *Skyy I* tells only half the story. The case soon returned to the court of appeals, and the court held that the defendant's photos, which differed in terms of angle, lighting, shadow, reflection, and background, did not infringe on the plaintiff's copyrights. *Ets-Hokin v. Skyy Spirits, Inc.*, 323 F.3d 763, 765 (9th Cir.2003) (*Skyy II*). Why? The only constant between the plaintiff's photographs and the defendant's photographs was the bottle itself, *id.* at 766, and an accurate portrayal of the unadorned bottle could not be copyrighted. . . .

The teaching of *Skyy I* and *II*, then, is that the vodka bottle, because it did not owe its origins to the photographers, had to be filtered out to determine what copyrightable expression remained. And, by analogy — though not perhaps the one Meshwerks had in mind — we hold that the unadorned images of Toyota's vehicles cannot be copyrighted by Meshwerks and likewise must be filtered out. To the extent that Meshwerks' digital wire-frame models depict only those unadorned vehicles, having stripped away all lighting, angle, perspective, and "other ingredients" associated with an original expression, we conclude that they have left no copyrightable matter.

Confirming this conclusion as well is the peculiar place where Meshwerks stood in the model-creation pecking order. On the one hand, Meshwerks had nothing to do with designing the appearance of Toyota's vehicles, distinguishing them from any other cars, trucks, or vans in the world. . . . On the other hand, how the models Meshwerks created were to be deployed in advertising — including the backgrounds, lighting, angles, and colors — were all matters left to those (G & W, Saatchi, and 3D Recon) who came after Meshwerks left the scene. . . . [8]

---

8. We are not called upon to, and do not, express any view on the copyrightability of the work products produced by those who employed and adorned Meshwerks' models.

It is certainly true that what Meshwerks accomplished was a peculiar kind of copying. It did not seek to recreate Toyota vehicles outright — steel, rubber, and all; instead, it sought to depict Toyota's three-dimensional physical objects in a two-dimensional digital medium. But we hold, as many before us have already suggested, that, standing alone, "[t]he fact that a work in one medium has been copied from a work in another medium does not render it any the less a 'copy.'" Nimmer on Copyright §8.01[B]. . . . After all, the putative creator who merely shifts the medium in which another's creation is expressed has not necessarily added anything beyond the expression contained in the original. . . .

In reaching this conclusion, we do not for a moment seek to downplay the considerable amount of time, effort, and skill that went into making Meshwerks' digital wire-frame models. But, in assessing the originality of a work for which copyright protection is sought, we look only at the final product, not the process, and the fact that intensive, skillful, and even creative labor is invested in the process of creating a product does not guarantee its copyrightability. *See Feist,* 499 U.S. at 359-60. . . .

2

Meshwerks' intent in making its wire-frame models provides additional support for our conclusion. "In theory, the originality requirement tests the putative author's state of mind: Did he have an earlier work in mind when he created his own?" Paul Goldstein, Goldstein on Copyright §2.2.1.1. If an artist affirmatively sets out to be unoriginal — to make a copy of someone else's creation, rather than to create an original work — it is far more likely that the resultant product will, in fact, be unoriginal. . . . Of course, this is not to say that the accidental or spontaneous artist will be denied copyright protection for not intending to produce art; it is only to say that authorial intent sometimes can shed light on the question of whether a particular work qualifies as an independent creation or only a copy.

In this case, the undisputed evidence before us leaves no question that Meshwerks set out to copy Toyota's vehicles, rather than to create, or even to add, any original expression. The purchase order signed by G & W asked Meshwerks to "digitize and model" Toyota's vehicles, and Meshwerks' invoice submitted to G & W for payment reflects that this is exactly the service Meshwerks performed. Aplt's App. at 113, 115. Meshwerks itself has consistently described digitization and modeling as an attempt accurately to depict real-world, three-dimensional objects as digital images viewable on a computer screen. *See, e.g., id.* at 369 ("the graphic sculptor is not intending to 'redesign' the product, he or she is attempting to depict that object in the most realistic way"). . . .

C

Although we hold that Meshwerks' digital, wire-frame models are insufficiently original to warrant copyright protection, we do not turn a blind eye to the fact that digital imaging is a relatively new and evolving technology and that Congress extended copyright protection to "original works of authorship fixed in any tangible medium of expression, *now known or later developed.*" 17 U.S.C. §102(a) (emphasis added). . . .

Digital modeling can be, surely is being, and no doubt increasingly will be used to create copyrightable expressions. Yet, just as photographs can be, but are not per se, copyrightable, the same holds true for digital models. There's little question that digital models can be devised of Toyota cars with copyrightable features, whether by virtue of unique shading, lighting, angle, background scene, or other choices. The problem for Meshwerks in this particular case is simply that the uncontested facts reveal that it wasn't involved in any such process. . . . For this reason, we do not envision any "chilling effect" on creative expression based on our holding today. . . .

Appendix A

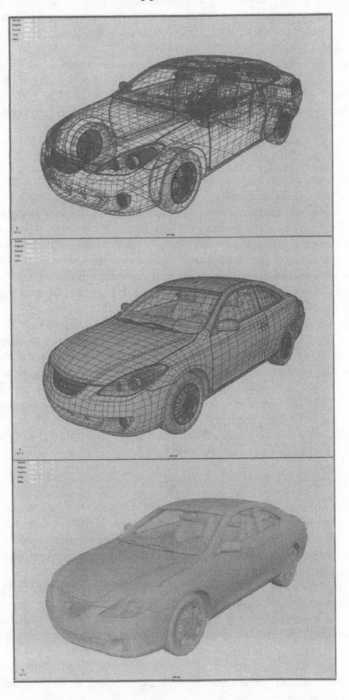

Mannion v. Coors Brewing Company

377 F. Supp. 2d 444 (S.D.N.Y. 2006)

KAPLAN, J.: . . .

Facts

Jonathan Mannion is a freelance photographer who specializes in portraits of celebrity athletes and musicians in the rap and rhythm-and-blues worlds. In 1999 he was hired by SLAM, a basketball magazine, to photograph basketball star Kevin Garnett in connection with an article. . . . The article, entitled "Above the Clouds," appeared as the cover story of the December 1999 issue of the magazine. It was accompanied by a number of Mannion's photographs of Garnett, including the one at issue here (the "Garnett Photograph"), which was printed on a two-page spread introducing the article.

The Garnett Photograph . . . is a three-quarter-length portrait of Garnett against a backdrop of clouds with some blue sky shining through. The view is up and across the right side of Garnett's torso, so that he appears to be towering above earth. He wears a white T-shirt, white athletic pants, a black close-fitting cap, and a large amount of platinum, gold, and diamond jewelry ("bling bling" in the vernacular), including several necklaces, a Rolex watch and bracelet on his left wrist, bracelets on his right wrist, rings on one finger of each hand, and earrings. His head is cocked, his eyes are closed, and his heavily-veined hands, nearly all of which are visible, rest over his lower abdomen, with the thumbs hooked on the waistband of the trousers. The light is from the viewer's left, so that Garnett's right shoulder is the brightest area of the photograph and his hands cast slight shadows on his trousers. As reproduced in the magazine, the photograph cuts off much of Garnett's left arm.

In early 2001, defendant Carol H. Williams Advertising ("CHWA") began developing ideas for outdoor billboards that would advertise Coors Light beer to young black men in urban areas. One of CHWA's "comp boards" — a "comp board" is an image created by an advertising company to convey a proposed design — used a manipulated version of the Garnett Photograph and superimposed on it the words "Iced Out" ("ice" being slang for diamonds) and a picture of a can of Coors Light beer (the "Iced Out Comp Board"). CHWA obtained authorization from Mannion's representative to use the Garnett Photograph for this purpose.

The Iced Out Comp Board . . . used a black-and-white, mirror image of the Garnett Photograph, but with the head cropped out on top and part of the fingers cropped out below. CHWA forwarded its comp boards to, and solicited bids for the photograph for the Coors advertising from, various photographers including Mannion, who submitted a bid but did not receive the assignment.

Coors and CHWA selected for a Coors billboard a photograph (the "Coors Billboard") . . . that resembles the Iced Out Comp Board. The Coors Billboard depicts, in black-and-white, the torso of a muscular black man, albeit a model other than Garnett, shot against a cloudy backdrop. The pose is similar to that in the Garnett Photograph, and the view also is up and across the left side of the torso. The model in the billboard photograph also wears a white T-shirt and white athletic pants. The model's jewelry is prominently depicted; it includes a necklace of platinum or gold and diamonds, a watch and two bracelets on the right wrist, and more bracelets on the left wrist. The light comes from the viewer's right, so that the left shoulder is the brightest part of the photograph, and the right arm and hand cast slight shadows on the trousers.

Mannion subsequently noticed the Coors Billboard at two locations in the Los Angeles area. He . . . brought this action for infringement in February of 2004. . . . The parties each move for summary judgment.

Garnett Photograph

Iced Out Comp Board   **Coors Billboard and Billboard Detail**

Original photograph of Kevin Garnett © Jonathan Mannion. Reproduced by permission.

Discussion . . .

Determining the Protectible Elements of the Garnett Photograph

The first question must be: in what respects is the Garnett Photograph protectible?

1. Protectible Elements of Photographs . . .

It sometimes is said that "copyright in the photograph conveys no rights over the subject matter conveyed in the photograph." But this is not always true. It of course is correct that the photographer of a building or tree or other pre-existing object has no right to prevent others from photographing the same thing. That is because originality depends upon independent creation, and the photographer did not create that object. By contrast, if a photographer arranges or otherwise creates the subject that his camera captures, he may have the right to prevent others from producing works that depict that subject.

Almost any photograph "may claim the necessary originality to support a copyright." Indeed, ever since the Supreme Court considered an 1882 portrait by the celebrity photographer Napoleon Sarony of the 27-year-old Oscar Wilde, courts have articulated lists of potential components of a photograph's originality. These lists, however, are somewhat unsatisfactory.

First, they do not deal with the issue, alluded to above, that the nature and extent of a photograph's protection differs depending on what makes that photograph original.

Second, courts have not always distinguished between decisions that a photographer makes in creating a photograph and the originality of the final product. Several cases, for example, have included in lists of the potential components of photographic originality "selection of film and camera," "lens and filter selection," and "the kind of camera, the kind of film, [and] the kind of lens." Having considered the matter fully, however, I think this is not sufficiently precise. Decisions about film, camera, and lens, for example, often bear on whether an image is original. But the fact that a photographer made such choices does not alone make the image original. "Sweat of the brow" is not the touchstone of copyright. Protection derives from the features of the work itself, not the effort that goes into it. . . .

A photograph may be original in three respects. They are not mutually exclusive.

a. Rendition

First, "there may be originality which does not depend on creation of the scene or object to be photographed . . . and which resides [instead] in such specialties as angle of shot, light and shade, exposure, effects achieved by means of filters, developing techniques etc." I will refer to this type of originality as originality in the rendition because, to the extent a photograph is original in this way, copyright protects not *what* is depicted, but rather *how* it is depicted. . . .

b. Timing

A photograph may be original in a second respect. "[A] person may create a worthwhile photograph by being at the right place at the right time." I will refer to this type of originality as originality in timing.

. . . A modern work strikingly original in timing might be *Catch of the Day,* by noted wildlife photographer Thomas Mangelsen, which depicts a salmon that appears to be jumping into the gaping mouth of a brown bear at Brooks Falls in Katmai National Park, Alaska. An older example is Alfred Eisenstaedt's photograph of a sailor kissing a young woman on VJ Day in Times Square, the memorability of which is attributable in significant part to the timing of its creation.

Copyright based on originality in timing is limited by the principle that copyright in a photograph ordinarily confers no rights over the subject matter. Thus, the copyright in *Catch of the Day* does not protect against subsequent photographs of bears feasting on salmon in the same location. Furthermore, if another photographer were sufficiently skilled and fortunate to capture a salmon at the precise moment that it appeared to enter a hungry bear's mouth—and others have tried, with varying degrees of success—that photographer, even if inspired by Mangelsen, would not necessarily have infringed his work because Mangelsen's copyright does not extend to the natural world he captured.

In practice, originality in timing gives rise to the same type of protection as originality in the rendition. In each case, the image that exhibits the originality, but not the underlying subject, qualifies for copyright protection.

c. Creation of the Subject

The principle that copyright confers no right over the subject matter has an important limitation. A photograph may be original to the extent that the photographer created "the scene or subject to be photographed." This type of originality, which I will refer to as originality in the creation of the subject, played an essential role in *Rogers v. Koons* [960 F.2d 301 (2d Cir. 1992)] and *Gross v. Seligman* [212 F. 930 (2d Cir. 1914)].

In *Rogers,* the court held that the copyright in the plaintiff's photograph *Puppies,* which depicted a contrived scene of the photographer's acquaintance, Jim Scanlon, and his wife on a park bench with eight puppies on their laps, protected against the defendants' attempt to replicate precisely, albeit in a three dimensional sculpture, the content of the photograph. Although the Circuit noted that *Puppies* was original because the artist "made creative judgments concerning technical matters with his camera and the use of natural light"—in other words, because it was original in the rendition—its originality in the creation of the subject was more salient. The same is true of the works at issue in *Gross v. Seligman,* in which the Circuit held that the copyright in a photograph named *Grace of Youth* was infringed when the same artist created a photograph named *Cherry Ripe* using "the same model in the identical pose, with the single exception that the young woman now wears a smile and holds a cherry stem between her teeth."

* * * * * *

To conclude, the nature and extent of protection conferred by the copyright in a photograph will vary depending on the nature of its originality. Insofar as a photograph is original in the rendition or timing, copyright protects the image but does not prevent others from photographing the same object or scene. . . .

By contrast, to the extent that a photograph is original in the creation of the subject, copyright extends also to that subject. Thus, an artist who arranges and then photographs a scene often will have the right to prevent others from duplicating that scene in a photograph or other medium.[65]

2. Originality of the Garnett Photograph

There can be no serious dispute that the Garnett Photograph is an original work. The photograph does not result from slavishly copying another work and therefore is original in the rendition. Mannion's relatively unusual angle and distinctive lighting strengthen that aspect of the photograph's originality. His composition—posing man against sky—evidences originality in the creation of the subject. Furthermore, Mannion instructed Garnett to wear simple and plain clothing and as much jewelry as possible, and "to look 'chilled out.'" His orchestration of the scene contributes additional originality in the creation of the subject.

Of course, there are limits to the photograph's originality and therefore to the protection conferred by the copyright in the Garnett Photograph. For example, Kevin Garnett's face, torso, and hands are not original with Mannion, and Mannion therefore may not prevent others from creating photographic portraits of Garnett. Equally obviously, the existence of a cloudy sky is not original, and Mannion therefore may not prevent others from using a cloudy sky as a backdrop.

The defendants, however, take this line of reasoning too far. They argue that it was Garnett, not Mannion, who selected the specific clothing, jewelry, and pose. In consequence, they maintain, the Garnett Photograph is not original to the extent of Garnett's clothing, jewelry, and pose. They appear to be referring to originality in the creation of the subject.

There are two problems with the defendants' argument. The first is that Mannion indisputably orchestrated the scene, even if he did not plan every detail before he met Garnett, and

---

65. I recognize that the preceding analysis focuses on a medium—traditional print photography—that is being supplanted in significant degree by digital technology. These advancements may or may not demand a different analytical framework.

then made the decision to capture it. The second difficulty is that the originality of the photograph extends beyond the individual clothing, jewelry, and pose viewed in isolation. It is the entire image — depicting man, sky, clothing, and jewelry in a particular arrangement — that is at issue here, not its individual components. . . .

NOTES AND QUESTIONS

1. Can *Meshwerks* and *Alfred Bell* be construed consistently?

2. Is it appropriate to consider intent in determining originality? If so, what type of intent counts? If Meshwerks had created its digital models for an art exhibit rather than for an advertising campaign, should the result change? Why, or why not?

3. How helpful is the *Mannion* court's taxonomy of originality in photographs? How distinct are the different dimensions of originality described by the court? Was the photograph in *Burrow-Giles* original in rendition, original in creation of the subject, or both?

4. Does assessment of originality in "rendition" or "creation of the subject" violate the *Bleistein* nondiscrimination principle?

5. Consider whether and to what extent copyright would (or should) protect the following:

    a. a photograph by acclaimed documentary photographer Walker Evans of riders on the New York City subway;

    b. photographs on a restaurant menu depicting dishes available at the restaurant;

    c. the photograph on your driver's license.

Is *Mannion* or *Feist* more helpful in analyzing these examples?

6. Should the *Mannion* taxonomy, or one like it, be used for other types of works? Would it have been helpful in evaluating the lithographs in *Bleistein*? How about the digital models in *Meshwerks*?

7. Are some creative products too insignificant to qualify as original? Current Copyright Office regulations deny copyright to, *inter alia*, titles, slogans, and other short phrases. 37 C.F.R. §202.1(a). Should copyright extend to small contributions to open source software projects or to Wikipedia entries? For discussion of the policy issues raised by these questions, see Justin Hughes, *Size Matters (or Should) in Copyright Law*, 74 Fordham L. Rev. 575 (2005).

3. The "Idea/Expression Distinction"

The third requirement for copyrightable subject matter is a negative one: Certain items are categorically excluded from receiving copyright protection. According to §102(b) of the Act: "In no case does copyright protection for an original work of authorship extend to any idea, procedure, process, system, method of operation, concept, principle, or discovery, regardless of the form in which it is described, explained, illustrated, or embodied in such work."

Courts and commentators often describe §102(b) as implementing a venerable precept of copyright law: An idea can never be copyrightable, but its expression may be. In fact, §102(b) seems to have two purposes: (1) to define the line between what is eligible for copyright protection and what belongs to the public domain; and (2) to define the line between copyrightable and patentable subject matter. (Which parts of §102(b) relate to each of these goals?) The term "idea/expression distinction" is thus shorthand for a rule requiring the exclusion of a variety of noncopyrightable elements.

As in the case of originality, many countries' laws have similar provisions. Unlike the originality requirement, however, the principle expressed in §102(b) is also enshrined in the major international copyright treaties. Both the TRIPS Agreement and WIPO Copyright Treaty state, in identical language, that copyright protection extends "to expressions and not to ideas, procedures, methods of operation or mathematical concepts as such." TRIPS Agreement, art. 9(2); WIPO Copyright Treaty, art. 2.

Why does the exclusion of ideas, procedures, methods of operation, and the like command such universal support? Both economic and non-economic approaches to copyright view the items listed in §102(b) as basic building blocks of copyrightable expression, and hold that granting copyright in these items would be counterproductive. Consider, for example, the idea of a pair of doomed lovers whose families oppose their marriage, or the scientific concepts embodied in Einstein's theory of relativity, or the steps that need to be performed to change a tire or bake an apple pie. Would it be efficient to give exclusive rights in any of these "ideas" to the first person to write about it? Would it be fair, or morally justifiable, to do so?

While the goal of protecting "expression" rather than "idea" is simple enough to state, how should a court implement §102(b) in practice? As in the case of §102(a)'s originality requirement, the legislative history of §102(b) is somewhat vague, indicating primarily that the provision was intended to continue the status quo: "Section 102(b) in no way enlarges or contracts the scope of copyright protection under the present law. Its purpose is to restate, in the context of the new single Federal system of copyright, that the basic dichotomy between expression and idea remains unchanged." H.R. Rep. No. 94-1476, 94th Cong., 2d Sess. 57 (1976), *reprinted in* 1976 U.S.C.C.A.N. 5659, 5670. Once again, therefore, the courts must develop their own guiding principles. As you read the cases in this section, keep §102(b)'s twofold purpose in mind, and think about whether that helps to explain the results in particular cases that might otherwise seem difficult to understand.

a. Form Versus Function Versus Fair Game

The landmark Supreme Court decision on the "idea/expression distinction" is *Baker v. Selden*, 101 U.S. 99 (1879). The legislative history of §102(b) indicates that Congress intended §102(b) in part to codify the holding of *Baker*. H.R. Rep. No. 94-1476, 94th Cong., 2d Sess. 57 (1976), *reprinted in* 1976 U.S.C.C.A.N. 5659, 5670. As you read the case, try to identify exactly where the Court draws the line between copyrightable and uncopyrightable subject matter.

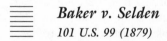

Baker v. Selden
101 U.S. 99 (1879)

BRADLEY, J.: Charles Selden, the testator of the complainant in this case, in the year 1859 took the requisite steps for obtaining the copyright of a book, entitled "Selden's Condensed Ledger, or Book-keeping Simplified," the object of which was to exhibit and explain a peculiar system of book-keeping. In 1860 and 1861, he took the copyright of several other books, containing additions to and improvements upon the said system. The bill of complaint was filed against the defendant, Baker, for an alleged infringement of these copyrights. The latter, in his answer, denied that Selden was the author or designer of the books, and denied the infringement charged, and contends on the argument that the matter alleged to be infringed is not a lawful subject of copyright. . . .

The book or series of books of which the complainant claims the copyright consists of an introductory essay explaining the system of book-keeping referred to, to which are annexed certain forms or blanks, consisting of ruled lines, and headings, illustrating the system and showing how it is to be used and carried out in practice. This system effects the same results as book-keeping by double entry; but, by a peculiar arrangement of columns and headings, presents the entire operation, of a day, a week, or a month, on a single page, or on two pages facing each other, in an account-book. The defendant uses a similar plan so far as results are concerned; but makes a different arrangement of the columns, and uses different headings. If the complainant's testator had the exclusive right to the use of the system explained in his book, it would be difficult to contend that the defendant does not infringe it, notwithstanding the difference in his form of arrangement; but if it be assumed that the system is open to public use, it seems to be equally difficult to contend that the books made and sold by the defendant are a violation of the copyright of the complainant's book considered merely as a book explanatory of the system. Where the truths of a science or the methods of an art are the common property of the whole world, any author has the right to express the one, or explain and use the other, in his own way. As an author, Selden explained the system in a particular way. It may be conceded that Baker makes and uses account-books arranged on substantially the same system; but the proof fails to show that he has violated the copyright of Selden's book, regarding the latter merely as an explanatory work; or that he has infringed Selden's right in any way, unless the latter became entitled to an exclusive right in the system.

The evidence of the complainant is principally directed to the object of showing that Baker uses the same system as that which is explained and illustrated in Selden's books. It becomes important, therefore, to determine whether, in obtaining the copyright of his books, he secured the exclusive right to the use of the system or method of book-keeping which the said books are intended to illustrate and explain. It is contended that he has secured such exclusive right, because no one can use the system without using substantially the same ruled lines and headings which he has appended to his books in illustration of it. In other words, it is contended that the ruled lines and headings, given to illustrate the system, are a part of the book, and, as such, are secured by the copyright; and that no one can make or use similar ruled lines and headings, or ruled lines and headings made and arranged on substantially the same system, without violating the copyright. And this is really the question to be decided in this case. Stated in another form, the question is, whether the exclusive property in a system of book-keeping can be claimed, under the law of copyright, by means of a book in which that system is explained? The complainant's bill, and the case made under it, are based on the hypothesis that it can be. . . .

There is no doubt that a work on the subject of book-keeping, though only explanatory of well-known systems, may be the subject of a copyright; but, then, it is claimed only as a book. Such a book may be explanatory either of old systems, or of an entirely new system; and, considered as a book, as the work of an author, conveying information on the subject of book-keeping, and containing detailed explanations of the art, it may be a very valuable acquisition to the practical knowledge of the community. But there is a clear distinction between the book, as such, and the art which it is intended to illustrate. The mere statement of the proposition is so evident, that it requires hardly any argument to support it. The same distinction may be predicated of every other art as well as that of book-keeping. A treatise on the composition and use of medicines, be they old or new; on the construction and use of ploughs, or watches, or churns; or on the mixture and application of colors for painting or dyeing; or on the mode of drawing lines to produce the effect of perspective — would be the subject of copyright; but no one would contend that the copyright of the treatise would give the exclusive right to the art or manufacture described therein. The copyright of the book, if not pirated from other works, would be valid without regard to the novelty, or want of novelty, of its subject-matter. The novelty of the art or thing described or explained has nothing to do with the validity of the copyright. To give to the author of the book an exclusive property in the art described therein, when no examination of its novelty has ever been officially made, would be a surprise and a fraud upon the public. That is the province of letters-patent, not of copyright. The claim to an invention or discovery of an art or manufacture must be subjected to the examination of the Patent Office before an exclusive right therein can be obtained; and it can only be secured by a patent from the government. . . .

. . . The very object of publishing a book on science or the useful arts is to communicate to the world the useful knowledge which it contains. But this object would be frustrated if the knowledge could not be used without incurring the guilt of piracy of the book. And where the art it teaches cannot be used without employing the methods and diagrams used to illustrate the book, or such as are similar to them, such methods and diagrams are to be considered as necessary incidents to the art, and given therewith to the public; not given for the purpose of publication in other works explanatory of the art, but for the purpose of practical application.

Of course, these observations are not intended to apply to ornamental designs, or pictorial illustrations addressed to the taste. Of these it may be said, that their form is their essence, and their object, the production of pleasure in their contemplation. This is their final end. They are as much the product of genius and the result of composition, as are the lines of the poet or the historian's periods. On the other hand, the teachings of science and the rules and methods of useful art have their final end in application and use; and this application and use are what the public derive from the publication of a book which teaches them. But as embodied and taught in a literary composition or book, their essence consists only in their statement. This alone is what is secured by the copyright. The use by another of the same methods of statement, whether in words or illustrations, in a book published for teaching the art, would undoubtedly be an infringement of the copyright.

Recurring to the case before us, we observe that Charles Selden, by his books, explained and described a peculiar system of book-keeping, and illustrated his method by means of ruled lines and blank columns, with proper headings on a page, or on successive pages. Now, whilst no one has a right to print or publish his book, or any material part thereof, as a book intended to convey instruction in the art, any person may practise and use the art itself which he has described and illustrated therein. The use of the art is a totally different thing from a publication of the book explaining it. The copyright of a book on book-keeping cannot secure the exclusive right to make, sell, and use account-books prepared upon the plan set forth in such book. Whether the art might or might not have been patented, is a question which is not before us. It was not patented, and is open and free to the use of the public. And, of course, in using the art, the ruled lines and headings of accounts must necessarily be used as incident to it.

[BAKER'S FORM.]

AUDITOR'S REGISTER.

RECEIPTS.

Date.	No.	From.	For.	County.		Total.
					Total	

BALANCE SHEET

FUNDS	Rec'd to 18_	[Dis'd] in 18_	To Rec. in 18_	To Dis. to 18_	Balance 18_	Ov'r Pd. 18_
County.						
Poor.						
Bridge.						
School.						
Township.						
Corporation.						
Redemption of Lands.						
Teachers' Institute.						
Show Licences.						
Peddlers' Licences.						
Volunteer Relief.						
Section 16.						
State Fund.						
Road Taxes.						
Building.						
Rail Road.						
Ministry.						
Soldiers' Pay.						
Bounty.						
Balance in Treasury.						
Total.						
County Treasurer-General Acct.						

ADDITIONAL RECEIPTS.

Floating Order.

RIGHT HAND PAGE

AUDITOR'S REGISTER.

DISBURSEMENTS.

Date.	No.	To.	For.	By.	County.	Poor.	Bridge.	Total.
				Total				

ADDITIONAL DISBURSEMENTS.

Exhibit.

LEFT HAND PAGE.

[SELDEN'S FORM]

AUDITOR'S RECORD. **CONDENSED LEDGER.**

DISBURSEMENTS.

RECEIPTS.

County Fund.

Date.	No.	Amount.	To.	For.	Authority.	Date.	No.	Amount.	Of.	For.	Authority.

Bro'ght Forward. — Dr. / Cr.

Distribution. — Dr. / Cr.

Date: from ...... to ...... inclusive.

Sundries to Sundries.

TREASURER.

Dr. | Cr. | Dr.

Total. — Dr. / Cr.

Balances. — Dr. / Cr.

$ County Fund.
Bridge Fund.
County Infirmary.
Building Fund.
Internal Fund.
Kind Fund.
Sale Redemptions.
Refunders.
Redemptions.
Tax Omissions.
Forfeitures.
Duplicate.
Section 16.
Section 29.
Peddlers' License.
Show License.
State Fund.
School Fund.
Corporation Fund.
Township Fund.
Treasurer's Fees.
State Relief Fund.
Soldiers' Fund.
Militia Fund.
Bounty Fund.
School Examiners' Fund.
CARRIED FORWARD.

Floating Order

LEFT HAND PAGE

RIGHT HAND PAGE

Selden's Condensed Ledger

The plausibility of the claim put forward by the complainant in this case arises from a confusion of ideas produced by the peculiar nature of the art described in the books which have been made the subject of copyright. In describing the art, the illustrations and diagrams employed happen to correspond more closely than usual with the actual work performed by the operator who uses the art. Those illustrations and diagrams consist of ruled lines and headings of accounts; and it is similar ruled lines and headings of accounts which, in the application of the art, the book-keeper makes with his pen, or the stationer with his press; whilst in most other cases the diagrams and illustrations can only be represented in concrete forms of wood, metal, stone, or some other physical embodiment. But the principle is the same in all. The description of the art in a book, though entitled to the benefit of copyright, lays no foundation for an exclusive claim to the art itself. The object of the one is explanation; the object of the other is use. The former may be secured by copyright. The latter can only be secured, if it can be secured at all, by letters-patent. . . .

NOTES AND QUESTIONS

1. What exactly is the *Baker* holding? Are the forms copyrightable or not? If Selden's book were still under copyright, how would you advise a client who wanted to do the following:

a. implement an accounting system that will require the client to use exact copies of the forms;
b. publish a book of blank forms containing exact copies of Selden's forms;
c. publish a book that compares different accounting systems. The book will include a description of Selden's system and reproduction of the forms as they appear in Selden's book and examples of how to modify the forms to meet different needs.

2. In *Baker* the defendant was a direct competitor of the copyright holder. Why didn't that affect the Supreme Court's decision in the case? Should a defendant's status as a competitor matter?

3. Does *Baker* mean that the more useful a work is, the less likely it is to be copyrightable? Would that make sense? If courts interpret *Baker* in that way, will they have to evaluate artistic merit?

4. Is *Baker* best described as a case about the uncopyrightability of "ideas"? Professor Pamela Samuelson argues that it is not: "[T]he main message the Court was trying to convey was that bookkeeping systems and other useful arts were beyond the scope of copyright protection in any text that might explain them or any drawing that might illustrate them." Pamela Samuelson, *Why Copyright Excludes Systems and Processes from the Scope of Its Protection*, 85 Tex. L. Rev. 1921, 1926 (2007). She argues that *Baker* provides a foundation for §102(b)'s exclusion of systems, methods, and processes, but not for its exclusion of ideas. Do you agree? Why might it matter? Reconsider this question after you read the remaining cases in this section.

5. Closely related to the exclusionary principle expressed in §102(b) is the doctrine of *merger*. Courts will sometimes state that if only one or a limited number of ways exist to express an idea, the idea and expression merge into an uncopyrightable whole. For example, in *Morrissey v. Procter & Gamble Co.*, 379 F.2d 675 (1st Cir. 1967), the court held that instructions for a sweepstakes contest could not be copyrighted:

When the uncopyrightable subject matter is very narrow, so that "the topic necessarily requires" . . . if not only one form of expression, at best only a limited number, to permit copyrighting would mean that a party or parties, by copyrighting a mere handful of forms, could exhaust all possibilities of future use of the substance. In such circumstances it does not seem accurate to say that any particular form of expression comes from the subject matter. However, it is necessary to say that the subject matter would be appropriated by permitting the copyrighting of its expression. We cannot recognize copyright as a game of chess in which the public can be checkmated. Cf. *Baker v. Selden.* . . .

379 F.2d at 679. Some courts regard the merger doctrine as a defense to copyright infringement liability, rather than as a bar to copyrightability at the outset. *See, e.g., Kregos v. Associated Press,* 937 F.2d 700, 705 (2d Cir. 1991) ("Assessing merger in the context of alleged infringement will normally provide a more detailed and realistic basis for evaluating the claim that protection of expression would invariably accord protection to an idea.").

Other courts are a bit more generous, holding that when there are few ways to express an idea, the particular expression may be copyrightable, but the scope of the copyright is "thin" — so thin that infringement only occurs in the case of a virtually identical copy. *See, e.g., Johnson Controls, Inc. v. Phoenix Control Sys., Inc.,* 886 F.2d 1173, 1175 (9th Cir. 1989) ("Where an idea and the expression 'merge,' or are 'inseparable,' the expression is not given copyright protection. . . . In addition, where an expression is, as a practical matter, indispensable, or at least standard, in the treatment of a given idea, the expression is protected only against verbatim, or virtually identical copying.").

What are the practical differences, if any, to litigants of these approaches? What incentives does the "thin copyright" approach create?

6. Section 101 of the Patent Act defines patentable subject matter: "Whoever invents or discovers any new and useful process, machine, manufacture, or composition of matter, or any new and useful improvement thereof, may obtain a patent therefor, subject to the conditions and requirements of this title." Selden described a process for bookkeeping. Was Selden's system therefore patentable subject matter? The answer in Selden's time was probably no, because methods of doing business were not considered patentable. The patentability of business methods remains unclear today. In 1998, the Federal Circuit characterized the judicially created exception to patentability as "ill-conceived," and ruled that a "hub-and-spoke" method of allocating costs and profits among a family of mutual funds was patentable subject matter. *See State Street Bank & Trust Co. v. Signature Financial Group, Inc.,* 149 F.3d 1368, 1375 (Fed. Cir. 1998). Recently, however, the Federal Circuit abrogated the test in *State Street* and ruled that a method of doing business could be patentable only if "(1) it is tied to a particular machine or apparatus, or (2) it transforms a particular article into a different state or thing." In re *Bilski,* 545 F.3d 943, 954 (Fed. Cir.), *cert. granted,* 129 S. Ct. 2735 (2009).

Are §101 of the Patent Act and §102(a) of the Copyright Act mutually exclusive? In other words, is §102(b) intended to draw a boundary line that prevents any overlap between the two systems of exclusive rights? If patent law changes by expanding the classes of patentable subject matter, should copyright law make any changes to its scope? We return to these questions in Chapter 4, which considers the copyrightability of computer software.

b. *Complications*

Baker and §102(b) might be read to suggest that information separates neatly into three categories: copyrightable, patentable, and public domain. The reality is more complicated. Within copyright law, the conceptual difficulties in separating excluded "idea" from protectable expression are substantial. Consider: Is §102(b) simply an elaboration of §102(a) or does it add something — i.e., could there be subject matter that qualifies for copyright protection under §102(a) that is nevertheless barred from such protection under §102(b)? Put differently, could there be an "original" theory or method of classification that would seem eligible for protection under §102(a) but that would be barred from such protection under §102(b)? The cases in this section consider this question.

First, where is the line between fact and fiction? Many historical novels blend the two, making the scope of copyright protection in such novels difficult to assess. Many nonfictional historical works, meanwhile, include some material that rests, at least in part, on hypothesis or conjecture. Additionally, many expressive works, both fictional and nonfictional, employ standard expressions to conjure up certain images. Should one author be permitted to claim a copyright in such a standard expression?

A.A. Hoehling v. Universal City Studios, Inc.
618 F.2d 972 (2d Cir.), cert. denied, 449 U.S. 841 (1980)

KAUFMAN, C.J.: A grant of copyright in a published work secures for its author a limited monopoly over the expression it contains. The copyright provides a financial incentive to those who would add to the corpus of existing knowledge by creating original works. Nevertheless, the protection afforded the copyright holder has never extended to history, be it documented fact or explanatory hypothesis. The rationale for this doctrine is that the cause of knowledge is best served when history is the common property of all, and each generation remains free to draw upon the discoveries and insights of the past. Accordingly, the scope of copyright in historical accounts is narrow indeed, embracing no more than the author's original expression of particular facts and theories already in the public domain. As the case before us illustrates, absent wholesale usurpation of another's expression, claims of copyright infringement where works of history are at issue are rarely successful.

I.

This litigation arises from three separate accounts of the triumphant introduction, last voyage, and tragic destruction of the Hindenburg, the colossal dirigible constructed in Germany during Hitler's reign. The zeppelin, the last and most sophisticated in a fleet of luxury airships, which punctually floated its wealthy passengers from the Third Reich to the United States, exploded into flames and disintegrated in 35 seconds as it hovered above the Lakehurst, New Jersey Naval Air Station at 7:25 P.M. on May 6, 1937. Thirty-six passengers and crew were killed but, fortunately, 52 persons survived. Official investigations conducted by both American and German authorities could ascertain no definitive cause of the disaster, but both suggested the plausibility of static electricity or St. Elmo's Fire, which could have ignited the highly explosive hydrogen that filled the airship. Throughout, the investigators refused to rule out the possibility of sabotage. . . .

The final pages of the airship's story marked the beginning of a series of journalistic, historical, and literary accounts devoted to the Hindenburg and its fate. Indeed, weeks of testimony by a plethora of witnesses before the official investigative panels provided fertile source material for would-be authors. Moreover, both the American and German Commissions issued official reports, detailing all that was then known of the tragedy. A number of newspaper and magazine articles had been written about the Hindenburg in 1936, its first year of trans-Atlantic service, and they, of course, multiplied many fold after the crash. In addition, two passengers Margaret Mather and Gertrud Adelt published separate and detailed accounts of the voyage, C.E. Rosendahl, commander of the Lakehurst Naval Air Station and a pioneer in airship travel himself, wrote a book titled *What About the Airship?*, in which he endorsed the theory that the Hindenburg was the victim of sabotage. In 1957, Nelson Gidding, who would return to the subject of the Hindenburg some 20 years later, wrote an unpublished "treatment" for a motion picture based on the deliberate destruction of the airship. In that year as well, John Toland published *Ships in the Sky* which, in its seventeenth chapter, chronicled the last flight of the Hindenburg. In 1962, Dale Titler released *Wings of Mystery*, in which he too devoted a chapter to the Hindenburg.[3]

Appellant A.A. Hoehling published *Who Destroyed the Hindenburg?*, a full-length book based on his exhaustive research in 1962. Mr. Hoehling studied the investigative reports, consulted previously published articles and books, and conducted interviews with survivors of the crash as well as others who possessed information about the Hindenburg. His book is presented as a factual account, written in an objective, reportorial style.

The first half recounts the final crossing of the Hindenburg, from Sunday, May 2, when it left Frankfurt, to Thursday, May 6, when it exploded at Lakehurst. Hoehling describes the airship, its role as an instrument of propaganda in Nazi Germany, its passengers and crew, the danger of hydrogen, and the ominous threats received by German officials, warning that the Hindenburg would be destroyed. The second portion, headed *The Quest*, sets forth the progress of the official investigations, followed by an account of Hoehling's own research. In the final chapter, spanning eleven pages, Hoehling suggests that all proffered explanations of the explosion, save deliberate destruction, are unconvincing. He concludes that the most likely saboteur is one Eric Spehl, a "rigger" on the Hindenburg crew who was killed at Lakehurst.

According to Hoehling, Spehl had motive, expertise, and opportunity to plant an explosive device, constructed of dry-cell batteries and a flashbulb, in "Gas Cell 4," the location of the initial explosion. An amateur photographer with access to flashbulbs, Spehl could have destroyed the Hindenburg to please his ladyfriend, a suspected communist dedicated to exploding the myth of Nazi invincibility.

Ten years later appellee Michael MacDonald Mooney published his book, *The Hindenburg*. Mooney's endeavor might be characterized as more literary than historical in its attempt to weave a number of symbolic themes through the actual events surrounding the tragedy. His dominant theme contrasts the natural beauty of the month of May, when the disaster occurred, with the cold, deliberate progress of "technology." The May theme is expressed not simply by the season, but also by the character of Spehl, portrayed as a sensitive artisan with needle and thread. The Hindenburg, in contrast, is the symbol of technology, as are its German creators and the Reich itself. The destruction is depicted as the ultimate triumph of nature over technology, as Spehl plants the bomb that ignites the hydrogen. Developing this theme from the outset, Mooney begins with an extended review of man's efforts to defy nature through flight, focusing on the evolution of the zeppelin. This story culminates in the construction of the Hindenburg, and the Nazis' claims of its indestructibility. Mooney then traces the fateful voyage, advising the reader almost immediately of Spehl's scheme. The book concludes with the airship's explosion.

Mooney acknowledges, in this case, that he consulted Hoehling's book, and that he relied on it for some details. He asserts that he first discovered the "Spehl-as-saboteur" theory when he read Titler's *Wings of Mystery*. Indeed, Titler concludes that Spehl was the saboteur, for essentially the reasons stated by Hoehling. Mooney also claims to have studied the complete

---

3. Titler's account was published after the release of appellant's book. In an affidavit in this litigation, Titler states that he copied Hoehling's theory of sabotage. Hoehling, however, has never instituted a copyright action against Titler.

National Archives and New York Times files concerning the Hindenburg, as well as all previously published material. Moreover, he traveled to Germany, visited Spehl's birthplace, and conducted a number of interviews with survivors.

After Mooney prepared an outline of his anticipated book, his publisher succeeded in negotiations to sell the motion picture rights to appellee Universal City Studios. Universal then commissioned a screen story by writers Levinson and Link, best known for their television series, *Columbo*, in which a somewhat disheveled, but wise detective unravels artfully conceived murder mysteries. In their screen story, Levinson and Link created a Columbo-like character who endeavored to identify the saboteur on board the Hindenburg. Director Robert Wise, however, was not satisfied with this version, and called upon Nelson Gidding to write a final screenplay. Gidding, it will be recalled, had engaged in preliminary work on a film about the Hindenburg almost twenty years earlier.

The Gidding screenplay follows what is known in the motion picture industry as a "Grand Hotel" formula, developing a number of fictional characters and subplots involving them. This formula has become standard fare in so-called "disaster" movies, which have enjoyed a certain popularity in recent years. In the film, which was released in late 1975, a rigger named "Boerth," who has an anti-Nazi ladyfriend, plans to destroy the airship in an effort to embarrass the Reich. Nazi officials, vaguely aware of sabotage threats, station a Luftwaffe intelligence officer on the zeppelin, loosely resembling a Colonel Erdmann who was aboard the Hindenburg. This character is portrayed as a likable fellow who soon discovers that Boerth is the saboteur. Boerth, however, convinces him that the Hindenburg should be destroyed and the two join forces, planning the explosion for several hours after the landing at Lakehurst, when no people would be on board. In Gidding's version, the airship is delayed by a storm, frantic efforts to defuse the bomb fail, and the Hindenburg is destroyed. The film's subplots involve other possible suspects, including a fictional countess who has had her estate expropriated by the Reich, two fictional confidence men wanted by New York City police, and an advertising executive rushing to close a business deal in America. . . .

[Hoehling sued Universal and Mooney for copyright infringement. The district court granted summary judgment in favor of the defendants.]

II.

A

Hoehling's principal claim is that both Mooney and Universal copied the essential plot of his book — *i.e.*, Eric Spehl, influenced by his girlfriend, sabotaged the Hindenburg by placing a crude bomb in Gas Cell 4. . . .

[A]ppellees . . . argue that Hoehling's plot is an "idea," and ideas are not copyrightable as a matter of law. *See Sheldon v. Metro-Goldwyn Pictures Corp.*, 81 F.2d 49, 54 (2d Cir.), *cert. denied*, 298 U.S. 669. . . .

Hoehling, however, correctly rejoins that while ideas themselves are not subject to copyright, his "expression" of his idea is copyrightable. *Id.* at 54. . . .

. . . But, where, as here, the idea at issue is an interpretation of an historical event, our cases hold that such interpretations are not copyrightable as a matter of law. In *Rosemont Enterprises, Inc. v. Random House, Inc.*, 366 F.2d 303 (2d Cir. 1966), *cert. denied*, 385 U.S. 1009 . . . , we held that the defendant's biography of Howard Hughes did not infringe an earlier biography of the reclusive alleged billionaire. Although the plots of the two works were necessarily similar, there could be no infringement because of the "public benefit in encouraging the development of historical and biographical works and their public distribution." *Id.* at 307; *accord, Oxford Book Co. v. College Entrance Book Co.*, 98 F.2d 688 (2d Cir. 1938). To avoid a chilling effect on authors who contemplate tackling an historical issue or event, broad latitude must be granted to subsequent authors who make use of historical subject matter, including theories or plots. Learned Hand counseled in *Myers v. Mail & Express Co.*, 36 C.O. Bull. 478, 479 (S.D.N.Y. 1919), "[t]here cannot be any such thing as copyright in the order of presentation of the facts, nor, indeed, in their selection."[5]

In the instant case, the hypothesis that Eric Spehl destroyed the Hindenburg is based entirely on the interpretation of historical facts, including Spehl's life, his girlfriend's anti-Nazi connections, the explosion's origin in Gas Cell 4, Spehl's duty station, discovery of a dry-cell battery among the wreckage, and rumors about Spehl's involvement dating from a 1938 Gestapo investigation. Such an historical interpretation, whether or not it originated with Mr. Hoehling, is not protected by his copyright and can be freely used by subsequent authors.

B

The same reasoning governs Hoehling's claim that a number of specific facts, ascertained through his personal research, were copied by appellees.[6] The cases in this circuit, however, make clear that factual information is in the public domain. *See, e.g., Rosemont Enterprises, Inc., supra*, 366 F.2d at 309; *Oxford Book Co., supra*, 98 F.2d at 691. Each appellee had the right to "avail himself of the facts contained" in Hoehling's book and to "use such information, whether correct or incorrect, in his own literary work." *Greenbie v. Noble*, 151 F. Supp. 45, 67 (S.D.N.Y. 1957). Accordingly, there is little consolation in relying on cases in other circuits holding that the fruits of original research are copyrightable. *See, e.g., Toksvig v. Bruce Publications Corp.*, 181 F.2d 664, 667 (7th Cir. 1950); *Miller v. Universal City Studios, Inc.*, 460 F. Supp. 984 (S.D. Fla. 1978). Indeed, this circuit has clearly repudiated *Toksvig* and its progeny. In *Rosemont Enterprises, Inc., supra*, 366 F.2d at 310, we refused to "subscribe to the view that an author is absolutely precluded from saving time and effort by referring to and relying upon prior published material. . . . It is just such wasted effort that the proscription against the copyright of ideas and facts . . . are designed to prevent." *Accord*, 1 Nimmer on Copyright §2.11 (1979).

C

The remainder of Hoehling's claimed similarities relate to random duplications of phrases and sequences of events. For example, all three works contain a scene in a German beer hall, in

---

5. This circuit has permitted extensive reliance on prior works of history. *See, e.g., Gardner v. Nizer*, 391 F. Supp. 940 (S.D.N.Y. 1975) (the story of the Rosenberg trial not copyrightable); *Fuld v. National Broadcasting Co.*, 390 F. Supp. 877 (S.D.N.Y. 1975) ("Bugsy" Siegel's life story not copyrightable); *Greenbie v. Noble*, 151 F. Supp. 45 (S.D.N.Y. 1957) (the life of Anna Carroll, a member of Lincoln's cabinet, not copyrightable). The commentators are in accord with this view. *See, e.g.,* 1, Nimmer on Copyright §2.11[A] (1979); Chafee, *Reflections on the Law of Copyright: I*, 45 Colum. L. Rev. 503, 511 (1945).

6. In detailed comparisons of his book with Mooney's work and Universal's motion picture, Hoehling isolates 266 and 75 alleged instances of copying, respectively. Judge Metzner correctly pointed out that many of these allegations are patently frivolous. The vast majority of the remainder deals with alleged copying of historical facts. It would serve no purpose to review Hoehling's specific allegations in detail in this opinion. The following ten examples, however, are illustrative: (1) Eric Spehl's age and birthplace; (2) Crew members had smuggled monkeys on board the Graf Zeppelin; (3) Germany's ambassador to the U.S. dismissed threats of sabotage; (4) A warning letter had been received from a Mrs. Rauch; (5) The Hindenburg's captain was constructing a new home in Zeppelinheim; (6) Eric Spehl was a photographer; (7) The airship flew over Boston; (8) The Hindenburg was "tail heavy" before landing; (9) A member of the ground crew had etched his name in the zeppelin's hull; and (10) The navigator set the Hindenburg's course by reference to various North Atlantic islands.

which the airship's crew engages in revelry prior to the voyage. Other claimed similarities concern common German greetings of the period, such as "Heil Hitler," or songs, such as the German National anthem. These elements, however, are merely *scenes à faire*, that is, "incidents, characters or settings which are as a practical matter indispensable, or at least standard, in the treatment of a given topic." *Alexander, supra*, 460 F. Supp. at 45; *accord, Bevan v. Columbia Broadcasting System, Inc.*, 329 F. Supp. 601, 607 (S.D.N.Y. 1971). Because it is virtually impossible to write about a particular historical era or fictional theme without employing certain "stock" or standard literary devices, we have held that *scenes à faire* are not copyrightable as a matter of law. *See Reyher v. Children's Television Workshop*, 533 F.2d 87, 91 (2d Cir.), *cert. denied*, 429 U.S. 980 (1976). . . .

D

All of Hoehling's allegations of copying, therefore, encompass material that is non-copyrightable as a matter of law, rendering summary judgment entirely appropriate. We are aware, however, that in distinguishing between themes, facts, and *scenes à faire* on the one hand, and copyrightable expression on the other, courts may lose sight of the forest for the trees. By factoring out similarities based on non-copyrightable elements, a court runs the risk of overlooking wholesale usurpation of a prior author's expression. A verbatim reproduction of another work, of course, even in the realm of nonfiction, is actionable as copyright infringement. *See Wainwright Securities, Inc. v. Wall Street Transcript Corp.*, 558 F.2d 91 (2d Cir. 1977), *cert. denied*, 434 U.S. 1014. . . . Thus, in granting or reviewing a grant of summary judgment for defendants, courts should assure themselves that the works before them are not virtually identical. In this case, it is clear that all three authors relate the story of the Hindenburg differently.

In works devoted to historical subjects, it is our view that a second author may make significant use of prior work, so long as he does not bodily appropriate the expression of another. *Rosemont Enterprises, Inc., supra*, 366 F.2d at 310. This principle is justified by the fundamental policy under girding the copyright laws — the encouragement of contributions to recorded knowledge. The "financial reward guaranteed to the copyright holder is but an incident of this general objective, rather than an end in itself." *Berlin v. E.C. Publications, Inc.*, 329 F.2d 541, 543-44 (2d Cir.), *cert. denied*, 379 U.S. 822 (1964). . . . Knowledge is expanded as well by granting new authors of historical works a relatively free hand to build upon the work of their predecessors. . . .

NOTES AND QUESTIONS

1. Why should the plot of a work receive copyright protection? Why isn't it enough for copyright to extend only to the literal textual wording?

2. The *Hoehling* court notes that it is attempting to avoid the wasted effort incurred when a secondcomer is required to research factual events anew. How is this wasted effort any different from that discussed in Question 3, *supra* page 66, in which two artists each had to travel to Colorado to depict the same landscape? They were each free to copy the original but the second artist was not free to copy the copy painted by the first. Why doesn't the same rule apply to historical facts? Why doesn't it apply to historical theories?

3. *Hoehling* might be understood as a case about the cost of errors. There is always a risk that a court will hold a defendant to be an infringer when he has, in fact, not infringed. Is that risk higher, or less acceptable, for works that are primarily factual?

4. Examine the text of §102(b) again. Which word or words in the statute exclude facts from copyright protection? As the Court explained in *Feist Publications, Inc. v. Rural Telephone Service Co.*, 499 U.S. 340 (1991), section 102(b) treats facts as uncopyrightable "discoveries":

> "No one may claim originality as to facts." . . . This is because facts do not owe their origin to an act of authorship. The distinction is one between creation and discovery: The first person to find and report a particular fact has not created the fact; he or she has merely discovered its existence. To borrow from *Burrow-Giles*, one who discovers a fact is not its "maker" or "originator." . . . "The discoverer merely finds and records." Nimmer §2.03[E]. Census takers, for example, do not "create" the population figures that emerge from their efforts; in a sense, they copy these figures from the world around them. Denicola, Copyright in Collections of Facts: A Theory for the Protection of Nonfiction Literary Works, 81 Colum. L. Rev. 516, 525 (1981). . . . Census data therefore do not trigger copyright because these data are not "original" in the constitutional sense. Nimmer §2.03[E]. The same is true of all facts — scientific, historical, biographical, and news of the day. "[T]hey may not be copyrighted and are part of the public domain available to every person."

Id. at 347-48. Are historical theories also "discoveries"? Are historians less creative than painters or novelists?

Note that historians are subject to separate ethical norms that prohibit plagiarism and require citation of sources. Do these norms serve the same purposes that copyright law serves?

5. Should a work that is held out to the public as a work of historical fiction receive stronger copyright protection for its plot than a work that is held out to the public as a work of history?

6. The merger doctrine applies when it is necessary for the secondcomer to use the words of the first because the idea may not be expressed in another way. The doctrine of *scenes à faire* protects a secondcomer's use of literary devices that are not literally necessary to express the idea, but which the audience has come to expect. What are the justifications for these doctrines? Are they equally compelling?

Next, how should the law separate unprotectable systems or processes from copyrightable expression? Many industries develop new methods of classifying information. What part, if any, of such a system, process, or method is copyrightable?

American Dental Association v. Delta Dental Plans Association
126 F.3d 977 (7th Cir. 1997)

EASTERBROOK, J.: This case presents the question whether a taxonomy is copyrightable. The American Dental Association has created the *Code on Dental Procedures and Nomenclature*. The first edition was published in 1969; the Code has been revised frequently since, in response to changes in dental knowledge and technology. All dental procedures are classified into groups; each procedure receives a number, a short description, and a long description. For example, number 04267 has been assigned to the short description "guided tissue regeneration — nonresorbable barrier, per site, per tooth (includes membrane removal)", which is classified with other surgical periodontic services. The Code made its first appearance in the *Journal of the American Dental Association*, covered by a general copyright notice; the

1991 and 1994 versions were submitted for copyright registration, which was granted by the Register of Copyrights. Delta Dental Association has published a work entitled *Universal Coding and Nomenclature* that includes most of the numbering system and short descriptions from the ADA's Code. In this suit for copyright infringement, Delta . . . argues [*inter alia*] that the Code is not copyrightable subject matter, and the district court granted summary judgment in its favor on this ground without reaching Delta's other arguments.

The district court held that the Code cannot be copyrighted because it catalogs a field of knowledge — in other words, that no taxonomy may be copyrighted. A comprehensive treatment cannot be selective in scope or arrangement, the judge believed, and therefore cannot be original either. Taxonomies are designed to be useful. The judge wrote that if "nothing remains after the 'useful' is taken away — if the primary function is removed from the form — the work is devoid of even that modicum of creativity required for protection, and hence is uncopyrightable." 39 U.S.P.Q.2d 1714, 1721. . . . No one would read the ADA's Code for pleasure; it was designed and is used for business (for records of patients' dental history or making insurance claims) rather than aesthetic purposes. The district court added that, as the work of a committee, the Code could not be thought original. Creation by committee is an oxymoron, the judge wrote.

The sweep of the district court's reasoning attracted the attention of many other suppliers of taxonomies. The American Medical Association, the American National Standards Institute, Underwriters Laboratories, and several other groups have filed a brief as *amici curiae* to observe that they, too, produce catalogs of some field of knowledge and depend on the copyright laws to enable them to recover the costs of the endeavor. Other groups or firms might say the same. The manuals issued by the Financial Accounting Standards Board to specify generally accepted accounting practices could not be copyrighted. Nor could the tests and answers devised by the Educational Testing Service. The district court's reasoning logically removes copyright protection from the West Key Number System, which is designed as a comprehensive index to legal topics, and *A Uniform System of Citation* (the *Bluebook*), a taxonomy of legal sources. Very little computer software could receive a copyright if the district judge is correct: no one reads, for pleasure, the source or object code of the word processing program on which this opinion was written, or of the operating system that runs the computer: take away the "useful" elements and these endeavors are worthless. Worse, most commercial software these days is written by committee, and authors receive less public credit than the gaffers on a movie set, whose names at least scroll by at the end after the audience has turned its collective back to head up the aisles. Blueprints for large buildings (more committee work), instruction manuals for repairing automobiles, used car value guides, dictionaries, encyclopedias, maps — all these, and many more, would flunk the district court's test of originality. Yet these items are routinely copyrighted, and challenges to the validity of these copyrights are routinely rejected. E.g., *Educational Testing Services v. Katzman*, 793 F.2d 533 (3d Cir. 1986) (Scholastic Aptitude Test); *CCC Information Services, Inc. v. Maclean Hunter Market Reports, Inc.*, 44 F.3d 61 (2d Cir. 1994) (list of used-car prices); *Lipton v. Nature Co.*, 71 F.3d 464 (2d Cir. 1995) (terms describing groups of animals). *See also* 17 U.S.C. §101 (including "architectural plans" within the definition of "pictoral, graphic and sculptural works" that are copyrightable); Paul Goldstein, *Copyright: Principles, Law and Practice* §2.15.2 (1989) (discussing copyright protection for computer programs). The American Medical Association's copyright in the *Physician's Current Procedural Terminology*, its catalog of medical procedures, was recently sustained, although against a challenge different from the district court's rationale. *Practice Management Information Corp. v. American Medical Association*, 121 F.3d 516 (9th Cir. 1997). Maps and globes are not only copyrightable, see *Rockford Map Publishers, Inc. v. Directory Service Co.*, 768 F.2d

145 (7th Cir. 1985), but also constituted two-thirds of the original scope of copyright. The Copyright Act of 1790 specified three protectable items: maps, charts, and books. Act of May 31, 1790, 1 Stat. 124. Like taxonomies, maps are valued to the extent they offer useful organizations of facts; like the Code, maps are produced by committees. (As are opinions of appellate courts, which despite this handicap, and the judges' effort to produce something useful, might occasionally have a modicum of originality.)

Any original literary work may be copyrighted. The necessary degree of "originality" is low, and the work need not be aesthetically pleasing to be "literary." *Feist Publications, Inc. v. Rural Telephone Service Co.*, 499 U.S. 340, 345-46. . . . Term papers by college sophomores are as much within the domain of copyright as Saul Bellow's latest novel. *See Bleistein v. Donaldson Lithographing Co.*, 188 U.S. 239. . . . Scholarship that explicates important facts about the universe likewise is well within this domain. Einstein's articles laying out the special and general theories of relativity were original works even though many of the core equations, such as the famous $E = mc^2$, express "facts" and therefore are not copyrightable. Einstein could have explained relativity in any of a hundred different ways; another physicist could expound the same principles differently.

So too with a taxonomy — of butterflies, legal citations, or dental procedures. Facts do not supply their own principles of organization. Classification is a creative endeavor. Butterflies may be grouped by their color, or the shape of their wings, or their feeding or breeding habits, or their habitats, or the attributes of their caterpillars, or the sequence of their DNA; each scheme of classification could be expressed in multiple ways. Dental procedures could be classified by complexity, or by the tools necessary to perform them, or by the parts of the mouth involved, or by the anesthesia employed, or in any of a dozen different ways. The Code's descriptions don't "merge with the facts" any more than a scientific description of butterfly attributes is part of a butterfly. Cf. *Nash v. CBS, Inc.*, 899 F.2d 1537 (7th Cir. 1990) (discussing the fact-expression dichotomy). There can be multiple, and equally original, biographies of the same person's life, and multiple original taxonomies of a field of knowledge. Creativity marks the expression even after the fundamental scheme has been devised. This is clear enough for the long description of each procedure in the ADA's Code. The long description is part of the copyrighted work, and original long descriptions make the work as a whole copyrightable. But we think that even the short description and the number are original works of authorship.

Number 04267 reads "guided tissue regeneration — nonresorbable barrier, per site, per tooth" but could have read "regeneration of tissue, guided by nonresorbable barrier, one site and tooth per entry." Or "use of barrier to guide regeneration of tissue, without regard to the number of sites per tooth and whether or not the barrier is resorbable." The first variation is linguistic, the second substantive; in each case the decision to use the actual description is original to the ADA, not knuckling under to an order imposed on language by some "fact" about dental procedures. Blood is shed in the ADA's committees about which description is preferable. The number assigned to any one of the three descriptions could have had four or six digits rather than five; guided tissue regeneration could have been placed in the 2500 series rather than the 4200 series; again any of these choices is original to the author of a taxonomy, and another author could do things differently. Every number in the ADA's Code begins with zero, assuring a large supply of unused numbers for procedures to be devised or reclassified in the future; an author could have elected instead to leave wide gaps inside the sequence. A catalog that initially assigns 04266, 04267, 04268 to three procedures will over time depart substantively from one that initially assigns 42660, 42670, and 42680 to the same three procedures. So all three elements of the Code — numbers, short descriptions, and long descriptions, are copyrightable subject matter under 17 U.S.C. §102(a). The *Maroon Book* and the

Bluebook offer different taxonomies of legal citations; Wotquenne and Helm devised distinct catalogs of C.P.E. Bach's oeuvre; Delta Dental Association could have written its own classification of dental procedures. . . .

Delta asks us to affirm the judgment on a ground that the district judge did not reach: that the Code is not copyrightable because it is a "system." Section 102(b) tells us that copyright protection even of an original work does not cover "any idea, procedure, process, system, method of operation, concept, principle, or discovery, regardless of the form in which it is described, explained, illustrated, or embodied in such work." But what could it mean to call the Code a "system"? This taxonomy does not come with instructions for use, as if the Code were a recipe for a new dish. Cf. *Publications International, Ltd. v. Meredith Corp.*, 88 F.3d 473 (7th Cir. 1996) (holding that recipes are not copyrightable). A dictionary cannot be called a "system" just because new novels are written using words, all of which appear in the dictionary. Nor is word-processing software a "system" just because it has a command structure for producing paragraphs. The Code is a taxonomy, which may be put to many uses. These uses may be or include systems; the Code is not.

Section 102(b) codifies the fact-expression dichotomy, which we have already considered, as well as the holding of *Baker v. Selden*, 101 U.S. (11 Otto) 99 . . . , that blank forms are not copyrightable, even if the structure of the forms captures the essence of an original work of literature. The book was protected as original literary expression, the Court held, but the form was a means of putting the book's ideas into practice — and copyright law, unlike patent law, covers only expression. Someone who buys a book full of ideas for new machines may build and sell one of the machines without infringing the author's copyright; *Baker* thought that the use of an accounting system described in a book is pretty much the same thing, even if practice of the system entails use of the author's forms. Baker rearranged Selden's forms, but if the original forms were copyrightable then the rearrangements were derivative works, which the original author had an exclusive right to produce. Protecting variations on the forms could have permitted the author of an influential accounting treatise to monopolize the practice of double-entry bookkeeping. Yet copyright law does not permit the author to monopolize the revenues to be derived from an improved system of accounting — or of reporting dental procedures. *See* William M. Landes & Richard A. Posner, *An Economic Analysis of Copyright Law*, 17 J. Legal Stud. 325, 350-53 (1989).

Few "how-to" works are "systems" in *Baker*'s sense. If they were, architectural blueprints could be freely copied, although the Berne Convention Implementation Act of 1988, Pub. L. 100-567, 102 Stat. 2854, adds protection for "architectural plans" to the statute. Descriptions of how to build or do something do not facilitate monopoly of the subject-matter being described, so the concern of *Baker* is not activated. Again consider blueprints: other architects can imitate the style of the completed building; they just can't copy the plans. What is more, a form that contains instructions for its completion is copyrightable in part (the instructions) and in the public domain in part (the lines and boxes). *Edwin K. Williams & Co. v. Edwin K. Williams & Co. East*, 542 F.2d 1053, 1061 (9th Cir. 1976); Goldstein at §2.15.1.b. So far as the ADA is concerned, any dentist, any insurer, anyone at all, may devise and use forms into which the Code's descriptions may be entered. The ADA encourages this use; standardization of language promotes interchange among professionals. (The fact that Delta used most of the Code but made modifications is the reason ADA objects, for variations salted through a convention impede communication.) Section 102(b) precludes the ADA from suing, for copyright infringement, a dentist whose office files record treatments using the Code's nomenclature. No field of practice has been or can be monopolized, given this constraint. Section 102(b) permits Delta to disseminate forms inviting dentists to use the ADA's Code when submitting bills to insurers. But it does not permit Delta to copy the Code itself, or make and distribute a derivative work based on the Code, any more than Baker could copy Selden's book. . . .

NOTES AND QUESTIONS

1. Was this case correctly decided? How did Delta Dental's conduct differ from that of Baker in *Baker v. Selden*? What did Delta Dental do wrong? Can you think of another, non–copyright-based legal theory that the ADA might have asserted?

2. Does the classification method developed by the ADA fall within any of the other categories listed in §102(b)? Might it be an unprotectable "process" or "method of operation"? How would the *ADA* court respond to such an argument?

3. Did the *ADA* court hold that the ADA's taxonomy is copyrightable because there exists a large number of possible variations on such a taxonomy? If so, is that reasoning sound? Consider, again, whether there could be subject matter that qualifies for copyright protection under §102(a) — because it is "original" — but is nevertheless barred from such protection under §102(b). Might there be such a thing as noncopyrightable originality? Is the ADA's taxonomy an example of that sort of originality?

4. According to the *ADA* court, *Baker* is a case holding "that blank forms are not copyrightable." Do you agree with that characterization of *Baker*? Read the following excerpt from the Copyright Office's regulations:

§202.1 Material not subject to copyright

The following are examples of works not subject to copyright and applications for registration of such works cannot be entertained:

(a) Words and short phrases such as names, titles, and slogans; familiar symbols or designs; mere variations of typographic ornamentation, lettering or coloring; mere listing of ingredients or contents;

(b) Ideas, plans, methods, systems, or devices, as distinguished from the particular manner in which they are expressed or described in a writing;

(c) Blank forms, such as time cards, graph paper, account books, diaries, bank checks, scorecards, address books, report forms, order forms and the like, which are designed for recording information and do not in themselves convey information;

(d) Works consisting entirely of information that is common property containing no original authorship, such as, for example: Standard calendars, height and weight charts, tape measures and rulers, schedules of sporting events, and lists or tables taken from public documents or other common sources.

(e) Typeface as typeface.

37 C.F.R. §202.1. Are these rules dictated by *Baker*? By some other principle?

A number of cases address blank forms. *Compare, e.g., Bibbero Sys., Inc. v. Colwell Sys., Inc.,* 893 F.2d 1104 (9th Cir. 1990) (holding billing forms that doctors used to obtain reimbursement from insurance companies were uncopyrightable blank forms), *with, e.g., Harcourt Brace & World, Inc. v. Graphic Controls Corp.,* 329 F. Supp. 517, 524 (S.D.N.Y. 1971) (holding test answer sheets copyrightable because they were "designed to guide the student in recording his answer" and therefore conveyed information).

5. Compare the different types of subject matter at issue in the three cases in this section. Is the ADA's taxonomy more creative than Selden's system of bookkeeping or Hoehling's

theory about the Hindenburg disaster? Does protecting the former, but not the latter two, promote the purposes of copyright?

6. Might Delta Dental have argued that the ADA's taxonomy was akin to a *scene à faire*— a standard that it was entitled to duplicate to satisfy customer expectations? Was Delta Dental well positioned to make this argument?

7. In *Southco, Inc. v. Kanebridge Corp.*, 390 F.3d 276 (3d Cir. 2004) (en banc) the defendant, a competitor of the plaintiff in the fastener business, was copying the plaintiff's part numbers in defendant's catalogs. Defendant asserted that the ability to reference the plaintiff's parts numbers was necessary to make competition viable. Plaintiff argued that its part numbers were highly creative, explaining that in its system of numbering each component of the part number represented a different aspect of each product (e.g. type of fastener, size, material, etc.). The court held that the part numbers in plaintiff's catalog were not original because the numbers were "rigidly dictated by the rules of the [plaintiff's] system." Is this result consistent with *ADA*?

4. Derivative Works and Compilations

In addition to the basic copyrightable subject matter provisions of §102, the Copyright Act contains a separate section that accords copyright protection to two special types of works:

§103. Subject matter of copyright: Compilations and derivative works

(a) The subject matter of copyright as specified by section 102 includes compilations and derivative works, but protection for a work employing preexisting material in which copyright subsists does not extend to any part of the work in which such material has been used unlawfully.

(b) The copyright in a compilation or derivative work extends only to the material contributed by the author of such work, as distinguished from the preexisting material employed in the work, and does not imply any exclusive right in the preexisting material. The copyright in such work is independent of, and does not affect or enlarge the scope, duration, ownership, or subsistence of, any copyright protection in the preexisting material.

As you read the following materials, consider whether authors of derivative works and compilations are or should be held to different standards of originality than authors of other works.

a. Derivative Works

U.S. copyright law has long recognized copyrights in works based on other works. Thus, for example, the Copyright Act of 1909 extended copyright protection to "[r]eproductions of a work of art" and to "abridgements, adaptations, arrangements, dramatizations, translations, or other versions" of preexisting works. Pub. L. No. 60-349, 60th Cong., 2d Sess. §§5(h), 6, 35 Stat. 1075, 1077 (1909). In the 1976 Act, Congress adopted the term *derivative work* and set forth a broad definition that encompasses any work based on or derived from another work:

A "derivative work" is a work based upon one or more preexisting works, such as a translation, musical arrangement, dramatization, fictionalization, motion picture version, sound recording, art reproduction, abridgement, condensation, or any other form in which a work may be recast, transformed, or adapted. A work consisting of editorial revisions, annotations, elaborations, or other modifications which, as a whole, represent an original work of authorship, is a "derivative work."

17 U.S.C. §101.

International copyright treaties similarly require protection of works based on other works, but the international copyright community has not adopted the "derivative" terminology. The Berne Convention mandates protection for "[t]ranslations, adaptations, arrangements of music and other alterations of a literary or artistic work." Berne Conv., art. 2(3). The TRIPS Agreement incorporates this provision.

Section 103(b) indicates that copyright in a derivative work subsists only in the new material contributed by the author of the derivative work. Neither this language nor the statutory definition, however, indicates when the derivative material is sufficiently distinguishable from the underlying original work to constitute a copyrightable work in its own right. Review the excerpt from *Feist, supra* pp. 58-60, which sets forth the standard that a work must satisfy to be considered an "original work of authorship." Then consider the standards of originality applied in the following cases.

L. Batlin & Son, Inc. v. Snyder
536 F.2d 486 (2d Cir.) (en banc), cert. denied, 429 U.S. 857 (1976)

OAKES, J.: . . . Uncle Sam mechanical banks have been on the American scene at least since June 8, 1886, when Design Patent No. 16,728, issued on a toy savings bank of its type. The basic delightful design has long since been in the public domain. The banks are well documented in collectors' books and known to the average person interested in Americana. . . . Uncle Sam, dressed in his usual stove pipe hat, blue full dress coat, starred vest and red and white striped trousers, and leaning on his umbrella, stands on a four- or five-inch wide base, on which sits his carpetbag. A coin may be placed in Uncle Sam's extended hand. When a lever is pressed, the arm lowers, and the coin falls into the bag, while Uncle Sam's whiskers move up and down. . . .

Appellant Jeffrey Snyder doing business as "J.S.N.Y." obtained a registration of copyright on a plastic "Uncle Sam bank" in Class G ("Works of Art") as "sculpture" on January 23, 1975. According to Snyder's affidavit, in January, 1974, he had seen a cast metal antique Uncle Sam bank with an overall height of the figure and base of 11 inches. In April 1974, he flew to Hong Kong to arrange for the design and eventual manufacture of replicas of the bank as Bicentennial items. . . . Snyder wanted his bank to be made of plastic and to be shorter than the cast metal sample "in order to fit into the required price range and quality and quantity of material to be used." The figure of Uncle Sam was thus shortened from 11 to nine inches, and the base shortened and narrowed. It was also decided, Snyder averred, to change the shape of the carpetbag and to include the umbrella in a one-piece mold for the Uncle Sam figure "so as not to have a problem with a loose umbrella or a separate molding process." . . .

[Batlin, a competing importer of novelty Uncle Sam mechanical banks, filed suit against Snyder after the U.S. Customs Service refused entry to a shipment of banks ordered by Batlin from a Hong Kong trading company. Batlin sought a declaration that Snyder's copyright was invalid. The district court granted Batlin a preliminary injunction.]

This court has examined both the appellants' plastic Uncle Sam bank made under Snyder's copyright and the uncopyrighted model cast iron mechanical bank which is itself a reproduction of the original public domain Uncle Sam bank. Appellant Snyder claims differences not only of size but also in a number of other very minute details: the carpetbag shape of the plastic bank is smooth, the iron bank rough; the metal bank bag is fatter at its base; the eagle on the front of the platform in the metal bank is holding arrows in his talons while in the plastic bank he clutches leaves, this change concededly having been made, however, because "the arrows did not reproduce well in plastic on a smaller size." The shape of Uncle Sam's face is supposedly different, as is the shape and texture of the hats, according to the Snyder affidavit. In the metal version the umbrella is hanging loose while in the plastic item it is included in the single mold. The texture of the clothing, the hairline, shape of the bow ties and of the shirt collar and left arm as well as the flag carrying the name on the base of the statue are all claimed to be different, along with the shape and texture of the eagles on the side. Many of these differences are not perceptible to the casual observer. Appellants make no claim for any difference based on the plastic mold lines in the Uncle Sam figure which are perceptible. . . .

The test of originality is concededly one with a low threshold in that "[a]ll that is needed . . . is that the 'author' contributed something more than a 'merely trivial' variation, something recognizably 'his own.'" *Alfred Bell & Co. v. Catalda Fine Arts, Inc.*, 191 F.2d at 103. But as this court said many years ago, "[w]hile a copy of something in the public domain will not, if it be merely a copy, support a copyright, a distinguishable variation will. . . ." *Gerlach-Barklow Co. v. Morris & Bendien, Inc.*, 23 F.2d 159, 161 (2d Cir. 1927). . . .

A reproduction of a work of art obviously presupposes an underlying work of art. . . . The underlying work of art may as here be in the public domain. But even to claim the more limited protection given to a reproduction of a work of art (that to the distinctive features contributed by the reproducer), the reproduction must contain "an original contribution not present in the underlying work of art" and be "more than a mere copy." 1 M. Nimmer, [The Law of Copyright (1975)], §20.2, at 93. . . .

Nor can the requirement of originality be satisfied simply by the demonstration of "physical skill" or "special training" . . . required for the production of the plastic molds that furnished the basis for appellants' plastic bank. A considerably *higher* degree of skill is required, true artistic skill, to make the reproduction copyrightable. . . . Here on the basis of appellants' own expert's testimony it took [Snyder's Hong Kong contractor] "[a]bout a day and a half, two days work" to produce the plastic mold sculpture from the metal Uncle Sam bank. If there be a point in the copyright law pertaining to reproductions at which sheer artistic skill and effort can act as a substitute for the requirement of substantial variation, it was not reached here.

Appellants rely heavily upon *Alva Studios, Inc. v. Winninger*, [177 F. Supp. 265 (S.D.N.Y. 1959)], the "Hand of God" case, where the court held that "great skill and originality [were required] to produce a scale reduction of a great work with exactitude." 177 F. Supp. at 267. There, the original sculpture [Auguste Rodin's *Hand of God*—EDS.] was, "one of the most intricate pieces of sculpture ever created" with "[i]nnumerable planes, lines and geometric patterns . . . interdependent in [a] multidimensional work." *Id*. Originality was found primarily by the district court to consist primarily in the fact that "[i]t takes 'an extremely skilled sculptor' many hours working directly in front of the original" to effectuate a scale reduction. *Id*. at 266. The court, indeed, found the exact replica to be so original, distinct, and creative as to constitute a work of art in itself. The complexity and exactitude there involved distinguishes [sic] that case amply from the one at bar. As appellants themselves have pointed out, there are a number of trivial differences or deviations from the original public domain cast iron bank in their plastic reproduction. Thus concededly the plastic version is not, and was scarcely meticulously produced to be, an exactly faithful reproduction. Nor is the creativity in the underlying work of art of the same order of magnitude as in the case of the "Hand of God." Rodin's sculpture is, furthermore, so unique and rare, and adequate public access to it such a problem

Uncle Sam Bank

that a significant public benefit accrues from its precise, artistic reproduction. No such benefit can be imagined to accrue here from the "knock-off" reproduction of the cast iron Uncle Sam bank. Thus appellants' plastic bank is neither in the category of exactitude required by *Alva Studios* nor in a category of substantial originality; it falls within what has been suggested by the amicus curiae is a copyright no-man's land. . . .

. . . To extend copyrightability to minuscule variations would simply put a weapon for harassment in the hands of mischievous copiers intent on appropriating and monopolizing public domain work. . . .

MESKILL, J., dissenting: . . . [T]he author's reasons for making changes should be irrelevant to a determination of whether the differences are trivial. As noted in *Alfred Bell, supra*, 191 F.2d at 105, even an inadvertent variation can form the basis of a valid copyright. After the fact speculation as to whether Snyder made changes for aesthetic or functional reasons should not be the basis of decision.

. . . Granting Snyder a copyright protecting [his] variations would ensure only that no one could copy his particular version of the bank now in the public domain, i.e., protection from someone using Snyder's figurine to slavishly copy and make a mold. . . .

This approach seems quite in accord with the purpose of the copyright statute to promote progress by encouraging individual effort through copyright protection. . . .

≣ **Entertainment Research Group, Inc. v. Genesis Creative Group, Inc.**
122 F.3d 1211 (9th Cir. 1997), cert. denied, 523 U.S. 1021 (1998)

REA, J.: . . . ERG designs and manufactures three-dimensional inflatable costumes that are used in publicity events, such as shopping mall openings. The costumes are approximately eight feet tall and are worn by a person who remains inside the costume. Various companies purchase and use these costumes to promote their products. The costumes are based upon these companies' cartoon characters.[2] . . .

[ERG and Genesis signed an agreement for Genesis to market and distribute ERG's costumes. Subsequently, Genesis entered into an agreement to market and distribute inflatable costumes designed by ERG's competitor, Aerostar. ERG sued Genesis and Aerostar for, *inter alia*, infringement of the copyrights in various ERG costumes. The district court granted summary judgment for defendants on ERG's copyright claim.]

. . . ERG contends that the district court should have applied the test created by a district court in the Central [sic] District of California. *Doran v. Sunset House Distributing Corp.*, 197 F. Supp. 940 (S.D. Cal. 1961), *aff'd*, *Sunset House Distributing Corp. v. Doran*, 304 F.2d 251 (9th Cir. 1962). In *Doran*, we affirmed the district court's decision that a three-dimensional, inflatable representation of Santa Claus was original and copyrightable. . . . [U]nder the *Doran* district court's test, if the form of the derivative work and the form of the underlying work—three-dimensional, two-dimensional, plastic, etc.—are sufficiently different, then the derivative work is original enough to be copyrightable.

. . . In the first place, the *Doran* test is inapplicable to the instant circumstances since *Doran* involved the copyrightability of a derivative work where the preexisting work was taken from the public domain and not copyrighted itself. Here, on the other hand, ERG's costumes were based on preexisting works that were copyrighted and owned by the ultimate purchasers. This difference is critical because in deciding whether to grant copyright protection to a derivative work, courts must be concerned about the impact such a derivative copyright will have on the copyright privileges and rights of the owner of the underlying work. *See* 17 U.S.C. §103(b). Indeed, the body of law regarding derivative copyrights is designed to strike a balance between the holder of a copyright in the underlying work and the creator of a work that is made by copying that underlying work. *See, e.g., Durham*, 630 F.2d at 910-11. Accordingly, because the *Doran* test completely fails to take into account the rights of the holder of the copyright for the underlying work, the *Doran* test should not be applied to determine the copyrightability of a derivative work that is based on a preexisting work that is itself copyrighted. . . .

. . . [W]e are satisfied that the test developed by the Second Circuit in *Durham* [*Industries, Inc. v. Tomy Corp.*, 630 F.2d 905 (2d Cir. 1980)] is the proper approach for us to apply in the instant circumstances to determine whether ERG's costumes are copyrightable as derivative works. The test contains two prongs:

First, to support a copyright the original aspects of a derivative work must be more than trivial. Second, the original aspects of a derivative work must reflect the degree to which it relies on preexisting material and must not in any way affect the scope of any copyright protection in that preexisting material.

Durham, 630 F.2d at 909. . . .

---

2. For example, Pillsbury purchased "Pillsbury Doughboy" costumes, Toys "R" Us purchased "Geoffrey the Giraffe" costumes, and Quaker Oats purchased "Cap'n Crunch" costumes.

. . . [The] second prong of the *Durham* test is necessary to ensure that copyright protection is not given to derivative works whose originality is merely trivial. . . . [I]f copyright protection were given to derivative works that are virtually identical to the underlying works, then the owner of the underlying copyrighted work would effectively be prevented from permitting others to copy her work since the original derivative copyright holder would have a de facto monopoly due to her "considerable power to interfere with the creation of subsequent derivative works from the same underlying work." *Gracen* [*v. Bradford Exchange*, 698 F.2d 300, 305 (7th Cir. 1983)]; *see also Durham*, 630 F.2d at 911. . . .

Viewing the three-dimensional costumes and the two-dimensional drawings upon which they are based, it is immediately apparent that the costumes are not exact replicas of the two-dimensional drawings. Indeed, as the district court observed with regard to the Toucan Sam costume, the proportions in the costumes are far different from those in the underlying drawings. However, as we discussed earlier, in evaluating the originality of ERG's costumes, any differences that exist because of functional or mechanical considerations should not be considered. The district court came to the conclusion that these differences in proportion were solely—or at least primarily—driven by the functional considerations necessitated by the fact that a human body must fit inside the costumes. . . .

. . . Although ERG is correct that there are some differences in the[ ] facial expressions, no reasonable trier of fact would see anything but the underlying copyrighted character when looking at ERG's costumes. . . .

In addition to concluding that ERG did not establish sufficient originality to warrant copyright protection for its derivative costumes, the district court also concluded that ERG failed to satisfy the second element of the *Durham* test. . . .

. . . [T]he district court was correct to conclude that granting ERG a copyright in its costumes would have the practical effect of providing ERG with a de facto monopoly on all inflatable costumes depicting the copyrighted characters also in ERG's costumes. Indeed, if ERG had copyrights for its costumes, any future licensee who was hired to manufacture costumes depicting these characters would likely face a strong copyright infringement suit from ERG. . . .

NOTES AND QUESTIONS

1. What standard of originality applies to derivative works? Is it the same as the basic standard set forth in *Feist, supra*? Should it be the same? Re-read the second prong of the *ERG* test. Is the Ninth Circuit attempting to state an additional threshold requirement that derivative works must meet? If not, what does the second prong of the test mean? Is the plaintiff really losing here because the court views its product as unworthy of protection? If so, is the court violating *Bleistein*'s nondiscrimination principle?

2. Both the *L. Batlin* court and the *ERG* court are anxious to avoid giving the first creator of a derivative work "a de facto monopoly" on all subsequent derivative works. *See also Gracen v. Bradford Exch.*, 698 F.2d 300, 304 (7th Cir. 1983) (Posner, J.) ("[E]specially as applied to derivative works, the concept of originality in copyright law has as one would expect a legal rather than aesthetic function—to prevent overlapping claims.") (citing *L. Batlin*). Is this concern well founded?

As discussed in *ERG*, the concern about de facto monopolies is based in part on a desire to protect the rights of the owner of copyright in the underlying work. Are there also reasons to be concerned about de facto monopolies on derivative works based on underlying public domain works? Recall *Alfred Bell v. Catalda*, *supra* page 67, which extended copyright protection to mezzotint reproductions of public domain paintings. Is that decision consistent with *L. Batlin* and *ERG*? Should a different standard apply depending on whether the underlying work is copyrighted or is in the public domain?

3. Are you persuaded by the Second Circuit's reconciliation of its decision in *L. Batlin* with the decision in *Alva Studios v. Winninger*? Is it appropriate to use one standard of originality for "ordinary" derivations and another for painstaking reproductions of works of fine art? Does either part of this standard survive the Supreme Court's decision in *Feist*? As we will see in Section A.4.b, *infra*, the *Feist* Court held that mere effort, or "sweat," does not automatically satisfy the originality requirement. Is *Alva Studios* still good law? What about *Alfred Bell*? Did those decisions protect mere effort?

4. Is a photograph of the Uncle Sam mechanical bank, or of the original Cap'n Crunch, a derivative work? Two recent decisions have considered this question. Both courts concluded that the photographs in question were copyrightable, but differed on the proper approach to determining whether the photographs might also qualify as derivative works. *See Ets-Hokin v. Skyy Spirits, Inc.*, 225 F.3d 1068 (9th Cir. 2000) (photograph of vodka bottle prepared for advertisement); *SHL Imaging, Inc. v. Artisan House, Inc.*, 117 F. Supp. 2d 301 (S.D.N.Y. 2000) (photographs of ornamental picture frames prepared for catalog). The *SHL Imaging* court explained its decision as follows:

> Recently, the Ninth Circuit addressed the question of whether a photograph is a derivative work of the object it depicts. *See Ets-Hokin v. Skyy Spirits, Inc.*, 225 F.3d 1068, 1077-1082 (9th Cir. 2000). Although the Ninth Circuit concluded that a photograph of a vodka bottle was not a derivative work of the bottle, it reached that holding only after determining that the bottle was not independently copyrightable. Thus, the Ninth Circuit reasoned that the bottle was not a preexisting work. *Ets-Hokin*, at 1077-1082. This Court respectfully believes that the *Ets-Hokin* court misconstrued the nature of derivative works. While the *Ets-Hokin* court correctly noted that a derivative work must be based on a "preexisting work," and that the term "work" refers to a "work of authorship" as set forth in 17 U.S.C. §102(a), it failed to appreciate that any derivative work must recast, transform or adopt [sic] the authorship contained in the preexisting work. A photograph of Jeff Koons' "Puppy" sculpture in Manhattan's Rockfeller Center, merely depicts that sculpture; it does not recast, transform, or adapt Koons' sculptural authorship. In short, the authorship of the photographic work is entirely different and separate from the authorship of the sculpture.

SHL Imaging, 117 F. Supp. 2d at 305-06. Do you agree with the court's analysis, or do you prefer the Ninth Circuit's approach? Should a photograph be considered a derivative work whenever the subject of the photograph is itself copyrightable? Are there reasons to treat photography differently than other methods of art reproduction?

5. Does adding harmony to a preexisting melody create a derivative work? *See Tempo Music, Inc. v. Morris*, 838 F. Supp. 162 (S.D.N.Y. 1994) (rejecting the argument that harmony simply expresses "common musical vocabulary" and holding that whether a particular harmony manifests sufficient originality to be copyrightable is a question of fact).

6. The definition of derivative works in §101 includes a reference to "translations." What does originality mean in the context of a translation? In *Merkos, L'Inyonei Chinuch, Inc. v. Otsar Sifrei Lubavitch, Inc.*, 312 F.3d 94 (2d Cir. 2002), the court held an English translation of a Hebrew prayer book copyrightable. The court stated, "The translation process requires exercise of careful literary and scholarly judgment. As the District Court commented, '[t]he translation of prayers . . . involves partly the precision of science but partly the sensitivity and spirit of art. Behind the words that are found in Hebrew and the words that are used in the

English are shades of meaning and subtlety that cannot be labeled functional.'" *Id.* at 97. Would the same rationale apply to translations of all types of works?

Note on Section 103(a)

In this chapter, we consider only the copyrightability of derivative works. As *ERG* indicates, the right to prepare or authorize preparation of derivative works is one of the exclusive rights of the copyright owner; therefore, unauthorized preparation of a derivative work may infringe the copyright. The two inquiries differ in focus. The copyrightability inquiry is primarily concerned with the extent to which the two works are different—i.e., with what the secondcomer has added. The infringement inquiry (which we consider in Chapter 5) is primarily concerned with the degree of similarity between the alleged derivative work and the underlying work—i.e., with what the secondcomer has taken. Infringement, however, also may bear on the question of copyrightability. Section 103(a) states: "[P]rotection for a work employing preexisting material in which copyright subsists does not extend to any part of the work in which such material has been used unlawfully."

In light of §103(a), can a derivative work prepared without the copyright owner's permission ever qualify for copyright protection? Courts have disagreed on the proper answer to this question. *Compare Pickett v. Prince*, 207 F.3d 402, 406 (7th Cir. 2000) (holding that "the right to make a derivative work does not authorize the maker to incorporate into it material that infringes someone else's copyright"), *with Eden Toys, Inc. v. Florelee Undergarment Co.*, 697 F.2d 27, 34 n.6 (2d Cir. 1982) (holding that a second-comer can assert copyright in a derivative work made without the copyright owner's permission if the original work does not "pervade" the derivative work). Which interpretation of §103(a) makes more sense? Are the efficiency concerns discussed in *ERG*, *supra*, relevant? Note also that use of underlying material can be lawful when authorized by the copyright owner, but it can also be lawful if authorized by other provisions of the Copyright Act, such as §107 concerning fair use. We consider fair use in Chapter 7, *infra*.

Note on Blocking Patents

The patent system follows a very different set of rules for allocating rights in initial inventions and subsequent patentable improvements. The secondcomer who invents a patentable improvement may apply for and receive a patent regardless of whether the first inventor authorized the improvement. The first inventor and the improver are said to hold "blocking patents." The improver may not practice his invention without permission from the original inventor, but the first inventor may not practice the improvement without permission from the improver. Such patents are frequently the subjects of cross-licensing agreements between the two inventors. *See Standard Oil Co. v. United States*, 283 U.S. 163, 172 n.5 (1931); *Carpet Seaming Tape Licensing v. Best Seam, Inc.*, 616 F.2d 1133, 1142 (9th Cir. 1980), *cert. denied*, 464 U.S. 818 (1983); 5 Donald S. Chisum, *Chisum on Patents* §16.02[1][a] (2001).

The blocking patents rule has been justified in terms of efficiency. According to Professor Merges, the rule encourages the original patentee to bargain with improvers, and therefore avoids potentially significant holdout costs that might impede valuable innovation. Robert

Merges, *Intellectual Property Rights and Bargaining Breakdown: The Case of Blocking Patents*, 62 Tenn. L. Rev. 75 (1994); *see generally* Ian Ayres & Eric Talley, *Solomonic Bargaining: Dividing a Legal Entitlement to Facilitate Coasean Trade*, 104 Yale L.J. 1027 (1995). More generally, a number of legal scholars have concluded that society benefits most when would-be improvers compete with one another and with the original patentee to produce and disclose to the public valuable inventions, even if this rule results in some duplicative research. *See, e.g.*, Robert P. Merges & Richard R. Nelson, *On the Complex Economics of Patent Scope*, 90 Colum. L. Rev. 839, 877-908 (1990); Mark A. Lemley, *The Economics of Improvement in Intellectual Property Law*, 75 Tex. L. Rev. 989 (1997).

Some commentators, however, have criticized the blocking patents rule. In an extremely influential article published in 1977, Professor Edmund Kitch argued that giving patentees broad rights to control subsequent improvements to their inventions would result in a more efficient allocation of research efforts. Kitch analogized such rights to nineteenth-century mining claims, which reserved for firstcomers the right to explore (or license others to explore) the land described in the claim deed. He argued that adopting a similar regime for patent law would reduce wasteful duplication and ensure optimal allocation of licenses to develop improvements, and therefore would promote greater overall progress. Edmund W. Kitch, *The Nature and Function of the Patent System*, 20 J.L. & Econ. 265, 276-78 (1977); *see also* Mark F. Grady & Jay I. Alexander, *Patent Law and Rent Dissipation*, 78 Va. L. Rev. 305 (1992). Professor Kitch's "prospect" model actually is quite similar to the copyright rule granting firstcomers the right to control the preparation of derivative works.

If blocking patents promote efficient bargaining between firstcomers and improvers, would not a regime of "blocking copyrights" also be efficient? Or is the "prospect" model more appropriate for copyright law? For an extended discussion of this question, see Lemley, *supra*.

b. Compilations

The Copyright Act of 1909 recognized copyright in "compilations," but did not supply a general definition of this term. The 1976 Act remedied this omission. Section 101 provides: "A 'compilation' is a work formed by the collection and assembling of preexisting materials or of data that are selected, coordinated, or arranged in such a way that the resulting work as a whole constitutes an original work of authorship." The definition of "compilation" further provides that "collective works" are a type of compilation. A collective work, in turn, "is a work, such as a periodical issue, anthology, or encyclopedia, in which a number of contributions, constituting separate and independent works in themselves, are assembled into a collective whole." 17 U.S.C. §101.

The difference between collective works and compilations more generally is also relevant to obligations that countries have under international treaties. Article 2 of the Berne Convention requires protection only for "[c]ollections of literary and artistic works such as encyclopedias and anthologies which, by reason of the selection and arrangement of their contents, constitute intellectual creations." Berne Conv., art. 2(5). The TRIPS Agreement mandates copyright protection for "[c]ompilations of data or other material . . . which by reason of the selection or arrangement of their contents constitute intellectual creations." TRIPS Agreement, art. 10(2). Thus, upon joining the WTO, countries that previously had complied with the Berne Convention were required to extend eligibility for copyright protection to compilations of all types, not just anthologies, encyclopedias, and the like.

In *Feist Publications, Inc. v. Rural Telephone Service Co.*, 499 U.S. 340 (1991), the Supreme Court sought to clarify the relationship between the Copyright Act's definition of an eligible "compilation" and the originality requirement:

Feist Publications, Inc. v. Rural Telephone Service Co.
499 U.S. 340 (1991)

[Review the facts of this case, pages 58-59 *supra*.]

O'CONNOR, J.: . . .

II

A

This case concerns the interaction of two well-established propositions. The first is that facts are not copyrightable; the other, that compilations of facts generally are. Each of these propositions possesses an impeccable pedigree. . . .

There is an undeniable tension between these two propositions. Many compilations consist of nothing but raw data — *i.e.*, wholly factual information not accompanied by any original written expression. On what basis may one claim a copyright in such a work? Common sense tells us that 100 uncopyrightable facts do not magically change their status when gathered together in one place. . . .

The key to resolving the tension lies in understanding why facts are not copyrightable. The *sine qua non* of copyright is originality. To qualify for copyright protection, a work must be original to the author. . . . Original, as the term is used in copyright, means only that the work was independently created by the author (as opposed to copied from other works), and that it possesses at least some minimal degree of creativity. 1 M. Nimmer & D. Nimmer, Copyright §§2.01[A], [B] (1990) (hereinafter Nimmer). To be sure, the requisite level of creativity is extremely low; even a slight amount will suffice. The vast majority of works make the grade quite easily, as they possess some creative spark, "no matter how crude, humble or obvious" it might be. *Id.*, §1.08[C][1]. . . .

Originality is a constitutional requirement. The source of Congress' power to enact copyright laws is Article I, §8, cl. 8, of the Constitution, which authorizes Congress to "secur[e] for limited Times to Authors . . . the exclusive Right to their respective Writings." In two decisions from the late 19th century — *The Trade-Mark Cases*, 100 U.S. 82 (1879); and *Burrow-Giles Lithographic Co. v. Sarony*, 111 U.S. 53 (1884) — this Court defined the crucial terms "authors" and "writings." In so doing, the Court made it unmistakably clear that these terms presuppose a degree of originality. . . .

It is this bedrock principle of copyright that mandates the law's seemingly disparate treatment of facts and compilations. "No one may claim originality as to facts." *Id.* [Nimmer], §2.11[A], p. 2-157. This is because facts do not owe their origin to an act of authorship. The distinction is one between creation and discovery: The first person to find and report a particular fact has not created the fact; he or she has merely discovered its existence. . . .

Factual compilations, on the other hand, may possess the requisite originality. The compilation author typically chooses which facts to include, in what order to place them, and how to arrange the collected data so that they may be used effectively by readers. These choices as to selection and arrangement, so long as they are made independently by the compiler and entail a minimal degree of creativity, are sufficiently original that Congress may protect such compilations through the copyright laws. . . .

This inevitably means that the copyright in a factual compilation is thin. Notwithstanding a valid copyright, a subsequent compiler remains free to use the facts contained in another's publication to aid in preparing a competing work, so long as the competing work does not feature the same selection and arrangement. . . .

It may seem unfair that much of the fruit of the compiler's labor may be used by others without compensation. As Justice Brennan has correctly observed, however, this is not "some unforeseen byproduct of a statutory scheme." *Harper & Row*, 471 U.S., at 589 (dissenting opinion). It is, rather, "the essence of copyright," *ibid.*, and a constitutional requirement. The primary objective of copyright is not to reward the labor of authors, but "[t]o promote the Progress of Science and useful Arts." Art. I, §8, cl. 8. Accord, *Twentieth Century Music Corp. v. Aiken*, 422 U.S. 151, 156 (1975). To this end, copyright assures authors the right to their original expression, but encourages others to build freely upon the ideas and information conveyed by a work. *Harper & Row, supra*, 471 U.S., at 556-557. This principle, known as the idea/expression or fact/expression dichotomy, applies to all works of authorship. As applied to a factual compilation, assuming the absence of original written expression, only the compiler's selection and arrangement may be protected; the raw facts may be copied at will. This result is neither unfair nor unfortunate. It is the means by which copyright advances the progress of science and art. . . .

B

As we have explained, originality is a constitutionally mandated prerequisite for copyright protection. The Court's decisions announcing this rule predate the Copyright Act of 1909, but ambiguous language in the 1909 Act caused some lower courts temporarily to lose sight of this requirement. . . .

[T]hese courts developed a new theory to justify the protection of factual compilations. Known alternatively as "sweat of the brow" or "industrious collection," the underlying notion was that copyright was a reward for the hard work that went into compiling facts. The classic formulation of the doctrine appeared in *Jeweler's Circular Publishing Co.* [*v. Keystone Publishing Co.*], 281 F. [83 (2d Cir. 1922)], at 88:

> The right to copyright a book upon which one has expended labor in its preparation does not depend upon whether the materials which he has collected consist or not of matters which are publici juris, or whether such materials show literary skill *or originality*, either in thought or in language, or anything more than industrious collection. The man who goes through the streets of a town and puts down the names of each of the inhabitants, with their occupations and their street number, acquires material of which he is the author (emphasis added).

The "sweat of the brow" doctrine had numerous flaws, the most glaring being that it extended copyright protection in a compilation beyond selection and arrangement — the compiler's original contributions — to the facts themselves. Under the doctrine, the only defense to infringement was independent creation. A subsequent compiler was "not entitled to take one word of information previously published," but rather had to "independently wor[k] out the matter for himself, so as to arrive at the same result from the same common sources of information." *Id.*, at 88-89. . . . "Sweat of the brow" courts thereby eschewed the most fundamental axiom of copyright law — that no one may copyright facts or ideas. . . .

Without a doubt, the "sweat of the brow" doctrine flouted basic copyright principles. Throughout history, copyright law has "recognize[d] a greater need to disseminate factual works than works of fiction or fantasy." *Harper & Row*, 471 U.S., at 563. Accord, Gorman, *Fact or Fancy: The Implications for Copyright*, 29 J. Copyright Soc. 560, 563 (1982). But "sweat of the brow" courts took a contrary view; they handed out proprietary interests in facts and declared that authors are absolutely precluded from saving time and effort by relying upon the facts contained in prior works. In truth, "[i]t is just such wasted effort that the proscription against the copyright of ideas and facts . . . [is] designed to prevent." *Rosemont Enterprises, Inc. v. Random House, Inc.*, 366 F.2d 303, 310 (CA2 1966), *cert. denied*, 385 U.S. 1009 (1967). "Protection for the fruits of such research . . . may in certain circumstances be available under a theory of unfair competition. But to accord copyright protection on this basis alone distorts basic copyright principles in that it creates a monopoly in public domain materials without the necessary justification of protecting and encouraging the creation of 'writings' by 'authors.' " Nimmer §3.04, p. 3-23.

C . . .

. . . In enacting the Copyright Act of 1976, Congress dropped the reference to "all the writings of an author" and replaced it with the phrase "original works of authorship." 17 U.S.C. §102(a). In making explicit the originality requirement, Congress announced that it was merely clarifying existing law. . . .

To ensure that the mistakes of the "sweat of the brow" courts would not be repeated, Congress took additional measures. For example, §3 of the 1909 Act had stated that copyright protected only the "copyrightable component parts" of a work, but had not identified originality as the basis for distinguishing those component parts that were copyrightable from those that were not. The 1976 Act deleted this section and replaced it with §102(b), which identifies specifically those elements of a work for which copyright is not available. . . . Section 102(b) is universally understood to prohibit any copyright in facts. . . .

Congress took another step to minimize confusion by deleting the specific mention of "directories . . . and other compilations" in §5 of the 1909 Act. As mentioned, this section had led some courts to conclude that directories were copyrightable *per se* and that every element of a directory was protected. In its place, Congress enacted two new provisions. First, to make clear that compilations were not copyrightable per se, Congress provided a definition of the term "compilation." Second, to make clear that the copyright in a compilation did not extend to the facts themselves, Congress enacted §103. . . .

The purpose of the statutory definition is to emphasize that collections of facts are not copyrightable *per se*. It conveys this message through its tripartite structure. . . . The statute identifies three distinct elements and requires each to be met for a work to qualify as a copyrightable compilation: (1) the collection and assembly of pre-existing material, facts, or data; (2) the selection, coordination, or arrangement of those materials; and (3) the creation, by virtue of the particular selection, coordination, or arrangement, of an "original" work of authorship. . . .

. . . It is not enough for copyright purposes that an author collects and assembles facts. To satisfy the statutory definition, the work must get over two additional hurdles. In this way, the plain language indicates that not every collection of facts receives copyright protection. Otherwise, there would be a period after "data." . . .

Not every selection, coordination, or arrangement will pass muster. This is plain from the statute. It states that, to merit protection, the facts must be selected, coordinated, or arranged "in such a way" as to render the work as a whole original. This implies that some "ways" will trigger copyright, but that others will not. . . .

As discussed earlier, however, the originality requirement is not particularly stringent. A compiler may settle upon a selection or arrangement that others have used; novelty is not required. Originality requires only that the author make the selection or arrangement independently (*i.e.*, without copying that selection or arrangement from another work), and that it display some minimal level of creativity. Presumably, the vast majority of compilations will pass this test, but not all will. There remains a narrow category of works in which the creative spark is utterly lacking or so trivial as to be virtually nonexistent. Such works are incapable of sustaining a valid copyright. Nimmer §2.01[B].

Even if a work qualifies as a copyrightable compilation, it receives only limited protection. This is the point of §103 of the Act. Section 103 explains that "[t]he subject matter of copyright . . . includes compilations," §103(a), but that copyright protects only the author's original contributions — not the facts or information conveyed:

> The copyright in a compilation . . . extends only to the material contributed by the author of such work, as distinguished from the preexisting material employed in the work, and does not imply any exclusive right in the preexisting material. §103(b).

As §103 makes clear, copyright is not a tool by which a compilation author may keep others from using the facts or data he or she has collected. . . . The 1909 Act did not require, as "sweat of the brow" courts mistakenly assumed, that each subsequent compiler must start from scratch and is precluded from relying on research undertaken by another. Rather, the facts contained in existing works may be freely copied because copyright protects only the elements that owe their origin to the compiler — the selection, coordination, and arrangement of facts.

In summary, the 1976 revisions to the Copyright Act leave no doubt that originality, not "sweat of the brow," is the touchstone of copyright protection in directories and other fact-based works. Nor is there any doubt that the same was true under the 1909 Act. The 1976 revisions were a direct response to the Copyright Office's concern that many lower courts had misconstrued this basic principle, and Congress emphasized repeatedly that the purpose of the revisions was to clarify, not change, existing law. The revisions explain with painstaking clarity that copyright requires originality, §102(a); that facts are never original, §102(b); that the copyright in a compilation does not extend to the facts it contains, §103(b); and that a compilation is copyrightable only to the extent that it features an original selection, coordination, or arrangement, §101. . . .

III . . .

The selection, coordination, and arrangement of Rural's white pages do not satisfy the minimum constitutional standards for copyright protection. As mentioned at the outset, Rural's white pages are entirely typical. . . . In preparing its white pages, Rural simply takes the data provided by its subscribers and lists it alphabetically by surname. The end product is a garden-variety white pages directory, devoid of even the slightest trace of creativity.

Rural's selection of listings could not be more obvious: It publishes the most basic information — name, town, and telephone number — about each person who applies to it for telephone service. This is "selection" of a sort, but it lacks the modicum of creativity necessary to transform mere selection into copyrightable expression. Rural expended sufficient effort to make the white pages directory useful, but insufficient creativity to make it original.

We note in passing that the selection featured in Rural's white pages may also fail the originality requirement for another reason. Feist points out that Rural did not truly "select" to publish the names and telephone numbers of its subscribers; rather, it was required to do so by the Kansas Corporation Commission as part of its monopoly franchise. See 737 F. Supp. at 612.

Accordingly, one could plausibly conclude that this selection was dictated by state law, not by Rural. . . .

_____

As the statutory definition indicates, a compilation may be made up of "data," but it also may be made up of other "materials." 17 U.S.C. §101. What other materials qualify? What types of works may plausibly be viewed as "compilations"? Consider the following cases.

Roth Greeting Cards v. United Card Co.
429 F.2d 1106 (9th Cir. 1970)

HAMLEY, J.: . . . Roth's claim involves the production and distribution by United of seven greeting cards which bear a remarkable resemblance to seven of Roth's cards on which copyrights had been granted. . . .

. . . [T]he trial court found that the art work in plaintiff's greeting cards was copyrightable, but not infringed by defendant. The trial court also found that, although copied by defendant, the wording or textual matter of each of the plaintiff's cards in question consist of common and ordinary English words and phrases which are not original with Roth and were in the public domain prior to first use by plaintiff.

Arguing that the trial court erred in ruling against it on merits, Roth agrees that the textual material involved in their greeting cards may have been in the public domain, but argues that this alone did not end the inquiry into the copyrightability of the entire card. Roth argues that "[I]t is the arrangement of the words, their combination and plan, together with the appropriate artwork . . ." which is original, the creation of Roth, and entitled to copyright protection. . . .

United argues, and we agree, that there was substantial evidence to support the district court's finding that the textual matter of each card, considered apart from its arrangement on the cards and its association with artistic representations, was not original to Roth and therefore not copyrightable.[4] However, proper analysis of the problem requires that all elements of each card, including text, arrangement of text, art work, and association between art work and text, be considered as a whole.

Considering all of these elements together, the Roth cards are, in our opinion, both original and copyrightable. In reaching this conclusion we recognize that copyright protection is not available for ideas, but only for tangible expression of ideas. *Mazer v. Stein,* 347 U.S. 201, 217 (1954). We conclude that each of Roth's cards, considered as a whole, represents a tangible expression of an idea and that such expression was, in totality, created by Roth. . . .

It appears to us that in total concept and feel the cards of United are the same as the copyrighted cards of Roth. With the possible exception of one United card . . . , the characters depicted in the art work, the mood they portrayed, the combination of art work conveying a particular mood with a particular message, and the arrangement of the words on the greeting card are substantially the same as in Roth's cards. In several instances the lettering is also very similar. . . .

The remarkable similarity between the Roth and United cards in issue . . . is apparent to even a casual observer. For example, one Roth card . . . has, on its front, a colored drawing of a

_____

4. Thus, if United had copied only the textual materials, which were not independently copyrightable, United might have been able to do so with impunity. . . .

Roth Cards (left) and United Cards (right)

cute moppet suppressing a smile and, on the inside, the words "i wuv you." With the exception of minor variations in color and style, defendant's card . . . is identical. Likewise, Roth's card entitled "I miss you already," depicts a forlorn boy sitting on a curb weeping, with an inside message reading ". . . and You Haven't even Left . . ." . . . , is closely paralleled by United's card with the same caption, showing a forlorn and weeping man, and with the identical inside message. . . .

KILKENNY, J., dissenting: The majority agrees with a specific finding of the lower court that the words on the cards are not the subject of copyright. By strong implication, it likewise accepts the finding of the trial court that the art work on the cards, although subject to copyright, was not infringed. Thus far, I agree.

I cannot, however, follow the logic of the majority in holding that the uncopyrightable words and the imitated, but not copied art work, constitutes such total composition as to be subject to protection under the copyright laws. The majority concludes that in the overall arrangement of the text, the art work and the association of the art work to the text, the cards were copyrightable and the copyright infringed. This conclusion, as I view it, results in the whole becoming substantially greater than the sum total of its parts. With this conclusion, of course, I cannot agree.

Feeling, as I do, that the copyright act is a grant of limited monopoly to the authors of creative literature and art, I do not think that we should extend a 56-year monopoly* in a situation where neither infringement of text, nor infringement of art work can be found. On these facts, we should adhere to our historic philosophy requiring freedom of competition. I would affirm.

Mason v. Montgomery Data, Inc.
967 F.2d 135 (5th Cir. 1992)

REAVLEY, J.: . . . Mason created and published 118 real estate ownership maps that, together, cover all of Montgomery County. The maps . . . pictorially portray the location, size, and shape

---

*[As described in detail in Chapter 3, copyright in a work created by an individual now lasts for the life of the author plus 70 years. — EDS.]

of surveys, land grants, tracts, and various topographical features within the county. Numbers and words on the maps identify deeds, abstract numbers, acreage, and the owners of the various tracts. Mason obtained the information that he included on the maps from a variety of sources.[3] Relying on these sources, Mason initially determined the location and dimensions of each survey in the county, and then drew the corners and lines of the surveys onto topographical maps of the county that were published by the United States Geological Survey (USGS). He then determined the location of the property lines of the real estate tracts within each survey and drew them on the USGS maps. Finally, Mason traced the survey and tract lines onto transparent overlays, enlarged clean USGS maps and the overlays, added names and other information to the overlays, and combined the maps and overlays to print the final maps. Mason testified that he used substantial judgment and discretion to reconcile inconsistencies among the various sources, to select which features to include in the final map sheets, and to portray the information in a manner that would be useful to the public. . . .

. . . [Defendant] Landata purchased a set of Mason's maps and reorganized them by cutting and pasting them into 72 map sheets. Landata then attached a transparent overlay to each of the 72 sheets, and depicted on these overlays numerous updates and corrections to the information on Mason's maps. . . . Landata created an inked mylar "master overlay" for each of the 72 reorganized map sheets. . . .

The district court determined that Mason's idea, "which includes drawing the abstract and tract boundaries, indicating the ownership name, the tract size, and the other factual information" on a map of Montgomery County, was "to create the maps, based on legal and factual public information." *Mason*, 765 F. Supp. at 356. Mason argues that the court clearly erred in finding that this idea can be expressed in only one or a limited number of ways. We agree. The record in this case contains copies of maps created by Mason's competitors that prove beyond dispute that the idea embodied in Mason's map is capable of a variety of expressions. . . . The record also contains affidavits in which licensed surveyors and experienced mapmakers explain that the differences between Mason's maps and those of his competitors are the natural result of each mapmaker's selection of sources, interpretation of those sources, discretion in reconciling inconsistencies among the sources, and skill and judgment in depicting the information. . . .

Landata contends that, even if the merger doctrine does not apply, Mason's maps are uncopyrightable because they are not "original" under *Feist*. . . .

Mason's maps pass muster under *Feist* because Mason's selection, coordination, and arrangement of the information that he depicted are sufficiently creative to qualify his maps as original "compilations" of facts. . . .

Mason's maps also possess sufficient creativity to merit copyright protection as pictorial and graphic works of authorship. . . .

NOTES AND QUESTIONS

1. In *Feist*, the standard the Court sets for originality is quite low. Do you think the fact that *Feist* involved a compilation had an effect on the Court's articulation of the standard?

---

3. These sources included tax, deed, and survey records from Montgomery County; data provided by the San Jacinto River Authority; survey records, maps, and abstracts of land titles from the Texas General Land Office; title data and subdivision information provided by Conroe Title; a map from the city of Conroe, Texas; and maps from the United States Coast and Geodetic Survey.

2. Do you agree with the *Feist* Court that the result it reached was "neither unfair nor unfortunate"? Is copyright an appropriate legal vehicle for protecting collections of information?

3. After *Feist*, what exactly must a compiler do to qualify the resulting collection of material for copyright protection? This question is a vital one for enterprises that seek to market, and protect, compilations of factual information. We consider the post-*Feist* jurisprudence concerning the copyrightability of databases in Chapter 4.

4. Do you agree with the *Mason* court that Mason's maps satisfied the *Feist* originality standard? Were the maps properly characterized as "compilations"? Note that the tradition of copyright protection for maps extends back to the first Copyright Act of 1790. In light of this tradition, and of the court's conclusion that the maps were protectible as "pictorial, graphic or sculptural works" anyway, why bother to characterize the maps as compilations?

5. Does *Roth Greeting Cards* effectively treat the greeting cards as "compilations"? If copyright did not protect compilations, would these works be considered copyrightable under §102(a)? Under §102(b)? If copyright protected only collective works but not compilations, would these works be copyrightable?

Although *Roth Greeting Cards* predates *Feist*, courts within the Ninth Circuit frequently cite and rely on its "total concept and feel" standard. *See, e.g., Apple Computer, Inc. v. Microsoft Corp.*, 35 F.3d 1435, 1446 (9th Cir. 1994); *Litchfield v. Spielberg*, 736 F.2d 1352, 1357 (9th Cir. 1984), *cert. denied*, 470 U.S. 1052 (1985); *Sid & Marty Krofft Television Prods., Inc. v. McDonald's Corp.*, 562 F.2d 1157, 1167 (9th Cir. 1977). Is this standard consistent with *Feist*? Does viewing a textual or graphic work as a compilation of its elements, rather than simply as a literary or pictorial work, make a finding of originality more or less likely? While the total concept and feel test can be relevant for determining originality for the purposes of the threshold question of copyrightability, courts also employ this test in the infringement analysis. *See* Chapter 5.B.1 *infra*.

6. Do you think that Mason's maps or the greeting cards in *Roth Greeting Cards* would have qualified as copyrightable "[c]ollections of literary and artistic works" under the Berne Convention?

7. Is there a minimum number of preexisting elements that a creator must combine in order for there to be originality? The Compendium II of Copyright Office Practices ¶307.01 (1984) states that "[a]ny compilation consisting of less than four selections is considered to lack the requisite original authorship." The Ninth Circuit has also held that the combination of four preexisting elements in a lamp did not result in an original work of authorship. *Lamps Plus, Inc. v. Seattle Lighting Fixture Co.*, 345 F.3d 1140 (9th Cir. 2003); *see also Satava v. Lowry*, 323 F.3d 805 (9th Cir. 2003) (finding combination of six unprotectible elements in glass-in-glass jellyfish sculptures did not rise to the level of originality sufficient to merit copyright protection).

8. In *Darden v. Peters*, 488 F.3d 277 (4th Cir. 2007), the plaintiff had taken a U.S. Census map, added color and shading to give the map a three-dimensional effect, selected a font for labeling the states, and added additional labels as well. The Copyright Office rejected the application for registration and the Fourth Circuit agreed, concluding that: "Additions to the preexisting maps such as color, shading, and labels using standard fonts and shapes fall within the narrow category of works that lack even a minimum level of creativity. . . ." *Id.* at 287. The court noted that the contributions Darden alleged to constitute original authorship elements resembled the examples set forth in regulations issued by the Copyright Office of the types of works that lack a minimum level of creativity: "[w]ords and short phrases such as names, titles, and slogans; familiar symbols or designs; mere variations of typographic ornamentation, lettering or coloring; mere listing of ingredients or contents." 37 C.F.R. §202.1(a);

see supra page 98. Why was Darden's map denied protection when Mason's maps were granted protection? In his application for registration Darden described his work as "a derivative work that . . . was based on preexisting 'US Census black and white outline maps.'" Does the difference in treatment lie solely in Darden's designation of his map as a "derivative work" instead of a compilation?

9. In *Atari Games Corp. v. Oman*, 979 F.2d 242 (D.C. Cir. 1992), the D.C. Circuit reversed the Register of Copyrights' decision to deny registration as an audiovisual work to an early video game — Atari's BREAKOUT. The game was fairly simple. Players would move a paddle to hit a square ball against a wall built of rectangles. *See id.* at 243. The size of the wall, paddle, and ball would change and the ball would increase in speed. *See id.* The court did not quarrel with the district court's finding that "simple geometric shapes and coloring alone are not per se copyrightable." *See id.* at 243-44. However, it emphasized that the Register should have focused on the "flow of the game as a whole," keeping in mind *Feist*'s statement that the standard for originality is not high. *See id.* at 244-45. Are audiovisual works always compilations because the statute defines them as "a series of related images"? 17 U.S.C. §101. Do you think that most video game displays are copyrightable compilations under the *Feist* standard?

B. WHO IS AN AUTHOR?

Thus far, we have considered the requirements that flow from the constitutional authorization to grant exclusive rights in "Writings." The Intellectual Property Clause also specifies that these rights are to be granted to "Authors." Does this wording impose additional threshold requirements for the grant of copyright? What does it mean to be an "author"? The present Copyright Act suggests several different answers, depending on the circumstances of a work's creation.

The Copyright Act recognizes three kinds of authorship: sole authorship, joint or co-authorship, and employer authorship of "works made for hire." The determination of authorship has considerable practical importance, because the Act assigns initial ownership of the copyright to the party or parties deemed to be the "author" or "authors" of the work:

§201. Ownership of copyright

(a) **Initial ownership.** Copyright in a work protected under this title vests initially in the author or authors of the work. The authors of a joint work are co-owners of copyright in the work.

(b) **Works made for hire.** In the case of a work made for hire, the employer or other person for whom the work was prepared is considered the author for purposes of this title, and, unless the parties have expressly agreed otherwise in a written instrument signed by them, owns all of the rights comprised in the copyright.

As you will see, the "works made for hire" provisions of the U.S. Copyright Act stand in stark contrast to the copyright laws of many other countries, which recognize only natural persons as authors. The major international copyright treaties — the Berne Convention, the TRIPS Agreement, and the WIPO treaties — refer simply to "authors," and do not specify how authorship is to be defined.

As you read the second part of this chapter, identify the different understandings of authorship embodied in the Copyright Act's categories and consider the extent to which they are consistent with each other and with the policies incorporated in the Intellectual Property Clause of the Constitution.

1. Sole Authorship

The Copyright Act does not define the term *author*, nor did any of the previous Copyright Acts define this term. Is a definition necessary? Consider the following decision:

Lindsay v. The Wrecked and Abandoned Vessel R.M.S. Titanic
52 U.S.P.Q.2d 1609 (S.D.N.Y. 1999)

BAER, J.: . . . In 1994, the plaintiff, under contract with a British television company, filmed and directed the British documentary film, "Explorers of the Titanic," a chronicle of [defendant] RMST's third salvage expedition of the Titanic. . . . To film this documentary, Lindsay sailed with RMST and the salvage expedition crew to the wreck site and remained at sea for approximately one month. . . . The plaintiff alleges that during and after filming this documentary in 1994, he conceived a new film project for the Titanic wreck using high illumination lighting equipment. . . .

As part of his pre-production efforts, the plaintiff created various story boards for the film, a series of drawings which incorporated images of the Titanic by identifying specific camera angles and shooting sequences "that reflected Planitff's [sic] creative inspiration and force behind his concept for shooting the Subject Work." . . . The plaintiff also alleges that he, along with members of his film team, designed the huge underwater light towers that were later used to make the film. . . . Lindsay also "personally constructed the light towers" and thereafter "for approximately 3-4 weeks directed, produced, and acted as the cinematographer of the Subject Work, underwater video taping of the Titanic wreck site, and otherwise participated in the 1996 salvage operation." . . . He also directed the filming of the wreck site from on board the salvage vessel "Ocean Voyager" after leading daily planning sessions with the crew of the Nautile, the submarine used to transport the film equipment and photographers to the underwater wreck site. . . . The purpose of the sessions was to provide the photographers with "detailed instructions for positioning and utilizing the light towers." . . .

[Plaintiff asserted a copyright infringement claim against defendants based on their licensing of the footage to The Discovery Channel. The court denied defendants' motion to dismiss this claim.]

The defendants first argue that the plaintiff cannot have any protectable right in the illuminated footage since he did not dive to the ship and thus did not himself actually photograph the wreckage. This argument, however, does not hold water. . . .

For over 100 years, the Supreme Court has recognized that photographs may receive copyright protection in "so far as they are representatives of original intellectual conceptions of the author." *Burrow-Giles Lithographic Co. v. Sarony*, 111 U.S. 53, 58 (1884). An individual claiming to be an author for copyright purposes must show "the existence of those facts of originality, of intellectual production, of thought, and conception." . . . Taken as true, plaintiff's allegations meet this standard. Lindsay's alleged storyboards and the specific directions he provided to the film crew regarding the use of the lightowers [sic] and the angles from which to shoot the wreck all indicate that the final footage would indeed be the product of Lindsay's "original intellectual conceptions." . . .

All else being equal, where a plaintiff alleges that he exercised such a high degree of control over a film operation — including the type and amount of lighting used, the specific camera angles to be employed, and other detail-intensive elements of a film — such that the final product duplicates his conceptions and visions of what the film should look like, the plaintiff may be said to be an "author" within the meaning of the Copyright Act. . . .

NOTES AND QUESTIONS

1. Recall the engraver in *Alfred Bell & Co. v. Catalda Fine Arts, supra* page 67, who claimed copyright in his reproductions of paintings by Old Masters. Would the engravings in that case satisfy the definition of authorship articulated above? Is there a difference between "originality" and "authorship"?

2. If "originality" and "authorship" are indeed distinct concepts, does the requirement of authorship translate into a separate, and perhaps higher, threshold for copyright protection? Should it? *Feist* notwithstanding, should the constitutional reference to "Authors" be read to require this result?

3. Professor Peter Jaszi has observed:

> The "author" has been the main character in a drama played out on the parallel stages of literary and legal culture. By the mid-seventeenth century, well before the English enacted the 1709 Statute of Anne, writers began to assert claims to special status by designating themselves as "authors." During the eighteenth century, "authorship" became intimately associated with the Romantic movement in literature and art, expressing "an extreme assertion of the self and the value of individual experience . . . together with the sense of the infinite and the transcendental."

Peter Jaszi, *Toward a Theory of Copyright: The Metamorphoses of "Authorship,"* 1991 Duke L.J. 455, 455. Professor Jaszi argues that this individualistic understanding of authorship played, and continues to play, an important role in shaping Anglo-American copyright law. In particular, he argues that "[t]he 'authorship' concept, with its roots in notions of individual self-proprietorship, provided the rationale for thinking of literary productions as personal property with various associated attributes including alienability." *Id.* at 472. As a result of this process of abstraction and commodification, however, modern copyright law — the law that protects Viacom as well as Toni Morrison — confronts a tension between protecting economic rights in "works" and protecting "authors." As you read on, consider whether you agree.

2. Joint Authorship

Section 101 defines a "joint work" as "a work prepared by two or more authors with the intention that their contributions be merged into inseparable or interdependent parts of a unitary whole." 17 U.S.C. §101. Under this definition, what level of contribution is sufficient to qualify a party as a co-author?

Erickson v. Trinity Theatre, Inc.
13 F.3d 1061 (7th Cir. 1994)

RIPPLE, J.: . . . [Karen Erickson, a founding member of the Trinity Theatre, prepared three plays for the company. After a dispute developed between the parties, Trinity stopped paying royalties to Erickson for performances of the plays. Trinity argued that it was a co-author and co-owner of copyright in the plays because various Trinity actors had made suggestions that Erickson incorporated during development of the plays.]

Even if two or more persons collaborate with the intent to create a unitary work, the product will be considered a "joint work" only if the collaborators can be considered "authors." Courts have applied two tests to evaluate the contributions of authors claiming joint authorship status: Professor Nimmer's de minimis test and Professor Goldstein's copyrightable subject matter ("copyrightability") test. The de minimis and copyrightability tests differ in one fundamental respect. The de minimis test requires that only the combined product of joint efforts must be copyrightable. By contrast, Professor Goldstein's copyrightability test requires that each author's contribution be copyrightable. . . .

[Professor Nimmer's] position has not found support in the courts. . . . [It] is not consistent with one of the Act's premises: ideas and concepts standing alone should not receive protection. Because the creative process necessarily involves the development of existing concepts into new forms, any restriction on the free exchange of ideas stifles creativity to some extent. Restrictions on an author's use of existing ideas in a work, such as the threat that accepting suggestions from another party might jeopardize the author's sole entitlement to a copyright, would hinder creativity. Second, contribution of an idea is an exceedingly ambiguous concept. Professor Nimmer provides little guidance to courts or parties regarding when a contribution rises to the level of joint authorship except to state that the contribution must be "more than a word or a line." . . .

We agree that the language of the Act supports the adoption of a copyrightability requirement. Section 101 of the Act defines a "joint work" as a "work prepared by two or more *authors*" (emphasis added). To qualify as an author, one must supply more than mere direction or ideas. . . .

. . . This test also enables parties to predict whether their contributions to a work will entitle them to copyright protection as a joint author. . . .

[Because Trinity could not identify any specific copyrightable contributions made by its actors, the court concluded that Trinity could not qualify as a joint author of the plays.]

Some works, like motion pictures, incorporate the copyrightable contributions of many people, each of whom intends that his or her contribution be merged with the others to form a unitary whole. Is each of these individuals therefore an "author"?

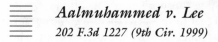

Aalmuhammed v. Lee
202 F.3d 1227 (9th Cir. 1999)

KLEINFELD, J.: . . . In 1991, Warner Brothers contracted with Spike Lee and his production companies to make the movie *Malcolm X*, to be based on the book, *The Autobiography of Malcolm X*. Lee co-wrote the screenplay, directed, and co-produced the movie, which starred Denzel Washington as Malcolm X. Washington asked Jefri Aalmuhammed to assist him in his preparation for the starring role because Aalmuhammed knew a great deal about Malcolm X and Islam. Aalmuhammed, a devout Muslim, was particularly knowledgeable about the life of Malcolm X, having previously written, directed, and produced a documentary film about Malcolm X.

. . . [Aalmuhammed] reviewed the shooting script for Spike Lee and Denzel Washington and suggested extensive script revisions. Some of his script revisions were included in the released version of the film; others were filmed but not included in the released version. Most of the revisions Aalmuhammed made were to ensure the religious and historical accuracy and authenticity of scenes depicting Malcolm X's religious conversion and pilgrimage to Mecca.

Aalmuhammed submitted evidence that he directed Denzel Washington and other actors while on the set, created at least two entire scenes with new characters, translated Arabic into English for subtitles, supplied his own voice for voice-overs, selected the proper prayers and religious practices for the characters, and edited parts of the movie during post production. Washington testified in his deposition that Aalmuhammed's contribution to the movie was "great" because "he helped to rewrite, to make more authentic." . . .

During the summer before *Malcolm X's* November 1992 release, Aalmuhammed asked for a writing credit as a co-writer of the film, but was turned down. When the film was released, it credited Aalmuhammed only as an "Islamic Technical Consultant," far down the list. . . .

[Aalmuhammed sought a declaratory judgment that the movie was a "joint work" and that he was a co-owner of the copyright and entitled to an accounting of the profits. The Ninth Circuit affirmed the district court's grant of summary judgment to defendants.]

. . . The statutory language establishes that for a work to be a "joint work" there must be (1) a copyrightable work, (2) two or more "authors," and (3) the authors must intend their contributions be merged into inseparable or interdependent parts of a unitary whole. A "joint work" in this circuit "requires each author to make an independently copyrightable contribution" to the disputed work. *Malcolm X* is a copyrightable work, and it is undisputed that the movie was intended by everyone involved with it to be a unitary whole. . . . Aalmuhammed has . . . submitted evidence that he rewrote several specific passages of dialogue that appeared in *Malcolm X*, and that he wrote scenes relating to Malcolm X's Hajj pilgrimage that were enacted in the movie. If Aalmuhammed's evidence is accepted, as it must be on summary judgment, these items would have been independently copyrightable. . . .

But there is another element to a "joint work." A "joint work" includes "two or more authors." Aalmuhammed established that he contributed substantially to the film, but not that he was one of its "authors." We hold that authorship is required under the statutory definition of a joint work, and that authorship is not the same thing as making a valuable and copyrightable contribution. . . .

Who, in the absence of contract, can be considered an author of a movie? The word is traditionally used to mean the originator or the person who causes something to come into being, or even the first cause, as when Chaucer refers to the "Author of Nature." For a movie, that might be the producer who raises the money. Eisenstein thought the author of a movie was the editor. The "auteur" theory suggests that it might be the director, at least if the director is able to impose his artistic judgments on the film. . . .

The Supreme Court dealt with the problem of defining "author" in new media in *Burrow-Giles Lithographic Co. v. Sarony.* . . . The Court decided that the photographer was the author, quoting various English authorities: "the person who has superintended the arrangement, who has actually formed the picture by putting the persons in position, and arranging the place where the people are to be — the man who is the effective cause of that"; " 'author' involves originating, making, producing, as the inventive or master mind, the thing which is to be protected"; "the man who really represents, creates, or gives effect to the idea, fancy, or imagination." The Court said that an "author," in the sense that the Founding Fathers used the term in the Constitution, was " 'he to whom anything owes its origin; originator; maker; one who completes a work of science or literature.' "

Answering a different question, what is a copyrightable "work," as opposed to who is the "author," the Supreme Court held in *Feist Publications* that "some minimal level of creativity" or "originality" suffices. But that measure of a "work" would be too broad and indeterminate to be useful if applied to determine who are "authors" of a movie. So many people might qualify as an "author" if the question were limited to whether they made a substantial creative contribution that that test would not distinguish one from another. Everyone from the producer and director to casting director, costumer, hairstylist, and "best boy" gets listed in the movie credits because all of their creative contributions really do matter. It is striking in *Malcolm X* how much the person who controlled the hue of the lighting contributed, yet no one would use the word "author" to denote that individual's relationship to the movie. A creative contribution does not suffice to establish authorship of the movie.

Burrow-Giles, in defining "author," requires more than a minimal creative or original contribution to the work. *Burrow-Giles* is still good law, and was recently reaffirmed in *Feist Publications*. *Burrow-Giles* and *Feist Publications* answer two distinct questions; who is an author, and what is a copyrightable work. . . .

The Second and Seventh Circuits have likewise concluded that contribution of independently copyrightable material to a work intended to be an inseparable whole will not suffice to establish authorship of a joint work.[24] Although the Second and Seventh Circuits do not base their decisions on the word "authors" in the statute, the practical results they reach are consistent with ours. These circuits have held that a person claiming to be an author of a joint work must prove that both parties intended each other to be joint authors. In determining whether the parties have the intent to be joint authors, the Second Circuit looks at who has decision making authority, how the parties bill themselves, and other evidence.

In *Thomson v. Larson*, an off-Broadway playwright had created a modern version of *La Boheme*, and had been adamant throughout its creation on being the sole author. He hired a drama professor for "dramaturgical assistance and research," agreeing to credit her as "dramaturg" but not author, but saying nothing about "joint work" or copyright. The playwright tragically died immediately after the final dress rehearsal, just before his play became the tremendous Broadway hit, *Rent*. The dramaturg then sued his estate for a declaratory judgment that she was an author of *Rent* as a "joint work," and for an accounting. The Second Circuit noted that the dramaturg had no decision making authority, had neither sought nor was billed as a co-author, and that the defendant entered into contracts as the sole author. On this reasoning, the Second Circuit held that there was no intent to be joint authors by the putative parties and therefore it was not a joint work. . . .

Aalmuhammed did not at any time have superintendence of the work. Warner Brothers and Spike Lee controlled it. . . .

Also, neither Aalmuhammed, nor Spike Lee, nor Warner Brothers, made any objective manifestations of an intent to be coauthors. Warner Brothers required Spike Lee to sign a "work for hire" agreement, so that even Lee would not be a co-author and co-owner with Warner Brothers. . . .

The Constitution establishes the social policy that our construction of the statutory term "authors" carries out. . . . Progress would be retarded rather than promoted, if an author could not consult with others and adopt their useful suggestions without sacrificing sole ownership of the work. Too open a definition of author would compel authors to insulate themselves and maintain ignorance of the contributions others might make. Spike Lee could not consult a scholarly Muslim to make a movie about a religious conversion to Islam, and the arts would be the poorer for that. . . .

---

24. *Thomson v. Larson*, 147 F.3d 195 (2d Cir. 1998); *Erickson v. Trinity Theatre, Inc.*, 13 F.3d 1061 (7th Cir. 1994); *Childress v. Taylor*, 945 F.2d 500 (2d Cir. 1991).

NOTES AND QUESTIONS

1. Review the questions posed following the excerpt from the *Lindsay* decision, *supra* page 118. Have your answers to any of these questions changed? Do the attributes of authorship identified by the *Aalmuhammed* court matter more when one is resolving claims of co-authorship? Why?

2. The Broadway hit *Rent*, the subject of the *Thomson v. Larson* dispute, was the culmination of a seven-year process of writing and rewriting. The Second Circuit's decision summarized the latter half of this process as follows:

> In the spring of 1993, [New York Theatre Workshop (NYTW) Artistic Director] Nicola urged Larson to allow the NYTW to hire a playwright or a bookwriter to help revamp the storyline and narrative structure of the play. But Larson "absolutely, vehemently and totally rejected [Nicola's] suggestion of hiring a bookwriter" and "was insistent on making RENT entirely his own project." Larson received a grant in the spring of 1994 to pay for a workshop production of *Rent*, which was presented to the public in the fall of 1994. . . . "[T]he professional consensus concerning the show, after the studio production, was that it was, at a minimum, very promising and that it needed a great deal of work." Artistic Director Nicola once again suggested to Larson that he consider working with a bookwriter, which Larson "adamantly and steadfastly refused, consistently emphasizing his intention to be the only author of RENT."
>
> In May 1995, in preparation for *Rent*'s off-Broadway opening scheduled for early 1996, Larson agreed to the NYTW's hiring of Lynn Thomson, a professor of advanced playwriting at New York University, as a dramaturg to assist him in clarifying the storyline of the musical. Thomson signed a contract with the NYTW, in which she agreed to provide her services. . . . The agreement stated that Thomson's "responsibilities shall include, but not be limited to: Providing dramaturgical assistance and research to the playwright and director." In exchange, the NYTW agreed to pay "a fee" of $2000, "[i]n full consideration of the services to be rendered" and to provide for billing credit for Thomson as "Dramaturg." The Thomson/NYTW agreement was silent as to any copyright interests or any issue of ownership with respect to the final work.
>
> [The "October Version" of *Rent* produced with Thomson's assistance] was characterized by experts as "a radical transformation of the show." [O]n November 3, 1995, Larson signed a contract with the NYTW for ongoing revisions to *Rent*. This agreement identified Larson as the "Author" of *Rent* and made no reference to Thomson. . . .

Thomson v. Larson, 147 F.3d 195, 197-98 (2d Cir. 1998). The court concluded that *Rent* was not a joint work. Which facts support the court's conclusion? Are there facts that support the opposite conclusion?

3. Recall the statutory definition of a joint work: "a work prepared by two or more authors with the intention that their contributions be merged into inseparable or interdependent parts of a unitary whole." 17 U.S.C. §101. Are *Erickson* and *Aalmuhammed* simply focusing on different elements of the definition, or are they interpreting the same element differently?

4. All authors of a joint work receive equal interests in the work. Thus, for example, if there are two joint authors, each author receives a one-half undivided interest. Upon an author's death, her interest passes to her heirs (see Chapter 3, *infra*). How might these rules have affected judicial evaluation of the co-authorship claims asserted in *Erickson*, *Thomson*, and *Aalmuhammed*?

5. Permission of all co-authors is required for an assignment or an exclusive license of the copyright in a joint work. In the U.S., however, any author of a joint work may grant a nonexclusive license without her co-authors' consent, subject to a duty to account to the co-authors for any profits received from the license. In contrast, some non-U.S. copyright

systems — e.g., France and the Republic of Korea — require that all co-authors consent to any exploitation of the work. Countries in this latter group, though, are more likely to furnish express safeguards against unreasonable behavior by co-authors. Thus, the Korean copyright law directs that consent may not be unreasonably withheld, while France authorizes its courts to resolve disagreements. What are the reasons to prefer one rule over another? Which rule do you think is more likely to promote progress?

6. The Second Circuit has held that a joint owner of a copyright cannot retroactively transfer his ownership interest to a defendant who has been sued by the other joint owner of the copyright. *Davis v. Blige*, 505 F.3d 90 (2d Cir. 2007). The court viewed the retroactive transfer as "an attempt to cut off the accrued rights of the other owner to sue for infringement," and concluded that permitting retroactive transfer would "violate basic principles of tort and contract law, and undermine the policies embodied by the Copyright Act." *Id.* at 97-98. It worried that permitting such retroactive assignments or even licenses would inject uncertainty and unpredictability into determinations of copyright ownership and authorization, creating "substantial mischief." *Id.* at 105. Do you agree? If such mischief resulted from a grant by one co-owner, would it be possible instead to require the authorizing co-owner to account to his other co-owners?

7. Should Aalmuhammed instead have claimed sole authorship in his separate contributions to *Malcolm X*? Thomson asserted such a claim, but the court declined to reach it because it had not been raised in the proceedings before the district court. *Thomson*, 147 F.3d at 206. How should such a claim be resolved?

8. The "intent to merge" requirement for a joint work creates difficulties for works that evolve over time with contributions from many individuals. The open source software movement presents an interesting case study. Open source computer programs are written and distributed with a license that allows others to make modifications to the program and further distribute the modified version to others to allow for still further modifications. Are the modified programs jointly authored by all of the different programmers in the chain? Or is each new modification simply a derivative work based on the previous program? Does it matter whether the underlying author intended, when she was writing her program, for others to modify and add to the program? Does the intention need to be specific to another author or to a particular contribution? Next, consider "Wikipedia" entries, which may be edited by many contributors on an ad hoc basis. Would your answers to any of the above questions change?

Collaborative art is another example that challenges the "joint work" definition contained in the Copyright Act. Modern art museums sometimes exhibit interactive installations that generate different patterns of images, lights, and/or sounds in response to viewer actions. Computer programs can be designed to generate complex, coherent stories and songs based in part on user input. Who is the "author" of each of these creations? What is the "work"? Are these questions meaningful ones?

At the other end of the technological spectrum, folklore and indigenous arts represent the cumulative creativity of generations. In addition, some indigenous images and stories have religious significance. The limitations of the definition of "joint work" can create problems for assertions of ownership in these types of works, and many of these works are also very old. Nonetheless, concerns about appropriation of their images and stories by outsiders who then claim broad copyright protection for "their" derivative works have led some indigenous peoples to turn to copyright protection as a way to maintain control over at least some parts of their heritage. In Australia, such claims have been recognized by the courts. *See Millpurrurru v. Indofurn Pty. Ltd.* (1994) 54 F.C.R. 240 (Austl.) (holding copyright in paintings of sacred Aboriginal designs infringed by depiction on carpets).

9. If no one qualifies as an "author," is the work a "work of authorship" at all? *See generally* Peter Jaszi, *On the Author Effect: Contemporary Copyright and Collective Creativity, in* Martha Woodmansee & Peter Jaszi, eds., *The Construction of Authorship: Textual Appropriation in Law and Literature* 29 (1994) (arguing that copyright law fails to comprehend the collaborative nature of creativity).

3. Works Made for Hire

In *Aalmuhammed*, the Ninth Circuit observed in passing that Warner Brothers, not Spike Lee, was the "author" of *Malcolm X* pursuant to a " 'work for hire' agreement." Given the court's description of the qualities necessary for authorship, that might seem to be a curious result. Warner Brothers' authorship status arises from the "work made for hire" provisions of the Copyright Act, to which we now turn.

The 1909 Copyright Act specified that "the word 'author' shall include an employer in the case of works made for hire," Copyright Act of 1909, §62, 17 U.S.C. §26 (1976 ed.), but did not define the term *works made for hire*. According to §101 of the 1976 Act:

A "work made for hire" is —
(1) a work prepared by an employee within the scope of his or her employment; or
(2) a work specially ordered or commissioned for use as a contribution to a collective work, as a part of a motion picture or other audiovisual work, as a translation, as a supplementary work, as a compilation, as an instructional text, as a test, as answer material for a test, or as an atlas, if the parties expressly agree in a written instrument signed by them that the work shall be considered a work made for hire. For the purpose of the foregoing sentence, a "supplementary work" is a work prepared for publication as a secondary adjunct to a work by another author for the purpose of introducing, concluding, illustrating, explaining, revising, commenting upon, or assisting in the use of the other work, such as forewords, afterwords, pictorial illustrations, maps, charts, tables, editorial notes, musical arrangements, answer material for tests, bibliographies, appendixes, and indexes, and an "instructional text" is a literary, pictorial, or graphic work prepared for publication and with the purpose of use in systematic instructional activities.

This definition, however, soon raised interpretative issues of its own.

a. Who Is an "Employee"?

Community for Creative Non-Violence v. Reid
490 U.S. 730 (1989)

MARSHALL, J.:

I

. . . In the fall of 1985, CCNV decided to participate in the annual Christmastime Pageant of Peace in Washington, D.C., by sponsoring a display to dramatize the plight of the homeless. As the District Court recounted:

[CCNV trustee Mitch] Snyder and fellow CCNV members conceived the idea for the nature of the display: a sculpture of a modern Nativity scene in which, in lieu of the traditional Holy Family, the two adult figures and the infant would appear as contemporary homeless people huddled on a streetside steam grate. The family was to be black (most of the homeless in Washington being black); the figures were to be life-sized, and the steam grate would be positioned atop a platform "pedestal," or base, within which special-effects equipment would be enclosed to emit simulated "steam" through the grid to swirl about the figures. They also settled upon a title for the work — "Third World America" — and a legend for the pedestal: "and still there is no room at the inn." 652 F. Supp. 1453, 1454 (DC 1987).

Snyder made inquiries to locate an artist to produce the sculpture. He was referred to respondent James Earl Reid, a Baltimore, Maryland, sculptor. In the course of two telephone calls, Reid agreed to sculpt the three human figures. CCNV agreed to make the steam grate and pedestal for the statue. Reid proposed that the work be cast in bronze, at a total cost of approximately $100,000 and taking six to eight months to complete. Snyder rejected that proposal because CCNV did not have sufficient funds, and because the statue had to be completed by December 12 to be included in the pageant. Reid then suggested, and Snyder agreed, that the sculpture would be made of a material known as "Design Cast 62," a synthetic substance that could meet CCNV's monetary and time constraints, could be tinted to resemble bronze, and could withstand the elements. The parties agreed that the project would cost no more than $15,000, not including Reid's services, which he offered to donate. The parties did not sign a written agreement. Neither party mentioned copyright.

After Reid received an advance of $3,000, he made several sketches of figures in various poses. At Snyder's request, Reid sent CCNV a sketch of a proposed sculpture showing the family in a creche-like setting: the mother seated, cradling the baby in her lap; the father standing behind her, bending over her shoulder to touch the baby's foot. Reid testified that Snyder asked for the sketch to use in raising funds for the sculpture. Snyder testified that it was also for his approval. Reid sought a black family to serve as a model for the sculpture. Upon Snyder's suggestion, Reid visited a family living at CCNV's Washington shelter but decided that only their newly born child was a suitable model. While Reid was in Washington, Snyder took him to see homeless people living on the streets. Snyder pointed out that they tended to recline on steam grates, rather than sit or stand, in order to warm their bodies. From that time on, Reid's sketches contained only reclining figures.

Throughout November and the first two weeks of December 1985, Reid worked exclusively on the statue, assisted at various times by a dozen different people who were paid with funds provided in installments by CCNV. On a number of occasions, CCNV members visited Reid to check on his progress and to coordinate CCNV's construction of the base. CCNV rejected Reid's proposal to use suitcases or shopping bags to hold the family's personal belongings, insisting instead on a shopping cart. . . .

On December 24, 1985, 12 days after the agreed-upon-date, Reid delivered the completed statue to Washington. There it was joined to the steam grate and pedestal prepared by CCNV and placed on display near the site of the pageant. Snyder paid Reid the final installment of the $15,000. The statue remained on display for a month. In late January 1986, CCNV members returned it to Reid's studio in Baltimore for minor repairs. Several weeks later, Snyder began making plans to take the statue on a tour of several cities to raise money for the homeless. Reid objected, contending that the Design Cast 62 material was not strong enough to withstand the ambitious itinerary. He urged CCNV to cast the statue in bronze at a cost of $35,000, or to create a master mold at a cost of $5,000. Snyder declined to spend more of CCNV's money on the project.

In March 1986, Snyder asked Reid to return the sculpture. Reid refused. He then filed a certificate of copyright registration for "Third World America" in his name and announced plans to take the sculpture on a more modest tour than the one CCNV had proposed. Snyder, acting in his capacity as CCNV's trustee, immediately filed a competing certificate of copyright registration.

Snyder and CCNV then commenced this action against Reid. . . . After a 2-day bench trial, the District Court declared that "Third World America" was a "work made for hire" under §101 of the Copyright Act. . . . The court reasoned that Reid had been an "employee" of CCNV within the meaning of §101(1) because CCNV was the motivating force in the statue's production. . . .

[The D.C. Circuit reversed and remanded, holding that under traditional principles of agency law, Reid was an independent contractor, and that therefore the work was not "prepared by an employee" as required by §101(1). The court further held that the statue could not be a "work made for hire" under §101(2).] We granted certiorari to resolve a conflict among the Courts of Appeals over the proper construction of the "work made for hire" provisions of the Act. . . . We now affirm.

II

A . . .

The dispositive inquiry . . . is whether "Third World America" is "a work prepared by an employee within the scope of his or her employment" under §101(1). The Act does not define these terms. In the absence of such guidance, four interpretations have emerged. The first holds that a work is prepared by an employee whenever the hiring party retains the right to control the product. . . . A second, and closely related, view is that a work is prepared by an employee under §101(1) when the hiring party has actually wielded control with respect to the creation of a particular work. This approach was formulated by the Court of Appeals for the Second Circuit, *Aldon Accessories Ltd. v. Spiegel, Inc.*, 738 F.2d 548, *cert. denied*, 469 U.S. 982 (1984), and adopted by the Fourth Circuit, *Brunswick Beacon, Inc. v. Schock-Hopchas Publishing Co.*, 810 F.2d 410 (1987), the Seventh Circuit, *Evans Newton, Inc. v. Chicago Systems Software*, 793 F.2d 889, *cert. denied*, 479 U.S. 949 (1986), and, at times, by petitioners. . . . A third view is that the term "employee" within §101(1) carries its common-law agency law meaning. This view was endorsed by the Fifth Circuit in *Easter Seal Society for Crippled Children & Adults of Louisiana, Inc. v. Playboy Enterprises*, 815 F.2d 323 (1987), and by the Court of Appeals below. Finally, respondent and numerous *amici curiae* contend that the term "employee" only refers to "formal, salaried" employees. The Court of Appeals for the Ninth Circuit recently adopted this view. *See Dumas v. Gommerman*, 865 F.2d 1093 (1989).

The starting point for our interpretation of a statute is always its language. *Consumer Product Safety Comm'n v. GTE Sylvania, Inc.*, 447 U.S. 102, 108 (1980). The Act nowhere defines the terms "employee" or "scope of employment." It is, however, well established that "[w]here Congress uses terms that have accumulated settled meaning under . . . the common law, a court must infer, unless the statute otherwise dictates, that Congress means to incorporate the established meaning of these terms." *NLRB v. Amax Coal Co.*, 453 U.S. 322, 329 (1981). . . . In the past, when Congress has used the term "employee" without defining it, we have concluded that Congress intended to describe the conventional master-servant relationship as understood by common-law agency doctrine. . . . Nothing in the text of the work for hire provisions indicates that Congress used the words "employee" and "employment" to describe anything other than " 'the conventional relation of employer and employee.' " . . . On the contrary, Congress' intent to incorporate the agency law definition is suggested by §101(1)'s use of the term, "scope of employment," a widely used term of art in agency law. *See* Restatement (Second) of Agency §228 (1958). . . .

In contrast, neither test proposed by petitioners is consistent with the text of the Act. The exclusive focus of the right to control the product test on the relationship between the hiring party and the product clashes with the language of §101(1), which focuses on the relationship between the hired and hiring parties. The right to control the product test also would distort the meaning of the ensuing subsection, §101(2). Section 101 plainly creates two distinct ways in which a work can be deemed for hire: one for works prepared by employees, the other for those specially ordered or commissioned works which fall within one of the nine enumerated categories and are the subject of a written agreement. The right to control the product test ignores this dichotomy by transforming into a work for hire under §101(1) any "specially ordered or commissioned" work that is subject to the supervision and control of the hiring party. Because a party who hires a "specially ordered or commissioned" work by definition has a right to specify the characteristics of the product desired, at the time the commission is accepted, and frequently until it is completed, the right to control the product test would mean that many works that could satisfy §101(2) would already have been deemed works for hire under §101(1). Petitioners' interpretation is particularly hard to square with §101(2)'s enumeration of nine specific categories of specially ordered or commissioned works eligible to be works for hire. . . .

The actual control test . . . fares only marginally better when measured against the language and structure of §101. . . . Under the actual control test, a work for hire could arise under §101(2), but not under §101(1), where a party commissions, but does not actually control, a product which falls into one of the nine enumerated categories. Nonetheless, we agree with the Court of Appeals for the Fifth Circuit that "[t]here is simply no way to milk the 'actual control' test . . . from the language of the statute." . . .

We therefore conclude that the language and structure of §101 of the Act do not support either the right to control the product or the actual control approaches.[8] The structure of §101 indicates that a work for hire can arise through one of two mutually exclusive means, one for employees and one for independent contractors, and ordinary canons of statutory interpretation indicate that the classification of a particular hired party should be made with reference to agency law.

This reading of the undefined statutory terms finds considerable support in the Act's legislative history. . . .

In 1961, the Copyright Office's first legislative proposal retained the distinction between works by employees and works by independent contractors. *See* Report of the Register of Copyrights on the General Revision of the U.S. Copyright Law, 87th Cong., 1st Sess. . . . After numerous meetings with representatives of the affected parties, the Copyright Office issued a preliminary draft bill in 1963. Adopting the Register's recommendation, it defined "work made for hire" as "a work prepared by an employee within the scope of the duties of his employment, but not including a work made on special order or commission." . . .

In response to objections by book publishers that the preliminary draft bill limited the work for hire doctrine to "employees," the 1964 revision bill expanded the scope of the work for hire classification to reach, for the first time, commissioned works. The bill's language,

---

8. We also reject the suggestion of respondent and *amici* that the §101(1) term "employee" refers only to formal, salaried employees. While there is some support for such a definition in the legislative history, . . . the language of §101(1) cannot support it. The Act does not say "formal" or "salaried" employee, but simply "employee." Moreover, respondent and those *amici* who endorse a formal, salaried employee test do not agree upon the content of this test. . . .

proposed initially by representatives of the publishing industry, retained the definition of work for hire insofar as it referred to "employees," but added a separate clause covering commissioned works, without regard to subject matter, "if the parties so agree in writing." Those representing authors objected that the added provision would allow publishers to use their superior bargaining position to force authors to sign work for hire agreements. . . .

In 1965, the competing interests reached a historic compromise, which was embodied in a joint memorandum submitted to Congress and the Copyright Office, incorporated into the 1965 revision bill, and ultimately enacted in the same form and nearly the same terms 11 years later. . . . The compromise retained as subsection (1) the language referring to "a work prepared by an employee within the scope of his employment." However, in exchange for concessions from publishers on provisions relating to the termination of transfer rights, the authors consented to a second subsection which classified four categories of commissioned works as works for hire if the parties expressly so agreed in writing: works for use "as a contribution to a collective work, as a part of a motion picture, as a translation, or as supplementary work." The interested parties selected these categories because they concluded that these commissioned works, although not prepared by employees and thus not covered by the first subsection, nevertheless should be treated as works for hire because they were ordinarily prepared "at the instance, direction, and risk of a publisher or producer." . . .

[The remaining five categories in current subsection (2) were added by the House Judiciary Committee during subsequent revisions.]

Finally, petitioners' construction of the work for hire provisions would impede Congress' paramount goal in revising the 1976 Act of enhancing predictability and certainty of copyright ownership. *See* H.R. Rep. No. 94-1476, *supra*, at 129. In a "copyright

Original artwork © James Earl Reid. Reprinted by permission.

Third World America: A Contemporary Nativity

marketplace," the parties negotiate with an expectation that one of them will own the copyright in the completed work. With that expectation, the parties at the outset can settle on relevant contractual terms, such as the price for the work and the ownership of reproduction rights.

To the extent that petitioners endorse an actual control test, CCNV's construction of the work for hire provisions prevents such planning. Because that test turns on whether the hiring party has closely monitored the production process, the parties would not know until late in the process, if not until the work is completed, whether a work will ultimately fall within §101(1). . . .

B

We turn, finally, to an application of §101 to Reid's production of "Third World America." In determining whether a hired party is an employee under the general common law of agency, we consider the hiring party's right to control the manner and means by which the product is accomplished. Among the other factors relevant to this inquiry are the skill required; the source of the instrumentalities and tools; the location of the work; the duration of the relationship between the parties; whether the hiring party has the right to assign additional projects to the hired party; the extent of the hired party's discretion over when and how long to work; the method of payment; the hired party's role in hiring and paying assistants; whether the work is part of the regular business of the hiring party; whether the hiring party is in business; the provision of employee benefits; and the tax treatment of the hired party. *See* Restatement §220(2) (setting forth a nonexhaustive list of factors relevant to determining whether a hired party is an employee). No one of these factors is determinative. . . .

[The Court concluded that in light of these factors, the court of appeals had correctly determined that Reid was an independent contractor rather than an employee of CCNV. It remanded for a determination of whether, under §101, the sculpture was nonetheless a joint work co-authored by Reid and CCNV.]

Aymes v. Bonelli
980 F.2d 857 (2d Cir. 1992)

ALTIMARI, J.: . . . [Bonelli hired Aymes to create computer programs for Island, Bonelli's swimming pool business. Aymes worked on the programs from 1980 to 1982.]

During that period, Aymes created a series of programs called "CSALIB" under the general direction of Bonelli, who was not a professional computer programmer. CSALIB was used by Island to maintain records of cash receipts, physical inventory, sales figures, purchase orders, merchandise transfers, and price changes. There was no written agreement between Bonelli and Aymes assigning ownership or copyright of CSALIB. . . .

Aymes did most of his programming at the Island office, where he had access to Island's computer hardware. He generally worked alone, without assistants or coworkers, and enjoyed considerable autonomy in creating CSALIB. This autonomy was restricted only by Bonelli who directed and instructed Aymes on what he wanted from the program. Bonelli was not, however, sufficiently skilled to write the program himself.

Although Aymes worked semi-regular hours, he was not always paid by the hour and on occasion presented his bills to Bonelli as invoices. At times, Aymes would be paid by the project and given bonuses for finishing the project on time. It is undisputed that Aymes never received any health or other insurance benefits from Island. It is similarly undisputed that Island never paid an employer's percentage of Aymes's payroll taxes and never withheld any of his salary for federal or state taxes. . . .

[After a bench trial, the district court ruled that Aymes had been Island's employee. The court of appeals disagreed.]

. . . *Reid* established that no one factor was dispositive, but gave no direction concerning how the factors were to be weighed. It does not necessarily follow that because no one factor is dispositive all factors are equally important. . . .

[T]here are some factors that will be significant in virtually every situation. These include: (1) the hiring party's right to control the manner and means of creation; (2) the skill required; (3) the provision of employee benefits; (4) the tax treatment of the hired party; and (5) whether the hiring party has the right to assign additional projects to the hired party. These factors will almost always be relevant and should be given more weight in the analysis. . . .

[T]he district court gave each factor equal weight and simply counted the number of factors for each side in determining that Aymes was an employee. In so doing, the district court overemphasized indeterminate and thus irrelevant factors having little or no bearing on Aymes's case. . . .

[The court found that although Bonelli had the right to control the manner of creation and the right to assign additional projects, the other three factors listed above dictated the conclusion that Aymes was an independent contractor, and that the remaining *Reid* factors were "relatively insignificant." Regarding the employee benefits and tax treatment factors, the court observed: "Island deliberately chose to deny Aymes two basic attributes of employment it presumably extended to its workforce. This undisputed choice is completely inconsistent with their defense." The court noted that "[t]he importance of these two factors is underscored by the fact that every case since *Reid* that has applied the test has found the hired party to be an independent contractor where the hiring party failed to extend benefits or pay social security taxes."]

NOTES AND QUESTIONS

1. To what extent does the test adopted by the *Reid* Court further the stated goals of predictability and certainty? Does the approach outlined in *Aymes v. Bonelli* further these goals?

2. Is the *Aymes* court's heavy emphasis on the employee benefits and tax treatment factors sensible? Would the *Reid* factors dictate a different result if Aymes had been hired by a software company? Should they do so?

3. In 2005 the American Law Institute adopted The Restatement (Third) of Agency, which is meant to supersede The Restatement (Second) of Agency. The wording of many of the sections has changed significantly and a different numbering scheme has been implemented. Section 7.07 is the parallel to old §220, and it no longer contains the list of factors that the Supreme Court discussed in *Reid*; instead, it simply states: "[A]n employee is an agent whose principal controls or has the right to control the manner and means of the agent's performance of work." Restatement (Third) of Agency, §7.07(3)(a) (2005). Should a change in the Restatement affect how courts analyze whether an individual is an employee or an independent contractor for purposes of determining whether a work is a work made for hire?

4. Examine carefully the second subsection of the "work made for hire" definition. Why did *Third World America* not qualify as a work made for hire under §101(2)? Why did *Malcolm*

X qualify as such a work? If Aalmuhammed had signed a work made for hire contract would that have put an end to his arguments concerning joint authorship?

5. In *Reid*, the Supreme Court remanded for consideration of CCNV's co-authorship claim. Following the remand, the district court assisted the parties in negotiating a settlement, under which Reid was credited with sole authorship of the work and CCNV received sole ownership of the original sculpture. Reid received the exclusive right to make three-dimensional reproductions, but the agreement authorized both parties to make two-dimensional reproductions. *See CCNV v. Reid*, 1991 Copr. L. Dec. (CCH) ¶26,753 (D.D.C. Jan. 7, 1991). Had the case not settled, how would you have resolved the co-authorship issue?

Following negotiation of the settlement and entry of the consent judgment by the district court, Reid requested access to the sculpture so that he could make a mold of it, but CCNV refused access. The parties returned to court again, where the district judge initially ordered that "Reid is entitled to a limited possessory right of his own, in the nature of an implied easement of necessity, to cause a master mold to be made of the sculpture" to enable him to exercise his rights under the consent judgment. *CCNV v. Reid*, Civ. A. No. 86-1507(TPJ), 1991 WL 370138 (D.D.C. Oct. 16, 1991), *superseded by* Civ. A. No. 86-1507(TPJ), 1991 WL 378209 (D.D.C. Oct. 29, 1991). The superseding opinion contained detail on the various matters involved in having a master mold produced.

Note on Works Prepared Outside the United States

Many of the world's other copyright regimes do not recognize a works made for hire doctrine. In countries such as France and Germany, the "author" of a work is the natural person (or persons) who created it, and initial ownership of copyright vests in that person. In contrast, countries such as Ecuador, Ghana, India, Japan, and the United Kingdom follow the works made for hire model and vest initial authorship of employee-created works in employers.

In the U.S. and other countries that follow the works made for hire model, the rationale for assigning authorship and initial ownership to employers is economic. When copyrightable material is prepared by an employee, the employer assumes the economic risk associated with developing and marketing the work. *See* I. Trotter Hardy, *An Economic Understanding of Copyright Law's Work-Made-for-Hire Doctrine*, 12 Colum.-VLA J.L. & Arts 181 (1988). Presumably, this is also true of employers in countries that lack a works made for hire rule. Notably, many of the countries that lack a works made for hire rule expressly provide that the initial ownership of copyright in an employee-created work may be varied by contract. What effects would you predict on the negotiation of employment contracts in these countries? The U.S., meanwhile, also allows employers and employees to vary initial ownership of copyright by contract. *See* 17 U.S.C. §201(b). Given this possibility, what effects would you predict on the negotiation of employment contracts in the U.S.?

Several countries have adopted hybrid regimes intended to protect the economic interests of employers and the moral rights of employees. In China, for example, the author of certain copyrighted works has the sole right to be credited as the author, while all other economic and moral rights belong to the employer. This rule applies to engineering designs, product designs, maps, and computer software. For those works, the employer is also required to reward the author for creating the work. For all other works, China vests copyright ownership in the employee but gives the employer a two-year exclusive right to exploit the work within the scope of the employer's business. Other countries provide varying exclusivity periods for the employer (e.g., Slovenia — 10 years, Bosnia and Herze-govina — 5 years).

NOTES AND QUESTIONS

1. Recall the *Aalmuhammed* court's discussion of the requirements for authorship. Can the works made for hire rule be reconciled with that discussion? Can it be reconciled with the constitutional language that authorizes copyright protection? For an insightful discussion of the tensions between economic and creative motivations for producing, distributing, and adapting works, see Rochelle Cooper Dreyfuss, *The Creative Employee and the Copyright Act of 1976*, 54 U. Chi. L. Rev. 590 (1987).

2. Is the U.S. works made for hire rule good economic policy? If the economic rationale for the rule is sound, wouldn't the same reasoning apply to any specially ordered or commis-sioned work? Would you support an amendment to §101 extending the works made for hire designation to all such works?

3. Would you recommend that the U.S. agree to a proposal that vests authorship in the employee, but grants to the employer the exclusive right to use the work "to the extent necessary in the sphere of his activities reasonably envisaged by the parties at the time of the creation of the work"? WIPO, *Report of the Committee of Governmental Experts on Model Provisions for National Laws on Employed Authors*, 22 Copyright 72, 76 (1986).

Professors Ian Ayres and Eric Talley have argued that, as a matter of general economic theory, dividing legal entitlements among parties sometimes can encourage them to reach efficient bargains. Ian Ayres & Eric Talley, *Solomonic Bargaining: Dividing a Legal Entitlement to Facilitate Coasean Trade*, 104 Yale L.J. 1027 (1995). In particular, they contend that "when two parties have private information about how much they value an entitlement, endowing each party with a partial claim to the entitlement can reduce the incentive to behave strategically during bargaining." *Id.* at 1029-30. Would you expect this insight to have any bearing on employer-employee bargaining over ownership of employee-created works?

4. When a lawsuit is filed alleging infringement of copyright in a work authored outside the U.S., what rule should the court use to determine the work's ownership status? *See Itar-Tass Russian News Agency v. Russian Kurier, Inc.*, 153 F.3d 82, 89-91 (2d Cir. 1998) (applying law of the work's country of origin to determine ownership); *see also infra* Chapter 11.F.

b. What Is the "Scope of Employment"?

For a work to be a "work made for hire" under the first definition provided in §101, the work must also have been created within the employee's "scope of employment." We turn now to this second requirement.

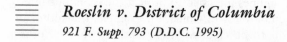

Roeslin v. District of Columbia
921 F. Supp. 793 (D.D.C. 1995)

GREENE, J.: In this action, plaintiff, an employee of the Department of Employment Services ("D.O.E.S.") of the District of Columbia, claims copyright infringement against the District for its use and copying of a computer software program (the "DC-790" system) that plaintiff devel-oped. The matter was tried, and it is now ripe for these findings of fact and conclusions of law.

Findings of Fact

D.O.E.S. is responsible for collecting and tabulating employment statistics for the District of Columbia and the D.C. metropolitan area. It collects the statistics by mailing the Current Employment Service ("CES") survey to area employers, and tabulating their responses. . . .

Plaintiff was hired by D.O.E.S. in November, 1986 for the position of a Labor Economist for a four year term. . . . He received a salary from the District and full benefits. At the time plaintiff was hired, he had no computer programming skills, nor was his supervisor, Mr. Groner, aware of whether plaintiff had any computer programming skills.

As a Labor Economist, plaintiff was charged with three tasks: (1) to improve employer response rate to the CES survey; (2) to expand the CES sample size; and (3) to develop industry and occupational employment projections. His job description listed his duties as: (1) planning and carrying out projects for collecting detailed economic data; (2) evaluating and adapting necessary statistical methods for the preparation of data; (3) planning, organizing and operating programs (i.e. projects) for the collection, verification and presentation of data; (4) selecting the most appropriate statistical methods; (5) preparing estimates of employment and unemployment; and (6) preparing various reports and studies. He had discretion in determining how to carry out these duties.

When plaintiff began working at D.O.E.S., employees manually collected the information from returned CES surveys and recorded the information on office record cards. A data processing staff would enter this data into the mainframe system. The estimates derived from this data were computed manually with the aid of a computer. The District anticipated the future development of the Automated Current Employment Statistics ("ACES") mainframe system.

Prior to developing the DC-790 system, plaintiff did use a computer to assist in the carrying out of his duties, although he did not do any computer programming. Plaintiff also assisted in the "automation" of the office, that is, in transferring some of the work that was done manually to already existing computer software applications. This task also did not involve any computer programming.

Plaintiff was motivated to create the DC-790 system in June 1988 when he attended a CES conference. Upon returning from the conference, plaintiff informed his supervisor, Mr. Groner, that he believed a personal computer ("PC") based system could be created for the District's CES surveys. Plaintiff testified that . . . Mr. Groner informed plaintiff that creation of a PC-based program was neither feasible nor desirable, and told plaintiff not to pursue the idea because he would be too busy with his other job duties, and because D.O.E.S. had already decided to eventually implement ACES, the mainframe system. Nonetheless, plaintiff informed Mr. Groner that he would create a PC-based system on his own time. Plaintiff testified that his motivation in creating the program was to prove that it could be done and to develop job opportunities for himself. Mr. Groner told the plaintiff that the program would be "in the public domain," which plaintiff took to mean that the system would not be owned by anybody. Mr. Groner actually believed that the District would own the program; he testified that he thought that the phrase "in the public domain" meant that the District would own the program.

In August 1988, plaintiff purchased a personal computer with his own funds. In October 1988, he purchased software using his own funds. Plaintiff taught himself how to program computers using books that he purchased with his own funds. He spent approximately 3,000 hours creating the various modules necessary to complete the DC-790 program, and creating enhancements to the system. . . . Plaintiff did all of this work at home. He also tested each module at home, using hypothetical data. Nobody at D.O.E.S. directed plaintiff to create the DC-790 system, supervised his doing so, or assisted him in doing so. He was not offered compensation for the creation of the system.

After testing each module at home, plaintiff brought each module into work to test with actual data. Some of the testing and debugging of various modules was done during office hours. Once each module worked properly, plaintiff incorporated the modules into the PC system operating at D.O.E.S. Shortly after the DC-790 system became operational, D.O.E.S. personnel ceased using office record cards. Plaintiff also created an operating manual for the DC-790 system in May 1990 in response to a request by an employee of the [Federal Bureau of Labor Statistics ("BLS")] Regional Office. Plaintiff received positive performance appraisals based, in part, on his development of the DC-790 system. Prior to April 1991, plaintiff attempted to promote the DC-790 system to BLS, and demonstrated the system to some of its personnel during office hours.

Throughout this period, according to plaintiff's testimony, he relied on Mr. Groner's statement to him that nobody would own the DC-790 system and that it would be in the public domain. Plaintiff stated that he first learned that the District asserted a proprietary interest in the program in April of 1991. At that time, he was provided with a copy of a letter from the District to the State of Maine, in which the District stated that it had a proprietary interest in the program. . . .

When plaintiff learned that the District claimed a proprietary interest in the DC-790 system, he confronted Mr. Groner. He told Mr. Groner that if anyone owned the system (rather than it being in the public domain), then he did, as the author of the program. Plaintiff and Mr. Groner met to discuss the issue, at which time plaintiff requested recognition by the District that he had independent ownership of the program, in exchange for which the District would be allowed free use and distribution of the software. He also requested a promotion.

In June of 1991, plaintiff placed a copyright notice on the initial screen of the DC-790 system. In June, through counsel, he notified the District's Corporation Counsel and the Mayor's office of his claim of copyright ownership. He also demanded that the District stop using the system. In December of that year, he filed for and received Copyright Registration No. TXu 514 262 for the DC-790 system. The District never filed an application to register a copyright for the system.

Despite plaintiff's notice of copyright ownership, employees of the District continued using the system. Mr. Groner never instructed his employees to cease using the system.

Plaintiff also gave notice that he would make no further modifications to the program if these modifications required programming. From November of 1992 until June or July of 1993, plaintiff was temporarily reassigned to the District's Office of Management, Information and Data Systems. During this time, plaintiff was working under a job description of computer programmer analyst. Plaintiff did not work on the DC-790 system while placed on this assignment. While the DC-790 system was rendered inoperable during this time period, due to an employee error, plaintiff was not asked to assist in correcting the problem.

In November of 1991, the District requested installation of the ACES system. The installation of this system was completed in January 1993. . . .

Conclusions of Law

I

The central issue in this case is whether plaintiff, as the author of the DC-790 system, or defendant, as plaintiff's employer, is the owner of the copyright on the DC-790 system. . . . The copyright statute defines a work made for hire as "a work prepared by an employee within the scope of his or her employment." *Id*. at §101. Because plaintiff has received a copyright registration for the DC-790 system, the presumption is that plaintiff owns the copyright. 17 U.S.C. §410(c). The burden is thus on the defendant to establish that the system is a work made for hire.

The Supreme Court has held that to determine whether an individual was an employee, and whether he created a work within the scope of his employment, courts should look to the general common law of agency. *Community for Creative Non-Violence v. Reid*, 490 U.S. 730, 740 (1989). There is no dispute in this case that plaintiff was an employee of defendant. The question is whether he created the DC-790 system within the scope of his employment.

The Restatement (Second) of Agency, which the Supreme Court cited in *Reid*, states that:

> (1) Conduct of a servant is within the scope of employment if, but only if:
>   (a) it is within the kind he is employed to perform;
>   (b) it occurs substantially within the authorized time and space limits; [and]
>   (c) it is actuated, at least in part, by a purpose to serve the master.

Restatement at §228. . . .

A.   With regard to the first prong, the Court finds that developing computer software is not the kind of work plaintiff was employed to perform. Plaintiff was hired as a labor economist, not as a computer programmer. There is no reference in his job description to computer programming; nor was his supervisor aware of whether plaintiff had any programming skills when he was hired. Plaintiff was hired to improve certain aspects of the CES survey and develop projections based on that survey. He was not hired to create a computer program that would assist the entire office and receive, process, and transmit the survey results.

Defendant makes much of the fact that plaintiff used computers at work, and that defendant allowed plaintiff, during work hours, to learn how to use computers. This, however, does not prove that computer programming was part of plaintiff's job duties or necessary to performing his job duties. Many people use computers in the work place, including plaintiff's coworkers, but do not program computers. The two skills are quite different—while many people operate computers, few have the technical ability or training necessary to program them.

To be sure, work that is incidental to the conduct authorized by the employer, even if it is not central to the employee's job duties, also falls within the scope of employment. Restatement at §229. To determine whether computer programming was incidental to plaintiff's employment, a court may consider such factors as whether this was the type of activity commonly done by labor economists, and whether it was likely that plaintiff would engage in such an activity. *Id.* The Court finds that while developing the DC-790 system did help the functioning of the work place, it was not the type of activity in which plaintiff would be reasonable [sic] expected to engage.

Moreover, it is disingenuous for the District now to claim that developing the DC-790 system was within the scope of plaintiff's job duties. Plaintiff originally approached Mr. Groner about writing a computer program that would perform the functions of the system. Plaintiff testifies, very credibly, that Mr. Groner discouraged him from doing so, stating that it would detract from his ability to perform his other job duties and that D.O.E.S. had already decided to implement the ACES system. It is unfair for the District to now claim that an activity it discouraged—developing the system—was within the scope of plaintiff's employment.

B.   Second, the Court must determine whether the development of the system "occurred substantially within the authorized time and space limits." The Court finds that it did not. Plaintiff credibly testified that he spent 3,000 hours outside of normal working hours creating the modules of the DC-790 system. He did this at home using a computer he purchased with his own funds. It is true that plaintiff tested each module at work. It is also true that once each module was operational, it was used in the work place. Nonetheless, the substantial amount of time plaintiff spent creating the DC-790 system, which is what is at issue in this case, was done on his own time outside of the office. . . .

C. Finally, the Court will address whether plaintiff was motivated to create the system, at least in part, by a purpose to serve the master. Plaintiff testified that he created the program for two reasons: (1) to create job opportunities for himself; and (2) to prove it could be done. The Court finds that plaintiff was motivated by each of these purposes. To be sure, the DC-790 system benefitted his employer, and the Court could fairly infer that part of plaintiff's motivation was to achieve this result. However, the Court finds that plaintiff was primarily motivated by self-fulfilling purposes. . . .

On the whole, then, the Court finds that defendant has not established that the DC-790 system was a work made for hire. . . .

Note on Employer Ownership of Trade Secrets

Many cases involving employee assertions of copyright ownership also present trade secrecy claims. As discussed in Chapter 3, although previous Copyright Acts generally required that a work be "published" to be eligible for federal copyright protection, the Copyright Act of 1976 abandoned that requirement. Under the present Act, copyright subsists in original, fixed works created after January 1, 1978 even if the works are concealed from the general public. In addition, as discussed in greater detail in Chapter 4, the 1976 Act extends copyright protection to computer software, a subject matter that frequently embodies economically valuable, nonpublic innovation.[1]

The standards used to determine whether a work is created within the scope of employment under copyright law and trade secret law are similar, but not identical. In copyright cases, courts have followed the three-step test set forth in *Roeslin v. District of Columbia, supra*, which is based on the general scope-of-employment provision of the Restatement (Second) of Agency, §228. In trade secrecy cases, courts have relied on a different test, originally set forth in §397 of the Restatement (Second), that focuses more narrowly on ownership of employee-developed inventions.[2] That test does not ask whether the employee was motivated in part by a desire to serve the employer, but only whether the invention relates to the type of work the employee was hired to perform, and in particular whether the employee's duties are "inventive" or "noninventive." Thus, if an employee "is employed to do experimental work for inventive purposes, it is inferred ordinarily . . . that patentable ideas arrived at through the experimentation are to be owned by the employer. This is even more clear where one is employed to achieve a particular result which the invention accomplishes. On the other hand, if one is employed merely to do work in a particular line in which he is an expert, there is no inference" of employer ownership. Restatement (Second) of Agency §397, cmt. a (1958); *see also* Restatement (Third) of Unfair Competition §42, cmt. e (1995) (adopting this

---

1. A trade secret is any information that derives independent economic or competitive value from not being generally known to the public or to competitors and is subject to reasonable measures to maintain its secrecy. *See* Uniform Trade Secrets Act §1; Restatement (Third) of Unfair Competition §39 (1995).
2. Patent rights, in contrast, always vest initially in the individual named in the patent as the inventor. Employment contracts routinely provide for assignment of any patents resulting from the employee's research.

test for ownership of trade secrets, whether or not patentable). Trade secrecy cases further distinguish between "specific inventive" and "general inventive" employees; employees hired for specific inventive purposes will retain ownership of innovations they make in other, unrelated fields, while "general inventive" employees will almost never retain ownership of their innovations. *See generally* Roger M. Milgrim, *Milgrim on Trade Secrets* §5.02[4] (1996). In addition, an employer may acquire an equitable "shop right" to use employee-owned innovations that were developed using the employer's facilities. *See id.* at §5.02[4][c].

Because of this difference in emphasis, the two tests would appear to require divergent results in, for example, a case involving an "inventive" employee who produces copyrighted material related to her work duties and then asserts, and can prove, that her efforts were not appreciably motivated by a desire to serve the employer. In such a case, the employer would own the trade secret, but the employee would own the copyright. Does that result make sense? If not, how might the law achieve greater consistency on the question of employer ownership?

The "scope of employment" nexus between copyright and trade secrecy claims implicates federal supremacy considerations. Should the outcome of a federal copyright claim be dictated by the outcome of a related state trade secrecy claim, or even more generally by state law? In *CCNV v. Reid, supra*, the Court observed:

> In past cases of statutory interpretation, when we have concluded that Congress intended terms such as "employee," "employer," and "scope of employment" to be understood in light of agency law, we have relied on the general common law of agency, rather than on the law of any particular State, to give meaning to these terms. . . . Establishment of a federal rule of agency, rather than reliance on state agency law, is particularly appropriate here given the Act's express objective of creating national, uniform copyright law. . . . We thus agree with the Court of Appeals that the term "employee" should be understood in light of the general common law of agency.

490 U.S. at 740-41. Did courts adjudicating scope of employment issues in copyright cases after *CCNV v. Reid* simply rely on the wrong section of the Restatement (Second) of Agency? Did you read the *Reid* opinion, *supra*, as requiring the federal courts to use §228 for this purpose?

The "scope of employment" question in copyright cases is now complicated by the fact that the Restatement (Third) of Agency, completed in 2005, no longer includes the test from §228 of the Restatement (Second). According to the new Restatement:

> An employee acts within the scope of employment when performing work assigned by the employer or engaging in a course of conduct subject to the employer's control. An employer's act is not within the scope of employment when it occurs within an independent course of conduct not intended by the employee to serve any purpose of the employer.

Restatement (Third) of Agency, §7.07(2) (2005). Apply this test to the facts of *Roeslin v. District of Columbia, supra*. Would it have produced a different outcome? Should a change to the Restatement prompt a parallel change to what has become the federal copyright standard?

Note on the "Teacher Exception"

One category of employees stands as a possible exception to the ordinary scope of employment rule. Traditionally, college and university teachers have been considered the owners of copyright in their scholarly writings and course materials, notwithstanding their status as full-time employees. Because the 1976 Act did not expressly preserve this exception, there is some debate about whether it still exists. Two decisions from the Seventh Circuit, both authored by former law professors, opine in dicta that the exception remains. *See Hays v. Sony Corp. of America*, 847 F.2d 412, 416 (7th Cir. 1988) (Posner, J.); *Weinstein v. University of Illinois*, 811 F.2d 1091, 1094 (7th Cir. 1987) (Easterbrook, J.). Judge Posner explained:

> The authority for [the pre-1976 Act rule] was in fact scanty, as explained in Simon, *Faculty Writings: Are They "Works for Hire" Under the 1976 Copyright Act?*, 9 J. College & University L. 485, 495-99 (1982) — but it was scanty not because the merit of the exception was doubted, but because, on the contrary, virtually no one questioned that the academic author was entitled to copyright his writings. Although college and university teachers do academic writing as a part of their employment responsibilities . . . [a] college or university does not supervise its faculty in the preparation of academic books and articles, and is poorly equipped to exploit their writings, whether through publication or otherwise. . . .
>
> The reasons for a presumption against finding academic writings to be work made for hire are as forceful today as they ever were. . . . To a literalist of statutory interpretation, the conclusion that the [1976] Act abolished the exception may seem inescapable. . . . But considering the havoc that such a conclusion would wreak in the settled practices of academic institutions, the lack of fit between the policy of the work-for-hire doctrine and the conditions of academic production, and the absence of any indication that Congress meant to abolish the teacher exception, we might, if forced to decide the issue, conclude that the exception had survived the enactment of the 1976 Act.

Hays, 847 F.2d at 416-17. *But see Vanderhurst v. Colorado Mountain Coll. Dist.*, 16 F. Supp. 2d 1297, 1307 (D. Colo. 1998) (ruling, based on §101(1) and *CCNV v. Reid*, that teaching outline created by instructor was work made for hire).

Do you agree with Judge Posner that, for policy reasons, a court "forced to decide the issue" should hold that the teacher exception persists? *See* Rochelle Cooper Dreyfuss, *The Creative Employee and the Copyright Act of 1976*, 54 U. Chi. L. Rev. 590 (1987). Is it relevant that the legislative history of the 1976 Act does not discuss the exception and gives no indication that Congress ever considered it?

In their published intellectual property policies, many colleges and universities have adopted, either explicitly or implicitly, the traditional presumption that academics retain copyright in their scholarly writings. *See, e.g., Weinstein*, 811 F.2d at 1094. Recently, however, many of these institutions have begun to reconsider their policies in light of the potential licensing revenues that faculty-developed software and digital distance learning materials can provide. Also, many university intellectual property policies routinely require faculty inventors of valuable *technologies* to assign patent and other rights to the institution. Indeed, universities obtain large amounts of revenue from the licensing of patents assigned to them by their faculties. Why should a university's copyright policy be any different from its patent policy? If you were counsel to such an institution, how would you advise it to proceed? What should be done about ownership of copyright in works whose production was supported in part by external funding?

c. Section 101(2) and "Specially Ordered or Commissioned" Works

Section 101(2) identifies nine categories of commissioned works that are eligible to be "works made for hire" if the parties so agree. How were these categories selected? Review the *CCNV v. Reid* Court's discussion of the legislative history of the statutory definition of "works made for hire." The Court describes a drafting process consisting largely of negotiation among the affected interest groups. As Professor Jessica Litman has documented, and as we discussed in Chapter 1.B.4 *supra*, this is the way that much of the 1976 Act was drafted. *See* Jessica D. Litman, *Copyright, Compromise, and Legislative History*, 72 Cornell L. Rev. 857, 871-79 (1987) ("As often as not, the reason a specific provision was deemed to be good was that industry representatives had agreed on it."). Is this an appropriate process for drafting copyright legislation? More narrowly, is it an appropriate process for determining which categories of works should be listed in §101(2)? Might there be another explanation for these categories? Consider the economics of the situation. Is there a transaction cost justification for these categories?

In 1999, Congress briefly added sound recordings to the list in §101(2). This time, the legislative process worked differently. At the request of the recording industry, the amendment was appended, without discussion or testimony, to an omnibus bill intended to amend the patent, trademark, and telecommunications laws. Intellectual Property and Communications Omnibus Reform Act of 1999, §1011(d), *as enacted by* Pub. L. 106-113, §1000(a)(9), 113 Stat. 1501A-521, -544 (1999). Recording artists greeted the news with outrage, and accused the recording industry of staging a copyright grab. Less than a year later, Congress repealed the amendment. Work Made for Hire and Copyright Corrections Act of 2000, Pub. L. 106-379, §2, 114 Stat. 1444, 1444 (2000).

So, if a recording artist signed a work-made-for-hire agreement in 2001, is his contribution to the sound recording a work made for hire? Unless the recording artist qualifies as an employee within the scope of his employment under §101(1), it is not. To be a work made for hire via contract under §101(2), the work must appear in the list of eligible works.

In fact, record labels typically require recording artists to sign contracts that state that their contributions are works made for hire, and (in the alternative) assign the copyrights in their sound recordings to the record company. Given this standard industry practice, why were recording artists so outraged at the designation of sound recordings as works made for hire? What difference would the change have made? Under other provisions of the Copyright Act, individual authors have the right to terminate transfers of their copyrights after a prescribed period of time. Individuals who create works made for hire have no such right, because they are not considered authors. *See* Chapter 3.C.2, *infra* (discussing termination of transfers).

The 2000 repeal of the 1999 sound recordings amendment directs courts and the Copyright Office to proceed as though both pieces of legislation had never been enacted. *See* Work Made for Hire and Copyright Corrections Act of 2000, Pub. L. 106-379, §2, 114 Stat. 1444, 1444 (2000). Why do you suppose Congress issued this curious instruction?

Note on the Mechanics of §101(2) Agreements

Although courts cannot control which specially ordered or commissioned works are eligible to be treated as works made for hire, they must determine whether the other requirements set forth in the definition have been satisfied. Section 101(2) states that the parties must "expressly agree in a written instrument signed by them." But when must the writing be executed, and what must it say? Predictably, both questions have inspired litigation.

Courts have disagreed on whether the writing must be prepared before or after the work is created. In *Schiller & Schmidt, Inc. v. Nordisco Corp.*, 969 F.2d 410 (7th Cir. 1992), the Seventh Circuit held that the writing must precede creation of the work. Writing for the court, Judge Posner commented: "The requirement of a written statement . . . is not merely a statute of frauds, although that is the purpose emphasized by the cases. . . . [The writing requirement also serves] to make the ownership of property rights in intellectual property clear and definite, so that such property will be readily marketable." *Id.* at 412. In *Eden Toys, Inc. v. Florelee Undergarment Co.*, 697 F.2d 27 (2d Cir. 1982), and again in *Playboy Enterprises, Inc. v. Dumas*, 53 F.3d 549 (2d Cir. 1995), however, the Second Circuit held that the parties could memorialize their agreement after the fact, so long as the evidence showed that they actually had agreed on a work for hire relationship before the work's creation. The *Dumas* court observed that in some circumstances, the rule adopted in *Schiller & Schmidt* " 'could frustrate the intent of the parties and cloud rather than serve the goal of certainty.' " *Dumas*, 53 F.3d at 559 (quoting 1 Melville B. Nimmer & David Nimmer, *Nimmer on Copyright* §5.03[B][2][b] (1994)). Which court has the better of this argument? Courts also have disagreed on whether the writing must actually use the words "work made for hire." According to the *Dumas* court, it must. *Dumas*, 53 F.3d at 560 (holding that language referring to an "assignment . . . of all right, title and interest" was insufficient to satisfy §101(2)). But in *Armento v. Laser Image, Inc.*, 950 F. Supp. 719 (W.D.N.C. 1996), the court concluded that given the circumstances surrounding the parties' relationship, the written agreement requirement was satisfied by language that provided that the commissioned maps and artwork "remain the sole property of [defendants], and cannot be reproduced or used for any other purpose by [the artist] without the written consent of [defendants]." *Id.* at 729. Echoing the *Dumas* court's own reasoning on the timing issue, the *Armento* court reasoned that a bright-line rule requiring the magic words might work injustice in some cases. *Id.* at 731-32. Again, which rule is better?

NOTES AND QUESTIONS

1. The recording industry has also asserted that recordings prepared for inclusion on an album are "contributions to a collective work." Does this argument have merit?

2. Hiring independent contractors is common practice in the software industry, and has recently come under sustained scrutiny for non–copyright-related reasons. Many of these programmers argue that they are de facto employees and should receive the same employee benefits and other advantages as their salaried co-workers. *See* Stanley Holmes, *Microsoft Policy May Jolt Temp Industry Labor*, L.A. Times, July 1, 2000, at C1. It is no surprise that Congress did not consider problems relating to works made for hire in the software industry when it drafted the 1976 Act. The software industry as we know it today did not exist, and as we discuss in Chapter 4, Congress was not even certain that computer programs were copyrightable subject matter. Today, however, many (if not most) computer programs are the work of many hands. Would you recommend that contributions to computer programs be added to the categories of works eligible for "work made for hire" status under §101(2)? *See* Matthew R. Harris, Note, *Copyright, Computer Software, and Work Made for Hire*, 89 Mich. L. Rev. 661 (1990). One commentator suggests that §101(2) already encompasses software (at least when the software in question is written by many contributors) because it includes "a contribution to a collective work." Jonathan Hudis, *Software "Made for Hire": Make Sure It's Really Yours*, 44 J. Copyright Soc'y U.S.A. 8, 21 (1996). Review the definition of "collective work" in §101. Do you agree?

4. U.S. Government Works

On its face, subsection (1) of the "works made for hire" definition would encompass works created by federal government employees in the scope of their employment. In fact, however, the Act excludes such works from copyright protection entirely:

§105. Subject matter of copyright: United States Government works

Copyright protection under this title is not available for any work of the United States Government, but the United States Government is not precluded from receiving and holding copyrights transferred to it by assignment, bequest, or otherwise.

At least two distinct policies underlie this provision. First, the rationale for assigning authorship to employers does not seem to apply in the case of federal government works. Indeed, federal government works are perhaps the paradigmatic example of works that are *not* subject to the public goods problem, because their production is funded by taxpayers. Second, the denial of copyright to federal government works reflects considerations of public access to the law. Recall *Wheaton v. Peters*, 33 U.S. (8 Pet.) 591 (1834), discussed in Chapter 1.B.2, *supra* pages 24-25, in which the former reporter for the Supreme Court attempted to assert a common law copyright to bar his successor from publishing volumes containing decisions that he had prepared. The Court noted without further analysis: "[T]he court are unanimously of opinion, that no reporter has or can have any copyright in the written opinions delivered by this court; and that the judges thereof cannot confer on any reporter any such right." *Id*. at 668.

Note on Model Codes

State and local legal systems and some federal agencies occasionally adopt laws or regulatory codes drafted by private organizations. In *Veeck v. Southern Building Code Congress Int'l* (SBCCI), 293 F.3d 791 (5th Cir. 2002) (en banc), *cert. denied*, 539 U.S. 969 (2003), the Fifth Circuit held that when a state adopts a privately drafted code as law, such law is not copyrightable. SBCCI promulgated model building codes, encouraging local governments to adopt them. The defendant Veeck posted on the web the building codes of two Texas towns that had adopted SBCCI's model. Veeck sued for a declaratory judgment of non-infringement and SBCCI counterclaimed for infringement

Citing *Wheaton v. Peters*, 33 U.S. (Pet.) 591 (1834), and its progeny, the *Veeck* court held that legislative enactments are not meaningfully different from judicial opinions with respect to copyrightability. In particular, the court rejected the argument that economic incentives should lead to different results and emphasized the nature of lawmaking in a democratic society:

> . . . SBCCI contends . . . that judges have no need of the Copyright Act's economic incentives in order to author judicial opinions. . . . SBCCI contrasts government employees with the private "authors" of model codes who allegedly depend on copyright incentives in order to perform their public service. . . .
>
> . . . However, the acceptance of SBCCI's and the dissent's theory, that nongovernmental employees who draft model statutes or regulations may be entitled to copyright protection, raises troubling issues. The complexities of modern life and the breadth of problems addressed by government entities necessitate continuous participation by private experts and interest groups in all aspects of statutory and regulatory lawmaking. . . . SBCCI offers no outer limit on claims of copyright prerogatives by nongovernmental persons who contribute to writing "the law."
>
> Not only is the question of authorship of "the law" exceedingly complicated by SBCCI's and the dissent's position, but in the end, the "authorship" question ignores the democratic process. Lawmaking bodies in this country enact rules and regulations only with the consent of the governed. The very process of lawmaking demands and incorporates contributions by "the people," in an infinite variety of individual and organizational capacities. Even when a governmental body consciously decides to enact proposed model building codes, it does so based on various legislative considerations, the sum of which produce its version of "the law."

In performing their function, the lawmakers represent the public will, and the public are the final "authors" of the law.

Id. at 796-99.

The court also held that the enacted codes were facts, ineligible for copyright protection:

> . . . The codes are "facts" under copyright law. They are the unique, unalterable expression of the "idea" that constitutes local law. . . . It should be obvious that for copyright purposes, laws are "facts": the U.S. Constitution is a fact; the Federal Tax Code and its regulations are facts; the Texas Uniform Commercial Code is a fact. Surely, in principle, the building codes of rural Texas hamlets are no less "facts" than the products of more august legislative or regulatory bodies. . . .
>
> We emphasize that in continuing to write and publish model building codes, SBCCI is creating copyrightable works of authorship. When those codes are enacted into law, however, they become to that extent "the law" of the governmental entities and may be reproduced or distributed as "the law" of those jurisdictions.

Id. at 801-02.

The court concluded by distinguishing cases in which the law requires citizens to refer to a copyrighted work. For example, a statute might refer to the Red Book, a car valuation guide. Citizens examining the statute would have to look outside of the statute itself—to the copyrighted Red Book—

> in the process of fulfilling their obligations. The copyrighted works do not "become law" merely because a statute refers to them. . . . Equally important, the referenced works or standards [in those cases] were created by private groups for reasons other than incorporation into law. To the extent incentives are relevant to the existence of copyright protection, the authors in these cases deserve incentives. . . . In the case of a model code, on the other hand, the text of the model serves no other purpose than to become law.

Id. at 804-05.

Do you agree with the *Veeck* decision? It was extremely close: 8-6. What arguments do you think the dissent made?

The majority emphasized that SBCCI held a copyright in its codes. *Id.* at 794. Of what value is that copyright if it disappears on enactment of the codes into law? In the case, Veeck did not copy the laws from the statute books of the Texas towns; rather, he copied it from a disk of model codes sold by SBCCI. *Id.* at 793. The court still found no infringement. Do you agree?

What are the implications of the *Veeck* decision for proposed uniform laws and accompanying reporters' notes drafted by the National Conference of Commissioners on Uniform State Laws (NCCUSL) and the American Law Insitute (ALI)? For example, NCCUSL and ALI promulgate the Uniform Commercial Code (UCC), which includes both proposed legislative text and comments by the relevant drafting committee. Some states adopt only the text as law; some also adopt the comments as law. Do NCCUSL and ALI have a copyright in anything? If not, will they have enough incentive to create model uniform laws?

NOTES AND QUESTIONS

1. What is the copyright status of works prepared pursuant to a contract with the federal government? The legislative history of §105 comments:

> The bill deliberately avoids making any sort of outright, unqualified prohibition against copyright in works prepared under Government contract or grant. There may well be cases where it would be in

the public interest to deny copyright in the writings generated by Government research contracts and the like; it can be assumed that, where a Government agency commissions a work for its own use merely as an alternative to having one of its own employees prepare the work, the right to secure a private copyright would be withheld. However, there are almost certainly many other cases where the denial of copyright protection would be unfair or would hamper the production and publication of important works. Where, under the particular circumstances, Congress or the agency involved finds that the need to have a work freely available outweighs the need of the private author to secure copyright, the problem can be dealt with by specific legislation, agency regulations, or contractual restrictions.

H.R. Rep. No. 94-1476, 94th Cong., 2d Sess. 59 (1976), *reprinted in* 1976 U.S.C.C.A.N. 5659, 5672. West Publishing Company and Mead Data Central, the publisher of LEXIS-NEXIS, claim copyright in both the print and electronic versions of their federal case reports. What do these copyrights cover? For further consideration of this question, see Chapter 4.E, *infra*. From time to time, smaller publishers of federal judicial decisions have challenged the wisdom of allowing private parties to claim copyright in published federal case reports, particularly where those reports have been given official status. Is there a "need to have [these] works freely available"?

2. Note that many foreign governments, including the British government, routinely claim copyright in works prepared by their employees. Under Article 2 of the Berne Convention (incorporated by reference in the TRIPS Agreement), the copyright status of official texts is for member countries to determine. Berne Conv., art. 2(4). International governance bodies, including the United Nations and WIPO, also routinely claim copyright in their documents.

Note on the Freedom of Information Act and Copyright

The Freedom of Information Act (FOIA) requires that U.S. government agencies make their records available for public inspection and copying. 5 U.S.C. §552(a). Private parties may own the copyright in documents that qualify as agency records subject to FOIA disclosure requirements. May the government disclose such copyrighted information without incurring copyright infringement liability?

The answer is unclear. FOIA provides for certain exemptions from its disclosure requirements, but none of those exemptions addresses copyright law specifically. Litigants have occasionally used 5 U.S.C. §552(b)(4) to attempt to prevent disclosure of copyrighted information. That section states that FOIA obligations do not apply to "matters that are . . . trade secrets and commercial or financial information obtained from a person and privileged or confidential."

Generally, courts seem unwilling to endorse either an agency's claim for a blanket exemption from FOIA requirements because of a private party's copyright interest or a private party's claim that FOIA trumps copyright law and requires an agency to release information regardless of the economic interests of copyright holders. In analyzing claims under exemption 4, courts balance "the public interest in disclosure against the interest Congress intended the exemption to protect." *Gilmore v. U.S. Dept. of Energy*, 4 F. Supp. 2d 912, 922 (N.D. Cal. 1998). In *Gilmore* the court held that computer software was not an agency record subject to FOIA's disclosure requirements while also noting that if the software were made available under FOIA, the value of the "copyright effectively [would be] reduced to zero." *Id.* at 923.

Matters can be even more complicated at the state level — many federal agency records are not protected by copyright because they are works of the U.S. government, barred from copyright protection by 17 U.S.C. §105. States and local governments, however, may assert copyright in their works. At the same time, many states have enacted FOIA-like disclosure requirements. How do such entities reconcile ownership of copyright with their FOIA-like obligations?

In *County of Suffolk v. First American Real Estate Solutions,* 261 F.3d 179 (2d Cir. 2001), the Second Circuit held that a New York county could own a copyright in its tax maps and that the New York Freedom of Information Law did not abrogate that copyright or prevent the county from enforcing it against a publisher who copied and distributed the maps. Is this decision consistent with *Veeck?* In other words, why shouldn't the court treat county tax maps like *Veeck* treated county building codes? Does the *First American* decision make sense as a policy matter? Is your answer to this question influenced by the fact that the defendant was a publisher who marketed the tax maps rather than a citizen trying to understand his or her tax liability? Would any copyright doctrine protect such a citizen? The court suggested that copyright law's fair use doctrine might protect some copiers. *Id.* at 193. We discuss the fair use doctrine in Chapter 7 of the casebook.

3

Acquiring and Maintaining Copyright

Copyright law has changed significantly since the enactment of the first Copyright Act. However, many of the rules contained in older copyright statutes still affect copyright law and practice. These rules primarily concern how copyright is obtained and maintained. In sum, they are rules that deal with the integrity of the copyright title. This chapter considers the development of these rules, and their influence on copyright law today.

A. FORMALITIES

Recall from Chapter 1 that until relatively recently, the U.S. did not play a significant role in the evolution of international copyright law. American isolationism from the international copyright system was most evident in statutory provisions, dating back to the Copyright Act of 1790, that required compliance with certain formalities as a quid quo pro for federal copyright protection. These formalities were: (1) publication; (2) notice; (3) registration; and (4) deposit of a copy of the copyrighted work with a designated entity. The Berne Convention expressly prohibits member countries from subjecting "the enjoyment and exercise of . . . rights" to any formality. *See* Berne Conv., art. 5(2). Accordingly, when it joined the Berne Convention in 1989, the U.S. eliminated these formalities as a condition of obtaining and preserving copyright protection. Today, failure to comply with copyright formalities no longer results in loss of copyright protection. Nevertheless, the four formalities listed above continue to complicate contemporary copyright analysis. First, the changes only apply prospectively, so some older works continue to be affected by the prior rules. Second, while failure to comply with formalities no longer affects any substantive rights, there are some practical reasons why these formalities remain important and should be observed. It is thus necessary to learn both the old and the new rules.

Finally, it is important to note that before January 1, 1978 (the effective date of the 1976 Act), if a work did not qualify for federal statutory protection, it may have been eligible for state protection (either statutory or common law), although certain activities would result in the loss of that protection as well.

1. An Overview

In 1790, Congress enacted the first Copyright Act to provide statutory protection to authors of maps, charts, and books. As a condition of protection, the Act prescribed certain requirements. First, for works that had been printed or published before the Act, the Act required that the author or proprietor deposit a copy of the title of the work, but not the work itself, with the clerk's office in the district court of the place where the author or proprietor resided. For works published after enactment, deposit was to be made before publication. The clerk was required to maintain a book of record in which the title of the protected work would be entered. Second, the Act required the author or proprietor to give notice of copyright to the public by publishing a copy of the record of copyright received from the clerk in at least one domestic newspaper within two months from the date of the record, and to maintain this newspaper notice for a period of four weeks. In 1802, Congress amended the 1790 Act by adding another notice requirement. Section 1 of the 1802 amendment required that the copy of record published in the newspapers also be inserted in the title page or in the page immediately following the title of *every* book. Third, the 1790 Act required that the author or proprietor deposit a copy of the work in the office of the Secretary of State within six months of its publication. Each of these three formalities was essential to perfecting the title of the copyright owner under the 1790 Act. *See Wheaton v. Peters*, 33 U.S. (8 Pet.) 591 (1834).

The basic copyright framework established by the 1790 Act was amended many times throughout the nineteenth century. However, none of the amendments resulted in substantial changes to the formalities required for copyright protection.

The first significant changes to the formalities required by copyright law occurred with passage of the Copyright Act of 1909. This Act abandoned the requirement of notice in a newspaper, and provided that copyright protection would subsist upon publication of the work with proper notice of copyright attached to the work itself. Such notice was required on each copy of the work published or offered for sale in the U.S. As specified by the Act, proper notice consisted of the word "Copyright" or "Copr.," and the name of the copyright proprietor. Printed literary, musical, and dramatic works also had to include the year copyright was secured by publication, and notice had to appear on the title page or the page immediately following. For all other works eligible for protection under the Act (maps, works of art such as models or designs and their reproductions, scientific or technical drawings, photographs and prints/pictorial illustrations), proper notice consisted of the symbol "©" accompanied by an identifying mark, symbol, or initials of the copyright owner. Further, the owner's full name had to appear on some accessible part of the work. For example, in the case of maps or drawings, the owner's full name could appear on the margin of the work; for models the owner's full name could be placed on the permanent base or pedestal on which the work was mounted. The Act demanded strict compliance with the notice requirements in order to preserve copyright protection. The Act also required prompt deposit of "two complete copies of the best [published] edition" of the work with the Copyright Office. The Act authorized the Copyright Office to demand deposit. Failure to timely comply with such a demand resulted not only in a fine but also in forfeiture of the copyright.

Under the 1909 Act a copyright owner was entitled to register his or her claim with the Copyright Office and obtain a certificate of registration. Although registration was optional during the first term of the copyright, failure to register and deposit copies of the work created a bar to any action for copyright infringement. In addition, the owner was required to register in order to receive a renewal term. (We discuss copyright duration and renewal in Sections B and C, *infra*.) Finally, under the 1909 Act, certain unpublished works that were "not reproduced for sale" could be registered, thus bringing such works under federal statutory protection. Section 12 of the 1909 Act indicated that the types of unpublished works eligible for statutory protection through registration were lectures and similar productions, dramatic compositions, musical compositions, dramatico-musical compositions, motion picture photoplays, motion pictures other than photoplays, photographs, works of art, and plastic works and drawings.

Like its predecessor Acts, the 1909 Act did not provide a definition of "publication." Yet, unless a work was eligible for registration as an unpublished work "not reproduced for sale," this concept was now central to determining whether or not an author or proprietor was entitled to statutory protection. The absence of a statutory definition meant that it was up to the courts to determine when exactly publication occurred.[1] Over time, judicial construction yielded several different rules about what might constitute publication and, even more important, what kinds of actions did *not* result in a publication for copyright purposes. For example, it became settled case law that the public nature of a particular use of a copyrighted work, such as a public performance or public delivery of a lecture or speech, did not necessarily constitute a publication of the work. *See, e.g., Ferris v. Frohman*, 223 U.S. 424 (1912); *McCarthy & Fischer, Inc. v. White*, 259 F.364 (S.D.N.Y. 1919); *Nutt v. National Inst. Inc. for the Improvement of Memory*, 31 F.2d 236 (2d Cir. 1929). Instead, "publication" seemed to turn on the degree to which a large number of people had both access to and control over multiple tangible copies of the work, or whether the public was given unrestricted access to copy the work. *See Burke v. National Broad. Co.*, 598 F.2d 688, 693 (1st Cir. 1979); *Patterson v. Century Prods.*, 93 F.2d 489, 492 (2d Cir. 1937). However, with the advent of the new broadcast technologies of radio and television, the focus on access to and control over physical copies began to seem more and more artificial.

In 1976, Congress enacted a new copyright statute. Several prior attempts to revise the copyright law had failed, in part because of disagreement about whether the U.S. should join the Berne Convention with its high substantive standards of protection. As discussed in Chapter 1, among other concerns, the U.S. did not wish to wholly abandon formalities as a prerequisite for copyright protection, and ultimately did not do so in the 1976 Act. Nonetheless, the legislative history of the 1976 Act indicates that Congress was sensitive to the hardship placed on authors and proprietors who failed to comply with the formalities required by the 1909 Act. In addition, other issues, such as the difficulty of defining the threshold concept of "publication," signaled the need for a general revision of these requirements.

The 1976 Act abandoned the requirement of publication as a condition of statutory protection and replaced it with the requirement of "fixation" in a tangible medium of expression. The change effectively abolished the dual system of protection, under which unpublished works were protected by state common law and published works by federal statutory copyright. The House Report asserted the following rationale for this fundamental shift:

> "Publication," perhaps the most important single concept under the . . . [1909 Act] also represents its most serious defect. Although at one time, when works were disseminated almost exclusively through printed copies, "publication" could serve as a practical dividing line between common law and statutory protection, this is no longer true. With the development of the 20th-century communications revolution, the concept of publication has become increasingly artificial and obscure. To cope with the legal consequences of an established concept that has lost much of its meaning and justification, the courts have given "publication" a number of diverse interpretations, some of them radically different. Not unexpectedly, the results in individual cases have become unpredictable and often unfair.

---

1. The Act did provide guidelines to determine the precise moment that publication occurred for the purpose of calculating the term of copyright protection. Section 26 stated that the date of publication for a work "of which copies are reproduced for sale or distribution . . . shall be held to be the earliest date when copies of the first authorized edition were placed on sale, sold, or publicly distributed by the proprietor of the copyright or under his authority." However, at least one case held that this provision should not be construed to provide a general definition of "publication." *See Cardinal Film Corp. v. Beck*, 248 F. 368 (S.D.N.Y. 1918).

H.R. Rep. No. 94-1476, 94th Cong., 2d Sess., 129-30 (1976), *reprinted in* 1976 U.S.C.C.A.N. 5659, 5741-43. Further, the House Report stated that abolishing the publication requirement would facilitate fidelity to the constitutional requirement that protection should be afforded to authors only for "limited times." According to the Report, "[c]ommon law protection in 'unpublished' works is now perpetual, no matter how widely they may be disseminated by means other than 'publication'; the bill would place a time limit on the duration of exclusive rights in them. The provision would also aid scholarship and the dissemination of historical materials by making unpublished, undisseminated manuscripts available for publication after a reasonable period." *Id.* at 130. Finally, the House Report noted that having a uniform copyright system would facilitate U.S. adherence to international copyright treaties because "[n]o other country has anything like our present dual system." *Id.*

Although publication is no longer a threshold requirement for federal copyright protection, the concept of publication continues to have some importance under the 1976 Act. We discuss the importance of publication for copyright duration and termination of transfers later in this chapter. The difference between published and unpublished works also has some bearing on the notice and deposit provisions of the 1976 Act, which are discussed below.

The 1976 Act retained a notice requirement, but here too it mitigated the harshness of the 1909 Act. In explaining Congress' decision to retain the requirement, the House Report identified four principal functions of the notice formality: (1) it had the effect of placing in the public domain a substantial body of published material that no one was interested in copyrighting, because the authors of such material could simply omit the required notice; (2) it informed the public whether a particular work was copyrighted; (3) it identified the copyright owner; and (4) it showed the date of publication. Accordingly, the Act required that notice of copyright be included on works published by authority of the copyright owner. Congress retained the basic form of notice: (1) the word "Copyright" or its abbreviated version, "Copr.," or the symbol "©"; (2) the year of first publication; and (3) the name of the copyright owner. Errors in the name or date could be corrected without forfeiting copyright protection. Further, the requirement regarding the location of notice on a copyrighted work was relaxed to allow notice to be placed on copies "in such manner and location as to give reasonable notice of the claim of copyright." 17 U.S.C. §401(c). In addition, the 1976 Act provided that protection would not be lost by omission of copyright notice, whether intentional or not, if "no more than a relatively small number" of copies or phonorecords were distributed without notice, or if registration of the work occurred within five years of publication and a reasonable effort was made to cure the earlier omission. *Id.* §405.

Like the 1909 Act, the 1976 Act required deposit of published works with the Copyright Office. The 1976 Act authorized the Register of Copyright to demand that an author comply with the deposit requirements. Failure to comply within three months of the demand no longer resulted in forfeiture but rather only in a civil fine.

The 1976 Act made registration of copyright voluntary and provided that registration could take place at any time during the copyright term. The 1976 Act, like the 1909 Act before it, requires the copyright owner to register and deposit copies of the work before filing an infringement lawsuit. Registration under the 1976 Act was effected by depositing two complete copies or phonorecords of the best edition of a published work or one complete copy or phonorecord of an unpublished work, along with a registration form and the required fee. This deposit for registration purposes could also be used to satisfy the deposit requirement. However, the Act treated registration and deposit separately, making it possible to satisfy the deposit requirement without registering the copyrighted work. *See id.* §§407-408.

In 1988, when the U.S. joined the Berne Convention, Congress modified both the notice and the registration requirements to comply with the terms of this important international treaty. Consistent with the requirements of the Berne Convention, notice is no longer a condition of protection for works published after March 1, 1989, the effective date of the domestic statute implementing U.S. accession. Instead, notice "may" be placed on publicly distributed copies of the copyrighted work. *See id.* §401(a). Note, however, that there still remains an important reason for copyright owners to satisfy the "optional" notice provisions in a post-Berne environment: The presence of a copyright notice will defeat a defendant's assertion of "innocent infringement," which affects the damages that may be recovered. *See id.* §401(d). In addition, the pre-1989 notice rules (and the concept of "publication") continue to have significance because the Berne Convention Implementation Act (BCIA) only applies prospectively to copies of works publicly distributed after March 1, 1989. The notice requirements of the 1909 and 1976 Copyright Acts remain in effect for copies publicly distributed before January 1, 1978, and March 1, 1989, respectively.

The BCIA also modified the rule that made registration of copyright a precondition of commencing an infringement suit. Here, Congress drew a distinction between works of U.S. origin and works originating from countries that belonged to the Berne Convention. For works originating from a Berne Convention country, an infringement action may be initiated without registering the work with the Copyright Office. However, for works of U.S. origin, the copyright owner still must register before filing suit. *See id.* §411.

As in the case of notice, there are good reasons that foreign works from Berne Convention countries should be registered even though the 1976 Act makes registration optional. First, a copyright owner may not elect to recover statutory damages, and is not eligible to receive an award of attorneys' fees, unless registration occurs before the start of the infringing activity or within three months of first publication. *See id.* §412. In addition, the certificate of registration of a work issued before or within five years of first publication will serve as presumptive, albeit rebuttable, proof of the dates of creation and publication, the identity of the copyright owner, and the validity of the copyright. *See id.* §410(c).

Finally, in 1993 under implementing legislation for the North American Free Trade Agreement (NAFTA), and in 1994 under the implementing legislation for the TRIPS Agreement, Congress remedied the loss of U.S. copyright protection for certain works of foreign origin due to failure to comply with the notice requirement and/or the registration and deposit requirements under the 1909 and 1976 Acts. These restoration provisions are discussed in Section 3.A.6, *infra*.

Having reviewed the history of formalities in U.S. law, we turn now to the current rules regarding each of them.

2. What Is Publication?

Before the effective date of the 1976 Copyright Act, unpublished creative works of authorship were protected by state common law copyright. Publication of a work destroyed the common law rights, and at the same time marked the point at which federal statutory protection became a viable option for authors. An author who chose to receive protection under the statutory regime received the benefit of federal copyright so long as she complied with the formalities. However, an author who upon publication failed to comply with the statutory formalities, or whose attempts at compliance were defective in some way, lost both common law protection and statutory protection. Courts countered the harshness of this rule by developing a definitional balancing test, applied on a case-by-case basis, to ameliorate the consequences of publication without proper notice. This test consisted of distinguishing between a "general" publication that would divest the author of her common law copyright and a "limited" publication that was nondivesting.

Estate of Martin Luther King, Jr., Inc. v. CBS, Inc.
194 F.3d 1211 (11th Cir. 1999)

ANDERSON, C.J.: . . . The facts underlying this case form part of our national heritage and are well-known to many Americans. On the afternoon of August 28, 1963, the Southern Christian Leadership Conference ("SCLC") held the March on Washington ("March") to promote the growing civil rights movement. The events of the day were seen and heard by some 200,000 people gathered at the March, and were broadcast live via radio and television to a nationwide audience of millions of viewers. The highlight of the March was a rousing speech that Dr. Martin Luther King, Jr., the SCLC's founder and president, gave in front of the Lincoln Memorial ("Speech"). The Speech contained the famous utterance, "I have a dream . . . ," which became symbolic of the civil rights movement. The SCLC had sought out wide press coverage of the March and the Speech, and these efforts were successful; the Speech was reported in daily newspapers across the country, was broadcast live on radio and television, and was extensively covered on television and radio subsequent to the live broadcast.

On September 30, 1963, approximately one month after the delivery of the Speech, Dr. King took steps to secure federal copyright protection for the Speech under the Copyright Act of 1909, and a certificate of registration of his claim to copyright was issued by the Copyright Office on October 2, 1963. Almost immediately thereafter, Dr. King filed suit in the Southern District of New York to enjoin the unauthorized sale of recordings of the Speech and won a preliminary injunction on December 13, 1963.

For the next twenty years, Dr. King and the Estate enjoyed copyright protection in the Speech and licensed it for a variety of uses, and renewed the copyright when necessary. In 1994, CBS entered into a contract with the Arts & Entertainment Network to produce a historical documentary series entitled "The 20th Century with Mike Wallace." One segment was devoted to "Martin Luther King, Jr. and The March on Washington." That episode contained material filmed by CBS during the March and extensive footage of the Speech (amounting to about 60% of its total content). CBS, however, did not seek the Estate's permission to use the Speech in this manner and refused to pay royalties to the Estate. The instant litigation ensued.

On summary judgment, the district court framed the issue as "whether the public delivery of Dr. King's speech . . . constituted a general publication of the speech so as to place it in the public domain." 13 F. Supp. 2d at 1351. After discussing the relevant case law, the District Court held that Dr. King's "performance coupled with such wide and unlimited reproduction and dissemination as occurred concomitant to Dr. King's speech during the March on Washington can be seen only as a general publication which thrust the speech into the public domain." *Id*. at 1354.[2] Thus, the District Court granted CBS's motion for summary judgment. The Estate now appeals to this Court. . . .

---

2. The district court noted that there potentially was some additional evidence of general publication. First, the SCLC published a newsletter of wide circulation containing the full text of the Speech. Second, an advance text of the Speech may have been freely available to the public in a press tent at the March. However, the district court disregarded both of these items of evidence because the procedural posture of the case was one of summary judgment, and "material facts [were] in dispute as to whether the use of Dr. King's speech in the newsletter was authorized and also as to the actual availability of the advance text." 13 F. Supp. 2d at 1353 n.5.

Because of the dates of the critical events, the determinative issues in this case are properly analyzed under the Copyright Act of 1909 ("1909 Act"), rather than the Copyright Act of 1976 ("1976 Act") that is currently in effect. The question is whether Dr. King's attempt to obtain statutory copyright protection on September 30, 1963 was effective, or whether it was a nullity because the Speech had already been forfeited to the public domain via a general publication.

Under the regime created by the 1909 Act, an author received state common law protection automatically at the time of creation of a work. This state common law protection persisted until the moment of a general publication. When a general publication occurred, the author either forfeited his work to the public domain, or, if he had therebefore complied with federal statutory requirements, converted his common law copyright into a federal statutory copyright.

In order to soften the hardship of the rule that publication destroys common law rights, courts developed a distinction between a "general publication" and a "limited publication." Only a general publication divested a common law copyright. A general publication occurred "when a work was made available to members of the public at large without regard to their identity or what they intended to do with the work." Conversely, a non-divesting limited publication was one that communicated the contents of a work to a select group and for a limited purpose, and without the right of diffusion, reproduction, distribution or sale. The issue before us is whether Dr. King's delivery of the Speech was a general publication.

Numerous cases stand for the proposition that the performance of a work is not a general publication.

It appears from the case law that a general publication occurs only in two situations. First, a general publication occurs if tangible copies of the work are distributed to the general public in such a manner as allows the public to exercise dominion and control over the work. Second, a general publication may occur if the work is exhibited or displayed in such a manner as to permit unrestricted copying by the general public. However, the case law indicates that restrictions on copying may be implied, and that express limitations in that regard are deemed unnecessary.

The case law indicates that distribution to the news media, as opposed to the general public, for the purpose of enabling the reporting of a contemporary newsworthy event, is only a limited publication. For example, in *Public Affairs Assoc., Inc. v. Rickover*, 284 F.2d 262 (D.C. Cir. 1960), *vacated on other grounds*, 369 U.S. 111 (1962), the court said that general publication occurs only when there is "a studied effort not only to secure publicity for the contents of the addresses through the channels of information, but to *go beyond customary sources of press or broadcasting* in distributing the addresses to any interested individual." Although the *Rickover* court ultimately held that a general publication had occurred, it contrasted the "limited use of the addresses by the press for fair comment," i.e., limited publication, with "the unlimited distribution to anyone who was interested," i.e., general publication. This rule comports with common sense; it does not force an author whose message happens to be newsworthy to choose between obtaining news coverage for his work and preserving his common-law copyright. As the dissenting judge in the *Rickover* case remarked . . . "[t]here is nothing in the law which would compel this court to deprive the creator of the right to reap financial benefits from these efforts because, at the time of their creation, they had the added virtue of being newsworthy events of immediate public concern." *Rickover*, 284 F.2d at 273 (Washington J., dissenting).

With the above principles in mind, in the summary judgment posture of this case and on the current state of this record, we are unable to conclude that CBS has demonstrated beyond any genuine issue of material fact that Dr. King, simply through his oral delivery of the Speech, engaged in a general publication making the Speech "available to members of the public at large without regard to their identity or what they intended to do with the work." A performance, no matter how broad the audience, is not a publication; to hold otherwise would be to upset a long line of precedent. This conclusion is not altered by the fact that the Speech was broadcast live to a broad radio and television audience and was the subject of extensive contemporaneous news coverage. We follow . . . case law indicating that release to the news media for contemporary coverage of a newsworthy event is only a limited publication. . . .

The district court held that "the circumstances in this case take the work in question outside the parameters of the 'performance is not a publication' doctrine." These circumstances included "the overwhelmingly public nature of the speech and the fervent intentions of the March organizers to draw press attention." Certainly, the Speech was one of a kind — a unique event in history. However, the features that make the Speech unique — e.g., the huge audience and the Speech's significance in terms of newsworthiness and history — are features that, according to the case law, are not significant in the general versus limited publication analysis. . . .

Because there exist genuine issues of material fact as to whether a general publication occurred, we must reverse the district court's grant of summary judgment for CBS. . . .

NOTES AND QUESTIONS

1. It is important to remember that the timing of the alleged publication determines which notice rules apply. In *Estate of Martin Luther King, Jr., Inc.*, the question was whether Dr. King's speech in August 1963 constituted a "publication." Thus, the 1909 Act was applicable even though the case was decided in 1999.

2. Section 101 of the 1976 Act defines publication as follows:

> "Publication" is the distribution of copies or phonorecords of a work to the public by sale or other transfer of ownership, or by rental, lease, or lending. The offering to distribute copies or phonorecords to a group of persons for purposes of further distribution, public performance, or public display, constitutes publication. A public performance or display of a work does not of itself constitute publication.

Does this language clarify the definition of "publication" that subsisted before passage of the 1976 Act? What do you think are the reasons for the rule that public performance or display does not, alone, constitute publication?

3. Generally, courts have held that posting material to a web site, such as photographs, music files, and computer software, constitutes publication. In *Getaped.com Inc. v. Cangemi*, 188 F. Supp. 2d 398 (S.D.N.Y. 2002), the court held that a web page itself is also published when it "goes live" because at that time an Internet user can make a copy of the web page. This approach is consistent with the Berne Convention, which provides that published works are those that, regardless of their mode of manufacture, are reasonably available to the public. *See* Berne Conv. art. 3(3).

4. Recall the discussion of the fixation requirement in Chapter 2.A.1. Does the fixation requirement accomplish the goals of copyright more effectively than the concept of publication?

3. Notice of Copyright

As discussed above, under the Copyright Act of 1909, works published in the U.S. without strict compliance with the notice requirements prescribed by the Act lost copyright protection. The 1976 Act kept the form of notice prescribed by the 1909 Act, but afforded opportunities to cure inadequate notice. After accession to the Berne Convention, Congress amended the 1976 Act to eliminate completely the requirement of copyright notice, but notice remains an important consideration for practical reasons.

Read §§401-406 of the 1976 Act, which contain the new optional notice provisions for the different categories of copyrightable works. Keeping in mind that before March 1, 1989, these requirements were mandatory, consider the following problems:

a. In 1985, Tom published his first novel. What should the copyright notice contain?

b. Assume that notice was omitted from the first edition of Tom's novel. What are the consequences of this error? What are the consequences if, in 1986, Tom's publisher alerts bookstores that have purchased copies of the novel, and gets the bookstores to paste a notice of copyright inside all the copies that still remain on their shelves?

c. Janice is a freelance writer. In 1991, she wrote an op-ed article for the *Sun Times*, a weekly periodical. The *Sun Times* affixes notice to the periodical. Does Janice also need to affix notice to her article?

d. What result if neither Janice nor the *Sun Times* affixes notice to their respective works?

An additional consequence of elimination of the notice requirement relates to abandonment of copyright. The default status of a work lacking a copyright notice has flipped: Before 1989, the lack of a copyright notice indicated no copyright in the work, sometimes referred to as a forfeiture or "abandonment" of copyright. Today, lack of a copyright notice does not result in abandonment. Abandonment can now only occur as a result of an "intentional relinquishment of a known right" by the copyright owner. *See, e.g., A&M Records, Inc. v. Napster, Inc.*, 239 F.3d 1004 (9th Cir. 2001). Certainly, including a statement such as "I dedicate this work to the public domain" on the work in place of a copyright notice would suffice. Mere failure to enforce one's rights does not result in an abandonment, although it may support an equitable defense based on laches or estoppel. *See, e.g., Kling v. Hallmark Cards, Inc.*, 225 F.3d 1030 (9th Cir. 2000). Creative Commons offers a "Public Domain Dedication" option that is clearly an express abandonment of copyright. *See http://creativecommons.org/licenses/publicdomain/*.

4. Deposit Requirements

The 1976 Copyright Act requires copyright owners to deposit two complete copies of the "best edition" of their published works with the Copyright Office. *See* 17 U.S.C. §407. The Act provides special deposit requirements for works first published outside the U.S., as well as for particular categories of works such as collective works, sound recordings, and recordings of transmission programs. *See id.* §§407-408. In addition, the registration requirement (which we examine next) requires a deposit of copies of the work. Thus, a work is not properly registered unless the deposit requirement is met.

The deposit requirement serves two important policy objectives. First, as discussed in Chapter 1, it enriches the resources of the Library of Congress, the largest library in the world. In recent years, the Copyright Office has encouraged deposits of digital copies in place of physical copies. Second, and important for practical reasons, the deposit requirement facilitates the ongoing development of a comprehensive record of copyright claims through the optional registration system codified in §408 of the 1976 Act.

Despite these objectives, the Copyright Act provides that the Register of Copyrights may issue regulations modifying the deposit requirements for any category of copyrightable works. The Register is authorized to consider the nature of the work and, in the case of individual authors of pictorial, graphic, or sculptural works produced in limited editions, the copyright owner's financial condition. *See id.* §407. For the regulations, see 37 C.F.R. §§202.19-202.242 (2001).

5.   Registration

As discussed above, registration is no longer a requirement for copyright protection. However, registration, or at least attempted registration, for U.S. works is required to commence an infringement action. *See* 17 U.S.C. §411(a). To preserve the ability to elect statutory damages as opposed to actual damages (which must be proved) and eligibility to receive an award of attorneys' fees, registration must have been made before the infringement commences. *Id.* at §412. For newly published works, copyright owners have three months in which to register their work and remain eligible for statutory damages and attorneys' fees even if the infringement commences before registration. *Id.* Additionally, registration permits a copyright owner to seek the assistance of U.S. Customs and Border Protection agents in seizing infringing items at the border. Finally, registration within five years of publication constitutes prima facie evidence of the validity of the copyright and of the facts stated in the certificate. *Id.* at §410.

Registration is effected by submitting a registration form to the Copyright Office along with the required fee and deposit copies. Recent changes in the Copyright Office now provide applicants with several options. First, the Copyright Office has implemented an online filing system for registration, the advantages of which include faster processing time and the ability to upload some deposits as electronic files. Alternatively, applicants can electronically complete a new single form (Form CO) for most categories of copyrighted works and submit the form, together with the requisite deposit and fees, by regular mail. The third option is to register with the traditional, category-specific paper forms. An applicant who chooses this route must write the Copyright Office to request the appropriate form for the category of work being registered. These forms are relatively simple and many individuals complete and file them without the assistance of an attorney. The online registration system has the lowest fees and applicants who choose this process may also check the status of their registration online. For a current list of fees associated with the different types of filings, see *http://www.copyright.gov/docs/fees.html.*

In some instances, the Copyright Office may deny registration after all the requirements, such as deposit, application, and fee, have been met. An author in this situation may nevertheless institute an infringement lawsuit, but will not have the evidentiary presumptions that accompany registration. Additionally, a copy of the complaint must be served on the Register of Copyrights, and the Register may choose to join the case with regard to the issue of registrability. Alternatively, the party whose registration has been denied can file suit against the Register of Copyrights to compel issuance of the registration. The Copyright Act provides that "all actions taken by the Register of Copyrights under this title are subject to the provisions of the Administrative Procedure Act." 17 U.S.C. §701(e). As provided in the Administrative Procedure Act, an agency action may be set aside only if "arbitrary, capricious, an abuse of discretion, or otherwise not in accordance with law." 5 U.S.C. §706(2)(A); *see, e.g. Darden v. Peters*, 488 F.3d 277 (4th Cir. 2007) (rejecting argument that a *de novo* standard should be applied to review of Copyright Office decisions). Unlike the Patent Act and the Lanham Act (trademark), the Copyright Act does not contain any mechanism for cancelling a registration once issued.

In 2005, a set of amendments enacted as part of the Family Entertainment and Copyright Act (FECA) modified the registration requirements for certain categories of works thought to need additional protection before their release for commercial distribution. One impetus for these amendments was the regular availability of first-run, not-yet-released movies for download through Internet swarming distribution software such as BitTorrent. In addition to making it a felony to make such works available for distribution on a publicly accessible computer network, see Chapter 6.E, *infra*, FECA directs the Copyright Office to establish abbreviated procedures for "preregistration" for any class of works determined to have "a history of infringement prior to authorized commercial distribution." 17 U.S.C. §408(f)(2). The Copyright Office currently permits preregistration of motion pictures, sound recordings, and software. Preregistration requires only a form and a fee; no deposit copy is required.

Preregistration provides the copyright owner with the ability to bring an infringement lawsuit as though full registration had been made. *See id.* §411(a). Preregistration, however, should be followed by a full registration within three months of first publication or within one month of learning of the infringement (whichever is *earlier*). Failure to file the full registration within that time frame has two consequences. First, such a failure will result in dismissal of any action for an infringement that commenced less than two months after publication. *See id.* §408(f)(4). Second, it will render the copyright owner ineligible to receive statutory damages and attorneys' fees. *See id.* §412.

NOTES AND QUESTIONS

1. The U.S. is well known for its elaborate copyright administration system. What policy goals does this system serve? How might you argue that they are consistent (or not) with the utilitarian underpinnings of the U.S. copyright system? What changes, if any, would you recommend to this system and why?

2. If a registration has been rejected by the Copyright Office, under what circumstances would you counsel a client to pursue an action against the Register of Copyrights rather than pursuing a suit for infringement? Some courts have held that in the context of an infringement action the Copyright Office's refusal to register a work based on insufficient originality is entitled to "some deference," while others have concluded that the issue should be reviewed *de novo*. *Compare Paul Morelli Design, Inc. v. Tiffany & Co.*, 200 F. Supp. 2d 482 (E.D. Pa. 2002) (some deference required) *with Ward v. National Geographic Soc'y*, 208 F. Supp. 2d 429 (S.D.N.Y. 2002) (*de novo* review of copyrightability). Note that either of these standards constitute less deference than is accorded the registration decision if it is challenged directly.

3. Compliance with the deposit rules can affect the validity of a registration. For example, submitting a later revised version of the work sought to be registered can result in a lack of copyright registration. *See, e.g,. Geoscan, Inc. v. Geotrace Techs., Inc.*, 226 F.3d 387, 393 (5th Cir. 2000) (dismissing lawsuit for failure to submit deposit copies of the source code of the original program). This deposit requirement can pose practical problems for authors of works that are updated frequently, such as computer programs or web sites.

4. Among other special exceptions to the deposit rules, the Copyright Office has issued special deposit rules for computer programs. For published or unpublished computer programs, the first 25 pages and the last 25 pages of the source code must be deposited either

on paper or in microform. *See* 37 C.F.R §202.20. For a program that is less than 50 pages, the entire source code must be deposited. *Id.* If a computer program contains a trade secret, the owner should write a letter stating this fact, and may block out portions of the code that contain the trade secret. What do you think is the reason for this rule? Is it consistent with the purposes of copyright discussed in Chapter 1?

5. Recall that countries that have joined the Berne Convention are required to provide copyright protection without subjecting "the enjoyment and the exercise of these rights" to any formality. *See* Berne Conv., art. 5(2). The TRIPS Agreement incorporates this provision as part of the mandatory obligations imposed on members of the World Trade Organization (WTO). Most countries have eliminated registration systems entirely, while others retain a non-mandatory registration system. A few countries, including the U.S., impose some measure of mandatory registration. *See, e.g.*, Article 63 of the Argentina Copyright Act (failure to register results in suspension of the author's economic rights). Argentina, like the U.S., imposes the formalities on its own nationals, and excludes foreign authors from these requirements to the extent that they may be inconsistent with international obligations. As an international matter, this bifurcated treatment is permissible. The nondiscrimination requirements of the Berne Convention and the TRIPS Agreement prohibit treating foreign authors worse than national authors, not vice versa. Why might a nation elect such discriminatory treatment of its own authors?

6. Recall that §412 limits *all* authors' eligibility to recover statutory damages and attorneys' fees when infringement occurs before registration. Is the U.S. in compliance with its international obligations?

7. Article 4.1 of the Chinese copyright law provides that "[w]orks the publication and/or dissemination of which are prohibited by law shall not be protected by this Law." The U.S. initiated a formal complaint at the WTO against China, claiming that Article 4.1 denies copyright protection to certain categories of works, including those that fail to satisfy "content review." *See China — Measures Affecting the Protection and Enforcement of Intellectual Property Rights*, WT/DS362/R ¶7.16 (Jan. 26, 2009). The U.S. also claimed that such content review is, in effect, a "formality" to which copyrighted works in China are subject. *Id.* ¶7.145. In response, China argued that Article 4.1 merely denies "copyright protection" with respect to enforceability of such works, but not "copyright," which vests at the moment of creation. *Id.* ¶¶7.17, 7.21, 7.54. China also argued that Article 4.1 denies protection to, *inter alia*, works whose contents are unconstitutional or immoral. *Id.* ¶¶7.17, 7.53.

The WTO Panel found that China's law violated the TRIPS Agreement. It noted that the Chinese administrative regulations prohibit content that "jeopardize[s] the unification, sovereignty and territorial integrity of the State"; "propagate[s] cults and superstition"; or "jeopardize[s] social ethics or fine national cultural traditions." *Id.* Under the plain language of Article 4.1, authors of works that are prohibited from publication or distribution in China are denied the full panoply of rights required by the Berne Convention and TRIPS Agreement. The Panel concluded that China's copyright law denies protection to certain classes of works in violation of Article 5(1) of the Berne Convention, as incorporated by Article 9 (1) of the TRIPS Agreement. *Id.* ¶¶7.50, 7. 60. Do you agree?

Having already ruled that Article 4.1 of China's copyright law has the effect of denying copyright protection to certain classes of works, the WTO Panel chose to exercise "judicial economy" and did not rule directly on the question whether submission of an authorial work to content review constitutes a formality under the Berne Convention and TRIPS Agreement. *Id.* ¶¶7.191, 7.192. Are content restrictions "formalities" proscribed under Article 5(2) of the Berne Convention? Australia, Canada, and the European Community joined the U.S. to argue that content review is an impermissible formality. *Id.* ¶¶7.149, 7.151, 7.152.

Note on Copyright's Default Rules and the Google Book Search Project

When Congress adopted the first federal Copyright Act in 1790, it selected a regime that required affirmative steps on the copyright owner's part to obtain a federal copyright—publication with proper notice and registration. This required copyright owners to "opt in" in order to obtain protection. Today, protection is automatic: Upon fixation of an original work of authorship, federal copyright protection vests in the author. A copyright owner must take affirmative steps to "opt out" of such protection. This significant change in the copyright system leads to many more works being subject to protection, but automatic protection can also lead to problems, including difficulty locating copyright owners. Works whose owners cannot be located are referred to as "orphan works." A system that requires someone to take affirmative steps to obtain a copyright reduces the number of "orphans," because only those copyright owners that care enough about protection will bother to obtain copyrights. Such copyright owners are also more likely to maintain adequate records with the Copyright Office, making it easier to locate them.

In 2004, Google announced the Google Book Search (GBS) project, the goal of which was to create a searchable database containing every book that it could find. Under the original design for the project, users would be able to search the database for specific books or for books about topics of interest to them. Unlike a digital catalog, which relies on titles and keywords, the database would allow searches on the full text of included works, and would have the capability to return full-text search results. Several leading university libraries, including those at Harvard, the University of Michigan, and Oxford University, granted Google access to scan their collections. Google stated that it would accommodate copyright interests by designing its system to return full-text search results only for public domain works. For books still under copyright, searches would return only small excerpts. If a copyright owner entered into an agreement with Google, the search could return several pages of text in response to a search request. As of 2009, over 20,000 publishers and authors had entered into agreements with Google.

After Google launched the GBS project and began scanning books, several publishers complained to Google. They asserted that inclusion of their works in the databases violated their copyrights, even if searches returned only small excerpts. In response, Google offered any copyright owner that objected to the inclusion of its works the opportunity to have them excluded entirely from the search results. Essentially, Google's offer adopted an opt-in approach to copyright protection: Copyright owners must affirmatively invoke copyright to prevent their works from being included.

The Authors Guild and several of its individual members, unsatisfied with Google's proposal, filed a class action lawsuit against Google arguing that the preparation of digitally scanned copies infringed their members' copyrights. Subsequently, five member companies of the Association of American Publishers filed a separate lawsuit against Google. To these plaintiffs, a system requiring them to opt out of Google's database and into full copyright protection ignored their copyright rights. Before the disputes could be litigated, the parties agreed on a settlement and submitted it to the court for approval. The initial proposed settlement engendered a flurry of commentary and objection, leading to its eventual withdrawal. A subsequent amended settlement agreement met with many similar objections. As of this writing, the fate of the proposed settlement is uncertain. For more information, *see http://www.googlebooksettlement.com*; *see also generally http://thepublicindex.org* (collecting court documents).

The GBS project holds the potential to significantly expand access to a vast array of written works. It also raises many interesting and complicated copyright questions. As you continue through the book, we will refer back to the GBS project and this Note, seeking to deepen your understanding of what is at stake in building a comprehensive database of written works.

NOTES AND QUESTIONS

1. In response to copyright owner complaints, Google argued that the procedure it offered for objecting to inclusion was simple and fully protected those copyright owners who did not want their works included in the database. If copyright protection is automatic, arising without the need for any affirmative action on the part of the copyright owner, should a private party such as Google be allowed to convert that protection into something that requires an affirmative step on the copyright owner's part? Should the Copyright Act be amended to allow some types of copying subject to an opt-in rule? For discussion of this question, see Oren Bracha, *Standing Copyright Law on Its Head? The Googlization of Everything and the Many Faces of Property*, 85 Tex. L. Rev. 1799 (2007).

2. If you were a book copyright owner, would you want your work included in the database? Remember that Google's default policy for books still under copyright is to display only short excerpts in response to search inquiries. If you were interested in permitting several pages to be displayed, you could enter into an agreement with Google. Would you be willing to enter into such an agreement? Why, or why not?

6. Restoration of Copyright Protection for Certain Works of Foreign Authors

Recall that before Berne accession, failure to comply with copyright formalities led to loss of U.S. copyright protection for a number of works. Both foreign and domestic authors were affected. Although Article 18 of the Berne Convention requires retroactive protection of foreign works that have lost copyright for failure to satisfy formalities imposed by domestic laws, the U.S. did not comply with this requirement immediately. The North American Free Trade Agreement Implementation Act of 1993 added §104A to the Copyright Act to restore copyright protection in Canadian and Mexican motion picture works that had lost protection for failure to comply with copyright formalities. In 1994, domestic legislation implementing the TRIPS Agreement extended restoration to all types of works by authors from all WTO countries.

The Uruguay Round Agreement Implementation Act amended §104A by expanding the provisions for copyright restoration to conform with the requirements of the Berne Convention. The effective date of restoration was January 1, 1996 for works whose source countries (defined in 17 U.S.C. §104A(h)(8)) were members of the Berne Convention or the WTO on that date. *See id.* §104A(h)(2). The Act defines a "restored work" to include foreign works that lost copyright protection because of: (1) failure to include a copyright notice; (2) noncompliance with other formalities imposed at any time by U.S. copyright law, including failure to renew or failure to comply with manufacturing requirements (discussed in Chapter 1.C.1, *supra*); (3) lack of subject matter protection in the case of sound recordings fixed before February 15, 1972; or (4) lack of national eligibility.[1] *See id.* §104A(h)(6)(C). To be eligible for restoration in the U.S., the work's copyright must not have expired in the source country before the date of restoration in the U.S. It is

---

1. If an author was a national of a country with which the U.S. had no treaty related to copyright, that author's work would not have been protected by U.S. copyright law at all.

important to note that §104A vests ownership of a restored work "initially in the author or initial rightholder in the work as determined by the law in the source country of the work." *See id.* §104A(b).

The length of protection for a restored copyright is the remainder of the term of copyright that the work would have been granted had it not lost protection. The owner of a restored copyright is entitled to full remedies for any infringing act that occurs on or after the date of restoration. *See id.* §104A(d)(1).

As you might imagine, restoration of lapsed copyright protection had serious consequences for individuals who had invested in the restored work in reliance on its public domain status. Section 104A provides special rules for these "reliance parties" including a period of immunity to wind down otherwise infringing activity. Before the owner of a restored copyright can bring an infringement action against a reliance party, the owner must give a notice of intent to enforce the restored copyright. The notice requirements are complicated and require attention to the detailed provisions spelled out in the statute. There already have been several cases involving copyright in restored works. *See, e.g., Dam Things from Denmark v. Russ Berrie & Co.*, 290 F.3d 548 (3d Cir. 2002) (finding, *inter alia*, restoration of Danish toy manufacturer's copyright in troll doll under §104A and discussing the effect of defendant's reliance party status); *Van Cleef & Arpels Logistics, S.A. v. Landau Jewelry*, 583 F. Supp. 2d 461, 465 (S.D.N.Y. 2008) (failure to file a notice of intent under the URAA "does not alter the legal inevitability of restoration"); *Hoepker v. Kruger*, 200 F. Supp. 2d 340 (S.D.N.Y. 2002) (dismissing claim against reliance party due to copyright owner's inadequate notice of intent to enforce restored copyright).

NOTES AND QUESTIONS

1. To test your understanding of the restoration rules, try to answer the following problems:

   a. In 1935, copies of a novel by German novelist Hans Schmidt were published in the U.S. without copyright notice. Is he eligible to take advantage of the restoration provisions?

   b. In 1998, French playwright Nicole Guilleme discovered that a company based in Dallas, Texas publishes unauthorized translations of her play *La Maison*. *La Maison* lost U.S copyright protection in 1957 for failure to file renewal registration for the work. What steps should Nicole take to enforce her copyright in *La Maison*?

   c. In 1991, Tom and Jerry started a business that specializes in digitally mastered reprints of old posters featuring medieval costumes. One of these posters is the work of Carmella Fabrosio, a Spanish photographer and artist. The original poster, created in 1930, did not have the name of the artist, or any other identifying information. In 1996, Fabrosio's great-granddaughter Rosa discovered copies of the remastered posters for sale over the Internet. Although the Spanish copyright has expired, Rosa, who inherited the Spanish copyright in 1943, wishes to file a notice of intent to enforce with the Copyright Office. Is her great-grandmother's work eligible for restoration of copyright protection under §104A?

2. What policy reasons might be articulated for Congress' failure to extend restoration under §104A to U.S. works?

3. A federal district court in Colorado has ruled that that the restoration provision is unconstitutional, *Golan v. Holder*, 611 F. Supp. 2d 1165 (D. Colo. Apr. 3, 2009), while

the D.C. Circuit has rejected a similar challenge, *Luck's Music Library, Inc. v. Gonzales*, 407 F.3d 1262 (D.C. Cir. 2005). These challenges are discussed in more detail in Section 3.B.2, *infra*.

B. DURATION

Now that you have been exposed to the rules governing the types of works that qualify for protection ("original works of authorship fixed in a tangible medium of expression"), who obtains initial copyright ownership (the "author" as defined by the Copyright Act), and the formalities needed to secure copyright (no publication, notice, or registration is required), we turn to the issue of how long copyright protection lasts. First, this section describes the complicated rules governing the duration of copyright. After we explain these rules, we explore the policy impetus for, and the implications of, the ever-increasing duration of copyright protection.

1. The Basics of Duration

It would be nice if we could simply say that copyright lasts for the life of the author plus 70 years. Unfortunately, a more complex set of rules governs the duration of copyright. To assist in understanding these rules and keeping them straight, it will help if you remember that they stem from two different regimes, one under the 1909 Act and one under the 1976 Act. Additionally, in 1998 Congress passed the Sonny Bono Copyright Term Extension Act (CTEA), which amended the 1976 Act. Regardless of which set of rules is applicable, all copyright durations run until the end of the calendar year. *See* 17 U.S.C. §305. To understand some of the rules discussed later in this section and in the cases that you will read, it is important to know that as a result of the CTEA, the current duration of copyright protection is 20 years longer than that initially adopted in the 1976 Act. The 1976 Act originally provided for a basic term of protection of the life of the author plus 50 years, and for works made for hire and anonymous or pseudonymous works, a term of either 100 years from creation or 75 years from publication, whichever is shorter.

a. *Works Created on or After January 1, 1978*

The easiest duration rules to understand are for those works first fixed on or after January 1, 1978 (recall that this is the effective date of the 1976 Act). For these works, the duration rules of the 1976 Act, as modified by the CTEA, apply:

a. The copyright in a work created by a single author endures for the life of the author plus 70 years.

b. The copyright in a work created by joint authors who did not create the work as a work made for hire endures for the life of the last surviving author plus 70 years.

c. The copyright in a work that is an anonymous work, a pseudonymous work, or a work made for hire endures for a term of 120 years from the year of creation or 95 years from the year of publication, *whichever expires first. See* 17 U.S.C. §302.

b. Works First Published Before January 1, 1978

The more complicated durations are for those works published before January 1, 1978. As you learned in the first section of this chapter, under the 1909 Act, publication with proper notice marked the moment at which federal copyright protection began. Published works displaying the proper copyright notice were granted a 28-year term of copyright protection. Additionally, a copyright owner could extend copyright protection for a renewal term of 28 years, for a total of 56 years, by filing a renewal certificate with the Copyright Office (and by registering the copyright if it had not previously been registered). The renewal certificate had to be filed during the final year of the initial term of protection. If the author had assigned the copyright in its first term, copyright would revert to the author once the second term began. If the copyright owner failed to file the renewal, copyright protection ended after 28 years.

Under this dual term scheme of protection, the date of death of the author was irrelevant for purposes of copyright duration. What mattered was the date of publication, the use of proper notice, and the filing of a renewal certificate.

It is not, however, accurate to say that copyrights in all works published before 1978 had a maximum duration of 56 years. The 1976 Act extended protection for these works by an additional 19 years so that the duration would be more comparable to the life plus 50 being adopted for works created after January 1, 1978. The way in which the 1976 Act accomplishes this extension is by adding 19 years to the renewal term. Thus, if the copyright owner secured a renewal term by the timely filing of a renewal certificate, the owner ultimately received an additional 47 years of protection (28 renewal + 19 extension) beyond the initial 28-year term. This led to a total possible term of protection of 75 years.

In 1998, Congress once again extended the duration of protection by 20 more years. As in the 1976 Act, Congress accomplished this extension by adding these additional years to the renewal term. Thus, the longest duration possible for works *published* before 1978 is now 95 years (28 initial + 28 renewal + 19 extension + 20 extension).

You might be tempted to think that this is not all that complicated; after all, the bottom line is that copyright duration in works published before 1978 is 95 years from publication. Under this rationale, works published in 1915 would remain subject to protection until the year 2010. But as a result of the timing of the CTEA, adopted in 1998, there were works that had already entered the public domain because of the expiration of the 75-year term in or before 1997. The CTEA did not grant new protection for these works. This means that works published before 1923 are in the public domain (1997 − 75 = 1922). Beginning with works first published with proper copyright notice in 1923, copyright in works published before January 1, 1978, will have a potential total duration of 95 years.

There is one further complicating matter related to the renewal requirement under the 1909 Act. As stated above, if a renewal certificate was not filed in the final year of the first term of copyright protection (i.e., the 28th year), copyright protection ceased at the end of the initial term. This requirement caught more than a few authors off guard and resulted in the loss of copyright protection for some rather famous works, including, among others, the holiday classic *It's a Wonderful Life* and the movie *Pygmalion*. In 1992, Congress decided to eliminate the requirement of the renewal certificate, making all renewals automatic. However, Congress did not revive protection for works that had passed into the public domain due to a failure to file the renewal certificate. Thus, in 1992, Congress could reach back only 28 years to make renewals automatic for those works published in or after 1964 (1992 − 28 = 1964). For works published before 1964, actual filing of a renewal certificate with the Copyright Office was required to obtain protection for the renewal term.

Below is a graphic depiction of these rules.

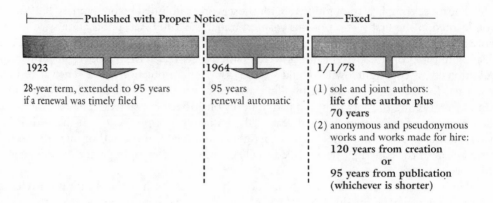

| ├———————Published with Proper Notice ———————┤ | ├——Fixed——┤ |

1923 — 28-year term, extended to 95 years if a renewal was timely filed

1964 — 95 years renewal automatic

1/1/78 —
(1) sole and joint authors: **life of the author plus 70 years**
(2) anonymous and pseudonymous works and works made for hire: **120 years from creation** or **95 years from publication** (whichever is shorter)

c. Works Created but Unpublished Before January 1, 1978

As the above chart indicates and as discussed in an earlier portion of this chapter, the 1909 Act only protected *published* works,[2] yet the 1976 Act protects both published and unpublished works so long as they are fixed. Works created but not published before January 1, 1978 (the effective date of the 1976 Act) were subject to common law or state statutory copyright protection. Not all of these sources of law provided for a finite term of protection. In adopting the 1976 Act, Congress decided to grant previously unpublished works federal copyright protection. These works were, after all, *fixed*; they just had not yet been published. Granting previously unpublished works federal copyright protection, coupled with broad pre-emption provisions barring all state laws that granted copyright-like protection, would bring all fixed works under one system of protection. On the issue of duration for these previously unpublished works, Congress determined that the same duration rules used for works created after January 1, 1978, should apply — i.e., life of the author plus 50 (now 70) years.

There was a problem in applying these same duration rules to unpublished works, however. Calculating the duration of copyright based on the date of death of the authors would divest some works of federal copyright protection at the same moment that all state law protection was extinguished. For example, a work created in 1920 by an author who died in 1925, and never published, would be granted federal copyright protection under the 1976 Act, but such protection lasted only until 1975 (life + 50 years, the original duration under the 1976 Act). Some commentators expressed concern about the unfairness of this treatment as well as the potential "takings" arguments that might be raised.

Congress solved this problem by providing a minimum term of federal copyright protection for these previously unpublished works. Federal copyright protection for works created before 1978 but not yet published as of January 1, 1978, endures for the term otherwise provided for newly created works, except that in no event would copyright expire before

---

2. As noted earlier in this chapter, under the 1909 Act unpublished works that were "not reproduced for sale" could be registered, thus bringing the unpublished work under federal statutory protection. The statute indicated that the types of unpublished works eligible to elect for statutory protection through registration were: "lectures and similar productions, dramatic compositions, musical compositions, dramatico-musical compositions, motion picture photoplays, motion pictures other than photoplays, photographs, works of art and plastic works and drawings." Section 12, 1909 Act. The discussion here assumes that no registration took place.

December 31, 2002. Congress also provided an additional incentive to publish those unpublished works by granting an additional 25 (now 45) years of protection if the work were published before December 31, 2002.

Below is a graphic representation of these rules.

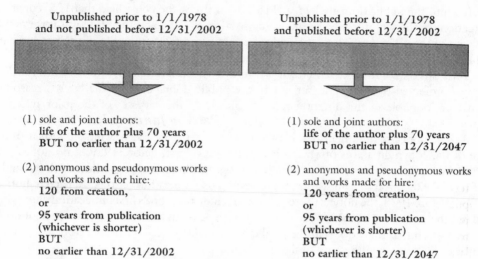

Unpublished prior to 1/1/1978 and not published before 12/31/2002

Unpublished prior to 1/1/1978 and published before 12/31/2002

(1) sole and joint authors:
life of the author plus 70 years
BUT no earlier than 12/31/2002

(1) sole and joint authors:
life of the author plus 70 years
BUT no earlier than 12/31/2047

(2) anonymous and pseudonymous works and works made for hire:
120 from creation,
or
95 years from publication
(whichever is shorter)
BUT
no earlier than 12/31/2002

(2) anonymous and pseudonymous works and works made for hire:
120 years from creation,
or
95 years from publication
(whichever is shorter)
BUT
no earlier than 12/31/2047

NOTES AND QUESTIONS

1. The explanation of the rules governing copyright duration shows that for works published before January 1, 1978, the date of publication is the important date for determining the expiration of copyright. At first blush, for works created after January 1, 1978, the date of first publication is not relevant to determining duration; what matters for these works is the date of death of the author of the work, and copyright in those works will last for 70 years after the date of death. However, the Copyright Act provides that 95 years after the year of first publication, there is a presumption that the death of the author occurred at least 70 years earlier. *See* 17 U.S.C. §302(e). This presumption can only be applied if the Copyright Office records contain no indication of the life status of the author. Additionally, for works that are made for hire or published anonymously or under a pseudonym, the date of first publication remains an important date: As described above, copyright in those works will last for 95 years from publication (or 120 years from creation if that date results in a shorter copyright duration). Thus, the year of first publication also can be relevant for works created after January 1, 1978.

2. For foreign works, the duration rules may sometimes be more complicated, particularly since important consideration must be given to events that took place outside the U.S. For example, in *Societe Civile Succession v. Renoir*, 549 F.3d 1182 (9th Cir. 2008), the plaintiff, a French trust, sued for copyright infringement of sculptures co-authored by the famous French artist Pierre-Auguste Renoir and one of his assistants, Richard Guino. Societe Civile Succession (SCS) obtained the copyrights pursuant to a settlement agreement between Renoir's family and Guino's family. However, Renoir's great-grandson, a defendant in this case, was not part of the settlement agreement. The sculptures were first published in France no later than 1917 in Renoir's name, but there was no American-style notice affixed to the works. In 1984, SCS obtained U.S. copyright registrations for the sculptures and indicated that they

were either first published in England in 1983 or unpublished. The court held that publication without copyright notice in a foreign country does not place a work in the public domain in the U.S. Further, because the sculptures were never published with a copyright notice, they did not fall under the 1909 Act. Consequently, "the sculptures were neither protected by copyright nor injected into the public domain." *Id.* at 1187. Ultimately, the court held that U.S. copyright protection for the sculptures began upon registration in 1984 and therefore was governed by the rules of the 1976 Act. Thus, the sculptures are protected for the life of the last surviving author, Guino, who died in 1973, plus 70 years (i.e., until 2043).

Does this outcome make sense? Is it possible that a work can be "neither fish nor fowl" — i.e., not protected by copyright but not in the public domain? Does the court's reasoning point to a loophole in the duration rules or merely to the excesses of the prior system of formalities?

3. The notice requirement that existed in U.S. law before 1989 facilitated public knowledge of the copyright status of a work in several ways. First, before 1989, if no notice were included on copies of the work, the work was not protected by copyright (although remember that from 1978 through 1989, there were some possibilities for "curing" defective notice). Second, before 1978, the notice was required to include the work's first publication date, which enabled the public to determine the duration of the copyright. Today, the absence of notice does not mean that the work is in the public domain. Also, without proper notice, the public cannot easily determine the date of first publication.

As discussed in note 1, the duration for some works created today is measured, at least in part, from the date of publication. If there is no copyright notice indicating a publication date, examining the records of the Copyright Office may help because the registration form requires the date of first publication. For those works whose duration is measured based on the life of the author, the registration form also requires information that would assist future researchers in determining the date of death of an author, such as the place and year of birth of the author.

But remember, registration is not required for copyright protection. Thus, despite someone's best intentions, it may be impossible to obtain the information necessary to determine whether a work remains under copyright protection. In such cases, a would-be user of a work may need to seek that information from the copyright owner directly. Of course, the copyright owner may have an interest in not being entirely forthcoming about facts relating to the copyright status of a work.

Is it appropriate to have a system for intangible property that allows individuals to assert claims of ownership without any registration or public notice of ownership claims? Compare this system with the elaborate systems of registration for real property in the U.S. Are there characteristics of copyright that justify this difference?

4. To test your understanding of these rules, determine the date on which the following works entered, or will enter, the public domain. The answers are in note 5, *infra*.

a. A novel, written by Alice Author, first published with proper copyright notice on July 1, 1930. Alice Author died December 1, 1931.

b. A novel, written by Benjamin Author, never published. Benjamin Author died in 1900. Would the answer be different if the work were first published in 1980? Would it matter whether the work bore proper copyright notice?

c. A computer software program written by Patience Programmer, an employee of Data-Systems, Inc., in 1988. Copies of the program were sold to the public, with no copyright notice, from November 1989 through January 1992. Patience Programmer died in 1990.

d. A song written in 2001 by the mother/daughter team of Mamma Moore and Cindy Moore, copies of which were distributed beginning on January 1, 2010. Mamma Moore died in 2002, Cindy Moore dies in 2040.

5. After you have completed the problems in note 4, check your answers with the following:

a. Answer: Copyright protection would have expired on July 1, 1958, unless proper renewal registration was filed in the 28th year of protection. With proper renewal registration, the work would enter the public domain on January 1, 2026. Remember, under the 1976 Act, unlike the 1909 Act, copyright duration runs until the end of the calendar year. The date of Alice's death is irrelevant because the work was created and published before 1978.

b. Answer: Although this author is entitled to the term of life + 70 years, that term would have already expired (1900 + 70 = 1970). Thus, the work is subject to the minimum term Congress provided under the 1976 Act. Remember that under the 1976 Act works created before 1978 but previously unpublished were brought under federal statutory protection (eliminating any state common law protection) and given protection until the end of 2002. The unpublished novel would have entered the public domain on January 1, 2003. If the work were published in 1980, its copyright would extend until the end of 2047. *See* 17 U.S.C. §303. The published copies would need to have proper copyright notice because publication occurred prior to March 1, 1989, the effective date of the Berne Convention Implementation Act.

c. Answer: This work will be in the public domain on January 1, 2085. Because this work is a work for hire, Patience's date of death is not relevant. The duration rule that applies is 120 years from creation: 1988 + 120 = 2108, or 95 years from publication: 1989 + 95 = 2084, whichever expires first = 12/31/2084. That the work was published without notice does not matter because the publications all occurred after March 1, 1989.

d. Answer: This work will be in the public domain on January 1, 2111. This is a joint work; its duration is therefore measured by the life of the last surviving author plus 70 years. Remember, copyright duration runs to the end of the calendar year.

2. The Policy Behind Copyright Duration

The Constitution requires that the exclusive rights granted to authors be "for limited Times." The first Copyright Act provided for a duration of 14 years with the possibility of an additional 14-year term, a total of 28 years. That duration was doubled in 1909 to a total possible term of protection of 56 years. Today, as you have just learned, copyright lasts far longer. · /

The lengthening duration of copyright results in the slower entry of works into the public domain. The change from a dual term system to a unitary term also significantly slowed the growth of the public domain. Under a system requiring an affirmative step on the part of the copyright owner to extend the duration of copyright (i.e., registration and the filing of a renewal certificate), many works entered the public domain after a mere 14 or 28 years. Today, as a result of the further term extensions granted by the Sonny Bono Copyright Term Extension Act of 1998 (CTEA), no additional works of authorship will enter the public domain as the result of the expiration of copyright protection until January 1, 2019.

In large measure, the shift in duration from a dual term to a unitary term resulted from an increased desire to harmonize U.S. law with copyright protection schemes in other countries. The Berne Convention requires a minimum term of protection of life plus 50 years. While the U.S. was not prepared to become a member of the Berne Convention at the time of the 1976 Act, adopting a term consistent with that treaty helped pave the way for U.S. ratification of it. Supporters of the adoption of the CTEA also pointed to international harmonization as a justification for increasing the term of protection in the U.S. Copyright protection in many European countries lasts for life plus 70 years, exceeding the Berne Convention's minimum requirement.

In the U.S., the various extensions of copyright duration have applied not only to new works created after the passage of each new duration extension, but also to works already created. In fact, the copyright industries lobby Congress hard to get these extensions in order to protect works already in existence. For example, the first film in which Mickey Mouse appears, *Steamboat Willy,* was copyrighted in 1928 and was facing the expiration of copyright protection in 2003. Disney executives testified before Congress in support of the CTEA.

After the passage of the CTEA, Eric Eldred filed a lawsuit to challenge its constitutionality. Since 1995, Eldred has maintained a web site devoted to literary works that are in the public domain. Each year, on December 31, an entire year's worth of new material would enter the public domain, and Eldred would begin the process of making those works freely available through his web site. In 1997, the National Endowment for the Humanities recognized his web site as one of the 20 best humanities sites. Daren Fonda, *Copyright Crusader*, Boston Globe, Aug. 29, 1999 (Magazine), at 12. The passage of the CTEA, however, meant that Eldred would have to wait 20 years for any new works to enter the public domain. With the assistance of Harvard Law School's Berkman Center for Internet and Society, Eldred and others filed a declaratory judgment action, alleging that the CTEA violated the First Amendment and the originality and "limited Times" requirements of the Intellectual Property Clause. Below is the Supreme Court's opinion in that case.

Eldred v. Ashcroft
537 U.S. 186 (2003)

GINSBURG, J.: . . . Petitioners . . . seek a determination that the [Copyright Term Extension Act (CTEA), Pub. L. 105-298, §102(b) and (d), 112 Stat. 2827-2828] fails constitutional review under both the Copyright Clause's "limited Times" prescription and the First Amendment's free speech guarantee. . . .

I

A

. . . The Nation's first copyright statute, enacted in 1790, provided a federal copyright term of 14 years from the date of publication, renewable for an additional 14 years if the author survived the first term. The 1790 Act's renewable 14-year term applied to existing works (i.e., works already published and works created but not yet published) and future works alike. Congress expanded the federal copyright term to 42 years in 1831 (28 years from publication, renewable for an additional 14 years), and to 56 years in 1909 (28 years from publication, renewable for an additional 28 years). Both times, Congress applied the new copyright term to existing and future works; to qualify for the 1831 extension, an existing work had to be in its initial copyright term at the time the Act became effective.

In 1976, Congress altered the method for computing federal copyright terms. 1976 Act §§302-304. For works created by identified natural persons, the 1976 Act provided that federal copyright protection would run from the work's creation, not — as in the 1790, 1831, and 1909 Acts — its publication; protection would last until 50 years after the author's death. §302(a). In these respects, the 1976 Act aligned United States copyright terms with the then-dominant international standard adopted under the Berne Convention for the Protection of Literary and Artistic Works. . . .

These new copyright terms, the 1976 Act instructed, governed all works not published by its effective date of January 1, 1978, regardless of when the works were created. §§302-303. For published works with existing copyrights as of that date, the 1976 Act granted a copyright term of 75 years from the date of publication, §304(a) and (b), a 19-year increase over the 56-year term applicable under the 1909 Act.

The measure at issue here, the CTEA, installed the fourth major duration extension of federal copyrights. Retaining the general structure of the 1976 Act, the CTEA enlarges the terms of all existing and future copyrights by 20 years. For works created by identified natural persons, the term now lasts from creation until 70 years after the author's death. 17 U.S.C. §302(a). This standard harmonizes the baseline United States copyright term with the term adopted by the European Union in 1993. . . .

. . . [I]n common with the 1831, 1909, and 1976 Acts, the CTEA's new terms apply to both future and existing copyrights. . . .

II

A

We address first the determination of the courts below that Congress has authority under the Copyright Clause to extend the terms of existing copyrights. Text, history, and precedent, we conclude, confirm that the Copyright Clause empowers Congress to prescribe "limited Times" for copyright protection and to secure the same level and duration of protection for all copyright holders, present and future.

The CTEA's baseline term of life plus 70 years, petitioners concede, qualifies as a "limited Tim[e]" as applied to future copyrights. Petitioners contend, however, that existing copyrights extended to endure for that same term are not "limited." Petitioners' argument essentially reads into the text of the Copyright Clause the command that a time prescription, once set, becomes forever "fixed" or "inalterable." The word "limited," however, does not convey a meaning so constricted. At the time of the Framing, that word meant what it means today: "confine[d] within certain bounds," "restrain[ed]," or "circumscribe[d]." S. Johnson, A Dictionary of the English Language (7th ed. 1785). Thus understood, a time span appropriately "limited" as applied to future copyrights does not automatically cease to be "limited" when applied to existing copyrights. And as we observe, *infra* . . . , there is no cause to suspect that a purpose to evade the "limited Times" prescription prompted Congress to adopt the CTEA.

. . . History reveals an unbroken congressional practice of granting to authors of works with existing copyrights the benefit of term extensions so that all under copyright protection will be governed evenhandedly under the same regime. . . .

Because the Clause empowering Congress to confer copyrights also authorizes patents, congressional practice with respect to patents informs our inquiry. We count it significant that early Congresses extended the duration of numerous individual patents as well as copyrights.

The courts saw no "limited Times" impediment to such extensions; renewed or extended terms were upheld in the early days. . . .

Satisfied that the CTEA complies with the "limited Times" prescription, we turn now to whether it is a rational exercise of the legislative authority conferred by the Copyright Clause. On that point, we defer substantially to Congress.

The CTEA reflects judgments of a kind Congress typically makes, judgments we cannot dismiss as outside the Legislature's domain. . . . [A] key factor in the CTEA's passage was a 1993 European Union (EU) directive instructing EU members to establish a copyright term of life plus 70 years. Consistent with the Berne Convention, the EU directed its members to deny this longer term to the works of any non-EU country whose laws did not secure the same extended term. By extending the base-line United States copyright term to life plus 70 years, Congress sought to ensure that American authors would receive the same copyright protection in Europe as their European counterparts. The CTEA may also provide greater incentive for American and other authors to create and disseminate their work in the United States.

In addition to international concerns, Congress passed the CTEA in light of demographic, economic, and technological changes,[14] and rationally credited projections that longer terms would encourage copyright holders to invest in the restoration and public distribution of their works. . . . [15]

In sum, we find that the CTEA is a rational enactment; we are not at liberty to second-guess congressional determinations and policy judgments of this order, however debatable or arguably unwise they may be. . . .

B . . .

Petitioners dominantly advance a series of arguments all premised on the proposition that Congress may not extend an existing copyright absent new consideration from the author. . . .

. . . [P]etitioners contend that the CTEA's extension of existing copyrights does not "promote the Progress of Science" as contemplated by the preambular language of the Copyright Clause. Art. I, §8, cl. 8. . . . [Petitioners] maintain that the preambular language identifies the sole end to which Congress may legislate. . . . The CTEA's extension of existing copyrights categorically fails to "promote the Progress of Science," petitioners argue, because it does not stimulate the creation of new works but merely adds value to works already created.

As petitioners point out, we have described the Copyright Clause as "both a grant of power and a limitation," *Graham v. John Deere Co. of Kansas City*, 383 U.S. 1, 5 (1966), and have said that "[t]he primary objective of copyright" is "[t]o promote the Progress of Science," *Feist*, 499 U.S., at 349. The "constitutional command," we have recognized, is that Congress, to the

---

14. Members of Congress expressed the view that, as a result of increases in human longevity and in parents' average age when their children are born, the pre-CTEA term did not adequately secure "the right to profit from licensing one's work during one's lifetime and to take pride and comfort in knowing that one's children — and perhaps their children — might also benefit from one's posthumous popularity." 141 Cong. Rec. 6553 (1995) (statement of Sen. Feinstein).

15. JUSTICE BREYER urges that the economic incentives accompanying copyright term extension are too insignificant to "mov[e]" any author with a "rational economic perspective." Calibrating rational economic incentives, however, like "fashion[ing] . . . new rules [in light of] new technology," Sony, 464 U.S., at 431, is a task primarily for Congress, not the courts. Congress heard testimony from a number of prominent artists; each expressed the belief that the copyright system's assurance of fair compensation for themselves and their heirs was an incentive to create. *See, e.g.*, House Hearings 233-239 (statement of Quincy Jones); Copyright Term Extension Act of 1995: Hearings before the Senate Committee on the Judiciary, 104th Cong., 1st Sess., 55-56 (1995) (statement of Bob Dylan); *id.*, at 56-57 (statement of Don Henley); *id.*, at 57 (statement of Carlos Santana). We would not take Congress to task for crediting this evidence which, as JUSTICE BREYER acknowledges, reflects general "propositions about the value of incentives" that are "undeniably true." . . .

extent it enacts copyright laws at all, create a "system" that "promote[s] the Progress of Science." *Graham*, 383 U.S., at 6.

We have also stressed, however, that it is generally for Congress, not the courts, to decide how best to pursue the Copyright Clause's objectives. The justifications we earlier set out for Congress' enactment of the CTEA provide a rational basis for the conclusion that the CTEA "promote[s] the Progress of Science."

On the issue of copyright duration, Congress, from the start, has routinely applied new definitions or adjustments of the copyright term to both future works and existing works not yet in the public domain. . . . Congress' unbroken practice since the founding generation thus overwhelms petitioners' argument that the CTEA's extension of existing copyrights fails *per se* to "promote the Progress of Science."

Closely related to petitioners' preambular argument, or a variant of it, is their assertion that the Copyright Clause "imbeds a quid pro quo." They contend, in this regard, that Congress may grant to an "Autho[r]" an "exclusive Right" for a "limited Tim[e]," but only in exchange for a "Writin[g]." Congress' power to confer copyright protection, petitioners argue, is thus contingent upon an exchange: The author of an original work receives an "exclusive Right" for a "limited Tim[e]" in exchange for a dedication to the public thereafter. Extending an existing copyright without demanding additional consideration, petitioners maintain, bestows an unpaid-for benefit on copyright holders and their heirs, in violation of the *quid pro quo* requirement.

We can demur to petitioners' description of the Copyright Clause as a grant of legislative authority empowering Congress "to secure a bargain — this for that." But the legislative evolution earlier recalled demonstrates what the bargain entails. Given the consistent placement of existing copyright holders in parity with future holders, the author of a work created in the last 170 years would reasonably comprehend, as the "this" offered her, a copyright not only for the time in place when protection is gained, but also for any renewal or extension legislated during that time. Congress could rationally seek to "promote . . . Progress" by including in every copyright statute an express guarantee that authors would receive the benefit of any later legislative extension of the copyright term. Nothing in the Copyright Clause bars Congress from creating the same incentive by adopting the same position as a matter of unbroken practice. . . .

We note, furthermore, that patents and copyrights do not entail the same exchange, and that our references to a *quid pro quo* typically appear in the patent context. This is understandable, given that immediate disclosure is not the objective of, but is *exacted from*, the patentee. It is the price paid for the exclusivity secured. For the author seeking copyright protection, in contrast, disclosure is the desired objective, not something exacted from the author in exchange for the copyright. Indeed, since the 1976 Act, copyright has run from creation, not publication.

Further distinguishing the two kinds of intellectual property, copyright gives the holder no monopoly on any knowledge. A reader of an author's writing may make full use of any fact or idea she acquires from her reading. The grant of a patent, on the other hand, does prevent full use by others of the inventor's knowledge. In light of these distinctions, one cannot extract from language in our patent decisions — language not trained on a grant's duration — genuine support for petitioners' bold view. Accordingly, we reject the proposition that a quid pro quo requirement stops Congress from expanding copyright's term in a manner that puts existing and future copyrights in parity.[22] . . .

---

22. The fact that patent and copyright involve different exchanges does not, of course, mean that we may not be guided in our "limited Times" analysis by Congress' repeated extensions of existing patents. If patent's *quid pro quo* is more exacting than copyright's, then Congress' repeated extensions of existing patents without constitutional objection suggests even more strongly that similar legislation with respect to copyrights is constitutionally permissible.

it becomes difficult, if not impossible, even to dispute these characterizations, Congress' "choice is clearly wrong." *Helvering v. Davis*, 301 U.S. 619, 640 (1937).

First, the present statute primarily benefits the holders of existing copyrights, *i.e.*, copyrights on works already created. And a Congressional Research Service (CRS) study prepared for Congress indicates that the added royalty-related sum that the law will transfer to existing copyright holders is large. E. Rappaport, CRS Report for Congress, Copyright Term Extension: Estimating the Economic Values (1998) (hereinafter CRS Report). In conjunction with official figures on copyright renewals, the CRS Report indicates that only about 2% of copyrights between 55 and 75 years old retain commercial value — *i.e.*, still generate royalties after that time. But books, songs, and movies of that vintage still earn about $400 million per year in royalties. CRS Report 8, 12, 15. Hence, (despite declining consumer interest in any given work over time) one might conservatively estimate that 20 extra years of copyright protection will mean the transfer of several billion extra royalty dollars to holders of existing copyrights — copyrights that, together, already will have earned many billions of dollars in royalty "reward." See *id.*, at 16.

The extra royalty payments will not come from thin air. Rather, they ultimately come from those who wish to read or see or hear those classic books or films or recordings that have survived. . . .

A second, equally important, cause for concern arises out of the fact that copyright extension imposes a "permissions" requirement — not only upon potential users of "classic" works that still retain commercial value, but also upon potential users of any other work still in copyright. Again using CRS estimates, one can estimate that, by 2018, the number of such works 75 years of age or older will be about 350,000. . . . Because the Copyright Act of 1976 abolished the requirement that an owner must renew a copyright, such still-in-copyright works (of little or no commercial value) will eventually number in the millions. . . .

. . . [T]he permissions requirement can inhibit or prevent the use of old works (particularly those without commercial value): (1) because it may prove expensive to track down or to contract with the copyright holder, (2) because the holder may prove impossible to find, or (3) because the holder when found may deny permission either outright or through misinformed efforts to bargain. The CRS, for example, has found that the cost of seeking permission "can be prohibitive." CRS Report 4. . . .

. . . The costs to the users of nonprofit databases, now numbering in the low millions, will multiply as the use of those computer-assisted databases becomes more prevalent. And the qualitative costs to education, learning, and research will multiply as our children become ever more dependent for the content of their knowledge upon computer-accessible databases — thereby condemning that which is not so accessible, say, the cultural content of early 20th-century history, to a kind of intellectual purgatory from which it will not easily emerge. . . .

The majority also invokes the "fair use" exception, and it notes that copyright law itself is restricted to protection of a work's expression, not its substantive content. Neither the exception nor the restriction, however, would necessarily help those who wish to obtain from electronic databases material that is not there . . .

What copyright-related benefits might justify the statute's extension of copyright protection? First, no one could reasonably conclude that copyright's traditional economic rationale applies here. . . . Using assumptions about the time value of money provided us by a group of economists (including five Nobel prize winners), Brief for George A. Akerlof et al. as *Amici Curiae* 5-7, it seems fair to say that, for example, a 1% likelihood of earning $100 annually for 20 years, starting *75 years into the future*, is worth less than seven cents today.

What potential Shakespeare, Wharton, or Hemingway would be moved by such a sum? What monetarily motivated Melville would not realize that he could do better for his grandchildren by putting a few dollars into an interest-bearing bank account? . . .

. . . Of course Congress did not intend to act unconstitutionally. But it may have sought to test the Constitution's limits. After all, the statute was named after a Member of Congress, who, the legislative history records, "wanted the term of copyright protection to last forever." 144 Cong. Rec. H9952 (daily ed. Oct. 7, 1998) (statement of Rep. Mary Bono). See also Copyright Term, Film Labeling, and Film Preservation Legislation: Hearings on H.R. 989 et al. before the Subcommittee on Courts and Intellectual Property of the House Judiciary Committee, 104th Cong., 1st Sess., 94 (1995) (hereinafter House Hearings) (statement of Rep. Sonny Bono) (questioning why copyrights should ever expire); *ibid.* (statement of Rep. Berman) ("I guess we could . . . just make a permanent moratorium on the expiration of copyrights"); *id.*, at 230 (statement of Rep. Hoke) ("Why 70 years? Why not forever? Why not 150 years?"); . . . *id.*, at 234 (statement of Quincy Jones) ("I'm particularly fascinated with Representative Hoke's statement. . . . [W]hy not forever?"); *id.*, at 277 (statement of Quincy Jones) ("If we can start with 70, add 20, it would be a good start"). . . .

Second, the Court relies heavily for justification upon international uniformity of terms. . . . [I]n this case the justification based upon foreign rules is surprisingly weak. . . .

Despite appearances, the statute does *not* create a uniform American-European term with respect to the lion's share of the economically significant works that it affects — *all* works made "for hire" and *all* existing works created prior to 1978. With respect to those works the American statute produces an extended term of 95 years while comparable European rights in "for hire" works last for periods that vary from 50 years to 70 years to life plus 70 years. Neither does the statute create uniformity with respect to anonymous or pseudonymous works. . . .

Third, several publishers and filmmakers argue that the statute provides incentives to *those who act as publishers* to republish and to redistribute older copyrighted works. This claim cannot justify this statute, however, because the rationale is inconsistent with the basic purpose of the Copyright Clause — as understood by the Framers and by this Court. The Clause assumes an initial grant of monopoly, designed primarily to encourage creation, followed by termination of the monopoly grant in order to promote dissemination of already-created works. It assumes that it is the *disappearance* of the monopoly grant, not its *perpetuation*, that will, on balance, promote the dissemination of works already in existence. . . .

I share the Court's initial concern, about intrusion upon the decisionmaking authority of Congress. . . . But I do not believe it intrudes upon that authority to find the statute unconstitutional on the basis of (1) a legal analysis of the Copyright Clause's objectives; (2) the total implausibility of any incentive effect; and (3) the statute's apparent failure to provide significant international uniformity. Nor does it intrude upon congressional authority to consider rationality in light of the expressive values underlying the Copyright Clause, related as it is to the First Amendment, and given the constitutional importance of correctly drawing the relevant Clause/Amendment boundary. . . .

. . . Even if it is difficult to draw a single clear bright line, the Court could easily decide (as I would decide) that this particular statute simply goes too far. . . .

NOTES AND QUESTIONS

1. Who has the better argument about the significance of past copyright and patent extensions, the majority or Justice Stevens?

2. The majority and Justice Stevens also disagreed about the level of deference owed to Congress under Art. I, §8, cl. 8. Who has the better argument there?

The majority pointed to international uniformity in copyright duration as a permissible policy choice supporting passage of the CTEA. Did you find the majority's reasoning on this point persuasive? The Berne Convention requires a copyright term of life plus 50 years, but it permits countries to adopt longer terms. Berne Conv., art. 7. It is worth considering how different views about the underlying justification for copyright affect a country's choice of the appropriate copyright duration. If copyright protection in one country (e.g., France) is based on a natural rights rationale, might the duration chosen be different than in a country that justifies copyright protection on utilitarian grounds? How should these different policies be reconciled in the context of global harmonization? Is it appropriate to accord greater deference to Congress in such circumstances?

Life plus 70 years may become the de facto international rule of copyright duration as the U.S. and EU pursue bilateral and regional agreements that export this term to other countries. Reconciling different national copyright policies usually results in stronger protection since countries with higher standards are usually unwilling to engage in the politically costly endeavor of withdrawing a benefit already given.

3. In upholding the CTEA as a rational exercise of Congress' copyright power, the Court noted the incentive effects of the extra 20 years in light of "demographic, economic, and technological" changes. Was the majority or Justice Breyer more persuasive on this point? Do you think the majority agreed or disagreed with Congress' conclusion that the CTEA represented sound policy?

4. Do Justice Breyer's arguments about the economic rationality of the CTEA concern the deference owed to Congress under Art. I, §8, cl. 8, or under the First Amendment? On what basis does Justice Breyer argue for more rigorous review of the CTEA? Are his First Amendment concerns well founded? Did the majority adequately answer these concerns? Revisit this question after you have read Chapter 7, which discusses the fair use doctrine.

5. The Court rejected plaintiff's argument that the Constitution requires a quid pro quo for the grant of a copyright and that giving existing works 20 additional years of protection violated this requirement. Do you agree with the majority's reasoning? Is Congress' decision to omit the quid pro quo of publication from the 1976 Act relevant to determination of the constitutional question? Why, or why not?

Justice Stevens, in contrast, argued that the grant of a patent or a copyright is similar to a contract between the inventor or author and the public. He asserted that it would be unfair to the public to change the terms of that bargain by lengthening the term of protection. *Eldred v. Ashcroft*, 537 U.S. 186, 223-40 (2003) (Stevens, J., dissenting). What is the majority's answer to this argument? In a footnote omitted from the edited opinion, the majority asserted that "copyright law serves public ends by providing individuals with an incentive to pursue private ones." *Id.* at 212 n.18. Will providing individuals with incentives to pursue private ends always serve public ends?

6. In *United States v. Lopez*, 514 U.S. 549, 552 (1995), the Supreme Court held that "congressional power under the Commerce Clause . . . is subject to outer limits." One way to determine if a particular law has exceeded that outer limit is to examine whether the rationale offered in support of Congressional authority has any stopping point or if the rationale offered would support regulation of all human activity. In the appeals court in *Eldred*, Judge Sentelle in dissent expressed the view that the rationale offered in support of the CTEA leads to an unlimited view of the copyright power. *Eldred v. Reno*, 239 F.3d 372, 381 (D.C. Cir. 2001) (Sentelle, J., dissenting), *aff'd sub nom. Eldred v. Ashcroft*, 537 U.S. 186 (2003). Does the Supreme Court's majority opinion address the "outer limit" of Congressional

power under the intellectual property clause? Do you think the Court would have reached a different decision if petitioners had also challenged the constitutionality of prospective term extension? Note that in *Gonzales v. Raich*, 545 U.S. 1, 23 (2005), the Supreme Court cautioned against reading *Lopez* in isolation from the "larger context of modern-era Commerce Clause jurisprudence."

7. Two lawsuits filed on behalf of different plaintiffs have raised constitutional challenges to §104A of the Copyright Act, which restores copyright to eligible foreign works. In the first, *Lucks' Music Library, Inc. v. Gonzales*, 407 F.3d 1262 (D.C. Cir. 2005), the court rejected the plaintiff's constitutional challenges to §104A, relying heavily on the Supreme Court's opinion in *Eldred*. In the second lawsuit, the courts relied on *Eldred* to reach the opposite result.

The lead plaintiff in the second lawsuit, Mr. Lawrence Golan, conducted a small college orchestra that, following enactment of §104A, had to pay royalties to perform restored works by Shostakovich, Prokofiev, and others. The district court initially rejected Golan's constitutional arguments, but the Tenth Circuit reversed the district court's First Amendment holding. The court instructed that a law removing works from the public domain "alters the traditional contours of copyright protection and requires first amendment scrutiny." *Golan v. Gonzales*, 501 F.3d 1179, 1187 (10th Cir. 2007). On remand, the district court concluded that §104A is content-neutral, and therefore subject to only intermediate constitutional scrutiny, but that the restoration rules are "'substantially broader than necessary'" to effectuate the important government goal of achieving compliance with the Berne Convention. *Golan v. Holder*, 611 F. Supp. 2d 1165, 1175 (D. Colo. Apr. 3, 2009) (quoting *Ward v. Rock Against Racism*, 491 U.S. 781, 800 (1989)). According to the court, the Berne Convention imposes no requirement that restored copyrights be given protection perfectly equivalent to that given copyrights still in force; therefore, Congress could have granted much broader protection to reliance parties than §104A provides. *See id.* An appeal of the district court's ruling is expected.

8. Are there other steps that Congress might take to ensure that some works continue to pass into the public domain? Under patent law, the patentee must pay periodic maintenance fees. 35 U.S.C. §41(b) (providing for fees to be paid at four-year intervals, beginning three years and six months after the patent grant and ending with the payment eleven years and six months after the grant). Failure to do so results in expiration of the patent. Would a similar system be desirable in copyright law? A bill proposed in the 109th Congress, called the Public Domain Enhancement Act, provided that "The Register of Copyrights shall charge a fee of $1 for maintaining in force the copyright in any published United States work. The fee shall be due 50 years after the date of first publication or on December 31, 2006, whichever occurs later, and every 10 years thereafter until the end of the copyright term. Unless payment of the applicable maintenance fee is received in the Copyright Office on or before the date the fee is due or within a grace period of 6 months thereafter, the copyright shall expire as of the end of that grace period." H.R. 2408, 109th Cong., 1st Sess., §3(c). If you were a member of Congress, what types of evidence would help you to make a decision on such a bill? Would it comply with U.S. obligations under international treaties?

9. Are there other ways of dealing with the transactional difficulties presented by long copyright terms? In January 2005, several members of Congress requested that the Copyright Office undertake a review of potential problems posed by orphan works, which Congress described generally as "copyrighted works whose owners are difficult or even impossible to locate." They expressed a concern that public access to such works might be impeded because of the high transaction costs involved in locating the copyright owners and the uncertainty associated with using the works without permission. In January 2006, the Copyright Office submitted a final report to Congress in which it concluded that sufficient ground exists for a "meaningful legislative solution" to address the orphan works problem. Among other things,

the Report recommended that Congress amend the Copyright Act to limit the scope of monetary remedies and injunctive relief available for infringement of copyright in an orphan work. *See* Report on Orphan Works, *http://www.copyright.gov/orphan/ orphan-report-full.pdf.* Do you think these recommendations effectively address disincentives to use orphan works? If adopted, would they sufficiently ameliorate the concerns associated with long copyright terms? What other recommendations would you suggest? Recall the GBS project described on pages 157-58. Google's approach to scanning old books that might still be within copyright was to put the burden on the copyright owners to come forward and object to the use of those works. Is this a workable solution for other kinds of works? For other kinds of uses?

C. RENEWALS AND TERMINATIONS OF TRANSFERS

1. Renewals

As discussed earlier in this chapter, the 1909 Act granted copyright protection for an initial 28-year term with the possibility for a renewal term of 28 years. To obtain protection for that renewal term, the author had to file a renewal certificate with the Copyright Office. The Supreme Court's decision in *Stewart v. Abend*, excerpted below, addresses the reasons for and effects of this dual term system. While you might be tempted to disregard the importance of this case because the 1976 Act uses a unitary term, remember that the 1909 Act's duration scheme applies to works created before the effective date of the 1976 Act (January 1, 1978). The renewal terms of these works will be in force until the year 2072 $(1977 + 95)$!

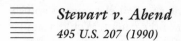

Stewart v. Abend

495 U.S. 207 (1990)

O'Connor, J.: The author of a pre-existing work may assign to another the right to use it in a derivative work. In this case the author of a pre-existing work agreed to assign the rights in his renewal copyright term to the owner of a derivative work, but died before the commencement of the renewal period. The question presented is whether the owner of the derivative work infringed the rights of the successor owner of the pre-existing work by continued distribution and publication of the derivative work during the renewal term of the pre-existing work.

I

Cornell Woolrich authored the story "It Had to Be Murder," which was first published in February 1942 in Dime Detective Magazine. . . . In 1945, Woolrich agreed to assign the rights to make motion picture versions of six of his stories, including "It Had to Be Murder," to B. G. De Sylva Productions for $9,250. He also agreed to renew the copyrights in the stories at the appropriate time and to assign the same motion picture rights to De Sylva Productions for the 28-year renewal term. In 1953, actor Jimmy Stewart and director Alfred Hitchcock formed a production company, Patron, Inc., which obtained the motion picture rights in "It Had to Be Murder" from De Sylva's successors in interest for $10,000.

In 1954, Patron, Inc., along with Paramount Pictures, produced and distributed "Rear Window," the motion picture version of Woolrich's story "It Had to Be Murder." Woolrich died in 1968 before he could obtain the rights in the renewal term for petitioners as promised and without a surviving spouse or child. He left his property to a trust administered by his executor, Chase Manhattan Bank, for the benefit of Columbia University. On December 29, 1969, Chase Manhattan Bank renewed the copyright in the "It Had to Be Murder" story pursuant to 17 U.S.C. §24 (1976 ed.). Chase Manhattan assigned the renewal rights to respondent Abend for $650 plus 10% of all proceeds from exploitation of the story.

"Rear Window" was broadcast on the ABC television network in 1971. Respondent then notified petitioners Hitchcock (now represented by cotrustees of his will), Stewart, and MCA Inc., the owners of the "Rear Window" motion picture and renewal rights in the motion picture, that he owned the renewal rights in the copyright and that their distribution of the motion picture without his permission infringed his copyright in the story. Hitchcock, Stewart, and MCA nonetheless entered into a second license with ABC to rebroadcast the motion picture. In 1974, respondent filed suit against these same petitioners, and others, in the United States District Court for the Southern District of New York, alleging copyright infringement. Respondent dismissed his complaint in return for $25,000.

Three years later, the United States Court of Appeals for the Second Circuit decided *Rohauer v. Killiam Shows, Inc.*, 551 F.2d 484, cert. denied, 431 U.S. 949 (1977), in which it held that the owner of the copyright in a derivative work may continue to use the existing derivative work according to the original grant from the author of the pre-existing work even if the grant of rights in the pre-existing work lapsed. Several years later, apparently in reliance on Rohauer, petitioners re-released the motion picture in a variety of media, including new 35 and 16 millimeter prints for theatrical exhibition in the United States, videocassettes, and videodiscs. They also publicly exhibited the motion picture in theaters, over cable television, and through videodisc and videocassette rentals and sales.

Respondent then brought the instant suit in the United States District Court for the Central District of California against Hitchcock, Stewart, MCA, and Universal Film Exchanges, a subsidiary of MCA and the distributor of the motion picture. Respondent's complaint alleges that the re-release of the motion picture infringes his copyright in the story because petitioners' right to use the story during the renewal term lapsed when Woolrich died before he could register for the renewal term and transfer his renewal rights to them. Respondent also contends that petitioners have interfered with his rights in the renewal term of the story in other ways. He alleges that he sought to contract with Home Box Office (HBO) to produce a play and television version of the story, but that petitioners wrote to him and HBO stating that neither he nor HBO could use either the title, "Rear Window" or "It Had to Be Murder." Respondent also alleges that petitioners further interfered with the renewal copyright in the story by attempting to sell the right to make a television sequel and that the re-release of the original motion picture itself interfered with his ability to produce other derivative works. . . .

II

A . . .

Since the earliest copyright statute in this country, the copyright term of ownership has been split between an original term and a renewal term. Originally, the renewal was intended merely to serve as an extension of the original term; at the end of the original term, the renewal could be effected and claimed by the author, if living, or by the author's executors, administrators, or assigns. In 1831, Congress altered the provision so that the author could assign his contingent interest in the renewal term, but could not, through his assignment, divest the rights of his widow or children in the renewal term. . . . In this way, Congress attempted to give the author a second chance to control and benefit from his work. Congress also intended to secure to the author's family the opportunity to exploit the work if the author died before he could register for the renewal term. "The evident purpose of [the renewal provision] is to provide for the family of the author after his death. Since the author cannot assign his family's renewal rights, [it] takes the form of a compulsory bequest of the copyright to the designated persons." *De Sylva v. Ballentine*, 351 U.S. 570, 582 (1956).

In its debates leading up to the Copyright Act of 1909, Congress elaborated upon the policy underlying a system comprised of an original term and a completely separate renewal term. "It not infrequently happens that the author sells his copyright outright to a publisher for a comparatively small sum." H.R. Rep. No. 2222, 60th Cong., 2d Sess., 14 (1909). The renewal term permits the author, originally in a poor bargaining position, to renegotiate the terms of the grant once the value of the work has been tested. "[U]nlike real property and other forms of personal property, [a copyright] is by its very nature incapable of accurate monetary evaluation prior to its exploitation." 2 M. Nimmer & D. Nimmer, Nimmer on Copyright §9.02, p. 9-23 (1989) (hereinafter Nimmer). "If the work proves to be a great success and lives beyond the term of twenty-eight years, . . . it should be the exclusive right of the author to take the renewal term, and the law should be framed . . . so that [the author] could not be deprived of that right." H.R. Rep. No. 2222, supra, at 14. With these purposes in mind, Congress enacted the renewal provision of the Copyright Act of 1909, 17 U.S.C. §24 (1976 ed.). With respect to works in their original or renewal term as of January 1, 1978, Congress retained the two-term system of copyright protection in the 1976 Act.

Applying these principles in *Miller Music Corp. v. Charles N. Daniels, Inc.*, 362 U.S. 373 (1960), this Court held that when an author dies before the renewal period arrives, his executor is entitled to the renewal rights, even though the author previously assigned his renewal rights to another party. "An assignment by an author of his renewal rights made before the original copyright expires is valid against the world, if the author is alive at the commencement of the renewal period. *[Fred] Fisher Co. v. [M.] Witmark & Sons*, 318 U.S. 643, [1943] so holds." *Id.*, at 375. If the author dies before that time, the "next of kin obtain the renewal copyright free of any claim founded upon an assignment made by the author in his lifetime. These results follow not because the author's assignment is invalid but because he had only an expectancy to assign; and his death, prior to the renewal period, terminates his interest in the renewal which by §24 vests in the named classes." *Ibid.* . . . Thus, the renewal provisions were intended to give the author a second chance to obtain fair remuneration for his creative efforts and to provide the author's family a "new estate" if the author died before the renewal period arrived.

. . . If the assignee of all of the renewal rights holds nothing upon the death of the assignor before arrival of the renewal period, then, *a fortiori*, the assignee of a portion of the renewal rights, *e.g.*, the right to produce a derivative work, must also hold nothing. Therefore, if the author dies before the renewal period, then the assignee may continue to use the original work only if the author's successor transfers the renewal rights to the assignee. This is the rule adopted by the Court of Appeals below and advocated by the Register of Copyrights. Application of this rule to this case should end the inquiry. Woolrich died before the commencement of the renewal period in the story, and, therefore, petitioners hold only an unfulfilled expectancy. Petitioners have been "deprived of nothing. Like all purchasers of contingent interests, [they took] subject to the possibility that the contingency may not occur." *Miller Music, supra*, at 378.

B

The reason that our inquiry does not end here, and that we granted certiorari, is that the Court of Appeals for the Second Circuit reached a contrary result in *Rohauer v. Killiam Shows, Inc.*, 551 F.2d 484 (1977). Petitioners' theory is drawn largely from *Rohauer*. The Court of Appeals in *Rohauer* attempted to craft a "proper reconciliation" between the owner of the pre-existing work, who held the right to the work pursuant to *Miller Music*, and the owner of the derivative work, who had a great deal to lose if the work could not be published or distributed. 551 F.2d, at 490. Addressing a case factually similar to this case, the court concluded that even if the death of the author caused the renewal rights in the pre-existing work to revert to the statutory successor, the owner of the derivative work could continue to exploit that work. The court reasoned that the 1976 Act and the relevant precedents did not preclude such a result and that it was necessitated by a balancing of the equities:

> [T]he equities lie preponderantly in favor of the proprietor of the derivative copyright. In contrast to the situation where an assignee or licensee has done nothing more than print, publicize and distribute a copyrighted story or novel, a person who with the consent of the author has created an opera or a motion picture film will often have made contributions literary, musical and economic, as great as or greater than the original author. . . . [T]he purchaser of derivative rights has no truly effective way to protect himself against the eventuality of the author's death before the renewal period since there is no way of telling who will be the surviving widow, children or next of kin or the executor until that date arrives. Id., at 493. . . .

Though petitioners do not, indeed could not, argue that its language expressly supports the theory they draw from *Rohauer*, they implicitly rely on §6 of the 1909 Act, 17 U.S.C. §7 (1976 ed.), which states that "dramatizations . . . of copyrighted works when produced with the consent of the proprietor of the copyright in such works . . . shall be regarded as new works subject to copyright under the provisions of this title." Petitioners maintain that the creation of the "new," *i.e.*, derivative, work extinguishes any right the owner of rights in the pre-existing work might have had to sue for infringement that occurs during the renewal term.

We think, as stated in Nimmer, that "[t]his conclusion is neither warranted by any express provision of the Copyright Act, nor by the rationale as to the scope of protection achieved in a derivative work. It is moreover contrary to the axiomatic copyright principle that a person may exploit only such copyrighted literary material as he either owns or is licensed to use." 1 Nimmer §3.07[A], pp. 3-23 to 3-24 (footnotes omitted). The aspects of a derivative work added by the derivative author are that author's property, but the element drawn from the pre-existing work remains on grant from the owner of the pre-existing work. So long as the pre-existing work remains out of the public domain, its use is infringing if one who employs the work does not have a valid license or assignment for use of the pre-existing work. It is irrelevant whether the pre-existing work is inseparably intertwined with the derivative work. Indeed, the plain language of [§7 of the 1909 Act] supports the view that the full force of the copyright in the pre-existing work is preserved despite incorporation into the derivative work. This well-settled rule also was made explicit in the 1976 Act:

> The copyright in a compilation or derivative work extends only to the material contributed by the author of such work, as distinguished from the preexisting material employed in the work, and does not imply any exclusive right in the preexisting material. The copyright in such work is independent of, and does not affect or enlarge the scope, duration, ownership, or subsistence of, any copyright protection in the preexisting material. 17 U.S.C. §103(b) [1988 ed.].

Properly conceding there is no explicit support for their theory in the 1909 Act, its legislative history, or the case law, petitioners contend, as did the court in Rohauer, that the termination provisions of the 1976 Act, while not controlling, support their theory of the case. For works existing in their original or renewal terms as of January 1, 1978, the 1976 Act added 19 years to the 1909 Act's provision of 28 years of initial copyright protection and 28 years of renewal protection. See 17 U.S.C. §§304(a) and (b) [1988 ed.]. For those works, the author has the power to terminate the grant of rights at the end of the renewal term and, therefore, to gain the benefit of that additional 19 years of protection. See §304(c). In effect, the 1976 Act provides a third opportunity for the author to benefit from a work in its original or renewal term as of January 1, 1978. Congress, however, created one exception to the author's right to terminate: The author may not, at the end of the renewal term, terminate the right to use a derivative work for which the owner of the derivative work has held valid rights in the original and renewal terms. See §304(c)(6)(A). The author, however, may terminate the right to create new derivative works. Ibid. For example, if petitioners held a valid copyright in the story throughout the original and renewal terms, and the renewal term in "Rear Window" were about to expire, petitioners could continue to distribute the motion picture even if respondent terminated the grant of rights, but could not create a new motion picture version of the story. Both the court in Rohauer and petitioners infer from this exception to the right to terminate an intent by Congress to prevent authors of pre-existing works from blocking distribution of derivative works. In other words, because Congress decided not to permit authors to exercise a third opportunity to benefit from a work incorporated into a derivative work, the Act expresses a general policy of undermining the author's second opportunity. We disagree.

The process of compromise between competing special interests leading to the enactment of the 1976 Act undermines any such attempt to draw an overarching policy out of §304(c)(6)(A), which only prevents termination with respect to works in their original or renewal copyright terms as of January 1, 1978, and only at the end of the renewal period. . . .

In fact, if the 1976 Act's termination provisions provide any guidance at all in this case, they tilt against petitioners' theory. The plain language of the termination provision itself indicates that Congress assumed that the owner of the pre-existing work possessed the right to sue for infringement even after incorporation of the preexisting work in the derivative work.

> A derivative work *prepared* under authority of the grant before its termination may continue to be utilized under the terms of the grant after its termination, but this privilege does not extend to the preparation after the termination of other derivative works based upon the copyrighted work covered by the terminated grant. §304(c)(6)(A) (emphasis added).

Congress would not have stated explicitly in §304(c)(6)(A) that, at the end of the renewal term, the owner of the rights in the pre-existing work may not terminate use rights in existing derivative works unless Congress had assumed that the owner continued to hold the right to sue for infringement even after incorporation of the preexisting work into the derivative work.

Accordingly, we conclude that neither the 1909 Act nor the 1976 Act provides support for the theory set forth in Rohauer. . . .

Finally, petitioners urge us to consider the policies underlying the Copyright Act. They argue that the rule announced by the Court of Appeals will undermine one of the policies of the Act — the dissemination of creative works — by leading to many fewer works reaching the public. *Amicus* Columbia Pictures asserts that "[s]ome owners of underlying work renewal copyrights may refuse to negotiate, preferring instead to retire their copyrighted works, and all derivative works based thereon, from public use. Others may make demands — like respondent's demand for 50% of petitioners' future gross proceeds in excess of advertising expenses . . . —which are so exorbitant that a negotiated economic accommodation will be impossible." Brief for Columbia Pictures et al. as *Amici Curiae* 21. These arguments are better addressed by Congress than the courts.

In any event, the complaint that respondent's monetary request in this case is so high as to preclude agreement fails to acknowledge that an initially high asking price does not preclude bargaining. Presumably, respondent is asking for a share in the proceeds because he wants to profit from the distribution of the work, not because he seeks suppression of it.

Moreover, although dissemination of creative works is a goal of the Copyright Act, the Act creates a balance between the artist's right to control the work during the term of the copyright protection and the public's need for access to creative works. The copyright term is limited so that the public will not be permanently deprived of the fruits of an artist's labors. But nothing in the copyright statutes would prevent an author from hoarding all of his works during the term of the copyright. In fact, this Court has held that a copyright owner has the capacity arbitrarily to refuse to license one who seeks to exploit the work. *See Fox Film Corp. v. Doyal,* 286 U.S. 123, 127 (1932).

The limited monopoly granted to the artist is intended to provide the necessary bargaining capital to garner a fair price for the value of the works passing into public use. When an author produces a work which later commands a higher price in the market than the original bargain provided, the copyright statute is designed to provide the author the power to negotiate for the realized value of the work. That is how the separate renewal term was intended to operate. At heart, petitioners' true complaint is that they will have to pay more for the use of works they have employed in creating their own works. But such a result was contemplated by Congress and is consistent with the goals of the Copyright Act. . . .

NOTES AND QUESTIONS

1. As mentioned in the introduction before the *Stewart* case, renewals will remain a part of our copyright system until 2072. A copyright lawyer in 2020 will still need to know the rules concerning renewals to determine whether a work published in 1950 remains subject to protection, whether a renewal certificate for such work had to be filed, and who owns the rights in the renewal term. Additionally, as explained in the next section of this chapter, assignments of interests in the renewal term can be terminated insofar as those assignments also assign the extensions to the 28-year renewal term granted by Congress. These two extensions are the 19 years added by the 1976 Act and the 20 years added by the CTEA.

2. As the Court explains in *Stewart,* the renewal term was meant to give the author and her family a chance to recapture the value of a previously assigned copyright. The Court's interpretation of the right to a second bite at the apple given to authors and their families was not entirely protective, however, because it permitted the renewal right to be sold. Indeed, it became standard practice in many form agreements not only for the author to assign the initial and renewal terms of copyright, but also for the author's spouse to sign the agreement as well, thereby assigning any rights the spouse might have in the renewal term (see note 4, below). Do you think that judicial enforcement of such agreements was faithful to the policies underlying the renewal rules? Note that the transfer of rights in the renewal period had to be explicitly stated. Generally, transfers of "all rights, title and interests" during the initial copyright term did not transfer such rights for the renewal term.

3. In 1992, Congress passed the Copyright Renewal Act (CRA), which made renewal automatic. Previously, the requirement of filing a renewal certificate meant that many works

that no longer had commercial significance lost their copyright protection because the owner did not take the affirmative step required to extend it. After passage of the CRA, no affirmative action was required for copyright protection to extend the full 75 (now 95) years. Works that routinely had passed into the public domain after 28 years now receive protection for 95 years. After the Supreme Court decided *Eldred v. Ashcroft*, pages 166-73, Internet archivists filed a constitutional challenge to the CRA. They asserted that the change from an opt-in system of renewal to one of automatic renewal altered the "traditional contours of copyright protection" and therefore required First Amendment scrutiny. *Kahle v. Gonzales*, 487 F.3d 697 (9th Cir. 2007). The Ninth Circuit dismissed the plaintiffs' claims holding that the CRA "placed existing copyrights in parity with those of future works." *Id.* at 700.

4. In *Stewart*, Cornell Woolrich died without any widow or children to claim an interest in his copyrights and so the renewal term vested in the executor of his estate, Chase Manhattan Bank. Section 304 of the Copyright Act dictates the succeeding claimants to the renewal term in the event of an author's death. If the author is not still living, the first class of successor claimants is the widow, widower, or children of the author. The statute does not specify how the interest is to be divided among members of this class. One court has held that if both a widow or widower and children survive the author, 50 percent of the interest belongs to the widow or widower and the remaining 50 percent is divided among the children. *BMI, Inc. v. Roger Miller Music, Inc.*, 396 F.3d 762 (6th Cir.) *cert. denied*, 546 U.S. 871 (2005). If no widow, widower, or children are living, the next class of claimants is the author's executor as fiduciary to the beneficiaries under the author's will. If the author fails to leave a will, the final class of claimants is the author's next of kin, as determined by state intestacy rules. *See DeSylva v. Ballentine*, 351 U.S. 570 (1956).

The vesting of the renewal term may not be varied by the author's will or state laws of intestate succession. Thus, if an author dies before the vesting of the renewal term, it is irrelevant that her will leaves all of her copyrights to her best friend and not her husband or children. This results because of the rules described in *Stewart*, i.e., the author has no interest to pass on, only a mere expectancy that is extinguished upon her dying before the vesting of the renewal term. The best friend will own the copyrights, but only until their first terms of protection expire; the statutory beneficiaries will take the renewal terms. This aspect of renewal term vesting has caused some commentators to describe the renewal rules as forced inheritance rules. If the author survives long enough to have the renewal term vest in her, then her will or the laws of intestate succession will determine who owns any remaining years of copyright protection.

5. *Stewart* does not address the issue of when the right to the renewal term vests. Because the renewal certificate could be filed at any point during the final year of the first term of protection, an issue arose as to the timing of the vesting of the renewal term, with three possible options: the beginning of the final year of protection, the date of the filing of the renewal certificate, or the first day of the renewal term. *Compare Marascalco v. Fantasy, Inc.*, 953 F.2d 469 (9th Cir. 1991) (vesting occurred upon commencement of the renewal term), with *Frederick Music Co. v. Sickler*, 708 F. Supp. 587 (S.D.N.Y. 1989) (vesting occurred upon registration of the renewal certificate). If an author died during the final year of the first term, the timing of the vesting of the renewal right had important implications.

Congress addressed this previously complicated question in the CRA of 1992, which abolished the renewal certificate requirement. As described earlier in this chapter, works first covered by federal copyright protection in or after 1964 obtained protection for the full 95 years without the requirement of filing a renewal certificate. However, Congress encouraged renewal certificates to be filed by providing certain benefits in exchange for filing. One of those benefits is certainty of vesting. If a renewal certificate is timely filed in the final year of the first term, the renewal term interest vests in the appropriate person(s) measured as of the date of the filing of the renewal certificate. If the renewal certificate is not filed, then the renewal vests in the appropriate person(s) measured as of the first day of the renewal term. *See* 17 U.S.C. §304(a)(2).

Another incentive to file the renewal relates to the ability to bring the kind of infringement claim like the one at issue in *Stewart v. Abend*. Section 304(a)(4)(A) provides that if the renewal application is not filed, then a derivative work prepared under authority of a grant or license from the copyright owner may continue to be used "under the terms of the grant." This effectively changes the result of *Stewart v. Abend* in situations where the renewal is not filed. The section provides that while new derivative works may not be prepared during the renewal term, the copyright owner cannot stop the exploitation of authorized derivative works that were created prior to end of the first term. Requiring that the exploitation of the derivative work be "under the terms of the grant" may mean that royalties will need to be paid, if the transfer or license requires such payments.

6. *Stewart* addressed the renewal rights issue in the context of an assignment that permitted the assignee to make a derivative work, namely a movie based on the book. The Court's conclusion that the renewal term properly vested in the estate and that Abend had the right to sue for infringement seemingly would have put him in a very good bargaining position to negotiate a royalty agreement that would allow the defendants to keep distributing their derivative work. Without such an arrangement, Abend could seek to enjoin any subsequent distribution of the film. In fact, Abend had sought an injunction barring the ongoing distribution and performance of *Rear Window*. The Ninth Circuit had ruled that the case was not an appropriate case for an injunction, but rather that royalties, fixed by the district court, should be awarded for the continued use of the derivative work. The Supreme Court did not grant certiorari on the remedy issue. Does the remedy prescribed by the Ninth Circuit amount to a forced license? Is this appropriate? We discuss the remedies available to a copyright owner in Chapter 11.

2. Termination of Transfers

As the Court in *Stewart* describes, the 1976 Act includes provisions for terminating transfers of copyright interests. Specifically, the Act speaks of terminating a "grant of a transfer or license of a copyright." In this section we will use the traditional phrase "termination of transfers" to encompass terminations of both transfers and licenses. The Act contains two different provisions concerning terminations of transfers: (1) transfers made prior to January 1, 1978, that convey an interest in the renewal term, and (2) transfers made after January 1, 1978. These two types of termination provisions are motivated by different policy concerns. The latter termination provisions, codified in §203, have a policy rationale similar to that for the renewal term: Congress wanted to provide authors with a second opportunity to obtain remuneration for their creative endeavors. The former set of termination provisions relating to transfers of interests in the renewal term, codified in §304(c)-(d), reflect a different policy decision concerning who should benefit from the lengthening of the renewal term by 19 years under the 1976 Act and by 20 additional years under the CTEA. Should these added years of protection benefit creators and their families, or assignees of the renewal term? The termination provisions favor creators and their families, if they are interested in recapturing the value of the copyright by following the procedure set forth in the Act for terminating transfers.

The termination provisions contain complex rules about what kinds of transfers may be terminated and the procedures and timing that must be followed to effect a termination. Keeping the underlying policy rationales in mind assists in understanding these rules. Note also that, while courts had enforced assignments of contingent interests in renewal terms executed by authors, spouses, and even children, Congress expressly prohibited any assignment or waiver of termination rights. Under both sections, the statute provides that termination "may be effected notwithstanding any agreement to the contrary, including an agreement to make a will or to make any future grant." 17 U.S.C. §§203(a)(5), 304(c)(5). Therefore, an author may exercise the right to terminate even when she has agreed by contract not to do so.

a. Terminations of Transfers Made after January 1, 1978 — Section 203

Types of Transfers that Can Be Terminated. The provisions that allow for the termination of transfers executed on or after January 1, 1978, are meant to allow an author, who may have been in a poor bargaining position initially, an opportunity to recapture the value of her work. Thus, these termination provisions do not apply to works made for hire, and they only apply to transfers made by the author, not any subsequent transfer of copyright interests by those in the chain of title. Both exclusive and nonexclusive licenses, as well as outright transfers of copyright interest, can be terminated. Transfers by will are not subject to termination.

Who May Exercise the Termination Right. In the case of a grant executed by one author, termination may be exercised by the author, or if the author is dead, by those who own at least 51 percent of the author's termination interest. In the case of grants executed by more than one author, a majority of the authors must act together to terminate the grant, with each author's interest being exercised as a unit. If the author is dead, his or her termination interest is owned first by the widow or widower. If in addition to the widow or widower there are surviving children or grandchildren, then the widow or widower owns one half of the termination interest and the children and grandchildren divide the other half on a *per stirpes*[1] basis. If only children or grandchildren remain, with no widow or widower surviving, then the children or grandchildren divide the termination interest based on the number of children represented on a *per stirpes* basis. The share of a deceased child represented by grandchildren (the children of that deceased child) may only be exercised by the action of the majority of those grandchildren. In the event that there is no widow, widower, children, or grandchildren, the author's executor, administrator, personal representative, or trustee owns the author's entire termination interest.

When Termination May Be Effected. The termination may be effected at any time during a five-year window, which begins at the end of 35 years from the date of execution of the grant. For example, a grant executed on February 1, 2000, could be terminated anytime between February 1, 2035, and January 31, 2040. The only exception to this rule is where the grant covers the right of publication of the work, in which case the five-year window begins

---

1. *Per stirpes* denotes a method of dividing interests in an estate. Under this method, a class or group of distributees takes the share to which their deceased ancestor would have been entitled. For example, if author *A* had two children, *B* and *C*, now deceased, and *B* had two children and *C* had four children, the termination interest will not be divided equally among the six grandchildren. Instead, two will exercise their parent *B*'s one-half interest, and four will exercise their parent *C*'s one-half interest. The opposite of a *per stirpes* distribution is a *per capita* distribution.

35 years from the date of publication or 40 years from the date of execution, whichever is earlier.

How Termination Is Effected. Notice of termination must be given by serving advance notice on the grantee or the grantee's successor in title. The notice must state the effective date of termination (which must fall within the five-year window described above) and must be served not less than two or more than ten years prior to that effective date. The statute further provides that a copy of the notice shall be recorded with the Copyright Office before the effective date of termination as a condition to its taking effect.

The Effect of Termination. Upon the effective date of a properly exercised termination, all rights that were covered by the grant revert to the author or the person(s) owning termination interests. Those ownership rights vest as of the date the notice of termination was served and vest in the same proportionate shares as the termination right was divided (i.e., on a *per stirpes* basis). Further grants of the terminated rights, or agreements to make a further grant, are only valid if they are made after the effective date of termination. However, further valid grants to the grantees whose rights are being terminated may be made after notice of termination has been served.

The Act does provide that derivative works prepared under authority of the grant before its termination may continue to be utilized after the termination, but that use remains subject to the terms of the grant. For example, if the grant required annual royalty payments based on gross sales of the derivative work, termination would not extinguish the obligation to make those royalty payments. This exception for derivative works applies only to derivative works prepared prior to the termination date. It does not extend to permit preparation of other derivative works after such termination date.

b. Terminations of Transfers Made Before January 1, 1978 — Sections 304(c) & (d)

Types of Transfers That Can Be Terminated. For transfers made before January 1, 1978, only those transfers that convey any interest in the renewal term can be terminated. Thus, a transfer made in 1975 of "all right title and interest during the initial term of copyright" is not terminable. As with the termination provision under §203, the termination provisions of §304 apply to exclusive and nonexclusive licenses as well as outright transfers. Because these termination provisions focus on allowing recapture of the extended renewal term by the statutorily designated beneficiaries of the original renewal term, transfers that can be terminated include not only those made by the author but those made by a widow, widower, children, executor, or next of kin. Also, given the underlying policy reasons for these termination provisions, transfers concerning works made for hire are not terminable, nor are transfers made by will.

Who May Exercise the Termination Right. When the transfer sought to be terminated is a grant by someone other than the author, termination can only be exercised by the surviving person or persons that executed that grant. Thus, a transfer executed by a widow who dies before timely notice of termination can be sent is no longer terminable. Termination of transfer by the author, on the other hand, can be exercised by the author, or, if the author is deceased, by a majority of those owning termination interests. The ownership of termination interests and the majority requirements under the §304 termination provisions are identical to those under the §203 termination provision.

When Termination May Be Effected. The termination right granted under §304(c) concerns the additional 19 years added to the renewal term by the 1976 Act. Termination can be effected during a five-year window that begins 56 years from the date copyright protection was originally secured (typically upon publication with proper notice). The termination provisions under §304(d) concern the additional 20 years provided by the CTEA. Termination can be effected during the five-year window that begins at the end of 75 years from the date copyright was originally secured. Note, however, that the provisions of §304(d) can be used only if the termination right under §304(c) expired prior to the effective date of the CTEA (which was October 27, 1998), and if the termination right provided in §304(c) had not previously been exercised.

How the Termination Is Effected. Similar to terminations under §203, notice of termination must be given by serving advance notice on the grantee or the grantee's successor in title. The notice must state the effective date of termination (which must fall within the five-year windows described above) and must be served not less than two or more than ten years before that effective date. As with terminations under §203, a copy of the notice must be recorded with the Copyright Office before the effective date of termination as a condition to its taking effect.

The Effect of Termination. The effect of termination under §304(c) or (d) is similar to the effect of termination under §203, including the requirements for valid subsequent grants and for ongoing use of derivative works prepared before termination.

NOTES AND QUESTIONS

1. Are authors better off under the 1976 Act's termination of transfer provisions than under the 1909 Act's dual term scheme? Recall that the Court's interpretation of the renewal term rules permitted authors, and even the statutory heirs, to assign their contingent interests in the renewal term at any time. The termination of transfer provisions, on the other hand, make the right to terminate a transfer inalienable. Is this a sensible policy?

2. Test your understanding of the termination provisions by answering the following hypotheticals. The answers are in note 3 *infra*.

    a. Arthur created a work in 1950 and first published it with proper copyright notice on July 10, 1955. In 1954, Arthur assigned "all right title and interest" to the copyright in the work, including "any and all rights in the renewal term," to Bob. Arthur died on December 1, 1982, leaving his widow, Carol. Arthur's will bequeathed all his copyrights to Denise, his secretary. Assume a renewal registration was properly filed. Who owns copyright in the work today? Can any rights be terminated by anyone? By whom and when?

    b. Same facts as in a., except Arthur lived until December 1, 1985. Who owns copyright in the work today? Can any rights be terminated by anyone? By whom and when?

    c. Flora comes to your office to talk to you about an upcoming merger of her company. Before the meeting starts, Flora tells you that she wrote and recorded a song back in 1975 that went platinum in 1990 but she received only $2,000 because she had assigned the copyright to a company, Giga, Inc., in 1979. She tells you that this song recently has been included in a blockbuster hit movie and is on the soundtrack that is a hot-selling album. She is quite proud of her big hit and that's why she told you the story. Is there anything to which you should alert her?

   d. Henry created a play, titled *Georgia's Garden*, in 2001. Henry died in 2002, leaving
       two sons, Leo and Mike. His will leaves all his literary property including all his copy-
       rights to his long-time companion, Orin. Leo and Mike would like to regain control
       over the play; can they?

   3. Below are the answers to the problems in note 2. Be sure that you tried your best to
answer them before checking!

   a. Arthur's assignment to Bob was adequate to assign the renewal term if Arthur lived
       long enough for the renewal term to vest in him. Under the 1909 Act, copyright
       protection began on the day of publication with notice, July 10, 1955, so the first
       term expired 28 years later, $7/10/1955 + 28 = 12/31/1983$. (The first term ended
       on December 31 because the 1976 Act changed the computation of all terms to the
       end of the calendar year.) Assuming the renewal registration was properly filed, the
       renewal term vested on the next day, January 1, 1984. Arthur did not live long
       enough, so the assignment to Bob was only an assignment of a contingent interest
       that never vested. Under §304, the renewal term vested in Arthur's widow, who now
       owns the copyright in the work. The will has no effect because a will cannot override
       the forced inheritance rules of the Copyright Act. There is no transfer agreement to be
       terminated.
   b. In this case, Arthur lived long enough for the renewal term to vest in him; therefore,
       the earlier assignment transferred the vested interest to Bob, who owns the copyright
       today. It is irrelevant what Arthur's will says, because Arthur had already assigned his
       rights in the renewal term to Bob. (Note: If the renewal had not been assigned to
       Bob, then the will would have been effective to transfer the remaining years of
       copyright protection to Denise.) However, the assignment to Bob, because it was
       (1) before January 1, 1978, and (2) an assignment of a renewal interest, may be
       subject to a §304 termination. Carol, Arthur's widow, may retake the final 39 years
       of the copyright term, the years added onto the basic 56 years from the 1909 Act. $7/10/1955 + 56 = 7/10/2011$ would mark the beginning of the five-year window,
       with 7/9/2016 marking the end of that window. Notice of termination could be
       served on Bob as early as July 10, 2001 (ten years before the earliest termination date
       possible) or as late as July 9, 2014 (two years prior to the latest termination date).
       Note that §304 authorizes termination starting 56 years from the date that copyright
       was first secured. Thus, unlike duration, which runs to the end of the calendar year,
       termination may occur during the calendar year once the 56th year date is completed.
   c. You should alert Flora to her termination possibilities. Because the transfer was exe-
       cuted after January 1, 1978, §203 is the termination provision that applies. This is true
       even though the work was created and probably published before 1978. Section
       203 would allow Flora to terminate the transfer to Giga, Inc. 35 years after the transfer
       date. The opening of the five-year window is $1979 + 35 = 2014$ with 2019 being the
       end of the five-year window. Flora could send notice of termination as early as 2004
       and as late as 2017. Once notice was sent, Flora could renegotiate her agreement with
       Giga, Inc., but would have to wait until after the termination date to enter into an
       agreement with any other company. As under §304, §203 termination periods are also
       computed from the date of the grant and not the end of the calendar year. Therefore,
       to know the exact beginning and end of the termination window, you would need the
       exact date of the assignment to Giga.
   d. Leo and Mike cannot regain control because transfers by will cannot be terminated.

Note on "Agreements to the Contrary"

Recall that the renewal term provided by the 1909 Act was meant to provide authors with an opportunity to renegotiate assignments made before the full value of a work was known. However, the ability to transfer the contingent interest in the renewal term meant that such transfers became standard in industry contracts and significantly undermined the purpose of the renewal term as a second bite at the apple. With the termination provisions, Congress provided a stronger right for authors and their statutory heirs. Both §203 and §304 provide that "termination of the grant may be effected notwithstanding any agreement to the contrary, including any agreement to make a will or to make any future grant." 17 U.S.C. §§203(a)(5), 304(c)(5), 304(d)(1). The Supreme Court has characterized the termination right as inalienable. *Stewart v. Abend*, 495 U.S. 207, 230 (1990).

Just what constitutes an "agreement to the contrary"? It seems clear that an agreement that the author will not seek to exercise her termination rights would qualify. What if the parties to an oral agreement dispute copyright ownership many years later and, in settling that dispute, agree that the work was created as a "work made for hire"? Recall that works made for hire are not subject to termination rights. Should the settlement agreement characterizing the work as a work made for hire be considered "an agreement to the contrary"? The Second Circuit has concluded that "an agreement made subsequent to a work's creation that declares that it is a work created for hire" is an agreement to the contrary and, therefore, does not bar a subsequent lawsuit seeking to terminate the oral assignment of copyright. *Marvel Characters Inc. v. Simon*, 310 F.3d 280 (2d Cir. 2002). The court determined that:

> Any other construction of §304(c) would thwart the clear legislative purpose and intent of the statute. If an agreement between an author and publisher that a work was created for hire were outside the purview of §304(c)(5), the termination provision would be rendered a nullity; litigation-savvy publishers would be able to utilize their superior bargaining position to compel authors to agree that a work was created for hire in order to get their works published.

Id. at 290-91.

Questions about what constitutes an "agreement to the contrary" also arise when the parties to a transfer of copyright renegotiate their agreement without using the formal statutory process for terminating the initial transfer. If the purpose of the statute is to permit authors and their heirs an opportunity to renegotiate the terms once the full value of the work is known, would it be appropriate to characterize that newly renegotiated agreement as "an agreement to the contrary" because it effectively cuts off the statutory termination right? Should it matter how many years had passed since the time of the first agreement or whether the terms of the new agreement are more favorable to the author?

In *Milne ex rel. Coyne v. Stephen Slesinger, Inc.*, 430 F.3d 1036 (9th Cir. 2005), *cert. denied*, 548 U.S. 904 (2006), the granddaughter and heir to the copyrights of A.A. Milne relating to the character Winnie the Pooh sought to terminate an agreement made by Milne in 1930. In 1983, however, the granddaughter's father (Christopher Robin Milne) had entered into a new agreement with the assignee that expressly acknowledged the potential right to terminate the 1930 agreement and sought to replace that agreement with the new one. The Ninth Circuit held that the 1930 agreement had been contractually terminated by the 1983 agreement. The court rejected the argument that the 1983 agreement was "an agreement to the contrary." Citing the Act's legislative history, it reasoned that Congress "did not intend for the statute to 'prevent the parties to a transfer or license from voluntarily agreeing at any time to terminate an existing grant and negotiating a new one.'" *Id*. at 1045 (quoting H.R.

Rep. No. 94-1476, 94th Cong., 2d Sess. 127 (1976), *reprinted in* 1976 U.S.C.C.A.N. 5659, 5743). The court noted that the terms of the 1983 agreement were far more favorable to the heirs and that the granddaughter had benefited from this new agreement.

The Second Circuit reached a similar conclusion in *Penguin Group v. Steinbeck*, 537 F.3d 193 (2d Cir. 2008), concerning a 1994 agreement in which John Steinbeck's third wife and widow terminated a 1938 agreement and re-granted rights to the publisher. In a lawsuit brought by Steinbeck's descendants from a prior marriage seeking to terminate the 1938 agreement and recapture the copyrights, the court determined that the 1994 agreement was not an "agreement to the contrary" but was, instead, a valid contractual termination that ended the 1938 agreement. The 1994 agreement was not only more favorable to the widow, but it also obligated the publisher to publish some of her writings. As with the 1938 agreement, the 1994 agreement did not provide any royalties to the descendants.

The statute provides that a further grant "of any right covered by a terminated grant is valid only if it is made after the effective date of the termination." 17 U.S.C. §§203(b)(4), 304(c)(6)(D), 304(d)(1). An exception is made for a further grant to the original grantee or the original grantee's successor in interest, so long as such further grant is made "after the notice of termination has been served." *Id.* §§203(b)(4), 304(c)(6)(D), 304(d)(1). Should these statutory provisions affect interpretation of agreements that are voluntarily renegotiated outside the formalities of the termination process? The *Steinbeck* court relied on the fact that the authors' heirs renegotiated the agreements "while wielding the threat of termination," even though the statutory formalities for vesting the termination rights through service of notice were not completed prior to the execution of the renegotiated agreement. *Steinbeck*, 537 F.3d at 202; *see also Milne*, 430 F.3d at 1045 (noting that while Christopher Robin Milne "presumably could have served a termination notice, he elected instead to use his leverage to obtain a better deal").

4

Protected Works and Boundary Problems

This chapter considers copyrightability from a different perspective, by examining the increasing breadth of subject matter to which copyright protection applies, and by exploring the different tests that courts have developed to assess the presence of original expression in different kinds of works. The topics covered in this chapter also raise questions about the proper scope of the copyright system.

The Copyright Act defines broad categories of content that are copyrightable regardless of the form or medium in which the work is expressed:

§102. Subject matter of copyright: In general

(a) Copyright protection subsists, in accordance with this title, in original works of authorship fixed in any tangible medium of expression, now known or later developed, from which they can be perceived, reproduced, or otherwise communicated, either directly or with the aid of a machine or device. Works of authorship include the following categories:

(1) literary works;
(2) musical works, including any accompanying words;
(3) dramatic works, including any accompanying music;
(4) pantomimes and choreographic works;
(5) pictorial, graphic, and sculptural works;
(6) motion pictures and other audiovisual works;
(7) sound recordings; and
(8) architectural works.

The definitions of these categories, set forth in §101, illustrate some of the kinds of works that fall within each category. A "literary work" can be a book or a poem, but also any other kind of work that is "expressed in words, numbers, or other verbal or numerical symbols or indicia," such as a computer program or a database. (Limits on the copyrightability of computer programs and databases are explored in Sections 4.B and 4.E, *infra*.) The statutory definition of "literary works," however, expressly excludes "audiovisual works," which are listed separately in §102(a)(6).

"Audiovisual works" include motion pictures, which §101 defines as "a series of related images," with or without accompanying sounds, that "when shown in succession, impart an impression of motion." This definition encompasses both live-action footage and works of animation. Audiovisual works also include any other works consisting of a series of related images, with or without accompanying sounds, that are intended to be shown via a machine or device. Such works would include, for example, a slide or Power-Point presentation made up entirely of text and numbers, even though the same content in print format would be considered a literary work. They also would include a slide or PowerPoint presentation made up entirely of charts and diagrams, even though the same content in print format would be considered a pictorial or graphic work. *See* H.R. Rep. No. 94-1476, 94th Cong., 2d Sess. 56 (1976), *reprinted in* 1976 U.S.C.C.A.N. 5659, 5669.

Other kinds of works are classified as "pictorial, graphic, and sculptural works." This category includes maps and diagrams as well as drawings, paintings, and photographs. It also includes three-dimensional objects, ranging from classically inspired statuary to globes that depict the Earth. Finally, this category includes "the design of a useful article," such as a clock or a lamp, but only in some circumstances. We explore these circumstances in Section 4.A, *infra*.

Although architectural works might be considered "sculptural" in nature, the legislative history of §102 indicates that Congress did not intend to extend copyright protection to buildings, but only to "[p]urely nonfunctional or monumental structures" and "artistic sculpture or decorative ornamentation or embellishment added to a structure." H.R. Rep. No. 94-1476 at 55, *reprinted in* 1976 U.S.C.C.A.N. at 5668. Thus, for example, if both the Statue of Liberty and the Empire State Building had been constructed after January 1, 1978, copyright protection might extend to the Statue of Liberty as a monumental work, but not to the Empire State Building because of its functionality. In addition, the House Report notes that architectural *plans* would be considered protectible drawings. The addition of "architectural works" to §102(a) came later, in 1990. *See* Architectural Works Copyright Protection Act of 1990, Pub. L. 101-650, 104 Stat. 5133. We discuss architectural works in Section 4.C, *infra*.

"Sound recordings" are works consisting of the fixation of a series of sounds. Yo-Yo Ma performing Bach's "Suites for Unaccompanied Cello," Aretha Franklin singing "Respect," Patrick Stewart reading "A Christmas Carol," and a "sound collage" consisting of animal noises recorded at the zoo all qualify as sound recordings. Motion picture soundtracks, however, do not; according to §101, soundtracks are protected as part of the motion picture that they accompany.

Several of the categories—musical works, dramatic works, pantomimes, and choreographic works—are not defined at all in §101. The legislative history of §102 states that these categories "have fairly settled meanings." H.R. Rep. No. 94-1476 at 53, *reprinted in* 1976 U.S.C.C.A.N. at 5666-67. Do you agree? How would you classify a rap composition?

As we described in Chapter 1.B.3, the categories listed in §102(a) were intended to withstand changes in form or medium. However, the increasing volume and variety of content available in digital form poses novel problems for the classification scheme devised by Congress in 1976. Ultimately, every digital work including, for example, .doc, .mp3, .gif, and .jpg files, consists of a (very long) string of binary coded symbols. Is every such work therefore a "literary work"? At the same time, however, every literary work that requires more than one screen to display—e.g., a long article or a novel—is analogous to the PowerPoint presentation described above; it is a series of related images that is intended to be shown via a machine or device. Are all such works therefore "audiovisual works"?

The problem of determining in which category a work belongs is significant only if the categorization makes any difference. Indeed, the categorizations do matter. Congress and the courts have developed different approaches to identifying copyrightable and uncopyrightable content within different subject matter categories. As you study the material in this chapter, consider whether these differences are warranted, and whether they affect the ultimate determination of the scope of copyright protection afforded to different kinds of works. As discussed in Chapter 5, the Copyright Act grants some rights only for certain categories of works, and also grants some exemptions that are category specific. Thus, determining in which category a work falls is not merely an academic exercise.

Finally, it is important to note that the list of categories of protectible works in §102 is introduced with the word "include," defined by the Copyright Act to be "illustrative and not limitative." *See* §101 (defining "including"). If the categories do, in fact, matter, what happens when a work is determined to be protectible but not within any of the listed categories of works?

Each section of this chapter is designed to explore some of the more difficult determinations relating to the copyrightability of certain categories of works. As you read this chapter, consider also two more basic questions. First, is the incentive of copyright really needed to produce more of a given type of work? For example, product labels, advertisements, and portrait photographs all can be protected under copyright, yet is copyright protection necessary to encourage the creation of these types of works? Second, is copyright the proper protection for the type of work at issue? For example, assuming that some form of legal protection is needed for, say, the design of a lamp or the innovations embodied in a computer program, should that legal protection be copyright? In this chapter you will learn more about the emergence of "hybrid" models of intellectual property protection both in the U.S. and abroad, which resemble copyright protection in some respects. As you read, consider whether the various kinds of subject matter discussed are better protected under copyright law, a regime modeled after copyright law, or a different sort of regime altogether.

A. USEFUL ARTICLES WITH PICTORIAL, GRAPHIC, OR SCULPTURAL ASPECTS

As the introduction to this chapter made clear, many types of works are the subject of copyright. For example, three-dimensional works of art that are original and fixed are copyrightable. Does eligibility for copyright change when the work is incorporated into a product with a utilitarian function? For example, is a Mickey Mouse telephone copyrightable? Under modern copyright law, the answer depends on the extent to which a product's expressive aspects are separable from its useful ones. This section traces the evolution of the separability requirement.

1. "Kitsch" or "Progress"?

The Supreme Court addressed the question of copyright protection for useful articles with expressive aspects in the following case, decided before the enactment of the 1976 Act.

Mazer v. Stein
347 U.S. 201 (1954)

REED, J.: . . . Respondents are partners in the manufacture and sale of electric lamps. One of the respondents created original works of sculpture in the form of human figures by traditional clay-model technique. From this model, a production mold for casting copies was made. The resulting statuettes, without any lamp components added, were submitted by the respondents to the Copyright Office for registration as "works of art" or reproductions thereof under §5(g) or §5(h) of the copyright law, and certificates of registration issued. Sales (publication in accordance with the statute) as fully equipped lamps preceded the applications for copyright registration of the statuettes. Thereafter, the statuettes were sold in quantity throughout the country both as lamp bases and as statuettes. The sales in lamp form accounted for all but an insignificant portion of respondents' sales. . . .

[Petitioners Mazer, et al., copied the statuettes and sold their own lamps embodying the copies. They contended that the statuettes, when "intended primarily to [be] use[d] . . . in the form of lamp bases to be made and sold in quantity," were not proper subject matter of copyright. Respondents brought a copyright infringement lawsuit.] The District Court dismissed the complaint. The Court of Appeals reversed and held the copyrights valid. It said: "A subsequent utilization of a work of art in an article of manufacture in no way affects the right of the copyright owner to be protected against infringement of the work of art itself." 204 F.2d at page 477.

. . . The case requires an answer, not as to a manufacturer's right to register a lamp base but as to an artist's right to copyright a work of art intended to be reproduced for lamp bases. . . . Petitioners question the validity of a copyright of a work of art for "mass" production. "Reproduction of a work of art" does not mean to them unlimited reproduction. Their position is that a copyright does not cover industrial reproduction of the protected article. . . .

[The Court reviewed the history of legislation defining categories of copyrightable subject matter, beginning with the Act of 1790 and ending with the 1909 Copyright Act. We summarize this history at page 26 *supra*.] . . . In 1909 Congress again enlarged the scope of the copyright statute. . . . Significant for our purposes was the deletion of the fine-arts clause of the 1870 Act. Verbal distinctions between purely aesthetic articles and useful works of art ended insofar as the statutory copyright language is concerned. . . .

The successive acts, the legislative history of the 1909 Act and the practice of the Copyright Office unite to show that "works of art" and "reproductions of works of art" are terms that were intended by Congress to include the authority to copyright these statuettes. Individual perception of the beautiful is too varied a power to permit a narrow or rigid concept of art. . . .

The economic philosophy behind the clause empowering Congress to grant patents and copyrights is the conviction that encouragement of individual effort by personal gain is the best way to advance public welfare through the talents of authors and inventors in "Science and useful Arts." Sacrificial days devoted to such creative activities deserve rewards commensurate with the services rendered.

Affirmed.

Lamp Base

Opinion of DOUGLAS, J., in which BLACK, J., concurs: . . . The Copyright Office has supplied us with a long list of such articles which have been copyrighted — statuettes, book ends, clocks, lamps, door knockers, candlesticks, inkstands, chandeliers, piggy banks, sundials, salt and pepper shakers, fish bowls, casseroles, and ash trays. Perhaps these are all "writings" in the constitutional sense. But to me, at least, they are not obviously so. It is time that we came to the problem full face. I would accordingly put the case down for reargument.

NOTES AND QUESTIONS

1. Are door knockers, fish bowls, and the other things that Justice Douglas lists "art" (or "Science")? Are they "Writings" or "Discoveries"? Is protection of these items the inevitable consequence of the nondiscrimination principle articulated by Justice Holmes in *Bleistein, supra* pages 64-65?

2. In the face of obvious congressional determination to broaden the scope of copyright, would it have been appropriate for the Court to order briefing and reargument on whether it is

within the scope of congressional power to protect the lamps in *Mazer* and the articles listed in the *Mazer* concurrence? Does protection advance the goals of copyright law discussed in Chapter 1, *supra*? Recall *Eldred v. Ashcroft, supra* Chapter 3. What standard does the Court use there in defining the scope of congressional power, and what implications does it have for the constitutional issues raised by *Mazer*?

2. Defining Useful Articles and Determining Separability

Congress sought to codify *Mazer*'s holding in the 1976 Act's definitions. The definition of "pictorial, graphic, and sculptural works" provided in §101 states, in part:

> Such works shall include works of artistic craftsmanship insofar as their form but not their mechanical or utilitarian aspects are concerned; the design of a useful article, as defined in this section, shall be considered a pictorial, graphic, or sculptural work only if, and only to the extent that, such design incorporates pictorial, graphic, or sculptural features that can be identified separately from, and are capable of existing independently of, the utilitarian aspects of the article.

Section 101 defines a "useful article" as "an article having an intrinsic utilitarian function that is not merely to portray the appearance of the article or to convey information."

Congress subjected pictorial, graphic, and sculptural elements of useful articles to an "extra" test of copyrightability beyond originality and fixation: that of separability. Why? What is the separability test intended to do? In an attempt to provide some guidance on these questions, the House Report noted:

> The Committee has added language to the definition of "pictorial, graphic, and sculptural works" in an effort to make clearer the distinction between works of applied art protectible under the bill and industrial designs not subject to copyright protection. . . .
>
> In adopting this amendatory language, the Committee is seeking to draw as clear a line as possible between copyrightable works of applied art and uncopyrighted works of industrial design. A two-dimensional painting, drawing, or graphic work is still capable of being identified as such when it is printed on or applied to utilitarian articles such as textile fabrics, wallpaper, containers, and the like. The same is true when a statue or carving is used to embellish an industrial product or, as in the *Mazer* case, is incorporated into a product without losing its ability to exist independently as a work of art. On the other hand, although the shape of an industrial product may be aesthetically satisfying and valuable, the Committee's intention is not to offer it copyright protection under the bill. Unless the shape of an automobile, airplane, ladies' dress, food processor, television set, or any other industrial product contains some element that, physically or conceptually, can be identified as separable from the utilitarian aspects of that article, the design would not be copyrighted under the bill. The test of separability and independence from "the utilitarian aspects of the article" does not depend upon the nature of the design — that is, even if the appearance of an article is determined by esthetic (as opposed to functional) considerations, only elements, if any, which can be dentified separately from the useful article as such are copyrightable. And, even if the three-dimensional design contains some such element (for example, a carving on the back of a chair or a floral relief design on silver flatware), copyright protection would extend only to that element, and would not cover the over-all configuration of the utilitarian article as such.

H.R. Rep. No. 94-1476, 94th Cong., 2d Sess. 54-55 (1976), *reprinted in* 1976 U.S.C.C.A.N. 5659, 5667-68.

How well do the statutory definitions and the accompanying legislative history delineate the dividing line between copyrightable "applied art" and uncopyrightable "industrial design"? Think first about how the 1976 Act's approach implements the *Mazer* holding. The lamps fit the definition of "useful article" because they have an "intrinsic utilitarian function"—providing light. The next question, then, is whether the lamps' design incorporated pictorial, graphic, or sculptural features that could be separately identified. One could separately identify the Balinese dancer forming the lamps' bases; indeed, the lamps and bases were physically separated when the bases were submitted for registration. *Mazer*, then, is the paradigmatic case of the *physical separability* to which the House Report refers.

Other cases, however, raise difficult line-drawing questions. Think of the variety of other decorative techniques that you have seen employed in lamps, clocks, or the other items listed in Justice Douglas' opinion in *Mazer*. Many of these techniques are nonrepresentational, and many incorporate design elements into the overall configuration of the article. In such cases, it can be quite difficult to identify the precise location of the line between form and function, and thus to determine whether separable, copyrightable features exist. These cases require courts to determine what is meant by the other kind of separability mentioned in the House Report: *conceptual separability*. Read the following cases and consider how the courts resolve the separability questions raised.

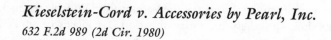

Kieselstein-Cord v. Accessories by Pearl, Inc.
632 F.2d 989 (2d Cir. 1980)

OAKES, J.: . . . Appellant Barry Kieselstein-Cord designs, manufactures exclusively by hand-craftsmanship, and sells fashion accessories. To produce the two [belt] buckles in issue here, the "Winchester" and the "Vaquero," he worked from original renderings which he had conceived and sketched. He then carved by hand a waxen prototype of each of the works from which molds were made for casting the objects in gold and silver. Difficult to describe, the buckles are solid sculptured designs. . . .

The Vaquero buckle, created in 1978, was part of a series of works that the designer testified was inspired by a book on design of the art nouveau school and the subsequent viewing of related architecture on a trip to Spain. The buckle was registered with the Copyright Office . . . as "jewelry," although the appellant's contribution was listed on the certificate as "original sculpture and design." Explaining why he named the earlier buckle design "Winchester," the designer said that he saw "in [his] mind's eye a correlation between the art nouveau period and the butt of an antique Winchester rifle" and then "pulled these elements together graphically." The registration, which is recorded on a form used for works of art, or models or designs for works of art, specifically describes the nature of the work as "sculpture."

The Winchester buckle in particular has had great success in the marketplace. . . . A shortened version of the belt with the small Winchester buckle is sometimes worn around the neck or elsewhere on the body rather than around the waist. Sales of both buckles were made primarily in high fashion stores and jewelry stores, bringing recognition to appellant as a "designer." The recognition included a 1979 Coty American Fashion Critics' Award for his work in jewelry design as well as election in 1978 to the Council of Fashion Designers of America. Both the Winchester and the Vaquero buckles, donated by appellant after this lawsuit was commenced, have been accepted by the Metropolitan Museum of Art for its permanent collection. . . .

[The appellee made and sold exact, but far cheaper, copies of the buckles. Appellee admitted to the copying, but argued that the buckles were not copyrightable because they had no separately identifiable pictorial, graphic, or sculptural features. The district court agreed with this argument and granted the appellee summary judgement. Kieselstein-Cord appealed.]

Discussion . . .

We are left nevertheless with the problem of determining when a pictorial, graphic, or sculptural feature "can be identified separately from, and [is] capable of existing independently of, the utilitarian aspects of the article," 17 U.S.C. §101. This problem is particularly difficult because, according to the legislative history explored by the court below, such separability may occur either "physically or conceptually," *House Report* at 55. . . . Examples of conceptual separateness as an artistic notion may be found in many museums today and even in the great outdoors. Professor Nimmer cites Christo's "Running Fence" as an example of today's "conceptual art." . . .

We see in appellant's belt buckles conceptually separable sculptural elements, as apparently have the buckles' wearers who have used them as ornamentation for parts of the body other than the waist. The primary ornamental aspect of the Vaquero and Winchester buckles is conceptually separable from their subsidiary utilitarian function. . . . Pieces of applied art, these buckles may be considered jewelry, the form of which is subject to copyright protection. . . .

Appellant's designs are not, as the appellee suggests in an affidavit, mere variations of "the well-known western buckle." As both the expert witnesses for appellant testified and the Copyright Office's action implied, the buckles rise to the level of creative art. Indeed, body ornamentation has been an art form since the earliest days, as anyone who has seen the Tutankhamen or Scythian gold exhibits at the Metropolitan Museum will readily attest. The basic requirements of originality and creativity, which the two buckles satisfy and which all works of art must meet to be copyrighted, would take the vast majority of belt buckles wholly out of copyrightability. . . .

WEINSTEIN, J., dissenting: . . . The works sued on are, while admirable aesthetically pleasing examples of modern design, indubitably belt buckles and nothing else; their innovations of form are inseparable from the important function they serve—helping to keep the tops of trousers at waist level.

The conclusion that affirmance [of the district court] is required is reached reluctantly. The result does deny protection to designers who use modern three-dimensional abstract works artfully incorporated into a functional object as an inseparable aspect of the article while granting it to those who attach their independent representational art, or even their trite gimmickry, to a useful object for purposes of enhancement. Moreover, this result enables the commercial pirates of the marketplace to appropriate for their own profit, without any cost to themselves, the works of talented designers who enrich our lives with their intuition and skill. The crass are rewarded, the artist who creates beauty is not. All of us are offended by the flagrant copying of another's work. This is regrettable, but it is not for this court to twist the law in order to achieve a result Congress has denied. . . .

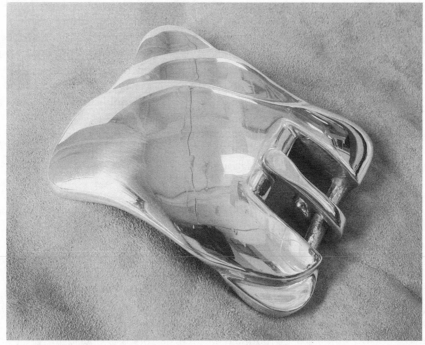

Vaquero Buckle

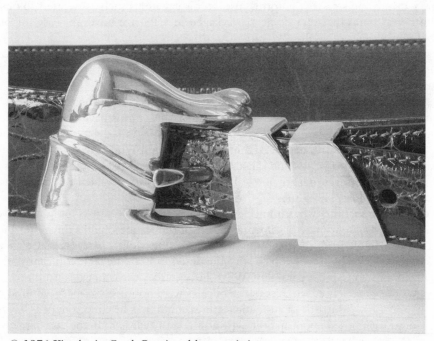

Winchester Buckle

[Judge Weinstein quoted the portion of the legislative history excerpted *supra* pages 196-97, and argued that it clearly required a denial of copyrightability.]

Congress considered and declined to enact legislation that would have extended copyright protection to "[t]he 'design of a useful article' . . . including its two-dimensional or three-dimensional features of shape and surface, which make up the appearance of the article." Passage of this provision was recommended by the Register of Copyrights. It was opposed by the Department of Justice on policy grounds . . . [that] it would charge the public a fee for the use of improved and pleasing new designs and styles in useful articles. . . .

Thus far Congress and the Supreme Court have answered in favor of commerce and the masses, rather than the artists, designers and the well-to-do. Any change must be left to those higher authorities. The choices are legislative not judicial.

Carol Barnhart Inc. v. Economy Cover Corp.
773 F.2d 411 (2d Cir. 1985)

MANSFIELD, J.: . . . The bones of contention are four human torso forms designed by Barnhart, each of which is life-size, without neck, arms, or a back, and made of expandable white styrene. Plaintiff's president created the forms in 1982 by using clay, buttons, and fabric to develop an initial mold, which she then used to build an aluminum mold into which the poly-styrene is poured to manufacture the sculptural display form. There are two male and two female upper torsos. One each of the male and female torsos is unclad for the purpose of displaying shirts and sweaters, while the other two are sculpted with shirts for displaying sweaters and jackets. All the forms, which are otherwise life-like and anatomically accurate, have hollow backs designed to hold excess fabric when the garment is fitted onto the form. Barnhart's advertising stresses the forms' uses to display items such as sweaters, blouses, and dress shirts, and states that they come "[p]ackaged in UPS-size boxes for easy shipping and [are] sold in multiples of twelve." . . .

[Economy Cover Corp. copied Barnhart's forms, and Barnhart sued for copyright infringement. The district court granted Economy's motion for summary judgment, and Barnhart appealed.]

. . . Appellant emphasizes that clay sculpting, often used in traditional sculpture, was used in making the molds for the forms. It also stresses that the forms have been responded to as sculptural forms, and have been used for purposes other than modeling clothes, e.g., as decorating props and signs without any clothing or accessories. While this may indicate that the forms are "aesthetically satisfying and valuable," it is insufficient to show that the forms possess aesthetic or artistic features that are physically or conceptually separable from the forms' use as utilitarian objects to display clothes. . . .

In concluding that the two belt buckles [in *Kieselstein-Cord*] were copyrightable we relied on the fact that "[t]he primary ornamental aspect of the Vaquero and Winchester buckles is conceptually separable from their subsidiary utilitarian function." *Id.* at 993. A glance at the pictures of the two buckles . . . coupled with the description in the text, confirms their highly ornamental dimensions and separability. What distinguishes those buckles from the Barnhart forms is that the ornamented surfaces of the buckles were not in any respect required by their utilitarian functions; the artistic or aesthetic features could thus be conceived of as having been added to, or superimposed upon, an otherwise utilitarian article. . . . In the case of the Barnhart forms, on the other hand, the features claimed to be aesthetic or artistic, e.g., the life-size configuration of the breasts and the width of the shoulders, are inextricably intertwined with the utilitarian feature, the display of clothes. Whereas a model of a human torso, in order to serve its utilitarian function, must have some configuration of the chest and some width of shoulders, a belt buckle can serve its function satisfactorily without any ornamentation of the type that renders the *Kieselstein-Cord* buckles distinctive.[5] . . .

NEWMAN, J., dissenting: . . . What must be carefully considered is the meaning and application of the principle of "conceptual separability." Initially, it may be helpful to make the obvious point that this principle must mean something other than "physical separability." That latter principle is illustrated by the numerous familiar examples of useful objects ornamented by a drawing, a carving, a sculpted figure, or any other decorative embellishment that could physically appear apart from the useful article. Professor Nimmer offers the example of the sculptured jaguar that adorns the hood of and provides the name for the well-known British automobile. . . .

. . . In my view, the answer derives from the word "conceptual." For the design features to be "conceptually separate" from the utilitarian aspects of the useful article that embodies the design, the article must stimulate in the mind of the beholder a concept that is separate from the concept evoked by its utilitarian function. . . .

I think the relevant beholder must be that most useful legal personage — the ordinary, reasonable observer. This is the same person the law enlists to decide other conceptual issues in copyright law. . . .

The "separateness" of the utilitarian and non-utilitarian concepts engendered by an article's design is itself a perplexing concept. I think the requisite "separateness" exists whenever the design creates in the mind of the ordinary observer two different concepts that are not inevitably entertained simultaneously. . . . [T]he example of the artistically designed chair displayed in a museum may be helpful. The ordinary observer can be expected to apprehend the design of a chair whenever the object is viewed. He may, in addition, entertain the concept of a work of art, but, if this second concept is engendered in the observer's mind simultaneously with the concept of the article's utilitarian function, the requisite "separateness" does not exist. The test is not whether the observer fails to recognize the object as a chair but only whether the concept of the utilitarian function can be displaced in the mind by some other concept. . . . The separate concept will normally be that of a work of art.

Some might think that the requisite separability of concepts exists whenever the design of a form engenders in the mind of the ordinary observer any concept that is distinct from the concept of the form's utilitarian function. Under this approach, the design of an artistically designed chair would receive copyright protection if the ordinary observer viewing it would entertain the concept of a work of art in addition to the concept of a chair. This approach, I fear, would subvert the Congressional effort to deny copyright protection to designs of useful articles that are aesthetically pleasing. . . .

In endeavoring to draw the line . . . courts will inevitably be drawn into some minimal inquiry as to the nature of art. . . . Of course, courts must not assess the *quality* of art, but a determination of whether a design engenders the concept of a work of art, separate from the concept of an article's utilitarian function, necessarily requires some consideration of whether the object *is* a work of art. . . .

---

5. [The majority characterized the test proposed in Judge Newman's dissent as "a standard so ethereal as to amount to a 'non-test.'"] . . . [I]t is the object, not the form of display, for which copyright protection is sought. Congress has made it reasonably clear that copyrightability of the object should turn on its ordinary use as viewed by the average observer, not by a temporary flight of fancy that could attach to any utilitarian object, including an automobile engine, depending on how it is displayed. . . . However, regardless of which standard is applied we disagree with the proposition that the mannequins here . . . could be viewed by the ordinary observer as anything other than objects having a utilitarian function as mannequins. . . .

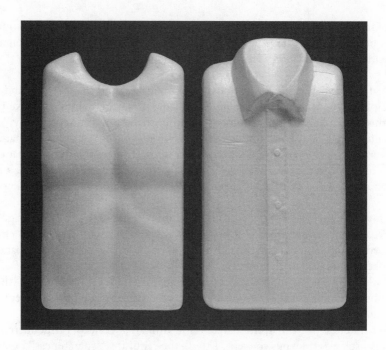

Torso Forms

Our case involving the four styrene chest forms seems to me a much easier case than *Kieselstein-Cord*. An ordinary observer . . . who views the two unclothed forms . . . would be most unlikely even to entertain, from visual inspection alone, the concept of a mannequin with the utilitarian function of displaying a shirt or blouse. . . . As appellant contends, with pardonable hyperbole, the design of Michelangelo's "David" would not cease to be copyrightable simply because cheap copies of it were used by a retail store to display clothing. . . . [Judge Newman concluded, however, that a triable question of fact existed as to the ordinary observer's perception of the two clothed forms.]

Brandir International, Inc. v. Cascade Pacific Lumber Co.
834 F.2d 1142 (2d Cir. 1987)

OAKES, J.: [The lawsuit concerned a bicycle rack made of bent metal tubing, developed by Brandir's owner and subsequently copied by Cascade Pacific. The Copyright Office denied registration. The district court agreed with this conclusion, and granted summary judgment to Cascade Pacific; the court of appeals affirmed.]

Perhaps the differences between the majority and the dissent in *Carol Barnhart* might have been resolved had they had before them the Denicola article on *Applied Art and Industrial Design: A Suggested Approach to Copyright in Useful Articles*, [67 Minn. L. Rev. 707 (1983)]. . . . Denicola argues that "the statutory directive requires a distinction between works of industrial design and works whose origins lie outside the design process, despite the utilitarian environment in which they appear." He views the statutory limitation of copyrightability as "an attempt to identify elements whose form and appearance reflect the unconstrained perspective of the artist," such features not being the product of industrial design. . . . To state the Denicola test in the language of conceptual separability, if design elements reflect a merger of aesthetic and functional considerations, the artistic aspects of a work cannot be said to be conceptually separable from the utilitarian elements. Conversely, where design elements can be identified as reflecting the designer's artistic judgment exercised independently of functional influences, conceptual separability exists.

We believe that Professor Denicola's approach provides the best test for conceptual separability and, accordingly, adopt it here for several reasons. First, the approach is consistent with the holdings of our previous cases. . . . Second, the test's emphasis on the influence of utilitarian concerns in the design process may help, as Denicola notes, to "alleviate the de facto discrimination against nonrepresentational art that has regrettably accompanied much of the current analysis." *Id.* at 745. Finally, and most importantly, we think Denicola's test will not be too difficult to administer in practice. The work itself will continue to give "mute testimony" of its origins. In addition, the parties will be required to present evidence relating to the design process and the nature of the work. . . .

Turning now to the facts of this case, we note first that Brandir contends, and its chief owner [Steven] Levine testified, that the original design of the RIBBON Rack stemmed from wire sculptures that Levine had created, each formed from one continuous undulating piece of wire. . . . He also created a wire sculpture in the shape of a bicycle and states that he did not give any thought to the utilitarian application of any of his sculptures until he accidentally juxtaposed the bicycle sculpture with one of the self-standing wire sculptures. . . . [A friend] informed him that the sculptures would make excellent bicycle racks. . . .

. . . The RIBBON Rack has been featured in *Popular Science, Art and Architecture*, and *Design 384* magazines, and it won an Industrial Designers Society of America design award in the spring of 1980. In the spring of 1984 the RIBBON Rack was selected from 200 designs to be included . . . in an exhibition entitled "The Product of Design: An Exploration of the Industrial Design Process," an exhibition that was written up in the New York Times. . . .

. . . [W]e find that the rack is not copyrightable. It seems clear that the form of the rack is influenced in significant measure by utilitarian concerns and thus any aesthetic elements cannot be said to be conceptually separable from the utilitarian elements. . . .

Had Brandir merely adopted one of the existing sculptures as a bicycle rack, neither the application to a utilitarian end nor commercialization of that use would have caused the object to forfeit its copyrighted status. Comparison of the RIBBON Rack with the earlier sculptures, however, reveals that while the rack may have been derived in part from one of [sic] more "works of art," it is in its final form essentially a product of industrial design. In creating the RIBBON Rack, the designer has clearly adapted the original aesthetic elements to accommodate and further a utilitarian purpose. These altered design features of the RIBBON Rack, including the spacesaving, open design achieved by widening the upper loops to permit parking under as well as over the rack's curves, the straightened vertical elements that allow in- and above-ground installation of the rack, the ability to fit all types of bicycles and mopeds, and the heavy-gauged tubular construction of rustproof galvanized steel are all features that combine to make for a safe, secure, and maintenance-free system of parking bicycles and mopeds. Its undulating shape is said in *Progressive Architecture*, January 1982, to permit double the storage of conventional bicycle racks. . . .

It is unnecessary to determine whether to the art world the RIBBON Rack properly would be considered an example of minimalist sculpture [as plaintiff had asserted]. The result under the copyright statute is not changed. Using the test we have adopted, it is not enough that, to paraphrase Judge Newman, the rack may stimulate in the mind of the reasonable observer a concept separate from the bicycle rack concept. While the RIBBON Rack may be worthy of admiration for its aesthetic qualities alone, it remains nonetheless the product of industrial design. Form and function are inextricably intertwined in the rack, its ultimate design being as much the result of utilitarian pressures as aesthetic choices. Indeed, the visually pleasing proportions and symmetricality of the rack represent design changes made in response to functional concerns. Judging from the awards the rack has received, it would seem in fact that Brandir has achieved with the RIBBON Rack the highest goal of modern industrial design, that is, the harmonious fusion of function and aesthetics. Thus there remains no artistic element of the RIBBON Rack that can be identified as separate and "capable of existing independently, of, the utilitarian aspects of the article." . . .

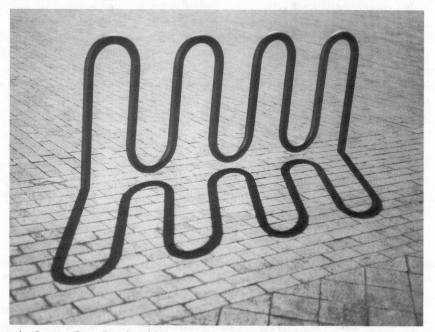

Photo by Joanne Gere. Reprinted by permission.

RIBBON Rack in Shadow

RIBBON is a registered trademark of Brandir International, Inc.

RIBBON Rack in Use as Bike Rack

WINTER, J., dissenting: . . . [M]y colleagues' adaptation of Professor Denicola's test diminishes the statutory concept of "conceptual separability" to the vanishing point. . . .

. . . [T]he relevant question is whether the design of a useful article, however intertwined with the article's utilitarian aspects, causes an ordinary reasonable observer to perceive an aesthetic concept not related to the article's use. The answer to this question is clear in the instant case because any reasonable observer would easily view the Ribbon Rack as an ornamental sculpture. Indeed, there is evidence of actual confusion over whether it is strictly ornamental in the refusal of a building manager to accept delivery until assured by the buyer that the Ribbon Rack was in fact a bicycle rack. Moreover, Brandir has received a request to use the Ribbon Rack as environmental sculpture, and has offered testimony of art experts. . . .

. . . Copyright protection, which is intended to generate incentives for designers by according property rights in their creations, should not turn on purely fortuitous events. For that reason, the Copyright Act expressly states that the legal test is how the final article is perceived, not how it was developed through various stages. . . .

NOTES AND QUESTIONS

1. Are the three cases reconcilable? How would each case be decided under the approach taken in the other cases? Which approach to defining conceptual separability do you think is best, and why? Which is most faithful to the language of the House Report? Which approach adheres best to the nondiscrimination principle articulated by Justice Holmes in *Bleistein*?

2. What standard of review was applied in each of the above cases? Is conceptual separability more appropriately considered a question of fact or a question of law?

3. In *Esquire v. Ringer*, 591 F.2d 796 (D.C. Cir. 1978), the D.C. Circuit read the House Report's reference to "conceptually" separable features much more narrowly: "[A]ny possible ambiguity raised by this isolated reference disappears when the excerpt is considered in its entirety. The [surrounding] passages indicate unequivocally that the overall design or configuration of a utilitarian object, even if it is determined by aesthetic as well as functional considerations, is not eligible for copyright." *Id.* at 803-04. The *Esquire* court held that the Copyright Office did not abuse its discretion in denying registration to a set of modernistic, rounded designs for lighting fixtures. *Esquire*, however, arose under the 1909 Copyright Act; the court looked to the 1976 Act and its legislative history only as additional evidence to support its conclusion that denial of registration was consistent with Copyright Office regulations and established practice. In a later decision concerning registrability under the 1976 Act, the D.C. Circuit cited the "notable lack of agreement among courts and commentators on the very meaning of 'conceptual separability,'" and deferred judgment on the question. *Oddzon Prods., Inc. v. Oman*, 924 F.2d 346, 349-50 (D.C. Cir. 1991). Do you think the *Esquire* court got it right? *See also Norris Indus., Inc. v. Int'l Tel. & Tel. Corp.*, 696 F.2d 918 (11th Cir. 1983) (finding that wheel covers "did not contain a superfluous sculptured design, serving no function, that can be identified apart from the wheel covers themselves").

4. Professor Alfred Yen has argued that it is impossible to undertake a conceptual separability analysis without making judgments about what is art and what is not. He notes that within the field of aesthetic theory, there are several different schools of opinion on this subject:

> Aestheticians have . . . spilled a fair amount of ink on the subject, but their efforts have not created a uniformly accepted definition of art. However, three contrasting approaches to defining art are particularly relevant to this Article. First, formalism emphasizes the physical configuration of a work. Second, intentionalism focuses on the behavior of an object's creator. Third, institutionalism prefers a contextual approach that concentrates on how members of a cultural tradition called "the artworld" treat a work.

Alfred C. Yen, *Copyright Opinions and Aesthetic Theory*, 71 S. Cal. L. Rev. 247, 252-53 (1998). He observes that leading copyright decisions reflect this lack of consensus:

> Leading cases adopt analytical perspectives that are equivalent to major branches of aesthetic theory. In fact, the very effort to avoid aesthetics has led courts to adopt these varying perspectives because the facts of individual cases often make one analytical perspective seem more or less subjective and aesthetically controversial than others. . . . [C]ourts are essentially swapping one set of aesthetic premises for others in response to the facts of particular cases. Copyright opinions therefore amount to the judicial declaration of preference for one aesthetic perspective over others. Indeed, copyright opinions rendered today *necessarily require* the judicial declaration of such preference.

Id. at 298 (see BB Rule 5.2(d)(iii)). The solution to this problem, he argues, is more, not less, subjectivity in judging. Judges should be more explicit about which aesthetic biases and presumptions they hold:

> [J]udges can take steps that will diminish (but not eliminate) the importance of their personal aesthetic biases. A judge must realize that he is not an objective, disinterested observer of the works under consideration. His initial intuitions inevitably come from the peculiar set of circumstances that make up his life. These intuitions may fortuitously be "ordinary" or similar to those held by other people. However, a judge must realize that this fortuity does not make, and cannot make, his intuitions correct in the strongest sense of the word. At best, his intuitions can be correct in a culturally relative way. In short, a judge must know that his intuition which "seems right" probably stands on highly contestable intellectual premises. Reflexive rejection of other possibilities represents the very sort of subjective censorship that Holmes warned against.
>
> A judge who is conscious of this problem can guard against it by being particularly open-minded to alternate aesthetic sensibilities. For example, a dedicated formalist should listen particularly carefully to arguments based in intentionalism or reader-response theory. Traditionally oriented judges should listen carefully to avant-garde arguments. . . . The net result is that courts will wind up embracing a broader set of aesthetic conventions by openly thinking about aesthetics than they would by simply applying doctrine that embodies existing dogma.

Id. at 300-01.

Consider the three Second Circuit cases you have just read. Do they support Professor Yen's observations? Which aesthetic perspective does each opinion adopt? Do you agree with Professor Yen's proposal for addressing the problem of unconscious judicial bias? Would some other solution be more desirable?

5. Is a degree of discrimination against nonrepresentational art an appropriate part of the conceptual separability analysis? In another portion of his *Carol Barnhart* dissent, Judge Newman observed: "Any concern that copyright protection may accord a monopoly to advances in functional design . . . is adequately met by confining the scope of copyright protection to the precise expression of the proprietor's design." 773 F.2d at 421 n.1 (Newman, J., dissenting). Do you agree?

Section 113 of the Copyright Act places some additional limits on the scope of copyright in a pictorial, graphic, or sculptural work. Examine §113(a)-(c) now. Do any of these provisions address the concern discussed by Judge Newman? Section 113(c) does not allow the copyright owners of designs of useful articles to prevent photographs of those articles from being made and used in advertisements or commentaries about the articles. Why do you think Congress enacted this limitation on the rights of copyright owners for this category of works?

6. Remember that the threshold determination of whether something is a "useful article" is important, because something that is not a "useful article" need not be subjected to a

separability analysis. Do the belt buckles, mannequin forms, and bicycle racks from the cases you have read satisfy the §101 definition of "useful article"? How about masks designed to resemble animals' noses? *See Masquerade Novelty, Inc. v. Unique Indus., Inc.*, 912 F.2d 663 (3d Cir. 1990) (no).

Might a collection of blank forms in a personal organizer — e.g., calendar forms, address book forms, and "to do" lists — qualify as a useful article? *See Harper House, Inc. v. Thomas Nelson, Inc.*, 889 F.2d 197, 203 (2d Cir. 1989) (holding that no matter how useful a work is, the useful article rule does not affect the copyrightability of an integrated work of text and blank forms, but only that of pictorial, graphic, or sculptural works).

Remember also that other limitations on copyrightability, such as those discussed in Chapter 2, still apply in cases involving useful articles. *See, e.g., Past Pluto Prods. Corp. v. Dana*, 627 F. Supp. 1435 (S.D.N.Y. 1986) (uniform, machine-manufactured "spikes" on Statue of Liberty foam novelty hat lacked sufficient originality to be copyrightable).

7. While courts generally consider clothing a "useful article," some cases raise interesting questions. Consider whether the clothing in the following hypotheticals is a "useful article":

    a. clothing for stuffed bears (*See Boyds Collection, Ltd. v. Bearington Collection, Inc.*, 365 F. Supp. 2d 612 (M.D. Pa. 2005) (holding, on motion for summary judgment, that clothes for a doll might be shown not to be a useful article)).

    b. a "jeweled" bikini made of clear plastic and crushed rock (*See Poe v. Missing Persons*, 745 F.2d 1238 (9th Cir. 1984) (reversing a grant of summary judgment and remanding for evidence on the question of usefulness)).

    c. the exterior design of a slipper shaped as a whimsical bear foot (*See Animal Fair, Inc. v. Amfesco Indus., Inc.*, 620 F. Supp. 175 (D. Minn. 1985) (assuming on a motion for a preliminary injunction that the slipper would be a useful article, and holding its "entire exterior design" protectible because "wholly unrelated to function"), *aff'd mem.*, 794 F.2d 678 (8th Cir. 1986)).

In almost all other cases, courts have found the artistic elements of the clothing's design to be inextricably interwoven with the clothing's function of covering parts of the human body. Thus, in the case of most clothing there is nothing that the Copyright Act will protect. *See, e.g., Morris v. Buffalo Chips Bootery, Inc.*, 160 F. Supp. 2d 718 (S.D.N.Y. 2001) (finding leather vests and dresses to be useful articles without separable artistic elements). Note, however, that the pattern or design printed on fabric can qualify as a graphic work.

8. Unlike the U.S., European countries protect clothing designs under both copyright and independent design protection statutes. The most recent EU directive concerning design protection is discussed in the Note on Industrial Design Protection in the EU, *infra* pages 210-11. Article 17 of this directive also expressly provides that such design protection does not foreclose protection under copyright law.

3. New Paradigms?

The murky contours of the "conceptual separability" test create uncertainty for those seeking copyright protection for the designs of useful articles. As you have seen, industries unsure about the availability or scope of copyright protection tend to lobby for more protection; thus, the materials covered in the preceding subsection raise the question whether Congress should accede to such requests by rewriting the definition of "pictorial, graphic, and sculptural works" to give it a broader (or at least clearer) scope. They also raise the question whether the design of useful articles might more appropriately be protected via a different legal regime, as some other countries have done.

More concretely, the TRIPS Agreement obligates signatory countries to provide a minimum level of protection for industrial designs:

Article 25. Requirements for Protection

1. Members shall provide for the protection of independently created industrial designs that are new or original. Members may provide that designs are not new or original if they do not significantly differ from known designs or combinations of known design features. Members may provide that such protection shall not extend to designs dictated essentially by technical or functional considerations.

2. . . . Members shall be free to meet this obligation through industrial design law or through copyright law.

TRIPS Agreement, art. 25. The U.S. has stated that it already provides adequate protection to satisfy the TRIPS standard. As you read the following materials, consider whether this is so, and whether any of the regimes described are (or would be) good complements to, or substitutes for, copyright protection in this area.

Note on Design Patents

The first of the alternatives for design protection that we discuss is not new. At the time of the *Mazer* decision, design patents had existed in the U.S. for over a century. Under the Patent Act, a design patent is available for "any new, original, and ornamental design for an article of manufacture." 35 U.S.C. §171. If granted, the design patent lasts for 14 years from the date of issuance. During that period, the patentee may prevent others from making, using, importing, or selling an article embodying the patented design. *Id*. §271.

There are few limitations on the subject matter of design patents. *In re Koehring*, 37 F.2d 421 (C.C.P.A. 1930), is illustrative. There, the Court of Customs and Patent Appeals ordered the Patent Office to grant a patent on the design of a cement mixer truck. The court rejected the Patent Office's arguments that a machine with moving parts could not qualify as an "article of manufacture" under the Patent Act and could not be "inventively ornamental" as required by the design patent portion of the Act. It reasoned that in enacting design patent protection, Congress "had in mind the elimination of much of the unsightly repulsiveness that characterizes many machines and mechanical devices which have a tendency to depress rather than excite the esthetic sense." *Id*. at 422. The court concluded that the statutory grant of protection could extend to any man-made article, with or without moving parts, as long as the appearance of that article was "a matter of concern to anybody." *Id*. at 423. The design, however, cannot be governed solely by function. *See Seiko Epson Corp. v. Nu-Kote Int'l, Inc.*, 190 F.3d 1360, 1368 (Fed. Cir. 1999).

Until recently, the Copyright Office denied registration for any work that was already the subject of a design patent while the Patent Office and the Court of Customs and Patent Appeals (the predecessor to the U.S. Court of Appeals for the Federal Circuit) permitted design patents to issue on copyrighted designs. The Copyright Office relied on pre-*Mazer* cases such as *Korzybski v. Underwood & Underwood*, 36 F.2d 727 (2d Cir. 1929), which held that "[e]verything disclosed in the patent became a part of the public domain, except the monopoly of the patentee to make, use, and vend the patented device for a limited time." *Id*. at 728. The Court of Customs and Patent Appeals, in contrast, concluded that "[i]f anything, the concurrent availability of both modes of securing exclusive rights aids in achieving the stated purpose of the constitutional provision." *In re Yardley*, 493 F.2d 1389, 1396 (C.C.P.A. 1974). In 1995, the Copyright Office, bowing to widespread criticism, reversed its policy and now allows registration for works that are also the subject of an issued design patent. 37 C.F.R. §202.10.

Although the numbers of design patent applications and issued design patents have increased significantly in recent years, reliance on copyright protection is far more common. Given the stronger protection afforded by a design patent and, now, the ability to elect both forms of protection simultaneously, this might strike the student of intellectual property law as curious. The reasons for this pattern are largely practical. First, infringement is difficult to prove, although the Federal Circuit recently modified the test for infringement in *Egyptian Goddess, Inc. v. Swisa, Inc.*, 543 F.3d 665 (Fed. Cir. 2008) (en banc), which should make proving infringement somewhat easier. *See* James Juo, *Egyptian Goddess: Rebooting Design Patents and Resurrecting* Whitman Saddle, 18 Fed. Circuit B.J. 429, 450 (2009). More significantly, obtaining design patent protection is expensive and time-consuming. Before a design patent can issue, the Patent Office must examine it for novelty and originality, and must determine that the design is ornamental rather than functional. If the design is functional, the inventor might be entitled to obtain a utility patent, but a design patent is foreclosed. The average examination time is 16 months, U.S. Patent & Trademark Office, Design Patents: January 1977 — December 2008 (2009), and protection does not attach until the patent is granted. Many mass-marketed products have relatively short life cycles. Submitting a design patent application before a design proves profitable may not make sense, but marketing the product while the application is pending invites copying before legal protection is available.

Note on Trade Dress Protection

In the last several decades, at the same time that developers of industrial designs were testing the bounds of the Copyright Act's protection for pictorial, graphic, and sculptural works, they also were exploring the scope of federal unfair competition law. The Lanham Act, which protects federally registered trademarks, also protects against use in commerce of unregistered marks or "false designation[s] of origin" if such use is likely to confuse consumers as to the source or sponsorship of the goods or services. 15 U.S.C. §1125(a). Originally, the "false designation of origin" part of this provision had been understood to prohibit only misleading indications of geographic origin. In 1992, however, the Supreme Court upheld a jury verdict in favor of Taco Cabana, a Mexican restaurant chain that charged a competitor with imitating its "trade dress" — the external and internal decor of its restaurants — thereby creating an impression of joint ownership or affiliation. Importantly, the Court held that Taco Cabana did not need to prove that its trade dress had acquired "secondary meaning" — i.e., that customers in its target market recognized the decor as an indicator of source. *Two Pesos, Inc. v. Taco Cabana, Inc.*, 505 U.S. 763 (1992).

Two Pesos set off a torrent of trade dress infringement litigation, but the boom was short-lived. Almost immediately, courts were confronted with novel questions about what features of a product could be protected as trade dress. Historically, trade dress had been understood to mean the packaging of a product or service — e.g., the design of a bottle to hold liquor or laundry detergent. Increasingly, however, manufacturers began to assert trade dress protection in the design of products themselves — e.g., the design of clothing or lawn furniture. A split developed among the federal circuit courts over the proper way to handle these latter cases. The Second and Third Circuits held that if a trade dress claim concerned product configuration, as opposed to the design of packaging, the party claiming protection for a particular feature must prove secondary meaning. *Knitwaves, Inc. v. Lollytogs Ltd.*, 71 F.3d 996 (2d Cir. 1995); *Duraco Prods., Inc. v. Joy Plastic Enters. Ltd.*, 40 F.3d 1431 (3d Cir. 1994). The Eighth Circuit, on the other hand, read *Two Pesos* as prohibiting such a requirement. *Stuart Hall Co. v. Ampad Corp.*, 51 F.3d 780 (8th Cir. 1995).

Ultimately, in *Wal-Mart Stores, Inc. v. Samara Bros., Inc.*, 529 U.S. 205 (2000), the Supreme Court sided with the Second and Third Circuits, and substantially limited the scope of its earlier *Two Pesos* decision. The Court distinguished product design from words or packaging that might be attached to a product, reasoning that although consumers might be "predisposed" to regard the latter as symbols of source, the same predisposition did not exist with respect to product features. It observed: "Consumers should not be deprived of the benefits of competition with regard to the utilitarian and esthetic purposes that product design ordinarily serves by a rule of law that facilitates plausible threats of suit against new entrants. . . ." *Id.* at 213. The Court concluded that secondary meaning must be proven for trade dress protection to apply to product configuration.

In addition, as is the case with design patent protection, trade dress protection is not permitted for functional features of product design. In trademark parlance, trade dress is considered functional if it is essential to the use or purpose of the product or if it affects the cost or quality of the article, or, in the words of the Supreme Court, "if exclusive use of the feature would put competitors at a significant non-reputation-related disadvantage," *Qualitex Co. v. Jacobson Prod. Co.*, 514 U.S. 159, 165 (1995). The Court has also held that a manufacturer that wished to claim trade dress protection for a product feature disclosed in an expired patent (utility, not design) must overcome a strong presumption that the feature was functional and not protectible as trade dress. *TrafFix Devices, Inc. v. Marketing Displays, Inc.*, 532 U.S. 23 (2001).

Note on Industrial Design Protection in the EU

Because neither a copyright nor a patent nor a trade dress model seems well suited to protecting industrial designs, many nations have adopted sui generis industrial design protection laws. Of these laws, the EU's 1998 Directive on the Legal Protection of Designs ("EU Design Directive") is perhaps the most important. *See* Directive 98/71/EC of the European Parliament and of the Council of 13 Oct. 1998 on the Legal Protection of Designs, 1998 O.J. (L 289) 28. Although many EU member countries had adopted some form of design protection, those laws were inconsistent. The EU Design Directive was intended to harmonize legal protection for designs throughout the EU, and to provide a model for protection of industrial designs worldwide. *See* Graeme B. Dinwoodie, *Federalized Functionalism: The Future of Design Protection in the European Union*, 24 AIPLA Q.J. 611 (1996).

Under the EU Design Directive, EU member countries must provide a registration-based system of protection for designs that are new and of "individual character." A design qualifies under the latter standard "if the overall impression it produces on the informed user differs from the overall impression produced on such a user by any design which has been made available to the public before the date of filing of the application for registration." EU Design Directive, art. 5(1). Design features that are "solely dictated by [the product's] technical function," or that are necessary for mechanical interoperability with another product, are ineligible for protection. *Id.* art. 7. Protection must subsist for five years from the date of filing, and be renewable in five-year increments for a total of 25 years. *Id.* art. 10. The design right includes the right to control "the making, offering, putting on the market, importing, exporting or using of a product in which the design is incorporated or to which it is applied, or stocking such a product for those purposes." *Id.* art. 12. However, the EU Design Directive specifically exempts private, noncommercial uses, experimental uses, and "acts of reproduction for the purposes of making citations or of teaching, provided that such acts are compatible with fair trade practice and do not unduly prejudice the normal exploitation of the design, and that mention is made of the source." *Id.* art. 13(1).

Laws such as the EU Design Directive offer clear advantages, and some disadvantages, to developers of industrial designs. Compared to copyright law, the directive provides a relatively clear standard of eligibility for protection that does not require the registering body or the courts to determine whether the design is "art." Compared to patent law, it establishes a less rigorous threshold for protection, which likely will translate into much shorter processing time for applications to register. All of these features, however, benefit firstcomers only, and every company that is a repeat player in its market will be a secondcomer at least some of the time.

Whether the model developed in the EU Design Directive is the best possible model is more debatable. Professor Dinwoodie observes that the "dictated solely by function" provision may be interpreted as allowing protection whenever other possible designs for the product are available; if so, he argues, "there remains a danger that the few designs that will enable the product to function may be depleted by the successive grant of design rights in those respective possibilities to a small number of producers." Dinwoodie, *supra*, at 673-74. In addition, he notes that the provision allowing copying for mechanical interoperability (e.g., of moving parts) probably does not extend to copying for "aesthetic interoperability" (e.g., spare parts that match the original product in visual appearance), and worries about the potential anti-competitive effects on industries such as the automobile parts industry. *Id.* at 682-97. It is worth noting, moreover, that the EU Design Directive specifically allows for cumulative protection under design protection law and copyright law, as well as under any other applicable laws. *Id.* at 710-18.

Note on Industrial Design Protection Efforts in the U.S.

The last several decades have witnessed repeated attempts to secure passage of industrial design protection legislation by Congress. Until quite recently these attempts were uniformly unsuccessful. Design protection legislation has never commanded universal support among U.S. manufacturers. Although substantial interests have supported the creation of federal design protection, equally powerful lobbies have opposed these proposals. Independent manufacturers of automobile parts, for example, have sought to preserve their current freedom to supply parts for any type of automobile. Automobile insurers support this competitive market, which avoids monopolistic pricing for replacement parts. Other industries, such as the fashion industry, have been divided on the question of design protection; firms serving haute couture markets support such legislation, while those serving discount fashion markets do not.

Resistance to a hybrid industrial design regime may be weakening, however. Congress has shown greater willingness to enact sui generis protection for specific subcategories of industrial design that are perceived to merit special attention. This, in turn, may pave the way for a general design protection law. Additionally, Congress' increased willingness to amend the copyright, patent, and trademark laws to harmonize them with those of major trading partners may make Congress more inclined to follow these countries' lead in other areas of intellectual property protection as well.

Not surprisingly, given its economic importance, the computer industry was the first beneficiary of efforts to establish industry-specific design protection. By the early 1980s, newly developed techniques enabled relatively inexpensive copying of the integrated circuit designs embedded in semiconductor chips, which required great effort and expense to develop. Congress found that existing intellectual property law did not offer an appropriate level of protection. Patent law often would not protect layouts and design work "because the creativity involved does not rise to the inventive level required by the patent laws." H.R. Rep. No. 98-781, 98th Cong., 2d Sess. 3, *reprinted in* 1984 U.S.C.C.A.N. 5750, 5752. Additionally, "it was uncertain whether the copyright law could protect against copying of the pattern on the chip itself, if the pattern was deemed inseparable from the utilitarian function of the chip." *Brooktree Corp. v. Advanced Micro Devices, Inc.*, 977 F.2d 1555, 1562 (Fed. Cir. 1992). In 1984, Congress enacted the first sui generis design protection law, the Semiconductor Chip Protection Act (SCPA), Pub. L. No. 98-620, 98 Stat. 3335 (1984) (codified at 17 U.S.C. §§901-914), which granted limited protection for the designs of semiconductor chips, also known as "mask works."

Under the SCPA the owner of an original mask work has the exclusive right to reproduce the work and to import or distribute a semiconductor chip product that embodies the work. 17 U.S.C. §905. Prompt registration is required for protection, with the rights having a ten-year duration. The SCPA contained a prohibition against extending protection to "any idea, procedure, process, system, method of operation, concept, principle, or discovery," essentially replicating §102(b) of the Copyright Act. *Id.* §902(c).

Despite the legislative history indicating that Congress believed the Act to be vital to ensuring the continued prosperity of the semiconductor industry, only the *Brooktree* case cited above was decided under the Act. Commentators often claim that technology rendered the Act obsolete almost before its enactment. The process of transforming a mask work into a chip is a complex one. As chip fabrication processes became more complex, would-be copiers found it much more difficult to move from the mask to the chip without knowledge of the processing technology.

Outside the computer and semiconductor industries the pace of technological change has also quickened. More traditional manufacturing industries also began to confront the threat of rapid, perfect copying of their designs, and some industries redoubled their efforts to secure legal protection. In particular, the boat manufacturing industry worried about a new technology, known as "direct molding" or "plug molding," which allowed secondcomers to copy the shape of a hull cheaply and easily. Initial efforts to secure protection targeted state legislatures. In 1983, at the behest of the local boat industry, the Florida legislature passed a law that prohibited use of the direct molding process to copy boat hulls. The U.S. Supreme Court struck down the Florida statute, holding it preempted by the federal patent laws. We will consider this decision, *Bonito Boats, Inc. v. Thunder Craft Boats, Inc.*, 489 U.S. 141 (1989), in Chapter 10.

Undeterred by this setback, the boat manufacturers renewed their efforts at the federal level, and finally prevailed. In 1998, the House Judiciary Committee's Subcommittee on Courts and Intellectual Property was chaired by Rep. Howard Coble of North Carolina, home to a strong boat-building industry. That year, Congress enacted the Vessel Hull Design Protection Act (VHDPA), Pub. L. No. 105-304, Title V, 112 Stat. 2860, 2906 (1998) (codified at 17 U.S.C. §§1301-1332), which extended federal protection to the design of a "vessel hull." The description of the subject matter of this law reads as follows:

§1301. Designs protected

(a) Designs protected

(1) In general. The designer or other owner of an original design of a useful article which makes the article attractive or distinctive in appearance to the purchasing or using public may secure the protection provided by this chapter. . . .

(b) Definitions. For the purpose of this chapter, the following terms have the following meanings:

(1) A design is "original" if it is the result of the designer's creative endeavor that provides a distinguishable variation over prior work pertaining to similar articles which is more than merely trivial and has not been copied from another source.

(2) A "useful article" is a vessel hull or deck, including a plug or mold, which in normal use has an intrinsic utilitarian function that is not merely to portray the appearance of the article or to convey information. An article which normally is part of a useful article shall be deemed to be a useful article. . . .

The VHDPA establishes a ten-year term of protection, during which the owner of a protected design has the exclusive rights to make or import the design and to sell or distribute it. 17 U.S.C. §§1305, 1308. It is worth noting that despite the almost complete abandonment of formalities in the copyright context, Congress evidently did not feel comfortable dispensing with formalities for the new regime. A design eligible for protection must be registered within two years after it is first made public. *Id.* §1310(a). Notice of registration is required, and omission of notice insulates a secondcomer from liability unless that party has received actual written notice from the design owner before beginning its own manufacture. *Id.* §§1306-1307.

The VHDPA supplies Congress with a template for industrial design protection consistent with efforts seeking international harmonization. As you have seen, during the 1990s, Congress enacted legislation to extend the term of copyright from life plus 50 years to match the longer term of life plus 70 years recognized by some European countries. It also abandoned the traditional practice of granting patentees a term of 17 years from the date of patent issuance in favor of the model followed by Europe and Japan that grants a term of 20 years from the date the patent application is filed. On the trademark side, it has acceded to the Madrid Protocol, a major international agreement that provides for harmonized registration procedures. Whether Congress will also follow the European lead with regard to industrial design protection remains to be seen.

NOTES AND QUESTIONS

1. Why do you think Congress chose to enact a free-standing law to protect the design of semiconductor chips rather than modifying the Copyright Act? Under what constitutional power do you think Congress enacted the SCPA? Wouldn't the technical drawings representing the mask work be copyrightable subject matter? If so, why wouldn't copyright law suffice?

2. The VHDPA includes a provision, §1302, that reflects some of the same concerns embodied in sections 102(b) and 902(c) (limiting protection of mask works under the SCPA) of the Copyright Act, and Article 7 of the EU Design Directive, which limits the scope of protection for semiconductor chips. Examine §1302. Among other things, it excludes from protection designs that are "dictated solely by a utilitarian function of the article that embodies it." 17 U.S.C. §1302(4). Elsewhere, however, the VHDPA states that "[t]he design of a vessel hull, deck, or combination of a hull and deck, including a plug or a mold, is subject to protection under this chapter, notwithstanding section 1302(4)." *Id.* §1301(a)(2). What, then, is the point of §1302(4)?

3. Examine carefully the portions of §1301 quoted above. If Congress wished to amend the VHDPA to extend protection to industrial designs generally, how might it do so? In the 110th session of Congress, bills were introduced that would have amended the VHDPA to provide protection for registered fashion designs for a three-year period. H.R. 2033, 110th

Cong. 1st Sess., S. 1957, 110th Cong., 2d Sess. The bills demonstrate how Congress could use the VHDPA as a template for extending protection to other types of design. They proposed to amend §1301 by defining "fashion design" as "the appearance as a whole of an article of apparel, including its ornamentation," and extending the protections in §1301(a) to "fashion design."

Reread Notes 7-8 on page 207. Is VHDPA-type protection for fashion designs desirable as a policy matter? For a discussion of that question, see Kal Raustiala & Christopher Sprigman, *The Piracy Paradox: Innovation and Intellectual Property in Fashion Design*, 92 Va. L. Rev. 1687 (2006) (examining why the fashion industry thrives despite the lack of protection and arguing that copying may promote innovation there), and Randal C. Picker, *Of Pirates and Puffy Shirts: A Comment on "The Piracy Paradox: Innovation and Intellectual Property in Fashion Design,"* available at http://ssrn.com/abstract_id=959727 (2007) (arguing that the situation is more complex than Raustiala & Sprigman suggest and expressing skepticism that copying of fashion design leads to more innovation).

4. Are new models of intellectual property protection necessary, or is deviation from the traditional patent/copyright paradigm unwise? Consider the following excerpt:

> The legal hybrid solutions override the negative economic premises of the traditional paradigms in several ways. In contrast to the patent regime, the hybrid legal institutions have lower thresholds for eligibility. All the hybrids typically fail the nonobviousness test and thereby fail to deliver the kind of path-breaking technical achievements that reconciled economic thought with legal monopoly in the first instance. For example, plant varieties, integrated circuit designs, engineering projects, and certain commercial designs need only show some form of "novelty" to qualify under their respective hybrid regimes. . . .
>
> Additionally, in contrast to the tenets of the copyright model, the hybrid legal institutions violate the negative economic premise that limits copyright protection to cultural goods. For example, the source code of a computer program or a drawing of an industrial object may resemble literary or artistic production when portrayed as two-dimensional representations of functional or factual matter; it may then receive copyright protection under the principle prohibiting discrimination on the basis of merit. Yet if embodied in three-dimensional products, the hybrid regime would extend protection to markets in which industrial, not cultural, exploitation occurs. . . .
>
> The paradigmatic intellectual property regimes . . . evolved with strict limitations and exceptions to balance the public interest in competition against specific incentives to create. In contrast, the hybrid legal regimes appear to have been crafted without comparable inhibitions. As improvised responses to sectoral protectionist demands, they lack coherent theoretical foundations and reflect different economic premises.

J.H. Reichman, *Legal Hybrids Between the Patent and Copyright Paradigms*, 94 Colum. L. Rev. 2432, 2500, 2502-03 (1995). What kinds of limitations are appropriate for sui generis protection regimes? Is cumulative protectionist bias inevitable when hybrid regimes for protection are adopted? *See id.*

5. In your opinion, would a general European-style industrial design protection regime be desirable for the U.S.? Why, or why not? Given what you have learned thus far about the values underlying the U.S. intellectual property system, how would you design a regime of intellectual property protection for industrial designs? Does the SCPA or the VHDPA provide a satisfactory template for such a regime? Does the EU Design Directive provide an acceptable model? Under what constitutional power would Congress enact such sui generis protection?

6. Is the U.S. in compliance with its obligations under Article 25 of the TRIPS Agreement to "provide for the protection of independently created industrial designs that are new or original"? Trade representatives for the U.S. have asserted that copyright protects a substantial subset of industrial designs. Yet recall the distinction made in the House Report when

describing the separability requirement for useful articles: "[T]he Committee is seeking to draw as clear a line as possible between copyrightable works of applied art and uncopyrighted works of industrial design." H.R. Rep. No. 94-1476, 94th Cong., 2d Sess. 54-55 (1976), *reprinted in* 1976 U.S.C.C.A.N. 5659, 5667-68.

7. If Congress were to enact a general design protection law, what, if anything, should it do about designs that are also eligible for protection under copyright law and/or design patent law? Some commentators argue that allowing a designer to claim protection under more than one legal regime results in overprotection. Do you agree? Should Congress draw boundaries between different legal regimes, or require claimants to elect one form of protection or the other? A different kind of overlapping protection can also occur when state law attempts to provide certain kinds of protection for works subject to copyright protection. When the overlap is between federal law and state law, issues of preemption must be considered. We explore these issues in Chapter 10.

B. COMPUTER SOFTWARE

Computer software presents difficulties akin to those raised by pictorial, graphic, and sculptural works, but also poses unique questions. Software, as a functional work, is unlike other works traditionally protected by copyright. At the same time, a programmer's written code is analogous, at least at some level, to the text of a novel. Indeed, Congress itself seized on this analogy, choosing to protect computer programs as "literary works." While the Berne Convention does not mention computer programs, the TRIPS Agreement reflects the U.S. model, requiring that computer programs, whether in source code or object code, be protected as literary works. TRIPS Agreement, art. 10. As we will see, however, the analogy to literary works is somewhat strained, and has presented difficulties for courts.

As you read the following materials, consider the implications of treating software as a literary work rather than as a pictorial, graphic, or sculptural work. Think also about whether the underlying policy justifications for copyright law discussed in Chapter 1 apply to software. Consider whether the law might more effectively address software under a regime specific to it, rather than under the more general copyright law.

1. Text or Machine?

In the early days of computer technology, copyright law did not clearly protect computer software. Firms relied on trade secret law to protect the code as written by programmers (source code), and contract law to define the terms of use of the machine-readable version of the code (object code) that they distributed to customers. In 1964, the Register of Copyrights began accepting computer programs for registration. Few firms wished to deposit source code because disclosing the code to the Copyright Office would destroy the secrecy required for trade secret protection. The Copyright Office would, however, accept submissions of object code if the applicant indicated that the program contained original authorship. The Office would then register the code under a "rule of doubt," with the registration certificate indicating that the Office had not determined whether copyrightable authorship existed. See U.S. Congress, Office of Technology Assessment, *Finding a Balance: Computer Software, Intellectual Property, and the Challenge of Technological Change* 66, OTA-TCT-527 (1992).

In 1955, well before the full-fledged computer revolution that brought a personal computer into almost every home, Congress authorized the Copyright Office to conduct a study recommending changes to the 1909 Act to address new technologies. It quickly became evident that any revision must address computer uses of copyrighted works. At the end of 1974, Congress passed a bill establishing the Commission on New Technological Uses of Copyrighted Works (CONTU). CONTU's initial agenda was, among other things, to study issues associated with the reproduction and use of copyrighted works in computers and computer-generated works.

Shortly thereafter, Congress passed the 1976 Copyright Act. The Act's legislative history suggested that programs could be copyrightable as literary works: "The term 'literary works' does not connote any criterion of literary merit or qualitative value: it includes . . . computer programs to the extent that they incorporate authorship in the programmer's expression of original ideas, as distinguished from the ideas themselves." H.R. Rep. No. 94-1476, 94th Cong., 2d Sess. 54 (1976), *reprinted in* 1976 U.S.C.C.A.N. 5659, 5667. Pending CONTU's report, Congress, as part of the 1976 Act, enacted a "status quo" provision in §117 that was intended to preserve the law — whatever it was — with respect to computer programs.[1]

After conducting its research, CONTU concluded that Congress could appropriately find computer programs to be "writings" within the meaning of the Constitution's Intellectual Property Clause:

> [A] program is created, as are most copyrighted works by placing symbols in a medium. In this respect it is the same as a novel, poem, play, musical score, blueprint, advertisement, or telephone directory. It is not the same as a phonorecord or videotape. Those works are created by shaping physical grooves or electromagnetic fields so that when they are moved past sensing devices electric currents are created which, when amplified, do physical work. Notwithstanding these apparent differences, all these works are writings in the constitutional sense, and eligible for copyright if the Congress so provides.

CONTU's Final Report and Recommendations 28 (published in Copyright, Congress and Technology: The Public Record, vol. 5, Oryx Press 1980) (hereinafter CONTU Report). The Commission also argued that §102(b) (which, as you recall, bars copyright protection for processes) did not stand as an obstacle to copyright protection because copyright "protects the program as long as it remains fixed in a tangible medium of expression but [does not protect] the electro-mechanical functioning of [the] machine." *Id.* at 39. According to CONTU:

> Programs should no more be considered machine parts than videotapes should be considered parts of projectors. . . . When a program is copied into the memory of a computer it still exists in a form in which a human-readable version may be produced. . . . Only when the program is inserted, instruction by instruction, into the processing element of the computer and electrical impulses are sent through the circuitry of the processor to initiate work is the ability to copy lost.

Id. at 41, 45.

---

1. Section 117 stated: "Notwithstanding the provisions of sections 106 through 116 and 118, this title does not afford to the owner of copyright in a work any greater or lesser rights with respect to the use of the work in conjunction with automatic systems capable of storing, processing, retrieving, or transferring information, or in conjunction with any similar device, machine, or process than those afforded to works under the law, whether title 17 or the common law or statutes of a State, in effect on December 31, 1976, as held applicable and construed by a court in an action brought under this title."

CONTU also considered whether affording computer programs copyright protection would comport with copyright policy. It noted that computer programs suffer from the classic public goods problem discussed in Chapter 1 and thus concluded that "some form of protection is necessary to encourage the creation and broad distribution of computer programs in a competitive market." *Id.* at 20-21. While noting that the laws of patent, trade secret, and unfair competition might protect certain aspects of software, CONTU expressed concern about these other approaches because "[e]ach of these forms of protection may inhibit the dissemination of information and restrict competition to a greater extent than copyright." *Id.* at 32. CONTU also rejected fears that copyright in programs would lead to dominant software firms. It emphasized that new firms could cheaply and easily enter the market, and argued that such low barriers to entry made the existence of a monopoly unlikely.

CONTU eventually made two recommendations for statutory change that were implemented by Congress in 1980. Congress repealed §117's placeholder, replacing it with what is now §117(a)-(b). It also adopted a definition of computer program in §101: "A 'computer program' is a set of statements or instructions to be used directly or indirectly in a computer in order to bring about a certain result."

CONTU's recommendations were not, however, unanimous. Commissioner John Hersey, then president of the Authors' League, wrote a strong dissent. Hersey cast a skeptical eye on the need for copyright protection, noting that the prime supporters of such protection for software were large corporations. He feared that large companies would "lock their software into their own hardware," adversely affecting independent software vendors who would like to sell programs to run on all hardware. CONTU Report at 73. Hersey particularly objected to copyright protection for the machine-readable version of programs: "To call a machine control element a copy of a literary work flies in the face of common sense." *Id.* at 67. He argued:

> Programs are profoundly different from the various forms of "works of authorship" secured under the Constitution by copyright. Works of authorship have always been intended to be circulated to human beings and to be used by them—to be read, heard, or seen, for either pleasurable or practical ends. Computer programs, in their mature phase, are addressed to machines. . . . [T]he program itself, in its mature and usable form, is a machine control element, a mechanical device, having no purpose beyond being engaged in a computer to perform mechanical work. . . . [The CONTU majority's] metaphor [treating programs like ordinary printed instructions] does not hold up beyond a certain point. Descriptions and printed instructions tell human beings how to use materials or machinery to produce desired results. In the case of computer programs, <u>the instructions themselves eventually become an essential part of the machinery that produces the results</u>. . . . Printed instructions tell how to do; programs are able to do.

Id. at 56-58 (emphasis in original).

Commissioner Hersey's dissent reminds us that not all, even those in the computer industry, advocated copyright protection for software. But while Hersey emphasized the utilitarian nature of a program, others embraced the analogy to a literary work, pointing to the creativity inherent in designing and coding a program as a justification for copyright protection. Programmers make a number of design decisions that reflect individual creativity: "Out of [ ] elementary logic expressions . . . computer programs of great elegance and complexity can be written. The choice of logic elements, their pattern, sequence, and significance are as fundamental to programmers' expression as the choice of words, their sequence and significance are to the poets' expression. . . . [C]omputer programming is a kind of creative writing." Anthony L. Clapes et al., *Silicon Epics and Binary Bards: Determining the Proper Scope of Copyright Protection for Computer Programs*, 34 UCLA L. Rev. 1493, 1533, 1538 (1987). Clapes and his coauthors even compared a computer program to a symphony: "A typical customer perceives computer programs as things that cause computers to act in a particular way. In a sense, this perspective is similar to the concertgoer's impression of a symphony. . . . Yet the concertgoer knows that the symphony, as created by its composer, is in fact a sequence of instructions that must be processed by an instrumentality, the orchestra, to produce the 'symphony' heard by the listener." *Id.* at 1510-11.

This confusion over whether the law should consider programs to be text or a machine eventually led to litigation. In the early cases, courts pondered questions such as whether both source and object code should be protected by copyright, and whether operating system software should be treated the same as application programs.

Apple Computer, Inc. v. Franklin Computer Corp.
714 F.2d 1240 (3d Cir. 1983), cert. dismissed, *464 U.S. 1033 (1984)*

SLOVITER, J.: . . . Franklin [Computer Corp.], the defendant below, manufactures and sells the ACE 100 personal computer and at the time of the hearing employed about 75 people and had sold fewer than 1,000 computers. The ACE 100 was designed to be "Apple compatible," so that peripheral equipment and software developed for use with the Apple II computer could be used in conjunction with the ACE 100. Franklin's copying of Apple's operating system computer programs in an effort to achieve such compatibility precipitated this suit. . . . [The district court denied plaintiff Apple Computer's request for a preliminary injunction and Apple appealed.]

There are three levels of computer language in which computer programs may be written. High level language, such as the commonly used BASIC or FORTRAN, uses English words and symbols, and is relatively easy to learn and understand (e.g., "GO TO 40" tells the computer to skip intervening steps and go to the step at line 40). A somewhat lower level language is assembly language, which consists of alphanumeric labels (e.g., "ADC" means "add with carry"). Statements in high level language, and apparently also statements in assembly language, are referred to as written in "source code." The third, or lowest level computer language, is machine language, a binary language using two symbols, 0 and 1, to indicate an open or closed switch (e.g., "01101001" means, to the Apple, add two numbers and save the result). Statements in machine language are referred to as written in "object code."

The CPU [(Central Processing Unit)] can only follow instructions written in object code. However, programs are usually written in source code which is more intelligible to humans. Programs written in source code can be converted or translated by a "compiler" program into object code for use by the computer. Programs are generally distributed only in their object code version stored on a memory device.

A computer program can be stored or fixed on a variety of memory devices, two of which are of particular relevance for this case. The ROM (Read Only Memory) is an internal permanent memory device consisting of a semi-conductor "chip" which is incorporated into the circuitry of the computer. A program in object code is embedded on a ROM before it is incorporated in the computer. Information stored on a ROM can only be read, not erased or rewritten. The ACE 100 apparently contains EPROMS (Erasable Programmable Read Only Memory) on which the stored information can be erased and the chip reprogrammed, but the district court found that for purposes of this proceeding, the difference between ROMs and EPROMs is inconsequential. 545 F. Supp. at 813 n. 3. The other device used for storing the programs at issue is a diskette or "floppy disk," an auxiliary memory device consisting of a flexible magnetic disk resembling a phonograph record, which can be inserted into the computer and from which data or instructions can be read.

Computer programs can be categorized by function as either application programs or operating system programs. Application programs usually perform a specific task for the computer user, such as word processing, checkbook balancing, or playing a game. In contrast, operating system programs generally manage the internal functions of the computer or facilitate use of application programs. The parties agree that the fourteen computer programs at issue in this suit are operating system programs. . . .

Franklin did not dispute that it copied the Apple programs. . . . [Franklin's Vice President David] McWherter concluded that use of the identical signals was necessary in order to ensure 100 percent compatibility with application programs created to run on the Apple computer. . . . Franklin made no attempt to rewrite any of the programs prior to the lawsuit except for [one]. . . . Apple introduced evidence that Franklin could have rewritten programs, . . . and that there are in existence operating programs written by third parties which are compatible with Apple II.

Franklin's principal defense . . . is primarily a legal one, directed to its contention that the Apple operating system programs are not capable of copyright protection. . . .

Copyrightability of a Computer Program Expressed in Object Code

Certain statements by the district court suggest that programs expressed in object code, as distinguished from source code, may not be the proper subject of copyright. We find no basis in the statute for any such concern. Furthermore, our decision in *Williams Electronics, Inc. v. Artic International, Inc.*, [685 F.2d 870 (3d Cir. 1982)], laid to rest many of the doubts expressed by the district court. . . .

The district court also expressed uncertainty as to whether a computer program in object code could be classified as a "literary work."[7] However, the category of "literary works," one of the seven copyrightable categories, is not confined to literature in the nature of Hemingway's *For Whom the Bell Tolls*. The definition of "literary works" in section 101 includes expression not only in words but also "numbers, or other . . . numerical symbols or indicia," thereby expanding the common usage of "literary works." . . . Thus a computer program, whether in object code or source code, is a "literary work" and is protected from unauthorized copying, whether from its object or source code version. . . .

Copyrightability of Computer Operating System Programs

We turn to the heart of Franklin's position on appeal which is that computer operating system programs, as distinguished from application programs, are not the proper subject of copyright "regardless of the language or medium in which they are fixed." Brief of Appellee at 15 (emphasis deleted). . . . [W]e consider [this] as a matter of first impression.

Franklin contends that operating system programs are *per se* excluded from copyright protection under the express terms of section 102(b) of the Copyright Act, and under the precedent and underlying principles of *Baker v. Selden*, 101 U.S. 99 . . . (1879). These separate grounds have substantial analytic overlap. . . .

---

7. The district court stated that a programmer working directly in object code appears to think more as a mathematician or engineer, that the process of constructing a chip is less a work of authorship than the product of engineering knowledge, and that it may be more apt to describe an encoded ROM as a pictorial three-dimensional object than as a literary work. 545 F. Supp. at 821-22. . . . Apple does not seek to protect the ROM's architecture but only the program encoded upon it.

1. "Process," "System" or "Method of Operation"...

Franklin's attack on operating system programs as "methods" or "processes" seems inconsistent with its concession that application programs are an appropriate subject of copyright. Both types of programs instruct the computer to do something. Therefore, it should make no difference for purposes of section 102(b) whether these instructions tell the computer to help prepare an income tax return (the task of an application program) or to translate a high level language program from source code into its binary language object code form (the task of an operating system program such as "Applesoft"). Since it is only the instructions which are protected, a "process" is no more involved because the instructions in an operating system program may be used to activate the operation of the computer than it would be if instructions were written in ordinary English in a manual which described the necessary steps to activate an intricate complicated machine. There is, therefore, no reason to afford any less copyright protection to the instructions in an operating system program than to the instructions in an application program.

Franklin's argument, receptively treated by the district court, that an operating system program is part of a machine mistakenly focuses on the physical characteristics of the instructions. But the medium is not the message. We have already considered and rejected aspects of this contention.... The mere fact that the operating system program may be etched on a ROM does not make the program either a machine, part of a machine or its equivalent. Furthermore, as one of Franklin's witnesses testified, an operating system does not have to be permanently in the machine in ROM, but it may be on some other medium, such as a diskette or magnetic tape, where it could be readily transferred into the temporary memory space of the computer. In fact, some of the operating systems at issue were on diskette. As the CONTU majority stated,

> Programs should no more be considered machine parts than videotapes should be considered parts of projectors or phonorecords parts of sound reproduction equipment.... That the words of a program are used ultimately in the implementation of a process should in no way affect their copyrightability.

CONTU Report at 21....

Perhaps the most convincing item leading us to reject Franklin's argument is that the statutory definition of a computer program as a set of instructions to be used in a computer in order to bring about a certain result, 17 U.S.C. §101, makes no distinction between application programs and operating programs. Franklin can point to no decision which adopts the distinction it seeks to make....

2. Idea/Expression Dichotomy...

We ... focus on whether the idea is capable of various modes of expression. If other programs can be written or created which perform the same function as an Apple's operating system program, then that program is an expression of the idea and hence copyrightable. In essence, this inquiry is no different than that made to determine whether the expression and idea have merged, which has been stated to occur where there are no or few other ways of expressing a particular idea.

The district court made no findings as to whether some or all of Apple's operating programs represent the only means of expression of the idea underlying them. Although there seems to be a concession by Franklin that at least some of the programs can be rewritten, we do not believe that the record on that issue is so clear that it can be decided at the appellate level. Therefore, if the issue is pressed on remand, the necessary finding can be made at that time.

Franklin claims that whether or not the programs can be rewritten, there are a limited "number of ways to arrange operating systems to enable a computer to run the vast body of Apple-compatible software," Brief of Appellee at 20. This claim has no pertinence to either the idea/expression dichotomy or merger. The idea which may merge with the expression, thus making the copyright unavailable, is the idea which is the subject of the expression. The idea of one of the operating system programs is, for example, how to translate source code into object code. If other methods of expressing that idea are not foreclosed as a practical matter, then there is no merger. Franklin may wish to achieve total compatibility with independently developed application programs written for the Apple II, but that is a commercial and competitive objective which does not enter into the somewhat metaphysical issue of whether particular ideas and expressions have merged. . . .

NOTES AND QUESTIONS

1. The *Franklin* case explains the different "levels" of computer languages. A compiler is a program that translates a high-level language (source code) version of a program into machine language (object code). As the case also notes, programmers represent compiled code using the numbers zero and one to represent the "on" and "off" states of the hardware switches in the computer. Note, however, that compiled code does not necessarily — or even usually — have the same sequence as the source code from which it was derived. A program does not usually execute its steps in the same order in which the programmer wrote them down in source code. For example, programs often present users with options such as "Print" or "Save As." If the user selects "Print," the program will jump to the instructions relating to that command, which may or may not be the next line of instructions in the source code. Moreover, the compiled code is not necessarily stored in computer memory in the same sequence or organization as the source code form. Are these differences relevant to the policy question of the appropriateness of protection and/or the "correct" level of protection afforded source code versus object code?

2. Recall the excerpt from the Clapes *et al.* article, *supra* page 217, analogizing a computer program to a symphony. Should creativity automatically equal protection? Few would dispute that Albert Einstein was creative, but could he have obtained copyright protection for $E = mc^2$? Is a symphony different from a computer program in ways that should influence the copyright analysis?

3. Did the CONTU majority reply adequately to Commissioner Hersey's argument that programs are fundamentally different from other copyrightable works because they are addressed to machines? Are computer programs in their executable form different from songs recorded in digital form on a CD or motion pictures stored on videotape?

In an influential article, Professors Pamela Samuelson, Randall Davis, J.H. Reichman, and the founder of Lotus Corp., Mitchell Kapor, discussed the differences between programs and conventional copyrighted works, arguing that those differences were so great that computer programs could not plausibly be considered just another kind of "literary work" protectible by copyright:

1.1.1 Computer Programs Are Not Only Texts; They Also Behave . . .

Behavior is not a secondary by-product of a program, but rather an essential part of what programs are. To put the point starkly: No one would want to buy a program that did not behave, i.e., that did nothing, no matter how elegant the source code "prose" expressing that nothing. . . .

1.1.2 Text and Behavior Are Largely Independent . . .

The independence of text and behavior is one important respect in which programs differ from other copyrighted works. Imagine trying to create two pieces of music that have different notes, but that sound indistinguishable. Imagine trying to create two plays with different dialogue and characters, but that appear indistinguishable to the audience. Yet, two programs with different texts can be indistinguishable to users.

1.1.3 Behavior is Valuable . . .

All this stands in sharp contrast to traditional literary works which are valued because of their expression (i.e., what they say and how well they say it). Programs have almost no value to users as texts. Rather, their value lies in behavior.

Pamela Samuelson et al., *A Manifesto Concerning the Legal Protection of Computer Programs,* 94 Colum. L. Rev. 2308, 2316-19 (1994).[2] Are these insights also arguments against providing copyright protection for computer programs? Why, or why not?

2. Distinguishing Idea from Expression in Software

After a few years, it became settled law that both source and object code, whether for operating systems or applications, are protected by copyright. However, the same limiting doctrines that apply to literary works generally also apply to computer programs. For example, as the case below notes, the merger doctrine applies to computer programs.

As Chapter 2 revealed, it is difficult enough to separate idea from expression when dealing with literal text. It is even more difficult when the work is a computer program. Rather than copying literal elements of the code, another programmer could copy the structure of a program and write code in a different language from the original. That code would perform exactly the same function in exactly the same way as the original, but the new product's literal code did not copy that of the first. Indeed, it would not look remotely like the literal code of the first program. Is this secondcomer a copyist or a legitimate competitor? In part, this is a question about defining the protectible expression in a computer program. In addition to protecting the literal lines of code, should copyright also protect the structure of a computer program? Should that structure be analogized to a detailed plot for a literary work? Or is the more appropriate analogy to a process or method of operation, which is excluded from copyright protection?

Courts have been grappling for a number of years with the question whether the structure of a program is protected by copyright law. They have taken varying approaches to answering that question. As you read the following cases, consider the policy arguments on both sides. Focus too on the defendants — are they slavish copiers or are they bringing something new to the market? Should it matter?

Computer Associates International, Inc. v. Altai, Inc.
982 F.2d 693 (2d Cir. 1992)

WALKER, J.: . . . Among other things, this case deals with the challenging question of whether and to what extent the "non-literal" aspects of a computer program, that is, those aspects that are not reduced to written code, are protected by copyright. . . .

---

2. Reprinted by permission of the authors and the Columbia Law Review.

Background . . .

I. Computer Program Design

Certain elementary facts concerning the nature of computer programs are vital to the following discussion. The Copyright Act defines a computer program as "a set of statements or instructions to be used directly or indirectly in a computer in order to bring about a certain result." 17 U.S.C. §101. In writing these directions, the programmer works "from the general to the specific." *Whelan Assocs., Inc. v. Jaslow Dental Lab., Inc.,* 797 F.2d 1222, 1229 (3d Cir. 1986), *cert. denied,* 479 U.S. 1031(1987). *See generally* Steven R. Englund, Note, *Idea, Process, or Protected Expression?: Determining the Scope of Copyright Protection of the Structure of Computer Programs,* 88 Mich. L. Rev. 866, 867-73 (1990) (hereinafter "Englund"); Peter S. Menell, *An Analysis of the Scope of Copyright Protection for Application Programs,* 41 Stan. L. Rev. 1045, 1051-57 (1989) (hereinafter "Menell"); Mark T. Kretschmer, Note, *Copyright Protection For Software Architecture: Just Say No!,* 1988 Colum. Bus. L. Rev. 823, 824-27 (1988) (hereinafter "Kretschmer"); Peter G. Spivack, Comment, *Does Form Follow Function? The Idea/Expression Dichotomy in Copyright Protection of Computer Software,* 35 UCLA L. Rev. 723, 729-31 (1988) (hereinafter "Spivack").

The first step in this procedure is to identify a program's ultimate function or purpose. An example of such an ultimate purpose might be the creation and maintenance of a business ledger. Once this goal has been achieved, a programmer breaks down or "decomposes" the program's ultimate function into "simpler constituent problems or 'subtasks,' " Englund, at 870, which are also known as subroutines or modules. *See* Spivack, at 729. In the context of a business ledger program, a module or subroutine might be responsible for the task of updating a list of outstanding accounts receivable. Sometimes, depending upon the complexity of its task, a subroutine may be broken down further into sub-subroutines.

Having sufficiently decomposed the program's ultimate function into its component elements, a programmer will then arrange the subroutines or modules into what are known as organizational or flow charts. Flow charts map the interactions between modules that achieve the program's end goal. *See* Kretschmer, at 826.

In order to accomplish these intra-program interactions, a programmer must carefully design each module's parameter list. A parameter list, according to the expert appointed and fully credited by the district court, Dr. Randall Davis, is "the information sent to and received from a subroutine." *See* Report of Dr. Randall Davis, at 12. The term "parameter list" refers to the form in which information is passed between modules (e.g. for accounts receivable, the designated time frame and particular customer identifying number) and the information's actual content (e.g. 8/91-7/92; customer No. 3). *Id.* With respect to form, interacting modules must share similar parameter lists so that they are capable of exchanging information.

"The functions of the modules in a program together with each module's relationships to other modules constitute the 'structure' of the program." Englund, at 871. . . .

In fashioning the structure, a programmer will normally attempt to maximize the program's speed, efficiency, as well as simplicity for user operation, while taking into consideration certain externalities such as the memory constraints of the computer upon which the program will be run. *See id.;* Kretschmer, at 826; Menell, at 1052. "This stage of program design often requires the most time and investment." Kretschmer, at 826.

Once each necessary module has been identified, designed, and its relationship to the other modules has been laid out conceptually, the resulting program structure must be embodied in a written language that the computer can read. This process is called "coding," and requires two steps. *Whelan,* 797 F.2d at 1230. First, the programmer must transpose the program's structural blue-print into a source code. . . . Once the source code has been completed, the second step is to translate or "compile" it into object code. . . .

After the coding is finished, the programmer will run the program on the computer in order to find and correct any logical and syntactical errors. This is known as "debugging" and, once done, the program is complete. *See* Kretschmer, at 826-27.

II. Facts

[Computer Associates (CA) developed and marketed a program called CA-SCHEDULER, which was intended to schedule when the computer should perform certain functions, and to control the computer's operation while it executed the schedule. Another program, ADAPTER, was a module within CA-SCHEDULER that translated CA-SCHEDU-LER's language to allow it to run on the operating system installed on the user's computer. This saved CA the time and expense of writing different versions of CA-SCHEDULER for different operating systems, and saved its customers the expense of buying multiple copies for each operating system their machines might use. Altai sought to modify its own scheduling software, ZEKE, to run on operating systems other than the one for which it was designed. Altai hired a programmer (Arney) away from CA, not knowing that Arney had worked on ADAPTER and also brought home a copy of its source code. Arney copied about 30 percent of ADAPTER's source code into OSCAR 3.4, Altai's first implementation of a compatibility component analogous to ADAPTER's. The lower court found copyright infringement and Altai did not appeal that holding. On discovering the infringement, Altai gave eight new programmers who had not worked on OSCAR 3.4 a description of what functionality the software required. These programmers wrote new code, replacing OSCAR 3.4 with a new compatibility component, OSCAR 3.5. The district court held that Altai's OSCAR 3.5 did not infringe any CA copyrights. CA appealed. The portion of the opinion that we have reproduced here focuses on determining the protectible elements of CA's program. Chapter 5 contains the portion of the opinion considering whether Altai infringed.] . . .

Discussion . . .

I. Copyright Infringement

. . . As a general matter, and to varying degrees, copyright protection extends beyond a literary work's strictly textual form to its non-literal components. As we have said, "[i]t is of course essential to any protection of literary property . . . that the right cannot be limited literally to the text, else a plagiarist would escape by immaterial variations." *Nichols v. Universal Pictures Co.*, 45 F.2d 119, 121 (2d Cir. 1930) (L. Hand, J.), *cert. denied*, 282 U.S. 902 (1931). Thus, where "the fundamental essence or structure of one work is duplicated in another," 3 Nimmer, §13.03[A][1], at 13-24, courts have found copyright infringement. This black-letter proposition is the springboard for our discussion.

A. Copyright Protection for the Non-literal Elements of Computer Programs . . .

CA argues that, despite Altai's rewrite of the OSCAR code, the resulting program remained substantially similar to the structure of its ADAPTER program. . . . In addition to these aspects, CA contends that OSCAR 3.5 is also substantially similar to ADAPTER with respect to the list of services that both ADAPTER and OSCAR obtain from their respective operating systems. We must decide whether and to what extent these elements of computer programs are protected by copyright law. . . .

[The court noted that the Copyright Act protects original works of authorship, including literary works, and that Congress intended to protect computer programs as literary works.]

The syllogism that follows from the foregoing premises is a powerful one: if the non-literal structures of literary works are protected by copyright; and if computer programs are literary works, as we are told by the legislature; then the non-literal structures of computer programs are protected by copyright. . . .

1) Idea vs. Expression Dichotomy . . .

The essentially utilitarian nature of a computer program . . . complicates the task of distilling its idea from its expression. *See SAS Inst. [Inc. v. S & H Computer Sys., Inc.],* 605 F. Supp. [816,] 829 [(M.D. Tenn. 1985)]; *cf.* Englund, at 893. In order to describe both computational processes and abstract ideas, its content "combines creative and technical expression." *See* Spivack, at 755. The variations of expression found in purely creative compositions, as opposed to those contained in utilitarian works, are not directed towards practical application. For example, a narration of Humpty Dumpty's demise, which would clearly be a creative composition, does not serve the same ends as, say, a recipe for scrambled eggs — which is a more process oriented text. Thus, compared to aesthetic works, computer programs hover even more closely to the elusive boundary line described in §102(b).

The doctrinal starting point in analyses of utilitarian works, is the seminal case of *Baker v. Selden,* 101 U.S. 99 (1879). In *Baker,* the Supreme Court faced the question of "whether the exclusive property in a system of bookkeeping can be claimed, under the law of copyright, by means of a book in which that system is explained?" . . .

To the extent that an accounting text and a computer program are both "a set of statements or instructions . . . to bring about a certain result," 17 U.S.C. §101, they are roughly analogous. In the former case, the processes are ultimately conducted by human agency; in the latter, by electronic means. In either case, as already stated, the processes themselves are not protectable. But the holding in *Baker* goes farther. The Court concluded that those aspects of a work, which "must necessarily be used as incident to" the idea, system or process that the work describes, are also not copyrightable. 101 U.S. at 104. . . . From this reasoning, we conclude that those elements of a computer program that are necessarily incidental to its function are similarly unprotectable.

While *Baker v. Selden* provides a sound analytical foundation, it offers scant guidance on how to separate idea or process from expression, and moreover, on how to further distinguish protectable expression from that expression which "must necessarily be used as incident to" the work's underlying concept. In the context of computer programs, the Third Circuit's noted decision in *Whelan* has, thus far, been the most thoughtful attempt to accomplish these ends.

The court in *Whelan* faced substantially the same problem as is presented by this case. There, the defendant was accused of making off with the non-literal structure of the plaintiff's copyrighted dental lab management program, and employing it to create its own competitive version. In assessing whether there had been an infringement, the court had to determine which aspects of the programs involved were ideas, and which were expression. In separating the two, the court settled upon the following conceptual approach:

[T]he line between idea and expression may be drawn with reference to the end sought to be achieved by the work in question. In other words, *the purpose or function of a utilitarian work would be the work's idea, and everything that is not necessary to that purpose or function would be part of the expression of the idea. . . .* Where there are various means of achieving the desired purpose, then the particular means chosen is not necessary to the purpose; hence, there is expression, not idea.

797 F.2d at 1236 (citations omitted). The "idea" of the program at issue in *Whelan* was identified by the court as simply "the efficient management of a dental laboratory." *Id.* at n. 28. . . .

Whelan has [been adopted by some courts and rejected by others, and has] fared even more poorly in the academic community, where its standard for distinguishing idea from expression has been widely criticized for being conceptually overbroad. *See, e.g.*, Englund, at 881; Menell, at 1074, 1082; Kretschmer, at 83739; Spivack, at 747-55; Thomas M. Gage, Note, Whelan Associates v. Jaslow Dental Laboratories: *Copyright Protection for Computer Software Structure — What's the Purpose?*, 1987 Wis. L. Rev. 859, 860-61 (1987). The leading commentator in the field has stated that "[t]he crucial flaw in [*Whelan's*] reasoning is that it assumes that only one 'idea,' in copyright law terms, underlies any computer program, and that once a separable idea can be identified, everything else must be expression." 3 Nimmer §13.03(F), at 13-62.34. This criticism focuses not upon the program's ultimate purpose but upon the reality of its structural design. As we have already noted, a computer program's ultimate function or purpose is the composite result of interacting subroutines. Since each subroutine is itself a program, and thus, may be said to have its own "idea," *Whelan's* general formulation that a program's overall purpose equates with the program's idea is descriptively inadequate. . . .

2) Substantial Similarity Test for Computer Program Structure: Abstraction-Filtration-Comparison

We think that *Whelan's* approach to separating idea from expression in computer programs relies too heavily on metaphysical distinctions and does not place enough emphasis on practical considerations. As the cases that we shall discuss demonstrate, a satisfactory answer to this problem cannot be reached by resorting, *a priori*, to philosophical first principals [sic]. . . .

Step One: Abstraction

. . . [T]he theoretic framework for analyzing substantial similarity expounded by Learned Hand in the *Nichols* case is helpful in the present context. In *Nichols*, we enunciated what has now become known as the "abstractions" test for separating idea from expression:

> Upon any work . . . a great number of patterns of increasing generality will fit equally well, as more and more of the incident is left out. The last may perhaps be no more than the most general statement of what the [work] is about, and at times might consist only of its title; but there is a point in this series of abstractions where they are no longer protected, since otherwise the [author] could prevent the use of his "ideas," to which, apart from their expression, his property is never extended.

Nichols, 45 F.2d at 121.

. . . In contrast to the *Whelan* approach, the abstractions test "implicitly recognizes that any given work may consist of a mixture of numerous ideas and expressions." 3 Nimmer §13.03[F], at 13-62.34-63.

As applied to computer programs, the abstractions test will comprise the first step in the examination for substantial similarity. Initially, in a manner that resembles reverse engineering on a theoretical plane, a court should dissect the allegedly copied program's structure and isolate each level of abstraction contained within it. This process begins with the code and ends with an articulation of the program's ultimate function. Along the way, it is necessary essentially to retrace and map each of the designer's steps — in the opposite order in which they were taken during the program's creation. *See* Background: Computer Program Design, *supra.* As an anatomical guide to this procedure, the following description is helpful:

> At the lowest level of abstraction, a computer program may be thought of in its entirety as a set of individual instructions organized into a hierarchy of modules. At a higher level of abstraction, the instructions in the lowest-level modules may be replaced conceptually by the functions of those modules. At progressively higher levels of abstraction, the functions of higher-level modules conceptually replace the implementations of those modules in terms of lower-level modules and instructions, until finally, one is left with nothing but the ultimate function of the program. . . . A program has structure at every level of abstraction at which it is viewed. At low levels of abstraction, a program's structure may be quite complex; at the highest level it is trivial.

Englund, at 897-98; *cf.* Spivack, at 774

Step Two: Filtration

. . . Professor Nimmer suggests, and we endorse, a "successive filtering method" for separating protectable expression from non-protectable material. *See generally* 3 Nimmer §13.03[F]. This process entails examining the structural components at each level of abstraction to determine whether their particular inclusion at that level was "idea" or was dictated by considerations of efficiency, so as to be necessarily incidental to that idea; required by factors external to the program itself; or taken from the public domain and hence is nonprotectable expression. *See also* Kretschmer, at 844-45 (arguing that program features dictated by market externalities or efficiency concerns are unprotectable). The structure of any given program may reflect some, all, or none of these considerations. Each case requires its own fact specific investigation. . . .

(a)   *Elements Dictated by Efficiency*

The portion of *Baker v. Selden*, discussed earlier, . . . appears to be the cornerstone for what has developed into the doctrine of merger. The doctrine's underlying principle is that "[w]hen there is essentially only one way to express an idea, the idea and its expression are inseparable and copyright is no bar to copying that expression." Under these circumstances, the expression is said to have "merged" with the idea itself. In order not to confer a monopoly of the idea upon the copyright owner, such expression should not be protected. . . .

[W]hen one considers the fact that programmers generally strive to create programs "that meet the user's needs in the most efficient manner," Menell, at 1052, the applicability of the merger doctrine to computer programs becomes compelling. In the context of computer program design, the concept of efficiency is akin to deriving the most concise logical proof or formulating the most succinct mathematical computation. Thus, the more efficient a set of modules are, the more closely they approximate the idea or process embodied in that particular aspect of the program's structure.

While, hypothetically, there might be a myriad of ways in which a programmer may effectuate certain functions within a program, — i.e., express the idea embodied in a given subroutine — efficiency concerns may so narrow the practical range of choice as to make only one or two forms of expression workable options. *See* 3 Nimmer §13.03[F][2], at 13-63; *see also*

Whelan, 797 F.2d at 1243 n. 43 ("It is true that for certain tasks there are only a very limited number of file structures available, and in such cases the structures might not be copyrightable. . . ."). Of course, not all program structure is informed by efficiency concerns. *See* Menell, at 1052 (besides efficiency, simplicity related to user accommodation has become a programming priority). It follows that in order to determine whether the merger doctrine precludes copyright protection to an aspect of a program's structure that is so oriented, a court must inquire "whether the use of *this particular set* of modules is necessary efficiently to implement that part of the program's process" being implemented. Englund, at 902. If the answer is yes, then the expression represented by the programmer's choice of a specific module or group of modules has merged with their underlying idea and is unprotected. *Id*. at 902-03. . . .

(b)   Elements Dictated By External Factors

We have stated that where "it is virtually impossible to write about a particular historical era or fictional theme without employing certain 'stock' or standard literary devices," such expression is not copyrightable. *Hoehling v. Universal City Studios, Inc.*, 618 F.2d 972, 979 (2d Cir.), *cert. denied*, 449 U.S. 841(1980). . . .

Professor Nimmer points out that "in many instances it is virtually impossible to write a program to perform particular functions in a specific computing environment without employing standard techniques." 3 Nimmer §13.03[F][3], at 13-65. This is a result of the fact that a programmer's freedom of design choice is often circumscribed by extrinsic considerations such as (1) the mechanical specifications of the computer on which a particular program is intended to run; (2) compatibility requirements of other programs with which a program is designed to operate in conjunction; (3) computer manufacturers' design standards; (4) demands of the industry being serviced; and (5) widely accepted programming practices within the computer industry. *Id*. at 13-66-71. . . .

Building upon . . . existing case law, we conclude that a court must also examine the structural content of an allegedly infringed program for elements that might have been dictated by external factors.

(c)   Elements taken From the Public Domain

Closely related to the non-protectability of *scenes a faire*, is material found in the public domain. Such material is free for the taking and cannot be appropriated by a single author even though it is included in a copyrighted work. . . .

Step Three: Comparison

The third and final step of the test for substantial similarity that we believe appropriate for non-literal program components entails a comparison. Once a court has sifted out all elements of the allegedly infringed program which are "ideas" or are dictated by efficiency or external factors, or taken from the public domain, there may remain a core of protectible expression. In terms of a work's copyright value, this is the golden nugget. . . .

3)   Policy Considerations

CA and some amici argue against th[is] type of approach. . . . At bottom, they claim that if programmers are not guaranteed broad copyright protection for their work, they will not invest the extensive time, energy and funds required to design and improve program structures. While they have a point, their argument cannot carry the day. The interest of the copyright law is not in simply conferring a monopoly on industrious persons, but in advancing the public welfare through rewarding artistic creativity, in a manner that permits the free use and development of non-protectable ideas and processes. . . .

Feist teaches that substantial effort alone cannot confer copyright status on an otherwise uncopyrightable work. As we have discussed, despite the fact that significant labor and expense often goes into computer program flow-charting and debugging, that process does not always result in inherently protectable expression. Thus, *Feist* implicitly undercuts the *Whelan* rationale, "which allow[ed] copyright protection beyond the literal computer code . . . [in order to] provide the proper incentive for programmers by protecting their most valuable efforts. . . ." *Whelan*, 797 F.2d at 1237 (footnote omitted). We note that *Whelan* was decided prior to *Feist* when the "sweat of the brow" doctrine still had vitality. In view of the Supreme Court's recent holding, however, we must reject the legal basis of CA's disincentive argument.

Furthermore, we are unpersuaded that the test we approve today will lead to the dire consequences for the computer program industry that plaintiff and some *amici* predict. To the contrary, serious students of the industry have been highly critical of the sweeping scope of copyright protection engendered by the *Whelan* rule, in that it "enables first comers to 'lock up' basic programming techniques as implemented in programs to perform particular tasks." Menell, at 1087; *see also* Spivack, at 765 (*Whelan* "results in an inhibition of creation by virtue of the copyright owner's quasi-monopoly power").

To be frank, the exact contours of copyright protection for non-literal program structure are not completely clear. We trust that as future cases are decided, those limits will become better defined. Indeed, it may well be that the Copyright Act serves as a relatively weak barrier against public access to the theoretical interstices behind a program's source and object codes. This results from the hybrid nature of a computer program, which, while it is literary expression, is also a highly functional, utilitarian component in the larger process of computing.

Generally, we think that copyright registration — with its indiscriminating availability — is not ideally suited to deal with the highly dynamic technology of computer science. Thus far, many of the decisions in this area reflect the courts' attempt to fit the proverbial square peg in a round hole. The district court, *see Computer Assocs.*, 775 F. Supp. at 560, and at least one commentator have suggested that patent registration, with its exacting up-front novelty and non-obviousness requirements, might be the more appropriate rubric of protection for intellectual property of this kind. *See* Randell M. Whitmeyer, Comment, *A Plea for Due Processes: Defining the Proper Scope of Patent Protection for Computer Software*, 85 Nw. U. L. Rev. 1103, 1123-25 (1991). In any event, now that more than 12 years have passed since CONTU issued its final report, the resolution of this specific issue could benefit from further legislative investigation — perhaps a CONTU II.

In the meantime, Congress has made clear that computer programs are literary works entitled to copyright protection. Of course, we shall abide by these instructions, but in so doing we must not impair the overall integrity of copyright law. . . .

Softel, Inc. v. Dragon Medical and Scientific Communications, Inc.

118 F.3d 955 (2d Cir. 1997), cert. denied, *523 U.S. 1020 (1998)*

[Softel and Dragon had a longstanding relationship under which Softel provided video imaging software to Dragon. Softel owned the copyright in the code it supplied. The relationship soured. Dragon retrieved files that Softel had attempted to delete from Dragon's system and used Softel's image retrieval modules to create new programs. After Softel sued for copyright infringement, Dragon created new programs written in a different language to run on different hardware (the "post-litigation" programs). The judge below found that the pre-litigation programs infringed Softel's copyrights, but the post-litigation ones did not. The appeal addresses Softel's claims regarding the post-litigation programs.]

PARKER, J.: . . . On this appeal, Softel renews its claim that Dragon's post-litigation programs infringed copyrights held by Softel. Softel argues that it claimed in the district court that its software combined certain computer programming design elements in an expressive way and that Dragon had copied that expression, but that Judge Cannella ignored this claim and instead addressed (and rejected) a claim that Softel had not made, to wit, that each of the design elements, *taken individually*, was protectible expression.

It is well-established in this Circuit that non-literal similarity of computer programs can constitute copyright infringement. *See Altai*, 982 F.2d at 702. We have prescribed an "abstraction-filtration-comparison" method of analysis for determining whether a program has been infringed. *See id.* at 706-12. . . .

Our application of this method of analysis to the facts of *Altai* demonstrates that an allegation of infringement based on similarities in architecture cannot be ignored merely because many or all of the design elements that make up that architecture are not protectible when considered at a lower level of abstraction. In *Altai*, the district court held many aspects of the program at issue in that case to be not protectible for various reasons (e.g., because they were in the public domain or were computer *scenes a faire*). Nevertheless, the court proceeded to a higher level of abstraction and responded to the plaintiff's claim of infringement based on alleged similarities between the two programs' "organizational charts." *Computer Assocs. Int'l. Inc. v. Altai, Inc.*, 775 F. Supp. 544, 562 (E.D.N.Y. 1991). In reviewing that claim, the trial court made no effort to remove from its analysis those elements of the program that had been found unprotectible at the lower level of abstraction. Instead, analyzing the program at the higher level of abstraction, it rejected the organizational claim on the grounds that the structure alleged to have been infringed was "simple and obvious to anyone exposed to the operation of the program[s]." *Id.* This Court approved that approach, adding only that the district court's use of the word "obvious" should be understood to be a holding that the purportedly infringed structure was a *scene a faire*. *See Altai*, 982 F.2d at 714-15.

The foregoing approach is consistent with the Supreme Court's decision in *Feist Publications, Inc. v. Rural Telephone Service Co.*, 499 U.S. 340 (1991), discussed by this Court in *Altai*, 982 F.2d at 711-12. In *Feist*, the Court made quite clear that a compilation of non-protectible elements can enjoy copyright protection even though its constituent elements do not. *See Feist*, 499 U.S. at 344-51 A district court in another circuit has illustrated the danger of overlooking this aspect of copyright law with an astute hypothetical:

> Suppose defendant copied plaintiff's abstract painting composed entirely of geometric forms arranged in an original pattern. The alleged infringer could argue that each expressive element (i.e., the geometric forms) is unprotectible under the functionality, merger, scenes a faire, and unoriginality theories and, thus, all elements should be excluded prior to the substantial similarity of expression analysis. Then, there would be nothing left for purposes of determining substantial similarity of expression. In this example, elimination of "unprotectible" elements would result in a finding of no copyright infringement, which would be clearly inconsistent with the copyright law's purpose of providing incentives to authors of original works.

Apple Computer, Inc. v. Microsoft Corp., 779 F. Supp. 133, 136 (N.D. Cal. 1991), aff'd in relevant part and rev'd and remanded in part, 35 F.3d 1435, 1444 (9th Cir. 1994). Scholars agree: ["] . . . An original arrangement of uncopyrightable or public domain works—even facts — is as copyrightable as a compilation in the computer context as it is elsewhere in copyright law. Thus, individual program elements that are "filtered" out at one level may be copyrightable when viewed as part of an aggregate of elements at another level of abstraction.["] Arthur R. Miller, *Copyright Protection for Computer Programs, Databases, and Computer-Generated Works: Is Anything New Since CONTU?*, 106 Harv. L. Rev. 977, 1003 (1993) (footnote omitted); *see also* 3 Melville B. Nimmer & David Nimmer, *Nimmer on Copyright* §13.03[F][5], at 13-145 (1996) ("*Nimmer*") ("In performing the filtering, the court should be sensitive to the myriad ways in which copyrightable creativity can manifest itself; the analysis should not proceed mechanically simply by isolating physical elements out of the copyrightable work."). Indeed, when applied to the context of literary works, this point becomes quite obvious: taken individually, the words that constitute a literary work are not copyrightable, yet this fact does not prevent a literary text, i.e., a collection of words, from enjoying copyright protection. *See Nimmer* §13.03[F][5], at 13145 n. 345.1 (explaining that the fact that Hamlet's soliloquy can be atomized into unprotectible words does not mean that the soliloquy as a whole lacks originality for copyright purposes). . . .

[Softel's president] testified regarding relationships between all four of the design elements at issue: apparently, the menus cued external files which read English language commands into the main program, where the commands cued modules of code. Standing alone, these allegations may not help answer the question of how many ways existed to design a computer program with the same functionality as Softel's. However, when they are combined with an allegation that the specific commands used by Dragon were nearly identical with Softel's, they do appear to establish at least a colorable claim that there was a modicum of expression in the design of the program and that Dragon infringed that expression. That is, even if there were few ways to design such a program, it does not seem likely that Dragon would have to use an identical structure *and* copy approximately fifteen out of fifteen commands.

Softel presented an argument, supported by some evidence, that the manner in which it had combined certain computer design elements was expressive for purposes of copyright law, and that Dragon had copied this expression. Keeping in mind that the requisite level of originality for copyright protection is "minimal" and "extremely low," *Feist*, 499 U.S. at 345 we cannot say that Softel's claim was without merit on its face. However, several aspects of Judge Cannella's opinion reveal that he either ignored or misanalyzed Softel's argument, and consequently failed to perform the *Altai* analysis at the highest level of abstraction — here, the interrelationships among the four identified elements. . . .

[The district] court's findings of fact and conclusions of law address each element individually, but not in relation to each other. For example, the court credited Dragon's expert testimony that each of the four design elements was pervasively used in the computer industry, but did not address the issue of whether the choice and manner of combination of the four elements was commonplace. Similarly, the court found that the programmer at Dragon who was responsible for the post-litigation programs had learned to use external files from another source, and that certain code is required whenever a screen touchpoint is used, but did not address the question of where Dragon's programmer learned to combine external files, or touch-point finger-finding algorithms, with the other design elements. . . .

The district court's dismissal of Softel's claim [ ] of non-literal infringement . . . [is] vacated and remanded for further consideration consistent with this opinion. . . .

NOTES AND QUESTIONS

1. Does the court's decision in *Altai* make theoretical sense? Does it make technological sense? Do you think courts will be able to implement it as a practical matter? Is it an

improvement over the *Whelan* test to which it refers? Would you argue that it, like *Hoehling* (review note 3, *supra* page 93), is about the cost of errors?

2. The *Altai* court points out that much, if not most, of the investment in creating a program is made in designing it. Actual coding is not that pricey. If *Altai* practically means that copyright protects the literal code but little of the design structure, is this result consistent with the policy bases for copyright discussed in Chapter 1? How does the *Altai* court respond to the argument that its decision provides "too little" protection to program design?

3. Does the syllogism employed by the *Altai* and *Whelan* courts — computer programs are protected as literary works; literary works are protected against nonliteral infringement; therefore, computer programs are protected against nonliteral infringement — make sense? Consider the following:

> The copyright question is usually posed as whether [Sequence, Structure, and Organization (SSO)] is protected as a "nonliteral element" of the protected program code. The analogy is to the copyright in a novel or play, which has long been recognized to extend beyond the verbatim language to more or less detailed elements of plot sequence. Most of the proponents of broad program copyrights conveniently forget that copyright in other types of literary works, such as histories, fact works, rule books, and technical works, is much "thinner," limited to verbatim language and close paraphrases thereof. They also usually forget that computer programs are only literary works in form; in substance they are the technology for using computers. Consequently, reasoning by analogy to traditional (nonfunctional) works without resort to policy cannot be expected to lead to sensible results, unless one is a strong believer in luck.

Dennis S. Karjala, *The Relative Roles of Patent and Copyright in the Protection of Computer Programs*, 17 J. Marshall J. Computer & Info. L. 41, 53 (1998).

Professor Karjala argues that policy considerations do not support copyright protection for a program's structure. Nevertheless, he applauds the *Altai* decision. In his view, "[i]n fact, a court that applies the *Computer Associates* filters honestly will soon realize that *everything* in the SSO is present for the purpose of making the program function better, that is, for efficiency reasons. Consequently, under *Computer Associates*, after filtering for efficiency there is very little, if anything, to protect besides the code." *Id.* at 54.

Do you agree? Are efficiency considerations monolithic? Put differently, programmers make efficiency trade-offs. Some might choose to optimize use of memory; others the usability of the program. Program structure varies depending on those choices. Recall the Clapes excerpt, *supra* page 217. Do such choices evidence creativity and justify copyright protection?

4. Is the court's decision in *Softel* consistent with Professor Karjala's interpretation of *Altai* and its likely consequences for copyright protection of program structure? Is *Softel* consistent with *Altai* generally? Does it make sense to treat the structure of a program as a compilation? (Review note 9 on page 116 discussing the *Atari Games Corp. v. Oman* case.)

5. Recall the *Franklin* case, *supra*, and the last sentence of the case excerpt: "Franklin may wish to achieve total compatibility with independently developed application programs written for the Apple II, but that is a commercial and competitive objective which does not enter into the somewhat metaphysical issue of whether particular ideas and expressions have merged." *Apple Computer, Inc. v. Franklin Computer Corp.*, 714 F.2d 1240, 1253 (3d Cir. 1983), *cert. dismissed*, 464 U.S. 1033 (1984). The court in *Altai* indicated that elements of a program required for compatibility should be filtered out. Is this consistent with *Franklin*?

Alternatively, might compatibility considerations preclude copyrightability altogether rather than serving as one "filter" in the infringement analysis? In *Lexmark International, Inc. v. Static Control Components, Inc.*, 387 F.3d 522 (6th Cir. 2004), the court addressed the copyrightability of a short program consisting of only eight commands. Noting the brief-ness of the plaintiff's program, the court observed that "unless a creative flair is shown, a very brief program is less likely to be copyrightable because it affords fewer opportunities for original expression." *Id.* at 542-43. The court found that plaintiff's code functioned as a "lock-out" code that prevented communication between two devices unless the exact code was copied. The court held that "[t]o the extent compatibility requires that a particular code sequence be included in the component device to permit its use, the merger and scenes a faire doctrines generally preclude the code sequence from obtaining copyright protection." *Id.* at 536. Which approach is better — *Franklin*'s, *Altai*'s, or *Lexmark*'s?

6. From whose perspective should compatibility requirements be assessed? In *Dun & Bradstreet Software Services, Inc. v. Grace Consulting, Inc.*, 307 F.3d 197 (3d Cir. 2002), *cert. denied*, 538 U.S. 1032 (2003), the defendant, a computer consulting corporation formed to provide services to plaintiff's licensees, began to offer competing software programs to the licensees. Defendant used copy and call commands to access the plaintiff's software so that its programs would interoperate with the plaintiff's program. It argued that industry practice justified duplication of copy and call commands for this purpose. The court rejected the argu-ment, holding that in determining whether program elements are dictated by external factors, including interoperability, a court must examine the program from the viewpoint of its creator, not that of the alleged infringer. Is this consistent with *Altai*? What policy goals might be furthered by using the alleged infringer's viewpoint rather than the creator's?

7. Note that a court's decision about what elements of a work are copyrightable influences the answer to the ultimate question whether infringement has occurred. We revisit this issue in Chapter 5.

≡ ***Lotus Development Corporation v. Borland International, Inc.***
≡ *49 F.3d 807 (1st Cir. 1995),* **aff'd by an equally divided court,** *516 U.S. 233 (1996)*

STAHL, J:. . . .

This appeal requires us to decide whether a computer menu command hierarchy is copy-rightable subject matter. In particular, we must decide whether, as the district court held, plaintiff-appellee Lotus Development Corporation's copyright in Lotus 1-2-3, a computer spreadsheet program, was infringed by defendant-appellant Borland International, Inc., when Borland copied the Lotus 1-2-3 menu command hierarchy into its Quattro and Quattro Pro computer spreadsheet programs.

I. Background

Lotus 1-2-3 is a spreadsheet program that enables users to perform accounting functions electronically on a computer. Users manipulate and control the program via a series of menu commands, such as "Copy," "Print," and "Quit." Users choose commands either by high-lighting them on the screen or by typing their first letter. In all, Lotus 1-2-3 has 469 commands arranged into more than 50 menus and submenus.

Lotus 1-2-3, like many computer programs, allows users to write what are called "macros." By writing a macro, a user can designate a series of command choices with a single macro keystroke. Then, to execute that series of commands in multiple parts of the spreadsheet, rather than typing the whole series each time, the user only needs to type the single pre-programmed macro keystroke, causing the program to recall and perform the designated series of commands automatically. Thus, Lotus 1-2-3 macros shorten the time needed to set up and operate the program.

Borland released its first Quattro program to the public in 1987, after Borland's engineers had labored over its development for nearly three years. Borland's objective was to develop a spreadsheet program far superior to existing programs, including Lotus 1-2-3. In Borland's words, "[f]rom the time of its initial release . . . Quattro included enormous innovations over competing spreadsheet products."

. . . Borland included in its Quattro and Quattro Pro version 1.0 programs "a *virtually identical* copy of the entire 1-2-3 menu tree." *Borland III*, 831 F. Supp. at 212 (emphasis in original). In so doing, Borland did not copy any of Lotus's underlying computer code; it copied only the words and structure of Lotus's menu command hierarchy. Borland included the Lotus menu command hierarchy in its programs to make them compatible with Lotus 1-2-3 so that spreadsheet users who were already familiar with Lotus 1-2-3 would be able to switch to the Borland programs without having to learn new commands or rewrite their Lotus macros.

In its Quattro and Quattro Pro version 1.0 programs, Borland achieved compatibility with Lotus 1-2-3 by offering its users an alternate user interface, the "Lotus Emulation Interface." By activating the Emulation Interface, Borland users would see the Lotus menu commands on their screens and could interact with Quattro or Quattro Pro as if using Lotus 1-2-3, albeit with a slightly different looking screen and with many Borland options not available on Lotus 1-2-3. In effect, Borland allowed users to choose how they wanted to communicate with Borland's spreadsheet programs: either by using menu commands designed by Borland, or by using the commands and command structure used in Lotus 1-2-3 augmented by Borland-added commands. . . .

[Lotus sued Borland for copyright infringement. Both parties moved for summary judgement.] [T]he district court denied Borland's motion and granted Lotus's motion in part. The district court ruled that the Lotus menu command hierarchy was copyrightable expression because

> [a] very satisfactory spreadsheet menu tree can be constructed using different commands and a different command structure from those of Lotus 1-2-3. In fact, Borland has constructed just such an alternate tree for use in Quattro Pro's native mode. Even if one holds the arrangement of menu commands constant, it is possible to generate literally millions of satisfactory menu trees by varying the menu commands employed.

Borland II, 799 F. Supp. at 217. The district court demonstrated this by offering alternate command words for the ten commands that appear in Lotus's main menu. *Id*. For example, the district court stated that "[t]he 'Quit' command could be named 'Exit' without any other modifications." . . . Because so many variations were possible, the district court concluded that the Lotus developers' choice and arrangement of command terms, reflected in the Lotus menu command hierarchy, constituted copyrightable expression. . . .

Immediately following the district court's summary judgment decision, Borland removed the Lotus Emulation Interface from its products. . . . Borland retained what it called the "Key Reader" in its Quattro Pro programs. Once turned on, the Key Reader allowed Borland's programs to understand and perform some Lotus 1-2-3 macros. . . . Accordingly, people who wrote or purchased macros to shorten the time needed to perform an operation in Lotus 1-2-3 could still use those macros in Borland's programs. The district court permitted Lotus to file a supplemental complaint alleging that the Key Reader infringed its copyright. . . .

. . . [T]he district court found that Borland's Key Reader file included "a virtually identical copy of the Lotus menu tree structure, but represented in a different form and with first letters of menu command names in place of the full menu command names." . . . The district court held that "the Lotus menu structure, organization, and first letters of the command names . . . constitute part of the protectible expression found in [Lotus 1-2-3]." Accordingly, the district court held that with its Key Reader, Borland had infringed Lotus's copyright. . . . The district court then entered a permanent injunction against Borland from which Borland appeals.

This appeal concerns only Borland's copying of the Lotus menu command hierarchy into its Quattro programs. . . .

II. Discussion

On appeal, Borland does not dispute that it factually copied the words and arrangement of the Lotus menu command hierarchy. Rather, Borland argues that it "lawfully copied the unprotectible menus of Lotus 1-2-3." . . .

B. *Matter of First Impression*

Whether a computer menu command hierarchy constitutes copyrightable subject matter is a matter of first impression in this court. . . .

Borland vigorously argues, however, that the Supreme Court charted our course more than 100 years ago when it decided *Baker v. Selden*, 101 U.S. 99 (1879). . . . Borland argues:

> The facts of *Baker v. Selden*, and even the arguments advanced by the parties in that case, are identical to those in this case. The only difference is that the "user interface" of Selden's system was implemented by pen and paper rather than by computer.

. . . Borland even supplied this court with a video that, with special effects, shows Selden's paper forms "melting" into a computer screen and transforming into Lotus 1-2-3.

We do not think that *Baker v. Selden* is nearly as analogous to this appeal as Borland claims. . . . [U]nlike Selden, Lotus does not claim to have a monopoly over its accounting system. Rather, this appeal involves Lotus's monopoly over the commands it uses to operate the computer. Accordingly, this appeal is not, as Borland contends, "identical" to *Baker v. Selden*.

C. *Altai* . . .

In the instant appeal, we are not confronted with alleged nonliteral copying of computer code. Rather, we are faced with Borland's deliberate, literal copying of the Lotus menu command hierarchy. Thus, we must determine not whether nonliteral copying occurred in some amorphous sense, but rather whether the literal copying of the Lotus menu command hierarchy constitutes copyright infringement.

While the *Altai* test may provide a useful framework for assessing the alleged nonliteral copying of computer code, we find it to be of little help in assessing whether the literal copying of a menu command hierarchy constitutes copyright infringement. . . .

D. *The Lotus Menu Command Hierarchy: A "Method of Operation"*

Borland argues that the Lotus menu command hierarchy is uncopyrightable because it is a system, method of operation, process, or procedure foreclosed from copyright protection by 17 U.S.C. §102(b). . . .

We think that "method of operation," as that term is used in §102(b), refers to the means by which a person operates something, whether it be a car, a food processor, or a computer. Thus a text describing how to operate something would not extend copyright protection to the method of operation itself; other people would be free to employ that method and to describe it in their own words. Similarly, if a new method of operation is used rather than described, other people would still be free to employ or describe that method.

We hold that the Lotus menu command hierarchy is an uncopyrightable "method of operation." The Lotus menu command hierarchy provides the means by which users control and operate Lotus 1-2-3. If users wish to copy material, for example, they use the "Copy" command. If users wish to print material, they use the "Print" command. Users must use the command terms to tell the computer what to do. Without the menu command hierarchy, users would not be able to access and control, or indeed make use of, Lotus 1-2-3's functional capabilities.

The Lotus menu command hierarchy does not merely explain and present Lotus 1-2-3's functional capabilities to the user; it also serves as the method by which the program is operated and controlled. The Lotus menu command hierarchy is different from the Lotus long prompts, for the long prompts are not necessary to the operation of the program; users could operate Lotus 1-2-3 even if there were no long prompts.[9] The Lotus menu command hierarchy is also different from the Lotus screen displays, for users need not "use" any expressive aspects of the screen displays in order to operate Lotus 1-2-3; because the way the screens look has little bearing on how users control the program, the screen displays are not part of Lotus 1-2-3's "method of operation."[10] The Lotus menu command hierarchy is also different from the underlying computer code, because while code is necessary for the program to work, its precise formulation is not. In other words, to offer the same capabilities as Lotus 1-2-3, Borland did not have to copy Lotus's underlying code (and indeed it did not); to allow users to operate its programs in substantially the same way, however, Borland had to copy the Lotus menu command hierarchy. Thus the Lotus 1-2-3 code is not an uncopyrightable "method of operation." . . .

Accepting the district court's finding that the Lotus developers made some expressive choices in choosing and arranging the Lotus command terms, we nonetheless hold that that expression is not copyrightable because it is part of Lotus 1-2-3's "method of operation." We do not think that "methods of operation" are limited to abstractions; rather, they are the means by which a user operates something. If specific words are essential to operating something, then they are part of a "method of operation" and, as such, are unprotectable. This is so whether they must be highlighted, typed in, or even spoken, as computer programs no doubt will soon be controlled by spoken words.

The fact that Lotus developers could have designed the Lotus menu command hierarchy differently is immaterial to the question of whether it is a "method of operation." In other words, our initial inquiry is not whether the Lotus menu command hierarchy incorporates any expression. Rather, our initial inquiry is whether the Lotus menu command hierarchy is a "method of operation." Concluding, as we do, that users operate Lotus 1-2-3 by using the Lotus menu command hierarchy, and that the entire Lotus menu command hierarchy is essential to operating Lotus 1-2-3, we do not inquire further whether that method of operation could have been designed differently. The "expressive" choices of what to name the command

9. As the Lotus long prompts [(short text appearing under the highlighted menu command that explains what the command does)] are not before us on appeal, we take no position on their copyrightability, although we do note that a strong argument could be made that the brief explanations they provide "merge" with the underlying idea of explaining such functions.

10. As they are not before us on appeal, we take no position on whether the Lotus 1-2-3 screen displays constitute original expression capable of being copyrighted.

terms and how to arrange them do not magically change the uncopyrightable menu command hierarchy into copyrightable subject matter. . . .

In many ways, the Lotus menu command hierarchy is like the buttons used to control, say, a video cassette recorder ("VCR"). . . . Users operate VCRs by pressing a series of buttons that are typically labelled "Record, Play, Reverse, Fast Forward, Pause, Stop/Eject." That the buttons are arranged and labeled does not make them a "literary work," nor does it make them an "expression" of the abstract "method of operating" a VCR via a set of labeled buttons. Instead, the buttons are themselves the "method of operating" the VCR.

When a Lotus 1-2-3 user chooses a command, either by highlighting it on the screen or by typing its first letter, he or she effectively pushes a button. . . .

That the Lotus menu command hierarchy is a "method of operation" becomes clearer when one considers program compatibility. Under Lotus's theory, if a user uses several different programs, he or she must learn how to perform the same operation in a different way for each program used. For example, if the user wanted the computer to print material, then the user would have to learn not just one method of operating the computer such that it prints, but many different methods. We find this absurd. The fact that there may be many different ways to operate a computer program, or even many different ways to operate a computer program using a set of hierarchically arranged command terms, does not make the actual method of operation chosen copyrightable; it still functions as a method for operating the computer and as such is uncopyrightable.

Consider also that users employ the Lotus menu command hierarchy in writing macros. Under the district court's holding, if the user wrote a macro to shorten the time needed to perform a certain operation in Lotus 1-2-3, the user would be unable to use that macro to shorten the time needed to perform that same operation in another program. Rather, the user would have to rewrite his or her macro using that other program's menu command hierarchy. This is despite the fact that the macro is clearly the user's own work product. . . .

We also note that in most contexts, there is no need to "build" upon other people's expression, for the ideas conveyed by that expression can be conveyed by someone else without copying the first author's expression. In the context of methods of operation, however, "building" requires the use of the precise method of operation already employed; otherwise, "building" would require dismantling, too. Original developers are not the only people entitled to build on the methods of operation they create; anyone can. Thus, Borland may build on the method of operation that Lotus designed and may use the Lotus menu command hierarchy in doing so. . . .

BOUDIN, J., concurring:. . . .

I

Most of the law of copyright and the "tools" of analysis have developed in the context of literary works such as novels, plays, and films. In this milieu, the principal problem — simply stated, if difficult to resolve — is to stimulate creative expression without unduly limiting access by others to the broader themes and concepts deployed by the author. The middle of the spectrum presents close cases; but a "mistake" in providing too much protection involves a small cost: subsequent authors treating the same themes must take a few more steps away from the original expression.

The problem presented by computer programs is fundamentally different in one respect. The computer program is a *means* for causing something to happen; it has a mechanical utility, an instrumental role, in accomplishing the world's work. Granting protection, in other words, can have some of the consequences of *patent* protection in limiting other people's ability to perform a task in the most efficient manner. Utility does not bar copyright (dictionaries may be copyrighted), but it alters the calculus.

Of course, the argument *for* protection is undiminished, perhaps even enhanced, by utility: if we want more of an intellectual product, a temporary monopoly for the creator provides incentives for others to create other, different items in this class. But the "cost" side of the equation may be different where one places a very high value on public access to a useful innovation that may be the most efficient means of performing a given task. Thus, the argument for extending protection may be the same; but the stakes on the other side are much higher. . . .

Requests for the protection of computer menus present the concern with fencing off access to the commons in an acute form. A new menu may be a creative work, but over time its importance may come to reside more in the investment that has been made by *users* in learning the menu and in building their own mini-programs — macros — in reliance upon the menu. Better typewriter keyboard layouts may exist, but the familiar QWERTY keyboard dominates the market because that is what everyone has learned to use. . . .

Thus, to assume that computer programs are just one more new means of expression, like a filmed play, may be quite wrong. The "form" — the written source code or the menu structure depicted on the screen — look hauntingly like the familiar stuff of copyright; but the "substance" probably has more to do with problems presented in patent law or, as already noted, in those rare cases where copyright law has confronted industrially useful expressions. Applying copyright law to computer programs is like assembling a jigsaw puzzle whose pieces do not quite fit. . . .

II

. . . [I]t is very hard to see that Borland has shown any interest in the Lotus menu except as a fall-back option for those users already committed to it by prior experience or in order to run their own macros using 1-2-3 commands. At least for the amateur, accessing the Lotus menu in the Borland Quattro or Quattro Pro program takes some effort.

Put differently, it is unlikely that users who value the Lotus menu for its own sake — independent of any investment they have made themselves in learning Lotus' commands or creating macros dependent upon them — would choose the Borland program in order to secure access to the Lotus menu. Borland's success is due primarily to other features. Its rationale for deploying the Lotus menu bears the ring of truth.

Now, any use of the Lotus menu by Borland is a commercial use and deprives Lotus of a portion of its "reward," in the sense that an infringement claim if allowed would increase Lotus' profits. But this is circular reasoning: broadly speaking, every limitation on copyright or privileged use diminishes the reward of the original creator. Yet not every writing is copyrightable or every use an infringement. The provision of reward is one concern of copyright law, but it is not the only one. If it were, copyrights would be perpetual and there would be no exceptions.

The present case is an unattractive one for copyright protection of the menu. The menu commands (*e.g.*, "print," "quit") are largely for standard procedures that Lotus did not invent and are common words that Lotus cannot monopolize. What is left is the particular combination and sub-grouping of commands in a pattern devised by Lotus. This arrangement may have a more appealing logic and ease of use than some other configurations; but there is a certain arbitrariness to many of the choices.

If Lotus is granted a monopoly on this pattern, users who have learned the command structure of Lotus 1-2-3 or devised their own macros are locked into Lotus, just as a typist who has learned the QWERTY keyboard would be the captive of anyone who had a monopoly on the production of such a keyboard. Apparently, for a period Lotus 1-2-3 has had such sway in the market that it has represented the *de facto* standard for electronic spreadsheet commands. So long as Lotus is the superior spreadsheet—either in quality or in price—there may be nothing wrong with this advantage.

But if a better spreadsheet comes along, it is hard to see why customers who have learned the Lotus menu and devised macros for it should remain captives of Lotus because of an investment in learning made by the users and not by Lotus. Lotus has already reaped a substantial reward for being first; assuming that the Borland program is now better, good reasons exist for freeing it to attract old Lotus customers: to enable the old customers to take advantage of a new advance, and to reward Borland in turn for making a better product. If Borland has not made a better product, then customers will remain with Lotus anyway.

Thus, for me the question is not whether Borland should prevail but on what basis. . . .

A different approach would be to say that Borland's use is privileged because, in the context already described, it is not seeking to appropriate the advances made by Lotus' menu; rather, having provided an arguably more attractive menu of its own, Borland is merely trying to give former Lotus users an option to exploit their own prior investment in learning or in macros. . . .

. . . Some solutions (*e.g.*, a very short copyright period for menus) are not options at all for courts but might be for Congress. In all events, the choices are important ones of policy, not linguistics, and they should be made with the underlying considerations in view.

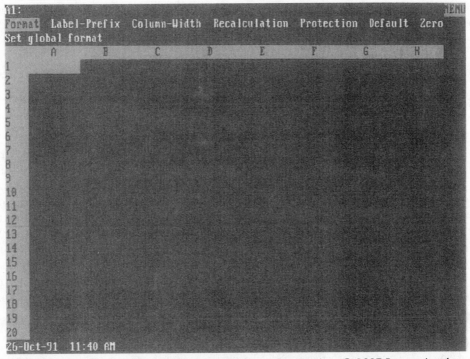

Reprint Courtesy of International Business Machines Corporation, © 1987 International Business Machines Corporation.

Screen Shot of Lotus 1-2-3 2.01

Note on Protecting Interfaces

The question of copyright protection for program interfaces has bedeviled courts, commentators, and software firms. The term *interface* encompasses, first, the manner in which modules communicate with each other and with other programs (*see Altai* and *Softel*). End users never see these interfaces. The term also includes user interfaces that are visible to the outside world (*see Lotus*).

The economics of the software industry may help to inform the debate about whether copyright policy supports protection for program interfaces. Economic and legal commentators often describe the software market as characterized by network effects. In its simplest terms, a network market is one in which the value of a product grows as more people purchase it. For example, a telephone has no value unless a person can use it to talk to others. The more people who connect to the system, the more valuable the phone becomes. Note that the telephone industry in the U.S. historically has been heavily regulated, in part because of its network effects.

Consider the market for operating system software. Every operating system has an interface to which an application programmer must write in order for its application to run on the operating system. Generally, an application can run only on the system for which it was designed (because different systems have different interfaces). As the number of applications running on an operating system increases, the value of the system goes up, causing more developers to write applications for it and more consumers to adopt it, and so on. Commentators call this phenomenon a "positive feedback effect," and that effect helps to explain why large first-mover advantages characterize network markets. (For a more detailed description of network effects, see Mark A. Lemley & David McGowan, *Legal Implications of Network Economic Effects*, 86 Cal. L. Rev. 479 (1998).)

Recall the cases you have just read. In the *Apple* case, Franklin's argument that it needed its system to be compatible with the Apple II has the flavor of a network effects rationale. In *Altai*, many similarities between the programs at issue were dictated by a third party not involved in the litigation — IBM. IBM had the dominant share of the mainframe operating system market and both Altai and Computer Associates sought to have their programs run on the most popular IBM systems. Thus, both had to write their scheduling programs to fit with IBM's interfaces, necessitating at least some similarities between the two programs.

As the *Lotus* case showed, somewhat weaker network effects characterize the market for applications. Customers invest time and money in acquiring the skills necessary to operate a system and store files in its format. If the customer cannot transfer her investment to another system, she will not incur the costs to switch even to a superior system. The *Lotus* court thought such a result would be "absurd." Some commentators argue that at least certain interfaces are not the proper subject matter of copyright as traditionally interpreted. "[I]nternal interface compilations [are] unprotectable by copyright law because they are industrial compilations of applied know-how, information equivalents to the gears that allow physical machines to interoperate." Pamela Samuelson et al., *A Manifesto Concerning the Legal Protection of Computer Programs*, 94 Colum. L. Rev. 2308, 2402 (1994). Professor Dennis Karjala observes:

> [Courts'] treatment [of interfaces as nonliteral elements of a program] assumes away the fundamental question of whether a particular interface, as such, constitutes copyright subject matter. In fact the definition of a computer program in the Copyright Act clearly distinguishes between the set of statements or instructions constituting the program and the "certain results" that are achieved by execution of those statements and instructions. All program interfaces, moreover,

are a crucial part of what the actual program *does*, that is, a part of the "certain result" that operation of the program brings about. . . . Consequently, under the statutory definition, interfaces are *not* covered by the program copyright.

Dennis Karjala, *The Relative Roles of Patent and Copyright in the Protection of Computer Programs*, 17 J. Marshall J. Computer & Info. L. 41, 55 (1998). Courts seem to be moving toward concluding that at least those interfaces that other programmers must use to write applications that run on the particular system are not copyrightable. Some would also hold that a competitor may implement another's interfaces to market a directly competing product. Should courts evaluate these two different uses of another's interfaces in the same way? (See Chapter 7.B.2. for a more detailed discussion of this question.)

User interfaces or some elements of them, at least, are more clearly copyrightable. As Professor Karjala notes, "[Some] aspects of screen displays can independently qualify as §102(a) copyright subject matter, for example, as pictorial works (e.g., video game characters), graphic works (e.g., spreadsheet formats), or literary works (e.g., help screens). These graphic, literary, and pictorial displays produced by programs are traditional subject matter of copyright to the extent that they have no function other than to inform or to portray an appearance." *Id.* at 70.

NOTES AND QUESTIONS

1. How is the approach of the *Lotus* court different from that of the *Altai* court? Do you agree with the *Lotus* court that *Altai*'s analysis was not relevant in its case? Should *Altai*'s test extend to cases of literal infringement? *See Bateman v. Mnemonics, Inc.*, 79 F.3d 1532 (11th Cir. 1996) (yes); *Gates Rubber Co. v. Bando Chem. Indus., Ltd.*, 9 F.3d 823 (10th Cir. 1993) (same). Should the law use different tests for the copyrightability of interfaces within a program, program-to-program interfaces, and user interfaces?

2. What is the difference between the approaches of the majority and the concurrence in the *Lotus* case? Which makes more sense? What are the trade-offs involved?

3. Does the First Circuit's analysis mean that the Lotus Emulation Interface also was not copyrightable? Should the Lotus Emulation Interface have been analyzed as a graphic work, separate from the software that generated the display? Video game displays are categorized as audiovisual works. *See, e.g., Williams Elecs., Inc. v. Artic Int'l, Inc.*, 685 F.2d 870 (3d Cir. 1982), *supra* Chapter 2. Should the displays for more utilitarian programs be treated similarly? Do you think most text-based user interfaces would receive copyright protection under this analysis?

4. Many user interfaces use icons instead of words — consider the trash can icon on a MacIntosh operating system, or the recycle bin icon on a Windows system. What if Lotus had used fancifully designed icons instead of words on its menus for program commands, and a competitor copied those icons? Should the result of a copyrightability analysis change? An entire industry is devoted to analyzing the most efficient way to design user interfaces. Would idea and expression inevitably merge?

5. Note that it disturbs both the majority and the concurrence in the *Lotus* case that consumers may be locked into using Lotus 1-2-3 if another program cannot offer compatibility. What are the reasons for this lock-in? Why should it have any relevance to the copyright analysis? Does permitting another firm to copy the user interface and to run macros written for the dominant program penalize the first company for its success in writing a program that became a market leader? Reread Question 5, *supra* page 232-33. Is the *Lotus* court's approach to compatibility consistent with *Franklin, Altai*, or *Lexmark*?

6. Think about the market for PC operating systems. Can an operating system succeed if it cannot run all of the applications that Microsoft Windows runs? Can an application succeed if it cannot run on Windows?

Recall the debate between the CONTU majority and Commissioner Hersey about whether the software market would tend toward monopoly. Who was right? Do the economics of the software industry militate against copyright protection for internal program interfaces and/or user interfaces? Do developers need a legal incentive to create innovative interfaces? Is the problem that copyright protection would last too long given market conditions?

7. For an excellent discussion of the *Lotus* case and the problems of "user holdup" and lock-in, see Robert P. Merges, *Who Owns the Charles River Bridge?: Intellectual Property and Competition in the Software Industry* (working paper, April 2, 1999), *http://www.law.berkeley.edu/institutes/bclt/pubs/merges/criver.pdf*.

3. New Paradigms?

The preceding sections show at least some of the difficulty courts have had in applying copyright law to computer programs. Much of that trouble arises from computer programs' particular characteristics as works that behave and perform a useful function. In *Altai*, the court suggested that patent protection for software might be more suitable than copyright. Another alternative would be for Congress to enact sui generis legislation that specifically addresses software. Read the following materials and then consider what, if anything, Congress should do.

Note on Patent Protection for Software

Even before cases such as *Altai* and *Lotus* seemed to signal that copyright law might not protect computer programs to the extent that software firms might have desired and expected, those firms had been filing patent applications. The Patent Act provides that "processes" meeting the Act's requirements fall within the class of patentable subject matter. 35 U.S.C. §101. Initially, however, both legal precedent and policy considerations presented barriers to patenting software. Courts had long held that neither mathematical algorithms nor methods of doing business were patentable subject matter. A program is, of course, a type of mathematical algorithm, and many programs implemented methods of doing business. On the policy side, many commentators, including CONTU, questioned whether patent protection for software might unduly restrict competition and inhibit desirable dissemination of information. *See* Pamela Samuelson, Benson *Revisited: The Case Against Patent Protection for Computer Programs and Other Computer-Related Inventions*, 39 Emory L.J. 1025 (1990); CONTU Report at 32-33. Yet what is a computer program if not a "process" for accomplishing a useful result? Courts now recognize at least some computer programming innovations as patentable subject matter, but the extent of patent protection for these inventions remains unresolved.

The Supreme Court case that paved the way for recognition of computer programs as patentable subject matter was *Diamond v. Diehr*, 450 U.S. 175 (1981). In *Diehr*, the Court upheld a patent on a process that used a well-known equation (i.e., a mathematical algorithm) to monitor the temperature inside a synthetic rubber mold. The Court emphasized that the algorithm eventually produced a useful result — cured rubber. For a number of years after *Diehr*, applicants effectively patented software, but drafted their claims to look like those in the *Diehr* case by emphasizing the utility of their inventions in improving traditional industrial processes. *See* Julie E. Cohen & Mark A. Lemley, *Patent Scope and Innovation in the Software Industry*, 89 Cal. L. Rev. 1 (2001).

A series of decisions from the exclusive court for patent appeals, the Court of Appeals for the Federal Circuit, gradually whittled away at *Diehr*'s ostensible requirement that a process including a software-based algorithm must produce a physical result to be patentable. This trend culminated in *State Street Bank & Trust Co. v. Signature Financial Group*, 149 F.3d 1368 (Fed. Cir. 1998), in which the court upheld a patent for a computerized accounting system that allocated costs and fees within a family of mutual funds. The court found the resulting numbers to be "a useful, concrete, and tangible result" that justified classifying the process as patentable subject matter. *Id.* at 1373. Subsequently, however, in *In re Bilski*, the Federal Circuit returned to the approach in *Diehr* and earlier cases, holding that the test for whether a process is within the subject matter of patent law is whether: ("(1) it is tied to a particular machine or apparatus, or (2) it transforms a particular article into a different state or thing." 545 F.3d 943, 954 (Fed. Cir. 2008), *cert. granted*, 129 S.Ct. 2735 (2009) (citation omitted). The implications of this test for computer program–related innovations are unclear.

Other countries also face difficulties in addressing the patentability of these types of innovations. Article 52C of the European Patent Convention prohibits patents on "programs for computers." At the same time, however, the European Patent Office considers inventions implemented on a computer patentable if they meet general patentability requirements. The issue of patenting software itself remains under discussion, leaving the global future of software patents uncertain.

Note on Trade Secret Protection for Software

As already noted, from the early years of the software industry, firms have sought to keep the design specifications and source code of their programs a trade secret. Indeed, CONTU indicated that the availability of copyright protection was not intended to preclude trade secret protection. CONTU Report at 35. The 1976 Act's abandonment of the publication requirement for copyright protection enabled software firms to claim both copyright and trade secret protection simultaneously. The Copyright Office took an additional step to help firms maintain secrecy by adopting less rigorous deposit requirements for computer programs. *See* 37 C.F.R. §202.20.

Trade secrecy law protects only against misappropriation of the secret. This includes discovery of the secret by "improper means" such as corporate espionage or inducing breach of contract, but it does not include independent creation. It also does not include discovery of the information through reverse engineering of a publicly available product. *See* Unif. Trade Secrets Act §1 (defining misappropriation).

The rule allowing reverse engineering creates difficulties for software firms that distribute their product on a widespread basis, even if the program is distributed in object code form. CONTU believed that this was a significant problem that militated in favor of allowing copyright protection for software:

> Because secrecy is paramount, [trade secret law] is inappropriate for protecting works that contain the secret and are designed to be widely distributed. Although this matters little in the case of unique programs prepared for large commercial customers, it substantially precludes the use of trade secrecy with respect to programs sold in multiple copies over the counter to small businesses, schools, consumers and hobbyists.

CONTU Report at 34.

More recently, courts have held that copyright law allows reverse engineering of software in certain circumstances. *See Sega Enterprises Ltd. v. Accolade, Inc., infra* Chapter 7, page 566. Note, finally, that a grant of patent protection precludes continued trade secret protection because the public disclosures required by the patent law eliminate the secrecy required under trade secrecy law.

For all of these reasons, many modern software firms have adopted the tactic of attempting to prevent reverse engineering by attaching licenses to every copy of their programs. Software firms also use contracts to control what departing employees can take with them to their new employers. The interaction of federal copyright law and state trade secrecy and contract laws raises difficult questions, which are addressed in Chapter 9.

Note on the EU Software Directive

In Europe, the Member States of what is now the EU did not have uniform laws to protect intellectual property rights in software. Germany, Spain, the United Kingdom, France, and Denmark provided statutory protection for programs, but the content of that protection varied. *See* Paul Bruno Arenas, *Comment: Implementation, Compliance and Enforcement: The European Community Directive for the Legal Protection of Computer Software*, 5 Transnat'l Law. 803 (1992). Other countries like Italy, the Netherlands, and Greece provided protection under judicial interpretations of existing legislation. *See id.* at 827. Still other countries provided little or no protection to programs. *See id.* at 829-30.

In 1991, the European Community adopted its Directive on the Legal Protection of Computer Programs, to harmonize the disparate approaches and ensure adequate protection. *See* Council Directive of 14 May 1991 on the Legal Protection of Computer Programs, 1991 O.J. (L-122) 42. Keep in mind also that the software industry in Europe lagged behind that of the U.S. The large software firms operating in Europe were primarily U.S.-based. One goal of the EU in seeking to harmonize the law of its Member States was to create a legal environment that would encourage the growth of a European software industry. In 2009, the 1991 directive was repealed and replaced with a substantially similar one. *See* Council Directive 2009/24, Legal Protection of Computer Programs, 2009 O.J. (L 111) 16 (EC) (EU Software Directive).

Many provisions of the EU Software Directive resemble U.S. law. The EU Software Directive provides that Member States must protect computer programs as literary works under copyright law. *See id.*, art. 1(1). Computer programs must be original to merit protection but the originality standard does not include an assessment of "the qualitative or aesthetic merits of the program. . . . " *See id.*, pmbl. As in the U.S., the idea/expression distinction applies to computer programs as to other copyrighted works. *See id.*, art. 1(2).

The EU Software Directive contains some other provisions that do not have direct statutory counterparts in U.S. law. For example, it lists certain acts that a licensor of computer software may not forbid. A licensor may not restrict the right of a person to make a back-up copy. *See id.*, art. 5(2). Nor, ostensibly, may it restrict a person's right to observe, study, and test the functioning of a program to understand its ideas so long as such person is engaging in a permitted act. *See id.*, art. 5(3). Under certain circumstances, the EU Software Directive also permits a person in rightful possession of the program to reverse engineer the program by decompiling[2] it to obtain information necessary to ensure interoperability between the

---

2. Decompilation, a form of reverse engineering, is the reverse of compilation. Recall that compiling a program involves using software to translate it from source code to object code. *See Apple Computer, Inc. v. Franklin Computer Corp., supra* page 218. Decompilation is a process that uses software (called a decompiler) to translate object code into human-readable commands.

decompiled program and another independently created one. *See id.*, art. 6. The right to engage in such conduct is limited to cases in which the necessary information is not available elsewhere. *See id.*, art. 6(1). We consider this provision of the EU Software Directive again in Chapter 7.

NOTES AND QUESTIONS

1. Software patents also pose difficulties for the Patent and Trademark Office (PTO). The abstract nature of the claimed inventions makes software patent applications particularly difficult to evaluate. For a number of reasons, the PTO's prior art database, against which it determines nonobviousness, remains inadequate, although as more software patents issue, that database should improve. Also, the PTO has had difficulty simply processing the flood of patent applications claiming software inventions. *See generally* James Bessen & Michael J. Meurer, *Patent Failure: How Judges, Bureaucrats, and Lawyers Put Innovators at Risk* 187-214 (2008). Estimates of the number of software patents vary, but they surely number in the hundreds of thousands. *See* Julie E. Cohen & Mark A. Lemley, *Patent Scope and Innovation in the Software Industry*, 89 Cal. L. Rev. 1, 11-14 (2001)) (noting that as of the year 2000, the PTO had granted about 100,000 patents on software and software-related inventions, with thousands more issuing each year); Wendy Schascht, *Patent Reform: Issues in the Biomedical and Software Industries*, 27 Biotechnology L. Rep. 153, 158 (2009) (noting that over 20,000 software patents are issued each year). Many argue that the sheer number of applications, combined with a lack of examiner expertise, has resulted in the grant of some patents that are invalid — i.e., the invention claimed does not, in fact, meet the Patent Act's requirements of novelty, utility, and nonobviousness. Rather than challenging such patents, however, many companies will pay to license them. Why do you think that is the case? What is the cost to society of invalid patents?

2. If copyright law is moving toward protecting only the literal code, does permitting patents on features such as interfaces make sense? The *Altai* case suggests that the differences between the patent and copyright regimes may make a case for patenting software because patent law has higher threshold requirements for protection than copyright law.

3. In many cases involving software, courts express concern about how to draw the appropriate line between patent and copyright law. A computer may be "hardwired" to perform the same functions as software. Does this make a case for or against copyright protection for software? For or against patent protection? What do you think influences a firm's choice of the relative balance between wiring the machine to perform functions and writing software that performs those functions?

4. What are the pros and cons of trade secret protection from a software firm's perspective and from the public's perspective?

5. Why do you think the EU permits the limited copying involved in decompilation when the decompiler's goal is to achieve interoperability? What behavior on the part of dominant providers might the decompilation provision of the EU Software Directive be intended to induce?

6. Consider the following excerpt that explores what a sui generis regime to protect software might look like. In this article, the authors use the word *clone* to refer to a program copied from a preexisting program, functionally indistinguishable from that preexisting program, and whose internal design is substantially identical to the preexisting program's internal design:

A[n] . . . approach [modeled on the Semiconductor Chip Protection Act discussed in Section 4.A, *supra*], tailored to market-preservation principles, might be worth considering. Such an approach might provide a period of automatic anti-cloning protection and an opportunity to register inno-vative software compilations or subcompilations in order to get a longer period of blockage or a period of compensation under a standard licensing arrangement. A software developer might register, for example, a new user interface design, a macro language, a new algorithm, or the like, without having to register the product as a whole. . . .

[R]egistration should probably be required within a year or two of the first commercial dis-tribution of a product. . . . [T]he regime should employ a light, copyright-like registration process, rather than a patent-like examination process, although it should allow later opportunities to challenge whether the registered material qualifies for protection. This would minimize the up-front costs associated with gaining protection, in accordance with the market-oriented principles discussed above. . . .

[R]egistration might bring with it a longer period of blockage, or alternatively, an automatic royalty-bearing license available on standard terms after expiration of the unregistered design pro-tection right. Of the two alternatives, we favor the latter because it would remove the transaction costs of licensing. Reasonable fixed fees would encourage second comers to compensate the inno-vator rather than duplicating effort. They would also prevent the innovator from getting hit by its own hardball in licensing negotiations.

Pamela Samuelson et al., *A Manifesto Concerning the Legal Protection of Computer Programs*, 94 Colum. L. Rev. 2308, 2417-18 (1994).[3]

What do you think of this proposal? Can you think of other alternatives to existing intellectual property regimes that would work well for software?

C. ARCHITECTURAL WORKS

As described at the beginning of this chapter, §102 provides a list of eight different cat-egories of works of authorship eligible for protection. Before the addition of architectural works to that list in 1990, architectural *plans* were protected as graphic works, but finished *buildings* were not. Finished buildings generally were not considered protected because, no matter how aesthetically pleasing, buildings are functional. More precisely, as useful articles, buildings would be subject to the separability analysis we discussed in Section A above. Congress and the courts refused to acknowledge any separability that would permit protection for a building itself, although particular nonfunctional features like gargoyles might be protected.

The pre-1990 exclusion of buildings from copyright protection had an important conse-quence for owners of copyrights in architectural plans: Although copying the plans themselves would infringe the copyrights, courts held that building from the plans would not.

The copyright status of buildings changed in 1990 following U.S. accession to the Berne Convention. Article 2 of the Berne Convention defines literary and artistic works to include "illustrations, maps, plans, sketches and three dimensional works relative to geography, topog-raphy, architecture or science." Without modifying the protection that was already available for architectural plans, in 1990 Congress passed the Architectural Works Copyright Protection Act (AWCPA), which amended the Copyright Act to comply with this Berne requirement by adding architectural works as the eighth category of works in §102(a). Section 101 defines an "architectural work" as

---

3. Reprinted by permission of the authors and the Columbia Law Review.

the design of a building as embodied in any tangible medium of expression, including a building, architectural plans, or drawings. The work includes the overall form as well as the arrangement and composition of spaces and elements in the design, but does not include individual standard features.

17 U.S.C. §101.

Note two important consequences that result from this addition. First, an author of architectural plans now can use those plans as deposit copies to register an architectural work. Because Congress did not exclude architectural plans from the definition of "pictorial, graphic, and sculptural works," the plans can also be registered as graphic works. Using the plans to register the architectural work protects against another's building the structure described in the plans; registering the plans as graphic works does not. Second, when a building is protected as an architectural work it is not subject to the statutorily mandated separability analysis employed for useful articles. Does the last sentence of the definition of "architectural work" achieve the same purpose as the separability analysis? Consider the following cases and the notes and questions, and chart for yourself the differences pre- and post-1990.

1.   What Is a "Building"?

The Copyright Act defines architectural work as "the design of a building," §101, but does not define "building." The House Report accompanying the AWCPA states that the term encompasses "habitable structures such as houses and office buildings. It also covers structures that are used, but not inhabited, by human beings, such as churches, pergolas, gazebos, and garden pavilions." *See* H.R. Rep. 101-735, *reprinted in* 1990 U.S.C.C.A.N. 6935, 6951. The regulations pertinent to architectural work registration promulgated by the Copyright Office pursuant to its authority under section 702 of the Act implements that language:

> The term building means humanly habitable structures that are intended to be both permanent and stationary, such as house and office buildings, and other permanent and stationary structures designed for human occupancy, including but not limited to churches, museums, gazebos, and garden pavilions.

37 C.F.R. §202.11(b)(2) (1997). The regulations further prohibit registration of "[s]tructures other than buildings, such as bridges, cloverleafs, dams, walkways, tents, recreational vehicles, mobile homes, and boats." 37 C.F.R. §202.11(d)(1) (1997).

NOTES AND QUESTIONS

1. While in many cases it may be clear that the work at issue qualifies as a building, in other cases it is not so clear. Consider whether the following structures qualify as a "building":

a.   A shopping mall store located within the larger structure of the shopping mall. *See The Yankee Candle Co. v. New England Candle Co.*, 14 F. Supp. 2d 154 (D. Mass. 1998), *vacated by settlement*, 29 F. Supp. 2d 44 (1998) (no).

b.   A multi-story parking garage with stairwells and areas for vending machines. *See Moser Pilon Nelson Architects, LLC v. HNTB Corp.*, 80 U.S.P.Q. 2d 1085 (D. Conn. 2006) (yes).

c.   A modular home designed to be built in a factory, transported on flatbed trailers to a homesite, and permanently affixed to a cement foundation. *See Patriot Homes, Inc. v. Forest River Housing, Inc.*, 548 F. Supp. 2d 647 (N.D. Ind. 2008) (yes).

2. The two types of works associated with architecture—the plans and the building itself—create interesting cases in copyright law even after the addition of architectural works to the list of categories of protectible works. Copyright Office regulations specifically state that any claim to copyright protection for the technical drawings must be registered separately from the registration for architectural work protection. The protection for architectural plans as graphic works, separate from protection for the architectural works, is supposedly equivalent to the level of protection such plans were given before the AWCPA. As noted in the introduction to this section, the copyright in such architectural plans is not infringed by the construction of a structure based on those plans, but can be infringed by copying the plans in other plans. In effect, the copyright owner of architectural plans obtains something less than full copyright protection: Certain kinds of derivative works, namely three-dimensional structures that are created based on preexisting architectural plans, do not infringe. Does this holdover rule from pre-Berne era case law make sense?

3. Understanding the law prior to 1990 will remain important for years to come. Architectural works created before the AWCPA are protected by copyright if they were unconstructed or embodied only in unpublished plans or drawings on December 1, 1990 (the effective date of the Act). Works that were actually constructed before that date, or that were based on plans published before that date, are not eligible for protection as architectural works. The only copyright protection available is the protection afforded the plans as graphic works. While such plans may not be copied, the buildings themselves may be. At least one court has held that a building was "constructed" when it was "built to the extent that it was no longer an idea or plan, but a tangible structure." *Zitz v. Pereira*, 119 F. Supp. 2d 133, 148 (E.D.N.Y. 1999), *aff'd*, 225 F.3d 646 (2d Cir. 2000) (rejecting the argument that the structure needed to be "finished" or "habitable" and instead adopting a "substantially constructed" standard).

2.   Are Buildings "Compilations"?

Once the issue of what constitutes a building has been resolved, how is the originality required of all copyrightable works to be judged? Again, the definition of architectural works is helpful: "The work includes the overall form as well as the arrangement and composition of spaces and elements in the design, but does not include individual standard features." §101. How this definition works in practice is the issue to which we now turn.

Nelson-Salabes, Inc. v. Morningside Holdings

2001 WL 419002 (D. Md. 2001), aff'd in part, rev'd in part on other grounds, 284 F.3d 505 (4th Cir. 2002)

[Plaintiff, Nelson-Salabes, Inc., was hired by developers to provide architectural design work for a proposed assisted living facility, Satyr Hill Catered Living (Satyr Hill). Nelson-Salabes created four drawings depicting the footprint, floor plans, and elevations of the Satyr Hill site. These drawings were integrated into the overall development plan and submitted to Baltimore County for approval of the required special exception, a lengthy but necessary step in the development of any assisted living center in Baltimore County. Subsequent to the county's approval, the original developers sold the project to the defendant, Morningside Holdings, a company that already owned other assisted living centers. Morningside Holdings was particularly interested in the site because it had an approved development plan. After being told that they were not going to be retained as architects on the project, Nelson-Salabes informed the managing agent for Morningside that it "could proceed with another architect, but if he did so, he could not use Nelson-Salabes's design, including the footprint and elevations." The new architects that Morningside hired were told to design Satyr Hill to conform to another of Morningside's assisted living centers. The new plans were submitted to the county for approval as amended development plans, stating the reasons for the amendment as "minor footprint revisions" and "minor changes to architectural elevations of buildings."]

BLACK, J.: . . . As designed by Nelson-Salabes, the Satyr Hill site has a three-story building configured in "Y" shape. The front elevation features an octagonal shaped silo in the center, where two arms of the "Y" intersect. The first floor of the silo serves as an entrance. A porte-cochere extends from the entrance to a traffic circle in front of the building. The second and third floors of the silo serve as common areas and contain large windows. The first floor of the vertical element is brick, and the remainder of the building is vinyl siding. Both ends of the front elevation contain a vertical element protruding from the building with bay windows and a gable roof. There are also vertical elements with gable roofs located between the silo and the ends of the building. These elements protrude from the building and aesthetically break up the length of the building. . . .

. . . Nelson-Salabes presented a certificate of registration for its architectural work for the Satyr Hill site.* Consequently, the burden shifts to the defendants to rebut plaintiff's *prima facie* case of validity.

The defendants assert that neither the footprint of the building, nor the elevations are copyrightable. More specifically, defendants assert that the Y-shaped footprint is neither original nor an expression of artistic merit. Rather, they argue that it is utilitarian and within the public domain. According to the defendants, the "Y" shape is commonly used for architectural structures and, in this case, was dictated by zoning regulations, building codes, and physical attributes of the site. Similarly, the defendants assert that the various elements of the front elevation, such as brick, siding, gables, the octagonal entrance, and bay windows are common features of similar buildings in the area. Defendants further assert that the height of the building and the elevations were dictated by the Baltimore County zoning ordinance.

The Court agrees that Nelson-Salabes's use of certain individual features, such as the bay windows or the octagonal entrance, is neither original nor an expression of artistic merit. Nonetheless, "[t]he mere fact that component parts of a collective work are neither original to the plaintiff nor copyrightable by the plaintiff does not preclude a determination that the combination of such component parts as a separate entity is both original and copyrightable." Moreover, 17 U.S.C. §101 provides that an "architectural work" includes "the overall form as well as the arrangement and composition of spaces and elements in the design, but does not include individual standard features." 17 U.S.C. §101.

---

* [As authorized by the definition of "architectural work," Nelson-Salabes obtained the registration based on the design as embodied in its plans. — EDS.]

Defendants' Nursing Home, as Built

Computer Simulation Based on Nelson-Salabes Design

Here, the Court finds that Nelson-Salabes's combination of common features such as a Y-shaped footprint, bay windows, the octagonal silo entrance, and gables created a unique design. To be sure, Paul Seiben, plaintiff's expert in architecture, testified that he had never seen the same combination of elements used by Nelson-Salabes on any other building. Further, the footprint and front elevation used by Nelson-Salabes were not the only feasible designs. Consequently, the Court further finds that the defendants have failed to rebut the *prima facie* validity of plaintiff's copyright, and that Nelson-Salabes's selection and arrangement of common architectural features is unique and exhibits artistic expression. Therefore, the Court further finds that Nelson-Salabes owns a valid copyright in its architectural work for the Satyr Hill site. . . .

[The court determined that the defendants had infringed the plaintiff's copyrighted architectural work.] [T]he Court finds that both works contain the same unique combination of design elements including the use of an octagonal entrance, protruding gables, and bay windows on the ends of the building. The Court recognizes that differences do exist between the two designs. . . . Further supporting the Court's conclusion is the fact that Turner [Morningside's managing agent] told his architect that he wanted the design to fit within the approved plan. It is also undisputed that only minor changes could be made to the plan or it would require a new special exception. Moreover, the defendants noted on their amended development plans that they only made "minor" changes to the footprint and elevations. . . .

Intervest Construction, Inc. v. Canterbury Estate Homes, Inc.
554 F.3d 914 (11th Cir. 2008)

Birch, J.: In this copyright infringement action the appellant contends that the district court erred when it examined the two floor-plans at issue . . . emphasizing the differences between the two. . . .

I. Background

. . . [T]he floor plan for The Westminster was created in 1992 as a work-made-for-hire by Intervest Construction, Inc. ("Intervest"). The putatively infringing floor-plan, The Kensington, was created in 2002 by Canterbury Estate Homes, Inc. ("Canterbury"). Each floor plan depicts a four-bedroom house, with one bedroom being denominated as a "master" bedroom or suite. Each floor plan includes a: two-car garage; living room; dining room; "family" room; foyer; "master" bathroom; kitchen; second bathroom; nook; and porch/patio. Each floor-plan also reflects certain "elements" common to most houses: doors; windows; walls; bathroom fixtures (toilet, tub, shower, and sink); kitchen fixtures (sink, counter, refrigerator, stovetop, and pantry/cabinets); utility rooms and fixtures (washer, dryer, and sink); and closets. A cursory examination of the two floor-plans reveals that the square footage of both is approximately the same. Also, as is common to houses, there are placements of entrances, exits, hallways, openings, and utilities (furnace, air conditioner, hot water heater, and telephone hardware).

After identifying all of these unassigned components and elements of the floor-plans, the district court undertook a careful comparative analysis of the selection, coordination, and arrangement of these common components and elements. The district court focused upon the dissimilarities in such coordination and arrangement: [The court then proceeded with a lengthy comparison of the floor plans. A few excerpts from that comparison are included below.]

First, Canterbury represents that the square footage of the rooms in the two designs is different, and visual examination of the floor plans appears to confirm that. . . .

Second, the garage in The Westminster has a front entrance, while The Kensington's has a side entrance. Further, Intervest's design has an attic access from the garage, while Canterbury's version has a "bonus room" above the garage, something The Westminster lacks entirely. Moreover, the inside air conditioning unit and water heater are placed differently in the two floor plans. Additionally, The Kensington has two windows in the garage, while The Westminster has none. In The Westminster, there is a bedroom closet to the left of the utility room, whereas in The Kensington, there is a hallway in that location. . . .

Proceeding to the center portion of the homes, the nooks in the two plans are markedly different. In that regard, [The Westminster's] nook feeds into a ninety degree angle adjacent to the Porch and has windows looking both to the outside and to the Porch. On the other hand, [The Kensington's] design is rounded into the porch and is completely made of glass. There is no window to the outside or into the Covered Patio. Moreover, the entrance from the Nook into the Living Room in [The Westminster's] design has an elongated wall which travels much further into the Living Room than in [The Kensington's] design, and also fails to break inward at a ninety degree angle like in [The Kensington's] design. . . .

The kitchens in the two plans are also substantially different. In that connection, the wall placement in the southeast corner of the kitchens is significantly different. [The Kensington's] design pushes this wall further into the Living Room and pushes the Kitchen Counter much further north than in [The Westminster's] design. This allows [The Kensington's] design to have a much larger Pantry than [The Westminster's] design. . . .

. . . Additionally, in The Kensington's master bath, "the doors to the walk-in closets . . . are solid and open in different directions than those [in The Westminster], which uses a retractable door." Finally, the sinks in the master bath are placed differently in the two designs. In The Kensington, the sinks are centered; in The Westminster, they are not." [Eds. — Internal citations have been omitted.] . . .

II. Discussion

Since we are dealing with a specific type of copyrightable work, here an architectural work, we begin by examining the statutory definition of an "architectural work," to wit: "the design of a building as embodied in any tangible medium of expression, including a building, architectural plans or drawings. The work includes the overall form as well as the arrangement and composition of spaces and elements in the design, but does not include individual standard features." 17 U.S.C. §101 (2008). A review of the legislative history discloses that such "individual standard features" include "common windows, doors, and other staple building components." H.R.Rep. No. 101-735 (1990) *as reprinted in* 1990 U.S.C.C.A.N. 6935, 6949. Including the phrase "the arrangement and composition of spaces and elements in the design" demonstrates Congress' appreciation that "creativity in architecture frequently takes the form of a selection, coordination, or arrangement of unprotectible elements into an original, protectible whole." *Id.* Accordingly, while individual standard features and architectural elements classifiable as ideas or concepts are not themselves copyrightable, an architect's original combination or arrangement of such elements may be. Thus, the definition of an architectural work closely parallels that of a "compilation" under the statute, that is: "[A] work formed by the collection and assembling of preexisting materials or of data that are selected, coordinated, or arranged in such a way that the resulting work as a whole constitutes an original work of authorship." 17 U.S.C. §101. The Supreme Court . . . and our court . . . [have] indicated that the compiler's choices as to selection[,] coordination, or arrangement are the only portions of a compilation, or here, architectural work, that are even entitled to copyright protection. Accordingly, any similarity comparison of the works at issue here must be accomplished at the level of protected expression — that is, the *arrangement* and *coordination* of those common elements ("selected" by the market place, i.e., rooms, windows, doors, and "other staple building components"). In undertaking such a comparison it should be recalled that the copyright protection in a compilation is "thin." Moreover, as the Second Circuit has noted, the substantial similarity inquiry is "narrowed" when dealing with a compilation.

Thus, when viewed through the narrow lens of compilation analysis only the original, and thus protected arrangement and coordination of spaces, elements and other staple building components should be compared.[3] . . . [A]s noted above, while a creative work is entitled to the most protection, a compilation is entitled to the least, narrowest or "thinnest" protection. Accordingly, when courts have examined copyright infringement claims involving compilations the definition of "substantial similarity" has been appropriately modified to accentuate the narrower scope of protection available. . . .

III. Conclusion

. . . Given that the plans at issue were protected by compilation copyrights which were "thin," the district court correctly determined that the differences in the protectable expression were so significant that, as a matter of law, no reasonable properly-instructed jury of lay observers could find the works substantially similar. . . .

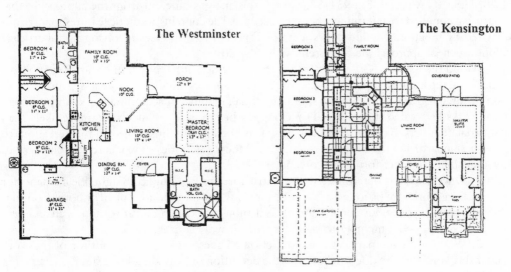

Westminster and Kensington Floor Plans

---

3. There are three types of work that are entitled to copyright protection — creative, derivative, and compiled. Copyrights in these three distinct works are known as creative, derivative, and compilation copyrights. An example of a creative work is a novel. An example of a derivative work is a screenplay based on a novel; it is called "derivative" because it is based on a preexisting work that has been recast, transformed, or adapted. An example of a compilation is [the floor plans at issue in this case.] The [Copyright] Act has

NOTES AND QUESTIONS

1. The standard employed for determining the copyrightability of architectural works again highlights the significance of the categories listed in §102. The definition of architectural work clearly envisions a compilation analysis: an architectural work "includes the overall form as well as the arrangement and composition of spaces and elements in the design, but does not include individual standard features." 17 U.S.C. §101. The legislative history to the AWCPA states:

> The phrase "arrangement and composition of spaces and elements" recognizes that:
> (1) creativity in architecture frequently takes the form of a selection, coordination, or arrangement of unprotectible elements into an original, protectible whole; (2) an architect may incorporate new, protectible design elements into otherwise standard, unprotectible building features; and (3) interior architecture may be protected.

H.R. Rep. No. 101-735, 101st Cong., 2d Sess. 20-21 (1990), *reprinted in* 1990 U.S.C.C.A.N. 6935, 6949. The legislative history of the AWCPA also indicates a two-step analysis for determining copyrightability:

> First, an architectural work should be examined to determine whether there are original design elements present, including overall shape and interior architecture. If such design elements are present, a second step is reached to examine whether the design elements are functionally required. If the design elements are not functionally required, the work is protectible without regard to physical or conceptual separability.

H.R. Rep. No. 101-735, 101st Cong., 2d Sess. 20-21 (1990), *reprinted in* 1990 U.S.C.C.A.N. 6935, 6951-52. How is this analysis different from the approaches that courts have applied to determine whether a useful article contains aesthetic features that are not dictated by function? Should courts employ this approach in cases involving useful articles? Would such an approach be consistent with the statute?

Would the issue in *Nelson-Salabes* have been decided differently if the court had applied a conceptual separability approach as opposed to the approach indicated by the statute's definition of "architectural works"? Why should pictorial, graphic, or sculptural works and architectural works be treated differently? Did Congress believe that architects are more likely than industrial designers to create original works of authorship and thus subjected their creations to a lower standard? Do the different standards for these categories of works relate somehow to the availability of other forms of protection?

2. Once the court determines that the structure is a building, copyrightable elements for architectural works can be found in the exterior plans, the interior floor plan, or both. Consider the floor plan of your house or apartment. Is it subject to copyright protection as an architectural work? Did you remember to consider when it was "constructed"?

3. Why wasn't the party that hired Nelson-Salabes considered the author of the work under the work-for-hire doctrine? Review the definition of "work made for hire" contained in §101. Because most architects are not employees of the individual or entity for whom

---

> created a hierarchy in terms of the protection afforded to these different types of copyrights. A creative work is entitled to the most protection, followed by a derivative work, and finally by a compilation. This is why the Feist Court emphasized that the copyright protection in a factual compilation is "thin."

Warren Publishing, Inc. v. Microdos Data Corp., 115 F.3d 1509, 1515 n. 16 (11th Cir. 1997) (citation omitted) [brackets in original — EDS.].

architectural services are rendered, the second prong of the definition is the only way for these works to qualify as "works made for hire." Recall that under this prong the work must be within one of the listed nine types. Architectural works are not included in this list. Thus, the architect (or the architectural firm for which she works) remains the author of the architectural work, and, unless the contract provides otherwise, the architect (or architectural firm) is the copyright owner.

Most, although certainly not all, architecture projects are undertaken pursuant to contracts, the vast majority of which are based on standard form agreements created by the American Institute of Architects (AIA). The AIA Agreement used by the parties in the *Nelson-Salabes* case provided:

> The Architect's Drawings, Specifications or other documents shall not be used by the Owner or others on other projects, for additions to this Project, or for completion of this Project by others unless the Architect is adjudged to be in default under this Agreement, except by agreement in writing and with appropriate compensation to the Architect. . . .

The Standard Form of Agreement Between Owner and Architect used by AIA members (B141 1997 Edition) makes it clear that the architect is granting the owner only a nonexclusive license to reproduce the documents created by the architect, and that if the architect's services are terminated before the completion of the project, the license is terminated. Only if the architect is in default of the agreement may the documents be used by another credentialed design professional for the sole purpose of completing and maintaining the project. Do you think most individuals who hire architects to custom-design a home realize that if they fire their architect they may have serious copyright problems in completing their home? Do they realize that the exact same home could be built next door or down the block?

Note on Limitations on the Protection Granted to Architectural Works

Categorizing works can matter not only in determining copyrightability, but also in determining the scope of rights granted to a copyright owner. Classifying a work as an "architectural work" carries with it important limitations on the rights granted by the Act. Section 120 provides:

§120. Scope of exclusive rights in architectural works

(a) Pictorial Representations Permitted. — The copyright in an architectural work that has been constructed does not include the right to prevent the making, distributing, or public display of pictures, paintings, photographs, or other pictorial representations of the work, if the building in which the work is embodied is located in or ordinarily visible from a public place.

(b) Alterations to and Destruction of Buildings. — Notwithstanding the provisions of section 106(2), the owners of a building embodying an architectural work may, without the consent of the author or copyright owner of the architectural work, make or authorize the making of alterations to such building, and destroy or authorize the destruction of such building.

Do these limitations seem appropriate? Do they seem fair to the author/copyright owner? To the owner of a copy of the work? To the public? Recall the different policy justifications for copyright protection. Are these limitations on the scope of rights granted to owners of copyrights in architectural works consistent with the utilitarian justification for copyright law, with Lockean labor theory, or with a natural rights approach to copyright? Does economic theory, particularly the role of transaction costs, provide a rationale for these limitations?

Before the AWCPA it was clear that monuments were to be protected, if at all, as sculptural works. Now that architectural works are granted protection, it is unclear whether the classification for certain monumental works has changed or whether dual categorization is possible. Looking to the legislative history of the AWCPA is not particularly helpful: "Monumental, nonfunctional works of architecture are currently protected under §102(a)(5) of title 17 as sculptural works. These works are, nevertheless, architectural works, and as such, will not be protected exclusively under section 102(a)(8)." H.R. Rep. No. 101-735, 101st Cong., 2d Sess. 20 n.43 (1990), *reprinted in* 1990 U.S.C.C.A.N. 6935, 6951. This would indicate that the dual categorization possible for such works would be something the courts would need to sort out. However, Professor Patry, the former Policy Advisor to the Register of Copyrights, states that the word "not" was a typographical error and was intended to read "now." This one-letter correction would take works previously protected as sculptural works and subject them to the more limited protection granted architectural works. Given that the purpose behind the AWCPA was to bring U.S. law into compliance with the Berne Convention, do you think that Congress intended the statute to have this effect?

The implications of this debate about categorization are significant. Consider the Statue of Liberty, the St. Louis Arch, or the Vietnam Veterans Memorial in Washington D.C. Are these and similar works copyrightable as sculptural works? As architectural works? Selecting the proper category may not influence the determination of copyrightability, but the scope of protection afforded the copyright owner, and correspondingly the rights of the public to make certain uses of the work, will vary significantly depending on the category in which the work is placed. Section 120 permits photographs of architectural works that are in public view to be taken, sold, and exhibited without infringing the reproduction right of the copyright owner. Section 120 does not apply to sculptural works. How should courts resolve this question of categorization? For a further exploration of the issues related to monumental works of architecture, see Melissa M. Mathis, Note, *Function, Nonfunction, and Monumental Works of Architecture: An Interpretive Lens in Copyright Law*, 22 Cardozo L. Rev. 595 (2001).

3. New Paradigms?

Copyright protection is not the only type of protection that might be relevant to an architectural work. As you have seen with the other categories of works explored in this chapter, when authors seek protection for nontraditional creative works, copyright is but one place they look. For architectural works, trademark law can also provide a measure of relief from certain kinds of copying. The Federal Circuit has defined trade dress as "the overall combination and arrangement of design elements into the total image by which the product is perceived by the consuming public." *L.A. Gear, Inc. v. Thom McAn Shoe Co.*, 988 F.2d 1117, 1129 (Fed. Cir. 1993); *see also Two Pesos, Inc. v. Taco Cabana, Inc.*, 505 U.S. 763 (1992) (discussing the requirements for protecting the trade dress of a restaurant). The PTO has registered many different building designs as trademarks, including the Guggenheim Museum, Pizza Hut, and a number of McDonald's restaurants. One court has also recognized the interior layout of a store as protectible trade dress. *Best Cellars Inc. v. Grape Finds at Dupont, Inc.*, 90 F. Supp. 2d 431, 453-54 (S.D.N.Y. 2000) (interior construction of wine store).

Similar, in some ways, to the limits on copyrightability for architectural works, trademark law also attempts to prevent functional features from being monopolized. As discussed *supra* pages 209-210, trade dress is considered functional if exclusive use of the feature would put competitors at a significant non–reputation-related disadvantage. This is a different standard than the standard set forth in the definition of architectural works. In one case, the court determined that the plaintiff did not have a protectible trade dress in its shopping mall store using a motif of a New England colonial home, in part because "[g]ranting exclusive use of generic features found in colonial era homes and buildings across New England to create the concept of a colonial shop would severely disadvantage others looking to compete in the retail industry by employing a colonial motif." *The Yankee Candle Co. v. New England Candle Co.*, 14 F. Supp. 2d 154, 163 (D. Mass. 1998).

Even if an architectural work is distinctive and nonfunctional in the trademark sense, the owner must use the architectural work as a trademark to obtain protection. This means the building must function, in the eyes of the consuming public, as a source identifying feature of the product or service sold. Merely existing is not sufficient to garner trademark protection. The Rock and Roll Hall of Fame and Museum, located in Cleveland, Ohio, learned this lesson the hard way. The Sixth Circuit ruled that the museum had failed to use the image of its highly unique structure, designed in 1991 by world-renowned architect I.M. Pei, as a trademark. Rather, the museum had merely sold souvenirs that depicted the building. *Rock and Roll Hall of Fame and Museum, Inc. v. Gentile Prod.*, 134 F.3d 749 (6th Cir. 1998). In that case, the Rock and Roll Hall of Fame sought to enjoin a photographer from selling posters that contained a photograph of the building against a colorful sunset.

If an architectural work qualifies for trademark protection, an individual such as the defendant in the *Rock and Roll Hall of Fame* case should be wary of the commercial activity in which he engages. Selling photographs of a building that has achieved both copyright and trademark status will not violate copyright law because of the limitations codified in §120. However, an individual selling those same photographs could encounter problems under trademark law. To infringe a trademark there must be a likelihood that the consuming public will be confused as to the source, sponsorship, or affiliation of the goods. 15 U.S.C. §1125. If that likelihood of confusion is present, the limitations in §120 of the Copyright Act will not provide a defense to *trademark* infringement.

NOTES AND QUESTIONS

1. Does overlapping protection for buildings make sense? Recall what you thought about the appropriate nature of the limits contained in §120. Has your opinion changed? Should there be similar limits for trademark rights?

2. Although required by the Berne Convention, does it make sense to have *any* protection for the design of buildings? In what way is protection for only the plans inadequate?

D. CHARACTERS

Characters, like architectural works before their addition to the Copyright Act, do not seem to fall neatly within any of the §102(a) categories. Characters certainly are an element of many different kinds of works, including literary works, motion pictures, graphic works such as comic strips, and even video games. Are characters separately copyrightable?

1.   Expression or Idea?

Metro-Goldwyn-Mayer, Inc. v. American Honda Motor Co.
900 F. Supp. 1287 (C.D. Cal. 1995)

KENYON, J.: . . . This case arises out of Plaintiffs Metro-Goldwyn-Mayer's and Dan-jaq's claim that Defendants American Honda Motor Co. and its advertising agency Rubin Postaer and Associates, violated Plaintiffs' "copyrights to sixteen James Bond films and the exclusive intellectual property rights to the James Bond character and the James Bond films" through Defendants' recent commercial for its Honda del Sol automobile.

Premiering last October 1994, Defendants' "Escape" commercial features a young, well-dressed couple in a Honda del Sol being chased by a high-tech helicopter. A grotesque villain with metal-encased arms[2] jumps out of the helicopter onto the car's roof, threatening harm. With a flirtatious turn to his companion, the male driver deftly releases the Honda's detachable roof (which Defendants claim is the main feature allegedly highlighted by the commercial), sending the villain into space and effecting the couple's speedy get-away.

Plaintiffs move to enjoin Defendants' commercial pending a final trial on the merits, and Defendants move for summary judgment. . . .

[I]n an effort to accommodate Plaintiffs' demands without purportedly conceding liability, Defendants changed their commercial by: (1) altering the protagonists' accents from British to American; and (2) by changing the music to make it less like the horn-driven James Bond theme. This version of the commercial was shown during the Superbowl, allegedly the most widely viewed TV event of the year. . . .

a.   Plaintiffs' Ownership Of The Copyrights

Plaintiffs claim that the Honda commercial: (1) "infringes [P]laintiffs' copyrights in the James Bond films by intentionally copying numerous specific scenes from the *films*"; and (2) "independently infringes [P]laintiffs' copyright in the *James Bond character as expressed and delineated in those films.*"

Neither side disputes that Plaintiffs own registered copyrights to each of the sixteen films which Plaintiffs claim "define and delineate the James Bond character." However, Defendants argue that because Plaintiffs have not shown that they own the copyright to the James Bond character in particular, Plaintiffs cannot prevail. Specifically, Defendants claim that James Bond has appeared in two films in which Plaintiffs hold no copyright — "Casino Royale" and "Never Say Never Again" — and therefore, Plaintiffs cannot have exclusive rights to the James Bond character.

It appears that Defendants misconstrue Plaintiffs' claim. First, Plaintiffs do not allege that Defendants have violated Plaintiffs' copyright in the James Bond character itself, but rather in the James Bond character *as expressed and delineated in Plaintiffs' sixteen films.* To the extent

---

2. Defense counsel argued at the hearing that the villain's arms were normal and merely gloved. The Court's review of the commercial indicates that at the very least, the gloves contained some sort of metal in them as indicated by the scraping and clanging sounds made by the villain as he tries to get into, and hold onto, the Honda's roof.

that copyright law only protects original *expression*, not *ideas*, Plaintiffs' argument is that the James Bond character as developed in the sixteen films is the copyrighted work at issue, not the James Bond character generally. *See, e.g., Anderson v. Stallone*, 11 U.S.P.Q.2d 1161, 1989 WL 206431, *6 (C.D. Cal. 1989) (holding that Rocky characters as developed in three "Rocky" movies "constitute expression protected by copyright independent from the story in which they are contained"). Second, there is sufficient authority for the proposition that a plaintiff who holds copyrights in a film series acquires copyright protection as well for the expression of any significant characters portrayed therein. *See, e.g., New Line Cinema Corp. v. Bertlesman Music Group*, 693 F. Supp. 1517, 1521 n.5 (S.D.N.Y. 1988) ("Because New Line has valid copyrights in the Nightmare [on Elm Street film] series, it is clear that it has acquired copyright protection as well *for the character of Freddy.*") (emphasis added). And third, the *Sam Spade* case, [*Warner Bros. Pictures, Inc. v. Columbia Broad. Sys., Inc.*, 216 F.2d 945, 949-50 (9th Cir. 1954), *cert. denied*, 348 U.S. 971 (1955)] on which Defendants' rely, is distinguishable on its facts because *Sam Spade* dealt specifically with the transfer of rights from author to film producer rather than the copyrightability of a character as developed and expressed in a series of films.

Accordingly, Plaintiffs will likely satisfy the "ownership" prong of the test.

b. What Elements Of Plaintiffs' Work Are Protectible Under Copyright Law

Plaintiffs contend that Defendants' commercial infringes in two independent ways: (1) by reflecting specific scenes from the 16 films; and (2) by the male protagonist's possessing James Bond's unique character traits as developed in the films.

Defendants respond that Plaintiffs are simply trying to gain a monopoly over the "action/spy/police hero" genre which is contrary to the purposes of copyright law. Specifically, Defendants argue that the allegedly infringed elements identified by Plaintiffs are not protectible because: (1) the helicopter chase scene in the Honda commercial is a common theme that naturally flows from most action genre films, and the woman and villain in the film are but stock characters that are not protectable; and (2) under the Ninth Circuit's *Sam Spade* decision, the James Bond character does not constitute the "story being told," but is rather an unprotected dramatic character.

(1) Whether Film Scenes Are Copyrightable

[The court found that the plaintiffs were likely to succeed in their claim of copyright for the action film sequence common to the James Bond movies, noting that a "filmmaker could produce a helicopter chase scene in practically an indefinite number of ways, but only James Bond films bring the various elements [described by one of plaintiffs' experts] together in a unique and original way." Those elements were identified as "hybridiz[ing] the spy thriller with the genres of adventure, comedy (particularly, social satire and slapstick), and fantasy."]

(2) Whether James Bond Character Is Copyrightable

The law in the Ninth Circuit is unclear as to when visually-depicted characters such as James Bond can be afforded copyright protection. In the landmark *Sam Spade* case, *Warner Bros.*, 216 F.2d at 950, the Ninth Circuit held that the *literary* character Sam Spade was not copyrightable because he did not constitute "the story being told." The court opined: "It is conceivable that the character really constitutes the story being told, but if the character is only the chessman in the game of telling the story he is not within the area of the protection afforded by the copyright." *Id*.

Two subsequent Ninth Circuit decisions have cast doubt on the continued viability of the *Sam Spade* holding as applied to graphic characters. In *Walt Disney Productions v. Air Pirates*, 581 F.2d 751, 755 (9th Cir. 1978), *cert. denied*, 439 U.S. 1132 (1979), the circuit panel held that several Disney comic book characters were protected by copyright. In acknowledging the *Sam Spade* opinion, the court reasoned that because "comic book characters . . . are distinguishable from literary characters, the [*Sam Spade*] language does not preclude protection of Disney's characters." *Id*. The *Air Pirates* decision may be viewed as either: (1) following *Sam Spade* by implicitly holding that Disney's graphic characters constituted the story being told; or (2) applying a less stringent test for the protectability of graphic characters. One rationale for adopting the second view is that, "[a]s a practical matter, a graphically depicted character is much more likely than a literary character to be fleshed out in sufficient detail so as to warrant copyright protection." *Anderson*, 1989 WL 206431, at *7. However, as one district court warned, "this fact does not warrant the creation of separate analytical paradigms for protection of characters in the two mediums." *Id*. A second Ninth Circuit opinion issued in 1988 did little to clarify *Air Pirates'* impact on the *Sam Spade* test. In *Olson v. National Broadcasting Co.*, 855 F.2d 1446, 1451-52 n.6 (9th Cir. 1988), the court cited with approval the *Sam Spade* "story being told" test and declined to characterize this language as dicta. Later in the opinion, the court cited the *Air Pirates* decision along with Second Circuit precedent,[9] recognizing that "cases subsequent to [the *Sam Spade* decision] have allowed copyright protection for characters who are especially distinctive." *Id*. at 1452. *Olson* also noted that "copyright protection may be afforded to characters visually depicted in a television series or in a movie." *Id*. However, later in the opinion, the court distanced itself from the character delineation test applied by these other cases, referring to it as "the more lenient standard[ ] adopted elsewhere." *Id*.

There have been no Ninth Circuit cases on the protectability of visually-depicted characters since *Olson*, and therefore, it behooves this Court to analyze James Bond's status under the *Sam Spade/Olson*/Ninth Circuit "story being told" test, as well as under the *Air Pirates/* Second Circuit "character delineation" test.

Predictably, Plaintiffs claim that under either test, James Bond's character as developed in the sixteen films is sufficiently unique and deserves copyright protection, just as Judge Keller ruled that Rocky and his cohorts were sufficiently unique. *See Anderson*, 1989 WL 206431, at *7-8. Plaintiffs point to various character traits that are specific to Bond—i.e. his cold-bloodedness; his overt sexuality; his love of martinis "shaken, not stirred"; his marksmanship; his "license to kill" and use of guns; his physical strength; his sophistication—some of which, Plaintiffs' claim, appear in the Honda commercial's hero.

On the other hand, Defendants assert that, like Sam Spade, James Bond is not the "story being told," but instead "has changed enormously from film to film, from actor to actor, and from year to year." Moreover, Defendants contend that even if Bond's character is sufficiently delineated, there is so little character development in the Honda commercial's hero that Plaintiffs cannot claim that Defendants copied more than the broader outlines of Bond's personality. *See, e.g., Smith v. Weinstein*, 578 F. Supp. 1297, 1303 (S.D.N.Y.), *aff'd*, 738 F.2d 419 (2d Cir. 1984) ("no character infringement claim can succeed unless plaintiff's original conception

---

9. The Second Circuit has adopted an alternate test for determining whether dramatic characters are protectable under copyright law. In the landmark case of *Nichols*, 45 F.2d at 121, the court held that copyright protection is granted to a character if it is developed with enough specificity so as to constitute protectable expression. This has been viewed to be a less stringent standard than *Sam Spade's* "story being told" test.

sufficiently developed the character, and defendants have copied this development and not merely the broader outlines").

Reviewing the evidence and arguments, the Court believes that James Bond is more like Rocky than Sam Spade — in essence, that James Bond is a copyrightable character under either the *Sam Spade* "story being told test" or the Second Circuit's "character delineation" test. Like Rocky, Sherlock Holmes, Tarzan, and Superman, James Bond has certain character traits that have been developed over time through the sixteen films in which he appears. Contrary to Defendants' assertions, because many actors can play Bond is a testament to the fact that Bond is a unique character whose specific qualities remain constant despite the change in actors. *See* Pfeiffer and Lisa, *The Incredible World of 007*, at 8 ("[Despite the different actors who have played the part] James Bond is like an old reliable friend."). Indeed, audiences do not watch Tarzan, Superman, Sherlock Holmes, or James Bond for the story, they watch these films to see their heroes at work. A James Bond film without James Bond is *not* a James Bond film. Moreover, as discussed more specifically below, the Honda Man's character, from his appearance to his grace under pressure, is substantially similar to Plaintiffs' Bond. . . .

Titan Sports, Inc. v. Turner Broadcasting Systems, Inc.
981 F. Supp. 65 (D. Conn. 1997)

DORSEY, C.J.: . . . Titan Sports, Inc., etc., ("Plaintiff") . . . promotes live, and on cable, syndicated, and pay-per-view television, professional wrestling under its registered service mark "World Wrestling Federation" ("WWF").

[Defendant Turner Broadcasting Systems, Inc. ("TBS")] owns and operates several cable networks. . . . [Defendant World Championship Wrestling, Inc., ("WCW") is] a majority owned subsidiary of TBS. WCW competes directly with WWF in televising professional wrestling, associated merchandising, and licensing programs. . . .

Plaintiff contends that success in the professional wrestling business depends upon the development of interesting wrestling characters and story lines. Characters must have names, personalities, histories, relationships, personas, and visual appearances that appeal to consumers. Plaintiff alleges that WWF programming combines character-driven story lines with skillful wrestling while WCW has no reputation for creativity. TBS proposed interpromotional matches in order to associate WCW with WWF, but Plaintiff rejected this idea.

After wrestling unsuccessfully with WCW, Scott Hall contracted to wrestle for Plaintiff. Plaintiff created a wrestling character for Hall called "Razor Ramon," alias "The Bad Guy," with a distinctive Hispanic accent, slicked back hair in a ponytail with a curl in the front, a toothpick in his mouth, a vest, and multiple chains around his neck. . . . The contract provided that Plaintiff retained exclusive ownership of the character's name and likeness and the exclusive right to distribute copyrightable materials based on the character. . . .

Plaintiff developed Razor Ramon into one of its most popular characters. He has appeared in television broadcasts, live events, a two-hour videotape, several magazines, and is the subject of merchandise devoted to the character. He won WWF's Intercontinental Championship at least four times. The character is well-recognized by wrestling fans.

Plaintiff developed another character using wrestler Kevin Nash who wrestled unsuccessfully with defendant WCW. Nash and Plaintiff entered into a contract with provisions similar to Hall's contract. Nash's character was "Diesel," alias "Big Daddy Cool." Diesel's trade dress included a goatee beard and moustache, black leather pants, a black leather vest decorated with silver studs and tassels, a black low cut tank-top shirt, a black fingerless glove on the right hand, black elbow pads, black wrist bands, sunglasses, and black leather boots. Diesel is visibly different from the characters previously portrayed by Nash at WCW.

Diesel was added to Plaintiff's story lines and appeared in television broadcasts, commercial videotapes, magazines, and became the subject of merchandise. Like Razor Ramon, Diesel also became widely recognized and popular, winning the WWF Heavyweight Championship in 1995. . . .

In 1996, enticed by WCW's promise of lucrative, guaranteed contracts, Hall and Nash contracted to wrestle with WCW. [Hall and Nash subsequently appeared on WCW broadcasts, although defendants did not refer to them by any name.] . . .

In Counts I and II of the Amended Complaint, Plaintiff alleges copyright infringement of the characters Razor Ramon and Diesel. Defendants move to dismiss Counts I and II as they pertain to Plaintiffs Diesel character on the basis that Plaintiff failed to plead sufficient character development to establish a copyrightable character.

. . . The owner of a copyright in various works embodying a character can acquire copyright protection for the character itself.

A plaintiff, however, must still demonstrate that the character was "distinctively delineated in the plaintiff's work, and such delineation was copied in the defendant's work." 1 Melville B. Nimmer, *Nimmer on Copyright* §2.12, at 2-172.34 (1996).[1] The protection is limited to the character as defined by performances in the copyrighted works. "[O]nly a uniquely developed character with some degree of novelty is copyrightable." *Jones v. CBS, Inc.*, 733 F. Supp. 748, 753 (S.D.N.Y. 1990). "'[T]he less developed the characters, the less they can be copyrighted. . . .'" *Williams* [*v. Crichton*], 84 F.3d [581] at 589, [(2d Cir. 1996)] (citation omitted). *Accord: Hoehling v. Universal City Studios, Inc.*, 618 F.2d 972, 979 (2d Cir. 1980), *cert. denied*, 449 U.S. 841 . . . (1980) (copyright law does not protect "'characters . . . which are as a practical matter indispensable, or at least standard, in the treatment of a given topic.'") (citations omitted).

Plaintiff does not have a registered copyright in the character Diesel. Plaintiff has obtained copyright registration in numerous broadcasts, videos, and magazines in which its Diesel character has appeared. Defendants contend, however, that Plaintiff has failed to plead that the character of Diesel exhibits the uniqueness or distinctiveness necessary to obtain copyright protection. Plaintiff sufficiently alleges that the Diesel character is a developed and distinctive character worthy of copyright protection. Plaintiff described in detail Diesel's trade dress, costumes, hair color, and style, all of which were unique among wrestlers and recognizable by wrestling fans. Plaintiff devoted almost three pages of the Amended Complaint to explaining how the Diesel character developed into a fully independent character and ultimately became integral to the story lines of many televised events. Construing all allegations in favor of plaintiff, it cannot be said that there is no set of facts upon which relief could be granted to Plaintiff. Defendants' motion to dismiss Counts I and II is denied. . . .

---

1. Although the language in *Warner Bros.* suggests that if a plaintiff owns a valid copyright in a work the plaintiff automatically obtains a copyright in the characters, all characters embodied in a copyrighted work are not necessarily protected. Instead, the character still must be sufficiently developed in the work to be worthy of copyright protection. To hold otherwise would provide copyright protection to any insubstantial and undeveloped character.

NOTES AND QUESTIONS

1. Under what §102 category of work did these courts find the plaintiffs' characters copyrightable? Were they literary works? Pictorial or graphic works? Audiovisual works? Does it matter?

2. Determining which characters are independently copyrightable is difficult. When does a character transform itself from a mere idea into expression? As is often the case, the two extremes are relatively easy to identify. Minor characters or stock characters, those necessary to tell a story of a certain time period or genre, are not protectible. On the other hand, copyright law protects highly delineated characters that are central to a story or, in the words of the *Sam Spade* case, characters that constitute the "story being told." The middle ground is where most of the disputes over copyrightability occur. Is there a difference between the two tests described and applied by the court in the James Bond case? What does the *Titan Sports* court mean when it states that "the less developed the characters, the less they can be copyrighted"?

3. The *Sam Spade* case, in which the Second Circuit articulated the "story being told" test, involved a claim by Warner Brothers against Dashiell Hammett, the author of the mystery-detective story entitled "The Maltese Falcon." *Warner Bros. Pictures, Inc. v. Columbia Broadcasting System, Inc.*, 216 F.2d 945, 949-50 (9th Cir. 1954), *cert. denied*, 348 U.S. 971 (1955). Hammett had previously assigned the copyright in the work to Warner Brothers, which made the famous movie of the same name starring Humphrey Bogart and Mary Astor. When Hammett used the characters from "The Maltese Falcon" in subsequent works and authorized others to do so, Warner Brothers sued for infringement. The court noted that "[i]f Congress had intended that the sale of the right to publish a copyrighted story would foreclose the author's use of its characters in subsequent works for the life of the copyright, it would seem Congress would have made specific provision therefor." *Id.* at 950. It was in this context that the court employed the requirement that the characters constitute the "story being told" in order to be a part of the copyright that was conveyed. Should the factual context influence which standard a court employs?

4. As described in the James Bond case, it appears that there may be a different standard for copyrightability when the character is visually depicted versus described in a literary work. Is a picture really worth a thousand words? There may even be a difference in the standard applied depending on the nature of the visual depiction. Graphically depicted characters, those that are drawn, garner a kind of graphic work protection. Visually depicted characters in movies employing actors to portray the characters may have more difficulty in obtaining protection.

Additionally, a character in a movie takes on the physical attributes of the actor portraying the character. Are those attributes then part of the character? *Titan Sports* exemplifies a situation in which a character, portrayed by a single actor, appears to have sufficient originality. In that case, the issue of copyright ownership was handled through a contract providing that the character was a work for hire (permissible under the second prong of the definition of works made for hire in §101 as a contribution to a motion picture or audiovisual work). In the absence of a contract, who is the "author" of such a character? In addition to copyright, there may be issues concerning the actor's rights of publicity. We consider these issues below.

5. Is it possible to infringe a copyrighted character without copying the general context in which the character is usually found? For example, if a James Bond-like character were hosting a cooking show, with no bad guys jumping out of helicopters to steal the filet mignon, would that still constitute infringement of the James Bond character? Can we say that setting and other accompanying characters, even ones so undelineated as to be just "bad guys," are some of the attributes that contribute to the copyrightability of literary characters? How about graphically

depicted characters? If Mickey Mouse is speeding around in a spaceship with three unsightly one-eyed slimy alien creatures, will we still recognize Mickey and find Disney's copyright infringed? Perhaps graphically depicted characters do not need the same level of, or for that matter, any contextual support for the copyrights to be infringed.

6. In the late 1990s and early 2000s online real-time interactive role-playing games such as Everquest and World of Warcraft became increasingly popular. In these games, individuals begin their life in a fantasy world by selecting a character type, for example, a sorcerer or a warrior, and as they play, their character takes on new attributes based on experiences and other actions in the fantasy world. Entrepreneurial gamers use online auction sites such as eBay to sell their characters, some of which they may have spent hundreds of hours developing. Sony Online Entertainment, the copyright owner of the Everquest game, asked eBay to halt those sales, asserting that the sale of the characters violated its copyrights, among other rights. eBay complied with the request. *See* Monty Phan, *Defining Their Own Reality*, Newsday, Feb. 13, 2001, at C08. Do you think Sony's copyright claim was a strong one? Why would eBay agree to halt those sales?

Note on Fan Fiction on the Internet

Many fans of particular movies, televisions shows, and popular novels write new scenes, stories, episodes, and even entire movie plots utilizing the characters from their favorite shows. These pieces of fan fiction are then shared with other fans, typically for free, through various means including Internet listservs and the World Wide Web. No question exists concerning copying; these activities clearly copy the characters from copyrighted works. It is also clear that these fan fiction stories copy fully delineated characters; after all, that is the point. They do not, typically, copy the plot of existing shows; instead, they create new story lines and plots. Courts have held, although not in the context of fan fiction, that unauthorized sequels are infringements. *Anderson v. Stallone*, 11 U.S.P.Q.2d 1161, 1989 WL 206431, *6 (C.D. Cal. 1989); *Microstar v. FormGen, Inc.*, 154 F.3d 1107 (9th Cir. 1998) (holding that new levels of the Duke Nukem video games are like sequels and sequels infringe the derivative work right granted to copyright owners). *But see Suntrust Bank v. Houghton Mifflin Co.*, 268 F.3d 1257 (11th Cir. 2001) (recognizing the likelihood of a successful fair use defense, and reversing a preliminary injunction blocking the publication of *The Wind Done Gone*, a novel based on *Gone With the Wind* but told from a different perspective).

The art of storytelling has been around for thousands of years, and during the same thousands of years storytellers have been using the characters in stories they hear to create new stories. Today's storytellers often use characters from television shows and movies as raw material for their expressive activity; in the modern era, these characters constitute a significant portion of our shared culture. Today, large corporations, with bottom lines and shareholders to worry about, own copyrights in that cultural raw material.

Should copyright owners be able to put an end to fan fiction? Many copyright owners have certainly tried, although some have permitted fan fiction to flourish, hoping that the enthusiasm generated by such activity will increase their profits. Those copyright owners that have tried to put an end to fan sites or fan fiction have sometimes faced significant backlash from their customer base. If certain uses of these shared cultural images are permitted under copyright law, is copyright law penalizing the copyright owners of creative works that become the most successful and famous?

It is customary for individuals to place copyright disclaimers on their fan fiction. These disclaimers may indicate that the author does not have permission from the owners of the television show or movie. They often assert that because the fan fiction writer is not making any money the work does not infringe. *See* Rebecca Tushnet, *Payment in Credit: Copyright Law and Subcultural Creativity*, 70 Law & Contemp. Probs. 135 (2007). Chapter 7 explores the critically important doctrine of fair use and why the noncommercial nature of a use can matter significantly in finding a use to be a fair one. Without knowing much about fair use yet, do you think fan fiction should be permitted? What factors contribute to your decision? Where would you draw the line in allowing fan fiction to be created and distributed? Given that fan fiction is so widespread, should copyright law be interpreted (or amended, if necessary) to conform to ordinary people's general expectations concerning the level of protection? Alternatively, should large sections of society conform their behavior to a law that might seem counterintuitive? For a discussion of this issue, see Jessica Litman, *Revising Copyright Law for the Information Age*, 75 Or. L. Rev. 19 (1996). Be sure to revisit the issue of fan fiction after you have completed the readings on fair use in Chapter 7.

2. New Paradigms?

As with other categories of works examined in this chapter, copyright is not the only body of law that grants protection to the creator or owner of a work embodying a character. Trademark and unfair competition law plays a significant role in protecting characters. Additionally, when real people portray characters, rights of publicity may also provide a certain kind of protection.

Note on Trademark and Unfair Competition Law

As described earlier in this chapter, trademark and unfair competition law protects signals used to identify goods or services against use by others that is likely to cause confusion among consumers as to the source or sponsorship of the products or services. Characters often function as those signals, sometimes having been created especially for that purpose. The Energizer Bunny, Betty Crocker, and the Michelin Man are examples of characters specifically created to market products. Other times, however, courts have recognized characters developed in the context of novels, movies, television shows, and even video games as protectible trademarks. In both the James Bond and professional wrestling cases discussed earlier, the plaintiffs asserted trademark infringement claims as well as copyright claims. Plaintiffs argued that defendants' use of their characters would create a false impression of affiliation and was likely to cause consumers to believe that the plaintiffs sponsored or approved of the defendants' products. In the context of the advertisement for the Honda del Sol, this claim may seem logical — consumers may believe that James Bond, their reliable old friend, is endorsing this car. In the context of professional wrestling shows, however, should a claim of trademark infringement be recognized? What are the products that plaintiffs and defendants are selling?

Note on Rights of Publicity

Many states grant individuals protection against certain unauthorized uses of their likenesses or personal attributes. Generally, laws protecting rights of publicity, both common law and statutory, prohibit using a person's likeness to sell a product or gain other advantages. An individual's *persona*, his or her name, likeness, and attributes, is not a copyrightable work. When an actor portrays a character, the actor's individual attributes become intermingled with the character contained in an audiovisual work. Who then owns the character, or the character with the physical attributes of the actor? Usually these gray areas are handled through contracts, but not always.

The case of actors George Wendt and John Ratzenberger, who played Norm and Cliff on the long-running television series "Cheers," exemplifies the problems that can arise. The actors' contracts with the studio, Paramount, specified that the studio owned the characters Norm and Cliff. When Paramount authorized two animatronic robots, named Hank and Bob, to be placed in "Cheers," look-alike bars owned by Host International, Wendt and Ratzenberger sued both Host and Paramount, alleging a violation of their rights of publicity. The court concluded that the actors' participation in the television show "Cheers" did not result in a loss of their rights to control the commercial exploitation of their likenesses. *Wendt v. Host Int'l, Inc.*, 125 F.3d 806, 811 (9th Cir. 1997). The court required an examination of the robots, outside the contextual setting of the "Cheers"-like bar, to determine if they were sufficiently similar to the actors to constitute their likenesses. The court relied on an earlier case in which Vanna White had succeeded in suing over the use of a robot dressed in an evening gown depicted next to a game board recognizable as that used on the "Wheel of Fortune" game show. *White v. Samsung Elecs. Am., Inc.*, 971 F.2d 1395 (9th Cir. 1992). In *Wendt*, the court concluded that there was a genuine issue of material fact concerning the degree to which the robots in this case, one heavyset and one dressed as a mailman, looked like the actors.

The defendants' petition for rehearing en banc was denied. Judge Kozinski, not a member of the original panel that heard the appeal, dissented from the denial of rehearing en banc:

> The right of publicity, as defined by the state courts, is limited to using a celebrity's name, voice, face or signature. A copyright holder can generally avoid using any of these tangible elements in exploiting its copyright. *White* exploded the right of publicity to include anything that brings the celebrity to mind. It's inevitable that so broad and ill-defined a property right will trench on the rights of the copyright holder. According to the panel, Paramount and Host may not use Norm and Cliff in a way that reminds people of the actors who played them and whose identity is therefore fused in the public mind. This is a daunting burden. Can Warner Brothers exploit Rhett Butler without also reminding people of Clark Gable? Can Paramount cast Shelly Long in *The Brady Bunch Movie* without creating a triable issue of fact as to whether it is treading on Florence Henderson's right of publicity? How about Dracula and Bela Lugosi? Ripley and Sigourney Weaver? Kramer and Michael Richards?

Wendt v. Host Int'l Inc., 197 F.3d 1284, 1286 (9th Cir. 1999) (J. Kozinski, dissenting). In the future, how do you think television and movie studios will handle this precedent?

One way to view the result in *Wendt* is that Paramount, the owner of the copyrighted works in which Norm and Cliff are highly delineated characters, was unable to authorize the making of derivative works (i.e., the animatronic robots) because of state law protections for the actors' rights of publicity. The Ninth Circuit addressed whether these state law claims should be barred by federal copyright law. The court concluded that the rights protected by state law were not the same as those protected by federal law, although it noted that the case would be different if Wendt and Ratzenberger were attempting to preclude Paramount from exhibiting the copyrighted works in the "Cheers" series. *Wendt*, 125 F.3d at 810. Although federal preemption of state law claims under copyright law is not covered in detail until Chapter 9, it is important to consider the effect of the Ninth Circuit's decision permitting such state law claims to proceed. Can these state law protections be reconciled with federal copyright protection?

Rights of publicity claims can also be asserted against third parties who do not have authorization from any copyright owners. In *KNB Enterprises v. Matthews*, 92 Cal. Rptr. 2d 713 (Cal. App. 2000), the California Court of Appeals allowed plaintiff to proceed with its claims of misappropriation of models' likenesses when the defendant reproduced erotic photographs of the models on the Internet. While the plaintiff also owned the copyright in those photographs, it only asserted the right of publicity claims that it had acquired through contracts with the models. The court held that because a human likeness is not copyrightable, even if captured in a copyrighted photograph, the models' claims were not preempted by copyright law.

NOTES AND QUESTIONS

1. The combined protection of copyright law and trademark law available for characters creates relatively thick armor to protect these fictional characters. Is this appropriate? Consider the following:

[I]t is in general important to make sure that our copyright law does not provide protection so strong that it enables the Disney Company, and other current stakeholders, to block—or even delay—the creation of new works and the exploitation of new media by tying up the raw material everyone needs to use. For that reason, copyright law has, and needs, limitations on the nature and scope of the rights we give to the copyright holder. It can undermine the system to make exceptions to those limitations for the sake of a tremendously appealing and lucrative character. It can also undermine the system to ask the courts to go outside copyright and make up a quasi-property right, nominally derived from unwritten, unarticulated state law, that omits the limitations built into the copyright system. Trying to stretch the Lanham Act around this whole set of problems and opportunities avoids any problems of federal preemption of state law, but raises the very same policy issues. If the reasons we have limits on the scope of rights under copyright are sound, then we need to be very careful whenever we recognize a new set of rights designed to circumvent those limits.

Jessica Litman, *Mickey Mouse Emeritus: Character Protection and the Public Domain*, 11 U. Miami Ent. & Sports L. Rev. 429, 435 (1994).

2. Copyright is meant to provide an incentive for the creation and dissemination of new works. What do you think is the purpose behind providing a right of publicity? Does providing a right of publicity interfere with or assist in achieving the goals of copyright?

E. DATABASES

Compilations of data are another category of "new" works that complicates copyright law. Although the Copyright Act has protected compilations for a long time, the question of copyright protection for compilations of factual information only recently has become the subject of heated debate. The TRIPS Agreement requires members to provide protection for databases under the standard set forth in Article 10(2) for compilations generally: "Compilations of data or other material, whether in machine readable or other form, which by reason of the selection or arrangement of their contents constitute intellectual creations shall be protected as such. . . ."

As discussed in Chapter 2, the Copyright Act defines a compilation as "a work formed by the collection and assembling of preexisting materials or of data that are selected, coordinated, or arranged in such a way that the resulting work as a whole constitutes an original work of authorship." 17 U.S.C. §101. Because copyright does not protect the facts contained within a particular work, the copyrightablity of a compilation of facts depends on the selection and arrangement of those facts. Recall that in *Feist*, the Supreme Court denied copyright protection to a "white pages" telephone directory on the grounds that an alphabetical arrangement of facts lacks sufficient originality to justify copyright protection. The Supreme Court rejected the "sweat of the brow" theory as a basis for copyright protection, and held that the originality requirement in U.S. copyright law, although de minimis, is nevertheless an indispensable constitutional requirement. (Recall from Chapter 2 that some countries have a higher standard of originality.) Even when the arrangement or selection of data is sufficiently original, copyright protection in factual compilations is described as "thin," meaning that in order to infringe, the defendant must copy the compilation's original elements (i.e., its selection or arrangement) exactly or almost exactly. See *Feist*, Chapter 2, *supra*.

Compilations of data that lack the originality in selection or arrangement necessary for copyright protection are nonetheless susceptible to the public goods problem. Compilers may spend substantial sums collecting the data, yet if others can freely copy it, the compiler will not be able to recoup his expenses, let alone make a profit. In addition, in the information age databases are invaluable to the public, and an important part of the infrastructure for electronic commerce. Many commentators therefore conclude that compilers of such works should receive some sort of protection to provide them with an incentive to collect and aggregate data. The critical inquiry, then, is what form such protection should take—copyright law, sui generis protection based on an unfair competition model, or some other regulatory/statutory regime.

1. Selection, Arrangement, and Utility

This section explores the application of *Feist* and §102(b) to compilations of information. The utility of databases, like that of other useful works discussed earlier in this chapter, makes distinguishing creative from "garden variety" selection or arrangement of database contents an arduous task for courts. In addition, the idea/expression dichotomy plays a critical role in determining what, if anything, is protectible within a given compilation. Separating the idea of a particular compilation's selection or arrangement from its expression can be a particularly vexing problem.

The use of the disjunctive "or" in the definition of a compilation indicates that original expression can be found in the selection of the works or data to include in the compilation, regardless of their coordination or arrangement. Originality can also subsist in the arrangement of the items selected, regardless of whether the selection itself is also original. In the cases that follow, be sure to understand whether it is the selection or the arrangement that the plaintiff asserts is sufficiently original. Finally, consider whether databases produced in a digital form that allows users to manipulate the contents can really be said to have an "arrangement" or "coordination."

Bellsouth Advertising & Publishing Corp. v. Donnelley Information Publishing, Inc.

999 F.2d 1436 (11th Cir. 1993) (en banc), cert. denied, *510 U.S. 1101 (1994)*

BIRCH, J.:

I. Introduction

In this appeal, we must decide whether acts of copying infringed the compilation copyright registered in a "yellow pages" classified business directory. . . . [W]e are called upon to apply *Feist Publications, Inc. v. Rural Tel. Serv. Co.,* 499 U.S. 340 (1991), which addressed copyright protection for a "white pages" telephone directory, to resolve the infringement claims presented to us concerning a directory of a different color.

The pivotal issue in this case is whether that which was copied by the alleged infringer was protected by the registered claim of compilation copyright. The parties agree that the only elements of a work entitled to compilation copyright protection are the selection, arrangement or coordination as they appear in the work as a whole. The parties dispute what elements of a classified directory constitute such selection, arrangement or coordination. Mindful that the protection afforded to a whole work by a compilation copyright is "thin," the determination as to whether an infringement of a compilation copyright has occurred is particularly difficult where less than the entire work is copied.

II. Background

BellSouth Advertising & Publishing Corporation ("BAPCO") is a wholly owned subsidiary of BellSouth Corporation ("BellSouth") created for the purpose of preparing, publishing and distributing telephone directories. Using telephone listing information supplied by Southern Bell Telephone and Telegraph Company ("Southern Bell"), another wholly owned subsidiary of BellSouth, BAPCO publishes a classified, "yellow pages," advertising directory for the Greater Miami area. . . .

After BAPCO published its 1984 directory for the Greater Miami area, Donnelley Information Publishing, Inc. and Reuben H. Donnelley Corp. (collectively "Donnelley") began promoting and selling classified advertisements to be placed in a competitive classified directory for the Greater Miami area. To generate a list of business telephone subscribers to be solicited for placement in its directory, Donnelley gave copies of BAPCO's directory to Appalachian Computer Services, Inc. ("ACS"), a data entry company. Donnelley first marked each listing in the BAPCO directory with one alphanumeric code indicating the size and type of advertisement purchased by the subscriber and a similar code indicating the type of business represented by the BAPCO heading under which the listing appeared. For each listing appearing in the BAPCO directory, ACS created a computer data base containing the name, address, and telephone number of the subscriber as well as the codes corresponding to business type and unit of advertising. From this data base, Donnelley printed sales lead sheets, listing this information for each subscriber, to be used to contact business telephone subscribers to sell advertisements and listings in the Donnelley directory. Relying on this information copied from the BAPCO directory, Donnelley ultimately prepared its own competitive directory for the Greater Miami area. . . .

... From the process by which Donnelley prepared its competitive yellow pages directory, the district court identified three acts of copying: (1) the entry of subscriber information into the computer data base by ACS; (2) the printout of sales lead sheets from this data base; and (3) the publication of Donnelley's directory. . . . [Pre-*Feist*, the district court granted summary judgment to BAPCO on its copyright infringement claim, and the court of appeals affirmed. On petition for certiorari, the Supreme Court vacated that decision and remanded for reconsideration given its intervening decision in *Feist*.]

III. Discussion ...

B. *BAPCO's Claim of Infringement*

To establish its claim of copyright infringement, BAPCO must prove "(1) ownership of a valid copyright, and (2) copying of constituent elements of the work that are original." 499 U.S. at—, 111 S. Ct. at 1296. The validity of BAPCO's copyright in its directory, considered as a whole, was conceded by Donnelley. To demonstrate the second element of infringement, BAPCO must prove that Donnelley, by taking the material it copied from the BAPCO directory, appropriated BAPCO's *original* selection, coordination or arrangement.

The district court found that BAPCO engaged in a number of acts of selection in compiling its listings. For example, BAPCO determined the geographic scope of its directory and the closing date after which no changes in the listing would be included. The district court erred, however, in implicitly determining that these selective acts were sufficiently original to merit copyright protection. Rural obviously established a geographic scope and closing date for its white pages, which were held uncopyrightable as a matter of law in *Feist*. The district court's analysis would protect such factual elements of every compilation; any collection of facts "fixed in any tangible medium of expression" will by necessity have a closing date and, where applicable, a geographic limit selected by the compiler. . . . The district court also focused on a number of marketing techniques employed by BAPCO to generate its listings, such as the determination of the number of free listings offered to each subscriber, the selection of which customers to contact by an on-premise visit from sales personnel, the selection of the date of commencement of its advertisement sales campaign, and the procedure used to recommend the purchase of listings under multiple headings. . . .

. . . [T]hese acts are not acts of authorship, but techniques for the discovery of facts. In *Feist*, the Court emphasized the distrinction "between creation and discovery: the first person to find and report a particular fact has not created the fact; he or she has merely discovered its existence." 499 U.S. at—, 111 S. Ct. at 1288. By employing its sales strategies, BAPCO discovered that certain subscribers describe their businesses in a particular fashion and were willing to pay for certain number listings under certain available business descriptions. To be sure, BAPCO employed a set of strategies or techniques for discovering this data. Any useful collection of facts, however, will be structured by a number of decisions regarding the optimal manner in which to collect the pertinent data in the most efficient and accurate manner. If this were sufficient, then the protection of copyright would extend to census data, cited in *Feist* as a paradigmatic example of a work that lacks the requisite originality. 499 U.S. at—, 111 S. Ct. at 1288. Just as the Copyright Act does not protect "industrious collection," it affords no shelter to the resourceful, efficient, or creative collector. . . .

In addition to these acts of selection, the district court found that BAPCO engaged in feats of coordination and arrangement to generate its yellow pages directory. The court explains that BAPCO arranged its directory in an alphabetized list of business types, with individual businesses listed in alphabetical order under the applicable headings. . . . BAPCO's arrangement and coordination is "entirely typical" for a business directory. With respect to business telephone directories, such an arrangement "is not only unoriginal, it is practically inevitable." 499 U.S. at—, 111 S. Ct. at 1297. . . .

The district court's suggestion that BAPCO could have arranged its headings according to the number of advertisers or to list its subscribers under each heading according to the length of time for which that subscriber had appeared under that heading misapprehends the question. The relevant inquiry is not whether there is some imaginable, though manifestly less useful, method of arranging business telephone listings. . . . The pertinent inquiry is whether the compiler has demonstrated originality, the "*sine qua non*" of copyright, in *its* arrangement or coordination. The arrangement of BAPCO's yellow pages, like that of Rural's white pages is "entirely typical" of its respective type.

The district court also identified acts of coordination and arrangement in the particular system of headings used in the BAPCO directory. The district court appears to find that, when Donnelley entered the listing information from the BAPCO directory, it also copied the particular heading under which that listing appeared in the BAPCO directory. 719 F. Supp. at 1558-59. BAPCO, however, failed to introduce evidence sufficient to establish a genuine dispute of material fact as to whether Donnelley copied the particular heading structure employed by BAPCO. Donnelley stipulated that it obtained the "business type" for each listing from the BAPCO directory. The evidence submitted to the district court in the form of affidavit, deposition, and witness testimony reveals that Donnelley established its own system of headings and that, in constructing its data base, Donnelley entered an alphanumeric code that corresponded to the Donnelley heading with each BAPCO listing. Further, the sales lead sheets generated by Donnelley from its database, as well as pages of the respective directories submitted to the district court, illustrate that Donnelley selected a somewhat different category of headings to describe the listings originally appearing in the BAPCO directory. Considering the extent to which the heading structure of a classified business directory is dictated by functional considerations and common industry practice, the differences apparent in the glossary of headings employed by Donnelley are sufficient to rebut any inference of copying that otherwise might be drawn from those terms that are common to both directories. In sum, the evidence before the district court requires the conclusion that, by determining the type of business of each subscriber by observation of the BAPCO directory and translating that business type into an encoded heading of its own creation, Donnelley extracted uncopyrightable information regarding the business activities of BAPCO's subscribers without appropriating any arguably original, protectible expressive element in the BAPCO glossary of headings. . . .

We note that Donnelley did not copy, nor was alleged to have copied, the text or graphic material from the advertisements in the BAPCO directory, the positioning of these advertisements, the typeface, or the textual material included by BAPCO to assist the user. Unlike the infringer in *Southern Bell Tel. & Tel. Co. v. Associated Tel. Directory Publishers*, 756 F.2d 801 (11th Cir. 1985), Donnelley did not photocopy, or reproduce by any equivalent means, the page by page arrangement or appearance of its competitor's directory in the process of creating its own work. . . . Given that the copyright protection of a factual compilation is "thin," a competitor's taking the bulk of the factual material from a preexisting compilation without infringement of the author's copyright is not surprising. *Feist*, 499 U.S. at—, 111 S. Ct. at 1289. While it may seem unfair for a compiler's labor to be used by a competitor without compensation, the Court noted in *Feist* that "[t]he primary objective of copyright is not to reward the labor of authors, but '[t]o promote the Progress of Science and useful Arts.'" 499 U.S. at—, 111 S. Ct. at 1290 (quoting U.S. Const. art. I, §8, cl. 8). "To this end, copyright assures authors the right to their *original* expression, but encourages others to build freely upon the ideas and information conveyed by a work." *Id.* (emphasis added); *see also Harper & Row, Publishers v. Nation Enterprises*, 471 U.S. 539, 545-46 (1985).

IV. Conclusion

By copying the name, address, telephone number, business type, and unit of advertisement purchased for each listing in the BAPCO directory, Donnelley copied no original element of selection, coordination or arrangement; Donnelley thus was entitled to summary judgment on BAPCO's claim of copyright infringement. . . .

HATCHETT, J., dissenting: . . . The clearest example of BAPCO's original selection is its choice of the classified headings that would be included in the *1984 Yellow Pages*. BAPCO selected the approximately 7,000 classified headings in the *1984 Yellow Pages* from the 4,700 primary headings and approximately 34,000 related headings in the BAPCO headings book. BAPCO presented the undisputed testimony . . . that the BAPCO headings book is not standardized to coincide with the menu of classified headings used in the National Yellow Pages Sales Association (NYPSA) publications. Moreover, even if BAPCO's selection of classified headings is similar to other NYPSA publications, it would still be copyrightable under *Feist* so long as BAPCO selected [its headings] independently. . . .

CCC Information Services, Inc. v. Maclean Hunter Market Reports, Inc.

44 F.3d 61 (2d Cir. 1994), cert. denied, *516 U.S. 817 (1995)*

LEVAL, J.: . . .

Background

. . . The appellant is Maclean Hunter Market Reports, Inc. ("Maclean"). Since 1911, Maclean, or its predecessors, have published the *Automobile Red Book — Official Used Car Valuations* (the "Red Book"). The Red Book, which is published eight times a year, in different versions for each of three regions of the United States (as well as a version for the State of Wisconsin), sets forth the editors' projections of the values for the next six weeks of "average" versions of most of the used cars (up to seven years old) sold in that region. These predicted values are set forth separately for each automobile make, model number, body style, and engine type. Red Book also provides predicted value adjustments for various options and for mileage in 5,000 mile increments.

The valuation figures given in the Red Book are not historical market prices, quotations, or averages; nor are they derived by mathematical formulas from available statistics. They represent, rather, the Maclean editors' predictions, based on a wide variety of informational sources and their professional judgment, of expected values for "average" vehicles for the upcoming six weeks in a broad region. The introductory text asserts, "You, the subscriber, must be the final judge of the actual value of a particular vehicle. Any guide book is a supplement to and not a substitute for expertise in the complex field of used vehicle valuation."

. . . Appellee CCC Information Services, Inc. ("CCC"), is also in the business of providing its customers with information as to the valuation of used vehicles. Rather than publishing a book, however, CCC provides information to its customers through a computer data base. Since at least 1988, CCC has itself been systematically loading major portions of the Red Book onto its computer network and republishing Red Book information in various forms to its customers.

. . . CCC's "VINguard Valuation Service" ("VVS") provides subscribers with the average of a vehicle's Red Book valuation and its valuation in the NADA Official Used Car Guide (the "Bluebook"), the other leading valuation book, published by the National Automobile Dealers Association ("NADA"). The offer of this average of Red Book and Bluebook satisfies a market because the laws of certain states use that average figure as a minimum for insurance payments upon the "total loss" of a vehicle. . . .

. . . CCC brought this action in 1991, seeking, inter alia, a declaratory judgment that it incurred no liability to Maclean under the copyright laws by taking and republishing material from the Red Book. Maclean counterclaimed alleging infringement. . . . [The district court granted summary judgment of noninfringement for CCC; Maclean appealed.]

Discussion

1. *Does the Red Book manifest originality so as to be protected by the copyright laws?* The first significant question raised by this appeal is whether Maclean holds a protected copyright interest in the Red Book. CCC contends, and the district court held, that the Red Book is nothing more than a compilation of unprotected facts, selected and organized without originality or creativity, and therefore unprotected under the Supreme Court's teachings in *Feist*. We disagree. . . .

The protection of compilations is consistent with the objectives of the copyright law, which are . . . dictated by the Constitution. . . . Compilations that devise new and useful selections and arrangements of information unquestionably contribute to public knowledge by providing cheaper, easier, and better organized access to information. Without financial incentives, creators of such useful compilations might direct their energies elsewhere, depriving the public of their creations and impeding the advance of learning. . . .

The thrust of the Supreme Court's ruling in *Feist* was not to erect a high barrier of originality requirement. It was rather to specify, rejecting the strain of lower court rulings that sought to base protection on the "sweat of the brow," that *some* originality is essential to protection of authorship, and that the protection afforded extends only to those original elements. Because the protection is so limited, there is no reason under the policies of the copyright law to demand a high degree of originality. To the contrary, such a requirement would be counterproductive. The policy embodied into law is to encourage authors to publish innovations for the common good — not to threaten them with loss of their livelihood if their works of authorship are found insufficiently imaginative. . . .

The district court was simply mistaken in its conclusion that the Red Book valuations were, like the telephone numbers in *Feist*, pre-existing facts that had merely been discovered by the Red Book editors. To the contrary, Maclean's evidence demonstrated without rebuttal that its valuations were neither reports of historical prices nor mechanical derivations of historical prices or other data. Rather, they represented predictions by the Red Book editors of future prices estimated to cover specified geographic regions.[6] According to Maclean's evidence, these predictions

---

6. That they are expressed in numerical form is immaterial to originality. . . . The Act broadly defines literary works to include "works, other than audiovisual works, expressed in words, numbers, or other verbal or numerical symbols. . . ."

were based not only on a multitude of data sources, but also on professional judgment and expertise. The testimony of one of Maclean's deposition witnesses indicated that fifteen considerations are weighed; among the considerations, for example, is a prediction as to how traditional competitor vehicles, as defined by Maclean, will fare against one another in the marketplace in the coming period. The valuations themselves are original creations of Maclean.

Recognizing that "[o]riginality may also be found in the selection and ordering of particular facts or elements," the district court concluded that none had been shown. . . . This was because the Red Book's selection and arrangement of data represents "a logical response to the needs of the vehicle valuation market." . . . The fact that an arrangement of data responds *logically* to the needs of the market for which the compilation was prepared does not negate originality. To the contrary, the use of logic to solve the problems of how best to present the information being compiled is independent creation. . . .

We find that the selection and arrangement of data in the Red Book displayed amply sufficient originality to pass the low threshold requirement to earn copyright protection. This originality was expressed, for example, in Maclean's division of the national used car market into several regions, with independent predicted valuations for each region depending on conditions there found. A car model does not command the same value throughout a large geographic sector of the United States; used car values are responsive to local conditions and vary from place to place. A 1989 Dodge Caravan will not command the same price in San Diego as in Seattle. In furnishing a single number to cover vast regions that undoubtedly contain innumerable variations, the Red Book expresses a loose judgment that values are likely to group together with greater consistency within a defined region than without. The number produced is necessarily both approximate and original. Several other aspects of the Red Book listings also embody sufficient originality to pass *Feist's* low threshold. These include: (1) the selection and manner of presentation of optional features for inclusion; (2) the adjustment for mileage by 5,000 mile increments (as opposed to using some other breakpoint and interval); (3) the use of the abstract concept of the "average" vehicle in each category as the subject of the valuation; and (4) the selection of the number of years' models to be included in the compilation.

We conclude for these reasons that the district court erred in ruling that the Red Book commands no copyright protection by reason of lack of originality.

2. *The idea-expression dichotomy and the merger of necessary expression with the ideas expressed.* CCC's strongest argument is that it took nothing more than ideas, for which the copyright law affords no protection to the author. According to this argument, (1) each entry in the Red Book expresses the authors' *idea* of the value of a particular vehicle; [and] (2) to the extent that "expression" is to be found in the Red Book's valuations, such expression is indispensable to the statement of the idea and therefore merges with the idea. . . .

The argument is not easily rebutted, for it does build on classically accepted copyright doctrine. . . .

Given the nature of compilations, it is almost inevitable that the original contributions of the compilers will consist of *ideas*. Originality in *selection*, for example, will involve the compiler's idea of the utility to the consumer of a limited selection from the particular universe of available data. One compiler might select out of a universe of all businesses those he believes will be of interest to the Chinese-American community, *see Key Publications, [Inc. v. Chinatown Today Pub'l Enterp., Inc.,]* 945 F.2d [509] 514 [(2d Cir. 1991)], another will select those statistics as to racehorses or pitchers that are believed to be practical to the consumers in helping to pick winners, *see Kregos v. Associated Press*, 937 F.2d [700,] 706-07 [(2d Cir. 1991)]; another will offer a list of restaurants he suggests are the best, the most elegant, or offer the best value within a price range. Each of these exercises in selection represents an *idea*.

In other compilations, the original contribution of the compiler will relate to ideas for the coordination, or arrangement of the data. Such ideas for arrangement are generally designed to serve the consumers' needs . . . [such as] a listing of New York restaurants . . . broken down by geographic areas of the city, specialty or type (e.g., seafood, steaks and chops, vegetarian, kosher, Chinese, Indian); price range; handicapped accessibility, etc.

It is apparent that virtually any independent creation of the compiler as to selection, coordination, or arrangement will be designed to add to the usefulness or desirability of his compendium for targeted groups of potential customers, and will represent an idea. In the case of a compilation, furthermore, such structural ideas are likely to be expressed in the most simple, unadorned, and direct fashion. If, as CCC argues, the doctrine of merger permits the wholesale copier of a compilation to take the individual expression of such ideas, so as to avoid the risk that an idea will improperly achieve protection, then the protection explicitly conferred on compilations by Section 103 of the U.S. Copyright Act will be illusory.

We addressed precisely this problem in *Kregos*, 937 F.2d 700. The plaintiff Kregos had created a form to be used to help predict the outcome of a baseball game by filling in nine statistics of the competing pitchers. . . .

[*Kregos* described] different categories of ideas. It distinguished between, on the one hand, those ideas that undertake to advance the understanding of phenomena or the solution of problems, such as the identification of the symptoms that are the most useful in identifying the presence of a particular disease; and those, like the pitching form there at issue, that do not undertake to explain phenomena or furnish solutions, but are infused with the author's taste or opinion. *Kregos* postulated that the importance of keeping ideas free from private ownership is far greater for ideas of the first category. . . .

. . . To the extent that protection of the Red Book would impair free circulation of any ideas, these are ideas of the weaker category, infused with opinion; the valuations explain nothing, and describe no method, process, or procedure. Maclean Hunter makes no attempt, for example, to monopolize the basis of its economic forecasting or the factors that it weighs. . . . As noted above, the Red Book specifies in its introduction that "[y]ou, the subscriber, must be the final judge of the actual value of a particular vehicle." . . .

The balancing of interests suggested by *Kregos* leads to the conclusion that we should reject CCC's argument seeking the benefit of the merger doctrine. . . .

Conclusion

Because Maclean has demonstrated a valid copyright, and an infringement thereof, we direct the entry of judgment in Maclean's favor. We remand to the district court for further proceedings.

NOTES AND QUESTIONS

1. Which of these two cases does the better job of applying Supreme Court precedent?

2. In *Bellsouth*, the majority frames the case as one concerning an arrangement that lacks originality, but the dissent sees it as one concerning original selection of the categories to be employed in the work. Which view is more persuasive? In *CCC*, is it selection or arrangement that leads to a finding of originality?

3. Could BAPCO's selection or arrangement of business listings be characterized as the expression of an idea, as in *CCC*? Could BAPCO's selection or arrangement be characterized as a system? How do you think the *CCC* court would respond to the argument that Maclean

Hunter's Red Book is a "system"? Compare *American Dental Association v. Delta Dental*, Chapter 2, page 94 *supra*.

4. Recall the *Lotus* case earlier in this chapter concerning the lack of copyright protection for the menu command hierarchy of the Lotus 1-2-3 spreadsheet program. Should Lotus have argued that the menu command structure was really a compilation that evidenced originality either in its selection of which commands to include, or in its arrangement of those commands?

2. What Is a "Fact"?

If facts are not copyrightable, it is important to know what constitutes a "fact" for copyright purposes. As you can see from the previous pair of cases, the stakes are high for individuals who may have exerted labor and expense in creating a work that has significant utility, but that is deemed to be an unoriginal compilation of facts. As the following cases suggest, what constitutes a fact may be in the eye of the beholder.

CDN Inc. v. Kapes
197 F.3d 1256 (9th Cir. 1999)

O'SCANNLAIN, J.: We must decide whether prices listed in a wholesale coin price guide contain sufficient originality to merit the protection of the copyright laws.

I

Kenneth Kapes operates a coin business, Western Reserve Numismatics, in Ohio. In response to many inquiries he received regarding the price of coins, Kapes developed "The Fair Market Coin Pricer," which listed on his internet web page the retail prices of many coins. In order to generate the prices he listed, Kapes used a computer program he developed to create retail prices from wholesale prices. The exact process is unclear, but Kapes acknowledges using appellee CDN, Inc.'s wholesale price lists.

CDN publishes the Coin Dealer Newsletter, a weekly report of wholesale prices for collectible United States coins, as well as the Coin Dealer Newsletter Monthly Supplement and the CDN Quarterly. The Newsletter, or "Greysheet" as it is known in the industry, includes prices for virtually all collectible coins and is used extensively by dealers. In December 1996, CDN discovered the existence of Kapes' internet site and list of current retail prices. CDN filed a complaint on February 21, 1997 in the U.S. District Court for the Central District of California, alleging that Kapes infringed CDN's copyrights by using CDN's wholesale prices as a baseline to arrive at retail prices. . . . [The district court granted summary judgment for CDN on the threshold issue of copyrightability, and the court of appeals affirmed.]

Discoverable facts, like ideas, are not copyrightable. But compilations of facts are copyrightable even where the underlying facts are not. *See Feist Publications, Inc. v. Rural Tel. Serv. Co.*, 499 U.S. 340, 344 (1991). The distinction between facts and non-facts, and between discovery and creation, lies at the heart of this case. The essential ingredient present in creations, but absent in facts, is originality, "the sine qua non of copyright." *Id.* at 345. Subject matter created by and original to the author merits copyright protection. Items not original to the author, i.e., not the product of his creativity, are facts and not copyrightable. . . . In order to warrant protection, compilations and other works must contain a minimal amount of originality or creativity. . . .

Appellant's attempt to equate the phone number listings in *Feist* with CDN's price lists does not withstand close scrutiny. First, Kapes conflates two separate arguments: (1) that the listing, selection, and inclusion of prices is not original enough to merit protection; and (2) that the prices themselves are not original creations. Whether CDN's selection and arrangement of the price lists is sufficiently original to merit protection is not at issue here. CDN does not allege that Kapes copied the entire lists, as the alleged infringer had in *Feist*. Rather, the issue in this case is whether the prices themselves are sufficiently original as compilations to sustain a copyright. Thus Kapes' argument that the selection is obvious or dictated by industry standards is irrelevant.

Although the requirement of originality is a constitutional one inherent in the grant to Congress of the power to promote science and the useful arts, the required level of originality is "minimal." . . . "The vast majority of works make the grade quite easily, as they possess some creative spark, 'no matter how crude, humble or obvious' it might be." *Feist*, 499 U.S. at 345 (quoting 1 M. Nimmer & D. Nimmer, *Copyright* §1.08[C][1] (1990)). This spark glows in CDN's prices, which are compilations of data chosen and weighed with creativity and judgment. . . .

. . . [CDN] begins with examining the major coin publications to find relevant retail price information. CDN then reviews this data to retain only that information it considers to be the most accurate and important. Prices for each grade of coin are determined with attention to whether the coin is graded by a professional service (and which one). CDN also reviews the online bid and ask prices posted by dealers. . . . CDN also considers the impact of public auctions and private sales, and analyzes the effect of the economy and foreign policies on the price of coins. As the district court found, CDN does not republish data from another source or apply a set formula or rule to generate prices. . . .

Our holding that the prices are copyrightable is consistent with that of the Second Circuit in *CCC Info. Servs., Inc. v. Maclean Hunter Mkt. Reports*, 44 F.3d 61 (2d Cir. 1994). . . . [There, t]he court held that the [Red Book] valuations were not "pre-existing facts that had merely been discovered by the Red Book editors," but instead "represented predictions by the Red Book editors of future prices estimated to cover specified geographic regions." *CCC*, 44 F.3d at 67. Like CDN's prices, the prices in the Red Book granted copyright protection by the Second Circuit, are "based not only on a multitude of data sources, but also on professional judgment and expertise." *Id.*

Kapes attempts to distinguish *CCC* by arguing that the prices in the Red Book were projections of future values, while the prices in the Greysheet are estimates of present value. But the distinction between present and future values is not important to this case. What is important is the fact that both Maclean and CDN arrive at the prices they list through a process that involves using their judgment to distill and extrapolate from factual data. It is simply not a process through which they discover a preexisting historical fact, but rather a process by which they create a price which, in their best judgment, represents the value of an item as closely as possible. If CDN merely listed historical facts of actual transactions, the guides would be long, cumbersome, and of little use to anyone. Dealers looking through such data would have to use their own judgment and expertise to estimate the value of a coin. What CDN has done is use its own judgment and expertise in arriving at that value for the dealers. This process imbues the prices listed with sufficient creativity and originality to make them copyrightable. . . .

≡ *Matthew Bender & Co. v. West Publishing Co.*
≡ *158 F.3d 693 (2d Cir. 1998)*, cert. denied, 526 U.S. 1154 (1999)

JACOBS, C.J.: Defendants-appellants West Publishing Co. and West Publishing Corp. (collectively "West") create and publish printed compilations of federal and state judicial opinions. Plaintiff-appellee Matthew Bender & Company, Inc. and intervenor-plaintiff-appellee Hyper-Law, Inc. (collectively "plaintiffs") manufacture and market compilations of judicial opinions stored on compact disc-read only memory ("CD-ROM") discs, in which opinions they embed (or intend to embed) citations that show the page location of the particular text in West's printed version of the opinions (so-called "star pagination").[1] Bender and HyperLaw seek judgment declaring that star pagination will not infringe West's copyrights in its compilations of judicial opinions. West now appeals from a judgment of the United States District Court for the Southern District of New York (Martin, J.), granting summary judgment of noninfringement to Bender and partial summary judgment of noninfringement to HyperLaw.

West's primary contention on appeal is that star pagination to West's case reporters allows a user of plaintiffs' CD-ROM discs (by inputting a series of commands) to "perceive" West's copyright-protected arrangement of cases, and that plaintiffs' products (when star pagination is added) are unlawful copies of West's arrangement. We reject West's argument. . . .

Discussion . . .

. . . [C]opyright protection in compilations "may extend only to those components of a work that are original to the author." [*Feist*, 499 U.S. 340,] 348. The "originality" requirement encompasses requirements both "that the work was independently created . . . , *and* that it possesses at least some minimal degree of creativity." *Id.* at 345 (emphasis added). At issue here are references to West's volume and page numbers distributed through the text of plaintiffs' versions of judicial opinions. West concedes that the pagination of its volumes — *i.e.*, the insertion of page breaks and the assignment of page numbers — is determined by an automatic computer program, and West does not seriously claim that there is anything original or creative in that process. As Judge Martin noted, "where and on what particular pages the text of a court opinion appears does not embody any original creation of the compiler." Because the internal pagination of West's case reporters does not entail even a modicum of creativity, the volume and page numbers are not original components of West's compilations and are not themselves protected by West's compilation copyright.[9]

Because the volume and page numbers are unprotected features of West's compilation process, they may be copied without infringing West's copyright. However, West proffers an alternative argument based on the fact (which West has plausibly demonstrated) that plaintiffs have inserted or will insert *all* of West's volume and page numbers for certain case reporters. West's alternative argument is that even though the page numbering is not (by itself) a protectible element of West's compilation, (i) plaintiffs' star pagination to West's case reporters embeds West's arrangement of cases in plaintiffs' CD-ROM discs, thereby allowing a user to

---

1. This cross-reference method is called "star pagination" because an asterisk and citation or page number are inserted in the text of the judicial opinion to indicate when a page break occurs in a different version of the case.

9. The same conclusion can be arrived at using a different chain of reasoning. There is a fundamental distinction under the Copyright Act between the original work of authorship and the physical embodiment of that work in a tangible medium. The embedding of the copyrightable work in a tangible medium does not mean that the features of the tangible medium are also copyrightable. Thus, here, the original element of West's compilation, its arrangement of cases, is protectable, while the features of the physical embodiment of the work, *i.e.*, the page numbers, are not.

perceive West's protected arrangement[11] through the plaintiffs' file-retrieval programs, and (ii) that under the Copyright Act's definition of "copies," 17 U.S.C. §101, a work that allows the perception of a protectible element of a compilation through the aid of a machine amounts to a copy of the compilation. We reject this argument. . . .

. . . West's definition of a copy, as applied to a CD-ROM disc, would expand the embedded work to include all arrangements and *re*arrangements that could be made by a third-party user who manipulates the data on his or her own initiative. But the relevant statutory wording refers to material objects in which "a work" readable by technology "is fixed," not to another work or works that can be created, unbidden, by using technology to alter the fixed embedding of the work, by rearrangement or otherwise. The natural reading of the statute is that the arrangement of the work is the one that can be perceived by a machine without an uninvited manipulation of the data. . . .

Conclusion

We hold that Bender and HyperLaw will not infringe West's copyright by inserting star pagination to West's case reporters in their CD-ROM disc version of judicial opinions. The judgement of the district court is affirmed.

SWEET, J., dissenting: . . . The majority concludes that because the volume and page numbers are "unprotected features" of West's compilation process, they may be copied without infringing West's copyright. The majority reasons that, pursuant to the Copyright Act, the "embedding of the copyrightable work in a tangible medium does not mean that the features of the tangible medium are also copyrightable." Therefore, West's arrangement of cases is protectible, but the page numbers are not. The classification of page numbers as physical embodiment rather than the result of originality is the foundation stone of the majority's interpretation of the authorities dealing with the copyright statute.

In my view West's case arrangements, an essential part of which is page citations, are original works of authorship entitled to copyright protection. Comprehensive documentation of West's selection and arrangement of judicial opinions infringes the copyright in that work.

This reasoning is consistent with *Feist*. As discussed above, the majority notes that the compiler's copyright is "thin." *Feist*, 499 U.S. 340, 350-51. Therefore, "a subsequent compiler remains free to use the facts contained in another's publication to aid in preparing a competing work, *so long as the competing work does not feature the same selection and arrangement*." *Id*. at 349, (emphasis added). In this case, allowing plaintiffs to use the page numbers contained in West's publication enables them to feature West's same selection and arrangement. Indeed, were it not for the ability to reproduce West's arrangement, its pagination would be of limited (if any) use. . . .

[T]he pagination results from West's arrangements, selections, syllabi, headnotes, key numbering, citations and descriptions. The page number, arbitrarily determined, is the sole

---

11. . . . [B]ecause we find that West's arrangement has not been copied through the insertion of star pagination to West's case reporters, we can assume without deciding that West's case reporters contain an original and copyrightable arrangement.

In addition, this opinion will not address any copying by plaintiffs of the *selection* of cases included in West's case reporters. First, West argued below that Bender had copied West's arrangement of cases, not its selection. Second, it is uncontested that plaintiffs' compilations include many more opinions than West's case reporters. . . . Accordingly, we cannot find that the selection of cases in plaintiffs' compilations is substantially similar to West's selection. . . .

result of the West system, appears nowhere else, and is essential to its coordinated method of citation. It is, so to speak, an original fact resulting from West's creativity. . . .

According to the majority, a more fundamental reason to reject West's argument that plaintiffs have copied its arrangement is that the arrangement can be perceived only after a person uses the machine to rearrange the material.

Some of the most seminal developments in copyright law have been driven by technological change. There was a time when people questioned whether photographs, *see Burrow-Giles Lithographic Co. v. Sarony*, 111 U.S. 53 (1884), or advertisements, *see Bleistein v. Donaldson Lithographing Co.*, 188 U.S. 239 (1903), were copyrightable. Here again it is necessary to reconcile technology with pre-electronic principles of law. Clearly, plaintiffs' CD-ROM disks are not "copies" in the traditional sense. Yet, plaintiffs provide the ability for a user to push a button or two and obtain West's exact selection and arrangement. This technological capacity presents a new question. The majority's answer threatens to eviscerate copyright protection for compilations. . . .

NOTES AND QUESTIONS

1. So . . . what is a "fact"? Do the cases in this section use the same standard for identifying original expression and distinguishing this from "fact"? Compare *CDN v. Kapes* and *CCC v. Maclean Hunter, supra*, with *Hoehling v. Universal City Studios*, Chapter 2, *supra*, which concerned the copyrightability of historical research and theories. Are these cases reconcilable? In *CCC* the defendant argued that the selection of variables factoring into the price of used vehicles was itself a fact. Why did the court reject that argument? When do numbers (e.g., prices) based on a selection of variables become facts? In *Matthew Bender*, is the court saying that the arrangement of cases has become a fact?

2. How can a price itself be a compilation of data? Have some of these decisions confused the subject matter of copyright and patent law? Didn't *Baker v. Selden, supra* Chapter 2, say that systems or algorithms are not protected by copyright? If courts protect the end result of a formula under copyright law — like the price in *Kapes* — is that the same as protecting the formula itself? Should the system for valuing coins in *Kapes* be patented rather than the prices copyrighted? In another case involving the copyrightability of prices, the Second Circuit considered whether commodity futures prices circulated by the commodity exchange at the close of each day's trading were meant to reflect "how the market *should* value . . . or *will* value" the commodity futures as "an empirical reality, an economic fact about the world that [the plaintiff was] seeking to discover," or whether the plaintiff was "creating predictions or estimates." *New York Mercantile Exch., Inc. v. Intercontinental Exch., Inc.*, 497 F.3d 109, 115 (2d Cir. 2007) (emphasis in original). Recognizing that it is often difficult to determine the line between *creation*, which would be copyrightable, and *discovery*, which would not, the court ruled that even if the prices were copyrightable, the merger doctrine barred plaintiff's infringement claim.

3. Does digital technology make it harder or easier for an arrangement to satisfy the originality requirement? Should the capabilities of the technology have any role in determining whether a particular selection or arrangement has the requisite level of creativity? Where is the "copyrightable" arrangement in a digital database that can be rearranged at the push of a button?

4. Are databases more like "useful articles" than literary works? If we value databases and desire to see them produced at optimal levels, is copyright the best mechanism to utilize? The most efficient? What other approaches might you suggest Congress consider and why?

3. New Paradigms?

Factual compilations have significant economic value to their creators as well as to the public. Consequently, optimal production is a desired goal for both databases that meet the statutory requirements for copyright protection and those that do not. If copyright protection is not available due to a lack of originality, what alternatives are there? What about a sui generis regime for the protection of databases? This solution has been adopted by the EU and has been considered in the U.S.

Note on the EU Database Directive

Directive 96/9/EC of the European Parliament and of the Council of March 11, 1996 on the Legal Protection of Databases, 1996 O.J. (L 77) 20, more commonly known as the EU Database Directive, is aimed at protecting substantial investments (or "sweat of the brow") expended in creating a database. A database is defined as "a collection of independent works, data or other materials arranged in a systematic or methodical way and individually accessible by electronic or other means." *Id.*, art. 1(2). This definition includes "paper" databases. However, it also specifically excludes computer programs used to make or operate a database.

The EU Database Directive establishes a two-tier system of protection for databases. First, Article 3 requires EU Member States to provide copyright protection for databases that "by reason of the selection or arrangement of their contents, constitute the author's own intellectual creation." The exclusive copyright rights granted to the author of a database are: temporary or permanent reproduction; translation, adaptation, arrangement, and any other alteration; any form of distribution to the public of the database or copies thereof; any communication, display, or performance to the public; any reproduction, distribution, communication, display, or performance to the public of any alteration, translation, adaptation, or other arrangement of the database. *See id.*, art. 5.

Second, the EU Database Directive also established a new right to prevent unauthorized extraction or re-utilization of the contents of the database. This sui generis right gives the author of a database the ability to control any uses of the information in the database, distinct from use of the database as a whole. Member States are required to provide protection to "prevent extraction and/or re-utilization of the whole or of a substantial part . . . of the contents of the database."[1]

The EU Database Directive does not define what amount of investment is required (i.e., what is substantial) to qualify for protection but, instead, provides that the investment may be "qualitative" or "quantitative." Article 7(1) requires that the substantial investment be made "in either the obtaining, verification or presentation of the contents." Even with this circumscription, however, Recital 40 states that the "object of this sui generis right is to ensure protection in *any*[2] investment in obtaining, verifying or presenting the contents of the database. . . ." It is likely that most databases will satisfy the quantitative test because database production typically entails investing significant amounts of human and/or financial resources in any of the listed activities. *Id.*, recital 40.

---

1. Extraction is "the permanent or temporary transfer of all or a substantial part of the contents of a database to another medium by any means or in any form." Directive 96/9/EC of the European Parliament and of the Council of March 11, 1996 on the Legal Protection of Databases, 1996 O.J. (L 77) 20, art. 7(2)(a). Re-utilization is "any form of making available to the public all or a substantial part of the contents of a database by the distribution of copies, by renting, by on-line or other forms of transmission." *Id.*, art. 7(2)(b).
2. Emphasis added.

The EU Database Directive recognizes a limited number of exceptions to the database right. These exceptions apply to: (a) use of nonelectronic databases for private purposes; (b) extraction for purposes of illustration and teaching, so long as the source is indicated and the extraction is justified by a noncommercial purpose; and (c) extraction or re-utilization that occurs for the purposes of public security or an administrative or judicial procedure. *See id.*, art. 9.

Article 10 provides for a 15-year term of protection. Upon additional investment in the database, a new 15-year term arises. This results in the potential for perpetual protection for databases that are continually updated.

From an international perspective, the most important aspect of the EU Database Directive is its reciprocity provision. Recital 56 states that the benefits required by the Directive should extend only to nationals or residents of Member States of the EU; to companies and firms incorporated under the laws of a Member State and having their registered office, central administration, or principal place of business within the Community; and to nationals or residents of countries that offer comparable protection to databases produced by nationals or residents of the European Community. Thus, unless the U.S. adopts protection for databases that is viewed as comparable to that provided under the EU Database Directive, the EU's sui generis rights will not be available to database manufacturers from the U.S.

Note on Database Protection in the U.S.

In the U.S., legal protection for uncopyrightable collections or compilations of information is still unsettled. The reciprocity provisions of the EU Database Directive have added weight to the argument that the U.S. should adopt sui generis federal database protection. In general, efforts to protect information goods currently are taking place at both the state and federal levels.

At the state level, there exists a patchwork of legal theories, arising under unfair competition, contract, and trade secret laws, that could be used to protect noncopyrightable collections of information. Many, however, consider these legal regimes insufficient for protecting the full value of these compilations, particularly in a digital networked environment. One particularly important unresolved issue is the extent to which copyright preempts state law regimes for protection for databases. We return to this question in Chapter 9.

At the federal level, Congress has considered a number of proposals to create a sui generis law to protect collections of data. In 1996, a bill for database protection modeled very closely on the EU Database Directive was introduced. Because this bill proposed an absolute property right, with no attendant limitations or exceptions and potentially perpetual protection, it evoked strong adverse reactions from groups such as the National Education Association, the National Academy of Sciences, and the American Library Association. These "user groups" argued that granting property rights in facts would be detrimental to research and education. Consequently, the bill remained tabled until the end of the 104th Congress.

Database protection bills introduced during the 105th, 106th, and 108th sessions of Congress eschewed the property model of the EU approach and proposed, instead, a misappropriation tort prohibiting conduct that threatened an actual or potential market for a database and allowing some "reasonable uses" by educational, scientific, and research organizations. These bills failed, however.

Throughout the debates over database protection, the scientific and educational communities, joined by several government agencies, have expressed a number of concerns. They have argued, among other things, that unless appropriately circumscribed, database protection legislation would increase transaction costs for data users, deter value-added uses of protected databases, and undermine First Amendment freedoms. In addition, they have noted the prospect of anticompetitive conduct by sole-source data providers and the accompanying (even if unintended) adverse effects on innovation and competition. Some question whether these costs are outweighed by the benefits that would accompany protection. Prospects for legislated database protection in the U.S. are thus unclear.

A recurring issue in the controversy over sui generis database protection is whether Congress can constitutionally provide protection to "unoriginal" compilations of data. Given that originality is a constitutional requirement for protection of the "writings" of authors, Congress cannot rely on the Intellectual Property Clause as the basis of its authority to enact such protection. If Congress passes database protection legislation, the courts will need to determine whether Congress may rely on the Commerce Clause instead.

Jane C. Ginsburg, No "Sweat"? Copyright and Other Protection of Works of Information After Feist v. Rural Telephone
92 Colum. L. Rev. 338, 371-72, 378, 387-88 (1992)[3]

[O]ne may argue that a Commerce Clause-derived statute barring misappropriation of compiled information would not conflict with the Patent-Copyright Clause as long as the protective law departs in significant ways from the copyright model. Appropriate and meaningful departures might be made with respect to duration of protection and, more significantly, with respect to scope of protection. Copyright protection lasts for the life of the author plus fifty years, or in the case of a work made for hire (as many information compilations are likely to be), for at least seventy-five years from creation of the work.* The duration of statutory protection of compiled information might be made considerably shorter — for example, ten years from dissemination. The scope of protection might be limited by imposition of compulsory licenses. An elaborated system of compulsory licenses heightens the dissimilarities between the proposed compiled information protection statute and the copyright model of "exclusive Right[s]." In its most basic form, a federal misappropriation statute would accord no exclusive right of control over the compiled information, but would merely guarantee the information gatherer the right to be paid for third-party use of the information. Distinguished in this way from conventional copyright legislation, a federal misappropriation statute might avoid a clash between the provisions of Article 1, Section 8. . . .

Decisions as to what constitutes knowledge and how to achieve its progress seem particularly ill-adapted to the judicial branch. A judgment that, under the Constitution, a given work or class of works does not promote knowledge seems implausible as a matter of fact, and extravagant, if not overreaching, as a matter of technique. Even the *Feist* Court did not suggest that unoriginal compilations fail to promote knowledge; the Court's acknowledgment of these works' utility suggests the contrary. . . .

In *Feist*, the Supreme Court rejected the "sweat of the brow" basis for copyright protection, stressing instead a constitutional standard of creative originality and a constitutional principle of free riding on uncreative efforts. The Court thereby sought to promote wide and cheap public access to information. Ironically, the elimination of "sweat" copyright may require information providers to restrict access to compilations in order to maintain a

---

3. Reprinted by permission of the author and the Columbia Law Review.
* [Copyright protection now lasts for life of the author plus 70 years, or in the case of a work made for hire, at least 95 years from creation. — EDS.]

contractual or technological hold on the material. Similarly, the costs of "added value" of subjective elements to make the compilation copyrightable as a whole will be passed along to consumers, many or most of whom may not have wished these features in the first place. As a result, *Feist* may make access to information both more burdensome and more expensive than had copyright protection been available.

This observation heightens the desirability of an alternative form of protection.

J.H. Reichman & Pamela Samuelson, Intellectual Property Rights in Data?
50 Vand. L. Rev. 51, 144-46 (1997)

Feist recognized that the public's right to appropriate data and information from copyrighted works implemented an important constitutional principle. Under the Commerce Clause of the Constitution, one might nonetheless reconcile this principle with a minimalist approach to regulating data appropriations that sounded in unfair competition law. In contrast, an exclusive intellectual property right in data that interfered with the underlying purposes of both copyright law and the First Amendment appears to violate the Constitution on its face. This tension with the purpose and subject matter limitations of the constitutional Enabling Clause is then magnified by the prospects for perpetual protection of databases under all the current protection schemes, which violate the "limited times" provision of that same clause. . . .

An alternative approach that would protect the contents of databases on modified liability principles draws upon studies that perceive an affinity between the needs of the database industry and those of other producers of commercially important information products. The common denominator facing all these industries is that the fruits of their investment usually consist of aggregates of valuable information that are embodied on or near the face of products sold in the open market. Because trade secret law does not normally cover such products, third parties who rapidly duplicate the embodied information they contain deprive innovators of the lead time needed to recoup their investments, without contributing, directly or indirectly, to the overall costs of research and development. Investors in information goods thus may lack any functional equivalent of the lead-time protection that trade secrecy laws historically conferred on compilations of applied know-how in the manufacturing era.

A legal regime devised to fill this gap would emulate the economic functions of the liability principles that underlie classical trade secret law, and would not grant exclusive property rights in data. It would instead provide

> those who invest in industrial applications of advanced technical know-how with artificial lead-time to overcome market failure, with a menu of users' fees that sensibly allocates contributions to the costs of research and development among members of the relevant technical community, and with a common set of pro-competitive ground rules that also make it possible for the relevant technical communities to take collective action to enforce and adjust the liability framework eventually adopted.[432]

---

432. [J.H. Reichman, *Legal Hybrids Between the Patent and Copyright Paradigms*, 94 Colum. L. Rev. 2432,] 2545.

NOTES AND QUESTIONS

1. Professors Ginsburg, Reichman, and Samuelson all agree that protection for databases is important for society. However, Professor Ginsburg seems to have a less favorable view of the *Feist* decision than Professors Reichman and Samuelson, who seem at least tacitly to endorse the decision and its labeling of originality as a constitutional requirement. *See also* Yochai Benkler, *Constitutional Bounds of Database Protection: The Role of Judicial Review in the Creation and Definition of Private Rights in Information*, 15 Berkeley Tech. L.J. 535 (2000). Recall the purposes of copyright. In what ways does originality promote the "Progress of Science and the useful Arts"? Would providing protection against misappropriation of unoriginal compilations of facts interfere with this goal?

2. Are you persuaded that there is a need for legal protection for collections of data? In *Feist*, the Supreme Court stated that copyright "encourages others to build freely upon the ideas and *information* conveyed by a work." *Feist Publ'ns. Inc. v. Rural Tel. Serv. Co.*, 499 U.S. 340, 350 (1991). How might sui generis protection for insufficiently original works affect this important copyright objective? If, as Professor Ginsburg suggests, Congress adopts a database statute under the Commerce Clause, should it matter whether it advances the "Progress of Science and useful Arts"? Might database protection, even under a different constitutional authority, retard "progress"? Resolution of this question raises issues of federal preemption and interaction among different constitutional provisions, a subject to which we turn in Chapter 10.

3. Note that database protection will not necessarily preclude copyright protection where the compilation satisfies the *Feist* standard. Would an overlap between copyright and a new sui generis right be efficient, or would it amount to overprotection?

4. If you were a Senator, would you vote for a database protection statute? What kind of limitations and exceptions to database protection do you think are necessary at a minimum? Does the EU Directive provide a good model? How about the alternative suggested by Professor Ginsburg? Professors Reichman and Samuelson provide some more detail to their proposal to implement what they refer to as "a market-preserving form of relief." The proposal would implement two different mechanisms for preserving markets. The first mechanism is a blocking period:

> During this period, no second comer could appropriate the contents of the database as a whole or of any component substantial enough to represent a threat of market failure. The database provider, meanwhile, would freely determine the rates charged for other uses during this same period, subject to public interest limitations favoring science and education that would likely become mandatory in this environment. Further investigation, however, might persuade policymakers not to award an initial blocking period to certain databases of great public interest at all. They might also decide to confine it to those databases that were distributed in markets that are, or would readily become, competitive.

Reichman & Samuelson, *supra*, at 146. The second mechanism is an automatic licensing scheme:

> In the database milieu, one can plausibly implement this device in different ways. For example, the European Commission initially proposed putting sole-source database producers under an obligation to license their data to second comers on fair and nondiscriminatory terms. This solution included provisions calling for arbitration to resolve disputes in the event that the parties to the nonvoluntary license could not agree on terms. Alternatively, the automatic license could become

universally available at the end of the initial blocking period, in which case it would last for a second period to be determined.

Id. at 146-47. They recognize that determining how long the blocking and automatic licensing periods should last would be complicated:

> Because the goal of a modified liability regime is to provide artificial lead time while precluding opportunities for rent-seeking, it is preferable to adopt short rather than long blocking periods in most technological sectors. The database environment presents a more complex set of variables than some other industries, however, because entry costs often appear formidable and the sole-source market structure is deeply ingrained. An initial blocking period must, therefore, not be so short as further to discourage existing entrants. At the same time, assuming that the existence of multiple providers is otherwise feasible, both the existing entrant and would-be or potential competitors know that an automatic license will ultimately facilitate direct competition on the same market segment, subject to the second comer's payment of reasonable royalties for the second period. . . .

Id. at 147.

Does this proposal adequately balance the interests at stake? Is it too complicated to implement?

III COPYRIGHT SCOPE AND ENFORCEMENT

5

The Statutory Rights of Copyright Owners

In previous chapters, we considered the subject matter that copyright does and does not protect and the rules that govern the inception and duration of copyright ownership. We now explore the important and complex question of what copyright ownership means. Formally, copyright law concerns the study of the exclusive rights, or entitlements, conferred by Title 17 of the U.S. Code, the provisions of which also reflect obligations established by the various international treaties to which the U.S. is a party. Creators do not rely solely on Title 17 to protect their creations, however. Instead, they use a variety of means other than copyright, including contracts and technological measures, to secure what they perceive to be the optimal level of protection for their works. Reliance on these other sources of protection is increasing as the technology to make and distribute copies improves and as copyright owners more routinely distribute works in digital form. Thus, in recent years, the study of these protection mechanisms has become essential to understanding the rights of copyright owners and the debates about the appropriate scope of those rights.

The second half of this book undertakes an integrated study of the different modes of protection available to copyright owners and the relationships among them. At the same time, it is important to remember that the rights in Title 17 establish a baseline understanding of the extent of protection to which copyright owners are — and are not — entitled. Also remember that many works are not prepared or distributed in digital form. Generally, contracts and special-purpose technological restrictions provide much less effective protection for non-digital works than digital ones. Presently, then, the statutory rights of copyright owners remain the most important means of protection. We begin our exploration there.

The exclusive rights of a copyright owner are set forth in §106 of the Copyright Act:

§106. Exclusive rights in copyrighted works

Subject to sections 107 through 122, the owner of copyright under this title has the exclusive rights to do and to authorize any of the following:

(1) to reproduce the copyrighted work in copies or phonorecords;

(2) to prepare derivative works based upon the copyrighted work;

(3) to distribute copies or phonorecords of the copyrighted work to the public by sale or other transfer of ownership, or by rental, lease, or lending;

(4) in the case of literary, musical, dramatic, and choreographic works, pantomimes, and motion pictures and other audiovisual works, to perform the copyrighted work publicly;

(5) in the case of literary, musical, dramatic, and choreographic works, pantomimes, and pictorial, graphic, or sculptural works, including the individual images of a motion picture or other audiovisual work, to display the copyrighted work publicly; and

(6) in the case of sound recordings, to perform the copyrighted work publicly by means of a digital audio transmission.

17 U.S.C. §106.

This chapter first considers the elements of a copyright owner's claim for infringement of one or more of the §106 exclusive rights. It then examines the scope of each §106 right. In Chapter 6, we will explore the rules governing who may be held liable for copyright infringement.

A.   THE ELEMENTS OF INFRINGEMENT

In addition to alleging facts that would establish infringement of one or more of the §106 rights, all copyright infringement claims must include other elements. We begin by examining these elements.

1.   The Prima Facie Case of Infringement

A prima facie claim of copyright infringement has two main elements. The plaintiff has the initial burden of producing sufficient evidence of each element.

First, the plaintiff must allege and prove ownership of a valid copyright. As discussed in Chapter 3, a certificate of registration issued either before publication or within five years after first publication of the work is prima facie evidence of both ownership of the copyright and its validity. *See* 17 U.S.C. §410. This presumption is an important benefit of timely registration. Even if the presumption is no longer available because more than five years have elapsed since publication, copyright owners of U.S. works (*see id.* §101 for a definition of "United States work") still must register before filing an infringement lawsuit. *Id.* §411.

Second, the plaintiff must prove that the defendant violated one of the exclusive rights reserved to the copyright owner by §106 — e.g., the right to reproduce the copyrighted work in copies or phonorecords, §106(1), or the right to publicly perform the copyrighted work, §106(4). We will consider each of the §106 rights in subsequent sections of this chapter.

Sometimes, however, this second element requires an additional, preliminary inquiry. Because copyright law affords the copyright owner no rights against the author of an independently created work, the plaintiff must show that the defendant in fact obtained protected expression of the plaintiff's and used that expression in the defendant's work. Put differently, the plaintiff must show that the defendant's allegedly infringing work does not simply represent expression originated by the defendant that coincidentally resembles the expression in the copyrighted work. As a shorthand, we use the term copying in fact to describe this showing. In many cases, especially those involving parties formerly in a contractual relationship with one another, the defendant's copying in fact is clear and undisputed. In other cases, however, proving copying in fact can be quite difficult. The cases that follow explore those difficulties.

A word of caution before you begin reading the cases that follow: Throughout this chapter there will be discussions in the cases of the similarities between plaintiff's and defendant's works. The term "similarity" is used by courts, sometimes in combination with other factors, to determine two different parts of the infringement analysis: (1) whether the defendant copied from the plaintiff (copying in fact) and (2) whether the defendant copied enough of plaintiff's protected expression to constitute infringement (most relevant for claims of violations of the right to reproduce the work, §106(1), and the right to prepare derivative works, §106(2)). Beware of this dual use of "similarity" as it can be confusing both to students of copyright law and to judges.

2. Copying in Fact

Suppose that the defendant in a copyright infringement case has produced a novel that is similar, but not identical, to the plaintiff's, and that the defendant denies ever having read the plaintiff's novel. Discovery requests have failed to turn up any direct evidence of copying—e.g., evidence that the defendant purchased and read the plaintiff's book immediately before writing his own—but there are other ways that the defendant might have encountered the book. Is this a case of independent creation, or is the defendant lying (or simply forgetful)? How should the law decide? In general, one can imagine two kinds of circumstantial evidence that might be relevant to this question: (1) evidence suggesting that the defendant had *access* to the plaintiff's work; and (2) the degree of *similarity* between the two works. Should either kind of circumstantial evidence be sufficient to establish copying in fact? Consider the following cases.

Three Boys Music Corp. v. Michael Bolton
212 F.3d 477 (9th Cir. 2000), cert. denied, 531 U.S. 1126 (2001)

D. NELSON, J.: . . .

I. Background

The Isley Brothers, one of this country's most well-known rhythm and blues groups, have been inducted into the Rock and Roll Hall of Fame. They helped define the soul sound of the 1960s with songs such as "Shout," "Twist and Shout," and "This Old Heart of Mine," and they mastered the funky beats of the 1970s with songs such as "Who's That Lady," "Fight the Power," and "It's Your Thing." In 1964, the Isley Brothers wrote and recorded "Love is a Wonderful Thing" for United Artists. . . . The following year, they switched to the famous Motown label and had three top-100 hits including "This Old Heart of Mine."

Hoping to benefit from the Isley Brothers' Motown success, United Artists released "Love is a Wonderful Thing" in 1966. The song was not released on an album, only on a 45-record as a single. Several industry publications predicted that "Love is a Wonderful Thing" would be a hit. . . . On September 17, 1966, Billboard listed "Love is a Wonderful Thing" at number 110 in a chart titled "Bubbling Under the Hot 100." The song was never listed on any other Top 100 charts. In 1991, the Isley Brothers' "Love is a Wonderful Thing" was released on compact disc. *See* Isley Brothers, *The Isley Brothers—The Complete UA Sessions*, (EMI 1991).

Michael Bolton is a singer/songwriter who gained popularity in the late 1980s and early 1990s by reviving the soul sound of the 1960s. Bolton has orchestrated this soul-music revival in part by covering* old songs such as Percy Sledge's "When a Man Loves a Woman" and Otis Redding's "(Sittin' on the) Dock of the Bay." Bolton also has written his own hit songs. In early 1990, Bolton and [songwriting partner Andrew] Goldmark wrote a song called "Love is a Wonderful Thing." Bolton released it as a single in April 1991, and as part of Bolton's album, "Time, Love and Tenderness." Bolton's "Love is a Wonderful Thing" finished 1991 at number 49 on Billboard's year-end pop chart. . . .

[Three Boys Music Corp., the owner of the copyright in the Isley Brothers' song, sued Bolton, Goldmark, and their record companies for copyright infringement. After a jury trial, Three Boys was awarded $5.4 million.]

II. Discussion

Proof of copyright infringement is often highly circumstantial, particularly in cases involving music. A copyright plaintiff must prove (1) ownership of the copyright; and (2) infringement — that the defendant copied protected elements of the plaintiff's work. Absent direct evidence of copying, proof of infringement involves fact-based showings that the defendant had "access" to the plaintiff's work and that the two works are "substantially similar."

Given the difficulty of proving access and substantial similarity, appellate courts have been reluctant to reverse jury verdicts in music cases. . . .

Proof of access requires "an opportunity to view or to copy plaintiff's work." This is often described as providing a "reasonable opportunity" or "reasonable possibility" of viewing the plaintiff's work. We have defined reasonable access as "more than a 'bare possibility.' " *Jason* [*v. Fonda*, 698 F.2d 966, 967 (9th Cir. 1983)]. Nimmer has elaborated on our definition: "Of course, reasonable opportunity as here used, does not encompass any bare possibility in the sense that anything is possible. Access may not be inferred through mere speculation or conjecture. There must be a reasonable possibility of viewing the plaintiff's work — not a bare possibility." 4 Nimmer, §13.02[A], at 13-19. "At times, distinguishing a 'bare' possibility from a 'reasonable' possibility will present a close question." *Id.* at 13-20.

Circumstantial evidence of reasonable access is proven in one of two ways: (1) a particular chain of events is established between the plaintiff's work and the defendant's access to that work (such as through dealings with a publisher or record company), or (2) the plaintiff's work has been widely disseminated. *See* 4 Nimmer, §13.02[A], at 13-20-13-21; 2 Paul Goldstein, *Copyright: Principles, Law, and Practice* §8.3.1.1., at 90-91 (1989). Goldstein remarks that in music cases the "typically more successful route to proving access requires the plaintiff to show that its work was widely disseminated through sales of sheet music, records, and radio performances." 2 Goldstein, §8.3.1.1, at 91. . . .

Proof of widespread dissemination is sometimes accompanied by a theory that copyright infringement of a popular song was subconscious. Subconscious copying has been accepted since Learned Hand embraced it in a 1924 music infringement case: "Everything registers somewhere in our memories, and no one can tell what may evoke it. . . . Once it appears that another has in fact used the copyright as the source of this production, he has invaded the author's rights. It is no excuse that in so doing his memory has played him a trick."

---

* A "cover" is a recording by an artist of a musical work written by someone else and previously released on an album by a different recording artist. As we discuss in Section G, *infra*, covers are the subject of a compulsory license under §115 of the Copyright Act. — EDS.

Fred Fisher, Inc. v. Dillingham, 298 F. 145, 147-48 (S.D.N.Y. 1924). In *Fred Fisher*, Judge Hand found that the similarities between the songs "amount[ed] to identity" and that the infringement had occurred "probably unconsciously, what he had certainly often heard only a short time before." *Id.* at 147.

In modern cases, however, the theory of subconscious copying has been applied to songs that are more remote in time. *ABKCO Music, Inc. v. Harrisongs Music, Ltd.*, 722 F.2d 988 (2d Cir. 1983) is the most prominent example. In *ABKCO*, the Second Circuit affirmed a jury's verdict that former Beatle George Harrison, in writing the song "My Sweet Lord," subconsciously copied The Chiffons' "He's So Fine," which was released six years earlier. *See id.* at 997, 999. Harrison admitted hearing "He's So Fine" in 1963, when it was number one on the Billboard charts in the United States for five weeks and one of the top 30 hits in England for seven weeks. *See id.* at 998. The court found: "the evidence, standing alone, 'by no means compels the conclusion that there was access . . . it does not compel the conclusion that there was not.' " . . . In *ABKCO*, however, the court found that "the similarity was so striking and where access was found, the remoteness of that access provides no basis for reversal." *Id.* . . .

The Isley Brothers' access argument was based on a theory of widespread dissemination and subconscious copying. They presented evidence supporting four principal ways that Bolton and Goldmark could have had access to the Isley Brothers' "Love is a Wonderful Thing":

(1) Bolton grew up listening to groups such as the Isley Brothers and singing their songs. In 1966, Bolton and Goldmark were 13 and 15, respectively, growing up in Connecticut. Bolton testified that he had been listening to rhythm and blues music by black singers since he was 10 or 11, "appreciated a lot of Black singers," and as a youth was the lead singer in a band that performed "covers" of popular songs by black singers. . . .

(2) Three disk jockeys testified that the Isley Brothers' song was widely disseminated on radio and television stations where Bolton and Goldmark grew up. . . .

(3) Bolton confessed to being a huge fan of the Isley Brothers and a collector of their music. Ronald Isley testified that when Bolton saw Isley at the Lou Rawls United Negro College Fund Benefit concert in 1988, Bolton said, "I know this guy. I go back with him. I have all his stuff." . . .

(4) Bolton wondered if he and Goldmark were copying a song by another famous soul singer. Bolton produced a work tape attempting to show that he and Goldmark independently created their version of "Love is a Wonderful Thing." On that tape of their recording session, Bolton asked Goldmark if the song they were composing was Marvin Gaye's "Some Kind of Wonderful."

. . . [T]his is a more attenuated case of reasonable access and subconscious copying than *ABKCO*. In this case, the appellants never admitted hearing the Isley Brothers' "Love is a Wonderful Thing." . . . Nor did the Isley Brothers ever claim that Bolton's and Goldmark's song is so "strikingly similar" to the Isley Brothers' that proof of access is presumed and need not be proven.

Despite the weaknesses of the Isley Brothers' theory of reasonable access, the appellants had a full opportunity to present their case to the jury. Three rhythm and blues experts (including legendary Motown songwriter Lamont Dozier of Holland-Dozier-Holland fame) testified that they had never heard of the Isley Brothers' "Love is a Wonderful Thing." . . . Bolton also pointed out that 129 songs called "Love is a Wonderful Thing" are registered with the Copyright Office, 85 of them before 1964.

The Isley Brothers' reasonable access arguments are not without merit. Teenagers are generally avid music listeners. It is entirely plausible that two Connecticut teenagers obsessed with rhythm and blues music could remember an Isley Brothers' song that was played on the radio and television for a few weeks, and subconsciously copy it twenty years later. . . .

Although we might not reach the same conclusion as the jury regarding access, we find that the jury's conclusion about access is supported by substantial evidence. . . .

Bolton and Goldmark also contend that their witnesses rebutted the Isley Brothers' prima facie case of copyright infringement with evidence of independent creation. By establishing reasonable access and substantial similarity, a copyright plaintiff creates a presumption of copying. The burden shifts to the defendant to rebut that presumption through proof of independent creation. . . .

The appellants' case of independent creation hinges on three factors: the work tape demonstrating how Bolton and Goldmark created their song, Bolton and Goldmark's history of songwriting, and testimony that their arranger, Walter Afanasieff, contributed two of five unprotectible elements that they allegedly copied. The jury, however, heard the testimony of Bolton, Goldmark, Afanasieff, and [appellants' expert, Anthony] Ricigliano about independent creation. The work tape revealed evidence that Bolton may have subconsciously copied a song that he believed to be written by Marvin Gaye. Bolton and Goldmark's history of songwriting presents no direct evidence about this case. And Afanasieff's contributions to Bolton and Goldmark's song were described by the appellants' own expert as "very common." Once again, we refuse to disturb the jury's determination about independent creation. The substantial evidence of copying based on access and substantial similarity was such that a reasonable juror could reject this defense. . . .

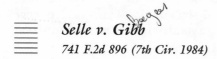

Selle v. Gibb

741 F.2d 896 (7th Cir. 1984)

CUDAHY, J.: The plaintiff, Ronald H. Selle, brought a suit against three brothers, Maurice, Robin and Barry Gibb, known collectively as the popular singing group, the Bee Gees, alleging that the Bee Gees, in their hit tune, "How Deep Is Your Love," had infringed the copyright of his song, "Let It End." . . . [The jury found liability, but the district court granted the Bee Gees' motion for judgment notwithstanding the verdict.]

I

Selle composed his song, "Let It End," in one day in the fall of 1975. . . . He played his song with his small band two or three times in the Chicago area and sent a tape and lead sheet of the music to eleven music recording and publishing companies. Eight of the companies returned the materials to Selle; three did not respond. . . .

The Bee Gees are internationally known performers and creators of popular music. They have composed more than 160 songs; their sheet music, records and tapes have been distributed worldwide, some of the albums selling more than 30 million copies. The Bee Gees, however, do not themselves read or write music. In composing a song, their practice was to tape a tune, which members of their staff would later transcribe and reduce to a form suitable for copyrighting, sale and performance by both the Bee Gees and others.

In addition to their own testimony at trial, the Bee Gees presented testimony by their manager, Dick Ashby, and two musicians, Albhy Galuten and Blue Weaver, who were on the Bee Gees' staff at the time "How Deep Is Your Love" was composed. These witnesses described in detail how, in January 1977, the Bee Gees and several members of their staff went to a recording studio in the Chateau d'Herouville about 25 miles northwest of Paris. There the group composed at least six new songs and mixed a live album. Barry Gibb's testimony included a detailed explanation of a work tape which was introduced into evidence and played in court. This tape preserves the actual process of creation during which the brothers, and particularly Barry, created the tune of the accused song while Weaver, a keyboard player, played the tune which was hummed or sung by the brothers. Although the tape does not seem to preserve the very beginning of the process of creation, it does depict the process by which ideas, notes, lyrics and bits of the tune were gradually put together. . . .

The only expert witness to testify at trial was Arrand Parsons, a professor of music at Northwestern University who has had extensive professional experience primarily in classical music. He has been a program annotator for the Chicago Symphony Orchestra and the New Orleans Symphony Orchestra and has authored works about musical theory. Prior to this case, however, he had never made a comparative analysis of two popular songs. . . .

Dr. Parsons testified that, in his opinion, "the two songs had such striking similarities that they could not have been written independent of one another." . . . However, on several occasions he declined to say that the similarities could only have resulted from copying. . . .

III

Selle's primary contention on this appeal is that the district court misunderstood the theory of proof of copyright infringement on which he based his claim. Under this theory, copyright infringement can be demonstrated when, even in the absence of any direct evidence of access, the two pieces in question are so strikingly similar that access can be inferred from such similarity alone. . . .

One difficulty with plaintiff's theory is that no matter how great the similarity between the two works, it is not their similarity *per se* which establishes access; rather, their similarity tends to prove access in light of the nature of the works, the particular musical genre involved and other circumstantial evidence of access. . . .

As a threshold matter, therefore, it would appear that there must be at least some other evidence which would establish a reasonable possibility that the complaining work was *available* to the alleged infringer. . . .

Judge Leighton thus based his decision on what he characterized as the plaintiff's inability to raise more than speculation that the Bee Gees had access to his song. The extensive testimony of the defendants and their witnesses describing the creation process went essentially uncontradicted, and there was no attempt even to impeach their credibility. . . .

IV

. . . This decision is also supported by a more traditional analysis of proof of access based only on the proof of "striking similarity" between the two compositions. The plaintiff relies almost exclusively on the testimony of his expert witness, Dr. Parsons, that the two pieces were, in fact, "strikingly similar."[3] Yet formulating a meaningful definition of "striking similarity" is no simple task, and the term is often used in a conclusory or circular fashion. . . .

"Striking similarity" is not merely a function of the number of identical notes that appear in both compositions. An important factor in analyzing the degree of similarity of two compositions is the uniqueness of the sections which are asserted to be similar.

---

3. Plaintiff also relies on the fact that both songs were played on numerous occasions in open court for the jury to hear and on the deposition testimony of one of the Bee Gees, Maurice, who incorrectly identified Theme B of Selle's song as the Bee Gees' composition, "How Deep Is Your Love."

If the complaining work contains an unexpected departure from the normal metric structure or if the complaining work includes what appears to be an error and the accused work repeats the unexpected element or the error, then it is more likely that there is some connection between the pieces. . . .

Finally, the similarities should appear in a sufficiently unique or complex context as to make it unlikely that both pieces were copied from a prior common source, *Sheldon v. Metro-Goldwyn Pictures Corp.*, 81 F.2d 49, 54 (2d Cir.), *cert. denied*, 298 U.S. 669 (1936), or that the defendant was able to compose the accused work as a matter of independent creation, *Nichols v. Universal Pictures Corp.*, 45 F.2d 119, 122 (2d Cir. 1930), *cert. denied*, 282 U.S. 902 (1931). *See also Darrell v. Joe Morris Music Co.*, 113 F.2d 80 (2d Cir. 1940) ("simple, trite themes . . . are likely to recur spontaneously . . . and [only few] . . . suit the infantile demands of the popular ear"). . . .

. . . [T]o bolster the expert's conclusion that independent creation was not possible, there should be some testimony or other evidence of the relative complexity or uniqueness of the two compositions. Dr. Parsons' testimony did not refer to this aspect of the compositions and, in a field such as that of popular music in which all songs are relatively short and tend to build on or repeat a basic theme, such testimony would seem to be particularly necessary. . . .

[The court affirmed the district court's grant of judgment notwithstanding the verdict, concluding that the plaintiff had failed to establish a basis from which the jury could infer access by the defendants to his song, and also had not met his burden of proving striking similarity.]

Ty, Inc. v. GMA Accessories, Inc.
132 F.3d 1167 (7th Cir. 1997)

POSNER, C.J.: Ty, the manufacturer of the popular "Beanie Babies" line of stuffed animals, has obtained a preliminary injunction under the Copyright Act against the sale by GMA . . . of "Preston the Pig" and "Louie the Cow." These are bean-bag animals manufactured by GMA that Ty contends are copies of its copyrighted pig ("Squealer") and cow ("Daisy"). Ty began selling the "Beanie Babies" line, including Squealer, in 1993, and it was the popularity of the line that induced GMA to bring out its own line of bean-bag stuffed animals three years later. GMA does not contest the part of the injunction that enjoins the sale of Louie, but asks us on a variety of grounds to vacate the other part, the part that enjoins it from selling Preston.

We have appended to our opinion five pictures found in the appellate record. The first shows Squealer (the darker pig, actually pink) and Preston (white). The second is a picture of two real pigs. The third and fourth are different views of the design for Preston that Janet Salmon submitted to GMA several months before Preston went into production. The fifth is a picture of the two bean-bag cows; they are nearly identical. A glance at the first picture shows a striking similarity between the two bean-bag pigs as well. The photograph was supplied by GMA and actually understates the similarity (the animals themselves are part of the record). The "real" Preston is the same length as Squealer and has a virtually identical snout. The difference in the lengths of the two animals in the picture is a trick of the camera. The difference in snouts results from the fact that the pictured Preston was a manufacturing botch. And GMA put a ribbon around the neck of the Preston in the picture, but the Preston that it sells doesn't have a ribbon. . . .

. . . [C]opying entails access. If, therefore, two works are so similar as to make it highly probable that the later one is a copy of the earlier one, the issue of access need not be addressed separately, since if the later work was a copy its creator must have had access to the original.

Selle v. Gibb, [741 F.2d 896, 901 (7th Cir. 1984)]; *Gaste v. Kaiserman*, [863 F.2d 1061, 1068 (2d Cir. 1988)]; *Ferguson v. National Broadcasting Co.*, [584 F.2d 111 (5th Cir. 1978)]. Of course the inference of access, and hence of copying, could be rebutted by proof that the creator of the later work could not have seen the earlier one or (an alternative mode of access) a copy of the earlier one. But . . . we do not read our decision in *Selle* to hold or imply, in conflict with the *Gaste* decision, that no matter how closely the works resemble each other, the plaintiff must produce some (other) evidence of access. He must produce evidence of access, all right — but, as we have just said, and as is explicit in *Selle* itself, a similarity that is so close as to be highly unlikely to have been an accident of independent creation *is* evidence of access.

What troubled us in *Selle* but is not a factor here is that two works may be strikingly similar — may in fact be identical — not because one is copied from the other but because both are copies of the same thing in the public domain. In such a case — imagine two people photographing Niagara Falls from the same place at the same time of the day and year and in identical weather — there is no inference of access to anything but the public domain, and, equally, no inference of copying from a copyrighted work. A similarity may be striking without being suspicious.

But here it is both. GMA's pig is strikingly similar to Ty's pig but not to anything in the public domain — a real pig, for example, which is why we have included in our appendix a photograph of real pigs. The parties' bean-bag pigs bear little resemblance to real pigs even if we overlook the striking anatomical anomaly of Preston — he has three toes, whereas real pigs have cloven hooves. We can imagine an argument that the technology of manufacturing bean-bag animals somehow prevents the manufacturer from imitating a real pig. But anyone even slightly familiar with stuffed animals knows that there are many lifelike stuffed pigs on the market. . . .

Real pigs are not the only pigs in the public domain. But GMA has not pointed to any fictional pig in the public domain that Preston resembles. . . . In rebuttal all that GMA presented was the affidavit of the designer, Salmon, who swears, we must assume truthfully, that she never looked at a Squealer before submitting her design. But it is not her design drawing that is alleged to infringe the copyright on Squealer; it is the manufactured Preston, the soft sculpture itself, which, as a comparison of the first with the third and fourth pictures in the appendix reveals, is much more like Squealer than Salmon's drawing is. And remember that the manufactured Preston *in the photograph* is a sport, with its stubby snout and its ribbon. Interestingly, these are features of Salmon's drawing but not of the production-model Preston, suggesting design intervention between Salmon's submission and actual production.

It is true that only a few months elapsed between Salmon's submission of the drawing to GMA and the production of Preston. But the record is silent on how long it would have taken to modify her design to make it more like Squealer. For all we know, it might have been done in hours — by someone who had bought a Squealer. The Beanie Babies are immensely popular. They are also, it is true, sometimes hard to find. . . . But it is unbelievable that a substantial company like GMA which is in the same line of business as Ty could not have located and purchased a Squealer if it wanted to copy it. A glance at the last picture in the appendix shows an identity between Louie the Cow and Ty's Daisy that is so complete (and also not explainable by reference to resemblance to a real cow or other public domain figure) as to compel an inference of copying. If GMA thus must have had access to Louie, it is probable, quite apart from any inference from the evidence of similarity, that it had access to Squealer as well.

This discussion shows how . . . the true relation between similarity and access [can be] expressed. Access (and copying) may be inferred when two works are so similar to each other and not to anything in the public domain that it is likely that the creator of the second work copied the first, but the inference can be rebutted by disproving access or otherwise showing independent creation. . . .

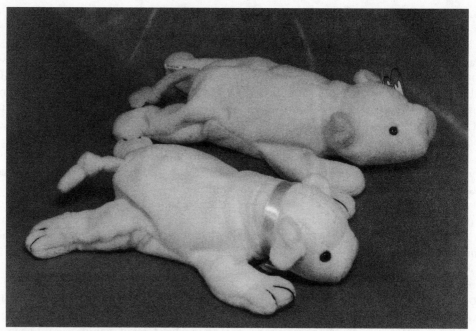

Squealer © 1993 Ty, Inc. Reprinted by permission. Photograph provided by Banner & Witcoff, Ltd., attorneys for GMA, Inc.

Preston and Squealer

NOTES AND QUESTIONS

1. As we cautioned earlier, the terminology that courts use in assessing claims for infringement of the reproduction right, §106(1) and the derivative work right, §106(2), can be confusing. Some courts do not use the term "copying-in-fact," instead labeling the first part of the inquiry as whether the defendant "copied" the plaintiff's work. They then proceed to consider whether the defendant also engaged in "infringing copying" or "improper appropriation" — i.e., copying prohibited by §106(1).

As discussed in Section B.1 of this chapter, in evaluating whether copying is prohibited by §106(1), most courts use a "substantial similarity" standard, finding infringement if the defendant's work is substantially similar to the protected elements of the plaintiff's work. Such similarity proves infringing copying or improper appropriation. Unfortunately, courts may also use the term "substantial similarity" (or "probative similarity") to describe the degree of similarity required to show copying in fact. This similarity is analytically distinct from the substantial similarity required to prove a violation of §106(1). Make sure that you understand which aspect of the copyright infringement claim the court is discussing when it uses terms like "copying" and "substantial similarity."

2. Do "subconscious copying" claims serve copyright law's ultimate purpose of promoting progress? Should there be a distinct statute of limitations on such claims, or should courts impose conditions regarding when such claims can be asserted?

3. The British case *Francis Day & Hunter v. Bron*, [1963] 2 All. E. R. 16 (Eng. C.A.), involved an infringement claim brought by the music publishers of the song "In a Little Spanish

Town," composed in 1926. "In a Little Spanish Town" had been extensively disseminated in the U.S. by sheet music, broadcasting, and distribution of records. The plaintiffs alleged that another song, "Why," composed in 1959 by an individual who had lived most of his life in the U.S., copied a substantial part of "In a Little Spanish Town." The composer of "Why" testified that despite playing various instruments in bands he had never, to his knowledge, seen, studied, or played the music of "In a Little Spanish Town," nor to his recollection had he ever heard the song. The composer admitted, however, that it was possible he had heard "In a Little Spanish Town" at a younger age, because he listened to a lot of music and had started composing at the age of 11. The trial court denied the infringement claim, holding that the similarities could have been coincidental. According to the court, the evidence was insufficient to draw an inference of access in the absence of direct evidence and in face of the composer's denial. The judge outlined a six-factor test to determine whether the defendant had copied the plaintiff's song: "[1] The degree of familiarity (if proved at all, or properly inferred) with the plaintiffs' work, [2] the character of the work, particularly its qualities of impressing the mind and memory, [3] the objective similarity of the defendants' work, [4] the inherent probability that such similarity as is found could be due to coincidence, [5] the existence of other influences on the defendant composer, and . . . [6] the quality of the defendant composer's own evidence on the presence or otherwise in his mind of the plaintiff's work."

Would consideration of these factors have changed the result in *Three Boys Music Corp.*? Do you think these factors would have made a difference in *Selle*?

4. Are *Selle* and *Ty* consistent? If the similarities between "Let It End" and "How Deep Is Your Love" could be the fortuitous result of popular culture, why not the similarities between Squealer and Preston? If you had represented GMA, what arguments might you have made?

5. Do you agree with the *Ty* court that when similarities between two works can be attributed to public domain elements, the threshold for access should be higher? Should the threshold also be higher when the similarities can be attributed to the pervasiveness of popular culture more generally?

6. In *Three Boys Music Corp.*, the court found that widespread dissemination is one way to prove reasonable access when trying to establish copying by the defendant. Does that approach unduly favor songs that are popular over those that never achieve any measure of success? In the digital era, how useful is the standard of widespread dissemination? For example, should the mere fact that a song is available on the Internet count as widespread dissemination? Is downloading in itself evidence of dissemination? If so, what number of downloads do you think should trigger a determination of widespread dissemination?

7. How well does the "independent creation" doctrine survive cases like *Three Boys Music Corp., Selle,* and *Ty*? As the court in *Three Boys Music Corp.* explains, after the plaintiff has introduced sufficient evidence to support an inference of access, the burden shifts to the defendant to rebut that inference by proving independent creation. Practically, do the rules about proof of access articulated in the cases you read allow for such proof? In *Sheldon v. Metro-Goldwyn Pictures Corp.*, 81 F.2d 49 (2d Cir.), *cert. denied*, 298 U.S. 669 (1936), Judge Learned Hand famously observed, "[I]f by some magic a man who had never known it were to compose anew Keats's Ode on a Grecian Urn, he would be an 'author,' and, if he copyrighted it, others might not copy that poem, though they might of course copy Keats's." *Id.* at 54. Under the rules set forth in the cases above, if Keats's original Ode on a Grecian Urn were still protected under copyright today, would Judge Hand's hypothetical poet be considered an author or a presumptive infringer? Which result comports more closely with the policies underlying copyright law? How would you draw the evidentiary line between subconscious copying and independent creation with such popular works as *Star Wars* or the *Harry Potter* series?

As discussed in Chapter 2, *supra*, pages 70-71, in patent law, an inventor who independently develops something that is covered by an enforceable patent still infringes that patent. Why do you think copyright law has a different rule? Should independent creation be considered a defense? Or should proving a lack of independent creation be part of the plaintiff's prima facie case?

8. The Music Genome Project is a comprehensive database of songs identified by their distinct characteristics or "genes," ranging from melody and lyrics to rhythm, tempo, harmony (including vocal harmony), arrangement, and instrumentation. Founded in 2000, its goal is to establish a taxonomy of all of the musical attributes of songs to facilitate listeners' ability to identify a body of music unique to their tastes and preferences. Pandora Radio is a digital music service that relies exclusively on technology licensed from the Music Genome Project to help users identify new songs similar to the music they already enjoy. Should courts admit evidence of "genetic similarities" when considering copying in fact? In what ways might such evidence be relevant? Should such evidence trump the opinion of an expert? Of an ordinary listener? For discussion of some of the issues raised by "genetic analysis" of music, see Yvette Joy Liebesman, *Using Innovative Technologies to Analyze For similarity Between Musical Works in Copyright Infringement Disputes*, 35 AIPLA Q.J. 331 (2007).

9. When a case involves musical works, listening to the two compositions and viewing their musical scores can be helpful in evaluating the similarities. The Copyright Infringement Project sponsored by the UCLA Intellectual Property Project and Columbia Law School has collected many sound files and musical scores from copyright cases involving musical works, including the works at issue in *Three Boys Music Corp.*, *Selle*, and *Arnstein*. See *http://www.ccnmtl.columbia.edu/projects/law/library/introduction.html*.

Note on Access and Independent Creation in the Corporate Context

As cases like *Three Boys Music Corp.* and *Selle* suggest, documenting independent creation after the fact can be a daunting task for individual creators. The Bee Gees were able to defeat Selle's infringement claim because they could document their recording procedures, and because they and Selle traveled in very different circles. Similarly, in *Repp v. Webber*, 132 F.3d 882 (2d Cir. 1997), British composer Andrew Lloyd Webber was able to rely on geographic and social differences to defeat an infringement claim brought by an American composer of liturgical folk music. Many authors, however, cannot establish that they created their works while secluded in a French chateau or a British manor, and cannot comprehensively document their creation processes. Typically, then, when an individual defendant raises independent creation, he is arguing that the plaintiff has failed to establish the prima facie case of infringement because the plaintiff has not shown that copying in fact occurred.

Corporate creators confront a slightly different set of problems. Even large companies with organized production processes cannot document every step in that process. In *Grubb v. KMS Patriots, L.P.*, 88 F.3d 1 (1st Cir. 1996), the court held that timesheets submitted by the designer who created the new logo for the New England Patriots football team established that he had created the logo before the Patriots received the plaintiff's proposed new logo via unsolicited submission. Had the timing of plaintiff's submission been different, however, it would have been much more difficult for the Patriots to prove that the plaintiff's logo had not somehow made its way to their design firm. In *Bouchat v. Baltimore Ravens, Inc.*, 241 F.3d 350 (4th Cir. 2001), another logo design case, the plaintiff could not prove that the particular piece of paper he submitted to the chairman of the Maryland Stadium Authority (MSA) had ever made its way to the Ravens. Instead, he submitted evidence regarding the routine practice by which papers received at the MSA's offices were forwarded to the chairman's law office, and of regular contact between that office and the office of the Ravens' team owner, which was located in the same building. The jury returned a verdict for the plaintiff, and the court of appeals ruled that the striking similarity of plaintiff's and defendants' designs, together with the evidence establishing that defendants' internal procedures created a reasonable possibility of access, sufficed to sustain the verdict. In the face of decisions like *Bouchat*, establishing procedures to document the creative process has become a matter of pressing concern for companies that create and commission copyrighted works.

One judicially created tool, the "corporate receipt doctrine," suggests that, at a minimum, companies should establish procedures for handling the receipt and disposition of unsolicited or solicited submissions of copyrightable works. Under the corporate receipt doctrine, possession of a work by one employee of a corporation implies possession by another employee who allegedly infringed the work. *See* 4 Melville B. Nimmer & David Nimmer, *Nimmer on Copyright* §13.02[A] (2008).

In *Jones v. Blige*, 558 F.3d 485 (6th Cir. 2009), Leonard Jones, one of the plaintiffs, had submitted a demo CD with a cover letter and other information regarding his client, an aspiring rap artist, to the office of the Senior Vice President of Artists and Repertoire for Universal Music Enterprises. Jones later spoke to an assistant who allegedly informed him that the CD was on the desk of the vice president, who was planning to listen to it. After some time, when no response was forthcoming from Universal, Jones requested that the assistant return the package. The materials were returned to Jones in a different envelope and without the cover letter, indicating that the package had been opened. In August 2001, Jones heard "Family Affair" by Mary J. Blige on the radio and believed it to be very similar to the song he had submitted to Universal. He sued Universal, Blige's publisher, and Blige herself for copyright infringement. Relying on the corporate receipt doctrine, Jones tried to prove access by arguing that somebody at the vice president's office had opened the package containing the CD and that Blige had access to the CD as a result of her business relationship with Universal. The Sixth Circuit ruled that Jones had established no more than an "attenuated corporate connection" between the defendants, and that "to find a reasonable possibility of access, a jury would be required to make an implausible leap, unsupported by evidence other than bare corporate receipt." *Id.* at 493. Because the two songs were not so strikingly similar as to give rise to an inference of copying, the court affirmed the district court's grant of summary judgment to the defendants.

Other circuits also have rejected a "bare corporate receipt" rule. *See e.g.*, *Towler v. Sayles*, 76 F.3d 579, 583 (4th Cir. 1996) (close relationship required for the corporate receipt doctrine to apply); *Jorgensen v. Epic/Sony Records*, 351 F.3d 46, 48 (2d Cir. 2003) (bare corporate receipt insufficient to raise a triable issue of access in the absence of a nexus between the recipients and the alleged infringers).

Software companies have developed special procedures for documenting independent creation. As we discussed in Chapter 4.B, *supra*, because software is more valuable to the extent that it is compatible, or interoperable, with other software, some degree of access to competitors' products is often an indispensable part of the development process. If the functional specifications for an existing program are not publicly available from its developer, another developer who wants access to that information may reverse engineer the program by decompiling the object code version of the program into its human-readable commands. (Courts have ruled that this procedure, which entails copying, can be a fair use of copyrighted software. *See* Chapter 7.) Often, however, the developer will segregate the programmers responsible for writing the new program from those responsible for decompiling and understanding the existing program. This "clean room" process involves placing the first set of programmers in a separate room or facility and monitoring all of the technical information that goes into that room or facility. In particular, the competitor's decompiled code is excluded from the clean room. Instead, the programmers responsible for decompiling the code must produce a set of specifications that simply describe the functionality that the new program must have. These specifications are sent into the clean room, and constitute the only form of access to the competitor's product that the programming team actually writing the code of the new product will have. Altai used just such an approach in *Computer Associates International, Inc. v. Altai, Inc.*, excerpted in Chapter 4.B.2, pages 222-29 *supra*.

NOTES AND QUESTIONS

1. In the patent system, documentation of inventive work is routine. Priority of invention is critical to establishing patent rights, and investigators keep detailed laboratory notebooks for precisely this purpose. Another researcher typically countersigns the notebook when the data is entered to provide additional verification of the content and date of laboratory results. Do you think that problems of proving and rebutting access would be more easily solved if authors of copyrighted works kept similar notebooks? Why, or why not?

2. What other steps might individual authors take during the creative process to bolster a defense of independent creation in case they are sued for infringement?

3. Is the practical effect of the cases on corporate receipt that plaintiffs have a higher evidentiary burden to satisfy than is typical for proceedings at the summary judgment stage? It was apparent in *Jones* that somebody at Universal Music opened the package containing the CD sent by the plaintiffs. Why is that fact, combined with Universal's business relationship with Mary J. Blige, an insufficient basis from which to infer access?

4. The manner in which an author documents independent creation may vary depending on the type of work. Assume that you represent a client that produces programs for television. Your client routinely receives unsolicited submissions of screenplays, proposals for new series, and the like. What procedures would you advise your client to adopt for handling these submissions?

B. THE REPRODUCTION RIGHT

We begin our consideration of §106 with the right that historically has been the "core" right of the copyright owner — the right to reproduce, and authorize others to reproduce, the copyrighted work in copies, codified in §106(1) of the 1976 Copyright Act. Section 106(1) covers, most obviously, the creation of exact copies of the copyrighted work. It also, however, covers the creation of nonexact or "substantially similar" copies. These cases raise some of the most complex questions in §106(1) infringement proceedings, and we begin with them. We consider the exact copy in subsection B.2 *infra*.

1. The "Substantially Similar" Copy

Among the most difficult issues in any copyright infringement case is determining whether the defendant has engaged in actionable copying (i.e., copying in violation of §106(1)) by taking "too much" of the plaintiff's work. The plaintiff must show that the defendant copied protectible — i.e., copyrightable — expression. Courts often refer to this inquiry as whether the defendant's and plaintiff's works are "substantially similar." If they are, then the defendant is liable for copyright infringement unless his conduct is authorized under the statute or he otherwise has a viable defense. The substantial similarity question is one of fact.

While easily stated, the substantial similarity test has proved quite difficult to apply, in part because similarity is also relevant to the threshold question of copying in fact (*see* Section A.2, *supra*, page 291). When we refer to "substantial similarity," we are discussing a level of "sameness" between the works that supports a finding of infringement.

In the following materials, we explore the application of the substantial similarity test to determine whether copying is wrongful and thus infringing. As you read the following materials, identify how different courts implement the test. Consider also how they guard against the risk of finding liability when the defendant has only taken unprotected material such as ideas and *scenes à faire* from the plaintiff. Finally, think about how you would formulate a substantial similarity test that can be effectively communicated in jury instructions.

a. Classic Cases

We begin with two classic cases that should be part of every copyright student's store of knowledge. As you read the cases, try to identify what test (if any) the court is using in determining wrongful appropriation.

Nichols v. Universal Pictures Corp.
45 F.2d 119 (2d Cir. 1930), cert. denied, 282 U.S. 902 (1931)

L. HAND, J.: [The plaintiff sued the defendant for copyright infringement. The district court entered a decree of dismissal from which the plaintiff appealed.]

The plaintiff is the author of a play, "Abie's Irish Rose," which it may be assumed was properly copyrighted. . . . The defendant produced publicly a motion picture play, "The Cohens and The Kellys," which the plaintiff alleges was taken from it. As we think the defendant's play too unlike the plaintiff's to be an infringement, we may assume, arguendo, that in some details the defendant used the plaintiff's play, as will subsequently appear, though we do not so decide. It therefore becomes necessary to give an outline of the two plays.

"Abie's Irish Rose" presents a Jewish family living in prosperous circumstances in New York. The father, a widower, is in business as a merchant, in which his son and only child helps him. The boy has philandered with young women, who to his father's great disgust have always been Gentiles, for he is obsessed with a passion that his daughter-in-law shall be an orthodox Jewess. When the play opens the son, who has been courting a young Irish Catholic girl, has already married her secretly before a Protestant minister, and is concerned to soften the blow for his father, by securing a favorable impression of his bride, while concealing her faith and race. To accomplish this he introduces her to his father at his home as a Jewess, and lets it appear that he is interested in her, though he conceals the marriage. The girl somewhat reluctantly falls in with the plan; the father takes the bait, becomes infatuated with the girl, concludes that they must marry, and assumes that of course they will, if he so decides. He calls in a rabbi, and prepares for the wedding according to the Jewish rite.

Meanwhile the girl's father, also a widower, who lives in California, and is as intense in his own religious antagonism as the Jew, has been called to New York, supposing that his daughter is to marry an Irishman and a Catholic. Accompanied by a priest, he arrives at the house at the moment when the marriage is being celebrated, but too late to prevent it and the two fathers, each infuriated by the proposed union of his child to a heretic, fall into unseemly and grotesque antics. The priest and the rabbi become friendly, exchange trite sentiments about religion, and agree that the match is good. Apparently out of abundant caution, the priest celebrates the marriage for a third time, while the girl's father is inveigled away. The second act closes with each father, still outraged, seeking to find some way by which the union, thus trebly insured, may be dissolved.

The last act takes place about a year later, the young couple having meanwhile been abjured by each father, and left to their own resources. They have had twins, a boy and a girl, but their fathers know no more than that a child has been born. At Christmas each, led by his craving to see his grandchild, goes separately to the young folks' home, where they encounter each other, each laden with gifts, one for a boy, the other for a girl. After some slapstick comedy, depending upon the insistence of each that he is right about the sex of the grandchild, they become reconciled when they learn the truth, and that each child is to bear the given name of a grandparent. The curtain falls as the fathers are exchanging amenities, and the Jew giving evidence of an abatement in the strictness of his orthodoxy.

"The Cohens and The Kellys" presents two families, Jewish and Irish, living side by side in the poorer quarters of New York in a state of perpetual enmity. The wives in both cases are still living, and share in the mutual animosity, as do two small sons, and even the respective dogs. The Jews have a daughter, the Irish a son; the Jewish father is in the clothing business; the Irishman is a policeman. The children are in love with each other, and secretly marry, apparently after the play opens. The Jew, being in great financial straits, learns from a lawyer that he has fallen heir to a large fortune from a great-aunt, and moves into a great house, fitted luxuriously. Here he and his family live in vulgar ostentation, and here the Irish boy seeks out his Jewish bride, and is chased away by the angry father. The Jew then abuses the Irishman over the telephone, and both become hysterically excited. The extremity of his feelings make the Jew sick, so that he must go to Florida for a rest, just before which the daughter discloses her marriage to her mother.

On his return the Jew finds that his daughter has borne a child; at first he suspects the lawyer, but eventually learns the truth and is overcome with anger at such a low alliance. Meanwhile, the Irish family who have been forbidden to see the grandchild, go to the Jew's house, and after a violent scene between the two fathers in which the Jew disowns his daughter, who decides to go back with her husband, the Irishman takes her back with her baby to his own poor lodgings. The lawyer, who had hoped to marry the Jew's daughter, seeing his plan foiled, tells the Jew that his fortune really belongs to the Irishman, who was also related to the dead woman, but offers to conceal his knowledge, if the Jew will share the loot. This the Jew repudiates, and, leaving the astonished lawyer, walks through the rain to his enemy's house to surrender the property. He arrives in great dejection, tells the truth, and abjectly turns to leave. A reconciliation ensues, the Irishman agreeing to share with him equally. The Jew shows some interest in his grandchild, though this is at most a minor motive in the reconciliation, and the curtain falls while the two are in their cups, the Jew insisting that in the firm name for the business, which they are to carry on jointly, his name shall stand first.

It is of course essential to any protection of literary property, whether at common-law or under the statute, that the right cannot be limited literally to the text, else a plagiarist would escape by immaterial variations. That has never been the law, but, as soon as literal appropriation ceases to be the test, the whole matter is necessarily at large, so that, as was recently well said by a distinguished judge, the decisions cannot help much in a new case. . . . Upon any work, and especially upon a play, a great number of patterns of increasing generality will fit equally well, as more and more of the incident is left out. The last may perhaps be no more than the most general statement of what the play is about, and at times might consist only of its title; but there is a point in this series of abstractions where they are no longer protected, since otherwise the playwright could prevent the use of his "ideas," to which, apart from their expression, his property is never extended. . . . Nobody has ever been able to fix that boundary, and nobody ever can. . . . As respects plays, the controversy chiefly centers upon the characters and sequence of incident, these being the substance.

. . . [W]e do not doubt that two plays may correspond in plot closely enough for infringement. How far that correspondence must go is another matter. Nor need we hold that the same may not be true as to the characters, quite independently of the "plot" proper, though, as far as we know, such a case has never arisen. If Twelfth Night were copyrighted, it is quite possible that a second comer might so closely imitate Sir Toby Belch or Malvolio as to infringe, but it would not be enough that for one of his characters he cast a riotous knight who kept wassail to the discomfort of the household, or a vain and foppish steward who became amorous of his mistress. These would be no more than Shakespeare's "ideas" in the play, as little capable of monopoly as Einstein's Doctrine of Relativity, or Darwin's theory of the Origin of Species. It follows that the less developed the characters, the less they can be copyrighted; that is the penalty an author must bear for marking them too indistinctly.

In the two plays at bar we think both as to incident and character, the defendant took no more — assuming that it took anything at all — than the law allowed. The stories are quite different. One is of a religious zealot who insists upon his child's marrying no one outside his faith; opposed by another who is in this respect just like him, and is his foil. Their difference in race is merely an obbligato to the main theme, religion. They sink their differences through grandparental pride and affection. In the other, zealotry is wholly absent; religion does not even appear. It is true that the parents are hostile to each other in part because they differ in race; but the marriage of their son to a Jew does not apparently offend the Irish family at all, and it exacerbates the existing animosity of the Jew, principally because he has become rich, when he learns it. They are reconciled through the honesty of the Jew and the generosity of the Irishman; the grandchild has nothing whatever to do with it. The only matter common to the two is a quarrel between a Jewish and an Irish father, the marriage of their children, the birth of grandchildren and a reconciliation.

If the defendant took so much from the plaintiff, it may well have been because her amazing success seemed to prove that this was a subject of enduring popularity. Even so, granting that the plaintiff's play was wholly original, and assuming that novelty is not essential to a copyright, there is no monopoly in such a background. Though the plaintiff discovered the vein, she could not keep it to herself; so defined, the theme was too generalized an abstraction from what she wrote. It was only a part of her "ideas."

Nor does she fare better as to her characters. It is indeed scarcely credible that she should not have been aware of those stock figures, the low comedy Jew and Irishman. The defendant has not taken from her more than their prototypes have contained for many decades. If so, obviously so to generalize her copyright, would allow her to cover what was not original with her. But we need not hold this as matter of fact, much as we might be justified. Even though we take it that she devised her figures out of her brain de novo, still the defendant was within its rights.

There are but four characters common to both plays, the lovers and the fathers. The lovers are so faintly indicated as to be no more than stage properties. They are loving and fertile; that is really all that can be said of them, and anyone else is quite within his rights if he puts loving and fertile lovers in a play of his own, wherever he gets the cue. The plaintiff's Jew is quite unlike the defendant's. His obsession is his religion, on which depends such racial animosity as he has. He is affectionate, warm and patriarchal. None of these fit the defendant's Jew, who shows affection for his daughter only once, and who has none but the most superficial interest in his grandchild. He is tricky, ostentatious and vulgar, only by misfortune redeemed into honesty. Both are grotesque, extravagant and quarrelsome; both are fond of display; but these common qualities make up only a small part of their simple pictures, no more than any one might lift if he chose. The Irish fathers are even more unlike; the plaintiff's a mere symbol for religious fanaticism and patriarchal pride, scarcely a character at all. Neither quality appears in the defendant's, for while he goes to get his grandchild, it is rather out of a truculent determination not to be forbidden, than from pride in his progeny. For the rest he is only a grotesque hobbledehoy, used for low comedy of the most conventional sort, which any one might borrow, if he chanced not to know the exemplar.

. . . A comedy based upon conflicts between Irish and Jews, into which the marriage of their children enters, is no more susceptible of copyright than the outline of Romeo and Juliet.

The plaintiff has prepared an elaborate analysis of the two plays, showing a "quadrangle" of the common characters, in which each is represented by the emotions which he discovers. She presents the resulting parallelism as proof of infringement, but the adjectives employed are so general as to be quite useless. Take for example the attribute of "love" ascribed to both Jews. The plaintiff has depicted her father as deeply attached to his son, who is his hope and joy; not so, the defendant, whose father's conduct is throughout not actuated by any affection for his daughter, and who is merely once overcome for the moment by her distress when he has violently dismissed her lover. "Anger" covers emotions aroused by quite different occasions in each case; so do "anxiety," "despondency" and "disgust." It is unnecessary to go through the catalogue for emotions are too much colored by their causes to be a test when used so broadly. This is not the proper approach to a solution; it must be more ingenuous, more like that of a spectator, who would rely upon the complex of his impressions of each character. . . .

The *Nichols* case emphasizes the importance of determining which elements of the plaintiff's work are copyrightable and which are not. The defendant cannot be liable for infringement if he takes only uncopyrightable elements of the plaintiff's work. Only if the plaintiff shows that the defendant took protected material does the inquiry proceed to assess whether the defendant took "too much" — i.e., whether the defendant's work is substantially similar to the plaintiff's. The next case, while not using the term "substantial similarity," attempts to explain both what constitutes improper copying and the perspective from which the jury is to assess similarity between works.

Arnstein v. Porter
154 F.2d 464 (2d Cir. 1946), cert. denied, 330 U.S. 851 (1947)

Plaintiff, a citizen and resident of New York, brought this suit, charging infringement by defendant, a citizen and resident of New York, of plaintiff's copyrights to several musical compositions, infringement of his rights to other uncopyrighted musical compositions, and wrongful use of the titles of others. . . .

Plaintiff alleged that defendant's "Begin the Beguine" is a plagiarism from plaintiff's "The Lord Is My Shepherd" and "A Mother's Prayer." Plaintiff testified, on deposition, that "The Lord Is My Shepherd" had been published and about 2,000 copies sold, that "A Mother's Prayer" had been published, over a million copies having been sold. In his depositions, he gave no direct evidence that defendant saw or heard these compositions. He also alleged that defendant's "My Heart Belongs to Daddy" had been plagiarized from plaintiff's "A Mother's Prayer."

Plaintiff also alleged that defendant's "I Love You" is a plagiarism from plaintiff's composition "La Priere," stating in his deposition that the latter composition had been sold. He gave no direct proof that plaintiff knew of this composition.

He also alleged that defendant's song "Night and Day" is a plagiarism of plaintiff's song "I Love You Madly," which he testified had not been published but had once been publicly performed over the radio, copies having been sent to divers radio stations but none to defendant; a copy of this song, plaintiff testified, had been stolen from his room. He also alleged that "I Love You Madly" was in part plagiarized from "La Priere." He further alleged that defendant's "You'd Be So Nice To Come Home To" is plagiarized from plaintiff's "Sadness Overwhelms My Soul." He testified that this song had never been published or publicly performed but that copies had been sent to a movie producer and to several publishers. He also alleged that defendant's "Don't Fence Me In" is a plagiarism of plaintiff's song "A Modern Messiah" which has not been published or publicly performed; in his deposition he said that about a hundred copies had been sent to divers radio stations and band leaders but that he sent no copy to defendant. Plaintiff said that defendant "had stooges right along to follow me, watch me, and live in the same apartment with me," and that plaintiff's room had been ransacked on several occasions. Asked how he knew that defendant had anything to do with any of these "burglaries," plaintiff said, "I don't know that he had to do with it, but I only know that he could have." He also said ". . . many of my compositions had been published. No one had to break in to steal them. They were sung publicly."

Defendant in his deposition categorically denied that he had ever seen or heard any of plaintiff's compositions or had had any acquaintance with any persons said to have stolen any of them. . . .

FRANK, J.: . . . The principal question on this appeal is whether the lower court . . . properly deprived plaintiff of a trial of his copyright infringement action. The answer depends on whether "there is the slightest doubt as to the facts." . . . In applying that standard here, it is important to avoid confusing two separate elements essential to a plaintiff's case in such a suit: (a) that defendant copied from plaintiff's copyrighted work and (b) that the copying (assuming it to be proved) went so far as to constitute improper appropriation.

As to the first — copying — the evidence may consist (a) of defendant's admission that he copied or (b) of circumstantial evidence — usually evidence of access — from which the trier of the facts may reasonably infer copying. Of course, if there are no similarities, no amount of evidence of access will suffice to prove copying. If there is evidence of access and similarities exist, then the trier of the facts must determine whether the similarities are sufficient to prove copying. On this issue, analysis ("dissection") is relevant, and the testimony of experts may be received to aid the trier of the facts. If evidence of access is absent, the similarities must be so striking as to preclude the possibility that plaintiff and defendant independently arrived at the same result.

If copying is established, then only does there arise the second issue, that of illicit copying (unlawful appropriation). On that issue (as noted more in detail below) the test is the response of the ordinary lay hearer; accordingly, on that issue, "dissection" and expert testimony are irrelevant. . . .

[The court held that the defendant was not entitled to summary judgment because the record showed that more than a million of one of the plaintiff's compositions were sold and others were publicly performed. It reasoned that the credibility of the plaintiff and his sometimes "fantastic" story was a matter for the jury to evaluate.]

Assuming that adequate proof is made of copying, that is not enough; for there can be "permissible copying," copying which is not illicit. Whether (if he copied) defendant unlawfully appropriated presents, too, an issue of fact. The proper criterion on that issue is not an analytic or other comparison of the respective musical compositions as they appear on paper or in the judgment of trained musicians. The plaintiff's legally protected interest is not, as such, his reputation as a musician but his interest in the potential financial returns from his compositions which derive from the lay public's approbation of his efforts. The question, therefore, is whether defendant took from plaintiff's works so much of what is pleasing to the ears of lay listeners, who comprise the audience for whom such popular music is composed, that defendant wrongfully appropriated something which belongs to the plaintiff.

Surely, then, we have an issue of fact which a jury is peculiarly fitted to determine.[22] Indeed, even if there were to be a trial before a judge, it would be desirable (although not necessary) for him to summon an advisory jury on this question.

We should not be taken as saying that a plagiarism case can never arise in which absence of similarities is so patent that a summary judgment for defendant would be correct. Thus suppose that Ravel's "Bolero" or Shostakovitch's "Fifth Symphony" were alleged to infringe "When Irish Eyes Are Smiling." But this is not such a case. For, after listening to the playing of the respective compositions, we are, at this time, unable to conclude that the likenesses are so trifling that, on the issue of misappropriation, a trial judge could legitimately direct a verdict for defendant.

At the trial, plaintiff may play, or cause to be played, the pieces in such manner that they may seem to a jury to be inexcusably alike, in terms of the way in which lay listeners of such music would be likely to react. The plaintiff may call witnesses whose testimony may aid the jury in reaching its conclusion as to the responses of such audiences. Expert testimony of musicians may also be received, but it will in no way be controlling on the issue of illicit copying, and should be utilized only to assist in determining the reactions of lay auditors. The impression made on the refined ears of musical experts or their views as to the musical excellence of plaintiff's or defendant's works are utterly immaterial on the issue of misappropriation; for the views of such persons are caviar to the general — and plaintiff's and defendant's compositions are not caviar. . . .

. . . [R]eversed and remanded.

NOTES AND QUESTIONS

1. What is the primary purpose of Judge Hand's "abstractions" analysis? How is it helpful in assessing substantial similarity? Does it tell us how much similarity is "substantial"?

2. The *Arnstein* court indicates that "dissection" is relevant to deciding the issue of copying in fact, but not to deciding the issue of substantial similarity. What do you think the court means by "dissection"? Why is expert testimony relevant to the issue of copying in fact but not to the issue of wrongfulness? Alternatively, why not just apply the "ordinary observer" test to both the issue of copying in fact and that of its wrongfulness? Would Judge Hand agree with the *Arnstein* court's view of the appropriate use of experts?

Do you think that a jury often finds for the defendant once the plaintiff has satisfied the first prong of the test by establishing copying in fact? If not, is this an argument against the bifurcated test?

22. It would, accordingly, be proper to exclude tone-deaf persons from the jury. . . .

3. How does the *Arnstein* court guard against the risk of finding the defendant liable for taking only that which is unprotected? Is the jury to compare only the protected elements the defendant took with the protected elements in plaintiff's work? Is "whether defendant took from plaintiff's works so much of what is pleasing to the ears of lay listeners" the appropriate comparison?

4. Would Judge Hand have approved the denial of defendant's motion for summary judgment in *Arnstein*? Under *Arnstein*'s rule, how likely is it that a copyright infringement case in the Second Circuit will be disposed of on summary judgment? Keep in mind that *Arnstein* was decided prior to major Supreme Court decisions establishing the modern standard for summary judgment motions. *See Anderson v. Liberty Lobby, Inc.*, 477 U.S. 242 (1986); *Celotex Corp. v. Catrett*, 477 U.S. 317 (1986).

---

b. One Contemporary Approach: The Second Circuit

By now it should be apparent that the test for infringement is less exact than one might expect. In this section and the following section, we focus on more recent cases in the Second and Ninth Circuits. These circuits and their lower courts tend to be leaders in the copyright field because so many important publishing, entertainment, and software companies are located in their jurisdictions. As you read these cases, which apply the test in diverse subject matter settings ranging from illustrations to software, consider whether they are consistent with the classic cases as well as with each other. Think also about exactly what comparison the court should instruct the fact-finder to conduct.

We begin with a group of cases arising in the Second Circuit.

Steinberg v. Columbia Pictures Industries, Inc.
663 F. Supp. 706 (S.D.N.Y. 1987)

STANTON, J.: In these actions for copyright infringement, plaintiff Saul Steinberg is suing the producers, promoters, distributors and advertisers of the movie "Moscow on the Hudson" ("Moscow"). Steinberg is an artist whose fame derives in part from cartoons and illustrations he has drawn for *The New Yorker* magazine. Defendant Columbia Pictures Industries, Inc. (Columbia) is in the business of producing, promoting and distributing motion pictures, including "Moscow." [The other defendants include affiliates of Columbia and newspapers publishing the alleging infringing advertisement.] . . .

Plaintiff alleges that defendants' promotional poster for "Moscow" infringes his copyright on an illustration that he drew for *The New Yorker* and that appeared on the cover of the March 29, 1976 issue of the magazine. . . .

. . . [T]his court . . . grants summary judgment on the issue of copying to plaintiff.

I

. . . Summary judgment is often disfavored in copyright cases, for courts are generally reluctant to make subjective comparisons and determinations. Recently, however, this circuit has "recognized that a court may determine non-infringement as a matter of law on a motion for summary judgment." "When the evidence is so overwhelming that a court would be justified in ordering a directed verdict at trial, it is proper to grant summary judgment."

II

. . . On March 29, 1976, *The New Yorker* published as a cover illustration the work at issue in this suit, widely known as a parochial New Yorker's view of the world. The magazine registered this illustration with the United States Copyright Office and subsequently assigned the copyright to Steinberg. . . .

Defendants' illustration was created to advertise the movie "Moscow on the Hudson," which recounts the adventures of a Muscovite who defects in New York. In designing this illustration, Columbia's executive art director, Kevin Nolan, has admitted that he specifically referred to Steinberg's poster, and indeed, that he purchased it and hung it, among others, in his office. Furthermore, Nolan explicitly directed the outside artist whom he retained to execute his design, Craig Nelson, to use Steinberg's poster to achieve a more recognizably New York look. Indeed, Nelson acknowledged having used the facade of one particular edifice, at Nolan's suggestion that it would render his drawing more "New York-ish." While the two buildings are not identical, they are so similar that it is impossible, especially in view of the artist's testimony, not to find that defendants' impermissibly copied plaintiff's.[1] . . .

III

. . . Defendants' access to plaintiff's illustration is established beyond peradventure. Therefore, the sole issue remaining with respect to liability is whether there is such substantial similarity between the copyrighted and accused works as to establish a violation of plaintiff's copyright. The central issue of "substantial similarity," which can be considered a close question of fact, may also validly be decided as a question of law.

The definition of "substantial similarity" in this circuit is "whether an average lay observer would recognize the alleged copy as having been appropriated from the copyrighted work." . . .

There is no dispute that defendants cannot be held liable for using the *idea* of a map of the world from an egocentrically myopic perspective. . . .

Even at first glance, one can see the striking stylistic relationship between the posters, and since style is one ingredient of "expression," this relationship is significant. Defendants' illustration was executed in the sketchy, whimsical style that has become one of Steinberg's hallmarks. Both illustrations represent a bird's eye view across the edge of Manhattan and a river bordering New York City to the world beyond. Both depict approximately four city blocks in detail and become increasingly minimalist as the design recedes into the background. Both use the device of a narrow band of blue wash across the top of the poster to represent the sky, and both delineate the horizon with a band of primary red.[3]

The strongest similarity is evident in the rendering of the New York City blocks. Both artists chose a vantage point that looks directly down a wide two-way cross street that intersects two avenues before reaching a river. Despite defendants' protestations, this is not an inevitable way of depicting blocks in a city with a grid-like street system, particularly since

---

1. Nolan claimed also to have been inspired by some of the posters that were inspired by Steinberg's; such secondary inspiration, however, is irrelevant to whether or not the "Moscow" poster infringes plaintiff's copyright by having impermissibly copied it.

3. Defendants claim that since this use of thin bands of primary colors is a traditional Japanese technique, their adoption of it cannot infringe Steinberg's copyright. This argument ignores the principle that while "[o]thers are free to copy the original . . . [t]hey are not free to copy the copy." . . .

Original Artwork by Saul Steinberg, *View of the World from 9th Avenue.* © 1976
The Saul Steinberg Foundation/Artists Rights Society (ARS), New York. Cover reprinted
with permission of *The New Yorker* magazine. All rights reserved.

"Moscow on the Hudson" Poster

most New York City cross streets are one-way. Since even a photograph may be copyrighted because "no photograph, however simple, can be unaffected by the personal influence of the author," *Time Inc. v. Bernard Geis Assoc.*, 293 F. Supp. 130, 141 (S.D.N.Y. 1968), *quoting Bleistein, supra,* one can hardly gainsay the right of an artist to protect his choice of perspective and lay-out in a drawing, especially in conjunction with the overall concept and individual details. Indeed, the fact that defendants changed the names of the streets while retaining the same graphic depiction weakens their case: had they intended their illustration realistically to depict the streets labeled on the poster, their four city blocks would not so closely resemble plaintiff's four city blocks. Moreover, their argument that they intended the jumble of streets and landmarks and buildings to symbolize their Muscovite protagonist's confusion in a new city does not detract from the strong similarity between their poster and Steinberg's.

While not all of the details are identical, many of them could be mistaken for one another; for example, the depiction of the water towers, and the cars, and the red sign above a parking lot, and even many of the individual buildings. The shapes, windows, and configurations of various edifices are substantially similar. The ornaments, facades and details of Steinberg's buildings appear in defendants', although occasionally at other locations. In this context, it is significant that Steinberg did not depict any buildings actually erected in New York; rather, he was inspired by the general appearance of the structures on the West Side of Manhattan to create his own New York-ish structures. Thus, the similarity between the buildings depicted in the "Moscow" and Steinberg posters cannot be explained by an assertion that the artists happened to choose the same buildings to draw. The close similarity can be explained only by the defendants' artist having copied the plaintiff's work. Similarly, the locations and size, the errors and anomalies of Steinberg's shadows and streetlight, are meticulously imitated.

In addition, the Columbia artist's use of the childlike, spiky block print that has become one of Steinberg's hallmarks to letter the names of the streets in the "Moscow" poster can be explained only as copying. There is no inherent justification for using this style of lettering to label New York City streets as it is associated with New York only through Steinberg's poster.

While defendants' poster shows the city of Moscow on the horizon in far greater detail than anything is depicted in the background of plaintiff's illustration, this fact alone cannot alter the conclusion. "Substantial similarity" does not require identity, and "duplication or near identity is not necessary to establish infringement." Neither the depiction of Moscow, nor the eastward perspective, nor the presence of randomly scattered New York City landmarks in defendants' poster suffices to eliminate the substantial similarity between the posters. As Judge Learned Hand wrote, "no plagiarist can excuse the wrong by showing how much of his work he did not pirate."

Defendants argue that their poster could not infringe plaintiff's copyright because only a small proportion of its design could possibly be considered similar. This argument is both factually and legally without merit. "[A] copyright infringement may occur by reason of a substantial similarity that involves only a small portion of each work." Moreover, this case involves the entire protected work and an iconographically, as well as proportionately, significant portion of the allegedly infringing work.

The process by which defendants' poster was created also undermines this argument. The "map," that is, the portion about which plaintiff is complaining, was designed separately from the rest of the poster. The likenesses of the three main characters, which were copied from a photograph, and the blocks of text were superimposed on the completed map.

I also reject defendants' argument that any similarities between the works are unprotectible *scenes a faire*, or "incidents, characters or settings which, as a practical matter, are indispensable or standard in the treatment of a given topic." It is undeniable that a drawing of New York City blocks could be expected to include buildings, pedestrians, vehicles, lampposts and water towers. Plaintiff, however, does not complain of defendants' mere use of these elements in their poster; rather, his complaint is that defendants copied his *expression* of those elements of a street scene.

While evidence of independent creation by the defendants would rebut plaintiff's prima facie case, "the absence of any countervailing evidence of creation independent of the copyrighted source may well render clearly erroneous a finding that there was not copying."

Moreover, it is generally recognized that ". . . since a very high degree of similarity is required in order to dispense with proof of access, it must logically follow that where proof of access is offered, the required degree of similarity may be somewhat less than would be necessary in the absence of such proof." As defendants have conceded access to plaintiff's copyrighted illustration, a somewhat lesser degree of similarity suffices to establish a copyright infringement than might otherwise be required. Here, however, the demonstrable similarities are such that proof of access, although in fact conceded, is almost unnecessary. . . .

≡ *Boisson v. Banian, Ltd.*
≡ *273 F.3d 262 (2d Cir. 2001)*

CARDAMONE, J.: . . . [P]laintiff [Judi Boisson] . . . designed and produced two alphabet quilts entitled "School Days I" and "School Days II." . . . [E]ach consists of square blocks containing the capital letters of the alphabet, displayed in order. The blocks are set in horizontal rows and vertical columns, with the last row filled by blocks containing various pictures or icons. The letters and blocks are made up of different colors, set off by a white border and colored edging. . . .

Defendant Vijay Rao is the president and sole shareholder of defendant Banian Ltd. . . . [H]e imported from India each of the three alphabet quilts at issue in this case[:] . . . "ABC Green Version I," . . . "ABC Green Version II" [and] "ABC Navy". . . .

[Boisson and her wholly owned company, American Country Quilts and Linens, Inc., sued Rao and Banian, alleging that the defendants had infringed the plaintiffs' copyrights in the two School Days quilts. Following a bench trial, the trial court denied the claims, ruling that Banian's quilts were not substantially similar to plaintiffs'. The court of appeals noted that the defendants had conceded the validity of the plaintiffs' copyrights and did not dispute the district court's finding of copying in fact. It then engaged in a lengthy discussion of what elements of plaintiffs' quilts were original and therefore protected by copyright, using the clearly erroneous standard to assess the district court's findings. The court found that although the alphabet itself is not copyrightable, the plaintiffs' layout was. Additionally, it held that the choice of color in combination with other creative elements can be copyrightable.]

. . . We review *de novo* the district court's determination with respect to substantial similarity because credibility is not at stake and all that is required is a visual comparison of the products — a task we may perform as well as the district court.

Generally, an allegedly infringing work is considered substantially similar to a copyrighted work if "the ordinary observer, unless he set out to detect the disparities, would be disposed to overlook them, and regard their aesthetic appeal as the same." *Folio Impressions*, [*Inc. v. Byer Cal.,*] 937 F.2d [759] at 765 [(2d Cir. 1991)]. Yet in *Folio Impressions*, the evidence at trial showed the plaintiff designer had copied the background for its fabric from a public domain document and "contributed nothing, not even a trivial variation." 937 F.2d at 764. Thus, part of the plaintiff's fabric was not original and therefore not protectible. We articulated the need for an ordinary observer to be "more discerning" in such circumstances.

[T]he ordinary observer would compare the finished product that the fabric designs were intended to grace (women's dresses), and would be inclined to view the entire dress — consisting of protectible and unprotectible elements — as one whole. Here, since only some of the design enjoys copyright protection, the observer's inspection must be more discerning.

Id. at 765-66. Shortly after *Folio Impressions* was decided, we reiterated that a "more refined analysis" is required where a plaintiff's work is not "wholly original," but rather incorporates elements from the public domain. *Key Publ'ns, Inc. v. Chinatown Today Publ'g Enters., Inc.*, 945 F.2d 509, 514 (2d Cir. 1991). In these instances, "[w]hat must be shown is substantial similarity between those elements, and only those elements, that provide copyrightability to the allegedly infringed compilation." *Id.* . . . In the case at hand, because the alphabet was taken from the public domain, we must apply the "more discerning" ordinary observer test.

In applying this test, a court is not to dissect the works at issue into separate components and compare only the copyrightable elements. To do so would be to take the "more discerning" test to an extreme, which would result in almost nothing being copyrightable because original works broken down into their composite parts would usually be little more than basic unprotectible elements like letters, colors and symbols. This outcome — affording no copyright protection to an original compilation of unprotectible elements — would be contrary to the Supreme Court's holding in *Feist Publications [Inc. v. Rural Tel. Serv. Co.,* 499 U.S. 340 (1991)].

Although the "more discerning" test has not always been identified by name in our case law, we have nevertheless always recognized that the test is guided by comparing the "total concept and feel" of the contested works. For example, in *Streetwise Maps [Inc. v. Vandam, Inc.],* 159 F.3d [739] at 748 [(2d Cir. 1998)], we found no infringement — not because the plaintiff's map consisted of public domain facts such as street locations, landmasses, bodies of water and landmarks, as well as color — but rather "because the total concept and overall feel created by the two works may not be said to be substantially similar." . . .

. . . [W]hen evaluating claims of infringement involving literary works, we have noted that while liability would result only if the protectible elements were substantially similar, our examination would encompass "the similarities in such aspects as the total concept and feel, theme, characters, plot, sequence, pace, and setting of the [plaintiff's] books and the [defendants'] works." *Williams [v. Crichton],* 84 F.3d [581] at 588 [(2d Cir. 1996)]; . . .

In the present case, while use of the alphabet may not provide a basis for infringement, we must compare defendants' quilts and plaintiffs' quilts on the basis of the arrangement and shapes of the letters, the colors chosen to represent the letters and other parts of the quilts, the quilting patterns, the particular icons chosen and their placement. Our analysis of the "total concept and feel" of these works should be instructed by common sense. It is at this juncture that we part from the district court, which never considered the arrangement of the whole when comparing plaintiffs' works with defendants'. With this concept in mind, we pass to a comparison of the quilts at issue.

. . . Comparison

. . . "School Days I" consists of six horizontal rows, each row containing five blocks, with a capital letter or an icon in each block. The groupings of blocks in each row are as follows: A-E; F-J; K-O; P-T; U-Y; and Z with four icons following in the last row. The four icons are a cat, a house, a single-starred American flag and a basket. "ABC Green Version I" displays the capital letters of the alphabet in the same formation. The four icons in the last row are a cow jumping over the moon, a sailboat, a bear and a star. "ABC Green Version II" is identical to "ABC Green Version I," except that the picture of the cow jumping over the moon is somewhat altered, the bear is replaced by a teddy bear sitting up and wearing a vest that looks like a single-starred American flag, and the star in the last block is represented in a different color.

All three quilts use a combination of contrasting solid color fabrics or a combination of solid and polka-dotted fabrics to represent the blocks and letters. The following similarities are observed in plaintiffs' and defendants' designs: "A" is dark blue on a light blue background; "B" is red on a white background; "D" is made of polka-dot fabric on a light blue background; "F" on plaintiffs' "School Days I" is white on a pink background, while the "F" on defendants' "ABC Green" versions is pink on a white background; "G" has a green background; "H" and "L" are each a shade of blue on a white background; "M" in each quilt is a shade of yellow on a white background; "N" is green on a white background; "O" is blue on a polka-dot background; "P" is polka-dot fabric on a yellow background; "Q" is brown on a light background; "R" is pink on a gray/purple background, "S" is white on a red background; "T" is blue on a white background; "U" is gray on a white background; "V" is white on a gray background; "W" is pink on a white background; "X" is purple in all quilts, albeit in different shades, on a light background; "Y" is a shade of yellow on the same light background; and "Z" is navy blue or black, in all the quilts.

Boisson also testified that defendants utilized the same unique shapes as she had given to the letters "J," "M," "N," "P," "R" and "W." With respect to the quilting patterns, "School Days I" and the "ABC Green" versions feature diamond-shaped quilting within the blocks and a "wavy" pattern in the plain white border that surrounds the blocks. The quilts are also edged with a 3/8″ green binding.

From this enormous amount of sameness, we think defendants' quilts sufficiently similar to plaintiffs' design as to demonstrate illegal copying. In particular, the overwhelming similarities in color choices lean toward a finding of infringement. Although the icons chosen for each quilt are different and defendants added a green rectangular border around their rows of blocks, these differences are not sufficient to cause even the "more discerning" observer to think the quilts are other than substantially similar insofar as the protectible elements of plaintiffs' quilt are concerned. . . . Moreover, the substitution in "ABC Green Version II" of the teddy bear wearing a flag vest as the third icon causes this version of defendants' quilt to look even more like plaintiffs' quilt that uses a single-starred American flag as its third icon. Consequently, both of defendants' "ABC Green" quilts infringed plaintiffs' copyright on its "School Days I" quilt. . . .

[The court further held that Banian's "ABC Navy" quilt did not infringe "School Days I" because the icons and colors were different. It held that the "ABC Green" quilts did not infringe "School Days II" because the "total concept and feel" were different: The letters were arranged differently and the colors (red, white, and blue in plaintiffs' quilt versus green in the defendants') did not create the same impression.]

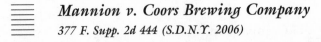

Mannion v. Coors Brewing Company
377 F. Supp. 2d 444 (S.D.N.Y. 2006)

[Review the excerpt from the Mannion case, pages 77-81 *supra*, paying special attention to the images reproduced there. Recall that the court identified three different ways originality can be expressed in photographs. In the excerpt below, the court considers how to compare photographs to determine if they are substantially similar.]

Kaplan J.: . . .

The Idea/Expression Difficulty

Notwithstanding the originality of the Garnett Photograph, the defendants argue that the Coors Billboard does not infringe because the two, insofar as they are similar, share only "the generalized idea and concept of a young African American man wearing a white T-shirt and a large amount of jewelry."

It is true that an axiom of copyright law is that copyright does not protect "ideas," only their expression. Furthermore, when "a given idea is inseparably tied to a particular expression" so that "there is a 'merger' of idea and expression," courts may deny protection to the expression in order to avoid conferring a monopoly on the idea to which it inseparably is tied. But the defendants' reliance on these principles is misplaced.

The "idea" (if one wants to call it that) postulated by the defendants does not even come close to accounting for all the similarities between the two works, which extend at least to angle, pose, background, composition, and lighting. It is possible to imagine any number of depictions of a black man wearing a white T-shirt and "bling bling" that look nothing like either of the photographs at issue here.

This alone is sufficient to dispose of the defendants' contention that Mannion's claims must be rejected because he seeks to protect an idea rather than its expression. But the argument reveals an analytical difficulty in the case law about which more ought to be said. One of the main cases upon which the defendants rely is *Kaplan v. Stock Market Photo Agency, Inc.*, [133 F. Supp. 2d 317 (S.D.N.Y. 2001)] in which two remarkably similar photographs of a businessman's shoes and lower legs, taken from the top of a tall building looking down on a street below . . . were held to be not substantially similar as a matter of law because all of the similarities flowed only from an unprotected idea rather than from the expression of that idea.

But what is the "idea" of Kaplan's photograph? Is it (1) a businessman contemplating suicide by jumping from a building, (2) a businessman contemplating suicide by jumping from a building, seen from the vantage point of the businessman, with his shoes set against the street far below, or perhaps something more general, such as (3) a sense of desperation produced by urban professional life?

If the "idea" is (1) or, for that matter, (3), then the similarities between the two photographs flow from something much more than that idea, for it would have been possible to convey (1) (and (3)) in any number of ways that bear no obvious similarities to Kaplan's photograph. (Examples are a businessman atop a building seen from below, or the entire figure of the businessman, rather than just his shoes or pants, seen from above.) If, on the other hand, the "idea" is (2), then the two works could be said to owe much of their similarity to a shared idea. . . .

The idea/expression distinction arose in the context of literary copyright. . . . And it makes sense to speak of the idea conveyed by a literary work and to distinguish it from its expression. To take a clear example, two different authors each can describe, with very different words, the theory of special relativity. The words will be protected as expression. The theory is a set of unprotected ideas.

In the visual arts, the distinction breaks down. For one thing, it is impossible in most cases to speak of the particular "idea" captured, embodied, or conveyed by a work of art because every observer will have a different interpretation.[80] Furthermore, it is not clear that there is any

---

80. In cases dealing with toys or products that have both functional and design aspects, courts sometimes use "idea" to refer to a gimmick embodied in the product. . . . This case does not concern any kind of gimmick, and the Court ventures no opinion about the applicability of the idea/expression dichotomy to any product that embodies a gimmick, including toys or other objects that combine function and design.

real distinction between the idea in a work of art and its expression. An artist's idea, among other things, is to depict a particular subject in a particular way. As a demonstration, a number of cases from this Circuit have observed that a photographer's "conception" of his subject is copyrightable. By "conception," the courts must mean originality in the rendition, timing, and creation of the subject — for that is what copyright protects in photography. But the word "conception" is a cousin of "concept," and both are akin to "idea." In other words, those elements of a photograph, or indeed, any work of visual art protected by copyright, could just as easily be labeled "idea" as "expression." . . .

. . . [A]t what point do the similarities between two photographs become sufficiently general that there will be no infringement even though actual copying has occurred? . . . [T]his question is precisely the same, although phrased in the opposite way, as one that must be addressed in all infringement cases, namely whether two works are substantially similar with respect to their protected elements. It is nonsensical to speak of one photograph being substantially similar to another in the rendition and creation of the subject but somehow not infringing because of a shared idea. Conversely, if the two photographs are not substantially similar in the rendition and creation of the subject, the distinction between idea and expression will be irrelevant because there can be no infringement. The idea/expression distinction in photography, and probably the other visual arts, thus achieves nothing beyond what other, clearer copyright principles already accomplish. . . .

Comparison of the Coors Billboard and the Garnett Photograph

The next step is to determine whether a trier of fact could or must find the Coors Billboard substantially similar to the Garnett Photograph with respect to their protected elements.

Substantial similarity ultimately is a question of fact. "The standard test for substantial similarity between two items is whether an 'ordinary observer, unless he set out to detect the disparities, would be disposed to overlook them, and regard [the] aesthetic appeal as the same.'" The Second Circuit sometimes has applied a "more discerning observer" test when a work contains both protectible and unprotectible elements. The test "requires the court to eliminate the unprotectible elements from its consideration and to ask whether the protectible elements, standing alone, are substantially similar." The Circuit, however, is ambivalent about this test. In several cases dealing with fabric and garment designs, the Circuit has cautioned that:

> "a court is not to dissect the works at issue into separate components and compare only the copyrightable elements. . . . To do so would be to take the 'more discerning' test to an extreme, which would result in almost nothing being copyrightable because original works broken down into their composite parts would usually be little more than basic unprotectible elements like letters, colors and symbols." [Boisson, 273 F.3d at 272.]

Dissecting the works into separate components and comparing only the copyrightable elements, however, appears to be exactly what the "more discerning observer" test calls for.

The Circuit indirectly spoke to this tension in the recent case of *Tufenkian Import/Export Ventures, Inc. v. Einstein Moomjy, Inc.*[, 338 F.3d 127 (2d Cir. 2003)]. There the trial court purported to use the more discerning observer test but nonetheless compared the "total-concept-and-feel" of carpet designs. . . .

In light of these precedents, the Court concludes that it is immaterial whether the ordinary or more discerning observer test is used here because the inquiries would be identical. The cases agree that the relevant comparison is between the protectible elements in the Garnett Photograph and the Coors Billboard, but that those elements are not to be viewed in isolation.

The Garnett Photograph is protectible to the extent of its originality in the rendition and creation of the subject. Key elements of the Garnett Photograph that are in the public domain — such as Kevin Garnett's likeness — are not replicated in the Coors Billboard. Other elements arguably in the public domain — such as the existence of a cloudy sky, Garnett's pose, his white T-shirt, and his specific jewelry — may not be copyrightable in and of themselves, but their existence and arrangement in this photograph indisputably contribute to its originality. Thus the fact that the Garnett Photograph includes certain elements that would not be copyrightable in isolation does not affect the nature of the comparison. The question is whether the aesthetic appeal of the two images is the same.

The two photographs share a similar composition and angle. The lighting is similar, and both use a cloudy sky as backdrop. The subjects are wearing similar clothing and similar jewelry arranged in a similar way. The defendants, in other words, appear to have recreated much of the subject that Mannion had created and then, through imitation of angle and lighting, rendered it in a similar way. The similarities here thus relate to the Garnett Photograph's originality in the rendition and the creation of the subject and therefore to its protected elements.

There of course are differences between the two works. The similarity analysis may take into account some, but not all, of these. It long has been the law that "no plagiarist can excuse the wrong by showing how much of his work he did not pirate." [*Id.* at 132-33 (quoting *Sheldon v. Metro-Goldwyn Pictures Corp.*, 81 F.2d 49, 56 (2d Cir. 1936)) (internal quotation marks omitted)]. Thus the addition of the words "Iced Out" and a can of Coors Light beer may not enter into the similarity analysis.

Other differences, however, are in the nature of changes rather than additions. One image is black and white and dark, the other is in color and bright. One is the mirror image of the other. One depicts only an unidentified man's torso, the other the top three-fourths of Kevin Garnett's body. The jewelry is not identical. One T-shirt appears to fit more tightly than the other. These changes may enter the analysis because "[i]f the points of dissimilarity not only exceed the points of similarity, but indicate that the remaining points of similarity are, within the context of plaintiff's work, of minimal importance . . . then no infringement results."

The parties have catalogued at length and in depth the similarities and differences between these works. In the last analysis, a reasonable jury could find substantial similarity either present or absent. . . .

NOTES AND QUESTIONS

1. Are "style" and "choice of perspective and lay-out" properly considered aspects of protectible expression? Before answering, consider whether Impressionism, for example, would have been regarded as a style when it was first developed. If style is properly copyrightable, can imitating one's own style constitute copyright infringement? For example, assume an artist paints a canvas that depicts the Brooklyn Bridge. He paints the bridge in the Cubist style. He then assigns ownership of the copyright in the painting to another. Can he paint the Brooklyn Bridge again in the same style without incurring liability for copyright infringement? Can he paint other bridges in that style?

Is "rendition," as described in *Mannion*, the same as *Steinberg*'s "style" and "choice of perspective and lay-out," or is it different?

2. Do you agree with the *Mannion* court's conclusion that "other, clearer copyright principles" render the idea/expression distinction superfluous in cases involving visual artworks?

What are those principles? How does the court separate protectible and unprotectible elements of the Garnett photograph? How should a jury do this?

3. What is the purpose of *Boisson*'s "more discerning observer" test? Do you think it will achieve its purpose? Do you agree with the *Mannion* court's observation that the Second Circuit seems "ambivalent" about the test? Can you think of any rationale for employing both a "more discerning observer" test and the "total concept and feel" test as the *Boisson* court does? What do you make of the *Boisson* court's reference to *Feist*? When a plaintiff asserts infringement of a copyright in a pictorial, graphic, or sculptural work, is a compilation analysis appropriate?

Should the *Mannion* and *Steinberg* courts have applied a "more discerning observer" test instead? Would *Boisson*'s test have changed the result in either case? Would it have changed the result in *Nichols* or *Arnstein*?

4. The *Boisson* court describes the ordinary observer test as focusing on aesthetic appeal: "Generally, an allegedly infringing work is considered substantially similar to a copyrighted work if the 'ordinary observer, unless he set out to detect the disparities, would be disposed to overlook them, and regard [the] aesthetic appeal [of the two works] as the same.'" *Boisson*, 273 F.3d at 272. Do you think the earlier *Arnstein* court would have agreed with this definition? Would Judge Hand have agreed with this definition? Does either *Nichols* or *Arnstein* use or endorse a "total concept and feel" test? For a more recent decision involving literary works that considers total concept and feel, see *Williams v. Crichton*, 84 F.3d 581 (2d Cir. 1996) (holding that defendants' Jurassic Park stories did not infringe earlier Dinosaur World books).

5. Consider all of the decisions from courts in the Second Circuit that you have read: *Nichols, Arnstein, Steinberg, Boisson,* and *Mannion.* Are the decisions consistent? Can differences be accounted for by the different subject matters involved: a literary work in *Nichols,* music in *Arnstein,* and pictorial, graphic, or sculptural works in *Steinberg, Boisson,* and *Mannion*?

6. In *Boisson*, the Second Circuit reversed findings of no improper appropriation made following a bench trial, made its own assessment of plaintiffs' and defendants' works, and directed that a judgment of infringement be issued. In light of what you have learned about the standard of review in copyright cases, was this appropriate? Did the court essentially conclude that the plaintiffs were entitled to judgment as a matter of law? In *Steinberg*, the district court did so conclude. Was that decision proper? Under the test articulated in *Boisson*, how likely is it that a copyright infringement case in the Second Circuit will result in summary judgment for the plaintiff? What about summary judgment for the defendant?

7. Review the final paragraph of the *Steinberg* opinion. Should courts require a "somewhat lesser degree of similarity" when the defendant admits using the plaintiff's work for "inspiration"? Is the court confusing the two kinds of similarity at issue in a copyright infringement case?

8. Should there be both qualitative and quantitative aspects to substantial similarity? In *Castle Rock Entertainment, Inc. v. Carol Publishing Group, Inc.*, the Second Circuit observed: "'[S]ubstantial similarity' requires that the copying [be] quantitatively and qualitatively sufficient to support the legal conclusion that infringement (actionable copying) has occurred." 150 F.3d 132, 138 (2d Cir. 1998). How then do you think courts could have found the following to be infringing: (a) copying 300 words from a 200,000-word manuscript (*Harper & Row, Publishers, Inc. v. The Nation Enters.*, 471 U.S. 539 (1985), *see* Chapter 7, pages 535-40 *infra*), and (b) copying three sentences of a scientific treatise (*Henry Holt & Co. v. Liggett & Myers Tobacco Co.*, 23 F. Supp. 302 (E.D. Pa. 1938)). *See* Paul Goldstein, 2 Copyright §7.3.1, at 7:25 (2d ed. Supp. 2001) (collecting these cases).

c. Another Contemporary Approach: The Ninth Circuit

Courts in the Ninth Circuit take a somewhat different approach to the problem of substantial similarity. Consider the following group of cases.

Sid & Marty Krofft Television Productions, Inc. v. McDonald's Corp.
562 F.2d 1157 (9th Cir. 1977)

[Sid and Marty Krofft had created a children's TV show called H.R. Pufnstuf that featured a fantasy land and costumed characters. Needham, Harper & Steers, Inc. (Needham) designed an ad campaign for the McDonald's fast food chain that featured fanciful costumed characters inhabiting McDonaldland. The lower court held that the McDonaldland television commercials infringed the plaintiffs' copyright in the H.R. Pufnstuf television show. The court's judgment was based on the jury's answers to special interrogatories.]

CARTER, J.: This is a copyright infringement action . . . alleg[ing] inter alia, that the McDonald land advertising campaign infringed the copyrighted H.R. Pufnstuf television episodes as well as various copyrighted articles of Pufnstuf merchandise. . . .

. . . The jurors were shown for their consideration on the question of infringement: (1) two H.R. Pufnstuf television episodes; (2) various items of H.R. Pufnstuf merchandise, such as toys, games, and comic books; (3) several 30 and 60 second McDonaldland television commercials; and (4) various items of McDonaldland merchandise distributed by McDonald's, such as toys and puzzles. . . .

The real task in a copyright infringement action . . . is to determine whether there has been copying of the expression of an idea rather than just the idea itself. "[N]o one infringes, unless he descends so far into what is concrete [in a work] as to invade . . . [its] expression." Only this expression may be protected and only it may be infringed.

The difficulty comes in attempting to distill the unprotected idea from the protected expression. No court or commentator . . . has been able to improve upon Judge Learned Hand's famous "abstractions test" articulated in *Nichols v. Universal Pictures Corporation.* . . .

The test for infringement . . . has been given a new dimension. There must be ownership of the copyright and access to the copyrighted work. But there also must be substantial similarity not only of the general ideas but of the expressions of those ideas as well. Thus two steps in the analytic process are implied by the requirement of substantial similarity.

The determination of whether there is substantial similarity in ideas may often be a simple one. [For] example . . . the idea . . . embodied [in a plaster statue of a nude] is a simple one — a plaster recreation of a nude human figure. A statue of a horse or a painting of a nude would not embody this idea and therefore could not infringe. The test for similarity of ideas is still a factual one, to be decided by the trier of fact.

We shall call this the "extrinsic test." It is extrinsic because it depends not on the responses of the trier of fact, but on specific criteria which can be listed and analyzed. Such criteria include the type of artwork involved, the materials used, the subject matter, and the setting for the subject. Since it is an extrinsic test, analytic dissection and expert testimony are appropriate. Moreover, this question may often be decided as a matter of law.

The determination of when there is substantial similarity between the forms of expression is necessarily more subtle and complex. As Judge Hand candidly observed, "Obviously, no principle can be stated as to when an imitator has gone beyond copying the 'idea,' and has borrowed its 'expression.' Decisions must therefore inevitably be ad hoc." If there is substantial similarity in ideas, then the trier of fact must decide whether there is substantial similarity in the expressions of the ideas so as to constitute infringement.

The test to be applied in determining whether there is substantial similarity in expressions shall be labeled an intrinsic one — depending on the response of the ordinary reasonable person. . . . It is intrinsic because it does not depend on the type of external criteria and analysis which marks the extrinsic test. As this court stated in *Twentieth Century-Fox Film Corp. v. Stonesifer*, 140 F.2d 579, 582 (9th Cir. 1944):

> "The two works involved in this appeal should be considered and tested, not hypercritically or with meticulous scrutiny, but by the observations and impressions of the average reasonable reader and spectator."

Because this is an intrinsic test, analytic dissection and expert testimony are not appropriate. . . .

The Tests Applied

In the context of this case, the distinction between these tests is important. Defendants do not dispute the fact that they copied the idea of plaintiffs' Pufnstuf television series — basically a fantasyland filled with diverse and fanciful characters in action. They argue, however, that the expressions of this idea are too dissimilar for there to be an infringement. They come to this conclusion by dissecting the constituent parts of the Pufnstuf series — characters, setting, and plot — and pointing out the dissimilarities between these parts and those of the McDonaldland commercials.

This approach ignores the idea-expression dichotomy alluded to in *Arnstein* and analyzed today. Defendants attempt to apply an extrinsic test by the listing of dissimilarities in determining whether the expression they used was substantially similar to the expression used by plaintiffs. That extrinsic test is inappropriate; an intrinsic test must here be used. . . . Analytic dissection, as defendants have done, is therefore improper. . . .

The present case demands an even more intrinsic determination because both plaintiffs' and defendants' works are directed to an audience of children. This raises the particular factual issue of the impact of the respective works upon the minds and imaginations of young people. As the court said in *Ideal Toy Corp. v. Fab-Lu Ltd.*, 261 F. Supp. 238, 241-42 (S.D.N.Y. 1966), *aff'd*, 360 F.2d 1021 (2 Cir. 1966):

> "In applying the test of the average lay observer, (children) are not to be excluded — indeed they are the 'far-flung faithful . . . audience.' The television advertising campaign of plaintiff was directed toward acquainting these youngsters with . . . its [product]. . . . It is the youngsters who, on the basis of this impression, go to the stores with their parents or at home make their wishes known for the [products] they desire after television has made its impact upon them. In their enthusiasm to acquire . . . the [products] they certainly are not bent upon 'detecting disparities' or even readily observing upon inspection [ ] fine details. . . ." . . .

The H. R. Pufnstuf series became the most popular children's show on Saturday morning television. This success led several manufacturers of children's goods to use the Pufnstuf characters. It is not surprising, then, that McDonald's hoped to duplicate this peculiar appeal to children in its commercials. It was in recognition of the subjective and unpredictable nature of children's responses that defendants opted to recreate the H. R. Pufnstuf format rather than use an original and unproven approach.

Defendants would have this court ignore that intrinsic quality which they recognized to embark on an extrinsic analysis of the two works. For example, in discussing the principal characters — Pufnstuf and Mayor McCheese — defendants point out:

> " 'Pufnstuf' wears what can only be described as a yellow and green dragon suit with a blue cummerbund from which hangs a medal which says 'mayor'. 'McCheese' wears a version of pink formal dress 'tails' with knicker trousers. He has a typical diplomat's sash on which is written 'mayor', the 'M' consisting of the McDonald's trademark of an 'M' made of golden arches."

So not only do defendants remove the characters from the setting, but dissect further to analyze the clothing, colors, features, and mannerisms of each character. We do not believe that the ordinary reasonable person, let alone a child, viewing these works will even notice that Pufnstuf is wearing a cummerbund while Mayor McCheese is wearing a diplomat's sash. Duplication or near identity is not necessary to establish infringement. . . .

We have viewed representative samples of both the H. R. Pufnstuf show and McDonaldland commercials. It is clear to us that defendants' works are substantially similar to plaintiffs'. They have captured the "total concept and feel" of the Pufnstuf show. *Roth Greeting Cards v. United Card Co.*, 429 F.2d 1106, 1110 (9th Cir. 1970). We would so conclude even if we were sitting as the triers of fact. There is no doubt that the findings of the jury in this case are not clearly erroneous. . . .

NOTES AND QUESTIONS

1. How does *Krofft* compare to *Arnstein*? Is *Krofft*'s "extrinsic" test, which allows for dissection and expert testimony, the same as *Arnstein*'s test for copying in fact? Under *Krofft*'s approach, similarity of "general ideas" seems intended to serve as a preliminary "filter" in the improper appropriation analysis. Does that approach make sense? Why, or why not? Is a similarity-of-general-ideas test likely to eliminate a meaningful number of cases of alleged infringement? In the end, do *Krofft* and *Arnstein* use the same test for improper appropriation of copyrightable expression?

2. The *Krofft* court also refers to the "total concept and feel" test developed by the Ninth Circuit in *Roth Greeting Cards*, Chapter 2, pages 112-13 *supra*, to evaluate the similarity of compilations of otherwise unprotectible elements. Is this simply another way of restating the "intrinsic" ordinary observer test? Is there a significant difference between assessing similarity of ideas and assessing similarity of concepts? Is saying that two works are similar in "feel" a good way of describing similarity of protected expression?

At some level, all works can be viewed as "compilations" of their constituent elements. Copyright law sometimes strains to provide appropriate protection for the compiler without extending protection to mere ideas. Should the degree of similarity required to prove infringement be higher or lower in the case of a "total concept and feel" analysis?

3. Do you think juries using the *Krofft* test are equipped to guard against the risk of holding a defendant liable when he has taken only unprotected material? How would you frame the issue for the fact-finder to lessen the chances of finding liability mistakenly? How would you write the jury instructions in *Krofft*?

4. Recall the *Arnstein* court's observation in footnote 22 that it would be appropriate to exclude the tone-deaf from the jury in a case involving musical compositions. To what extent

should the ordinary observer test dictate jury selection? Because children cannot serve on juries, should the parties in *Krofft* have been required to test for wrongful copying using focus groups of seven-year-olds?

Cavalier v. Random House, Inc.
297 F.3d 815 (9th Cir. 2002)

FLETCHER, J.: . . .

A. Background

[The Cavaliers developed children's stories based on a character called] Nicky Moonbeam, an anthropomorphic moon . . .

From 1995 through 1998, the Cavaliers submitted more than 280 pages of material, including their copyrighted works, to Random House and [Children's Television Workshop ("CTW")]. The first submission consisted of two stories — *Nicky Moonbeam: The Man in the Moon* and *Nicky Moonbeam Saves Christmas* — and the design for a "moon night light" to be built directly into the back cover of a "board book." A "board book" is a book with sturdy, thick pages, designed for use by young children. Later submissions in 1996 and 1998 consisted of "pitch materials," which included detailed illustrations, ideas for general story lines and television programs, specific traits of the Nicky Moonbeam characters, and goals for the Nicky Moonbeam stories.

After face-to-face meetings with the Cavaliers regarding their submissions, Random House and CTW rejected their works. Soon thereafter, in February 1999, Random House and CTW jointly published the books *Good Night, Ernie* and *Good Night, Elmo*, . . .

C. Trial Court Proceedings . . .

[The Cavaliers sued Random House and CTW for infringement of their copyrights in the Nicky Moonbeam characters, illustrations, text, and night light.]

The trial court granted Random House and CTW's motion for summary judgment on the following grounds: (1) The Cavaliers' general story lines in which anthropomorphic moon and stars ease children's fears of sleeping in the dark, and the depiction of related scenes and stock characters ("scenes-a-faire"), are not protectible by copyright; [and] (2) *Good Night, Ernie*, [and] *Good Night, Elmo* . . . were not substantially similar to the copyright-protectible material in the Cavaliers' works. . . .

II

. . . Whether a particular work is subject to copyright protection is a mixed question of fact and law subject to de novo review. "Although summary judgment is not highly favored on questions of substantial similarity in copyright cases, summary judgment is appropriate if the court can conclude, after viewing the evidence and drawing inferences in a manner most favorable to the non-moving party, that no reasonable juror could find substantial similarity of ideas and expression. . . . Where reasonable minds could differ on the issue of substantial similarity, however, summary judgment is improper." *Shaw v. Lindheim*, 919 F.2d 1353, 1355 (9th Cir. 1990) (quotation marks and citations omitted).

III

[The court noted that defendants did not dispute ownership or access.] . . . The sole issue before us is whether any of Random House's or CTW's works were substantially similar to the Cavaliers' submissions.

We employ a two-part analysis in this circuit — an extrinsic test and an intrinsic test — to determine whether two works are substantially similar. *Id.* The "extrinsic test" is an objective comparison of specific expressive elements. "[T]he test focuses on articulable similarities between the plot, themes, dialogue, mood, setting, pace, characters, and sequence of events in two works." Although originally cast as a "test for similarity of ideas," *Sid & Marty Krofft Television Prods., Inc. v. McDonald's Corp.*, 562 F.2d 1157, 1164 (9th Cir. 1977), the extrinsic test, now encompassing all objective manifestations of *expression*, no longer fits that description. The "intrinsic test" is a subjective comparison that focuses on "whether the ordinary, reasonable audience" would find the works substantially similar in the "total concept and feel of the works."

A court "must take care to inquire only whether 'the *protectible elements, standing alone, are substantially similar.*' " *Williams v. Crichton*, 84 F.3d 581, 588 (2d Cir. 1996) (emphasis in original) (citation omitted); *accord Apple Computer, Inc. v. Microsoft Corp.*, 35 F.3d 1435, 1442-43 (9th Cir. 1994). Therefore, when applying the extrinsic test, a court must filter out and disregard the non-protectible elements in making its substantial similarity determination. . . .

A. Good Night, Ernie *and* Good Night, Elmo

The Cavaliers allege that the following elements of *Good Night, Ernie* were copied by Random House and CTW from their submissions:

(1) A built-in night light with an "on" button on the inside back cover of a board book, with the light appearing as a moon with eyes, nose, and smiling benevolent expression;
(2) A character looking into the sky, wondering who and what the stars are;
(3) A character interacting with smiling, rosy-faced, bright yellow, five-pointed stars;
(4) A character sitting on a crescent moon;
(5) Smiling, bright yellow, rosy-cheeked, five-pointed stars playing and lounging on the clouds during the day and wearing colorful woolen hats;
(6) A character polishing a star with a cloth;
(7) Smiling, bright yellow, rosy-cheeked, five-pointed stars floating in a child's bedroom, glowing and comforting the child;
(8) Stars trailed by a distinctive "moondust."

The Cavaliers allege that the following elements of *Good Night, Elmo* were copied:

(1) A built-in night light comparable to that in *Good Night, Ernie;*
(2) Moonbeams shining through a window;
(3) A character saying "hop on a moonbeam and take a ride";
(4) A character interacting with smiling, yellow, rosy-cheeked, five-pointed stars trailing sparkling dust and surrounded by other stars.

We first compare the *Good Night* books to the Nicky Moonbeam stories as literary works, taken as a whole. We then compare individual art work from the *Good Night* books to that in the Cavaliers' submissions.

1. Comparison of Literary Works as a Whole

On summary judgment, only the extrinsic test matters for comparison of literary works. If the Cavaliers can show that there is a triable issue of fact under the extrinsic test, the intrinsic test's subjective inquiry must be left to the jury and Random House and CTW's motion for summary judgment must be denied. . . . Conversely, if the Cavaliers cannot show a triable issue of fact under the extrinsic test, Random House and CTW necessarily prevail on summary judgment. A jury could not find copyright infringement because there can be no substantial similarity without evidence under both the extrinsic and intrinsic tests. . . . We now apply the objective factors of the extrinsic test, considering only the protectible material, to determine whether *Good Night, Ernie* and/or *Good Night, Elmo*, taken as a whole, are sufficiently similar to the Cavaliers' works to raise a triable issue of fact.

The Cavaliers' Nicky Moonbeam stories and *Good Night, Elmo* share the general premise of a child, invited by a moon-type character, who takes a journey through the night sky and returns safely to bed to fall asleep. But basic plot ideas, such as this one, are not protected by copyright law. . . .

Otherwise, the actual narratives in *Good Night, Ernie* and *Good Night, Elmo* do not share much in common with the Nicky Moonbeam stories. The Nicky Moonbeam stories (2000-4000 words each) involve relatively elaborate story lines, while the text in the *Good Night* books (roughly 100 words each) describes a simple, discrete group of scenes. The stories do not share any detailed sequence of events. Moreover, although some of the Cavaliers' illustrations appear to depict events in the Nicky Moonbeam stories, the allegedly copied illustrations appear in a different context in the *Good Night* books.

The principal setting in the *Good Night* books is the night sky, which is also prevalent in the Nicky Moonbeam stories. However, this setting naturally and necessarily flows from the basic plot premise of a child's journey through the night sky; therefore, the night sky setting constitutes scenes-a-faire and cannot support a finding of substantial similarity. Furthermore, neither of the *Good Night* books involves the beach or the North Pole, the venues for significant parts of the Nicky Moonbeam stories.

The pace, dialogue, mood, and theme of the *Good Night* books differ markedly from those of the Nicky Moonbeam stories. In the *Good Night* books, the entire night journey is completed in five simple pages. There is no dialogue in *Good Night, Ernie*, and the dialogue in *Good Night, Elmo* is limited to two simple exchanges. The district court correctly characterized their mood as "fun" and "very lighthearted." There is no focused theme or message in either story.

In contrast, the Nicky Moonbeam stories progress more deliberately, with several contemplative scenes developing thematic details. There is extensive dialogue. . . . Although also written for children, the mood in the Nicky Moonbeam stories is more serious and instructional. They contain explicit messages for children. . . .

[T]he main characters in the *Good Night* books are different — Sesame Street Muppets (Ernie and Elmo) rather than Nicky Moonbeam. Although *Good Night, Elmo* features Mr. Moon, he does not share any of the anthropomorphic characteristics of Nicky Moonbeam, except the ability to talk. Moreover, a moon character can be considered a stock character for children's literature, and directly flows from the idea of a journey in the night sky. None of the other characters in the Nicky Moonbeam stories are found in the *Good Night* books.

Random House and CTW contend that even if their *Good Night* books contain some protectible elements, such commonalities would not justify a finding of substantial similarity of the works. . . . We agree. . . . [A] compilation of "random similarities scattered throughout the works" is "inherently subjective and unreliable." Th[is] argument is especially strong here since the alleged similarities are selected from over 280 pages of submissions. Further, "[c]onsideration of the total concept and feel of a work, rather than specific inquiry into plot and character development, is especially appropriate in an infringement action involving children's works[.]" Since the "total concept and feel" of the Cavaliers' stories are, as discussed above, more serious and instructional than defendants' books, a finding of infringement is disfavored in this case. In sum, there is no triable issue of fact on the issue of whether either *Good Night, Ernie* or *Good Night, Elmo* is a substantially similar literary work to the Nicky Moonbeam stories under the extrinsic test.

2. Comparison of Individual Art Works

Even though we hold that the *Good Night* stories, taken as a whole, do not infringe the Cavaliers' copyright, the question remains whether protected parts of the Cavaliers' works have been copied. . . . We therefore consider whether there exists a triable issue of substantial similarity between any of the isolated art work, as freestanding work divorced from the stories. Indeed, almost all of the allegedly copied elements are found in the Cavaliers' art work rather than in the narratives. Three of the art works present a close question of substantial similarity for summary judgment purposes: (1) the moon night light design on the extended inside back cover; (2) the illustration of stars relaxing on clouds; and (3) the illustration of stars being polished.

The basic mode of analysis for comparison of the literary elements applies to comparison of the art work. As with literary works, unprotectible elements should not be considered when applying the extrinsic test to art work. "This does not mean that at the end of the day, when the works are considered under the intrinsic test, they should not be compared as a whole. Nor does it mean that infringement cannot be based on original selection and arrangement of unprotected elements. However, the unprotectable elements have to be identified, or filtered, before the works can be considered as a whole." *Apple Computer*, 35 F.3d at 1446 (citations omitted). The precise factors evaluated for literary works do not readily apply to art works. Rather, a court looks to the similarity of the objective details in appearance. . . . Although we do not attempt here to provide an exhaustive list of relevant factors for evaluating art work, the subject matter, shapes, colors, materials, and arrangement of the representations may be considered in determining objective similarity in appearance. . . .

A comparison of the night light designs reveals obvious similarities. The basic idea — a night light built into the inside back cover of a board book — is the same. In *Good Night, Elmo*, the night light is in the shape of a smiling moon face with pinkish cheeks and black eyes. In *Good Night, Ernie*, the exterior outline of the face on the night light is a star rather than a moon, but the features are the same. Both the moon and star faces in the *Good Night* books share these characteristics with the moon face in the Cavaliers' stories. In both of the *Good Night* books, the stars surround the night light faces in much the same manner as in the Cavaliers' stories. Both lights are positioned in the upper portion of the projecting inside back cover, as they are in the Cavaliers' design. The shape (a star enclosed in a circle) and positioning of the "on" button to the lower-right is the same. Although the concept of a built-in night light is not protectible under copyright law, the choice of a smiling moon or star face with pinkish cheeks surrounded by stars in a specific configuration, and situated above an encircled star "on" button, constitutes protectible expression. The differences — mainly that the facial features of Random House and

CTW's moon and star lights have ping-pong ball-shaped eyes and bulbous nose, compared to plaintiffs' black circles and no nose — are relatively minor and do not support a grant of summary judgment for the defendant on the issue of substantial similarity.

A comparison of the two depictions of stars relaxing on clouds also reveals obvious similarities. The basic concept — stars situated on clouds — is the same. As expressed in their accompanying texts, both illustrations share the theme of exploring the stars' activities during daytime: The Cavaliers' drawing aims "to give you an idea of what stars do during the day when they are 'off work' dressing up or involved in any activity until night"; the text in *Good Night, Ernie* reads "Ernie wonders what the stars do during the day. He thinks about visiting them." Several of the stars in both illustrations are resting on clouds, appearing ready to fall asleep. Most strikingly, several of the stars in both illustrations are wearing red and green woolen (striped and solid) winter or sleeping caps. On the other hand, some of the other details differ. The stars in the Cavaliers' drawing are engaged in various activities — one is wearing a costume, one is dancing in a top hat, one is lounging, and one is yawning. In contrast, none of Random House and CTW's stars are dressed up, and all have sleepy gazes (eyelids drooping). Furthermore, the main characters in each illustration are different (*Nicky Moonbeams* v. *Ernie*) and are doing different things (reading vs. flying). Finally, as stated above, the facial features and curves of the stars are different. Despite these differences, the striking similarities in the details of the subject matter, and arrangement of the stars and the clouds, dress of the stars, and accompanying text are sufficient to survive summary judgment on the question of substantial similarity.

Finally, we compare the two depictions of stars being polished. Obvious similarities again appear. The subject matter — a star being polished — is the same. Furthermore, the stars being polished are both five-pointed, yellowish, and smiling. But the basic idea of polishing a star and the depiction of the common features of stars are unprotectible, and the two works differ significantly in the protectible details. Ernie polishes the entire star in *Good Night, Ernie*, while four smaller stars simultaneously polish the points of the star in the Cavaliers' illustration. The curves and facial details of the stars differ, as the *Good Night, Ernie* stars are rounder and have ping-pong ball-shaped eyes and red bulbous noses; moreover, there is a long line of "dirty" stars, as indicated by their brownish tint, waiting to be polished. Ernie also uses sun rays to help him polish. These significant elements are absent from the Cavaliers' work. Thus, we do not find a triable issue of substantial similarity as to this illustration. . . .

Swirsky v. Carey
376 F.3d 841 (9th Cir. 2004)

CANBY, J.: . . .

Factual Background

This case concerns the alleged similarity between the choruses of two popular and contemporary rhythm and blues ("R & B") songs: plaintiffs' "One of Those Love Songs" (*"One"*) and Mariah Carey's "Thank God I Found You" (*"Thank God"*). *One* was jointly composed by plaintiffs Seth Swirsky and Warryn Campbell (collectively "Swirsky") in 1997. . . . *One* was recorded by the musical group Xscape and released in May 1998 on Xscape's album "Traces of My Lipstick." *Thank God* was composed by defendants Carey, James Harris III, and Terry Lewis in 1999 and was released on Carey's album "Rainbow" in November 1999.

One and *Thank God* have generally dissimilar lyrics and verse melodies, but they share an allegedly similar chorus that Swirsky claims as an infringement of *One*'s copyright. Swirsky filed this action in district court against Carey, Harris, Lewis, and a number of music companies that had financial interests in *Thank God* (collectively "Carey") for copyright infringement and related claims. The defendants moved for summary judgment, contending that Swirsky had failed to present a triable issue on the required first, or "extrinsic," part of our circuit's two-part test for the establishment of substantial similarity necessary to sustain a claim of copyright infringement. . . . The district court agreed . . . and granted summary judgment to Carey. . . . This appeal followed.

Substantial Similarity . . .

[Carey conceded Swirsky's ownership of a valid copyright and] a high degree of access to *One*. Swirsky's burden of proof of substantial similarity is thus commensurately lowered.

In determining whether two works are substantially similar, we employ a two-part analysis: an objective extrinsic test and a subjective intrinsic test. . . .

The extrinsic test considers whether two works share a similarity of ideas and expression as measured by external, objective criteria. The extrinsic test requires "analytical dissection of a work and expert testimony." *Three Boys*, 212 F.3d at 485. "Analytical dissection" requires breaking the works "down into their constituent elements, and comparing those elements for proof of copying as measured by 'substantial similarity.'" Because the requirement is one of substantial similarity to *protected* elements of the copyrighted work, it is essential to distinguish between the protected and unprotected material in a plaintiff's work.

The expert testimony on which Swirsky relied was that of Dr. Robert Walser, chair of the Musicology Department at the University of California at Los Angeles. On the basis of his aural assessment of *One* and *Thank God*, Dr. Walser opined that the two songs had substantially similar choruses.

Dr. Walser . . . stated that the two songs' choruses shared a "basic shape and pitch emphasis" in their melodies, which were played over "highly similar basslines and chord changes, at very nearly the same tempo and in the same generic style." Dr. Walser also noted that it was a "suspicious coincidence" that the two songs' choruses were both sung in B-flat. Dr. Walser further testified that the choruses in both *One* and *Thank God* shared a similar structure in that measures five through seven of each chorus were "almost exactly" the same as the first three measures of each chorus.

Dr. Walser also noted a number of differences between the two songs' choruses. Dr. Walser found that the fourth measures of the choruses were "dramatically different" from each other and noted that while the "basic, emphasized pitches and rhythms" of the basslines were alike, the basslines to both choruses were "ornamented and played slightly differently from chorus to chorus." Dr. Walser also found that certain "text-setting choices" created differences between the two songs' choruses. For example, he noted that in *Thank God*, Carey sings "D, scale degree three, for a full beat on the first beat of the first measure" while Xscape in *One* sings the same pitch "divided into two eight–note pulses." Dr. Walser ultimately concluded, however, that these differences were not enough to differentiate the songs because the overall emphasis on musical notes was the same, which "contribute[d] to the impression of similarity one hears when comparing the two songs." . . .

The district court found this evidence insufficient to survive a motion for summary judgment for four reasons. First, the district court found that Dr. Walser's expert methodology was flawed. Second, the district court, using its own analysis, found that no triable issue was raised as to the substantial similarity of measures two, three, six, seven, and eight of the two choruses. Third, the district court held that measures one and five of *One* were *scenes a faire*, and thus incapable of supporting a finding of infringement. Finally, the district court discounted any similarity between the two choruses based on key, harmony, tempo, or genre because it found no precedent for substantial similarity to be "founded solely on similarities in key, harmony, tempo or genre, either alone or in combination." We disagree with much of the district court's reasoning on all four points and conclude that Swirsky has satisfied the extrinsic test because he has provided "indicia of a sufficient disagreement concerning the substantial similarity of [the] two works." *Brown Bag*, 960 F.2d at 1472 (internal quotations and citation omitted).

A. Dr. Walser's Methodology

There is nothing inherently unsound about Dr. Walser's musicological methodology in this case. The district court is correct that Dr. Walser's methodology is "selective," in as much as it discounts notes that he characterizes as "ornamental." Dr. Walser, however, explained that the melody (pitch and rhythm) and bassline of a song cannot be divorced from the harmonic rhythm of a song. According to Dr. Walser, notes falling on the beat will be more prominent to the ear than notes falling off the beat. Thus, Dr. Walser opined that, even though measure three of both choruses were not identical in numerical pitch sequence or note selection, they both "emphasize[d] the second scale degree, C, over an A in the bass, resolving to the third scale degree, D, over a D in the bass in the last half of the measure." Dr. Walser provided a comparable analysis for measures one, three, and eight.

Similarly, Dr. Walser explained that some artists will ornament their notes in ways that others do not. Dr. Walser testified at deposition that both Carey and Xscape ornament their notes with "melismas" and "appoggiaturas," both of which are technical terms for moving up to the next note and then back again. Dr. Walser testified that he did not notate these ornaments in his transcriptions, or take them into account in his opinion, because he "took that to be a matter of the singer customizing the song and regarded those notes as not structural; they are ornamental." As we said in *Newton v. Diamond*, 349 F.3d 591 (2003), we can "consider only [the defendant's] appropriation of the song's compositional elements and must remove from consideration all the elements unique to [Plaintiff's] performance." Id. at 595. Dr. Walser's methodology sought to remove notes he perceived as performance-related.

To a certain extent, Dr. Walser's methodology does concentrate on how the two choruses sound to his expert ears, which led the district court to conclude that his testimony related to intrinsic and not extrinsic similarity. We do not agree, however, that Dr. Walser's testimony was an intrinsic rather than extrinsic analysis. He was not testifying, as the intrinsic test would require, as to whether subjectively the "ordinary, reasonable person would find the total concept and feel of the [two choruses] to be substantially similar." *Three Boys*, 212 F.3d at 485 (quoting *Pasillas v. McDonald's Corp.*, 927 F.2d 440, 442 (9th Cir. 1991)). Instead, he was stating that, although the two choruses are not exactly identical on paper, when examined in the structural context of harmony, rhythm, and meter, they are remarkably similar. We, therefore, cannot accept the district court's conclusion that Dr. Walser did not "adequately explain, based on objective criteria, why [his] particular subset of notes is more important, or more appropriately analyzed, than the other notes present in the songs." The district court erred in completely discounting Dr. Walser's expert opinion.

B. The District Court's Measure-by-Measure Analysis

The district court also erred by basing its comparison of the two choruses almost entirely on a measure-by-measure comparison of melodic note sequences from the full transcriptions of the choruses. Objective analysis of music under the extrinsic test cannot mean that a court may simply compare the numerical representations of pitch sequences and the visual representations of notes to determine that two choruses are not substantially similar, without regard to other elements of the compositions. Under that approach, expert testimony would not be required at all, for any person untrained in music could conclude that "2-2-2-2-2-2-1-2-1-3" did not match "2-2-4-3-2-3" or that a half-note is not identical to an eighth-note. Certainly, musicological experts can disagree as to whether an approach that highlights stressed notes, as Dr. Walser's does, is the most appropriate way to break down music for substantial-similarity comparison, but no approach can completely divorce pitch sequence and rhythm from harmonic chord progression, tempo, and key, and thereby support a conclusion that compositions are dissimilar as a matter of law. It is these elements that determine what notes and pitches are heard in a song and at what point in the song they are found. To pull these elements out of a song individually, without also looking at them in combination, is to perform an incomplete and distorted musicological analysis.

Furthermore, to disregard chord progression, key, tempo, rhythm, and genre is to ignore the fact that a substantial similarity can be found in a combination of elements, even if those elements are individually unprotected. Thus, although chord progressions may not be individually protected, if in combination with rhythm and pitch sequence, they show the chorus of *Thank God* to be substantially similar to the chorus of *One*, infringement can be found. *See Three Boys*, 212 F.3d at 485.

We recognize the difficulties faced by the district court in this case. . . . The application of the extrinsic test, which assesses substantial similarity of ideas and expression, to musical compositions is a somewhat unnatural task, guided by relatively little precedent. . . . The extrinsic test provides an awkward framework to apply to copyrighted works like music or art objects, which lack distinct elements of idea and expression. Nevertheless, the test is our law and we must apply it. The extrinsic test does serve the purpose of permitting summary judgment in clear cases of non-infringement, and it informs the fact-finder of some of the complexities of the medium in issue while guiding attention toward protected elements and away from unprotected elements of a composition.

In analyzing musical compositions under the extrinsic test, we have never announced a uniform set of factors to be used. We will not do so now. Music, like software programs and art objects, is not capable of ready classification into only five or six constituent elements; music is comprised of a large array of elements, some combination of which is protectable by copyright. . . . Other courts have taken account of additional components of musical compositions, including melody, harmony, rhythm, pitch, tempo, phrasing, structure, chord progressions, and lyrics. . . . In addition, commentators have opined that timbre, tone, spatial organization, consonance, dissonance, accents, note choice, combinations, interplay of instruments, basslines, and new technological sounds can all be elements of a musical composition. . . .

There is no one magical combination of these factors that will automatically substantiate a musical infringement suit; each allegation of infringement will be unique. So long as the plaintiff can demonstrate, through expert testimony that addresses some or all of these elements and supports its employment of them, that the similarity was "substantial" and to "protected elements" of the copyrighted work, the extrinsic test is satisfied. Swirsky has met that standard here. . . .

C. Scenes a Faire Analysis

The district court erred in finding the first and fifth measures of *One* to be unprotectable by reason of the *scenes a faire* doctrine. *Scenes a faire* analysis requires the court to examine whether "motive" similarities that plaintiffs attribute to copying could actually be explained by the common-place presence of the same or similar "motives" within the relevant field. Under the *scenes a faire* doctrine, when certain commonplace expressions are indispensable and naturally associated with the treatment of a given idea, those expressions are treated like ideas and therefore not protected by copyright. The district court held that the first and fifth measures of *One* were not protected by copyright because Dr. Walser admitted in his deposition that the pitch sequence of the first measure of *One*'s chorus was more similar to the pitch sequence in the first measure of the folk song "For He's a Jolly Good Fellow" ("*Jolly Good*") than to the pitch sequence in the first measure of *Thank God*'s chorus.

The evidence does not support the district court's ruling that the first measure of *One* is a *scene a faire* as a matter of law. The songs *One* and *Jolly Good* are not in the same relevant "field" of music; *One* is in the hip-hop/R & B genre and *Jolly Good* is in the folk music genre. Thus, comparing the first measure of *One*'s chorus to the first measure of *Jolly Good* does not tell the court whether the first measure of *One*'s chorus is an indispensable idea within the field of hip-hop/R & B. Further, even if *One* and *Jolly Good* were in the same genre of music, a musical measure cannot be "common-place" by definition if it is shared by only two songs. *One* and *Jolly Good* are also written in different time signatures. . . .

The district court also erred in finding the fifth measure of *One* to be a *scene a faire* as a matter of law. Carey introduced no independent evidence showing that measure five of *One* was more similar to *Jolly Good* than *Thank God;* she relied exclusively on Dr. Walser's opinion that measure five was "almost identical" to measure one of *One*. As we have already pointed out, on summary judgment, "almost identical" and "identical" are not equivalents. . . . It is inappropriate to grant summary judgment on the basis of *scenes a faire* without independent evidence, unless the allegation of *scenes a faire* is uncontested. It was contested here.

Conclusion

We conclude that Swirsky's expert adequately explained his methodology and provided "indicia of a sufficient disagreement concerning the substantial similarity of two works" so that the issue of the substantial similarity of the two choruses should have been presented to a jury. . . .

NOTES AND QUESTIONS

1. The *Cavalier* court notes that the extrinsic test has expanded to include all "objective manifestations of expression." Why would the Ninth Circuit make this change? In *Shaw v. Lindheim*, 919 F.2d 1353 (9th Cir. 1990), the case in which the Ninth Circuit formally announced the change, the court discussed several of its prior opinions affirming grants of summary judgment to infringement defendants. It observed: "By creating a discrete set of standards for determining the objective similarity of literary works, the law of this circuit has implicitly recognized the distinction between situations in which idea and expression merge in representational objects and those in which the idea is distinct from the written expression of a concept by a poet, a playwright, or a writer." *Id.* at 1360. The court seemed to suggest that literary and dramatic works must be compared along more dimensions to determine whether observed similarities extend beyond ideas. Do you agree? Do you think that such a comparison is a proper first step for the court to undertake?

2. Is the Ninth Circuit consistent in its substantial similarity analysis in *Cavalier* and *Swirsky?* How would the *Boisson* court have resolved the two appeals? Do you read the Second

Circuit's test(s) for substantial similarity of expression as giving district courts permission to engage in an inquiry comparable to the Ninth Circuit's revised extrinsic analysis?

3. How should courts treat *scenes a faire* in an infringement proceeding? In a portion of the opinion not reproduced above, the *Cavalier* court addressed the claim that the defendants infringed the plaintiffs' copyright in a series about a friendly dragon, and noted that "[t]he themes of teaching children to have confidence, to overcome their fears, and to try are not only too general to be protected but are also standard topics in children's literature." *Cavalier v. Random House, Inc.*, 297 F.3d 815, 828 (9th Cir. 2002). Similarity to these elements therefore would not constitute infringement. *See also Williams v. Crichton*, 84 F.3d 581, 589 (2d Cir. 1996) (noting that "electrified fences, automated tours, dinosaur nurseries, and uniformed workers are classic *scenes a faire* that flow from the uncopyrightable concept of a dinosaur zoo").

Would a court applying the *Boisson* test agree with the *Cavalier* court that similarity to *scenes a faire* cannot support an infringement claim?

4. In *Swirsky*, the Ninth Circuit emphasized the importance of the expert testimony regarding the substantial similarity of the songs. Review carefully the portion of the opinion that deals with the expert's methodology. How does this methodology differ from the analysis in *Cavalier*? Do you think the expert in *Swirsky* added any substantive analysis that a court could not undertake on its own? What was the procedural benefit to having an expert testify about substantial similarity? Were there procedural costs? Did the expert's involvement mean that the district court was accorded less authority to conduct its own analysis? Is that result appropriate? Note also the *Swirsky* court's reliance on experts to identify *scenes a faire*. Is it easier to identify *scenes a faire* in a literary work than in music?

5. The *Swirsky* court agreed with the expert that performance-related elements of the songs could not be considered in determining substantial similarity. *Swirsky*, 376 F.3d 841 at 847. Aren't such performance-related elements part of an artist's style and expression? If the Second Circuit had adopted a similar approach, do you think the outcome in *Steinberg* would have been different?

6. For many years, the rule was that experts could testify on the issue of probative copying (copying in fact) but not on the wrongfulness of that copying (substantial similarity). In recent years, however, as the Ninth Circuit has developed its extrinsic test, it has become more willing to allow trial courts to admit expert testimony on the substantial similarity issue. In *Swirsky*, the Ninth Circuit relied on expert testimony to reverse a grant of summary judgment. The court noted that, like software, music comprises a large array of elements, any combination of which could be copyrightable, and expert testimony on substantial similarity should not be casually dismissed. *Swirsky v. Carey*, 376 F.3d 841, 849 (9th Cir. 2004). If expert testimony is important for surviving summary judgment, then the use of experts in infringement litigation may become increasingly common. Is that a desirable state of affairs? Why, or why not?

7. Of the various tests you have studied, which do you find most faithful to copyright's goals and objectives? Does your answer depend on whether you judge the risks of overprotection to be greater than the risks of underprotection?

d. Technology Cases

In technology cases, expert testimony is essential to evaluating infringement claims. Review the excerpt from the *Altai* case in Chapter 4, pages 222-29 *supra*. Recall both the factual context (a suit alleging infringement of non-literal elements of computer software) and the court's adoption of a three-step abstraction-filtration-comparison test for distinguishing idea from expression and determining infringement. In the following excerpt, the court considers how to assess substantial similarity.

Computer Associates International, Inc. v. Altai, Inc.
982 F.2d 693 (2d Cir. 1992)

WALKER, J.: . . . Step Three: Comparison

The third and final step of the test for substantial similarity that we believe appropriate for non-literal program components entails a comparison. Once a court has sifted out all elements of the allegedly infringed program which are "ideas" or are dictated by efficiency or external factors, or taken from the public domain, there may remain a core of protectable expression. In terms of a work's copyright value, this is the golden nugget. At this point, the court's substantial similarity inquiry focuses on whether the defendant copied any aspect of this protected expression, as well as an assessment of the copied portion's relative importance with respect to the plaintiff's overall program. . . .

B.   The District Court Decision . . .

1)   Use of Expert Evidence in Determining Substantial Similarity Between Computer Programs

. . . [I]n deciding the limits to which expert opinion may be employed in ascertaining the substantial similarity of computer programs, we cannot disregard the highly complicated and technical subject matter at the heart of these claims. Rather we recognize the reality that computer programs are likely to be somewhat impenetrable by lay observers — whether they be judges or juries — and, thus, seem to fall outside the category of works contemplated by those who engineered the *Arnstein* test. . . .

. . . [W]e leave it to the discretion of the district court to decide to what extent, if any, expert opinion, regarding the highly technical nature of computer programs, is warranted in a given case.

In so holding, we do not intend to disturb the traditional role of lay observers in judging substantial similarity in copyright cases that involve the aesthetic arts, such as music, visual works or literature.

In this case, [the expert's] opinion was instrumental in dismantling the intricacies of computer science so that the court could formulate and apply an appropriate rule of law. While [the expert's] report and testimony undoubtedly shed valuable light on the subject matter of the litigation, Judge Pratt remained, in the final analysis, the trier of fact. The district court's use of the expert's assistance, in the context of this case, was entirely appropriate.

2)   Evidentiary Analysis

The district court had to determine whether [defendant] Altai's OSCAR 3.5 program was substantially similar to [plaintiff] CA's ADAPTER. We note that Judge Pratt's method of analysis effectively served as a road map for our own, with one exception — Judge Pratt filtered out the non-copyrightable aspects of OSCAR 3.5 rather than those found in ADAPTER, the allegedly infringed program. We think that our approach — i.e., filtering out the unprotected aspects of an allegedly infringed program and then comparing the end product to the structure of the suspect program — is preferable, and therefore believe that district courts should proceed in this manner in future cases.

We opt for this strategy because, in some cases, the defendant's program structure might contain protectable expression and/or other elements that are not found in the plaintiff's program. Since it is extraneous to the allegedly copied work, this material would have no bearing on any potential substantial similarity between the two programs. Thus, its filtration would be wasteful and unnecessarily time consuming. Furthermore, by focusing the analysis on the infringing rather than on the infringed material, a court may mistakenly place too little emphasis on a quantitatively small misappropriation which is, in reality, a qualitatively vital aspect of the plaintiff's protectable expression.

The fact that the district court's analysis proceeded in the reverse order, however, had no material impact on the outcome of this case. Since Judge Pratt determined that OSCAR effectively contained no protectable expression whatsoever, the most serious charge that can be levelled against him is that he was overly thorough in his examination.

The district court took the first step in the analysis set forth in this opinion when it separated the program by levels of abstraction. The district court stated:

> As applied to computer software programs, this abstractions test would progress in order of "increasing generality" from object code, to source code, to parameter lists, to services required, to general outline. In discussing the particular similarities, therefore, we shall focus on these levels. . . .

Moving to the district court's evaluation of OSCAR 3.5's structural components, we agree with Judge Pratt's systematic exclusion of non-protectable expression. With respect to code, the district court observed that after the rewrite of OSCAR 3.4 to OSCAR 3.5, "there remained virtually no lines of code that were identical to ADAPTER." Accordingly, the court found that the code "present[ed] no similarity at all."

Next, Judge Pratt addressed the issue of similarity between the two programs' parameter lists and macros. He concluded that, viewing the conflicting evidence most favorably to CA, it demonstrated that "only a few of the lists and macros were similar to protected elements in ADAPTER; the others were either in the public domain or dictated by the functional demands of the program." As discussed above, functional elements and elements taken from the public domain do not qualify for copyright protection. With respect to the few remaining parameter lists and macros, the district court could reasonably conclude that they did not warrant a finding of infringement given their relative contribution to the overall program. . . .

The district court also found that the overlap exhibited between the list of services required for both ADAPTER and OSCAR 3.5 was "determined by the demands of the operating system and of the applications program to which it [was] to be linked through ADAPTER or OSCAR. . . ." In other words, this aspect of the program's structure was dictated by the nature of other programs with which it was designed to interact and, thus, is not protected by copyright.

Finally, in his infringement analysis, Judge Pratt accorded no weight to the similarities between the two programs' organizational charts, "because [the charts were] so simple and obvious to anyone exposed to the operation of the program[s]." CA argues that the district court's action in this regard "is not consistent with copyright law" — that "obvious" expression is protected, and that the district court erroneously failed to realize this. However, to say that elements of a work are "obvious," in the manner in which the district court used the word, is to say that they "follow naturally from the work's theme rather than from the author's creativity." This is but one formulation of the *scenes a faire* doctrine, which we have already endorsed as a means of weeding out unprotectable expression. . . .

Since we accept Judge Pratt's factual conclusions and the results of his legal analysis, we affirm his denial of CA's copyright infringement claim based upon OSCAR 3.5. We emphasize that, like all copyright infringement cases, those that involve computer programs are highly fact specific. The amount of protection due structural elements, in any given case, will vary according to the protectable expression found to exist within the program at issue.

NOTES AND QUESTIONS

1. Should cases like *Altai* go to the jury at all?

2. Does the *Altai* court conduct the correct comparison? If you were Computer Associates, what would you argue is the correct comparison? Review *Softel, Inc. v. Dragon Medical & Scientific Communications, Inc.*, pages 229-31 *supra*, before you answer.

3. Is the *Altai* court's abstraction-filtration-comparison test for substantial similarity consistent with the tests established by prior Second Circuit precedent (*Nichols* and *Arnstein*)? With the Ninth Circuit's approach to substantial similarity? In *Brown Bag Software v. Symantec Corp.*, 960 F.2d 1465 (9th Cir. 1992), decided the same year as *Altai*, the Ninth Circuit approved rigorous "analytic dissection" of computer software as part of the modified "extrinsic" inquiry elaborated in its post-*Krofft* decisions.

4. In technology cases, the approach of filtering out unprotected elements before conducting a comparison has gained widespread currency among the courts. At least one Ninth Circuit panel has warned that eliminating unprotectible elements from the substantial similarity inquiry in such cases may also create dangers:

> Because there ought to be copyright protection for an innovative melding of elements from pre-existing works, elements which have been deemed "unprotectible" should not be eliminated prior to the substantial similarity of expression analysis. Suppose defendant copied plaintiff's abstract painting composed entirely of geometric forms arranged in an original pattern. The alleged infringer could argue that each expressive element (i.e., the geometric forms) is unprotectible under the functionality, merger, scenes a faire, and unoriginality theories and, thus, all elements should be excluded prior to the substantial similarity of expression analysis. Then, there would be nothing left for purposes of determining substantial similarity of expression. . . .
>
> [I]f it is determined that the defendant used the unprotectible elements in an arrangement which is not substantially similar to the plaintiff's work, then no copyright infringement can be found. If, on the other hand, the works are deemed substantially similar, then copyright infringement will be established even though the copyrighted work is composed of unprotectible elements. There is simply no other logical way of protecting an innovative arrangement or "look and feel" of certain works.

Apple Computer, Inc. v. Microsoft Corp., 779 F. Supp. 133, 135-36 (N.D. Cal. 1991).

The *Apple v. Microsoft* court, however, ultimately applied a quite rigorous dissection analysis to the works at issue. Those works were not computer programs, but rather competing desktop graphical user interfaces for personal computer operating systems—i.e., PGS works. *Apple Computer, Inc. v. Microsoft Corp.*, 799 F. Supp. 1006 (N.D. Cal. 1992). The Ninth Circuit affirmed in an opinion suggesting that analytical dissection is appropriate for all works. *Apple Computer, Inc. v. Microsoft Corp.*, 35 F.3d 1435, 1445-46 (9th Cir. 1994), *cert. denied*, 513 U.S. 1184 (1995). The court explained that such dissection does not "run afoul" of *Krofft*'s admonition to assess the "total concept and feel" of the work, because "the unprotectable elements have to be identified, or filtered, before the works can be considered as a whole." *Id.* at 1446. The Ninth Circuit also endorsed the district court's holding that because the two works were composed primarily of unprotectible elements, the defendant's work should not be found to infringe unless it was "virtually identical" to the plaintiff's work. *Id.* at 1446-47. The court explained:

> Having dissected the alleged similarities and considered the range of possible expression, the court must define the scope of the plaintiff's copyright — that is, decide whether the work is entitled to "broad" or "thin" protection. Depending on the degree of protection, the court must set the appropriate standard for a subjective comparison of the works to determine whether, as a whole, they are sufficiently similar to support a finding of illicit copying.

Id. at 1443. Does the Ninth Circuit's *Apple v. Microsoft* opinion successfully reconcile the competing imperatives of dissection and holistic comparison? How does the "virtually identical" test compare to the "more discerning observer" test described in *Boisson*, pages 314-16 *supra*?

5. What are the advantages and disadvantages of using different tests of substantial similarity for different types of works? Does this practice violate the nondiscrimination principle enunciated by Justice Holmes in *Bleistein v. Donaldson*, pages 64-65 *supra*?

6. Should the "virtually identical" test be applied to all works with significant amounts of non-copyrightable content? How would the court in *Boisson* answer that question? *See also BUC Int'l Corp. v. International Yacht Council Ltd.*, 489 F.3d 1129 (11th Cir. 2007) (holding that the "virtually identical" test should apply only to "claims of compilation copyright infringement of nonliteral elements of a computer program," and not to claimed infringement of the copyright in a compilation of yacht listings).

2. The Exact Copy

As we noted at the start of this section, §106(1) covers the creation of both "substantially similar" copies and exact copies of the copyrighted work. We turn now to the exact copying cases.

Traditionally, exact copying cases have included two groups. In the first group are the cases sometimes called "piracy" cases — e.g., those involving the defendant who has burned 5,000 unauthorized copies of a chart-topping album onto CDs, or has replicated 10,000 unauthorized copies of a popular software program. For cases in this group, infringement liability is usually quite clear. The difficult issues, if any, are procedural or remedial, including discovery issues that arise during the process of tracing the infringing copies back to their source, issues concerning the computation of damages, and so on.

The second group of exact copying cases concerns very different sorts of conduct. The defendants are not "pirates," but rather are engaged in arguably privileged conduct, and infringement liability hinges on the rules that govern the various defenses afforded by the copyright laws. For example, a defendant might assert that her copying is excused by §108, which allows certain acts of copying by nonprofit libraries and archives, or that her copying was a fair use under §107 of the Act, or that it is excused by the plaintiff's misuse of its copyright. We consider fair use and misuse in Chapters 7 and 8, *infra*. Read §108 now. What justifications can you identify for the privileges set forth there?

More recently, the advent of digital technologies has created two additional groups of exact copying cases. Cases in the third group involve copies that are made automatically during the processes of reading, viewing, hearing, and using an authorized copy of the work. Recall *MAI Systems v. Peak Computer Corp.*, pages 50-53 *supra*, in which the Ninth Circuit held that temporary reproduction of a computer program in RAM creates a "copy" for purposes of the Copyright Act. Section 117 of the Act permits certain reproductions of computer programs but its scope is limited, sheltering only the "owner of a copy of a computer program" and certain maintenance organizations. Moreover, §117's exceptions apply only to computer programs. It provides no protection for routine reproductions in RAM of other digital works like music, text, and graphics. The conclusion that reproductions in RAM are statutory "copies" has been adopted by courts across the country. This legal doctrine has had sweeping implications for the ordinary practices of computer and Internet users with respect to all kinds of copyrighted works.

The final group of exact copying cases involves private individuals who upload and download copies of files containing copyrighted content to and from publicly accessible web sites and file-sharing platforms. In these cases, defendants sometimes argue that the content did not contain a copyright notice, and that any infringement therefore was innocent. The Act does provide an "innocent infringement" defense, but it is narrower than that argument suggests:

> Any person who innocently infringes a copyright, in reliance upon an authorized copy or phonorecord from which the copyright notice has been omitted and which was publicly distributed by authority of the copyright owner before the effective date of the Berne Convention Implementation Act of 1988, incurs no liability for actual or statutory damages . . . before receiving actual notice that registration for the work has been made . . . if such person proves that he or she was misled by the omission of notice.

17 U.S.C. §405(b). Would you expect this defense to be available to many defendants in this fourth group of cases?

NOTES AND QUESTIONS

1. Have you ever downloaded or uploaded content from or to the Internet that did not contain a copyright notice — e.g., a screensaver, a piece of clip art, or a photograph? Did you think you were committing copyright infringement? Should an innocent infringement defense be available in such circumstances? Would allowing such a defense effectively reinstate a copyright notice requirement for works posted on the Internet?

2. Should Congress enact a provision that would shield browsing by Internet users? The ordinary conduct of users of licensed software? The EU has enacted such a provision, providing an exception for "[t]emporary acts of reproduction . . . which are transient or incidental [and] an integral and essential part of a technological process" when the sole purpose is to enable either "a transmission in a network between third parties by an intermediary" or "a lawful use of a work," and when the temporary reproductions "have no independent economic significance." Directive 2001/29/EC of the European Parliament and of the Council of 22 May 2001 on the harmonisation of certain aspects of copyright and related rights in the Information Society, 2001 O.J. (L. 167) 10, art. 5(1). In the U.S., some scholars argue that temporary copying by users is shielded by implied license, while others argue that it is fair use. You will learn about these doctrines in Chapters 7 and 8.

3. Re-read §117 now. Then examine the license agreement for the operating system or word processing program installed on your personal computer. According to the license agreement, do you "own" your copy of that software?

As originally written, §117 excluded nonowners — e.g., those who possess authorized copies subject to a license agreement that reserves ownership to the copyright owner — from its benefits. Thus, the *MAI* court ruled that §117 did not allow a licensee to authorize a third-party service organization to make a RAM copy of a computer operating system while performing repairs on the system. *MAI Systems v. Peak Computer Corp.*, 991 F.2d 511, 518-19 (9th Cir. 1993), *cert. dismissed*, 510 U.S. 1033 (1994).

Congress subsequently amended §117 to authorize third-party service organizations to maintain or repair any computer "that lawfully contains an authorized copy" of the software if certain conditions are met; therefore, the specific conduct at issue in *MAI* no longer constitutes infringement. During the process that led to enactment of this amendment, Congress considered, but ultimately declined to adopt, broader language that would have extended the privileges authorized by §117 to any "rightful possessor" of a copy of a computer program. Should Congress have adopted this language instead?

4. In *Storage Technology Corp. v. Custom Hardware Engineering & Consulting Inc.*, 421 F.3d 1307 (Fed. Cir. 2005), the defendant service company left copies of plaintiff's code in its customer's RAM for the duration of its maintenance contract. The court held that "maintenance" as used in §117(c) has a "much broader temporal connotation" than "repair" as used in §117(d). According to the court, "maintenance, or servicing, was meant to encompass monitoring systems for problems, not simply fixing a single, isolated malfunction." *Id.* at 1312. Concluding that the protection of §117 ceases only when maintenance ends, the court stated that "[i]t would run counter to [Congress's] objective to construe section 117(c) narrowly to apply only to companies that performed repair in discrete, temporally isolated stages, rather than to construe the statute to apply to repair and maintenance services generally, so long as the companies' only reason for copying the software at issue was to fix and maintain the machines on which the software was running." *Id.* at 1313.

Note on Ephemeral Copies

The copyright problems caused by automatic reproduction in computer memory are not entirely unprecedented. Within the broadcast industries, simultaneous recording of broadcast transmissions has been common practice for decades. Although such reproduction is not technically inevitable, as it is in the case of RAM copies, it serves a variety of purposes that are important from a business perspective. (Can you think of what these might be?) Congress responded to this practice by enacting §112 and §118 of the 1976 Act, which exclude qualifying broadcasters from infringement liability for making certain "ephemeral" copies.

According to the legislative history of §112, Congress considered ephemeral recordings to include "copies or phonorecords of a work made for purposes of later transmission by a broadcasting organization legally entitled to transmit the work." H.R. Rep. No. 94-1476, 94th Cong., 2d Sess. 101 (1976), *reprinted in* 1976 U.S.C.C.A.N. 5659, 5716. The issue, as Congress framed it, was whether a broadcaster licensed to perform or display a work should be able to record the performance or display to aid in its transmission. *See id.* Congress concluded that "practical exigencies of broadcasting" supported an exemption from liability for such a copy but that the *scope* of that exemption remained controversial. *Id.*

Section 112(a) exempts a "transmitting organization" entitled to transmit a display or performance of the work to the public from liability for making one copy or phonorecord of a "transmission program" (defined in §101) embodying the display or performance. This exemption from liability is conditioned on the transmitting organization's refraining from making any other copy, and is limited to use of the authorized copy solely for the "transmitting organization's own transmissions within its local service area." 17 U.S.C. §112(a). The transmitting organization may not retain the copy of the transmission program for more than six months after the date of the transmission program's first broadcast to the public unless that copy is used solely for archival purposes. *See id.* The exemption does not apply to motion pictures and audiovisual works. Furthermore, under §112(g), the transmission program is not eligible for copyright protection as a derivative work under §103 unless the owner of the copyright in the preexisting material consents. Subsections 112(b)-(d) define more lenient exemptions for the reproduction of ephemeral copies by governmental bodies and other nonprofit organizations in certain circumstances. In 1998, as part of its enactment of the Digital Millennium Copyright Act (DMCA), Congress amended §112 by adding special provisions governing ephemeral copies of sound recordings. The rules governing reproduction and performance of sound recordings are considered in Section G.2 and 3, *infra*.

Section 118(d) provides an additional exemption for ephemeral recordings made by a public broadcasting entity. The legislative history explains that "encouragement and support of noncommercial broadcasting is in the public interest." H.R. Rep. No. 94-1476, 94th Cong., 2d Sess. 117 (1976), *reprinted in* 1976 U.S.C.C.A.N. 5659, 5732. It also emphasizes that "public broadcasting may encounter problems not confronted by commercial broadcasting enterprises, due to such factors as the special nature of programming, repeated use of programs, and, of course, limited financial resources." *Id.*

The §118 exemption applies only to "published nondramatic musical works and published pictorial, graphic, and sculptural works." 17 U.S.C. §118(b). As under §112, the public broadcasting entity must be entitled to transmit the work to qualify for the exemption. However, if the public broadcasting entity cannot reach a voluntary license agreement with the copyright owner, it may broadcast the work pursuant to a compulsory license, with rates and terms set by the Copyright Royalty Judges (CRJs) who are charged with administering the statutory and compulsory licenses under the Act. *Id.* §118(b); *see also* 37 C.F.R. §§253.1-253.11 (2005) (setting forth royalty rates for certain activities entered into by public broadcasting entities). Unlike §112, §118 does not limit the number of copies or phonorecords that may be made of the transmission program embodying the work; does not restrict the exchange of copies or phonorecords between various public broadcasting companies; and does not require destruction of the copies after a period of time. Thus, these recordings are not "ephemeral" in the ordinary sense of the word. Finally, §118 permits a governmental body or nonprofit institution to record a program transmitted by a public broadcasting company for use in connection with classroom teaching activities so long as the recording entity destroys the copy within seven days from the date of transmission. *See* 17 U.S.C. §118(c).

NOTES AND QUESTIONS

1. Why do you think Congress excluded motion pictures and audiovisual works from §112? Why did it limit the §118 exemption to an even narrower class of works?

2. Is the statute's different treatment of commercial and public broadcast entities warranted in light of the underlying purposes of copyright law? Why or why not?

3. Do the ephemeral copying exemptions lend support to arguments that Congress should enact some sort of exemption from infringement liability for automatic reproduction in a computer's RAM?

4. The Copyright Royalty and Distribution Reform Act of 2004 amended the Copyright Act's system for administering its statutory and compulsory licenses, including those of §118. Pub. L. No. 108-419, 118 Stat. 2341 (2004). The amendment replaced the former process of using ad hoc Copyright Arbitration Royalty Panels (CARPs) consisting of arbitrators and convened by the Librarian of Congress. Under the new system, the Librarian of Congress

appoints three attorneys to serve as full-time Copyright Royalty Judges (CRJs) for a statutorily defined time period. *See* 17 U.S.C. §§801-804. The CRJs oversee rate-setting procedures under §§112(e), 114, 115, 116, 118, 119, and 1004. *See id.* §801.

C. THE DISTRIBUTION RIGHT

Section 106(3) gives copyright owners the exclusive right "to distribute copies or pho-norecords of the copyrighted work to the public by sale or other transfer of ownership, or by rental, lease, or lending." 17 U.S.C. §106(3). Under U.S. copyright law, this right of public distribution has always gone hand-in-hand with the right to reproduce the work. The first copyright statute, the Act of 1790, granted the copyright owner the right to "print, reprint, publish or vend" the work. Act of 1790, §1, 1 Stat. 124, 124 (1790). As a practical matter, however, enumeration of the distribution right as a separate right also gives the copyright owner the flexibility to pursue entities that are distributing unauthorized copies reproduced by others. When do you think the copyright owner would find it preferable to sue the distrib-utor rather than the copier? Although the distribution right applies to any "copy" of a copy-righted work, it is most often invoked in cases involving exact copies.

1. What Is a "Distribution"?

Capitol Records, Inc. v. Thomas
579 F. Supp. 2d 1210 (D. Minn. 2008)

DAVIS, C.J.:

I. Introduction

. . . The Court has sua sponte raised the issue of whether it erred in instructing the jury that making sound recordings available for distribution on a peer-to-peer network, regardless of whether actual distribution was shown, qualified as distribution under the Copyright Act. . . .

II. Background

Plaintiffs are recording companies that owned or controlled exclusive rights to copyrights in sound recordings, including 24 at issue in this lawsuit. On April 19, 2006, Plaintiffs filed a Complaint against Defendant Jammie Thomas alleging that she infringed Plaintiffs' copy-righted sound recordings pursuant to the Copyright Act, 17 U.S.C. §§101, 106, 501-505, by illegally downloading and distributing the recordings via the online peer-to-peer file sharing application known as Kazaa. Plaintiffs sought injunctive relief, statutory damages, costs, and attorney fees. . . .

In Jury Instruction No. 15, the Court instructed: "The act of making copyrighted sound recordings available for electronic distribution on a peer-to-peer network, without license from the copyright owners, violates the copyright owners' exclusive right of distribution, regardless of whether actual distribution has been shown."

On October 4, 2007, the jury found that Thomas had willfully infringed on all 24 of Plaintiffs' sound recordings at issue, and awarded Plaintiffs statutory damages in the amount of $9,250 for each willful infringement. On October 5, the Court entered judgment on the jury's verdict. . . .

On May 15, 2008, the Court issued an Order stating that it was contemplating granting a new trial on the grounds that it had committed a manifest error of law in giving Jury Instruction No. 15. . . .

III.   Discussion . . .

B.   *Prejudicial Effect of Any Error of Law* . . .

2.   **Reproduction Right**

Plaintiffs argue that regardless of the correctness of Jury Instruction No. 15, Plaintiffs had an indisputably valid reproduction claim, so even an erroneous instruction did not mislead the jury or prejudice Thomas.

The Special Verdict Form provides no insight as to whether the jurors found Thomas liable because of Jury Instruction No. 14, dealing with Plaintiffs' reproduction right, or because of Jury Instruction No. 15, dealing with Plaintiffs' distribution right. The Court cannot know whether the jury reached its verdict on permissible or impermissible grounds. Additionally, even if Thomas were liable under the reproduction right, there is no way for the Court to determine if the jury would have granted the same high statutory damage award based solely on violation of the reproduction right.

3.   **Distribution to MediaSentry**

The parties agree that the only evidence of actual dissemination of copyrighted works was that Plaintiffs' agent, MediaSentry, copied songs. Plaintiffs argue that even if distribution requires an actual transfer, the trial evidence established transfers of copyrighted works to MediaSentry. Thomas retorts that dissemination to an investigator acting as an agent for the copyright owner cannot constitute infringement.

"It is well-established that the lawful owner of a copyright cannot infringe its own copyright." *Olan Mills, Inc. v. Linn Photo Co.*, 23 F.3d 1345, 1348 (8th Cir. 1994) (citation omitted). However, the Eighth Circuit holds that a copyright owner's authorization of an investigator to pursue infringement does "not authorize the investigator to validate [the third party's] unlawful conduct." *Id.* "Indeed, the investigator's assignment [i]s part of [the copyright owner's] attempt to stop . . . infringement." *Id. See also RCA/Ariola Int'l Inc. v. Thomas & Grayston Co.*, 845 F.2d 773, 781-82 (8th Cir. 1988) (holding retailer liable for actively assisting in reproduction of copyrighted works at request of authorized investigative agent of copyright owners).

Plaintiffs further argue that even if the law required a defendant's active involvement in making distributions, Thomas is liable because she took the active steps of willfully reproducing copyrighted works without authorization and affirmatively choosing to place them in a shared folder making them available to anyone who wanted them on a computer network dedicated to the illegal distribution of copyrighted works. . . .

The Court holds that distribution to MediaSentry can form the basis of an infringement claim. Eighth Circuit precedent clearly approves of the use of investigators by copyright owners. While Thomas did not assist in the copying in the same manner as the retail defendant in *Olan Mills*—by actually completing the copying for the investigator—or as the retail defendants in *RCA/Ariola*—by assisting in selecting the correct tape on which to record and helping customers copy—she allegedly did assist in a different, but substantial manner. Plaintiffs presented evidence that Thomas, herself, provided the copyrighted works for copying and placed them on a network specifically designed for easy, unauthorized copying. These actions would constitute more substantial participation in the infringement than the actions of the defendants in the Eighth Circuit cases who merely assisted in copying works provided by the investigators.

Although the Court holds that distribution to an investigator, such as MediaSentry, can constitute unauthorized distribution, in light of Jury Instruction No. 15, it is impossible to determine upon which basis the jury entered its verdict or how the erroneous jury instruction affected the jury's damage calculation. Therefore, if the Court determines that Jury Instruction No. 15 was incorrect, it will grant a new trial.

C. Statutory Framework

The Copyright Act provides that "the owner of copyright under this title has the exclusive rights to do and to authorize any of the following: . . . (3) to distribute copies or phonorecords of the copyrighted work to the public by sale or other transfer of ownership, or by rental, lease, or lending." 17 U.S.C. §106(3). The Act does not define the term "distribute." . . .

D. Plain Meaning of the Term "Distribution"

. . . Each party asserts that the Court should adopt the plain meaning of the term "distribution;" however, they disagree on what that plain meaning is. Thomas and her supporters argue that the plain meaning of the statute compels the conclusion that merely making a work available to the public does not constitute a distribution. Instead, a distribution only occurs when a defendant actually transfers to the public the possession or ownership of copies or phonorecords of a work. Plaintiffs and their supporters assert that making a work available for distribution is sufficient. . . .

Starting with the language in §106(3), the Court notes that Congress explains the manners in which distribution can be effected: sale, transfer of ownership, rental, lease, or lending. The provision does not state that an offer to do any of these acts constitutes distribution. Nor does §106(3) provide that making a work available for any of these activities constitutes distribution. An initial reading of the provision at issue supports Thomas's interpretation. . . .

The ordinary dictionary meaning of the word "distribute" necessarily entails a transfer of ownership or possession from one person to another. *See, e.g., Merriam-Webster's Collegiate Dictionary* (10th ed. 1999) (defining "distribute" as, among other things, "1: to divide among several or many: APPORTION . . . 2 . . . b: to give out or deliver esp. to members of a group").

Additionally, the leading copyright treatises conclude that making a work available is insufficient to establish distribution. *See, e.g.,* 2-8 *Nimmer on Copyright,* §8.11[A] (2008); 4 *William F. Patry, Patry on Copyright,* §13.11.50 (2008). . . .

Register of Copyrights, Marybeth Peters, has opined to Congress that making a copyrighted work available violates the distribution right. . . . However, opinion letters from the Copyright Office to Congress on matters of statutory interpretation are not binding. . . .

As Plaintiffs note, in other provisions of federal copyright law, Congress has explicitly defined "distribute" to include offers to distribute. *See* 17 U.S.C. §901(a)(4) (stating, in context of copyright protection of semiconductor chip products, that "to 'distribute' means to sell, or to lease, bail, or otherwise transfer, or to offer to sell, lease, bail, or otherwise transfer"); 17 U.S.C. §506(a)(1)(C) (imposing criminal penalties for "the distribution of a work being prepared for commercial distribution, by making it available on a computer network accessible to members of the public"). . . .

The differing definitions of "distribute" within copyright law demonstrate that there is not one uniform definition of the term throughout copyright law. . . . However, the Court notes that when Congress intends distribution to encompass making available or offering to transfer, it has demonstrated that it is quite capable of explicitly providing that definition within the statute. In this case, Congress provided the means by which a distribution occurs — "by sale or other transfer of ownership, or by rental, lease, or lending" — without also providing that a distribution occurs by an offer to do one of those actions, as it did in §901(a)(4). While the Copyright Act does not offer a uniform definition of "distribution," the Court concludes that, in light of the examined provisions, Congress's choice to not include offers to do the enumerated acts or the making available of the work indicates its intent that an actual distribution or dissemination is required in §106(3). . . .

The Court does not find the definitive interpretation of the term "distribute" in other titles of the U.S. Code. However, the Court does note that, while Congress has not added "offer to distribute" to §106(3) of the Copyright Act, it has added "offers to sell" in the related field of patent law. 35 U.S.C. §271(a). *See also Eldred v. Ashcroft*, 537 U.S. 186, 201-02 (2003) (citing patent practice as persuasive precedent in a copyright case). Before Congress amended the Patent Act to expressly include "offers to sell," courts strictly interpreted the statutory language, which expressly forbade sales but not offers to sell, as requiring proof of an actual sale. Court and congressional actions with regard to the Patent Act demonstrate two principles; 1) in the absence of a statutory definition that explicitly includes or excludes offers to sell or distribute, courts interpret liability narrowly to not include offers; and 2) Congress can and will amend a statute, when necessary, to explicitly include liability for an offer to do a prohibited act.

The Court's examination of the use of the term "distribution" in other provisions of the Copyright Act, as well as the evolution of liability for offers to sell in the analogous Patent Act, lead to the conclusion that the plain meaning of the term "distribution" does not including making available and, instead, requires actual dissemination. . . .

E.   *Whether "Distribution" Is Synonymous with "Publication"*

Plaintiffs advocate that, within the Copyright Act, the term "distribution" is synonymous with the term "publication."

> "Publication" is the distribution of copies or phonorecords of a work to the public by sale or other transfer of ownership, or by rental, lease, or lending. The offering to distribute copies or phonorecords to a group of persons for purposes of further distribution, public performance, or public display, constitutes publication. A public performance or display of a work does not of itself constitute publication.

17 U.S.C. §101. Under this definition, making sound recordings available on Kazaa could be considered distribution.

The first sentence of the definition of "publication" and §106(3) are substantially identical. However, there is additional language in the definition of "publication." Relying primarily on legislative history, Plaintiffs assert that the sentence defining publication as "[t]he offering to distribute copies or phonorecords to a group of persons for purposes of further distribution, public performance, or public display" should also apply to the definition of distribution.

Plaintiffs note that the text of §106 grants a copyright owner the following five exclusive rights: "(1) to reproduce the copyrighted work . . . (2) to prepare derivative works . . . (3) to distribute copies of the work . . . (4) . . . to perform the copyrighted work publicly; and (5) . . . to display the work publicly." 17 U.S.C. §106. However, the House and Senate Committees evaluating the Copyright Act, described the following five rights: "the exclusive rights of reproduction, adaptation, *publication*, performance, and display." *Elektra Entm't Group, Inc. v. Barker*, 551 F. Supp. 2d 234, 241 (S.D.N.Y. 2008) (quoting H.R. Rep. No. 94-1476, at 61 (1976); S.Rep. No. 94-473, at 57 (1976)) (emphasis added in *Barker*). The Committee Reports identified the "Rights of Reproduction, Adaptation, and Publication" as "[t]he first three clauses of section 106." *Id.* (quoting H.R. Rep. at 61; S. Rep. at 57). Also, the House Committee Report stated that §106(3) " 'establishes the exclusive right of publication' and governs 'unauthorized public distribution' — using the words 'distribution' and 'publication' interchangeably within a single paragraph." *Id.* (citing H.R. Rep. at 62; S. Rep. at 58). The Court does not find these snippets of legislative history to be dispositive of the definition of distribution. Nowhere in this legislative history does Congress state that distribution should be given the same broad meaning as publication. In any case, even if the legislative history indicated that some members of Congress equated publications with distributions under §106(3), that fact cannot override the plain meaning of the statute. . . .

The Court concludes that simply because all distributions within the meaning of §106(3) are publications does not mean that all publications within the meaning of §101 are distributions. . . .

Congress's choice to use both terms within the Copyright Act demonstrates an intent that the terms have different meanings. . . .

F. *Existence of a Protected Right to Authorize Distribution*

Plaintiffs and their supporters also take the position that authorizing distribution is an exclusive right protected by the Copyright Act. They base this argument on the fact that §106 states "the owner of copyright under this title has the exclusive rights **to do** and **to authorize** any of the following . . . (3) to distribute. . . ." (emphasis added). Plaintiffs claim that the statute grants two separate rights — the right to "do" distribution and the right to "authorize" distribution. Therefore, making sound recordings available on Kazaa violates the copyright owner's exclusive right to authorize distribution.

The Court concludes that the authorization clause merely provides a statutory foundation for secondary liability, not a means of expanding the scope of direct infringement liability. . . .

H. *Hotaling v. Church of Jesus Christ of Latter-Day Saints*

In *Hotaling*, the Fourth Circuit held that "a library distributes a published work, within the meaning of the Copyright Act, when it places an unauthorized copy of the work in its collection, includes the copy in its catalog or index system, and makes the copy available to the public." *Id.* at 201 (citation omitted).

The Fourth Circuit noted, "In order to establish 'distribution' of a copyrighted work, a party must show that an unlawful copy was disseminated 'to the public.' " *Id.*, at 203. In *Hotaling*, there was no evidence in the record "showing specific instances within the limitations period in which the libraries loaned the infringing copies to members of the public." *Id.* at 203. The court concluded,

When a public library adds a work to its collection, lists the work in its index or catalog system, and makes the work available to the borrowing or browsing public, it has completed all the steps necessary for distribution to the public. At that point, members of the public can visit the library and use the work. Were this not to be considered distribution within the meaning of §106(3), a copyright holder would be prejudiced by a library that does not keep records of public use, and the library would unjustly profit by its own omission.

Id. at 203. As demonstrated by the quotation above, the Fourth Circuit did not analyze any case law to support its conclusion that making the copyrighted materials available for distribution constituted distribution. Nor did it conduct any analysis of §106(3). Instead, the court was guided by equitable concerns.

Some courts have applied the principle articulated in *Hotaling* to conclude that merely making a work available for others to download over a peer-to-peer network may constitute a distribution. *See, e.g., Warner Bros. Records, Inc. v. Payne,* Civil Action No. W-06-CA-051, 2006 WL 2844415, at *3-4 (W.D.Tex. July 17, 2006) ("Listing unauthorized copies of sound recordings using an online file-sharing system constitutes an offer to distribute those works, thereby violating a copyright owner's exclusive right of distribution.") (citing, e.g., *Hotaling,* 118 F.3d at 203).

Amici conclude that *Hotaling's* deemed distributed liability should apply to peer-to-peer file sharing because a contrary rule would reward infringers who use technology configured to not retain direct evidence of wrongdoing. *See Warner Bros. Records, Inc.,* 2006 WL 2844415, at *3 ("[T]he same evidentiary concerns that were present in *Hotaling* are also present in a case involving peer-to-peer file sharing programs. As Plaintiffs note, '[p]iracy typically takes place behind closed doors and beyond the watchful eyes of a copyright holder.'") (citations omitted).

. . . [*Hotaling* is not] consistent with the logical statutory interpretation of §106(3), the body of Copyright Act case law, and the legislative history of the Copyright Act. Nonetheless, it is appropriate to note that this Court's rejection of *Hotaling* in favor of the plain meaning of §106(3) does not leave copyright holders without redress. The specter of impossible-to-meet evidentiary standards raised by amici is overstated. A person who makes an unauthorized copy or phonorecord of a copyrighted work for the purposes of uploading it onto a peer-to-peer network, absent a defense such as fair use, violates the reproduction right. 17 U.S.C. §106(a). That person might also be liable for indirect infringement to the extent that her conduct caused others to engage in unauthorized reproduction, adaptation, public distribution, public performance, or public display of another's copyrighted work.

The end user who accesses or downloads the unauthorized copy or phonorecord may be liable for direct infringement, depending on the facts of the case and the applicability of defenses, such as the fair use defense. . . .

Finally, while the Court does not adopt the deemed-disseminated theory based on *Hotaling,* it notes that *direct* proof of actual dissemination is not required by the Copyright Act. Plaintiffs are free to employ circumstantial evidence to attempt to prove actual dissemination. Overall, it is apparent that implementation of Congress's intent through a plain meaning interpretation of §106(3) will not leave copyright holders without recourse when infringement occurs over a peer-to-peer network.

I. *Implications of International Law*

1. U.S. Treaty Obligations Regarding the Making-Available Right

The United States is party to the World Intellectual Property Organization ("WIPO") Copyright Treaty ("WCT") and the WIPO Performances and Phonograms Treaty ("WPPT"). S. Rep. No. 105-190, 5, 9 (1998). It is undisputed that the WCT and the WPPT recognize a making-available right that is not dependent on proof that copies were actually transferred to particular individuals. WCT art. 6(1), art. 8; WPPT art. 12(1), art. 14. Additionally, by ratifying and adopting the treaties, the legislative and executive branches indicated that U.S. law complied with the treaties by protecting that making-available right.

Amici also note that the United States has entered various Free Trade Agreements ("FTA") that require the United States to provide a making-available right. *See, e.g.*, U.S.-Australia Free Trade Agreement, art. 17.5, May 18, 2004.

2. *Charming-Betsy* Doctrine . . .

Amici assert that under the *Charming Betsy* rule, the Court must adopt any reasonable interpretation of the Copyright Act that would grant Plaintiffs a making-available right to ensure that the U.S. complies with its treaty obligations.

The Supreme Court has explained:

> [T]his Court ordinarily construes ambiguous statutes to avoid unreasonable interference with the sovereign authority of other nations. This rule of construction reflects principles of customary international law-law that (we must assume) Congress ordinarily seeks to follow.

F. Hoffmann-La Roche Ltd. v. Empagran S.A., 542 U.S. 155, 164 (2004). *See Murray v. Schooner Charming Betsy*, 6 U.S. (2 Cranch) 64, 118 (1804) ("[A]n act of Congress ought never to be construed to violate the law of nations if any other possible construction remains. . . ."). . . .

The WIPO treaties are not self-executing and lack any binding legal authority separate from their implementation through the Copyright Act. . . . Therefore, the fact that the WIPO treaties protect a making-available right does not create an enforceable making-available right for Plaintiffs in this Court. *See, e.g., Guaylupo-Moya v. Gonzales*, 423 F.3d 121, 137 (2d Cir. 2005). . . . Rather, the contents of the WIPO treaties are only relevant insofar as §106(3) is ambiguous and there is a reasonable interpretation of §106(3) that aligns with the United States' treaty obligations. . . .

The Court acknowledges that past Presidents, Congresses, and the Register of Copyrights have indicated their belief that the Copyright Act implements WIPO's make-available right. The Court also acknowledges that, given multiple reasonable constructions of U.S. law, the *Charming Betsy* doctrine directs the Court to adopt the reasonable construction that is consistent with the United States' international obligations. However, after reviewing the Copyright Act itself, legislative history, binding Supreme Court and Eighth Circuit precedent, and an extensive body of case law examining the Copyright Act, the Court concludes that Plaintiffs' interpretation of the distribution right is simply not reasonable. . . . Here, concern for U.S. compliance with the WIPO treaties and the FTAs cannot override the clear congressional intent in §106(3). . . .

NOTES AND QUESTIONS

1. Do you agree with the *Capitol Records* court's interpretation of §106(3)? *Capitol Records* reflects the majority position among courts that have considered what constitutes "distribution" in the digital context. Most courts have held that merely making files available for sharing via a peer-to-peer network does not violate the distribution right. *See, e.g., Atlantic v. Howell*, 554 F. Supp. 2d 976 (D. Ariz. 2008); *London Sire-Records Inc., v. Doe 1*, 542 F. Supp. 2d 153 (D. Mass. 2008).

2. Neither the Berne Convention nor the TRIPS Agreement enumerates a separate right to distribute copies of copyrighted works, although a distribution right appears to be implicit in, *inter alia*, the reproduction right afforded under Article 9 of the Berne Convention (and incorporated into the TRIPS Agreement). The WIPO Copyright Treaty (WCT) seeks to remedy this omission in two separate provisions. Article 6 of the WCT provides for a right to control "the making available to the public of the original and copies of [copyrighted] works through sale or other transfer of ownership." WCT, art. 6. This right applies to "fixed copies that can be put into circulation as tangible objects." Agreed Statements Concerning the WIPO Copyright Treaty, adopted by the Diplomatic Conference on Dec. 20, 1996, WIPO CRNR/DC/96, Statement Concerning Article 6. Article 8 of the WCT provides an additional right of communication to the public: "[A]uthors of literary and artistic works shall enjoy the exclusive right of authorizing any communication to the public of their works . . . including the making available to the public of their works. . . ." WCT, art. 8. According to the accompanying Agreed Statement, however, "the mere provision of physical facilities for enabling or making a communication does not in itself amount to communication. . . ."Agreed Statements, *supra*, Statement Concerning Article 8. Under the *Capitol Records* interpretation of §106(3), is the U.S. in compliance with its obligations under the WCT? *See Arista Records LLC v. Greubel*, 453 F. Supp. 2d 961, 969 n.10 (N.D. Tex. 2006) (acknowledging the treaty compliance question but declining to address it while ruling on a motion to dismiss).

3. Should the *Capitol Records* court have relied on the *Charming Betsy* canon to reach the interpretation of §106(3) urged by the plaintiffs? *See also* Restatement (Third) of Foreign Relations Law of the United States §114 (1987) ("Where fairly possible, a United States statute is to be construed so as not to conflict with international law or with an international agreement of the United States."). In fact, courts do not often rely on this canon when interpreting statutes. Why do you think that is the case?

4. What do you think of the ruling allowing Capitol Records to satisfy its burden of proving actual distribution of an unauthorized copy by showing distribution to plaintiff's investigator, MediaSentry? Does that ruling represent good policy? Would universal adoption of that rule suffice to establish treaty compliance?

On retrial, plaintiffs used the MediaSentry evidence to establish unauthorized distribution of copies of 24 copyrighted songs. The jury awarded statutory damages of $80,000 per song, for a total of $1.92 million. The court subsequently issued an order remitting damages to $54,000. We discuss statutory damages in Chapter 11 *infra*.

5. At several places in its opinion, the *Capitol Records* court discusses the relative ease of proving infringement of the reproduction right. Does that option provide adequate recourse for the copyright owner who cannot prove actual distribution? You will learn about indirect infringement, another potential avenue of recourse mentioned by the court, in Chapter 6.

6. As a matter of policy, should Congress amend §106(3) to broaden its scope? Why, or why not? How would you draft such an amendment?

7. In 2004, a Canadian court held: "The mere fact of placing a copy on a shared directory in a computer where that copy can be accessed via a P2P service does not amount to distribution. Before it constitutes a distribution, there must be a positive act by the owner of the shared directory, such as sending out the copies or advertising that they are available for copying." *BMG Canada Inc. v. John Doe*, 2004 F.C. 488, 2004 Fed. Ct. Trial LEXIS 321, *21-*22.

In part as a result of this decision, the U.S. placed Canada on the Special 301 Watch List (see Chapter 1 *supra* for a discussion of Special 301), and began pressuring that country to "ratify and implement the WIPO Internet Treaties as soon as possible, and to reform its copyright law so that it provides adequate and effective protection of copyrighted works in

digital works); Mark A. Lemley, *Dealing with Overlapping Copyrights on the Internet,* 22 U. Dayton L. Rev. 547, 575, 584 (1997) (suggesting a rule "permitting the transfer of an electronic work to a single party provided the sender deletes her copies of the work within a reasonable time").

To date, Congress has shown little inclination to amend §109 to provide special rules for electronic transfers. Indeed, in reporting to Congress, the Register of Copyrights recommended against amending §109 to provide for a first sale right to transmit digital copies. According to the Report,

> [t]he transmission of a work from one person to another over the Internet results in a reproduction on the recipient's computer, even if the sender subsequently deletes the original copy of the work. This activity therefore entails an exercise of an exclusive right that is not covered by section 109. . . .
>
> Physical copies degrade with time and use; digital information does not. . . . Digital transmissions can adversely [a]ffect the market for the original to a much greater degree than transfers of physical copies. Additionally, unless a "forward-and-delete" technology is employed to automatically delete the sender's copy, the deletion of a work requires an additional affirmative act on the part of the sender subsequent to the transmission. This act is difficult to prove or disprove, as is a person's claim to have transmitted only a single copy, thereby raising complex evidentiary concerns. . . .
>
> . . . The tangible nature of a copy is a defining element of the first sale doctrine and critical to its rationale. The digital transmission of a work does not implicate the alienability of a physical artifact. . . . The benefits to further expansion [of §109] simply do not outweigh the likelihood of increased harm.

Executive Summary, Digital Millennium Copyright Act, Section 104 Report. To access the Report, visit *http://www.loc.gov/copyright/reports* and click on the "Digital Millennium Copyright Act §104 Study" link.

NOTES AND QUESTIONS

1. Should Congress amend §109 to provide special rules for electronic transfers of copies of copyrighted works by their owners? Do you agree with the Register's reasoning in recommending against such an amendment?

2. Consider carefully the various exceptions to the U.S. first sale doctrine that have been codified in §109(b), and the problem of digital works. Is the U.S. first sale doctrine becoming obsolete? Does the doctrine represent sound public policy? Does the first sale doctrine with its exceptions accord with ordinary consumer expectations regarding the use(s) they may make of the copyrighted material they purchase?

In *Brilliance Audio, Inc. v. Haights Cross Communications,* 474 F.3d 365 (6th Cir. 2007), the court considered whether the record rental exception to the first sale doctrine applies to all sound recordings or only to sound recordings of musical works. The defendants purchased and repackaged retail editions of plaintiff's audio books and then distributed the works by, among other things, renting them in direct competition with the plaintiff. The court reviewed the legislative history of §109 and determined that Congress intended to address only concerns related to rental of musical recordings. *Id.* at 371-73. It reasoned, further, that an exception to the first sale doctrine "should be construed narrowly because it upsets the traditional bargain between the rights of copyright owners and the personal property rights of an individual who owns a particular copy." *Id.* at 373. Do you agree that audiobooks are distinguishable enough from sound recordings of musical works to justify excluding them from the ambit of §109(b)(1)(A)? Should Congress expand the scope of the record rental exception?

3. In deciding how, or whether, to adapt the first sale doctrine to the digital environment, it is important to return to first principles and consider what purposes the first sale doctrine serves. According to Professor R. Anthony Reese, purposes of the traditional first sale doctrine include "making access to copyrighted works more affordable . . . and helping to ensure that works of authorship remain available to the public over time." R. Anthony Reese, *The First Sale Doctrine in the Era of Digital Networks*, 44 B.C. L. Rev. 577, 578 (2003). Do those goals militate in favor of extending the first sale doctrine to the electronic context?

4. Most other countries use the term *exhaustion* to describe what the U.S. copyright system refers to as the first sale doctrine. As the Berne Convention does not expressly address distribution rights, it is perhaps not surprising that it also does not address exhaustion of those rights. The TRIPS Agreement specifies that "nothing in this Agreement shall be used to address the issue of exhaustion of intellectual property rights." TRIPS Agreement, art. 6. Article 6 of the WCT also indicates that exhaustion, or lack thereof, is a matter for member countries to determine. Why do you think the negotiators of these agreements did not include a uniform rule covering this issue?

5. With the advent of digital works and distribution media and the perceived threat of widespread copying that these technologies create, copyright owners again began experimenting with blanket restrictions on resale or other transfer of copies of works. Software manufacturers were the first to do so, employing so-called shrinkwrap restrictions—asserted license terms printed on the physical package containing the software, accompanied by notice to the purchaser that opening the package constituted consent to the restrictions. In part because of doubts about the enforceability of shrinkwrap provisions, many producers of software and other digital works now use the digital medium itself to convey asserted license terms to consumers. The terms are displayed during the installation process—or, if the work is purchased via the Internet, during the purchase process—and the purchaser must click on a button indicating assent in order to proceed. These digital "contracts" have become known as "clickwrap" agreements. How do you think the *Bobbs-Merrill* Court would view these efforts? We consider the implications of clickwrap agreements in Chapters 8 and 10.

Note on Libraries, the First Sale Doctrine, and §108

As discussed above, the first sale doctrine allows libraries that have purchased copies of works to lend those copies, repeatedly, to members of the public. Nonprofit libraries and archives also enjoy some unique distribution privileges under copyright law. Section 108 authorizes certain acts of copying by these entities, and clearly allows some distribution of the resulting copies.

The privileges established by §108 include reproduction of single copies for the library itself or for library patrons for purposes of private study, scholarship, or research; reproduction and distribution for purposes of preservation, security, or research use by another library; reproduction to replace a damaged, deteriorating, or lost copy; and reproduction and distribution for patrons of other libraries within an interlibrary loan system. *See* 17 U.S.C. §108(a)-(e). These provisions, however, include limitations designed to ensure that none of these activities can become a market substitute for purchases of copyrighted works. Thus, for example, a library may not make copies for patrons if it has substantial reason to believe that it is facilitating "the related or concerted reproduction or distribution of multiple copies or phonorecords of the same material." *Id.* §108(g). In addition, it may not make copies of musical works, motion pictures, or pictorial, graphic, or sculptural works (other than illustrations) for purposes other than preservation, security, or replacement of a deteriorating or damaged copy—i.e., it may not make such copies for the personal use of library patrons. *See id.* §108(i). Finally, a library may not make replacement copies unless it has "after a reasonable effort, determined that an unused replacement cannot be obtained at a fair price." *Id.* §108(c)(1).

Like §109(a), §108 has come under pressure in the digital environment. In the Digital Millennium Copyright Act of 1998, Congress amended §108 to restrict libraries' abilities to distribute copies of works in their collections to members of the public in digital format. As amended, §108 allows a library to reproduce copies or phonorecords in digital format, but prohibits them from making such copies available to the public outside the library's own premises. *See id.* §108(b)(2), (c)(2).

Note on the EU Rental Rights Directive and the Public Lending Right

Like the U.S., the countries of the EU generally recognize principles of first sale, or "exhaustion." Unlike the U.S., however, the EU has in place a directive that comprehensively regulates the rental, lease, and lending of all types of copyrighted works. The EU Rental Rights Directive, adopted in 1992 by the then-European Community, establishes an exclusive right to authorize or prohibit rental, lease, or lending of all works other than buildings and works of applied art. Council Directive 92/100/EEC of 19 November 1992 on rental right and lending right and on certain rights related to copyright in the field of intellectual property, 1992 O.J. (L. 346) 61, art. 2(1), (3). In addition, another directive separately provides a right to control the rental of computer programs. Directive 2009/24, Legal Protection of Computer Programs, art. 4, 2009 O.J. (L 111) 16(EC). For a legislative history and early critique of the EU Rental Rights Directive, see Robert A. Rosenbloum, *The Rental Rights Directive: A Step in the Right and Wrong Directions*, 15 Loy. L.A. Ent. L.J. 547 (1995).

How do libraries fare under a comprehensive rental rights regime? The EU Rental Rights Directive authorizes member states to derogate from the exclusive rental right for public lending, provided that authors receive some remuneration. The impetus for this provision was the "public lending right" developed by Denmark in the mid-twentieth century, and subsequently adopted by Australia, Finland, Great Britain, Iceland, the Netherlands, New Zealand, Norway, Sweden, and the former West Germany. See Daniel Y. Mayer, Note, *Literary Copyright and Public Lending Right*, 18 Case W. Res. J. Int'l L. 483, 485-86 (1986).

Under the public lending right, the author of a copyrighted work receives a small royalty each time a member of the public borrows the work, or alternatively, based on a census of titles in stock and available for public borrowing or usage. The right to receive this royalty belongs to authors, as distinct from subsequent assignees of the authors' copyright interests, although some countries also provide for separate payments to publishers. Unlike the exclusive rights afforded under §106 of the U.S. Copyright Act, or under the EU Rental Rights Directive, the public lending right does not entitle an author to prohibit the public lending of a work. In the language of law and economics, the right is a liability rule rather than a property rule; it entitles the author only to be paid. Payments to authors are financed by taxpayers via the administrative budget for the public library system. *See* Mayer, *supra*, at 488-97; Jennifer M. Schneck, Note, *Closing the Book on the Public Lending Right*, 63 N.Y.U. L. Rev. 878, 887-99 (1988).

In the wake of the EU Rental Rights Directive, a number of other countries both within and outside the EU have adopted or are considering adopting such a right. *See* Joshua H. Foley,

Comment, *Enter the Library: Creating a Digital Lending Right*, 16 Conn. J. Int'l L. 369, 385 & n.115 (2001). Bills to enact a public lending right in the U.S. were introduced in Congress several times during the 1970s and 1980s, but neither the House nor the Senate has ever approved such a bill.

NOTES AND QUESTIONS

1. Does §108's carefully qualified group of exceptions strike you as generally sensible, or as too complicated? If the latter, what rules for libraries would you propose?

2. Is the European "rental right plus public lending right" model superior to the all-or-nothing approach taken by U.S. copyright law? Why, or why not? Would you recommend that the U.S. give all copyright owners the exclusive right to control rental or lending of their works? Would you recommend that the U.S. adopt a public lending right for noncommercial lending? How about a liability rule model for rentals of copyrighted works generally?

3. How should the public lending right apply to digital works held by libraries? Should distribution of digital works outside the physical premises of a library be prohibited, as it is under the amendments to §108 of the U.S. Copyright Act? Are those amendments necessary to prevent abuse of library privileges, or do they undermine the potential of digital libraries? Is there another solution? For one proposal for a royalty-bearing "digital lending right" modeled after the public lending right, see Joshua H. Foley, Comment, *Enter the Library: Creating a Digital Lending Right*, 16 Conn. J. Int'l L. 369 (2001).

4. Professor Jane Ginsburg argues that in the digital age, access to content rather than ownership of copies is the essence of what copyright should protect. Jane C. Ginsburg, *From Having Copies to Experiencing Works: The Development of an Access Right in U.S. Copyright Law*, 50 J. Copyright Soc'y U.S.A. 113 (2003). Do you agree? What are the implications of this view for the first sale doctrine? What are the implications for other exceptions, such as §108, under which the distribution of exact copies is privileged?

5. In addition to special privileges for libraries, the 1976 Act also contains an exception to the §106 reproduction and distribution rights for copies or phonorecords prepared "in specialized formats exclusively for use by blind or other persons with disabilities." 17 U.S.C. §121. The exception applies only to nondramatic literary works, and only to those works that previously have been published in some other format.

6. The Copyright Office recently completed a study of the challenges that digital technologies raise for libraries, and issued a report recommending a series of amendments designed to harmonize §108 with the library community's emerging consensus about "best practices" in the digital age. The Section 108 Study Group Report is available at *http://www.section108.gov/*.

7. Review the Note on Copyright's Default Rules and the Google Book Search (GBS) project, pages 157-58 *supra*. The GBS project implicates the rights to reproduce not only those books that qualify as "orphan works," but also all other books still under copyright. Essentially, the GBS project would offer a new type of online library with full-text search capability. Google is a for-profit entity that plans to realize advertising and subscription revenues from the GBS project, so it is not eligible for the exemptions in §108. Instead, Google hopes to enjoy the privilege of exercising copyright rights pursuant to the terms of the proffered settlement agreement, which would implement a form of collective licensing. Would-be readers, for their part, would enjoy access to books stored by the GBS project on the terms set by Google.

Do you think the GBS project represents a good solution to the problem of access in a digital age? Has your answer to the question whether you would opt out of the settlement agreement changed (see Question 2, page 158 *supra*)? Are there restrictions that you would like to see included in the settlement agreement?

3. Unauthorized Importation and the First Sale Doctrine

An important adjunct of the distribution right is the right to prevent the unauthorized importation of copies of the copyrighted work into the U.S. *See* 17 U.S.C. §602. As discussed in Chapter 1, copyright law has always been concerned with the territorial origin of copies of protected works. Recall the Manufacturing Clause, page 34 *supra*, which required that copyrighted works be printed within the U.S. The purpose of the Manufacturing Clause, however, was to protect U.S. printers, not U.S. copyright owners. Modern copyright law, in contrast, is concerned with whether the copies are infringing, and whether the importation is authorized by the copyright owner. For example, copies made without the authority of any copyright owner (U.S. or foreign) clearly violate the importation right.

Copyrights can be divided geographically, however. Sometimes, the foreign copyright holder is completely unrelated to and unaffiliated with the U.S. copyright owner of the same work. This might happen, for example, when the author of the work sells or licenses the U.S. rights and the foreign rights (or, more likely, the European rights, the Asian rights, and so on) to different publishers. It might also happen if a U.S. company owns the entire copyright, but sells or licenses the rights to exploit the work outside the U.S. to a foreign company, or vice versa. In other cases, the U.S. and foreign copyright holders have a parent/subsidiary relationship or are sibling companies.

Foreign licensees or affiliates typically agree not to distribute the work within each other's territory, and also agree to impose these geographic restrictions on their distributors. However, the temptation to violate such restrictions is strong. Copyrighted products (like most other products) command much higher prices in the U.S. and other industrialized countries than they do in developing countries. In an era of global trade and currency fluctuation, this is a recipe for arbitrage (buying in one country at a low price that the seller set in expectation that the buyer would distribute in that country and reselling in another country for a higher price). Recall, moreover, that the first sale doctrine allows the owner of a lawfully made copy of a work to resell it. Under these circumstances, just what is an unauthorized copy for purposes of the importation right is an important question.

Quality King Distributors, Inc. v. L'anza Research International, Inc.
523 U.S. 135 (1998)

STEVENS, J.: . . .

I

Respondent, L'anza Research International, Inc. (L'anza), is a California corporation engaged in the business of manufacturing and selling shampoos, conditioners, and other hair care products. L'anza has copyrighted the labels that are affixed to those products. In the United States, L'anza sells exclusively to domestic distributors who have agreed to resell within limited geographic areas and then only to authorized retailers such as barber shops, beauty salons, and professional hair care colleges. L'anza has found that the American "public is generally unwilling to pay the price charged for high quality products, such as L'anza's products, when they are sold along with the less expensive lower quality products that are generally carried by supermarkets and drug stores." App. 54 (declaration of Robert Hall). . . .

L'anza also sells its products in foreign markets. In those markets, however, it does not engage in comparable advertising or promotion; its prices to foreign distributors are 35% to 40% lower than the prices charged to domestic distributors. . . .

[Three shipments of hair care products manufactured by L'anza were purchased by a distributor in Malta. The goods subsequently "found their way back to the United States," where they were purchased by petitioner Quality King and sold to "unauthorized retailers." L'anza sued Quality King and others in the chain of distribution for copyright infringement. The district court granted summary judgment to L'anza, and the Court of Appeals for the Ninth Circuit affirmed. Several years earlier, the Third Circuit had reached the opposite result, holding that the first sale doctrine supplied a complete defense to conduct like Quality King's. The Supreme Court granted certiorari to resolve the circuit conflict.]

II

This is an unusual copyright case because L'anza does not claim that anyone has made unauthorized copies of its copyrighted labels. Instead, L'anza is primarily interested in protecting the integrity of its method of marketing the products to which the labels are affixed. Although the labels themselves have only a limited creative component, our interpretation of the relevant statutory provisions would apply equally to a case involving more familiar copyrighted materials such as sound recordings or books. Indeed, we first endorsed the first sale doctrine in a case involving a claim by a publisher that the resale of its books at discounted prices infringed its copyright on the books. *Bobbs-Merrill Co. v. Straus*, 210 U.S. 339 (1908). . . .

The *Bobbs-Merrill* opinion emphasized the critical distinction between statutory rights and contract rights. In this case, L'anza relies on the terms of its contracts with its domestic distributors to limit their sales to authorized retail outlets. Because the basic holding in *Bobbs-Merrill* is now codified in §109(a) of the Act, and because those domestic distributors are owners of the products that they purchased from L'anza (the labels of which were "lawfully made under this title"), L'anza does not, and could not, claim that the statute would enable L'anza to treat unauthorized resales by its domestic distributors as an infringement of its exclusive right to distribute copies of its labels. L'anza does claim, however, that contractual provisions are inadequate to protect it from the actions of foreign distributors who may resell L'anza's products to American vendors unable to buy from L'anza's domestic distributors, and that §602(a) of the Act, properly construed, prohibits such unauthorized competition. . . .

III

The most relevant portion of §602(a) provides:

"Importation into the United States, without the authority of the owner of copyright under this title, of copies or phonorecords of a work that have been acquired outside the United States is an infringement of the exclusive right to distribute copies or phonorecords under section 106, actionable under section 501. . . ."[11]

11. The remainder of §602(a) reads as follows: "This subsection does not apply to — (1) importation of copies or phonorecords under the authority or for the use of the Government of the United States or of any State or political subdivision of a State, but not including copies or phonorecords for use in schools, or copies of any audiovisual work imported for purposes other than archival use; (2) importation, for the private use of the importer and not for distribution, by any person with respect to no more than one copy or phonorecord of any one work at any one time, or by any person arriving from outside the United States with respect to copies or phonorecords forming part of such person's

It is significant that this provision does not categorically prohibit the unauthorized importation of copyrighted materials. Instead, it provides that such importation is an infringement of the exclusive right to distribute copies "under section 106." Like the exclusive right to "vend" that was construed in *Bobbs-Merrill*, the exclusive right to distribute is a limited right. The introductory language in §106 expressly states that all of the exclusive rights granted by that section — including, of course, the distribution right granted by subsection (3) — are limited by the provisions of §§107 through 120 [now 122 — Eds.]. One of those limitations, as we have noted, is provided by the terms of §109(a), which expressly permit the owner of a lawfully made copy to sell that copy "[n]otwithstanding the provisions of section 106(3)."

After the first sale of a copyrighted item "lawfully made under this title," any subsequent purchaser, whether from a domestic or from a foreign reseller, is obviously an "owner" of that item. Read literally §109(a) unambiguously states that such an owner "is entitled, without the authority of the copyright owner, to sell" that item. Moreover, since §602(a) merely provides that unauthorized importation is an infringement of an exclusive right "under section 106," and since that limited right does not encompass resales by lawful owners, the literal text of §602(a) is simply inapplicable to both domestic and foreign owners of L'anza's products who decide to import them and resell them in the United States.[14] . . .

IV

L'anza advances two primary arguments based on the text of the Act: (1) that §602(a), and particularly its three exceptions, are superfluous if limited by the first sale doctrine; and (2) that the text of §501 defining an "infringer" refers separately to violations of §106, on the one hand, and to imports in violation of §602. . . .

The Coverage of §602(a)

Prior to the enactment of §602(a), the Act already prohibited the importation of "piratical," or unauthorized, copies. Moreover, that earlier prohibition is retained in §602(b) of the present Act.[17] L'anza therefore argues (as do the Solicitor General and other *amici curiae*) that §602(a) is superfluous unless it covers nonpiratical ("lawfully made") copies sold by the copyright owner, because importation nearly always implies a first sale. There are several flaws in this argument.

First, even if §602(a) did apply only to piratical copies, it at least would provide the copyright holder with a private remedy against the importer, whereas the enforcement of §602(b) is vested in the Customs Services. Second, because the protection afforded by §109(a) is available only to the "owner" of a lawfully made copy (or someone authorized by

---

personal baggage; or (3) importation by or for an organization operated for scholarly, educational, or religious purposes and not for private gain, with respect to no more than one copy of an audiovisual work solely for its archival purposes, and no more than five copies or phonorecords of any other work for its library lending or archival purposes, unless the importation of such copies or phonorecords is part of an activity consisting of systematic reproduction or distribution, engaged in by such organization in violation of the provisions of section 108(g)(2)."

14. Despite L'anza's contention to the contrary . . . the owner of goods lawfully made under the Act is entitled to the protection of the first sale doctrine in an action in a United States court even if the first sale occurred abroad. Such protection does not require the extraterritorial application of the Act any more than §602(a)'s "acquired abroad" language does.

17. Section 602(b) provides in relevant part: "In a case where the making of the copies or phonorecords would have constituted an infringement of copyright if this title had been applicable, their importation is prohibited. . . ." The first sale doctrine of §109(a) does not protect owners of piratical copies, of course, because such copies were not "lawfully made."

the owner), the first sale doctrine would not provide a defense to a §602(a) action against any nonowner such as a bailee, a licensee, a consignee, or one whose possession of the copy was unlawful. Third, §602(a) applies to a category of copies that are neither piratical nor "lawfully made under this title." That category encompasses copies that were "lawfully made" not under the United States Copyright Act, but instead, under the law of some other country.

The category of copies produced lawfully under a foreign copyright was expressly identified in the deliberations that led to the enactment of the 1976 Act. . . . In a report to Congress, the Register of Copyrights stated, in part:

> "When arrangements are made for both a U.S. edition and a foreign edition of the same work, the publishers frequently agree to divide the international markets. The foreign publisher agrees not to sell his edition in the United States, and the U.S. publisher agrees not to sell his edition in certain foreign countries. It has been suggested that the import ban on piratical copies should be extended to bar the importation of the foreign edition in contravention of such an agreement." Copyright Law Revision: Report of the Register of Copyrights on the General Revision of the U.S. Copyright Law, 87th Cong., 1st Sess., 125-126 (H. R. Judiciary Comm. Print 1961).

Even in the absence of a market allocation agreement between, for example, a publisher of the United States edition and a publisher of the British edition of the same work, each such publisher could make lawful copies. If the author of the work gave the exclusive United States distribution rights — enforceable under the Act — to the publisher of the United States edition and the exclusive British distribution rights to the publisher of the British edition, however, presumably only those made by the publisher of the United States edition would be "lawfully made under this title" within the meaning of §109(a). . . .

The argument that the statutory exceptions to §602(a) are superfluous if the first sale doctrine is applicable rests on the assumption that the coverage of that section is coextensive with the coverage of §109(a). But since it is, in fact, broader because it encompasses copies that are not subject to the first sale doctrine — *e.g.*, copies that are lawfully made under the law of another country — the exceptions do protect the traveler who may have made an isolated purchase of a copy of a work that could not be imported in bulk for purposes of resale. . . .

Section 501's Separate References to §§106 and 602

The text of §501 does lend support to L'anza's submission. In relevant part, it provides:

> "(a) Anyone who violates any of the exclusive rights of the copyright owner as provided by sections 106 through 118 or of the author as provided in section 106A(a), or who imports copies or phonorecords into the United States in violation of section 602, is an infringer of the copyright or right of the author, as the case may be. . . ."

The use of the words "*or* who imports," rather than words such as "*including* one who imports," is more consistent with an interpretation that a violation of §602 is distinct from a violation of §106 (and thus not subject to the first sale doctrine set out in §109(a)) than with the view that it is a species of such a violation. Nevertheless, the force of that inference is outweighed by other provisions in the statutory text.

Most directly relevant is the fact that the text of §602(a) itself unambiguously states that the prohibited importation is an infringement of the exclusive distribution right "under section 106, actionable under section 501." . . .

Of even greater importance is the fact that the §106 rights are subject not only to the first sale defense in §109(a), but also to all of the other provisions of "sections 107 through 120."

If §602(a) functioned independently, none of those sections would limit its coverage. For example, the "fair use" defense embodied in §107 would be unavailable to importers if §602(a) created a separate right not subject to the limitations on the §106(3) distribution right. Under L'anza's interpretation of the Act, it presumably would be unlawful for a distributor to import copies of a British newspaper that contained a book review quoting excerpts from an American novel protected by a United States copyright. Given the importance of the fair use defense to publishers of scholarly works, as well as to publishers of periodicals, it is difficult to believe that Congress intended to impose an absolute ban on the importation of all such works containing any copying of material protected by a United States copyright. . . .

V

The parties and their *amici* have debated at length the wisdom or unwisdom of governmental restraints on what is sometimes described as either the "gray market" or the practice of "parallel importation." In *K Mart Corp. v. Cartier, Inc.*, 486 U.S. 281 (1988), we used those terms to refer to the importation of foreign-manufactured goods bearing a valid United States trademark without the consent of the trademark holder. . . . We are not at all sure that those terms appropriately describe the consequences of an American manufacturer's decision to limit its promotional efforts to the domestic market and to sell its products abroad at discounted prices that are so low that its foreign distributors can compete in the domestic market. But even if they do, whether or not we think it would be wise policy to provide statutory protection for such price discrimination is not a matter that is relevant to our duty to interpret the text of the Copyright Act.

Equally irrelevant is the fact that the Executive Branch of the Government has entered into at least five international trade agreements that are apparently intended to protect domestic copyright owners from the unauthorized importation of copies of their works sold in those five countries.[30] The earliest of those agreements was made in 1991; none has been ratified by the Senate. Even though they are of course consistent with the position taken by the Solicitor General in this litigation, they shed no light on the proper interpretation of a statute that was enacted in 1976.

GINSBURG, J., concurring: This case involves a "round trip" journey, travel of the copies in question from the United States to places abroad, then back again. I join the Court's opinion recognizing that we do not today resolve cases in which the allegedly infringing imports were manufactured abroad. . . .

NOTES AND QUESTIONS

1. Are you satisfied with the Court's explanation of the coverage of §602(a)? Are you satisfied with its interpretation of §501?

2. Review the brief excerpt from Justice Ginsburg's concurrence. If a copy is lawfully made abroad, is §109(a) a defense to a claim of unlawful importation under §602? According to the Ninth Circuit, the answer is "no." *See Omega S.A. v. Costco Wholesale Corp.*, 541 F.3d 982 (9th Cir. 2008), *cert. granted*. No. 08-1423, 559 U.S. (Apr. 19, 2010). Omega manufactured watches in Switzerland with a copyrighted design engraved on the underside, and sold them

---

30. The Solicitor General advises us that such agreements have been made with Cambodia, Trinidad and Tobago, Jamaica, Ecuador, and Sri Lanka.

to authorized distributors overseas. Some of the watches made their way to Costco, which sold them to consumers at discount prices. Ruling that Costco could not invoke §109(a), the court reasoned that ". . . the application of §109(a) to foreign-made copies would impermissibly apply the Copyright Act extraterritorially in a way that the application of the statute after foreign sales does not." *Id.* at 988.

Is the *Omega* decision consistent with *L'anza?* Consistent with the wording of §§109 and 602? Note that in the PRO-IP Act of 2008, Congress revised and reorganized §602. It amended the language in §602(b), concerning what the Court terms "piratical" copies, to focus more narrowly on interception of such copies at the U.S. border. It then created a new §602(a)(2)(B) encompassing those "piratical" copies within the subsection defining acts of infringement. Review the portion of the *L'anza* opinion discussing the scope of §602(a), and read the current version of §602. Do the PRO-IP Act amendments strengthen Omega's position on what §602(a) prohibits?

3. Should Omega, as the copyright owner and manufacturer of the watches at issue, be able to use copyright law to prevent their resale in the U.S.? Should copyright law respect market allocation agreements between domestic and foreign copyright holders? Consider, for example, the popular *Harry Potter* series of children's books. The American editions of these books differ from the original British editions. The spelling is Americanized — e.g., "color" instead of "colour" and "realize" instead of "realise" — and the language altered to reflect American terminology and usage — e.g., "vacation" for "holiday" and "bathroom" for "toilet" or "loo." If a market exists within the U.S. for the "authentic" British editions of the *Harry Potter* books, why not allow an enterprising importer to satisfy the demand?

4. If a fan of the *Harry Potter* series purchases copies of the British editions while visiting London and brings them back with her to the U.S., has she committed copyright infringement? Study §602 carefully before you answer. If after finishing the books, the *Harry Potter* fan decides to resell her copies of the British editions on eBay, does §109(a) allow her to do so? May someone who purchases a Swiss-made Omega watch from an authorized U.S. distributor resell it pursuant to §109(a)? To avoid providing "greater copyright protection to foreign-made copies than to their domestically-made counterparts," the Ninth Circuit had earlier held that "the copyright owner's voluntary sale of the copies within the United States exhausted the exclusive right of distribution." *Omega S.A.,* 541 F. 3d at 986. Because the facts before it did not implicate that judicially-created rule, the *Omega* court declined to disturb it. Can the exhaustion rule that the court describes be reconciled with an interpretation of §109(a) that prohibits extraterritorial application?

5. The rules that apply in trademark cases involving gray market goods are similar to those that apply in copyright cases, but not identical. In trademark cases, the statute that proscribes unauthorized importation is the Tariff Act of 1930 (as amended), which provides in relevant part: "[I]t shall be unlawful to import into the United States any merchandise of foreign manufacture if such merchandise . . . bears a trademark owned by a citizen of, or by a corporation or association organized within, the United States." 19 U.S.C. §1526(a). In its implementing regulations, the Customs Service interpreted this language to allow importation of goods manufactured by the foreign parent of the U.S. trademark holder, on the reasoning that in this case the mark is "owned by" the foreign parent. It also interpreted the statute to permit importation of goods manufactured abroad for the U.S. trademark holder or its foreign subsidiary, on the reasoning that in these cases the merchandise is not "of foreign manufacture." In a rather confusing plurality opinion, the Supreme Court declined to hold the Customs Service's reading of the statute unreasonable. *K Mart Corp. v. Cartier, Inc.,* 486 U.S. 281 (1988). The result is that gray market imports are prohibited under the Tariff Act only if the U.S. and foreign trademark owners lack common ownership or control — e.g., if

the U.S. trademark holder has licensed the use of the mark abroad by an independent foreign manufacturer, or vice versa. (In another part of the *K Mart* decision, a majority of the Court struck down other provisions of the Customs regulations that allowed importation as long as the U.S. trademark holder had authorized the use of the mark.)

U.S. trademark owners were bitterly unhappy with the common ownership or control aspects of the *K Mart* decision, but were unable to secure relief in Congress. Subsequently, however, the federal courts of appeals have interpreted the domestic trademark law, the Lanham Act, to afford some relief against imported goods manufactured by foreign affiliates. Section 42 of the Lanham Act, 15 U.S.C. §1124, prohibits the importation of goods "which shall copy or simulate the name of any domestic manufacture, or manufacturer, or trader." Courts have held that this provision bars the importation of goods that bear an identical trademark to the valid U.S. trademark, but that are physically different from the U.S. trademark holder's goods, regardless of the trademark's genuine character abroad and regardless of any affiliation between the U.S. and foreign trademark holders. The rationale for this rule is that "[t]rademarks applied to physically different foreign goods are not genuine from the viewpoint of the American consumer." *Lever Bros. v. United States*, 981 F.2d 1330, 1338 (D.C. Cir. 1993) (holding that Sunlight brand detergent originally manufactured for use in the United Kingdom was not genuine, and therefore could not be imported, because it produced fewer suds than the version of Sunlight marketed in the U.S.); *see also Societe des Produits Nestle, S.A. v. Casa Helvetia, Inc.*, 982 F.2d 633 (1st Cir. 1992) (holding that Perugina brand chocolate bars intended for sale in Venezuela and containing different ingredients than the Perugina brand chocolate bars ordinarily imported for sale in the U.S. were materially different from U.S. bars, and therefore could not be imported into, and sold in, the U.S.).

L'anza did not pursue any trademark claims against Quality King under either the Tariff Act or the Lanham Act. Why not?

6. Internationally, rules regarding the effect of exhaustion principles on gray market imports vary. (Recall that the TRIPS Agreement does not mandate that countries adopt rules on exhaustion.) In *Silhouette International Schmied GmbH & Co. KG v. Hartlauer Handelgesellschaft mbH*, 2 C.M.L.R. 953 (1998), a trademark case, the European Court of Justice (ECJ) interpreted the governing law as requiring pure territoriality. The plaintiff, Silhouette, an Austrian company, produces high-end eyeglasses. Silhouette sold a consignment of eyeglass frames in a discontinued style to a Bulgarian company, which agreed that the frames would be sold only in Bulgaria or other former Eastern bloc countries. Instead, the frames were purchased by Hartlauer, a discount retailer operating within Austria. The Austrian courts ruled that under traditional principles of Austrian law, Silhouette's sale of the frames would have exhausted its trademark rights. However, they referred to the ECJ (the high court of the then European Community) the question whether an intervening European trademark directive, now incorporated into Austrian law, had altered the operation of exhaustion principles. The ECJ concluded that under the directive, exhaustion applied only if the goods were sold within the countries of the European Community, but not if they were sold in a country outside the Community.

The language of the more recent EU directive on copyright harmonization suggests that the same principles will apply to exhaustion of rights under copyright law. Directive 2001/29/EC of the European Parliament and of the Council of 22 May 2001 on the harmonisation of certain aspects of copyright and related rights in the information society, 2001 O.J. (L. 167) 10, art. 4(2).

7. Some academics argue that gray markets in copyrighted and/or trademarked goods can be efficient because they promote the acquisition of these goods by more consumers and at lower prices. *See, e.g.*, Nancy T. Gallini & Aidan Hollis, *A Contractual Approach to the*

Gray Market, 19 Int'l Rev. L. & Econ. 1 (1999); Shubha Ghosh, *An Economic Analysis of the Common Control Exception to Gray Market Exclusion*, 15 U. Pa. J. Int'l Bus. L. 373 (1994). Other commentators respond that copyright and trademark protection are territorial by design, and that this is appropriate because the price discrimination that territoriality enables — that is, charging relatively affluent consumers in the U.S. and other industrialized countries more for the same goods — enables producers and distributors to provide consumers in these countries with "extras" such as warranty service, and increases incentives to produce, distribute, and promote products. Copyright owners also argue that gray-market goods unfairly constrain their profit margins by forcing them to compete against their own products. *See, e.g.*, Richard S. Higgins & Paul H. Rubin, *Counterfeit Goods*, 29 J.L. & Econ. 211 (1986); William M. Landes & Richard A. Posner, *Trademark Law: An Economic Perspective*, 30 J.L. & Econ. 265 (1987); Elin Dugan, Note, *United States of America, Home of the Cheap and the Gray: A Comparison of Recent Court Decisions Affecting the U.S. and European Gray Markets*, 33 Geo. Wash. Int'l L. Rev. 397, 409-11 (2001) (summarizing manufacturers' arguments). Who has the better argument? If you agree with the gray-market critics, are you more persuaded by territoriality concerns or by the price discrimination argument? (If the latter, have you ever shopped at a discount store like Costco, Sam's Club, or Price Club?)

8. How should copyright law respond to distribution of copies across national borders via the Internet? Digital delivery is increasingly the mechanism of choice for distribution of a wide variety of types of works. Does §602(a) as currently worded allow such distribution by foreign copyright holders? Should it?

9. In the digital era, some of the copyright industries have taken matters into their own hands and are selling "region-coded" entertainment goods. The technology for region-coding was developed by the video game industry to combat large-scale counterfeiting that was perceived as particularly acute in Southeast Asia and China. The industry reasoned that if video game cartridges purchased in Asia would not play on video game consoles sold in North America or Europe, counterfeiters would have more difficulty gaining a foothold in the industry's most lucrative markets. Subsequently, a number of the copyright industries implemented region-coding technologies more widely to control gray-market imports. The movie industry, for example, sells region-coded DVDs and Blu-ray discs under a series of cooperative licensing agreements with manufacturers of home DVD and Blu-ray players. Under the region-coding agreements, regions perceived as harboring counterfeiters are no longer the exclusive targets. DVDs manufactured in Europe will not work on DVD players sold in North America, and vice versa.

What do you think of these arrangements? If copyright law does not prohibit the imports, is it good policy to allow the affected industries to adopt technological protections that have that effect?

10. In addition to the amendments described in Question 2 *supra*, the PRO-IP Act amended §602(a) to provide that unauthorized *exportation* of copies or phonorecords is an infringement of copyright actionable under §501. Why do you think Congress made this change? Is it good policy?

D. THE RIGHT TO PREPARE DERIVATIVE WORKS

Very closely related to the "core" right of reproduction is the right to prepare derivative works based on the copyrighted work. 17 U.S.C. §106(2). The Copyright Act of 1870 was the first to introduce formally a version of the right to prepare derivative works. It provided that authors could reserve the right to dramatize or translate their own works. The 1909 Act changed this right of reservation to an outright grant, and also expanded derivative rights beyond dramatizations and translations to include the rights to make "any other version thereof, if it be a literary work; . . . to convert it into a novel or other nondramatic work if it be a drama; to arrange or adapt it if it be a musical work; to complete, execute, and finish it if it be a model or design for a work of art. . . ." 1909 Copyright Act, §1(b). While the language of the 1909 Act represented the first codification of derivative rights, judicial construction of the exclusive right to reproduce had already established protection beyond the literal copy of a protected work. Indeed, the legislative history of the 1909 Act indicated that Congress intended simply to codify existing case law. *See* H.R. Rep. No. 60-2222, App. 13-1, at 13-6 (1909).

In 1976, Congress further extended the right to prepare derivative works to all categories of copyrightable subject matter. Section 103(a) of the Copyright Act makes clear that derivative works meeting the statutory standards of §102 are themselves independently copyrightable, and the examples in the definition supplied by §101 indicate that the de minimis transformation of the underlying work can result in a derivative work. In Chapter 2, we discussed what constitutes originality sufficient to support the grant of a copyright in a derivative work. In this section, we focus on a different question: the scope of the exclusive right of the author to prepare and to authorize others to prepare derivative works based upon the copyrighted work.

The addition of a right to prepare derivative works has made the determination of infringement even more difficult for courts. Recall the importance of showing substantial similarity in establishing infringement of the reproduction right. Because a derivative work, by definition, is based upon a preexisting copyrighted work, some degree of copying has inevitably taken place whenever a derivative work has been prepared. This overlap makes it difficult to determine which right has been infringed — the exclusive right to reproduce the work or the exclusive right to prepare derivative works. Indeed, courts often conflate the analysis of these two rights in disposing of an infringement case. This section explores the different ways that courts have defined the scope of the right to prepare derivative works and the various approaches used to determine when infringement of this right has occurred.

1. Defining "Derivative"

The 1976 Copyright Act defines a derivative work as follows:

> A derivative work is a work based upon one or more preexisting works, such as a translation, musical arrangement, dramatization, fictionalization, motion picture version, sound recording, art reproduction, abridgement, condensation, or any other form in which a work may be recast, transformed, or adapted. A work consisting of editorial revisions, annotations, elaborations, or other modifications which, as a whole, represent an original work of authorship is a "derivative work."

17 U.S.C. §101.

According to the House Report accompanying the 1976 Act:

> The exclusive right to prepare derivative works . . . overlaps the exclusive right of reproduction to some extent. It is broader than that right, however, in the sense that reproduction requires fixation in copies or phonorecords, whereas the preparation of a derivative work, such as a ballet, pantomime, or improvised performance, may be an infringement even though nothing is ever fixed in tangible form. . . .

. . . [T]o constitute a violation of section 106(2), the infringing work must incorporate a portion of the copyrighted work in some form; for example, a detailed commentary on a work or a programmatic musical composition inspired by a novel would not normally constitute infringements under this clause.

H.R. Rep. No. 94-1476, 94th Cong., 2d Sess. 62 (1976), *reprinted in* 1976 U.S.C.C.A.N. 5659, 5675. Although the legislative history seems rather straightforward, defining what constitutes a derivative work raises some difficult questions. What is the rationale for giving copyright owners the exclusive right to prepare derivative works, and how broadly should the grant be construed? In particular, how does one apply the §101 definition in real cases? Additionally, how does the derivative works right differ from the exclusive right of reproduction?

We begin with a scholarly excerpt discussing the policy underpinnings of the derivative works right, and then move to cases in which courts have addressed these questions.

Paul Goldstein, *Derivative Rights and Derivative Works in Copyright*
30 J. Copr. Soc'y 209, 217, 227 (1983)

Taken together, sections 102(a) and 103, and sections 106(1) and 106(2), give a prospective copyright owner the incentive to make an original, underlying work, the exclusive right to make new, successive works incorporating expressive elements from the underlying work, and the incentive and exclusive right to make still newer, successive works based on these. The continuum may stretch from an underlying novel or story to the work's adaptation into a motion picture, its transformation into a television series, and the eventual embodiment of its characters in dolls, games and other merchandise. The works at the outer reaches of this continuum, and some intermediate works as well, will frequently bear scant resemblance to the expression *or* the ideas of the seminal work and will often be connected only by a license authorizing use of a title or character name.

This analysis offers some help in identifying the point at which the right "to reproduce the copyrighted work in copies" leaves off and the right "to prepare derivative works based upon the copyrighted work" begins: It is that point at which the contribution of independent expression to an existing work effectively creates a new work for a different market. . . .

Derivative rights affect the *level* of investment in copyrighted works by enabling the copyright owner to proportion its investment to the level of expected returns from all markets, not just the market in which the work first appears, as is generally the case with reproduction rights. The publisher who knows that it can license, and obtain payment for, the translation, serialization, condensation and motion picture rights for a novel will invest more in purchasing, producing and marketing the novel than it would if its returns were limited to revenues from book sales in the English language.

Derivative rights also affect the *direction* of investments in copyrighted works. By spreading the duty to pay over different markets, section 106(2) tends to perfect the information available to the copyright owner respecting the value of its works to different groups of users. It also enables choices in light of that information. Knowing that the French and German language markets belong exclusively to it, a publisher of English language works may decide to invest in works that, once translated, will appeal to these audiences as well. The publisher can acquire a work because of its motion picture potential and can comfortably invest in the work's development and marketing to increase that potential. . . .

≣≣ *Castle Rock Entertainment, Inc. v. Carol Publishing*
≣≣ *Group, Inc.*
≣   *150 F.3d 132 (2d Cir. 1998)*

WALKER, J.: This case presents two interesting and somewhat novel issues of copyright law. The first is whether *The Seinfeld Aptitude Test*, a trivia quiz book devoted exclusively to testing its readers' recollection of scenes and events from the fictional television series *Seinfeld*, takes sufficient protected expression from the original, as evidenced by the book's substantial similarity to the television series, such that, in the absence of any defenses, the book would infringe the copyright in *Seinfeld*. The second is whether *The Seinfeld Aptitude Test* (also referred to as *The SAT*) constitutes fair use of the *Seinfeld* television series.

[The district court granted summary judgment to plaintiffs and enjoined publication of *The SAT*; defendants appealed.]

Background

The material facts in this case are undisputed. Plaintiff Castle Rock is the producer and copyright owner of each episode of the *Seinfeld* television series. The series revolves around the petty tribulations in the lives of four single, adult friends in New York: Jerry Seinfeld, George Costanza, Elaine Benes, and Cosmo Kramer. Defendants are Beth Golub, the author, and Carol Publishing Group, Inc., the publisher, of *The SAT*, a 132-page book containing 643 trivia questions and answers about the events and characters depicted in *Seinfeld*. These include 211 multiple choice questions, in which only one out of three to five answers is correct; 93 matching questions; and a number of short-answer questions. The questions are divided into five levels of difficulty, labeled (in increasing order of difficulty) "Wuss Questions," "This, That, and the Other Questions," "Tough Monkey Questions," "Atomic Wedgie Questions," and "Master of Your Domain Questions." Selected examples from level 1 are indicative of the questions throughout *The SAT*:

1. To impress a woman, George passes himself off as
    a) a gynecologist
    b) a geologist
    c) a marine biologist
    d) a meteorologist

11. What candy does Kramer snack on while observing a surgical procedure from an operating-room balcony?
12. Who said, "I don't go for those nonrefundable deals . . . I can't commit to a woman . . . I'm not committing to an airline."?
    a) Jerry
    b) George
    c) Kramer

The book draws from 84 of the 86 *Seinfeld* episodes that had been broadcast as of the time *The SAT* was published. Although Golub created the incorrect answers to the multiple choice questions, every question and correct answer has as its source a fictional moment in a *Seinfeld* episode. Forty-one questions and/or answers contain dialogue from *Seinfeld*. The single episode most drawn upon by *The SAT*, "The Cigar Store Indian," is the source of 20 questions that directly quote between 3.6% and 5.6% of that episode (defendants' and plaintiff's calculations, respectively).

The name "Seinfeld" appears prominently on the front and back covers of *The SAT*, and pictures of the principal actors in *Seinfeld* appear on the cover and on several pages of the book. On the back cover, a disclaimer states that "This book has not been approved or licensed by any entity involved in creating or producing *Seinfeld*." The front cover bears the title "The Seinfeld Aptitude Test" and describes the book as containing "[h]undreds of spectacular questions of minute details from TV's greatest show about absolutely nothing." . . .

Golub has described *The SAT* as a "natural outgrowth" of *Seinfeld* which, "like the *Seinfeld* show, is devoted to the trifling, picayune and petty annoyances encountered by the show's characters on a daily basis." According to Golub, she created *The SAT* by taking notes from *Seinfeld* programs at the time they were aired on television and subsequently reviewing videotapes of several of the episodes, as recorded by her or various friends.

The SAT's publication did not immediately provoke a challenge. The National Broadcasting Corporation, which broadcasted *Seinfeld*, requested free copies of *The SAT* from defendants and distributed them together with promotions for the program. *Seinfeld's* executive producer characterized *The SAT* as "a fun little book." There is no evidence that *The SAT's* publication diminished *Seinfeld's* profitability, and in fact *Seinfeld's* audience grew after *The SAT* was first published.

Castle Rock has nevertheless been highly selective in marketing products associated with *Seinfeld*, rejecting numerous proposals from publishers seeking approval for a variety of projects related to the show. Castle Rock licensed one *Seinfeld* book, *The Entertainment Weekly Seinfeld Companion*, and has licensed the production of a CD-ROM product that includes discussions of *Seinfeld* episodes; the CD-ROM allegedly might ultimately include a trivia bank. Castle Rock claims in this litigation that it plans to pursue a more aggressive marketing strategy for *Seinfeld*-related products, including "publication of books relating to *Seinfeld*."

In November 1994, Castle Rock notified defendants of its copyright and trademark infringement claims. In February 1995, after defendants continued to distribute *The SAT*, Castle Rock filed this action alleging federal copyright and trademark infringement and state law unfair competition. . . .

A. "Substantial Similarity"

We have stated that "substantial similarity"

requires that the copying [be] quantitatively *and* qualitatively sufficient to support the legal conclusion that infringement (*actionable* copying) has occurred. The qualitative component concerns the copying of expression, rather than ideas[, facts, expression in the public domain, or any other non-protectable elements]. . . . The quantitative component generally concerns the amount of the copyrighted work that is copied, which must be more than "*de minimis*."

Ringgold v. Black Entertainment Television, Inc., 126 F.3d 70, 75 (2d Cir. 1997) (emphasis added).

As to the quantitative element, we conclude that *The SAT* has crossed the *de minimis* threshold. At the outset, we observe that the fact that the copying appears in question and answer form is by itself without particular consequence: the trivia quiz copies fragments of *Seinfeld* in the same way that a collection of *Seinfeld* jokes or trivia would copy fragments of the series. . . .

As to *Ringgold's* qualitative component, each *SAT* trivia question is based directly upon original, protectable expression in *Seinfeld*. As noted by the district court, *The SAT* did not copy from *Seinfeld* unprotected facts, but, rather, creative expression. . . . Unlike the facts in a phone book, which "do not owe their origin to an act of authorship," . . . each "fact" tested by *The SAT* is in reality fictitious expression created by *Seinfeld*'s authors. *The SAT* does not quiz such true facts as the identity of the actors in *Seinfeld*, the number of days it takes to shoot an episode, the biographies of the actors, the location of the *Seinfeld* set, etc. Rather, *The SAT* tests whether the reader knows that the character Jerry places a Pez dispenser on Elaine's leg during a piano recital, that Kramer enjoys going to the airport because he's hypnotized by the baggage carousels, and that Jerry, opining on how to identify a virgin, said "It's not like spotting a toupee." Because these characters and events spring from the imagination of *Seinfeld*'s authors, *The SAT* plainly copies copyrightable, creative expression. . . .

B. *Other Tests*

As defendants note, substantial similarity usually "arises out of a claim of infringement as between comparable works . . . [where] because of the equivalent nature of the competing works, the question of similarity can be tested conventionally by comparing comparable elements of the two works." Because in the instant case the original and secondary works are of different genres and to a lesser extent because they are in different media, tests for substantial similarity other than the quantitative/qualitative approach are not particularly helpful to our analysis. . . .

Under the "total concept and feel" test, urged by defendants, we analyze "the similarities in such aspects as the total concept and feel, theme, characters, plot, sequence, pace, and setting" of the original and the allegedly infringing works. . . . Defendants contend that *The SAT* and the *Seinfeld* programs are incomparable in conventional terms such as plot, sequence, themes, pace, and setting. For example, *The SAT* has no plot; "[t]he notion of pace . . . cannot be said even to exist in the book"; *The SAT*'s "sequence has no relationship to the sequences of any of the *Seinfeld* episodes, since it is a totally random and scattered collection of questions relating to events that occurred in the shows"; and *The SAT*'s only theme "is how much a *Seinfeld* fan can remember of 84 different programs." The total concept and feel test, however, is simply not helpful in analyzing works that, because of their different genres and media, must necessarily have a different concept and feel. Indeed, many "derivative" works of different genres, in which copyright owners have exclusive rights . . . may have a different total concept and feel from the original work. . . .

[The court then discussed and rejected the defendants' fair use defense. (You will read that portion of the opinion in Chapter 7 — EDS.)]

. . . Although derivative works that are subject to the author's copyright transform an original work into a new mode of presentation, such works — unlike works of fair use — take expression for purposes that are not "transformative."[9] . . .

. . . Because *The SAT* borrows exclusively from *Seinfeld* and not from any other television or entertainment programs, *The SAT* is likely to fill a market niche that Castle Rock would in general develop. Moreover, as noted by the district court, this "*Seinfeld* trivia game is not critical of the program, nor does it parody the program; if anything, *SAT* pays homage to *Seinfeld*." *Castle Rock*, 955 F. Supp. at 271-72. Although Castle Rock has evidenced little if any interest in exploiting this market for derivative works based on *Seinfeld*, such as by creating and publishing *Seinfeld* trivia books (or at least trivia books that endeavor to "satisfy" the

---

9. Indeed, if the secondary work sufficiently transforms the expression of the original work such that the two works cease to be substantially similar, then the secondary work is not a derivative work and, for that matter, does not infringe the copyright of the original work. *See* 1 Nimmer §3.01, at 3-3 (stating that "a work will be considered a derivative work only if it would be considered an infringing work" if it were unauthorized).

"between-episode cravings" of *Seinfeld* lovers), the copyright law must respect that creative and economic choice. "It would . . . not serve the ends of the Copyright Act — *i.e.*, to advance the arts — if artists were denied their monopoly over derivative versions of their creative works merely because they made the artistic decision not to saturate those markets with variations of their original." . . .

Warner Bros. Entertainment, Inc. v. RDR Books
575 F. Supp. 2d 513 (S.D.N.Y. 2008)

PATTERSON, J.: . . .

Findings of Fact

I. The Copyrighted Works

Plaintiff J.K. Rowling ("Rowling") is the author of the highly acclaimed *Harry Potter* book series. . . . Written for children but enjoyed by children and adults alike, the *Harry Potter* series chronicles the lives and adventures of Harry Potter and his friends as they come of age at the Hogwarts School of Witchcraft and Wizardry and face the evil Lord Voldemort. It is a tale of a fictional world filled with magical spells, fantastical creatures, and imaginary places and things. . . .

Rowling published the first of seven books in the series, *Harry Potter and the Philosopher's Stone*, in the United Kingdom in 1997. In 1998, the first book was published in the United States as *Harry Potter and the Sorcerer's Stone*. Over the next ten years, Rowling wrote and published the remaining six books in the *Harry Potter* series (*Id.*): *Harry Potter and the Chamber of Secrets* (1998), *Harry Potter and the Prisoner of Azkaban* (1999), *Harry Potter and the Goblet of Fire* (2000), *Harry Potter and the Order of the Phoenix* (2003), and *Harry Potter and the Half-Blood Prince* (2005). The seventh and final book, *Harry Potter and the Deathly Hallows* was released on July 21, 2007. Rowling owns a United States copyright in each of the *Harry Potter* books.

The *Harry Potter* series has achieved enormous popularity and phenomenal sales. The books have won numerous awards, including children's literary awards and the British Book Award. Most gratifying to Rowling is that the *Harry Potter* series has been credited with encouraging readership among children.

As a result of the success of the *Harry Potter* books, Plaintiff Warner Bros. Entertainment Inc. ("Warner Brothers") obtained from Rowling the exclusive film rights to the entire seven-book *Harry Potter* series. . . .

In addition, Rowling wrote two short companion books to the *Harry Potter* series (the "companion books"), the royalties from which she donated to the charity Comic Relief. The first, *Quidditch Through the Ages* (2001), recounts the history and development of "quidditch," an imaginary sport featured in the *Harry Potter* series that involves teams of witches and wizards on flying broomsticks. The second, *Fantastic Beasts & Where to Find Them* (2001), is an A-to-Z encyclopedia of the imaginary beasts and beings that exist in *Harry Potter*'s fictional world. Both appear in the *Harry Potter* series as textbooks that the students at Hogwarts use in their studies, and the companion books are marketed as such. Neither of the companion books is written in narrative form; instead each book chronicles and expands on the fictional facts that unfold in the *Harry Potter* series. The companion books are both registered with the

United States Copyright Office. Although the market for the companion books is not nearly as large as the market for the *Harry Potter* series, Rowling's companion books have earned more than $30 million to date.

Rowling has stated on a number of occasions since 1998 that, in addition to the two companion books, she plans to publish a "*Harry Potter* encyclopedia" after the completion of the series and again donate the proceeds to charity. . . .

II.   The Allegedly Infringing Work

Defendant RDR Books is a Michigan-based publishing company that seeks to publish a book entitled "The Lexicon," the subject of this lawsuit. Steven Vander Ark, a former library media specialist at a middle school in Michigan, is the attributed author of the Lexicon. . . . He is also the originator, owner, and operator of "The Harry Potter Lexicon" website . . . , a popular *Harry Potter* fan site from which the content of the Lexicon is drawn.

A.   *The Origins of the Lexicon* . . .

Vander Ark began work on his website, "The Harry Potter Lexicon" (the "website" or "Lexicon website"), in 1999 and opened the website in 2000. His purpose in establishing the website was to create an encyclopedia that collected and organized information from the *Harry Potter* books in one central source for fans to use for reference. At its launch, the website featured Vander Ark's descriptive lists of spells, characters, creatures, and magical items from *Harry Potter* with hyperlinks to cross-referenced entries. In response to feedback from users of the website, Vander Ark developed an A-to-Z index to each list to allow users to search for entries alphabetically.

The website presently features several indexed lists of people, places, and things from *Harry Potter*, including the "Encyclopedia of Spells," "Encyclopedia of Potions," "Wizards, Witches, and Beings," "The Bestiary," and "Gazetteer of the Wizarding World." In addition to these reference features, the website contains a variety of supplemental material pertaining to *Harry Potter*, including fan art, commentary, essays, timelines, forums, and interactive data. The website is currently run by a staff of seven or eight volunteers, including four primary editors, all of whom were recruited to help update and expand the website's content after the publication of the fifth book in the *Harry Potter* series. The website uses minimal advertising to offset the costs of operation. Use of the website is free and unrestricted.

Vander Ark has received positive feedback, including from Rowling and her publishers, about the value of the Lexicon website as a reference source. In May 2004, Vander Ark read a remark by Rowling posted on her website praising his Lexicon website as follows: "This is such a great site that I have been known to sneak into an internet cafe while out writing and check a fact rather than go into a bookshop and buy a copy of Harry Potter (which is embarrassing). A website for the dangerously obsessive; my natural home." . . . In July 2005, Vander Ark received a note from Cheryl Klein, a Senior Editor at Scholastic Inc., American publisher of the *Harry Potter* series, thanking him and his staff "for the wonderful resource [his] site provides for fans, students, and indeed editors & copyeditors of the Harry Potter series," who "referred to the Lexicon countless times during the editing of [the sixth book in the series], whether to verify a fact, check a timeline, or get a chapter & book reference for a particular event." In September 2006, Vander Ark was invited by Warner Brothers to the set of the film *The Order of the Phoenix*, where he met David Heyman, the producer of all the *Harry Potter* films. Heyman told Vander Ark that Warner Brothers used the Lexicon website almost every day. . . .

Prior to any discussions with RDR Books about publishing portions of the Lexicon website as a book, Vander Ark was aware of Rowling's public statements regarding her intention to write a *Harry Potter* encyclopedia upon completion of the seventh book in the series. In June 2007, just before the release of the seventh book, Vander Ark emailed Christopher Little Literary Agency, Rowling's literary agent in the United Kingdom, and suggested that he would be "a good candidate for work as an editor, given [his] work on the Lexicon," should Rowling start working on an encyclopedia or other reference to the *Harry Potter* series. The literary agency advised him that Rowling intended to work alone and did not require a collaborator.

B. RDR Books' Acquisition and Marketing of the Lexicon

Roger Rapoport is the president of Defendant RDR Books. Rapoport learned of Vander Ark and the Lexicon website when he read an article in his local newspaper dated July 23, 2007, profiling Vander Ark as a well known figure within the *Harry Potter* fan community and the proprietor of the Lexicon website who "holds the key to all things 'Harry Potter.'" . . .

At his first meeting with Rapoport in August 2007, Vander Ark raised his concerns regarding the permissibility of publishing the Lexicon in view of Rowling's plan to publish an encyclopedia and her copyrights in the *Harry Potter* books. . . . Prior to August 2007, Vander Ark had developed and circulated the opinion that publishing "any book that is a guide to [the *Harry Potter*] world" would be a violation of Rowling's intellectual property rights. Vander Ark had even stated on a public internet newsgroup that he would not publish the Lexicon "in any form except online" without permission because Rowling, not he, was "entitled to that market." Vander Ark changed his mind about publishing the Lexicon after Rapoport reassured him that he had looked into the legal issue and determined that publication of content from the Lexicon website in book form was legal. Rapoport agreed to stand by this opinion by adding an atypical clause to the publishing contract providing that RDR would defend and indemnify Vander Ark in the event of any lawsuits. . . .

. . . The idea was to publish the first complete guide to the *Harry Potter* series that included information from the seventh and final *Harry Potter* novel. Vander Ark believed that there was an advantage to being the first reference guide on the market to cover all seven *Harry Potter* books. . . .

D. The Content of the Lexicon

The Lexicon is an A-to-Z guide to the creatures, characters, objects, events, and places that exist in the world of *Harry Potter*. As received by the Court in evidence, the Lexicon manuscript is more than 400 type-written pages long and contains 2,437 entries organized alphabetically. . . .

The Lexicon manuscript was created using the encyclopedia entries from the Lexicon website. Because of space limitations for the printed work, which seeks to be complete but also easy to use, about half of the material from the website was not included in the Lexicon manuscript. . . .

The Lexicon entries cull every item and character that appears in the *Harry Potter* works, no matter if it plays a significant or insignificant role in the story. The entries cover every spell (e.g., Expecto Patronum, Expelliarmus, and Incendio), potion (e.g., Love Potion, Felix Felicis, and Draught of Living Death), magical item or device (e.g., Deathly Hallows, Horcrux, Cloak of Invisibility), form of magic (e.g., Legilimency, Occlumency, and the Dark Arts), creature (e.g., Blast-Ended Skrewt, Dementors, and Blood-Sucking Bugbears), character (e.g., Harry Potter, Hagrid, and Lord Voldemort), group or force (e.g., Aurors, Dumbledore's Army,

Death Eaters), invented game (e.g., Quidditch), and imaginary place (e.g., Hogwarts School of Witchcraft and Wizardry, Diagon Alley, and the Ministry of Magic) that appear in the *Harry Potter* works. . . .

Each entry, with the exception of the shortest ones, gathers and synthesizes pieces of information relating to its subject that appear scattered across the *Harry Potter* novels, the companion books, . . . and published interviews of Rowling. The types of information contained in the entries include descriptions of the subject's attributes, role in the story, relationship to other characters or things, and events involving the subject. Repositories of such information, the entries seek to give as complete a picture as possible of each item or character in the *Harry Potter* world, many of which appear only sporadically throughout the series or in various sources of *Harry Potter* material.

The snippets of information in the entries are generally followed by citations in parentheses that indicate where they were found within the corpus of the *Harry Potter* works. The thoroughness of the Lexicon's citation, however, is not consistent; some entries contain very few citations in relation to the amount material provided. . . . When the Lexicon cites to one of the seven *Harry Potter* novels, the citation provides only the book and chapter number. Vander Ark explained that page numbers were excluded from the citations because the various editions of the *Harry Potter* books have different pagination, but the chapter numbers remain consistent. The Lexicon neither assigns a letter to each edition nor specifies a standard edition while providing a conversion table for other editions, practices which Plaintiffs' expert Jeri Johnson testified were common for reference guides.

While not its primary purpose, the Lexicon includes commentary and background information from outside knowledge on occasion. For example, the Lexicon contains sporadic etymological references. . . . The Lexicon also points to the very few "flints," or errors in the continuity of the story, that appear in the *Harry Potter* series.

While there was considerable opining at trial as to the type of reference work the Lexicon purports to be and whether it qualifies as such (no doubt in part due to its title), the Lexicon fits in the narrow genre of non-fiction reference guides to fictional works. As Defendant's expert testified, the *Harry Potter* series is a multi-volume work of fantasy literature, similar to the works of J.R.R. Tolkien and C.S. Lewis. Such works lend themselves to companion guides or reference works because they reveal an elaborate imaginary world over thousands of pages, involving many characters, creatures, and magical objects that appear and reappear across thousands of pages. (Tr. (Sorensen) at 504:16-23; *id.* at 507:1-5 (testifying that she found 19 or 20 companion guides to J.R.R. Tolkien's works, and about 15 guides to C.S. Lewis's works).) Fantasy literature spawns books having a wide variety of purposes and formats, as demonstrated by the books about *Harry Potter* that Plaintiffs entered into evidence. (Pl. Exs. 73, 74, 75, 192; 13E-13G.) The Lexicon, an A-to-Z guide which synthesizes information from the series and generally provides citations for location of that information rather than offering commentary, is most comparable to the comprehensive work of Paul F. Ford, *Companion to Narnia: A Complete Guide to the Magical World of C.S. Lewis's* The Chronicles of Narnia (Pl. Ex. 62). . . . [4] . . .

Although it is difficult to quantify how much of the language in the Lexicon is directly lifted from the *Harry Potter* novels and companion books, the Lexicon indeed contains at least a troubling amount of direct quotation or close paraphrasing of Rowling's original language.[6] The Lexicon occasionally uses quotation marks to indicate Rowling's language, but more often

---

4. The *Companion to Narnia*, however, is far more erudite and informative than the Lexicon . . .

6. Some of the most extensive direct quotation occurs where the Lexicon reproduces a song or poem that appears in the novels. . . .

the original language is copied without quotation marks, often making it difficult to know which words are Rowling's and which are Vander Ark's.

For example, in the entry for "armor, goblin made," the Lexicon uses Rowling's poetic language nearly verbatim without quotation marks.[7] The original language from *Harry Potter and the Deathly Hallows* reads:

> "Muggle-borns," he said. "Goblin-made armour does not require cleaning, simple girl. Goblins' silver repels mundane dirt, imbibing only that which strengthens it."

(Pl. Ex. 10 at 303.) The Lexicon entry for "armor, goblin made" reads in its entirety:

> Some armor in the wizarding world is made by goblins, and it is quite valuable. (e.g., HBP20) According to Phineas Nigellus, goblin-made armor does not require cleaning, because goblins' silver repels mundane dirt, imbibing only that which strengthens it, such as basilisk venom. In this context, "armor" also includes blades such as swords.

Although the Lexicon entry introduces Rowling's language with the phrase, "According to Phineas Nigellus," it does not use quotation marks.

The Lexicon entry for "Dementors" reproduces Rowling's vivid description of this creature sometimes using quotation marks and sometimes quoting or closely paraphrasing without indicating which language is original expression. The original language appears in Chapters 5 and 10 of *Harry Potter and the Prisoner of Azkaban* as follows:

> . . . Its face was completely hidden beneath its hood. . . . There was a hand protruding from the cloak and it was glistening, grayish, slimy-looking, and scabbed, like something dead that had decayed in water . . .
>
> And then the thing beneath the hood, whatever it was, drew a long, slow, rattling breath, as though it were trying to suck something more than air from its surroundings.
>
> * * *
>
> "Dementors are among the foulest creatures to walk this earth. They infest the darkest, filthiest places, they glory in decay and despair, they drain peace, hope, and happiness out of the air around them. Even Muggles feel their presence, though they can't see them. Get too near a dementor and every good feeling, every happy memory will be sucked out of you. If it can, the dementor will feed on you long enough to reduce you to something like itself . . . soulless and evil. . . ."

(Pl. Ex. 6 at 83, 187.) The Lexicon entry for "Dementors" reads in its entirety:

> Dementors are some of the most terrible creatures on earth, flying tall black spectral humanoid things with flowing robes. They "infest the darkest, filthiest places, they glory in decay and despair, they drain peace, hope, and happiness out of the air around them," according to Lupin (PA10). Dementors affect even Muggles, although Muggles can't see the foul, black creatures. Dementors feed on positive human emotions; a large crowd is like a feast to them. They drain a wizard of his power if left with them too long. They were the guards at Azkaban and made that place horrible indeed. The Ministry used Dementors as guards in its courtrooms as well (GF30, DH13). There are certain defenses one can use against Dementors, specifically the Patronus Charm. A Dementor's breath sounds rattling and like it's trying to suck more than air out of a room. Its hands are "glistening, grayish, slimy-looking, and scabbed". It exudes a biting, soul-freezing cold (PA5).

---

7. [In the Lexicon, i]talics are used in the block quotations to highlight the original language that is copied or paraphrased. The italics do not appear in the originals.

Another example of verbatim copying and close paraphrase can be found in the Lexicon entry for "Mirror of Erised." The original language from *Harry Potter and the Sorcerer's Stone* reads:

> It was a magnificent mirror, as high as the ceiling, with an ornate gold frame, standing on two clawed feet. There was an inscription carved around the top: Erised stra ehru oyt ube cafru oyt on wohsi.
>
> * * *
>
> . . . "It shows us nothing more or less than the deepest desire of our hearts. You [Harry Potter], who have never known your family, see them standing around you. Ronald Weasley, who has always been overshadowed by his brothers, sees himself standing alone, the best of all of them. However, this mirror will give us neither knowledge or truth. Men have wasted away before it, entranced by what they have seen, or been driven mad, not knowing if what it shows is real or even possible."

(Pl. Ex. 4 at 207, 213). The first paragraph of the Lexicon entry reads:

> A magnificent mirror, as high as a classroom ceiling, with an ornate gold frame, standing on two clawed feet. The inscription carved around the top reads "Erised stra ehru oyt ube cafru oyt on wohsi," which is "I show you not your face but your heart's desire" written backwards (that is, in what is called 'mirror writing'). When you look into the mirror you see the deepest, most desperate desire of your heart. The mirror has trapped people who can't bear to stop staring into it, unsure if what they see is going to actually happen. Harry sees his family in the Mirror; Ron sees himself as Head Boy and Quidditch champion (PS12). . . .

An example of particularly extensive direct quotation is found in the Lexicon entry for "Trelawney, Sibyll Patricia," the professor of Divination at the Hogwarts School who tells two important prophecies in the story. The Lexicon not only reproduces her prophecies word-for-word in their entirety, but in doing so, reveals dramatic plot twists and how they are resolved in the series. For example, the first prophecy reads:

> "The one with the power to vanquish the Dark Lord approaches. . . . Born to those who have thrice defied him, born as the seventh month dies . . . and the Dark Lord will mark him as his equal, but he will have power the Dark Lord knows not . . . and either must die at the hand of the other for neither can live while the other survives. . . . The one with the power to vanquish the Dark Lord will be born as the seventh month dies. . . ."

(Pl. Ex. 8 at 841 (ellipses in original).) The Lexicon entry reproduces this prophecy exactly but in italics and indented. (Pl. Ex. 1, entry for "Trelawney, Sibyll Patricia.") The Lexicon entry continues by discussing what happens as a result of this prophecy: "Severus Snape was eavesdropping on this conversation and he reported the first part of the Prophecy to the Dark Lord. Voldemort immediately began searching for this threat, and centered his attention on the child of Lily and James Potter. (OP 37)." The entry then quotes the second prophecy, but without a citation to where it appears in the *Harry Potter* series.

A number of Lexicon entries copy Rowling's artistic literary devices that contribute to her distinctive craft as a writer. . . .

. . . [T]he Lexicon entry for "Marchbanks, Madam Griselda" uses an artful simile from the original works to describe this character. Rowling's language in *Harry Potter and the Order of the Phoenix* reads:

> . . . Harry thought Professor Marchbanks must be the tiny, stooped witch with a face so lined it looked as though it had been draped in cobwebs; Umbridge was speaking to her very deferentially. . . .

(Pl. Ex. 8 at 710.) The Lexicon entry reads in part:

> . . . Madam Marchbanks in June 1996 was tiny and stooped, her face so lined it appeared draped in cobwebs. . . .

The Lexicon's close paraphrasing is not limited to the seven *Harry Potter* novels, but can be found in entries drawn from the companion books as well. For example, the entry for "Montrose Magpies" uses language from *Quidditch Through the Ages*. The original language reads:

> The Magpies are the most successful team in the history of the British and Irish League, which they have won thirty-two times. Twice European Champions. . . . The Magpies wear black and white robes with one magpie on the chest and another on the back.

(Pl. Ex. 2 at 35-36.) The Lexicon entry reads:

> The most successful Quidditch team in history, which has won the British and Irish league thirty-two times and the European Cup twice. Their robes are black and white, with one magpie on the chest and another on the back (QA7). . . .

Aside from verbatim copying, another factual issue of contention at trial was the Lexicon entries that contain summaries of certain scenes or key events in the *Harry Potter* series. Most frequently, these are the longer entries that describe important objects, such as the "Deathly Hallows," or momentous events, such as the "Triwizard Tournament," or that trace the development of an important character, such as Harry Potter, Lord Voldemort, Severus Snape, and Albus Dumbledore. Plaintiffs' expert testified at length that in her opinion these entries constitute "plot summaries," . . . while Defendant's expert characterized them as character studies or analysis.

Neither of these characterizations is exactly apt. Without endorsing one characterization or another, such entries in the Lexicon do encapsulate elements of the very elaborate and wide ranging plot (sometimes in chronological order, sometimes not) confined to the subject of the entry. In the entries for significant characters, these plot elements are occasionally used to support an observation about the character's nature or development. . . .

Conclusions of Law . . .

B. *Copying*

. . . While acknowledging actual copying, Defendant disputes that the copying amounts to an improper or unlawful appropriation of Rowling's works. . . .

The appropriate inquiry under the substantial similarity test is whether "the copying is quantitatively and qualitatively sufficient to support the legal conclusion that infringement (actionable copying) has occurred." *Ringgold [v. Black Entertainment Television, Inc.]*, 126 F.3d [70,] at 75 [2d Cir. 1997]. . . .

In evaluating the quantitative extent of copying in the substantial similarity analysis, the Court "considers the amount of copying not only of direct quotations and close paraphrasing, but also of all other protectable expression in the original work." *Castle Rock-Castle Rock [Entertainment, Inc. v. Carol Publ'g Group, Inc.]*, 150 F.3d [132,] at 140 n. 6 [2d Cir. 1997]. . . .

Plaintiffs have shown that the Lexicon copies a sufficient quantity of the *Harry Potter* series . . . to support a finding of substantial similarity between the Lexicon and Rowling's novels. The Lexicon draws 450 manuscript pages worth of material primarily from the 4,100-page *Harry Potter* series. . . . Most of the Lexicon's 2,437 entries contain direct quotations or paraphrases, plot details, or summaries of scenes from one or more of the *Harry Potter* novels. As Defendant admits, "the Lexicon reports thousands of fictional facts from the Harry Potter works." (Def's Post-trial Br. at 35). Although hundreds of pages or thousands of fictional facts may amount to only a fraction of the seven-book series, this quantum of copying is sufficient to support a finding of substantial similarity where the copied expression is entirely the product of the original author's imagination and creation. . . .

The quantitative extent of the Lexicon's copying is even more substantial with respect to *Fantastic Beasts* and *Quidditch Through the Ages*. Rowling's companion books are only fifty-nine and fifty-six pages long, respectively. The Lexicon reproduces a substantial portion of their content, with only sporadic omissions, across hundreds of entries. . . .

As to the qualitative component of the substantial similarity analysis, Plaintiffs have shown that the Lexicon draws its content from creative, original expression in the *Harry Potter* series and companion books. Each of the 2,437 entries in the Lexicon contains "fictional facts" created by Rowling, such as the attributes of imaginary creatures and objects, the traits and undertakings of major and minor characters, and the events surrounding them. . . .

Defendant . . . argues that while a substantial similarity may be found where invented facts are "reported and arranged in such a way as to tell essentially the same story" as the original, "the order in which the fictional facts are presented in the Lexicon bears almost no resemblance to the order in which the fictional facts are arranged to create the story of Harry Potter and the universe he inhabits." (Def. Post-trial Br. at 34, 36). Reproducing original expression in fragments or in a different order, however, does not preclude a finding of substantial similarity. . . . Here, the Lexicon's rearrangement of Rowling's fictional facts does not alter the protected expression such that the Lexicon ceases to be substantially similar to the original works. . . .

. . . Under these circumstances, Plaintiffs have established a prima facie case of infringement.

C. Derivative Work

Plaintiffs allege that the Lexicon not only violates their right of reproduction, but also their right to control the production of derivative works. The Copyright Act defines a "derivative work" as "a work based upon one or more preexisting works, such as a translation, musical arrangement, dramatization, fictionalization, motion picture version, sound recording, art reproduction, abridgment, condensation, or any other form in which a work may be *recast, transformed, or adapted*" 17 U.S.C. §101 (emphasis added). A work "consisting of editorial revisions, annotations, elaborations, or other modifications which, as a whole, represents an original work of authorship" is also a derivative work. *Id.*

A work is not derivative, however, simply because it is "based upon" the preexisting works. . . . If that were the standard, then parodies and book reviews would fall under the definition, and certainly "ownership of copyright does not confer a legal right to control public evaluation of the copyrighted work." *Ty, Inc. v. Publ'ns Int'l Ltd.*, 292 F.3d 512, 521 (7th Cir. 2002). The statutory language seeks to protect works that are "recast, transformed, or adapted" into another medium, mode, language, or revised version, while still representing the "original work of authorship." *See Castle Rock*, 150 F.3d at 143 n. 9 (stating that "derivative works that are subject to the author's copyright transform an original work into a new mode of presentation"); *Twin Peaks [Prods., Inc. v.Publ'ns Int'l, Ltd.]*, 996 F.2d [1366,] at 1373 [2d Cir. 1993] (finding a derivative work where a guidebook based on the *Twin Peaks* television series "contain[ed] a substantial amount of material from the teleplays, transformed from one medium to another"). Thus in *Ty, Inc. v. Publications International Ltd.*, Judge Posner concluded, as the parties had stipulated, that a collectors' guide to Beanie Babies was not a derivative work because "guides don't *recast, transform, or adapt* the things to which they are guides." 292 F.3d at 520 (emphasis added).

Plaintiffs argue that based on the *Twin Peaks* decision "companion guides constitute derivative works where, as is the case here, they 'contain a substantial amount of material from the underlying work.'" (Pl. Post-trial Br. ¶288, at 88-89.) This argument inaccurately states the holding of *Twin Peaks* and overlooks two important distinctions between the Lexicon and the guidebook in *Twin Peaks*. First, as mentioned earlier, the portions of the Lexicon that encapsulate plot elements or sketch plotlines bear no comparison with the guidebook in *Twin Peaks*, whose plot summaries giving "elaborate recounting of plot details" were found to constitute an "abridgement" of the original work. *See Twin Peaks*, 996 F.2d at 1373 n. 2 (reproducing an excerpt of the infringing book containing a high degree of detail). Given that the Lexicon's use of plot elements is far from an "elaborate recounting" and does not follow the same plot structure as the *Harry Potter* novels, Plaintiffs' suggestion that these portions of the Lexicon are "unauthorized abridgements" is unpersuasive. Second, and more importantly, although the Lexicon "contain[s] a substantial amount of material" from the *Harry Potter* works, the material is not merely "transformed from one medium to another," as was the case in *Twin Peaks*. *Id.* at 1373. By condensing, synthesizing, and reorganizing the preexisting material in an A-to-Z reference guide, the Lexicon does not recast the material in another medium to retell the story of *Harry Potter*, but instead gives the copyrighted material another purpose. . . . That purpose is to give the reader a ready understanding of individual elements in the elaborate world of *Harry Potter* that appear in voluminous and diverse sources. As a result, the Lexicon no longer "represents [the] original work[s] of authorship." 17 U.S.C. §101. Under these circumstances, and because the Lexicon does not fall under any example of derivative works listed in the statute, Plaintiffs have failed to show that the Lexicon is a derivative work . . .

NOTES AND QUESTIONS

1. How meaningful is the concept of substantial similarity in distinguishing between the right to reproduce and the right to prepare a derivative work? The *Castle Rock* court notes that *The SAT* is a work in a different genre and a different medium than the *Seinfeld* television show but concludes, nevertheless, that *The SAT* is "substantially similar" to the show, and therefore an infringing derivative work. According to the *Warner Brothers* court, however, a work that "gives the copyrighted material another purpose" is not a derivative work (though it may still be a work that infringes the reproduction right). Are the two decisions consistent? Which approach to the scope of the derivative work right do you prefer? Why?

2. As described by Professor Goldstein, the right to prepare derivative works is primarily a means of granting the author of the underlying work an incentive to invest even more in the creation of the underlying work in return for exclusive control over all markets related to the copyrighted work. Do you agree with his analysis? What value does the right to prepare derivative works add to the incentive of the author of the underlying work? Which approach to the scope of the derivative work right best encompasses the rationale for derivative rights posited by Professor Goldstein?

3. Do you agree with the *Castle Rock* court that the decision not to enter certain markets is an "artistic" one consistent with copyright's goal of promoting creativity? If the copyright owner's control does not extend to all subsidiary markets, how does one decide which markets

a copyright owner is (or should be) entitled to exploit? What justifications can you state for deciding that a copyright owner is entitled only to some markets and not all? Where on Professor Goldstein's continuum of derivative works/markets would you draw the line? We return to these questions in Chapter 7.

4. If the result under either the *Castle Rock* approach or the *Warner Brothers* approach is a judgment of infringement, does it matter which test courts use to determine whether something is a derivative work? There are places in the Copyright Act where it matters whether someone has reproduced a work or created a derivative work. For example, recall from Chapter 3, pages 183-87 *supra*, that under the rules governing termination of transfers, authors of derivative works are shielded from infringement actions in certain circumstances. *See* 17 U.S.C. §§203(b)(1), 304(a)(4)(A). Whether an individual has created a derivative work versus a mere reproduction is also important for foreign works with restored copyrights. "Reliance parties" who prepared derivative works based on the foreign work prior to restoration may continue to exploit such derivative works upon payment to the copyright owner. If the restored copyright owner and the reliance party cannot agree on a price, the statute empowers the court to set the price. *Id.* §104A(d)(3). *See, e.g., Dam Things From Denmark v. Russ Berrie & Co., Inc.*, 290 F.3d 548 (3d Cir. 2002). Thus, for these copyright owners, the derivative work right is protected by a liability rule, not a property rule. The reproduction right, however, remains protected by a property rule.

5. As you learned in Chapter 2, pages 106-07 *supra*, in the patent system secondcomers are allowed to apply for and receive patents on their improvements to the underlying invention. These "blocking patents" may encourage cross-licensing between the two inventors, and some scholars argue that that rule promotes efficiency. Should copyright law adopt a similar rule, allowing secondcomers to make derivative works but preventing either author from using the "improvement" without authorization from the other? Alternatively, should copyright law adopt a rule that allows anyone to make and use derivative works so long as compensation is paid to the author of the underlying work, as is the case currently under §104A?

6. One leading commentator described the right to prepare derivative works as "completely superfluous," and argued that it is subsumed by the exclusive rights of reproduction and public performance:

> [U]nder the Section 101 definition of a derivative work, it must be "based upon one or more pre-existing works." Unless sufficient of the pre-existing work is contained in the later work so as to constitute the latter an infringement of the former, the latter by definition is not a derivative work. Therefore, if the latter work does not incorporate sufficient of the pre-existing work as to constitute an infringement of either the reproduction right, or of the performance right, then it likewise will not infringe the right to make derivative works because no derivative work will have resulted.

2 Melville B. Nimmer & David Nimmer, Nimmer on Copyright §8.09[A] (2004).

Another commentator argued that a single grant of rights that encompasses derivative rights is preferable to an approach enumerating separate, overlapping rights: "The essential principle is the author's right to control all the channels through which his work or any fragments of his work reach the market. It should be one right, and not just a bundle of separate rights. . . ." Zechariah Chafee, *Reflections on the Law of Copyright*, 45 Colum. L. Rev. 505 (1945).

The development of the right to prepare derivative works was in fact a deliberate response to the narrowness with which the law originally defined copies. As technology evolved and new markets opened, opportunities arose to exploit works in forms different from their originals. Early courts interpreting the right to reproduce the work held that these new expressions did not constitute "copies" under the law and thus were not infringements of the underlying work.

See, e.g., *White-Smith Music Publ'g Co. v. Apollo Co.*, 209 U.S. 1 (1908) (holding that a perforated player-piano roll that would produce the sounds of the underlying copyrighted musical composition when used with a player piano did not constitute an infringing copy of the musical composition); *Stowe v. Thomas*, 23 F. Cas. 201 (C.C.E.D. Pa. 1853) (holding that a translation of *Uncle Tom's Cabin* into German was not an infringement of the copyrighted English language version). Over time, courts noted the tension this practice created. In a special concurrence in *White-Smith*, Justice Holmes noted: "The restraint (of copyright) is directed against reproduction of this collocation. . . . [T]he restriction is combined to specific form . . . but one would expect that, if it was to be protected at all, that collocation would be protected according to what was its essence. . . ." *White-Smith*, 209 U.S. at 19. A year later, §1 of the 1909 Copyright Act granted exclusive rights to the copyright owner to make "any other version" of the copyrighted work.

As this history demonstrates, Professors Nimmer and Chafee are both correct. The right of reproduction is now broad enough to encompass derivative rights. This broad reproduction right often serves the function Chafee describes, especially in a case where the works are very similar. As you continue through this section, consider whether the reproduction right serves this function in all cases.

2. Modes of Transformation

As noted earlier, it is difficult to draw a line between a "copy" of a protected work and a noninfringing transformation of the work. Often the question turns on the degree to which the underlying work has been transformed. However, courts disagree on a number of issues, including whether the standard for what constitutes a *copyrightable* derivative work is the same as for what constitutes an *infringing* derivative work. Put differently, while a derivative work must be original and fixed to be copyrightable, must it also be original and fixed to infringe? Consider the following cases.

a. "Recasting" and Originality

Mirage Editions, Inc. v. Albuquerque A.R.T. Company
856 F.2d 1341 (9th Cir. 1988), cert. denied, 489 U.S. 1018 (1989)

BRUNETTI, J.: Albuquerque A.R.T. (appellant or A.R.T.) appeals the district court's granting of summary judgment in favor of appellees Mirage, Dumas, and Van Der Marck (Mirage). . . .

Patrick Nagel was an artist whose works appeared in many media including lithographs, posters, serigraphs, and as graphic art in many magazines, most notably Playboy. Nagel died in 1984. His widow Jennifer Dumas owns the copyrights to the Nagel art works which Nagel owned at the time of his death. Mirage is the exclusive publisher of Nagel's works and also owns the copyrights to many of these works. . . . No one else holds a copyright in any Nagel work. Appellee Alfred Van Der Marck Editions, Inc. is the licensee of Dumas and Mirage and the publisher of the commemorative book entitled *NAGEL: The Art of Patrick Nagel* ("the book"), which is a compilation of selected copyrighted individual art works and personal commentaries.

Since 1984, the primary business of appellant has consisted of: 1) purchasing artwork prints or books including good quality artwork page prints therein; 2) gluing each individual print or page print onto a rectangular sheet of black plastic material exposing a narrow black margin around the print; 3) gluing the black sheet with print onto a major surface of a rectangular white ceramic tile; 4) applying a transparent plastic film over the print, black sheet and ceramic tile surface; and 5) offering the tile with artwork mounted thereon for sale in the retail market.

It is undisputed, in this action, that appellant did the above process with the Nagel book. The appellant removed selected pages from the book, mounted them individually onto ceramic tiles and sold the tiles at retail. . . .

The district court concluded appellant infringed the copyrights in the individual images through its tile-preparing process and also concluded that the resulting products comprised derivative works.

Appellant contends that there has been no copyright infringement because (1) its tiles are not derivative works, and (2) the "first sale" doctrine precludes a finding of infringement. . . .

The protection of derivative rights extends beyond mere protection against unauthorized copying to include the right to make other versions of, perform, or exhibit the work. . . .

What appellant has clearly done here is to make another version of Nagel's art works . . . and that amounts to preparation of a derivative work. By borrowing and mounting the preexisting, copyrighted individual art images without the consent of the copyright proprietors — Mirage and Dumas as to the art works and Van Der Marck as to the book — appellant has prepared a derivative work and infringed the subject copyrights.

Appellant's contention that since it has not engaged in "art reproduction" and therefore its tiles are not derivative works is not fully dispositive of this issue. Appellant has ignored the disjunctive phrase "or any other form in which a work may be recast, transformed or adapted." The legislative history of the Copyright Act of 1976 indicates that Congress intended that for a violation of the right to prepare derivative works to occur "the infringing work must incorporate a portion of the copyrighted work in *some form*." 1976 U.S. Code Cong. & Admin. News 5659, 5675 (emphasis added). The language "recast, transformed or adapted" seems to encompass other alternatives besides simple art reproduction. By removing the individual images from the book and placing them on the tiles, perhaps the appellant has not accomplished reproduction. We conclude, though, that appellant has certainly recast or transformed the individual images by incorporating them into its tile-preparing process. . . .

We recognize that, under the "first sale" doctrine as enunciated at 17 U.S.C. §109(a) . . . appellant can purchase a copy of the Nagel book and subsequently alienate its ownership in that book. However, the right to transfer applies only to the particular copy of the book which appellant has purchased and nothing else. The mere sale of the book to the appellant without a specific transfer by the copyright holder of its exclusive right to prepare derivative works, does not transfer that [derivative] right to appellant. The derivative works right, remains unimpaired and with the copyright proprietors — Mirage, Dumas and Van Der Marck. As we have previously concluded that appellant's tile-preparing process results in derivative works and as the exclusive right to prepare derivative works belongs to the copyright holder, the "first sale" doctrine does not bar the appellees' copyright infringement claims. . . .

Lee v. A.R.T. Company
125 F.3d 580 (7th Cir. 1997)

EASTERBROOK, J.: Annie Lee creates works of art, which she sells through her firm Annie Lee & Friends. Deck the Walls, a chain of outlets for modestly priced art, is among the buyers of her works, which have been registered with the Register of Copyrights. One Deck the Walls store sold some of Lee's notecards and small lithographs to A.R.T. Company, which mounted the works on ceramic tiles (covering the art with transparent epoxy resin in the process) and resold the tiles. Lee contends that these tiles are derivative works, which under 17 U.S.C. §106(2) may not be prepared without the permission of the copyright proprietor. She seeks both monetary and injunctive relief. . . .

Now one might suppose that this is an open and shut case under the doctrine of first sale, codified at 17 U.S.C. §109(a). A.R.T. bought the work legitimately, mounted it on a tile, and resold what it had purchased. Because the artist could capture the value of her art's contribution to the finished product as part of the price for the original transaction, the economic rationale for protecting an adaptation as "derivative" is absent. See William M. Landes & Richard A. Posner, *An Economic Analysis of Copyright Law*, 17 J. Legal Studies 325, 353-57 (1989). An alteration that includes (or consumes) a complete copy of the original lacks economic significance. One work changes hands multiple times, exactly what §109(a) permits, so it may lack legal significance too. But §106(2) creates a separate exclusive right, to "prepare derivative works," and Lee believes that affixing the art to the tile is "preparation," so that A.R.T. would have violated §106(2) even if it had dumped the finished tiles into the Marianas Trench. For the sake of argument we assume that this is so and ask whether card-on-a-tile is a "derivative work" in the first place.

. . . The district court concluded that A.R.T.'s mounting of Lee's works on tile is not an "original work of authorship" because it is no different in form or function from displaying a painting in a frame or placing a medallion in a velvet case. No one believes that a museum violates §106(2) every time it changes the frame of a painting that is still under copyright, although the choice of frame or glazing affects the impression the art conveys, and many artists specify frames (or pedestals for sculptures) in detail. . . . *Mirage Editions* acknowledge[s] that framing and other traditional means of mounting and displaying art do not infringe authors' exclusive right to make derivative works. Nonetheless, the ninth circuit held, what A.R.T. does creates a derivative work because the epoxy resin bonds the art to the tile. Our district judge thought this a distinction without a difference, and we agree. If changing the way in which a work of art will be displayed creates a derivative work, and if Lee is right about what "prepared" means, then the derivative work is "prepared" when the art is mounted; what happens later is not relevant, because the violation of the §106(2) right has already occurred. If the framing process does not create a derivative work, then mounting art on a tile, which serves as a flush frame, does not create a derivative work. . . .

Lee wages a vigorous attack on the district court's conclusion that A.R.T.'s mounting process cannot create a derivative work because the change to the work "as a whole" is not sufficiently original to support a copyright. Cases such as *Gracen v. The Bradford Exchange, Inc.*, 698 F.2d 300 (7th Cir. 1983), show that neither A.R.T. nor Lee herself could have obtained a copyright in the card-on-a-tile, thereby not only extending the period of protection for the images but also eliminating competition in one medium of display. After the ninth circuit held that its mounting process created derivative works, A.R.T. tried to obtain a copyright in one of its products; the Register of Copyrights sensibly informed A.R.T. that the card-on-a-tile could not be copyrighted independently of the note card itself. But Lee says that this is irrelevant — that a change in a work's appearance may infringe the exclusive right under §106(2) even if the alteration is too trivial to support an independent copyright. Pointing to the word "original" in the second sentence of the statutory definition, the district judge held that "originality" is essential to a derivative work. This understanding has the support of both cases and respected commentators. Pointing to the fact that the first sentence in the statutory definition omits any reference to originality, Lee insists that a work may be derivative despite the mechanical nature of the transformation. This view, too, has the support of both cases and respected commentators.

Fortunately, it is not necessary for us to choose sides. Assume for the moment that the first sentence recognizes a set of non-original derivative works. To prevail, then, Lee must show that A.R.T. altered her works in one of the ways mentioned in the first sentence. The tile is not an "art reproduction"; A.R.T. purchased and mounted Lee's original works. That leaves the residual clause: "any other form in which a work may be recast, transformed, or adapted." None of these words fits what A.R.T. did. Lee's works were not "recast" or "adapted." "Transformed" comes closer and gives the ninth circuit some purchase for its view that the permanence of the bond between art and base matters. Yet the copyrighted note cards and lithographs were not "transformed" in the slightest. The art was bonded to a slab of ceramic, but it was not changed in the process. It still depicts exactly what it depicted when it left Lee's studio. If mounting works is a "transformation," then changing a painting's frame or a photograph's mat equally produces a derivative work. Indeed, if Lee is right about the meaning of the definition's first sentence, then *any* alteration of a work, however slight, requires the author's permission. We asked at oral argument what would happen if a purchaser jotted a note on one of the note cards, or used it as a coaster for a drink, or cut it in half, or if a collector applied his seal (as is common in Japan); Lee's counsel replied that such changes prepare derivative works, but that as a practical matter artists would not file suit. A definition of derivative work that makes criminals out of art collectors and tourists is jarring despite Lee's gracious offer not to commence civil litigation.

If Lee (and the ninth circuit) are right about what counts as a derivative work, then the United States has established through the back door an extraordinarily broad version of authors' moral rights, under which artists may block any modification of their works of which they disapprove. No European version of *droit moral* goes this far. . . . We . . . decline to follow . . . *Mirage Editions*.

NOTES AND QUESTIONS

1. Do you agree with *Mirage Editions* or with *Lee*? Do the tiles represent a market that copyright law reserves to the owner of the underlying work, or have the artists already "captured the value" of their art? How should the law determine the answer to this question?

2. Recall what you learned in Chapter 2 about the requirements for copyright protection. Do the tiles in *Mirage Editions* and *Lee* satisfy the requirement of originality? If the tiles are not "original," should they be considered infringing derivative works? Should originality be relevant to determining the *copyrightability* of a derivative work but not to deciding the issue of whether the derivative work *infringes*?

3. Consider the following hypotheticals.

a. Anne is an artist who engages in oil painting. She licenses a company to sell poster reproductions of her paintings. David purchases a number of her posters and then makes and resells oil painting "replicas" of the posters. David prepares each replica by taking a poster he bought; applying acrylic paint to it; mounting it on a canvas; applying oil paint to match the original colors and style; applying varnish; and framing and selling the result. Has David created a derivative work under the reasoning of *Mirage Editions*? Under *Lee*?

b. Cesar is an artist who works in the medium of collage. He purchases magazines and newspapers and combines the cover images and headlines with other "found objects." For example, one of his most well-known works combines the cover of *People* magazine's annual "50 Most Beautiful People" issue with other materials that address issues of appearance, weight, diet, and self-image. Under the reasoning of *Mirage Editions*, has Cesar created a derivative work based on the *People* cover? Under *Lee*?

    c. Family Video, a Utah-based chain of video rental stores, purchases videotapes of Hollywood films from authorized distributors and then edits them to remove profanity, violence, and sexual situations. Has Family Video created unauthorized derivative works? *See Clean Flicks of Colo., LLC v. Soderbergh*, 433 F. Supp. 2d 1236 (D. Colo. 2006) (holding that edited movies are unauthorized copies but not unauthorized derivative works because the infringing copies were not used in a transformative manner).

    4. One scholar has suggested that protection for derivative works should depend on the nature of the use by the secondcomer. One type of use is "consumptive," that is, it incorporates a copy of the underlying work into the derivative work. In such cases, the derivative user could argue that the copyright owner of the underlying work has already been compensated by receiving the price on the first sale of the work. Because this kind of use does not necessarily create a "new" market, the copyright owner should not be able to preclude others from using the work in this way. A second type of use is a "productive" or "public goods use." Such uses create products related to the copyrighted work, effectively exploiting a single copy of the work in a new form and creating a new market for the derivative work. In such cases, the copyright owner of the underlying work should be able to claim the lost value of the use of the work in such a manner because its price at first sale would not have compensated for the productive or public goods use. *See* Amy B. Cohen, *When Does a Work Infringe the Derivative Works Right of a Copyright Owner?*, 17 Cardozo Arts & Ent. L.J. 623 (1999).

    Do you agree with this analysis? Was the use at issue in both *Mirage Editions* and *Lee* "consumptive" or "productive"? How significant to this question is the definition of the copyrighted work's market? In *Mirage* and *Lee* is the relevant market that for "works of art" or that for "decorative tiles"? What should be the appropriate factors in defining the market(s) at issue?

b. Required Form?

    Mirage Editions and *Lee* reveal a disagreement about whether an infringing derivative work must satisfy the originality requirement that applies to copyrightable derivative works. We now ask the same question in the fixation context: Must an *infringing* derivative work meet the fixation requirement that applies to *copyrightable* derivative works?

    The following cases also address the question of how to define what constitutes an infringing derivative work in a digital environment. Computer games are popular entertainment products and many users seek to enhance their experience when playing. This opens a market for companies who make the user's experience of a game more rewarding. However, these enhancements often modify the game in some way. Do they therefore create infringing derivative works? Who should control the market for enhancements of computer games and other digital works? Consider the following cases.

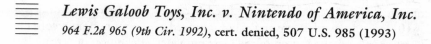

Lewis Galoob Toys, Inc. v. Nintendo of America, Inc.

964 F.2d 965 (9th Cir. 1992), cert. denied, 507 U.S. 985 (1993)

FARRIS, J.: Nintendo of America appeals the district court's judgment following a bench trial (1) declaring that Lewis Galoob Toys' Game Genie does not violate any Nintendo copyrights and dissolving a temporary injunction and (2) denying Nintendo's request for a permanent injunction enjoining Galoob from marketing the Game Genie. . . . We affirm. . . .

The Nintendo Entertainment System is a home video game system marketed by Nintendo. To use the system, the player inserts a cartridge containing a video game that Nintendo produces or licenses others to produce. By pressing buttons and manipulating a control pad, the player controls one of the game's characters and progresses through the game. The games are protected as audiovisual works under 17 U.S.C. §102(a)(6).

The Game Genie is a device manufactured by Galoob that allows the player to alter up to three features of a Nintendo game. For example, the Game Genie can increase the number of lives of the player's character, increase the speed at which the character moves, and allow the character to float above obstacles. The player controls the changes made by the Game Genie by entering codes provided by the Game Genie Programming Manual and Code Book. The player also can experiment with variations of these codes.

The Game Genie functions by blocking the value for a single data byte sent by the game cartridge to the central processing unit in the Nintendo Entertainment System and replacing it with a new value. If that value controls the character's strength, for example, then the character can be made invincible by increasing the value sufficiently. The Game Genie is inserted between a game cartridge and the Nintendo Entertainment System. The Game Genie does not alter the data that is stored in the game cartridge. Its effects are temporary.

Discussion

1. Derivative Work

A derivative work must incorporate a protected work in some concrete or permanent "form." The Copyright Act defines a derivative work as follows:

> A "derivative work" is a work based upon one or more preexisting works, such as a translation, musical arrangement, dramatization, fictionalization, motion picture version, sound recording, art reproduction, abridgment, condensation, *or any other form in which a work may be recast, transformed, or adapted.* . . .

17 U.S.C. §101 (emphasis added). The examples of derivative works provided by the Act all physically incorporate the underlying work or works. The Act's legislative history similarly indicates that "the infringing work must incorporate a portion of the copyrighted work in some form." 1976 U.S. Code Cong. & Admin. News 5659, 5675. . . .

Our analysis is not controlled by the Copyright Act's definition of "fixed." The Act defines copies as "material objects, other than phonorecords, in which a work is *fixed* by any method." 17 U.S.C. §101 (emphasis added). The Act's definition of "derivative work," in contrast, lacks any such reference to fixation. *See id.* Further, we have held in a copyright infringement action that "[i]t makes no difference that the derivation may not satisfy certain requirements for statutory copyright registration itself." . . . A derivative work must be fixed to be *protected* under the Act, *see* 17 U.S.C. §102(a), but not to *infringe*.

The argument that a derivative work must be fixed because "[a] 'derivative work' is a work," 17 U.S.C. §101, and "[a] work is 'created' when it is fixed in a copy or phonorecord for the first time," *id.*, relies on a misapplication of the Copyright Act's definition of "created":

> A work is 'created' when it is fixed in a copy or phonorecord for the first time; where a work is prepared over a period of time, the portion of it that has been fixed at any particular time constitutes

the work as of that time, and where the work has been prepared in different versions, each version constitutes a separate work. *Id.*

The definition clarifies the *time* at which a work is *created*. If the provision were a definition of "work," it would not use that term in such a casual manner. The Act does not contain a definition of "work." Rather, it contains specific definitions: "audiovisual works," "literary works," and "pictorial, graphic and sculptural works," for example. The definition of "derivative work" does not require fixation.

The district court's finding that no independent work is created, *see Galoob*, 780 F. Supp. at 1291, is supported by the record. The Game Genie merely enhances the audiovisual displays (or underlying data bytes) that originate in Nintendo game cartridges. The altered displays do not incorporate a portion of a copyrighted work in some concrete or permanent *form*. Nintendo argues that the Game Genie's displays are as fixed in the hardware and software used to create them as Nintendo's original displays. Nintendo's argument ignores the fact that the Game Genie cannot produce an audiovisual display; the underlying display must be produced by a Nintendo Entertainment System and game cartridge. Even if we were to rely on the Copyright Act's definition of "fixed," we would similarly conclude that the resulting display is not "embodied," *see* 17 U.S.C. §101, in the Game Genie. It cannot be a derivative work. . . .

Nintendo asserted at oral argument that the existence of a $150 million market for the Game Genie indicates that its audiovisual display must be fixed. We understand Nintendo's argument; consumers clearly would not purchase the Game Genie if its display was not "sufficiently permanent or stable to permit it to be perceived . . . for a period of more than transitory duration." 17 U.S.C. §101. But, Nintendo's reliance on the Act's definition of "fixed" is misplaced. Nintendo's argument also proves too much; the existence of a market does not, and cannot, determine conclusively whether a work is an infringing derivative work. For example, although there is a market for kaleidoscopes, it does not necessarily follow that kaleidoscopes create unlawful derivative works when pointed at protected artwork. The same can be said of countless other products that enhance, but do not replace, copyrighted works.

Nintendo also argues that our analysis should focus exclusively on the audiovisual displays created by the Game Genie, i.e., that we should compare the altered displays to Nintendo's original displays. Nintendo emphasizes that " '[a]udiovisual works' are works that consist of a series of related images . . . *regardless of the nature of the material objects . . . in which the works are embodied.*" 17 U.S.C. §101 (emphasis added). The Copyright Act's definition of "audiovisual works" is inapposite; the *only* question before us is whether the audiovisual displays created by the Game Genie are "derivative works." The Act does not similarly provide that a work can be a derivative work regardless of the nature of the material objects in which the work is embodied. A derivative work must incorporate a protected work in some concrete or permanent form. We cannot ignore the actual source of the Game Genie's display. . . .

In holding that the audiovisual displays created by the Game Genie are not derivative works, we recognize that technology often advances by improvement rather than replacement. Some time ago, for example, computer companies began marketing spell-checkers that operate within existing word processors by signaling the writer when a word is misspelled. These applications, as well as countless others, could not be produced and marketed if courts were to conclude that the word processor and spell-checker combination is a derivative work based on the word processor alone. The Game Genie is useless by itself, it can only enhance, and cannot duplicate or recaste [sic], a Nintendo game's output. It does not contain or produce a Nintendo game's output in some concrete or permanent form, nor does it supplant demand for Nintendo game cartridges. Such innovations rarely will constitute infringing derivative works under the Copyright Act. . . .

Micro Star v. FormGen Inc.
154 F.3d 1107 (9th Cir. 1998)

KOZINSKI, J.: Duke Nukem routinely vanquishes Octabrain and the Protozoid Slimer. But what about the dreaded Micro Star? . . .

FormGen Inc., GT Interactive Software Corp. and Apogee Software, Ltd. (collectively FormGen) made, distributed and own the rights to Duke Nukem 3D (D/N-3D), an immensely popular (and very cool) computer game. D/N-3D is played from the first-person perspective; the player assumes the personality and point of view of the title character, who is seen on the screen only as a pair of hands and an occasional boot, much as one might see oneself in real life without the aid of a mirror. Players explore a futuristic city infested with evil aliens and other hazards. The goal is to zap them before they zap you, while searching for the hidden passage to the next level. The basic game comes with twenty-nine levels, each with a different combination of scenery, aliens, and other challenges. The game also includes a "Build Editor," a utility that enables players to create their own levels. With FormGen's encouragement, players frequently post levels they have created on the Internet where others can download them. Micro Star, a computer software distributor, did just that: It downloaded 300 user-created levels and stamped them onto a CD, which it then sold commercially as Nuke It (N/I). N/I is packaged in a box decorated with numerous "screen shots," pictures of what the new levels look like when played.

Micro Star filed suit in district court, seeking a declaratory judgment that N/I did not infringe on any of FormGen's copyrights. FormGen counterclaimed, seeking a preliminary injunction barring further production and distribution of N/I. Relying on *Lewis Galoob Toys, Inc. v. Nintendo of Am., Inc.*, 964 F.2d 965 (9th Cir. 1992), the district court held that N/I was not a derivative work and therefore did not infringe FormGen's copyright. The district court did, however, grant a preliminary injunction as to the screen shots, finding that N/I's packaging violated FormGen's copyright by reproducing pictures of D/N-3D characters without a license. The court rejected Micro Star's fair use claims. Both sides appeal their losses. . . .

FormGen alleges that its copyright is infringed by Micro Star's unauthorized commercial exploitation of user-created game levels. In order to understand Form-Gen's claims, one must first understand the way D/N-3D works. The game consists of three separate components: the game engine, the source art library and the MAP files.[2] The game engine is the heart of the computer program; in some sense, it *is* the program. It tells the computer when to read data, save and load games, play sounds and project images onto the screen. In order to create the audiovisual display for a particular level, the game engine invokes the MAP file that corresponds to that level. Each MAP file contains a series of instructions that tell the game engine (and, through it, the computer) what to put where. For instance, the MAP file might say scuba gear goes at the bottom of the screen. The game engine then goes to the source art library, finds the image of the scuba gear, and puts it in just the right place on the screen.[3] The MAP file describes the level in painstaking detail, but it does not actually contain any of the copyrighted art itself; everything that appears on the screen actually comes from the art library. Think of the game's

---

2. So-called because the files all end with the extension ".MAP." Also, no doubt, because they contain the layout for the various levels.

3. Actually, this is all a bit metaphorical. Computer programs don't actually go anywhere or fetch anything. Rather, the game engine receives the player's instruction as to which game level to select and instructs the processor to access the MAP file corresponding to that level. The MAP file, in turn, consists of a series of instructions indicating which art images go where. When the MAP file calls for a particular art image, the game engine tells the processor to access the art library for instructions on how each pixel on the screen must be colored in order to paint that image.

audiovisual display as a paint-by-numbers kit. The MAP file might tell you to put blue paint in section number 565, but it doesn't contain any blue paint itself; the blue paint comes from your palette, which is the low-tech analog of the art library, while you play the role of the game engine. When the player selects one of the N/I levels, the game engine references the N/I MAP files, but still uses the D/N-3D art library to generate the images that make up that level.

FormGen points out that a copyright holder enjoys the exclusive right to prepare derivative works based on D/N-3D. *See* 17 U.S.C. §106(2) (1994). According to FormGen, the audiovisual displays generated when D/N-3D is run in conjunction with the N/I CD MAP files are derivative works that infringe this exclusivity. . . .

. . . [W]e have developed certain criteria a work must satisfy in order to qualify as a derivative work. One of these is that a derivative work must exist in a "concrete or permanent form," *Galoob*, 964 F.2d at 967 (internal quotation marks omitted), and must substantially incorporate protected material from the preexisting work. Micro Star argues that N/I is not a derivative work because the audiovisual displays generated when D/N-3D is run with N/I's MAP files are not incorporated in any concrete or permanent form, and the MAP files do not copy any of D/N-3D's protected expression. It is mistaken on both counts.

The requirement that a derivative work must assume a concrete or permanent form was recognized without much discussion in *Galoob*. There, we noted that all the Copyright Act's examples of derivative works took some definite, physical form and concluded that this was a requirement of the Act. *See Galoob*, 964 F.2d at 967-68. . . . Obviously, N/I's MAP files themselves exist in a concrete or permanent form; they are burned onto a CD-ROM. But what about the audiovisual displays generated when D/N-3D runs the N/I MAP files — i.e., the actual game level as displayed on the screen? Micro Star argues that, because the audiovisual displays in *Galoob* didn't meet the "concrete or permanent form" requirement, neither do N/I's. . . .

Micro Star argues that the MAP files on N/I are a more advanced version of the Game Genie, replacing old values (the MAP files in the original game) with new values (N/I's MAP files). But, whereas the audiovisual displays created by Game Genie were never recorded in any permanent form, the audiovisual displays generated by D/N-3D from the N/I MAP files are in the MAP files themselves. In *Galoob*, the audiovisual display was defined by the original game cartridge, not by the Game Genie; no one could possibly say that the data values inserted by the Game Genie described the audiovisual display. In the present case the audiovisual display that appears on the computer monitor when a N/I level is played is described — in exact detail — by a N/I MAP file.

This raises the interesting question whether an exact, down to the last detail, description of an audiovisual display (and — by definition — we know that MAP files do describe audiovisual displays down to the last detail) counts as a permanent or concrete form for purposes of *Galoob*. We see no reason it shouldn't. What, after all, does sheet music do but describe in precise detail the way a copyrighted melody sounds? To be copyrighted, pantomimes and dances may be "described in sufficient detail to enable the work to be performed from that description." Similarly, the N/I MAP files describe the audiovisual display that is to be generated when the player chooses to play D/N-3D using the N/I levels. Because the audiovisual displays assume a concrete or permanent form in the MAP files, *Galoob* stands as no bar to finding that they are derivative works. . . .

Micro Star further argues that the MAP files are not derivative works because they do not, in fact, incorporate any of D/N-3D's protected expression. In particular, Micro Star makes much of the fact that the N/I MAP files reference the source art library, but do not actually contain any art files themselves. Therefore, it claims, nothing of D/N-3D's is reproduced in the MAP files. In making this argument, Micro Star misconstrues the protected work. The work that Micro Star infringes is the D/N-3D story itself—a beefy commando type named Duke who wanders around post-Apocalypse Los Angeles, shooting Pig Cops with a gun, lobbing hand grenades, searching for medkits and steroids, using a jetpack to leap over obstacles, blowing up gas tanks, avoiding radioactive slime. A copyright owner holds the right to create sequels, *see Trust Co. Bank v. MGM/UA Entertainment Co.*, 772 F.2d 740 (11th Cir. 1985), and the stories told in the N/I MAP files are surely sequels, telling new (though somewhat repetitive) tales of Duke's fabulous adventures. A book about Duke Nukem would infringe for the same reason, even if it contained no pictures.[5] . . .

NOTES AND QUESTIONS

1. Do you agree with the *Galoob* court's statement that "[a] derivative work must be fixed to be *protected* . . . but not to *infringe*"? Although this statement is consistent with the legislative history excerpted on pages 366-67 *supra*, is it consistent with the wording of the statute? Keep in mind that under rules of statutory construction, a court may not resort to the legislative history when the wording of the statute is clear. Does the court's interpretation of the "form" requirement from §101 make sense given its conclusion that a derivative work need not be fixed to infringe? Given the legislative history? Should the court have accepted the market-based argument made by Nintendo?

2. Do you agree with the *Micro Star* court that *Galoob* does not bar the finding that the audiovisual displays generated by the N/I MAP files are derivative works? Micro Star did not create any game levels of its own; it simply downloaded existing user-created levels that Form-Gen had authorized. Is the mere redistribution of a preexisting, authorized derivative work a violation of §106(3)?

3. What test did the *Micro Star* court apply to determine whether the defendants had created a derivative work? How does this test compare to the substantial similarity test applied by the *Castle Rock* court? How does it compare to the originality test applied by the *Warner Brothers Entertainment* court?

4. ClearPlay provides filtering technology for DVD players that allows users to program their players to skip certain scenes in movies. Each movie has its own filter file that can be downloaded from ClearPlay's website and installed on the DVD player. Once the filter is installed, a user inserts her copy of the movie and, when the movie is played, the scenes containing the objectionable content are not seen. No modified version of the movie is created in any separate fixed copy. In 2002, ClearPlay filed a declaratory judgment action against eight movie studios and the Directors Guild of America, arguing that its technology did not infringe any of the studios' copyrights. *Huntsman v. Soderbergh*, No. 02-M-1662 (D. Colo., filed Aug. 29, 2002). In response, the studios claimed that the ClearPlay technology creates unauthorized derivative works. What do you think of this claim?

While the case was pending, Congress passed the Family Movie Act as part of the Family Entertainment and Copyright Act of 2005. Included in the legislation was a new exemption from copyright liability, discussed in Section F.4, *infra*, for technologies such as ClearPlay's.

5. Should the right to prepare derivative works be construed differently when the allegedly "derivative" work is a by-product of new technology? Should the level of innovation

---

5. We note that the N/I MAP files can only be used with D/N-3D. If another game could use the MAP files to tell the story of a mousy fellow who travels through a beige maze, killing vicious saltshakers with paper-clips, then the MAP files would not incorporate the protected expression of D/N-3D because they would not be telling a D/N-3D story.

achieved by the defendant, or efficiency considerations associated with a new technology, make a difference? If all rights to ancillary products are reserved to the owner of the underlying work, how do you think that will influence the development of new technologies?

Note on Linking and Framing

As *Galoob* and *Microstar* illustrate, determining the proper scope of the right to prepare derivative works becomes even more challenging when one considers the capabilities of networked digital technologies. Consider, for example, the basic linking technology of the Web. Linking allows a web site to provide its visitors with access to other web sites. A "link" is essentially an address embedded in a web site's HTML code that points a user to another location on the Web. When a user clicks on a link, the user's browser reads the address embedded in the HTML code, finds the location on the Web, and requests a copy of that web page. The hosting computer for that page responds by sending a copy of the requested page to the browser, which then displays it on the user's screen.

There are several different ways in which users can access and view the linked web page. A deep link is a link to a subsidiary page of a web site that allows users to go directly to a specific file or location within that web site without first visiting the home page of the site. This might be analogized to reading the end of a novel first, simply to know how the story ended, or to a "pin cite" that tells the reader of a law review article on which page of the cited source a quotation is located. On the Internet, however, the link may alter the way that the user experiences the site to which the link connects. Framing is a type of linking that allows a web page to be split by a web browser into multiple, independent scrollable windows with each window containing different content. This technique also allows content from one web site to be inset within another. In this sense, framing may broadly be analogized to an earlier (though not as popular) technology, the picture-within-a-picture television screen. Because framing technology is versatile, it may be used with varying degrees of added creative expression.

Copyright owners of web-based content have made repeated efforts to deploy their exclusive copyright rights to prevent linking and framing. The first wave of efforts relied principally on the rights to reproduce and to prepare derivative works. In *Futuredontics Inc. v. Applied Anagramics Inc.*, 45 U.S.P.Q.2d 2005 (C.D. Cal.), *aff'd*, 152 F.3d 925 (9th Cir. 1998), the defendant's web page framed the plaintiff's web page with a border that included advertising sold by the defendant. The court held that *Mirage Editions* might allow the plaintiff to establish that the defendant's web page was an infringing derivative work. It therefore denied the defendant's motion to dismiss the lawsuit. The parties later settled their dispute.

Later court decisions, however, cast doubt on the *Futuredontics* ruling. A number of these lawsuits arose in the context of pop-up advertisements. Many consumers have software installed on their desktops that enables "behavioral marketing." The software works by studying a user's activity as he or she browses the Internet. Based on the user's perceived interests, the software triggers the display of one or more pop-up ads. The ad itself may or may not overlay the content of the web site the user was visiting. Often, the pop-up ad may present the products or services of the site's competitor. Does the pop-up ad create a derivative work? Courts have unanimously concluded that it does not. In *Wells Fargo & Co. v. WhenU.Com, Inc.*, 293 F. Supp. 2d 734 (E.D. Mich. 2003), the court reasoned that:

> WhenU's conduct affects plaintiff's sites in a comparable manner [to the way in which the Game Genie affected Nintendo's product]. It only temporarily changes the way the sites are viewed by consumers. As soon as the advertisements are "disconnected" — that is closed or

minimized — plaintiffs' sites revert to their original form. If anything, WhenU's advertisements modify their sites far less that [sic] the Game Genie altered users' NES video game experiences.

Id. at 770; *see also 1-800 Contacts, Inc. v. When U. Com*, 309 F. Supp. 2d 467, 487-88 (S.D.N.Y. 2003) ("A definition of 'derivative work' that sweeps within the scope of the copyright law a multi-tasking Internet shopper whose word-processing program obscures the screen display of Plaintiff's website is indeed 'jarring,' and not supported by the definition set forth at 17 U.S.C. §101."), *rev'd on other grounds*, 414 F.3d 400 (2d Cir.), *cert denied*, 546 U.S. 1033 (2005); *U-Haul Int'l, Inc. v. When U. Com, Inc.*, 279 F. Supp. 2d 723, 731 (E.D. Va. 2003) (articulating the same concern).

Scholarly commentators have disagreed on whether and when linking and framing might violate the derivative work right. Professor Maureen O'Rourke has argued that either an implied license or the fair use doctrine may shelter users who engage in linking and framing from liability for copyright infringement. *See* Maureen A. O'Rourke, *Fencing Cyberspace: Drawing Borders in a Virtual World*, 82 Minn. L. Rev. 609, 660-62, 669-70 (1998). She concludes, however, that the implied license argument is less persuasive in cases involving deep linking. *Id*. at 669. Other commentators argue that owners of web sites should have a duty to employ technological measures first (such as, for example, using code to detect a deep link and refusing to grant access to the deep linker) as alternatives to copyright claims.

Is the case against linking and framing any stronger than that against pop-up ads? Does framing a web site constitute "recasting," "transforming," or "adapting" the underlying site? Is it analogous to defendant's conduct in *Mirage Editions* (or in *Lee*)? Do linking and framing satisfy the "form" requirement as interpreted by *Galoob*? Would either the *Galoob* court or the *Micro Star* court conclude that these practices create derivative works? Should courts treat deep linking differently, as Professor O'Rourke recommends? Should they treat framing differently, because of the uses of advertising that it allows? Do the cases interpreting the scope of the derivative work right support either distinction? Do theoretical rationales for the derivative work right offer support? Would either result be desirable as a policy matter?

E.   MORAL RIGHTS: THE AMERICAN VERSION

This section departs briefly from an analysis of the enumerated exclusive rights in §106 to consider "moral rights," a different category of rights that serve to augment the classic set of rights designed to protect an author's economic interests. Because one aspect of moral rights is protection against distortion of one's work, it is logical to consider moral rights after exploring the scope of the derivative work right in U.S. copyright law.

Moral rights originated in French law, and are commonly viewed as a central and distinguishing feature of the continental European copyright tradition. Today, however, most other countries also afford protection for moral rights pursuant to the requirements of the Berne Convention. Article 6bis of the Berne Convention provides:

(1) Independently of the author's economic rights, and even after the transfer of the said rights, the author shall have the right to claim authorship of the work and to object to any distortion, mutilation or other modification of, or other derogatory action in relation to, the said work, which would be prejudicial to his honor or reputation.

Two rights flow from the provisions of Article 6bis: (1) the right to claim paternity of the work (known in the U.S. as the right of attribution) and (2) the right to the work's integrity. The Berne Convention specifies that protection for these rights should be granted at least until the expiration of the author's economic rights (*e.g.* life + 70 years in the U.S.). However, countries may opt to cease protection of moral rights after the death of the author. *See* Berne Conv., art. 6bis(2).

Section 106 of the Copyright Act does not specify protection for moral rights; nevertheless, moral rights do enjoy some protection under U.S. law. The scope and sufficiency of such protection, however, are the subjects of considerable debate. Recall from Chapter 1 that the U.S. was the last major industrialized country to join the Berne Convention. Recall, also, that among the reasons for the U.S.' recalcitrance was concern over the requirement that members of the Berne Convention afford protection for the "moral rights" of authors. Congress did not provide direct protection for moral rights in the Berne Convention Implementation Act (BCIA). Instead, §2(3) of the BCIA stated that existing U.S. law was sufficient to satisfy U.S. obligations under the Berne Convention. According to the legislative history, "[t]his existing U.S. law includes various provisions of the Copyright Act and the Lanham Act, various state statutes, and common law principles such as libel, defamation, misrepresentation, and unfair competition. . . ." S. Rep. No. 352, 100th Cong., 2d Sess. 9-10 (1988), *reprinted in* 1988 U.S.C.C.A.N. 3706, 3714-15. The TRIPS Agreement, however, explicitly excluded the protection of moral rights primarily at the insistence of the U.S. *See* TRIPS Agreement, art. 9(1).[1]

This section considers whether the congressional judgment expressed in the legislative history of the BCIA was correct, and whether U.S. reluctance to accept moral rights is justified.

1. Theories for the Protection of Moral Rights Under U.S. Law

Just what are the "various provisions of the Copyright Act" and the other statutory and common law protections that, according to Congress, already provide protection for the moral rights of an author? Consider the following case, decided under the provisions of the 1909 Act.

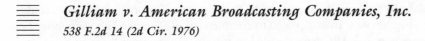

Gilliam v. American Broadcasting Companies, Inc.

538 F.2d 14 (2d Cir. 1976)

LUMBARD, J.: Plaintiffs, a group of British writers and performers known as "Monty Python,"[2] appeal from a denial by Judge Lasker in the Southern District of a preliminary injunction to restrain the American Broadcasting Company (ABC) from broadcasting edited versions of three separate programs originally written and performed by Monty Python for broadcast by the British Broadcasting Corporation (BBC). We agree with Judge Lasker that the appellants have demonstrated that the excising done for ABC impairs the integrity of the original work. We further find that the countervailing injuries that Judge Lasker found might have

---

1. Note, however, that the WIPO Performances and Phonograms Treaty requires that member states grant to performers the rights of paternity and integrity in their "live aural performances or performances fixed in phonograms." *See* WPPT, art. 5(1).

2. Appellant Gilliam is an American citizen residing in England.

accrued to ABC as a result of an injunction at a prior date no longer exist. We therefore direct the issuance of a preliminary injunction by the district court.

Since its formation in 1969, the Monty Python group has gained popularity primarily through its thirty-minute television programs created for BBC as part of a comedy series entitled "Monty Python's Flying Circus." In accordance with an agreement between Monty Python and BBC, the group writes and delivers to BBC scripts for use in the television series. This scriptwriters' agreement recites in great detail the procedure to be followed when any alterations are to be made in the script prior to recording of the program. The essence of this section of the agreement is that, while BBC retains final authority to make changes, appellants or their representatives exercise optimum control over the scripts consistent with BBC's authority and only minor changes may be made without prior consultation with the writers. Nothing in the scriptwriters' agreement entitles BBC to alter a program once it has been recorded. The agreement further provides that, subject to the terms therein, the group retains all rights in the script.

Under the agreement, BBC may license the transmission of recordings of the television programs in any overseas territory. The series has been broadcast in this country primarily on non-commercial public broadcasting television stations, although several of the programs have been broadcast on commercial stations in Texas and Nevada. In each instance, the thirty-minute programs have been broadcast as originally recorded and broadcast in England in their entirety and without commercial interruption.

In October 1973, Time-Life Films acquired the right to distribute in the United States certain BBC television programs, including the Monty Python series. Time-Life was permitted to edit the programs only "for insertion of commercials, applicable censorship or governmental . . . rules and regulations, and National Association of Broadcasters and time segment requirements." No similar clause was included in the scriptwriters' agreement between appellants and BBC. Prior to this time, ABC had sought to acquire the right to broadcast excerpts from various Monty Python programs in the spring of 1975, but the group rejected the proposal for such a disjointed format. Thereafter, in July 1975, ABC agreed with Time-Life to broadcast two ninety-minute specials each comprising three thirty-minute Monty Python programs that had not previously been shown in this country.

Correspondence between representatives of BBC and Monty Python reveals that these parties assumed that ABC would broadcast each of the Monty Python programs "in its entirety." On September 5, 1975, however, the group's British representative inquired of BBC how ABC planned to show the programs in their entirety if approximately 24 minutes of each 90 minute program were to be devoted to commercials. BBC replied on September 12, "we can only reassure you that ABC have decided to run the programmes 'back to back,' and that there is a firm undertaking not to segment them." ABC broadcast the first of the specials on October 3, 1975. Appellants did not see a tape of the program until late November and were allegedly "appalled" at the discontinuity and "mutilation" that had resulted from the editing done by Time-Life for ABC. Twenty-four minutes of the original 90 minutes of recording had been omitted. Some of the editing had been done in order to make time for commercials; other material had been edited, according to ABC, because the original programs contained offensive or obscene matter.

In early December, Monty Python learned that ABC planned to broadcast the second special on December 26, 1975. The parties began negotiations concerning editing of that program and a delay of the broadcast until Monty Python could view it. These negotiations were futile, however, and on December 15 the group filed this action to enjoin the broadcast and for damages. Following an evidentiary hearing, Judge Lasker found that "the plaintiffs have established an impairment of the integrity of their work" which "caused the film or program . . . to lose its iconoclastic verve." According to Judge Lasker, "the damage that has been caused to the plaintiffs is irreparable by its nature." Nevertheless, the judge denied the motion for the preliminary injunction on the grounds that it was unclear who owned the copyright in the programs produced by BBC from the scripts written by Monty Python. . . .

Judge Lasker granted Monty Python's request for more limited relief by requiring ABC to broadcast a disclaimer during the December 26 special to the effect that the group dissociated itself from the program because of the editing. A panel of this court, however, granted a stay of that order until this appeal could be heard and permitted ABC to broadcast, at the beginning of the special, only the legend that the program had been edited by ABC. . . .

Judge Lasker denied the preliminary injunction in part because he was unsure of the ownership of the copyright in the recorded program. Appellants first contend that the question of ownership is irrelevant because the recorded program was merely a derivative work taken from the script in which they hold the uncontested copyright. Thus, even if BBC owned the copyright in the recorded program, its use of that work would be limited by the license granted to BBC by Monty Python for use of the underlying script. We agree.

Section 7 of the Copyright Law, 17 U.S.C. §7, provides in part that "adaptations, arrangements, dramatizations . . . or other versions of . . . copyrighted works when produced with the consent of the proprietor of the copyright in such works . . . shall be regarded as new works subject to copyright. . . ." Manifestly, the recorded program falls into this category as a dramatization of the script, and thus the program was itself entitled to copyright protection. However, section 7 limits the copyright protection of the derivative work, as works adapted from previously existing scripts have become known, to the novel additions made to the underlying work, and the derivative work does not affect the "force or validity" of the copyright in the matter from which it is derived. . . . Thus, any ownership by BBC of the copyright in the recorded program would not affect the scope or ownership of the copyright in the underlying script.

Since the copyright in the underlying script survives intact despite the incorporation of that work into a derivative work, one who uses the script, even with the permission of the proprietor of the derivative work, may infringe the underlying copyright. . . .

If the proprietor of the derivative work is licensed by the proprietor of the copyright in the underlying work to vend or distribute the derivative work to third parties, those parties will, of course, suffer no liability for their use of the underlying work consistent with the license to the proprietor of the derivative work. Obviously, it was just this type of arrangement that was contemplated in this instance. The scriptwriters' agreement between Monty Python and BBC specifically permitted the latter to license the transmission of the recordings made by BBC to distributors such as Time-Life for broadcast in overseas territories.

One who obtains permission to use a copyrighted script in the production of a derivative work, however, may not exceed the specific purpose for which permission was granted. Most of the decisions that have reached this conclusion have dealt with the improper extension of the underlying work into media or time, i. e., duration of the license, not covered by the grant of permission to the derivative work proprietor. . . . Appellants herein do not claim that the broadcast by ABC violated media or time restrictions contained in the license of the script to BBC. Rather, they claim that revisions in the script, and ultimately in the program, could be made only after consultation with Monty Python, and that ABC's broadcast of a program edited after recording and without consultation with Monty Python exceeded the scope of any license that BBC was entitled to grant. . . .

. . . Whether intended to allow greater economic exploitation of the work, as in the media and time cases, or to ensure that the copyright proprietor retains a veto power over revisions desired for the derivative work, the ability of the copyright holder to control his work remains paramount in our copyright law. We find, therefore, that unauthorized editing of the underlying work, if proven, would constitute an infringement of the copyright in that work similar to any other use of a work that exceeded the license granted by the proprietor of the copyright. . . .

II

It also seems likely that appellants will succeed on the theory that, regardless of the right ABC had to broadcast an edited program, the cuts made constituted an actionable mutilation of Monty Python's work. This cause of action, which seeks redress for deformation of an artist's work, finds its roots in the continental concept of droit moral, or moral right, which may generally be summarized as including the right of the artist to have his work attributed to him in the form in which he created it. See 1 M. Nimmer, supra, at §110.1.

American copyright law, as presently written, does not recognize moral rights or provide a cause of action for their violation, since the law seeks to vindicate the economic, rather than the personal, rights of authors. Nevertheless, the economic incentive for artistic and intellectual creation that serves as the foundation for American copyright law cannot be reconciled with the inability of artists to obtain relief for mutilation or misrepresentation of their work to the public on which the artists are financially dependent. Thus courts have long granted relief for misrepresentation of an artist's work by relying on theories outside the statutory law of copyright, such as contract law . . . or the tort of unfair competition. . . . Although such decisions are clothed in terms of proprietary right in one's creation, they also properly vindicate the author's personal right to prevent the presentation of his work to the public in a distorted form. . . .

Here, the appellants claim that the editing done for ABC mutilated the original work and that consequently the broadcast of those programs as the creation of Monty Python violated the Lanham Act §43(a), 15 U.S.C. §1125(a). This statute, the federal counterpart to state unfair competition laws, has been invoked to prevent misrepresentations that may injure plaintiff's business or personal reputation, even where no registered trademark is concerned. It is sufficient to violate the Act that a representation of a product, although technically true, creates a false impression of the product's origin. . . .

These cases cannot be distinguished from the situation in which a television network broadcasts a program properly designated as having been written and performed by a group, but which has been edited, without the writer's consent, into a form that departs substantially from the original work. "To deform his work is to present him to the public as the creator of a work not his own, and thus makes him subject to criticism for work he has not done." [Martin A.] Roeder, [*The Doctrine of Moral Rights*, 53 Harv. L. Rev. 554, 569 (1940)]. In such a case, it is the writer or performer, rather than the network, who suffers the consequences of the mutilation, for the public will have only the final product by which to evaluate the work. Thus, an allegation that a defendant has presented to the public a "garbled," . . . distorted version of plaintiff's work seeks to redress the very rights sought to be protected by the Lanham Act, 15 U.S.C. §1125(a), and should be recognized as stating a cause of action under that statute. . . .

. . . We find that the truncated version at times omitted the climax of the skits to which appellants' rare brand of humor was leading and at other times deleted essential elements in the schematic development of a story line. We therefore agree with Judge Lasker's conclusion that the edited version broadcast by ABC impaired the integrity of appellants' work and represented to the public as the product of appellants what was actually a mere caricature of their talents. We believe that a valid cause of action for such distortion exists and that therefore a preliminary injunction may issue to prevent repetition of the broadcast prior to final determination of the issues. . . .

NOTES AND QUESTIONS

1. How effective were the alternative theories of protection posited by the plaintiffs in *Gilliam*? Does *Gilliam* support Congress' statement that at the time of U.S. ratification of the Berne Convention existing law provided sufficient protection for moral rights as required by the Berne Convention?

2. *Gilliam* suggests that the right to prepare derivative works may also provide protection for the non-economic interests of authors. Should derivative rights be construed this way? Recall the economic rationale for derivative rights articulated by Professor Goldstein and by the court in *Castle Rock*. Are derivative rights an appropriate vehicle for complying with the Berne Convention's requirements for the protection of moral rights? Are there any reasons that moral rights should not be protected as part of the derivative work right? Why protect an author's non-economic interests? We return to these questions in Chapter 7.

3. Review Question 3.c in Section 5.D.2.a, page 385 *supra*. If the studios that own the copyrights in the films object to Family Video's actions, can they rely on *Gilliam* to support a claim for violation of their right to create derivative works? Why, or why not?

4. Owners of copyrights in certain classic black and white films have begun colorizing them. The owner of the copyright to a black and white film directed by John Huston, entitled *Asphalt Jungle*, colorized the film and licensed it for broadcast on French television. Huston's successors sued, claiming that the broadcast of the colorized version infringed Huston's right of integrity. Under U.S. law, the author of the film would be the movie studio under its work for hire agreement with Huston. French law does not recognize such agreements. The French Supreme Court held that French law governed the question of authorship, and thus that Huston was the author. As the author, Huston was entitled to the full range of moral rights. The Versailles Court of Appeal enjoined the broadcast. Is this an appropriate result? Would it make any difference to your answer if Huston shot the movie in black and white not because of technical limitations, but for artistic reasons?

Does colorization of a motion picture violate the derivative work right? If the copyright is no longer owned by the creator of the film, are there any other claims under U.S. law that the creator might bring to halt the colorization?

5. In *United States v. Microsoft Corp.*, 253 F.3d 34 (D.C. Cir.), *cert. denied*, 534 U.S. 952 (2001), defendant Microsoft argued that its licensing clauses, which prohibited Original Equipment Manufacturers (OEMs) from removing certain icons (such as the icon for Microsoft's "Internet Explorer" browser) from the "desktop" visible to users, were justified by its copyright rights. Microsoft did not identify the exact rights that it claimed were infringed, but the court engaged in a discussion of the *Gilliam* decision before rejecting Microsoft's argument. Does either *Gilliam* or the European notion of moral rights provide support for Microsoft's argument?

6. In addition to the rights of paternity (attribution) and integrity secured by the Berne Convention, many countries recognize a moral right of divulgation or disclosure and a moral right to withdraw the work from circulation if it no longer represents the author's views. The right of divulgation allows an author to control the terms under which his or her works may first be disclosed to the public. Can you think of any existing laws in the U.S. that might provide comparable protection to authors? How about comparable protection for the right of withdrawal?

7. Many countries provide copyright owners with a right called the *droit de suite* (also called a "neighboring" right to that of copyright). Generally, the *droit de suite* gives an artist the right to receive a part of the proceeds that arise from the resale of the artist's work. The right is particularly useful to painters and graphic artists. Historically, copies of works of art have not provided a significant source of income for visual artists. Their income comes instead from the sale of the original artwork itself. This distinguishes visual artists from authors of literary works who derive significant income from the sale of copies of their works. The value of an original work of art often appreciates significantly over time. In the absence of some mechanism to allow the artist to receive some of the proceeds on resale, artwork may be underproduced. (Recall the discussion of the "public goods" problem in Chapter 1.) The Berne Convention provides that "The author . . . shall, with respect to original works of art and original manuscripts of writers and composers, enjoy the inalienable right to an interest in any sale of the work subsequent to the first transfer by the author of the work." Berne Conv., art. 14ter. However, another provision of the Berne Convention, by seemingly providing that an author can claim *droit de suite* in a foreign country only to the extent legislation in her home country recognizes the right, implies that it may be permissible for a member country not to implement the *droit de suite*. *See id.*, art. 14ter(2) ("The [resale rights] protection . . . may be claimed in a country of the Union only if legislation in the country to which the author belongs so permits, and to the extent permitted by the country where this protection is claimed"). The U.S. has not implemented the *droit de suite* at the federal level, although one state, California, recognizes it. The California Resale Royalties Act, enacted in 1976, provides for payment to the artist on the resale of a "work of fine art," and applies to sellers who reside in California as well as sales taking place there. The artist is entitled to a royalty of 5 percent of the gross sale price. *See* Cal. Civ. Code §986 (2005).

What do you think of the *droit de suite*? What would be the costs and benefits of implementing it as part of the federal copyright scheme?

2. The Visual Artists Rights Act

Two years after the U.S. acceded to the Berne Convention, Congress enacted the Visual Artists Rights Act of 1990 ("VARA"), Pub. L. No. 101-650, tit. VI, 104 Stat. 5089, 5128-33 (1990), which provides a limited and unique set of moral rights protections. VARA grants the author of a "work of visual art" the right of attribution; the right to prevent any intentional distortion, mutilation, or other modification of the work that would be prejudicial to his or her reputation; and, in the case of works of art of "recognized stature," the right to prevent destruction. 17 U.S.C. §106A. VARA also provides for damages and addresses the moral rights concerns associated with removing works of visual art from buildings.

The rights granted by §106A are granted only to authors of works of visual art. The definition of "works of visual art," one of the longest definitions contained in §101, provides both a positive definition of what such works *are* and a negative definition of what such works *are not*. A "work of visual art" includes "a painting, drawing, print, or sculpture, existing in a single copy, in a limited edition of 200 copies or fewer that are signed and consecutively numbered by the author. . . ." 17 U.S.C. §101. Thus, unlike the rights granted in §106, which are granted in the intangible work, as distinct from the "copy" in which the intangible work is embodied, the rights granted by §106A pertain only to certain physical embodiments—works existing in single copies or in less than 200 copies if they are signed and consecutively numbered. A "work of visual art" does not include any uncopyrighted work or work made for hire or "any poster, map, globe, chart, technical drawing, diagram, model, applied art, motion picture or other audiovisual work, book, magazine, newspaper, periodical, data base, electronic information service, electronic publication, or similar publication; . . . any merchandising item or advertising, promotional, descriptive, covering, or packaging material or container; . . . ." *Id.*

Read §106A and the definition of a "work of visual art" found in §101 of the Copyright Act, and then consider the following cases.

≡ *Lilley v. Stout*
≡ *384 F. Supp. 2d 83 (D.D.C. 2005)*

FRIEDMAN, J.: This case arises from a disputed collaboration between the two named parties in the production of a work of art. . . .

I. Background

. . . Lilley is a "photographer [who] has been taking photographs since at least 1992." . . . From 1993 to mid-2000, he and defendant Renee Stout, who is also an artist, "collaborated on several projects." For an unspecified period of time during that period, they also were "involved in a personal relationship," . . . the failure of which has led, at least in part, to this dispute.

In the summer of 1998, Stout asked Lilley to "take some photographs at a friend's home . . . as studies for paintings [Stout] planned to create." . . . At the friend's home, Lilley photographed a "red" room using his own camera and choosing the subject matter of each photograph. After the photographs were developed, Stout "reviewed [them] with [Lilley] and discussed which frames would make good studies" for her paintings. After this review session, Lilley allowed Stout to keep the photographic prints and negatives so that she could finalize her project.

Stout created one painting from the photographs and decided to use the photographs themselves as part of an artwork. This resulting work, entitled "Red Room at Five," is central to the parties' dispute. . . .

"Red Room at Five" consists of six of Lilley's photographs that had been "selected and arranged by [Stout] and placed in a binder with a red cover and illustration." When Lilley received the work, it did not include a colophon, "a notice that accompanies a work and provides information relating to the publication and authorship." Lilley subsequently requested a copy of the colophon but was told it was incomplete. The personal relationship between the parties ended in August 2000, and Lilley continued to request copies of the colophon to no avail. Finally, in April 2001, Lilley received a draft colophon that stated: "Photographs by the artist and by Gary Lilley at the direction of the artist." Lilley contends that the language of the colophon amounts to improper attribution of his "work[s] of visual art" under VARA. In addition, Lilley claims that Stout is selling both "Red Room at Five" and individual photographs taken by Lilley as her own works, thereby violating the Copyright Act. . . .

II. Discussion . . .

A. *Visual Artists Rights Act of 1990*

Plaintiff has alleged a claim under the Visual Artists Rights Act of 1990 ("VARA"). Congress enacted VARA to "protect[ ] both the reputations of certain visual artists and the works of art they create." H.R. Rep No. 101-514, at 7, *reprinted in* 1990 U.S.C.C.A.N. 6915 ("House Report"). These protections are enumerated in the individual rights of "attribution" and "integrity," known collectively as "moral rights." *Id.* As described in the House Report accompanying the legislation, "[t]he former ensures that artists are correctly identified with the works of art they create, and that they are not identified with works created by others. The latter allows artists to protect their works against modifications and destructions that are prejudicial to their honors or reputations." *Id.* Specifically, the rights of attribution include the right to (a) claim authorship of a work he or she created, and (b) prevent the use of one's name as the author of a work that he or she did not create. *See* 17 U.S.C. §106A(a)(1)-(2). The rights of integrity permit an author to (a) prevent any intentional distortion, mutilation, or other modification of his or her work, and (b) prevent any destruction of a work of recognized stature. *See* 17 U.S.C. §106A(a)(3).

As "moral rights" legislation, VARA vested immutable rights in an author that generally could not be assigned or transferred . . . and that are "independent of the exclusive rights provided in [Section] 106." Thus, ownership of the copyright in a work is irrelevant to an author's standing to bring a VARA claim. Indeed, even if an author wishes to waive his or her rights under VARA, such a waiver can be effected only by a written instrument signed by the author that specifically identifies the work and the specific uses of that work.

Absent this waiver, a court must consider whether the artistic work qualifies as a "work of visual art." Recognizing the broad scope of protections afforded to eligible authors, Congress created a tightly circumscribed definition for qualified works. Thus, VARA established a new and distinct genus of art: "work[s] of visual art," which differs in many respects from the pre-existing categories in Section 102(a) of the Copyright Act. *See* 3-8D Nimmer on Copyright §8D.06(A)(1) (2004).

For a photographic work to qualify for protection as a "work of visual art" under VARA, it must meet the statutory definition: "a still photographic image produced for exhibition purposes only, existing in a single copy that is signed by the author, or in a limited edition of 200 copies or fewer that are signed and consecutively numbered by the author." 17 U.S.C. §101. The Court concludes that the statutory term "still photographic image" in Section 101 has a plain and unambiguous meaning. It is clear from a plain reading of the statute and the specific context in which the language is used that both photographic prints and negatives qualify as "still photographic image[s]" and that both therefore are eligible for protection as "work[s] of visual art" under VARA. *See* House Report at 6921 (definition of a "still photographic image" encompasses a wide range of artistic works, including "positives (for example, prints, contact sheets, and transparencies such as slides) and negatives (negative photographic images or transparent material used for printing positives) of a photograph.").

In addition to demonstrating that photographs or negatives are "works of visual art," a plaintiff to succeed under VARA also must satisfy the remaining statutory requirements under the Visual Artists Rights Act: intent to exhibit, uniqueness, and signing. *See* 17 U.S.C. §101. Defendant argues that plaintiff's complaint fails to make a sufficient intent to exhibit allegation under the statute — that is, that his prints or negatives were "produced for exhibition purposes only" — or that the prints and negatives in question have been "signed by the author." According to the defendant, plaintiff's claim that the photographs at issue were taken "as studies for paintings defendant planned to create" is sufficient to demonstrate that they fall outside the relevant definition of a "work of visual art." Plaintiff replies that he has averred the facts necessary to demonstrate the proper intent to exhibit and that "community standards" should be applied to the signing requirement.

The question of intent to exhibit is especially challenging in the realm of photography. While it may appear simple to distinguish between an amateur photographer taking snapshots on vacation and an artist producing photographs "for exhibition only," few artists would characterize their work as the latter. Indeed, many notable "fine art" photographers pursued their work in quite utilitarian contexts. *See* Jennifer T. Olsson, *Note: Rights in Fine Art Photography: Through a Lens Darkly*, 70 Tex. L. Rev. 1489, 1499-1500 (1992) ("Eugune Atget's revered photographs of a vanishing Paris were initially made as reference documents for painters to copy. Weegee photographed crime scenes in the service of photojournalism. . . . August Sander's self imposed mission was to create a virtual catalog of the German people.")

The technical realities of photography also complicate the question. At least three distinct phases comprise the photographic process that results in a positive print: practical camera handling, negative development, and printing. Thus, in the course of creating her art, a photographer almost always will create two images, first a negative and then a print, for which VARA protection may be justified. As plaintiff Lilley notes, the term "for exhibition purposes only" cannot be limited to the author's "purpose" at the moment she clicks the camera's shutter. If that were the case, then only the photographic negative would ever be protected, as its production and purpose were contemporaneous with the click of the shutter. Instead, it seems more reasonable that the intent or purpose of the author be examined as of the time the unique work in question is "produced."

This method of analysis comports with the uncertain time frame expressed in the term "produced" in Section 101 and responds to the reality that a negative "produced" in one instant and a print "produced" in another may correspond to different intentions or purposes of the author. While courts have expounded on how the process of practical camera handling "imbue[s] the medium with almost limitless creative potential," *SHL Imaging, Inc. v. Artisan House, Inc.*, 117 F. Supp. 2d 301, 310 (S.D.N.Y. 2000), few opportunities have arisen for courts to explore the opportunity for creativity in the process of developing negatives or producing prints. As many professional photographers and artists recognize, however, the process of producing a print from a negative contains room for originality. Thus, plaintiff Lilley's intent when clicking the shutter of his camera and creating the negatives is irrelevant to his claim. His probably different purpose in developing the negatives to produce the prints is the real issue. Were they "produced for exhibition purposes only"?

Plaintiff's case presents a good example of the potential for the fact that a single work of visual art may be created for a variety of purposes. As a result, it may be difficult to assign a specific intent. Plaintiff Lilley admits that the photographs were taken to serve "as studies for paintings defendant [Stout] planned to create." Contrary to defendant's assertion, VARA does not pose a *per se* bar to protection for preparatory works, such as studies. *See, e.g., Flack v. Friends of Queen Catherine Inc.*, 139 F. Supp. 2d 526 at 533 (holding that a clay model, which was part of a larger, unfinished b[r]onze sculpture, qualified as a "work of visual art.") In addition, it may be fair to infer from the facts plaintiff alleges—at least on a motion to dismiss for failure to state a claim—that, when taking the photographs of the "red" room, Lilley intended to exhibit the resulting prints. This inference could be drawn from plaintiff's artistic background, past experience as a photographer, and previous collaboration with the defendant to create art for exhibition. While these inferences might be relevant if the issue before the Court related to the negatives Lilley produced, the circumstances of the photographic prints can be resolved more easily.

Plaintiff's own assertions demonstrate quite clearly that the discrete photographic prints at issue were not "produced for exhibition purposes *only*." 17 U.S.C. §101 (emphasis added). His complaint states that once the photographs were developed, he and the defendant "reviewed the photographs . . . and discussed which frames would make good studies for a series of paintings." The photographic prints at issue—those that were "reviewed" with defendant and comprise "Red Room at Five"—therefore were not "produced for exhibition purposes only." Rather, they had the primary purpose of assisting defendant Stout in her artistic endeavor. Indeed, the only suggestion that plaintiff had any alternative motivation for producing the images comes from a statement in his opposition to the motion that he "alleged that the photographs were intended for 'exhibition purposes only.'" This statement, however, appears nowhere in plaintiff's amended complaint. . . .

But even if the claim had been pled in the complaint, it is belied by plaintiff's acts of reviewing the photographs with defendant and turning over possession to her. It is difficult to conceive how plaintiff could have exhibited these prints once they were incorporated into "Red Room at Five." Because plaintiff's own assertions demonstrate that the discrete photographs at issue were not produced solely for exhibition purposes, his photographic prints fail to satisfy the definition of "work[s] of visual art" in Section 101, and his amended complaint thus fails to state a claim under VARA. . . .

Martin v. City of Indianapolis
192 F.3d 608 (7th Cir. 1999)

WOOD, J.: We are not art critics, do not pretend to be and do not need to be to decide this case. A large outdoor stainless steel sculpture by plaintiff Jan Martin, an artist, was demolished by the defendant as part of an urban renewal project. Plaintiff brought a one-count suit against the City of Indianapolis (the "City") under the Visual Artists Rights Act of 1990 ("VARA"), 17 U.S.C. §101 *et seq.* . . .

I. Background

Plaintiff is an artist, but in this instance more with a welding torch than with a brush. He offered evidence to show, not all of it admitted, that his works have been displayed in museums, and other works created for private commissions, including a time capsule for the Indianapolis Museum of Art Centennial. He has also done sculptured jewelry for the Indiana Arts Commission. In 1979, at the Annual Hoosier Salem Art Show, plaintiff was awarded the prize for best of show in any medium. He holds various arts degrees from Purdue University, the Art Institute of Chicago and Bowling Green State University in Ohio. Plaintiff had been employed as production coordinator for Tarpenning-LaFollette Co. (the "Company"), a metal contracting firm in Indianapolis. It was in this position that he turned his artistic talents to metal sculpture fabrication. . . .

Plaintiff went to work on the project and in a little over two years it was completed. He named it "Symphony #1," but as it turns out in view of this controversy, a more suitable musical name might have been "1812 Overture." Because of the possibility that the sculpture might someday have to be removed, as provided for in the Project Agreement, Symphony #1 was engineered and built by plaintiff so that it could be disassembled for removal and later reassembled. The sculpture did not go unnoticed by the press, public or art community. . . .

[The City subsequently acquired the land on which Symphony #1 was located. During the negotiations that led to the sale the City was repeatedly told that the sculpture could be moved if the City did not want it. The City promised to notify the plaintiff if it planned to remove the sculpture. Despite these assurances, shortly after the City acquired the land, it had the sculpture demolished without notice to the plaintiff.] . . . . This lawsuit resulted in which summary judgment was allowed for plaintiff. However, his victory was not entirely satisfactory to him, nor was the City satisfied. The City appealed, and plaintiff cross-appealed.

II. Analysis

Although recognized under the Berne Convention, the legal protection of an artist's so-called "moral rights" was controversial in this country. The United States did not join the Berne Convention until 1988 when it did so in a very limited way. Then Congress followed up by enacting VARA in 1990, with this explanation found in the House Reports:

> An artist's professional and personal identity is embodied in each work created by that artist. Each work is a part of his or her reputation. Each work is a form of personal expression (oftentimes painstakingly and earnestly recorded). It is a rebuke to the dignity of the visual artist that our copyright law allows distortion, modification and even outright permanent destruction of such efforts.

H.R. Rep. No. 101-514, at 15 (1990), *reprinted in* 1990 U.S.C.C.A.N. 6915, 6925.

. . . VARA provides: "[T]he author of a work of visual art . . . shall have the right . . . to prevent any destruction of a work of *recognized stature*, and any intentional or grossly negligent destruction of that work is a violation of that right." 17 U.S.C. §106A(a)(3)(B) (emphasis added). The district court considered Symphony #1 to be of "recognized stature" under the evidence presented and thus concluded that the City had violated plaintiff's rights under VARA. That finding is contested by the City.

"Recognized stature" is a necessary finding under VARA in order to protect a work of visual art from destruction. In spite of its significance, that phrase is not defined in VARA, leaving its intended meaning and application open to argument and judicial resolution. The only case found undertaking to define and apply "recognized stature" is *Carter v. Helmsley-Spear, Inc.*, 861 F. Supp. 303 (S.D.N.Y. 1994), *aff'd in part, vacated in part, rev'd in part*, 71 F.3d 77 (2d Cir. 1995). . . . Although the Second Circuit reversed the district court and held that the work was not a work of visual art protected by VARA, *id.* at 88, the district court presented an informative discussion in determining whether a work of visual art may qualify as one of "recognized stature." *See Carter I*, 861 F. Supp. at 324-26. That determination is based greatly on the testimony of experts on both sides of the issue, as would ordinarily be expected.

The stature test formulated by the New York district court required:

> (1) that the visual art in question has "stature," i.e. is viewed as meritorious, and (2) that this stature is "recognized" by art experts, other members of the artistic community, or by some cross-section of society. In making this showing, plaintiffs generally, but not inevitably, will need to call expert witnesses to testify before the trier of fact.

Carter I, 861 F. Supp. at 325.

Even though the district court in this present case found that test was satisfied by the plaintiff's evidence, plaintiff argues that the *Carter v. Helmsley-Spear* test may be more rigorous than Congress intended. That may be, but we see no need for the purposes of this case to endeavor to refine that rule. Plaintiff's evidence, however, is not as complete as in *Carter v. Helmsley-Spear*, possibly because Symphony #1 was destroyed by the City without the opportunity for experts to appraise the sculpture in place.

The City objects to the "stature" testimony that was offered by plaintiff as inadmissible hearsay. If not admitted, it would result in plaintiff's failure to sustain his burden of proof. . . . Plaintiff's evidence of "stature" consisted of certain newspaper and magazine articles, and various letters, including a letter from an art gallery director and a letter to the editor of *The Indianapolis News*, all in support of the sculpture, as well as a program from the show at which a model of the sculpture won "Best of Show." After reviewing the City's objection, the district court excluded plaintiff's "programs and awards" evidence as lacking adequate foundation . . . but nevertheless found Martin had met his "stature" burden of proof with his other evidence.

Included in the admitted evidence, for example, was a letter dated October 25, 1982 from the Director of the Herron School of Art, Indiana University, Indianapolis. It was written to the Company and says in part, "The proposed sculpture is, in my opinion, an interesting and aesthetically stimulating configuration of forms and structures." *The Indianapolis Star*, in a four-column article by its visual arts editor, discussed public sculpture in Indianapolis. This article included a photograph of Symphony #1. The article lamented that the City had "been graced by only five pieces of note," but that two more had been added that particular year, one being plaintiff's sculpture. It noted, among other things, that Symphony #1 had been erected without the aid of "federal grants" and without the help of any committee of concerned citizens. Other public sculptures came in for some criticism in the article. However, in discussing Symphony #1, the author wrote: "Gleaming clean and abstract, yet domestic in scale and reference, irregularly but securely cabled together, the sculpture shows the site what it might be. It unites the area, providing a nexus, a marker, a designation, an identity and, presumably, a point of pride."

The district judge commented on the City's hearsay objection to plaintiff's admitted evidence as follows:

> The statements contained within the proffered newspaper and magazine articles and letters are offered by Martin to show that respected members of the art community and members of the public at large consider Martin's work to be socially valuable and to have artistic merit, and to show the newsworthiness of Symphony #1 and Martin's work. *These statements are offered by Martin to show that the declarants said them*, not that the statements are, in fact, true. . . . The statements contained within the exhibits show how art critics and the public viewed Martin's work, particularly Symphony #1, and show that the sculpture was a matter worth reporting to the public. Therefore, the statements contained within these challenged exhibits are not hearsay because they are not being offered for the truth of the matters asserted therein.

Martin I, 982 F. Supp. at 630 (emphasis added).

We agree with the assessment made by the district court. . . .

[The City also claimed that the plaintiff had waived his VARA rights because he had signed a Project Agreement that specifically acknowledged that the City might acquire the property and require that the sculpture be removed.]

. . . Under 17 U.S.C. §106A(e)(1), an artist may waive VARA rights "in a written instrument signed by the author," specifying to what the waiver applies. There is no written waiver instrument in this case which falls within the VARA requirements. We regard this argument to be without merit.

In spite of the City's conduct resulting in the intentional destruction of the sculpture, we do not believe under all the circumstances, particularly given the fact that the issue of VARA rights had not been raised until this suit, that the City's conduct was "wilful," as used in VARA, 17 U.S.C. §504(c)(2), so as to entitle the plaintiff to enhanced damages. This appears to be a case of bureaucratic failure within the City government, not a wilful violation of plaintiff's VARA rights. As far as we can tell from the record, those VARA rights were unknown to the City. . . .

MANION, J., concurring in part and dissenting in part: . . . I begin with the well-worn adage that one man's junk is another man's treasure. . . . For the Martin sculpture to receive protection under the Visual Artists Rights Act (VARA), it has to rise to the statutory level of "recognized stature." Because at this summary judgment stage, at least, it has clearly not merited the protection that goes with that description, I respectfully dissent. . . .

. . . VARA was . . . designed . . . to protect great works of art from destruction and mutilation, among other things. 17 U.S.C. §106A(a). In order to restrict VARA's reach, the Act was limited to preventing destruction of works of art that had attained a "recognized stature." 17 U.S.C. §106A(a)(3)(B). . . . As the district court in *Carter v. Helmsley-Spear, Inc.* stated: "the recognized stature requirement is best viewed as a gate-keeping mechanism — protection is afforded only to those works of art that art experts, the art community, or society in general views as possessing stature." 861 F. Supp. 303, 325 (S.D.N.Y. 1994), *rev'd in part and aff'd in part*, 71 F.3d 77 (2d Cir. 1995). . . .

I dissent . . . because summary judgment is not appropriate here. A plaintiff cannot satisfy his burden of demonstrating recognized stature through old newspaper articles and unverified letters, some of which do not even address the artwork in question. Rather, as the district court stated in *Carter*, in "making this showing [of recognized stature] plaintiffs generally, but not inevitably, will need to call expert witnesses to testify before the trier of fact." 861 F. Supp. at 325. Instances where expert testimony on this point is not necessary will be rare, and this is not one of those exceptional cases where something of unquestioned recognition and stature was destroyed. Furthermore, where newspaper articles are admitted into evidence only to acknowledge recognition but not for the truth of the matter asserted (that the art in question was good or bad), a plaintiff needs more to overcome *a defendant's* motion for summary judgment on a VARA claim, much less prevail on his own summary judgment motion. While the very

Original artwork © Jan Martin. Reprinted by Permission.

Symphony #1

8. VARA provides that the rights granted by §106A apply to works created before the effective date of the Act only if title to those works is transferred by the author *after* the effective date of the Act. Pub. L. No. 101-650, 104 Stat. 5089, §610 (1990). Does this limitation on the effect of VARA for previously created works make sense? For works created after the effective date of VARA (June 1, 1991), the rights granted to the author of a work of visual art under §106A last for the life of the author, no matter how many times the artwork is sold or transferred. If you were advising a client who is commissioning a sculpture for inclusion in the lobby of a new building, what might you suggest be included in the contract with the sculptor?

9. In addition to the right to prevent certain destructions or mutilations of qualified works, §106A gives an author the right to be compensated in the event such destruction or mutilation has already occurred. Like a successful copyright infringement plaintiff, a successful VARA plaintiff can recover actual damages or statutory damages, as well as attorneys' fees. Unlike copyright infringement plaintiffs, however, VARA plaintiffs need not have registered their works prior to the violations in order to be eligible for an award of statutory damages or attorneys' fees, nor is registration required to institute a lawsuit for violations of §106A rights. 17 U.S.C. §§411, 412. Why might Congress have exempted VARA claims from the registration requirements?

In the *Martin* case, the lower court awarded Mr. Martin his attorneys' fees as well as $20,000 in statutory damages, the maximum amount of statutory damages permissible at that time for non-willful violations. *Martin v. City of Indianapolis*, 4 F. Supp. 2d 808 (S.D. Ind. 1998) *aff'd*, 192 F.3d 608 (7th Cir. 1999). Currently, maximum statutory damages permissible are $30,000 for non-willful violations and $150,000 for willful violations. 17 U.S.C. §504. We discuss the topics of damages and attorneys' fees in more detail in Chapter 11.

3. The Right of Attribution Revisited

Review the discussion of the legislative history of the BCIA, page 393 *supra*. Does VARA reflect a congressional judgment to deny rights of attribution to authors of other types of works? Consider the following case.

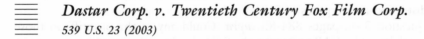

Dastar Corp. v. Twentieth Century Fox Film Corp.
539 U.S. 23 (2003)

SCALIA, J.: In this case, we are asked to decide whether §43(a) of the Lanham Act, 15 U.S.C. §1125(a), prevents the unaccredited copying of a work. . . .

I

In 1948, three and a half years after the German surrender at Reims, General Dwight D. Eisenhower completed Crusade in Europe, his written account of the allied campaign in Europe during World War II. Doubleday published the book, registered it with the Copyright Office in 1948, and granted exclusive television rights to an affiliate of respondent Twentieth Century Fox Film Corporation (Fox). Fox, in turn, arranged for Time, Inc., to produce a television series, also called Crusade in Europe, based on the book, and Time assigned its copyright in the series to Fox. The television series, consisting of 26 episodes, was first broadcast in 1949. . . . In 1975, Doubleday renewed the copyright on the book as the "proprietor of copyright in a work made for hire." Fox, however, did not renew the copyright on the Crusade television series, which expired in 1977, leaving the television series in the public domain. . . .

. . . In 1995, Dastar decided to expand its product line from music compact discs to videos. Anticipating renewed interest in World War II on the 50th anniversary of the war's end, Dastar released a video set entitled World War II Campaigns in Europe. To make Campaigns, Dastar purchased eight beta cam tapes of the *original* version of the Crusade television series, which is in the public domain, copied them, and then edited the series. . . . Dastar substituted a new opening sequence, credit page, and final closing for those of the Crusade television series; inserted new chapter-title sequences and narrated chapter introductions; moved the "recap" in the Crusade television series to the beginning and retitled it as a "preview"; and removed references to and images of the book. Dastar created new packaging for its Campaigns series and . . . a new title.

Dastar manufactured and sold the Campaigns video set as its own product. The advertising states: "Produced and Distributed by: *Entertainment Distributing*" (which is owned by Dastar), and makes no reference to the Crusade television series. Similarly, the screen credits state "DASTAR CORP presents" and "an ENTERTAINMENT DISTRIBUTING Production," and list as executive producer, producer, and associate producer, employees of Dastar. The Campaigns videos themselves also make no reference to the Crusade television series, New Line's Crusade videotapes, or the book. . . .

In 1998, respondents Fox, SFM, and New Line brought this action alleging that Dastar's sale of its Campaigns video set infringes Doubleday's copyright in General Eisenhower's book and, thus, their exclusive television rights in the book. Respondents later amended their complaint to add claims that Dastar's sale of Campaigns "without proper credit" to the Crusade television series constitutes "reverse passing off" in violation of §43(a) of the Lanham Act . . . and in violation of state unfair-competition law. . . .

[The District Court found for respondents on all three counts, awarded Dastar's profits to the respondents and doubled them pursuant to §35 of the Lanham Act. . . . The Ninth Circuit affirmed the judgment for respondents on the Lanham Act claim, but reversed as to the copyright claim.]

II

The Lanham Act was intended to make "actionable the deceptive and misleading use of marks," and "to protect persons engaged in . . . commerce against unfair competition." While much of the Lanham Act addresses the registration, use, and infringement of trademarks and related marks, §43(a), . . . is one of the few provisions that goes beyond trademark protection. As originally enacted, §43(a) created a federal remedy against a person who used in commerce either "a false designation of origin, or any false description or representation" in connection with "any goods or services."

. . . [A]s it comes to us, the gravamen of respondents' claim is that, in marketing and selling Campaigns as its own product without acknowledging its nearly wholesale reliance on the Crusade television series, Dastar has made a "false designation of origin, false or misleading description of fact, or false or misleading representation of fact, which . . . is likely to cause confusion . . . as to the origin . . . of his or her goods." That claim would undoubtedly be sustained if Dastar had bought some of New Line's Crusade videotapes and merely repackaged them as its own. Dastar's alleged wrongdoing, however, is vastly different: it took a creative work in the public domain — the Crusade television series — copied it, made modifications (arguably minor), and produced its very own series of videotapes. If "origin" refers only to the manufacturer or producer of the physical "goods" that are made available to the public (in this case the videotapes), Dastar was the origin. If, however, "origin" includes the creator of the underlying work that Dastar copied, then someone else (perhaps Fox) was the origin of Dastar's product. At bottom, we must decide what §43(a)(1)(A) of the Lanham Act means by the "origin" of "goods."

III

. . . We think the most natural understanding of the "origin" of "goods" — the source of wares — is the producer of the tangible product sold in the marketplace, in this case the physical Campaigns videotape sold by Dastar. The concept might be stretched . . . to include not only the actual producer, but also the trademark owner who commissioned or assumed responsibility for ("stood behind") production of the physical product. But as used in the Lanham Act, the phrase "origin of goods" is in our view incapable of connoting the person or entity that originated the ideas or communications that "goods" embody or contain. Such an extension would not only stretch the text, but it would be out of accord with the history and purpose of the Lanham Act and inconsistent with precedent. . . .

. . . The right to copy, and to copy without attribution, once a copyright has expired, like "the right to make [an article whose patent has expired] — including the right to make it in precisely the shape it carried when patented — passes to the public." The rights of a patentee or copyright holder are part of a "carefully crafted bargain," . . . under which, once the patent or copyright monopoly has expired, the public may use the invention or work at will and without attribution. Thus, in construing the Lanham Act, we have been "careful to caution against misuse or over-extension" of trademark and related protections into areas traditionally occupied by patent or copyright. . . . Assuming for the sake of argument that Dastar's representation of itself as the "Producer" of its videos amounted to a representation that it originated the creative work conveyed by the videos, allowing a cause of action under §43(a) for that representation would create a species of mutant copyright law that limits the public's "federal right to 'copy and to use'" expired copyrights. . . .

When Congress has wished to create such an addition to the law of copyright, it has done so with much more specificity than the Lanham Act's ambiguous use of "origin." The Visual Artists Rights Act of 1990 . . . provides that the author of an artistic work "shall have the right . . . to claim authorship of that work." That express right of attribution is carefully limited and focused: It attaches only to specified "work[s] of visual art," . . . is personal to the artist, . . . and endures only for "the life of the author". . . . Recognizing in §43(a) a cause of action for misrepresentation of authorship of noncopyrighted works (visual or otherwise) would render these limitations superfluous. . . .

In sum, reading the phrase "origin of goods" in the Lanham Act in accordance with the Act's common-law foundations (which were *not* designed to protect originality or creativity), and in light of the copyright and patent laws (which *were*), we conclude that the phrase refers to the producer of the tangible goods that are offered for sale, and not to the author of any idea, concept, or communication embodied in those goods. . . . To hold otherwise would be akin to finding that §43(a) created a species of perpetual patent and copyright, which Congress may not do. . . .

. . . For merely saying it is the producer of the video . . . no Lanham Act liability attaches to Dastar. . . .

NOTES AND QUESTIONS

1. Consider the changes made by Dastar to the original *Crusade* television series. Are these changes sufficient to give Dastar copyright in *World War II Campaigns*? If so, then didn't Dastar accurately credit itself? If Dastar had credited Fox, would that have given Fox different grounds for complaint under the Lanham Act?

2. *Dastar* dealt with a work in which copyright had expired. Does its holding also apply to works still within their copyright terms? Several courts have said yes. *See, e.g., General Universal Sys. v. Lee*, 379 F.3d 131 (5th Cir. 2004) (software); *Zyla v. Wadsworth*, 360 F.3d 243 (1st Cir. 2004) (textbook). What is the "origin" of these types of works? *See Bob Creeden & Assocs., Ltd., v. Infosoft, Inc.*, 362 F. Supp. 2d 876 (N.D. Ill. 2004) (holding that the "origin" of a software system is the company that produces and markets the tangible product); *Williams v. UMG Recordings*, 281 F. Supp. 2d 1177 (C.D. Cal. 2003) (holding that the origin of a film is its producer). Does *Dastar* also apply to works that are not eligible for copyright protection?

3. In *Gilliam*, the court recognized a right of relief under §43(a) of the Lanham Act for artists whose works have been mutilated before presentation to the public. How did the claims by the plaintiffs in *Dastar* differ from the claims made by the plaintiffs in *Gilliam*? Does *Dastar* overrule *Gilliam*?

4. A significant effect of the Supreme Court's holding in *Dastar* is that works in which copyright has expired can be copied without attribution to the author(s). Examine Berne Conv., art. 6bis and TRIPS Agreement, art. 9(1) carefully. After *Dastar*, is the U.S. in compliance with its international obligations?

5. On remand, the district court found Dastar liable for infringement of Doubleday's copyright in the Eisenhower book and the Ninth Circuit affirmed. *See Twentieth Century Fox Film Corp. v. Entertainment Distrib.*, 429 F.3d 869 (9th Cir. 2005), *cert. denied*, 548 U.S. 919 (2006).

F. THE PUBLIC PERFORMANCE AND PUBLIC DISPLAY RIGHTS

U.S. copyright law first recognized the right to publicly perform a work in 1856, but the right applied only to a "dramatic composition, designed or suited for public representation." In 1831, Congress granted copyright protection to musical compositions, but it was not until 1897 that it granted a public performance right in such works. In addition to providing for civil penalties, the 1897 Act made unauthorized public performance of dramatic or musical compositions criminal, if engaged in willfully and for profit. The 1909 Act continued the tradition of acknowledging a public performance right only for dramatic works and musical compositions. The 1909 Act also limited the scope of the copyright owner's right to control public performances to those engaged in for profit.

In 1913, the newly formed American Society of Composers, Authors, and Publishers (ASCAP) attempted to convince businesses that they needed to pay royalties for the right to play music in their establishments. The businesses refused to pay for any license from ASCAP, arguing that the music played as background entertainment was not "for profit" because the patrons were not charged an admission fee. In 1914, ASCAP filed suit against the operator of a restaurant in a hotel at which an orchestra played in the background. The defendant asserted that the performance was not for profit because the restaurant's patrons were not charged a separate fee to hear the orchestra play. In 1917, the Supreme Court delivered its unanimous opinion in *Herbert v. Shanley*, and rejected this argument:

> If the rights under the copyright are infringed only by a performance where money is taken at the door they are very imperfectly protected. . . . The defendants' performances are not eleemosynary. They are part of a total for which the public pays, and the fact that the price of the whole is attributed to a particular item which those present are expected to order, is not important. It is true that the music is not the sole object, but neither is the food, which probably could be got cheaper elsewhere. The object is a repast in surroundings that to people having limited powers of conversation or disliking the rival noise give a luxurious pleasure not to be had from eating a silent meal. If music did not pay it would be given up. If it pays it pays out of the public's pocket. Whether it pays or not the purpose of employing it is profit, and that is enough.

242 U.S. 591, 594-95 (1917).

The 1976 Act removed the for-profit limitation, and also expanded the categories of works to which the public performance and display rights apply. The right of public performance is granted to copyright owners of "literary, musical, dramatic, and choreographic works, pantomimes, and motion pictures and other audiovisual works." 17 U.S.C. §106(4). Copyright owners of sound recordings are not granted this general public performance right, but instead are granted a separate public performance right in §106(6). The §106(6) right is limited to digital audio transmissions, as we discuss in Section G, *infra*. Excluded from the list of works in §106(4) are pictorial, graphic, and sculptural works, as well as architectural works, for which a right of public performance would not be meaningful.

The 1976 Act grants a right of public display to copyright owners of "literary, musical, dramatic, and choreographic works, pantomimes, and pictorial, graphic, or sculptural works, including the individual images of a motion picture or other audiovisual work." *Id.* §106(5). The Act does not grant copyright owners of either architectural works or sound recordings a public display right.

1. Public Performance

Just what does it mean to *publicly perform* a copyrighted work? A right to control the public performance of a work was first recognized at a time when the only types of performances possible were live performances. As technology evolved, allowing performances to occur in locations remote from where the listener or viewers were located, determining what constituted a "public performance" became difficult. The 1909 Act did not contain a definition of public performance and the courts struggled with the concept. Would playing a radio station in a business open to the public be a public performance? That the radio station was engaged in a public performance might be clear, but would the business also be engaged in a public performance? If both the radio station and the business were engaged in a public performance for which the copyright owner was entitled to compensation, would the copyright owner effectively receive double compensation for a single performance?

In 1975, the Supreme Court issued its decision in *Twentieth Century Music Corp. v. Aiken*, 422 U.S. 151 (1975). Mr. Aiken owned a small fast-food shop in Pittsburgh known as "George Aiken's Chicken," in which he played a radio over four speakers in the ceiling. The Court held that Mr. Aiken's turning on the radio was not a "performance" of a copyrighted work. Instead, it held that Mr. Aiken was the audience, not the performer, for the performance engaged in by the radio station.

Congress, in §101 of the 1976 Act, promptly overturned the *Aiken* Court's interpretation of "performance":

> To "perform" a work means to recite, render, play, dance, or act it, either directly or by means of any device or process or, in the case of a motion picture or other audiovisual work, to show its images in any sequence or to make the sounds accompanying it audible.

17 U.S.C. §101. Thus, turning on a radio or a television constitutes a "performance" of the works being broadcast.

While a wide range of actions constitute performance under the definition given in the Act, only public performances are within the control of the copyright owner. While we all may agree that a radio station performs a work, is that performance a "public" performance if the radio station is only broadcast into private homes? The Act provides the following definition:

> To perform or display a work "publicly" means—
>
> (1) to perform or display it at a place open to the public or at any place where a substantial number of persons outside of a normal circle of a family and its social acquaintances is gathered; or
>
> (2) to transmit or otherwise communicate a performance or display of the work to a place specified by clause (1) or to the public, by means of any device or process, whether the members of the public capable of receiving the performance or display receive it in the same place or in separate places and at the same time or at different times.

Id. Thus, the radio station is engaged in a public performance, but the person who turns on the radio in the privacy of her home is not. The next two cases consider the two clauses of the statutory definition in greater detail: What attributes must a place, or a transmission, possess to render a performance "public"?

Columbia Pictures Indus. v. Redd Horne, Inc.
749 F.2d 154 (3d Cir. 1984)

RE, C.J.: . . . Maxwell's Video Showcase, Ltd., operates two stores in Erie, Pennsylvania. At these two facilities, Maxwell's sells and rents video cassette recorders and prerecorded video cassettes, and sells blank video cassette cartridges. These activities are not the subject of the plaintiffs' complaint. The copyright infringement issue in this case arises from defendants' *exhibition* of video cassettes of the plaintiffs' films, or what defendants euphemistically refer to as their "showcasing" or "in-store rental" concept.

Each store contains a small showroom area in the front of the store, and a "showcase" or exhibition area in the rear. The front showroom contains video equipment and materials for sale or rent, as well as dispensing machines for popcorn and carbonated beverages. Movie posters are also displayed in this front area. In the rear "showcase" area, patrons may view any of an assortment of video cassettes in small, private booths with space for two to four people. There are a total of eighty-five booths in the two stores. Each booth or room is approximately four feet by six feet and is carpeted on the floor and walls. In the front there is a nineteen inch color television and an upholstered bench in the back.

The procedure followed by a patron wishing to utilize one of the viewing booths or rooms is the same at both facilities. The customer selects a film from a catalogue which contains the titles of available films. The fee charged by Maxwell's depends on the number of people in the viewing room, and the time of day. The price is $5.00 for one or two people before 6 p.m., and $6.00 for two people after 6 p.m. There is at all times a $1.00 surcharge for the third and fourth person. The fee also entitles patrons to help themselves to popcorn and soft drinks before entering their assigned rooms. Closing the door of the viewing room activates a signal in the counter area at the front of the store. An employee of Maxwell's then places the cassette of the motion picture chosen by the viewer into one of the video cassette machines in the front of the store and the picture is transmitted to the patron's viewing room. The viewer may adjust the light in the room, as well as the volume, brightness, and color levels on the television set.

Access to each room is limited to the individuals who rent it as a group. Although no restriction is placed on the composition of a group, strangers are not grouped in order to fill a particular room to capacity. Maxwell's is open to any member of the public who wishes to utilize its facilities or services.

Maxwell's advertises on Erie radio stations and on the theatre pages of the local newspapers. Typically, each advertisement features one or more motion pictures, and emphasizes Maxwell's selection of films, low prices, and free refreshments. The advertisements do not state that these motion pictures are video cassette copies. At the entrance to the two Maxwell's facilities, there are also advertisements for individual films, which resemble movie posters.

Infringement of Plaintiffs' Copyright

It may be stated at the outset that this is not a case of unauthorized taping or video cassette piracy. The defendants obtained the video cassette copies of plaintiffs' copyrighted motion pictures by purchasing them from either the plaintiffs or their authorized distributors. The sale or rental of these cassettes to individuals for home viewing is also not an issue. Plaintiffs do not contend that in-home use infringes their copyright.

The plaintiffs' complaint is based on their contention that the exhibition or showing of the video cassettes in the private booths on defendants' premises constitutes an unauthorized public performance in violation of plaintiffs' exclusive rights under the federal copyright laws. . . .

"To perform a work means . . . in the case of a motion picture or other audiovisual work, to show its images in any sequence or to make the sounds accompanying it audible." 17 U.S.C. §101 (1982). Clearly, playing a video cassette results in a sequential showing of a motion picture's images and in making the sounds accompanying it audible. Thus, Maxwell's activities constitute a performance under section 101.

The remaining question is whether these performances are public. Section 101 also states that to perform a work "publicly" means "[t]o perform . . . it at a place open to the public or at any place where a substantial number of persons outside of a normal circle of a family and its social acquaintances is gathered." *Id.* The statute is written in the disjunctive, and thus two categories of places can satisfy the definition of "to perform a work publicly." The first category is self-evident; it is "a place open to the public." The second category, commonly referred to as a semi-public place, is determined by the size and composition of the audience.

The legislative history indicates that this second category was added to expand the concept of public performance by including those places that, although not open to the public at large, are accessible to a significant number of people. *See* H.R. Rep. No. 1476, 94th Cong., 2d Sess. 64, *reprinted in* 1976 U.S. Code Cong. & Ad. News 5659, 5677-78 (hereinafter cited as *House Report*). Clearly, if a place is public, the size and composition of the audience are irrelevant. However, if the place is not public, the size and composition of the audience will be determinative.

We find it unnecessary to examine the second part of the statutory definition because we agree with the district court's conclusion that Maxwell's was open to the public. On the composition of the audience, the district court noted that "the showcasing operation is not distinguishable in any significant manner from the exhibition of films at a conventional movie theater." 568 F. Supp. at 500. Any member of the public can view a motion picture by paying the appropriate fee. The services provided by Maxwell's are essentially the same as a movie theatre, with the additional feature of privacy. The relevant "place" within the meaning of section 101 is each of Maxwell's two stores, not each individual booth within each store. Simply because the cassettes can be viewed in private does not mitigate the essential fact that Maxwell's is unquestionably open to the public.

The conclusion that Maxwell's activities constitute public performances is fully supported by subsection (2) of the statutory definition of public performance:

> (2) to transmit or otherwise communicate a performance . . . of the work to a place specified by clause (1) or to the public, by means of any device or process, whether the members of the public capable of receiving the performance . . . receive it in the same place or in separate places and at the same time or at different times.

17 U.S.C. §101 (1982). As explained in the House Report which accompanies the Copyright Revision Act of 1976, "a performance made available by transmission to the public at large is 'public' even though the recipients are not gathered in a single place. . . . The same principles apply whenever the potential recipients of the transmission represent a limited segment of the public, such as the occupants of hotel rooms . . . ." *House Report, supra,* at 64-65, U.S. Code Cong. & Admin. News, p. 5678. Thus, the transmission of a performance to members of the public, even in private settings such as hotel rooms or Maxwell's viewing rooms, constitutes a public performance. As the statutory language and legislative history clearly indicate, the fact that members of the public view the performance at different times does not alter this legal consequence.

Professor Nimmer's examination of this definition is particularly pertinent: "*if the same copy* . . . of a given work is repeatedly played (*i.e.*, 'performed') by different members of the public, albeit at different times, this constitutes a 'public' performance." 2 M. Nimmer, §8.14[C][3], at 8-142 (emphasis in original). Indeed, Professor Nimmer would seem to have envisaged Maxwell's when he wrote:

> [O]ne may anticipate the possibility of theaters in which patrons occupy separate screening rooms, for greater privacy, and in order not to have to await a given hour for commencement of a given film. These too should obviously be regarded as public performances within the underlying rationale of the Copyright Act.

Id. at 8-142. Although Maxwell's has only one copy of each film, it shows each copy repeatedly to different members of the public. This constitutes a public performance.

The First Sale Doctrine

The defendants also contend that their activities are protected by the first sale doctrine. . . . Section 109(a) is an extension of the principle that ownership of the material object is distinct from ownership of the copyright in this material. The first sale doctrine prevents the copyright owner from controlling the future transfer of a particular copy once its material ownership has been transferred. The transfer of the video cassettes to the defendants, however, did not result in the forfeiture or waiver of all of the exclusive rights found in section 106. The copyright owner's exclusive right "to perform the copyrighted work publicly" has not been affected; only its distribution right as to the transferred copy has been circumscribed.

In essence, the defendants' "first sale" argument is merely another aspect of their argument that their activities are not public performances. For the defendants' argument to succeed, we would have to adopt their characterization of the "showcasing" transaction or activity as an "in-store rental." The facts do not permit such a finding or conclusion. The record clearly demonstrates that showcasing a video cassette at Maxwell's is a significantly different transaction than leasing a tape for home use. Maxwell's never disposed of the tapes in its showcasing operations, nor did the tapes ever leave the store. At all times, Maxwell's maintained physical dominion and control over the tapes. Its employees actually played the cassettes on its machines. The charges or fees received for viewing the cassettes at Maxwell's facilities are analytically indistinguishable from admission fees paid by patrons to gain admission to any public theater. Plainly, in their showcasing operation, the appellants do not sell, rent, or otherwise dispose of the video cassette. On the facts presented, Maxwell's "showcasing" operation is a public performance, which, as a matter of law, constitutes a copyright infringement. . . .

Cartoon Network LP v. CSC Holdings, Inc.
536 F.3d 121 (2d Cir. 2008), cert. denied, 129 S. Ct. 2890 (2009)

WALKER, J.: . . . In March 2006, Cablevision, an operator of cable television systems, announced the advent of its new "Remote Storage DVR System." As designed, the RS-DVR allows Cablevision customers who do not have a stand-alone DVR to record cable programming on central hard drives housed and maintained by Cablevision at a "remote" location. RS-DVR customers may then receive playback of those programs through their home television sets, using only a remote control and a standard cable box equipped with the RS-DVR software. Cablevision notified its content providers, including plaintiffs, of its plans to offer RS-DVR, but it did not seek any license from them to operate or sell the RS-DVR.

Plaintiffs, which hold the copyrights to numerous movies and television programs, sued Cablevision for declaratory and injunctive relief. They alleged that Cablevision's proposed operation of the RS-DVR would directly infringe their exclusive rights to both reproduce and publicly perform their copyrighted works. . . .

I. Operation of the RS-DVR System

Cable companies like Cablevision aggregate television programming from a wide variety of "content providers"—the various broadcast and cable channels that produce or provide individual programs—and transmit those programs into the homes of their subscribers via coaxial cable. At the outset of the transmission process, Cablevision gathers the content of the various television channels into a single stream of data. Generally, this stream is processed and transmitted to Cablevision's customers in real time. Thus, if a Cartoon Network program is scheduled to air Monday night at 8pm, Cartoon Network transmits that program's data to Cablevision and other cable companies nationwide at that time, and the cable companies immediately re-transmit the data to customers who subscribe to that channel.

Under the new RS-DVR, this single stream of data is split into two streams. The first is routed immediately to customers as before. The second stream flows into a device called the Broadband Media Router ("BMR") . . . which buffers the data stream, reformats it, and sends it to the "Arroyo Server," which consists, in relevant part, of two data buffers and a number of high-capacity hard disks. The entire stream of data moves to the first buffer (the "primary ingest buffer"), at which point the server automatically inquires as to whether any customers want to record any of that programming. If a customer has requested a particular program, the data for that program move from the primary buffer into a secondary buffer, and then onto a portion of one of the hard disks allocated to that customer. As new data flow into the primary buffer, they overwrite a corresponding quantity of data already on the buffer. The primary ingest buffer holds no more than 0.1 seconds of each channel's programming at any moment. Thus, every tenth of a second, the data residing on this buffer are automatically erased and replaced. The data buffer in the BMR holds no more than 1.2 seconds of programming at any time. While buffering occurs at other points in the operation of the RS-DVR, only the BMR buffer and the primary ingest buffer are utilized absent any request from an individual subscriber.

As the district court observed, "the RS-DVR is not a single piece of equipment," but rather "a complex system requiring numerous computers, processes, networks of cables, and facilities staffed by personnel twenty-four hours a day and seven days a week." To the customer, however, the processes of recording and playback on the RS-DVR are similar to that of a standard set-top DVR. Using a remote control, the customer can record programming by selecting a program in advance from an on-screen guide, or by pressing the record button while viewing a given program. A customer cannot, however, record the earlier portion of a program once it has begun. To begin playback, the customer selects the show from an on-screen list of previously recorded programs. The principal difference in operation is that, instead of sending signals from the remote to an onset box, the viewer sends signals from the remote, through the cable, to the Arroyo Server at Cablevision's central facility. In this respect, RS-DVR more closely resembles a VOD [Video on Demand] service, whereby a cable subscriber uses his remote and cable box to request transmission of content, such as a movie, stored on computers at the cable company's facility. But unlike a VOD service, RS-DVR users can only play content that they previously requested to be recorded.

Cablevision has some control over the content available for recording: a customer can only record programs on the channels offered by Cablevision (assuming he subscribes to them). Cablevision can also modify the system to limit the number of channels available and considered doing so during development of the RS-DVR.

II. The District Court's Decision

In the district court, plaintiffs successfully argued that Cablevision's proposed system would directly infringe their copyrights in three ways. First, by briefly storing data in the primary ingest buffer and other data buffers integral to the function of the RS-DVR, Cablevision would make copies of protected works and thereby directly infringe plaintiffs' exclusive right of reproduction under the Copyright Act. Second, by copying programs onto the Arroyo Server hard disks (the "playback copies"), Cablevision would again directly infringe the reproduction right. And third, by transmitting the data from the Arroyo Server hard disks to its RS-DVR customers in response to a "playback" request, Cablevision would directly infringe plaintiffs' exclusive right of public performance. Agreeing with all three arguments, the district court awarded summary declaratory judgment to plaintiffs and enjoined Cablevision from operating the RS-DVR system without obtaining licenses from the plaintiff copyright holders. . . .

Discussion . . .

[The court of appeals held that the data stored in the buffers were not "fixed" because they were not embodied in the storage medium for a period of more than transitory duration. As to the copies stored on the Arroyo Server hard disks, it held that they were "made" by Cablevision's customers, who supplied the volitional conduct that caused them to be created. You will learn about the role of volitional conduct in distinguishing between direct infringers and parties liable, if at all, on a theory of indirect infringement, in Chapter 6. — Eds.]

III.   Transmission of RS-DVR Playback

Plaintiffs' final theory is that Cablevision will violate the Copyright Act by engaging in unauthorized public performances of their works through the playback of the RS-DVR copies. . . . Section 101, the definitional section of the Act, explains that

> [t]o perform or display a work "publicly" means (1) to perform or display it at a place open to the public or at any place where a substantial number of persons outside of a normal circle of a family and its social acquaintances is gathered; or (2) to transmit or otherwise communicate a performance or display of the work to a place specified by clause (1) or to the public, by means of any device or process, whether the members of the public capable of receiving the performance or display receive it in the same place or in separate places and at the same time or at different times.

[17 U.S.C.] §101.

The parties agree that this case does not implicate clause (1). Accordingly, we ask whether these facts satisfy the second, "transmit clause" of the public performance definition: Does Cablevision "transmit . . . a performance . . . of the work . . . to the public"? *Id.* No one disputes that the RS-DVR playback results in the transmission of a performance of a work — the transmission from the Arroyo Server to the customer's television set. Cablevision contends that . . . the transmission is not "to the public" under the transmit clause. . . .

The statute itself does not expressly define the term "performance" or the phrase "to the public." It does explain that a transmission may be "to the public . . . whether the members of the public capable of receiving the performance . . . receive it in the same place or in separate places and at the same time or at different times." *Id.* This plain language instructs us that, in determining whether a transmission is "to the public," it is of no moment that the potential recipients of the transmission are in different places, or that they may receive the transmission at different times. The implication from this same language, however, is that it is relevant, in determining whether a transmission is made to the public, to discern who is "capable of receiving" the performance being transmitted. . . .

The legislative history of the transmit clause supports this interpretation. The House Report on the 1976 Copyright Act states that

> [u]nder the bill, as under the present law, a performance made available *by transmission to the public at large* is "public" even though the recipients are not gathered in a single place, and even if there is no proof that any of the *potential recipients* was operating his receiving apparatus at the time of the transmission. The same principles apply whenever the *potential recipients of the transmission* represent a limited segment of the public, such as the occupants of hotel rooms or the subscribers of a cable television service.

H.R. Rep. No. 94-1476, at 64-65 (1976), *reprinted in* 1976 U.S.C.C.A.N. 5659, 5678 (emphases added). . . .

From the foregoing, it is evident that the transmit clause directs us to examine who precisely is "capable of receiving" a particular transmission of a performance. Cablevision argues that, because each RS-DVR transmission is made using a single unique copy of a work, made by an individual subscriber, one that can be decoded exclusively by that subscriber's cable box, only one subscriber is capable of receiving any given RS-DVR transmission. This argument accords with the language of the transmit clause. . . .

The district court, in deciding whether the RS-DVR playback of a program to a particular customer is "to the public," apparently considered all of Cablevision's customers who subscribe to the channel airing that program and all of Cablevision's RS-DVR subscribers who request a copy of that program. Thus, it concluded that the RS-DVR playbacks constituted public performances because "Cablevision would transmit the *same program* to members of the public, who may receive the performance at different times, depending on whether they view the program in real time or at a later time as an RS-DVR playback." In essence, the district court suggested that, in considering whether a transmission is "to the public," we consider not the potential audience of a particular transmission, but the potential audience of the underlying work (i.e., "the program") whose content is being transmitted.

We cannot reconcile the district court's approach with the language of the transmit clause. That clause speaks of people capable of receiving a particular "transmission" or "performance," and not of the potential audience of a particular "work." Indeed, such an approach would render the "to the public" language surplusage. Doubtless the *potential* audience for every copyrighted audiovisual work is the general public. As a result, any transmission of the content of a copyrighted work would constitute a public performance under the district court's interpretation. But the transmit clause obviously contemplates the existence of non-public transmissions; if it did not, Congress would have stopped drafting that clause after "performance."

On appeal, plaintiffs offer a slight variation of this interpretation. They argue that both in its real-time cablecast and via the RS-DVR playback, Cablevision is in fact transmitting the "same performance" of a given work: the performance of the work that occurs when the programming service supplying Cablevision's content transmits that content to Cablevision and the service's other licensees.

Thus, according to plaintiffs, when Congress says that to perform a work publicly means to transmit . . . a performance . . . to the public, they really meant "transmit . . . the 'original performance' . . . to the public." The implication of this theory is that to determine whether a given transmission of a performance is "to the public," we would consider not only the potential audience of that transmission, but also the potential audience of any transmission of the same underlying "original" performance.

Like the district court's interpretation, this view obviates any possibility of a purely private transmission. Furthermore, it makes Cablevision's liability depend, in part, on the actions of legal strangers. Assume that HBO transmits a copyrighted work to both Cablevision and Comcast. Cablevision merely retransmits the work from one Cablevision facility to another, while Comcast retransmits the program to its subscribers. Under plaintiffs' interpretation, Cablevision would still be transmitting the performance to the public, solely because Comcast has transmitted the same underlying performance to the public. . . .

We do not believe Congress intended such odd results. Although the transmit clause is not a model of clarity, we believe that when Congress speaks of transmitting a performance to the public, it refers to the performance created by the act of transmission. Thus, HBO transmits its own performance of a work when it transmits to Cablevision, and Cablevision transmits its own performance of the same work when it retransmits the feed from HBO. . . .

In sum, none of the arguments advanced by plaintiffs or the district court alters our conclusion that, under the transmit clause, we must examine the potential audience of a given transmission by an alleged infringer to determine whether that transmission is "to the public." And because the RS-DVR system, as designed, only makes transmissions to one subscriber using a copy made by that subscriber, we believe that the universe of people capable of receiving an RS-DVR transmission is the single subscriber whose self-made copy is used to create that transmission.

Plaintiffs contend that it is "wholly irrelevant, in determining the existence of a public performance, whether 'unique' *copies* of the same work are used to make the transmissions." But plaintiffs cite no authority for this contention. And our analysis of the transmit clause suggests that, in general, any factor that limits the *potential* audience of a transmission is relevant. . . .

Indeed, we believe that *Columbia Pictures Industries, Inc. v. Redd Horne, Inc.*, 749 F.2d 154 (3d Cir.1984), relied on by both plaintiffs and the district court, supports our decision to accord significance to the existence and use of distinct copies in our transmit clause analysis. . . .

. . . In concluding that Maxwell's violated the transmit clause, that court explicitly relied on the fact that defendants showed the same copy of a work seriatim to its clientele, and it quoted [the Nimmer] treatise emphasizing the same fact. . . .

Unfortunately, neither the *Redd Horne* court nor Prof. Nimmer explicitly explains *why* the use of a distinct copy affects the transmit clause inquiry. But our independent analysis confirms the soundness of their intuition: the use of a unique copy may limit the potential audience of a transmission and is therefore relevant to whether that transmission is made "to the public." . . .

Given that each RS-DVR transmission is made to a given subscriber using a copy made by that subscriber, we conclude that such a transmission is not "to the public," . . . .

This holding, we must emphasize, does not generally permit content delivery networks to avoid all copyright liability by making copies of each item of content and associating one unique copy with each subscriber to the network, or by giving their subscribers the capacity to make their own individual copies. We do not address whether such a network operator would be able to escape any other form of copyright liability, such as liability for unauthorized reproductions or liability for contributory infringement. . . .

[The court directed that summary judgment be granted in favor of Cablevision.]

NOTES AND QUESTIONS

1. Consider the following hypotheticals. Which clause(s) of the statutory definition of "publicly" does each implicate, and how should each be decided? Do the *Redd Horne* analysis and the *Cartoon Network* analysis appear to dictate different outcomes in any of the hypotheticals?

 a. Rentals from the store desk of videotapes that are then taken by customers to individual viewing booths, placed in separate video players located in each booth, and played under the control of the customers.

 b. Rentals from a hotel desk of DVDs for viewing in the individual hotel rooms, when each room is equipped with a DVD player and the guest controls the playing of the DVD.

 c. Rentals from a hotel desk of DVDs for viewing in the individual hotel rooms, when the DVD player is located at the front desk.

 d. Rentals of DVDs and portable DVD players in airports, when the DVDs are watched in-flight and then returned, along with the players, at travelers' destination airports.

2. In *Cartoon Network*, why shouldn't the characterization of a performance depend on "the potential audience of any transmission of the same underlying 'original' performance"? From the perspective of the content provider, what distinguishes Cablevision's RS-DVR service from a video-on-demand service?

3. In determining whether particular transmissions are public, is it appropriate to consider whether or not unique copies were used? Why or why not? Based on the legislative history quoted in the *Redd Horne* opinion, how do you think the 1976 Congress would have answered that question? Should any performance transmitted over a one-to-many infrastructure count as "public"?

4. Why do you think the plaintiffs in *Redd Horne* and *Cartoon Network* objected to the services that the defendants provided? From a practical standpoint, how would each defendant's service affect the market for the copyrighted works?

5. As the *Redd Horne* court observes, the first sale doctrine of §109(a) limits only the copyright owner's right of public distribution, not the right of public performance. Therefore, when someone rents or even purchases a copy of a music or a motion picture, lawful possession of that copy does not give him the right to publicly perform the copyrighted work embodied in it. The notion that "It's my copy; I can do with it what I want" is thus not entirely true. There are other limiting doctrines in copyright law that may allow for certain public performances, see page 413 *supra* and Chapter 7 *infra*, but the first sale doctrine will not.

2. Public Display

In addition to a public performance right, §106 grants a right of public display to copyright owners of literary, musical, dramatic, and choreographic works, as well as pantomimes. Additionally, individual images of a motion picture and other audiovisual work are protected by the public display right. Section 101 defines "display" as follows:

> To "display" a work means to show a copy of it, either directly or by means of a film, slide, television image, or any other device or process or, in the case of a motion picture or other audiovisual work, to show individual images nonsequentially.

The definition of "publicly" quoted on page 413 *supra* also applies to the public display right. Thus, displaying a work at a place open to the public or at any place where a substantial number of persons outside of the normal circle of a family and its social acquaintances is gathered constitutes a public display. Additionally, a public display can occur by transmitting the display to a place open to the public or to a place where sufficient numbers of people are gathered, even if those people are not in the same place or do not receive the transmitted display at the same time.

Relatively few cases discuss the public display right, and those that do only do so in passing. For example, in *Ringgold v. Black Entertainment Television*, 126 F.3d 70 (2d Cir. 1997), plaintiff, Faith Ringgold, asserted a violation of her public display right when an authorized poster depicting her work was used in the background of a scene for a television program. The court acknowledged that there was no dispute about "copying" the plaintiff's work as it was "displayed on the set of defendant's television program," and thus focused its discussion on the defendants' arguments of "de minimis" use and fair use. *See also Triangle Publ'ns Inc. v. Knight-Ridder Newspapers, Inc.*, 445 F. Supp. 875 (S.D. Fla. 1978) (finding that defendant's use of a copy of a *TV Guide* magazine in a television advertisement for a competing television program guide constituted an infringing "display" as defined by §101, but refusing to grant an injunction because the First Amendment encourages comparative advertising of the sort at issue). Excluding cases concerning transmissions over computer networks (discussed below), there have been remarkably few cases alleging violation of the public display right since its recognition in 1976. One author identified only eight reported cases as of 2001. *See* R. Anthony Reese, *The Public Display Right: The Copyright Act's Neglected Solution to the Controversy over RAM "Copies,"* 2001 U. Ill. L. Rev. 83, 104.

A major reason for the lack of cases may be the rights granted to an owner of a copy of a copyrighted work by §109. Recall that §109(a) codifies the first sale doctrine, which permits someone who has rightfully acquired a copy of a copyrighted work to resell, or even rent, that copy, notwithstanding the public distribution right of the copyright owner. Section 109(c), in turn, permits someone who owns a copy of a copyrighted work to publicly display that work, notwithstanding the public display right of the copyright owner. Specifically, §109(c) provides:

> Notwithstanding the provisions of section 106(5), the owner of a particular copy lawfully made under this title, or any person authorized by such owner, is entitled, without the authority of the copyright owner, to display that copy publicly, either directly or by the projection of no more than one image at a time, to viewers present at the place where the copy is located.

Section 109(d) provides that the authorization in §109(c) does not "extend to any person who has acquired possession of the copy . . . from the copyright owner, by rental, lease, loan, or otherwise, without acquiring ownership of it." Thus, someone who rents or licenses a copy of the copyrighted work from the copyright owner does not have the right to publicly display that copy. Once the copyright owner has *sold* a copy of the work, however, the purchaser and others authorized by the purchaser may display the copy publicly. For example, if a museum buys a painting, it can display it in the gallery.

If most individuals who are in possession of lawfully made copies of a work can publicly display those copies without violating the public display right of the copyright owner, what is the point of the public display right? First, if the copy is not "lawfully made under this title," then publicly displaying that copy may be an infringement of the public display right.[1] (Additionally, there may be an infringement of the reproduction right.) More important, however, is the final qualification placed on the §109(c) privilege to authorize public display. If the display is accomplished by projecting an image of the lawfully acquired copy to viewers located in a place other than where the copy is located, then §109(c) will not immunize the display from infringement liability. Thus, with the exception of unlawfully made copies, the §109(c) exemption effectively limits the reach of the public display right to those displays that are made by transmission.

3. Public Performance, Public Display, and the Internet

As you may have guessed by now, the exclusive rights of public performance and public display have been invoked to support allegations of infringement when material is transmitted over the Internet or posted on a web site. The definition of "publicly," which includes transmissions to individuals in their own homes (television broadcasts, for example), clearly encompasses transmissions that occur over networked computers. The legislative history of the

---

1. Note that §109(c) uses the same phrase — "lawfully made under this title" — that is used in §109(a) and that was discussed in connection with the importation right. *See Quality King*, Section C, pages 358-62 *supra*.

1976 Act indicates that as early as 1965, Congress was alerted to the potential of a network of computers like the Internet:

> Equally if not more significant for the future are the implications of information storage and retrieval devices; when linked together by communications satellites or other means, these could eventually provide libraries and individuals throughout the world with access to a single copy of a work by transmission of electronic images. It is not inconceivable that, in certain areas at least, "exhibition" may take over from "reproduction" of "copies" as the means of presenting authors' works to the public, and we are now convinced that a basic right of public exhibition should be expressly recognized in the statute.

House Comm. on the Judiciary, 87th Cong., Copyright Law Revision Part 6: Supplementary Report of the Register of Copyrights on the General Revision of the U.S. Copyright Law: 1965 Revision Bill 20 (Comm. Print 1965). Early cases concerning the Internet acknowledged the public displays facilitated by computer bulletin board postings. *See Playboy Enters., Inc. v. Frena*, 839 F. Supp. 1552, 1556-57 (M.D. Fla. 1993); usenet newsgroup postings, *Religious Tech. Ctr. v. Netcom On-Line Communication Servs.*, 907 F. Supp. 1361 (N.D. Cal. 1995); and web sites, *Marobie-FL, Inc. v. National Ass'n of Fire and Equip. Distribs.*, 983 F. Supp. 1167, 1173 n.4 (N.D. Ill. 1997).

If material on a web site constitutes a public display then there are literally millions of public displays occurring every day. Thus, one might expect that after the Internet boom, there would have been many court decisions concerning the public display right. This, however, has yet to occur. Most infringement cases concerning material transmitted over the Internet have alleged a violation of the reproduction right. As discussed earlier in this chapter, Internet transmissions, including web browsing, involve the creation of multiple RAM copies. Such transmissions also involve the distribution of copies, at least as interpreted by some courts. Allegations of infringement based on the public performance and public display rights may be raised, but are rarely addressed by the courts once they find infringement of another right.

A notable exception is *Video Pipeline Inc. v. Buena Vista Home Entertainment, Inc.*, 192 F. Supp. 2d 321 (D.N.J. 2002), *aff'd*, 342 F. 3d 191 (3d Cir. 2003), *cert. denied*, 540 U.S. 1178 (2004). Video Pipeline compiled and marketed previews of motion pictures available for home video distribution to home video wholesalers and retailers. When it began making authorized preview clips supplied by the studios available to its customers via Internet streaming, the studios demanded the return of the preview materials. Video Source then used authorized copies of the motion pictures owned by its customers to prepare its own, unauthorized preview clips. The court held that Internet streaming of both the authorized and the unauthorized previews violated the public performance and public display rights.

As we discuss in more detail in Chapter 8, the different exclusive rights granted to a copyright owner by the Copyright Act are severable and separately transferable. On the Internet, however, the same activity may implicate more than one right. For example, posting a work on the Web may implicate the exclusive rights of reproduction, public distribution, and public display. This overlap of rights can lead to problems. One author has suggested the creation of a new "transmission" right to deal with this overlap. *See* Mark A. Lemley, *Dealing with Overlapping Copyrights on the Internet*, 22 U. Dayton L. Rev. 547 (1997). Another has recommended rejecting the RAM copy doctrine, and reinvigorating the public display right as a solution. Professor R. Anthony Reese argues:

> Although alternative copyright approaches to controlling transmissions over computer networks have emerged, the public display right is in many ways superior to those alternatives and would allow

courts to avoid some troublesome and unnecessary results from applying other exclusive rights to such transmissions. It avoids many of the problems of divided ownership of copyright rights, and it may ease the problem of potentially excessive copyright control that the RAM copy doctrine presents.

In addition, the display right has two less concrete advantages over the distribution and RAM copy alternatives. First, it is more faithful to the language and intent of the Copyright Act than either of the alternatives. Second, insisting that the specific rights implicated by a particular activity (such as transmitting images over the World Wide Web) be properly identified emphasizes that copyright owners do not simply "own" their "works" but, rather, they have exclusive control over certain specified uses of those works, while other uses — for example, reading or viewing a copy of a work, privately performing a work, or using a work's uncopyrightable elements — are not under the copyright owner's control.

R. Anthony Reese, *The Public Display Right: The Copyright Act's Neglected Solution to the Controversy over RAM "Copies,"* 2001 U. Ill. L. Rev. 83, 149.

Perfect 10, Inc. v. Amazon.com, Inc.
508 F.3d 1146 (9th Cir. 2007)

IKUTA, J.: . . .

Google operates a search engine, a software program that automatically accesses thousands of websites . . . and indexes them within a database stored on Google's computers. When a Google user accesses the Google website and types in a search query, Google's software searches its database for websites responsive to that search query. Google then sends the relevant information from its index of websites to the user's computer. . . .

The Google search engine that provides responses in the form of images is called "Google Image Search." In response to a search query, Google Image Search identifies text in its database responsive to the query and then communicates to users the images associated with the relevant text. Google's software cannot recognize and index the images themselves. Google Image Search provides search results as a webpage of small images called "thumbnails," which are stored on Google's servers. The thumbnail images are reduced, lower-resolution versions of full-sized images stored on third-party computers.

When a user clicks on a thumbnail image, the user's browser program interprets HTML instructions on Google's webpage. These HTML instructions direct the user's browser to cause a rectangular area (a "window") to appear on the user's computer screen. The window has two separate areas of information. The browser fills the top section of the screen with information from the Google webpage, including the thumbnail image and text. The HTML instructions also give the user's browser the address of the website publisher's computer that stores the full-size version of the thumbnail. By following the HTML instructions to access the third-party webpage, the user's browser connects to the website publisher's computer, downloads the full-size image, and makes the image appear at the bottom of the window on the user's screen. Google does not store the images that fill this lower part of the window and does not communicate the images to the user; Google simply provides HTML instructions directing a user's browser to access a third-party website. However, the top part of the window (containing the information from the Google webpage) appears to frame and comment on the bottom part of the window. Thus, the user's window appears to be filled with a single integrated presentation of the full-size image. . . . The processes by which the webpage directs a user's browser to incorporate content from different computers into a single window is referred to as "in-line linking." . . .

Google also stores webpage content in its cache. For each cached webpage, Google's cache contains the text of the webpage as it appeared at the time Google indexed the page, but does not store images from the webpage. Google may provide a link to a cached webpage in response to a user's search query. However, Google's cache version of the webpage is not automatically updated when the webpage is revised by its owner. So if the webpage owner updates its webpage to remove the HTML instructions for finding an infringing image, a browser communicating directly with the webpage would not be able to access that image. However, Google's cache copy of the webpage would still have the old HTML instructions for the infringing image. Unless the owner of the computer changed the HTML address of the infringing image, or otherwise rendered the image unavailable, a browser accessing Google's cache copy of the website could still access the image where it is stored on the website publisher's computer. In other words, Google's cache copy could provide a user's browser with valid directions to an infringing image even though the updated webpage no longer includes that infringing image.

In addition to its search engine operations, Google generates revenue through a business program called "AdSense." Under this program, the owner of a website can register with Google to become an AdSense "partner." The website owner then places HTML instructions on its webpages that signal Google's server to place advertising on the webpages that is relevant to the webpages' content. Google's computer program selects the advertising automatically by means of an algorithm. AdSense participants agree to share the revenues that flow from such advertising with Google. . . .

Google also generated revenues through an agreement with Amazon.com that allowed Amazon.com to in-line link to Google's search results. Amazon.com gave its users the impression that Amazon.com was providing search results, but Google communicated the search results directly to Amazon.com's users. Amazon.com routed users' search queries to Google and automatically transmitted Google's responses (i.e., HTML instructions for linking to Google's search results) back to its users.

Perfect 10 markets and sells copyrighted images of nude models. Among other enterprises, it operates a subscription website on the Internet. Subscribers pay a monthly fee to view Perfect 10 images in a "members' area" of the site. Subscribers must use a password to log into the members' area. Google does not include these password-protected images from the members' area in Google's index or database. Perfect 10 has also licensed Fonestarz Media Limited to sell and distribute Perfect 10's reduced-size copyrighted images for download and use on cell phones.

Some website publishers republish Perfect 10's images on the Internet without authorization. Once this occurs, Google's search engine may automatically index the webpages containing these images. . . .

III. Direct Infringement . . .

The district court held that Perfect 10 was likely to prevail in its claim that Google violated Perfect 10's display right with respect to the infringing thumbnails. . . . However, the district court concluded that Perfect 10 was not likely to prevail on its claim that Google violated . . . [Perfect 10's display right] with respect to its full-size infringing images. . . .

A. *Display Right* . . .

We have not previously addressed the question when a computer displays a copyrighted work for purposes of section 106(5). Section 106(5) states that a copyright owner has the exclusive right "to display the copyrighted work publicly." The Copyright Act explains that "display" means "to show a copy of it, either directly or by means of a film, slide, television image, or any other device or process. . . ." 17 U.S.C. §101. Section 101 defines "copies" as "material objects, other than phonorecords, in which a work is fixed by any method now known or later developed, and from which the work can be perceived, reproduced, or otherwise communicated, either directly or with the aid of a machine or device." *Id*. Finally, the Copyright Act provides that "[a] work is 'fixed' in a tangible medium of expression when its embodiment in a copy or phonorecord, by or under the authority of the author, is sufficiently permanent or stable to permit it to be perceived, reproduced, or otherwise communicated for a period of more than transitory duration." *Id*.

We must now apply these definitions to the facts of this case. A photographic image is a work that is " 'fixed' in a tangible medium of expression," for purposes of the Copyright Act, when embodied (i.e., stored) in a computer's server (or hard disk, or other storage device). . . . The computer owner shows a copy "by means of a . . . device or process" when the owner uses the computer to fill the computer screen with the photographic image stored on that computer, or by communicating [sic] the stored image electronically to another person's computer. In sum, based on the plain language of the statute, a person displays a photographic image by using a computer to fill a computer screen with a copy of the photographic image fixed in the computer's memory. There is no dispute that Google's computers store thumbnail versions of Perfect 10's copyrighted images and communicate copies of those thumbnails to Google's users. Therefore, Perfect 10 has made a prima facie case that Google's communication of its stored thumbnail images directly infringes Perfect 10's display right.

Google does not, however, display a copy of full-size infringing photographic images for purposes of the Copyright Act when Google frames in-line linked images that appear on a user's computer screen. Because Google's computers do not store the photographic images, Google does not have a copy of the images for purposes of the Copyright Act. In other words, Google does not have any "material objects . . . in which a work is fixed . . . and from which the work can be perceived, reproduced, or otherwise communicated" and thus cannot communicate a copy. 17 U.S.C. §101.

. . . Providing the[] HTML instructions is not equivalent to showing a copy. First, the HTML instructions are lines of text, not a photographic image. Second, HTML instructions do not themselves cause infringing images to appear on the user's computer screen. The HTML merely gives the address of the image to the user's browser. The browser then interacts with the computer that stores the infringing image. It is this interaction that causes an infringing image to appear on the user's computer screen. . . .

Perfect 10 argues that Google displays a copy of the full-size images by framing the full-size images, which gives the impression that Google is showing the image within a single Google webpage. While in-line linking and framing may cause some computer users to believe they are viewing a single Google webpage, the Copyright Act, unlike the Trademark Act, does not protect a copyright holder against acts that cause consumer confusion. . . .[7]

---

7. Perfect 10 also argues that Google violates Perfect 10's right to display full-size images because Google's in-line linking meets the Copyright Act's definition of "to perform or display a work 'publicly.'" 17 U.S.C. §101. This phrase means "to transmit or otherwise communicate a performance or display of the work to . . . the public, by means of any device or process, whether the members of the public capable of receiving the performance or display receive it in the same place or in separate places and at the same time or at different times." *Id*. Perfect 10 is mistaken. Google's activities do not meet this definition because Google transmits or communicates only an address which directs a user's browser to the location where a copy of the full-size image is displayed. Google does not communicate a display of the work itself.

Nor does our ruling that a computer owner does not display a copy of an image when it communicates only the HTML address of the copy erroneously collapse the display right in section 106(5) into the reproduction right set forth in section 106(1). Nothing in the Copyright Act prevents the various rights protected in section 106 from overlapping. . . .

Because Google's cache merely stores the text of webpages, our analysis of whether Google's search engine program potentially infringes Perfect 10's display and distribution rights is equally applicable to Google's cache. Perfect 10 is not likely to succeed in showing that a cached webpage that in-line links to full-size infringing images violates such rights. For purposes of this analysis, it is irrelevant whether cache copies direct a user's browser to third-party images that are no longer available on the third party's website, because it is the website publisher's computer, rather than Google's computer, that stores and displays the infringing image. . . .

[The court also concluded that Google's display of thumbnail images was fair use. For that portion of the opinion, see page 427, *infra*.]

V. Amazon.Com

. . . The district court concluded that Perfect 10 was unlikely to succeed in proving that Amazon.com was a direct infringer, because it merely in-line linked to the thumbnails on Google's servers and to the full-size images on third-party websites. . . .

We agree that Perfect 10 has not shown a likelihood that it would prevail on the merits of its claim that Amazon.com directly infringed its images. Amazon.com communicates to its users only the HTML instructions that direct users' browsers to Google's computers (for thumbnail images) or to a third party's computer (for full-size infringing images). Therefore, Amazon.com does not display . . . a copy of the thumbnails or full-size images to its users. . . .

NOTES AND QUESTIONS

1. Do you agree that the plain language of the Act mandates rejection of Perfect 10's claims for direct infringement with respect to the full-size images? The district court reached the same conclusion, but used a different approach. The court considered two possible tests for what constitutes a display. The "server" test defines "'display' as the act of *serving* content over the web"—i.e., physically sending ones and zeroes over the Internet to the user's browser. *Perfect 10 v. Google, Inc.*, 416 F. Supp. 2d 828, 839 (C.D. Cal. 2006) (emphasis in original). The "incorporation" test defines "'display' as the mere act of incorporating content into a webpage that is then pulled up by the browser." *Id.* The court found the server test preferable because it "is based on what happens at the technological-level[;] . . . neither invites copyright infringing activity by a search engine . . . nor flatly precludes liability for such activity[;] . . . website operators can readily understand the server test and courts can apply it relatively easily[; and it] . . . maintains, however uneasily, the delicate balance for which copyright law strives— i.e., between encouraging the creation of creative works and encouraging the dissemination of information." *Id.* at 843-44. Which approach do you prefer, the district court's or the Ninth Circuit's? Do you agree with the district court that a server test is preferable as a matter of policy?

2. Review *Capitol Records v. Thomas*, pages 341-47 *supra*. Perfect 10 also asserted a claim against Google for direct infringement of its distribution right. It argued that, like users of peer-to-peer file-sharing services, Google made the infringing full-size images "available" to its users. The court rejected that argument, reasoning that "Google does not own a collection

of Perfect 10's full-size images and does not communicate these images to the computers of people using Google's search engine." It concluded that therefore "the 'deemed distribution' rule does not apply to Google." *Perfect 10, Inc. v. Amazon.com, Inc.,* 508 F.3d at 1162. If copyright law were to adopt a "deemed distribution" rule, how broadly should such a rule extend? Would you agree that a "deemed distribution" rule should not extend to search engines? Why or why not? What about "Web 2.0" platforms such as Facebook and YouTube?

3. Review the Note on Linking and Framing, pages 391-92 *supra*, which describes efforts by some copyright owners to use the derivative work right to restrict linking to and framing of their online content. The *Perfect 10* litigation is part of a second wave of cases based on the right of public display. Linking and framing occur in many contexts other than searching. Are there contexts in which courts should scrutinize linking and framing more closely? Would any of the tests described by the Ninth Circuit and the district court in *Perfect 10* facilitate such scrutiny?

4. Review the Note on Copyright's Default Rules and the Google Book Search Project, page 157 *supra*, and Question 7, page 357 *supra*. The GBS project also implicates book copyright owners' rights of public display, because Google directly displays excerpts from their works, hosted on its own servers, to members of the public. The GBS project thus offers a good example of the overlap identified by Prof. Lemley, page 423 *supra*.

5. Do you favor a rejection of the RAM copy doctrine in favor of increased reliance on the public display right, as Prof. Reese recommends? Will relying on the public display right provide sufficient protection for copyright owners in the digital age? Is rejecting the RAM copy doctrine all that is necessary? What about the cached copies created during an Internet user's browsing activities that are stored in more permanent computer memory?

6. Does a public performance or display of a work via the Internet inevitably implicate the reproduction right? Sometimes, depending on the nature of the work and the nature of the transmission, a strong argument can be made that no reproduction has occurred, but that there has been a public performance. Consider streaming technology that works by allowing only small portions of a streamed broadcast to be "copied" onto a browser's computer. Each small portion is erased as the next small portion is loaded. Never is a complete copy of the work transmitted or retained. If streaming transmissions were deemed to involve both public performances and reproductions, the difficulties involved in obtaining the necessary permission from the different copyright owners would increase significantly. *See infra* Section G; *see also* R. Anthony Reese, *Copyright and Internet Music Transmissions: Existing Law, Major Controversies, Possible Solutions,* 55 U. Miami L. Rev. 237, 250-57 (2001) (discussing the statutory interpretation and transaction cost issues associated with streaming).

4. Limitations on the Public Performance and Public Display Rights

As with the other rights granted to copyright owners, the public performance and public display rights are subject to express limitations contained in the Act. The concept of "publicness" embodied in the definition of "publicly" limits the breadth of these rights in the first instance. Consider the following hypotheticals and determine whether any of them involve activities constituting "public performances" or "public displays":

a. Molly purchases a copy of *Jurassic Park 3* as a gift for her ten-year-old son, Johnny, on his birthday. Johnny opens the gift at his party, held at his house with ten of his friends. He immediately inserts the DVD into the player and all the kids start watching.

b. Same facts as in a., but instead of just ten friends, Johnny invited his entire fourth-grade class, all 27 of them, to his house for his party.

c. The student ACLU group at your law school rents a copy of *Dead Man Walking* from the local video store and shows it for "Movie Night" in the student lounge.

d. Jack Jackson works for a large computer chip manufacturer and is a huge fan of the cartoon strip *Dilbert*. He has clipped several of his favorite strips from the newspaper and posted them on the outside of his cubicle where everyone who walks by can see them.

e. Same facts as in d., but Jack scans the cartoons and posts copies on his Facebook page.

f. Your copyright professor brings to class a poster depicting a painting by Mondrian that she purchased at the local bookstore to discuss the copyrightable elements in the painting.

g. Same facts as in f., but your professor locates an image of the poster online and posts a copy on the Web discussion site for the course.

h. Sally brings her portable stereo to the beach and plays her favorite CDs loud enough for those around her to hear.

i. Each night, the 50 girls at a Girl Scout summer camp sing "Puff the Magic Dragon" around the campfire.

j. Wee-Care Daycare plays movies during quiet hour each afternoon.

Even if a particular activity meets the definition of a public performance or public display, the Copyright Act contains various additional limitations that may be relevant. First, were any of the public displays you found in items a. through j. excused by §109(c)? Second, the fair use doctrine, which we cover in Chapter 7, applies to all of the rights granted in §106. Finally, §110 contains many additional limitations designed to shelter certain nonprofit public performances and public displays.

Recall that the 1909 Act granted copyright owners the right to control only for-profit performances of a work. When the 1976 Act removed the for-profit qualification, the exemptions contained within §110 were considered necessary for certain nonprofit uses. Section 110 contains 11 separate subsections, each permitting certain kinds of public performances and public displays. These separate subsections are extremely specific. Sometimes a subsection only applies to certain types of works, sometimes a subsection only applies to certain establishments, and sometimes an exemption in §110 applies only if certain individuals are the ones engaged in the performance or hosting the event. Read through the limitations contained in §110 and then revisit hypotheticals a. through j., posed above. For those that you found were "public performances," which ones are placed outside of the copyright owner's control by §110? Be sure to pay close attention to the details of each exemption.

Many of the exemptions contained in §110 are the direct result of lobbying groups' efforts to protect their interests. *See* Jessica Litman, *Copyright, Compromise, and Legislative History*, 72 Cornell L. Rev. 857 (1987). Section 110 is also a convenient place for Congress to create additional exemptions when it desires. When industry groups tried to require the Girl Scouts and day care centers to agree to licenses, they were met with legislators' threats that if they continued to press their rights, new exemptions would be added to §110. Examine §110(4). Are new exemptions necessary for the activities described in hypotheticals i. and j.?

Section 110(5) exempts, *inter alia*, certain small businesses from infringement liability when they play the radio or television set in their establishments. We discuss this exemption, and the EU's allegation that it violates the TRIPS Agreement, in Section G.3.c, pages 458-60 *infra*.

Note on Distance Education Issues

Section 110(1) contains an exemption for public performances and public displays relating to teaching activities. Specifically, it exempts:

> performance or display of a work by instructors or pupils in the course of face-to-face teaching activities of a nonprofit educational institution, in a classroom or similar place devoted to instruction, unless, in the case of a motion picture or other audiovisual work, the performance, or the display of individual images, is given by means of a copy that was not lawfully made under this title, and that the person responsible for the performance knew or had reason to believe was not lawfully made; . . .

Note that the requirement of a lawfully made copy applies only to motion pictures or audiovisual works. Thus, teachers can explore infringing paintings by displaying them in their classrooms, but §110(1) does not immunize performing infringing movies or even infringing television commercials during class. It is possible that other exemptions, specifically fair use, might apply.

The requirement in §110(1) that the performance or display occur in the course of face-to-face teaching in a classroom or similar place excludes transmissions that might be used in distance learning activites. In 2002, Congress passed the Technology, Education, and Copyright Harmonization Act of 2002 (TEACH Act), which expanded a previous, narrower exemption for distance learning codified in §110(2). Currently, to qualify for the §110(2) exemption, the transmission of a performance or display of a work must be limited to "students officially enrolled" in a course offered by "an accredited nonprofit educational institution."[1] The exemption applies to transmissions of "nondramatic literary or musical works," as well as "reasonable and limited portions of any other works." Not eligible for the exemption are works that are "produced or marketed primarily for performance or display as part of mediated instructional activities transmitted via digital networks," a limitation argued to be essential by the publishing industry. Section 110(2) requires that the performance or display be related and of material assistance to the teaching content of the transmission, and further requires that the performance or display relate to "systematic mediated instructional activities," another limitation urged by the publishing industry. 17 U.S.C. §110(2)(A)-(B). The use of the copyrighted works must be an integral part of the class experience and be controlled by or under the actual supervision of the instructor.

The TEACH Act also provides that if temporary copies ("ephemeral" copies) are necessary to make the exempt transmissions, such reproductions may be made without infringing the reproduction right of the copyright owner. This exemption for ephemeral copies is codified in §112, which contains exemptions for other kinds of ephemeral copies and which we discussed in more detail in Section B, pages 339-40 *supra*. It expressly allows conversion of print or other analog versions of works into digital formats if no digital version of the work is available to the institution, or if the digital version that is available contains technological protections that prevent its use. *See Id.*

An important part of making the TEACH Act acceptable to publishers was the requirement that the transmitting body apply technological measures that reasonably prevent retention of the work in accessible form by the recipients of the transmission after the class session has ended, and prevent unauthorized further dissemination of the work in accessible form by the

---

1. Section 110(2) also exempts receptions "by officers or employees of governmental bodies as a part of their official duties or employment."

recipients to others. *See id.* §110(2)(D). Additionally, institutions must not interfere with technological measures used by copyright owners to prevent such retention and further dissemination. We discuss technological protections for copyrighted works and the legal protections granted to them by the Digital Millennium Copyright Act in Chapter 9.

NOTES AND QUESTIONS

1. Does §110(2) represent a good balance between the interests of educators and publishers? Does it do a good job of preserving the benefits of technologically aided distance learning?

2. The newest addition to §110 is §110(11), added in 2005, which specifies that the following is not an infringement of copyright:

> the making imperceptible, by or at the direction of a member of a private household, of limited portions of audio or video content of a motion picture, during a performance in or transmitted to that household for private home viewing, from an authorized copy of the motion picture, or the creation or provision of a computer program or other technology that enables such making imperceptible and that is designed and marketed to be used, at the direction of a member of a private household, for such making imperceptible, if no fixed copy of the altered version of the motion picture is created by such computer program or other technology.

This provision shields technologies such as the one developed by ClearPlay and discussed in Section D.2, page 390 *supra.* Copyright owners asserted that the technology ClearPlay was distributing, which was designed to permit individuals to skip objectionable content while watching authorized copies of movies on DVDs, infringed their derivative work right. The title of §110 indicates that it provides exemptions from infringement liability for "certain performances and displays." The new exemption in §110(11) does not mention the term "derivative work." In hearings on the bill, the Register of Copyrights had testified that the exemption was unnecessary because infringement of the derivative work right requires creation of a fixed copy. Does the addition of §110(11) reinforce the opposite argument?

More generally, is the derivative work right really an independent right of a copyright owner? Or, does infringement of the derivative work right necessarily involve infringement of one of the other rights of the copyright owner, i.e., the right to reproduce the work in copies or to engage in a public performance? *See* Tyler Ochoa, *Copyright, Derivative Works and Fixation: Is* Galoob *a Mirage, or Does the* Form(gen) *of the Alleged Derivative Work Matter?*, 20 Santa Clara Computer & High Tech. L.J. 991 (2004) (arguing that the derivative work right should be interpreted as dependent upon the other rights). Section 110(11) provides an exemption from infringement liability for activity that occurs during a performance of a work, but not necessarily during a public performance. In that case, is §110(11) unnecessary after all?

Note on Cable and Satellite Retransmission Rights

Television is an extremely significant means of conveying performances of many different copyrighted works, including literary works, musical works, motion pictures, and other audiovisual works. Before the 1950s, if your television antennae were not strong enough to pick up the signals transmitted through the air, you were out of luck. In rural areas, far from the closest signal tower, perhaps separated from that tower by hills or even mountains, the limited range of antennae reception meant no television reception. Community Antennae Television (CATV) was an attempt to remedy this problem by having large towers erected to receive the signals and then pass those signals on through wires to individual homes. This was the beginning of cable television. Copyright owners asserted that these operations were publicly performing their works for profit without authorization. In a pair of cases, the Supreme Court agreed with the cable system operators that they were not engaged in a public performance of the works they transmitted. The Court held that a CATV system merely "enhances the viewer's capacity to receive the broadcaster's signals . . . ." *Fortnightly Corp. v. United Artists Television, Inc.*, 392 U.S. 390, 399 (1968); *see also Teleprompter Corp. v. Columbia Broad. Sys., Inc.*, 415 U.S. 394 (1974).

During the lengthy revision process that led to the 1976 Act, cable television had become more pervasive: Approximately 3,500 cable operators were servicing 7,700 communities, reaching 10.8 million homes and earning revenues of almost $770 million. H.R. Rep. No. 94-1476, 94th Cong., 2d Sess. 88 (1976), *reprinted in* 1976 U.S.C.C.A.N. 5659, 5703. Given that the Act's broad definition of "perform" would now clearly encompass these cable systems, the need for some reconciliation between copyright owners and cable television operators was apparent. Congress balanced these interests by placing certain retransmissions of television signals over cable systems within the scope of the exclusive rights granted to copyright owners, but making them subject to a compulsory license. The 1976 Act provided that cable television operators are not liable for copyright infringement if they file periodic accountings of their broadcast operations and pay a license fee based on a formula in the statute. This mechanism is called a compulsory license because while the copyright owners are compensated through the payment of a fee, they are not permitted to refuse to license their works. A compulsory license is a compromise between giving the copyright owner complete control over certain uses and granting users a complete exemption from liability. The compulsory license provision for cable retransmission, a lengthy and complex provision, is codified in §111 of the Act. *See also* 37 C.F.R. §201.17 (2005) (setting forth certain regulations governing compulsory licenses for secondary transmissions).

In large measure, the details of the retransmission rules reflect concern for both the threat that cable systems pose to local broadcast stations and the need for competition in the marketplace. In the early years of cable television, it was the cable operators that needed assistance in participating in the market for providing television signals to homes. Thus, retransmission of local signals and network programming does not require any fee. Cable retransmission of these signals and programs is thought not to invade the market for the underlying copyrighted work, because the rates charged for advertising take into account households that receive these broadcasts over cable as well. Additionally, cable systems are required by the Communications Act to carry local broadcast stations (sometimes referred to as the "must carry" rule). *See* 47 U.S.C. §§534-535. The retransmission of distant non-network programs, however, is not required by Federal Communications Commission (FCC) regulations, and may potentially harm the market for programs by making it less likely that new stations in distant markets will pay to carry these programs if viewers can already see those shows through cable retransmission. Thus, retransmission of distant non-networked programs requires payment of a license fee. These compulsory royalty fees are paid to the Copyright Office and subsequently divided and paid to program suppliers, professional sports leagues, and individual copyright claimants. Additionally, FCC network nonduplication, syndicated exclusivity, and sports blackout rules limit the ability of a cable company to import a distant broadcast that duplicates certain local broadcasts.

The 1976 Copyright Act only addressed cable television systems. The next technological innovation, satellite systems, struggled to develop in a marketplace where such systems were at a clear disadvantage. In order to broadcast any stations, the provider of the satellite system had to negotiate licenses individually. In 1988, Congress enacted the Satellite Home Viewer Act, codifying a compulsory license scheme for satellite retransmissions in §119. This amendment permitted the compulsory license to be used by satellite systems, but only to deliver signals to individuals in "unserved households" that could not receive a "grade B" signal over the air from their local broadcast stations with roof-top antennae. Court cases beginning in 1998 found that satellite television providers were systematically ignoring the "unserved household" requirement. *See, e.g., Primetime 24 Joint Venture v. NBC, Inc.*, 219 F.3d 92, 97-98 (2d Cir. 2000). In these cases, courts issued injunctions to terminate subscriber access to satellite signals if the individuals did not meet the unserved household requirement.

Responding to these cases and to tension in the industry, Congress passed the Satellite Home Viewer Improvement Act (SHVIA) in 1999. That Act "grandfathered" in existing satellite television customers, avoiding any termination of service that would have resulted from the court injunctions. SHVIA authorizes satellite providers to retransmit local broadcasts into local market areas royalty free. In return for exemption from copyright liability, SHVIA requires that if a satellite provider retransmits any local broadcast station, it must carry them all. This carry-one/carry-all provision is codified in the Communications Act, and, like the must-carry rules applicable to cable television, dovetails with exemptions from public performance infringement liability in the Copyright Act. A satellite provider can avoid the carry-one/carry-all requirement by negotiating private retransmission agreements with those stations it desires to broadcast instead of relying on the exemption in the Copyright Act for its authorization to retransmit stations. Each commercial station had to elect whether it desired to maintain control over all satellite retransmissions by requiring individually negotiated retransmission consent or whether it desired to be included in the mandatory carriage rules. This election could be changed after four years, with any new election lasting for three years. The grandfathering provision was set to expire on December 31, 2004, but Congress extended it to December 31, 2009. *See* Satellite Home Viewer Extension and Reauthorization Act of 2004 (SHVERA), 47 U.S.C. §325(b)(2)(C). While SHVERA modified SHVIA in several ways, the provisions discussed above remain the same. As of the writing of the third edition of this book, another reauthorization bill, the Satellite Home Viewer Update and Reauthorization Act of 2009 (SHVURA), was making its way through Congress. Once again, the provisions discussed above would remain unchanged, but the bill directs the Copyright Office to conduct a study on phasing out the compulsory license for retransmission of distant broadcast signals.

As Congress and the FCC were struggling to craft rules concerning satellite retransmission of television broadcasts, retransmission of television broadcast signals over the Internet began to concern the established players in the television broadcast market. One company that attempted to retransmit broadcast signals through its web site was iCraveTV.com, located in Canada. Canada's retransmission rules differ from those in the U.S., and the operator of iCraveTV.com believed that its behavior was lawful under Canadian copyright law. Copyright owners, however, successfully sued in the U.S. and obtained an injunction because the court found that individuals in the U.S. were able to obtain retransmissions through the iCraveTV web site. The court held that "because plaintiffs seek relief under U.S. law for infringements of the U.S. Copyright Act, there is no need for this Court to address any issue of Canadian law." *National Football League v. TVRadioNow Corp.*, 53 U.S.P.Q.2d 1831, 1837 (W.D. Pa. 2000). Following this case, Congress held hearings to consider the status of Internet retransmissions, and whether compulsory licenses should encompass such retransmissions. To date, Congress has not passed any legislation concerning Internet retransmissions.

NOTES AND QUESTIONS

1. Consider how the rules concerning retransmission adopted in both the Copyright Act and the Communications Act affect competition in the marketplace for television system services. Using compulsory licenses to balance the needs of new communication technologies and the rights of copyright owners, a step first implemented in response to the player piano under the 1909 Act, is alive and well. Are the uses of the compulsory license in the television broadcast market explained above appropriate? Why not require cable system and satellite providers to negotiate licenses with each individual broadcast station? Note that the use of compulsory licenses also represents a means for encouraging competition in the marketplace as new technologies change the method of delivery of copyrighted works and thus threaten entrenched market players.

2. Should a compulsory license be available for entities that desire to retransmit television broadcasts over the Internet?

3. The retransmission involved in cable systems and satellite systems requires the creation of temporary copies of these broadcasts, thus implicating not just the public performance rights of copyright owners, but the reproduction right as well. As we explained in Section B, pages 339-40 *supra*, §112 of the Copyright Act grants a limited exemption to allow for these "ephemeral copies."

5. International Treatment of Public Performances and Public Displays

The U.S. is unusual in including both in-person performance and performance by transmission within the single "public performance" right. In many countries, the right to communicate a work to the public is divided into as many as three separate rights: (1) the right of public performance, encompassing the right to control the performance of the work in the presence of the public either by live performance or by means of a recording; (2) the right of wireless transmission, encompassing transmission by radio waves including satellite broadcasts; and (3) the right of "cabling," encompassing the transmission by cable or wire. In some countries, a broadcast right encompasses both wireless and "wired" transmissions.

Currently, the Berne Convention requires member countries to grant the following rights relating to what U.S. law refers to as "public performance":

1. To authors of dramatic, dramatico-musical, and musical works, the exclusive right of publicly performing their work by any means or process and communicating a performance of the work to the public (Berne Conv., art. 11).
2. To authors of literary and artistic works, the exclusive right of broadcasting and communicating their works to the public by means of "wireless diffusion of signs, sounds, or images"; controlling rebroadcasting of such a communication; and controlling public communication through loudspeakers or similar equipment (*id.*, art. 11bis).
3. To authors of literary works, the exclusive right to control "the public recitation of their works . . . by any means or process," and to control "any communication to the public of the recitation of their works." (*id.*, art. 11ter).

Recall that the TRIPS Agreement incorporates Articles 1-21 (except 6bis) of the Berne Convention. These requirements therefore are part of the mandatory international minimum standards of copyright protection.

Pursuant to Article 11bis(2) of the Berne Convention (incorporated by reference into TRIPS), countries are allowed to limit the three public performance rights listed above so long as "equitable remuneration" is paid to owners. Many of the exceptions to the public performance right in U.S. law that we have discussed in this section do not involve any remuneration; they are outright exemptions from copyright infringement liability. Historically, countries were given wide latitude in implementing the Berne Convention's requirements. In fact, the dispute referral mechanisms contained in the Berne Convention have never been utilized. But with the incorporation of the Berne Convention into the dispute settlement process of the World Trade Organization (WTO), resolving the issue of whether various exemptions comport with the treaties' requirements has become serious business. The TRIPS Agreement permits member countries to limit the rights granted to copyright owners, but requires that those limitations be confined "[1] to certain special cases which [2] do not conflict with a normal exploitation of the work and [3] do not unreasonably prejudice the legitimate interest of the right holder." TRIPS Agreement, art. 13. This provision is often referred to as the "three-step test." Whether the various limitations and exceptions in U.S. copyright law comply with either Article 11bis(2) or the TRIPS three-step test is the subject of much debate. A ruling by the WTO that one of the exemptions in §110 of the Copyright Act exceeds the limits of Article 13 is discussed in more detail in the next section of this chapter.

In addition to the Berne Convention and the TRIPS Agreement, there are two other agreements that relate to the public performance and public display rights: the WIPO Copyright Treaty (WCT) and the WIPO Performances and Phonograms Treaty (WPPT). The U.S. is a member of both agreements. With respect to the public performance right, the WCT requires countries to grant to authors

> the exclusive right of authorizing any communication to the public of their works, by wire or wireless means, including the making available to the public of their works in such a way that members of the public may access these works from a place and at a time individually chosen by them.

WCT, art. 8. The WCT also contains a provision similar to Article 13 of TRIPS, allowing limitations on the required rights that meet the three-step test. *Id.*, art. 10. The WPPT requires that performers and producers "shall enjoy the right to a single equitable remuneration for the direct or indirect use of phonograms published for commercial purposes for broadcasting or for any communication to the public." WPPT, art. 15. This treaty allows countries to enact legislation establishing terms that require the performers and producers to share a single equitable remuneration. However, countries may choose not to comply with Article 15, or may choose to comply with Article 15 only for certain kinds of uses, by notifying WIPO.

The EU has implemented its own balance of rights and limitations in its directive on copyright harmonization, adopted in 2001. The Directive requires member countries to provide authors with an "exclusive right to authorise or prohibit any communication to the public of their works, by wire or wireless means . . . ." Directive 2001/29/EC of the European Parliament and of the Council of 22 May 2001 on the harmonisation of certain aspects of copyright and related rights in the Information Society, 2001 O.J. (L. 167) 10, art. 3(1). Member states may provide for exceptions to the rights required by Article 3, as detailed in a long list of permissible exceptions contained in Article 5(3). These exceptions do not require any remuneration, but the final clause of Article 5 requires that any exceptions adopted by a member country "shall only be applied in certain special cases which do not conflict with normal exploitation of the work or other subject-matter and do not unreasonably prejudice the legitimate interests of the rightholder." *Id.*, art. 5(5).

The international requirements for protection of the broadcasting right are highly relevant in the case of wireless transmissions such as television and radio broadcasts. While copyright laws are geographically bounded, applying only to activities within the territory of each country, wireless transmissions can cross national borders. Currently, there are no technological means for stopping such border-crossing wireless broadcasts. The infringement disputes that can result from cross-border reception may require examining the copyright rights granted under multiple countries' laws. In 1998, WIPO began work on a treaty to update broadcast protection for the digital age. As currently proposed, the WIPO Broadcast Treaty would give broadcasting organizations many exclusive rights in their broadcasts, including the rights of fixation, retransmission, communication to the public, and distribution. There are also proposed terms dealing with technological protection measures and rights management information, topics you will learn more about in Chapter 9. The scope of protection for broadcasting organizations and the duration of the rights proposed under the Broadcast Treaty are the subjects of considerable debate, however. WIPO has spent nearly a decade conducting regional consultations on the various disputed issues.

G. COPYRIGHT AND THE MUSIC INDUSTRY

Copyright in the music industry is both particularly complex and particularly important. This section provides an overview of how copyright issues affect the industry, and is designed to help you appreciate how the different §106 rights granted to a copyright owner can be utilized by the various industry players. Finally, this section explores in more depth how Congress has responded to the needs of existing market players whose business models, established around the then-existing copyright law, have been threatened by new technologies.

There are two copyrights in any recorded piece of music: the copyright in the musical work, which can involve both musical notes and lyrics, and the copyright in the sound recording. Despite the advent of recorded sound in the late 1800s and the commercial introduction of the first "victrola" phonograph machine in 1906, sound recordings were not granted federal copyright protection until 1971.[1] Previously, some states recognized a state-law copyright in sound recordings.

The sound recording copyright protects the elements of original authorship that inhere in a fixed recording of sounds, whether it is a recording of a musical performance, a dramatic reading, or a sequence of railroad whistles. In the music industry, this sound recording copyright creates an important second layer of protection, even though this protection is limited in various ways that we discuss below. Whereas most copyrighted works are fixed in "copies," sound recordings are fixed in "phonorecords," which the Copyright Act defines as

material objects in which sounds, other than those accompanying a motion picture or other audio-visual work, are fixed by any method now known or later developed, and from which the sounds can be perceived, reproduced, or otherwise communicated, either directly or with the aid of a machine or device.

1. Congress enacted protection for sound recordings in 1971. Sound Recording Act of 1971 (the "SRA"), Pub. L. 92-140, 85 Stat. 391. The protection was effective February 15, 1972.

17 U.S.C. §101. Thus, phonorecords include vinyl albums, cassettes, and CDs, as well as digital files.

Understanding copyright issues in the music industry requires keeping straight both the layers of copyright protection involved and various interested parties. On the next page is a chart depicting the various rights in musical works and sound recordings and the entities that administer each right. It may be helpful to refer back to this chart as you read through the following materials.

1. Introduction to the "Players" in the Music Industry

Almost everyone understands the role of the songwriter and also the role of the recording artist who performs and records a musical work. But in between these two known players are several other important entities. First, there is the music publisher. The music publisher is really the "middleman" between the songwriter and other industry players. Other industry players include performing artists, record companies, and collective rights organizations, as well as other entities that might license a songwriter's musical works, whether for performance, recording and distributing in phonorecords, or "synchronizing" with images in a television commercial, movie, or video game. While a songwriter is not required to engage a music publisher, he or she usually does so because the music publisher knows the business and can therefore be a significant asset to the songwriter. To a large extent, the genre of music determines how active a role the publisher plays. In country music, it is common for recording artists to perform and record musical works written by others, and thus a role of the music publisher is to promote a songwriter's songs. In rock music, it is more common for the artist to write most, if not all, of his or her songs. In that case, the publishing company's role is to administer the catalog of that artist's musical works, including licensing the use of the musical works by others. In general, music publishing companies require that the copyright in the musical work be assigned to them, but agree to split royalties earned on the musical work 50/50 with the songwriter.

When a performing artist creates a sound recording, often there is a recording company that works with the recording artist to produce, distribute, and promote the recorded songs, whether through sales of copies or through licensing of the recording for audio streaming. Typically, the recording artist will assign all copyright interest in the sound recording to the recording company. The contract often specifies that the sound recording is created as a work made for hire and that, to the extent that it is not a work made for hire, the artist assigns "all right, title, and interest" to the recording company. By now, you should understand the significance of the way in which the recording company obtains copyright ownership. If not, review Chapter 3.C.2, *supra*.

Phonorecords of recorded songs reproduce both the sound recording and the underlying musical work. If the recording artist is recording a musical work written by someone else, he or she will need permission. The songwriter will be the proper person from whom to obtain permission only if the songwriter has not contracted with a music publisher. Even the music publisher may not be the only proper entity from whom to obtain authorization, however, because a majority of music publishers contract with the Harry Fox Agency. Harry Fox licenses the right to record and reproduce in phonorecords millions of musical works, as well as the right to publicly distribute those phonorecords. As explained in more detail below, such licenses are referred to in the industry as "mechanicals" because they originally involved the mechanical reproduction of musical works. Distributors of recorded music enter the music industry picture as well. Sales of CDs at brick and mortar stores rely on the first sale doctrine, which permits stores to purchase authorized copies of those CDs and resell those copies without further

	Reproduction and Distribution in Phonorecords	Other Reproduction/ Creation of Derivative Works	Public Performance
Musical Works	**Statutory right:** §106(1) & (3)	**Statutory right:** §106(1) & (2)	**Statutory right:** §106(4)
	Specific limitations on §106 rights: §115 — compulsory license §§1001-1008 — Audio Home Recording Act (AHRA)		**Specific limitations on §106 rights:** §110 — various limitations
	Rights Administered by: —Music Publishers —Copyright Office (§115; AHRA) —Harry Fox Agency	**Rights Administered by:** —Music Publishers	**Rights Administered by:** —ASCAP, BMI, or SESAC
Sound Recordings	**Statutory right:** §106(1) & (3)	**Statutory right:** §106(1) & (2)	**Statutory right:** §106(6)
	Specific limitations on §106 rights: §114(b) — "sound alikes" not covered §§1001-1008 — AHRA	**Specific limitations on §106 rights:** §114(b) — actual sounds must be reproduced	**Specific limitations on §106 rights:** §§106(6) & 114(a) — digital audio transmission only §114(d)-(j) — exemptions
	Rights Administered by: —Record Labels —Copyright Office (AHRA)	**Rights Administered by:** —Record Labels	**Rights Administered by:** —Record Labels —Sound Exchange (§114 statutory license)

concern for copyright rights. Digital distributors, such as Apple's iTunes and Rhaspody, are engaged in what the Copyright Act deems a "digital phonorecord delivery," or DPD. The statutory duties surrounding DPDs are discussed in more detail in this section.

Radio stations broadcasting over the Internet or over the airwaves, and concert venues, nightclub owners, and other businesses that "play" music must also be considered part of the music industry. As you know from Section F *supra*, these entities are all engaging in "public performances." Because the musical work copyright owners have a public performance right, permission from them will be needed, assuming no specific exemption applies (e.g., §110). Obtaining authorization from each individual copyright owner of each musical work performed, or even from each music publisher, would involve insurmountable transaction costs. However, collective rights organizations (CROs) exist that have licensed the right to administer public performance rights from the music publishers, and can authorize public performances for millions of copyrighted works through a blanket license. The American Society of Composers, Authors, and Publishers (ASCAP), Broadcast Music, Inc. (BMI), and the Society of European Stage Authors and Composers (SESAC) are the three main CROs. The creation and evolution of these CROs are explored later in this section.

Radio stations and nightclubs are also engaged in public performances of sound recordings. As discussed in Section F *supra*, the Copyright Act does not grant copyright owners of sound recordings a general public performance right. However, when the public performance is by means of a digital audio transmission — for example, streamed from an online site, in addition to authorization for public performance of the musical work, the online site will need authorization to publicly perform the sound recording. *See* 17 U.S.C. §106(6). The required authorization for the sound recording can come from the statute, which exempts certain digital public performances of sound recordings. *See id.* §114(d). Authorization can also come from a statutory license provided by §114, so long as the user entity complies with detailed statutory requirements and pays a fee currently collected and distributed by SoundExchange, an entity created by the trade organization for the recording companies, the Recording Industry Association of America (RIAA). If neither the exemption nor the statutory license applies, the entity engaged in a public performance by means of a digital audio transmission will need the permission of the copyright owners in the sound recordings being performed.

Follow-on creators that license musical works and sound recordings, such as movie studios and video game producers, also are players in the music industry. Their uses of musical works can implicate the reproduction right, the derivative work right, and often the public performance right as well.

NOTES AND QUESTIONS

1. Where, at the end of the day, are the creative individuals, that is, the songwriters and the performers? How big a role do these individuals play in the operation of the music industry?

2. And, of course, there are individuals who listen to music, play music, make their own creative works using other people's recordings, and upload the resulting works to blogs and websites like Facebook and YouTube. The music landscape has shifted dramatically in the last decade, challenging the legal structure that was mostly established for a different technological reality. As you continue through this section, consider whether the structure as a whole is well designed for the digital world in which individuals can play a far more direct and integral role in the creation, dissemination, and use of recorded music.

2. Reproduction, Public Distribution, and Derivative Work Issues

Like all of the other categories of works, musical works and sound recordings are protected by the exclusive rights granted to copyright owners in §106. In music, however, each of the exclusive rights seems to take at least one special twist or turn.

a. Musical Works and Section 115

The first twist in music copyright occurred in the 1909 Act. Around the turn of the last century, player pianos and phonograph record players gained popularity. Before the advent of the player piano, sales of sheet music were the main source of revenue for musical work copyright owners. Initially, the makers of player piano rolls and phonograph records did not pay royalties for embodying musical works in the rolls and records. After an unsuccessful challenge to this practice in the Supreme Court (*White-Smith Music Publishing Co. v. Apollo Co.*, 209 U.S. 1 (1908); see Chapter 2.A, *supra*), Congress granted musical work copyright owners the right to control the "mechanical reproduction" of their works. Congress, however, was suspicious of the market power of one piano roll company, the Aeolian Company, and so, for the first time in the history of the Copyright Act, Congress adopted a compulsory license system. Any manufacturer of piano rolls could use any musical composition without negotiating with the copyright owner for permission, so long as the musical work had been previously licensed to someone else for mechanical reproduction and the manufacturer paid a statutory royalty. The statutory royalty rate was set at 2 cents per mechanical copy distributed.

The compulsory license for mechanical reproductions of musical works, sometimes called simply "mechanicals," remains a part of the Copyright Act today, and allows recording artists to record what are commonly known in the industry as "covers" — musical works written by someone else and previously released on an album by a different recording artist. Codified in §115, the compulsory license applies not just to player piano rolls, but also to CDs, cassettes, and any other "phonorecord" that mechanically reproduces the musical work. In 1998, Congress amended §115 to make clear that it applied to distribution of phonorecords by means of digital downloads. The Act uses the term *digital phonorecord delivery* (DPD) and defines it as "each individual delivery of a phonorecord by a digital transmission of a sound recording which results in a specifically identifiable reproduction." 17 U.S.C. §115(d). The definition specifically excludes real-time transmissions "where no reproduction of the sound recording or the musical work embodied therein is made from the inception of the transmission through to its receipt by the transmission recipient in order to make the sound recording audible." *Id.* Therefore, web streaming is not considered a DPD. For example, if a web site allows individuals to download copies of an MP3 file, the downloaded file is a "phonorecord" and the entity running the web site has engaged in a DPD. If the web site owner is paying the mechanical royalty fees, there is no infringement liability for the reproduction of the musical work. Remember, however, that the compulsory mechanical license authorizes only the reproduction of the musical work, not the sound recording. Unless the web site owner is the copyright owner or a licensee of the sound recording embodied in the MP3 file, the web site owner may be violating the copyright in the sound recording.

Section 115 retains the requirement that, to be subject to the compulsory license, the musical work must have been previously distributed to the public, embodied in a phonorecord created under the authority of the copyright owner. The compulsory license allows for reproduction in phonorecords, and even allows for a new arrangement of the work to conform it to the style of the recording artist. The new arrangement is expressly excluded from obtaining protection as a derivative work, however, unless the entity creating the new arrangement obtains the consent of the copyright owner. *See id.* §115(a)(2). The license does not allow for a change in the "basic melody or fundamental character of the work." *Id.* The statutory royalty rate for phonorecords made and distributed after January 1, 2006 is 9.1 cents or 1.75 cents per minute of playing time or fraction thereof, whichever is greater. The responsibility for setting rates lies with the panel of Copyright Royalty Judges (CRJs) that replaced the previous system of Copyright Arbitration Royalty Panels. *See* Note 4, pages 340-41 *supra*. For regulations regarding how to file a notice of intent to obtain a compulsory license and account for copies distributed under that license, see 37 C.F.R. §§201.18-201.19 (2005).

The compulsory license in §115 is not, however, the way in which most creators of sound recordings obtain permission to use musical works. If one recording artist desires to record a performance of a musical work that has already been the subject of an authorized recording, instead of complying with the requirements of §115, a representative for the later recording artist typically contacts the Harry Fox Agency. Established in New York City in 1927 as a wholly owned subsidiary of the National Music Publishing Company, Harry Fox serves as an agent on behalf of music publishers, licensing musical works for reproduction and distribution in phonorecords — i.e., granting "mechanical" licenses. Other types of musical licenses must be negotiated with the music publisher, including synchronization ("synch") licenses that allow the musical work to be included in an audiovisual work such as a video game, television commercial, or movie. Of course, the Harry Fox Agency has authority to grant licenses only for those musical works for which the Agency itself has a license. The number of copyright owners that have entered into licensing agreements with Harry Fox is staggering: Harry Fox represents over 27,000 music publishers, who collectively own more than 2.5 million copyrighted musical works.

Although the compulsory license is not utilized for most recordings that are made, the availability of the compulsory mechanical license does affect the rate paid. In effect, the parties to the licenses administered by Harry Fox are negotiating in the shadow of a compulsory license that both parties know could be used instead. Thus, it is rare that the agreed license rate exceeds the rate set by the CRJs.

NOTES AND QUESTIONS

1. Songs first made popular in the late 1970s and the 1980s are being "remade" by the recording artists of today. Roland Orzabal wrote the song "Mad World." The song was recorded and released by Orzabal's band, Tears for Fears, in 1982. The song was covered by a standard music publishing agreement with music publisher Chrysalis Music Group, which has agreements with Harry Fox and BMI. The song has been covered by several different recording artists, including Gary Jules in 2003 and American Idol finalist Adam Lambert in 2009. What rights did these artists need to obtain to record the song? What were their options for obtaining those rights? Could Orzabal or Chrysalis Music Group have stopped Jules or Lambert from recording and releasing the song?

2. The Copyright Office has ruled that cellular phone ringtones that are excerpts of pre-existing sound recordings "fall squarely within the scope of the statutory license" under §115 and constitute DPDs. *In the Matter of Mechanical & Digital Phonorecord Delivery Rate Adjustment Proceeding*, U.S. Copyright Office, No. RF 2006-1 (Oct. 16, 2006). If additional material is included, the ringtone may be a derivative work and thus ineligible for the §115 mechanical license. *Id.* Songwriters, represented by the National Music Publishers Association, the Songwriters Guild of America, and the Nashville Songwriters Association International, had argued that all ringtones are derivative works. Why do you think the Copyright Office ruled as it did? Do you think the ruling is a sound one?

3. What types of licenses would be needed to create the video games Rock Band and Guitar Hero? Reproducing a work in the context of audiovisual works has long been viewed to fall outside the scope of the mechanical license authorized by §115, and instead to require a "synch" license. For example, the song "Mad World" (see Note 1, above) was used in the movie *Donnie Darko* and also in the video game *Gears of War*. What licenses did the movie and video game creators need and from whom could they obtain them?

Imagine that you are a manufacturer of a karaoke product, which you hope to sell for use in restaurants and bars. What kinds of licenses do you need, and from whom? Does it make a difference whether you put the recordings on cassettes or compact discs or embed them in a microchip, which, when plugged into a television, displays the lyrics of the song on the television screen in real time? Does it matter whether, while the song plays, your product displays only the lyrics and no other images? Does a mechanical license entitle you to print or display the song lyrics in real time? *Compare Leadsinger Inc. v. BMG Music Publ'g*, 512 F.3d 522 (9th Cir. 2008) (holding that a karaoke device that displays lyrics is not a phonorecord but is an audiovisual work excluded from §115's compulsory licensing scheme), with *EMI Entm't World, Inc. v. Priddis Music, Inc.*, 505 F. Supp. 2d 1217 (D. Utah 2007) (finding that mere display of lyrics as a song is played does not amount to an audiovisual work and does not require a synch license).

4. Because web streaming is not considered a DPD, the compulsory license in §115 does not confer the right to conduct web streaming, or to make server copies as part of a streaming operation. *See The Rodgers & Hammerstein Org. v. UMG Recordings, Inc.*, 60 U.S.P.Q.2d 1354 (S.D.N.Y. 2001). Web streaming implicates rights of public performance for both musical works and sound recordings. We discuss those rights in Section G.3 *infra*.

5. The Berne Convention contemplates that certain uses of copyrighted works may be the subject of compulsory licensing. Specifically, Article 13 allows countries to permit the recording of musical works that have already been recorded with permission of the copyright owner. These permissible recordings must not "be prejudicial to the rights of these authors to obtain equitable remuneration which, in the absence of agreement, shall be fixed by competent authority." Berne Conv., art. 13(3). This provision clearly sanctions the compulsory license of §115.

b. Sound Recordings and Section 114

While the Act grants copyright owners of sound recordings a reproduction right, it does not protect against imitation, but only against direct duplication of the recorded sounds. Put differently, "sound alikes" do not infringe the sound recording owner's reproduction right. Why do you think this is the case? After all, other copyrighted works are protected against imitation as well as exact duplication. What is different about sound recordings? At least two considerations may have influenced Congress. First, Congress was focusing primarily on stopping record piracy, not imitations. Second, there is some indication in the legislative history that Congress was concerned about safeguarding our musical heritage. How does permitting sound alike recordings help to do this?

The limitations on the rights of sound recording copyright owners are codified in §114. That section provides that the §106(1) right "is limited to the right to duplicate the sound recording in the form of phonorecords or copies that directly or indirectly recapture the actual sounds fixed in the recording." 17 U.S.C. §114(b). While one might expect the derivative work right to cover sound alikes, it too is limited by §114. Section 114 requires that "the actual sounds fixed in the sound recording [be] rearranged, remixed, or otherwise altered in sequence or quality" to qualify as a derivative work of a sound recording. *Id*. To further clarify both of these limitations, §114 provides that neither the reproduction nor the derivative work right extends to the making of "an independent fixation of other sounds, even though such sounds imitate or simulate those in the copyrighted sound recording." *Id*.

c. Sampling Musical Works and Sound Recordings

In rap music, "sampling" is a common practice in which one recording artist will digitally copy and remix sounds from previously recorded albums. As you now know, this practice may implicate two copyrights. When should sampling require the permission of the musical work copyright owner? When should it require the permission of the sound recording copyright owner?

≡ **Newton v. Diamond**
≡ *388 F.3d 1189 (9th Cir. 2004)*

SCHROEDER, J.: . . .

Background and Procedural History

The plaintiff and appellant in this case, James W. Newton, is an accomplished avant-garde jazz flutist and composer. In 1978, he composed the song "Choir," a piece for flute and voice intended to incorporate elements of African-American gospel music, Japanese ceremonial court music, traditional African music, and classical music, among others. According to Newton, the song was inspired by his earliest memory of music, watching four women singing in a church in rural Arkansas. In 1981, Newton performed and recorded "Choir" and licensed all rights in the sound recording to ECM Records for $5000. The license covered only the sound recording, and it is undisputed that Newton retained all rights to the composition of "Choir." . . .

The defendants and appellees include the members of the rap and hip-hop group Beastie Boys, and their business associates. In 1992, Beastie Boys obtained a license from ECM Records to use portions of the sound recording of "Choir" in various renditions of their song "Pass the Mic" in exchange for a one-time fee of $1000. Beastie Boys did not obtain a license from Newton to use the underlying composition.

The portion of the composition at issue consists of three notes, C — D flat — C, sung over a background C note played on the flute. The score to "Choir" also indicates that the entire song should be played in a "largo/senza-misura" tempo, meaning "slowly/without-measure." The parties disagree about whether two additional elements appear in the score. First, Newton argues that the score contains an instruction that requires overblowing the background C note that is played on the flute. Second, Newton argues that multiphonics are part of the composition because they are necessarily created when a performer follows the instructions on the score to simultaneously play the flute note and sing the vocal notes. Because we review the district court's grant of summary judgment to the Beastie Boys, we must construe the evidence in Newton's favor. We therefore assume that these two elements are part of the "Choir" composition. . . .

The dispute between Newton and Beastie Boys centers around the copyright implications of the practice of sampling, a practice now common to many types of popular music. Sampling entails the incorporation of short segments of prior sound recordings into new recordings. The practice originated in Jamaica in the 1960s, when disc jockeys (DJs) used portable sound systems to mix segments of prior recordings into new mixes, which they would overlay with chanted or "scatted" vocals. *See* Robert M. Szymanski, *Audio Pastiche: Digital Sampling, Intermediate Copying, Fair Use*, 3 U.C.L.A. Ent. L. Rev. 271, 277 (Spring 1996). Sampling migrated to the United States and developed throughout the 1970s, using the analog technologies of the time. *Id.* The digital sampling involved here developed in the early 1980s with the advent of digital synthesizers having MIDI (Musical Instrument Digital Interface) keyboard controls. These digital instruments allowed artists digitally to manipulate and combine sampled sounds, expanding the range of possibilities for the use of pre-recorded music. Whereas analog devices limited artists to "scratching" vinyl records and "cutting" back and forth between different sound recordings, digital technology allowed artists to slow down, speed up, combine, and otherwise alter the samples. *See id.*

Pursuant to their license from ECM Records, Beastie Boys digitally sampled the opening six seconds of Newton's sound recording of "Choir." Beastie Boys repeated or "looped" this six-second sample as a background element throughout "Pass the Mic," so that it appears over forty times in various renditions of the song. In addition to the version of "Pass the Mic" released on their 1992 album, "Check Your Head," Beastie Boys included the "Choir" sample in two remixes, "Dub the Mic" and "Pass the Mic (Pt. 2, Skills to Pay the Bills)." It is unclear whether the sample was altered or manipulated, though Beastie Boys' sound engineer stated that alterations of tone, pitch, and rhythm are commonplace, and Newton maintains that the pitch was lowered slightly.

Newton filed the instant action in federal court on May 9, 2000, alleging violations of his copyright in the underlying composition. . . . The district court granted summary judgment in favor of Beastie Boys. . . . The district court held that the three-note segment of the "Choir" composition could not be copyrighted because, as a matter of law, it lacked the requisite originality. . . . The court also concluded that even if the segment were copyrightable, Beastie Boys' use of the work was de minimis and therefore not actionable. . . .

Whether Defendants' Use Was De Minimis

. . . Assuming that the sampled segment of the composition was sufficiently original to merit copyright protection, we nevertheless affirm on the ground that Beastie Boys' use was de minimis and therefore not actionable.

For an unauthorized use of a copyrighted work to be actionable, the use must be significant enough to constitute infringement. . . . This means that even where the fact of copying is conceded, no legal consequences will follow from that fact unless the copying is substantial. . . . The principle that trivial copying does not constitute actionable infringement has long been a part of copyright law. . . .

A leading case on de minimis infringement in our circuit is *Fisher v. Dees*, 794 F.2d 432 (9th Cir. 1986), where we observed that a use is de minimis only if the average audience would not recognize the appropriation. *See id.* at 434 n.2. This observation reflects the relationship between the de minimis maxim and the general test for substantial similarity, which also looks to the response of the average audience, or ordinary observer, to determine whether a use is infringing. . . . To say that a use is de minimis because no audience would recognize the appropriation is thus to say that the use is not sufficiently significant.

This case involves not only use of a composition, . . . but also use of a sound recording of a particular performance of that composition. Because the defendants were authorized to use the sound recording, our inquiry is confined to whether the unauthorized use of the composition itself was substantial enough to sustain an infringement claim. Therefore, we may consider only Beastie Boys' appropriation of the song's compositional elements and must remove from consideration all the elements unique to Newton's performance. Stated another way, we must "filter out" the licensed elements of the sound recording to get down to the unlicensed elements of the composition, as the composition is the sole basis for Newton's infringement claim. . . . *See Cavalier* [*v. Random House, Inc.*, 297 F.3d 815] at 822 [(9th Cir. 2002)]; *Apple Computer, Inc. v. Microsoft Corp.*, 35 F.3d 1435, 1446 (9th Cir. 1994).

In filtering out the unique performance elements from consideration, and separating them from those found in the composition, we find substantial assistance in the testimony of Newton's own experts. . . . Newton's experts . . . reveal the extent to which the sound recording of "Choir" is the product of Newton's highly developed performance techniques, rather than the result of a generic rendition of the composition. As a general matter, according to Newton's expert Dr. Christopher Dobrian, "[t]he contribution of the performer is often so great that s/he in fact provides as much musical content as the composer." This is particularly true with works like "Choir," given the improvisational nature of jazz performance and the minimal scoring of the composition. Indeed, as Newton's expert Dr. Oliver Wilson explained:

> [T]he copyrighted score of "Choir," as is the custom in scores written in the jazz tradition, does not contain indications for all of the musical subtleties that it is assumed the performer-composer of the work will make in the work's performance. The function of the score is more mnemonic in intention than prescriptive.

And it is clear that Newton goes beyond the score in his performance. For example, Dr. Dobrian declared that "Mr. Newton blows and sings in such a way as to emphasize the upper partials of the flute's complex harmonic tone, [although] such a modification of tone color is not explicitly requested in the score." Dr. Dobrian also concludes that Newton "uses breath control to modify the timbre of the sustained flute note rather extremely" and "uses portamento to glide expressively from one pitch to another in the vocal part." Dr. Dobrian concedes that these elements do not appear in the score, and that they are part of Newton's performance of the piece. . . .

. . . [R]egardless of whether the average audience might recognize the "Newton technique" at work in the sampled sound recording, those performance elements are beyond consideration in Newton's claim for infringement of his copyright in the underlying composition.

Once we have isolated the basis of Newton's infringement action — the "Choir" composition, devoid of the unique performance elements found only in the sound recording — we turn to the nub of our inquiry: whether Beastie Boys' unauthorized use of the composition, as opposed to their authorized use of the sound recording, was substantial enough to sustain an infringement action. . . . The practice of music sampling will often present cases where the degree of similarity is high. Indeed, unless the sample has been altered or digitally manipulated, it will be identical to the sampled portion of the original recording. Yet as Nimmer explains, "[if] the similarity is only as to nonessential matters, then a finding of no substantial similarity should result." 4 Nimmer §13.03[A][2], at 13-48; *cf. Warner Bros. v. Am. Broad. Cos.,* 720 F.2d 231, 242 (2d Cir. 1983). This reflects the principle that the substantiality requirement applies throughout the law of copyright, including cases of music sampling, even where there is a high degree of similarity.

The high degree of similarity between the works here (i.e., "Pass the Mic" and "Choir"), but the limited scope of the copying, place Newton's claim for infringement into the class of cases that allege what Nimmer refers to as "fragmented literal similarity." 4 Nimmer §13.03[A][2], at 13-45. Fragmented literal similarity exists where the defendant copies a portion of the plaintiff's work exactly or nearly exactly, without appropriating the work's overall essence or structure. *Id.* Because the degree of similarity is high in such cases, the dispositive question is whether the copying goes to trivial or substantial elements. Substantiality is measured by considering the qualitative and quantitative significance of the copied portion in relation to the plaintiff's work as a whole. . . . This focus on the sample's relation to the plaintiff's work as a whole embodies the fundamental question in any infringement action. . . . Courts also focus on the relationship to the plaintiff's work because a contrary rule that measured the significance of the copied segment in the defendant's work would allow an unscrupulous defendant to copy large or qualitatively significant portions of another's work and escape liability by burying them beneath non-infringing material in the defendant's own work, even where the average audience might recognize the appropriation. . . .

On the undisputed facts of this record, no reasonable juror could find the sampled portion of the composition to be a quantitatively or qualitatively significant portion of the composition as a whole. Quantitatively, the three-note sequence appears only once in Newton's composition. It is difficult to measure the precise relationship between this segment and the composition as a whole, because the score calls for between 180 and 270 seconds of improvisation. When played, however, the segment lasts six seconds and is roughly two percent of the four-and-a-half-minute "Choir" sound recording licensed by Beastie Boys. Qualitatively, this section of the composition is no more significant than any other section. Indeed, with the exception of two notes, the entirety of the scored portions of "Choir" consist of notes separated by whole and half-steps from their neighbors and is played with the same technique of singing and playing the flute simultaneously; the remainder of the composition calls for sections of improvisation that range between 90 and 180 seconds in length.

The Beastie Boys' expert, Dr. Lawrence Ferrara, concludes that the compositional elements of the sampled section do not represent the heart or the hook of the "Choir" composition, but rather are "simple, minimal and insignificant." . . . Newton has failed to offer any evidence, . . . to rebut Dr. Ferrara's testimony and to create a triable issue of fact on the key question, which is whether the sampled section is a qualitatively significant portion of the "Choir" composition as a whole. Instead, Newton's experts emphasize the uniqueness of the "Newton technique," which is found throughout the "Choir" composition and in Newton's other work. . . .

Because Newton conceded that "Choir" and "Pass the Mic" "are substantially dissimilar in concept and feel, that is, in [their] overall thrust and meaning" and failed to offer any evidence to rebut Dr. Ferrara's testimony that the sampled section is not a quantitatively or qualitatively significant portion of the "Choir" composition, the Beastie Boys are entitled to prevail on summary judgment. . . . [A]n average audience would not discern Newton's hand as a composer, apart from his talent as a performer, from Beastie Boys' use of the sample. The copying was not significant enough to constitute infringement. Beastie Boys' use of the "Choir" composition was de minimis. . . .

GRABER, J., dissenting: . . . As the majority observes, a use is de minimis only if an average audience would not recognize the appropriation. *Fisher v. Dees*, 794 F.2d 432, 434 n.2 (9th Cir. 1986). The majority is correct that James Newton's considerable skill adds many recognizable features to the performance sampled by Beastie Boys. Even after those features are "filtered out," however, the composition, standing alone, is distinctive enough for a fact-finder reasonably to conclude that an average audience would recognize the appropriation of the sampled segment and that Beastie Boys' use was therefore not de minimis.

Newton has presented evidence that the compositional elements of "Choir" are so compositionally distinct that a reasonable listener would recognize the sampled segment even if it were performed by the featured flautist of a middle school orchestra. It is useful to begin by observing that the majority's references to the sampled segment of "Choir" as a "3 note-sequence" are overly simplified. The sampled segment is actually a three-note sequence sung above a fingered held C note, for a total of four separate tones. Even passages with relatively few notes may be qualitatively significant. The opening melody of Beethoven's Fifth Symphony is relatively simple and features only four notes, but it certainly is compositionally distinctive and recognizable.

The majority, while citing the correct standard of review, fails fully to apply it. First, the majority usurps the function of the fact-finder by weighing the opinions of the various experts and emphasizing some parts of their testimony over others. . . . The majority also fails to interpret the evidence in Newton's favor when, for example, it asserts that Newton's experts failed to distinguish between the sound recording and the composition. . . . To the contrary, Newton presented expert evidence that the composition alone is distinctive and recognizable.

. . . Professor Wilson acknowledges that much of the distinctiveness of the sampled material is due to Newton's performance and that the copyrighted score does not fully convey the quality of the piece as performed. Nevertheless, Professor Wilson concludes that the score

> clearly indicates that the performer will simultaneously sing and finger specific pitches, gives a sense of the rhythm of the piece, and also provides the general structure of this section of the piece. Hence, in my opinion, the digital sample of the performance . . . is clearly a realization of the musical score filed with the copyright office.

. . . [The letter from Professor Christopher Dobrian] concludes:

> Applying traditional analysis to this brief excerpt from Newton's "Choir" — i.e., focusing solely on the notated pitches — a theorist could conclude (erroneously, in my opinion) that the excerpt contains an insignificant amount of information because it contains a simple "neighboring-tone" figure: C to D-flat and back to C. . . . If, on the other hand, one considers the special playing technique *described in* the score (holding one fingered note constant while singing the other pitches) and the resultant complex, expressive effect that results, it is clear that the "unique expression" of this excerpt is not solely in the pitch choices, but is actually in those particular pitches performed in that particular way on that instrument. These components in this particular combination are not found anywhere else in the notated music literature, and they are *unique and distinctive* in their sonic/musical result.

Professor Dobrian is not talking about Newton's performance of the sampled portion. Rather, he is speaking of the distinctiveness of the underlying composition. The "playing technique" is not a matter of personal performance, but is a built-in feature of the score itself. In essence, Dobrian is stating that *any* flautist's performance of the sampled segment would be distinctive and recognizable, because the score itself is distinctive and recognizable. . . .

The majority also asserts that Newton failed to offer evidence to rebut Beastie Boys' expert on the question whether the sampled section of "Choir" is qualitatively significant. . . . Again, the majority improperly discounts, or improperly interprets, Dr. Dobrian's unequivocal description of the sampled passage: "These components in this particular combination are not found anywhere else in the notated music literature, and they are unique and distinctive in their sonic/musical result." A fact-finder would be entitled to find either that the sampled passage is trivial and trite (Beastie Boys' expert) or, instead, that it is "unique and distinctive" in the musical literature (Newton's expert).

Because Newton has presented evidence establishing that reasonable ears differ over the qualitative significance of the composition of the sampled material, summary judgment is inappropriate in this case. . . .

Bridgeport Music, Inc. v. Dimension Films
410 F.3d 792 (6th Cir. 2005)

GUY, J.: . . . This action arises out of the use of a sample from the composition and sound recording "Get Off Your Ass and Jam" ("Get Off") in the rap song "100 Miles and Runnin" ("100 Miles"), which was included in the sound track of the movie *I Got the Hook Up*

(*Hook Up*). Specifically, [plaintiff] Westbound [Records, Inc.] appeals from the district court's decision to grant summary judgment to defendant on the grounds that the alleged infringement was *de minimis*. . . .

I. . . .

Bridgeport and Westbound claim to own the musical composition and sound recording copyrights in "Get Off Your Ass and Jam" by George Clinton, Jr. and the Funkadelics. We assume, as did the district court, that plaintiffs would be able to establish ownership in the copyrights they claim. There seems to be no dispute either that "Get Off" was digitally sampled or that the recording "100 Miles" was included on the sound track of *I Got the Hook Up*. Defendant No Limit Films, in conjunction with Priority Records, released the movie to theaters on May 27, 1998. The movie was apparently also released on VHS, DVD, and cable television. Fatal to Bridgeport's claims of infringement [of the musical work copyright] was the Release and Agreement it entered into with two of the original owners of the composition "100 Miles," . . . granting a sample use license. . . . Finding that No Limit Films had previously been granted an oral synchronization license to use the composition "100 Miles" in the sound track of *Hook Up*, the district court concluded Bridgeport's claims against No Limit Films were barred by the unambiguous terms of the Release and Agreement. . . .

Westbound's claims are for infringement of the sound recording "Get Off." . . . Because defendant does not deny it, we assume that the sound track of *Hook Up* used portions of "100 Miles" that included the allegedly infringing sample from "Get Off." The recording "Get Off" opens with a three-note combination solo guitar "riff" that lasts four seconds. According to one of plaintiffs' experts, Randy Kling, the recording "100 Miles" contains a sample from that guitar solo. Specifically, a two-second sample from the guitar solo was copied, the pitch was lowered, and the copied piece was "looped" and extended to 16 beats. Kling states that this sample appears in the sound recording "100 Miles" in five places; specifically, at 0:49, 1:52, 2:29, 3:20 and 3:46. By the district court's estimation, each looped segment lasted approximately 7 seconds. As for the segment copied from "Get Off," the district court described it as follows:

> The portion of the song at issue here is an arpeggiated chord — that is, three notes that, if struck together, comprise a chord but instead are played one at a time in very quick succession — that is repeated several times at the opening of "Get Off." The arpeggiated chord is played on an unaccompanied electric guitar. The rapidity of the notes and the way they are played produce a high-pitched, whirling sound that captures the listener's attention and creates anticipation of what is to follow.

Bridgeport, 230 F. Supp. 2d at 839. . . .

II. . . .

. . . After listening to the copied segment, the sample, and both songs, the district court found that no reasonable juror, even one familiar with the works of George Clinton, would recognize the source of the sample without having been told of its source. This finding, coupled with findings concerning the quantitatively small amount of copying involved and the lack of qualitative similarity between the works, led the district court to conclude that Westbound could not prevail on its claims for copyright infringement of the sound recording. . . .

Westbound does not challenge the district court's characterization of either the segment copied from "Get Off" or the sample that appears in "100 Miles." . . . The heart of Westbound's arguments is the claim that no substantial similarity or *de minimis* inquiry should be undertaken at all when the defendant has not disputed that it digitally sampled a copyrighted sound recording. We agree. . . .

B.   *Analysis* . . .

Section 114(b) provides that "[t]he exclusive right of the owner of copyright in a sound recording under clause (2) of section 106 is limited to the right to prepare a derivative work in which the actual sounds fixed in the sound recording are rearranged, remixed, or otherwise altered in sequence or quality." Further, the rights of sound recording copyright holders under clauses (1) and (2) of section 106 "do not extend to the making or duplication of another sound recording that consists *entirely* of an independent fixation of other sounds, even though such sounds imitate or simulate those in the copyrighted sounds recording." 17 U.S.C. §114(b) (emphasis added). The significance of this provision is amplified by the fact that the Copyright Act of 1976 added the word "entirely" to this language. . . . In other words, a sound recording owner has the exclusive right to "sample" his own recording. We find much to recommend this interpretation. . . .

To begin with, there is ease of enforcement. Get a license or do not sample. We do not see this as stifling creativity in any significant way. It must be remembered that if an artist wants to incorporate a "riff" from another work in his or her recording, he is free to duplicate the sound of that "riff" in the studio. Second, the market will control the license price and keep it within bounds. . . . The sound recording copyright holder cannot exact a license fee greater than what it would cost the person seeking the license to just duplicate the sample in the course of making the new recording. Third, sampling is never accidental. It is not like the case of a composer who has a melody in his head, perhaps not even realizing that the reason he hears this melody is that it is the work of another which he had heard before. When you sample a sound recording you know you are taking another's work product.

This analysis admittedly raises the question of why one should, without infringing, be able to take three notes from a musical composition, for example, but not three notes by way of sampling from a sound recording. . . . Our first answer to this question is what we have earlier indicated. We think this result is dictated by the applicable statute. Second, even when a small part of a sound recording is sampled, the part taken is something of value. . . . No further proof of that is necessary than the fact that the producer of the record or the artist on the record intentionally sampled because it would (1) save costs, or (2) add something to the new recording, or (3) both. For the sound recording copyright holder, it is not the "song" but the sounds that are fixed in the medium of his choice. When those sounds are sampled they are taken directly from that fixed medium. It is a physical taking rather than an intellectual one.

This case also illustrates the kind of mental, musicological, and technological gymnastics that would have to be employed if one were to adopt a *de minimis* or substantial similarity analysis. . . . We would want to emphasize, however, that considerations of judicial economy are not what drives this opinion. If any consideration of economy is involved it is that of the music industry. As this case and other companion cases make clear, it would appear to be cheaper to license than to litigate. . . .

. . . The record companies and performing artists are not all of one mind, however, since in many instances, today's sampler is tomorrow's samplee. The incidence of "live and let live" has been relatively high, which explains why so many instances of sampling go unprotested and why so many sampling controversies have been settled.

. . . [T]o pursue further the subject of stifling creativity, many artists and record companies have sought licenses as a matter of course. . . . Since there is no record of those instances of sampling that either go unnoticed or are ignored, one cannot come up with precise figures, but it is clear that a significant number of persons and companies have elected to go the licensing route. Also there is a large body of pre-1972 sound recordings that is not subject to federal copyright protection. . . . Additionally, just as many artists and companies choose to sample and take their chances, it is likely that will continue to be the case.

. . . [T]he record industry, including the recording artists, has the ability and know-how to work out guidelines, including a fixed schedule of license fees, if they so choose. . . .

. . . Since the district judge found no infringement, there was no necessity to consider the affirmative defense of "fair use." On remand, the trial judge is free to consider this defense and we express no opinion on its applicability to these facts. . . .

NOTES AND QUESTIONS

1. Do you agree with the majority in *Newton* that the use of the plaintiff's score was de minimis? What do you think of the implication from *Newton* that what was copied from the plaintiff's work is indistinguishable to an average audience? Isn't the point of sampling to copy portions that at least some members of an audience *will* recognize?

2. Is the *Newton* court's explicit recognition of a "de minimis use" shelter for sampling desirable? Why, or why not? Once copying is admitted, how much copying is needed to meet the improper appropriation requirement in a "fragmented literal similarity" analysis? Does the *Newton* court's opinion help to define the line between permissible copying and improper appropriation?

3. While the sound recording copyright owner's reproduction right is narrower than the reproduction right for musical works because it does not extend to sound alikes, under the *Bridgeport* approach it may also be significantly broader. Do you agree with the *Bridgeport* court's interpretation of §114(b)? In the statutory structure, is §114 meant to limit or expand the rights granted in §106?

4. The *Bridgeport* court concluded that its bright-line rule, "[g]et a license or do not sample," was also sound policy. Do you agree? In deciding this question, would it be important to understand why recording artists sample when, as the court notes, they are free to make sound alike recordings? Consider the following excerpt:

> Cultural judgments about borrowing, repetition and originality are central to understanding legal evaluations of both sampling and hip hop. Repetition expressed through sampling and looping has been, for much of the history of hip hop, an inherent part of what makes hip hop music identifiably hip hop. Consequently, the question of whether and how sampling should be permitted is in some measure an inquiry about how and to what extent hip hop can and should continue to exist as a musical form. Copyright standards, particularly in the music area, must have greater flexibility to accommodate varying styles and types of musical production, whether based on an African American aesthetic of repetition and revision, a postmodern style, transformative imitation and borrowing in the manner of Handel, allusion as practiced by Brahms or another aesthetic that fails to conform to the Romantic author ideal that has to this point been integral to copyright.
>
> Musical borrowing is not necessarily antithetical to originality or creativity. The conceptions of creativity and originality that pervade copyright discussions are incomplete or inaccurate models of actual musical production, particularly the collaborative aspects of musical practice evident in borrowing. Similarly, views of past musical composition should be tempered with a recognition of the operation of invented traditions and cultural ideals that play a powerful role in shaping both representations and contemporary beliefs and attitudes.

Olufunmilayo B. Arewa, *From J.C. Bach to Hip Hop: Musical Borrowing, Copyright, and Cultural Context*, 84 N.C. L. Rev. 547, 630-31 (2006); *see also* K.J. Greene, *Copyright, Culture & Black Music: A Legacy of Unequal Protection*, 21 Hastings Comm. & Ent. L.J. 339 (1999) (exploring how African-American music artists, as a group, were routinely deprived of copyright protection). Should reform in the standards for permissible borrowing be developed by Congress or by the courts?

5. Arguably, the problem in *Newton* was that it was impossible to use the licensed sound recording without also using the composition. Does the de minimis use rule in effect allow a royalty-free license for underlying musical works under limited circumstances? If so, why shouldn't the same rule apply when the underlying musical work is licensed but the sound recording is not, as in *Bridgeport*?

6. The *Bridgeport* court noted that "a large body of pre-1972 sound recordings . . . is not subject to federal copyright protection." Recall that Congress did not extend federal copyright protection to sound recordings until 1971. Section 301(c) of the Act, which we discuss in more detail in Chapter 10, expressly preserves state law protection for sound recordings fixed before February 15, 1972, the effective date of the Sound Recording Amendment. Therefore, these recordings are not necessarily available for sampling. *See Capitol Records, Inc. v. Naxos of America, Inc.*, 372 F.3d 471 (2d Cir. 2004) (holding that pre-1972 recordings that had passed into the public domain in their country of origin, Britain, were not necessarily unprotected in the U.S., and that their copyright status depended on New York state law).

7. It is important to remember that while a sound alike may be free from claims of copyright infringement of the sound recording copyright, other claims may exist. *See, e.g., Waits v. Frito-Lay, Inc.*, 978 F.2d 1093, 1098 (9th Cir. 1992) (imitation of singer's voice in radio commercial violated singer's right of publicity under California law), *cert. denied*, 506 U.S. 1080 (1993); *Midler v. Ford Motor Co.*, 849 F.2d 460, 461 (9th Cir. 1988) (use in television car commercial of sound alike rendition of song Bette Midler had recorded violated her right of publicity under California law), *cert. denied*, 503 U.S. 951 (1992). We consider copyright preemption challenges to right of publicity actions in Chapter 10.

d. The Audio Home Recording Act

In 1992, after industry negotiation, Congress enacted the Audio Home Recording Act (AHRA) to address digital audio tape (DAT) technology. The AHRA itself is interesting largely for historical purposes, because DAT technology never became widely used by individuals. However, it is important to study the AHRA approach to DAT technology because it represents a different way of balancing the interests of the various stakeholders when new technology changes the copyright landscape. Codified in Chapter 10 of Title 17, the AHRA contains three key elements.

First, manufacturers of digital audio recorders and tapes agreed to embed in the technology a Serial Copy Management System (SCMS) that allows first-generation copies to be created but prevents subsequent-generation copying. This mandated copy-protection technology was an attempt to reduce the attractiveness of DAT. Unlike prior analog tapes, DAT copies did not degrade in quality over multiple generations, and the music industry worried that the technology would facilitate widespread infringement. The AHRA also includes prohibitions on circumventing the SCMS and on marketing technology designed to circumvent the SCMS.

The second key element of the AHRA is a royalty-pooling scheme that requires manufacturers to pay a royalty of 2 percent of the transfer price for each digital audio recording device (DARD) sold and a royalty of 3 percent for each unit of digital audio recording media sold.

These royalties must be paid regardless of the manner in which the consumer uses the device or tapes. Thus, the price a consumer pays for a DAT includes the royalty fee even if the consumer plans to use the tape to record birds outside her window. (Significantly, the SCMS technology will prevent her from making anything other than first-generation copies of her recording.) These royalties are then pooled and subsequently divided among copyright owners of musical works, copyright owners of sound recordings, and featured recording artists, with a small percentage of the fund paid to non-featured musicians and vocalists. The mechanical license of §115, described above, represents one method for balancing the competing interests in the copyright landscape as technology evolves. The royalty pool of the AHRA represents another approach. Perhaps unfortunately, it never became possible to determine if the approach was a successful one. In 1994, the first royalty pool generated by the AHRA totaled just under $450,000. As DAT technology began its push into homes, home computing and the Internet burst onto the scene as a preferred technology. What remains of the DAT market are primarily devices made for professional use, which are statutorily exempt from both the SCMS and the royalty pooling scheme. For the regulations implementing the royalty pooling system, see 37 C.F.R. §§201.27-201.28 (2005).

The final key element of the AHRA is an exemption from copyright infringement liability for consumers engaged in certain activities, as well as for manufacturers of certain devices and media. Section 1008 provides:

> No action may be brought under this title alleging infringement of copyright based on the manufacture, importation, or distribution of a digital audio recording device, a digital audio recording medium, an analog recording device, or an analog recording medium, or based on the noncommercial use by a consumer of such a device or medium for making digital musical recordings or analog musical recordings.

17 U.S.C. §1008. Before the AHRA, whether individual copying of an album for personal use (for example, on cassette tape) constituted an infringement was not a settled issue. The recording industry's position was that such copies were infringing, while others asserted that fair use permitted such noncommercial copying. The legislative history of the Sound Recording Amendment of 1971 included a statement that granting copyright protection for sound recordings was not intended "to restrain the home recording, from broadcast or from tapes or records, of recorded performances, where home recording is for private use and with no purpose of reproducing or otherwise capitalizing commercially on it." H.R. Rep. No. 487, 92d Cong., 1st Sess. 7 (1971), *reprinted in* 1971 U.S.C.C.A.N. 1566, 1572. No case had ever directly addressed the issue. Section 1008 made an exemption explicit.

Considering that the AHRA is concerned with digital reproduction, it is perhaps surprising that the Act specifically exempted general purpose computers from its coverage. During the negotiations leading up to the AHRA, the computer industry made clear that it would not agree to a law that would require computers to incorporate the SCMS or the payment of royalties on computers and disks. If the computer industry opposed the law, the other interested parties knew passage was unlikely. The quickest route to passage of the law was to exempt the entire computer industry from its coverage. Congress drafted a set of nested definitions for the terms "digital music recording" and "digital audio recording device" that had the effect of excluding computers from the definitions of the devices covered by the AHRA.

While Congress clearly intended to exempt general purpose computers from the SCMS requirement and the royalty payments, questions remain concerning §1008's exemption for personal copies. Does this exemption reach digital copies made using computers?

The Ninth Circuit has twice addressed this issue, with varying results. In *Recording Industry Ass'n of America v. Diamond Multimedia Systems, Inc.*, 180 F.3d 1072, 1076 (9th Cir. 1999), the court concluded that one of the first handheld MP3 players, the Rio, was not subject to the AHRA and thus did not have to contain the SMCS or pay the required royalty. The court reasoned that because the Rio could "only make copies from a computer hard drive, it was not a digital audio recording device" as defined by the statute. *Id*. at 1081. After closely parsing the AHRA's definitions, the court cited the AHRA's legislative history to support its holding:

> [T]he Rio's operation is entirely consistent with the [AHRA's] main purpose — the facilitation of personal use. As the Senate Report explains, "[t]he purpose of [the Act] is to ensure the right of consumers to make analog or digital audio recordings of copyrighted music for their *private, noncommercial use*." S. Rep. 102-294, at *86 (emphasis added). The Act does so through its home taping exemption, *see* 17 U.S.C. §1008, which "protects all noncommercial copying by consumers of digital and analog musical recordings," H.R. Rep. 102-873(I), at *59. The Rio merely makes copies in order to render portable, or "space-shift," those files that already reside on a user's hard drive. *Cf. Sony Corp. of America v. Universal City Studios*, 464 U.S. 417 (1984) (holding that "time-shifting" of copyrighted television shows with VCR's constitutes fair use under the Copyright Act, and thus is not an infringement). Such copying is paradigmatic noncommercial personal use entirely consistent with the purposes of the Act.

Id. at 1079.

The second case in which the Ninth Circuit addressed the provisions of the AHRA involved the file-sharing software known as Napster. This time, however, the court was not as enamored with the AHRA's personal use exemption:

> Napster contends that MP3 file exchange is the type of "noncommercial use" protected from infringement actions by the statute. Napster asserts it cannot be secondarily liable for users' non-actionable exchange of copyrighted musical recordings. The district court rejected Napster's argument, stating that the Audio Home Recording Act is "irrelevant" to the action because: (1) plaintiffs did not bring claims under the Audio Home Recording Act; and (2) the Audio Home Recording Act does not cover the downloading of MP3 files.
>
> We agree with the district court that the Audio Home Recording Act does not cover the downloading of MP3 files to computer hard drives. First, [the court agreed with the holding in *Diamond Multimedia* above that the Act's definition of "digital audio recording devices" does not encompass computers]. Second, notwithstanding Napster's claim that computers are "digital audio recording devices," computers do not make "digital music recordings" as defined by the Audio Home Recording Act. *Id*. at 1077 (citing S. Rep. 102-294) ("There are simply no grounds in either the plain language of the definition or in the legislative history for interpreting the term 'digital musical recording' to include songs fixed on computer hard drives.").

A&M Records, Inc. v. Napster, Inc., 239 F.3d 1004, 1024-25 (9th Cir. 2001).

If computers and personal digital music players do not qualify as DARDs, it would appear that the AHRA's provision for freedom from liability for copyright infringement does not have lasting significance in the era of digital copying.

NOTES AND QUESTIONS

1. Compulsory licensing is one approach to balancing the competing interests of copyright owners and those who desire to use copyrighted works in certain ways. With

compulsory licensing, individual copyright owners are compensated directly for the use of their works, albeit at a rate set either by statute or by some statutorily defined method. Royalty pooling, on the other hand, is not a direct payment of royalties to the copyright owners of the works used. Rather, as the name implies, the pool of royalty payments is divided in an attempt at a rough estimate of the level of use of any particular copyrighted work. Consider the online distribution of music. Does either a compulsory license or a royalty pooling scheme seem appropriate? How would such a license fee or royalty payment be computed, and on whom (or what) would it be levied? Personal computers? CD burners and recording media? Internet service contracts?

2. The U.S. is not alone in experimenting with royalty pools. France, for example, imposes a royalty on the sale of all copying media, such as blank audio and video tapes. The royalty, called a levy, is based on the running time of the medium with an administrative commission determining which media require payment of the levy. The funds collected as a result of this levy are distributed by allotting 25 percent to a cultural fund meant to sponsor creative activities, live performances, and training for artists, and dividing the remaining 75 percent among authors, producers, and performers. Many other countries have imposed royalties on blank media. *See* Glynn S. Lunney Jr., *The Death of Copyright: Digital Technology, Private Copying, and the Digital Millennium Copyright Act*, 87 Va. L. Rev. 813, 852-58 (2001).

3. The EU's 2001 directive on copyright harmonization authorizes member countries to provide exceptions and limitations to the reproduction right "in respect of reproductions on any medium made by a natural person for private use and for ends that are neither directly nor indirectly commercial," but only "on condition that the rightholders receive fair compensation." Directive 2001/29/EC of the European Parliament and of the Council of 22 May 2001 on the harmonisation of copyright and related rights in the Information Society, 2001 O.J. (L. 167) 10, art. 5(2)(b). Do you think that it is possible to create an exception for downloaded digital music files under this provision? How would fair compensation be achieved? Would a royalty pooling arrangement suffice?

4. Should the AHRA's exemption from infringement liability be expressly extended to cover MP3 or other digital file formats and personal computers?

5. XM, a licensed satellite radio broadcaster, offered a new service to its subscribers called "XM+MP3." The service was facilitated by special devices that made it possible for subscribers to receive XM radio broadcasts, make digital downloads for private personal use, store MP3 files that subscribers already own or had acquired from a third party, and store up to 50 hours of broadcast music (about 1,000 songs) for unlimited replay so long as the users maintained a subscription with XM. Users of the service could also transfer music files from their personal computer onto the XM+MP3 player to create indexed personal libraries of sound recordings and personalized playlists. In a lawsuit filed against XM by major record labels, XM asserted that it was statutorily immune from suit for copyright infringement based on the AHRA. The parties disputed whether the XM+MP3 players were DARDs under the definitions contained in the AHRA. According to the court, however, even if the devices qualified as DARDs, the AHRA only offers immunity for actions based on the distribution of such devices and not "absolute immunity" from copyright litigation. *Atlantic Recording Corp. v. XM Satellite Radio*, 81 U.S.P.Q.2d 1407, 1411 (S.D.N.Y. 2007). A license to broadcast music is not "a wholesale, blanket protection for any and all conduct." *Id.* at 1412. The court noted that the allegations by the plaintiffs were not based on the XM+MP3 players, but on the fact that XM was acting as an unauthorized content deliverer to those devices. *See id.* Do you agree with the court's interpretation of the AHRA? Is there any way XM can offer these services without violating the Copyright Act? What other defenses might you raise on behalf of XM?

3.   Public Performance

a.   Musical Works, ASCAP, and BMI

Section 106 grants copyright owners of musical works, but not sound recordings, a general right to perform the work publicly. (In 1995 Congress granted copyright owners of sound recordings a more limited public performance right, explored in Section G.3.b, *infra*.) While the public performance right was first granted in 1897, it was not until almost 20 years later that this right began to have significant revenue potential. The problem concerned transaction costs: How were all of the different copyright owners realistically going to be able to detect and collect royalties for each public performance of their works in restaurants, dance halls, and theaters?

To solve the transaction cost problem, a group of nine music business luminaries, headed by attorney Nathan Burkan, established the American Society of Composers, Authors, and Publishers in 1913. After its successful litigation of *Herbert v. Shanley*, 242 U.S. 591 (1917), see page 412 *supra*, which established that licenses were needed, ASCAP began the business of collective licensing. By bringing together thousands of musical works and offering to license them under a blanket license agreement, ASCAP significantly reduced the transaction costs involved in complying with the requirements of the Copyright Act. Today, a license from ASCAP will allow a business to publicly perform all of the musical works in ASCAP's catalog. In 2010, this catalog contained over 8.5 million copyrighted works. Payments made by ASCAP are split 50/50 between the songwriter and the music publisher. Different licenses are available from ASCAP depending on the nature of the business. For example, ASCAP has license agreements for restaurants, dance schools, bowling alleys, festivals, private clubs, funeral establishments, and music on hold, as well as licenses covering the performance of musical works through web sites. More information about ASCAP, its licenses, and its operations can be found on its web site, *www.ascap.com*.

As radio increased in popularity during the 1930s, ASCAP initially established that music performed on the radio was for profit and for the public; thus, the radio stations needed authorization from the copyright owners of the musical works they played, which, conveniently, could be obtained through ASCAP. In 1939, after ASCAP began raising its fees considerably, radio broadcasters formed their own collective rights organization (CRO), Broadcast Music, Inc. (BMI). Some of ASCAP's less distinguished members had developed a general sense that ASCAP's distribution of royalty payments was unjust, and agreed to join the new organization. However, BMI managed to lure away only one major music publisher, and its signing of new and less established artists was accomplished mainly through the use of advance payments against future royalties. Nonetheless, on January 1, 1941, radio stations began a boycott of ASCAP music, instead broadcasting almost exclusively Latin music, which ASCAP had thus far ignored. ASCAP was forced to the bargaining table, and signed a new deal with the radio broadcasters in October 1941. After establishing a foothold in Latin music, BMI expanded its representation. Today, BMI, in affiliation with foreign performing rights organizations, represents the copyright holders of nearly 6.5 million musical works. More information about BMI can be found at *www.bmi.com*. Most songwriters and music publishers have entered into agreements with ASCAP, BMI, or SESAC, the third CRO, established in 1930 and headquartered in Nashville, Tennessee. Look at the copyright information accompanying your favorite CDs or DPDs to determine which entity you would need to contact if you wanted to publicly perform the musical works recorded on them, either by singing them yourself or by playing the recorded version.

Over the years, ASCAP's and BMI's practice of pooling thousands of copyrights and then offering a blanket license to publicly perform those works on an all-or-nothing basis has raised claims of antitrust violations. Cases filed in the 1940s and 1950s by the Justice Department's Antitrust Division resulted in consent decrees that continue to govern aspects of the operations of both ASCAP and BMI. One of the requirements of those consent decrees is that a potential licensee may apply to a federal court for a binding determination of "reasonable fees" in the event that the licensee and the CRO cannot come to an agreement on the fee to be paid.

Musical works can be performed by a variety of means, including live performances and the playing of pre-recorded music. Jukeboxes, referred to in the 1976 Copyright Act as "coin-operated phonorecord players," were once an extremely popular means of playing music in an establishment in no small part because of an exemption from the musical work public performance right under the 1909 Act. Beginning in the 1920s, music publishers repeatedly attempted to eliminate this exemption. Jukebox operators argued that the royalties received because of the mechanical reproductions used by jukeboxes were more than sufficient compensation for the copyright owners. Not until the revisions that led to the 1976 Act was the jukebox exemption finally eliminated. At one point, the dispute between music publishers and jukebox operators threatened to hold up the entire revision process. Instead, Congress and the Copyright Office urged a compromise that was finally accepted. By now, you should recognize that a "compromise" in the Copyright Act is likely to be a compulsory license. That was the case with jukeboxes. Codified in §116, this compulsory license permitted operators of jukeboxes to engage in public performances of copyrighted musical works so long as they paid a set fee and attached a certificate to the jukebox. The annual fee was originally $8 per jukebox. It rose to $50 in 1984, with further cost-of-living adjustments beginning in 1987.

The compulsory license for jukeboxes was never a great success. In 1988, the Copyright Office concluded that two-thirds of jukeboxes were unlicensed. Additionally, many viewed subjecting the public performance right to a compulsory license as inconsistent with the Berne Convention. Thus, the Berne Convention Implementation Act of 1988 (BCIA) encouraged industry negotiation and agreement, with compulsory licensing available only if an agreement were not reached. Following the BCIA, ASCAP, BMI, and SESAC established the Jukebox Licensing Office, a joint venture that allows "one-stop shopping" for jukebox licenses authorizing public performances on jukeboxes of all songs in the ASCAP, BMI, and SESAC repertoires.

NOTES AND QUESTIONS

1. Review Question 1, page 441 *supra*. If Adam Lambert wants permission to publicly perform his version of "Mad World," from whom must he obtain permission? If a third party wants permission to publicly perform Lambert's recording of "Mad World," from whom must that party obtain permission?

2. As discussed above, streaming music over the Internet does not constitute a digital phonorecord delivery and thus is not covered by the §115 mechanical license. *See* Note 4, page 442, *supra*. Web streaming is, instead, a public performance requiring authorization for both the musical work and sound recording copyrights. ASCAP, BMI, and SESAC offer webcasting licenses that authorize the public performance of the musical works in their respective catalogs. In some circumstances, rights to publicly perform the sound recordings must be negotiated separately; those licenses are discussed below.

When someone downloads a digital copy of a song over the Internet, should it be considered a public performance as well as a reproduction? Recall that the definition of public performance includes "to transmit or otherwise communicate a performance . . . to the public, by means of any device or process, whether the members of the public capable of receiving the performance or display receive it in the same place or in separate places and at the same time or at different times." 17 U.S.C. §101. Does it matter if the receiving computer is set up to automatically play the downloaded song? In *United States v. ASCAP*, 485 F. Supp. 2d 438 (S.D.N.Y. 2008), the court expressly rejected ASCAP's argument that downloading constitutes a public performance, instead characterizing such activity as a reproduction. The court concluded that "in light of the distinct classification and treatment of performances and reproductions under the Act . . . Congress did not intend the two uses to overlap to the extent proposed by ASCAP. . . ." *Id.* at 447. Should the result change if the DPD is a ringtone delivered to a mobile phone, and the individual then programs the phone to play the ringtone whenever a call is received? *See In re Application of Cellco Partnership*, 663 F. Supp. 2d 363 (S.D.N.Y. 2009) (rejecting ASCAP's claims that the download of a ringtone to a cell phone is a public performance and holding that, in general, if the playing of a ringtone on a cell phone when a phone call is received constitutes a public performances, it is exempted by the §110(4) limitation for nonprofit performances).

3. Unlike compulsory licenses and royalty pooling, CROs are not the result of any congressional action. Which is the better approach? Compulsory licenses reduce transaction costs by setting the terms of the agreement and by providing administrative support in the form of record keeping, royalty collection, and distribution. CROs also reduce transaction costs, but do so in a different way.

> In a CRO, knowledgeable industry participants set the rules of exchange. These rules are not likely to be uniform, one-size-fits-all terms as in a statutory compulsory license; they often vary according to the broad features of the rights. Individual works covered by discrete [intellectual property rights] are assigned to categories based on the members' knowledge and experience. Through this expert tailoring, CROs produce an intermediate level of contract detail, reflecting not only collective industry expertise but also the need for efficiency in carrying out a high volume of transactions.
>
> An important component of expert tailoring, then, is the use of royalty rates as set by experts. But the statutory compulsory licenses often begin with rational royalty rates as well. What separates private CROs from compulsory licensing schemes is that the former have proven to be more flexible over time. ASCAP, for example, frequently adjusts the rates it charges radio and television stations. Statutes, on the other hand, are difficult to change. Because interested parties can often spend enough to veto a change in legislation, compulsory licenses in the [intellectual property rights] field are subject to "legislative lock-in." CROs avoid this problem.

Robert P. Merges, *Contracting into Liability Rules: Intellectual Property Rights and Collective Rights Organizations*, 84 Cal. L. Rev. 1293, 1295-96 (1996). While legislative lock-in is certainly a problem for statutorily established rights, the lock-in associated with licensing rates has been tempered through the use of panels of copyright royalty judges to periodically revise rates. Do these rate revisions affect your evaluation of Professor Merges' argument?

4. CROs can reset the rates they charge to whatever the market will accept. When the market power of these organizations becomes too large, their activities may come under the scrutiny of antitrust regulators, as ASCAP's and BMI's did. Absent government intervention, a collective action problem exists for potential licensees. Is the collective action problem as significant as the legislative lock-in problem associated with compulsory licensing? When government antitrust regulators intervene, are we merely trading one form of government market intervention (i.e., compulsory licensing) for another (i.e., antitrust regulation)?

b. Section 110 Limitations Revisited

While much of the contemporary domestic debate surrounding music copyright issues has involved digital music services, a different kind of debate involving traditional radio and television broadcasts took center stage internationally. Recall from Section F, *supra*, that §110 contains many different exemptions to the public performance rights of copyright owners, several of which apply to musical work copyright owners.

Before 1998, §110(5) provided an exemption from liability for public performances of all types of works when those performances consisted of turning on a publicly available broadcast (e.g., radio or television) using equipment typically used in a home. This exemption, sometimes referred to as the "homestyle" exemption, had been the subject of many court opinions attempting to define which businesses could rely on this exemption. Those opinions often focused not only on the type of equipment used, but also on the number of speakers and the physical size of the establishment, despite no mention of these factors in the statute.

In 1998, Congress passed the Fairness in Music Licensing Act (FIMLA), Pub. L. No. 105-298, 112 Stat. 2830, title II. The FIMLA created, for the first time, bright-line requirements concerning square footage and equipment type for businesses to be able to play nondramatic musical works by turning on the radio or television without having to pay a license fee. The National Restaurant Association and the National Federation of Independent Businesses strongly supported the passage of this Act. Not surprisingly, ASCAP and BMI vehemently opposed what they viewed as a significant expansion of the homestyle exemption. The FIMLA passed as part of a bill that increased the duration of all copyrights by 20 years — the Sonny Bono Copyright Term Extension Act, discussed in Chapter 3. Many in Congress expressed the view that the FIMLA balanced out the lengthening of copyright duration by giving small businesses a slight break from having to pay license fees when they wanted to play the radio. Additionally, because the exemption created by the FIMLA only applies to *licensed* radio and television broadcasts of musical works, a royalty already has been paid to the copyright owner for the broadcast.

The FIMLA amended §110(5), but retained the homestyle exemption as subsection (A). In simple terms, the exemption that existed before the FIMLA, now codified at §110(5)(A), permits anyone to turn on the radio or television in a public place so long as three conditions are met: (1) the receiving device is of a kind commonly used in private homes; (2) no direct charge is made to see or hear the transmission; and (3) the transmission is not further transmitted to the public. This exemption ostensibly applies to all categories of works.

The FIMLA also added a new exemption, §110(5)(B), which applies only to nondramatic musical works. Small business establishments — those of less than 2,000 square feet (or less than 3,750 square feet if the business is a food service or drinking establishment) — can use any kind of equipment and stay within the bounds of the exemption. Establishments that exceed these square footage limits may not have more than a total of six loudspeakers and may have no more than four loudspeakers in any one room or adjoining outdoor space. If the business also communicates a visual portion of the work, the business must have no more than four audiovisual devices, such as television sets, and no more than one such device in any one room. Additionally, the screen size for these televisions sets must not exceed a diagonal width of 55 inches. 17 U.S.C. §110(5)(B)(i)(II) & (ii)(II). The FIMLA also allows a business to challenge the proposed rate charged by a CRO such as ASCAP or BMI in the business's local federal court rather than the Rate Court in New York, which administers the ASCAP and BMI consent decrees.

Shortly after the passage of the FIMLA, the EU commenced sanction proceedings against the U.S. before the WTO, asserting that both exemptions in §110(5) violated the TRIPS

Agreement. This was the first time that the U.S. had been accused of violating its TRIPS obligations. The U.S. argued that Article 13 of TRIPS permitted the §110(5) exemptions. As you already know, Article 13 allows countries to adopt exceptions to the rights of copyright owners so long as they meet the three-step test discussed on page 435 *supra*. Permissible exceptions are limited to "certain special cases which do not conflict with a normal exploitation of the work and do not unreasonably prejudice the legitimate interests of the right holder." In July 2000, the WTO dispute settlement body (DSB) held that the §110(5)(B) exemption codified by the FIMLA violated the TRIPS Agreement.

The DSB determined that the §110(5)(B) exemption was not limited to "certain special cases" because, while it had a specific policy objective, it exempted a majority of the users that were specifically intended to be covered by the minimum performance rights required by Article 11bis. The DSB also concluded that the exemption contained in §110(5)(B) conflicted with "normal exploitation" of copyrighted musical works. Concerning the third element required for an exemption to meet the three-step test of Article 13, the DSB focused on the economic interests of the copyright owners and held that "prejudice to the legitimate interest of right holders reaches an unreasonable level if an exception or limitation causes or has the potential to cause an unreasonable loss of income to the copyright owner." United States — Section 110(5) of the US Copyright Act, WT/DS160/R (15 June 2000), ¶6.229. The DSB found that the §110(5)(B) exemptions would unreasonably prejudice the legitimate interests of copyright owners.

The decision found that the homestyle exemption, now codified in §110(5)(A), was limited enough not to violate the TRIPS Agreement. The panel decision found that the homestyle exemption was narrowed by the FIMLA:

> [T]he homestyle exemption was originally intended to apply to performances of all types of works. However, given that the present subparagraph (B) applies to "a performance or display of a non-dramatic musical work," the parties agree, by way of an *a contrario* interpretation, that the effect of the introductory phrase "except as provided in subparagraph (B)," that was added to the text in subparagraph (A), is that it narrows down the application of subparagraph (A) to works other than "nondramatic musical works."

Id. ¶2.7. If this interpretation of the homestyle exemption is correct, turning on the radio in a public place — e.g., a boombox at the beach — would not be exempted from liability by §110(5).

The WTO gave the U.S. 12 months, until July 27, 2001, to comply with its decision by amending U.S. law. So far, however, Congress has made no changes to §110(5)(B). On June 23, 2003, the U.S. and the EU agreed to a temporary arrangement pursuant to which the U.S. would make a lump-sum payment of $3.3 million to the EU, to a fund established to finance activities of general interest to European music copyright holders, including promoting copyright awareness activities. That temporary arrangement ended on December 21, 2004. The parties continue to report that they are engaged in consultations in order to reach a mutually satisfactory resolution.

NOTES AND QUESTIONS

1. In determining that the "homestyle" exemption of §110(5), currently codified in subsection (5)(A), was consistent with the TRIPS Agreement, the panel noted that the U.S. had agreed that after the passage of the FIMLA, subsection (5)(A) did not apply to

"nondramatic musical works." In proceedings before the WTO, the U.S. is represented by the U.S. Trade Representative (USTR). Does the USTR's interpretation of the scope of the home-style exemption bind U.S. courts? Does it matter that the WTO panel expressly relied on the USTR's narrow interpretation?

2. Why do you think the EU would bring a complaint against the U.S.? Persons or corporations of U.S. origin probably own the copyrights in most of the sound recordings played in the establishments sheltered under §110(5). According to Professor Laurence Helfer, "The EC [acted] on a complaint by the Irish Music Rights Organization that the FIMLA is causing its members to lose $1.36 million annually in licensing royalties. Canada, Australia and Switzerland soon joined the EC in seeking formal consultations with the United States, alleging that their songwriters and music publishers [would] also be denied . . . performance royalties." Laurence R. Helfer, *World Music on a U.S. Stage: A Berne/TRIPs and Economic Analysis of the Fairness in Music Licensing Act*, 80 B.U. L. Rev. 93, 99 (2000).

3. How likely is Congress to change the §110(5) exemption? On the one hand, many members of Congress opposed the FIMLA, and it only passed after procedural maneuvering tied its fate to legislation that increased the duration of copyright by 20 years (the Sonny Bono Copyright Term Extension Act) and that a solid majority of Congress favored. On the other hand, some members of Congress have a certain disdain for altering domestic legislation solely because the WTO requires it. However, the potential imposition of trade sanctions "makes the option of resistance far less likely or palatable." Graeme B. Dinwoodie, *The Development and Incorporation of International Norms in the Formation of Copyright Law*, 62 Ohio St. L.J. 733, 764 (2001).

c. *Sound Recordings and Public Performance by Means of a Digital Audio Transmission*

Because sound recordings are not protected by a general public performance right, no license is required to publicly perform those sound recordings in most cases, whether the performance is by a DJ playing music in a nightclub, piped-in music in an elevator, or jukeboxes blasting out the latest hits. Following the recognition of a sound recording copyright in 1971, copyright owners lobbied for a public performance right, but strong opposition from broadcasters thwarted any attempted legislation. The potential of digital audio transmissions to supplant the purchase of CDs by individuals finally outweighed objections by the broadcast industry, and Congress enacted the Digital Performance Right in Sound Recordings Act of 1995 (DPRA), Pub. L. No. 104-39, 109 Stat. 336 (1995), effective February 1, 1996. The regulations implementing the DPRA are contained primarily in 37 C.F.R. §§260-62 (2005).

While §106(4) grants copyright owners of musical works the right to publicly perform their works, §106(6) grants a more limited public performance right to sound recording copyright owners. Only if the public performance occurs "by means of a digital audio transmission" is it within the control of the sound recording copyright owner. This right is qualified by a number of exemptions and statutory licenses, which are codified in §114 of the Copyright Act.

Many viewed the DPRA as a compromise because it granted a more limited public performance right in sound recordings than in other categories of works. The limited nature of the right was intended to address the concerns of the recording industry without "upsetting the longstanding business and contractual relationships among record producers and performers, music composers and publishers and broadcasters that have served all of these industries well for decades." S. Rep. No. 104-128, at 13 (1995), *reprinted in* 1995 U.S.C.C.A.N. 356, 360. Compromise also was built into the law in the form of a three-tiered system for categorizing digital transmissions based on their likelihood of affecting phonorecord sales: Those transmissions that are least likely to affect sales are exempt entirely. Other transmissions that might harm phonorecord sales are within the scope of the right, but are subject to a statutory license (a new term used by DPRA to describe a compulsory license). The final category of transmissions, those that have the most potential to reduce phonorecord sales, are fully within the control of the copyright owner, requiring authorization for any digital performance.

Almost immediately advances in webcasting technology complicated the interpretation and application of the DPRA. In 1998, Congress significantly amended the provisions relating to the exemptions and statutory license originally enacted in the DPRA "to create fair and efficient licensing mechanisms that address the complex issues facing copyright owners and copyright users as a result of the rapid growth of digital audio services." H.R. Conf. Rep. No. 105-796, at 79-80 (1998). The amendments, part of the Digital Millennium Copyright Act, retained the three-tiered structure, with some digital transmissions exempt, some within a statutory license scheme, and some within complete control of the copyright owner. However, the amendments narrowed the exempt category and brought more activities within copyright owners' control, requiring more individual licensing.

Understanding the exemptions from the §106(6) right and the types of activities for which a statutory license is available is easier if one keeps the policy behind the law in mind. The purpose of granting sound recording copyright owners a limited public performance right is to guard against harm to the market for sales of phonorecords. If an individual can hear the songs she wants at any time she wants by dialing up a celestial jukebox, she will be unlikely to purchase her own phonorecords, either by digitally downloading them or by obtaining them at a record store. Thus, those digital transmissions that are "interactive" — i.e., that allow recipients to choose what music will be played or to predict with some specificity the music that will be played — are not exempt, nor are they eligible for statutory licensing; permission from the sound recording copyright owner must be obtained. *See* 17 U.S.C. §114(d)(2). (Remember, permission from the musical work copyright owner will also be necessary.) Archived programs that allow individuals to effectively rewind and fast forward through the program are also considered "interactive."

Services that digitally perform sound recordings but are not interactive can utilize the statutory license codified in §114(d) if they, *inter alia*, (1) do not use a signal that causes the receiver to change from one program channel to another; (2) do not pre-announce the broadcast of particular songs; (3) include various information about the recording being transmitted if feasible; and (4) do not violate the "sound recording performance complement." *See id.* The sound recording performance complement requires, in any three-hour period, the transmission of no more than:

> (A) 3 different selections of sound recordings from any one phonorecord lawfully distributed for public performance or sale in the United States, if no more than 2 such selections are transmitted consecutively; or
>> (B) 4 different selections of sound recordings —
>>> (i) by the same featured recording artist; or
>>> (ii) from any set or compilation of phonorecords lawfully distributed together as a unit for
>> public performance or sale in the United States,
>
> if no more than three such selections are transmitted consecutively:

Provided, That the transmission of selections in excess of the numerical limits provided for in clauses (A) and (B) from multiple phonorecords shall nonetheless qualify as a sound recording performance complement if the programming of the multiple phonorecords was not willfully intended to avoid the numerical limitations prescribed in such clauses.

Id. §114(j)(13). The process for setting the royalty fee for this statutory license is similar to that for jukeboxes; voluntary industry negotiation and agreement with royalties set by a panel of Copyright Royalty Judges if no agreement can be achieved. *Id.* §§114(j), 804(a).

The vast majority of webcasting stations attempt to stay in this category so that they can use the statutory license scheme. The rates for statutory licenses have been hotly disputed, however. A panel of CRJs issued a decision in March 2007 that established a per-performance, per-listener escalating royalty rate for all stations that exceed a monthly aggregate tuning-hours threshold. Additionally, it imposed a $500 per-channel fee on all commercial webcasters. Webcasters derided the panel's royalty rate determination, asserting that the rates favored the music industry and would drive them out of business. In response, Congress passed the Webcaster Settlement Act of 2008, Public Law 110-435, and the Webcaster Settlement Act of 2009, Public Law 111-36, which authorized SoundExchange, an entity created by record labels to administer the sound recording performance royalties, to enter into webcasting licenses on behalf of all copyright owners and performers. In 2009, the Copyright Office announced a series of agreements that SoundExchange had reached with a wide variety of webcasting entities. *See* U.S. Copyright Office, *Notification of Agreements Under the Webcaster Settlement Act of 2008*, 74 Fed. Reg. 9293 (Mar. 3, 2009), U.S. Copyright Office, *Notification of Agreements Under the Webcaster Settlement Act of 2009*, 74 Fed. Reg. 34796 (July 17, 2009), and 74 Fed. Reg. 40614 (Aug. 12, 2009). The Copyright Office published the different agreements as appendices to the official notice appearing in the Federal Register and indicated that the rates and terms in the agreements are "available to any webcasters meeting the respective eligibility conditions of the agreements as an alternative to the rates and terms of any determination by the Copyright Royalty Judges." *Notification of 2008*, 74 Fed. Reg. at 9293. Thus, entities engaged in webcasting that need to obtain a statutory license can elect to comply with the terms of the agreements for which they are eligible and pay the negotiated rates, instead of the rates set by the March 2007 panel of CRJs.

The third category in the three-tiered structure established in §114 include those entities that are exempt from having to pay a license fee, either statutory or negotiated. The main exemption contained in §114(d) is the broadcast exemption. "[N]on-subscription broadcast transmission[s]" are exempt from the §106(6) rights of sound recording copyright owners. 17 U.S.C. §114(d)(1)(A)-(B). Subsequent to the enactment of the DPRA, thousands of radio stations began transmitting their broadcasts over the Internet through streaming technology. In 2000, the Recording Industry Association of America (RIAA) petitioned the Copyright Office to clarify whether AM/FM broadcasters who simultaneously stream their broadcasts over the Internet could claim the §114(d)(1)(A) exemption. The Copyright Office issued rules interpreting the broadcasting exemption not to extend to such transmissions, and requiring radio stations that want to transmit their broadcasts over the Internet either to obtain permission directly from the copyright owners of the sound recordings or to comply with the requirements for the statutory license. Radio station owners immediately challenged the rulemaking, but the court upheld the Copyright Office's interpretation of the statute. *Bonneville Int'l Corp. v. Peters*, 347 F.3d 485 (3d Cir. 2003). The court concluded that the DPRA's provisions clearly limited the scope of the broadcasting exemption to over-the-air digital transmissions by FCC-licensed broadcasters. *Id.* at 495. It also relied on the legislative history of the DPRA, which indicated congressional intent not to alter the existing relationship between the recording industry and broadcasters, and which characterized the broadcasting exemption as intended to shelter "free-over-the-air broadcast services." *Id.* at 498. This ruling effectively categorized all radio stations broadcasting over the web into one of the other two tiers, thus requiring a license.

The significance of being able to rely on the statutory license versus needing to clear each public performance on an individual basis cannot be understated. Consider webcasting stations with which you are familiar, ranging from your local college radio station to the digital stations available through services like Yahoo!Music and Pandora. Whether they are eligible to rely on the statutory licenses turns on their diligent compliance with the complicated provisions of the statute.

Arista Records, LLC v. Launch Media, Inc.,
578 F.3d 148 (2d Cir. 2009), cert. denied, 130 S. Ct. 1290 (2010)

WESLEY, J.: We are the first federal appellate court called upon to determine whether a webcasting service that provides users with individualized internet radio stations — the content of which can be affected by users' ratings of songs, artists, and albums — is an interactive service within the meaning of 17 U.S.C. §114(j)(7). If it is an interactive service, the webcasting service would be required to pay individual licensing fees to those copyright holders of the sound recordings of songs the webcasting service plays for its users. If it is not an interactive service, the webcasting service must only pay a statutory licensing fee set by the Copyright Royalty Board. . . .

Background[2]

On May 24, 2001 Arista Records, LLC, Bad Boy Records, BMG Music, and Zomba Recording LLC (collectively, "BMG") brought suit against Launch Media, Inc. ("Launch") alleging that Launch . . . willfully infring[ed] sound recording copyrights of BMG from 1999 to 2001. . . .

Launch operates an internet radio website, or "webcasting" service, called LAUNCHcast, which enables a user to create "stations" that play songs that are within a particular genre or similar to a particular artist or song the user selects. BMG holds the copyrights in the sound recordings of some of the songs LAUNCHcast plays for users. . . .

An "interactive service" according to the statute "is one that enables a member of the public to receive a transmission of a program specially created for the recipient, or on request, a transmission of a particular sound recording, whether or not as part of a program, which is selected by or on behalf of the recipient." 17 U.S.C. §114(j)(7). The statute provides little guidance as to the meaning of its operative term "specially created." According to Merriam-Webster's Collegiate Dictionary, "specially" means: (1) "in a special manner"; (2) "for a special purpose"; (3) "in particular" or "specifically"; or (4) "especially." Create, the root of "created," means: (1) "to bring into existence"; (2) "to produce"; (3) to "cause" or "occasion"; or (4) to "design."

These definitions indicate that a "specially created" program is a program produced or designed specifically for the user — not much help defining the terms of the statute in this case. BMG sees the issue as a simple one. BMG argues that any service that reflects user input is specially created for and by the user and therefore qualifies as an interactive service. But we should not read the statute so broadly. Justice Oliver Wendell Holmes once wrote that "[a] word is not a crystal, transparent and unchanged, it is the skin of a living thought and may vary greatly in color and content according to the circumstances and the time in which it is used." *Towne v. Eisner,* 245 U.S. 418, 425 (1918). Holmes's observation seems pertinent here.

---

2. Plaintiffs-Appellants appeal the judgment of the United States District Court for the Southern District of New York (Owen, *J.*), entered on May 16, 2007, and from interlocutory orders merged into the judgment, finding in favor of Defendant-Appellee Launch Media, Inc., now owned by Yahoo!, Inc. ("Yahoo").

The meaning of the phrase in question must significantly depend on the context in which Congress chose to employ it. . . .

With the inception and public use of the internet in the early 1990s, the recording industry became concerned that existing copyright law was insufficient to protect the industry from music piracy. At the time, the United States Register of Copyrights referred to the internet as "the world's biggest copying machine." Stephen Summer, *Music on the Internet: Can the Present Laws and Treaties Protect Music Copyright in Cyberspace?*, 8 CURRENTS: INT' L. TRADE L.J. 31, 32 (1999). What made copying music transmitted over the internet more dangerous to recording companies than traditional analog copying with a tape recorder was the fact that there is far less degradation of sound quality in a digital recording than an analog recording. *See id.* . . . If an internet user could listen to music broadcast over, or downloaded from, the internet for free, the recording industry worried that the user would stop purchasing music. Jason Berman, president of the Recording Industry Association of America (the "RIAA"), the lobbying arm of the recording industry, . . . warned that "digital delivery would siphon off and eventually eliminate the major source of revenue for investing in future recordings" and that "[o]ver time, this [would] lead to a vast reduction in the production of recorded music." Digital Performance Right in Sound Recording: Hearing on H.R. 1506 Before the H. Comm. on the Judiciary, Subcomm. on Courts & Intellectual Prop., 104th Cong. (1995) (statement of Jason Berman, President, RIAA). . . .

In light of these concerns, and recognizing that "digital transmission of sound recordings [were] likely to become a very important outlet for the performance of recorded music," Congress enacted the Digital Performance Right in Sound Recordings Act of 1995 (the "DPSR"), giving sound recording copyright holders an exclusive but "narrow" right to perform—play or broadcast—sound recordings via a digital audio transmission. H.R.Rep. No. 104-274, at 12, 13-14. The right was limited to exclusive performance of digital audio transmissions through paid subscriptions services and "interactive services." *See* 17 U.S.C. §114(d) (1995). While non-interactive subscription services qualified for statutory licensing, interactive services were required to obtain individual licenses for each sound recording those interactive services played via a digital transmission. *See* Lydia Pallas Loren, *Untangling the Web of Music Copyrights*, 53 CASE W. RES. L.REV. 673, 692 (2003). . . .

The House report noted that the DPSR was enacted to address two related concerns. First, without "appropriate copyright protection in the digital environment, the creation of new sound recordings and musical works could be discouraged, ultimately denying the public some of the potential benefits of the new digital transmission technologies." H.R.Rep. No. 104-274, at 13. Second, "certain types of subscription and interaction audio services might adversely affect sales of sound recordings and erode copyright owners' ability to control and be paid for use of their work." *Id.* With regard to the latter concern, the House noted that "interactive services are most likely to have a significant impact on traditional record sales, and therefore pose the greatest threat to the livelihoods of those whose income depends upon revenues derived from traditional record sales." *Id.* at 14. . . .

Fairly soon after Congress enacted the DPSR, critics began to call for further legislation, charging that the DPSR was too narrowly drawn and did not sufficiently protect sound recording copyright holders from further internet piracy. For instance, webcasting services, which provide free—i.e., nonsubscription—services that do not provide particular sound recording on request and are therefore not interactive within the meaning of term under the DPSR, at that time fell outside the sound recording copyright holder's right of control. . . .

In light of these concerns, Congress enacted the current version of §114 under the DMCA in 1998. The term "interactive service" was expanded to include "those that are specially created for a particular individual." H.R.Rep. No. 105-796, at 87 (1998) (Conf.Rep.).

As enacted, the definition of "interactive service" was now a service "that enables a member of the public to receive a transmission of a program specially created for the recipient, or on request, a transmission of a particular sound recording, whether or not as part of a program, which is selected by or on behalf of the recipient." 17 U.S.C. §114(j)(7).

According to the House conference report,

> The conferees intend that the phrase "program specially created for the recipient" be interpreted reasonably in light of the remainder of the definition of "interactive service." For example, a service would be interactive if it allowed a small number of individuals to request that sound recordings be performed in a program specially created for that group and not available to any individuals outside of that group. In contrast, a service would not be interactive if it merely transmitted to a large number of recipients of the service's transmissions a program consisting of sound recordings requested by a small number of those listeners.

H.R.Rep. No. 105-796, at 87-88 (Conf.Rep.).

The House report continued that a transmission is considered interactive "if a transmission recipient is permitted to select particular sound recordings in a prerecorded or predetermined program." *Id.* at 88. "For example, if a transmission recipient has the ability to move forward and backward between songs in a program, the transmission is interactive. It is not necessary that the transmission recipient be able to select the actual songs that comprise the program." *Id.* . . .

In sum, from the SRA to the DMCA, Congress enacted copyright legislation directed at preventing the diminution in record sales through outright piracy of music or new digital media that offered listeners the ability to select music in such a way that they would forego purchasing records.

Armed with the statute's text and context, we must examine the complex nature of the service LAUNCHcast provided. . . .[8]

After creating a username and password, and entering basic information and preferences unrelated to the music LAUNCHcast provides, a LAUNCHcast user is able to create and modify personalized radio stations. First, the user is prompted to select artists whose music the user prefers. The user is then asked which music genres the user enjoys and asked to rate the genres on a scale. The user is also asked the percentage of new music — songs the user has not previously rated — the user would like to incorporate into the user's station (the "unrated quota") and whether the user permits playing songs with profane lyrics. The minimum unrated quota is 20%, meaning no less than 20% of the songs played can be unrated.

Once LAUNCHcast begins playing music based on the user's preferred artists and genres, the user rates the songs, artists, or albums LAUNCHcast plays between zero and 100, with 100 being the best rating. Below the rating field are hyperlinks termed "history," "share," and "buy." The history hyperlink allows the user to see a list of the songs previously played, and the buy hyperlink facilitates the user's purchase of the songs. The share hyperlink allows the user to share the station with other users. This feature facilitates the "subscription" of one user to another user's station. When user A subscribes to the station of user B, user B becomes a "DJ" for user A. . . . While a song is playing, the user has the ability to pause the song, skip the song, or delete the song from the station by rating the song zero. Notably, the user may not go back to restart the song that is playing, or repeat any of the previously played songs in the playlist.

---

8. Federal judges are appointed for life. U.S. CONST. art. III, §1. Our familiarity with the ever-changing terms and technology of the digital age is, to say the least, varied. We have attempted to portray the processes and procedures of LAUNCHcast in lay terms, understandable to ourselves and the public.

Whenever the user logs into LAUNCHcast and selects a station, LAUNCHcast generates a playlist of fifty songs based on several variables. LAUNCHcast does not provide a list of the pool of songs or of the songs in the generated playlist, and therefore, the user does not know what songs might be played. LAUNCHcast selects the songs by first looking to the unrated quota and whether to exclude songs with profane lyrics or songs that cannot be transmitted over the user's bandwidth. Next LAUNCHcast creates a list of all the potential songs that can be put in the playlist (called a "hashtable"). LAUNCHcast then generates a list of all songs played for the user within the last thirty days, a list of all DJs, genres, and radio stations to which the user subscribes, and a list of all the ratings of all the songs, artists, and albums rated by either the user or any DJ to which the user subscribes. Songs that the user has rated are "explicitly rated" songs. LAUNCHcast "implicitly rates" songs that appear in an album that the user or a subscribed-to DJ has rated and songs that appear in the same album as another song the user has already rated.[12] All of these songs are initially added to the hashtable. LAUNCHcast then excludes: (1) all songs that the user, or a DJ to which the user subscribes, requests be skipped permanently (rated as zero) and (2) songs played within the last three hours for the user on any LAUNCHcast station. This yields approximately 4,000 songs.

LAUNCHcast then adds to the hashtable the 1,000 most popular songs—songs most highly rated by all LAUNCHcast users—in the bandwidth specified by the user, provided those songs are not already on the hashtable. [The court describes in detail the creation of the hashtable, which eventually contains approximately 10,000 songs. To create a playlist of 50 songs LAUNCHcast randomly selects songs from the hashtable and tests each song to determine if it should be discarded based on a set of rules.—EDS.] . . .

. . . . LAUNCHcast does not play the same song twice in a playlist [and] LAUNCHcast excludes a song from a playlist if three other songs by that artist have already been selected for the playlist. In other words, if the Beatles' "Here Comes the Sun," "A Day in the Life," and "Eleanor Rigby" have already been selected for the playlist, no other Beatles' song could be added to the playlist. . . . LAUNCHcast excludes a song from a playlist if two other songs from the same album have already been selected for the playlist. . . .

Finally, once all fifty songs are selected for the playlist, LAUNCHcast orders the playlist. The ordering of the songs is random, provided LAUNCHcast does not play more than two songs in the same album or three songs by the same artist consecutively.[17]

It is hard to think of a more complicated way to "select songs," but this is the nature of webcast music broadcasting in the digital age. Given LAUNCHcast's format, we turn to the question of whether LAUNCHcast is an interactive service as a matter of law. As we have already noted, a webcasting service such as LAUNCHcast is interactive under the statute if a user can either (1) request—and have played—a particular sound recording, or (2) receive a transmission of a program "specially created" for the user. A LAUNCHCAST user cannot request and expect to hear a particular song on demand; therefore, LAUNCHcast does not meet the first definition of interactive. But LAUNCHcast may still be liable if it enables the user to receive a transmission of a program "specially created" for the user. It comes as no surprise to us that the district court, the parties, and others have struggled with what Congress meant by this term. . . .

---

12. In other words, if the user rates the band U2 or U2's album The Joshua Tree, then U2's song "With or Without You" on the album will be implicitly rated. Likewise, if the user rates Gordon Lightfoot's song "Rainy Day People" but does not rate Lightfoot's iconic song "Canadian Railroad Trilogy"—found on a different album—"Rainy Day People" will be explicitly rated while "Canadian Railroad Trilogy" will be implicitly rated.

17. This brings LAUNCHcast into compliance with the "sound recording performance complement," which limits webcasters to playing no more than three selections from a given record in a three-hour period. 17 U.S.C. §114(d)(2)(C)(i), (j)(13).

Launch does not deny that each playlist generated when a LAUNCHcast user selects a radio station is unique to that user at that particular time. However, this does not necessarily make the LAUNCHcast playlist specially created for the user. Based on a review of how LAUNCHcast functions, it is clear that LAUNCHcast does not provide a specially created program within the meaning of §114(j)(7) because the webcasting service does not provide sufficient control to users such that playlists are so predictable that users will choose to listen to the webcast in lieu of purchasing music, thereby — in the aggregate — diminishing record sales.

First, the rules governing what songs are pooled in the hashtable ensure that the user has almost no ability to choose, let alone predict, which specific songs will be pooled in anticipation for selection to the playlist. At least 60% of the songs in the hashtable are generated by factors almost entirely beyond the user's control. The playlist — a total of fifty songs — is created from a pool of approximately 10,000 songs, at least 6,000 of which (1,000 of the most highly rated LAUNCHcast songs among all users and 5,000 randomly selected songs) are selected without any consideration for the user's song, artist, or album preferences. The user has control over the genre of songs to be played for 5,000 songs, but this degree of control is no different from a traditional radio listener expressing a preference for a country music station over a classic rock station. LAUNCHcast generates this list with safeguards to prevent the user from limiting the number of songs in the list eligible for play by selecting a narrow genre. . . .

Even the ways in which songs are rated include variables beyond the user's control. For instance, the ratings by all of the user's subscribed-to DJs are included in the playlist selection process. When the user rates a particular song, LAUNCHcast then implicitly rates all other songs by that artist, subjecting the user to many songs the user may have never heard or does not even like.[23] There are restrictions placed on the number of times songs by a particular artist or from a particular album can be played, and there are restrictions on consecutive play of the same artist or album. Finally, because each playlist is unique to each user each time the user logs in, a user cannot listen to the playlist of another user and anticipate the songs to be played from that playlist, even if the user has selected the same preferences and rated all songs, artists, and albums identically as the other user. . . .

Finally, after navigating these criteria to pool a hashtable and generate a playlist, LAUNCHcast randomly orders the playlist. This randomization is limited by restrictions on the consecutive play of artists or albums, which further restricts the user's ability to choose the artists or albums they wish to hear. LAUNCHcast also does not enable the user to view the unplayed songs in the playlist, ensuring that a user cannot sift through a playlist to choose the songs the user wishes to hear.

It appears the only thing a user can predict with certainty — the only thing the user can control — is that by rating a song at zero the user will not hear that song on that station again. But the ability not to listen to a particular song is certainly not a violation of a copyright holder's right to be compensated when the sound recording is played.

In short, to the degree that LAUNCHcast's playlists are uniquely created for each user, that feature does not ensure predictability. Indeed, the unique nature of the playlist helps Launch ensure that it does not provide a service so specially created for the user that the user ceases to purchase music. LAUNCHcast listeners do not even enjoy the limited predictability that once graced the AM airwaves on weekends in America when "special requests" represented love-struck adolescents' attempts to communicate their feelings to "that special friend." Therefore, we cannot say LAUNCHcast falls within the scope of the DMCA's definition of an interactive service created for individual users. . . .

---

23. It would be wrong, for instance, to assume that because a user likes the Beatles' album A Hard Day's Night the user would also like The White Album.

NOTES AND QUESTIONS

1. Why did the court need to detail the manner in which LAUNCHcast selected the music to be played for a listener? Do you agree with the court's determination that LAUNCHcast was not an interactive service? Recognize what is at stake in the determination: The defendant will need to pay some license fee; the question is whether it will be able to use the statutory licenses negotiated by SoundExchange and published by the Copyright Office, or whether it will need to obtain individually negotiated licenses.

2. How interactive are music webcasting services like Pandora or Yahoo!Music? How would an entity seeking to be more interactive go about negotiating all of the required licenses? Would the transaction costs involved make such a venture prohibitive for all but the entities that already own vast collections of rights in sound recordings?

3. Review Question 1, page 441 *supra*. If a third party wants to stream Adam Lambert's version of "Mad World" over the Internet, from whom must it obtain permission? Do you want to know in what context the streaming will occur? What if there are moving images accompanying the sounds, such as a video posted on YouTube?

4. Radio broadcasts made over traditional analog sound waves obviously do not infringe the §106(6) right because they are not *digital* transmissions. If the radio station converted the over-the-air signal to a digital one, it can rely on the broadcast exemption in §114 for the performance of the sound recordings. Note that the station will still need authorization to publicly perform the musical works. When the station simultaneously transmits its broadcast via the Web, that broadcast is not exempt. Should it be? How would that affect competition in the webcasting market?

5. A Performance Rights Act has been pending in Congress for the past several years. The legislation would provide owners of sound recording copyrights with full performance rights covering the use of their sound recordings by over-the-air broadcasters. If enacted, the proposed Performance Rights Act would remove a longstanding limitation that benefits conventional radio stations. The proposed bill would amend §106(6) of the Copyright Act to read as follows: "in the case of sound recordings, to perform the copyrighted work publicly by means of an audio transmission." As drafted, the bill provides relief for noncommercial radio stations, including public, educational, and religious stations, by giving those stations the option of a nominal annual flat fee. It provides similar relief for commercial stations whose annual revenue is under $1.25 million, which currently comprise approximately three-fourths of all music radio stations. Finally, the proposed legislation seeks to amend the §114 statutory license for digital public performances to ensure the preservation of royalties payable to songwriters or copyright owners of underlying musical works. Most other industrialized countries already provide similar protection for performance rights for sound recordings. The bill has enjoyed broad support, including from quarters traditionally resistant to the expansion of copyright rights. However, the National Association of Broadcasters has attacked the legislation, calling it a "performance tax" and seeking pledges from legislators to oppose the bill. If you were a legislator, how would you vote?

6

The Different Faces of Infringement

In Chapter 5, we focused primarily on identifying what activities constitute infringement rather than on the equally important questions of who is an infringer and what is the nature of her liability. In many cases, the infringer's identity is obvious. For example, if you were to copy a Dan Brown novel with pen and paper, you would liable for infringement unless you had some defense to liability. More advanced technology, however, complicates the question. Because copying by hand is quite laborious, you would likely use a photocopier to reproduce the book. Now the law must face the additional question whether the company that manufactures the photocopier and/or the company that operates the photocopying business are also infringers. You might then scan your photocopy of the book into your laptop, log on to the Internet, and post the copy to a web site for others to access and download. Or, instead of posting the copy, you might use file-sharing software to make it available to others. The question then arises whether the Internet access provider, the web site operator, and/or the provider of file-sharing software are also liable for copyright infringement.

Copyright law has developed doctrines of direct and secondary liability to address the varying ways that infringement can occur and the liability of parties other than those who commit the act of infringement. As you read the following materials, consider the differences among the various theories of secondary liability. Think too about how well courts have adapted these doctrines to high-technology settings.

A. DIRECT INFRINGEMENT

Religious Technology Center v. Netcom On-Line Communication Services, Inc.
907 F. Supp. 1361 (N.D. Cal. 1995)

WHYTE, J.: This case concerns an issue of first impression regarding intellectual property rights in cyberspace. Specifically, this order addresses whether the operator of a computer bulletin

469

board service ("BBS"), and the large Internet access provider that allows that BBS to reach the Internet, should be liable for copyright infringement committed by a subscriber of the BBS.

Plaintiffs Religious Technology Center ("RTC") and Bridge Publications, Inc. ("BPI") hold copyrights in the unpublished and published works of L. Ron Hubbard, the late founder of the Church of Scientology ("the Church"). Defendant Dennis Erlich ("Erlich") is a former minister of Scientology turned vocal critic of the Church, whose pulpit is now the Usenet newsgroup alt.religion.scientology ("a.r.s."), an online forum for discussion and criticism of Scientology. Plaintiffs maintain that Erlich infringed their copyrights when he posted portions of their works on a.r.s. Erlich gained his access to the Internet through defendant Thomas Klemesrud's ("Klemesrud's") BBS "support.com." Klemesrud is the operator of the BBS, which is run out of his home and has approximately 500 paying users. Klemesrud's BBS is not directly linked to the Internet, but gains its connection through the facilities of defendant Netcom On-Line Communications, Inc. ("Netcom"), one of the largest providers of Internet access in the United States.

After failing to convince Erlich to stop his postings, plaintiffs contacted defendants Klemesrud and Netcom. Klemesrud responded to plaintiffs' demands that Erlich be kept off his system by asking plaintiffs to prove that they owned the copyrights to the works posted by Erlich. However, plaintiffs refused Klemesrud's request as unreasonable. Netcom similarly refused plaintiffs' request that Erlich not be allowed to gain access to the Internet through its system. Netcom contended that it would be impossible to prescreen Erlich's postings and that to kick Erlich off the Internet meant kicking off the hundreds of users of Klemesrud's BBS. Consequently, plaintiffs named Klemesrud and Netcom in their suit against Erlich. . . .

1.   Direct Infringement

Infringement consists of the unauthorized exercise of one of the exclusive rights of the copyright holder delineated in section 106. 17 U.S.C. §501. Direct infringement does not require intent or any particular state of mind, although willfulness is relevant to the award of statutory damages. 17 U.S.C. §504(c). . . .

a.   Undisputed Facts

The parties do not dispute the basic processes that occur when Erlich posts his allegedly infringing messages to a.r.s. Erlich connects to Klemesrud's BBS using a telephone and a modem. Erlich then transmits his messages to Klemesrud's computer, where they are automatically briefly stored. According to a prearranged pattern established by Netcom's software, Erlich's initial act of posting a message to the Usenet results in the automatic copying of Erlich's message from Klemesrud's computer onto Netcom's computer and onto other computers on the Usenet. In order to ease transmission and for the convenience of Usenet users, Usenet servers maintain postings from newsgroups for a short period of time—eleven days for Netcom's system and three days for Klemesrud's system. Once on Netcom's computers, messages are available to Netcom's customers and Usenet neighbors, who may then download the messages to their own computers. Netcom's local server makes available its postings to a group of Usenet servers, which do the same for other servers until all Usenet sites worldwide have obtained access to the postings, which takes a matter of hours. . . .

Unlike some other large on-line service providers, such as CompuServe, America Online, and Prodigy, Netcom does not create or control the content of the information available to its subscribers. It also does not monitor messages as they are posted. It has, however, suspended the accounts of subscribers who violated its terms and conditions, such as where they had

commercial software in their posted files. Netcom admits that, although not currently configured to do this, it may be possible to reprogram its system to screen postings containing
particular words or coming from particular individuals. Netcom, however, took no action
after it was told by plaintiffs that Erlich had posted messages through Netcom's system that
violated plaintiffs' copyrights, instead claiming that it could not shut out Erlich without shutting out all of the users of Klemesrud's BBS.

b.   Creation of Fixed Copies

. . . In the present case, there is no question after *MAI* [*Systems Corp. v. Peak Computer,
Inc.*] that "copies" were created, as Erlich's act of sending a message to a.r.s. caused reproductions of portions of plaintiffs' works on both Klemesrud's and Netcom's storage devices. Even
though the messages remained on their systems for at most eleven days, they were sufficiently
"fixed" to constitute recognizable copies under the Copyright Act. . . .

c.   Is Netcom Directly Liable for Making the Copies?

Accepting that copies were made, Netcom argues that Erlich, and not Netcom, is directly
liable for the copying. *MAI* did not address the question raised in this case: whether possessors
of computers are liable for incidental copies automatically made on their computers using their
software as part of a process initiated by a third party. . . . Netcom's actions, to the extent that
they created a copy of plaintiffs' works, were necessary to having a working system for transmitting Usenet postings to and from the Internet. Unlike the defendants in *MAI*, neither
Netcom nor Klemesrud initiated the copying. . . . Thus, unlike *MAI*, the mere fact that Netcom's system incidentally makes temporary copies of plaintiffs' works does not mean Netcom
has caused the copying. The court believes that Netcom's act of designing or implementing a
system that automatically and uniformly creates temporary copies of all data sent through it is
not unlike that of the owner of a copying machine who lets the public make copies with it.
Although some of the people using the machine may directly infringe copyrights, courts analyze the machine owner's liability under the rubric of contributory infringement, not direct
infringement. . . . Plaintiffs' theory would create many separate acts of infringement and, carried to its natural extreme, would lead to unreasonable liability. It is not difficult to conclude
that Erlich infringes by copying a protected work onto his computer and by posting a message
to a newsgroup. However, plaintiffs' theory further implicates a Usenet server that carries
Erlich's message to other servers regardless of whether that server acts without any human
intervention beyond the initial setting up of the system. It would also result in liability for every
single Usenet server in the worldwide link of computers transmitting Erlich's message to every
other computer. These parties, who are liable under plaintiffs' theory, do no more than operate
or implement a system that is essential if Usenet messages are to be widely distributed. There is
no need to construe the Act to make all of these parties infringers. Although copyright is a strict
liability statute, there should still be some element of volition or causation which is lacking
where a defendant's system is merely used to create a copy by a third party.

Plaintiffs point out that the infringing copies resided for eleven days on Netcom's computer and were sent out from it onto the "Information Superhighway." However, under
plaintiffs' theory, any storage of a copy that occurs in the process of sending a message to
the Usenet is an infringement. While it is possible that less "damage" would have been done if
Netcom had heeded plaintiffs' warnings and acted to prevent Erlich's message from being
forwarded, this is not relevant to its *direct* liability for copying. The same argument is true
of Klemesrud and any Usenet server. Whether a defendant makes a direct copy that constitutes
infringement cannot depend on whether it received a warning to delete the message. . . .

Playboy Enterprises, Inc. v. Frena involved a suit against the operator of a small BBS whose system contained files of erotic pictures. 839 F. Supp. 1552, 1554 (M.D. Fla. 1993). A subscriber of the defendant's BBS had uploaded files containing digitized pictures copied from the plaintiff's copyrighted magazine, which files remained on the BBS for other subscribers to download. *Id.* The court did not conclude, as plaintiffs suggest in this case, that the BBS is itself liable for the unauthorized *reproduction* of plaintiffs' work; instead, the court concluded that the BBS operator was liable for violating the plaintiff's right to publicly *distribute and display* copies of its work. *Id.* at 1556-57. . . .

[T]his court holds that the storage on a defendant's system of infringing copies and retransmission to other servers is not a direct infringement by the BBS operator of the exclusive right to *reproduce* the work where such copies are uploaded by an infringing user. *Playboy* does not hold otherwise. . . .

NOTES AND QUESTIONS

1. Does the *Netcom* court's holding on Netcom's liability for direct infringement apply equally to Klemesrud? Who is (are) the direct infringer(s) in *Netcom*? Why do you think the plaintiffs are not satisfied with recovering against the direct infringer(s)?

2. The *Netcom* court notes that "copyright is a strict liability statute." What does this mean? Consider the following hypothetical: A book publisher infringes an author's copyright. It markets the infringing book through major retail chains that stock tens of thousands of titles. The chains sell the books to their customers. Are the chains liable for direct infringement? Of which exclusive right of the copyright owner? Does their likely lack of both knowledge of the infringement and an intent to infringe insulate them from liability? Would it be fair to hold them liable for infringement? How is *Netcom* different from this hypothetical?

3. Is the *Netcom* decision consistent with *MAI Systems Corp. v. Peak Computer, Inc.*, 991 F.2d 511 (9th Cir. 1993), *cert. dismissed*, 510 U.S. 1033 (1994), Chapter 2 *supra*? In *CoStar Group, Inc. v. LoopNet, Inc.*, 373 F.3d 544 (4th Cir. 2004), the court distinguished *MAI* as follows:

> . . . [C]onstruing the Copyright Act to require some aspect of volition and meaningful causation — as distinct from passive ownership and management of an electronic Internet facility — receives additional support from the Act's concept of "copying." . . . When an electronic infrastructure is designed and managed as a *conduit* of information and data that connects users over the Internet, the owner and manager of the conduit hardly "copies" the information and data in the sense that it fixes a copy in its system of more than transitory duration. Even if the information and data are "downloaded" onto the owner's RAM or other component as part of the transmission function, that downloading is a temporary, automatic response to the user's request, and the entire system functions solely to transmit the user's data to the Internet. Under such an arrangement, the ISP provides a system that automatically transmits users' material but is itself totally indifferent to the material's content. In this way, it functions as does a traditional telephone company when it transmits the contents of its users' conversations. . . .
>
> In concluding that an ISP has not itself fixed a copy in its system of more than transitory duration when it provides an Internet hosting service to its subscribers, we do not hold that a computer owner who downloads copyrighted software onto a computer cannot infringe the software's copyright. *See, e.g., MAI Systems Corp. v. Peak Computer, Inc.*, 991 F.2d 511, 518-19 (9th Cir. 1993). When the computer owner downloads copyrighted software, it possesses the software, which then functions in the service of the computer or its owner, and the copying is no longer of a

transitory nature. . . . "Transitory duration" is thus both a qualitative and quantitative character-ization. It is quantitative insofar as it describes the period during which the function occurs, and it is qualitative in the sense that it describes the status of transition. . . .

Id. at 550-51. Are you persuaded by the court's analysis?

4. The *Netcom* court also held that Netcom was not a direct infringer of either the plain-tiffs' exclusive right of public display or their exclusive right of public distribution. Do you agree? Is it possible to distinguish *Netcom* from *Frena*? In declining to find Cablevision liable for direct infringement of the reproduction right based on copies of programming stored at the request of customers of its remote DVR service (*see* pages 416-20 *supra*), the Second Circuit offered a slightly different analysis of the direct liability problem presented by networked digital services:

> There are only two instances of volitional conduct in this case: Cablevision's conduct in designing, housing, and maintaining a system that exists only to produce a copy, and a customer's conduct in ordering that system to produce a copy of a specific program. In the case of a VCR, it seems clear — and we know of no case holding otherwise — that the operator of the VCR, the person who actually presses the button to make the recording, supplies the necessary element of volition, not the person who manufactures, maintains, or, if distinct from the operator, owns the machine. We do not believe that an RS-DVR customer is sufficiently distinguishable from a VCR user to impose liability as a direct infringer on a different party for copies that are made automatically upon that customer's command.
>
>   . . . In determining who actually "makes" a copy, a significant difference exists between mak-ing a request to a human employee, who then volitionally operates the copying system to make the copy, and issuing a command directly to a system, which automatically obeys commands and engages in no volitional conduct. . . . Here, by selling access to a system that automatically pro-duces copies on command, Cablevision more closely resembles a store proprietor who charges customers to use a photocopier on his premises, and it seems incorrect to say, without more, that such a proprietor "makes" any copies when his machines are actually operated by his customers. . . .
>
>   Our refusal to find Cablevision directly liable on these facts is buttressed by the existence and contours of the Supreme Court's doctrine of contributory liability in the copyright context. After all, the purpose of any causation-based liability doctrine is to identify the actor (or actors) whose "conduct has been so significant and important a cause that [he or she] should be legally responsible." W. Page Keeton et al., *Prosser and Keeton on Torts* §42, at 273 (5th ed.1984). But here, to the extent that we may construe the boundaries of direct liability more narrowly, the doctrine of contributory liability stands ready to provide adequate protection to copyrighted works.

Cartoon Network LP v. CSC Holdings, Inc., 536 F.3d 121, 131-32 (2d Cir. 2008), *cert. denied*, 129 S.Ct. 2890 (2009). Is the Second Circuit's analysis more persuasive than the Fourth Circuit's in *Loopnet* (*see* note 3 *supra*)? Do you agree that the nature of Cablevision's involve-ment in the recording of copies makes an indirect liability inquiry more appropriate? Revisit this question after you read the next two sections of this chapter.

5. Who is the direct infringer in the employment context? According to *Nimmer on Copyright*, an employee is not personally liable for infringement if the infringing "act was required of him as a part of the duties of his employment, and if, further, he was not permitted to exercise discretion, judgment or responsibility in the conduct of such duties." 3 Melville B. Nimmer & David Nimmer, *Nimmer on Copyright* §12.04[A][3][d], at 12-100 (2004). Nimmer also notes, however, that absent these elements, the general rule is that "an employee who in the exercise of his authority commits or determines that his employer (corporate or

otherwise) shall commit an act that constitutes an infringement will be held jointly and severally liable with his employer." *Id.* at 12-93.

Note on Infringement by Authorization

A brief reading of §§501 and 106 of the Copyright Act might lead one to conclude that a person who authorizes another to infringe is himself a direct infringer. Section 501 defines an infringer as "[a]nyone who violates any of the exclusive rights of the copyright owner as provided by section[ ] 106 . . . ." 17 U.S.C. §501. In turn, §106 states, "the owner of copyright has the *exclusive rights to do and to authorize. . . .*" *Id.* §106 (emphasis added). Thus, one might argue that among the copyright owner's exclusive rights is the right to authorize one of the acts (such as reproduction) enumerated in subsections (1)-(6) of §106. One who violates this right is therefore a direct infringer under §501.

The House Report accompanying the 1976 Act, however, indicates that Congress added the words "to authorize" to confirm its intent that contributory infringers be liable under the Act. The Report states, "[u]se of the phrase 'to authorize' [in §106] is intended to avoid any questions as to the liability of contributory infringers." H.R. Rep. No. 94-1476, 94th Cong., 2d Sess. 61 (1976), *reprinted in* 1976 U.S.C.C.A.N. 5659, 5674.

In many cases, the question whether authorization of an infringing act constitutes direct infringement is irrelevant. The court will hold the defendant liable for contributory infringement. Harder cases, however, arise when the authorization occurs in the U.S. but the act is committed abroad. For example, the defendant may enter into a license agreement in the U.S. under which it authorizes another to make infringing copies of a work, but the actual copying takes place in another country.

Traditionally, a country's copyright law has no extraterritorial effect; therefore, a copyright owner cannot sue for direct infringement in violation of U.S. copyright law based on conduct occurring wholly outside the U.S. Absent such direct infringement, an action in the U.S. based on contributory infringement would not succeed. If the copyright owner may not sue the U.S.-based "authorizer," it will have to journey to the country where the act occurred, hope that country's law prohibits the conduct, and seek a remedy there.

Courts are divided on whether a plaintiff may successfully sue for direct infringement based on the authorization to commit acts abroad. In *Subafilms, Ltd. v. MGM-Pathe Communications Co.*, 24 F.3d 1088 (9th Cir.) (en banc), *cert. denied*, 513 U.S. 1001 (1994), the court stated:

> Because the copyright laws do not apply extraterritorially, each of the rights conferred under the five section 106 categories must be read as extending "no farther than the [U.S.] borders." . . . In light of our . . . conclusion that the "authorization" right refers to the doctrine of contributory infringement, which requires that the authorized act *itself* could violate one of the exclusive rights listed in section 106(1)-(5) [now (1)-(6) — Eds.], we believe that "[i]t is simply not possible to draw a principled distinction" between an act that does not violate a copyright because it is not the type of conduct proscribed by section 106, and one that does not violate section 106 because the illicit act occurs overseas. . . . In both cases, the authorized conduct could not violate the exclusive rights guaranteed by section 106. In both cases, therefore, there can be no liability for "authorizing" such conduct. . . .
>
> To hold otherwise would produce the untenable anomaly, inconsistent with the general principles of third party liability, that a party could be held liable as an infringer for violating the "authorization" right when the party that it authorized could not be considered an infringer under the Copyright Act. Put otherwise, we do not think Congress intended to hold a party liable for

merely "authorizing" conduct that, had the *authorizing* party chosen to engage in itself, would have resulted in no liability under the Act. . . .

We are not persuaded by Appellees' parade of horribles.[10]

Id. at 1094-95.

A district court in Tennessee took issue with *Subafilms*. In *Curb v. MCA Records, Inc.*, 898 F. Supp. 586 (M.D. Tenn. 1995), the court stated:

> . . . *Subafilms* . . . reads the authorization right out of the Act in cases of foreign infringement.
>
> But piracy has changed since the Barbary days. Today, the raider need not grab the bounty with his own hands; he need only transmit his go-ahead by wire or telefax to start the presses in a distant land. *Subafilms* ignores this economic reality, and the economic incentives underpinning the Copyright Clause designed to encourage creation of new works, and transforms infringement of the authorization right into a requirement of domestic presence by a primary infringer. Under this view, a phone call to Nebraska results in liability; the same phone call to France results in riches. In a global marketplace, it is literally a distinction without a difference.
>
> A better view, one supported by the text, the precedents, and, ironically enough, the legislative history to which the *Subafilms* court cited, would be to hold that domestic violation of the authorization right is an infringement, sanctionable under the Copyright Act, whenever the authorizee has committed an act that would violate the copyright owner's §106 rights. . . .

Id. at 595.

NOTES AND QUESTIONS

1. Which court's reasoning do you find more persuasive?

2. The *Curb* court analogizes to phone calls, arguing that the *Subafilms* rule results in liability attaching for a call made to Nebraska but not one to France. How would you respond to this argument? Why do you think the plaintiffs are concerned about being able to bring suit in the U.S.?

3. The Berne Convention requires that authors be granted "the exclusive right of authorizing" exploitation of their works, but does not define what conduct the right of authorization encompasses. *See* Berne Conv., arts. 8, 9, 11-11ter, 12, 14.

B. VICARIOUS LIABILITY AND CONTRIBUTORY INFRINGEMENT

Review the introductory material to this chapter. There we raised the question of liability of parties other than the direct infringer — so-called secondary liability. What policies do you

---

10. As Appellants note, breach of contract remedies (such as those pursued in this case) remain available. Moreover, at least one court has recognized that actions under the copyright laws of other nations may be brought in United States courts. *See London Film Prods. Ltd. v. Intercontinental Communications, Inc.*, 580 F. Supp. 47, 48-50 (S.D.N.Y. 1984). . . . Finally, although we note that the difficulty of protecting American films abroad is a significant international trade problem, . . . the United States Congress, in acceding to the Berne Convention, has expressed the view that it is through increasing the protection afforded by *foreign* copyright laws that domestic industries that depend on copyright can best secure adequate protection. . . .

think should guide the liability of those who are not direct infringers but who nonetheless somehow participate in the infringing activity?

Courts rather than Congress have taken the lead in considering the relevant policies and developing theories of secondary liability. The 1909 Act did not mention liability for acts committed by one other than the direct infringer. As discussed above in the Note on Infringement by Authorization, the legislative history of the 1976 Act indicates that the addition of the words "to authorize" in §106 was intended to confirm congressional intent that secondary participants could be liable for copyright infringement under appropriate circumstances. Yet Congress still did not believe it necessary to codify those circumstances. This is in stark contrast to the congressional approach in the Patent Act. As we discuss below in Section C, the Patent Act specifies who may not be considered a contributory infringer (and, by inference, who may).

A line of cases decided under the 1909 Act developed two theories of indirect infringement—vicarious liability and contributory copyright infringement. Vicarious liability finds its theoretical basis in the respondeat superior doctrine developed under agency law. Under that doctrine, in certain circumstances, a principal may be held liable for acts of an agent. Courts looked to respondeat superior principles when addressing indirect infringement cases in the employer/employee and landlord/tenant contexts and in cases against owners of venues for infringement by performers. A leading case stating the test for vicarious liability in copyright infringement cases is *Shapiro, Bernstein & Co. v. H. L. Green Co.*, 316 F. 2d 304 (2d Cir. 1963). There, the court held a chain store owner vicariously liable for infringement by a record concessionaire operating on the store's premises. The court stated,

> When the *right and ability to supervise* coalesce with an obvious and *direct financial interest* in the exploitation of copyrighted materials — even in the absence of actual knowledge that the copyright monopoly is being impaired . . . the purposes of copyright law may be best effectuated by the imposition of liability upon the beneficiary of that exploitation.

Id. at 307 (emphasis added).

The store owner's retention of "the ultimate right of supervision" over the concessionaire and the right to "a proportionate share of the gross receipts from [record] sales" satisfied both prongs of the court's test. *Id.* at 308.

Contributory copyright infringement finds its theoretical basis in tort law, particularly principles of joint and several liability. In *Gershwin Publishing Corp. v. Columbia Artists Management, Inc.* (CAMI), 443 F.2d 1159 (2d Cir. 1971), the court addressed a claim of indirect infringement against CAMI. CAMI was directly involved in helping to set up local associations that sponsored community concerts at which copyrighted works were performed without a license. The performing artists were sometimes managed by CAMI and sometimes not. Regardless, artists would pay CAMI a portion of their fee to compensate it for its services in forming the local association. Artists managed by CAMI would pay an additional management fee. The court held, "[O]ne who, with *knowledge of the infringing activity, induces, causes or materially contributes* to the infringing conduct of another, may be held liable as a 'contributory' infringer," and found the facts of the case sufficient to support contributory liability. *Id.* at 1162 (emphasis added).

Although the elements of the two causes of action differ, as you will see, the dividing line between them can be blurry. Indeed, in many cases, a defendant may be held both vicariously and contributorily liable. *See id.* Further, the actions as stated above leave many open questions, including what the appropriate test is for someone who markets goods that are not themselves infringing but provide the means for others to infringe (e.g., a copier). Also, the traditional causes of action were developed in a different era. Courts continue to grapple with application of the tests to providers of on-line services.

We proceed as follows: We first consider the basic vicarious liability and contributory infringement doctrines in traditional and electronic settings. Next, we consider how courts should assess the secondary liability of manufacturers of devices and software, including peer-to-peer file sharing software. We conclude our discussion of secondary liability by considering the liability of on-line service providers (OSPs) for infringement by users of their services. In that section, we examine §512 of the Copyright Act in detail. Section 512 provides certain protections for OSPs against secondary liability.

As you read the material that follows, try to identify the tests that courts are using in different factual situations and think about whether you can reconcile the results in the cases. Consider also whether §512 represents an appropriate balancing of the interests involved in the on-line context.

Fonovisa, Inc. v. Cherry Auction, Inc.
76 F.3d 259 (9th Cir. 1996)

SCHROEDER, J.: This is a copyright and trademark enforcement action against the operators of a swap meet, sometimes called a flea market, where third-party vendors routinely sell counterfeit recordings that infringe on the plaintiff's copyrights and trademarks. The district court dismissed on the pleadings, holding that the plaintiffs, as a matter of law, could not maintain any cause of action against the swap meet for sales by vendors who leased its premises. . . .

Background

The plaintiff and appellant is Fonovisa, Inc., a California corporation that owns copyrights and trademarks to Latin/Hispanic music recordings. Fonovisa filed this action in district court against defendant-appellee, Cherry Auction, Inc., and its individual operators (collectively "Cherry Auction"). For purposes of this appeal, it is undisputed that Cherry Auction operates a swap meet in Fresno, California, similar to many other swap meets in this country where customers come to purchase various merchandise from individual vendors. . . . The vendors pay a daily rental fee to the swap meet operators in exchange for booth space. Cherry Auction supplies parking, conducts advertising and retains the right to exclude any vendor for any reason, at any time, and thus can exclude vendors for [copyright] and trademark infringement. In addition, Cherry Auction receives an entrance fee from each customer who attends the swap meet.

There is also no dispute for purposes of this appeal that Cherry Auction and its operators were aware that vendors in their swap meet were selling counterfeit recordings in violation of Fonovisa's trademarks and copyrights. . . .

. . . In this appeal, Fonovisa [challenges] the dismissal of its claims for contributory copyright infringement, vicarious copyright infringement and contributory trademark infringement.

The copyright claims are brought pursuant to 17 U.S.C. §§101 *et seq.* Although the Copyright Act does not expressly impose liability on anyone other than direct infringers, courts have long recognized that in certain circumstances, vicarious or contributory liability will be imposed. *See Sony Corp. of America v. Universal City Studios, Inc.*, 464 U.S. 417, 435 . . . (1984) (explaining that "vicarious liability is imposed in virtually all areas of the law, and the concept of contributory infringement is merely a species of the broader problem of identifying circumstances in which it is just to hold one individually accountable for the actions of another"). . . .

Vicarious Copyright Infringement

The concept of vicarious copyright liability was developed in the Second Circuit as an outgrowth of the agency principles of respondeat superior. The landmark case on vicarious liability for sales of counterfeit recordings is *Shapiro, Bernstein and Co. v. H.L. Green Co.*, 316 F.2d 304 (2d Cir. 1963). In *Shapiro*, the court was faced with a copyright infringement suit against the owner of a chain of department stores where a concessionaire was selling counterfeit recordings. . . .

The *Shapiro* court looked at the two lines of cases it perceived as most clearly relevant. In one line of cases, the landlord-tenant cases, the courts had held that a landlord who lacked knowledge of the infringing acts of its tenant and who exercised no control over the leased premises was not liable for infringing sales by its tenant. . . . In the other line of cases, the so-called "dance hall cases," the operator of an entertainment venue was held liable for infringing performances when the operator (1) could control the premises and (2) obtained a direct financial benefit from the audience, who paid to enjoy the infringing performance. . . .

From those two lines of cases, the *Shapiro* court determined that the relationship between the store owner and the concessionaire in the case before it was closer to the dance-hall model than to the landlord-tenant model. It imposed liability even though the defendant was unaware of the infringement. *Shapiro* deemed the imposition of vicarious liability neither unduly harsh nor unfair because the store proprietor had the power to cease the conduct of the concessionaire, and because the proprietor derived an obvious and direct financial benefit from the infringement. 316 F.2d at 307. The test was more clearly articulated in a later Second Circuit case as follows: "even in the absence of an employer-employee relationship one may be vicariously liable if he has the right and ability to supervise the infringing activity and also has a direct financial interest in such activities." *Gershwin Publishing Corp. v. Columbia Artists Management, Inc.*, 443 F.2d 1159, 1162 (2d Cir. 1971). . . .

The district court in this case agreed with defendant Cherry Auction that Fonovisa did not, as a matter of law, meet either the control or the financial benefit prong of the vicarious copyright infringement test articulated in *Gershwin, supra*. . . . In the district court's view, with respect to both control and financial benefit, Cherry Auction was in the same position as an absentee landlord who has surrendered its exclusive right of occupancy in its leased property to its tenants.

This analogy to [an] absentee landlord is not in accord with the facts as alleged in the district court and which we, for purposes of appeal, must accept. The allegations below were that vendors occupied small booths within premises that Cherry Auction controlled and patrolled. According to the complaint, Cherry Auction had the right to terminate vendors for any reason whatsoever and through that right had the ability to control the activities of vendors on the premises. In addition, Cherry Auction promoted the swap meet and controlled the access of customers to the swap meet area. In terms of control, the allegations before us are strikingly similar to those in *Shapiro*. . . .

In *Shapiro* . . . the concessionaire selling the bootleg recordings had a licensing agreement with the department store (H.L. Green Company) that required the concessionaire and its employees to "abide by, observe and obey all regulations promulgated from time to time by the H.L. Green Company," and H.L. Green Company had the "unreviewable discretion" to discharge the concessionaires' employees. 316 F.2d at 306. In practice, H.L. Green Company was not actively involved in the sale of records and the concessionaire controlled and supervised the individual employees. *Id*. Nevertheless, H.L. Green's ability to police its concessionaire — which parallels Cherry Auction's ability to police its vendors under Cherry Auction's similarly broad contract with its vendors — was sufficient to satisfy the control requirement. *Id*. at 308. . . .

We next consider the issue of financial benefit. The plaintiff's allegations encompass many substantive benefits to Cherry Auction from the infringing sales. These include the payment of a daily rental fee by each of the infringing vendors; a direct payment to Cherry Auction by each customer in the form of an admission fee, and incidental payments for parking, food and other services by customers seeking to purchase infringing recordings.

Cherry Auction nevertheless contends that these benefits cannot satisfy the financial benefit prong of vicarious liability because a commission, directly tied to the sale of particular infringing items, is required. They ask that we restrict the financial benefit prong to the precise facts presented in *Shapiro*, where defendant H.L. Green Company received a 10 or 12 percent commission from the direct infringers' gross receipts. Cherry Auction points to the low daily rental fee paid by each vendor, discounting all other financial benefits flowing to the swap meet, and asks that we hold that the swap meet is materially similar to a mere landlord. The facts alleged by Fonovisa, however, reflect that the defendants reap substantial financial benefits from admission fees, concession stand sales and parking fees, all of which flow directly from customers who want to buy the counterfeit recordings at bargain basement prices. The plaintiff has sufficiently alleged direct financial benefit.

Our conclusion is fortified by the continuing line of cases, starting with the dance hall cases, imposing vicarious liability on the operator of a business where infringing performances enhance the attractiveness of the venue to potential customers. . . . In this case, the sale of pirated recordings at the Cherry Auction swap meet is a "draw" for customers, as was the performance of pirated music in the dance hall cases and their progeny.

Plaintiffs have stated a claim for vicarious copyright infringement.

Contributory Copyright Infringement

Contributory infringement originates in tort law and stems from the notion that one who directly contributes to another's infringement should be held accountable. . . . Contributory infringement has been described as an outgrowth of enterprise liability . . . and imposes liability where one person knowingly contributes to the infringing conduct of another. The classic statement of the doctrine is in *Gershwin* . . . : "[O]ne who, with knowledge of the infringing activity, induces, causes or materially contributes to the infringing conduct of another, may be held liable as a 'contributory' infringer." . . .

There is no question that plaintiff adequately alleged the element of knowledge in this case. The disputed issue is whether plaintiff adequately alleged that Cherry Auction materially contributed to the infringing activity. We have little difficulty in holding that the allegations in this case are sufficient to show material contribution to the infringing activity. Indeed, it would be difficult for the infringing activity to take place in the massive quantities alleged without the support services provided by the swap meet. These services include, *inter alia*, the provision of space, utilities, parking, advertising, plumbing, and customers.

Here again Cherry Auction asks us to ignore all aspects of the enterprise described by the plaintiffs, to concentrate solely on the rental of space, and to hold that the swap meet provides nothing more. Yet Cherry Auction actively strives to provide the environment and the market for counterfeit recording sales to thrive. Its participation in the sales cannot be termed "passive," as Cherry Auction would prefer. . . .

[W]e agree with the Third Circuit's analysis in *Columbia Pictures Industries, Inc. v. Aveco, Inc.*, 800 F.2d 59 (3rd Cir. 1986) that providing the site and facilities for known infringing activity is sufficient to establish contributory liability. . . .

≡ *Perfect 10, Inc. v. Amazon.com, Inc.*
≡ *508 F.3d 1146 (9th Cir. 2007)*

IKUTA, J.: [Review the facts of this case set forth on pages 424-27, *supra*.]

Secondary Liability for Copyright Infringement

. . . [W]e must assess Perfect 10's arguments that Google is secondarily liable in light of the direct infringement that is undisputed by the parties: third-party websites' reproducing, displaying, and distributing unauthorized copies of Perfect 10's images on the Internet. . . .

A. Contributory Infringement

. . . We have adopted the general rule set forth in *Gershwin Publishing Corp. v. Columbia Artists Management, Inc.*, namely: "one who, with knowledge of the infringing activity, induces, causes or materially contributes to the infringing conduct of another, may be held liable as a 'contributory' infringer," 443 F.2d 1159, 1162 (2d Cir.1971). . . .

We have further refined this test in the context of cyberspace to determine when contributory liability can be imposed on a provider of Internet access or services. *See Napster*, 239 F.3d at 1019-20. In *Napster*, we considered claims that the operator of an electronic file sharing system was contributorily liable for assisting individual users to swap copyrighted music files stored on their home computers with other users of the system. *Napster*, 239 F.3d at 1011-13, 1019-22. We stated that "if a computer system operator learns of specific infringing material available on his system and fails to purge such material from the system, the operator knows of and contributes to direct infringement." *Id.* at 1021. Because Napster knew of the availability of infringing music files, assisted users in accessing such files, and failed to block access to such files, we concluded that Napster materially contributed to infringement. *Id.* at 1022.

The *Napster* test for contributory liability was modeled on the influential district court decision in *Religious Technology Center v. Netcom On-Line Communication Services, Inc. (Netcom)*, 907 F.Supp. 1361, 1365-66 (N.D.Cal.1995). *See Napster*, 239 F.3d at 1021. In *Netcom*, a disgruntled former Scientology minister posted allegedly infringing copies of Scientological works on an electronic bulletin board service. *Netcom*, 907 F.Supp. at 1365-66. The messages were stored on the bulletin board operator's computer, then automatically copied onto Netcom's computer, and from there copied onto other computers comprising "a worldwide community" of electronic bulletin board systems. *Id.* at 1366-67 & n. 4 (internal quotation omitted). *Netcom* held that if plaintiffs could prove that Netcom knew or should have known that the minister infringed plaintiffs' copyrights, "Netcom[would] be liable for contributory infringement since its failure to simply cancel [the former minister's] infringing message and thereby stop an infringing copy from being distributed worldwide constitute[d] substantial participation in [the former minister's] public distribution of the message." *Id.* at 1374.

. . . [B]oth decisions ruled that a service provider's knowing failure to prevent infringing actions could be the basis for imposing contributory liability. Under such circumstances, intent may be imputed. In addition, *Napster* and *Netcom* are consistent with the longstanding requirement that an actor's contribution to infringement must be material to warrant the imposition of contributory liability. *Gershwin*, 443 F.2d at 1162. Both *Napster* and *Netcom* acknowledge that services or products that facilitate access to websites throughout the world can significantly magnify the effects of otherwise immaterial infringing activities. *See Napster*, 239 F.3d at 1022; *Netcom*, 907 F.Supp. at 1375. . . . Moreover, copyright holders cannot protect their rights in a meaningful way unless they can hold providers of such services or products accountable for their actions pursuant to a test such as that enunciated in *Napster*. *See id.* at 929-30, 125 S.Ct. 2764 ("When a widely shared service or product is used to commit infringement, it may be impossible to enforce rights in the protected work effectively against all direct infringers, the only practical alternative being to go against the distributor of the copying device for secondary liability on a theory of contributory or vicarious infringement."). Accordingly, we hold that a computer system operator can be held contributorily liable if it "has *actual* knowledge that *specific* infringing material is available using its system," *Napster*, 239 F.3d at 1022, and can "take simple measures to prevent further damage" to copyrighted works, *Netcom*, 907 F.Supp. at 1375, yet continues to provide access to infringing works.

Here, the district court held that even assuming Google had actual knowledge of infringing material available on its system, Google did not materially contribute to infringing conduct because it did not undertake any substantial promotional or advertising efforts to encourage visits to infringing websites, nor provide a significant revenue stream to the infringing websites. *Perfect 10*, 416 F.Supp.2d at 854-56. This analysis is erroneous. There is no dispute that Google substantially assists websites to distribute their infringing copies to a worldwide market and assists a worldwide audience of users to access infringing materials. We cannot discount the effect of such a service on copyright owners, even though Google's assistance is available to all websites, not just infringing ones. Applying our test, Google could be held contributorily liable if it had knowledge that infringing Perfect 10 images were available using its search engine, could take simple measures to prevent further damage to Perfect 10's copyrighted works, and failed to take such steps.

The district court did not resolve the factual disputes over the adequacy of Perfect 10's notices to Google and Google's responses to these notices. Moreover, there are factual disputes over whether there are reasonable and feasible means for Google to refrain from providing access to infringing images. Therefore, we must remand this claim to the district court for further consideration . . .

B. Vicarious Infringement

Perfect 10 also challenges the district court's conclusion that it is not likely to prevail on a theory of vicarious liability against Google. *Perfect 10*, 416 F.Supp.2d at 856-58. . . . [T]o succeed in imposing vicarious liability, a plaintiff must establish that the defendant exercises the requisite control over the direct infringer and that the defendant derives a direct financial benefit from the direct infringement. . . . [A] defendant exercises control over a direct infringer when he has both a legal right to stop or limit the directly infringing conduct, as well as the practical ability to do so.

. . . In order to prevail at this preliminary injunction stage, Perfect 10 must demonstrate a likelihood of success [on these issues]. . . . Perfect 10 has not met this burden.

With respect to the "control" element . . . Perfect 10 has not demonstrated a likelihood of showing that Google has the legal right to stop or limit the direct infringement of third-party websites. Unlike *Fonovisa*, where by virtue of a "broad contract" with its vendors the defendant swap meet operators had the right to stop the vendors from selling counterfeit recordings on its premises, *Fonovisa*, 76 F.3d at 263, Perfect 10 has not shown that Google has contracts with third-party websites that empower Google to stop or limit them from reproducing, displaying, and distributing infringing copies of Perfect 10's images on the Internet. Perfect 10 does point to Google's AdSense agreement, which states that Google reserves "the right to monitor and terminate partnerships with entities that violate others' copyright[s]." *Perfect 10*, 416 F.Supp.2d at 858. However, Google's right to terminate an AdSense partnership does not give Google the right to stop direct infringement by third-party websites. An infringing third-party website can continue to reproduce, display, and distribute its infringing copies of Perfect 10 images after its participation in the AdSense program has ended. . . .

Moreover, the district court found that Google lacks the practical ability to police the third-party websites' infringing conduct. *Id.* at 857-58. Specifically, the court found that Google's supervisory power is limited because "Google's software lacks the ability to analyze every image on the [I]nternet, compare each image to all the other copyrighted images that exist in the world . . . and determine whether a certain image on the web infringes someone's copyright." *Id.* at 858. The district court also concluded that Perfect 10's suggestions regarding measures Google could implement to prevent its web crawler from indexing infringing websites and to block access to infringing images were not workable. *Id.* at 858 n. 25. Rather, the suggestions suffered from both "imprecision and overbreadth." *Id.* We hold that these findings are not clearly erroneous. Without image-recognition technology, Google lacks the practical ability to police the infringing activities of third-party websites. This distinguishes Google from the defendants held liable in *Napster* and *Fonovisa*. *See Napster*, 239 F.3d at 1023-24 (Napster had the ability to identify and police infringing conduct by searching its index for song titles); *Fonovisa*, 76 F.3d at 262 (swap meet operator had the ability to identify and police infringing activity by patrolling its premises).

Perfect 10 argues that Google could manage its own operations to avoid indexing websites with infringing content and linking to third-party infringing sites. . . . Google's failure to change its operations to avoid assisting websites to distribute their infringing content may constitute contributory liability. . . . However, this failure is not the same as declining to exercise a right and ability to make third-party websites stop their direct infringement. We reject Perfect 10's efforts to blur this distinction.

Because we conclude that Perfect 10 has not shown a likelihood of establishing Google's right and ability to stop or limit the directly infringing conduct of third-party websites, we agree with the district court's conclusion that Perfect 10 "has not established a likelihood of proving the [control] prong necessary for vicarious liability." *Perfect 10*, 416 F.Supp.2d at 858.[15] . . .

≡≡ *Perfect 10, Inc. v. Visa International Service Association*
≡≡ *494 F.3d 788 (9th Cir. 2007), cert. denied, 128 S. Ct. 2871 (2008)*

MILAN D. SMITH, JR., J.:

Perfect 10, Inc. (Perfect 10) sued Visa International Service Association, MasterCard International Inc., and several affiliated banks and data processing services (collectively, the

---

15. Having so concluded, we need not reach Perfect 10's argument that Google received a direct financial benefit.

Defendants), alleging secondary liability under federal copyright . . . law. . . . It sued because Defendants continue to process credit card payments to websites that infringe Perfect 10's intellectual property rights after being notified by Perfect 10 of infringement by those websites. The district court dismissed . . . under Federal Rule of Civil Procedure 12(b)(6) for failure to state a claim upon which relief can be granted. We affirm. . . .

Facts and Prior Proceedings

Perfect 10 publishes the magazine "PERFECT10" and operates the subscription website www.perfect10.com., both of which "feature tasteful copyrighted images of the world's most beautiful natural models." Appellant's Opening Brief at 1. Perfect 10 claims copyrights in the photographs published in its magazine and on its website . . . . Perfect 10 alleges that numerous websites based in several countries have stolen its proprietary images, altered them, and illegally offered them for sale online.

Instead of suing the direct infringers in this case, Perfect 10 sued Defendants, financial institutions that process certain credit card payments to the allegedly infringing websites. . . . Defendants collect fees for their services in these transactions. Perfect 10 alleges that it sent Defendants repeated notices specifically identifying infringing websites and informing Defendants that some of their consumers use their payment cards to purchase infringing images. Defendants admit receiving some of these notices, but they took no action in response to the notices after receiving them. . . .

Discussion

Secondary Liability Under Federal Copyright . . . Law

A. Secondary Liability for Copyright Infringement

. . . We evaluate Perfect 10's claims with an awareness that credit cards serve as the primary engine of electronic commerce and that Congress has determined it to be the "policy of the United States — (1) to promote the continued development of the Internet and other interactive computer services and other interactive media [and] (2) to preserve the vibrant and competitive free market that presently exists for the Internet and other interactive computer services, unfettered by Federal or State regulation." 47 U.S.C. §§230(b)(1), (2).

1. Contributory Copyright Infringement

. . . We have found that a defendant is a contributory infringer if it (1) has knowledge of a third party's infringing activity, and (2) "induces, causes, or materially contributes to the infringing conduct." *Ellison v. Robertson*, 357 F.3d 1072, 1076 (9th Cir.2004) (citing *Gershwin Publ'g Corp. v. Columbia Artists Mgmt., Inc.*, 443 F.2d 1159, 1162 (2d Cir.1971)). In an Internet context, we have found contributory liability when the defendant "engages in personal conduct that encourages or assists the infringement." *A & M Records, Inc. v. Napster, Inc.*, 239 F.3d 1004, 1019 (9th Cir.2001) (internal citations omitted). . . .

We understand these several criteria to be non-contradictory variations on the same basic test, i.e., that one contributorily infringes when he (1) has knowledge of another's infringement and . . . materially contributes to [it]. . . .

a.   Knowledge of the Infringing Activity

Because we find that Perfect 10 has not pled facts sufficient to establish that Defendants . . . materially contribute to the infringing activity, Perfect 10's contributory copyright infringement claim fails and we need not address the Defendants' knowledge of the infringing activity.

b.   Material Contribution, Inducement, or Causation

To state a claim of contributory infringement, Perfect 10 must allege facts showing that Defendants induce, cause, or materially contribute to the infringing conduct. . . . Perfect 10 argues that by continuing to process credit card payments to the infringing websites despite having knowledge of ongoing infringement, Defendants induce, enable and contribute to the infringing activity. . . . We disagree.

1. Material Contribution

The credit card companies cannot be said to materially contribute to the infringement in this case because they have no direct connection to that infringement. Here, the infringement rests on the reproduction, alteration, display and distribution of Perfect 10's images over the Internet. Perfect 10 has not alleged that any infringing material passes over Defendants' payment networks or through their payment processing systems, or that Defendants' systems are used to alter or display the infringing images. In *Fonovisa*, the infringing material was physically located in and traded at the defendant's market. Here, it is not. Nor are Defendants' systems used to locate the infringing images. The search engines in *Amazon.com* provided links to specific infringing images, and the service[ ] in *Napster* . . . allowed users to locate and obtain infringing material. Here, in contrast, the services provided by the credit card companies do not help locate and are not used to distribute the infringing images. While Perfect 10 has alleged that Defendants make it easier for websites to profit from this infringing activity, the issue here is reproduction, alteration, display and distribution, which can occur without payment. Even if infringing images were not paid for, there would still be infringement. *See Napster*, 239 F.3d at 1014 (Napster users infringed the distribution right by uploading file names to the search index for others to copy, despite the fact that no money changed hands in the transaction).

Our analysis is fully consistent with this court's recent decision in *Perfect 10 v. Amazon.com*. . . . The salient distinction is that Google's search engine itself assists in the distribution of infringing content to Internet users, while Defendants' payment systems do not. . . . [Defendants] in no way assist or enable Internet users to locate infringing material, and they do not distribute it. They do, as alleged, make infringement more profitable, and people are generally more inclined to engage in an activity when it is financially profitable. However, there is an additional step in the causal chain: Google may materially contribute to infringement by making it fast and easy for third parties to locate and distribute infringing material, whereas Defendants make it easier for infringement to be *profitable*, which tends to increase financial incentives to infringe, which in turn tends to increase infringement.

. . . Helping users to locate an image might substantially assist users to download infringing images, but processing payments does not. If users couldn't pay for images with credit cards, infringement could continue on a large scale because other viable funding mechanisms are available. For example, a website might decide to allow users to download some images for free and to make its profits from advertising, or it might develop other payment mechanisms that do not depend on the credit card companies. . . .

2. Vicarious Copyright Infringement

. . . To state a claim for vicarious copyright infringement, a plaintiff must allege that the defendant has (1) the right and ability to supervise the infringing conduct and (2) a direct financial interest in the infringing activity. *Ellison*, 357 F.3d at 1078; *Napster*, 239 F.3d at 1022 (citations omitted). . . .

a. Right and Ability to Supervise the Infringing Activity

In order to join a Defendant's payment network, merchants and member banks must agree to follow that Defendant's rules and regulations. These rules, among other things, prohibit member banks from providing services to merchants engaging in certain illegal activities and require the members and member banks to investigate merchants suspected of engaging in such illegal activity and to terminate their participation in the payment network if certain illegal activity is found. Perfect 10 has alleged that certain websites are infringing Perfect 10's copyrights and that Perfect 10 sent notices of this alleged infringement to Defendants. Accordingly, Perfect 10 has adequately pled that (1) infringement of Perfect 10's copyrights was occurring, (2) Defendants were aware of the infringement, and (3) on this basis, Defendants could have stopped processing credit card payments to the infringing websites. These allegations are not, however, sufficient to establish vicarious liability because even with all reasonable inferences drawn in Perfect 10's favor, Perfect 10's allegations of fact cannot support a finding that Defendants have the right and ability to control the infringing activity.

In reasoning closely analogous to the present case, the *Amazon.com* court held that Google was not vicariously liable for third-party infringement that its search engine facilitates. In so holding, the court found that Google's ability to control its own index, search results, and webpages does not give Google the right to control the infringing acts of third parties even though that ability would allow Google to affect those infringing acts to some degree. *Amazon.com*, 487 F.3d at 730-32. Moreover, and even more importantly, the *Amazon.com* court rejected a vicarious liability claim based on Google's policies with sponsored advertisers, which state that it reserves "the right to monitor and terminate partnerships with entities that violate others' copyright[s]." *Id.* at 730 (alteration in original). The court found that

> Google's right to terminate an AdSense partnership does not give Google the right to stop direct infringement by third-party websites. An infringing third-party website can continue to reproduce, display, and distribute its infringing copies of Perfect 10 images after its participation in the AdSense program has ended.

Id. This reasoning is equally applicable to the Defendants in this case. Just like Google, Defendants could likely take certain steps that may have the indirect effect of reducing infringing activity on the Internet at large. However, neither Google nor Defendants has any ability to directly control that activity, and the mere ability to withdraw a financial "carrot" does not create the "stick" of "right and ability to control" that vicarious infringement requires. A finding of vicarious liability here, under the theories advocated by the dissent, would also require a finding that Google is vicariously liable for infringement—a conflict we need not create, and radical step we do not take. . . .

b.   Obvious and Direct Financial Interest in the Infringing Activity

Because Perfect 10 has failed to show that Defendants have the right and ability to control the alleged infringing conduct, it has not pled a viable claim of vicarious liability. Accordingly, we need not reach the issue of direct financial interest. . . .

KOZINSKI, Circuit Judge, dissenting . . . :
   . . . Accepting the truth of plaintiff's allegations, as we must on a motion to dismiss, the credit cards are easily liable for indirect copyright infringement: They knowingly provide a financial bridge between buyers and sellers of pirated works, enabling them to consummate infringing transactions, while making a profit on every sale. If such active participation in infringing conduct does not amount to indirect infringement, it's hard to imagine what would. By straining to absolve defendants of liability, the majority leaves our law in disarray.

Contributory Infringement

   . . . Our recent opinion in *Perfect 10, Inc. v. Amazon.com, Inc.*, 487 F.3d 701 (9th Cir.2007), canvasses the caselaw in this area and concludes that Google "could be held contributorily liable if it had knowledge that infringing Perfect 10 images were available using its search engine, could take simple measures to prevent further damage to Perfect 10's copyrighted works, and failed to take such steps." *Amazon*, 487 F.3d at 729. Substitute "payment systems" for "search engine" in this sentence, and it describes defendants here: If a consumer wishes to buy an infringing image from one of the Stolen Content Websites, he can do so by using Visa or MasterCard, just as he can use Google to find the infringing images in the first place. . . .
   The majority struggles to distinguish *Amazon* by positing an "additional step in the causal chain" between defendants' activities and the infringing conduct. *Id.* at 797. . . . The majority is mistaken; there is no "additional step." Defendants participate in every credit card sale of pirated images; the images are delivered to the buyer only after defendants approve the transaction and process the payment. This is not just an economic incentive for infringement; it's an essential step in the infringement process.
   In any event, I don't see why it matters whether there is an "additional step." Materiality turns on how significantly the activity helps infringement, not on whether it's characterized as one step or two steps removed from it. . . . Taking the majority at its word, it sounds like defendants are providing very significant help to the direct infringers.
   My colleagues recognize, as they must, that helping consumers locate infringing content can constitute contributory infringement, but they consign the means of payment to secondary status. . . . But why is *locating* infringing images more central to infringement than *paying* for them? If infringing images can't be found, there can be no infringement; but if infringing images can't be paid for, there can be no infringement either. Location services and payment services are equally central to infringement. . . .
   The majority dismisses the significance of credit cards by arguing that "infringement could continue on a large scale [without them] because other viable funding mechanisms are available." . . . Of course, the same could be said about Google. [I]f Google were unwilling or unable to serve up infringing images, consumers could use Yahoo!, Ask.com, Microsoft Live Search, A9.com or AltaVista instead. . . . Even if none of these were available, consumers could still locate websites with infringing images through e-mails from friends, messages on discussion forums, . . . peer-to-peer networking using BitTorrent or eDonkey, offline and online

advertisements . . . , disreputable search engines hosted on servers in far-off jurisdictions or even old-fashioned word of mouth. . . .

Vicarious Infringement

. . . There is no doubt that defendants profit from the infringing activity of the Stolen Content Websites; after all, they take a cut of virtually every sale of pirated material. First Am. Compl. at 4 ¶13, 7 ¶25. The majority does not dispute this point so I need not belabor it. Maj. op. at 806.

Defendants here also have a right to stop or limit the infringing activity, a right they have refused to exercise. As the majority recognizes, "Perfect 10 . . . claims that Defendants' rules and regulations permit them to require member merchants to cease illegal activity—presumably including copyright infringement—as a condition to their continuing right to receive credit card payments from the relevant Defendant entities." Maj. op. at 804. Assuming the truth of this allegation, the cards have the authority, given to them by contract, to force the Stolen Content Websites to remove infringing images from their inventory as a condition for using defendants' payment systems. If the merchants comply, their websites stop peddling stolen content and so infringement is stopped or limited. If they don't comply, defendants have the right—and under copyright law the duty—to kick the pirates off their payment networks, forcing them to find other means of getting paid or go out of business. In that case, too, infringement is stopped or limited. The swap meet in *Fonovisa* was held vicariously liable precisely because it did not force the pirates to stop infringing or leave; there is no reason to treat defendants here differently.

That the pirates might find some other way of doing business is of no consequence; our cases make this perfectly clear. It didn't matter in *Fonovisa* that the infringers there could have continued their illegal sales by mail order or by hawking their unlawful merchandise on street corners. . . . Indeed, there is no case involving secondary infringement, going back to the dance hall cases of the last century, where the secondary infringer's refusal to do business with the direct infringer could have stopped infringement altogether and forever. Yet, courts have presumed that removing the particular means of infringement challenged in each case would make direct infringement more difficult and thereby diminish the scale of infringing activity. . . .

. . . [I]t makes no difference that defendants control only the means of payment, not the mechanics of transferring the material. Maj. op. at 802, 805, 806. In a commercial environment, distribution and payment are (to use a quaint anachronism) like love and marriage—you can't have one without the other. If cards don't process payment, pirates don't deliver booty. The credit cards, in fact, control distribution of the infringing material. . . .

NOTES AND QUESTIONS

1. How does each court: (1) define the elements of contributory and vicarious liability; and (2) apply the tests it defines to the facts before it? Are the cases consistent? In particular, do you agree with the majority in the *Visa* case that its decision is consistent with *Amazon.com*? Did the court apply more lenient standards to the credit card entities than it did to OSPs?

2. Are contributory infringement and vicarious liability truly distinct concepts? Do the courts implement them in that way? In particular, are knowledge and right to control synonymous? If one exists, must the other necessarily also exist? What is the disagreement between the majority and the dissent in *Visa* regarding the right to control? Which approach do you find more persuasive?

3. The *Amazon.com* court referenced the *Netcom* case that you read in Section A *supra*. How would you resolve claims that Netcom was contributorily and vicariously liable? In *Netcom*, the court observed:

> Netcom argues that its knowledge after receiving notice of Erlich's alleged infringing activities was too equivocal given the difficulty in assessing whether registrations are valid and whether use is fair. . . . Where a BBS operator cannot reasonably verify a claim of infringement, either because of a possible fair use defense, the lack of copyright notices on the copies, or the copyright holder's failure to provide the necessary documentation to show that there is a likely infringement, the operator's lack of knowledge will be found reasonable. . . .
>
> The first element of vicarious liability will be met if plaintiffs can show that Netcom has the right and ability to supervise the conduct of its subscribers. Netcom argues that it does not have the right to control its users' postings before they occur. Plaintiffs . . . argue that Netcom's terms and conditions, to which its subscribers must agree, specify that Netcom reserves the right to take remedial action against subscribers. . . .
>
> Netcom argues that it could not possibly screen messages before they are posted given the speed and volume of the data that goes through its system. Netcom further argues that it has never exercised control over the content of its users' postings. Plaintiffs' expert opines otherwise, stating that with an easy software modification Netcom could identify postings that contain particular words or come from particular individuals. . . . Plaintiffs further dispute Netcom's claim that it could not limit Erlich's access to Usenet without kicking off all 500 subscribers of Klemesrud's BBS. . . . Further evidence shows that Netcom can delete specific postings. . . . Whether such sanctions occurred before or after the abusive conduct is not material to whether Netcom can exercise control. . . .

Religious Tech. Ctr. v. Netcom On-Line Commc'n Servs., Inc., 907 F. Supp. 1361, 1374-76 (N.D. Cal. 1995). The court concluded that triable questions of fact remained as to both knowledge and right and ability to control. Do you agree with the court's reasoning? How would you evaluate knowledge (for contributory infringement) and right and ability to control (for vicarious liability) in the case of a web hosting service such as YouTube or Facebook?

4. Are the cases in this section consistent in their statement of what constitutes material contribution to the infringement for purposes of supporting a contributory infringement claim? Under the *Amazon.com* court's reasoning, does every on-line service inevitably materially contribute to infringement? If so, then contributory infringement cases involving on-line conduct would focus only on knowledge. Would that be appropriate? Does the majority approach in *Visa* offer a desirable way of limiting the material contribution doctrine in the case of OSPs, or do you agree with Judge Kozinski that the majority's analysis is deficient?

5. When might a fact-finder reasonably conclude that the availability of infringing material constitutes a "draw" for customers? For example, America Online (AOL) offers its subscribers a variety of services including Internet access, e-mail, and access to chat rooms and Usenet groups. Subscribers occasionally upload infringing materials to Usenet groups. Does the availability of this material constitute a "draw" sufficient to meet the requirements of vicarious liability? In *Ellison v. Robertson*, the court stated:

> AOL offers access to USENET groups as part of its service for a reason: it helps to encourage overall subscription to its services. Here, AOL's future revenue is directly dependent upon increases in its userbase. Certainly, the fact that AOL provides its subscribers access to certain USENET groups constitutes a small "draw" in proportion to its overall profits, but AOL's status as a behemoth online service provider, by itself, does not insulate it categorically from vicarious liability. Regardless of what fraction of AOL's earnings are considered a direct result of providing its subscribers access to the USENET groups that contained infringing material . . . they would be earnings nonetheless.

The essential aspect of the "direct financial benefit" inquiry is whether there is a causal relationship between the infringing activity and any financial benefit a defendant reaps, regardless of how substantial the benefit is in proportion to a defendant's overall profits. . . .

357 F.3d 1072, 1079 (9th Cir. 2004). Because the "record lack[ed] evidence that AOL attracted or retained subscriptions because of the infringement or lost subscriptions because of AOL's eventual obstruction of the infringement," the court affirmed a grant of summary judgment to AOL on the plaintiff's vicarious liability claim. *Id.* What do you think of this test as a practical matter? Suppose the plaintiff had produced evidence of two subscriptions attracted by the availability of infringing material on USENET groups accessible via AOL. Would summary judgment for AOL be improper? Doctrinally, does the court's formulation of the "direct financial benefit" inquiry make sense? (What kind of "causal relationship" is the court describing?)

6. Note that a court's definition of what constitutes sufficient benefit to satisfy the test for vicarious liability affects the prices that you pay. For example, Cherry Auction, Inc. will likely increase the fees it charges vendors to reflect its potential liability under the copyright law. These vendors will pass the increase on to their customers in the form of higher prices. Should this make any difference in formulating and/or applying a test for "financial benefit"?

7. Do the elements of contributory infringement and vicarious liability produce perverse incentives? It seems that the less one knows about the party with whom he is dealing, the less likely he will be liable for infringement under these theories. Should courts formulate a test for secondary liability specific to on-line conduct?

From a policy standpoint, would extending indirect liability to entities that provide financial services to alleged infringers be a good idea? Why or why not?

8. Should those who assist the secondarily liable party also be liable to the copyright owner for indirect infringement? For example, if a court holds the operator of an Internet search engine or an Internet access provider secondarily liable, would the venture capitalists who financed the Internet company also be liable for providing the funding that enables it to exist and therefore to infringe? In *UMG Recordings, Inc. v. Bertelsmann AG*, 222 F.R.D. 408 (N.D. Cal. 2004), the court addressed a similar question, and expressed "disfavor" toward the idea of liability for "vicarious or contributory assistance to a vicarious or contributory infringer." *Id.* at 412. The court concluded, however, that because the investors in the *UMG Recordings* case were alleged to be intimately involved in the indirect infringer's operations, it could assess the claim as it would any "traditional" secondary liability claim. It therefore declined to rule on "whether mere financial support of a contributing and vicarious infringer . . . would give rise to a claim for contributory or vicarious infringement against the party providing the funding" *Id.* at 413-14. Should providing financial support to a contributory or vicarious infringer itself give rise to liability? Why do you think the *UMG Recordings* court disfavors such "tertiary liability" claims? Why would plaintiffs bring such claims if they can also sue the direct and secondary infringers?

C. DEVICE MANUFACTURERS AND LIABILITY FOR INDUCING INFRINGEMENT

Many firms market equipment that could be used to infringe copyright, including photocopying machines, tape recorders, videocassette recorders (VCRs), and CD/DVD burners.

Practically, these firms know that at least some users of the equipment they sell will commit copyright infringement. The law thus has had to face the policy question whether to hold these firms liable for "indirect" infringement.

In *Sony Corp. of America v. Universal City Studios, Inc.*, 464 U.S. 417 (1984), the Supreme Court addressed an infringement claim premised on secondary liability. Owners of copyrights in television programs sued a manufacturer of VCRs for contributory copyright infringement. The Court, noting the "historic kinship between patent law and copyright law," turned to the Patent Act for guidance in formulating a test for contributory copyright infringement. *Id.* at 439. Unlike the Copyright Act, the Patent Act defines the scope of contributory infringement liability. Section 271 of the Patent Act provides that one who sells a "staple article or commodity of commerce suitable for substantial noninfringing use" is not liable for contributory infringement. 35 U.S.C. §271(c). The *Sony* Court emphasized that this rule reflects the Patent Act's balancing of the "public interest in access to [an] article of commerce" and the interest in providing appropriate incentives to the patentee. *Sony*, 464 U.S. at 440. Applying the patent rationale to copyright law, the Court stated:

> We recognize that there are substantial differences between the patent and copyright laws. But in both areas the contributory infringement doctrine is grounded on the recognition that adequate protection of a monopoly may require the courts to look beyond actual duplication of a device or publication to the products or activities that make such duplication possible. The staple article of commerce doctrine must strike a balance between a copyright holder's legitimate demand for effective — not merely symbolic — protection of the statutory monopoly, and the rights of others freely to engage in substantially unrelated areas of commerce. Accordingly, the sale of copying equipment, like the sale of other articles of commerce, does not constitute contributory infringement if the product is widely used for legitimate, unobjectionable purposes. Indeed, it need merely be capable of substantial noninfringing uses.

Id. at 442.

The Court found that the Betamax VCR at issue was capable of "commercially significant noninfringing uses." *Id.* First, many copyright owners do not object to an individual's taping their programs for purposes of time-shifting (enabling the taper to view the show at his convenience rather than at its scheduled time). Second, the Court held that individuals taping TV programs off the air for time-shifting purposes were sheltered by the fair use doctrine. (We excerpt that part of the opinion in Chapter 7.) Because the VCR was capable of being used in these noninfringing ways, the Court found Sony innocent of contributory infringement. The Court's holding allowed Sony to continue marketing its VCRs to the public without licenses from the copyright owners of the television programs that many VCR purchasers taped.

The *Sony* standard has presented interpretive difficulties for the courts, particularly in the context of digital technologies that permit reproduction and distribution of perfect copies of copyrighted works. The development of peer-to-peer file-sharing technology has posed especially thorny problems. Peer-to-peer technology enables Internet users to communicate directly with other users and access the files stored on each other's hard drives. This technology avoids the expense of maintaining a centralized server to store all of the files in which one might be interested, and opens up the hard drives of everyone using the same peer-to-peer networking program to each other. From the perspective of an Internet user, therefore, peer-to-peer technology vastly increases the Internet's potential as a tool for finding and sharing information. From the perspective of a copyright owner, however, centralized servers and the entities that operate them perform a valuable gatekeeping function: They provide a vantage point from which to guard against infringement. Copyright's secondary liability doctrines, in turn, supply third-party gatekeepers who meet certain threshold criteria of involvement with incentives to minimize infringing activity. The development of peer-to-peer file-sharing technology thus raises two important questions: (1) when do these secondary liability doctrines apply to developers of technologies that enable users to copy and share digital copyrighted content; and (2) exactly what must be shown, and by whom, for a technology developer to claim the protection of the *Sony* rule?

The first round of copyright infringement litigation over peer-to-peer technology involved the file-sharing service known as Napster. Napster's MusicShare software allowed users to search for MP3 music files stored on each others' computers and exchange the files directly with one another. The software maintained a dynamic directory of the files available from users currently logged on to the system. Each time a user logged on, the software would add that user's Internet Protocol (IP) address and list of available files to the directory. A logged-on user could then search the directory for desired files or recording artists, click on a file name in the list of search results, and download that file directly from whoever had offered it. (For a more detailed description of the operation of the Napster system, see page 506 *infra*.)

The Ninth Circuit held that once Napster had been notified of specific infringing files being traded on its system, it could be held contributorily liable for infringing the copyrights in those works. *A & M Records, Inc. v. Napster, Inc.*, 239 F.3d 1004, 1021-22 (9th Cir. 2001). Regarding *Sony*, it observed: "We are compelled to make a clear distinction between the architecture of the Napster system and Napster's conduct in relation to the operational capacity of the system. . . . [A]bsent specific information which identifies infringing activity, a computer system operator cannot be liable for contributory infringement merely because the structure of the system allows for the exchange of copyrighted material." *Id.* at 1020-21. Napster, however, had both specific knowledge and the ability to "purge" the infringing files. *Id.* The court ruled that Napster also could be held vicariously liable for infringement, because it received a direct financial benefit from advertising sales and had both the right and ability to control the infringement by filtering or otherwise blocking the exchange of files specifically identified as infringing. *Id.* at 1023-24.

The second round of copyright infringement litigation over peer-to-peer technology was *In re Aimster Copyright Litigation*, 334 F.3d 643 (7th Cir. 2003), *cert. denied*, 540 U.S. 1107 (2004), which involved a system designed to piggyback on America Online's Instant Messenger network. Unlike Napster, the Aimster system did not create a central directory of files offered for sharing by logged-in users, but simply created a dynamic listing of all users currently logged on to the system. An individual user could conduct file searches that would display to that user a list of all logged-on users who had the designated files available. In addition, the Aimster system automatically encrypted all communications between users.

The Seventh Circuit ruled that Aimster's encryption-based strategy amounted to willful blindness, and could not be used to avoid contributory infringement liability. In light of other facts, particularly an Aimster software tutorial that the court characterized as an "invitation to infringement," 334 F.3d at 651, the court held that Aimster had the burden to show that its service in fact currently had substantial noninfringing uses, and to provide "evidence concerning the frequency of such uses." *Id.* at 652-53. Because Aimster had produced no evidence of any actual non-infringing uses, it upheld a preliminary injunction shutting Aimster down. The court opined, however, that even if Aimster had produced sufficient evidence of noninfringing uses, to avoid liability it also would need to "show that it would have been disproportionately costly . . . to eliminate or at least reduce substantially the infringing uses." *Id.* at 653. The court expressed doubt about the applicability of vicarious liability to Aimster's conduct. It observed that vicarious liability is a theory that allows liability in "cases in which the only effective relief is obtainable from someone who bears a relation to the direct infringers that is analogous to the relation of a principal to an agent." *Id.* at 654. Ultimately, the court declined to rule on this question.

Both the *Napster* and *Aimster* disputes involved software-based systems whose providers played ongoing roles in their use. In a true peer-to-peer network, there is no support at all from a central server. The third round of copyright infringement litigation over peer-to-peer file-sharing involved two such systems, developed and distributed by Grokster and StreamCast after Napster's legal battles had begun. This litigation thus seemed to present both the secondary liability question and the *Sony* question in their purest forms: Should an entity that creates and releases true peer-to-peer software and exercises no ongoing control over its use, and that knows the software will be used on a widespread basis to infringe copyrights, be held secondarily liable for acts of copyright infringement committed by users of the software?

≡ ≡ ≡ **Metro-Goldwyn-Mayer Studios Inc. v. Grokster, Ltd.**
≡ ≡ ≡ *545 U.S. 913 (2005)*

SOUTER, J.: . . .

I

A

Respondents, Grokster, Ltd., and StreamCast Networks, Inc. . . . distribute free software products that allow computer users to share electronic files through peer-to-peer networks, so called because users' computers communicate directly with each other, not through central servers. . . .

. . . A group of copyright holders (MGM for short, but including motion picture studios, recording companies, songwriters, and music publishers) sued Grokster and StreamCast for their users' infringements, alleging that they knowingly and intentionally distributed their software to enable their users to reproduce and distribute the copyrighted works. . . .

. . . Grokster and StreamCast use no servers to intercept the content of the search requests or to mediate the file transfers conducted by users of the software, there being no central point through which the substance of the communications passes in either direction. . . .

Although Grokster and StreamCast do not therefore know when particular files are copied, a few searches using their software would show what is available on the networks the software reaches. MGM commissioned a statistician to conduct a systematic search, and his study showed that nearly 90% of the files available for download on [Grokster's] FastTrack system were copyrighted works. . . . Grokster and StreamCast dispute this figure, raising methodological problems and arguing that free copying even of copyrighted works may be authorized by the rightholders. They also argue that potential noninfringing uses of their software are significant in kind, even if infrequent in practice. . . .

. . . [T]he parties' anecdotal and statistical evidence entered thus far to show the content available on the . . . networks does not say much about which files are actually downloaded by users, and no one can say how often the software is used to obtain copies of unprotected material. But MGM's evidence gives reason to think that the vast majority of users' downloads are acts of infringement, and because well over 100 million copies of the software in question are known to have been downloaded, and billions of files are shared across the . . . networks each month, the probable scope of copyright infringement is staggering. . . .

Grokster and StreamCast concede the infringement in most downloads ... and it is uncontested that they are aware that users employ their software primarily to download copyrighted files. ... From time to time, moreover, the companies have learned about their users' infringement directly, as from users who have sent e-mail to each company with questions about playing copyrighted movies they had downloaded, to whom the companies have responded with guidance. ...

Grokster and StreamCast are not, however, merely passive recipients of information about infringing use. The record is replete with evidence that from the moment Grokster and Stream-Cast began to distribute their free software, each one clearly voiced the objective that recipients use it to download copyrighted works, and each took active steps to encourage infringement.

After the notorious file-sharing service, Napster, was sued by copyright holders for facilitation of copyright infringement ... StreamCast gave away a software program known as OpenNap, designed as compatible with the Napster program and open to Napster users for downloading files from other Napster and OpenNap users' computers. Evidence indicates that "[i]t was always [StreamCast's] intent to use [its OpenNap network] to be able to capture email addresses of [its] initial target market so that [it] could promote [its] StreamCast Morpheus interface to them," ...

StreamCast monitored both the number of users downloading its OpenNap program and the number of music files they downloaded. ... It also used the resulting OpenNap network to distribute copies of the Morpheus software and to encourage users to adopt it. ... Internal company documents indicate that StreamCast hoped to attract large numbers of former Napster users if that company was shut down by court order or otherwise. ... [I]t introduced itself to some potential advertisers as a company "which is similar to what Napster was," ...

The evidence that Grokster sought to capture the market of former Napster users is sparser but revealing, for Grokster launched its own OpenNap system called Swaptor and inserted digital codes into its Web site so that computer users using Web search engines to look for "Napster" or "[f]ree filesharing" would be directed to the Grokster Web site, where they could download the Grokster software. ... And Grokster's name is an apparent derivative of Napster. ...

StreamCast's executives monitored the number of songs by certain commercial artists available on their networks, and an internal communication indicates they aimed to have a larger number of copyrighted songs available on their networks than other file-sharing networks. ... Morpheus in fact allowed users to search specifically for "Top 40" songs. ... Similarly, Grokster sent users a newsletter promoting its ability to provide particular, popular copyrighted materials. ...

In addition to this evidence of express promotion, marketing, and intent to promote further, the business models employed by Grokster and StreamCast confirm that their principal object was use of their software to download copyrighted works. Grokster and StreamCast receive no revenue from users, who obtain the software itself for nothing. Instead both companies generate revenue by selling advertising space, and they stream the advertising to Grokster and Morpheus users while they are employing the programs. As the number of users of each program increases, advertising opportunities become worth more. ... Users seeking Top 40 songs, for example, or the latest release by Modest Mouse, are certain to be far more numerous than those seeking a free *Decameron*. ...

Finally, there is no evidence that either company made an effort to filter copyrighted material from users' downloads or otherwise impede the sharing of copyrighted files. ...

B

After discovery, the parties on each side of the case cross-moved for summary judgment. ... The District Court held that those who used the Grokster and Morpheus software to download copyrighted media files directly infringed MGM's copyrights, a conclusion not contested on appeal, but the court nonetheless granted summary judgment in favor of Grokster and StreamCast as to any liability arising from distribution of the then current versions of their software. Distributing that software gave rise to no liability in the court's view, because its use did not provide the distributors with actual knowledge of specific acts of infringement. . . .

The Court of Appeal affirmed. . . . [T]he court read *Sony Corp. of America v. Universal City Studios, Inc.*, 464 U.S. 417 (1984), as holding that distribution of a commercial product capable of substantial noninfringing uses could not give rise to contributory liability for infringement unless the distributor has actual knowledge of specific instances of infringement and failed to act on that knowledge. The fact that the software was capable of substantial noninfringing uses in the Ninth Circuit's view meant that Grokster and StreamCast were not liable, because they had no such actual knowledge, owing to the decentralized architecture of their software. The court also held that Grokster and StreamCast did not materially contribute to their users' infringement because . . . [there was] no involvement by the defendants beyond providing the software in the first place. . . .

[The Ninth Circuit also rejected MGM's vicarious liability argument because Grokster and StreamCast had no current right or ability to supervise the use of their software.]

II

A . . .

The argument for imposing indirect liability in this case is . . . a powerful one, given the number of infringing downloads that occur every day using StreamCast's and Grokster's software. When a widely shared service or product is used to commit infringement, it may be impossible to enforce rights in the protected work effectively against all direct infringers. . . .

One infringes contributorily by intentionally inducing or encouraging direct infringement . . . and infringes vicariously by profiting from direct infringement by declining to exercise a right to stop or limit it. . . . [9] Although "[t]he Copyright Act does not expressly render anyone liable for infringement committed by another," *Sony* . . . , 464 U.S., at 434, these doctrines of secondary liability emerged from common law principles and are well established in the law. . . .

B

. . . [T]his Court has dealt with secondary copyright infringement in only one recent case, and because MGM has tailored its principal claim to our opinion there, a look at our earlier holding is in order. . . . At the trial on the merits [in *Sony*], the evidence showed that the principal use of the VCR was for " 'time-shifting,' " or taping a program for later viewing at a more convenient time, which the Court found to be a fair, not an infringing, use. . . . There was no evidence that Sony had expressed an object of bringing about taping in violation of copyright or had taken active steps to increase its profits from unlawful taping. . . . Although Sony's advertisements urged consumers to buy the VCR to " 'record favorite shows' " or

---

9. We stated in *Sony* . . . that " 'the lines between direct infringement, contributory infringement and vicarious liability are not clearly drawn' . . . ," *id*. at 435, n.17. . . . Because we resolve th[is] case based on an inducement theory, there is no need to analyze separately MGM's vicarious liability theory.

" 'build a library' " of recorded programs, . . . neither of these uses was necessarily infringing, *id.* at 424, 454-55.

On those facts . . . the only conceivable basis for imposing liability was on a theory of contributory infringement arising from its sale of VCRs to consumers with knowledge that some of them would infringe. . . . But, because the VCR was "capable of substantial non-infringing uses," we held the manufacturer could not be faulted solely on the basis of its distribution. . . .

. . . [W]here an article is "good for nothing else" but infringement, . . . there is no legitimate public interest in its unlicensed availability and there is no injustice in presuming or imputing an intent to infringe. . . . Conversely, the [staple article of commerce] doctrine absolves the equivocal conduct of selling an item with substantial lawful as well as unlawful uses, and limits liability to instances of more acute fault than the mere understanding that some of one's products will be misused. It leaves breathing room for innovation and a vigorous commerce. . . .

The parties and many of the *amici* in this case think the key to resolving it is the *Sony* rule and, in particular, what it means for a product to be "capable of commercially significant noninfringing uses." . . . MGM advances the argument that granting summary judgment to Grokster and StreamCast as to their current activities gave too much weight to the value of innovative technology, and too little to the copyrights infringed by users of their software, given that 90% of works available on one of the networks was shown to be copyrighted. Assuming the remaining 10% to be its noninfringing use, MGM says this should not qualify as "substantial," and the Court should quantify *Sony* to the extent of holding that a product used "principally" for infringement does not qualify. . . .

We agree with MGM that the Court of Appeals misapplied *Sony*, which it read as limiting secondary liability quite beyond the circumstances to which the case applied. *Sony* barred secondary liability based on presuming or imputing intent to cause infringement solely from the design or distribution of a product capable of substantial lawful use, which the distributor knows is in fact used for infringement. The Ninth Circuit has read *Sony*'s limitation to mean that whenever a product is capable of substantial lawful use, the producer can never be held contributorily liable for third parties' infringing use of it . . . even when an actual purpose to cause infringing use is shown by evidence independent of design and distribution of the product. . . .

This view of *Sony*, however, was error, converting the case from one about liability resting on imputed intent to one about liability on any theory. Because *Sony* did not displace other theories of secondary liability . . . we do not revisit *Sony* further, as MGM requests, to add a more quantified description of the point of balance between protection and commerce when liability rests solely on distribution with knowledge that unlawful use will occur. . . .

C

Sony's rule limits imputing culpable intent as a matter of law from the characteristics or uses of a distributed product. But nothing in *Sony* requires courts to ignore evidence of intent if there is such evidence, and the case was never meant to foreclose rules of fault-based liability derived from the common law.[10] . . .

The classic case of direct evidence of unlawful purpose occurs when one induces commission of infringement by another, or "entic[es] or persuad[es] another" to infringe, Black's Law Dictionary 790 (8th ed. 2004), as by advertising. Thus at common law a copyright

---

10. Nor does the Patent Act's exemption from liability for those who distribute a staple article of commerce, 35 U.S.C. §271(c), extend to those who induce patent infringement, §271(b).

or patent defendant who "not only expected but invoked [infringing use] by advertisement" was liable for infringement. . . .

The rule on inducement of infringement as developed in the early cases is no different today. . . . [A]dvertising an infringing use or instructing how to engage in an infringing use, show[s] an affirmative intent that the product be used to infringe, and a showing that infringement was encouraged overcomes the law's reluctance to find liability when a defendant merely sells a commercial product suitable for some lawful use, see, *e.g.*, . . . *Fromberg, Inc. v. Thornhill*, 315 F.2d 407, 412-13 (5th Cir. 1963) (demonstrations by sales staff of infringing uses supported liability for inducement); *Haworth Inc. v. Herman Miller Inc.*, 37 U.S.P.Q.2d 1080, 1090 (W.D. Mich. 1994) (evidence that defendant "demonstrated and recommend[ed] infringing configurations" of its product could support inducement liability); *Sims v. Mack Trucks, Inc.*, 459 F. Supp. 1198, 1215 (E.D. Pa. 1978) (finding inducement where the use "depicted by the defendant in its promotional film and brochures infringes the . . . patent"). . . .

For the same reasons that *Sony* took the staple-article doctrine of patent law as a model for its copyright safe-harbor rule, the inducement rule, too, is a sensible one for copyright. We adopt it here, holding that one who distributes a device with the object of promoting its use to infringe copyright, as shown by clear expression or other affirmative steps taken to foster infringement, is liable for the resulting acts of infringement by third parties. We are, of course, mindful of the need to keep from trenching on regular commerce or discouraging the development of technologies with lawful and unlawful potential. Accordingly . . . mere knowledge of infringing potential or of actual infringing uses would not be enough here to subject a distributor to liability. Nor would ordinary acts incident to product distribution, such as offering customers technical support or product updates, support liability in themselves. The inducement rule, instead, premises liability on purposeful, culpable expression and conduct, and thus does nothing to compromise legitimate commerce or discourage innovation having a lawful promise.

III

A

The only apparent question about treating MGM's evidence as sufficient to withstand summary judgment under the theory of inducement goes to the need on MGM's part to adduce evidence that StreamCast and Grokster communicated an inducing message to their software users. . . . It is undisputed that StreamCast beamed onto the computer screens of users of Napster-compatible programs ads urging the adoption of its OpenNap program. . . . Those who accepted StreamCast's OpenNap program were offered software to perform the same services, which a factfinder could conclude would readily have been understood in the Napster market as the ability to download copyrighted music files. Grokster distributed an electronic newsletter containing links to articles promoting its software's ability to access popular copyrighted music. And anyone whose Napster or free file-sharing searches turned up a link to Grokster would have understood Grokster to be offering the same file-sharing ability as Napster . . . ; that would also have been the understanding of anyone offered Grokster's suggestively named Swaptor software, its version of OpenNap. And both companies communicated a clear message by responding affirmatively to requests for help in locating and playing copyrighted materials.

In StreamCast's case, of course, the evidence just described was supplemented by other unequivocal indications of unlawful purpose in . . . internal communications. . . . Whether the messages were communicated is not to the point on this record. . . .

Three features of this evidence of intent are particularly notable. First, each company showed itself to be aiming to satisfy a known source of demand for copyright infringement, the market comprising former Napster users. . . .

Second, this evidence of unlawful objective is given added significance by MGM's showing that neither company attempted to develop filtering tools or other mechanisms to diminish the infringing activity using their software. While the Ninth Circuit treated the defendants' failure to develop such tools as irrelevant because they lacked an independent duty to monitor their users' activity, we think this evidence underscores Grokster's and StreamCast's intentional facilitation of their users' infringement.[12]

Third, there is a further complement to the direct evidence of unlawful objective. . . . StreamCast and Grokster make money by selling advertising space, by directing ads to the screens of computers employing their software. . . . [T]he more the software is used, the more ads are sent out and the greater the advertising revenue becomes. . . . This evidence alone would not justify an inference of unlawful intent, but viewed in the context of the entire record its import is clear.

The unlawful objective is unmistakable.

B

In addition to intent to bring about infringement and distribution of a device suitable for infringing use, the inducement theory of course requires evidence of actual infringement by recipients of the device. . . . [T]here is no serious issue of the adequacy of MGM's showing on this point in order to survive the companies' summary judgment requests. . . .

GINSBURG, J., with whom REHNQUIST, C.J., and KENNEDY, J., join, concurring: . . . There is here at least a "genuine issue as to [a] material fact," . . . on the liability of Grokster or StreamCast, not only for actively inducing infringement, but also, or alternatively, based on the distribution of their software products, for contributory copyright infringement. . . .

This case differs markedly from *Sony*. . . . Here, there has been no finding of fair use and little beyond anecdotal evidence of noninfringing uses. . . . [T]he District Court and the Court of Appeals appear to have relied largely on declarations submitted by the defendants. These declarations include assertions (some of them hearsay) that a number of copyright owners authorize distribution of their works on the Internet and that some public domain material is available through peer-to-peer networks including those accessed through Grokster's and StreamCast's software. . . .

. . . Review of these declarations reveals mostly anecdotal evidence, sometimes obtained second-hand, of authorized copyrighted works or public domain works available online . . . and general statements about the benefits of peer-to-peer technology. . . . These declarations do not support summary judgment in the face of evidence, proffered by MGM, of overwhelming use of Grokster's and StreamCast's software for infringement.[3]

---

12. Of course, in the absence of other evidence of intent, a court would be unable to find contributory infringement liability merely based on a failure to take affirmative steps to prevent infringement, if the device otherwise was capable of substantial noninfringing uses. Such a holding would tread too close to the *Sony* safe harbor.

3. Justice Breyer finds support for summary judgment in this motley collection of declarations and in a survey conducted by an expert retained by MGM. . . . Even assuming, as Justice Breyer does, that the *Sony* Court would have absolved Sony of contributory liability solely on the basis of the use of the Betamax for authorized time-shifting . . . summary judgment is not inevitably appropriate here. *Sony* stressed that the plaintiffs there owned "well below 10%" of copyrighted television programming . . . and found, based on trial testimony from representatives of the four major sports leagues and other individuals authorized to consent to home-recording of their copyrighted broadcasts, that a

. . . [T]he District Court and the Court of Appeals did not sharply distinguish between uses of Grokster's and StreamCast's software products (which this case is about) and uses of peer-to-peer technology generally (which this case is not about). . . .

. . . On this record, the District Court should not have ruled dispositively on the contributory infringement charge by granting summary judgment to Grokster and StreamCast. . . .

BREYER, J., with whom STEVENS, J., and O'CONNOR, J., join, concurring: . . . The *Sony* Court had before it a survey . . . showing that roughly 9% of all VCR recordings were of the type — namely, religious, educational, and sports programming — owned by producers and distributors testifying on Sony's behalf who did not object to time-shifting. . . . A much higher percentage of VCR *users* had at one point taped an authorized program, in addition to taping unauthorized programs. And the plaintiffs — not a large class of content producers as in this case — owned only a small percentage of the total available *un*authorized programming. . . . But of all the taping actually done by Sony's customers, only around 9% was of the sort the Court referred to as authorized.

The Court found that the magnitude of authorized programming was "significant," and it also noted the "significant potential for future authorized copying." . . . The Court supported this conclusion by referencing the trial testimony of professional sports league officials and a religious broadcasting representative. . . . It also discussed (1) a Los Angeles educational station affiliated with the Public Broadcasting Service that made many of its programs available for home taping, and (2) Mr. Rogers' Neighborhood, a widely watched children's program. . . . On the basis of this testimony and other similar evidence, the Court determined that producers of this kind ha[ve] authorized duplication of their copyrighted programs "in significant enough numbers to create a *substantial* market for a noninfringing use of the" VCR. . . .

The Court, in using the key word "substantial," indicated that these circumstances alone constituted a sufficient basis for rejecting the imposition of secondary liability. . . .

As in *Sony*, witnesses here explained the nature of the noninfringing files on Grokster's network without detailed quantification. Those files include:

— Authorized copies of music by artists such as Wilco, Janis Ian, Pearl Jam, Dave Matthews, John Mayer, and others. . . .
— Free electronic books and other works from various online publishers, including Project Gutenberg. . . .
— Public domain and authorized software, such as WinZip. . . .
— Licensed music videos and television and movie segments distributed via digital video packaging with the permission of the copyright holder. . . .

The nature of these and other lawfully swapped files is such that it is reasonable to infer quantities of current lawful use roughly approximate to those at issue in *Sony*. . . .

Importantly, *Sony* also used the word "capable," asking whether the product is "*capable of*" substantial noninfringing uses. Its language and analysis suggest that a figure like 10%, if fixed for all time, might well prove insufficient, but that such a figure serves as an adequate foundation where there is a reasonable prospect of expanded legitimate uses over time. . . .

---

similar percentage of program copying was authorized. . . . Here, the plaintiffs allegedly control copyrights for 70% or 75% of the material exchanged through the Grokster and StreamCast software . . . and the District Court does not appear to have relied on comparable testimony about authorized copying from copyright holders.

And that is just what is happening. Such legitimate noninfringing uses are coming to include the swapping of *research information* . . . ; *public domain films* . . . ; *historical recordings and digital educational materials* . . . ; *digital photos* . . . ; *"shareware" and "freeware"* . . . ; *secure licensed music and movie files* . . . ; *news broadcasts past and present* . . . ; *user-created audio and video files* . . . ; *and all manner of free "open content" works collected by Creative Commons.* . . .

The real question here, I believe, is not whether the record evidence satisfies *Sony.* . . .

Instead, the real question is whether we should modify the *Sony* standard, as MGM requests, or interpret *Sony* more strictly, as I believe Justice Ginsburg's approach would do in practice. . . .

. . . [T]o determine whether modification, or a strict interpretation, of *Sony* is needed, I would ask whether MGM has shown that *Sony* incorrectly balanced copyright and new-technology interests. In particular: (1) Has *Sony* (as I interpret it) worked to protect new technology? (2) If so, would modification or strict interpretation significantly weaken that protection? (3) If so, would new or necessary copyright-related benefits outweigh any such weakening?

The first question is the easiest to answer. . . .

Sony's rule is clear. That clarity allows those who develop new products that are capable of substantial noninfringing uses to know, *ex ante*, that distribution of their product will not yield massive monetary liability. At the same time, it helps deter them from distributing products that have no other real function than — or that are specifically intended for — copyright infringement, deterrence that the Court's holding today reinforces. . . .

Sony's rule is strongly technology protecting. The rule deliberately makes it difficult for courts to find secondary liability where new technology is at issue. . . .

Sony's rule is forward looking. It does not confine its scope to a static snapshot of a product's current uses (thereby threatening technologies that have underdeveloped future markets). . . .

Sony's rule is mindful of the limitations facing judges where matters of technology are concerned. Judges have no specialized technical ability to answer questions about present or future technological feasibility or commercial viability where technology professionals, engineers, and venture capitalists themselves may radically disagree and where answers may differ depending upon whether one focuses upon the time of product development or the time of distribution. Consider, for example, the question whether devices can be added to Grokster's software that will filter out infringing files. . . .

[With respect to the second question,] [t]o require defendants to provide, for example, detailed evidence — say business plans, profitability estimates, projected technological modifications, and so forth — would doubtless make life easier for copyrightholder plaintiffs. But it would simultaneously increase the legal uncertainty that surrounds the creation or development of a new technology capable of being put to infringing uses. Inventors and entrepreneurs (in the garage, the dorm room, the corporate lab, or the boardroom) would have to fear (and in many cases endure) costly and extensive trials when they create, produce, or distribute the sort of information technology that can be used for copyright infringement. . . . The price of a wrong guess — even if it involves a good-faith effort to assess technical and commercial viability — could be large statutory damages (not less than $750 and up to $30,000 *per infringed work*). 17 U.S.C. §504(c)(1). . . .

The third question . . . I find the most difficult of the three. I do not doubt that a more intrusive *Sony* test would generally provide greater revenue security for copyright holders. But it is harder to conclude that the gains on the copyright swings would exceed the losses on the copyright roundabouts. . . .

Unauthorized copying likely diminishes industry revenues, though it is not clear by how much. . . .

The extent to which related production has actually and resultingly declined remains uncertain, though there is good reason to believe that the decline, if any, is not substantial. *See, e.g.*, M. Madden, Pew Internet & American Life Project, Artists, Musicians, and the Internet, p. 21, *http://www.pewinternet.org/pdfs/PIP_Artists. Musicians_Report.pdf* (nearly 70% of musicians believe that file sharing is a minor threat or no threat at all to creative industries); Benkler, *Sharing Nicely: On Shareable Goods and the Emergence of Sharing as a Modality of Economic Production*, 114 Yale L.J. 273, 351-52 (2004) ("Much of the actual flow of revenue to artists — from performances and other sources — is stable even assuming a complete displacement of the CD market by peer-to-peer distribution. . . . [I]t would be silly to think that music, a cultural form without which no human society has existed, will cease to be in our world [because of illegal file swapping]").

More importantly, copyright holders at least potentially have other tools available to reduce piracy and to abate whatever threat it poses to creative production. As today's opinion makes clear, a copyright holder may proceed against a technology provider where a provable specific intent to infringe (of the kind the Court describes) is present. . . .

. . . [S]ince September 2003, the Recording Industry of America has filed "thousands of suits against people for sharing copyrighted material." . . . These suits . . . apparently have had a real and significant deterrent effect. . . .

Further, copyright holders may develop new technological devices that will help curb unlawful infringement. . . .

At the same time, advances in lawful technology have discouraged unlawful copying by making *lawful* copying (*e.g.*, downloading music with the copyright holder's permission) cheaper and easier to achieve. . . .

Finally, as *Sony* recognized, the legislative option remains available. . . .

NOTES AND QUESTIONS

1. Both the petition for certiorari in *Grokster* and the respondents' opposition framed the case as presenting questions related to the *Sony* doctrine. Why do you think the Court decided the case on an inducement theory instead?

2. What is the reach of the inducement doctrine as outlined by *Grokster*? First, does the Court's opinion clearly separate the issues of intent and design? May design properly be considered in an inducement case? For what purpose? Second, what sort of advertising conduct constitutes evidence of inducement? Would Apple Computer's famous advertising slogan — "Rip. Mix. Burn." — establish a violation? If Apple were sued for contributory infringement of music and movie copyrights, would its use of the slogan preclude a grant of summary judgment based on the *Sony* rule?

3. Would it be appropriate to apply the approach in *Grokster* to claims of inducement to infringe in the *Perfect 10, Inc. v. Amazon.com, Inc.* and *Perfect 10, Inc. v. Visa International Service Ass'n* cases? How do you think each court would hold and why?

4. As it had in *Sony*, the Court in *Grokster* borrowed a secondary liability doctrine developed largely in the patent context. Is it appropriate to look to patent law to inform copyright law's content? Recall Chapter 2's discussion of some of the doctrinal differences between patent and copyright law, pages 70-71 *supra*. Might it be misleading to view patent law's secondary liability rules apart from its entire doctrinal system? Put differently, patent law may be forgiving toward manufacturers of staple articles of commerce because the patentee is adequately

protected by the broad rights it otherwise has. Alternatively, Congress may have codified the inducement doctrine in the patent context because the monopoly granted by the Patent Act lasts for a shorter duration. Should a court simply transplant doctrine from one system to another?

5. After *Grokster*, where does *Sony*'s test fit within the scheme of secondary liability? Where does *Grokster*'s inducement theory of liability fit?

6. Review footnote 9 of the Court's opinion. Would the *Sony* rule shield a technology developer against a vicarious liability claim? Should it? Is vicarious liability an appropriate theory of liability to use in device cases?

7. The two concurring opinions in *Grokster* indicate a deep division of opinion within the Court as to the precise content of the *Sony* rule. This division is not new. Although the decision in *Sony* may seem obvious 20 years after the fact, it was a 5-4 ruling. Four members of the Court would have held Sony liable for contributory infringement.

Absent sufficient evidence of intent to induce infringement, how should the *Sony* test apply to software like Grokster's and StreamCast's? Do you prefer Justice Ginsburg's approach, or Justice Breyer's, or some other approach?

Should the *Sony* rule ever shield a defendant that exercises ongoing control over a service related to its technology? Does the *Napster* court or the *Aimster* court offer a better answer to this question? How would an OSP like Netcom fare under the *Sony* test? What about a commercial photocopying store like FedEx Kinko's?

8. If Sony had been liable as a copyright infringer, those who owned the copyrights in the programs that VCR owners wanted to tape would essentially have the power to direct the VCR market. Between this group and Sony, who would be more likely to exploit the technology efficiently? Consider the following quote from *Sony*:

> It seems extraordinary to suggest that the Copyright Act confers upon all copyright owners collectively, much less the two respondents in this case, the exclusive right to distribute V[C]R's simply because they may be used to infringe copyrights. That, however, is the logical implication of their claim. The request for an injunction below indicates that respondents seek, in effect, to declare V[C]R's contraband.

Sony, 464 U.S. at 470 n. 21. If you were a copyright owner and your rights entitled you to control the distribution of VCRs, would you permit their distribution and, if so, under what terms? Why shouldn't you have control over that market? In Chapter 9, we will examine a similar question, namely whether copyright owners' rights entitle them to control the design and distribution of software that can be used to infringe copyrights.

9. If the law does not mandate that digital technologies be designed to minimize infringement, will technology developers do so anyway, to minimize the risks of secondary liability? Consider digital video recorders (DVRs), which allow users to record digital copies of television and cable programming. Although DVRs, like VCRs, generally allow fast-forwarding through recorded commercials during playback, one DVR, the RePlayTV, originally could be programmed to skip commercials entirely while recording. A service offered by the RePlayTV's manufacturer, SONICblue, could be used to send copied programs to other RePlayTV owners via the Internet. A group of movie and television studios sued SONICblue for contributory copyright infringement. While the litigation was in its discovery phase, SONICblue filed for bankruptcy and sold its RePlayTV business to a large consumer electronics company. After the purchaser agreed to remove the features to which the copyright plaintiffs objected, the secondary liability claims were settled. So far, no other DVR has offered comparable functionality, and no other DVR manufacturer has been sued for contributory copyright infringement.

10. Peer-to-peer technology continues to evolve to become more efficient. One popular technology, BitTorrent, allows for data transfer of a file in portions and among many users. An individual uses BitTorrent software to create a "seed" file that contains the entire work (e.g., a full-length motion picture) and a small "tracker" file. Others who obtain copies of the entire file can help BitTorrent function by leaving their computers open to sharing pieces of the file. Using BitTorrent software installed on a computer, users can obtain copies of the entire file by first searching for it through a torrent search engine web site. The search engine will point the user to the tracker file, which the user downloads from sites around the world. Once the tracker file has been downloaded, the torrent software takes over, communicating with other web servers and users to download all of the parts of the file until the software assembles the complete file on the user's computer. Torrent sharing allows for much quicker downloading than an exchange between just two users using early generation peer-to-peer file sharing software. The tracker server records who downloads the tracking file, but doesn't archive who trades what, and the server's tracker log can be deleted at any time. Adam V. Vickers, Comment, *Peering Beyond Today's Internet File Sharing Concerns: The Future of BitTorrent Technology*, 8 Tul. J. Tech. & Intell. Prop. 133, 135-38 (2006). How would you assess the liability of BitTorrent sites?

11. If you were a member of Congress, what sort of response to peer-to-peer technologies would you support? The dissent in *Sony* urged, "[C]ontinuing royalties, or even some form of limited injunction, may well be an appropriate means of balancing the equities in this case. . . . [If] a continuing royalty or other equitable relief is not feasible[, t]he [television] Studios then would be relegated to statutory damages for proved instances of infringement." *Sony*, 464 U.S. at 499-500 (Blackmun J., dissenting). Review the notes and questions on pages 453-54. Would a levy of some sort be a good solution? On which equipment or services would you impose such a levy? For one proposal, see Neil Weinstock Netanel, *Impose a Noncommercial Use Levy to Allow Free Peer-To-Peer File Sharing*, 17 Harv. J.L. & Tech. 1 (2003).

12. On remand in *Grokster*, the district court granted the copyright owners' motion for summary judgment against defendant StreamCast Networks on the question of liability, relying on the inducement theory outlined by the Supreme Court. (In a 2005 settlement, defendant Grokster agreed to cease distributing its client application and to stop supporting its existing network.) Plaintiffs then requested that the court permanently enjoin StreamCast from operating its Morpheus network or any similar network "until there is a 'robust and secure means exhaustively to' stop infringement," and require StreamCast to " 'use all technologically feasible means to prevent or inhibit' infringement" by users of existing versions of the Morpheus software. *Metro-Goldwyn-Mayer Studios, Inc. v. Grokster, Ltd.*, 518 F. Supp. 2d 1197 (C.D. Cal. 2007). In response, StreamCast asserted that plaintiffs' proposal effectively would require enjoining it from continued distribution of its software. It argued, further, that requiring filtering would be inconsistent with a line of patent cases in which, although defendants had been found liable for inducing infringement, courts refused to *enjoin* the sale of products that were staple articles of commerce suitable for substantial noninfringing use. *Id.* at 1231-32.

Observing that "[t]here is a distinction between forbidding distribution of a technology capable of substantial noninfringing uses and simply requiring sufficient efforts to minimize the prospective infringement that would otherwise be induced," the court rejected Stream-Cast's argument against a court-imposed filtering requirement. It reasoned that StreamCast's own actions had so closely associated the Morpheus software with copyright infringement that "continued distribution of Morpheus alone [, without filtering,] constitutes infringement." *Id.* at 1235. The court also noted that the Ninth Circuit had affirmed a district court order requiring Napster to implement acoustical fingerprinting and filtering technologies.

The court ruled, however, that since perfect filtering was not technically possible, plaintiffs' proposed wording set the bar too high. It ordered "StreamCast to reduce Morpheus' infringing capabilities, while preserving its core noninfringing functionality, as effectively as possible." *Id.* at 1236. It also ruled that StreamCast had no duty to filter out particular works until it had been given sufficient notice of those works' presence on its network. The court reserved authority to alter the injunction's terms in response to future events, and indicated that it would appoint a special master to oversee implementation. What do you think of the court's solution?

D. ON-LINE SERVICE PROVIDER LIABILITY

OSPs, whether providing access to a network or offering on-line services like search engines, were concerned about incurring secondary liability under traditional principles or under new adaptations of those principles to cases involving networks. *See, e.g., Sega Enters. Ltd. v. MAPHIA*, 857 F. Supp. 679 (N.D. Cal. 1994) (issuing a preliminary injunction against a bulletin board operator whose subscribers infringed by uploading copyrighted Sega video games). In any litigation, the OSP would usually be a deeper pocket than the direct infringer, making the OSP an attractive target. Because the infringing material could be distributed across the Internet, there existed the potential for large liability. Contractual solutions, like requiring subscribers to indemnify the OSP for infringement, were of little practical comfort because even if the OSP could enforce the contract against the subscriber, the subscriber would be unlikely to have the funds to indemnify it.

Against this background, Congress considered a number of proposals to provide OSPs with both greater certainty regarding the content of the law and a liability limitation. Strong lobbies represented each side, with telecommunications companies arguing for a broad exemption from infringement liability and copyright owners arguing for no — or at least a narrow — exemption. The eventual compromise is reflected in §512 of the Copyright Act, enacted in 1998 as Title II (Online Copyright Infringement Liability Limitation) of the Digital Millennium Copyright Act. Once again, because the legislation resulted from bargaining between interest groups, it is quite complex. Read §512 from the perspective of an OSP and consider how it would affect the manner in which you conduct your business. Then read the following materials for more detail on the workings of §512.

Note on §512

Generally, §512 establishes "safe harbors" that provide immunity from infringement liability under certain circumstances for a "service provider" that engages in the following activities: (1) transitory digital network communications; (2) system caching; (3) storing information on its systems at the direction of users; or (4) providing information location tools like hypertext links. The definition of "service provider," set forth in §512(k)(1), varies depending on which safe harbor is invoked.

An OSP must comply with detailed statutory requirements to take advantage of any of the safe harbors. Each safe harbor has its own requirements that the OSP must meet to qualify for immunity from liability. Also, to qualify under *any* exemption, the OSP must not interfere with "standard technical measures" applied by copyright owners to protect their works, and must adopt and reasonably implement a policy providing for termination of repeat infringers' accounts and must inform subscribers of this policy. 17 U.S.C. §512(i).

To avoid liability for transmitting or transiently storing infringing material, the transmission must be initiated by someone other than the OSP and must be carried out through an automatic process; the OSP must not select the recipient except through an automatic process; the OSP must not maintain a copy accessible to anyone other than the recipients; and the OSP must transmit the material without modifying its content. *Id.* §512(a). The OSP is not liable for infringement for caching copies if the material is made available by someone else, transmitted from that person to the recipient at the recipient's direction, and the storage is automatic. *Id.* §512(b). The caching OSP must further comply with "conditions" imposed by the copyright owner (including password protection and deadlines for refreshing or updating the cached copy), and must disable access to cached material upon notice that a court has ordered the cached material removed from the originating web site. *Id.* §512(b)(2).

The third safe harbor may be the most important to OSPs. It exempts an OSP from liability for infringing material "hosted" on its servers on behalf of subscribers, and for infringing material downloaded by its servers and retained for limited periods, such as Usenet postings. This exemption also covers the provision of server space for chatrooms and other fora in which users may direct the posting of material. To qualify for this safe harbor, the OSP must designate an agent to receive notification of claimed infringement from copyright owners, file that designation with the Copyright Office, and make it publicly available. *Id.* §512(c)(2). The OSP must not have "actual knowledge" that the material is infringing or "aware[ness]" of facts or circumstances from which infringing activity is apparent." If it does, it must "act[ ] expeditiously to remove, or disable access to, the material." *Id.* §512(c)(1)(A). Finally, the OSP must not obtain a "financial benefit directly attributable to the infringing activity, in a case in which the service provider has the right and ability to control such activity." *Id.* §512(c)(1)(B). Thus, this subsection does not shelter an OSP that would otherwise meet the requirements for vicarious liability.

The fourth safe harbor shelters OSPs that provide links, indexes, or other directories referencing infringing material. *Id.* §512(d). The requirements for qualifying under this section are essentially the same as those under the third safe harbor.

Under the third and fourth safe harbors, an OSP can obtain "actual knowledge" of infringing activity through a notice provided by a copyright owner to the OSP's designated agent. *Id.* §512(c)(3). Section 512(c)(3) provides detailed rules about the content and form of this notice and the OSP's obligations on its receipt. Among other things, the notice must provide contact information for the complaining party; must identify the allegedly infringing material with information sufficient to permit the OSP to locate it; and must state that the complaining party "has a good faith belief" that the material is unauthorized. The complaining party must state under penalty of perjury that he or she is authorized to act on behalf of the copyright owner, but none of the other required statements need be made under penalty of perjury. *See id.* However, if the complaining party "knowingly materially misrepresents . . . that material or activity is infringing," a court may award damages to the alleged infringer or the affected OSP. *Id.* §512(f).

If the OSP decides to remove the material, it must "take[ ] reasonable steps promptly to notify the subscriber" of the removal. *Id.* §512(g)(2)(A). The statute does not expressly require the OSP to furnish the subscriber with a copy of the notification from the complainant. If the subscriber wishes, he or she may furnish a counternotification that identifies the material; states under penalty of perjury that the subscriber has a good faith belief that it was removed by mistake; and consents to the jurisdiction of the federal district court where the subscriber's contact address is located or, for subscribers who reside outside the U.S., where the OSP is located. *Id.* §512(g)(3). Upon receipt of the counternotification, the OSP must notify the complainant, and must restore the material within 10 business days unless it first receives notice that a lawsuit has been filed. *Id.* §512(g)(2). If the OSP complies with all of these requirements, it is exempted from liability to the subscriber for any claim based on removal of the material. *Id.* §512(g)(1). A subscriber who "knowingly materially misrepresents" that material was removed by mistake will be liable for damages incurred by the copyright owner or its authorized licensee, or by the OSP. *Id.* §512(f).

Finally, §512(h) authorizes federal district court clerks, upon a copyright owner's request, to issue subpoenas for identification of subscribers who have posted allegedly infringing material, and OSPs receiving such subpoenas must "expeditiously disclose" the information. *Id.* §512(h).

There are a number of important things to keep in mind about §512. First, compliance with §512 is voluntary. An OSP may choose not to invoke the pertinent safe harbor and take its chances in the courts with any and all of the defenses otherwise available under copyright law. *Id.* §512(1). Second, even if an OSP that chooses to invoke §512 is not sheltered by it, the OSP's conduct may be excused under another section of the Copyright Act, like §107 on fair use. Finally, keep in mind that §512, which protects compliant OSPs from monetary remedies, affords only limited protection against injunctive and other equitable relief *See id.* §512(j).

NOTES AND QUESTIONS

1. What are the differences between §§512(a) and (b)? Would it make sense to exempt OSPs from liability by analogizing them to common carriers like phone companies? *See Netcom*, 907 F. Supp. at 1370 n.12 (raising the issue); *see also CoStar Group, Inc. v. Loop-Net, Inc.*, 373 F.3d 544, 551 (4th Cir. 2004) (same). No court has held a phone company liable for engaging in conduct like transmitting an infringing fax or storing an infringing recording on a voice-mail service. *See also* 17 U.S.C. §111(a)(3) of the Copyright Act (exempting a passive carrier from liability for infringement when it engages in a secondary transmission by providing solely "wires, cables, or other communications channels for the use of others"). Are there any relevant distinctions between common carriers like phone companies and OSPs, or do you find this analogy persuasive? Does either subsection (a) or (b) adopt a common carrier model?

2. What constitutes "transient storage" under §512(a)? In other words, how long may an OSP store material and still qualify for the §512(a) safe harbor? *See Ellison v. Robertson*, 357 F.3d 1072, 1081 (9th Cir. 2004) (holding that an OSP's storage of material contained in a Usenet newsgroup posting for 14 days was "transient"); *see also Field v. Google, Inc.*, 412 F. Supp. 2d 1106, 1124 (D. Nev. 2006) (Google's retention in cache of indexed pages for periods ranging from 14 to 20 days was "transient").

3. Why would the third safe harbor of §512 be the most important to an OSP? Recall that the safe harbors of §512(c) and (d) do not shelter an OSP that would otherwise meet the requirements for vicarious liability. Do they shelter an OSP that would otherwise meet the requirements for contributory infringement liability? Would §512(c) have sheltered Netcom? If not, what is the point of these subsections?

Assume that your client, an OSP, seeks your advice on avoiding liability for copyright infringement. Would you consider advising your client to ignore the requirements of §512 and rely on other defenses afforded under copyright law? Why, or why not?

4. Note that in certain situations nonprofit educational institutions that offer Internet service are subject to a slightly different set of requirements than other covered service providers. *See* 17 U.S.C. §512(e). In 2008, Congress passed the Higher Education Opportunity Act (HEOA), Pub. L. No. 110-315, which is directed at lowering tuition costs and streamlining the financial aid process. Buried in this lengthy piece of legislation is a provision requiring colleges to develop a plan to block peer-to-peer file-sharing and to offer students an alternative to illegal downloading as a condition of obtaining federal financial aid for students. *See* 20 U.S.C. §1094(a)(29). If you were a member of Congress, would you have voted for this provision? Why, or why not?

In part in response to HEOA, Stanford University has installed an automated system for students to respond to complaints about downloading. Failure to respond results in denial of access to the Internet, and students must clean their computers, pass a quiz, enter into a contract with the university, and/or pay a fine to have their Internet access reinstated. The fines increase with each violation, and on the third complaint, the matter is referred to the Office of Judicial Affairs (a so-called "three strikes" policy; *see also infra* page 514). Jane LePha, *Stanford punishes digital pirates*, *http://www.stanforddaily.com/cgi-bin/?p = 1035083*, Oct. 29, 2009. Indiana University has a similar system. *See http://filesharing.iu.edu/procedure* (last visited Oct. 30, 2009). What do you think of universities' use of their resources to implement such systems?

5. In the *Napster* litigation, discussed *supra* page 491, the district court summarized the operation of the Napster system as follows:

> [U]sing Napster typically involves the following basic steps: After downloading MusicShare software from the Napster website, a user can access the Napster system from her computer. The MusicShare software interacts with Napster's server-side software when the user logs on, automatically connecting her to one of some 150 servers that Napster operates. The MusicShare software reads a list of names of MP3 files that the user has elected to make available. This list is then added to a directory and index, on the Napster server, of MP3 files that users who are logged-on wish to share. If the user wants to locate a song, she enters its name or the name of the recording artist on the search page of the MusicShare program and clicks the "Find It" button. The Napster software then searches the current directory and generates a list of files responsive to the search request. To download a desired file, the user highlights it on the list and clicks the "Get Selected Song(s)" button. The user may also view a list of files that exist on another user's hard drive and select a file from that list. When the requesting user clicks on the name of a file, the Napster server communicates with the requesting user's and host user's MusicShare browser software to facilitate a connection between the two users and initiate the downloading of the file without any further action on either user's part.
>
> According to Napster, when the requesting user clicks on the name of the desired MP3 file, the Napster server routes this request to the host user's browser. The host user's browser responds that it either can or cannot supply the file. If the host user can supply the file, the Napster server communicates the host's address and routing information to the requesting user's browser, allowing the requesting user to make a connection with the host and receive the desired MP3 file. . . . The parties disagree about whether this process involves a hypertext link that the Napster server-side software provides. . . . However, plaintiffs admit that the Napster server gets the necessary IP address information from the host user, enabling the requesting user to connect to the host. . . . The MP3 file is actually transmitted over the Internet . . . but the steps necessary to make that connection could not take place without the Napster server. . . .

A&M Records, Inc. v. Napster, Inc., No. C 99-05183 MHP, 2000 WL 573136 (N.D. Cal. May 12, 2000). Early in the litigation, Napster moved for summary judgment, arguing that it was shielded from liability by its compliance with §512(a). How would you evaluate this argument? Was Napster eligible to invoke any of the other §512 safe harbors? Note that the peer-to-peer file-sharing technology at the heart of the *Napster* dispute had not yet been invented when Congress enacted §512. Should this technology be protected by its own statutory safe harbor? On what conditions?

6. In its directive on electronic commerce, the European Union adopted safe harbors for transmission, caching, and hosting services that are very similar to those provided in §512. *See* Directive 2000/31/EC of the European Parliament and of the Council of 8 June 2000 on certain legal aspects of information society services, in particular electronic commerce, in the Internal Market, 2000 O.J. (L 178) 1, arts. 12-15. The directive indicates that member countries may enact specific procedures for removing or disabling access to material that has been identified as infringing. *Id.*, arts. 12(3), 13(2), 14(3).

7. Remember that even if the OSP qualifies for monetary relief, it may still be subject to an injunction under §512(j). Read that subsection now. Consider particularly §512(j)(B)(ii) which allows a U.S. court to enter an injunction "restraining the service provider from providing access . . . to a specific, identified, online location outside the United States." 17 U.S.C. §512(j)(B)(ii). Does this solve the problem of infringing sites located offshore?

Understanding the interactions among the different provisions of §512 is a complex task. Work through the following set of questions to explore the way that §512 works in practice, and to assess how the statutory "notice and takedown" regime affects the interests of OSPs, copyright owners, and Internet users.

1. Section 512 does not shelter an OSP that fails to adopt and reasonably implement a policy for terminating repeat infringers. Read 17 U.S.C. §512(i) and identify its requirements. Are the OSPs in the following hypotheticals eligible to invoke §512's safe harbors?

    a. The OSP establishes a copyright policy but does not communicate the policy to its users until after it is sued for copyright infringement, and it terminates repeat infringers by blocking their passwords but not their IP addresses. *See A&M Records, Inc. v. Napster, Inc.*, No. C 99-05183 MHP, 2000 WL 573136 (N.D. Cal. May 12, 2000) (holding grant of summary judgment on the applicability of §512 inappropriate because genuine issues of material fact existed regarding the defendant's compliance with §512(i)).

    b. The OSP adopts a policy that does not use the term "repeat infringer" or otherwise track the statutory language but that prohibits violations of copyright law and provides for penalties ranging from removal of individual items to termination of service. Pursuant to the policy, the OSP has canceled "millions of listings," issued warnings of possible termination, and terminated some users. However, it has not "conduct[ed] active investigation of possible infringement or ma[de] a decision regarding difficult infringement issues." *See Corbis Corp. v. Amazon.com, Inc.*, 351 F. Supp. 2d 1090, 1101-04 (W.D. Wash. 2004) (OSP eligible to invoke §512).

    c. The OSP changes the e-mail address designated for receipt of notifications of claimed infringement but does not immediately inform the Copyright Office of the change. *See Ellison v. Robertson*, 357 F.3d 1072, 1080 (9th Cir. 2004) (delay of approximately six months raised a triable issue of material fact regarding the OSP's eligibility for a safe harbor, and also regarding whether the OSP should have known of the infringing activity).

d. The OSP does not respond to the plaintiff's takedown notices because they lack the required statement under penalty of perjury, but the OSP has received notices about the same allegedly infringing web sites from other copyright holders. *See Perfect 10, Inc. v. CCBill LLC,* 488 F.3d 1102 (9th Cir.) (lack of response to defective notices does not raise genuine issue of material fact concerning "reasonably implementing a repeat infringer policy," but court must consider how OSP responded to notices from other copyright owners), *cert. denied,* 552 U.S. 1062 (2007).

2. Obviously, whether an OSP has reasonably implemented a policy to terminate repeat infringers hinges in part on what the OSP knows about the activities of its subscribers. Section 512(c) defines three situations in which an OSP is charged with knowledge. Two of these situations — actual knowledge and receipt of a compliant takedown notice — are easily understood. The third situation, "awareness of facts or circumstances from which infringing activity is apparent," §512(c)(1)(A)(ii), is more difficult. Are there situations or "red flags" that should create a presumption of knowledge? In *Perfect 10, Inc. v. CCBill LLC,* the plaintiff argued that any of the following three conditions should be *per se* red flags: (1) defective takedown notices; (2) suspicious names of subscribers' web sites (such as "illegal.net" and "stolencelebritypics. com"); and (3) the presence of password-hacking information on subscribers' web sites. The court rejected all three of these arguments. It held that defective notices cannot be deemed to impart the required awareness. *CCBill,* 488 F.3d at 1114. Noting that sites that traffic in titillating pictures may attempt to increase their salacious appeal with words like "illegal" or "stolen," it refused to "place the burden of determining whether photographs are actually illegal on a service provider." *Id.* Finally, it noted that one could not know whether a site offering password-hacking information enabled infringement without verifying that the passwords worked. The court was unwilling to place such a burden on service providers. What do you think of the court's conclusions? Are there other situations that should create red flags?

The *CCBill* litigation involved a claim of §512 safe harbor immunity. Without the protection of the safe harbor, a court would analyze liability under contributory infringement doctrine, which requires a showing of knowledge of the infringing activity. Should the standard for what constitutes knowledge under contributory infringement doctrine be different from the standard for what constitutes knowledge under the statutory safe harbor? In *Amazon.com,* *supra* pages 480-82, the Ninth Circuit held that in light of the Supreme Court's opinion in *Grokster,* contributory infringement liability is for those who are actively encouraging infringement and that "a computer system operator can be held contributorily liable if it 'has *actual* knowledge that *specific* infringing material is available using its system'." *Id.* at 1172 (quoting *A&M Records, Inc. v. Napster,* 239 F.3d 1004, 1022 (9th Cir. 2001)). Does the standard in §512(c)(1)(A)(ii) mean that a defendant could lose the safe harbor protection but nonetheless avoid liability for contributory infringement because the requisite level of knowledge is not present? Does that result make sense? Why, or why not?

3. Is actual knowledge a concept that in fact is easily understood? In *UMG Recordings, Inc. v. Veoh Networks Inc.,* the court addressed the argument that hosting music and tagging videos as "music videos" gave Veoh actual knowledge of infringement: "If merely hosting user-contributed material capable of copyright protection [or assigning tags automatically] were enough to impute actual knowledge to a service provider, the *section 512(c)* safe harbor would be a dead letter . . .." No. CV 07-5744 AHM (AJWx), 2009 U.S. Dist. LEXIS 86932 (C.D. Cal. Sept. 11, 2009), at *25 (emphasis added).

When a notice lists the names of artists, is there a duty to seek out actual knowledge by searching for all items by them available at the site? *See id.* at *30 (finding no such duty and stating, "An artist's name is not 'information reasonably sufficient to permit the service provider to locate [such] material.' . . . Veoh presented undisputed evidence that simply searching for a name would not necessarily unearth only unauthorized material. Requiring Veoh to perform such searches would also conflict with the principle articulated in *CCBill* that ' . . . the burden of policing copyright infringement . . . [rests] squarely on the owners of copyright.' ") (citation omitted).

4. Does an OSP's implementation of a copyright compliance policy under §512 make its conduct "volitional" and therefore subject to a claim of direct infringement under *Netcom's* reasoning? In *CoStar Group, Inc. v. LoopNet, Inc.*, 373 F.3d 544 (4th Cir. 2004), which involved allegedly infringing copies of photographs of commercial real estate listings, the court concluded that it does not:

> . . . After expressly warranting that he has "all necessary rights and authorizations from the . . . copyright owner of the photographs," the subscriber uploads the photograph into a folder in LoopNet's system. The photograph is then transferred to the RAM of one of LoopNet's computers for review. A LoopNet employee reviews the photo for two purposes: (1) to block photographs that do not depict commercial real estate, and (2) to block photographs with obvious signs that they are copyrighted by a third party. If the photograph carries a copyright notice or represents subject matter other than commercial real estate, the employee deletes the photograph; otherwise, she clicks a button marked "accept," and LoopNet's system automatically associates the photograph with the subscriber's web page for the property listing, making it available for use. Unless a question arises, this entire process takes "a few seconds."
>
> Although LoopNet engages in volitional conduct to block photographs measured by two grossly defined criteria, this conduct, which takes only seconds, does not amount to "copying," nor does it add volition to LoopNet's involvement in storing the copy. The employee's look is so cursory as to be insignificant, and . . . tends only to lessen the possibility that LoopNet's automatic electronic responses will inadvertently enable others to trespass on a copyright owner's rights. . . . LoopNet can be compared to an owner of a copy machine who has stationed a guard by the door to turn away customers who are attempting to duplicate clearly copyrighted works. LoopNet has not by this screening process become engaged as a "copier" of copyrighted works. . . .
>
> To the extent that LoopNet's intervention in screening photographs goes further than the simple gatekeeping function described above, it is because of CoStar's complaints about copyright violations. Whenever CoStar has complained to LoopNet about a particular photograph, LoopNet has removed the photograph, and the property listing with which the photograph was associated has been marked. The next time the user tries to post a photograph to accompany that listing, LoopNet conducts a manual side-by-side review to make sure that the user is not reposting the infringing photograph. CoStar and other copyright holders benefit significantly from this type of response. If they find such conduct by an ISP too active, they can avoid it by adding a copyright notice to their photographs, which CoStar does not do. . . .

Id. at 556. What do you think of this reasoning?

5. Google uses automated tools called "bots" to index web sites. Google's bots copy pages and store them for up to 20 days in temporary storage called cache. When a user enters a query into Google for which an indexed page is relevant, the Google search engine will return both a link to the version of the page in the Google cache as well as a link to the actual page. A site owner can use certain codes to indicate to a bot that it does not wish the page to be indexed or does not wish the indexing site, i.e., Google, to use a cached link.

Does Google infringe web sites' copyrights when it copies pages into its cache or when it serves a user a copy of a cached page? In *Field v. Google, Inc.*, 412 F. Supp. 2d 1106 (D. Nev. 2006), the plaintiff challenged the latter practice, though not the initial copying. (Why not?) Citing *LoopNet*, the court reasoned: "[W]hen a user requests a Web page contained in the Google cache by clicking on a 'Cached' link, it is the user, not Google, who creates and downloads a copy of the cached Web page. Google is passive in this process. . . . The automated, non-volitional conduct by Google in response to a user's request does not constitute direct infringement under the Copyright Act." *Id.* at 1115. What do you think of this reasoning?

The court also held that even if Google had engaged in direct infringement, it could assert the defense of implied license. Plaintiff's failure to follow the industry standard (of which it was aware) of including certain code to indicate an unwillingness to have its web pages available from cache could be "reasonably interpreted as the grant of a license to Google for that use." *Id.* at 1116. Do you agree?

6. What does "storage at the direction of the user of material" mean in §512(c)(1)? Consider whether the web site operation in the following hypotheticals can take advantage of §512(c):

  a. Users upload video files to a web site that facilitates the sharing of the files. Some of the uploaded videos are infringing. When a user uploads a video file, the system automatically converts it into Flash format and copies a few still images from the video that are used to identify it in a search result. *See Io Group, Inc. v. Veoh Networks, Inc.,* 586 F. Supp. 2d 1132, 1148 (N.D. Cal. 2008) (holding §512(c) available to OSP and stating, ". . . Veoh does not itself actively participate [in] or supervise the uploading of files. Nor does it preview or select the files before the upload is completed. Instead, video files are uploaded through an automated process which is initiated entirely at the volition of Veoh's users."). Would the answer change if the process had not been automatic?

  b. Same facts as (a) but the software (i) automatically creates copies of small parts of the original file; (ii) allows users to access uploaded files by streaming; and (iii) allows users to download entire video files? *See UMG Recordings, Inc. v. Veoh Networks, Inc.,* 620 F.Supp. 2d 1081, 1088-89 (C.D. Cal. 2008) (holding §512(c) available to OSP and stating, ". . . §512(c) does not require that the infringing conduct constitute storage in its own right. Rather the infringing conduct must occur *as a result of the storage.* . . . [T]he language in the remainder of §512(c) "*presupposes* that the service provider will be providing access to the user's material.")

7. From the perspective of an Internet user, what do you make of the notification, counternotification, and subpoena procedures established by §512? Do they reflect an appropriate balancing of the various interests affected? If not, what changes would you recommend?

8. Now assess the notification requirements from the OSP's perspective. Consider first the requirement that the notification identify the allegedly infringing material and provide "information reasonably sufficient to permit the service provider to locate the material." 17 U.S.C. §512(c)(3)(A)(iii). What does this mean in practice? If you were in-house counsel to the OSP in each of the following hypotheticals, how would you respond?

  a. A letter sent to eBay.com states that counterfeit copies of a work are being traded on eBay, but does not provide the relevant eBay item numbers. *See Hendrickson v. eBay, Inc.,* 165 F. Supp. 2d 1082, 1090 (C.D. Cal. 2001) (notification insufficient).

  b. A letter sent to Amazon.com identifies "all *Manson* DVDs" as infringing. *See Hendrickson v. Amazon.com, Inc.,* 298 F. Supp. 2d 914, 916 (C.D. Cal. 2003) (notification sufficient).

  c. A letter sent to an on-line payment service that processes subscriptions to client sites offering pornographic content asserts that the client sites contain infringing images, but does not identify the precise sites or the precise images. *See Perfect 10, Inc. v. CCBill, LLC*, 340 F. Supp. 2d 1077 (C.D. Cal. 2004) (notification insufficient).

d. A letter sent to a provider of Internet hosting services identifies two hosted sites that it asserts were created for the sole purpose of displaying the copyrighted works, and states that essentially all of the images at those sites are infringing. *See ALS Scan, Inc. v. RemarQ Cmties., Inc.*, 239 F.3d 619, 625 (4th Cir. 2001) (notification sufficient).

Are all of these decisions consistent with each other?

When an OSP receives a notice that substantially complies with the statutory requirements, for how long must it monitor its system for the infringing material identified therein? *See Hendrickson*, 298 F. Supp. 2d at 917 (no obligation to detect items posted nine months after the date of the notice). The House Report accompanying §512 stated that the "legislation is not intended to discourage the service provider from monitoring its service for infringing material." H.R. Conf. Rep. No. 105-796, at 73, *reprinted in* 1998 U.S.C.C.A.N. 639, 649. Do you think OSPs will, in fact, monitor their services? Read §512(m) before you answer.

9. Finally, consider the notification requirements from the perspective of a copyright holder. First, what constitutes a "good faith belief" under §512(c)(3)(A)(v)? If a web site contains statements like " 'Join to download full length movies online now!' " followed by graphics depicting the copyright owner's films, must the copyright owner verify that, in fact, its material can be downloaded? *See Rossi v. Motion Picture Ass'n of Am.*, 391 F.3d 1000, 1002-06 (9th Cir. 2004) (good faith requirement is subjective, and copyright owner need not investigate whether its copyrighted movies were actually available for download before sending notification to the OSP), *cert. denied*, 544 U.S. 1018 (2005).

Second, what would constitute a "knowing[ ] material[ ] misrepresent[ation]" under §512(f)? How would you apply this standard in a case in which the copyright owner sends a notice knowing that parts of the material identified are not copyrighted, and that any infringement likely would be excused under the fair use doctrine? In *Online Policy Group v. Diebold, Inc.*, 337 F. Supp. 2d 1195 (N.D. Cal. 2004), the court assessed a notification sent by Diebold, a manufacturer of electronic voting machines, demanding the removal from the Internet of copied portions of an archive of e-mail exchanged among Diebold employees that revealed serious technical problems with Diebold's machines. The court concluded that Diebold had violated the statute:

> "Knowingly" means that a party actually knew, should have known if it acted with reasonable care or diligence, or would have had no substantial doubt had it been acting in good faith, that it was making misrepresentations. . . . "Material" means that the misrepresentation affected the ISP's response to a DMCA letter. . . .
>
> . . . No reasonable copyright holder could have believed that [the material] was protected by copyright, and there is no genuine issue of fact that Diebold knew — and indeed that it specifically intended . . . that its [notices] would result in prevention of publication of that content. The representations were material in that they resulted in removal of the content from websites. . . . The fact that Diebold never actually brought suit against any alleged infringer suggests strongly that Diebold sought to use [§512] . . . as a sword to suppress publication of embarrassing content rather than as a shield to protect its intellectual property.

Id. at 1204.

Are *Rossi* and *Online Policy Group* consistent with one another? Do the different standards they articulate for "good faith belief" and "knowing material misrepresentation," respectively, comport with the policy considerations animating §512?

10. Can failure to consider the applicability of fair use constitute a basis for a claim of knowing material misrepresentation under §512(f)? At least one court has answered "yes," making clear that there are constraints on a copyright owner's use of takedown notices. In *Lenz v. Universal Music Corp.*, 572 F. Supp. 2d 1150 (N.D. Cal. 2008), the court held that "to proceed under the DMCA with 'a good faith belief that use of the material in the manner complained of is not authorized by the copyright owner, its agent, or the law,' the owner *must* evaluate whether the material makes fair use of the copyright." *Id.* at 1154 (emphasis added).

11. At least two major Internet access providers appear to have deployed "deep packet inspection" technologies to analyze, and sometimes block, traffic passing through their networks. Deep packet inspection examines bits of digital information to determine which application generated the information, and can also be used to identify digital watermarks. After subscribers of the cable and Internet provider Comcast discovered a network utility that hampered use of the popular BitTorrent P2P file-sharing protocol, Comcast admitted that it had deliberately interfered with subscribers' BitTorrent downloads. According to Comcast, this helped it to manage competing demands for bandwidth. In March 2008, following an investigation by the Federal Communications Commission, Comcast announced that it would no longer engage in the challenged practice, and pledged to come up with other traffic management solutions, although it did not indicate what those solutions might be.

Is deep packet inspection by Internet access providers a good solution to the problem of on-line copyright infringement? Why, or why not? Review §512(a), the statutory safe harbor for transitory digital network communications. If an OSP engages in deep packet inspection, will it lose eligibility to claim the safe harbor? If so, is that result appropriate?

Note on OSPs and User-Generated Content

Many users rely on the Internet to distribute content that they have created. Web platforms like YouTube and Flickr, which did not exist when Congress enacted §512, were designed specifically as venues for such user-generated content (UGC). Today, those sites and many others like them receive millions of visitors daily. Those visits translate into substantial advertising revenue for the OSPs that operate the sites.

Often, UGC includes material drawn from preexisting copyrighted works. The uses of preexisting materials are so diverse as to defy description. Sometimes, the user-generated work is a mashup — a work that combines two preexisting works to create something that blends the two. Sometimes, users edit excerpts from single works, adding, deleting or substituting elements. Many users create works of "fan fiction," inserting new characters and storylines into the fictional universes of popular movies, television shows, and books. Others remix sounds and images from a variety of sources. In some user-generated works, copyrighted musical recordings provide soundtracks for video of users dancing, singing, or simply going about their daily activities. Sometimes, too, users simply repost snippets of copyrighted movies and television broadcasts that they find particularly interesting (or particularly annoying).

Web platforms for UGC have drawn considerable attention from the major copyright industries. Representatives of these industries argue that such sites function principally to enable uncontrolled distribution of infringing copies of their works, and that many of the user-generated works described above also infringe their copyrights.

In February 2007, Viacom served YouTube with 100,000 §512 takedown notices for allegedly infringing content uploaded by users. Some industry observers think Viacom expected the sheer number of notices to bring YouTube to the bargaining table, and hoped that YouTube would agree to use content filtering tools approved by Viacom. Instead, YouTube simply processed the notices and, where indicated, took down the infringing materials. Viacom then sued YouTube, asserting that YouTube should be held liable for repeated acts of copyright infringement committed by its users. Shortly after the lawsuit was filed, Google acquired YouTube, so the lawsuit now pits Viacom's resources against Google's. Discovery is underway, with no sign of an imminent settlement.

In addition, the major copyright industries have sought to engage the OSP industry in negotiations that would yield privately-agreed methods of policing for copyright infringement. In 2007, a group of major copyright owners including Disney, Fox, Microsoft, NBC Universal, and Viacom released a document titled "Copyright Principles for UGC Services," *http://www.ugcprinciples.com*. According to the proposed principles, Web platforms for UGC should implement "effective content identification technology . . . with the goal of eliminating from their services all infringing user-uploaded audio and video content for which Copyright Owners have provided Reference Material." *Id.* ¶3. The proposed principles define "effective content identification technology" as any technology that is both "commercially reasonable" and "highly effective, in relation to other technologies commercially available at the time of implementation." *Id.* The technology should automatically block user uploads for which a copyright owner has provided "reference data for content required to establish a match with user-uploaded content" unless the copyright owner has instructed that matches should be handled in some other way. *Id.* ¶3(a)-(c).

Pursuant to the proposed principles, a UGC service may undertake "manual (human) review of all user-uploaded audio and video content in lieu of, or in addition to, use of Identification Technology, if feasible and if such review is as effective as Identification Technology in achieving the goal of eliminating infringing content." *Id.* ¶3(f). UGC services also must give copyright owners that register with them access to "commercially reasonable enhanced searching and identification means" to search for infringing content themselves. *Id.* ¶5. The proposed principles state that "Copyright Owners and UGC services should cooperate to ensure that the Identification Technology is implemented in a manner that effectively balances legitimate interests in (1) blocking infringing user-uploaded content, (2) allowing wholly original and authorized uploads, and (3) accommodating fair use." *Id.* ¶3(d).

As of this writing, only a handful of OSPs have endorsed the proposed principles. Web platforms like YouTube argue that the provisions of §512 provide sufficient protection for copyright owner interests, and that they respond promptly to copyright owners' takedown notices.

NOTES AND QUESTIONS

1. Assume that discovery shows that YouTube has always acted promptly to process §512 takedown notices and remove infringing materials. How would you rule on Viacom's indirect copyright infringement claims against Google/YouTube, and why?

2. If you represented Google/YouTube in the Viacom lawsuit, what terms would you want included in any settlement? What terms would you want if you represented Viacom?

3. What do you think of the "Copyright Principles for UGC Services"? If you represented a Web platform for UGC, would you favor adoption? If UGC platforms all decided to adopt the copyright industries' filtering proposal, would that be an efficient solution to the problem of online copyright infringement? Would such a solution be fair to users? In response to the

Principles, a group of nonprofit organizations offered a competing proposal, titled "Fair Use Principles for User Generated Video Content." We will consider that proposal in Chapter 7, *infra*, after you have learned about fair use.

4. How are your answers to the questions above influenced by your view of the goals of the copyright system? For example, would you answer the questions differently if you subscribed primarily to an authors' rights view versus a users' rights view?

Note on Identifying and Suing the Direct Infringer

If an OSP cannot be sued for infringement, a copyright owner's remaining option for monetary redress is to sue the direct infringer. In 2003, the Recording Industry Association of America (RIAA) began a coordinated campaign to identify and sue individual music sharers. The RIAA employs sophisticated software tools to study file-sharing activities on peer-to-peer networks. The techniques allow the RIAA to identify the IP addresses used by individuals who are sharing files. Because IP addresses are assigned in blocks to the OSPs who provide Internet access, this enables the RIAA to identify the OSP whose services are being used. However, linking a particular IP address to a particular user requires access to the OSP's internal usage records.

Pursuant to §512(h), a copyright owner may obtain a subpoena requiring the OSP to reveal the subscriber's identity. The copyright owner need not file a lawsuit before seeking this information. Instead, it simply must file three items with a federal district court: (1) a proposed subpoena; (2) a copy of the "take down" notice described in §512(c)(3), *see* page 504 *supra*; and (3) a sworn declaration that the information is being sought solely to pursue "rights protected under this title." No judge reviews the requested subpoena; rather, §512(h) provides that the clerk "shall expeditiously issue" the subpoena if the required items are in proper form.

When the RIAA served Verizon with a §512(h) subpoena, Verizon refused to identify the subscriber and instead sought to quash the subpoena, arguing that §512(h) did not apply in situations in which the OSP was a mere conduit for arguably infringing transmissions. Ultimately, the D.C. Circuit agreed with Verizon's interpretation of the statute. It reasoned that §512(h) refers to documentation required under §512(c), and that "the cross-references to §512(c)(3) in §§512(b)-(d) demonstrate that §512(h) applies to an ISP storing infringing material on its servers in any capacity . . . ." *RIAA v. Verizon Internet Servs., Inc.*, 351 F.3d 1229, 1237 (D.C. Cir. 2003), *cert. denied*, 543 U.S. 924 (2004). The Eighth Circuit has agreed with the *Verizon* court's ruling. *See In re: Charter Commc'ns, Inc. Subpoena Enforcement Matter*, 393 F.3d 771 (8th Cir. 2005).

Without the ability to use the §512(h) subpoena to identify individuals engaged in file sharing, the RIAA turned to a mechanism available to any civil litigant who desires to file suit against an individual whose identity is unknown — a lawsuit filed against "John Doe." In the context of a John Doe lawsuit, the plaintiff may seek the assistance of the court in determining the defendant's identity. The plaintiff must file an ex parte request for a subpoena to a non-party in order to obtain the service provider's records. In *Sony Music Entertainment, Inc. v. Does 1-40*, 326 F. Supp. 2d 556 (S.D.N.Y. 2004), the court granted such a request but required that the service provider notify the subscribers whose identities would be disclosed with sufficient time to permit them to move to quash the subpoena. In addressing the subscribers' motion to quash, the court identified five considerations relevant in balancing First Amendment, privacy, and copyright interests: (i) whether the plaintiffs had established a prima facie case of copyright infringement; (ii) the specificity of the discovery request; (iii) the availability of alternative means of obtaining the information; (iv) the extent of the plaintiffs' need for the information;

and (v) the defendants' expectation of privacy. *Id.* at 564-67. It concluded that the first four considerations weighed strongly in favor of disclosure, and outweighed any privacy interest that the defendants might have. Courts across the country have generally agreed with this analysis.

Over time, the RIAA filed over 30,000 infringement lawsuits against individuals suspected of exchanging infringing files via peer-to-peer networks. *See http://www.usatoday.com/tech/news/2009-06-18-music-downloading_N.htm.* The RIAA did not attempt to proceed to judgment against most of these defendants, but instead encouraged settlement. In 2009, USA Today's on-line edition noted that "[t]he vast majority . . . settled for about $3,500 each," although in one case a jury awarded the record companies $1.92 million. *Id.; see also* note 4, Chapter 5, page 348 *supra.* The strategy of suing individuals, however, was expensive for the RIAA and resulted in some negative press. Moreover, according to most accounts, peer-to-peer file sharing has continued to increase both in the U.S. and outside. *See http://www.eff.org/wp/riaa-v-people-years-later#3.*

In 2008, the RIAA announced that it would de-emphasize suits against individuals and focus instead on negotiating so-called "three strikes" agreements with OSPs. Generally, under such an agreement, the RIAA will notify an OSP when it suspects the OSP's customer is infringing. The OSP in turn will inform its customer of the RIAA's notice and request that the customer cease its infringement (Strike 1). Failure to do so may result in additional notices and possibly slower service (Strike 2). Continued failure to end the infringement would result in a cessation of service (Strike 3). *See Music Industry to Drop Mass Suits,* Wall St. J., Dec. 27, 2008, *available at* 2008 WLNR 24774194. As of this writing, the RIAA has had limited success in convincing OSPs to enter into such agreements, although some OSPs appear to be taking a more aggressive stance toward the issuance of subscriber warning letters under their existing repeat-infringer policies.

NOTES AND QUESTIONS

1. With the availability of a John Doe lawsuit, do copyright owners need the §512(h) subpoena authority? How do the two procedural options compare? How do they compare from the defendant's perspective?

2. In challenging the §512(h) subpoenas, Verizon argued that under the Constitution, federal district courts lack Article III jurisdiction to issue subpoenas when there is no underlying "case or controversy," and that the First Amendment requires greater safeguards than §512(h) provides to protect an Internet user's ability to speak and associate with others anonymously. Because the court held that §512(h) could not be used in the case, it did not reach these constitutional challenges.

What should happen if constitutional challenges to §512(h) are raised by an OSP that *does* store the disputed material on its servers? Should a copyright owner be able to obtain a subpoena from a federal court without having to file a complaint? Should a copyright owner be able to obtain a subscriber's identity solely based on the information contained in the notice described in §512(c)(3)?

3. The EU's 2004 enforcement directive eschews balancing tests, and instead establishes a new "right of information" for intellectual property owners and directs member states to "ensure that . . . in response to a justified and proportionate request . . . judicial authorities may order that information on the origin and distribution networks of the goods or services which infringe . . . be provided." Corrigendum to Directive 2004/48/EC of the European Parliament and of the Council of 29 April 2004 on the enforcement of intellectual property rights, art. 8, ¶1, 2004 O.J. (L 195) 16. The court may issue a disclosure order to the alleged

infringer or any person who, on a commercial scale, is in possession of infringing goods, using infringing services, or providing services used in infringing activities. *Id*. The information to be disclosed includes names, addresses, quantities, and prices. *Id*. ¶2. Is this approach preferable? Why or why not?

4. According to the conventional wisdom when the RIAA began its litigation campaign, suing individual users was economically irrational. The average cost of filing each lawsuit was approximately $250, and the cost (including filing) of reaching a resolution likely totaled about $2,500. Justin Hughes, *On the Logic of Suing One's Customers and the Dilemma of Infringement-Based Business Models*, 22 Cardozo Arts & Ent. L.J. 725, 750 (2005). An average settlement of $3,500-$4,500 covers those costs. *See id*. at 749 & n. 89 (giving the $4,500 figure as the 2004 average); *http://www.usatoday.com/tech/news/2009-06-18-music-downloading_N.htm* (stating an average of $3,500). Was the conventional wisdom wrong? Does suing users create other disadvantages for copyright owners? For discussion of these questions, see Hughes, *supra*.

5. How do the advantages and disadvantages of suing direct infringers compare to the advantages and disadvantages of expanding the traditional theories of indirect liability? *Compare* Marybeth Peters, *Copyright Enters the Public Domain*, 51 J. Copyright Soc'y 701 (2004) (arguing that indirect infringement liability should be expanded so that the copyright industries would not need to resort to suing individual consumers) *with* Mark A. Lemley & R. Anthony Reese, *Reducing Digital Copyright Infringement Without Restricting Innovation*, 56 Stan. L. Rev. 1345 (2004) (advocating the creation of a relatively inexpensive, quasi-administrative procedure for suing direct infringers to take the pressure off third-party providers of multipurpose technologies).

6. What are the pros and cons of the three strikes approach from the RIAA's perspective? From the OSP's perspective? Why do you think OSPs have been reluctant to adopt this approach?

Partly as a result of HEOA (*see supra* note 4, page 506), some colleges and universities have adopted three strikes policies. Why might they be more willing to do so than other OSPs? Should they remit the fines they collect to the RIAA?

7. France has enacted three strikes legislation after lengthy discussion. The first version of the law called for the establishment of a High Authority for Diffusion of Works and Protection of Rights (HADOPI), and empowered the High Authority to issue fines and to block Internet access after two warnings. The French Constitutional Council, however, ruled that "only a court can authorize such action, because depriving a citizen of internet access could violate his or her fundamental right to communicate." *French Constitutional Panel OKs Piracy Law, Cutting Internet Access After 'Three-Strikes'*, 78 Pat. Trademark & Copyright J. (BNA), Oct. 30, 2009 at 804. The next version of the legislation, HADOPI 2, cured this defect by providing for judicial review of termination orders, and was upheld in virtually its entirety by the Constitutional Council. *Id*. Other countries are considering similar bills. Should the U.S.?

E.   CRIMINAL INFRINGEMENT

As the state of copying technology has developed over time to permit the making of ever-increasing numbers of perfect quality copies at the touch of a button, the copyright industries have pressured both Congress and law enforcement to respond by enhancing criminal sanctions in the Act and vigorously prosecuting those infringements defined as criminal. Prime movers in this effort include the computer software, sound recording, and motion picture industries.

We begin this section with a brief history of criminal copyright infringement—one that reveals progressively increasing penalties and some lowering of the standards that conduct must meet before the law will consider it criminal. We then explore the elements of a criminal case and the relationship between copyright law and non-copyright federal statutes. As you read these materials, consider whether Congress has struck the correct balance in deciding who should be called a "criminal" and who should not. Think too about your own conduct—how close have you ever come to being a copyright criminal?

Note on the History of Criminal Copyright Infringement

From the first Copyright Act of 1790 until 1897, copyright law lacked criminal penalties. In 1897, Congress amended the Act to provide for punishing as misdemeanors infringing public performances and representations of copyrighted dramatic or musical compositions conducted willfully and for profit. In 1909, Congress extended this liability to include all types of copyrighted works and infringement of any of the exclusive rights, while retaining the requirements that the infringement be committed "wilfully and for profit." The 1976 Act reworded the *mens rea* element slightly, providing for criminal liability for infringement done "willfully and for purposes of commercial advantage or private financial gain." The 1976 Act increased the maximum permissible penalties from one year in prison and a $1,000 fine to one year in prison for first-time offenders with a fine up to $10,000.[1] A court could increase the $10,000 fine to $25,000 in the case of infringement of the reproduction, public distribution, or performance rights in motion pictures, or of the reproduction, adaptation, or public distribution rights in sound recordings. A court could impose stiffer penalties on certain repeat offenders. The 1976 Act also provided for mandatory destruction of all infringing copies or phonorecords and the materials used in their production. *See* 17 U.S.C. §506(b).

In 1982, under pressure from the motion picture and recording industries, Congress designated certain categories of infringements as felonies, dividing them into two classes based on the number of infringing copies or phonorecords made or sold within a 180-day period. Congress defined the more serious felonies as those involving the reproduction or distribution of at least 1,000 copies or phonorecords of sound recordings and at least 65 of motion pictures or audiovisual works. A court could punish an infringer falling into this first category with up to five years in prison and $250,000.

Congress defined the second, less serious category of felonies as those involving threshold numbers of copies of at least 100 for sound recordings and seven for motion pictures or audiovisual works. The maximum sentence for committing this less serious felony was set at two years, but the court could impose a fine up to the same $250,000 applicable to more serious infringements.

All remaining criminal infringements were misdemeanors, subjecting the offender to up to $25,000 in fines and one year imprisonment. Thus, misdemeanor offenses included those infringements that were committed "willfully and for the purpose of commercial advantage or private financial gain," but (1) were not infringements of sound recordings, motion pictures, or audiovisual works, regardless of the magnitude of the infringement, (2) were infringements of those types of

---

1. The penalties for criminal infringement are set forth in Title 18 of the U.S. Code. *See* 18 U.S.C. §2319 (describing prison terms); *id.* §3571 (setting forth fines).

works through reproduction or distribution, but did not meet the threshold quantity of copies set out above, or (3) were infringements of sound recording, motion picture, or audiovisual works, but were infringements committed by the creation of a derivative work or by public performance [i.e., not reproduction or distribution].

Lydia Pallas Loren, *Digitization, Commodification, Criminalization: The Evolution of Criminal Copyright Infringement and the Importance of the Willfulness Requirement*, 77 Wash. U.L.Q. 835, 844 (1999).

The felony provisions of the 1982 amendments did not apply to infringement of any of a copyright owner's exclusive rights in computer software. However, the software industry was beset by large-scale piracy, claiming losses of $2.4 billion annually in testimony before the House Subcommittee on Intellectual Property and Judicial Administration. *See United States v. LaMacchia*, 871 F. Supp. 535, 540 (D. Mass. 1994). A proposal to extend felony treatment to certain infringements of computer software copyrights eventually became the Copyright Felony Act, enacted in 1992. This Act expanded the felony provisions to include *all* copyrighted works, not just computer software. The Copyright Felony Act also changed what would constitute a felony from the two categories above to "the reproduction or distribution, during any 180-day period, of at least 10 copies or phonorecords, of 1 or more copyrighted works with a retail value of more than $2,500." The penalties were those applicable to the most serious infringements under the 1982 amendments and could be enhanced for repeat offenders. The legislation retained the requirement that, to be criminal, the infringement must be willful and conducted for commercial advantage or private financial gain.

On the international front, Article 61 of the TRIPS Agreement requires members to provide:

> . . . criminal procedures and penalties to be applied at least in cases of wilful . . . copyright piracy on a commercial scale. Remedies available shall include imprisonment and mandatory fines sufficient to provide a deterrent, consistently with the level of penalties applied for crimes of a corresponding gravity. In appropriate cases, remedies available shall also include the seizure, forfeiture and destruction of the infringing goods and of any materials and implements the predominant use of which has been in the commission of the offences. Members may provide for criminal procedures and penalties to be applied in other cases of infringement of intellectual property rights, in particular where they are committed wilfully and on a commercial scale.

TRIPS Agreement, art. 61.

As you read the following, consider whether U.S. law goes beyond what TRIPS requires. The preceding brief history of U.S. law's provisions on criminal copyright infringement illustrates the trend of increasing penalties. Throughout, however, the *mens rea* requirement focused on willfulness and purposes of commercial advantage or private financial gain. First, we examine what "willfulness" means in the context of a criminal copyright prosecution.

United States v. Moran
757 F. Supp. 1046 (D. Neb. 1991)

KOPF, MAGISTRATE J.: . . . Dennis Moran (Moran), the defendant, is a full-time Omaha, Nebraska, police officer and the owner of a "mom-and-pop" movie rental business which rents video cassettes of copyrighted motion pictures to the public. On April 14, 1989, agents of the Federal Bureau of Investigation (FBI) executed a court-ordered search warrant on the premises of Moran's business. The FBI seized various video cassettes appearing to be unauthorized copies of copyrighted motion pictures, including "Bat 21," "Big," "Crocodile Dundee II," "The Fourth Protocol," "Hell-Bound: Hellraiser II," and "Mystic Pizza." The parties have stipulated that these six motion pictures are validly copyrighted motion pictures. The parties have further stipulated that each of the six motion pictures was distributed to Moran, with the permission of the copyright holder, between February 1, 1989, and April 14, 1989. The parties have further stipulated that at least one of the movies identified was reproduced by Moran onto a video cassette, without the authorization of the copyright holder, placed into inventory for rental, and subsequently rented. . . .

. . . Moran further advised the FBI agents that he would affix to the [ ] copies title labels for the copyrighted motion pictures and a copy of the FBI copyright warning label commonly found on video cassette tapes. Moran advised the FBI agents that he put the title labels and FBI warning on the tapes to stop customers from stealing or duplicating the tapes. . . .

Moran testified that he began to "insure" copyrighted video cassettes, meaning that he duplicated copyrighted video cassettes which he had validly purchased from distributors, when he realized copyrighted tapes were being vandalized. Moran testified he was under the impression that "insuring" tapes was legal whereas "pirating" tapes was not. For practical purposes, Moran defined "insuring" versus "pirating" as meaning that he could duplicate a copyrighted tape provided he had purchased the copyrighted tape and did not endeavor to rent both the copyrighted tape and the duplicate he had made. Moran testified that he formulated his belief about "insuring" versus "pirating" when talking with various colleagues in the business and from reading trade publications. However, Moran was not able to specifically identify the source of his information.

There was no persuasive evidence that Moran made multiple copies of each authorized version of the copyrighted material. The evidence indicates that Moran purchased more than one copyrighted tape of the same movie, but the persuasive evidence also reveals that Moran made only one copy of each copyrighted tape he purchased. There was no persuasive evidence that Moran endeavored to rent both the copyrighted tape and the duplicate. When Moran made the unauthorized copy, he put the unauthorized copy in a package made to resemble as closely as possible the package containing the original copyrighted motion picture Moran had purchased from an authorized distributor. . . .

A.

It must first be determined whether the word "willfully," as used in 17 U.S.C. §506(a), requires a showing of "bad purpose" or "evil motive" in the sense that there was an "intentional violation of a known legal duty." Adopting the research of the Motion Picture Association of America, the government argues that the term "willful" means only "an intent to copy and not to infringe." . . . On the other hand, Moran argues that the use of the word "willful" implies the kind of specific intent required to be proven in federal tax cases, which is to say, a voluntary, intentional violation of a known legal duty. . . .

Apparently no case has compared and analyzed the competing arguments, i.e., whether the word "willfully" requires either a showing of specific intent, as suggested by Moran, or the more generalized intent suggested by the government. Indeed, a leading text writer acknowledges that there are two divergent lines of cases, one of which requires specific intent and another which does not. . . .

I am persuaded that under 17 U.S.C. §506(a) "willfully" means that in order to be criminal the infringement must have been a "voluntary, intentional violation of a known legal duty." . . . I am so persuaded because I believe that in using the word "willful" Congress intended to soften the impact of the common-law presumption that ignorance of the law or mistake of the law is no defense to a criminal prosecution by making specific intent to violate the law an element of federal criminal copyright offenses. I came to this conclusion after examining the use of the word "willful" in the civil copyright infringement context and applying that use to the criminal statute. . . . (There is a general principle in copyright law of looking to civil authority for guidance in criminal cases). . . .

In the statutory damage context, a civil plaintiff is generally entitled to recover no less than $250.00 nor more than $10,000.00 per act of infringement.* 17 U.S.C. §504(c)(1). But where the infringement is committed "willfully," the court in its discretion may increase the award of statutory damages up to a maximum of $50,000.00 per act of infringement. 17 U.S.C. §504(c)(2). On the other hand, in the case of "innocent infringement," if the defendant sustains the burden of proving he/she was not aware, and had no reason to believe, that his/her acts constituted an infringement of the copyright, and the court so finds, the court may in its discretion reduce the applicable minimum to $100.00 per act of infringement.** 17 U.S.C. §504(c)(2). . . .

As noted text writers have concluded, the meaning of the term "willful," used in 17 U.S.C. §504, must mean that the infringement was with knowledge that the defendant's conduct constituted copyright infringement. *Nimmer, supra* p. 6, §14.04[B][3] at 14-40.3-14-40.4 (citations omitted). Otherwise, there would be no point in providing specially for the reduction of awards to the $100.00 level in the case of "innocent" infringement since any infringement which was nonwillful would necessarily be innocent.

The circuit courts of appeal which have considered the issue have all adopted *Nimmer's* formulation with regard to the meaning of the word "willful" for purposes of 17 U.S.C. §504(c)(2) and statutory civil damages. . . .

There is nothing in the text of the criminal copyright statute, the overall scheme of the copyright laws, or the legislative history to suggest that Congress intended the word "willful," when used in the criminal statute, to mean simply, as the government suggests, an intent to copy. Rather, since Congress used "willful" in the civil damage copyright context to mean that the infringement must take place with the defendant being knowledgeable that his/her conduct constituted copyright infringement, there is no compelling reason to adopt a less stringent requirement in the criminal copyright context. Accordingly, I find that "willfully," when used in 17 U.S.C. §506(a), means a "voluntary, intentional violation of a known legal duty." . . .

B.

[I]t is important to recognize that the rule does not require that a defendant's belief that his conduct is lawful be judged by an objective standard. Rather, the test is whether Moran truly believed that the copyright laws did not prohibit him from making one copy of a video cassette he had purchased in order to "insure" against vandalism. . . . Of course, the more unreasonable the asserted belief or misunderstanding, the more likely it is that the finder of fact will consider

---

* The court made an error here. At the time, a court could increase the award to a maximum of $10,000 with respect to any one work infringed, not per act of infringement. Now, the Act sets the amount at $150,000. *See* 17 U.S.C. §504(c)(2). — Eds.

** The court made the same error here. A court could decrease the award to a maximum of $100 with respect to any one work infringed, not per act of infringement. Now, the Act sets the amount at $200. *See id.* — Eds.

the asserted belief or misunderstanding to be nothing more than simple disagreement with known legal duties imposed by the law, and will find that the government has carried its burden of proving knowledge. . . .

In summary, when Moran's actions were viewed from the totality of the circumstances, the government failed to convince me beyond a reasonable doubt that Moran acted willfully. Moran is a long-time street cop who was fully cooperative with law enforcement authorities. He is obviously not sophisticated and, at least from the record, his business operation of renting movies to the public was not large or sophisticated. Rather, Moran's business appears to have been of the "mom-and-pop" variety. Moran's practice of "insuring," while obviously shifting the risk of loss from Moran to the copyright holder, was conducted in such a way as not to maximize profits, which one assumes would have been his purpose if he had acted willfully. For example, Moran purchased multiple authorized copies of the same movie, but he made only one unauthorized copy for each authorized version purchased. This suggests that Moran truly believed that what he was doing was in fact legal. I therefore find Moran not guilty.

NOTES AND QUESTIONS

1. Which interpretation of the willfulness requirement makes more sense to you?

2. Congress amended §506 in 1997 as part of the No Electronic Theft (NET) Act, which we discuss in more detail below. Under revised §506, "evidence of reproduction or distribution of a copyrighted work, by itself, shall not be sufficient to establish willful infringement." Does this resolve the controversy the *Moran* court discussed about the definition of "willfully"?

We next examine the 1976 Act's original requirement that the infringement be committed "for purposes of commercial advantage or private financial gain" before criminal liability may accrue. This requirement, as the next case shows, is ill suited to addressing the conduct of those who do not have an economic motive for infringing copyright.

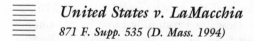

United States v. LaMacchia

871 F. Supp. 535 (D. Mass. 1994)

STEARNS, J.: This case presents the issue of whether new wine can be poured into an old bottle. The facts, as seen in the light most favorable to the government, are these. The defendant, David LaMacchia, is a twenty-one year old student at the Massachusetts Institute of Technology (MIT). LaMacchia, a computer hacker, used MIT's computer network to gain entree to the Internet. Using pseudonyms and an encrypted address, LaMacchia set up an electronic bulletin board which he named Cynosure. He encouraged his correspondents to upload popular software applications (Excel 5.0 and WordPerfect 6.0) and computer games (Sim City 2000). These he transferred to a second encrypted address (Cynosure II) where they could be downloaded by other users with access to the Cynosure password. Although LaMacchia was at pains to impress the need for circumspection on the part of his subscribers, the worldwide traffic generated by the offer of free software attracted the notice of university and federal authorities.

On April 7, 1994, a federal grand jury returned a one count indictment charging LaMacchia with conspiring with "persons unknown" to violate 18 U.S.C. §1343, the wire fraud statute. According to the indictment, LaMacchia devised a scheme to defraud that had as its object the facilitation "on an international scale" of the "illegal copying and distribution of copyrighted software" without payment of licensing fees and royalties to software manufacturers and vendors. The indictment alleges that LaMacchia's scheme caused losses of more than one million dollars to software copyright holders. The indictment does not allege that LaMacchia sought or derived any personal benefit from the scheme to defraud.

On September 30, 1994, the defendant brought a motion to dismiss, arguing that the government had improperly resorted to the wire fraud statute as a copyright enforcement tool in defiance of the Supreme Court's decision in *Dowling v. United States*, 473 U.S. 207 . . . (1985).

The *Dowling* Decision

Paul Edmond Dowling was convicted of conspiracy, interstate transportation of stolen property [ITSP], copyright violations and mail fraud in the Central District of California. Dowling and his co-conspirators sold bootleg Elvis Presley recordings by soliciting catalogue orders from post office boxes in Glendale, California. The infringing recordings were shipped in interstate commerce to Maryland and Florida. The eight ITSP counts on which Dowling was convicted involved thousands of phonograph albums. "[E]ach album contained performances of copyrighted musical compositions for the use of which no licenses had been obtained nor royalties paid. . . ." *Dowling, supra* at 212 . . . Dowling appealed his convictions (except those involving copyright infringement). The Ninth Circuit Court of Appeals affirmed. . . .

The Supreme Court granted certiorari only as to Dowling's convictions for interstate transportation of stolen property. The Court, in an opinion by Justice Blackmun, held that a copyrighted musical composition impressed on a bootleg phonograph record is not property that is "stolen, converted, or taken by fraud" within the meaning of the Stolen Property Act. Justice Blackmun emphasized that cases prosecuted under §2314 had traditionally involved "physical 'goods, wares [or] merchandise.'" The statute "seems clearly to contemplate a physical identity between the items unlawfully obtained and those eventually transported, and hence some prior physical taking of the subject goods" *Id*. at 216 . . . In Dowling's case there was no evidence "that Dowling wrongfully came by the phonorecords actually shipped or the physical materials from which they were made." *Dowling, supra* at 214. . . .

Justice Blackmun felt compelled, however, to answer the government's argument that the unauthorized use of the underlying musical compositions was itself sufficient to render the offending phonorecords property "stolen, converted or taken by fraud."

> [T]he Government's theory here would make theft, conversion, or fraud equivalent to wrongful appropriation of statutorily protected rights in copyright. The copyright owner, however, holds no ordinary chattel. A copyright, like other intellectual property, comprises a series of carefully defined and carefully delimited interests to which the law affords correspondingly exact protections. *Id*. at 216. . . .

A copyright, as Justice Blackmun explained, is unlike an ordinary chattel because the holder does not acquire exclusive dominion over the thing owned. . . . Justice Blackmun offered the "fair use" doctrine (17 U.S.C. §107) and the statutory scheme of compulsory licensing of musical compositions (17 U.S.C. §115) as examples of ways in which the property rights of a copyright holder are circumscribed by the Copyright Act. *Dowling, supra*, 473 U.S. at 217. . . .

> It follows that interference with copyright does not easily equate with theft, conversion or fraud. The Copyright Act even employs a separate term of art to define one who misappropriates a copyright: . . . "an infringer" . . . There is no dispute in this case that Dowling's unauthorized inclusion on his bootleg albums of performances of copyrighted compositions constituted infringement of those copyrights. It is less clear, however, that the taking that occurs when an infringer arrogates the use of another's protected work comfortably fits the terms associated with physical removal employed by §2314. The infringer invades a statutorily defined province guaranteed to the copyright holder alone. But he does not assume physical control over the copyright; nor does he wholly deprive its owner of its use. . . .

The ITSP statute, Justice Blackmun observed, had its roots in efforts by Congress to supplement the efforts of state authorities frustrated by jurisdictional problems arising from the transportation of stolen property across state lines. *Id.* at 219-220. . . .

> No such need for supplemental federal action has ever existed, however, with respect to copyright infringement, for the obvious reason that Congress always has had the bestowed authority to legislate directly in this area. . . . Given that power, it is implausible to suppose that Congress intended to combat the problem of copyright infringement by the circuitous route hypothesized by the government.
> . . . In sum, the premise of §2314 — the need to fill with federal action an enforcement chasm created by limited state jurisdiction — simply does not apply to the conduct the Government seeks to reach here. *Id.* at 220-221.

A review of the evolution of criminal penalties in the Copyright Act led Justice Blackmun to observe that:

> [T]he history of the criminal infringement provisions of the Copyright Act reveals a good deal of care on Congress' part before subjecting copyright infringement to serious criminal penalties. . . . In stark contrast, the Government's theory of this case presupposes a congressional decision to bring the felony provisions of §2314, which make available the comparatively light fine of not more than $10,000 but the relatively harsh term of imprisonment of up to 10 years, to bear on the distribution of a sufficient quantity of any infringing goods simply because of the presence here of a factor — interstate transportation — not otherwise thought relevant to copyright law. The Government thereby presumes congressional adoption of an indirect but blunderbuss solution to a problem treated with precision when considered directly. *Id.* at 225-226.

. . . Justice Blackmun concluded that "the deliberation with which Congress over the last decade has addressed the problem of copyright infringement for profit, as well as the precision with which it has chosen to apply criminal penalties in this area, demonstrates anew the wisdom of leaving it to the legislature to define crime and prescribe penalties. Here, the language of §2314 does not 'plainly and unmistakably' cover petitioner Dowling's conduct." *Id.* at 228. . . . Dowling's ITSP convictions were reversed.

The Copyright Law

. . . Since 1897, when criminal copyright infringement was first introduced into U.S. copyright law, the concept differentiating criminal from civil copyright violations has been that the infringement must be pursued for purposes of commercial exploitation. . . .

Discussion

The wire fraud statute, 18 U.S.C. §1343 was enacted in 1952. . . .

As the legislative history makes clear, the wire fraud statute was intended to complement the mail fraud statute by giving federal prosecutors jurisdiction over frauds involving the use of interstate (or foreign) wire transmissions. . . .

. . . Wire fraud offers an especially pleasing feature from the government's perspective that is particularly relevant to LaMacchia's case. Unlike the criminal copyright statute, 17 U.S.C. §506(a), the mail and wire fraud statutes do not require that a defendant be shown to have sought to personally profit from the scheme to defraud. . . .

[The court then reviewed three reasons why it found it difficult to permit a wire fraud prosecution under *Dowling*. Here, we concentrate only on the third.]

. . . Third, even were I to accept the argument made by the government in *Dowling*, that illegal conduct alone may suffice to satisfy the fraud element of [§1343], the holding would not cover LaMacchia's case for the simple reason that what LaMacchia is alleged to have done is not criminal conduct under §506(a) of the Copyright Act. . . .

What the government is seeking to do is to punish conduct that reasonable people might agree deserves the sanctions of the criminal law. But as Justice Blackmun observed in *Dowling*, copyright is an area in which Congress has chosen to tread cautiously, relying "chiefly . . . on an array of civil remedies to provide copyright holders protection against infringement," while mandating "studiously graded penalties" in those instances where Congress has concluded that the deterrent effect of criminal sanctions are required. *Dowling, supra* at 221, 225. . . . "This step-by-step, carefully considered approach is consistent with Congress' traditional sensitivity to the special concerns implicated by the copyright laws." *Id.* at 225. . . . Indeed, the responsiveness of Congress to the impact of new technology on the law of copyright, limned earlier in this opinion, confirms Justice Blackmun's conviction of "the wisdom of leaving it to the legislature to define crime and prescribe penalties." *Dowling, supra* at 228. . . .

> "The judiciary's reluctance to expand the protections afforded by the copyright without explicit legislative guidance is a recurring theme. Sound policy, as well as history, supports our consistent deference to Congress when major technological innovations alter the market for copyrighted materials. Congress has the institutional authority and the institutional ability to accommodate fully the varied permutations of competing interests that are inevitably implicated by such new technology."

Sony Corporation of America v. Universal City Studios, Inc., 464 U.S. 417, 431. . . .

While the government's objective is a laudable one, particularly when the facts alleged in this case are considered, its interpretation of the wire fraud statute would serve to criminalize the conduct of not only persons like LaMacchia, but also the myriad of home computer users who succumb to the temptation to copy even a single software program for private use. It is not clear that making criminals of a large number of consumers of computer software is a result that even the software industry would consider desirable. . . .

This is not, of course, to suggest that there is anything edifying about what LaMacchia is alleged to have done. If the indictment is to be believed, one might at best describe his actions as heedlessly irresponsible, and at worst as nihilistic, self-indulgent, and lacking in any fundamental sense of values. Criminal as well as civil penalties should probably attach to willful, multiple infringements of copyrighted software even absent a commercial motive on the part of the infringer. One can envision ways that the copyright law could be modified to permit such prosecution. But, " '[i]t is the legislature, not the Court which is to define a crime, and ordain its punishment.' " . . .

For the foregoing reasons, defendant LaMacchia's motion to dismiss is *ALLOWED*. . . .

Note on Internet-Era Amendments to the Copyright Felony Provisions

Congress responded to the *LaMacchia* case with the 1997 enactment of the NET Act. Indeed, the legislative history explicitly states that the purpose of the NET Act is "to reverse the practical consequences of *United States v. LaMacchia* . . . by criminaliz[ing] computer theft of copyrighted works, whether or not the defendant derives a direct financial benefit from the act(s) of misappropriation, thereby preventing such willful conduct from destroying businesses, especially small businesses, that depend on licensing agreements and royalties for survival." H.R. Rep. 105-339, 105th Cong., 1st Sess. 1997.

The NET Act retained the rule providing that an infringement conducted willfully for purposes of commercial advantage or private financial gain is criminal. However, it added a new definition to §101, defining "financial gain" to mean "receipt, or expectation of receipt, of anything of value, including the receipt of other copyrighted works." The NET Act also amended §506(a) to provide for a second type of criminal liability. An infringer may now be held criminally liable when the infringement involves the willful "reproduction or distribution, including by electronic means, during any 180-day period, of 1 or more copies or phonorecords of 1 or more copyrighted works with a total retail value of more than $1,000. . . ." 17 U.S.C. §506(a)(1)(B). Thus, after the NET Act, an infringer need not have a commercial motive to be a criminal. Note, however, that the NET Act did not amend the wire fraud statute, so the holding of *Dowling* continues to apply: a prosecutor cannot use the wire fraud statute to bring what is essentially a copyright infringement claim.

The NET Act did not change the criminal penalties applicable to "conventional" criminal infringements—i.e., those that meet the traditional prongs of willfulness and a purpose of commercial advantage or private financial gain. It did, however, provide a special menu of penalties for those without such economic motives who are convicted under the new crime of willfully reproducing or distributing copies or phonorecords with a total retail value of $1,000. In addition to the fines already applicable, the NET Act provides prison terms of: (1) up to three years for reproduction or distribution of ten or more copies or phonorecords of one or more copyrighted works with a total retail value of $2,500 or more; (2) up to six years for repeat offenses defined in (1); and (3) up to one year for reproduction or distribution of one or more copies or phonorecords with a total retail value of more than $1,000. 18 U.S.C. §2319(c). Offenses involving works with a total retail value over $2,500 are felonies; offenses involving works with a total retail value of $1,000 to $2,500 are misdemeanors.

The NET Act was not initially used much by prosecutors. There is no consensus on why this was the case. Some thought the expense of a criminal proceeding might not be worth incurring for small-scale infringements that nevertheless were labeled criminal by the Act. Others opined that the lack of sentencing guidelines was a disincentive to prosecution. In 1999, Congress held hearings to understand the reasons for the virtually complete lack of prosecutorial activity under the NET Act. Justice Department and industry representatives testified that the penalties under the then-current law were insufficient to deter infringement. *See* H.R. Rep. No. 106-216, at 4. Faced with evidence of continued large-scale infringement, Congress enacted the Digital Theft Deterrence and Copyright Damages Improvement Act of 1999. This Act authorized enhanced prison sentences based on the retail price of the item infringed and the number of infringing copies in certain circumstances. It also increased damages available in civil actions (see Chapter 10).

Neither the NET Act nor the penalty enhancements of 1999 proved effective to address a phenomenon that the motion picture industry perceived as particularly damaging: the availability of movies on the Internet before they are available for purchase on DVD and sometimes even before they are released to theaters. In 2005, Congress passed the Artists' Rights and Theft Prevention (ART) Act as part of the Family Entertainment and Copyright Act. The ART Act added two new criminal prohibitions, one to the general federal criminal laws and one to the Copyright Act. The first prohibition makes it a felony to knowingly use an audiovisual device to make a copy of a copyrighted movie "from a performance of such work in a motion picture exhibition facility," a practice sometimes referred to as "camcording" a movie. 18 U.S.C. §2319B. The second prohibition specifies another way in which willful infringement of a copyright rises to the level of criminal infringement: "by the distribution of a work being prepared for commercial distribution, by making it available on a computer network accessible to members of the public, if such person knew or should have known that the work was intended for commercial distribution." 17 U.S.C. §506(a)(1)(C). Although this legislation clearly was aimed at Internet availability of pre-release motion pictures, the statute defines "work being prepared for commercial distribution" to include computer programs, musical works and sound recordings, as well as motion pictures and other audiovisual works, that have not been commercially distributed. *Id.* §506(a)(3). It also expressly includes motion pictures that have "been made available for viewing in a motion picture exhibition facility" but have not yet been "made available in copies for sale to the general public in the United States in a format intended to permit viewing outside a motion picture exhibition facility." *Id.* §506(a)(3)(B). Violations of §506(a)(1)(C) are punishable with up to three years imprisonment, with enhancements for subsequent offenses and offenses "committed for purposes of commercial advantage or private financial gain." 18 U.S.C. §2319(d).

The push to strengthen criminal copyright enforcement next produced the Prioritizing Resources and Organization for Intellectual Property (PRO-IP) Act of 2008, which reorganized the Department of Justice to create the Intellectual Property Enforcement Division, headed by an enforcement officer reporting directly to the Deputy Attorney General; authorized the appointment of "intellectual property attachés" to be posted to U.S. embassies abroad; established the Office of the Intellectual Property Enforcement Representative within the Executive Office of the President; and gave the head of that office comprehensive advisory authority over domestic and international enforcement policy. In addition, the PRO-IP Act amended §411 to specify that registration of copyright is a prerequisite for filing a civil infringement lawsuit. By inference then, registration is *not* a prerequisite for commencing a criminal prosecution.

The coming years likely will see more legislative activity on the subject of criminal copyright infringement unless the problem of large-scale infringements is otherwise solved, perhaps through the use of technological protection devices (*see* Chapter 9). Be sure to check the latest statute when evaluating conduct and determining the applicable range of penalties.

NOTES AND QUESTIONS

1. Read §506 in its entirety. In what ways may a person be criminally liable for copyright infringement? Can an indirect infringer, i.e., one who is secondarily liable, be criminally liable?

Does the Copyright Act answer this question? If not, what do you think the answer should be?

Note that the Digital Millennium Copyright Act (DMCA), which we discuss in Chapter 9, contains its own section on criminal liability. *See* 17 U.S.C. §1204; *infra* Chapter 9. Section 1204 criminalizes violations of §§1201-02 that are willful and "for purposes of commercial advantage or private financial gain." 17 U.S.C. §1204(a). Section 1201 finds a violation, *inter alia*, when a person sells technology or a product that is "primarily designed or produced for the purpose of circumventing protection afforded by a technological measure that effectively protects a right of a copyright owner . . ." *Id.* §1201(b)(1)(A). Such a person is in a position somewhat analogous to an indirect infringer because the person does not actually conduct the circumvention but rather assists the circumventor. The statute expressly provides for criminal liability for such a person under §1204. Does this help to answer the question whether an indirect infringer should be held criminally liable under §506 or is it irrelevant?

2. Why do you think Congress added a definition of "financial gain" to the Copyright Act? Did LaMacchia have private financial gain, as that term is now defined, as his purpose? Why do you think Congress added a clause explicitly to include reproduction or distribution by electronic means?

3. Consider whether the infringers in the following hypotheticals are criminals under §506:

a. You download an article from the New York Times and make copies for 20 family members at a family reunion.

b. A teenager buys a CD for $17.99 at a retail store. He uploads it in MP3 format to a chat room or blog. Over the next three months, 10,000 Internet users download it. Would your answer change if only 10 users downloaded it? What about 100?

c. A group of academic researchers pools software by placing various software packages on a server to which all in the group have access. For example, an MIT researcher might post a copy of SAS, while someone from Wellesley posts a copy of Word. No one software package is worth $1,000, but the cumulative cost of the software posted exceeds that total.

Determining the "retail value" of a work is relevant for meeting the threshold requirement for certain types of criminal infringement, as well as for establishing whether the offense is a felony or a misdemeanor. The Fourth Circuit has determined that "retail value" refers to the greater of (1) the "prices assigned to commodities and goods for sale at the retail level at the time of sales at issue" or (2) "prices of commodities and goods determined by actual transactions between willing buyers and willing sellers at the retail level." *United States v. Armstead*, 524 F.3d 442, 446 (4th Cir. 2008). The court rejected the defendant's argument that because the defendant had sold bootleg copies of DVDs to undercover agents for $5 each, that was the "going rate" between willing buyers and willing sellers. The government had introduced evidence showing $19 as the minimum retail price for the DVDs at issue.

Whether bootleg sales have a one-for-one correspondence to lost retail sales for the copyright owner is a hotly debated issue. While the courts calculate the "retail value" for purposes of criminal liability based on the price of legitimate copies, they sometimes use different valuations in other contexts. For example, the Federal Mandatory Victims Restitution Act requires proof of the actual loss suffered. One court reasoned:

It is a basic principle of economics that as price increases, demand decreases. Customers who download music and movies for free would not necessarily spend money to acquire the same product. . . . I am skeptical that customers would pay $7.22 or $19 for something they got for free. Certainly 100% of the illegal downloads . . . did not result in the loss of a sale. . . .

United States v. Dove, 585 F. Supp. 2d 865, 870 (W.D. Va. 2008).

4. A bill proposed in the 108th Congress sought to attack the problem of infringements conducted through peer-to-peer file sharing by amending §506 to include the following:

> Any person who —
>
> . . . infringes a copyright by the knowing distribution, including by the offering for distribution to the public by electronic means, with reckless disregard of the risk of further infringement, during any 180-day period, of —
>
>   (A) 1,000 or more copies or phonorecords of 1 or more copyrighted works,
>
>   (B) 1 or more copies or phonorecords of 1 or more copyrighted works with a total retail value of more than $10,000, or
>
>   (C) 1 or more copies or phonorecords of 1 or more copyrighted pre-release works,
>
> shall be punished as provided under section 2319 of title 18. For purposes of this subsection, evidence of reproduction or distribution of a copyrighted work, by itself, shall not be sufficient to establish the necessary level of intent under this subsection.

Piracy Deterrence and Education Act of 2004, H.R. 4077, 108th Cong., 2d Sess. How would this have changed the standards for criminal liability?

5. In 1996, with virtually no debate, copyright infringement was added to the list of violations eligible to support liability under the Racketeer Influenced and Corrupt Organizations (RICO) Act. 18 U.S.C. §1961(1). If a civil RICO violation is proved, a court may treble the damages otherwise available under the law defining the underlying violation. *Id.* §1964(c). Defendants convicted of criminal RICO violations face imprisonment for up to 20 additional years, the fine set forth in Title 18 (currently up to $250,000) or "not more than twice the gross profits or other proceeds" from the violation, and forfeiture of all assets acquired or maintained in connection with the violation. *Id.* §1963(a).

Plaintiffs in civil copyright infringement lawsuits alleging large-scale infringement now have begun asserting civil RICO claims. Establishing a civil RICO violation requires proof of the underlying criminal violation (here, willful copyright infringement), an "enterprise," and a "pattern" of "racketeering activity" by the enterprise. *Id.* §1962. How should these terms be interpreted in the copyright context? Could the manufacture of a device that enables copyright infringement constitute an "enterprise," and could a "pattern" of indirect infringement constitute the required predicate activity?

7

Another Limitation on Copyright: Fair Use

Throughout the discussion of the different rights granted to copyright owners in §106 and to authors in §106A, you also learned of various statutory sections that limit those rights. Indeed, §106 begins with the cautionary note "*subject to* sections 107 through 122 . . . ," and §106A similarly indicates that the rights granted in that section are "*subject to* section 107." This chapter focuses on the statutory limitation that applies to all of the different §106 and §106A rights: fair use.

The statutory limitations on the rights of copyright owners generally fall into three categories. First, some limitations are simple, bright-line rules. For example, the reproduction and derivative work rights belonging to the copyright owner of a sound recording do not encompass sound alike recordings, §114(a), and, under the first sale doctrine codified in §109, the right of public distribution does not include subsequent sales or, for most works, rentals, after the copyright owner has parted with title to a particular copy.

The second category of limitations includes those that are very complex and technical. While these limitations also provide bright-line rules, they require careful attention to statutory sections that may cover many pages in the U.S. Code. Consider just a few of the examples from Chapters 5 and 6, each requiring compliance with several conditions in order for the limitation to apply:

- Section 110(5)(B), which allows certain small businesses to play nondramatic musical works by turning on the radio and television despite the public performance right. See pages 458-60 *supra*.
- Section 114(d), which allows certain types of digital audio transmissions of sound recordings despite the rights granted in §106(6). See pages 460-63 *supra*.
- Section 111, which allows for certain broadcast retransmissions despite the public performance right. See pages 431-34 *supra*.
- Section 512, which allows for certain temporary copies to be created by Internet service providers. See pages 503-05 *supra*.

The complexity of these limitations results from the way these provisions were drafted. As you are now aware, many of the detailed limitations in the Copyright Act were created through industry negotiation. When industry participants have material interests at stake, they desire certainty so that they may better structure their business dealings. Ex post decision making based on factors that are weighed by courts on a case-by-case basis does not lead to certainty in business planning. The need for certainty, however, explains only the perceived need for bright-line rules, not their complexity. This complexity results from allowing industry players on opposite sides (or even multiple sides) of the bargaining table to participate in the drafting process. The kind of dealmaking that results in these situations can lead to incredibly complex statutory provisions that resemble clauses that might be found in contracts.

The final category of limitations really consists of one limitation: fair use. The statutory section concerning fair use, §107 of the Act, does not provide bright-line rules, but rather confers upon courts the ability to decide whether a particular activity should be within the copyright owner's rights. Section 107 establishes factors for courts to consider in making such determinations, but ultimately it is the court that will decide whether a particular use is fair. One goal of this chapter is to help you understand why certain types of uses tend to survive this judicial scrutiny and why others do not. In addition, this chapter is designed to help you identify and critically evaluate the criteria, both statutory and nonstatutory, that courts employ in fair use cases.

A. FAIR USE IN COMPARATIVE PERSPECTIVE

Other countries also recognize a need for limitations on copyright owners' exclusive rights. Historically most other countries, however, have not relied on a doctrine like fair use to help define those limits. Instead, they designate specific types of uses that are permitted. The divergence between the U.S. fair use doctrine and other approaches to defining privileged uses of copyrighted works has become both increasingly apparent and increasingly problematic in a world where multilateral intellectual property treaties seek increasing harmonization of copyright norms.

The fair use doctrine began as a judge-made exception to the rights of copyright owners. In England, the "fair abridgement" doctrine had permitted, as the name implies, certain abridgements of the copyrighted works of others without liability for infringement. *See, e.g.,* *Cary v. Kearsley,* 170 Eng. Rep. 679, 680 (K.B. 1803) (recognizing a right to "fairly adopt part of the work of another" and noting that the court must not "put manacles upon science").

The first American case to consider the applicability of the fair abridgement doctrine was *Folsom v. Marsh,* 9 F. Cas. 342 (C.C.D. Mass. 1841). The plaintiff in that case had written a 12-volume, 7,000-page biography of President Washington. The defendant had copied 353 pages from the plaintiff's work to create a two-volume work. Writing for the court, Justice Story rejected the argument that the defendant's work was a fair abridgement.

[A] reviewer may fairly cite largely from the original work, if his design be really and truly to use the passages for the purposes of fair and reasonable criticism. On the other hand, it is as clear, that if he thus cites the most important parts of the work, with a view, not to criticise, but to supersede the use of the original work, and substitute the review for it, such a use will be deemed in law a piracy.

Id. at 344-45. In what has become the most cited passage in the history of fair use, Justice Story went on to describe how a court should examine a claim of fair abridgement:

In short, we must often, in deciding questions of this sort, look to the nature and objects of the selections made, the quantity and value of the materials used, and the degree in which the use may prejudice the sale, or diminish the profits, or supersede the objects, of the original work.

Id. at 348.

Justice Story's opinion in *Folsom* never used the phrase "fair use." That term did not appear in the case law until 28 years later. *See Lawrence v. Dana*, 15 F. Cas. 26, 60 (C.C.D. Mass. 1869). For the next hundred years after *Folsom*, however, courts continued to look to the factors identified by Justice Story as most relevant in resolving fair use cases.

During the extensive revision process that led to enactment of the 1976 Act, Congress determined that codification of the fair use doctrine was necessary, and drafted what became §107. The current version of §107 follows:

§107. Limitations on exclusive rights: Fair use

Notwithstanding the provisions of sections 106 and 106A, the fair use of a copyrighted work, including such use by reproduction in copies or phonorecords or by any other means specified by that section, for purposes such as criticism, comment, news reporting, teaching (including multiple copies for classroom use), scholarship, or research, is not an infringement of copyright. In determining whether the use made of a work in any particular case is a fair use the factors to be considered shall include—

(1) the purpose and character of the use, including whether such use is of a commercial nature or is for nonprofit educational purposes;

(2) the nature of the copyrighted work;

(3) the amount and substantiality of the portion used in relation to the copyrighted work as a whole; and

(4) the effect of the use upon the potential market for or value of the copyrighted work.

The fact that a work is unpublished shall not itself bar a finding of fair use if such finding is made upon consideration of all the above factors.

17 U.S.C. §107.

As in the case of §102(a) and (b), which you studied in Chapter 2, the legislative history of the 1976 Act indicates that §107 was meant to codify, not enlarge, the preexisting judge-made doctrine. Beyond the factors set forth in the statute, the legislative history provides little to guide courts in applying §107. "Although the courts have considered and ruled upon the fair use doctrine over and over again, no real definition of the concept has ever emerged. Indeed, since the doctrine is an equitable rule of reason, no generally applicable definition is possible, and each case raising the question must be decided on its own facts." H.R. Rep. No. 94-1476, 94th Cong., 2d Sess. 65 (1976), *reprinted in* 1976 U.S.C.C.A.N. 5659, 5679.

That the U.S. would delegate lawmaking authority to courts by directing them to apply inexact standards like those of §107 is not surprising because the U.S. legal tradition is based on a common law system in which law is primarily judge-made. Other parts of the world employ legal systems based on the civil law approach, in which a legislative body codifies the law with greater specificity.

Continental European copyright laws, for example, generally list detailed, specific exceptions to and limitations on the exclusive copyright rights. The enumerated exceptions often include permission for private noncommercial use, quotation, parody, news reporting and educational and research uses. Countries such as Belgium, France, Italy, Spain, Sweden, and Switzerland follow this approach. Germany also defines specific exceptions in its copyright statute and additionally employs a doctrine of "free utilization" that courts may use more flexibly. In all these countries courts rarely, if ever, depart from the statutes to find limitations of their own for other types of conduct not envisioned ex-ante by the legislature. Notwithstanding the difference in approach between common and civil law jurisdictions most countries permit at least some of the uses U.S. courts have traditionally labeled fair.

As discussed above, in the United Kingdom, courts initially developed common law principles for limiting copyright owners' rights. In 1911, the British Parliament codified certain of these limits, primarily by reference to the concept of "fair dealing." These included uses of copyrighted works for educational purposes, review, private study, research or news commentary, and public recitation. The British copyright acts of 1956 and 1988 continued these exceptions. In general, the concept of fair dealing has proved to be considerably narrower than the U.S. concept of fair use. *See* Paul Goldstein, International Copyright 293 (2001) (observing that the concept of fair dealing "does not give courts the same open-ended authority to resolve cases" that fall outside of the statutorily enumerated exceptions). British courts, and courts in some other common law countries, still sometimes recognize uncodified defenses to infringement liability, such as a claim that dissemination of a copyrighted work is in the "public interest." However, one British decision cautions against use of the public interest principle to expand the scope of the fair dealing defense. *See Hyde Park Residence Ltd. v. Yelland*, 97 (8) L.S.G. 35 (Eng. Ct. App. 2000).

Other countries vary, with some providing only narrow, specific limitations and others adopting a fair dealing model, while still others are moving toward the U.S. model. Brazil follows the Continental European model of specifying exceptions and limitations in the statute. Argentina does not formally recognize a fair use doctrine, but its courts have occasionally excused certain uses and others are specifically excepted by statute. Japan has codified limitations intended to balance the exclusive rights of authors and the public interest, and at least one of its limitations makes reference to "fair practice." *See* Japanese Copyright Act art. 32(1). Additionally, Japan has amended its copyright laws to enumerate certain Internet uses that will not require the permission of the copyright holder. These provisions became effective in January 2010. Canada has codified exceptions to the exclusive rights of copyright owners under the fair dealing principle. According to a leading treatise, "fair dealing is often given a grudging interpretation in Canada. Unlike the position relating to fair use in the United States, only a limited set of purposes fall under this defense in Canada, and they have not usually been broadly construed." 1 International Copyright Law and Practice, §8[2][a] at CAN-95 (Paul Geller, Gen. Ed. 2000). In 2007, Israel adopted a new copyright law that incorporates a U.S.-style fair use provision. In so doing, Israel joined Singapore, the Philippines, and Hong Kong (before its return to China) in modifying its law to more closely resemble that of the U.S.

Historically, the diverse approaches to limitations on the exclusive rights of copyright owners made it difficult for negotiators of multilateral treaties to settle on an approach acceptable to all signatories. The Berne Convention, which was drafted in the late 1800s by the major European powers without U.S. participation, *see* Chapter 1, pages 34-36 *supra*, generally follows a mixture of traditional Continental and British approaches to delineating permissible limitations and exceptions. For example, Article 10 permits quotations from published works "compatible with fair practice." Berne Conv., art. 10(1). Other provisions in Articles 10 and 10bis allow national legislation to permit specific uses, including uses for news reporting. Article 9(2), however, contains the "three-step test," which permits member countries to place additional limitations on the reproduction right: "It shall be a matter for legislation in the countries of the Union to permit the reproduction of such works in [1] certain special cases, provided that [2] such reproduction does not conflict with a normal exploitation of the work and [3] does not unreasonably prejudice the legitimate interests of the author." *Id.*, art. 9(2).

The negotiators of the TRIPS Agreement used the language of Article 9(2) of the Berne Convention as the basis for Article 13 of TRIPS: "Members shall confine limitations or exceptions to exclusive rights to certain special cases which do not conflict with a normal exploitation of the work and do not unreasonably prejudice the legitimate interests of the right holder."

TRIPS Agreement, art. 13. Because Article 13 applies to limitations on any of the exclusive copyright rights, some commentators view it as more restrictive than Article 9(2) of the Berne Convention, which applies only to limitations on the reproduction right.

Others argue, however, that courts should not interpret the TRIPS Agreement's version of the three-step test restrictively. The Max Planck Institute for Intellectual Property, Competition and Tax Law has issued a declaration that calls for a balanced interpretation of the test. *See http://www.ip.mpg.de/ww/en/pub/news/declaration_on_the_three_step_.cfm.* The Declaration emphasizes, *inter alia*, that the three steps do not require limitations to be interpreted narrowly, nor do they prevent either courts or legislatures from adopting open-ended limitations of reasonably foreseeable scope. *Id.* The Declaration also states:

> Limitations and exceptions do not conflict with a normal exploitation of protected subject matter, if they
>
> - are based on important competing considerations or
> - have the effect of countering unreasonable restraints on competition, notably on secondary makets, particularly where adequate compensation is ensured. . . .
> - The Three-Step Test should be interpreted in a manner that respects the legitimate interests of third parties, including
> - interests deriving from human rights and fundamental freedoms;
> - interests in competition, notably on secondary markets; and
> - other public interests, notably in scientific progress and cultural, social, or economic development.

Id. Many leading copyright scholars have signed the declaration. *See http://www.ip.mpg.de/ww/de/pub/aktuelles/declaration_on_the_three_step_/list_of_supporters.cfm.*

Negotiations over the WIPO Copyright Treaty (WCT) included proposals (made, interestingly, by the U.S.) to limit allowable exceptions in a way that would appear to contract the permissible sphere of U.S.-style fair use. However, the version of the WCT eventually signed contains language essentially similar to Article 13 of the TRIPS Agreement. *See* WCT, art. 10. The Agreed Statement for Article 10 indicates that the treaty is intended to permit signatories to "carry forward and appropriately extend into the digital environment limitations and exceptions in their national laws which have been considered acceptable under the Berne Convention. Similarly, these provisions should be understood to permit [signatory countries] to devise new exceptions and limitations that are appropriate in the digital network environment."

NOTES AND QUESTIONS

1. Which approach to defining privileged uses of copyrighted works seems to make more sense, the U.S. fair use doctrine, the Continental European approach, something in between, or a mixture? Consider this question as you continue through this chapter.

2. Compare the factors listed in §107 to those articulated by Justice Story in 1841. Are there any differences? Can you think of any other factors that might be relevant to the question whether a particular copyrighted work has been fairly copied, distributed, or publicly performed or displayed?

3. Do you read the TRIPS Agreement as permitting the type of interpretation that the Declaration suggests? Can you read the three-step test to authorize courts and legislatures to consider the interests of third parties when assessing limitations and exceptions to copyright rights?

4. Should the international copyright system adopt the U.S.-style fair use doctrine? Commentators have argued that the doctrine is another example of U.S. noncompliance with international standards. According to Professor Ruth Okediji:

> There are at least three potential arguments to support the supposition that the fair use doctrine violates Article 9(2) of the Berne Convention and, de facto, Article 13 of the TRIPS Agreement. First, the *indeterminacy* of the fair use doctrine violates the Berne Convention. Second, the *breadth* of the fair use doctrine violates the Berne Convention standard for permissible exceptions to authors' rights. Third, with particular reference to the TRIPS Agreement, the fair use doctrine may be challenged as a *nullification and impairment* of the expected benefits that trading partners reasonably should expect under the TRIPS Agreement.

Ruth Okediji, *Toward an International Fair Use Doctrine*, 39 Colum. J. Transnat'l L. 75, 117 (2000) (emphasis in original). Indeed, shortly after the conclusion of the TRIPS Agreement, Australia, New Zealand, and the European Community asked the U.S. to explain how its fair use doctrine is consistent with Article 13. The U.S. responded that Article 13 and the fair use doctrine share common goals, and that judicial interpretation of the doctrine is consistent with Article 13. As you read the materials in this chapter, consider whether the U.S. complies with Article 13 as written or as the Max Planck Institute would have it interpreted.

5. In the same article, Professor Okediji argues for the development of an international fair use standard. Okediji, *supra*, at 151-72. Do you think such a standard would be advisable? Consider this question again after you finish reading this chapter.

B. THE DIFFERENT FACES OF FAIR USE

Because courts apply the fair use doctrine on a case-by-case basis, predicting outcomes in fair use disputes can be difficult. Indeed, courts have deemed the doctrine "the most troublesome in the whole law of copyright." *Dellar v. Samuel Goldwyn, Inc.*, 104 F.2d 661, 662 (2d Cir. 1939). In practice, whether a particular use is deemed fair depends not only on the particular circumstances, but also on underlying normative theories. Here we present common fact patterns that arise in fair use cases and leading theories that one might employ to understand and resolve the ensuing disputes.

1. Cultural Interchange

Many of the illustrative uses listed in the preamble to §107 are those that further the development of a common culture. "[C]riticism, comment, news reporting, teaching . . . scholarship, [and] research" all promote the progress of learning and the arts. These uses also help to produce a public that is educated and informed not only about current events, but about shared values, interests, and debates. How far, though, should fair use privileges extend in the name of cultural progress and dissemination? At one end of the spectrum, it is reasonably clear that if you copy your neighbor's recent book on modern American politics and sell thousands of copies to the public at a discount below the retail price simply because you think everyone ought to read it, the fair use doctrine will not shield your conduct. At the other end, it is equally clear that if you publish a review of the book, whether flattering or harshly critical, and quote from it to illustrate your points, the quotations are fair use. For cases falling somewhere between these two extremes, however, determining the right outcome can be much harder.

Two of the Supreme Court's three post-1976 Act fair use decisions fall into this category of cases, which we call "cultural interchange" cases. As you read these decisions, identify the rules (or guidelines) that the Court develops to interpret, and to supplement, the §107 fair use factors and ask yourself whether these rules seem to strike the right balance.

Harper & Row, Publishers, Inc. v. Nation Enterprises
471 U.S. 539 (1985)

O'CONNOR, J.: . . . In February 1977, shortly after leaving the White House, former President Gerald R. Ford contracted with petitioners Harper & Row and Reader's Digest, to publish his as yet unwritten memoirs. The memoirs were to contain "significant hitherto unpublished material" concerning the Watergate crisis, Mr. Ford's pardon of former President Nixon and "Mr. Ford's reflections on this period of history, and the morality and personalities involved." . . . In addition to the right to publish the Ford memoirs in book form, the agreement gave petitioners the exclusive right to license prepublication excerpts, known in the trade as "first serial rights." Two years later, as the memoirs were nearing completion, petitioners negotiated a prepublication licensing agreement with Time, a weekly news magazine. Time agreed to pay $25,000, $12,500 in advance and an additional $12,500 at publication, in exchange for the right to excerpt 7,500 words from Mr. Ford's account of the Nixon pardon. The issue featuring the excerpts was timed to appear approximately one week before shipment of the full length book version to bookstores. Exclusivity was an important consideration; Harper & Row instituted procedures designed to maintain the confidentiality of the manuscript, and Time retained the right to renegotiate the second payment should the material appear in print prior to its release of the excerpts.

Two to three weeks before the Time article's scheduled release, an unidentified person secretly brought a copy of the Ford manuscript to Victor Navasky, editor of The Nation, a political commentary magazine. Mr. Navasky knew that his possession of the manuscript was not authorized and that the manuscript must be returned quickly to his "source" to avoid discovery. . . . He hastily put together what he believed was "a real hot news story" composed of quotes, paraphrases, and facts drawn exclusively from the manuscript. . . . Mr. Navasky attempted no independent commentary, research or criticism, in part because of the need for speed if he was to "make news" by "publish[ing] in advance of publication of the Ford book." App. 416-417. The 2,250-word article, reprinted in the Appendix to this opinion, appeared on April 3, 1979. As a result of The Nation's article, Time canceled its piece and refused to pay the remaining $12,500. . . .

[The district court found that The Nation's actions constituted copyright infringement. The Court of Appeals for the Second Circuit reversed.]

[T]here is no dispute that the unpublished manuscript of "A Time to Heal," as a whole, was protected by §106 from unauthorized reproduction. Nor do respondents dispute that verbatim copying of excerpts of the manuscript's original form of expression would constitute infringement unless excused as fair use. . . .

III.

A

Fair use was traditionally defined as "a privilege in others than the owner of the copyright to use the copyrighted material in a reasonable manner without his consent." H. Ball, Law of Copyright and Literary Property 260 (1944) (hereinafter Ball). . . .

"[T]he author's consent to a reasonable use of his copyrighted works ha[d] always been implied by the courts as a necessary incident of the constitutional policy of promoting the progress of science and the useful arts, since a prohibition of such use would inhibit subsequent writers from attempting to improve upon prior works and thus . . . frustrate the very ends sought to be attained." Ball 260. Professor Latman, in a study of the doctrine of fair use commissioned by Congress for the revision effort, . . . summarized prior law as turning on the "importance of the material copied or performed from the point of view of the reasonable copyright owner. In other words, would the reasonable copyright owner have consented to the use?"

[A. Latman, Fair Use of Copyrighted Works 15 (1958), reprinted as Study No. 14 in Copyright Law Revision Studies Nos. 14-16, prepared for the Senate Committee on the Judiciary, 86th Cong., 2d Sess. 7 (1960)]. . . .

Perhaps because the fair use doctrine was predicated on the author's implied consent to "reasonable and customary" use when he released his work for public consumption, fair use traditionally was not recognized as a defense to charges of copying from an author's as yet unpublished works. Under common-law copyright, "the property of the author . . . in his intellectual creation [was] absolute until he voluntarily part[ed] with the same." *American Tobacco Co. v. Werckmeister*, 207 U.S. 284 (1907). This absolute rule, however, was tempered in practice by the equitable nature of the fair use doctrine. In a given case, factors such as implied consent through *de facto* publication on performance or dissemination of a work may tip the balance of equities in favor of prepublication use. . . . But it has never been seriously disputed that "the fact that the plaintiff's work is unpublished . . . is a factor tending to negate the defense of fair use." . . . Publication of an author's expression before he has authorized its dissemination seriously infringes the author's right to decide when and whether it will be made public, a factor not present in fair use of published works. . . .

We also find unpersuasive respondents' argument that fair use may be made of a soon-to-be-published manuscript on the ground that the author has demonstrated he has no interest in nonpublication. This argument assumes that the unpublished nature of copyrighted material is only relevant to letters or other confidential writings not intended for dissemination. It is true that common-law copyright was often enlisted in the service of personal privacy. *See* Brandeis & Warren, *The Right to Privacy*, 4 Harv. L. Rev. 193, 198-199 (1890). In its commercial guise, however, an author's right to choose when he will publish is no less deserving of protection. The period encompassing the work's initiation, its preparation, and its grooming for public dissemination is a crucial one for any literary endeavor. The Copyright Act, which accords the copyright owner the "right to control the first public distribution" of his work, House Report, at 62, echos the common law's concern that the author or copyright owner retain control throughout this critical stage. . . .

B

Respondents, however, contend that First Amendment values require a different rule under the circumstances of this case. . . . Respondents advance the substantial public import of the subject matter of the Ford memoirs as grounds for excusing a use that would ordinarily not pass muster as a fair use — the piracy of verbatim quotations for the purpose of "scooping" the authorized first serialization. Respondents explain their copying of Mr. Ford's expression as essential to reporting the news story it claims the book itself represents. In respondents' view, not only the facts contained in Mr. Ford's memoirs, but "the precise manner in which [he] expressed himself [were] as newsworthy as what he had to say." . . . Respondents argue that the public's interest in learning this news as fast as possible outweighs the right of the author to control its first publication. . . .

Respondents' theory, however, would expand fair use to effectively destroy any expectation of copyright protection in the work of a public figure. Absent such protection, there would be little incentive to create or profit in financing such memoirs, and the public would be denied an important source of significant historical information. The promise of copyright would be an empty one if it could be avoided merely by dubbing the infringement a fair use "news report" of the book. . . .

In our haste to disseminate news, it should not be forgotten that the Framers intended copyright itself to be the engine of free expression. By establishing a marketable right to the use of one's expression, copyright supplies the economic incentive to create and disseminate ideas. . . .

It is fundamentally at odds with the scheme of copyright to accord lesser rights in those works that are of greatest importance to the public. . . . [A]s one commentator has noted: "If every volume that was in the public interest could be pirated away by a competing publisher, . . . the public [soon] would have nothing worth reading." Sobel, *Copyright and the First Amendment: A Gathering Storm?*, 19 ASCAP Copyright Law Symposium 43, 78 (1971). . . .

In view of the First Amendment protections already embodied in the Copyright Act's distinction between copyrightable expression and uncopyrightable facts and ideas, and the latitude for scholarship and comment traditionally afforded by fair use, we see no warrant for expanding the doctrine of fair use to create what amounts to a public figure exception to copyright. Whether verbatim copying from a public figure's manuscript in a given case is or is not fair must be judged according to the traditional equities of fair use.

IV.

Fair use is a mixed question of law and fact. *Pacific & Southern Co. v. Duncan*, 744 F.2d 1490, 1495, n.8 (CA11 1984). Where the district court has found facts sufficient to evaluate each of the statutory factors, an appellate court "need not remand for further factfinding . . . [but] may conclude as a matter of law that [the challenged use] do[es] not qualify as a fair use of the copyrighted work." *Id.*, at 1495. . . .

Purpose of the Use. The Second Circuit correctly identified news reporting as the general purpose of The Nation's use. News reporting is one of the examples enumerated in §107 to "give some idea of the sort of activities the courts might regard as fair use under the circumstances." Senate Report, at 61. This listing was not intended to be exhaustive, see *ibid.*; §101 (definition of "including" and "such as"), or to single out any particular use as presumptively a "fair" use. . . . The fact that an article arguably is "news" and therefore a productive use is simply one factor in a fair use analysis.

We agree with the Second Circuit that the trial court erred in fixing on whether the information contained in the memoirs was actually new to the public. As Judge Meskill wisely noted, "[c]ourts should be chary of deciding what is and what is not news." 723 F.2d, at 215 (dissenting). . . . "The issue is not what constitutes 'news,' but whether a claim of news reporting is a valid fair use defense to an infringement of *copyrightable expression*." [W. Patry, The Fair Use Privilege in Copyright Law 119 (1985).] The Nation has every right to seek to be the first to publish information. But The Nation went beyond simply reporting uncopyrightable information and actively sought to exploit the headline value of its infringement, making a "news event" out of its unauthorized first publication of a noted figure's copyrighted expression.

The fact that a publication was commercial as opposed to nonprofit is a separate factor that tends to weigh against a finding of fair use. . . . In arguing that the purpose of news reporting is not purely commercial, The Nation misses the point entirely. The crux of the profit/nonprofit distinction is not whether the sole motive of the use is monetary gain but whether the user stands to profit from exploitation of the copyrighted material without paying the customary price.

In evaluating character and purpose we cannot ignore The Nation's stated purpose of scooping the forthcoming hardcover and Time abstracts. The Nation's use had not merely the incidental effect but the *intended purpose* of supplanting the copyright holder's commercially valuable right of first publication. Also relevant to the "character" of the use is "the propriety of the defendant's conduct." 3 Nimmer §13.05[A], at 13-72. "Fair use presupposes 'good faith' and 'fair dealing.'" *Time Inc. v. Bernard Geis Associates*, 293 F. Supp. 130, 146 (SDNY 1968), quoting Schulman, *Fair Use and the Revision of the Copyright Act*, 53 Iowa L. Rev. 832 (1968). The trial court found that The Nation knowingly exploited a purloined manuscript. . . .

Nature of the Copyrighted Work. Second, the Act directs attention to the nature of the copyrighted work. "A Time to Heal" may be characterized as an unpublished historical narrative or autobiography. The law generally recognizes a greater need to disseminate factual works than works of fiction or fantasy. *See* Gorman, *Fact or Fancy? The Implications for Copyright*, 29 J. Copyright Soc. 560, 561 (1982).

> "[E]ven within the field of fact works, there are gradations as to the relative proportion of fact and fancy. One may move from sparsely embellished maps and directories to elegantly written biography. The extent to which one must permit expressive language to be copied, in order to assure dissemination of the underlying facts, will thus vary from case to case." *Id.*, at 563.

Some of the briefer quotes from the memoirs are arguably necessary adequately to convey the facts; for example, Mr. Ford's characterization of the White House tapes as the "smoking gun" is perhaps so integral to the idea expressed as to be inseparable from it. . . . But The Nation did not stop at isolated phrases and instead excerpted subjective descriptions and portraits of public figures whose power lies in the author's individualized expression. Such use, focusing on the most expressive elements of the work, exceeds that necessary to disseminate the facts.

The fact that a work is unpublished is a critical element of its "nature." . . . Our prior discussion establishes that the scope of fair use is narrower with respect to unpublished works. While even substantial quotations might qualify as fair use in a review of a published work or a news account of a speech that had been delivered to the public or disseminated to the press, see House Report, at 65, the author's right to control the first public appearance of his expression weighs against such use of the work before its release. The right of first publication encompasses not only the choice whether to publish at all, but also the choices of when, where, and in what form first to publish a work. . . .

Amount and Substantiality of the Portion Used. Next, the Act directs us to examine the amount and substantiality of the portion used in relation to the copyrighted work as a whole. In absolute terms, the words actually quoted were an insubstantial portion of "A Time to Heal." The District Court, however, found that "[T]he Nation took what was essentially the heart of the book." 557 F. Supp., at 1072. We believe the Court of Appeals erred in overruling the District Judge's evaluation of the qualitative nature of the taking. *See, e.g., Roy Export Co. Establishment v. Columbia Broadcasting System, Inc.*, 503 F. Supp., at 1145 (taking of 55 seconds out of 1 hour and 29-minute film deemed qualitatively substantial). A Time editor described the chapters on the pardon as "the most interesting and moving parts of the entire manuscript." . . . The portions actually quoted were selected by Mr. Navasky as among the most powerful passages in those chapters. He testified that he used verbatim excerpts because simply reciting the information could not adequately convey the "absolute certainty with which [Ford] expressed himself," or show that "this comes from President Ford," . . . or carry the "definitive quality" of the original. . . . In short, he quoted these passages precisely because they qualitatively embodied Ford's distinctive expression.

As the statutory language indicates, a taking may not be excused merely because it is insubstantial with respect to the *infringing* work. As Judge Learned Hand cogently remarked, "no plagiarist can excuse the wrong by showing how much of his work he did not pirate." *Sheldon v. Metro-Goldwyn Pictures Corp.*, 81 F.2d 49, 56 (CA2), *cert. denied*, 298 U.S. 669 (1936). Conversely, the fact that a substantial portion of the infringing work was copied verbatim is evidence of the qualitative value of the copied material, both to the originator and to the plagiarist who seeks to profit from marketing someone else's copyrighted expression.

Stripped to the verbatim quotes, the direct takings from the unpublished manuscript constitute at least 13% of the infringing article. *See Meeropol v. Nizer*, 560 F.2d 1061, 1071 (CA2 1977) (copyrighted letters constituted less than 1% of infringing work but were prominently featured). The Nation article is structured around the quoted excerpts which serve as its dramatic focal points. . . . In view of the expressive value of the excerpts and their key role in the infringing work, we cannot agree with the Second Circuit that the "magazine took a meager, indeed an infinitesimal amount of Ford's original language." 723 F.2d, at 209.

Effect on the Market. Finally, the Act focuses on "the effect of the use upon the potential market for or value of the copyrighted work." This last factor is undoubtedly the single most important element of fair use. . . . "Fair use, when properly applied, is limited to copying by others which does not materially impair the marketability of the work which is copied." 1 Nimmer §1.10[D], at 1-87. The trial court found not merely a potential but an actual effect on the market. Time's cancellation of its projected serialization and its refusal to pay the $12,500 were the direct effect of the infringement. . . .

More important, to negate fair use one need only show that if the challenged use "should become widespread, it would adversely affect the *potential* market for the copyrighted work." *Sony Corp. of America v. Universal City Studios, Inc.*, 464 U.S., at 451 (emphasis added); *id.*, at 484, and n.36 (collecting cases) (dissenting opinion). This inquiry must take account not only of harm to the original but also of harm to the market for derivative works. . . .

It is undisputed that the factual material in the balance of The Nation's article, besides the verbatim quotes at issue here, was drawn exclusively from the chapters on the pardon. The excerpts were employed as featured episodes in a story about the Nixon pardon—precisely the use petitioners had licensed to Time. The borrowing of these verbatim quotes from the unpublished manuscript lent The Nation's piece a special air of authenticity—as Navasky expressed it, the reader would know it was Ford speaking and not The Nation. . . . Thus it directly competed for a share of the market for prepublication excerpts. The Senate Report states:

> "With certain special exceptions . . . a use that supplants any part of the normal market for a copyrighted work would ordinarily be considered an infringement." Senate Report, at 65.

Placed in a broader perspective, a fair use doctrine that permits extensive prepublication quotations from an unreleased manuscript without the copyright owner's consent poses substantial potential for damage to the marketability of first serialization rights in general. "Isolated instances of minor infringements, when multiplied many times, become in the aggregate a major inroad on copyright that must be prevented." *Ibid.* . . .

BRENNAN, J., with whom WHITE, J., and MARSHALL, J., join, dissenting: The Court holds that The Nation's quotation of 300 words from the unpublished 200,000-word manuscript of President Gerald R. Ford infringed the copyright in that manuscript, even though the quotations related to a historical event of undoubted significance — the resignation and pardon of President Richard M. Nixon. Although the Court pursues the laudable goal of protecting "the economic incentive to create and disseminate ideas," . . . this zealous defense of the copyright owner's prerogative will, I fear, stifle the broad dissemination of ideas and information copyright is intended to nurture. Protection of the copyright owner's economic interest is achieved in this case through an exceedingly narrow definition of the scope of fair use. The progress of arts and sciences and the robust public debate essential to an enlightened citizenry are ill served by this constricted reading of the fair use doctrine. . . . I therefore respectfully dissent. . . .

The "promotion of science and the useful arts" requires this limit on the scope of an author's control. Were an author able to prevent subsequent authors from using concepts, ideas, or facts contained in his or her work, the creative process would wither and scholars would be forced into unproductive replication of the research of their predecessors. . . . This limitation on copyright also ensures consonance with our most important First Amendment values. . . . Our "profound national commitment to the principle that debate on public issues should be uninhibited, robust, and wide-open," *New York Times Co. v. Sullivan*, 376 U.S. 254, 270 (1964), leaves no room for a statutory monopoly over information and ideas. "The arena of public debate would be quiet, indeed, if a politician could copyright his speeches or a philosopher his treatises and thus obtain a monopoly on the ideas they contained." *Lee v. Runge*, 404 U.S. 887, 893 (1971) (Douglas, J., dissenting from denial of certiorari). A broad dissemination of principles, ideas, and factual information is crucial to the robust public debate and informed citizenry that are "the essence of self-government." *Garrison v. Louisiana*, 379 U.S. 64, 74-75 (1964). And every citizen must be permitted freely to marshal ideas and facts in the advocacy of particular political choices.[4]

NOTES AND QUESTIONS

1. Focus first on the majority's analysis of the first and fourth statutory fair use factors. Does the majority treat these factors as distinct from one another, or as related? In particular, why should "whether the user stands to profit from exploitation of the copyrighted work without paying the customary price" be relevant to analysis of the purpose and character of the use? For a helpful discussion of these issues, see William W. Fisher III, *Reconstructing the Fair Use Doctrine*, 101 Harv. L. Rev. 1659, 1669-74 (1988).

2. Now focus on the interrelationship between the third and fourth statutory factors. As Justice Brennan's dissent notes, in total *The Nation* quoted only 300 words from the

---

4. It would be perverse to prohibit government from limiting the financial resources upon which a political speaker may draw, see *FEC v. National Conservative Political Action Committee*, 470 U.S. 480 (1985), but to permit government to limit the intellectual resources upon which that speaker may draw.

forthcoming book. As the example given in the introduction to this section, pages 534-35 *supra* indicates, quotations in a book review have long been considered a paradigmatic example of fair use. Why was this case different? What rules seem to be relevant to determining the "substantiality" of the quoted excerpts? Should it matter that a market for "prepublication rights" exists? Might one envision a similar market for post-publication quotation?

3. In its analysis of the second statutory factor, the majority acknowledges that the fair use doctrine generally affords more latitude to uses of works that are predominantly factual, but then downplays the importance of this consideration with respect to President Ford's manuscript. The dissenters, in contrast, view this attribute of the manuscript as extremely important. Who has the better argument? Does your conclusion depend at all on your view of the first factor, the purpose and character of *The Nation*'s use?

4. Did factors other than those expressly listed in §107 also influence the Court's decision? Many times in its opinion the Court refers to the "purloined" or "stolen" nature of the copy *The Nation* received. The Court also discusses the unpublished nature of the plaintiff's work. Was consideration of these factors appropriate? Was it inevitable given the circumstances under which *The Nation* had access to the work?

In the years following *Harper & Row*, several courts applied what almost amounted to a bright-line rule, refusing to find fair use when the copyrighted work was unpublished. *See, e.g., New Era Publ'ns Int'l, ApS v. Henry Holt & Co.*, 873 F.2d 576 (2d. Cir. 1989) (diaries and journals), *cert. denied*, 493 U.S. 1094 (1990); *Salinger v. Random House, Inc.*, 811 F.2d 90 (2d Cir.) (letters), *cert. denied*, 484 U.S. 890 (1987). In 1992, Congress enacted legislation to clarify that the unpublished nature of the copyrighted work did not bar a finding of fair use. This legislation added the final sentence of §107: "The fact that a work is unpublished shall not itself bar a finding of fair use if such finding is made upon consideration of all the above factors." Thus, the unpublished nature remains but one factor to consider in the determination of fair use. In light of this amendment, how should the unpublished character of a work weigh in the fair use balance? Should biographers who use unpublished materials receive special consideration?

5. Would the result in *Harper & Row* have been different if the case involved an author who wrote a biography of former President Ford using some material from the *Time* article after it was published? In *New Era Publications International, ApS v. Carol Publishing Group*, 904 F.2d 152 (2d. Cir.), *cert. denied*, 498 U.S. 921 (1990), the author had used segments of L. Ron Hubbard's published writings in authoring a critical biography of Hubbard, the founder of the Church of Scientology. Unlike the case involving Hubbard's unpublished works cited in note 4 above, here the court held the use fair:

> . . . [T]he book is an unfavorable biography. Section 107 provides that use of copyrighted materials for "purposes such as criticism, . . . scholarship, or research, is not an infringement of copyright." Our cases establish that biographies in general, and critical biographies in particular, fit "comfortably within" these statutory categories "of uses illustrative of uses that can be fair."
>
> . . . We have some hesitation in trying to characterize Hubbard's diverse body of writings as solely "factual" or "non-factual," but on balance, we believe that the quoted works — which deal with Hubbard's life, his views on religion, human relations, the Church, etc. — are more properly viewed as factual or informational.
>
> . . . Appellant calculates that the book quotes only a minuscule amount of 25 of the 48 works that appellee claimed were infringed, 5-6% of 12 other works and 8% or more of 11 works, each of the 11 being only a few pages in length. . . . In the context of quotation from published works, where a greater amount of copying is allowed, see *Harper & Row*, 471 U.S. at 564 . . . this is not so much as to be unfair. . . .

[W]e are skeptical here that potential customers for the authorized *favorable* biography of Hubbard in the future will be deterred from buying because the author's *unfavorable* biography quotes from Hubbard's works. Indeed, it is not "beyond the realm of possibility that" the book "might stimulate further interest" in the authorized biography. . . .

Furthermore, even assuming that the book discourages potential purchasers of the authorized biography, this is not necessarily actionable under the copyright laws. Such potential buyers might be put off because the book persuaded them (as it clearly hopes to) that Hubbard was a charlatan, but the copyright laws do not protect against that sort of injury. . . .

Id. at 155-60.

6. Do you agree with the dissenters that the majority should have given greater weight to First Amendment concerns? How might this be done without creating, in the majority's words, "a public figure exception to copyright"? Do you read the dissent as advocating such an exception? We return to the relationship between fair use and the First Amendment later in this section.

7. The majority begins its fair use discussion by noting that fair use was "traditionally defined" as being based on a theory of implied consent. If fair use is indeed based on implied consent, then wouldn't the plaintiff, who clearly has not consented to the use at issue, have an advantage going into the fair use analysis?

Slightly different from an implied consent theory of fair use is a customary use theory. Under this theory, a use should be found to be fair if it is "within . . . accepted norms and customary practice." Lloyd L. Weinreb, *Fair's Fair: A Comment on the Fair Use Doctrine*, 103 Harv. L. Rev. 1137, 1159-60 (1990) (characterizing this inquiry as "the most relevant inquiry"). Do you agree with Professor Weinreb? How would this theory apply to the use challenged in *Harper & Row*? What factors should guide a court in deciding that a use is "customary practice"? Professor Michael Madison argues that the fair use doctrine implicitly validates certain favored patterns and practices and that these practices should be more explicitly acknowledged in fair use analysis. *See* Michael J. Madison, *A Pattern-Oriented Approach to Fair Use*, 45 Wm. & Mary L. Rev. 1525 (2004). Should the fair use doctrine be used to endorse or reject particular social practices? How should courts decide which practices to endorse? Keep this question in mind as you read the next case.

≡ *Campbell v. Acuff-Rose Music, Inc.*
≡ *510 U.S. 569 (1994)*

SOUTER, J.: . . . In 1964, Roy Orbison and William Dees wrote a rock ballad called "Oh, Pretty Woman" and assigned their rights in it to respondent Acuff-Rose Music, Inc. Acuff-Rose registered the song for copyright protection.

Petitioners Luther R. Campbell, Christopher Wongwon, Mark Ross, and David Hobbs, are collectively known as 2 Live Crew, a popular rap music group. In 1989, Campbell wrote a song entitled "Pretty Woman," which he later described in an affidavit as intended, "through comical lyrics, to satirize the original work. . . ."

. . . On July 5, 1989, 2 Live Crew's manager informed Acuff-Rose that 2 Live Crew had written a parody of "Oh, Pretty Woman," that they would afford all credit for ownership and authorship of the original song to Acuff-Rose, Dees, and Orbison, and that they were willing to pay a fee for the use they wished to make of it. Enclosed with the letter were a copy of the lyrics and a recording of 2 Live Crew's song. . . . Acuff-Rose's agent refused permission, stating that "I am aware of the success enjoyed by 'The 2 Live Crews', but I must inform you that we cannot permit the use of a parody of 'Oh, Pretty Woman.'" . . . Nonetheless, in June or July 1989, 2 Live Crew released records, cassette tapes, and compact discs of "Pretty Woman" in a collection of songs entitled "As Clean As They Wanna Be." The albums and compact discs identify the authors of "Pretty Woman" as Orbison and Dees and its publisher as Acuff-Rose.

Almost a year later, after nearly a quarter of a million copies of the recording had been sold, Acuff-Rose sued 2 Live Crew and its record company, Luke Skyywalker Records, for copyright infringement. The District Court granted summary judgment for 2 Live Crew. . . .

The Court of Appeals for the Sixth Circuit reversed and remanded. . . .

II . . .

Congress meant §107 "to restate the present judicial doctrine of fair use, not to change, narrow, or enlarge it in any way" and intended that courts continue the common law tradition of fair use adjudication. H. R. Rep. No. 94-1476, p. 66 (1976) (hereinafter House Report); S. Rep. No. 94-473, p. 62 (1975) (hereinafter Senate Report). The fair use doctrine thus "permits [and requires] courts to avoid rigid application of the copyright statute when, on occasion, it would stifle the very creativity which that law is designed to foster." *Stewart v. Abend*, 495 U.S. 207, 236 (1990).

. . . [T]he four statutory factors [may not] be treated in isolation, one from another. All are to be explored, and the results weighed together, in light of the purposes of copyright. *See* Leval [, *Toward a Fair Use Standard*, 103 Harv. L. Rev. 1105,] 1110-1111 [(1990) (hereinafter Leval)]; Patry & Perlmutter, *Fair Use Misconstrued: Profit, Presumptions, and Parody*, 11 Cardozo Arts & Ent. L.J. 667, 685-687 (1993) (hereinafter Patry & Perlmutter).

A

The first factor in a fair use enquiry is "the purpose and character of the use, including whether such use is of a commercial nature or is for nonprofit educational purposes." §107(1). . . . The central purpose of this investigation is to see, in Justice Story's words, whether the new work merely "supersede[s] the objects" of the original creation, *Folsom v. Marsh, supra*, at 348; accord, *Harper & Row, supra*, at 562 ("supplanting" the original), or instead adds something new, with a further purpose or different character, altering the first with new expression, meaning, or message; it asks, in other words, whether and to what extent the new work is "transformative." Leval 1111. Although such transformative use is not absolutely necessary for a finding of fair use, *Sony* [*Corp. of America v. Universal City Studios, Inc.*, 464 U.S. 417 (1984)], *supra*, at 455, n.40,[11] the goal of copyright, to promote science and the arts, is generally furthered by the creation of transformative works. Such works thus lie at the heart of the fair use doctrine's guarantee of breathing space within the confines of copyright, see, e.g., *Sony, supra*, at 478-480 (BLACKMUN, J., dissenting), and the more transformative the new work, the less will be the significance of other factors, like commercialism, that may weigh against a finding of fair use.

. . . Suffice it to say now that parody has an obvious claim to transformative value, as Acuff-Rose itself does not deny. Like less ostensibly humorous forms of criticism, it can provide social benefit, by shedding light on an earlier work, and, in the process, creating a new one. . . .

The germ of parody lies in the definition of the Greek *parodeia*, quoted in Judge Nelson's Court of Appeals dissent, as "a song sung alongside another." 972 F.2d, at 1440, quoting

---

11. The obvious statutory exception to this focus on transformative uses is the straight reproduction of multiple copies for classroom distribution.

7 Encyclopedia Britannica 768 (15th ed. 1975). Modern dictionaries accordingly describe a parody as a "literary or artistic work that imitates the characteristic style of an author or a work for comic effect or ridicule," or as a "composition in prose or verse in which the characteristic turns of thought and phrase in an author or class of authors are imitated in such a way as to make them appear ridiculous." For the purposes of copyright law, the nub of the definitions, and the heart of any parodist's claim to quote from existing material, is the use of some elements of a prior author's composition to create a new one that, at least in part, comments on that author's works. . . . If, on the contrary, the commentary has no critical bearing on the substance or style of the original composition, which the alleged infringer merely uses to get attention or to avoid the drudgery in working up something fresh, the claim to fairness in borrowing from another's work diminishes accordingly (if it does not vanish), and other factors, like the extent of its commerciality, loom larger.[14] Parody needs to mimic an original to make its point, and so has some claim to use the creation of its victim's (or collective victims') imagination, whereas satire can stand on its own two feet and so requires justification for the very act of borrowing.[15] . . .

The fact that parody can claim legitimacy for some appropriation does not, of course, tell either parodist or judge much about where to draw the line. . . . [P]arody, like any other use, has to work its way through the relevant factors, and be judged case by case, in light of the ends of the copyright law.

Here, the District Court held, and the Court of Appeals assumed, that 2 Live Crew's "Pretty Woman" contains parody, commenting on and criticizing the original work, whatever it may have to say about society at large. As the District Court remarked, the words of 2 Live Crew's song copy the original's first line, but then "quickly degenerat[e] into a play on words, substituting predictable lyrics with shocking ones . . . [that] derisively demonstrat[e] how bland and banal the Orbison song seems to them." 754 F. Supp., at 1155 (footnote omitted). . . .

We have less difficulty in finding that critical element in 2 Live Crew's song than the Court of Appeals did, although having found it we will not take the further step of evaluating its quality. The threshold question when fair use is raised in defense of parody is whether a parodic character may reasonably be perceived. Whether, going beyond that, parody is in good taste or bad does not and should not matter to fair use. As Justice Holmes explained, "[i]t would be a dangerous undertaking for persons trained only to the law to constitute themselves final judges of the worth of [a work], outside of the narrowest and most obvious limits. At the one extreme some works of genius would be sure to miss appreciation. Their very novelty would make them repulsive until the public had learned the new language in which their author spoke." *Bleistein v. Donaldson Lithographing Co.*, 188 U.S. 239, 251 (1903) (circus posters have copyright protection); cf. *Yankee Publishing Inc. v. News America Publishing, Inc.*, 809 F. Supp. 267, 280 (SDNY 1992) (Leval, J.) ("First Amendment protections do not apply only to those who speak clearly, whose jokes are funny, and whose parodies succeed") (trademark case).

While we might not assign a high rank to the parodic element here, we think it fair to say that 2 Live Crew's song reasonably could be perceived as commenting on the original or

---

14. A parody that more loosely targets an original than the parody presented here may still be sufficiently aimed at an original work to come within our analysis of parody. If a parody whose wide dissemination in the market runs the risk of serving as a substitute for the original or licensed derivatives (see *infra*, . . . discussing factor four), it is more incumbent on one claiming fair use to establish the extent of transformation and the parody's critical relationship to the original. . . .

15. Satire has been defined as a work "in which prevalent follies or vices are assailed with ridicule," 14 Oxford English Dictionary, *supra*, at 500, or are "attacked through irony, derision, or wit," American Heritage Dictionary, *supra*, at 1604.

criticizing it, to some degree. 2 Live Crew juxtaposes the romantic musings of a man whose fantasy comes true, with degrading taunts, a bawdy demand for sex, and a sigh of relief from paternal responsibility. The later words can be taken as a comment on the naivete of the original of an earlier day, as a rejection of its sentiment that ignores the ugliness of street life and the debasement that it signifies. It is this joinder of reference and ridicule that marks off the author's choice of parody from the other types of comment and criticism that traditionally have had a claim to fair use protection as transformative works.[17]

The Court of Appeals, however, immediately cut short the enquiry into 2 Live Crew's fair use claim by confining its treatment of the first factor essentially to one relevant fact, the commercial nature of the use. The court then inflated the significance of this fact by applying a presumption ostensibly culled from *Sony*, that "every commercial use of copyrighted material is presumptively . . . unfair. . . ." *Sony*, 464 U.S., at 451. In giving virtually dispositive weight to the commercial nature of the parody, the Court of Appeals erred.

The language of the statute makes clear that the commercial or nonprofit educational purpose of a work is only one element of the first factor enquiry into its purpose and character. Section 107(1) uses the term "including" to begin the dependent clause referring to commercial use, and the main clause speaks of a broader investigation into "purpose and character." As we explained in *Harper & Row*, Congress resisted attempts to narrow the ambit of this traditional enquiry by adopting categories of presumptively fair use, and it urged courts to preserve the breadth of their traditionally ample view of the universe of relevant evidence. . . . Accordingly, the mere fact that a use is educational and not for profit does not insulate it from a finding of infringement, any more than the commercial character of a use bars a finding of fairness. If, indeed, commerciality carried presumptive force against a finding of fairness, the presumption would swallow nearly all of the illustrative uses listed in the preamble paragraph of §107, including news reporting, comment, criticism, teaching, scholarship, and research, since these activities "are generally conducted for profit in this country." *Harper & Row, supra*, at 592 (Brennan, J., dissenting). Congress could not have intended such a rule, which certainly is not inferable from the common-law cases, arising as they did from the world of letters in which Samuel Johnson could pronounce that "[n]o man but a blockhead ever wrote, except for money." 3 Boswell's Life of Johnson 19 (G. Hill ed. 1934).

Sony itself called for no hard evidentiary presumption. There, we emphasized the need for a "sensitive balancing of interests," 464 U.S., at 455 n.40, noted that Congress had "eschewed a rigid, bright-line approach to fair use," *id.*, at 449, n.31, and stated that the commercial or nonprofit educational character of a work is "not conclusive," *id.*, at 448-449, but rather a fact to be "weighed along with other[s] in fair use decisions." *Id.*, at 449, n.32, (quoting House Report, p. 66). The Court of Appeals's elevation of one sentence from *Sony* to a *per se* rule thus runs as much counter to *Sony* itself as to the long common-law tradition of fair use adjudication. Rather, as we explained in *Harper & Row*, *Sony* stands for the proposition that the "fact that a publication was commercial as opposed to nonprofit is a separate factor that tends to weigh against a finding of fair use." 471 U.S., at 562. But that is all, and the fact that even the force of that tendency will vary with the context is a further reason against elevating commerciality to hard presumptive significance. The use, for example, of a copyrighted work to advertise a product, even in a parody, will be entitled to less indulgence under the first factor of the fair

---

17. We note in passing that 2 Live Crew need not label its whole album, or even this song, a parody in order to claim fair use protection, nor should 2 Live Crew be penalized for this being its first parodic essay. Parody serves its goals whether labeled or not, and there is no reason to require parody to state the obvious (or even the reasonably perceived). *See* Patry & Perlmutter 716-717.

use enquiry, than the sale of a parody for its own sake, let alone one performed a single time by students in school. . . .[18]

B

The second statutory factor, "the nature of the copyrighted work," §107(2), draws on Justice Story's expression, the "value of the materials used." *Folsom v. Marsh*, 9 F. Cas., at 348. This factor calls for recognition that some works are closer to the core of intended copyright protection than others, with the consequence that fair use is more difficult to establish when the former works are copied. . . . [T]he Orbison original's creative expression for public dissemination falls within the core of the copyright's protective purposes. This fact, however, is not much help in this case, or ever likely to help much in separating the fair use sheep from the infringing goats in a parody case, since parodies almost invariably copy publicly known, expressive works.

C

The third factor asks whether "the amount and substantiality of the portion used in relation to the copyrighted work as a whole," §107(3) (or, in Justice Story's words, "the quantity and value of the materials used," *Folsom v. Marsh, supra,* at 348) are reasonable in relation to the purpose of the copying. Here, attention turns to the persuasiveness of a parodist's justification for the particular copying done, and the enquiry will harken back to the first of the statutory factors, for, as in prior cases, we recognize that the extent of permissible copying varies with the purpose and character of the use. . . . The facts bearing on this factor will also tend to address the fourth, by revealing the degree to which the parody may serve as a market substitute for the original or potentially licensed derivatives. *See* Leval 1123.

The District Court considered the song's parodic purpose in finding that 2 Live Crew had not helped themselves overmuch. 754 F. Supp., at 1156-1157. The Court of Appeals disagreed, stating that "[w]hile it may not be inappropriate to find that no more was taken than necessary, the copying was qualitatively substantial. . . . We conclude that taking the heart of the original and making it the heart of a new work was to purloin a substantial portion of the essence of the original." 972 F.2d, at 1438.

The Court of Appeals is of course correct that this factor calls for thought not only about the quantity of the materials used, but about their quality and importance, too. . . .

Where we part company with the court below is in applying these guides to parody, and in particular to parody in the song before us. Parody presents a difficult case. Parody's humor, or in any event its comment, necessarily springs from recognizable allusion to its object through distorted imitation. Its art lies in the tension between a known original and its parodic twin. When parody takes aim at a particular original work, the parody must be able to "conjure up" at least enough of that original to make the object of its critical wit recognizable. . . .

---

18. Finally, regardless of the weight one might place on the alleged infringer's state of mind, compare *Harper & Row*, 471 U.S., at 562 (fair use presupposes good faith and fair dealing) (quotation marks omitted), with *Folsom v. Marsh*, 9 F. Cas. 342, 349 (No. 4,901) (CCD Mass. 1841) (good faith does not bar a finding of infringement); Leval 1126-1127 (good faith irrelevant to fair use analysis), we reject Acuff-Rose's argument that 2 Live Crew's request for permission to use the original should be weighed against a finding of fair use. Even if good faith were central to fair use, 2 Live Crew's actions do not necessarily suggest that they believed their version was not fair use; the offer may simply have been made in a good faith effort to avoid this litigation. If the use is otherwise fair, then no permission need be sought or granted. Thus, being denied permission to use a work does not weigh against a finding of fair use. *See Fisher v. Dees*, 794 F.2d 432, 437 (CA9 1986).

We think the Court of Appeals was insufficiently appreciative of parody's need for the recognizable sight or sound when it ruled 2 Live Crew's use unreasonable as a matter of law. It is true, of course, that 2 Live Crew copied the characteristic opening bass riff (or musical phrase) of the original, and true that the words of the first line copy the Orbison lyrics. But if quotation of the opening riff and the first line may be said to go to the "heart" of the original, the heart is also what most readily conjures up the song for parody, and it is the heart at which parody takes aim. Copying does not become excessive in relation to parodic purpose merely because the portion taken was the original's heart. If 2 Live Crew had copied a significantly less memorable part of the original, it is difficult to see how its parodic character would have come through. . . .

This is not, of course, to say that anyone who calls himself a parodist can skim the cream and get away scot free. In parody, as in news reporting, see *Harper & Row, supra*, context is everything, and the question of fairness asks what else the parodist did besides go to the heart of the original. It is significant that 2 Live Crew not only copied the first line of the original, but thereafter departed markedly from the Orbison lyrics for its own ends. 2 Live Crew not only copied the bass riff and repeated it,[19] but also produced otherwise distinctive sounds, interposing "scraper" noise, overlaying the music with solos in different keys, and altering the drum beat. *See* 754 F. Supp., at 1155. This is not a case, then, where "a substantial portion" of the parody itself is composed of a "verbatim" copying of the original. It is not, that is, a case where the parody is so insubstantial, as compared to the copying, that the third factor must be resolved as a matter of law against the parodists.

Suffice it to say here that, as to the lyrics, we think the Court of Appeals correctly suggested that "no more was taken than necessary," 972 F.2d, at 1438, but just for that reason, we fail to see how the copying can be excessive in relation to its parodic purpose, even if the portion taken is the original's "heart." As to the music, we express no opinion whether repetition of the bass riff is excessive copying, and we remand to permit evaluation of the amount taken, in light of the song's parodic purpose and character, its transformative elements, and considerations of the potential for market substitution sketched more fully below.

D

The fourth fair use factor is "the effect of the use upon the potential market for or value of the copyrighted work." §107(4). . . . The enquiry "must take account not only of harm to the original but also of harm to the market for derivative works." *Harper & Row, supra*, at 568.

Since fair use is an affirmative defense, its proponent would have difficulty carrying the burden of demonstrating fair use without favorable evidence about relevant markets.[21] In moving for summary judgment, 2 Live Crew left themselves at just such a disadvantage when they failed to address the effect on the market for rap derivatives, and confined themselves to uncontroverted submissions that there was no likely effect on the market for the original. They did not, however, thereby subject themselves to the evidentiary presumption applied by the Court of Appeals. . . . [T]he court resolved the fourth factor against 2 Live Crew, just as it had the first, by applying a presumption about the effect of commercial use, a presumption which as applied here we hold to be error.

---

19. This may serve to heighten the comic effect of the parody, as one witness stated . . . or serve to dazzle with the original's music, as Acuff-Rose now contends.

21. Even favorable evidence, without more, is no guarantee of fairness. Judge Leval gives the example of the film producer's appropriation of a composer's previously unknown song that turns the song into a commercial success; the boon to the song does not make the film's simple copying fair. Leval 1124, n.84. This factor, no less than the other three, may be addressed only through a "sensitive balancing of interests." *Sony* . . . [at] 455, n.40. Market harm is a matter of degree, and the importance of this factor will vary, not only with the amount of harm, but also with the relative strength of the showing on the other factors.

No "presumption" or inference of market harm that might find support in *Sony* is applicable to a case involving something beyond mere duplication for commercial purposes. *Sony*'s discussion of a presumption contrasts a context of verbatim copying of the original in its entirety for commercial purposes, with the non-commercial context of *Sony* itself (home copying of television programming). In the former circumstances, what *Sony* said simply makes common sense: when a commercial use amounts to mere duplication of the entirety of an original, it clearly "supersede[s] the objects," *Folsom v. Marsh, supra,* at 348, of the original and serves as a market replacement for it, making it likely that cognizable market harm to the original will occur. *Sony, supra,* at 451. But when, on the contrary, the second use is transformative, market substitution is at least less certain, and market harm may not be so readily inferred. Indeed, as to parody pure and simple, it is more likely that the new work will not affect the market for the original in a way cognizable under this factor, that is, by acting as a substitute for it ("supersed[ing] [its] objects"). *See* Leval 1125; Patry & Perlmutter 692, 697-698. This is so because the parody and the original usually serve different market functions. . . .

We do not, of course, suggest that a parody may not harm the market at all, but when a lethal parody, like a scathing theater review, kills demand for the original, it does not produce a harm cognizable under the Copyright Act. Because "parody may quite legitimately aim at garroting the original, destroying it commercially as well as artistically," B. Kaplan, An Unhurried View of Copyright 69 (1967), the role of the courts is to distinguish between "[b]iting criticism [that merely] suppresses demand [and] copyright infringement[, which] usurps it." *Fisher v. Dees,* 794 F.2d, at 438.

This distinction between potentially remediable displacement and unremediable disparagement is reflected in the rule that there is no protectible derivative market for criticism. The market for potential derivative uses includes only those that creators of original works would in general develop or license others to develop. Yet the unlikelihood that creators of imaginative works will license critical reviews or lampoons of their own productions removes such uses from the very notion of a potential licensing market. "People ask . . . for criticism, but they only want praise." S. Maugham, Of Human Bondage 241 (Penguin ed. 1992). Thus, to the extent that the opinion below may be read to have considered harm to the market for parodies of "Oh, Pretty Woman," the court erred.[22] . . .

. . . 2 Live Crew's song comprises not only parody but also rap music, and the derivative market for rap music is a proper focus of enquiry, see *Harper & Row, supra,* at 568. . . . Evidence of substantial harm to it would weigh against a finding of fair use, because the licensing of derivatives is an important economic incentive to the creation of originals. *See* 17 U.S.C. §106(2) (copyright owner has rights to derivative works). Of course, the only harm to derivatives that need concern us, as discussed above, is the harm of market substitution. The fact that a parody may impair the market for derivative uses by the very effectiveness of its critical commentary is no more relevant under copyright than the like threat to the original market.[24]

Although 2 Live Crew submitted uncontroverted affidavits on the question of market harm to the original, neither they, nor Acuff-Rose, introduced evidence or affidavits addressing the likely effect of 2 Live Crew's parodic rap song on the market for a non-parody, rap version of "Oh, Pretty Woman." And while Acuff-Rose would have us find evidence of a rap market in the very facts that 2 Live Crew recorded a rap parody of "Oh, Pretty Woman" and another rap

22. We express no opinion as to the derivative markets for works using elements of an original as vehicles for satire or amusement, making no comment on the original or criticism of it.

24. In some cases it may be difficult to determine whence the harm flows. In such cases, the other fair use factors may provide some indicia of the likely source of the harm. A work whose overriding purpose and character is parodic and whose borrowing is slight in relation to its parody will be far less likely to cause cognizable harm than a work with little parodic content and much copying.

group sought a license to record a rap derivative, there was no evidence that a potential rap market was harmed in any way by 2 Live Crew's parody, rap version. . . . The evidentiary hole will doubtless be plugged on remand. . . .

Appendix A to Opinion of the Court

"Oh, Pretty Woman" by Roy Orbison and William Dees

> Pretty Woman, walking down the street,
> Pretty Woman, the kind I like to meet,
> Pretty Woman, I don't believe you, you're not the truth,
> No one could look as good as you
> Mercy

> Pretty Woman, won't you pardon me,
> Pretty Woman, I couldn't help but see,
> Pretty Woman, that you look lovely as can be
> Are you lonely just like me?

> Pretty Woman, stop a while,
> Pretty Woman, talk a while,
> Pretty Woman, give your smile to me
> Pretty Woman, yeah, yeah, yeah

> Pretty Woman, look my way,
> Pretty Woman, say you'll stay with me
> 'Cause I need you, I'll treat you right
> Come to me baby, Be mine tonight

> Pretty Woman, don't walk on by,
> Pretty Woman, don't make me cry,
> Pretty Woman, don't walk away,
> Hey, O.K.

> If that's the way it must be, O.K.
> I guess I'll go on home, it's late
> There'll be tomorrow night, but wait!

> What do I see
> Is she walking back to me?
> Yeah, she's walking back to me!

> Oh, Pretty Woman.

Appendix B to Opinion of the Court

"Pretty Woman" as Recorded by 2 Live Crew

> Pretty woman walkin' down the street
> Pretty woman girl you look so sweet
> Pretty woman you bring me down to that knee
> Pretty woman you make me wanna beg please
> Oh, pretty woman

> Big hairy woman you need to shave that stuff
> Big hairy woman you know I bet it's tough

Big hairy woman all that hair it ain't legit
'Cause you look like 'Cousin It'
Big hairy woman

Bald headed woman girl your hair won't grow
Bald headed woman you got a teeny weeny afro
Bald headed woman you know your hair could look nice
Bald headed woman first you got to roll it with rice
Bald headed woman here, let me get this hunk of biz for ya
Ya know what I'm saying you look better than rice a roni
Oh bald headed woman

Big hairy woman come on in
And don't forget your bald headed friend
Hey pretty woman let the boys
Jump in

Two timin' woman girl you know you ain't right
Two timin' woman you's out with my boy last night
Two timin' woman that takes a load off my mind
Two timin' woman now I know the baby ain't mine
Oh, two timin' woman

Oh pretty woman

NOTES AND QUESTIONS

1. How does the Court's analysis of the first and fourth statutory factors compare to that in *Harper & Row*? Are the two decisions consistent? Why not require 2 Live Crew to pay the "customary price" before profiting from its treatment of the song? Why wouldn't *The Nation*'s use of President Ford's manuscript also qualify as "transformative"?

The Court seems particularly anxious to correct what it characterizes as a misreading of its earlier opinion in *Sony Corp. of America v. Universal City Studios, Inc.*, 464 U.S. 417 (1984), to the effect that certain facts create bright-line presumptions against fair use. You will have a chance to judge for yourself what *Sony* says in subsection B.3, *infra*. Remember, however, that *Campbell* is the Supreme Court's most recent explication of the fair use factors.

2. Does the Court's distinction between parody and satire make sense? If the fair use doctrine prizes "transformative" uses, why bother to make this distinction? Is the distinction workable? Consider various examples with which you might be familiar: skits on *Saturday Night Live*, articles in *Mad Magazine* or *The Onion*, or certain episodes of *South Park*. Do these qualify as parody as defined by the Court, or are they more accurately described as satire?

Justice Kennedy's concurring opinion expressed doubt about whether 2 Live Crew's song was "legitimate parody," and noted that the Court's opinion left the issue open for the District Court on remand. Do you share Justice Kennedy's concern? How does one prove that the "parodic nature" of a work "may reasonably be perceived"? Whose perception matters? If it is the trier of fact's perception that matters, how does one apply the test laid out by the Court while remaining true to the aesthetic nondiscrimination principle that the Court articulates?

3. Does the Court's analysis of the third statutory factor make sense? Does this analysis seem to be informed by the analysis of the fourth factor, as in *Harper & Row*? By any other factor?

4. The *Campbell* Court states that fair use is an affirmative defense, and that the burden is on the defendant to prove facts that support the defense. Section 106 states that the rights

granted to copyright owners are "subject to" §107, while §107 states that a use that qualifies as fair "is not an infringement of copyright." Does this statutory language support the characterization of fair use as an affirmative defense? Do the policies underlying copyright law support placing the burden of proving fair use on the defendant? Should a copyright owner be required to prove a lack of fair use as part of his prima facie case of infringement?

The Court indicates that a defendant will have difficulty proving that the fourth fair use factor supports a finding of fair use without "favorable evidence about relevant markets." For the defendant, favorable evidence means evidence of little or no harm to the market for the plaintiff's work or to protectible derivative markets. How is the defendant to prove this? For example, how is 2 Live Crew to prove no harm to "the market for [non-parodic] rap derivatives"? Would it make more sense to put the burden of showing harm on the plaintiff, at least initially?

5. Note that *Campbell* was decided on defendants' motion for summary judgment. Fair use is a mixed question of law and fact. In many cases, the underlying facts — how much of the plaintiff's work has been copied, how many copies of defendant's work were sold, etc. — are not in dispute. The dispute involves how to characterize those activities and how to weigh them using the fair use factors. When will summary judgment on the issue of fair use be appropriate? The Court has held that the Seventh Amendment right to jury trial applies to copyright infringement cases. *Feltner v. Columbia Pictures Television*, 523 U.S. 340 (1998). In tort law, application of the law to undisputed facts is often reserved for the jury. *See, e.g., Sioux City & Pacific R.R. v. Stout*, 84 U.S. 657 (1873). Is determination of whether the defendant's use was fair similar to determination of whether the defendant's conduct was reasonable in tort law?

6. In each of the three fair use cases decided by the Supreme Court, the district courts ruled one way, only to be reversed by the courts of appeals, which rulings were, in each case, reversed by the Supreme Court. This kind of flip-flop on appeal is quite common in fair use cases.

Fair use cases thus obviously often entail close questions. Particularly in close cases, would a damages remedy be more likely to achieve copyright law's goals than the routine infringement remedy of an injunction? In a footnote in the *Campbell* opinion, the Court noted that "the goals of copyright law . . . are not always best served by automatically granting injunctive relief when parodists are found to have gone beyond the bounds of fair use." *Campbell v. Acuff-Rose Music, Inc.*, 510 U.S. 569, 578 n.10 (1994). Do you agree? Are there any costs to the copyright owner of a damages remedy rather than an injunction?

7. After remand from the Supreme Court, the parties in *Campbell* agreed to a settlement that gave 2 Live Crew a license to use "Oh, Pretty Woman." *See* Stan Soocher, They Fought the Law: Rock Music Goes to Court 189-91 (1999).

As *Campbell* illustrates, when a copyrighted work becomes widely popular or controversial, many later authors seek to imitate, interpret, or educate about the work as a cultural phenomenon. The popular television series "Star Trek," for example, has spawned both authorized derivative works — movies and several spinoff series — and a host of other creative responses from the public at large. These responses include imitations (e.g., the 1970s television series "Battlestar Galactica"); parodies (e.g., the 1999 movie *Galaxy Quest*); literary thought experiments (e.g., Stephen R. Boyett, *Treks Not Taken: What If Stephen King, Anne Rice, Bret Easton Ellis, and Other Literary Greats Had Written Episodes of* Star Trek: The Next Generation? (1996)); scholarly commentaries (e.g., Paul Joseph & Sharon Carton, *The Law of the Federation: Images of Law, Lawyers, and the Legal System in* "Star Trek: The Next Generation," 24 U. Tol. L. Rev. 43 (1992)); popular commentaries (e.g., Dave Marinaccio, *All I Really Need to Know I Learned from Watching Star Trek* (1994)); and fan web sites (e.g., *http://www.AllSciFi.com*). As *Harper & Row* illustrates, later authors may respond in similar ways to works by or about prominent individuals.

In many of these cases, reconciling fair use with the rights of copyright owners to prepare derivative works can be difficult. One way to view such works is that they are created and marketed to cash in on a cultural craze. This characterization clearly is not favorable to a finding of fair use. A different view is that these works are efforts at participating in and communicating about common experiences in society.

As you read the next group of cases, consider which characterization makes more sense, and how that characterization should affect the fair use analysis. Consider, too, whether the lower courts are drawing coherent, sensible rules from the Supreme Court's fair use decisions.

≡ *Castle Rock Entertainment v. Carol Publishing Group, Inc.*
≡ *150 F.3d 132 (2d Cir. 1998)*

[Review the facts of this case, Chapter 5.D, pages 368-71 *supra*.]

WALKER, JR., J.: . . . Defendants claim that, even if *The SAT*'s copying of *Seinfeld* constitutes *prima facie* infringement, *The SAT* is nevertheless a fair use of *Seinfeld*. . . .

A. Purpose/Character of Use . . .

. . . That *The SAT*'s use is commercial, at most, "tends to weigh against a finding of fair use." *Campbell*, 510 U.S. at 585. . . . But we do not make too much of this point. . . .

The more critical inquiry under the first factor and in fair use analysis generally is whether the allegedly infringing work "merely supersedes" the original work "or instead adds something new, with a further purpose or different character, altering the first with new . . . meaning [ ] or message," in other words "whether and to what extent the new work is 'transformative.'" *Id*. at 579 (quoting Leval at 1111). . . .

. . . [T]he fact that the subject matter of the quiz is plebeian, banal, or ordinary stuff does not alter the fair use analysis. Criticism, comment, scholarship, research, and other potential fair uses are no less protectable because their subject is the ordinary.

[D]efendants style *The SAT* as a work "decod[ing] the obsession with . . . and mystique that surround[s] 'Seinfeld,'" by "critically restructur[ing] [*Seinfeld*'s mystique] into a system complete with varying levels of 'mastery' that relate the reader's control of the show's trivia to knowledge of and identification with their hero, Jerry Seinfeld." Citing one of their own experts for the proposition that "[t]he television environment cannot speak for itself but must be spoken for and about," defendants argue that "*The SAT* is a quintessential example of critical text of the TV environment . . . expos[ing] all of the show's nothingness to articulate its true motive forces and its social and moral dimensions." . . . Castle Rock dismisses these arguments as post hoc rationalizations, claiming that had defendants been half as creative in creating *The SAT* as were their lawyers in crafting these arguments about transformation, defendants might have a colorable fair use claim.

Any transformative purpose possessed by *The SAT* is slight to non-existent. We reject the argument that *The SAT* was created to educate *Seinfeld* viewers or to criticize, "expose," or otherwise comment upon *Seinfeld*. *The SAT*'s purpose, as evidenced definitively by the statements of the book's creators and by the book itself, is to repackage *Seinfeld* to entertain *Seinfeld* viewers. *The SAT*'s back cover makes no mention of exposing *Seinfeld* to its readers, for example, as a pitiably vacuous reflection of a puerile and pervasive television culture, but rather urges *SAT* readers to "open this book to satisfy [their] between-episode [*Seinfeld*] cravings."

Golub, *The SAT*'s author, described the trivia quiz book not as a commentary or a *Seinfeld* research tool, but as an effort to "capture Seinfeld's flavor in quiz book fashion." Finally, even viewing *The SAT* in the light most favorable to defendants, we find scant reason to conclude that this trivia quiz book seeks to educate, criticize, parody, comment, report upon, or research *Seinfeld*, or otherwise serve a transformative purpose.[7] The book does not contain commentary or analysis about *Seinfeld*, nor does it suggest how *The SAT* can be used to research *Seinfeld*; rather, the book simply poses trivia questions. *The SAT*'s plain purpose, therefore, is not to expose *Seinfeld*'s "nothingness," but to satiate *Seinfeld* fans' passion for the "nothingness" that *Seinfeld* has elevated into the realm of protectable creative expression.

Although a secondary work need not necessarily transform the original work's expression to have a transformative purpose . . . the fact that *The SAT* so minimally alters *Seinfeld*'s original expression in this case is further evidence of *The SAT*'s lack of transformative purpose. To be sure, the act of testing trivia about a creative work, in question and answer form, involves some creative expression. While still minimal, it does require posing the questions and hiding the correct answer among three or four incorrect ones.[8] Also, dividing the trivia questions into increasing levels of difficulty is somewhat more original than arranging names in a telephone book in alphabetical order. *See Feist*, 499 U.S. at 362-63, 111. . . . *The SAT*'s incorrect multiple choice answers are also original. However, the work as a whole, drawn directly from the *Seinfeld* episodes without substantial alteration, is far less transformative than other works we have held not to constitute fair use. . . .

B. Nature of the Copyrighted Work

. . . Defendants concede that the scope of fair use is somewhat narrower with respect to fictional works, such as *Seinfeld*, than to factual works. . . . Although this factor may be of less (or even of no) importance when assessed in the context of certain transformative uses . . . the fictional nature of the copyrighted work remains significant in the instant case, where the secondary use is at best minimally transformative. Thus, the second statutory factor favors the plaintiff.

C. Amount and Substantiality of the Portion Used in Relation to the Copyrighted Work as a Whole . . .

In *Campbell* . . . the Supreme Court clarified that the third factor . . . must be examined in context. The inquiry must focus upon whether "[t]he extent of . . . copying" is consistent with or more than necessary to further "the purpose and character of the use." 510 U.S. at 586-87. . . .

In the instant case, it could be argued that *The SAT* could not expose *Seinfeld*'s "nothingness" without repeated, indeed exhaustive examples deconstructing *Seinfeld*'s humor, thereby emphasizing *Seinfeld*'s meaninglessness to *The SAT*'s readers. That *The SAT* posed as many as 643 trivia questions to make this rather straightforward point, however, suggests that *The SAT*'s purpose was entertainment, not commentary. Such an argument has not been

---

7. Had *The SAT*'s incorrect answer choices attempted to parody *Seinfeld*, for example, defendants would have a stronger case for fair use. . . .

8. In the time it took to write this last sentence, for example, one could have easily created the following trivia question about the film trilogy *Star Wars*: "Luke Skywalker was aghast to learn that Darth Vader was Luke's (a) father (b) father-in-law (c) best friend (d) Jerry Seinfeld," and innumerable other such trivia questions about original creative works.

advanced on appeal, but if it had been, it would not disturb our conclusion that, under any fair reading, *The SAT* does not serve a critical or otherwise transformative purpose. Accordingly, the third factor weighs against fair use.

D. Effect of Use Upon Potential Market for or Value of Copyrighted Work . . .

In considering the fourth factor, our concern is not whether the secondary use suppresses or even destroys the market for the original work or its potential derivatives, but whether the secondary use usurps or substitutes for the market of the original work. [*Campbell*, 510 U.S.] at 593. . . .

Unlike parody, criticism, scholarship, news reporting, or other transformative uses, *The SAT* substitutes for a derivative market that a television program copyright owner such as Castle Rock "would in general develop or license others to develop." *Campbell*, 510 U.S. at 592.[11] Because *The SAT* borrows exclusively from *Seinfeld* and not from any other television or entertainment programs, *The SAT* is likely to fill a market niche that Castle Rock would in general develop. Moreover, as noted by the district court, this "*Seinfeld* trivia game is not critical of the program, nor does it parody the program; if anything, *SAT* pays homage to *Seinfeld*." Although Castle Rock has evidenced little if any interest in exploiting this market for derivative works based on *Seinfeld*, such as by creating and publishing *Seinfeld* trivia books (or at least trivia books that endeavor to "satisfy" the "between-episode cravings" of *Seinfeld* lovers), the copyright law must respect that creative and economic choice. . . . The fourth statutory factor therefore favors Castle Rock.

E. Other Factors . . .

We also note that free speech and public interest considerations are of little relevance in this case, which concerns garden-variety infringement of creative fictional works. . . . [*C*]*f. Time Inc. v. Bernard Geis Assocs.*, 293 F. Supp. 130, 146 (S.D.N.Y. 1968) (discussing importance of access to information about President Kennedy's assassination in fair use analysis of home video of assassination). . . .

≡≡≡ *Núñez v. Caribbean International News Corp.*
≡≡≡ *(El Vocero de Puerto Rico)*
≡≡≡ 235 F.3d 18 (1st Cir. 2000)

TORRUELLA, C.J.: . . . Appellant Núñez, a professional photographer, took several photographs of Joyce Giraud (Miss Puerto Rico Universe 1997) for use in Giraud's modeling portfolio. Núñez then distributed the photographs to various members of the Puerto Rico modeling

---

11. Just as secondary users may not exploit markets that original copyright owners would "in general develop or license others to develop" even if those owners had not actually done so, copyright owners may not preempt exploitation of transformative markets, which they would not "*in general* develop or license others to develop," by actually developing or licensing others to develop those markets. Thus, by developing or licensing a market for parody, news reporting, educational or other transformative uses of its own creative work, a copyright owner plainly cannot prevent others from entering those fair use markets. *See* 4 Nimmer §13.05[A][4], at 13-181-13-182 (recognizing "danger of circularity" where original copyright owner redefines "potential market" by developing or licensing others to develop that market). . . .

community in accordance with normal practice. After the photographs had been taken, some controversy arose over whether they were appropriate for a Miss Puerto Rico Universe, based on the fact that Giraud was naked or nearly naked in at least one of the photos. A local television program displayed the photographs on screen and asked random citizens whether they believed the photographs were "pornographic." Giraud was interviewed by two local television stations as to her fitness to retain the Miss Universe Puerto Rico crown. El Vocero then obtained several of the photographs through various means. Over the next week, without Núñez's permission, three of his photographs appeared in El Vocero, along with several articles about the controversy.

Núñez claimed that the reprint of his photographs in El Vocero without his permission violated the Copyright Act of 1976. The district court applied the fair use test of 17 U.S.C. §107. Focusing on the "newsworthy" nature of the photographs, the difficulty of presenting the story without the photographs, and the minimal effect on Núñez's photography business, the court concluded that El Vocero had met the requirements of §107 and dismissed the complaint with prejudice. . . .

B.   The Purpose and Character of the Use . . .

The district court found that appellee . . . both sought to "inform" and "gain commercially," and that the two purposes offset each other in the fair use analysis. For a commercial use to weigh heavily against a finding of fair use, it must involve more than simply publication in a profit-making venture. . . . We agree with the district court that the commercial use here . . . constitutes more than mere reproduction for a profitable use. The photographs were used in part to create an enticing lead page that would prompt readers to purchase the newspaper. . . .

However, the district court also found that the pictures were shown not just to titillate, but also to inform. Puerto Ricans were generally concerned about the qualifications of Giraud for Miss Puerto Rico Universe, as is demonstrated by the several television shows discussing the photographs. This informative function is confirmed by the newspaper's presentation of various news articles and interviews in conjunction with the reproduction. Appellee reprinted the pictures not just to entice the buying public, but to place its news articles in context; as the district court pointed out, "the pictures were the story." . . .

. . . It suffices to say here that El Vocero did not manufacture newsworthiness, as it sought not to "scoop" appellant by publishing his photograph, but merely to provide news reporting to a hungry public. And the fact that the story is admittedly on the tawdry side of the news ledger does not make it any less of a fair use. . . .

Rather, what is important here is that plaintiffs' photographs were originally intended to appear in modeling portfolios, not in the newspaper; the former use, not the latter, motivated the creation of the work. Thus, by using the photographs in conjunction with editorial commentary, El Vocero did not merely "supersede[ ] the objects of the original creation[s]," but instead used the works for "a further purpose," giving them a new "meaning, or message." *Campbell*, 510 U.S. at 579. It is this transformation of the works into news—and not the mere newsworthiness of the works themselves—that weighs in favor of fair use under the first factor of §107. . . .

Appellee's good faith also weighs in its favor on this prong of the fair use test. . . . First, El Vocero attributed the photographs to Núñez. Although acknowledgment does not excuse infringement, the failure to acknowledge counts against the infringer. . . . Second, El Vocero obtained each of the photographs lawfully. An unlawful acquisition of the copyrighted work generally weighs against a finding of fair use; no such theft occurred here. . . .

In sum, the highlighting of the photograph on the front cover of El Vocero exposes the commercial aspect of the infringing use, and counts against the appellee. However, the informative nature of the use, appellee's good faith, and the fact that it would have been difficult to report the news without reprinting the photograph suggest that on the whole, this factor is either neutral or favors a finding of fair use.

C. Nature of the Copyrighted Work . . .

The district court suggested, and we agree, that Núñez's pictures could be categorized as either factual or creative: certainly, photography is an art form that requires a significant amount of skill; however, the photographs were not artistic representations designed primarily to express Núñez's ideas, emotions, or feelings, but instead a publicity attempt to highlight Giraud's abilities as a potential model. . . . Given the difficulty of characterizing the "nature" of the photographs, we find that the impact of their creativity on the fair use finding is neutral.

This reproduction, however, does not threaten Núñez's right of first publication. Although these photographs had not before been published in a book or public portfolio, they were hardly confidential or secret, as was the manuscript in *Harper & Row* prior to its serial publication. . . . Núñez had not sought to control further dissemination during his limited distribution: he had not registered the copyright prior to publication in El Vocero, required recipients to sign non-disclosure or no-resale agreements, or even sought oral promises from recipients not to re-distribute the photographs.

In sum, this factor favors appellee.

D. Amount and Substantiality of the Use . . .

. . . In this case, El Vocero admittedly copied the entire picture; however, to copy any less than that would have made the picture useless to the story. As a result, like the district court, we count this factor as of little consequence to our analysis. . . .

E. Effect on the Market . . .

. . . [W]e examine the effect of *this* publication on the market, and we also determine whether wide-scale reproduction of professional photographs in newspapers (for similar purposes) would in general affect the market for such photography. As to the first, we find little impact on the market for these specific pictures. The district court noted that the purpose of dissemination of the pictures in question is not to make money, but to publicize; they are distributed for free to the professional modeling community rather than sold for a profit. The fact that a relatively poor reproduction was displayed on the cover of a newspaper should not change the demand for the portfolio. If anything, it might increase it. . . .

However, the potential market for the photographs might also include the sale to newspapers for just this purpose: illustrating controversy. It is true that El Vocero's use of the photograph without permission essentially destroys this market. There is no evidence, however, that such a market ever existed in this case. Nuñez does not suggest that he ever tried to sell portfolio photographs to newspapers, or even that he had the right to do so under the contract with Giraud. . . .

. . . Because the only discernible effect of the publication in El Vocero was to increase demand for the photograph, and because any potential market for resale directly to the newspaper was unlikely to be developed, this factor favors a finding of fair use. . . .

≡ *Bill Graham Archives v. Dorling Kindersley Ltd.*
≡ *448 F.3d 605 (2d Cir. 2006)*

RESTANI, J.: . . .

Background

In October of 2003, [Dorling Kindersley ("DK")] published *Grateful Dead: The Illustrated Trip* ("Illustrated Trip"), in collaboration with Grateful Dead Productions, intended as a cultural history of the Grateful Dead. The resulting 480-page coffee table book tells the story of the Grateful Dead along a timeline running continuously through the book, chronologically combining over 2000 images representing dates in the Grateful Dead's history with explanatory text. A typical page of the book features a collage of images, text, and graphic art designed to simultaneously capture the eye and inform the reader. Plaintiff [Bill Graham Archives ("BGA" or "Appellant")] claims to own the copyright to seven images displayed in *Illustrated Trip*, which DK reproduced without BGA's permission.

Initially, DK sought permission from BGA to reproduce the images. In May of 2003, the CEO of Grateful Dead Productions sent a letter to BGA seeking permission. . . . BGA responded by offering permission in exchange for Grateful Dead Productions' grant of permission to BGA to make CDs and DVDs out of concert footage in BGA's archives. Next, DK directly contacted BGA seeking to negotiate a license agreement, but the parties disagreed as to an appropriate license fee. Nevertheless, DK proceeded with publication of *Illustrated Trip* without entering a license fee agreement with BGA. Specifically, DK reproduced seven artistic images originally depicted on Grateful Dead event posters and tickets. BGA's seven images are displayed in significantly reduced form and are accompanied by captions describing the concerts they represent.

When DK refused to meet BGA's post-publication license fee demands, BGA filed suit for copyright infringement. . . . [T]he district court determined that DK's reproduction of the images was fair use and granted DK's motion for summary judgment.

Discussion

I. Purpose and Character of Use . . .

. . . [W]e agree with the district court that DK's actual use of each image is transformatively different from the original expressive purpose. Preliminarily, we recognize, as the district court did, that *Illustrated Trip* is a biographical work documenting the 30-year history of the Grateful Dead. While there are no categories of presumptively fair use, *see Campbell v. Acuff-Rose Music, Inc.*, 510 U.S. at 584 . . . courts have frequently afforded fair use protection to the use of copyrighted material in biographies, recognizing such works as forms of historic scholarship, criticism, and comment that require incorporation of original source material for optimum treatment of their subjects. . . . No less a recognition of biographical value is warranted in this case simply because the subject made a mark in pop culture rather than some other area of human endeavor. . . .

In the instant case, DK's purpose in using the copyrighted images at issue in its biography of the Grateful Dead is plainly different from the original purpose for which they were created. Originally, each of BGA's images fulfilled the dual purposes of artistic expression and promotion. The posters were apparently widely distributed to generate public interest in the Grateful Dead and to convey information to a large number [of] people about the band's forthcoming concerts. In contrast, DK used each of BGA's images as historical artifacts to document and represent the actual occurrence of Grateful Dead concert events featured on *Illustrated Trip*'s timeline.

In some instances, it is readily apparent that DK's image display enhances the reader's understanding of the biographical text. In other instances, the link between image and text is less obvious; nevertheless, the images still serve as historical artifacts graphically representing the fact of significant Grateful Dead concert events selected by the *Illustrated Trip*'s author for inclusion in the book's timeline. We conclude that both types of uses fulfill DK's transformative purpose of enhancing the biographical information in *Illustrated Trip*, a purpose separate and distinct from the original artistic and promotional purpose for which the images were created. . . . [B]ecause DK's use of the disputed images is transformative both when accompanied by referencing commentary and when standing alone, we agree with the district court that DK was not required to discuss the artistic merits of the images to satisfy this first factor of fair use analysis.

This conclusion is strengthened by the manner in which DK displayed the images. First, DK significantly reduced the size of the reproductions. . . . While the small size is sufficient to permit readers to recognize the historical significance of the posters, it is inadequate to offer more than a glimpse of their expressive value. In short, DK used the minimal image size necessary to accomplish its transformative purpose.

Second, DK minimized the expressive value of the reproduced images by combining them with a prominent timeline, textual material, and original graphical artwork, to create a collage of text and images on each page of the book. To further this collage effect, the images are displayed at angles and the original graphical artwork is designed to blend with the images and text. Overall, DK's layout ensures that the images at issue are employed only to enrich the presentation of the cultural history of the Grateful Dead, not to exploit copyrighted artwork for commercial gain. . . .

Third, BGA's images constitute an inconsequential portion of *Illustrated Trip*. The extent to which unlicensed material is used in the challenged work can be a factor in determining whether a biographer's use of original materials has been sufficiently transformative to constitute fair use. . . . Although our circuit has counseled against considering the percentage the allegedly infringing work comprises of the copyrighted work in conducting *third-factor* fair use analysis, . . . several courts have done so, *see, e.g., Harper*, 471 U.S. at 565-66 . . . (finding the fact that quotes from President Ford's unpublished memoirs played a central role in the allegedly infringing magazine article, constituting 13% of that article, weighed against a finding of fair use). . . . We find this inquiry more relevant in the context of *first-factor* fair use analysis.

In the instant case, the book is 480 pages long, while the BGA images appear on only seven pages. Although the original posters range in size from $13'' \times 19''$ to more than $19'' \times 27''$, the largest reproduction of a BGA image in *Illustrated Trip* is less than $3'' \times 4^{1}/2''$, less than $^{1}/20$ the size of the original. And no BGA image takes up more than one-eighth of a page in a book or is given more prominence than any other image on the page. In total, the images account for less than one-fifth of one percent of the book. . . . [W]e are aware of no case where such an insignificant taking was found to be an unfair use of original materials.

Finally, as to this first factor, we briefly address the commercial nature of *Illustrated Trip*. Even though *Illustrated Trip* is a commercial venture, we recognize that "nearly all of the illustrative uses listed in the preamble paragraph of §107 . . . are generally conducted for profit. . . ." *Campbell*, 510 U.S. at 584. Moreover, "[t]he crux of the profit/nonprofit distinction is not whether the sole motive of the use is monetary gain but whether the user stands to profit from exploitation of the copyrighted material without paying the customary price." *Harper*, 471 U.S. at 562. Here, *Illustrated Trip* does not exploit the use of BGA's images as such for commercial gain. Significantly, DK has not used any of BGA's images in its commercial advertising or in any other way to promote the sale of the book. *Illustrated Trip* merely uses pictures and text to describe the life of the Grateful Dead. By design, the use of BGA's images is incidental to the commercial biographical value of the book. . . .

II. Nature of the Copyrighted Work . . .

We agree with the district court that the creative nature of artistic images typically weighs in favor of the copyright holder. We recognize, however, that the second factor may be of limited usefulness where the creative work of art is being used for a transformative purpose. . . . Here, we conclude that DK is using BGA's images for the transformative purpose of enhancing the biographical information provided in *Illustrated Trip*. Accordingly, we hold that even though BGA's images are creative works, which are a core concern of copyright protection, the second factor has limited weight in our analysis because the purpose of DK's use was to emphasize the images' historical rather than creative value.

III. Amount and Substantiality of the Portion Used . . .

The district court determined that even though the images are reproduced in their entirety, the third fair use factor weighs in favor of DK because the images are displayed in reduced size and scattered among many other images and texts. In faulting this conclusion, Appellant contends that the amount used is substantial because the images are copied in their entirety. Neither our court nor any of our sister circuits has ever ruled that the copying of an entire work *favors* fair use. At the same time, however, courts have concluded that such copying does not necessarily weigh against fair use because copying the entirety of a work is sometimes necessary to make a fair use of the image. *See . . . Núñez v. Caribbean Int'l News Corp.*, 235 F.3d 18, 24 (1st Cir. 2000). . . .

Here, DK used BGA's images because the posters and tickets were historical artifacts that could document Grateful Dead concert events and provide a visual context for the accompanying text. To accomplish this use, DK displayed reduced versions of the original images and intermingled these visuals with text and original graphic art. As a consequence, even though the copyrighted images are copied in their entirety, the visual impact of their artistic expression is significantly limited because of their reduced size. . . .

IV. Effect of the Use Upon the Market for or Value of the Original . . .

In the instant case, the parties agree that DK's use of the images did not impact BGA's primary market for the sale of the poster images. Instead, we look to whether DK's unauthorized use usurps BGA's potential to develop a derivative market. Appellant argues that DK interfered with the market for licensing its images for use in books. Appellant contends that there is an established market for licensing its images and it suffered both the loss of royalty revenue directly from DK and the opportunity to obtain royalties from others. . . .

. . . [W]e look at the impact on potential licensing revenues for "traditional, reasonable, or likely to be developed markets." [*American Geophysical Union v.*] *Texaco*, [*Inc.*] 60 F.3d [913,] at 930 [(2d Cir. 1995)]. In order to establish a traditional license market, Appellant points to the fees paid to other copyright owners for the reproduction of their images in *Illustrated Trip*. Moreover, Appellant asserts that it established a market for licensing its images, and in this case expressed a willingness to license images to DK. Neither of these arguments shows impairment to a traditional, as opposed to a transformative market. . . .

Here . . . we hold that DK's use of BGA's images is transformatively different from their original expressive purpose. In a case such as this, a copyright holder cannot prevent others from entering fair use markets merely "by developing or licensing a market for parody, news reporting, educational or other transformative uses of its own creative work." *Castle Rock*, 150 F.3d at 146 n. 11. "[C]opyright owners may not preempt exploitation of transformative markets. . . ." *Id.* Moreover, a publisher's willingness to pay license fees for reproduction of images does not establish that the publisher may not, in the alternative, make fair use of those images. *Campbell*, 510 U.S. at 585 n. 18 . . . (stating that "being denied permission to use [or pay license fees for] a work does not weigh against a finding of fair use"). Since DK's use of BGA's images falls within a transformative market, BGA does not suffer market harm due to the loss of license fees. . . .

NOTES AND QUESTIONS

1. Are these cases consistent with one another? Are they consistent with *Harper & Row* and *Campbell*? *Campbell* notwithstanding, do courts appear to be applying a standard based on aesthetic merit to determine which arguably "derivative" uses warrant protection under the fair use doctrine? Might aesthetic discrimination sometimes be appropriate in fair use cases?

2. In *Ty, Inc. v. Publications International Ltd.*, 292 F.3d 512 (7th Cir. 2002), *cert. denied*, 537 U.S. 1110 (2003), the manufacturer of "Beanie Babies" brought a copyright infringement action against a publisher of Beanie Babies collectors' guides. The court distinguished "copying that is complementary to the copyrighted work (in the sense that nails are complements of hammers)" from "copying that is a substitute for the copyrighted work (in the sense that nails are substitutes for pegs or screws), or for derivative works from the copyrighted work." *Id.* at 517. It held that complementary copying is fair use while substitutional copying is not. *Id.* at 517-18. Because the defendant had published a number of books that varied significantly from one another in content and tone, the court of appeals instructed the district court to conduct a detailed evaluation of each book. *Compare Ty, Inc.* with *Castle Rock*. What distinguishes *The SAT* from a Beanie Babies collectors' guide?

3. What are the limits of the "newsworthiness" reasoning applied in *Nuñez*? What if Nuñez had attempted to license the photographs to a different newspaper (the *National Enquirer*, for example), but after their publication in *El Vocero*, the other newspaper chose not to use them?

4. Do you agree that DK's use of BGA's images was transformative? Should courts treat the inclusion of images in a biographical account differently from the inclusion of text? Note the *BGA* court's conclusion that DK minimized its use of the expressive aspect of the images by reducing their size. Should this matter? If DK had reproduced full-page versions of the images, should the fair use analysis change?

Should the scope of fair use be the same for a biography of a pop culture movement (*BGA*) as for the biography of a religious (*New Era*) or political (*Harper & Row*) leader?

5. How should the fair use defense be applied when the work at issue has been kept secret? Specifically, how should a court weigh the fourth fair use factor in such cases, given that secrecy can positively enhance a work's value? In *Chicago Board of Education v. Substance, Inc.*, 354 F.3d 624 (7th Cir. 2003), *cert. denied*, 543 U.S. 816 (2004), the defendant, a public school teacher, published six standardized tests that had been created by the Chicago School Board. The tests were administered under secure conditions to maintain their reuse value. The defendant published the tests precisely to destroy the potential for reuse, claiming that the tests were "bad." The defendant raised an unsuccessful fair use defense to the copyright infringement claim. In addressing the fourth factor, the court held that the publication destroyed the value of the tests and the fact that this was not a market value was of no significance. *Id.* at 630. Do you agree that the fourth factor can be construed to encompass both the value of the work to the owner and the market for the work? Should the same reasoning apply when critical commentary succeeds in destroying the potential for an author to exploit a derivative market, such as turning the book into a movie?

6. How would you apply the fair use doctrine to the following not-so-imaginary hypotheticals? Do any of the uses described below qualify as parodies? Should the defendant's burden be higher if the challenged use is not considered a parody? Would it matter why the copyright owner has refused to authorize the use?

a.   Carla Cartoonist markets a "counterculture" comic book that portrays Mickey Mouse and Donald Duck as bawdy, promiscuous, recreational drug users. *See Walt Disney Productions Prods. v. Air Pirates*, 581 F.2d 751 (9th Cir. 1978), *cert. denied*, 439 U.S. 1132 (1979) (no fair use).

b.   Genevieve Goth repaints and re-costumes SuperStar Barbie dolls' heads as "Dungeon Dolls" and features them in sexually explicit stories. For example, one Dungeon Doll appearing on Ms. Goth's web site is Barbie re-costumed as "Lily, the Diva Dominatrix," the leading character in a story involving sexual slavery and torture. Mattel, Inc., owner of the copyright in the unadorned Barbie doll's head, sues for copyright infringement. *See Mattel, Inc. v. Pitt*, 229 F. Supp. 2d 315 (S.D.N.Y. 2002) (possible fair use). Is *Mattel* consistent with *Walt Disney* above?

c.   The manufacturers of Campari liqueur run a series of print ads interviewing celebrities about the first time they drank Campari. The ads use sexual double entendres, including the slogan, "You never forget your first time." *Hustler Magazine* runs a spoof ad that purports to document the recollections of Patrick Preacher, a prominent evangelical Christian minister, about his "first time" — with his mother, in an outhouse. Preacher distributes hundreds of thousands of photocopies of the ad as part of a direct mail campaign to raise money for his religious organization. *See Hustler Magazine Inc. v. Moral Majority Inc.*, 796 F.2d 1148 (9th Cir. 1986) (fair use).

d.   Marvin Minister writes a book, *The Truth*, which is used as scripture for some years by the Church of the Universe, which Minister founded. Later, after Minister's death, the Church discontinues use of *The Truth* on the ground that some of its teachings are outmoded and racist, and are no longer followed by the Church. The Chicago Church of the Universe, a breakaway movement founded by two former Church of the Universe members, adopts *The Truth* as its scripture and begins distributing copies to its members. *See Worldwide Church of God v. Philadelphia Church of God, Inc.*, 227 F.3d 1110 (9th Cir. 2000), *cert. denied*, 532 U.S. 958 (2001) (no fair use).

Mickey Mouse © Disney Enterprises, Inc. Reprinted by permission.

Air Pirates Cover

e. Review the facts of *Warner Brothers Entertainment Inc. v. RDR Books,* 575 F. Supp. 2d 513 (S.D.N.Y. 2008), Chapter 5.D.1 *supra.* RDR Books claims that even if *The Lexicon: An Unauthorized Guide to Harry Potter Fiction and Related Materials* is infringing, the infringement is excused as fair. *Id.* at 539-51 (no fair use).

f. Alice Randall writes a novel, *The Wind Done Gone,* that retells the story of Margaret Mitchell's classic novel, *Gone With the Wind,* from the perspective of Scarlett O'Hara's black half-sister, who is a slave on the family plantation. Mitchell's novel, which was enormously successful in its own right, was made even more popular by a series of authorized derivative works, including the movie starring Clark Gable and Vivien Leigh and a sequel, *Scarlett,* commissioned by Mitchell's estate. *See Suntrust Bank v. Houghton Mifflin Co.,* 268 F.3d 1257 (11th Cir. 2001) (probable fair use). (We also posed the *Gone With the Wind/The Wind Done Gone* hypothetical in Chapter 1, page 20 *supra.* Has your answer changed?)

g. Frederik Colting writes a book, *60 Years Later: Coming Through the Rye,* that tells the story of Mr. C, a 76-year old version of Holden Caulfield, the protagonist in J.D. Salinger's earlier work, *The Catcher in the Rye.* The same characteristics that made the original depressed and alienated make Mr. C a person of stunted emotional growth who is often miserable. The book includes Salinger as a character "in order to criticize his reclusive nature and alleged desire to exercise 'iron-clad control over his intellectual property, refusing to allow others to adapt any of his characters or stories in other media'. . . ." *Salinger v. Colting,* 641 F. Supp. 2d 250 (S.D.N.Y. 2009) (no fair use), *vacated,* No. 09-2878-cv, 2010 WL 1729126 (2d Cir. Apr. 30, 2010) (vacating preliminary injunction).

h. Jeff Koons is a visual artist who incorporates images from popular media and commercial advertising into his art. His painting "Niagara" depicts four pairs of women's lower legs and feet hovering over images of various confectionary treats like a brownie sundae. He adapted a photograph from a fashion magazine for one of the pairs of legs. According to Koons, the work is intended as a commentary on how popular images mediate basic needs. *See Blanch v. Koons,* 467 F.3d 244 (2d Cir. 2006) (fair use).

7. Recall from Chapter 5.E that, under the Berne Convention, the author of a protected work has the right to protect the integrity of the work. As described by Article 6bis, the right of integrity includes the right to object to modifications of the copyrighted work, and also to any "distortion" or "mutilation" of the work. Under U.S. copyright law, such modifications (and arguably distortions and mutilations as well) may result in the creation of derivative works, and may then be excused by the fair use doctrine. This overlap, and potential conflict, between the moral right of integrity and the fair use doctrine is a source of tension in U.S. copyright law. As the *Harper & Row* Court indicated, one of the important functions of the fair use doctrine is to safeguard First Amendment protections. Historically, U.S. ambivalence toward moral rights has stemmed partially from a perceived difficulty in reconciling moral rights with First Amendment concerns. Yet most European countries also have a strong commitment to freedom of expression. Further, the Berne Convention makes clear that countries may permit the reproduction of works by the press and for informational purposes. *See* Berne Conv. art. 2bis and art. 10bis. Review the discussion of U.S. protection for moral rights, Chapter 5.E, *supra,* and consider whether it might be possible to recognize stronger moral rights without violating First Amendment principles. Are moral rights in fact inconsistent with the First Amendment? Do moral rights protect the speech rights of authors at the expense of the public's speech rights? Would stronger moral rights protection affect authors' incentives to create?

Note on Fair Use and the First Amendment

"Cultural interchange" cases also implicate freedom of expression concerns. Recall that in *Harper & Row*, the Court rejected *The Nation*'s argument that the First Amendment should afford it a separate defense to copyright infringement, particularly for the press. It did so in part because of the unpublished nature of the work. The Court noted that "freedom of thought and expression 'includes both the right to speak freely and the right to refrain from speaking at all.'" *Harper & Row*, 471 U.S 539, 559 (quoting *Wooley v. Maynard*, 430 U.S. 705, 714 (1977)). Copyright law and the right of first publication in particular, the Court observed, serve "this countervailing First Amendment value." *Id*. at 560. The Court also noted, however, that both the idea-expression distinction and the fair use doctrine "embod[y]" First Amendment protections. *Id*. In *Eldred v. Ashcroft*, 537 U.S. 186 (2003), Chapter 3.B.2 *supra*, the Court reaffirmed this latter statement. It reasoned that "because copyright law contains built-in First Amendment accommodations," *id*. at 219-20, legislative amendments that do not "alter the traditional contours of copyright protection need not be subjected to heightened First Amendment scrutiny." *Id*. at 221.

What, exactly, do the Court's pronouncements on fair use and the First Amendment mean? One interpretation of *Harper & Row* and *Eldred* is that existing fair use doctrine sufficiently accommodates First Amendment values. On this view, there is no need for courts evaluating fair use cases expressly to consider First Amendment principles or doctrine.

A different view of the First Amendment's role in the fair use inquiry emerged in *Suntrust Bank v. Houghton Mifflin Co.*, 268 F.3d 1257 (11th Cir. 2001), which vacated a preliminary injunction barring publication of Alice Randall's book, *The Wind Done Gone*. Relying on *Campbell v. Acuff-Rose Music, Inc.*, the court held that the book was a highly transformative parody of *Gone With the Wind*, and that Suntrust, Margaret Mitchell's trustee, had not shown any likelihood of harm to the market for authorized derivative works. It further held that the issuance of the preliminary injunction "was at odds with the shared principles of the First Amendment and the copyright law, acting as a prior restraint on speech because the public had not had access to Randall's ideas or viewpoint in the form of expression that she chose." *Id*. at 1277. The court did not elaborate on this reasoning. In the introductory portion of its opinion, however, it characterized copyright and the First Amendment as working toward the shared goal of preventing censorship. *Id*. at 1263. Citing *Harper & Row*, it noted that "courts often need not entertain related First Amendment arguments in a copyright case," but that courts "must remain cognizant of the First Amendment protections interwoven into copyright law." *Id*. at 1265. What do you make of this approach? How would "remain[ing] cognizant" of the First Amendment affect the fair use analysis? For a useful discussion of this question, see Neil Weinstock Netanel, *Locating Copyright Within the First Amendment Skein*, 54 Stan. L. Rev. 1, 81-85 (2001).

Should the First Amendment ever provide a separate defense to a copyright infringement claim? Defendants in fair use cases have repeatedly raised First Amendment arguments to justify uses claimed to be in the public interest because of the "newsworthy" nature of the copied work. So far, courts have rejected these arguments, citing *Harper & Row*. *See, e.g.*, *Los Angeles News Serv. v. Tullo*, 973 F.2d 791 (9th Cir. 1992) (holding that "news clipping" service's unlicensed rebroadcast of excerpts from news services' videotapes of an airplane crash site and a train wreck site were not fair use); *see also Los Angeles News Serv. v. Reuters Television Int'l, Ltd.*, 149 F.3d 987 (9th Cir. 1998) (holding that television news agencies' unlicensed broadcast of copyrighted news footage of riots occurring in Los Angeles in April 1992 following the verdict in the Rodney King case was not fair use), *cert. denied*, 525 U.S. 1141 (1999). *But see Los*

Angeles News Serv. v. CBS Broadcasting, Inc., 305 F.3d 924 (9th Cir. 2002) (finding that Court TV's unlicensed rebroadcast of clips from such footage was fair). Should the Court's statements in *Harper & Row* and *Eldred* be read that broadly? Can you imagine a case in which the fair use doctrine and the idea-expression dichotomy would not suffice to protect speech concerns, and a separate First Amendment defense to a claim of copyright infringement would make sense? What about freedom of religion concerns? Review Question 6.d above. Should the First Amendment play a role there?

2. Technical Interchange

A recurring theme of this book, as of copyright law itself, has been the need to strike balances. Copyright law attempts to strike the optimal balance between providing authors with incentives to create and encouraging dissemination of works and information to the public. To achieve this goal, it also attempts to balance the needs of existing authors for protection with the needs of future authors to use the ideas and other raw materials needed to create. As you know from your reading, copyright law undertakes this balancing act in part by effectively granting more protection to highly creative works and less to factual or highly utilitarian works. Second generation authors generally have a greater need to access and use these latter types of works in creating new ones. *Harper & Row* and *Campbell* indicated that in general, the second statutory fair use factor is more likely to weigh in favor of fair use in cases involving factual works and against fair use if the work used is highly creative. Should the scope of fair use overall be greater for factual and utilitarian works?

Courts have addressed this question in the context of fair use cases involving computer software. Software is highly utilitarian, although some also consider software programming to be a very creative process. As you know from Chapter 4.B, of particular relevance for copyright law's treatment of computer software is that software also exhibits a high degree of interdependence. In order to accomplish the tasks desired by the computer user, software programs must interoperate with (or "talk to") one another, and must do so according to precise technical specifications. Thus, in Chapter 4, you studied a process for identifying copyrightable subject matter in computer software that involves "filtering out" program elements required for interoperability with other programs. *See* pages 222-29 *supra*. As electronic technologies, and particularly the Internet, have evolved, opportunities to develop new products that function with other computer programs, and other types of digital works, have multiplied.

As a practical matter, achieving interoperability between computer programs often requires copying protected elements of copyrighted programs. To understand how to write new programs that will interoperate with existing programs, many programmers engage in decompilation — converting the copyrighted software of others from the zeros and ones representing machine-readable object code into human-readable commands — so that they can understand the program's technical requirements. This process necessarily involves making copies of large portions of the copyrighted work. How should the fair use doctrine respond to this practice? The eventual new work of authorship that results may be a product that works with the copyrighted work (like Corel WordPerfect for Windows works with the Microsoft Windows operating system) or one that substitutes for the copyrighted work (like WordPerfect for Windows substitutes for Microsoft's own Word for Windows). Should it matter whether the defendant has designed a complementary or competing product? The next two cases address these questions. As you read them, consider whether the courts' rationales are equally persuasive in both cases.

Sega Enterprises Ltd. v. Accolade, Inc.
977 F.2d 1510 (9th Cir. 1992)

REINHARDT, J.: . . . Plaintiff-appellee Sega Enterprises, Ltd. ("Sega") . . . develop[s] and market[s] video entertainment systems, including the "Genesis" console . . . and video game cartridges. Defendant-appellant Accolade, Inc., is an independent developer, manufacturer, and marketer of computer entertainment software, including game cartridges that are compatible with the Genesis console, as well as game cartridges that are compatible with other computer systems.

Sega licenses its copyrighted computer code and its "SEGA" trademark to a number of independent developers of computer game software. . . . Accolade is not and never has been a licensee of Sega. Prior to rendering its own games compatible with the Genesis console, Accolade explored the possibility of entering into a licensing agreement with Sega, but abandoned the effort because the agreement would have required that Sega be the exclusive manufacturer of all games produced by Accolade.

Accolade used a two-step process to render its video games compatible with the Genesis console. First, it "reverse engineered" Sega's video game programs in order to discover the requirements for compatibility with the Genesis console. As part of the reverse engineering process, Accolade transformed the machine-readable object code contained in commercially available copies of Sega's game cartridges into human-readable source code using a process called "disassembly" or "decompilation." Accolade purchased a Genesis console and three Sega game cartridges, wired a decompiler into the console circuitry, and generated printouts of the resulting source code. Accolade engineers studied and annotated the printouts in order to identify areas of commonality among the three game programs. They then loaded the disassembled code back into a computer, and experimented to discover the interface specifications for the Genesis console by modifying the programs and studying the results. At the end of the reverse engineering process, Accolade created a development manual that incorporated the information it had discovered about the requirements for a Genesis-compatible game. According to the Accolade employees who created the manual, the manual contained only functional descriptions of the interface requirements and did not include any of Sega's code.

In the second stage, Accolade created its own games for the Genesis. According to Accolade, at this stage it did not copy Sega's programs, but relied only on the information concerning interface specifications for the Genesis that was contained in its development manual. Accolade maintains that with the exception of the interface specifications, none of the code in its own games is derived in any way from its examination of Sega's code. In 1990, Accolade released "Ishido," a game which it had originally developed and released for use with the Macintosh and IBM personal computer systems, for use with the Genesis console. . . .

In 1991, Accolade released five more games for use with the Genesis III. . . . With the exception of "Mike Ditka Power Football," all of those games, like "Ishido," had originally been developed and marketed for use with other hardware systems. . . .

[Sega brought a number of claims against Accolade, including a claim alleging that Accolade's disassembling of Sega's code constituted copyright infringement. The district court, holding that Sega would likely succeed on the merits of this claim, entered a preliminary injunction enjoining Accolade from disassembling Sega's code and from distributing any games developed through disassembly. The district court rejected Accolade's argument that the copying involved in its disassembly was sheltered by the fair use doctrine. The Ninth Circuit agreed that the disassembly process had reproduced Sega's code in copies for purposes of §106(1). The court then went on to consider Accolade's fair use argument.]

(a)

With respect to the first statutory factor, we observe initially that the fact that copying is for a commercial purpose weighs against a finding of fair use. *Harper & Row*, 471 U.S. at 562. . . .

. . . We must consider other aspects of "the purpose and character of the use" as well. As we have noted, the use at issue was an intermediate one only and thus any commercial "exploitation" was indirect or derivative.

The declarations of Accolade's employees indicate, and the district court found, that Accolade copied Sega's software solely in order to discover the functional requirements for compatibility with the Genesis console — aspects of Sega's programs that are not protected by copyright. 17 U.S.C. §102(b). With respect to the video game programs contained in Accolade's game cartridges, there is no evidence in the record that Accolade sought to avoid performing its own creative work. Indeed, most of the games that Accolade released for use with the Genesis console were originally developed for other hardware systems. Moreover, with respect to the interface procedures for the Genesis console, Accolade did not seek to avoid paying a customarily charged fee for use of those procedures, nor did it simply copy Sega's code; rather, it wrote its own procedures based on what it had learned through disassembly. Taken together, these facts indicate that although Accolade's ultimate purpose was the release of Genesis-compatible games for sale, its direct purpose in copying Sega's code, and thus its direct use of the copyrighted material, was simply to study the functional requirements for Genesis compatibility so that it could modify existing games and make them usable with the Genesis console. Moreover, as we discuss below, no other method of studying those requirements was available to Accolade. On these facts, we conclude that Accolade copied Sega's code for a legitimate, essentially non-exploitative purpose, and that the commercial aspect of its use can best be described as of minimal significance.

We further note that we are free to consider the public benefit resulting from a particular use notwithstanding the fact that the alleged infringer may gain commercially. . . . Public benefit need not be direct or tangible, but may arise because the challenged use serves a public interest. . . . In the case before us, Accolade's identification of the functional requirements for Genesis compatibility has led to an increase in the number of independently designed video game programs offered for use with the Genesis console. It is precisely this growth in creative expression, based on the dissemination of other creative works and the unprotected ideas contained in those works, that the Copyright Act was intended to promote. *See Feist Publications, Inc. v. Rural Tel. Serv. Co.*, [499] U.S. [340, 348] (1991) (citing *Harper & Row*, 471 U.S. at 556-57). The fact that Genesis-compatible video games are not scholarly works, but works offered for sale on the market, does not alter our judgment in this regard. We conclude that given the purpose and character of Accolade's use of Sega's video game programs, the presumption of unfairness has been overcome and the first statutory factor weighs in favor of Accolade.

(b)

As applied, the fourth statutory factor, effect on the potential market for the copyrighted work, bears a close relationship to the "purpose and character" inquiry in that it, too, accommodates the distinction between the copying of works in order to make independent creative expression possible and the simple exploitation of another's creative efforts. We must, of course, inquire whether, "if [the challenged use] should become widespread, it would adversely affect the potential market for the copyrighted work," *Sony Corp. v. Universal City Studios*,

464 U.S. 417, 451, by diminishing potential sales, interfering with marketability, or usurping the market. If the copying resulted in the latter effect, all other considerations might be irrelevant. The *Harper & Row* Court found a use that effectively usurped the market for the copyrighted work by supplanting that work to be dispositive. 471 U.S. at 567-69. However, the same consequences do not and could not attach to a use which simply enables the copier to enter the market for works of the same type as the copied work.

Unlike the defendant in *Harper & Row* . . . Accolade did not attempt to "scoop" Sega's release of any particular game or games, but sought only to become a legitimate competitor in the field of Genesis-compatible video games. Within that market, it is the characteristics of the game program as experienced by the user that determine the program's commercial success. As we have noted, there is nothing in the record that suggests that Accolade copied any of those elements.

By facilitating the entry of a new competitor, the first lawful one that is not a Sega licensee, Accolade's disassembly of Sega's software undoubtedly "affected" the market for Genesis-compatible games in an indirect fashion. We note, however, that while no consumer except the most avid devotee of President Ford's regime might be expected to buy more than one version of the President's memoirs, video game users typically purchase more than one game. There is no basis for assuming that Accolade's "Ishido" has significantly affected the market for Sega's "Altered Beast," since a consumer might easily purchase both; nor does it seem unlikely that a consumer particularly interested in sports might purchase both Accolade's "Mike Ditka Power Football" and Sega's "Joe Montana Football," particularly if the games are, as Accolade contends, not substantially similar. In any event, an attempt to monopolize the market by making it impossible for others to compete runs counter to the statutory purpose of promoting creative expression and cannot constitute a strong equitable basis for resisting the invocation of the fair use doctrine. Thus, we conclude that the fourth statutory factor weighs in Accolade's, not Sega's, favor, notwithstanding the minor economic loss Sega may suffer.

(c)

The second statutory factor, the nature of the copyrighted work, reflects the fact that not all copyrighted works are entitled to the same level of protection. . . . Works of fiction receive greater protection than works that have strong factual elements, such as historical or biographical works . . . or works that have strong functional elements, such as accounting textbooks, *Baker*, 101 U.S. at 104. Works that are merely compilations of fact are copyrightable, but the copyright in such a work is "thin." *Feist Publications*, [499] U.S. at [349]. . . .

Sega argues that even if many elements of its video game programs are properly characterized as functional and therefore not protected by copyright, Accolade copied protected expression. Sega is correct. The record makes clear that disassembly is wholesale copying. Because computer programs are also unique among copyrighted works in the form in which they are distributed for public use, however, Sega's observation does not bring us much closer to a resolution of the dispute.

The unprotected aspects of most functional works are readily accessible to the human eye. The systems described in accounting textbooks or the basic structural concepts embodied in architectural plans, to give two examples, can be easily copied without also copying any of the protected, expressive aspects of the original works. Computer programs, however, are typically distributed for public use in object code form, embedded in a silicon chip or on a floppy disk.

For that reason, humans often cannot gain access to the unprotected ideas and functional concepts contained in object code without disassembling that code — i.e., making copies. . . .

. . . [T]he record clearly establishes that disassembly of the object code in Sega's video game cartridges was necessary in order to understand the functional requirements for Genesis compatibility. The interface procedures for the Genesis console are distributed for public use only in object code form, and are not visible to the user during operation of the video game program. Because object code cannot be read by humans, it must be disassembled, either by hand or by machine. Disassembly of object code necessarily entails copying. Those facts dictate our analysis of the second statutory fair use factor. If disassembly of copyrighted object code is *per se* an unfair use, the owner of the copyright gains a *de facto* monopoly over the functional aspects of his work — aspects that were expressly denied copyright protection by Congress. 17 U.S.C. §102(b). In order to enjoy a lawful monopoly over the idea or functional principle underlying a work, the creator of the work must satisfy the more stringent standards imposed by the patent laws. *Bonito Boats, Inc. v. Thunder Craft Boats, Inc.*, 489 U.S. 141 (1989). Sega does not hold a patent on the Genesis console.

Because Sega's video game programs contain unprotected aspects that cannot be examined without copying, we afford them a lower degree of protection than more traditional literary works. . . . In light of all the considerations discussed above, we conclude that the second statutory factor also weighs in favor of Accolade.

(d)

As to the third statutory factor, Accolade disassembled entire programs written by Sega. Accordingly, the third factor weighs against Accolade. The fact that an entire work was copied does not, however, preclude a finding of fair use. *Sony Corp.*, 464.

U.S. at 449-50. . . . In fact, where the ultimate (as opposed to direct) use is as limited as it was here, the factor is of very little weight. . . .

(e)

In summary, careful analysis of the purpose and characteristics of Accolade's use of Sega's video game programs, the nature of the computer programs involved, and the nature of the market for video game cartridges yields the conclusion that the first, second, and fourth statutory fair use factors weigh in favor of Accolade, while only the third weighs in favor of Sega, and even then only slightly. Accordingly, Accolade clearly has by far the better case on the fair use issue.

We are not unaware of the fact that to those used to considering copyright issues in more traditional contexts, our result may seem incongruous at first blush. To oversimplify, the record establishes that Accolade, a commercial competitor of Sega, engaged in wholesale copying of Sega's copyrighted code as a preliminary step in the development of a competing product. However, the key to this case is that we are dealing with computer software, a relatively unexplored area in the world of copyright law. We must avoid the temptation of trying to force "the proverbial square peg in[to] a round hole." [*Computer Assocs. Int'l, Inc. v. Altai, Inc.*], 23 U.S.P.Q.2d at 1257.

In determining whether a challenged use of copyrighted material is fair, a court must keep in mind the public policy underlying the Copyright Act. . . . As discussed above, the fact that computer programs are distributed for public use in object code form often precludes public access to the ideas and functional concepts contained in those programs, and thus confers on the copyright owner a *de facto* monopoly over those ideas and functional concepts. That result defeats the fundamental purpose of the Copyright Act—to encourage the production of original works by protecting the expressive elements of those works while leaving the ideas, facts, and functional concepts in the public domain for others to build on. *Feist Publications*, [499] U.S. at [349-50]. . . .

Sega argues that the considerable time, effort, and money that went into development of the Genesis and Genesis-compatible video games militate against a finding of fair use. Borrowing from antitrust principles, Sega attempts to label Accolade a "free rider" on its product development efforts. In *Feist Publications*, however, the Court unequivocally rejected the "sweat of the brow" rationale for copyright protection. [499] U.S. at [353-54]. Under the Copyright Act, if a work is largely functional, it receives only weak protection. "This result is neither unfair nor unfortunate. It is the means by which copyright advances the progress of science and art." *Id*. at [350]. Here, while the work may not be largely functional, it incorporates functional elements which do not merit protection. The equitable considerations involved weigh on the side of public access. Accordingly, we reject Sega's argument.

(f)

We conclude that where disassembly is the only way to gain access to the ideas and functional elements embodied in a copyrighted computer program and where there is a legitimate reason for seeking such access, disassembly is a fair use of the copyrighted work, as a matter of law. Our conclusion does not, of course, insulate Accolade from a claim of copyright infringement with respect to its finished products. Sega has reserved the right to raise such a claim, and it may do so on remand. . . .

Sony Computer Entertainment, Inc. v. Connectix Corp.
203 F.3d 596 (9th Cir.), cert. denied, *531 U.S. 871 (2000)*

CANBY, J.: . . . Sony . . . produces and markets the Sony PlayStation console, a small computer with hand controls that connects to a television console and plays games that are inserted into the PlayStation on compact discs (CDs). Sony owns the copyright on the basic input-output system or BIOS, which is the software program that operates its PlayStation. Sony has asserted no patent rights in this proceeding. . . .

. . . The PlayStation console contains both (1) hardware components and (2) software known as firmware that is written onto a read-only memory (ROM) chip. The firmware is the Sony BIOS. . . .

Connectix's Virtual Game Station is software that "emulates" the functioning of the PlayStation console. That is, a consumer can load the Virtual Game Station software onto a computer, load a PlayStation game into the computer's CD-ROM drive, and play the Play-Station game. The Virtual Game Station software thus emulates both the hardware and firmware components of the Sony console. The Virtual Game Station does not play PlayStation games as well as Sony's PlayStation does. [Sony sued Connectix, claiming that when Connectix reverse engineered Sony's code during the course of creating the Virtual Game Station, it infringed Sony's copyrights. The district court granted an injunction in favor of Sony.] At the time of the injunction, Connectix had marketed its Virtual Game Station for Macintosh computer systems but had not yet completed Virtual Game Station software for Windows. . . .

C. Connectix's Reverse Engineering of the Sony BIOS

Connectix began developing the Virtual Game Station for Macintosh on about July 1, 1998. In order to develop a PlayStation emulator, Connectix needed to emulate both the PlayStation hardware and the firmware (the Sony BIOS).

Connectix first decided to emulate the PlayStation's hardware. In order to do so, Connectix engineers purchased a Sony PlayStation console and extracted the Sony BIOS from a chip inside the console. Connectix engineers then copied the Sony BIOS into the RAM of their computers and observed the functioning of the Sony BIOS in conjunction with the Virtual Game Station hardware emulation software as that hardware emulation software was being developed by Connectix. . . .

Once they had developed the hardware emulation software, Connectix engineers also used the Sony BIOS to "debug" the emulation software. In doing so, they repeatedly copied and disassembled discrete portions of the Sony BIOS.

Connectix also used the Sony BIOS to begin development of the Virtual Game Station for Windows. Specifically, they made daily copies to RAM of the Sony BIOS and used the Sony BIOS to develop certain Windows-specific systems for the Virtual Game Station for Windows. Although Connectix had its own BIOS at the time, Connectix engineers used the Sony BIOS because it contained CD-ROM code that the Connectix BIOS did not contain. . . .

During development of the Virtual Game Station, Connectix contacted Sony and requested "technical assistance". . . . Sony declined Connectix's request for assistance.

Connectix completed Virtual Game Station for Macintosh computers in late December 1998 or early January 1999. Connectix announced its new product at the MacWorld Expo on January 5, 1999. At MacWorld, Connectix marketed the Virtual Game Station as a "PlayStation emulator." The materials stated that the Virtual Game Station permits users to play "their favorite Playstation games" on a computer "even if you don't yet have a Sony PlayStation console." . . .

II.   Discussion . . .

A.   Fair Use . . .

1. Nature of the Copyrighted Work

Under our analysis of the second statutory factor, nature of the copyrighted work, we recognize that "some works are closer to the core of intended copyright protection than others." . . . Sony's BIOS lies at a distance from the core because it contains unprotected aspects that cannot be examined without copying. *See Sega*, 977 F.2d at 1526. We consequently accord it a "lower degree of protection than more traditional literary works." *Id*. As we have applied this standard, Connectix's copying of the Sony BIOS must have been "necessary" to have been fair use. *See id*. at 1524-26. We conclude that it was. . . .

We also reject the argument, urged by Sony, that Connectix infringed the Sony copyright by repeatedly observing the Sony BIOS in an emulated environment, thereby making repeated copies of the Sony BIOS. These intermediate copies could not have been "necessary" under *Sega*, contends Sony, because Connectix engineers could have disassembled the entire Sony BIOS first, then written their own Connectix BIOS, and used the Connectix BIOS to develop the Virtual Game Station hardware emulation software. We accept Sony's factual predicate for the limited purpose of this appeal. Our doing so, however, does not aid Sony.

Sony contends that Connectix's reverse engineering of the Sony BIOS should be considered unnecessary on the rationale that Connectix's decision to observe the Sony BIOS in an emulated environment required Connectix to make more intermediate copies of the Sony BIOS than if Connectix had performed a complete disassembly of the program. Under this logic, at least some of the intermediate copies were not necessary within the meaning of *Sega*. This construction stretches *Sega* too far. The "necessity" we addressed in *Sega* was the necessity of the method, i.e., disassembly, not the necessity of the number of times that method was applied. *See* 977 F.2d at 1524-26. In any event, the interpretation advanced by Sony would be a poor criterion for fair use. Most of the intermediate copies of the Sony BIOS were made by Connectix engineers when they booted up their computers and the Sony BIOS was copied into RAM. But if Connectix engineers had left their computers turned on throughout the period during which they were observing the Sony BIOS in an emulated environment, they would have made far fewer intermediate copies of the Sony BIOS (perhaps as few as one per computer). Even if we were inclined to supervise the engineering solutions of software companies in minute detail, and we are not, our application of the copyright law would not turn on such a distinction. Such a rule could be easily manipulated. More important, the rule urged by Sony would require that a software engineer, faced with two engineering solutions that each require intermediate copying of protected and unprotected material, often follow the *least efficient solution*. (In cases in which the solution that required the fewest number of intermediate copies was also the most efficient, an engineer would pursue it, presumably, without our urging.) This is precisely the kind of "wasted effort that the proscription against the copyright of ideas and facts . . . [is] designed to prevent." *Feist Publications, Inc. v. Rural Tel. Serv. Co.*, 499 U.S. 340, 354. . . . We decline to erect such a barrier in this case. If Sony wishes to obtain a lawful monopoly on the functional concepts in its software, it must satisfy the more stringent standards of the patent laws. *See Bonito Boats, Inc. v. Thunder Craft Boats, Inc.*, 489 U.S. 141, 160-61; *Sega*, 977 F.2d at 1526. This Sony has not done. The second statutory factor strongly favors Connectix.

2. Amount and Substantiality of the Portion Used

With respect to the third statutory factor, amount and substantiality of the portion used in relation to the copyrighted work as a whole, Connectix disassembled parts of the Sony BIOS and copied the entire Sony BIOS multiple times. This factor therefore weighs against Connectix. But as we concluded in *Sega*, in a case of intermediate infringement when the final product does not itself contain infringing material, this factor is of "very little weight." *Sega*, 977 F.2d at 1526-27. . . .

3. Purpose and Character of the Use

Under the first factor, purpose and character of the use, we inquire into whether Connectix's Virtual Game Station

> merely supersedes the objects of the original creation, or instead adds something new, with a further purpose or different character, altering the first with new expression, meaning, or message; it asks, in other words, whether and to what extent the new work is "transformative."

Campbell v. Acuff-Rose Music, Inc., 510 U.S. 569, 579 (1994) (internal quotation marks and citations omitted). . . .

We find that Connectix's Virtual Game Station is modestly transformative. The product creates a new platform, the personal computer, on which consumers can play games designed for the Sony PlayStation. This innovation affords opportunities for game play in new environments, specifically anywhere a Sony PlayStation console and television are not available, but a computer with a CD-ROM drive is. More important, the Virtual Game Station itself is a wholly new product, notwithstanding the similarity of uses and functions between the Sony Play-Station and the Virtual Game Station. . . .

Finally, we must weigh the extent of any transformation in Connectix's Virtual Game Station against the significance of other factors, including commercialism, that militate against fair use. . . . Connectix's commercial use of the copyrighted material was an intermediate one, and thus was only "indirect or derivative." *Sega,* 977 F.2d at 1522. Moreover, Connectix reverse-engineered the Sony BIOS to produce a product that would be compatible with games designed for the Sony PlayStation. We have recognized this purpose as a legitimate one under the first factor of the fair use analysis. *See id.* Upon weighing these factors, we find that the first factor favors Connectix. . . .

4. Effect of the Use upon the Potential Market . . .

. . . Whereas a work that merely supplants or supersedes another is likely to cause a substantially adverse impact on the potential market of the original, a transformative work is less likely to do so.

. . . [B]ecause the Virtual Game Station is transformative, and does not merely supplant the PlayStation console, the Virtual Game Station is a legitimate competitor in the market for platforms on which Sony and Sony-licensed games can be played. *See Sega,* 977 F.2d at 1522-23. For this reason, some economic loss by Sony as a result of this competition does not compel a finding of no fair use. Sony understandably seeks control over the market for devices that play games Sony produces or licenses. The copyright law, however, does not confer such a monopoly. . . .

NOTES AND QUESTIONS

1. Why shouldn't Accolade be required to enter a license agreement with Sega if it wishes to create games that can be played on the Sega consoles? Do you think that customers are likely to buy both Joe Montana Football and Mike Ditka Power Football? Should that decision be left to Sega, or to the market? Recall that in analyzing the fourth statutory fair use factor, the *Campbell* Court drew a "distinction between potentially remediable displacement and unremediable disparagement." *Campbell v. Acuff-Rose Music, Inc.,* 510 U.S. 569, 592. Where on this spectrum do Accolade's products lie? Does either end of the *Campbell* spectrum adequately capture the sort of competition at issue in *Sega*?

2. What is the ultimate holding of *Sega*? What would be an "illegitimate" reason for seeking access to functional elements of computer software? Do you agree with the court's conclusion that §107 may sometimes operate to privilege research by private-sector, commercial entities?

3. Is *Connectix* a necessary extension of the *Sega* holding? In particular, against which of the plaintiffs' products do the defendants in each case compete? Will consumers buy a Sony console if they can run PlayStation games on their PCs? The district court answered the latter question in the negative, ruling "that the Virtual Game Station was not transformative on the rationale that a computer screen and a television screen are interchangeable, and the Connectix product therefore merely 'supplants' the Sony Playstation console." *Connectix,* 203 F.3d at 607. Did the Ninth Circuit adequately answer this argument?

4. As you saw in subsection B.1, *supra,* the second fair use factor doesn't seem to drive the results in certain kinds of cases. In *Harper & Row,* President Ford's manuscript was highly

factual, yet the Court ultimately found *The Nation*'s use of that manuscript unfair. In *Campbell*, the parodied song was highly creative, yet the Court indicated that parody warrants considerable leeway. In both *Sega* and *Connectix*, in contrast, the second fair use factor was enormously important. Does it make sense to give special consideration to the nature of computer software, as both courts did? Do you agree with the Ninth Circuit's conclusion that denying fair use would threaten the boundary between copyright law and patent law? Should the second fair use factor have weighed equally strongly in both *Sega* and *Connectix*?

5. Recall Chapter 4.B's discussion addressing the suitability of copyright as the protective regime for software. Does the availability of the fair use doctrine make protecting software under copyright law more or less palatable?

The *Connectix* court stated, "If Sony wishes to obtain a lawful monopoly on the functional concepts in its software, it must satisfy the more stringent standards of the patent law." *Sony*, 203 F.3d at 605. After Sony lost its appeal of the denial of the preliminary injunction in the copyright case, it sued Connectix for patent infringement. (The parties eventually settled the case. *See Sony, Connectix Settle Claims, Plan Joint Software Products*, L.A. Times, Mar. 17, 2001, at C2.) Recall that the exclusive patent rights include the rights to make, use, and sell the patented invention. There is a good chance that if Sony's patents extend to the interfaces between its BIOS and other programs, including game programs, then at some point during Connectix' development process, it infringed those patents. If that is the case, then why do you think Sony chose to sue first for copyright infringement rather than patent infringement?

Should patent law and copyright law arrive at different results in decompilation cases? Would copyright doctrine matter much in this area if patent law protects facets of computer software, including interfaces (*see* Chapter 4, *supra* pages 240-41)? For arguments that patent law, too, should recognize some freedom to reverse engineer software to create interoperable products, see Julie E. Cohen & Mark A. Lemley, *Patent Scope and Innovation in the Software Industry*, 89 Cal. L. Rev. 1, 16-37 (2001); Maureen A. O'Rourke, *Toward a Doctrine of Fair Use in Patent Law*, 100 Colum. L. Rev. 1177 (2000).

6. How should courts address fair use claims by providers of products that help users modify copyrighted works to enhance their enjoyment? Re-read the facts of another pair of Ninth Circuit decisions: *Lewis Galoob Toys, Inc. v. Nintendo of America, Inc.*, 964 F.2d 965 (9th Cir. 1992), *cert. denied*, 507 U.S. 985 (1993), and *Micro Star v. FormGen, Inc.*, 154 F.3d 1107 (9th Cir. 1998), excerpted in Chapter 5.D.2. In *Galoob*, the Ninth Circuit held that the images produced by Galoob's Game Genie were not derivative works, but that even if they were, Galoob's use of Nintendo's copyrighted works was fair:

> The district court considered the potential market for derivative works based on Nintendo's game cartridges and found that: (1) "Nintendo has not, to date, issued or considered issuing altered versions of existing games," . . . and (2) Nintendo "has failed to show the reasonable likelihood of such a market." . . . The record supports the court's findings.

Galoob, 964 F.2d at 971.

In contrast, the *Micro Star* court rejected Micro Star's argument that its distribution of user-created "levels" for FormGen's Duke Nukem games was fair:

> Our examination of the section 107 factors yields straightforward results. Micro Star's use of FormGen's protected expression was made purely for financial gain. . . . The Supreme Court has explained that the second factor . . . is particularly significant because "some works are closer to the core of intended copyright protection than others, with the consequence that fair use is more difficult to establish when the former works are copied." *Campbell [v. Acuff-Rose Music, Inc.]*,

510 U.S. [569,] 586. The fair use defense will be much less likely to succeed when it is applied to fiction or fantasy creations, as opposed to factual works such as telephone listings. Duke-Nukem's world is made up of aliens, radioactive slime and freezer weapons — clearly fantasies, even by Los Angeles standards. N/I MAP files "expressly use [] the [D/N-3D] story's unique setting, characters, [and] plot,". . . . Only FormGen has the right to enter that market; whether it chooses to do so is entirely its business. . . . [Micro Star] is not protected by fair use.

Micro Star, 154 F.3d at 1113.

Are these decisions reconcilable? Do the facts of the two cases dictate opposite results?

7. In a portion of the opinion not excerpted above, the *Sega* court rejected three arguments that Accolade made to support the proposition that disassembly of object code is not copyright infringement. Specifically, Accolade argued that (1) infringement only occurred if the eventual end product resulting from disassembly violated one of the copyright owner's §106 rights; (2) §102(b) authorizes disassembly; and (3) §117 authorizes disassembly. Address each of these arguments and consider why the court ruled as it did.

Note on the Interoperability Provisions of the EU Software Directive

In Chapter 4.B, pages 244-45, *supra*, we briefly discussed the EU Software Directive. Directive 2009/24, Legal Protection of Computer Programs, 2009 O.J. (L 111) 16 (EC). Here we consider in more detail the steps that the directive takes to foster competition through interoperability.

According to Article 6 of the directive, entitled "Decompilation,"

> 1. The authorization of the rightholder shall not be required where reproduction of the code and translation of its form . . . are indispensable to obtain the information necessary to achieve the interoperability of an independently created computer program with other programs, provided that the following conditions are met:
> (a) those acts are performed by the licensee or by another person having a right to use a copy of a program . . .
> (b) the information necessary to achieve interoperability has not previously been readily available to the persons referred to in point (a); and
> (c) those acts are confined to the parts of the original program which are necessary in order to achieve interoperability.

Id., art. 6(1).

The recitals that serve as preface (and quasi-legislative history) to the EU Software Directive discuss what interoperability means. They define "interfaces" as "[t]he parts of the program which provide for . . . interconnection and interaction between elements of software and hardware. . . . " *Id.*, recital 10. "[I]nteroperability can be defined as the ability to exchange information and mutually to use the information which has been exchanged."

As discussed in Chapter 4, U.S. software companies have responded to the reverse engineering of their products by employing license agreements, including mass-market "shrinkwrap" or "clickwrap" agreements, that prohibit reverse engineering. The validity of these provisions is an unresolved question, as we discuss in Chapter 10. The EU Software Directive, in contrast, provides that "[a]ny contractual provisions contrary to Article 6 . . . shall be null and void." *Id.*, art. 8.

NOTES AND QUESTIONS

1. Does the EU Software Directive adopt *Sega*'s rule or is it different? What is the intent of Article 6? Would the directive shelter both a software vendor that decompiles an operating system to write an application that runs on the operating system and one that decompiles to write a competing operating system that implements the same interfaces? For a comparative discussion of U.S. and European law after the enactment of the first EU Software Directive in 1991 (which is substantially similar to the 2009 directive), see Pamela Samuelson, *Comparing the U.S. and E.C. Copyright Protection for Computer Programs: Are They More Different than They Seem?*, 13 J.L. & Com. 279 (1994).

2. Why should it make any difference whether means alternative to decompilation exist to allow the secondcomer to obtain the information it seeks? Both the cases and the EU Software Directive seem intended, at least in part, to induce software providers to disclose information sufficient to allow interoperability. Does that decision represent good policy? Professors Pamela Samuelson and Suzanne Scotchmer note that the expense of reverse engineering can be a factor influencing a company's decision whether to take a license instead. They argue that encouraging licensing can be beneficial because it enables innovators to recoup their research and development costs, and that reducing a secondcomer's costs of entry too far may harm innovation. Pamela Samuelson & Suzanne Scotchmer, *The Law and Economics of Reverse Engineering*, 111 Yale L.J. 1575 (2002). Is forcing secondcomers to engage in costly and laborious reverse engineering wasteful or efficient?

3. Does the EU's decision to invalidate license provisions contrary to the reverse engineering right make sense? Should the U.S. take a similar route? We return to this question in Chapters 8 and 10.

≡ ### *Perfect 10, Inc. v. Amazon, Inc.*
≡ *508 F.3d 1146 (9th Cir. 2007)*

[Review pages 424-27 *supra* for the facts of this case. The district court held that Google's display of thumbnail versions of infringing copies of Perfect 10's images most likely was not fair use. *Perfect 10 v. Google, Inc.*, 416 F. Supp. 2d 828 (C.D. Cal. 2006). The court concluded that "[t]he first, second, and fourth fair use factors weigh slightly in favor of P10. The third weighs in neither party's favor." *Id.* at 851. What follows is the Ninth Circuit's holding on the fair use issue.]

IKUTA, J.: . . .

Fair Use Defense

. . . Google contends that its use of thumbnails is a fair use of the images and therefore does not constitute an infringement of Perfect 10's copyright. . . .

In applying the fair use analysis in this case, we are guided by *Kelly v. Arriba Soft Corp.*, which considered substantially the same use of copyrighted photographic images as is at issue here. *See* 336 F.3d 811 [(9th Cir. 2003)]. In *Kelly*, a photographer brought a direct infringement claim against Arriba, the operator of an Internet search engine. The search engine provided thumbnail versions of the photographer's images in response to search queries. *Id.* at 815-16. We held that Arriba's use of thumbnail images was a fair use primarily based on the transformative nature of a search engine and its benefit to the public. *Id.* at 818-22. We also concluded that Arriba's use of the thumbnail images did not harm the photographer's market for his image. *Id*. at 821-22.

In this case, the district court determined that Google's use of thumbnails was not a fair use and distinguished *Kelly*. *Perfect 10*, 416 F. Supp. 2d [828, 845-51 (C.D. Cal. 2006)]. We consider these distinctions in the context of the four-factor fair use analysis.

Purpose and character of the use. . . . As noted in *Campbell*, a "transformative work" is one that alters the original work "with new expression, meaning, or message." *Campbell* [*v. Acuff-Rose Music, Inc.*], 510 U.S. [569, 579 (1994)]. . . .

Google's use of thumbnails is highly transformative. In *Kelly*, we concluded that Arriba's use of thumbnails was transformative because "Arriba's use of the images serve[d] a different function than Kelly's use — improving access to information on the [I]nternet versus artistic expression." *Kelly*, 336 F.3d at 819. Although an image may have been created originally to serve an entertainment, aesthetic, or informative function, a search engine transforms the image into a pointer directing a user to a source of information. Just as a "parody has an obvious claim to transformative value" because "it can provide social benefit, by shedding light on an earlier work, and, in the process, creating a new one," *Campbell*, 510 U.S. at 579, a search engine provides social benefit by incorporating an original work into a new work, namely, an electronic reference tool. Indeed, a search engine may be more transformative than a parody because a search engine provides an entirely new use for the original work, while a parody typically has the same entertainment purpose as the original work. . . . In other words, a search engine puts images "in a different context" so that they are "transformed into a new creation." [citation omitted].

The fact that Google incorporates the entire Perfect 10 image into the search engine results does not diminish the transformative nature of Google's use. As the district court correctly noted, *Perfect 10*, 416 F. Supp. 2d at 848-49, we determined in *Kelly* that even making an exact copy of a work may be transformative so long as the copy serves a different function than the original work, *Kelly*, 336 F.3d at 818-19. For example, the First Circuit has held that the republication of photos taken for a modeling portfolio in a newspaper was transformative because the photos served to inform, as well as entertain. *See [Núñ]ez v. Caribbean Int'l News Corp.*, 235 F.3d 18, 22-23 (1st Cir. 2000). . . . Here, Google uses Perfect 10's images in a new context to serve a different purpose.

The district court nevertheless determined that Google's use of thumbnail images was less transformative than Arriba's use of thumbnails in *Kelly* because Google's use of thumbnails superseded Perfect 10's right to sell its reduced-size images for use on cell phones. *See Perfect 10*, 416 F. Supp. 2d at 849. The district court stated that "mobile users can download and save the thumbnails displayed by Google Image Search onto their phones," and concluded "to the extent that users may choose to download free images to their phone rather than purchase [Perfect 10's] reduced-size images, Google's use supersedes [Perfect 10's]." *Id*.

Additionally, the district court determined that the commercial nature of Google's use weighed against its transformative nature. *Id*. Although *Kelly* held that the commercial use of the photographer's images by Arriba's search engine was less exploitative than typical commercial use, and thus weighed only slightly against a finding of fair use, *Kelly*, 336 F.3d at 818-20, the district court here distinguished *Kelly* on the ground that some website owners in the AdSense program had infringing Perfect 10 images on their websites, *Perfect 10*, 416 F. Supp. 2d at 846-47. The district court held that because Google's thumbnails "lead users to sites that directly benefit Google's bottom line," the AdSense program increased the commercial nature of Google's use of Perfect 10's images. *Id*. at 847. . . .

We note that the superseding use in this case is not significant at present: the district court did not find that any downloads for mobile phone use had taken place. *See Perfect 10*,

416 F. Supp. 2d at 849. Moreover, while Google's use of thumbnails to direct users to AdSense partners containing infringing content adds a commercial dimension that did not exist in *Kelly*, the district court did not determine that this commercial element was significant. *See id.* at 848-49. The district court stated that Google's AdSense programs as a whole contributed "$630 million, or 46% of total revenues" to Google's bottom line, but noted that this figure did not "break down the much smaller amount attributable to websites that contain infringing content." *Id.* at 847 & n. 12 (internal quotation omitted).

We conclude that the significantly transformative nature of Google's search engine, particularly in light of its public benefit, outweighs Google's superseding and commercial uses of the thumbnails in this case. . . .

. . . Therefore, this factor weighs heavily in favor of Google.

The nature of the copyrighted work. With respect to the second factor, "the nature of the copyrighted work," our decision in *Kelly* is directly on point. There we held that the photographer's images were "creative in nature" and thus "closer to the core of intended copyright protection than are more fact-based works." *Kelly*, 336 F.3d at 820 (internal quotation omitted). However, because the photos appeared on the Internet before Arriba used thumbnail versions in its search engine results, this factor weighed only slightly in favor of the photographer. *Id.*

Here, the district court found that Perfect 10's images were creative but also previously published. *Perfect 10*, 416 F. Supp. 2d at 850. The right of first publication is "the author's right to control the first public appearance of his expression." *Harpers & Row* [*Publishers v. Nation Enters.*] 471 U.S. [539, 564 (1985)]. Because this right encompasses "the choices of when, where, and in what form first to publish a work," *id.*, an author exercises and exhausts this one-time right by publishing the work in any medium. Once Perfect 10 has exploited this commercially valuable right of first publication by putting its images on the Internet for paid subscribers, Perfect 10 is no longer entitled to the enhanced protection available for an unpublished work. Accordingly the district court did not err in holding that this factor weighed only slightly in favor of Perfect 10. *See Perfect 10*, 416 F. Supp. 2d at 849-50.

The amount and substantiality of the portion used. . . . In *Kelly*, we held Arriba's use of the entire photographic image was reasonable in light of the purpose of a search engine. *Kelly*, 336 F.3d at 821. Specifically, we noted, "[i]t was necessary for Arriba to copy the entire image to allow users to recognize the image and decide whether to pursue more information about the image or the originating [website]. If Arriba only copied part of the image, it would be more difficult to identify it, thereby reducing the usefulness of the visual search engine." *Id.* Accordingly, we concluded that this factor did not weigh in favor of either party. *Id.* Because the same analysis applies to Google's use of Perfect 10's image, the district court did not err in finding that this factor favored neither party.

Effect of use on the market. . . . In *Kelly*, we concluded that Arriba's use of the thumbnail images did not harm the market for the photographer's full-size images. *See Kelly*, 336 F.3d at 821-22. We reasoned that because thumbnails were not a substitute for the full-sized images, they did not harm the photographer's ability to sell or license his full-sized images. *Id.* The district court here followed *Kelly's* reasoning, holding that Google's use of thumbnails did not hurt Perfect 10's market for full-size images. *See Perfect 10*, 416 F. Supp. 2d at 850-51. We agree.

Perfect 10 argues that the district court erred because the likelihood of market harm may be presumed if the intended use of an image is for commercial gain. However, this presumption does not arise when a work is transformative because "market substitution is at least less certain, and market harm may not be so readily inferred." *Campbell*, 510 U.S. at 591. As previously discussed, Google's use of thumbnails for search engine purposes is highly transformative, and so market harm cannot be presumed.

Perfect 10 also has a market for reduced-size images, an issue not considered in *Kelly*. The district court held that "Google's use of thumbnails likely does harm the potential market for the downloading of [Perfect 10's] reduced-size images onto cell phones." *Perfect 10*, 416 F. Supp. 2d at 851 (emphasis omitted). The district court reasoned that persons who can obtain Perfect 10 images free of charge from Google are less likely to pay for a download, and the availability of Google's thumbnail images would harm Perfect 10's market for cell phone downloads. *Id.* As we discussed above, the district court did not make a finding that Google users have downloaded thumbnail images for cell phone use. This potential harm to Perfect 10's market remains hypothetical. We conclude that this factor favors neither party.

Having undertaken a case-specific analysis of all four factors, we now weigh these factors together "in light of the purposes of copyright." *Campbell*, 510 U.S. at 578; *see also Kelly*, 336 F.3d at 818. . . . In this case, Google has put Perfect 10's thumbnail images (along with millions of other thumbnail images) to a use fundamentally different than the use intended by Perfect 10. In doing so, Google has provided a significant benefit to the public. Weighing this significant transformative use against the unproven use of Google's thumbnails for cell phone downloads, and considering the other fair use factors, all in light of the purpose of copyright, we conclude that Google's use of Perfect 10's thumbnails is a fair use. . . . [W]e vacate the preliminary injunction regarding Google's use of thumbnail images.

NOTES AND QUESTIONS

1. Did Arriba or Google transform the plaintiffs' works or simply their context? Should your answer to this question affect the fair use analysis?

2. Do *Arriba* and *Perfect 10* mean that search engines should never worry about copyright infringement claims? After *Perfect 10*, what arguments can a copyright owner make about a visual search engine's effects on the potential market for or value of its works? What evidence might demonstrate such effects? Should such evidence change the result of the fair use analysis?

What if the search engine is also a comparison shopping service — i.e., the search engine makes copies of web pages and extracts product and pricing information? When a user enters the name of a product, the engine returns a list of what sites are offering it for sale and at what price. *See Ticketmaster Corp. v. Tickets. com, Inc.*, No. 99CV7654, 2000 WL 1887522, at *3 (C.D. Cal. Aug. 10, 2000) (stating that it would likely excuse the copying of web pages as a step in creating the database containing uncopyrighted product and pricing information as fair, citing *Sony v. Connectix* and "certain prior cases" as authority for its view).

3. Is the *Perfect 10* court's analysis of the four factors consistent with the analysis of courts in the other cases you have read?

4. Many students have heard of the Turnitin software system. Schools using the system require students to submit electronic versions of papers to Turnitin and the Turnitin software performs a plagiarism analysis by comparing students' papers to certain other content. That content may include student papers previously submitted to and archived by Turnitin in digital form. Do these archival copies infringe the student authors' copyrights? *See Vanderhye v. IParadigms, LLC*, 562 F.3d 630, 638-45 (4th Cir. 2009) (finding fair use, adopting the district court's view that " 'Turnitin [] uses the papers for an entirely different purpose [than the original], namely, to prevent plagiarism and protect the students' written works from plagiarism . . . by archiving the students' works as digital code,' " and citing *Perfect 10* for support).

3.   Market Failure or "Productive Consumption"?

So far, our exploration of fair use in cultural and technological contexts has identified at least two underlying theories of fair use. First, a court is more likely to excuse a use as fair if it is productive, adding something new that enhances the benefit the public derives from the earlier copyrighted work. Second, a court is also more likely to take a favorable view of uses that are reasonable and customary, whether under an implied consent theory or under a more general theory of socially acceptable conduct.

Courts disagree, however, about how to treat certain acts of simple copying, such as copying for personal use or for research or classroom use, under these theories. Under the "productive use" theory, what makes a use productive enough to be fair? Must the use always "transform" the copyrighted work, or do other sorts of uses count? Specifically, can simple copying and consumption ever qualify as "productive"? Under the "reasonable and customary use" theory, should the fact that certain kinds of copying are widespread and customary be enough to insulate them, even as technological developments make such copying easier and easier?

The leading case involving copying for personal home use is the Supreme Court's decision in *Sony Corp. of America v. Universal City Studios, Inc.*, reproduced below. As you read the case, ask yourself whether the Court seems to adopt either of the above theories of fair use, or some other theory.

Sony Corporation of America v. Universal City Studios, Inc.
464 U.S. 417 (1984)

STEVENS, J.: Petitioners manufacture and sell home video tape recorders [called "Betamax" or "VTRs"]. Respondents own the copyrights on some of the television programs that are broadcast on the public airwaves. Some members of the general public use video tape recorders sold by petitioners to record some of these broadcasts, as well as a large number of other broadcasts. The question presented is whether the sale of petitioners' copying equipment to the general public violates any of the rights conferred upon respondents by the Copyright Act. . . .

[After a trial, the district court denied plaintiffs' claims. The Ninth Circuit reversed, finding defendants liable for contributory infringement.]

The respondents and Sony both conducted surveys of the way the Betamax machine was used by several hundred owners during a sample period in 1978. Although there were some differences in the surveys, they both showed that the primary use of the machine for most owners was "time-shifting," — the practice of recording a program to view it once at a later time, and thereafter erasing it. Time-shifting enables viewers to see programs they otherwise would miss because they are not at home, are occupied with other tasks, or are viewing a program on another station at the time of a broadcast that they desire to watch. Both surveys also showed, however, that a substantial number of interviewees had accumulated libraries of tapes. Sony's survey indicated that over 80% of the interviewees watched at least as much regular television as they had before owning a Betamax. Respondents offered no evidence of decreased television viewing by Betamax owners.

Sony introduced considerable evidence describing television programs that could be copied without objection from any copyright holder, with special emphasis on sports, religious, and educational programming. For example, their survey indicated that 7.3% of all Betamax use is to record sports events, and representatives of professional baseball, football, basketball, and hockey testified that they had no objection to the recording of their televised events for home use. . . .

[As discussed in Chapter 6.C, pages 489-92 *supra*, the Court looked to the Patent Act in formulating a standard for contributory liability of equipment manufacturers and distributors, and concluded that "the sale of copying equipment, like the sale of other articles of commerce, does not constitute contributory infringement if the product is widely used for legitimate, unobjectionable purposes. Indeed, it need merely be capable of substantial noninfringing uses."]

The question is thus whether the Betamax is capable of commercially significant non-infringing uses. In order to resolve that question, we need not explore *all* the different potential uses of the machine and determine whether or not they would constitute infringement. Rather, we need only consider whether on the basis of the facts as found by the district court a significant number of them would be non-infringing. Moreover, in order to resolve this case we need not give precise content to the question of how much use is commercially significant. For one potential use of the Betamax plainly satisfies this standard, however it is understood: private, noncommercial time-shifting in the home. It does so both (A) because respondents have no right to prevent other copyright holders from authorizing it for their programs, and (B) because the District Court's factual findings reveal that even the unauthorized home time-shifting of respondents' programs is legitimate fair use.

A. Authorized Time-Shifting

. . . [T]he findings of the District Court make it clear that time-shifting may enlarge the total viewing audience and that many producers are willing to allow private time-shifting to continue, at least for an experimental time period. . . .

. . . [T]wo items in the record deserve specific mention.

First is the testimony of John Kenaston, the station manager of Channel 58, an educational station in Los Angeles affiliated with the Public Broadcasting Service. He explained and authenticated the station's published guide to its programs. For each program, the guide tells whether unlimited home taping is authorized, home taping is authorized subject to certain restrictions (such as erasure within seven days), or home taping is not authorized at all. The Spring 1978 edition of the guide described 107 programs. Sixty-two of those programs or 58% authorize some home taping. Twenty-one of them or almost 20% authorize unrestricted home taping.

Second is the testimony of Fred Rogers, president of the corporation that produces and owns the copyright on Mister Rogers' Neighborhood. The program is carried by more public television stations than any other program. Its audience numbers over 3,000,000 families a day. He testified that he had absolutely no objection to home taping for noncommercial use and expressed the opinion that it is a real service to families to be able to record children's programs and to show them at appropriate times.

If there are millions of owners of VTR's who make copies of televised sports events, religious broadcasts, and educational programs such as Mister Rogers' Neighborhood, and if the proprietors of those programs welcome the practice, the business of supplying the equipment that makes such copying feasible should not be stifled simply because the equipment is used by some individuals to make unauthorized reproductions of respondents' works. The respondents do not represent a class composed of all copyright holders. . . .

Of course, the fact that other copyright holders may welcome the practice of time-shifting does not mean that respondents should be deemed to have granted a license to copy their programs. Third-party conduct would be wholly irrelevant in an action for direct infringement of respondents' copyrights. But in an action for *contributory* infringement against the seller of copying equipment, the copyright holder may not prevail unless the relief that he seeks affects only his programs, or unless he speaks for virtually all copyright holders with an interest in the outcome. . . .

B. Unauthorized Time-Shifting

Even unauthorized uses of a copyrighted work are not necessarily infringing. An unlicensed use of the copyright is not an infringement unless it conflicts with one of the specific exclusive rights conferred by the copyright statute. *Twentieth Century Music Corp. v. Aiken*, 422 U.S. 151, 154-155. Moreover, the definition of exclusive rights in §106 of the present Act is prefaced by the words "subject to sections 107 through 118." Those sections describe a variety of uses of copyrighted material that "are not infringements of copyright notwithstanding the provisions of §106." The most pertinent in this case is §107, the legislative endorsement of the doctrine of "fair use."

That section identifies various factors that enable a Court to apply an "equitable rule of reason" analysis to particular claims of infringement. Although not conclusive, the first factor requires that "the commercial or nonprofit character of an activity" be weighed in any fair use decision. If the Betamax were used to make copies for a commercial or profit-making purpose, such use would presumptively be unfair. The contrary presumption is appropriate here, however, because the District Court's findings plainly establish that time-shifting for private home use must be characterized as a noncommercial, nonprofit activity. Moreover, when one considers the nature of a televised copyrighted audiovisual work, see 17 U.S.C. §107(2) . . . and that time-shifting merely enables a viewer to see such a work which he had been invited to witness in its entirety free of charge, the fact that the entire work is reproduced, see §107(3), does not have its ordinary effect of militating against a finding of fair use.[33]

This is not, however, the end of the inquiry because Congress has also directed us to consider "the effect of the use upon the potential market for or value of the copyrighted work." §107(4). The purpose of copyright is to create incentives for creative effort. Even copying for noncommercial purposes may impair the copyright holder's ability to obtain the rewards that Congress intended him to have. But a use that has no demonstrable effect upon the potential market for, or the value of, the copyrighted work need not be prohibited in order

_____

33. It has been suggested that "consumptive uses of copyrights by home VTR users are commercial even if the consumer does not sell the homemade tape because the consumer will not buy tapes separately sold by the copyright holder." Home Recording of Copyrighted Works: Hearing before Subcommittee on Courts, Civil Liberties and the Administration of Justice of the House Committee on the Judiciary, 97th Congress, 2d Session, pt. 2, p. 1250 (1982) (memorandum of Prof. Laurence H. Tribe). Furthermore, "[t]he error in excusing such theft as noncommercial," we are told, "can be seen by simple analogy: jewel theft is not converted into a noncommercial veniality if stolen jewels are simply worn rather than sold." *Ibid.* The premise and the analogy are indeed simple, but they add nothing to the argument. The use to which stolen jewelery is put is quite irrelevant in determining whether depriving its true owner of his present possessory interest in it is venial; because of the nature of the item and the true owner's interests in physical possession of it, the law finds the taking objectionable even if the thief does not use the item at all. Theft of a particular item of personal property of course may have commercial significance, for the thief deprives the owner of his right to sell that particular item to any individual. Timeshifting does not even remotely entail comparable consequences to the copyright owner. Moreover, the time-shifter no more steals the program by watching it once than does the live viewer, and the live viewer is no more likely to buy prerecorded videotapes than is the time-shifter. Indeed, no live viewer would buy a prerecorded videotape if he did not have access to a VTR.

to protect the author's incentive to create. The prohibition of such noncommercial uses would merely inhibit access to ideas without any countervailing benefit.

Thus, although every commercial use of copyrighted material is presumptively an unfair exploitation of the monopoly privilege that belongs to the owner of the copyright, noncommercial uses are a different matter. A challenge to a noncommercial use of a copyrighted work requires proof either that the particular use is harmful, or that if it should become widespread, it would adversely affect the potential market for the copyrighted work. Actual present harm need not be shown; such a requirement would leave the copyright holder with no defense against predictable damage. Nor is it necessary to show with certainty that future harm will result. What is necessary is a showing by a preponderance of the evidence that *some* meaningful likelihood of future harm exists. If the intended use is for commercial gain, that likelihood may be presumed. But if it is for a noncommercial purpose, the likelihood must be demonstrated.

In this case, respondents failed to carry their burden with regard to home time-shifting. . . .

[The District Court] rejected respondents' "fear that persons 'watching' the original telecast of a program will not be measured in the live audience and the ratings and revenues will decrease," by observing that current measurement technology allows the Betamax audience to be reflected. *Id.*, at 466. It rejected respondents' prediction "that live television or movie audiences will decrease as more people watch Betamax tapes as an alternative," with the observation that "[t]here is no factual basis for [the underlying] assumption." *Ibid.* It rejected respondents' "fear that time-shifting will reduce audiences for telecast reruns," and concluded instead that "given current market practices, this should aid plaintiffs rather than harm them." *Ibid.* And it declared that respondents' suggestion that "theater or film rental exhibition of a program will suffer because of time-shift recording of that program" "lacks merit." *Id.*, at 467. . . .

The District Court's conclusions are buttressed by the fact that to the extent time-shifting expands public access to freely broadcast television programs, it yields societal benefits. In *Community Television of Southern California v. Gottfried*, 459 U.S. 458, 508 n. 12 (1983), we acknowledged the public interest in making television broadcasting more available. Concededly, that interest is not unlimited. But it supports an interpretation of the concept of "fair use" that requires the copyright holder to demonstrate some likelihood of harm before he may condemn a private act of time-shifting as a violation of federal law.

When these factors are all weighed in the "equitable rule of reason" balance, we must conclude that this record amply supports the District Court's conclusion that home time-shifting is fair use. In light of the findings of the District Court regarding the state of the empirical data, it is clear that the Court of Appeals erred in holding that the statute as presently written bars such conduct. . . .

BLACKMUN, J., with whom MARSHALL, J., POWELL, J., and REHNQUIST, J., join, dissenting: . . . *Two* kinds of Betamax usage are at issue here.[2] The first is "time-shifting," whereby the user records a program in order to watch it at a later time, and then records over it, and thereby erases the program, after a single viewing. The second is "library-building," in which the user records a program in order to keep it for repeated viewing over a longer term. Sony's advertisements, at various times, have suggested that Betamax users "record favorite shows" or

---

2. This case involves only the home recording for home use of television programs broadcast free over the airwaves. No issue is raised concerning cable or pay television, or the sharing or trading of tapes.

"build a library." Sony's Betamax advertising has never contained warnings about copyright infringement, although a warning does appear in the Betamax operating instructions. . . .

There are situations . . . in which strict enforcement of th[e copyright] monopoly would inhibit the very "Progress of Science and useful Arts" that copyright is intended to promote. An obvious example is the researcher or scholar whose own work depends on the ability to refer to and to quote the work of prior scholars. Obviously, no author could create a new work if he were first required to repeat the research of every author who had gone before him. The scholar, like the ordinary user, of course could be left to bargain with each copyright owner for permission to quote from or refer to prior works. But there is a crucial difference between the scholar and the ordinary user. When the ordinary user decides that the owner's price is too high, and forgoes use of the work, only the individual is the loser. When the scholar forgoes the use of a prior work, not only does his own work suffer, but the public is deprived of his contribution to knowledge. The scholar's work, in other words, produces external benefits from which everyone profits. In such a case, the fair use doctrine acts as a form of subsidy — albeit at the first author's expense — to permit the second author to make limited use of the first author's work for the public good. See Latman Fair Use Study 31; Gordon, Fair Use as Market Failure: A Structural Analysis of the *Betamax* Case and its Predecessors, 82 Colum. L. Rev. 1600, 1630 (1982).

A similar subsidy may be appropriate in a range of areas other than pure scholarship. The situations in which fair use is most commonly recognized are listed in §107 itself; fair use may be found when a work is used "for purposes such as criticism, comment, news reporting, teaching . . . scholarship, or research." The House and Senate Reports expand on this list somewhat, and other examples may be found in the case law. Each of these uses, however, reflects a common theme: each is a *productive* use, resulting in some added benefit to the public beyond that produced by the first author's work. The fair use doctrine, in other words, permits works to be used for "socially laudable purposes." See Copyright Office, Briefing Papers on Current Issues, reprinted in 1975 House Hearings 2051, 2055. I am aware of no case in which the reproduction of a copyrighted work for the sole benefit of the user has been held to be fair use. . . .

The making of a videotape recording for home viewing is an ordinary rather than a productive use of the Studios' copyrighted works. The District Court found that "Betamax owners use the copy for the same purpose as the original. They add nothing of their own." 480 F. Supp., at 453. Although applying the fair use doctrine to home VTR recording, as Sony argues, may increase public access to material broadcast free over the public airwaves, I think Sony's argument misconceives the nature of copyright. Copyright gives the author a right to limit or even to cut off access to his work. *Fox Film Corp. v. Doyal*, 286 U.S. 123, 127 (1932). A VTR recording creates no public benefit sufficient to justify limiting this right. Nor is this right extinguished by the copyright owner's choice to make the work available over the airwaves. Section 106 of the 1976 Act grants the copyright owner the exclusive right to control the performance and the reproduction of his work, and the fact that he has licensed a single television performance is really irrelevant to the existence of his right to control its reproduction. Although a television broadcast may be free to the viewer, this fact is equally irrelevant; a book borrowed from the public library may not be copied any more freely than a book that is purchased.

It may be tempting, as, in my view, the Court today is tempted, to stretch the doctrine of fair use so as to permit unfettered use of this new technology in order to increase access to television programming. But such an extension risks eroding the very basis of copyright law, by depriving authors of control over their works and consequently of their incentive to create. . . .

"NO MORE PACKING IN THE MIDDLE OF THE NIGHT! NO MORE RUNNING FROM THE BETAMAX PATROL! HERBERT, DARLING, WE'RE CLEAN!"

© 1984 King Features. Reprinted with special permission of King Features Syndicate.

NOTES AND QUESTIONS

1. Is the *Sony* majority correct in describing the use of VCRs for time-shifting as noncommercial? The majority notes that the practice of time-shifting does not affect the revenues of copyright owners. In an era in which many episodes of popular television series can be downloaded, purchased, or rented, would the fair use determination be the same? Would the fair use analysis differ if technology embedded in VCRs or digital video recorders (DVRs) either causes the devices not to record commercial advertisements in television broadcasts or allows users automatically to skip over any commercials that are recorded? Would the results of the fair use analysis differ if the plaintiff copyright owners could produce evidence that the devices are primarily used to create libraries of programs for repeat viewing? What obligations (if any) should device manufacturers have to discourage such conduct?

Recall *Cartoon Network LP v. CSC Holdings, Inc.*, 536 F.3d 121 (2d Cir. 2008), *cert. denied*, 129 S.Ct. 1890 (2009), Chapter 5.F.1 *supra*. There the court held that a cable company did not commit direct copyright infringement by storing programs at the instruction of customers using its remote DVR system. The court noted that any copies were actually made by the company's customers. Would the *Sony* Court view such customer copying as fair?

2. To what extent do considerations of productive use appear to play a role in the Court's decision? To what extent do considerations of reasonable and customary use appear to play a role?

3. Before the Court analyzed the fair use question, it pointed to some copyright owners that did not object to home taping of their television broadcasts. One of the copyright owners, Channel 58 in Los Angeles, gave express permission in its published program guides. Was such permission needed?

4. This first Supreme Court decision on fair use under the 1976 Act was decided 5-4. After oral arguments in 1983, the original vote was 5-4 in favor of infringement. As the

opinions were being circulated, with Justice Blackmun's proposed opinion as the majority, a shifting majority caused the Court to request reargument for the following term. Justice Blackmun's proposed majority opinion ultimately became the dissent. *See* Paul Goldstein, Copyright's Highway: From Gutenberg to the Celestial Jukebox 121-28 (rev. ed. 2003).

5. Some commentators have argued that if *Sony* had come out the other way, the copyright industries would have suppressed VCR technology and the lucrative video rental market would not have developed. Do you agree?

6. Should the fair use analysis shield personal uses or uses that occur in the privacy of the home? Why or why not? Exceptions to copyright for private or personal use have long been part of the copyright laws of many European countries. In particular, prior to the EU's 2001 directive on copyright harmonization, the copyright laws of France, Germany, the Netherlands, and Spain included broad private use exceptions.

Recall the "three-step test" of Article 9(2) of the Berne Convention and Article 13 of the TRIPS Agreement, pages 532-33 *supra*. Although the EU allows member states to provide exceptions or limitations to copyright, national discretion is limited by language that very closely tracks the three-step test. Exceptions "shall only be applied in certain special cases which do not conflict with a normal exploitation of the work or other subject-matter and do not unreasonably prejudice the legitimate interests of the rightholder." Directive 2001/29/EC of the European Parliament and of the Council of 22 May 2001 on the harmonisation of certain aspects of copyright and related rights in the information society, 2001 O.J. (L 167) 10, art. 5(5).

Some European courts have already confronted the challenge of reconciling the personal use exception with the directive's three-step test. In two cases, the plaintiffs had unknowingly purchased copy-protected DVDs. They sued the producers of the DVDs based on the personal copying exceptions afforded by the French and Belgian copyright laws. The French court held that the right of private copying in French copyright law does not violate the three-step test. Cour. d'appel Paris, No. RG:03/8500, *Stéphane P. v. Universal Pictures Video France* (Apr. 22, 2005). However, the Belgian court reasoned that the personal copying exception is simply "a granted immunity against prosecution," and not an affirmative right for users. *L'ASBL Association Belge des Consommateurs TestAchats/SE EMI Recorded Music Belgium*, Jugement du 25 mai 2004, No 2004/46/A du rôle des réferes, at 2. Would the courts have held the same way if they interpreted the three-step test as the Max Planck Institute suggests in its Declaration, *supra* page 533?

If Congress added language similar to art. 5(5) of the European copyright directive to the end of §107, would that assure U.S. compliance with international treaty obligations? Would such a sentence change the nature of the fair use inquiry?

Note on "Productive Consumption"

Critical to the question whether the copying in *Sony* was fair was whether it could be characterized as "productive" in some way related to the goals of copyright law. For the dissenters, the answer was clear. Justice Blackmun argued that the fair use doctrine permits copying only for socially valuable purposes that generate "external benefits" for everyone. *Sony*, 464 U.S. at 477-78 (Blackmun, J., dissenting). He concluded that this characterization does not apply to copying for personal home use, because if an ordinary user forgoes the use of a work because the price is too high, "only the individual is the loser." *Id.*

The majority addressed the question of "productive use," and responded to Justice Blackmun's arguments, in a footnote:

> Congress has plainly instructed us that fair use analysis calls for a sensitive balancing of interests. The distinction between "productive" and "unproductive" uses may be helpful in calibrating the balance, but it cannot be wholly determinative. Although copying to promote a scholarly endeavor certainly has a stronger claim to fair use than copying to avoid interrupting a poker game, the question is not simply two-dimensional. For one thing, it is not true that all copyrights are fungible. Some copyrights govern material with broad potential secondary markets. Such material may well have a broader claim to protection because of the greater potential for commercial harm. Copying a news broadcast may have a stronger claim to fair use than copying a motion picture. And, of course, not all uses are fungible. Copying for commercial gain has a much weaker claim to fair use than copying for personal enrichment. But the notion of social "productivity" cannot be a complete answer to this analysis. A teacher who copies to prepare lecture notes is clearly productive. But so is a teacher who copies for the sake of broadening his personal understanding of his specialty. Or a legislator who copies for the sake of broadening her understanding of what her constituents are watching; or a constituent who copies a news program to help make a decision on how to vote.

Sony, 464 U.S. at 455 n. 40.

The majority went on to identify examples of "productive" uses that involve no "transformation" of the copyrighted work and no addition of new creative expression:

> Making a copy of a copyrighted work for the convenience of a blind person is expressly identified by the House Committee Report as an example of fair use, with no suggestion that anything more than a purpose to entertain or to inform need motivate the copying. In a hospital setting, using a VTR to enable a patient to see programs he would otherwise miss has no productive purpose other than contributing to the psychological well-being of the patient. Virtually any time-shifting that increases viewer access to television programming may result in a comparable benefit. The statutory language does not identify any dichotomy between productive and nonproductive time-shifting, but does require consideration of the economic consequences of copying.

Id.

Note on Market Failure Theory

A different theory of fair use, which has garnered both widespread support and widespread criticism, downplays the emphasis on "productive" or "customary" uses and instead approaches the problem from an economic perspective. According to this theory, "market failure" both justifies a court's excusing certain infringements as fair and provides a unifying concept to explain the results in fair use cases. Briefly, the market failure argument goes something like this: In a perfectly competitive market, consensual transfers result in the movement of resources to those who value them the most. By according creators certain exclusive copyright rights, Congress has facilitated a market in copyrighted works in which copyright owners may license their creations to those who value them. Market flaws of various sorts, however, may prevent consensual exchanges from occurring. In such cases, a court may appropriately excuse infringing conduct as fair.

In a widely cited article (including by the dissent in *Sony*), Professor Wendy Gordon described the types of market failure that may exist in markets for copyrighted works:

> Copyright markets will not . . . always function adequately. . . . [A]t times bargaining may be exceedingly expensive or it may be impractical to obtain enforcement against nonpurchasers, or other market flaws might preclude achievement of desirable consensual exchanges. In those cases, the market cannot be relied on to mediate public interests in dissemination and private interests in remuneration. . . .
>
> 1. *Market Barriers.* . . . A particular type of market barrier is transaction costs. As long as the cost of reaching and enforcing bargains is lower than anticipated benefits from the bargains, markets will form. If transaction costs exceed anticipated benefits, however, no transactions will occur. . . . This may help explain why the "personal," "individual" nature of copying has been held relevant to fair use, and why "home use" may be relevant to the reach of copyright law. . . .
>
> 2. *Externalities.* . . . An analysis of the limitations of markets can also illuminate the special status that certain uses, such as scholarship, have in fair use tradition. The costs and benefits of the parties contracting for the uses often differ from the social costs and benefits at stake, so that transactions leading to an increase in social benefit may not occur. Thus, for example, a critic of the Warren Commission's investigation of the Kennedy assassination might write a "serious, thoughtful and impressive" book that will further public interest more than the revenues of his book alone would indicate. One might say that publication of his book gives an "external benefit" to persons who gain knowledge from the public debate sparked by the book without having purchased the book itself. . . .
>
> In cases of externalities, then, the potential user may wish to produce socially meritorious new works by using some of the copyright owner's material, yet be unable to purchase permission because the market structure prevents him from being able to capitalize on the benefits to be realized. . . .
>
> Distrust of the market may also be triggered when defendant's activities involve social values that are not easily monetized. . . . If the defendant's interest impinges on a first amendment interest, relying upon the market may become particularly inappropriate; constitutional values are rarely well paid in the marketplace. . . .
>
> 3. *Anti-Dissemination Motives.* . . . The case law has tended to grant fair use treatment where copyright owners seemed to be using their property right not for economic gain but to control the flow of information. . . .
>
> . . . Even if money were offered, the owner of a play is unlikely to license a hostile review or a parody. . . .

Wendy J. Gordon, *Fair Use as Market Failure: A Structural and Economic Analysis of the* Betamax *Case and Its Predecessors*, 82 Colum. L. Rev. 1600, 1613, 1627-33 (1982).[1]

Based on her analysis, Professor Gordon proposed a three-part test for when to label a use "fair": "Fair use should be awarded to the defendant in a copyright infringement action when (1) market failure is present; (2) transfer of the use to defendant is socially desirable; and (3) an award of fair use would not cause substantial injury to the incentives of the plaintiff copyright owner." *Id.* at 1614.

As Professor Gordon notes, market failure may manifest itself in a variety of ways. As time has passed, digital technologies have dramatically decreased the transaction costs of reaching bargained-for exchanges, in part by facilitating automated systems that charge for access to and use of copyrighted works. Other commentators, including Professor Lydia Pallas Loren, have

---

1. Reprinted by permission of the author.

cautioned against interpreting market failure theory as a theory that is simply about transaction costs: "A permission system can cure the market failure that results from high transaction costs. . . . [It] does not cure the market failure that exists when there are diffuse external benefits that cannot be efficiently internalized in any bargained-for exchange." Lydia Pallas Loren, *Redefining the Market Failure Approach to Fair Use in an Era of Copyright Permission Systems*, 5 J. Intell. Prop. L. 1, 33 (1997); *see also* Paul Goldstein, Copyright's Highway: From Gutenberg to the Celestial Jukebox, 207-08 (rev. ed. 2003) ("[S]ome of the 1976 Act's exemptions — indeed, some aspects of fair use itself — are there, not because of transaction costs, but because certain uses and users serve socially valuable ends. . . .").

NOTES AND QUESTIONS

1. Who has the better argument about what makes a use productive, the *Sony* majority or the *Sony* dissent? Is the notion of "productive consumption" sensible given the underlying purposes of copyright law, or simply incoherent? Review Question 4 in Chapter 5.D.2.a, page 385 *supra*, which discusses the distinction between "productive" and "consumptive" uses in the context of the right to prepare derivative works. Does the debate about this issue in *Sony* change your thinking about that distinction?

2. How would market failure theory resolve the dispute in *Sony*? Does your answer depend on whether there is a market mechanism in place to allow copyright owners of television programs to capture revenues from television viewers who seek to time-shift, or from advertisers who seek to reach this audience?

3. How would market failure theory resolve disputes about the other sorts of uses that the *Sony* majority discussed in its footnote about "productive" uses? Does the market failure rationale for fair use apply to a case like *Campbell v. Acuff-Rose Music, Inc.*, 510 U.S. 569 (1994), page 542 *supra*, which involves a parody of the copyrighted work? Does it apply to the hypothetical cases presented in Question 6, pages 561-63 *supra*?

4. Can you think of examples of socially desirable uses that are likely to generate the positive externalities to which Professors Gordon and Loren refer? Does §107's introductory reference to "criticism, comment, news reporting, teaching (including multiple copies for classroom use), scholarship, or research" answer this question?

Do you agree with Professor Gordon that fair use may appropriately protect users of copyrighted works who cannot afford to purchase permission because they cannot internalize the diffuse benefits their use produces?

Do you agree with Professor Loren that even if an efficient market forms such that users could easily seek permission from copyright owners, there may be cases in which it is "socially desirable" to allow a fair use claim anyway? Would the social desirability of such uses be easily quantified in economic terms? How should this concern be weighed against the other, more concrete concerns identified by market failure theory? Should the law ever consider the copyright *owner's* non-economic interests, as well?

5. Professor Goldstein argues that the appropriate response to private consumptive copying lies outside the bounds of the fair use inquiry:

[I]f pay-per-use becomes the dominant means for access to information, and if 'free' sources of information such as broadcasting and public libraries decline in quality and quantity, Congress will need to consider the distributional aspects of its copyright agenda and whether to carve out new exemptions, or provide overt subsidies, if the country's have-nots are to continue to receive these goods.

Paul Goldstein, Copyright's Highway: From Gutenberg to the Celestial Jukebox, 208 (rev. ed. 2003). Do you agree?

A critical question for market failure theory is whether holding the challenged use fair would frustrate development of a viable market for that use. In *Sony*, the copyright owners' expert had admitted that "time-shifting without librarying would result in 'not a great deal of harm.'" *Sony*, 480 F. Supp. at 467. With the passage of time, the evolution of both copying technologies and new business models based on copying have allowed copyright owners to present more concrete arguments about economic harm. Concurrently, market failure theory has moved from the pages of academic law reviews into court decisions.

The development of new markets and distribution methods raises a now familiar question: Which markets does copyright law reserve for the copyright owner? Put differently, what kinds of economic harm are cognizable under §107? Consider the following case.

A&M Records, Inc. v. Napster, Inc.
239 F.3d 1004 (9th Cir. 2001)

[Review the materials on peer-to-peer file-sharing in Chapter 6.C, pages 489-503, *supra*.]

BEEZER, J.: . . . Napster contends that its users do not directly infringe plaintiffs' copyrights because the users are engaged in fair use of the material. . . .

. . . The district court determined that Napster users engage in commercial use of the copyrighted materials largely because (1) "a host user sending a file cannot be said to engage in a personal use when distributing that file to an anonymous requester" and (2) "Napster users get for free something they would ordinarily have to buy." . . . The district court's findings are not clearly erroneous.

Direct economic benefit is not required to demonstrate a commercial use. Rather, repeated and exploitative copying of copyrighted works, even if the copies are not offered for sale, may constitute a commercial use. . . . In the record before us, commercial use is demonstrated by a showing that repeated and exploitative unauthorized copies of copyrighted works were made to save the expense of purchasing authorized copies. . . .

We also note that the definition of a financially motivated transaction for the purposes of criminal copyright actions includes trading infringing copies of a work for other items, "including the receipt of other copyrighted works." *See* No Electronic Theft Act ("NET Act"), Pub. L. No. 105-147, 18 U.S.C. §101 (defining "Financial Gain"). . . .

[Regarding the second and third fair use factors, the court noted that the works at issue were highly creative and that Napster users copied entire works.]

. . . [T]he district court concluded that Napster harms the market in "at least" two ways: it reduces audio CD sales among college students and it "raises barriers to plaintiffs' entry into the market for the digital downloading of music." . . . The district court relied on evidence plaintiffs submitted to show that Napster use harms the market for their copyrighted musical compositions and sound recordings. In a separate memorandum and order regarding the parties' objections to the expert reports, the district court examined each report, finding some more appropriate and probative than others. . . . Notably, plaintiffs' expert, Dr. E. Deborah Jay, conducted a survey (the "Jay Report") using a random sample of college and university students to track their reasons for using Napster and the impact Napster had on their music purchases. . . . The court recognized that the Jay Report focused on just one segment of the Napster user population and found "evidence of lost sales attributable to college use to be probative of irreparable harm for purposes of the preliminary injunction motion." . . .

Plaintiffs also offered a study conducted by Michael Fine, Chief Executive Officer of Soundscan, (the "Fine Report") to determine the effect of online sharing of MP3 files in order to show irreparable harm. Fine found that online file sharing had resulted in a loss of "album" sales within college markets. After reviewing defendant's objections to the Fine Report and expressing some concerns regarding the methodology and findings, the district court refused to exclude the Fine Report insofar as plaintiffs offered it to show irreparable harm. . . .

As for defendant's experts, plaintiffs objected to the report of Dr. Peter S. Fader, in which the expert concluded that Napster is *beneficial* to the music industry because MP3 music file-sharing stimulates more audio CD sales than it displaces. . . . The district court found problems in Dr. Fader's minimal role in overseeing the administration of the survey and the lack of objective data in his report. The court decided the generality of the report rendered it "of dubious reliability and value." The court did not exclude the report, however, but chose "not to rely on Fader's findings in determining the issues of fair use and irreparable harm." . . .

We, therefore, conclude that the district court made sound findings related to Napster's deleterious effect on the present and future digital download market. Moreover, lack of harm to an established market cannot deprive the copyright holder of the right to develop alternative markets for the works. . . . [T]he record supports the district court's finding that the "record company plaintiffs have already expended considerable funds and effort to commence Internet sales and licensing for digital downloads." . . . Having digital downloads available for free on the Napster system necessarily harms the copyright holders' attempts to charge for the same downloads. . . .

. . . We next address Napster's identified uses of sampling and space-shifting. . . .

The district court determined that sampling remains a commercial use even if some users eventually purchase the music. We find no error in the district court's determination. Plaintiffs have established that they are likely to succeed in proving that even authorized temporary downloading of individual songs for sampling purposes is commercial in nature. . . . The record supports a finding that free promotional downloads are highly regulated by the record company plaintiffs and that the companies collect royalties for song samples available on retail Internet sites. . . . Evidence relied on by the district court demonstrates that the free downloads provided by the record companies consist of thirty-to-sixty second samples or are full songs programmed to "time out," that is, exist only for a short time on the down-loader's computer. . . . In comparison, Napster users download a full, free and permanent copy of the recording. . . . The determination by the district court as to the commercial purpose and character of sampling is not clearly erroneous. . . .

Napster further argues that the district court erred in rejecting its evidence that the users' downloading of "samples" increases or tends to increase audio CD sales. The district court, however, correctly noted that "any potential enhancement of plaintiffs' sales . . . would not tip the fair use analysis conclusively in favor of defendant." . . . We agree that increased sales of copyrighted material attributable to unauthorized use should not deprive the copyright holder of the right to license the material. . . . Nor does positive impact in one market, here the audio CD market, deprive the copyright holder of the right to develop identified alternative markets, here the digital download market. . . .

Napster also maintains that space-shifting is a fair use. Space-shifting occurs when a Napster user downloads MP3 music files in order to listen to music he already owns on audio CD. . . .

We conclude that the district court did not err when it refused to apply the "shifting" analys[i]s of *Sony*. . . . *Sony* [is] inapposite because the methods of shifting in th[at] case[] did not also simultaneously involve distribution of the copyrighted material to the general public; the time or space-shifting of copyrighted material exposed the material only to the original user. . . .

NOTES AND QUESTIONS

1. Is the *Napster* court's fair use holding consistent with *Sony*? In particular, are the cases consistent in their definition of what constitutes a commercial use? Are they consistent in their view of what economic harm is relevant and what evidence should be considered in assessing economic harm?

2. Should *Napster* be understood as a case about market failure? It would indeed be difficult for Napster's numerous users to seek out the copyright owners of both the sound recordings and the underlying musical works to request permission to exchange songs. Does this argue for upholding Napster's fair use defense?

3. Should the activities of Napster users be considered "productive" in some sense? Why, or why not? If you conclude that these activities are productive, are there other factors that nonetheless weigh more heavily?

4. Would the *Napster* court have reached a different conclusion if Napster had shown that a substantial number of music copyright owners did not object to users distributing music through the Napster system? Would the court have concluded differently if Napster had shown that the music industry was attempting to suppress file-sharing technology rather than to develop business models allowing for widespread electronic distribution?

5. Review the Note on Copyright's Default Rules and the Google Book Search Project, *supra* Chapter 3. Are the copies that Google makes when it scans material into its system likely to be considered fair use? What about the short excerpts that it returns in search results? Should it matter to the fair use inquiry if a work is an orphan work?

Neither *Sony* nor *Napster* involved the types of uses that are traditionally viewed as implicating large positive externalities, like research and education. When, if ever, should courts excuse copying as fair when it occurs during the course of research or education? How, if at all, should the existence of permission systems affect the analysis? Consider the following case.

American Geophysical Union v. Texaco, Inc.
60 F.3d 913 (2d Cir. 1995)

[The plaintiffs were 83 publishers of scientific and technical journals. They brought a class action against Texaco, alleging that unauthorized copying of articles from their publications by Texaco's research scientists infringed their copyrights. Texaco subscribed to a number of journals. For example, it had had three subscriptions to the *Journal of Catalysis* (*Catalysis*) since 1988. It maintained a library of publications, and the library would route journals to interested scientists. The parties stipulated that, rather than inquire into the copying of all of Texaco's 400-500 researchers, they would select one researcher randomly as representative.

Dr. Donald H. Chickering was selected and the publishers took copies of eight articles from *Catalysis* from his files. The district court held that the photocopying of the eight articles was not fair use, and Texaco appealed.]

NEWMAN, C.J.: . . . The parties and many of the *amici curiae* have approached this case as if it concerns the broad issue of whether photocopying of scientific articles is fair use, or at least the only slightly more limited issue of whether photocopying of such articles is fair use when undertaken by a research scientist engaged in his own research. Such broad issues are not before us. Rather, we consider whether Texaco's photocopying by 400 or 500 scientists, as represented by Chickering's example, is a fair use. This includes the question whether such institutional, systematic copying increases the number of copies available to scientists while avoiding the necessity of paying for license fees or for additional subscriptions. . . .

II.   The Enumerated Fair Use Factors of Section 107 . . .

A.   *First Factor: Purpose and Character of Use*

. . . After noticing six of the[ ] articles when the original copy of the journal issue containing each of them was circulated to him, Chickering had them photocopied, at least initially, for the same basic purpose that one would normally seek to obtain the original — to have it available on his shelf for ready reference if and when he needed to look at it. The library circulated one copy and invited all the researchers to make their own photocopies. It is a reasonable inference that the library staff wanted each journal issue moved around the building quickly and returned to the library so that it would be available for others to look at. Making copies enabled all researchers who might one day be interested in examining the contents of an article in the issue to have the article readily available in their own offices. . . . Significantly, Chickering did not even have occasion to use five of the photocopied articles at all, further revealing that the photocopies of the eight *Catalysis* articles were primarily made just for "future retrieval and reference." . . .

It is true that photocopying these articles also served other purposes. The most favorable for Texaco is the purpose of enabling Chickering, if the need should arise, to go into the lab with pieces of paper that (a) were not as bulky as the entire issue or a bound volume of a year's issues, and (b) presented no risk of damaging the original by exposure to chemicals. And these purposes might suffice to tilt the first fair use factor in favor of Texaco if these purposes were dominant. . . . But [these purposes did not apply] to the six items copied from the circulated issues.

As to the other two articles, the circumstances are not quite as clear, but they too appear more to serve the purpose of being additions to Chickering's office "library" than to be spontaneous copying of a critical page that he was reading on his way to the lab. One was copied apparently when he saw a reference to it in another article, which was in an issue circulated to him. The most likely inference is that he decided that he ought to have copies of both items — again for placement on his shelf for later use if the need arose. The last article was copied, according to his affidavit, when he saw a reference to it "elsewhere." . . . What is clear is that this item too was simply placed "on the shelf." As he testified, "I kept a copy to refer to in case I became more involved in support effects research." *Id.*

The photocopying of these eight *Catalysis* articles may be characterized as "archival" — *i.e.*, done for the primary purpose of providing numerous Texaco scientists (for whom Chickering served as an example) each with his or her own personal copy of each article without

Texaco's having to purchase another original journal. The photocopying "merely 'supersede[s] the objects' of the original creation," . . . and tilts the first fair use factor against Texaco. . . .

Texaco criticizes three aspects of the District Court's analysis of the first factor. . . .

1. *Commercial use.* . . .

. . . [O]ur concern here is that the Court let the for-profit nature of Texaco's activity weigh against Texaco without differentiating between a direct commercial use and the more indirect relation to commercial activity that occurred here. Texaco was not gaining direct or immediate commercial advantage from the photocopying at issue in this case — *i.e.*, Texaco's profits, revenues, and overall commercial performance were not tied to its making copies of eight *Catalysis* articles for Chickering. . . . Rather, Texaco's photocopying served, at most, to facilitate Chickering's research, which in turn might have led to the development of new products and technology that could have improved Texaco's commercial performance. Texaco's photocopying is more appropriately labeled an "intermediate use." . . .

. . . [I]t would not be accurate to conclude that Texaco's copying of eight particular *Catalysis* articles amounted to "commercial exploitation," especially since the immediate goal of Texaco's copying was to facilitate Chickering's research in the sciences, an objective that might well serve a broader public purpose. . . . Still, we need not ignore the for-profit nature of Texaco's enterprise, especially since we can confidently conclude that Texaco reaps at least some indirect economic advantage from its photocopying. As the publishers emphasize, Texaco's photocopying for Chickering could be regarded simply as another "factor of production" utilized in Texaco's efforts to develop profitable products. Conceptualized in this way, it is not obvious why it is fair for Texaco to avoid having to pay at least some price to copyright holders for the right to photocopy the original articles.

2. *Transformative Use.* . . .

Texaco suggests that its conversion of the individual *Catalysis* articles through photocopying into a form more easily used in a laboratory might constitute a transformative use. However, Texaco's photocopying merely transforms *the material object* embodying the intangible article that is the copyrighted original work. . . . Texaco's making of copies cannot properly be regarded as a transformative use of the copyrighted material. . . .

Even though Texaco's photocopying is not technically a transformative use of the copyrighted material, we should not overlook the significant independent value that can stem from conversion of original journal articles into a format different from their normal appearance. . . . Before modern photocopying, Chickering probably would have converted the original article into a more serviceable form by taking notes, whether cursory or extended; today he can do so with a photocopying machine. Nevertheless, whatever independent value derives from the more usable format of the photocopy does not mean that every instance of photocopying wins on the first factor. In this case, the predominant archival purpose of the copying tips the first factor against the copier, despite the benefit of a more usable format.

3. *Reasonable and Customary Practice.*

Texaco contends that Chickering's photocopying constitutes a use that has historically been considered "reasonable and customary." We agree with the District Court that whatever validity this argument might have had before the advent of the photocopying licensing arrangements discussed below in our consideration of the fourth fair use factor, the argument today is insubstantial. . . .

B. *Second Factor: Nature of Copyrighted Work . . .*

Though a significant measure of creativity was undoubtedly used in the creation of the eight articles copied from *Catalysis*, even a glance at their content immediately reveals the predominantly factual nature of these works. Moreover, though we have previously recognized the importance of strong copyright protection to provide sufficient incentives for the creation of scientific works . . . nearly every category of copyrightable works could plausibly assert that broad copyright protection was essential to the continued vitality of that category of works.

Ultimately, then, the manifestly factual character of the eight articles precludes us from considering the articles as "within the core of the copyright's protective purposes," *Campbell*, [510] U.S. at [586]. . . . Thus, in agreement with the District Court, we conclude that the second factor favors Texaco.

C. *Third Factor: Amount and Substantiality of Portion Used . . .*

Texaco's suggestion that we consider that it copied only a small percentage of the total compendium of works encompassed within *Catalysis* is superficially intriguing, especially since *Catalysis* is traditionally marketed only as a periodical by issue or volume. However, as the District Court recognized, each of the eight articles in *Catalysis* was separately authored and constitutes a discrete "original work[ ] of authorship," . . . [E]ach article enjoys independent copyright protection, which the authors transferred to Academic Press, and what the publishers claim has been infringed is the copyright that subsists in each individual article — not the distinct copyright that may subsist in each journal issue or volume by virtue of the publishers' original compilation of these articles. . . .

Despite Texaco's claims that we consider its amount of copying "minuscule" in relation to the entirety of *Catalysis*, we conclude, as did the District Court, that Texaco has copied entire works. Though this conclusion does not preclude a finding of fair use, it militates against such a finding, *see Sony*, 464 U.S. at 449-50, . . . and weights the third factor in favor of the publishers. . . .

D. *Fourth Factor: Effect Upon Potential Market or Value . . .*

. . . [T]hough there is a traditional market for, and hence a clearly defined value of, *journal issues and volumes*, in the form of per-issue purchases and journal subscriptions, there is neither a traditional market for, nor a clearly defined value of, *individual journal articles*. . . . Like most authors, writers of journal articles do not directly seek to capture the potential financial rewards that stem from their copyrights by personally marketing copies of their writings. Rather, like other creators of literary works, the author of a journal article "commonly sells his rights to publishers who offer royalties in exchange for their services in producing and marketing the author's work." . . . In the distinctive realm of academic and scientific articles, however, the only form of royalty paid by a publisher is often just the reward of being published, publication being a key to professional advancement and prestige for the author. . . . The publishers in turn incur the costs and labor of producing and marketing authors' articles, driven by the prospect of capturing the economic value stemming from the copyrights in the original works, which the authors have transferred to them. . . .

Significantly, publishers have traditionally produced and marketed authors' individual articles only in a journal format, *i.e.*, in periodical compilations of numerous articles. . . . Publishers have not traditionally provided a simple or efficient means to obtain single copies of individual articles; reprints are usually available from publishers only in bulk quantities and with some delay. . . .

1. *Sales of Additional Journal Subscriptions, Back Issues, and Back Volumes. . . .*

. . . [I]n the unique world of academic and scientific articles, the effect on the marketability of the composite work in which individual articles appear is not obviously related to the effect on the market for or value of the individual articles. Since (1) articles are submitted unsolicited to journals, (2) publishers do not make any payment to authors for the right to publish their articles or to acquire their copyrights, and (3) there is no evidence in the record suggesting that publishers seek to reprint particular articles in new composite works, we cannot readily conclude that evidence concerning the effect of Texaco's use on the marketability of *journals* provides an effective means to appraise the effect of Texaco's use on the market for or value of *individual journal articles.*

These considerations persuade us that evidence concerning the effect of Texaco's photocopying of individual articles within *Catalysis* on the traditional market for *Catalysis* subscriptions is of somewhat limited significance in determining and evaluating the effect of Texaco's photocopying "upon the potential market for or value of" the individual articles. . . .

. . . [T]he evidence concerning sales of additional journal subscriptions, back issues, and back volumes does not strongly support either side with regard to the fourth factor. . . . At best, the loss of a few journal subscriptions tips the fourth factor only slightly toward the publishers because evidence of such loss is weak evidence that the copied articles themselves have lost any value.

2. *Licensing Revenues and Fees.* The District Court, however, went beyond discussing the sales of additional journal subscriptions in holding that Texaco's photocopying affected the value of the publishers' copyrights. Specifically, the Court pointed out that, if Texaco's unauthorized photocopying was not permitted as fair use, the publishers' revenues would increase significantly since Texaco would (1) obtain articles from document delivery services (which pay royalties to publishers for the right to photocopy articles), (2) negotiate photocopying licenses directly with individual publishers, and/or (3) acquire some form of photocopying license from the Copyright Clearance Center Inc. ("CCC").[16] Texaco claims that the District Court's reasoning is faulty because, in determining that the value of the publishers' copyrights was affected, the Court assumed that the publishers were entitled to demand and receive licensing royalties and fees for photocopying. Yet, continues Texaco, whether the publishers can demand a fee for permission to make photocopies is the very question that the fair use trial is supposed to answer.

It is indisputable that, as a general matter, a copyright holder is entitled to demand a royalty for licensing others to use its copyrighted work . . . and that the impact on potential licensing revenues is a proper subject for consideration in assessing the fourth factor.

However, not every effect on potential licensing revenues enters the analysis under the fourth factor. Specifically, courts have recognized limits on the concept of "potential licensing revenues" by considering only traditional, reasonable, or likely to be developed markets when examining and assessing a secondary use's "effect upon the potential market for or value of the copyrighted work". . . .

Though the publishers still have not established a conventional market for the direct sale and distribution of individual articles, they have created, primarily through the CCC, a workable market for institutional users to obtain licenses for the right to produce their own copies of individual articles via photocopying. The District Court found that many major corporations now subscribe to the CCC systems for photocopying licenses. . . . Indeed, it appears from the pleadings, especially Texaco's counterclaim, that Texaco itself has been paying royalties to the CCC. . . . Since the Copyright Act explicitly provides that copyright holders have the "exclusive rights" to "reproduce" and "distribute copies" of their works, *see* 17 U.S.C.

16. The CCC is a central clearing-house established in 1977 primarily by publishers to license photocopying. The CCC offers a variety of licensing schemes; fees can be paid on a per copy basis or through blanket license arrangements. Most publishers are registered with the CCC, but the participation of for-profit institutions that engage in photocopying has been limited, largely because of uncertainty concerning the legal questions at issue in this lawsuit. . . .

§106(1) & (3), and since there currently exists a viable market for licensing these rights for individual journal articles, it is appropriate that potential licensing revenues for photocopying be considered in a fair use analysis.

Despite Texaco's claims to the contrary, it is not unsound to conclude that the right to seek payment for a particular use tends to become legally cognizable under the fourth fair use factor when the means for paying for such a use is made easier. This notion is not inherently troubling: it is sensible that a particular unauthorized use should be considered "more fair" when there is no ready market or means to pay for the use, while such an unauthorized use should be considered "less fair" when there is a ready market or means to pay for the use. The vice of circular reasoning arises only if the availability of payment is conclusive against fair use. Whatever the situation may have been previously, before the development of a market for institutional users to obtain licenses to photocopy articles, . . . it is now appropriate to consider the loss of licensing revenues in evaluating "the effect of the use upon the potential market for or value of" journal articles. It is especially appropriate to do so with respect to copying of articles from *Catalysis*, a publication as to which a photocopying license is now available. We do not decide how the fair use balance would be resolved if a photocopying license for *Catalysis* articles were not currently available. . . .

Primarily because of lost licensing revenue, and to a minor extent because of lost subscription revenue, we agree with the District Court that "the publishers have demonstrated a substantial harm to the value of their copyrights through [Texaco's] copying," . . . and thus conclude that the fourth statutory factor favors the publishers.

E. *Aggregate Assessment*

We conclude that three of the four statutory factors, including the important first and the fourth factors, favor the publishers. . . . We . . . agree with the District Court's conclusion that Texaco's photocopying of eight particular articles from the *Journal of Catalysis* was not fair use. . . .

JACOBS, J., dissenting: . . . In this case the only harm to a market is to the supposed market in photocopy licenses. The CCC scheme is neither traditional nor reasonable; and its development into a real market is subject to substantial impediments. There is a circularity to the problem: the market will not crystallize unless courts reject the fair use argument that Texaco presents; but, under the statutory test, we cannot declare a use to be an infringement unless (assuming other factors also weigh in favor of the secondary user) there is a market to be harmed. At present, only a fraction of journal publishers have sought to exact these fees. I would hold that this fourth factor decisively weighs in favor of Texaco, because there is no normal market in photocopy licenses, and no real consensus among publishers that there ought to be one.

. . . [I]t is stipulated that (a) institutions such as Texaco subscribe to numerous journals, only 30 percent of which are covered by a CCC license; (b) not all publications of each CCC member are covered by the CCC licenses; and (c) not all the articles in publications covered by the CCC are copyrighted. It follows that no CCC license can assure a scientist that photocopying any given article is legal. . . .

Under a transactional license, the user must undertake copyright research every time an article is photocopied. First, one must consult a directory to determine whether or not the publisher of the journal is a member of the CCC. If it is, one must ascertain whether the particular publication is one that is covered by the CCC arrangement, because not all publications of participating publishers are covered. Then one must somehow determine whether the actual article is one in which the publisher actually holds a copyright, since there are many articles that, for such reasons as government sponsorship of the research, are not subject to copyright. The production director of plaintiff Springer-Verlag testified at trial that it is almost impossible to tell which articles might be covered by a copyright. Since even an expert has difficulty making such a determination, the transactional scheme would seem to require that an intellectual property lawyer be posted at each copy machine. Finally, once it is determined that the specific article is covered, the copyist will need to record in a log the date, name of publication, publisher, title and author of article, and number of pages copied.

It may be easier to hand copy the material. . . . Unless each publisher's licensing rights are made to depend upon whether or not that publisher participates in the CCC, we have the beginnings of a total market failure: with many thousands of scientific publications in circulation, a user cannot negotiate licensing fees individually with numerous publishers — unless it does nothing else. For many publications, licenses are simply not available. As to those, Dr. Chickering has the choice of hand copying, typescript, or the photocopying of selected pages only.

The blanket license fares no better. The CCC license cannot confer absolution for the photocopying of articles published by non-members of the CCC. Nor can the participating publishers properly collect fees for the photocopying of articles for which they do not hold the copyright. . . .

It is hard to escape the conclusion that the existence of the CCC — or the perception that the CCC and other schemes for collecting license fees are or may become "administratively tolerable" — is the chief support for the idea that photocopying scholarly articles is unfair in the first place. The majority finds it "sensible" that a use "should be considered 'less fair' when there is a ready market or means to pay for the use." . . . That view is sensible only to a point. There is no technological or commercial impediment to imposing a fee for use of a work in a parody, or for the quotation of a paragraph in a review or biography. Many publishers could probably unite to fund a bureaucracy that would collect such fees. The majority is sensitive to this problem, but concludes that "[t]he vice of circular reasoning arises only if the availability of payment is conclusive against fair use." . . . That vice is not avoided here. The majority expressly declines to "decide how the fair use balance would be resolved if a photocopying license for *Catalysis* articles were not currently available." . . . Moreover, the "important" fourth factor . . . tips in favor of the publishers (according to the majority) "[p]rimarily because of lost licensing revenue" and only "to a minor extent" on the basis of journal sales and subscriptions. . . .

I do not agree with the majority that the publishers "have created, primarily through the CCC, a workable market for institutional users to obtain licenses for the right to produce their own copies of individual articles via photocopying." . . . By the CCC's admission, in its correspondence with the Antitrust Division of the Justice Department, "the mechanism for the negotiation of a photocopy license fee is often not even in place. . . . Nor can it be said that CCC's current licensing programs have adequately met the market's needs." There is nothing workable, and there is no market. . . .

Note on *Princeton University Press v. Michigan Document Services, Inc.* and the Classroom Guidelines

In the wake of *Texaco*, the Sixth Circuit held that a commercial copyshop's reproduction of excerpts of copyrighted materials from a number of sources as part of coursepacks for students was not protected by fair use. *Princeton Univ. Press v. Michigan Document Servs., Inc.* (MDS),

99 F.3d 1381 (6th Cir. 1996) (en banc), *cert. denied*, 520 U.S. 1156 (1997). The plaintiffs were publishers who each maintained departments that would process permission requests. In assessing the four factors of §107, the court found the use non-transformative, and concluded that the lost permission fees constituted market harm. Relying on *Texaco*, the court rejected the notion that its reasoning was circular:

> [T]he circularity argument proves too much. Imagine that the defendants set up a printing press and made exact reproductions — asserting that such reproductions constituted 'fair use' — of a book to which they did not hold the copyright. Under the defendants' logic it would be circular for the copyright holder to argue market harm because of lost copyright revenues, since this would assume that the copyright holder had a right to such revenues. . . .
>
> The potential uses of the copyrighted works at issue . . . clearly include the selling of permission to reproduce portions of the works for inclusion in coursepacks — and the likelihood that publishers actually will license such reproduction is a demonstrated fact. A licensing market already exists here. . . . Thus there is no circularity in saying . . . that the potential for destruction of this market by widespread circumvention of the plaintiffs' permission fee system is enough, under the *Harper & Row* test, 'to negate fair use.'

Id. at 1387-88.

The court also found support for its decision in the "Agreement on Guidelines for Classroom Copying in Not-for-Profit Educational Institutions With Respect to Books and Periodicals" (Guidelines), which Congress incorporated into the legislative history of the 1976 Act. The Guidelines are limited to books and periodicals and are divided into two parts. Part I permits teachers to make single copies of book chapters, newspaper and periodical articles, short stories, and drawings in a book, periodical, or newspaper for "scholarly research or use in teaching or preparation to teach a class." H.R. Rep. No. 94-1476, at 72 (1976), *reprinted in* 1976 U.S.C.C.A.N. 5659, 5681-82. Part II permits multiple copies for classroom use provided that such copying meets defined tests of brevity and spontaneity. Copying is spontaneous if "[t]he inspiration and decision to use the work and the moment of its use for maximum teaching effectiveness are so close in time that it would be unreasonable to expect a timely reply to a request for permission." *Id.* at 5682. Additionally, the Guidelines limit copying from the same author, collective work or periodical volume and provide that "[t]here shall not be more than nine instances of . . . multiple copying during one class term." *Id.* at 5683. Each copy must contain a copyright notice, the student may not be charged more than the cost of copying, and the copying must not "substitute for the purchase of books, publishers' reprints or periodicals." *Id.* at 5682-83. According to the legislative history of the Act, the Guidelines are intended to " 'state the minimum and not the maximum standards of educational fair use.' " *Id.* at 5686.

The Guidelines are another example of Congress' reaching out to the copyright industries and some users of copyrighted works to help inform the drafting and interpretation of the statute. As is inevitably the case, not all affected parties were included in the discussion. Although some higher education groups were represented, neither the Association of American Law Schools (AALS) nor the American Association of University Professors (AAUP) participated. Both the AALS and the AAUP objected strongly to the guidelines as too restrictive and not reflective of already existing higher education practice. Their objections are expressly noted in the legislative history.

The *MDS* court concluded that the copying before it went "well beyond anything envisioned by the Congress that chose to incorporate the guidelines in the legislative history. . . ." *MDS*, 99 F.3d at 1390. It also stated that "changes in technology and teaching practices that have occurred over the last two decades [since the enactment of the 1976 Act] might conceivably make Congress more sympathetic to [the type of copying in this case]. If the law on this point is to be changed, however, we think the change should be made by Congress and not by the courts." *Id.* at 1391.

NOTES AND QUESTIONS

1. Do you think the *Texaco* and *MDS* cases were rightly decided? Who has the better argument about circularity in *Texaco*, the majority or the dissent? In his dissent in the *MDS* case, Judge Ryan distinguished between markets for the copyrighted work and the value of the work: "The plaintiffs certainly have not demonstrated that the coursepacks affected the market for the original copyrighted works [nor] their potential market for derivative works. . . . MDS's coursepacks would inflict 'market harm' if they damaged the *value* of the original work or the *value* of derivative products such as coursepacks the publishers might wish to market. . . ." *Princeton Univ. Press v. Michigan Document Servs., Inc.*, 99 F.3d 1381, 1407 (6th Cir. 1996) (en banc) (Ryan, J. dissenting), *cert. denied*, 520 U.S. 1156 (1997) (emphasis in original). Does this distinction offer a workable rule for deciding which markets fall within or outside the scope of the copyright owner's rights? Does the language of §107 support this distinction?

2. What accounts for the emphasis placed by the *Texaco* court on whether the challenged use is transformative? Section 107 does not mention this consideration as a factor relevant to the fair use inquiry. Does the Supreme Court's decision in *Campbell* require such a focus? Would you characterize the uses at issue in *Texaco* and *MDS* as "productive"? How would the *Sony* Court answer this question? Do either of the uses produce "external benefits" of the sort that Professor Gordon identifies as relevant to determining whether a market failure exists?

3. Is the *Bill Graham Archives* case, pages 557-60, *supra*, consistent with *Texaco*? The *BGA* court stated, "Here, unlike in *Texaco*, we hold that DK's use of BGA's images is transformatively different from their original expressive purpose." *Bill Graham Archives v. Dorling Kindersley Ltd.*, 448 F.3d 605, 614 (2d Cir. 2006). The *BGA* court also distinguished *Texaco* because that case "involved direct evidence that the allegedly infringing use [, copying by researchers,] would cause the owner [, the scientific journals,] to lose license revenues derived from a substantially similar use." *Id.* at n. 6. Do you find these distinctions persuasive? In particular, does the concept of "transformative markets" assist in determining what market harm is relevant under the fourth factor?

4. Should the *Texaco* court have given greater weight to considerations of reasonable and customary practice? Do you think that the result in *MDS* would have changed if the defendants had presented evidence that most campus copy-shops did not request permission or pay permission fees? For an argument that user expectations about reasonable and customary practice should continue to matter even in the face of changing technologies and markets, see Jessica Litman, *Copyright Noncompliance (or Why We Can't "Just Say Yes" to Licensing)*, 29 N.Y.U. J. Int'l L. & Pol. 239 (1997).

If reasonable and customary practice matters in defining the scope of fair use, it follows that ongoing user conduct shapes courts' perceptions about what is fair. Professor Ann Bartow has argued that therefore, it is important for individuals to continue to engage in copying in certain contexts without paying licensing fees, so that the uses will remain fair. *See* Ann Bartow, *Educational Fair Use in Copyright: Reclaiming the Right to Photocopy Freely*, 60 U. Pitt. L. Rev. 149, 229-30 (1998). Do you agree?

5. Is it appropriate for courts to rely on the Guidelines? According to Judge Ryan, dissenting in the *MDS* case, "That the Classroom Guidelines are not law should be reason enough . . . to refrain from using them to find infringement, but this is not the only reason

to reject out of hand arguments based on legislative history. Committee Reports are unreliable [and] do not accurately indicate congressional intent. . . ." *MDS*, 99 F.3d at 1411.

Keep in mind that the Guidelines expressly state that the proposed standards for educational copying are minimum standards for fair use, not upper limits on the amount of copying that would be fair. Practically, how likely do you think it is that a court would depart from the Guidelines by labeling more uses as fair? How much classroom copying do you think actually meets the criteria set forth in the Note above? One of the listed criteria is "spontaneity"; thus, a teacher who plans ahead is less likely to fall within the Guidelines!

6. How broad are the holdings of *Texaco* and *MDS*? Consider how these courts would resolve the following cases:

   a. A group of academic publishers sues a university, alleging that the university library routes new issues of journals to professors, who then make archival copies of articles relevant to their scholarly or teaching interests without remitting royalties to the CCC. A representative professor is selected, and archival copies of eight articles from the publishers' journals are discovered in her files.

   b. A group of academic publishers sues a university, alleging that the university library allows students to make photocopies of journal articles and book chapters for their personal use without remitting royalties to the CCC.

   c. A web site permits visitors to post news stories copied in their entirety from publications like the *Los Angeles Times*, and then append their own comments and criticisms. *See Los Angeles Times v. Free Republic*, 54 U.S.P.Q. 2d (BNA) 1453 (C.D. Cal. 2000) (no fair use).

   d. An Internet company allows individuals who have already purchased a particular compact disc to download the music on that CD in MP3 digital format for listening on their home or office computers. The download procedure requires the individual to place the original CD into his or her CD-ROM drive for verification. *See UMG Recordings, Inc. v. MP3.com, Inc.*, 92 F. Supp. 2d 349 (S.D.N.Y. 2000) (no fair use).

7. Who will bear the costs resulting from the holdings in *Texaco* and *MDS*? Does it matter who bears the costs? Is the cost of licensing reproduction of a copyrighted work simply another cost of production, like office supplies and equipment? Are there other ways that a publisher might make up the claimed shortfall in revenues?

8. One way to conceptualize fair use is as a compulsory license with a royalty rate of zero. Would it make sense to permit a court to excuse infringement as fair but require the infringer to pay something to the copyright owner other than statutory or actual damages? Is this any different from a court's finding infringement and opting to impose a judicially determined royalty? Revisit this question after you read Chapter 11 on remedies.

Recall from Chapter 5 that the Berne Convention allows countries to impose limitations on the rights of copyright owners of musical works, so long as the limitation is linked to a system of fair or equitable compensation. *See* Berne Conv., art. 13(1). Article 11bis(2) imposes a similar requirement for equitable remuneration with respect to limitations on the broadcast right. Would a rule that subjects all limitations to payment of reasonable compensation be consistent with U.S. copyright policy? With the TRIPS Agreement's three-step test? With the three-step test under the interpretation advocated by the Max Planck Institute (*see supra* page 533)?

9. Would a decision shielding personal copying after a viable licensing market has developed violate the three-step test in the TRIPS Agreement? The three-step test as interpreted according to the approach advocated by the Max Planck Declaration?

Note on Best Practices Statements

By now you have developed an appreciation for the difficulty of predicting the outcomes of fair use decisions. This uncertainty can present difficulties for copyright owners and users of copyrighted works alike. Indeed, Congress encouraged the development of the Classroom Guidelines (*see supra* pages 598-600) in part to provide educators with some certainty about what copying should be considered fair.

Over time, other groups have attempted to define the permissible contours of fair use in their industries. American University's Center for Social Media has been actively working to publicize codes of best practices in fair use for different industries. *See http://www.centerfor sssocialmedia.org/resources/fair_use/.* For example, certain documentary filmmakers have developed a "Statement of Best Practices in Fair Use" to address the most common situations such filmmakers face. *See id.* The authors of the Statement include a number of documentary producers, but they do not include other copyright owners in any appreciable number.

Review the *Note on OSPs and User-Generated Content,* pages 512-13 *supra,* which describes the Copyright Principles for UGC Services, an effort by certain copyright industries to define best practices for OSPs that provide "Web 2.0" content-sharing services. In response to the copyright industries' proposal, a group of nonprofit organizations issued a counterproposal titled "Fair Use Principles for User Generated Video Content," *http://www.eff.org/files/ UGC_Fair_Use_Best_Practices_0.pdf.* According to this proposal, automated content filters should be designed to incorporate protections for fair use. The proposal suggests a design for filtering technologies, so that user-generated video content would be removed only if:

(1) the video track matches the video track of a copyrighted work submitted by a content owner;

(2) the audio track matches the audio track of that *same* copyrighted work; and

(3) nearly the entirety (e.g., 90% or more) of the challenged content is comprised of a single copyrighted work (i.e., a "ratio test").

If filtering technologies are not reliably able to establish these three facts, further human review by the content owner should be required before content is taken down or blocked. Fair Use Principles, *supra,* ¶2(a).

In the future other groups may seek consensus on guidelines and best practices. While the legal effect of these documents remains to be tested in courts, there may be a role for such industry-based norm-shaping in the fair use area.

NOTES AND QUESTIONS

1. What probative value, if any, should courts accord efforts by private organizations to define the scope of fair use?

2. Consider the following examples of user-generated content, all available on YouTube as of this writing. If the creators of these video clips were sued for copyright infringement, could they successfully invoke the fair use doctrine? How would you analyze each example?

a. A short video of a toddler dancing to the song "Let's Go Crazy," by Prince;

b. A video of two students in a dorm room somewhere in China lipsynching to the song "That Way," by the Backstreet Boys;

c. A music video of Michael Jackson's "Thriller" performed by prison inmates in the Philippines;

    d. A mashup juxtaposing the soundtrack from *Brokeback Mountain* with clips from the *Back to the Future* movies in a way that suggests forbidden love between Marty McFly and Doc Brown;

    e. A video titled "Chad Vader, Day Shift Manager," that shows *Star Wars'* evil Lord Vader managing a supermarket;

    f. A mashup combining Apple Computer's famous "1984" Superbowl ad, which included Orwellian scenes of factory workers watching a video presentation by a demagogic leader, with footage of 2008 Democratic presidential candidate Hillary Clinton.

What is the difference between hypotheticals b. and c. above? Should the manner in which users engage with a copyrighted work make a difference to the fair use analysis?

3. If YouTube were to adopt the filtering protocols recommended in the copyright industry's "Copyright Principles for UGC Services," pages 512-13 *supra*, how would each of the videos in Question 2 be treated? Do the proposed principles appear to give a user-generated content (UGC) service the flexibility to manually review videos automatically selected for blocking and elect not to block certain of those videos? If you worked as in-house counsel for a UGC service that had adopted the proposed principles, would you recommend that approach? Why or why not?

4. What do you think of the "Fair Use Principles for User Generated Video Content"? If YouTube adopted the nonprofit organizations' proposed fair use principles, how would each of the videos in Question 2 be treated?

5. Under either proposal, manual review of the videos by the Web platform's legal staff might occur. (Do you see when and how this might happen under each proposal?) If you were responsible for manually reviewing and evaluating §512 takedown notices received by YouTube, how would you evaluate each of the videos in Question 2?

6. What other types of activities might benefit from developing a statement of best practices?

8

Copyright and Contract

In Chapter 1 you learned about the significant economic role of industries that depend heavily on copyright to sustain their business models. Those industries rely on the existence and enforcement of more or less intricate contractual arrangements to order their affairs. An effective understanding of copyright law therefore requires an appreciation of the many dimensions of the intersection of copyright and contract. To begin, there is the basic need for enforceable contracts to transfer title or interests in the intangible asset of a copyright itself. Contracts can also embody licenses authorizing a licensee to engage in an activity that would otherwise constitute infringement. Many contract issues relating to contract formation and interpretation are governed by state law. Other issues are governed by copyright-specific rules, some arising from the statute and others developed by courts.

The first part of this chapter introduces the basic rules that govern contracts and licenses involving copyrights that arise from the Copyright Act. It also addresses implied licenses and the revision "privilege" granted by the Copyright Act to the creators of collective works.

Because of the lengthy duration of copyrights and the ever-changing technological landscape, the language used in contracts can present interpretive problems as new means of exploiting a copyrighted work evolve. The second part of this chapter explores the tools for interpreting contract language in light of changing technologies and the underlying goals of copyright law.

The chapter then turns to an increasingly common practice: the ubiquitous use of shrink-wrap and clickwrap agreements. Some copyright owners seek to use these agreements to reorient the Copyright Act's default rules by restricting the activities that the purchaser or user may engage in, even if those activities otherwise would be authorized by fair use or other provisions of the Copyright Act. Certain licenses, such as open source and Creative Commons licenses, seek to reset the default rules provided by the Copyright Act by using rights granted under the Act to permit more copying and modification of copyrighted works. Both practices raise important questions about the nature of license obligations and require consideration of when a violation of the license terms constitutes copyright infringement rather than a breach of contract.

The chapter concludes with an exploration of the equitable doctrine of copyright misuse. Certain types of overreaching by copyright owners in their contracts can constitute a misuse of copyright. When a court holds that a copyright owner has engaged in misuse, the copyright itself is unenforceable until the conduct constituting misuse ceases. Thus, misuse is one means of limiting certain contract practices.

A. MODES OF TRANSFER

Section 106 of the Act grants a "bundle of rights" to the author of the work. Each right in the bundle may be transferred and owned separately. The owner of any particular right is entitled to the full protection and remedies afforded copyright owners under the Act. *See* §201(d)(2). An author may transfer an interest in the copyrighted work in a number of ways.

1. Writing and Recording "Transfers" of Copyright

Section 101 of the Copyright Act defines a "transfer of ownership" as "an assignment, mortgage, exclusive license, or any other conveyance, alienation, or hypothecation of a copyright or of any of the exclusive rights comprised in a copyright, whether or not it is limited in time or place of effect, but not including a nonexclusive license." 17 U.S.C. §101. Section 204 of the Copyright Act prescribes a particular form for the effective transfer of copyright ownership rights. This section states in part:

§204. Execution of Transfers and other Documents

(a) A transfer of copyright ownership, other than by operation of law, is not valid unless an instrument of conveyance, or a note or memorandum of the transfer, is in writing and signed by the owner of the rights conveyed or such owner's duly authorized agent.

In essence, §204 is a statute of frauds requirement, providing that any purported transfer of a copyright interest must be stated in writing, signed by the owner of the right being transferred. Because of the broad definition of "transfer of ownership" contained in §101, the Copyright Act's writing requirement applies not only to a complete transfer of copyright ownership, but also to exclusive licenses of some or all of the §106 rights and to the use of a copyright as security for a loan.

As you learned in your first-year Contracts class, putting agreements in writing is good practice: it requires the parties to articulate and clarify their thinking, minimizes misunderstandings, serves important evidentiary purposes, and emphasizes the seriousness of the promises undertaken. Courts have resisted suggestions that the Copyright Act's writing requirement should bend to arguments about industry custom:

> Section 204's writing requirement is not unduly burdensome; it necessitates neither protracted negotiations nor substantial expense. The rule is really quite simple: If the copyright holder agrees to transfer ownership to another party, that party must get the copyright holder to sign a piece of paper saying so. It doesn't have to be the Magna Charta; a one-line pro forma statement will do.

Effects Assocs., Inc. v. Cohen, 908 F.2d 555, 557 (9th Cir.1990) (rejecting defendant's "argument that . . . Moviemakers do lunch, not contracts").

Section 205 of the Act authorizes recordation of transfers with the Copyright Office and specifies procedures for recordation. Although recording a transfer with the Copyright office is not required, important benefits flow from proper and timely recording. Recordation provides constructive notice of the facts stated in the document so long as the document or attached materials identify the work in question and the work has been registered. Not only will such recordation provide information to potential licensees seeking to use a work, but recordation also establishes priority of ownership in the event of conflicting claims.

Section 205(d) sets forth the order for determining which claim prevails between two conflicting transferees. As a preliminary matter, the transfer first executed and recorded within one month of its execution (or within two months if executed outside the U.S.), and that satisfies the requirements of §205(c) (registration of the work and proper identification of the work), prevails. The first transfer will still prevail if, notwithstanding expiration of the time frame, it is nevertheless recorded before a later transfer. The later transfer will prevail if the recipient (1) properly recorded it before the earlier transfer was recorded; (2) took the transfer in good faith, for valuable consideration, or on the basis of a promise to pay a royalty; and (3) had no notice of the earlier transfer. Finally, §205 provides that whether recorded or not, a nonexclusive license prevails over a conflicting transfer of copyright ownership if the license is in writing and signed by the owner of the rights or her duly authorized agent, so long as the license was taken (1) in good faith before the conflicting transfer was recorded and (2) without notice of the conflicting transfer.

NOTES & QUESTIONS

1. Recall that the rights granted by §106 are intangible; accordingly, exclusive possession is difficult to secure and police. A copyright owner may grant many people the same right, such as the right to reproduce the copyrighted work. We typically refer to such grants as nonexclusive licenses. If a copyright owner grants license to one party that purports to be exclusive, what stops the copyright owner from granting a license to another party? Should an exclusive licensee simply trust that the copyright owner will not engage in subsequent transfers? The ability to record a transfer of ownership, including an exclusive license, with the Copyright Office is an important mechanism for policing exclusive grants.

2. In today's information economy, many companies' major assets are primarily intangible. Just like their counterparts with tangible assets, these firms may need to raise capital. If so, they may offer their intangible assets, including their copyrights, as security for a loan. If the firm fails to repay the loan, the secured party can "repossess" the collateral (the property serving as security). Because the Copyright Act defines a "transfer" to include the grant of a security interest (a "hypothecation" in the language of the Act), such a grant can be recorded with the Copyright Office. While state law, specifically Article 9 of the Uniform Commercial Code (UCC) as enacted by a state, governs the creation and enforcement of many, if not most, security interests, authorities generally agree that to perfect a security interest in a copyright, the secured party should file with the Copyright Office.

There are some instances in which a state UCC financing statement filing may be required. The Copyright Act provides that recording a transfer gives constructive notice only if the copyright has been registered. 17 U.S.C. §205(c)(2). The Ninth Circuit has held that because the Copyright Act provides "constructive notice" only for registered copyrights, the UCC governs perfection and priority of security interests in unregistered copyrights. *In re World Auxiliary Power Company*, 303 F.3d 1120 (9th Cir. 2002). Outside of the Ninth Circuit, however, such state filings may be insufficient. Ideally, then, a lender should always require that a copyright registration be filed before concluding the secured transaction. In some cases this is difficult because the work itself is in flux; for example, software under development changes daily. In those cases, filing under "regular" Article 9 rules may be sufficient, but it is not guaranteed.

Unfortunately, there are other complications. One controversial case held that even when the collateral is not the copyright itself, but rather the royalties generated by the copyright, the filing should still be made with the Copyright Office. *See In re National Peregrine, Inc.*

116 B.R. 194 (C.D. Cal. 1990). This conflicts with provisions of Article 9 that would label the royalties "accounts" and permit perfection in them to be achieved by a state law filing.

While various bodies have been working to clarify the relationship between Article 9 and the federal intellectual property laws, none of the efforts has yet borne fruit. In the meantime then, the best advice (at least outside of the Ninth Circuit) is to file in both the Copyright Office and the state location according to the provisions of the UCC to perfect a security interest in the copyright or the royalties generated by a copyright license.

3. In addition to §204's provisions requiring transfers to be written, a copyright also may be transferred by "operation of law." Section 201(d)(1) recognizes transfers by will (which would satisfy the writing requirement) as well as by intestate succession, which is governed by state law. Note, however, that intestate succession to the copyright is distinct from intestate succession to the termination interest, discussed in Chapter 3.C, which is governed by §§203 and 304.

4. In what ways is the Copyright Office recordation system similar to systems for recording transfers of interests in real property? In what ways is it different?

2. Implied Licenses

What happens if the writing requirement is not satisfied? Section 101's definition of "transfer of ownership" does not include nonexclusive licenses; therefore, no writing is required for such a license. When should a court imply a nonexclusive license? Other than being nonexclusive, what should the terms of that license be?

Asset Marketing Systems, Inc. v. Gagnon
542 F.3d 748 (9th Cir. 2008), cert. denied, 129 S.Ct. 2442 (2009)

SMITH, J.: . . . From May 1999 to September 2003, Gagnon [doing business as "Mister Computer"] was an at-will, independent contractor for [Asset Marketing Systems, Inc. (AMS)], hired to assist with its information technology needs. . . . Gagnon was asked to develop custom software for AMS. AMS was Gagnon's largest client, accounting for 98% of his business. Jay Akerstein, a partner at AMS who later became the Chief Operating Officer, was Gagnon's primary contact. Over the course of their four-year relationship, AMS paid Gagnon over $2 million, $250,000 of which was for custom software development and computer classes. Gagnon developed six computer programs for AMS.

In May 2000, AMS and Gagnon entered a Technical Services Agreement (TSA), which was scheduled to expire on April 30, 2001. The TSA, printed on Mister Computer letterhead, set forth Gagnon's fees and the services to be provided. The services included "Custom Application Programming—Consultant will provide Contractor with specific add-on products to enhance Contractor's current in-house database application," and mentioned nothing about a license. The TSA was not renewed, though the relationship continued.

AMS claims that on June 12, 2002, Gagnon signed a Vendor Nondisclosure Agreement (NDA).[1] The NDA would have given AMS ownership of all intellectual property developed for

---

1. The NDA was located and produced six months into the litigation.

AMS by Gagnon. Gagnon claims that the document is a forgery and that his signature cannot be authenticated.

In June 2003, Gagnon proposed that AMS execute an Outside Vendor Agreement (OVA). The OVA included a Proprietary Rights clause providing:

> Client agrees that all designs, plans, specifications, drawings, inventions, processes, and other information or items produced by Contractor while performing services under this agreement will be the property of Contractor and will be licensed to Client on a non-exclusive basis as will any copyrights, patents, or trademarks obtained by Contractor while performing services under this agreement. On request and at Contractor's expense, Client agrees to help Contractor obtain patents and copyrights for any new developments. This includes providing data, plans, specifications, descriptions, documentation, and other information, as well as assisting Contractor in completing any required application or registration. Any source code or intellectual property will remain the property of Contractor. Trademarks, service marks, or any items identifying said Company shall remain the Company's said property. Contractor will allow Company non exclusive, unlimited licensing of software developed for Company.

Akerstein declined to execute the OVA, but countered with a redlined version of the OVA, which substantially rewrote the Proprietary Rights clause to read:

> Contractor agrees that all designs, plans, specifications, drawings, inventions, processes, and other information or items produced by Contractor while performing services under this agreement will be the sole property of Client. Any source code or intellectual property agreed to and documented as Contractor's will remain the property of Contractor.

By the end of June 2003, AMS had decided to terminate Gagnon's services. AMS extended an employment offer to Gagnon, but he declined to accept the offer. AMS and Gagnon then discussed an exit strategy, and by late July, the parties had set a target exit date of September 15, 2003.

In August 2003, Gagnon responded to Akerstein's redlined OVA draft with a letter asserting that his "position has always been that Asset Marketing Systems shall be entitled to unlimited software licensing as long as my company had a business relationship with Asset Marketing Systems." The parties never executed the OVA.

In a letter to AMS dated September 18, 2003, Gagnon demanded $1.75 million for AMS to have the right to continue to use the programs and $2 million for Gagnon's agreement not to sell or disclose the programs to AMS's competitors.

In a letter dated September 23, 2003, AMS terminated its relationship with Gagnon. According to AMS, a consultant identified numerous problems with Gagnon's work. It also stated:

> Recently, we had discussed employee and intellectual property issues which have yet to be resolved. Despite the foregoing, I learned that we did not have copies of the source code for the software we developed and that copies of our SalesLogix software and our entire database may be maintained by you and your agents offsite.

The letter then demanded:

> In connection with that separation, you must immediately provide any and all copies of the source code for all software developed by and on behalf of Asset Marketing Systems immediately. You are not authorized to utilize that software which we believe is owned and all copyrights belong to Asset

Marketing Systems. Furthermore, despite your claimed ownership in that copyright, we believe that Asset Marketing Systems' trade secrets are embedded and utilized throughout that software which would preclude use by you as well.

We also demand that you return to us any copies of the SalesLogix software or Asset Marketing databases, programs or other materials that may have come into your possession during our relationship. . . .

In October 2003, Gagnon sent AMS a cease and desist letter, asserting that the use of the programs was unauthorized. . . . Gagnon demanded that AMS certify that it had undertaken to remove "all original and derivative source code" and all related files for the programs from AMS computers.

AMS responded by asserting that Gagnon could not unilaterally stop AMS from continuing to use and update the programs because it had an irrevocable license to use, copy, and modify the programs based on the course of conduct of the parties over the past two-and-a-half years. . . .

Gagnon alleges that AMS's continued use of the six programs constitutes copyright infringement because the programs were used by AMS without its obtaining a license or Gagnon's permission. AMS asserts three defenses to Gagnon's copyright infringement claim: an implied license, a transfer of copyright ownership via the NDA, and 17 U.S.C. §117. We hold that AMS has an implied unlimited license for the programs, and we do not reach the other defenses asserted by AMS.

Though exclusive licenses must be in writing, 17 U.S.C. §204, grants of nonexclusive licenses need not be in writing, and may be granted orally or by implication. *Foad Consulting Group, Inc. v. Azzalino*, 270 F.3d 821, 825-26 (9th Cir. 2001). We have previously considered the grant of an implied license in the context of movie footage and architectural drawings. *Id.; Effects Assocs., Inc. v. Cohen*, 908 F.2d 555, 558 (9th Cir. 1990).

In *Effects Associates*, a movie producer hired Effects Associates to create certain special effects for a movie. Though the film footage containing the special effects was used without the producer's obtaining a written license from Effects Associates, we found that an implied license had been granted because the footage was created at the producer's request with the intent that it be used in the film with no warning that use of the footage would constitute infringement. We determined that "[t]o hold that Effects did not at the same time convey a license to use the footage . . . would mean that plaintiff's contribution to the film was 'of minimal value,' a conclusion that can't be squared with the fact that Cohen paid Effects almost $56,000 for this footage." *Id.* at 559.

Thus, we have held that an implied license is granted when "(1) a person (the licensee) requests the creation of a work, (2) the creator (the licensor) makes that particular work and delivers it to the licensee who requested it,[4] and (3) the licensor intends that the licensee-requestor copy and distribute his work." *I.A.E., Inc. v. Shaver*, 74 F.3d 768, 776 (7th Cir. 1996) (citing *Effects*, 908 F.2d at 558-59) (footnote added). We apply the same analysis we did in *Effects* to implied licenses for computer programs. The last prong of the *Effects* test, however, is not limited to copying and distribution; instead we look at the protected right at issue — here, whether Gagnon intended that AMS use, retain, and modify the programs.

---

4. Though delivery of a copy of software does not compel the conclusion that Gagnon granted AMS a license, it is a relevant factor that we may consider. *See* 17 U.S.C. §202; *Effects*, 908 F.2d at 558 n.6 (recognizing that delivery is not dispositive, but "one factor that may be relied upon in determining that an implied license has been granted").

1. AMS Requested the Creation of the Programs

Gagnon argues that AMS never specifically requested that he create the programs, but "rather relayed its needs to Mr. Gagnon and he satisfied them by providing either computer hardware or computer software at his discretion." We find this interpretation of "request" to be strained. Gagnon did not create the programs on his own initiative and market them to AMS; rather, he created them in response to AMS's requests. Moreover, after prototype software was developed, he made changes to the programs in response to Akerstein and other AMS employees' requests. No genuine issue of material fact remains as to whether AMS requested the programs.

2. Gagnon Created the Software for AMS and Delivered It

Though Gagnon argues that the programs could be converted for use by another company, Gagnon admitted that the programs were created specifically for AMS and that AMS paid for the work related to drafting of the programs as well as some related costs. It is, therefore, undisputed that Gagnon created these programs for AMS.

The remaining question is whether Gagnon delivered the programs to AMS. We agree with the district court that Gagnon delivered them when he installed them onto the AMS computers and stored the source code on-site at AMS. Gagnon argues that even if he had installed the programs onto the AMS computers, he never delivered the source code so that AMS could modify the code. If AMS did not have the right to modify the code, it may have infringed Gagnon's copyright by exceeding the scope of its license. Gagnon primarily points to AMS's inability to locate the code on its own computer systems after his services were terminated to show that AMS did not possess the code. But, as we explain below, Gagnon's conduct manifested an objective intent to give AMS an unlimited license at the time of creation; thus, when he stored the source code at AMS, the code was delivered.

3. Gagnon's Intent as Manifested by His Conduct

Gagnon argues that he never intended that AMS would retain and modify the programs he delivered. Gagnon misunderstands the inquiry into intent, and we conclude that his conduct did manifest an intent to grant a license. The relevant intent is the licensor's objective intent at the time of the creation and delivery of the software as manifested by the parties' conduct. See *Effects*, 908 F.2d at 559 n.6 (noting that "every objective fact concerning the transaction" supported the finding that an implied license existed). The First and Fourth Circuits consider the following factors to determine such an intent:

> (1) whether the parties were engaged in a short-term discrete transaction as opposed to an ongoing relationship; (2) whether the creator utilized written contracts . . . providing that copyrighted materials could only be used with the creator's future involvement or express permission; and (3) whether the creator's conduct during the creation or delivery of the copyrighted material indicated that use of the material without the creator's involvement or consent was permissible.

[*John G. Danielson, Inc. v. Winchester-Conant Props., Inc.*, 322 F.3d 26, 41 (1st Cir. 2003).] We find this approach to be persuasive.

Gagnon and AMS had an ongoing service relationship in which Gagnon provided technical support for all computer-related problems at AMS; he also created certain custom software applications at AMS's request. The relationship of the parties indicates neither an intent to grant nor deny a license without Gagnon's future involvement.

Several documents exist, however, that reflect the parties' objective intent: the TSA, signed by both parties, the OVA submitted by Gagnon, and Gagnon's letter objecting to Akerstein's proposed changes to the OVA.[6] Courts have looked to contracts, even if unexecuted, as evidence of the intent of the party submitting the contract. *See Johnson v. Jones*, 149 F.3d 494, 501 (6th Cir.1998) (finding no license where architect submitted contracts containing express provision that drawings could not be used by others except with agreement and compensation).

The TSA, signed by both parties in 2000 and printed on Mister Computer letterhead, stated only that Gagnon "will provide" AMS "specific add-on products." Nothing in the TSA indicates Gagnon's understanding or intent that continued use of the custom application programming undertaken by Gagnon would be prohibited after the TSA terminated. . . . Like the special effects creators in *Effects Associates*, Gagnon was well paid for his services. Under the circumstances, it defies logic that AMS would have paid Gagnon for his programming services if AMS could not have used the programs without further payment pursuant to a separate licensing arrangement that was never mentioned in the TSA, and never otherwise requested at the time. This is especially so because custom software is far less valuable without the ability to modify it and because the TSA was set to expire in one year; one would expect some indication of the need for future licensing if the custom programs were to become unusable after the TSA expired.

The OVA submitted by Gagnon, but never executed, did not evidence any intent by Gagnon to limit AMS's use of the programs. Gagnon argues that the clause, "Client agrees that [intellectual property] produced by Contractor while performing services under this agreement will be the property of Contractor and will be licensed to Client on a non-exclusive basis as will any copyrights, patents, or trademarks obtained by Contractor while performing services under this agreement . . . ," means that his license was conditioned on a continuing relationship with AMS. We disagree. The clause "while performing services under this agreement" modifies the production of the intellectual property and the obtainment of copyrights. Furthermore, the contract then expressly stated, "Contractor will allow Company non-exclusive, unlimited licensing of software developed for Company," eliminating any ambiguity.

Moreover, Gagnon and AMS did not discuss a licensing agreement until their relationship was ending. Gagnon delivered the software without any caveats or limitations on AMS's use of the programs. Even if Gagnon and his employees maintained the software and had primary control over the code, they programmed on-site at AMS on AMS computers to which key AMS personnel had access—conduct that does not demonstrate an intent to retain sole control. The first time Gagnon expressed a contrary intent was in his letter to Aker[stein] sent after AMS had decided to terminate Gagnon's services. . . .

4. Scope and Irrevocability of Implied License

For the reasons outlined, we hold that Gagnon granted AMS an unlimited, nonexclusive license to retain, use, and modify the software. Furthermore, because AMS paid consideration, this license is irrevocable. *See Lulirama Ltd., Inc. v. Axcess Broad. Servs., Inc.*, 128 F.3d 872, 882 (5th Cir.1997). "[A] nonexclusive license supported by consideration is a contract."

---

6. We do not consider the NDA, allegedly signed by Gagnon, because Gagnon contests its validity and argues that his signature was forged, creating a factual dispute inappropriate for resolution on summary judgment.

Lulirama, 128 F.3d at 882; *see also Effects*, 908 F.2d at 559 n.7 (an implied license is a "creature of law, much like any other implied-in-fact contract"). If an implied license accompanied by consideration were revocable at will, the contract would be illusory. . . .

NOTES AND QUESTIONS

1. As *AMS* shows, parties do not always put their arrangements in writing. Is it good policy for courts to imply a nonexclusive license?

Are there other instances in which courts should imply licenses? Recall *Aalmuhammed v. Lee*, excerpted in Chapter 2.B.2. While the court there rejected Aalmuhammad's claim of joint authorship, it was clear that Aalmuhammed had contributed copyrightable expression to the film *Malcolm X*. It was also clear that the film's producers had neglected to secure a work made for hire agreement from Aalmuhammad, as authorized by §101(2). Is that an appropriate circumstance under which to imply a license?

2. Does the *AMS* decision set out appropriate criteria for determining under what circumstances such a license should be implied? In particular, the court treated delivery of tangible copies embodying the copyrighted work as a factor bearing on whether to imply a license. Does that make sense? Remember that copyright ownership is distinct from ownership of the underlying object in which the copyrightable expression is fixed. *See* 17 U.S.C. §202.

3. Recall *MAI Systems Corp. v. Peak Computer, Inc.*, 991 F.2d 511 (9th Cir. 1993), discussed in Chapter 2.A, in which the court held that a RAM copy, created by loading software from a hard disk into the CPU of a computer, satisfies the fixation requirement. Based on an extension of the *MAI* reasoning, routine activities such as forwarding e-mail and downloading documents from the web would each involve multiple acts of copying. Could courts hold that such activities are protected by an implied license? *See* Mark A. Lemley, *Dealing with Overlapping Copyrights on the Internet*, 22 U. Dayton L. Rev. 547 (1997). Would that be different than determining that a particular copying activity was fair use?

4. How should courts define the scope of an implied license? Should it be based on the parties' conduct? Industry practice? Should a court hold that an implied nonexclusive license to use a protected work encompasses all of the §106 rights?

5. The court in *AMS* determined that under contract law, because consideration was paid, the license should be irrevocable. Do you agree with that determination? The case law on duration and revocability of implied licenses is muddled. At least one court has held that an unspecified duration means a minimum duration of 35 years should be implied. *See Rano v. Sipa Press, Inc.*, 987 F.2d 580, 585 (9th Cir. 1993). *But see Korman v. HBC Florida, Inc.*, 182 F.3d 1291 (11th Cir. 1999) (holding that the Copyright Act does not impose a minimum 35-year term); *Walthal v. Rusk*, 172 F.3d 481 (7th Cir. 1999) (same). Which rule makes more sense? If the Copyright Act does not impose a minimum 35-year term, should an implied license nonetheless be subject to termination after 35 years under §203?

6. Sometimes even when there is a written contract courts must imply other terms of the contract. Silence on the issue of whether sublicensing is permitted is one example. A sublicense is a grant by a licensee to a third party, permitting that third party (the sublicensee) to engage in acts authorized by the initial grant from the copyright owner. Although an exclusive license constitutes a transfer of ownership, at least one court has ruled that an exclusive licensee is not equivalent to a copyright owner. *Gardner v. Nike, Inc.*, 279 F.3d 774 (9th Cir. 2002). In that case the Ninth Circuit held that an exclusive licensee may not transfer the licensed rights without the consent of the original licensor because "§201(d)(2) only conferred the 'protections and remedies' afforded a copyright owner under the 1976 Act, not the rights." *Id.* at 779.

A logical implication from *Gardner* is that rights obtained pursuant to any license, including an exclusive license, may not be sublicensed without authorization from the copyright owner. Would such a rule be good policy?

3. The Revision "Privilege" for Collective Works

In *Asset Marketing Systems* the court used a judicially created doctrine to determine whether to imply a license. The Copyright Act contains a provision that affords the creators of collective works an automatic, royalty-free license to republish copyrighted contributions to those works in certain circumstances. The scope of that privilege is the subject of the next case.

≡ *New York Times Company v. Tasini*
≡ *533 U.S. 483 (2001)*

GINSBURG, J.: . . . [Six freelance authors ("Authors") contributed 21 articles ("Articles") to three different periodicals, the *New York Times, Newsday,* and *Sports Illustrated,* each published by different companies. The publishers of these periodicals contracted with two different electronic database providers to include their periodicals in certain databases: LEXIS/NEXIS, the operator of the computerized database NEXIS, and University Microfilms, Inc. (UMI), the creator of two CD-ROM products, the New York Times OnDisc (NYTO) and General Periodicals OnDisc (GPO) ("Databases"). A computer program allows users to search the different databases using search criteria such as the author, headline, or date. The program then displays a list of results matching the search criteria. The user may then view each article and download or print a copy if the user desires.]

The freelance authors' complaint alleged that their copyrights had been infringed by the inclusion of their articles in the databases. The publishers, in response, relied on the privilege of reproduction and distribution accorded them by §201(c) of the Copyright Act. . . .

. . . When, as in this case, a freelance author has contributed an article to a "collective work" such as a newspaper or magazine, the statute recognizes two distinct copyrighted works: "Copyright in *each separate contribution to a collective work* is distinct from copyright in *the collective work as a whole. . . .*" §201(c) (emphasis added). Copyright in the separate contribution "vests initially in the author of the contribution" (here, the freelancer). *Ibid.* Copyright in the collective work vests in the collective author (here, the newspaper or magazine publisher) and extends only to the creative material contributed by that author, not to "the preexisting material employed in the work," §103(b). . . .

Section 201(c) both describes and circumscribes the "privilege" a publisher acquires regarding an author's contribution to a collective work:

> In the absence of an express transfer of the copyright or of any rights under it, the owner of copyright in the collective work is presumed to have acquired *only* the privilege of reproducing and distributing the contribution as part of that particular collective work, any revision of that collective work, and any later collective work in the same series. (Emphasis added.)

A newspaper or magazine publisher is thus privileged to reproduce or distribute an article contributed by a freelance author, absent a contract otherwise providing, only "as part of" any (or all) of three categories of collective works: (a) "that collective work" to which the author contributed her work, (b) "any revision of that collective work," or (c) "any later collective work in the same series." In accord with Congress' prescription, a "publishing company could reprint a contribution from one issue in a later issue of its magazine, and could reprint an article from a 1980 edition of an encyclopedia in a 1990 revision of it; the publisher could not revise the contribution itself or include it in a new anthology or an entirely different magazine or other collective work." H.R. Rep. 122-123, U.S. Code Cong. & Admin. News 1976, pp. 5659, 5738.

Essentially, §201(c) adjusts a publisher's copyright in its collective work to accommodate a freelancer's copyright in her contribution. If there is demand for a freelance article standing alone or in a new collection, the Copyright Act allows the freelancer to benefit from that demand; after authorizing initial publication, the freelancer may also sell the article to others. It would scarcely "preserve the author's copyright in a contribution" as contemplated by Congress, H.R. Rep. 122, U.S. Code Cong. & Admin. News 1976, pp. 5659, 5738, if a newspaper or magazine publisher were permitted to reproduce or distribute copies of the author's contribution in isolation or within new collective works. . . .

. . . When the user conducts a search, each article appears as a separate item within the search result. In NEXIS and NYTO, an article appears to a user without the graphics, formatting, or other articles with which the article was initially published. In GPO, the article appears with the other materials published on the same page or pages, but without any material published on other pages of the original periodical. In either circumstance, we cannot see how the Database perceptibly reproduces and distributes the article "as part of" either the original edition or a "revision" of that edition.

One might view the articles as parts of a new compendium — namely, the entirety of works in the Database. In that compendium, each edition of each periodical represents only a minuscule fraction of the ever-expanding Database. The Database no more constitutes a "revision" of each constituent edition than a 400-page novel quoting a sonnet in passing would represent a "revision" of that poem. "Revision" denotes a new "version," and a version is, in this setting, a "distinct form of something regarded by its creators or others as one work." Webster's Third New International Dictionary 1944, 2545 (1976). The massive whole of the Database is not recognizable as a new version of its every small part.

Alternatively, one could view the Articles in the Databases "as part of" no larger work at all, but simply as individual articles presented individually. That each article bears marks of its origin in a particular periodical (less vivid marks in NEXIS and NYTO, more vivid marks in GPO) suggests the article was *previously* part of that periodical. But the markings do not mean the article is *currently* reproduced or distributed as part of the periodical. The Databases' reproduction and distribution of *individual Articles* — simply as individual Articles — would invade the core of the Authors' exclusive rights under §106.

The Publishers press an analogy between the Databases, on the one hand, and microfilm and microfiche, on the other. We find the analogy wanting. Microforms typically contain continuous photographic reproductions of a periodical in the medium of miniaturized film. Accordingly, articles appear on the microforms, writ very small, in precisely the position in which the articles appeared in the newspaper. . . .

Invoking the concept of "media neutrality," the Publishers urge that the "transfer of a work between media" does not "alte[r] the character of" that work for copyright purposes. That is indeed true. But unlike the conversion of newsprint to microfilm, the transfer of articles to the Databases does not represent a mere conversion of intact periodicals (or revisions of periodicals) from one medium to another. The Databases offer users individual articles, not intact periodicals. In this case, media neutrality should protect the Authors' rights in the individual Articles to the extent those Articles are now presented individually, outside the collective work context, within the Databases' new media.[11] . . .

For the purpose at hand—determining whether the Authors' copyrights have been infringed—an analogy to an imaginary library may be instructive. Rather than maintaining intact editions of periodicals, the library would contain separate copies of each article. . . . The library would store the folders containing the articles in a file room, indexed based on diverse criteria, and containing articles from vast numbers of editions. In response to patron requests, an inhumanly speedy librarian would search the room and provide copies of the articles matching patron-specified criteria.

Viewing this strange library, one could not, consistent with ordinary English usage, characterize the articles "as part of" a "revision" of the editions in which the articles first appeared. In substance, however, the Databases differ from the file room only to the extent they aggregate articles in electronic packages (the LEXIS/NEXIS central discs or UMI CD-ROMs), while the file room stores articles in spatially separate files. The crucial fact is that the Databases, like the hypothetical library, store and retrieve articles separately within a vast domain of diverse texts. Such a storage and retrieval system effectively overrides the Authors' exclusive right to control the individual reproduction and distribution of each Article, 17 U.S.C. §§106(1), (3). . . .

The Publishers warn that a ruling for the Authors will have "devastating" consequences. The Databases, the Publishers note, provide easy access to complete newspaper texts going back decades. A ruling for the Authors, the Publishers suggest, will punch gaping holes in the electronic record of history. The Publishers' concerns are echoed by several historians, see Brief for Ken Burns et al. as *Amici Curiae*, but discounted by several other historians, see Brief for Ellen Schrecker et al. as *Amici Curiae*; Brief for Authors' Guild, Jacques Barzun et al. as *Amici Curiae*.

Notwithstanding the dire predictions from some quarters, see also *post*, at 520 (STEVENS, J., dissenting), it hardly follows from today's decision that an injunction against the inclusion of these Articles in the Databases (much less all freelance articles in any databases) must issue. *See* 17 U.S.C. §502(a) (court "may" enjoin infringement); *Campbell v. Acuff-Rose Music, Inc.*, 510 U.S. 569, 578, n.10 (1994) (goals of copyright law are "not always best served by automatically granting injunctive relief"). The parties (Authors and Publishers) may enter into an agreement allowing continued electronic reproduction of the Authors' works; they, and if necessary the courts and Congress, may draw on numerous models for distributing copyrighted works and remunerating authors for their distribution. *See, e.g.*, 17 U.S.C. §118(b); *Broadcast Music, Inc. v. Columbia Broadcasting System, Inc.*, 441 U.S. 1, 4-6, 10-12 (1979) (recounting history of blanket music licensing regimes and consent decrees governing their operation).[13] In any event, speculation about future harms is no basis for this Court to shrink authorial rights

---

11. The dissenting opinion apparently concludes that, under the banner of "media-neutrality," a copy of a collective work, even when considerably changed, must constitute a "revision" of that collective work so long as the changes were "necessitated by . . . the medium." We lack the dissent's confidence that the current form of the Databases is entirely attributable to the nature of the electronic media, rather than the nature of the economic market served by the Databases. In any case, we see no grounding in §201(c) for a "medium-driven" necessity defense to the Authors' infringement claims. Furthermore, it bears reminder here and throughout that these Publishers and all others can protect their interests by private contractual arrangement.

13. Courts in other nations, applying their domestic copyright laws, have also concluded that Internet or CD-ROM reproduction and distribution of freelancers' works violate the copyrights of freelancers. *See, e.g., Union Syndicale des Journalistes Français v. SDV Plurimedia* (T.G.I., Strasbourg, Fr., Feb. 3, 1998); *S.C.R.L. Central Station v. Association Generale des Journalistes Professionnels de Belgique* (CA, Brussels, Belg., 9e ch., Oct. 28, 1997), transl. and ed. in 22 Colum.-VLA J.L. & Arts 195 (1998); *Heg v. De Volskrant B.V.* (Dist. Ct., Amsterdam, Neth., Sept. 24, 1997), transl. and ed. in 22 Colum.-VLA J.L. & Arts, at 181. After the French *Plurimedia* decision, the journalists' union and the newspaper-defendant entered into an agreement compensating authors for the continued electronic reproduction of their works. *See FR3 v. Syndicats de Journalistes* (CA, Colmar, Sept. 15, 1998). . . .

Congress established in §201(c). Agreeing with the Court of Appeals that the Publishers are liable for infringement, we leave remedial issues open for initial airing and decision in the District Court. . . .

STEVENS, J., with whom BREYER, J. joins, dissenting: . . . I see no compelling reason why a collection of files corresponding to a single edition of the New York Times, standing alone, cannot constitute a "revision" of that day's New York Times. It might be argued, as respondents appear to do, that the presentation of each article within its own electronic file makes it impossible to claim that the collection of files as a whole amounts to a "revision." But the conversion of the text of the overall collective work into separate electronic files should not, by itself, decide the question. After all, one of the hallmarks of copyright policy, as the majority recognizes, is the principle of media neutrality.

No one doubts that the New York Times has the right to reprint its issues in Braille, in a foreign language, or in microform, even though such revisions might look and feel quite different from the original. Such differences, however, would largely result from the different medium being employed. Similarly, the decision to convert the single collective work newspaper into a collection of individual ASCII files can be explained as little more than a decision that reflects the different nature of the electronic medium. Just as the paper version of the New York Times is divided into "sections" and "pages" in order to facilitate the reader's navigation and manipulation of large batches of newsprint, so too the decision to subdivide the electronic version of that collective work into individual article files facilitates the reader's use of the electronic information. The bare-bones nature of ASCII text would make trying to wade through a single ASCII file containing the entire content of a single edition of the New York Times an exercise in frustration.[9] . . .

. . . I think that a proper respect for media neutrality suggests that the New York Times, reproduced as a collection of individual ASCII files, should be treated as a "revision" of the original edition, as long as each article explicitly refers to the original collective work and as long as substantially the rest of the collective work is, at the same time, readily accessible to the reader of the individual file. . . .

To see why an electronic version of the New York Times made up of a group of individual ASCII article-files, standing alone, may be considered a §201(c) revision, suppose that, instead of transmitting to NEXIS the articles making up a particular day's edition, the New York Times saves all of the individual files on a single floppy disk, labels that disk "New York Times, October 31, 2000," and sells copies of the disk to users as the electronic version of that day's New York Times. The disk reproduces the creative, editorial selection of that edition of the New York Times. The reader, after all, has at his finger tips substantially all of the relevant content of the October 31 edition of the collective work. Moreover, each individual article makes explicit reference to that selection by including tags that remind the reader that it is a part of the New York Times for October 31, 2000. Such a disk might well constitute "that particular collective work"; it would surely qualify as a "revision" of the original collective work. Yet all the features identified as essential by the majority and by the respondents would still be lacking. An individual looking at one of the articles contained on the disk would still see none of the original formatting context and would still be unable to flip the page.

---

9. An ASCII version of the October 31, 2000, New York Times, which contains 287 articles, would fill over 500 printed pages. Conversely, in the case of graphical products like GPO, the demands that memory-intensive graphics files can place on underpowered computers make it appropriate for electronic publishers to divide the larger collective work into manageably sized subfiles. The individual article is the logical unit. The GPO version of the April 7, 1996, New York Times Magazine, for example, would demand in the neighborhood of 200 megabytes of memory if stored as a single file, whereas individual article files range from 4 to 22 megabytes, depending on the length of the article.

Once one accepts the premise that a disk containing all the files from the October 31, 2000, New York Times can constitute a "revision," there is no reason to treat any differently the same set of files, stored in a folder on the hard disk of a computer at the New York Times. . . .

If my hypothetical October 31, 2000, floppy disk can be a revision, I do not see why the inclusion of other editions and other periodicals is any more significant than the placement of a single edition of the New York Times in a large public library or in a book store. Each individual file still reminds the reader that he is viewing "part of" a particular collective work. And the *entire* editorial content of that work still exists at the reader's fingertips. . . .

My reading of "revision," as encompassing products like the Electronic Databases, is not the only possible answer to the complex questions presented by this case. It is, nevertheless, one that is consistent with the statutory text and entirely faithful to the statute's purposes. . . .

The majority discounts the effect its decision will have on the availability of comprehensive digital databases, but I am not as confident. As petitioners' *amici* have persuasively argued, the difficulties of locating individual freelance authors and the potential of exposure to statutory damages may well have the effect of forcing electronic archives to purge freelance pieces from their databases. "The omission of these materials from electronic collections, for any reason on a large scale or even an occasional basis, undermines the principal benefits that electronic archives offer historians — efficiency, accuracy and comprehensiveness." Brief for Ken Burns et al. as *Amici Curiae* 13.

Moreover, it is far from clear that my position even deprives authors of much of anything (with the exception of perhaps the retrospective statutory damages that may well result from their victory today).[19] . . . The ready availability of that edition, both at the time of its first publication and subsequently in libraries and electronic databases, would be a benefit, not an injury, to most authors. . . .

NOTES AND QUESTIONS

1. The majority and the dissent differ in their interpretation of what constitutes a "revision" of a collective work in digital media. Reasoning by analogy can prove helpful in these types of cases, but finding the right analogy in cases involving new technology can be difficult. Is the majority's analogy to a library of file folders helpful?

2. In portions of the *Tasini* opinion not reproduced above, both the majority and dissent relied on other portions of the Copyright Act and its legislative history to support their interpretations. Under the 1909 Act copyrights were "indivisible"; to assign the right to publish a work, the entire copyright had to be assigned. This rule was especially harsh for authors of contributions to collective works. Additionally, to retain copyright in each separate contribution to the collective work a separate notice in the copyright owner's name was required. Publishers declined to print such notices, leaving authors with a choice between assigning their entire copyrights and having their works pass into the public domain upon publication of the collective work. The 1976 Act expressly rejected the indivisibility rule, allowing the different rights of a copyright owner to be transferred separately. The 1976 Act also adopted the rule that a single copyright notice on the collective work as a whole protected the individual contributions as well. 17 U.S.C. §404(c). The majority pointed to this history as evidencing the

---

19. It is important to remember that the prospect of payment by the Print Publishers was sufficient to stimulate each petitioner to create his or her part of the collective works, presumably with full awareness of its intended inclusion in the Electronic Databases.

importance of preserving the author's copyright in a contribution, while the dissent argued that a finding in favor of the publishers would not jeopardize the independent copyright in the contribution. What do you think?

3. In light of §201(c), an agreement by an author to publish his work in a collective work creates a default royalty-free license to include the work in revisions of that collective work. After *Tasini*, what factors should be relevant in determining the scope of the collective work publisher's revision privilege? In *Greenberg v. National Geographic Society*, 533 F.3d 1244 (11th Cir. 2008) (en banc), *cert. denied*, 129 S.Ct. 727 (2008), the court drew two fundamental lessons from *Tasini*: "First, the concept of 'revision' necessarily includes some elements of novelty or 'newness' . . . and second, consideration of the context in which the contributions are presented is critical in determining whether that novelty is sufficient to defeat the publisher's §201(c) privilege." *Id.* at 1251. The product at issue in the case was The Complete National Geographic (CNG), a series of CD-ROMs containing each monthly issue of the magazine as it was originally published from 1888 through 1996. The court rejected the plaintiff's argument that aggregating editions into a larger collective work took the new collective work outside the privilege. The product contained a 25-second introductory montage of individual cover images as a "virtual cover" for the product, allowed readers to flip through the pages of the magazine, to zoom in on a particular page, and to digitally search the magazine articles. The court concluded that these new elements did not take the CNG outside the §201(c) privilege. The individual author contributions were presented as digital replicas of the pages of the magazine, two pages at a time, with the fold in the middle and the page numbers in the exact same place as in the print version. The "new elements," the court noted, were a by-product of the digital medium. The court noted that "[a]s technology progresses and different mediums are created through which copyrightable works are introduced to the public, copyright law must remain grounded in the premise that a difference in form is not the same as a difference in substance." *Id.* at 1257; *see also Faulkner v. Nat'l Geographic Enters. Inc.*, 409 F.3d 26 (2d Cir. 2005), *cert. denied*, 546 U.S. 1076 (2005).

4. In *Tasini*, does the majority or the dissent have the better argument concerning the likely consequences of the Court's decision? Should the effect on current industry practice influence the Court's interpretation of the statute? Following the *Tasini* decision, the New York Times posted a notice on its web site stating that any freelance writer's work affected by the *Tasini* decision would be removed from the electronic databases unless the writer executed a release of all claims arising out of the New York Times' infringement in connection with that work. Jonathan Tasini again filed suit, this time alleging that the release agreement was unlawful and unenforceable. The court, however, dismissed that complaint, finding that Tasini lacked standing because he had not signed the release agreement. *Tasini v. New York Times Co., Inc.*, 184 F. Supp. 2d 350 (S.D.N.Y. 2002).

A settlement in a contemporaneous class action lawsuit shows one possible route to resolution. In that case, filed one year before the Supreme Court's decision in *Tasini* by the National Writers Union, the American Society of Journalists and Authors, and the Authors Guild against some of the nation's largest electronic publishers and database companies (including Reed Elsevier Inc., Thomson Corp., West Publishing Group, Dow Jones & Co., and Knight-Ridder Digital), the publishers agreed to set aside up to $18 million to provide payments for freelance authors whose works appear in the databases. *In re Literary Works in Electronic Databases Copyright Litigation*, MDL No. 1379 (S.D.N.Y. Sept. 27, 2005) (approving final settlement). The settlement established a two-tiered payment system: those freelance authors who obtained copyright registrations on their works received up to $1,500 per article to compensate for both past infringement and continued inclusion of the work in the database, while freelance authors who did not obtain registrations only received a maximum of $60 per article.

Some plaintiffs objected to the settlement, arguing that the named plaintiffs, who owned registered copyrights, failed adequately to represent the interests of unnamed class members, who owned unregistered copyrights. On appeal, the Second Circuit ruled that the district court lacked jurisdiction to certify a class consisting of claims arising from the infringement of unregistered copyrights and to approve a settlement with respect to those claims. *In re Literary Works in Electronic Databases Copyright Litigation*, 509 F.3d 116 (2d Cir. 2007). The Supreme Court reversed, holding that the lack of registration of some copyrights included in the class does not defeat federal subject matter jurisdiction. *Reed Elsevier, Inc. v. Muchnick*, 130 S. Ct. 1237 (2010). We discuss the Court's decision in Chapter 11 *infra*.

5. In *Tasini*, the majority indicates that perhaps an injunction is not an appropriate remedy. If the court fashions a remedy that permits the inclusion of articles in the databases without the consent of the copyright owners of the articles, but requires the publishers to pay a set amount to them, that amounts to a compulsory license. As the majority indicates, Congress has enacted certain compulsory license schemes in the Copyright Act. Which institution is better equipped to adopt such a regime, Congress or the courts? If Congress is the more appropriate institution, given what you know about copyright lawmaking, on whom should the Court place the burden of going to Congress to change the rules?

B. NEW USES AND OLD LANGUAGE

The dispute in *Tasini* arose in part because of technological change. CD-ROMs and massive networked databases did not exist at the time many of the articles at issue in *Tasini* were created. Understanding what constituted a "revision" in the new technological landscape challenged the parties and the Court. Interpreting the scope of a privilege can be equally difficult when that privilege is granted by contract. Unless the contract transfers "all right, title, and interest," selecting the language to memorialize the parties' intentions is a task to be undertaken with great care. The typical goal in contract drafting is to avoid ambiguity. If the contract is clear concerning the parties' respective rights and obligations, it is less likely that a dispute will arise and, if it does, that resort to the courts to interpret the contract will be necessary. Avoiding ambiguity may be simple enough for the uses of a particular copyrighted work contemplated by the parties, but, as you now know, copyrights can last for a very long time. What happens when the relevant technologies and distribution methods change? The two cases that follow illustrate this problem and explore the various contract interpretation methods employed by the courts.

Boosey & Hawkes Music Publishers, Ltd. v. The Walt Disney Company
145 F.3d 481 (2d Cir. 1998)

LEVAL, J.: Boosey & Hawkes Music Publishers Ltd., an English corporation and the assignee of Igor Stravinsky's copyrights for "The Rite of Spring," brought this action alleging that the Walt Disney Company's foreign distribution in video cassette and laser disc format ("video format") of the film "Fantasia," featuring Stravinsky's work, infringed Boosey's rights. . . .

I. Background

During 1938, Disney sought Stravinsky's authorization to use The Rite of Spring (sometimes referred to as the "work" or the "composition") throughout the world in a motion picture. Because under United States law the work was in the public domain, Disney needed no authorization to record or distribute it in this country, but permission was required for distribution in countries where Stravinsky enjoyed copyright protection. In January 1939 the parties executed an agreement (the "1939 Agreement") giving Disney rights to use the work in a motion picture in consideration of a fee to Stravinsky of $6000.

The 1939 Agreement provided that

> In consideration of the sum of Six Thousand ($6,000.) Dollars, receipt of which is hereby acknowledged, [Stravinsky] does hereby give and grant unto Walt Disney Enterprises, a California corporation . . . the nonexclusive, irrevocable right, license, privilege and authority to record in any manner, medium or form, and to license the performance of, the musical composition herein below set out. . . .

Under "type of use" in ¶3, the Agreement specified that

> The music of said musical composition may be used in one motion picture throughout the length thereof or through such portion or portions thereof as the Purchaser shall desire. The said music may be used in whole or in part and may be adapted, changed, added to or subtracted from, all as shall appear desirable to the Purchaser in its uncontrolled discretion. . . . The title "Rites of Spring" or "Le Sacre de Printemps," or any other title, may be used as the title of said motion picture and the name of [Stravinsky] may be announced in or in connection with said motion picture.

The Agreement went on to specify in ¶4 that Disney's license to the work "is limited to the use of the musical composition in synchronism or timed-relation with the motion picture." . . .

Finally, ¶7 of the Agreement provided that "the licensor reserves to himself all rights and uses in and to the said musical composition not herein specifically granted" (the "reservation clause").

Disney released Fantasia, starring Mickey Mouse, in 1940. The film contains no dialogue. It matches a pantomime of animated beasts and fantastic creatures to passages of great classical music, creating what critics celebrated as a "partnership between fine music and animated film." The soundtrack uses compositions of Bach, Beethoven, Dukas, Schubert, Tchaikovsky, and Stravinsky, all performed by the Philadelphia Orchestra under the direction of Leopold Stokowski. As it appears in the film soundtrack, The Rite of Spring was shortened from its original 34 minutes to about 22.5; sections of the score were cut, while other sections were reordered. For more than five decades Disney exhibited The Rite of Spring in Fantasia under the 1939 license. The film has been re-released for theatrical distribution at least seven times since 1940, and although Fantasia has never appeared on television in its entirety, excerpts including portions of The Rite of Spring have been televised occasionally over the years. Neither Stravinsky nor Boosey has ever previously objected to any of the distributions.

In 1991 Disney first released Fantasia in video format. The video has been sold in foreign countries, as well as in the United States. To date, the Fantasia video release has generated more than $360 million in gross revenue for Disney.

Boosey brought this action in February 1993. The complaint sought (1) a declaration that the 1939 Agreement did not include a grant of rights to Disney to use the Stravinsky work in video format; (2) damages for copyright infringement in at least 18 foreign countries. . . .

II.   Discussion . . .

1. *Whether the "motion picture" license covers video format.* Boosey contends that the license to use Stravinsky's work in a "motion picture" did not authorize distribution of the motion picture in video format, especially in view of the absence of an express provision for "future technologies" and Stravinsky's reservation of all rights not granted in the Agreement. Disputes about whether licensees may exploit licensed works through new marketing channels made possible by technologies developed after the licensing contract — often called "new-use" problems — have vexed courts since at least the advent of the motion picture.

In *Bartsch v. Metro-Goldwyn-Mayer, Inc.*, we held that "licensee[s] may properly pursue any uses which may reasonably be said to fall within the medium as described in the license." 391 F.2d 150, 155 (2d Cir. 1968) (Friendly, J. (quoting Nimmer)). We held in Bartsch that a license of motion picture rights to a play included the right to telecast the motion picture. We observed that "[i]f the words are broad enough to cover the new use, it seems fairer that the burden of framing and negotiating an exception should fall on the grantor," at least when the new medium is not completely unknown at the time of contracting. *Id.* at 154, 155.

The 1939 Agreement conveys the right "to record [the composition] in any manner, medium or form" for use "in [a] motion picture." We believe this language is broad enough to include distribution of the motion picture in video format. At a minimum, *Bartsch* holds that when a license includes a grant of rights that is reasonably read to cover a new use (at least where the new use was foreseeable at the time of contracting), the burden of excluding the right to the new use will rest on the grantor. The license "to record in any manner, medium or form" doubtless extends to videocassette recording and we can see no reason why the grant of "motion picture" reproduction rights should not include the video format, absent any indication in the Agreement to the contrary. If a new-use license hinges on the foreseeability of the new channels of distribution at the time of contracting — a question left open in *Bartsch* — Disney has proffered unrefuted evidence that a nascent market for home viewing of feature films existed by 1939. The *Bartsch* analysis thus compels the conclusion that the license for motion picture rights extends to video format distribution.

We recognize that courts and scholars are not in complete accord on the capacity of a broad license to cover future developed markets resulting from new technologies. The Nimmer treatise describes two principal approaches to the problem. According to the first view, advocated here by Boosey, "a license of rights in a given medium (*e.g.* 'motion picture rights') includes only such uses as fall within the unambiguous core meaning of the term (*e.g.*, exhibition of motion picture film in motion picture theaters) and excludes any uses that lie within the ambiguous penumbra (*e.g.* exhibition of motion picture on television)." Nimmer, §10.10[B] at 10-90; *see also Cohen v. Paramount Pictures Corp.*, 845 F.2d 851, 853-54 (9th Cir. 1988) (holding that license to use musical score in television production does not extend to use in videocassette release); *Rey v. Lafferty*, 990 F.2d 1379, 1390-91 (1st Cir. 1993) (holding that license to portray Curious George in animations for "television viewing" does not extend to videocassette release). Under this approach, a license given in 1939 to "motion picture" rights would include only the core uses of "motion picture" as understood in 1939 — presumably theatrical distribution — and would not include subsequently developed methods of distribution of a motion picture such as television videocassettes or laser discs. *See* Nimmer §10.10[B] at 10-90.

The second position described by Nimmer is "that the licensee may properly pursue any uses that may reasonably be said to fall within the medium as described in the license." *Id.* at 10-91. Nimmer expresses clear preferences for the latter approach on the ground that it is "less likely to prove unjust." *Id.* As Judge Friendly noted in *Bartsch*, "[S]o do we." 391 F.2d at 155.

We acknowledge that a result which deprives the author-licensor of participation in the profits of new unforeseen channels of distribution is not an altogether happy solution. Nonetheless, we think it more fair and sensible than a result that would deprive a contracting party of the rights reasonably found in the terms of the contract it negotiates. This issue is too often, and improperly, framed as one of favoritism as between licensors and licensees. Because licensors are often authors — whose creativity the copyright laws intend to nurture — and are often impecunious, while licensees are often large business organizations, there is sometimes a tendency in copyright scholarship and adjudication to seek solutions that favor licensors over licensees. . . .

In our view, new-use analysis should rely on neutral principles of contract interpretation rather than solicitude for either party. Although *Bartsch* speaks of placing the "burden of framing and negotiating an exception . . . on the grantor," 391 F.2d at 155, it should not be understood to adopt a default rule in favor of copyright licensees or any default rule whatsoever. What governs under *Bartsch* is the language of the contract. If the contract is more reasonably read to convey one meaning, the party benefitted by that reading should be able to rely on it; the party seeking exception or deviation from the meaning reasonably conveyed by the words of the contract should bear the burden of negotiating for language that would express the limitation or deviation. This principle favors neither licensors nor licensees. It follows simply from the words of the contract.

The words of Disney's license are more reasonably read to include than to exclude a motion picture distributed in video format. Thus, we conclude that the burden fell on Stravinsky, if he wished to exclude new markets arising from subsequently developed motion picture technology, to insert such language of limitation in the license, rather than on Disney to add language that reiterated what the license already stated.

Other significant jurisprudential and policy considerations confirm our approach to new-use problems. We think that our view is more consistent with the law of contract than the view that would exclude new technologies even when they reasonably fall within the description of what is licensed. Although contract interpretation normally requires inquiry into the intent of the contracting parties, intent is not likely to be helpful when the subject of the inquiry is something the parties were not thinking about. . . . Especially where, as here, evidence probative of intent is likely to be both scant and unreliable, the burden of justifying a departure from the most reasonable reading of the contract should fall on the party advocating the departure.[4]

Neither the absence of a future technologies clause in the Agreement nor the presence of the reservation clause alters that analysis. The reservation clause stands for no more than the truism that Stravinsky retained whatever he had not granted. . . .

---

4. We note also that an approach to new-use problems that tilts against licensees gives rise to antiprogressive incentives. Motion picture producers would be reluctant to explore and utilize innovative technologies for the exhibition of movies if the consequence would be that they would lose the right to exhibit pictures containing licensed works. *See Bartsch*, 391 F.2d at 155.

Nor do we believe that our approach disadvantages licensors. By holding contracting parties accountable to the reasonable interpretation of their agreements, we encourage licensors and licensees to anticipate and bargain for the full value of potential future uses. Licensors reluctant to anticipate future developments remain free to negotiate language that clearly reserves the rights to future uses. But the creation of exceptional principles of contract construction that places doubt on the capacity of a license to transfer new technologies is likely to harm licensors together with licensees, by placing a significant percentage of the profits they might have shared in the hands of lawyers instead.

Random House v. Rosetta Books, LLC

150 F. Supp. 2d 613 (S.D.N.Y. 2001), aff'd, 283 F.3d 490 (2d Cir. 2002)

STEIN, J.: . . . In the year 2000 and the beginning of 2001, Rosetta Books contracted with several authors to publish certain of their works — including *The Confessions of Nat Turner* and *Sophie's Choice* by William Styron; *Slaughterhouse-Five, Breakfast of Champions, The Sirens of Titan, Cat's Cradle,* and *Player Piano* by Kurt Vonnegut; and *Promised Land* by Robert B. Parker — in digital format over the internet. On February 26, 2001 Rosetta Books launched its ebook business, offering those titles and others for sale in digital format. The next day, Random House filed this complaint accusing Rosetta Books of committing copyright infringement and tortiously interfering with the contracts Random House had with Messrs. Parker, Styron and Vonnegut by selling its ebooks. It simultaneously moved for a preliminary injunction prohibiting Rosetta from infringing plaintiff's copyrights.

A. Ebooks

Ebooks are "digital book[s] that you can read on a computer screen or an electronic device." Ebooks are created by converting digitized text into a format readable by computer software. The text can be viewed on a desktop or laptop computer, personal digital assistant or handheld dedicated ebook reading device. . . .

Included in a Rosetta ebook is a book cover, title page, copyright page and "eforward" all created by Rosetta Books. Although the text of the ebook is exactly the same as the text of the original work, the ebook contains various features that take advantage of its digital format. . . .

B. Random House's licensing agreements

While each agreement between the author and Random House differs in some respects, each uses the phrase "print, publish and sell the work in book form" to convey rights from the author to the publisher.

1. Styron Agreements

Forty years ago, in 1961, William Styron granted Random House the right to publish *The Confessions of Nat Turner*. Besides granting Random House an exclusive license to "print, publish and sell the work in book form," Styron also gave it the right to "license publication of the work by book clubs," "license publication of a reprint edition," "license after book publication the publication of the work, in whole or in part, in anthologies, school books," and other shortened forms, "license without charge publication of the work in Braille, or photographing, recording, and microfilming the work for the physically handicapped," and "publish or permit others to publish or broadcast by radio or television . . . selections from the work, for publicity purposes. . . ." Styron demonstrated that he was not granting Random House the rights to license publication in the British Commonwealth or in foreign languages by crossing out these clauses on the form contract supplied by Random House.

The publisher agreed in the contract to "publish the work at its own expense and in such style and manner and at such a price as it deems suitable." The contract also contains a noncompete clause that provides, in relevant part, that "[t]he Author agrees that during the term of this agreement he will not, without the written permission of the Publisher, publish or permit to be published any material in book or pamphlet form, based on the material in the work, or which is reasonably likely to injure its sale." Styron's contract with Random House for the right to publish *Sophie's Choice*, executed in 1977, is virtually identical to his 1961 contract to publish *The Confessions of Nat Turner*.

2. Vonnegut Agreements

Kurt Vonnegut's 1967 contract granting Random House's predecessor-in-interest Dell Publishing Co., Inc. the license to publish *Slaughterhouse-Five* and *Breakfast of Champions* follows a similar structure to the Styron agreements. Paragraph #1 is captioned "grant of rights" and contains those rights the author is granting to the book publisher. Certain rights on the publisher's form contract are crossed out, indicating that the author reserved them for himself. One of the rights granted by the author includes the "[e]xclusive right to publish and to license the Work for publication, after book publication . . . in anthologies, selections, digests, abridgements, magazine condensations, serialization, newspaper syndication, picture book versions, microfilming, Xerox and other forms of copying, either now in use or hereafter developed."

Vonnegut specifically reserved for himself the "dramatic . . . motion picture (silent and sound) . . . radio broadcasting (including mechanical renditions and/or recordings of the text) . . . [and] television" rights. Unlike the Styron agreements, this contract does not contain a non-compete clause.

Vonnegut's 1970 contract granting Dell the license to publish *The Sirens of Titan, Cat's Cradle,* and *Player Piano* contains virtually identical grants and reservations of rights as his 1967 contract. However, it does contain a non-compete clause, which provides that "the Author . . . will not publish or permit to be published any edition, adaptation or abridgment of the Work by any party other than Dell without Dell's prior written consent." . . .

[The court then described the Parker Agreements, which are similar to the Styron and Vonnegut Agreements.]

[C.] Ownership of a Valid Copyright

Two elements must be proven in order to establish a prima facie case of infringement: "(1) ownership of a valid copyright, and (2) copying of constituent elements of the work that are original." *Feist Publications, Inc. v. Rural Tel. Serv. Co.,* 499 U.S. 340 (1991). In this case, only the first element—ownership of a valid copyright—is at issue, since all parties concede that the text of the ebook is identical to the text of the book published by Random House. . . .

1. Contract Interpretation of Licensing Agreements—Legal Standards

Random House claims to own the rights in question through its licensing agreements with the authors. Interpretation of an agreement purporting to grant a copyright license is a matter of state contract law. All of the agreements state that they "shall be interpreted according to the law of the State of New York."

In New York, a written contract is to be interpreted so as to give effect to the intention of the parties as expressed in the contract's language. The court must consider the entire contract and reconcile all parts, if possible, to avoid an inconsistency. . . .

These principles are in accord with the approach the U.S. Court of Appeals for the Second Circuit uses in analyzing contractual language in disputes, such as this one, "about whether licensees may exploit licensed works through new marketing channels made possible by technologies developed after the licensing contract—often called 'new use' problems."

Boosey & Hawkes Music Publishers, Ltd. v. Walt Disney Co., 145 F.3d 481, 486 (2d Cir. 1998). The two leading cases in this Circuit on how to determine whether "new uses" come within prior grants of rights are *Boosey* and *Bartsch v. Metro-Goldwyn-Mayer, Inc.*, 391 F.2d 150 (2d Cir. 1968), decided three decades apart. . . .

2. *Application of Legal Standards*

Relying on "the language of the license contract and basic principles of interpretation," *Boosey*, 145 F.3d at 487 n.3, as instructed to do so by *Boosey* and *Bartsch*, this Court finds that the most reasonable interpretation of the grant in the contracts at issue to "print, publish and sell the work in book form" does not include the right to publish the work as an ebook. At the outset, the phrase itself distinguishes between the pure content — *i.e.* "the work" — and the format of display — "in book form." The *Random House Webster's Unabridged Dictionary* defines a "book" as "a written or printed work of fiction or nonfiction, usually on sheets of paper fastened or bound together within covers" and defines "form" as "external appearance of a clearly defined area, as distinguished from color or material; the shape of a thing or person." *Random House Webster's Unabridged Dictionary* (2001), available in searchable form at *http://www.allwords.com*.

Manifestly, paragraph # 1 of each contract — entitled either "grant of rights" or "exclusive publication right" — conveys certain rights from the author to the publisher. In that paragraph, separate grant language is used to convey the rights to publish book club editions, reprint editions, abridged forms, and editions in Braille. This language would not be necessary if the phrase "in book form" encompassed all types of books. That paragraph specifies exactly which rights were being granted by the author to the publisher. Indeed, many of the rights set forth in the publisher's form contracts were in fact not granted to the publisher, but rather were reserved by the authors to themselves. For example, each of the authors specifically reserved certain rights for themselves by striking out phrases, sentences, and paragraphs of the publisher's form contract. This evidences an intent by these authors not to grant the publisher the broadest rights in their works.

Random House contends that the phrase "in book form" means to faithfully reproduce the author's text in its complete form as a reading experience and that, since ebooks concededly contain the complete text of the work, Rosetta cannot also possess those rights. While Random House's definition distinguishes "book form" from other formats that require separate contractual language — such as audio books and serialization rights — it does not distinguish other formats specifically mentioned in paragraph # 1 of the contracts, such as book club editions and reprint editions. Because the Court must, if possible, give effect to all contractual language in order to "safeguard against adopting an interpretation that would render any individual provision superfluous," *Sayers*, 7 F.3d at 1095, Random House's definition cannot be adopted. . . .

Random House also cites the non-compete clauses as evidence that the authors granted it broad, exclusive rights in their work. Random House reasons that because the authors could not permit any material that would injure the sale of the work to be published without Random House's consent, the authors must have granted the right to publish ebooks to Random House. This reasoning turns the analysis on its head. First, the grant of rights follows from the grant language alone. Second, non-compete clauses must be limited in scope in order to be enforceable in New York. Third, even if the authors did violate this provision of their Random House agreements by contracting with Rosetta Books — a point on which this Court does not opine — the remedy is a breach of contract action against the authors, not a copyright infringement action against Rosetta Books. . . .

Not only does the language of the contract itself lead almost ineluctably to the conclusion that Random House does not own the right to publish the works as ebooks, but also a reasonable person "cognizant of the customs, practices, usages and terminology as generally understood in the particular trade or business," *Sayers*, 7 F.3d at 1095, would conclude that the grant language does not include ebooks. "To print, publish and sell the work in book form" is understood in the publishing industry to be a "limited" grant. *See Field v. True Comics*, 89 F. Supp. 611, 613-14 (S.D.N.Y. 1950); *see also* Melville B. Nimmer & David Nimmer, *Nimmer on Copyright*, §10.14[C] (2001) (citing *Field*).

In *Field v. True Comics*, the court held that "the sole and exclusive right to publish, print and market *in book form*"—especially when the author had specifically reserved rights for himself—was "much more limited" than "the sole and exclusive right to publish, print and market *the book*." 89 F. Supp. at 612 (emphasis added). In fact, the publishing industry generally interprets the phrase "in book form" as granting the publisher "the exclusive right to publish a hardcover trade book in English for distribution in North America." 1 *Lindey on Entertainment, Publishing and the Arts* Form 1.01-1 (2d ed. 2000) (using the Random House form contract to explain the meaning of each clause). . . .

3. Comparison to Prior "New Use" Caselaw

The finding that the five licensing agreements at issue do not convey the right to publish the works as ebooks accords with Second Circuit and New York case law. Indeed, the two leading cases . . . that found that a particular new use was included within the grant language—*Boosey*, 145 F.3d 481 (2d Cir. 1998), and *Bartsch*, 391 F.2d 150 (2d Cir. 1968)—can be distinguished from this case on four grounds.

First, the language conveying the rights in *Boosey* and *Bartsch* was far broader than here. Second, the "new use" in those cases—*i.e.* display of a motion picture on television or videocassette—fell squarely within the same medium as the original grant. *See Boosey*, 145 F.3d at 486 (describing videocassettes and laser discs as "subsequently developed methods of distribution of a motion picture").

In this case, the "new use"—electronic digital signals sent over the internet—is a separate medium from the original use—printed words on paper. Random House's own expert concludes that the media are distinct because information stored digitally can be manipulated in ways that analog information cannot. Ebooks take advantage of the digital medium's ability to manipulate data by allowing ebook users to electronically search the text for specific words and phrases, change the font size and style, type notes into the text and electronically organize them, highlight and bookmark, hyperlink to specific parts of the text, and, in the future, to other sites on related topics as well, and access a dictionary that pronounces words in the ebook aloud. The need for a software program to interact with the data in order to make it usable, as well as the need for a piece of hardware to enable the reader to view the text, also distinguishes analog formats from digital formats. . . .

The third significant difference between the licensee in the motion picture cases cited above and the book publisher in this action is that the licensees in the motion picture cases have actually created a new work based on the material from the licensor. Therefore, the right to display that new work—whether on television or video—is derivative of the right to create that work. In the book publishing context, the publishers, although they participate in the editorial process, display the words written by the author, not themselves.

Fourth, the courts in *Boosey* and *Bartsch* were concerned that any approach to new use problems that "tilts against licensees [here, Random House] gives rise to antiprogressive incentives" insofar as licensees "would be reluctant to explore and utilize innovative technologies."

Boosey, 145 F.3d at 488, n.4; *see also Bartsch*, 391 F.2d at 155. However, in this action, the policy rationale of encouraging development in new technology is at least as well served by finding that the licensors—i.e., the authors—retain these rights to their works. In the 21st century, it cannot be said that licensees such as book publishers and movie producers are ipso facto more likely to make advances in digital technology than start-up companies. . . .

NOTES AND QUESTIONS

1. Which of these two cases has the better reasoning? Are these cases inconsistent, or does each case simply turn on the language of the contract at issue? If you had represented Random House in drafting and negotiating the author agreements, how would you have drafted the grant of rights provision to encompass ebooks? Remember, at the time those agreements were negotiated the computer industry was in its infancy.

2. As you know, a copyright owner is granted different rights under §106, including the right to reproduce the work, the right to prepare derivative works, the right to distribute copies of the work to the public, and the rights to publicly perform and display the work. The exact bundle of rights granted to a licensee can be extremely important, particularly as technology changes. If a licensee is granted the right to publicly perform the work, what happens when technologically enhanced means of engaging in that performance also result in copies being made? Should a license to make such copies ever be implied? Is that what the *Boosey & Hawkes* court did? For a helpful discussion of this problem, see Mark A. Lemley, *Dealing with Over-lapping Copyrights on the Internet*, 22 U. Dayton L. Rev. 547 (1997).

3. Contract interpretation is typically, although not always, governed by state law. There are many canons of construction that you learned in first-year Contracts class. For example, in certain situations the contract is said to be construed against the drafter. Should state law rules of contract interpretation apply to copyright contracts? Which principles of contract construction do the *Boosey & Hawkes* and *Random House* courts adopt?

Recall that in *CCNV v. Reid*, 490 U.S. 730 (1989), the Supreme Court held that a federal common law of agency, as opposed to the principles of agency law applied in each of the separate states, should be used to determine if the creator of a work is an employee. Are the arguments for using *federal* common law canons of contract interpretation as strong as the arguments for using a uniform federal agency test?

4. The problems associated with changing technologies and "old" contracts create a strong incentive on the part of the transferee simply to obtain the entire copyright. That way, there can be no dispute concerning what rights the transferee possesses. Subject only to termination rights, the transferee of "all right, title, and interest" in a particular copyright can exercise all of the rights of a copyright owner. Under what circumstances might a transferee be willing to accept less than the entire copyright?

5. Often members of the copyright industries (publishers, record companies, motion picture studios, and computer software companies) begin their contract negotiations seeking complete transfer of copyright ownership. For example, the publishers of this casebook sent the authors their standard publishing agreement, which contained the following copyright clause:

> The Authors grant the Publisher all right, title, and interest in and to the Work including the copyright thereto. The Authors acknowledge that as a result of this grant of ownership, the Publisher has throughout the world the exclusive right, among others, to reproduce the Work in any form or medium (now known or hereafter devised), to prepare derivative works based on the Work, to distribute copies of the Work in any form or medium (now known or later devised) to the public

by sale or other transfer of ownership, or by license, rental, lease or lending, and to perform and display the Work publicly.

Drafting the copyright clause in contracts (also referred to as the grant of rights clause) is, in part, an exercise in the possible. The authors of this casebook countered the original clause with this proposed clause:

The Authors grant the Publisher the exclusive right to reproduce the Work in print form and to prepare derivative works based upon the Work in print form. The Authors also grant to Publisher the exclusive right to distribute the Work in print form and any authorized derivative works thereof in print form to the public by sale or other transfer of ownership, or by license, rental, lease, or lending.

After negotiations, the parties finally agreed to the following clause:

The Authors grant the Publisher all right, title, and interest in and to the Work including the copyright thereto except that Authors expressly retain all exclusive rights to the Work in non-print form (including, but not limited to, electronic versions). The Authors acknowledge that as a result of this grant of ownership, the Publisher has throughout the world the exclusive rights, among others, to reproduce the Work in print form, to prepare derivative works based upon the Work in print form, and to distribute copies of the Work in print form to the public by sale or other transfer of ownership, or by license, rental, lease, or lending. The Authors further acknowledge that this grant to the Publisher of the ownership of the copyright to the Work includes the copyright to all derivative works in print form based upon the Work. Publisher shall have the right of first refusal of all remaining exclusive rights to the Work, including electronic rights, and the Authors agree to grant the Publisher all such rights, by separate instrument on mutually agreed terms, when Publisher develops a system for electronic distribution of the Work.

What did each of the parties give up? Given their initial positions, why might each side have agreed to this clause?

6. The problems of contract drafting can concern not just the phrasing of the grant of rights clause, but also the geographic scope of the grant. Is it sufficient for a license to grant rights "throughout the world"? Does your answer depend on how confident you are about the prospects for space travel in the next 120 years?

C. NEW LICENSING MODELS AND THE CONTRACT/LICENSE DISTINCTION

Negotiated contracts are an important piece of the contract and copyright puzzle. In more recent decades, a different type of contracting practice has taken on increased prominence in copyright law. The trend began in the software industry.

As you learned in Chapter 4, software is easily copied and, initially, software providers were uncertain whether they could successfully claim intellectual property protection for the information embodied in mass-marketed software products. They began to distribute their software with "end user license agreements" (EULAs) that prohibited end users from engaging in a variety of practices, some of which would be permissible under the Copyright Act.

More recently, other providers of digital content also have begun to adopt the practice of using EULAs. These take a variety of forms, including agreements printed on the package itself (shrinkwraps), electronic agreements to be "accepted" by the user's clicking "I agree" (click-wraps), and electronic agreements to be "accepted" by some act like downloading without having to click on a separate "I agree" button or box (browsewraps). Some early cases labeled shrinkwraps as contracts of adhesion and held them unenforceable in the absence of a state statute permitting enforcement. In recent years, however, courts have become increasingly willing to hold shrinkwrap and clickwrap agreements to be enforceable contracts under the common law of contract or the UCC.

In the late twentieth century, some authors began experimenting with a different use of mass license agreements. These authors sought to use licenses to ensure public availability of a rich supply of works. One way to attempt to ensure public availability of a work of authorship and to permit re-use of the expression the work embodies would be to abandon the work to the public domain. However, abandonment results in a complete loss of control; others may freely use the work's expression including as the basis for derivative works and may exercise their exclusive rights as copyright owners of those derivative works. If, instead of abandoning the underlying work, the author had retained copyright ownership and merely licensed the creation of derivative works, the license could insist on certain conditions.

The use of licenses as a means of ensuring ongoing public availability of expressive works began with what is known as the open source or free software movement. The best known open source license is the GNU General Public License (GNU GPL), under which the GNU/Linux computer operating system is distributed. This license authorizes others to copy, modify, and redistribute the software programs and to create and distribute new programs based on the initial ones. The license requires that if those new derivative programs are publicly distributed, they must be distributed subject to the same GNU GPL. The GNU GPL also requires that the program's source code must be distributed along with the object code. As you know from *Sega Enterprises Ltd. v. Accolade, Inc.*, and *Sony Computer Entertainment, Inc. v. Connectix Corp*, excerpted in Chapter 7 *supra*, access to the source code is critically important to understanding how a program functions and building interoperable programs. Thus, the open source movement uses copyright ownership and licenses to enforce social norms of sharing and openness. Open source licenses like the GNU GPL are also called "copyleft" licenses. The GNU GPL and other open source licenses are available at *http://www.fsf.org/licensing/licenses/*.

Inspired in part by the success of the open source movement in software, an organization called Creative Commons developed licensing tools with a similar aim — using "private rights to create public goods." *See http://creativecommons.org/about/history*. Creative Commons licenses allow authors of all types of works to place notices on their works that declare, with reference to specific licenses made available by Creative Commons, what rights are reserved and what rights users may exercise.

A brief note of caution before reading the cases in this section is in order. There is a conceptual difference between a contract and a license. A contract, as you learned in your first year class on the subject, must be supported by consideration to be enforceable. A license, on the other hand, need not involve such consideration. When a license is not supported by consideration it is sometimes referred to as a "bare license." Even if there are conditions placed on the license, a court could consider it to be similar to a gift with restrictions. In this sense a license is simply authorization to engage in an activity that requires permission from another person. In the copyright context, a license permits someone to engage in activity that, without the authorization of the copyright owner, would constitute infringement. Many times consideration is given to obtain that permission, making the license a contract.

NOTES & QUESTIONS

1. The requirement that publicly distributed works based on code available under the GPL must also be licensed under the GPL, thus allowing others to use that new work, has been characterized as "viral licensing": Once you "catch" the "virus," you can't get rid of it. Is the "viral" label a fair one?

2. Creative Commons licenses permit a copyright owner to customize aspects of the license she employs. Specifically, there are three different attributes that a copyright owner can select, each with a corresponding symbol that can be placed on the work:

![Noncommercial symbol]	Noncommercial:	Others may copy, distribute, publicly display, and publicly perform the work and derivative works based on it, but for noncommercial purposes only.
![No Derivative Works symbol]	No Derivative Works:	Others may copy, distribute, publicly display, and publicly perform only verbatim copies of the work, not derivative works based on it.
![Share Alike symbol]	Share Alike:	Others are allowed to distribute derivative works they create based on the copyright work, but only under a license identical to the license that governs the original work.

A copyright owner can pick and choose among the different attributes, but cannot select both the Share Alike and No Derivative Works options. Since its inception in 2001, the Creative Commons movement has spread to other countries. If you were an author, musician, or composer, would you distribute your works under a Creative Commons license? Which attributes would you select? Would your answer be different for different types of works? If so, why? Is there an attribute of the Creative Commons licenses that could be characterized as "viral"? To search for works available on the web under a Creative Commons license you can use the search engines linked by Creative Commons at *http://search.creativecommons.org/*.

3. A fourth license attribute is included in all Creative Commons licenses: The creator of the work must be given credit in any subsequent use of the work. The following symbol is used to notify users of the attribution requirement:

When Creative Commons first began, its licenses allowed authors to select whether they desired attribution as a condition of granting the permissions in the license. It found that 98% of individuals selected the attribution requirement. Creative Commons now includes the attribution provision as a standard element of all the licenses it provides for copyright owners to employ. Many open source licenses employ a similar provision.

What does the overwhelming desire for credit as a creator of a work indicate about the rights that are important to creators? Recall that the Copyright Act grants a right of attribution only to creators of "works of visual art" in §106A. Should an attribution right for all authors be added to §106?

4. Should open source and Creative Commons licenses be subject to termination rights? *See* Lydia Pallas Loren, *Building a Reliable Semicommons of Creative Works: Enforcement of Creative Commons Licenses and Limited Abandonment of Copyright*, 14 George Mason L. Rev. 271 (2007) (arguing that such licenses should be seen as a form of limited abandonment and

thus not subject to termination). Is there any reason to treat such licenses any differently than the clickwrap agreements that accompany other digital products? Remember that authorized derivative works created before termination can continue to be exploited, subject to the terms of the grant, even after termination.

5. Efforts to require greater institutional acceptance of "open" approaches to copyright licensing have been hotly contested by copyright interests. The National Institutes of Health (NIH) has adopted a policy requiring that all final manuscripts reporting the results of federally funded research be provided to the NIH in electronic form to be made available to the public "no later than 12 months after the official date of publication." See U.S. Dep't of Health & Human Services, National Institutes of Health, Revised Policy on Enhancing Public Access to Archived Publications Resulting from NIH-Funded Research, NOT-OD-08-033. Some scientific publishers have opposed that decision, arguing that members of the public may gain access to papers published in their journals from a variety of other sources. They have supported proposed legislation that would forbid federal agencies from imposing any condition requiring "the transfer or license to or for a Federal agency" of rights to make copyrighted works available to the public. Fair Copyright in Research Works Act, H.R. 6845, 110th Cong., 2d Sess. Would you support enactment of such a bill? Why, or why not?

The use of mass market licenses presents a host of challenging questions. Consider the following cases.

≣ **Vernor v. Autodesk, Inc.**
≣ *2009 WL 3187613 (W.D.Wash. Sept. 30, 2009)*

JONES, J.: . . . Mr. Vernor makes a living selling merchandise on eBay, the well-known internet marketplace. In 2005 and 2007, he attempted to sell what the court will refer to as "AutoCAD packages." Each AutoCAD package is an Autodesk-commissioned box, inside which is a "jewel case" containing a compact disk encoded with Autodesk's copyrighted AutoCAD software. The jewel case is sealed with a sticker advising that, among other things, "[t]his software is subject to the license agreement that appears during the installation process or is included in the package." The box also contains a copy of the Autodesk Software License Agreement (the "License"), and possibly other documentation as well.

Upon discovering Mr. Vernor's attempted eBay sale of AutoCAD packages, Autodesk invoked the "takedown" provisions of the Digital Millennium Copyright Act. Autodesk's 2005 takedown efforts delayed Mr. Vernor's sales. Its 2007 takedown efforts not only delayed one or more sales, they caused eBay to bar Mr. Vernor from selling anything for a month.

Autodesk directed its 2007 takedown notices at Mr. Vernor's attempted sales of AutoCAD packages that he acquired from a Seattle architecture firm, Cardwell/Thomas Associates ("CTA"), in a 2007 sale of office equipment. Although CTA had broken the sticker sealing the jewel case in each AutoCAD package, there is no dispute that the packages and their contents were authentic and otherwise identical to AutoCAD packages as Autodesk distributes them. There is no evidence or assertion that Mr. Vernor used AutoCAD software himself, or even installed it on his computer.

Mr. Vernor succeeded in selling two of the AutoCAD packages he acquired from CTA, and brought this action seeking a declaratory judgment that his sales of the other two

AutoCAD packages, and any other AutoCAD packages that he might acquire in the future, would not violate the Copyright Act. . . .

Autodesk obtained a consent judgment against CTA in the United States District Court for the Northern District of California. According to the recitals in the consent judgment, CTA agreed in 2002 to destroy all copies of AutoCAD software in the AutoCAD packages that it transferred to Mr. Vernor in 2007. CTA entered the 2002 agreement when upgrading its AutoCAD software. In the consent judgment, CTA agreed that it had breached its promise to destroy the AutoCAD packages, and that it had transferred those packages to Mr. Vernor in violation of Autodesk's copyright. . . .

. . . The parties disagree over whether Mr. Vernor has a first sale right to resell the Auto-CAD packages, and they disagree over whether Mr. Vernor's sales are contributory copyright infringement. The court answered both questions in Mr. Vernor's favor in May 2008, and for the reasons stated below, it does so again today.

III. Analysis . . .

A. *Rights Belonging to an "Owner" of a Copy of Copyrighted Material: The First Sale Doctrine of §109 and the Reproduction Exception of §117*

Some of the copyright principles bearing on this dispute are not controversial, and the court summarizes them here. No one disputes that Autodesk holds the copyright in the Auto-CAD software and the printed materials in the AutoCAD packages. . . . Exceptions to [the rights of a copyright owner] inure to an "owner" of a copy of copyrighted material. The first, commonly known as the "first sale" right, entitles the "owner of a particular copy" of copyrighted material to "sell or otherwise dispose of" that copy despite the copyright holder's distribution monopoly. 17 U.S.C. §109(a). The second is the privilege of the "owner of a copy of a computer program" to reproduce the program if doing so is an "essential step in the utilization of the computer program." 17 U.S.C. §117(a)(1). . . .

Mr. Vernor claims to be the "owner" of the copies of software in the AutoCAD packages in his possession, and seeks refuge in both §109 and §117. He contends that Autodesk transferred ownership of the AutoCAD packages to CTA, that CTA transferred ownership to him, and that he has a first sale right to sell those packages. For the same reason, he contends that anyone to whom he sells an AutoCAD package will become its owner, and will thus be privileged to use the software in his or her computer without violating Autodesk's right to control reproduction of the software.

Autodesk believes that it still owns the AutoCAD packages in Mr. Vernor's possession. It contends that it never transferred ownership of the AutoCAD packages to CTA. Indeed, in Autodesk's view, it never transfers ownership of AutoCAD packages to anyone. Instead, it licenses AutoCAD packages without transferring ownership of them, and thus remains the "owner" of the copies of copyrighted material contained therein. Autodesk claims that Mr. Vernor's sales of AutoCAD packages violate its distribution monopoly and contribute to violations of its reproduction monopoly by the persons to whom he sells. It thus claims that Mr. Vernor's sales constitute both direct and contributory copyright infringement.

B. *Autodesk's Transfer of AutoCAD Packages to CTA*

The key to resolving this dispute is determining whether Autodesk transferred ownership of the AutoCAD packages to CTA. Assuming that it did, no one disputes that CTA transferred whatever ownership it had to Mr. Vernor. Autodesk unquestionably transferred *possession* of ten AutoCAD packages to CTA in a 1999 settlement of a dispute. In the 1999 settlement agreement, CTA promised to "adhere to all terms of the Autodesk Software License Agreement." . . . .

The License governs both the use and disposition of the AutoCAD packages. It limits installation of AutoCAD software to two computers, with a ban on simultaneous use of the software on those computers. It prohibits modification or reverse engineering of the software. It bars any use or transfer of the software outside of the western hemisphere. It bars any transfer of the software without Autodesk's written permission. It also declares that "[t]itle and copyrights to the Software and accompanying materials and any copies made by you remain with Autodesk." Finally, the License dictates that a user who obtains the software via an upgrade from Autodesk must destroy any copies of older AutoCAD software in his possession.

The court also assumes for purposes of this order that in 2002 CTA upgraded the software contained in the AutoCAD packages that Autodesk transferred to it in the 1999 settlement agreement, and violated its agreement to destroy the copies of the software in those packages. . . . The court assumes that CTA agreed to destroy the AutoCAD 14 software in 2002 only because the assumption ultimately does not prejudice Mr. Vernor.

Importantly, however, CTA made no agreement to destroy the AutoCAD 14 software when it acquired it in 1999. It made that agreement in 2002 because CTA offered an enormous discount as an incentive to agree to destroy the software when it upgraded to AutoCAD 2000. . . . AutoCAD 2000 software retailed for $3750, but sold for $495 as an upgrade[].

There is no dispute that Autodesk licensed its software to CTA. The court makes this observation because the parties and their witnesses too often suggest that their dispute is about whether Autodesk "sold" rather than "licensed" its software. That dispute is not determinative, because the use of software copies can be licensed while the copies themselves are sold. Autodesk unquestionably licensed the software in that it limits the right to use it. For example, the License takes away fair use right to reverse engineer the software. The License also expands the right to use software. For example, it permits the licensee to install the software on two computers, whereas §117(a) would permit only a single installation. There is also no question that most software is transferred to consumers via licenses that restrict and expand their right to use it, although no party has presented competent evidence of the terms of any other software maker's license. The question before the court is whether the Autodesk License is a license that transfers ownership of the software copies included in AutoCAD packages. To capture that distinction, the court will use the terms "mere license" and "mere licensee" in reference to licenses that do not transfer ownership of any copies. The question before the court is whether Mr. Vernor is the "owner" of the copies of copyrighted material in the AutoCAD packages he acquired from CTA, or whether CTA was a mere licensee who had no ownership to transfer to Mr. Vernor.

C.   *Who is the "Owner" of the AutoCAD Packages? The Ninth Circuit Gives Two Different Answers.*

. . . Ninth Circuit precedent gives two different answers to the question of what distinguishes an "owner" from a mere licensee. . . .

1.   The *Wise* View: The Distinction Between a Transfer of Ownership and a Mere License Turns on the Terms of the Transfer Agreement.

[United States v.] Wise [, 550 F.2d 1180 (9th Cir.1977)] called upon the panel to examine several transfer agreements for movie prints. Many were generic distribution agreements transferring possession of prints to theaters and other outlets for display. Virtually all of the

distribution agreements "were designated as 'licenses'," and they transferred only "limited rights for the exhibition or distribution of the films for a limited purpose and for a limited period of time." *Wise*, 550 F.2d at 1190. The "[t]ypical" distribution agreement "reserved title to the film prints" in the studio and "required their return to [the studio] following expiration of the contract term." *Id.* . . .

The *Wise* panel noted that the "complicated" nature of agreements transferring rights in copyrighted works required an analysis of each transfer agreement before it. *Wise*, 550 F.2d at 1189. Designating an agreement as a "license" does not determine whether it transfers ownership. *Id.* at 1192. The panel noted several relevant characteristics of transfer agreements, but they were ambiguous in the sense that those characteristics were present in both transfers of ownership and mere licenses. For example, although an agreement that fails to include a clause reserving title in the transferred copy to the copyright holder is suggestive of an ownership transfer, that failure is not dispositive. *Id.* at 1191. Similarly, a single, up-front payment by the transferee for a particular copy is suggestive of a transfer of ownership, but not dispositive. An agreement requiring the transferee to destroy transferred copies is not dispositive of whether ownership transfers.

A clause in an agreement reserving title to the transferred copy in the copyright holder is also an ambiguous characteristic in *Wise*. With only one likely exception, in every agreement containing an express reservation of title in the copyright holder, the panel found a mere license. The likely exception was an agreement to transfer a print of "Camelot" to actress Vanessa Redgrave (the "Redgrave Contract."). Like all of the V.I.P. agreements, that agreement "reserved all rights and title in the studios, restricting the licensee to possession of the print for his own personal use." *Id.* at 1184. Nonetheless, when coupled with an upfront payment for the cost of the print and "the rest of the language of the agreement," the panel found the Redgrave Contract transferred ownership. *Id.* at 1192. It reached that conclusion despite restrictions that prevented the sale, lease, license, or loan of the print "to any other person," and eliminated all uses of the film except for Ms. Redgrave's in-home display. . . .

Only one characteristic was unambiguous in that it appeared only in agreements that the *Wise* panel deemed to be transfers of ownership. In each instance in which the transferee could, at his election, retain possession of the transferred copy indefinitely, and the copyright holder had no right to regain possession, the court found an ownership transfer. By contrast, the copyright holder's right to regain possession of the transferred copy was characteristic of a mere license.

The Autodesk License is a hodgepodge of terms that, standing alone, support both a transfer of ownership and a mere license. Autodesk expressly retains title to the "Software and accompanying materials," but it has no right to regain possession of the software or the "accompanying materials." Licensees pay a single up-front price for the software. Autodesk can require the destruction of the software, but only as consideration in the later purchase of an upgrade. The decision to upgrade, and thus the decision to accept Autodesk's destruction requirement, is entirely in the control of the licensee. Autodesk severely restricts the use and further transfer of the software.

. . . [T]he court concludes that *Wise* leads to the conclusion that the transfer of AutoCAD copies via the License is a transfer of ownership. Of all the agreements that the *Wise* panel analyzed, the License is most analogous to the Redgrave Contract. Like the License, the Redgrave Contract purported to reserve title in the copy to the copyright holder, but made no provision for the copyright holder to regain possession of the copy. Like Ms. Redgrave, Autodesk licensees pay a single price to the copyright holder at the outset of the transaction. Like the License, the Redgrave Contract severely restricts the use and transfer of the copy. But, like the panel in *Wise*, this court concludes that the License transferred ownership of the software copy despite those restrictions.

. . . *Wise* requires the court to look at a transaction holistically, and the court finds no basis for the conclusion that an agreement to permit perpetual possession of property can be construed as reserving ownership. Autodesk's attempt to establish the common understanding of "ownership" by citing a legal dictionary equating ownership with *unrestricted* ownership is consistent neither with *Wise* nor with common understanding. For example, a person who buys a home is nonetheless restricted in his use and subsequent transfer of the home by property laws, zoning ordinances, and fair housing statutes. No one would characterize the person's possession, however, as something other than ownership. Similarly, the court cannot characterize Autodesk's decision to let its licensees retain possession of the software forever as something other than a transfer of ownership, despite numerous restrictions on that ownership.

Autodesk did not regain ownership of the software copies it transferred to CTA when it upgraded CTA's software. Instead, years after Autodesk transferred ownership of the software copies to CTA, CTA agreed to destroy the copies as consideration for a discounted upgrade to new software. . . . As the court concluded in its prior order, "[t]here is no basis to distinguish this transaction from the salvage transactions that were found to be sales in *Wise*." *Vernor*, 555 F.Supp.2d at 1170 n.5. . . .

2. The *MAI* Trio: More Deference to a Copyright Holder's Characterization of a Transfer Agreement as a Mere License

More than 25 years after *Wise*, the *MAI [Sys. Corp. v. Peak Computer, Inc.*, 991 F.2d 511 (9th Cir. 1993)] panel took a more deferential view of the characterization of a transfer of copyrighted material as a mere license. The transfer agreement in *MAI* was a license that restricted the use of software. *MAI*, 991 F.2d at 517 n.3. The defendant in *MAI* was not a licensee, but rather a repair service that serviced computer systems on which licensed software had been installed. *Id.* at 513. The *MAI* panel was mainly concerned with whether the repair technicians' use of the computers entailed making an unauthorized copy of the software. *Id.* at 517-19. In a one-sentence footnote, the panel stated that because "MAI licensed its software, the [customers to whom it licensed the software] do not qualify as 'owners' of the software and are not eligible for protection under §117." *Id.* at 518 n.5. The panel did not cite *Wise*.

In *Triad [Sys. Corp. v. Southeastern Express Co.*, 64 F.3d 1330 (9th Cir. 1995)], a panel again confronted a copyright infringement claim against a repair service, this time considering three versions of a software transfer agreement. In the first, the copyright holder "sold its software outright." 64 F.3d at 1333. In the second version, it "began licensing" the software and prohibited duplication of the software or use of the software by third parties. *Id.* In the third, it added a requirement that licensees pay a "transfer fee" to sell computer systems on which the software had been installed. *Id.* The court concluded that customers who acquired software under the first agreement "own[ed] their software," and thus had the right under §117 to authorize repairs. *Id.* at 1333 & n.3. Transferees under the second and third agreements could not use §117 to authorize repairs, and thus the panel implicitly held that they were mere licensees. *Id.*

Most recently, in *Wall Data [Inc. v. Los Angeles County Sheriff's Dep't*, 447 F.3d 769 (9th Cir. 2006)], another panel considered the §117 defense of a computer software user. The transfer agreement in question prohibited the installation of the software in "multiple computer" or networked "multiple user arrangement[s]," and permitted transfers of the software between computers under the transferee's control only once every 30 days. *Wall Data*, 447 F.3d at 775 n.5. The agreement did not otherwise restrict resale or disposition of the software. The transferee, a large sheriff's department, purchased licenses permitting it to install approximately 3600 copies of the software. It instead installed copies of the software on more than

6000 computers, but used a password system to ensure that no more than 3600 users could access the software at one time. The *Wall Data* panel rejected the licensee's attempt to invoke §117 for two independent reasons. First, it followed *MAI* in concluding that a licensee who obtains a software copy with a license that "makes it clear that she or he is granting only a license to the copy of the software" and "imposes significant restrictions on the purchaser's ability to redistribute or transfer that copy" is "not an owner" of the copy. *Id*. at 785. It also cited *MAI* for the proposition that "if a software developer retains ownership of every copy of software, and merely licenses the use of those copies, §117 does not apply." *Id*. Second, the panel held that even if the licensee could rely on §117, it could not establish that its installation of more than 2000 unauthorized copies of the software was an "essential step" in the use of the software, as §117(a)(1) requires. . . . [T]he court cannot characterize either of *Wall Data*'s twin holdings as dicta. The *Wall Data* panel explained, however, that it had declined to revisit *MAI* despite substantial criticism from commentators and lower courts because the second of its two holdings made "any error [in the first holding] harmless." *Wall Data*, 447 F.3d at 786 n.9.

If the court were to follow the *MAI* Trio, Autodesk would prevail. . . .

D. Wise *and the* MAI *Trio Conflict Irreconcilably; this Court Must Follow* Wise.

With two sets of conflicting precedent before the court, the question becomes which to follow. That question, at least, has a simple answer. The court must follow the oldest precedent among conflicting opinions from three-judge Ninth Circuit panels. *United States v. Rodriguez-Lara*, 421 F.3d 932, 943 (9th Cir. 2005). This court is loath, however, to apply this rule unless there is no way to avoid the conflict between the opinions. As was the case in the prior order, the court finds the conflict unavoidable. . . .

Wise construed the statutory predecessor to §109, whereas each opinion in the *MAI* Trio construes §117. It is possible, then, that "owner" has a different meaning in each statute. Even on a casual analysis, this is unlikely. The court has already noted the presumption that identical terms within the same statute have the same meaning. *Vernor*, 555 F.Supp.2d at 1173 & n.8. At least in their briefs, Mr. Vernor and Autodesk agree that the phrases "owner of a copy" in §117 and "owner of a particular copy" in §109 have the same meaning. Autodesk Mot. At oral argument, Autodesk retreated from this position, suggesting that the court could reach the anomalous result that *Wise* and §109 permit Mr. Vernor to sell the AutoCAD packages whereas the *MAI* Trio and §117 deny him and the persons to whom he sells the right to use the software. This result is far from satisfactory. . . .

The lack of legislation addressing computer licensing leads the court to conclude with a discussion of the policy concerns that the parties have raised. Autodesk argues that this court's interpretation of "owner" will harm consumers and software producers alike. It suggests, for example, that software prices would rise if producers had to confront the possibility of resale, and that resale promotes piracy. Mr. Vernor contends that Autodesk's preferred interpretation of "owner" would give copyright holders of all stripes the ability to destroy secondary markets for their works by the simple expedient of declaring transfers of copies of their works to be "licenses" rather than sales. For example, a book publisher could transfer its wares pursuant to licenses retaining title and barring resale or use by other parties, effectively eliminating not only the secondhand market, but preventing a library from lending the book as well.

These contentions make for interesting debate. Autodesk's suggestion that consumers will be harmed by rising retail prices if software producers compensate for the resale market does not address the concomitant price benefit in the form of reduced resale prices. Although Autodesk would no doubt prefer that consumers' money reaches its pockets, that preference is not a basis for policy.

Autodesk's claim that Mr. Vernor promotes piracy is unconvincing. Mr. Vernor's sales of AutoCAD packages promote piracy no more so than Autodesk's sales of the same packages. Piracy depends on the number of people willing to engage in piracy, and a pirate is presumably just as happy to unlawfully duplicate software purchased directly from Autodesk as he is to copy software purchased from a reseller like Mr. Vernor. The court notes, moreover, that even if CTA had never opened its AutoCAD packages, never installed the software on its computer, and thus never raised the possibility of piracy, Autodesk would still take the position that CTA's resale of those packages was a copyright violation.

Mr. Vernor's fear of the destruction of established resale markets also seems misplaced. The court notes, for example, that widespread piracy of musical recordings from compact disks has not led the music industry to adopt a restrictive licensing regime like the one Autodesk advocates.

There is much more to say about such policy debates, but the court's decision today is not based on any policy judgment. Congress is both constitutionally and institutionally suited to render judgments on policy; courts generally are not. The parties' policy concerns might be of heightened importance had the Ninth Circuit not already addressed the dispositive legal questions in *Wise* and the *MAI* Trio. Precedent binds the court regardless of whether it would be good policy to ignore it. The court has followed *Wise* solely for the reasons stated in this order, not because of any policy judgment. . . . .

NOTES AND QUESTIONS

1. In *Vernor* the court had to determine whether the transaction was properly characterized as a sale or a license in order to decide whether an infringement claim would be permissible. Similarly, in *UMG Recordings, Inc. v. Augusto*, 558 F. Supp. 2d 1055 (C.D. Cal. 2008), the plaintiff had sent promotional CDs to music industry insiders. The CDs contained a label that stated:

> This CD is the property of the record company and is licensed to the intended recipient for personal use only. Acceptance of this CD shall constitute an agreement to comply with the terms of the license. Resale or transfer of possession is not allowed and may be punishable under federal and state laws.

The defendant had obtained copies of the CDs and, as in *Vernor*, was selling them on eBay, advertising them as "rare collectibles not available in stores." Nothing required the recipient to return the promotional CDs to UMG and there were no consequences if the CDs were lost or destroyed. The court looked past the copyright owner's characterization of the transaction as a "license" to the "economic realities of the transaction." *Id.* at 1061. Do you agree with the decision in these two cases to follow the *Wise* court's holistic approach? If so, which of the various reasons mentioned by the *Vernor* court do you find most persuasive?

2. There can be a lot at stake in determining who constitutes an owner of a copy and who constitutes a mere licensee. If copyright owners can control the subsequent transfer of copies of software, they will not need to compete with "used" copies of their own products. Should copyright owners be protected against such competition? The court in *Augusto, supra*, noted that the only benefit to the purported "license" was to restrain transfer, a purpose that the Supreme Court had rejected 100 years ago. *See* 558 F. Supp. 2d at 1061 (citing *Bobbs-Merrill Co. v. Straus*, 210 U.S. 339 (1908)). In *SoftMan Products Co. v. Adobe Software, Inc.*, 171 F. Supp. 2d 1075 (C.D. Cal. 2001), Adobe had entered into agreements with distributors

that restricted them from splitting apart packages of different software products. SoftMan purchased packages from authorized distributors, as if it were an end user, but then behaved as a reseller. In this way SoftMan avoided the contractual restrictions Adobe imposed on distributors as well as the restrictions imposed on an end user. The court held that the "the transfer of copies of Adobe software making up the distribution chain from Adobe to SoftMan are sales of the particular copies, but not of Adobe's intellectual rights in the computer program itself, which is protected by Adobe's copyright." The court found that the defendant was "an 'owner' of the copy and is entitled to the use and enjoyment of the software, with the rights that are consistent with copyright law." The court observed:

> This is an area fraught with conflicting policy considerations. Software publishers are desirous of augmenting the protections offered under copyright law. In this case, through the use of licensing, Adobe seeks a vast and seemingly unlimited power to control prices and all channels of distribution. On the other hand, in the absence of copyright law violations, the market can often best regulate prices and all subsequent transactions that occur after the first sale. Sound policy rationales support the analysis of those courts that have found shrinkwrap licenses to be unenforceable. A system of "licensing" which grants software publishers this degree of unchecked power to control the market deserves to be the object of careful scrutiny.

Id. at 1091.

Is there any reason to treat used copies of computer software differently than used books? What should be the rule when books are distributed in digital form with EULAs attached?

3. *Vernor* and *Softman* both involved the transfer of physical computer discs that contained copies of the software. Because they were embodied in physical copies that could be resold before being installed on a computer, the defendants did not confront the EULA with its "I agree" button. When copyrighted works are downloaded from the Internet, there is no tangible disk to be sold on the "used" market. Should a copyright owner be able, through contract, to insist that a user give up rights protected by the first sale doctrine to obtain access to the work?

4. Not all courts agree with the approach employed by *Vernor* and *Softman*. In *Adobe Systems, Inc. v. Stargate Software Inc.*, 216 F. Supp. 2d 1051 (N.D. Cal. 2002), the court found no "colorable reason" why Adobe and should not be free to characterize its agreements as it wished because the right to contract on mutually agreed terms is "[f]undamental to any free society." *Id.* at 1059. Further, the court reasoned that it would be "incongruous to conclude" that resellers are owners of the copies "while the end users who the resellers distribute to are granted a mere license." *Id.* at 1059-60 (quoting *Adobe Systems, Inc. v. One Stop Micro*, 84 F. Supp. 2d 1086, 1091 (N.D. Cal. 2000)). Consequently, the court construed the challenged transfer to a reseller as a license and not a sale.

Do you agree that it is "incongruous" that resellers may own the software while users are only licensees? Should resellers and users be subject to the same sort of treatment when considering whether a particular transaction is a "sale" or a "license"? Are the same copyright rights implicated? Are the same policy interests implicated?

5. Companies attempting to use contracts to restrict resale of copies of their software may be able to maintain actions for breach of contract against distributors who breach their distribution agreements. The company from which Vernor purchased the copies, CTA, had entered into a settlement agreement binding itself to the EULA. Should Autodesk also be able to pursue a claim of breach of contract against CTA? Would it matter how the settlement agreement was worded? Does the *Vernor* court's conclusion that CTA was an "owner" and not a licensee for purposes of §109(a) affect the viability of a copyright infringement claim by Autodesk against CTA?

6. Should other aspects of the balance of rights and limitations contained in the Copyright Act be open to recrafting by contract? Imagine that AutoDesk or Adobe had used a license agreement that purported to transfer copies subject to the proviso that recipients not publish negative reviews of the software. Would characterizing the transactions as sales rather than licenses assist a court in determining whether to enforce such a provision?

≡ *Jacobsen v. Katzer*
≡ *535 F.3d 1373 (Fed. Cir. 2008)*

HOCHBERG, J.: . . . Jacobsen manages an open source software group called Java Model Railroad Interface ("JMRI"). Through the collective work of many participants, JMRI created a computer programming application called DecoderPro, which allows model railroad enthusiasts to use their computers to program the decoder chips that control model trains. DecoderPro files are available for download and use by the public free of charge from an open source incubator website called SourceForge. . . . The downloadable files contain copyright notices and refer the user to a "COPYING" file, which clearly sets forth the terms of the Artistic License.

[Matthew Katzer and Kamind Associates, Inc. (collectively "Katzer/Kamind") offer] a competing software product, Decoder Commander, which is also used to program decoder chips. During development of Decoder Commander, one of Katzer/Kamind's predecessors or employees is alleged to have downloaded the decoder definition files from DecoderPro and used portions of these files as part of the Decoder Commander software. The Decoder Commander software files that used DecoderPro definition files did not comply with the terms of the Artistic License. Specifically, the Decoder Commander software did not include (1) the authors' names, (2) JMRI copyright notices, (3) references to the COPYING file, (4) an identification of SourceForge or JMRI as the original source of the definition files, and (5) a description of how the files or computer code had been changed from the original source code. The Decoder Commander software also changed various computer file names of DecoderPro files without providing a reference to the original JMRI files or information on where to get the Standard Version.

Jacobsen moved for a preliminary injunction, arguing that the violation of the terms of the Artistic License constituted copyright infringement. . . . The District Court found that Jacobsen had a cause of action only for breach of contract, rather than an action for copyright infringement based on a breach of the conditions of the Artistic License. . . .

II. . . .

A. . . .

Open Source software projects invite computer programmers from around the world to view software code and make changes and improvements to it. Through such collaboration, software programs can often be written and debugged faster and at lower cost than if the copyright holder were required to do all of the work independently. In exchange and in consideration for this collaborative work, the copyright holder permits users to copy, modify and distribute the software code subject to conditions that serve to protect downstream users and to keep the code accessible. By requiring that users copy and restate the license and attribution information, a copyright holder can ensure that recipients of the redistributed computer code know the identity of the owner as well as the scope of the license granted by the original owner. The Artistic License in this case also requires that changes to the computer code be tracked so that downstream users know what part of the computer code is the original code created by the copyright holder and what part has been newly added or altered by another collaborator.

Traditionally, copyright owners sold their copyrighted material in exchange for money. The lack of money changing hands in open source licensing should not be presumed to mean that there is no economic consideration, however. There are substantial benefits, including economic benefits, to the creation and distribution of copyrighted works under public licenses that range far beyond traditional license royalties. For example, program creators may generate market share for their programs by providing certain components free of charge. Similarly, a programmer or company may increase its national or international reputation by incubating open source projects. Improvement to a product can come rapidly and free of charge from an expert not even known to the copyright holder. . . .

B.

The parties do not dispute that Jacobsen is the holder of a copyright for certain materials distributed through his website. Katzer/Kamind also admits that portions of the DecoderPro software were copied, modified, and distributed as part of the Decoder Commander software. Accordingly, Jacobsen has made out a prima facie case of copyright infringement. Katzer/Kamind argues that they cannot be liable for copyright infringement because they had a license to use the material. Thus, the Court must evaluate whether the use by Katzer/Kamind was outside the scope of the license. The copyrighted materials in this case are downloadable by any user and are labeled to include a copyright notification and a COPYING file that includes the text of the Artistic License. The Artistic License grants users the right to copy, modify, and distribute the software:

> provided that [the user] insert a prominent notice in each changed file stating how and when [the user] changed that file, and provided that [the user] do at least ONE of the following:
>
> a) place [the user's] modifications in the Public Domain or otherwise make them Freely Available . . .
> b) use the modified Package only within [the user's] corporation or organization.
> c) rename any non-standard executables so the names do not conflict with the standard executables, which must also be provided, and provide a separate manual page for each nonstandard executable that clearly documents how it differs from the Standard Version, or
> d) make other distribution arrangements with the Copyright Holder.

The heart of the argument on appeal concerns whether the terms of the Artistic License are conditions of, or merely covenants to, the copyright license. Generally, a "copyright owner who grants a nonexclusive license to use his copyrighted material waives his right to sue the licensee for copyright infringement" and can sue only for breach of contract. *Sun Microsystems, Inc., v. Microsoft Corp.*, 188 F.3d 1115, 1121 (9th Cir.1999). If, however, a license is limited in scope and the licensee acts outside the scope, the licensor can bring an action for copyright infringement.

Thus, if the terms of the Artistic License allegedly violated are both covenants and conditions, they may serve to limit the scope of the license and are governed by copyright law. If they are merely covenants, by contrast, they are governed by contract law. . . .

III.

The Artistic License states on its face that the document creates conditions: "The intent of this document is to state the *conditions* under which a Package may be copied." (Emphasis added.) The Artistic License also uses the traditional language of conditions by noting that the rights to copy, modify, and distribute are granted "*provided that*" the conditions are met. Under California contract law, "provided that" typically denotes a condition.

The conditions set forth in the Artistic License are vital to enable the copyright holder to retain the ability to benefit from the work of downstream users. By requiring that users who modify or distribute the copyrighted material retain the reference to the original source files, downstream users are directed to Jacobsen's website. Thus, downstream users know about the collaborative effort to improve and expand the SourceForge project once they learn of the "upstream" project from a "downstream" distribution, and they may join in that effort.

The District Court interpreted the Artistic License to permit a user to "modify the material in any way" and did not find that any of the "provided that" limitations in the Artistic License served to limit this grant. The District Court's interpretation of the conditions of the Artistic License does not credit the explicit restrictions in the license that govern a downloader's right to modify and distribute the copyrighted work. The copyright holder here expressly stated the terms upon which the right to modify and distribute the material depended and invited direct contact if a downloader wished to negotiate other terms. These restrictions were both clear and necessary to accomplish the objectives of the open source licensing collaboration, including economic benefit. . . .

Copyright holders who engage in open source licensing have the right to control the modification and distribution of copyrighted material. As the Second Circuit explained in *Gilliam v. ABC*, 538 F.2d 14, 21 (2d Cir. 1976), the "unauthorized editing of the underlying work, if proven, would constitute an infringement of the copyright in that work similar to any other use of a work that exceeded the license granted by the proprietor of the copyright." Copyright licenses are designed to support the right to exclude; money damages alone do not support or enforce that right. The choice to exact consideration in the form of compliance with the open source requirements of disclosure and explanation of changes, rather than as a dollar-denominated fee, is entitled to no less legal recognition. Indeed, because a calculation of damages is inherently speculative, these types of license restrictions might well be rendered meaningless absent the ability to enforce through injunctive relief.

In this case, a user who downloads the JMRI copyrighted materials is authorized to make modifications and to distribute the materials "provided that" the user follows the restrictive terms of the Artistic License. A copyright holder can grant the right to make certain modifications, yet retain his right to prevent other modifications. Indeed, such a goal is exactly the purpose of adding conditions to a license grant. . . .

It is outside the scope of the Artistic License to modify and distribute the copyrighted materials without copyright notices and a tracking of modifications from the original computer files. If a downloader does not assent to these conditions stated in the COPYING file, he is instructed to "make other arrangements with the Copyright Holder." Katzer/Kamind did not make any such "other arrangements." The clear language of the Artistic License creates conditions to protect the economic rights at issue in the granting of a public license. These conditions govern the rights to modify and distribute the computer programs and files included in the downloadable software package. The attribution and modification transparency requirements directly serve to drive traffic to the open source incubation page and to inform downstream users of the project, which is a significant economic goal of the copyright holder that the law will enforce. Through this controlled spread of information, the copyright holder gains creative collaborators to the open source project; by requiring that changes made by downstream users be visible to the copyright holder and others, the copyright holder learns about the uses for his software and gains others' knowledge that can be used to advance future software releases.

IV.

. . . Having determined that the terms of the Artistic License are enforceable copyright conditions, we remand to enable the District Court to determine whether Jacobsen [is entitled to a preliminary injunction.] . . .

NOTES AND QUESTIONS

1. In what ways is *Jacobsen* similar to *Vernor*? In what ways are they different? Should a license authorizing activities that otherwise would be infringing be analyzed differently than a license prohibiting activities that otherwise would be authorized under the Copyright Act?

2. Because open source and Creative Commons licenses do not require the recipient of a covered work to click "I agree," some have argued that they do not create enforceable contracts. Another way to think about open source and Creative Commons licenses is as defenses to claims of infringement: The copyright owner could assert that a user of the work has engaged in an activity that constitutes infringement, but the user can point to the license as authorizing the activity. When the activity is outside the scope of the license, the defense of "licensed use" fails and the user is left to defend against the infringement claim. Some terms in open source and Creative Commons licenses, however, seek to create obligations that the Copyright Act would not create. Are such terms — for example, provisions requiring attribution — enforceable? On what theory?

3. According to the *Jacobsen* court, Katzer/Kamind did not simply receive a mere license — i.e., a grant of permission to use the copyrighted material — but instead had entered into an exchange for consideration. Why did the court so conclude? Do you agree with the court's characterization of the transaction as a contract? If a transaction subject to an open source or Creative Commons license is viewed as a mere license, should that affect the analysis of whether the license terms impose covenants or conditions?

4. Does *Jacobsen* provide sufficient guidance on how to distinguish covenants from conditions? In *Sun Microsystems, Inc. v. Microsoft Corp.*, 188 F.3d 1115 (9th Cir. 1999), cited by the court, Sun sued Microsoft for copyright infringement based on Microsoft's failure to comply with a license provision requiring Microsoft's products to be compatible with certain Sun specifications. The Ninth Circuit stated: "Whether this is a copyright or contract case turns on whether the compatibility provisions help define the scope of the license." *Id.* at 1121. On remand, the district court held that under California law the compatibility provisions were contractual covenants rather than license restrictions. The court relied on the language and structure of the agreement: the license was not conditional on compliance with the compatibility requirements, and the agreement's remedial scheme that provided for notice and a right to cure in the event of breach would have been frustrated if Sun could sue immediately for copyright infringement. *Sun Microsystems, Inc. v. Microsoft Corp.*, 81 F. Supp. 2d 1026, 1032-33 (N.D. Cal. 2000). The appropriate cause of action was thus breach of contract rather than copyright infringement. Does the *Sun Microsystems* approach provide more guidance?

5. Should the question whether a particular contractual provision is a covenant or condition be decided as a matter of federal copyright law or under state contract law? Courts generally apply state law to this question, but remember *CCNV v. Reid*, Chapter 2.B *supra*, in which the Court emphasized the importance of uniformity in the treatment of works made for hire and articulated the basis for a federal common law standard.

6. The court in *Jacobsen* seems to categorize cases neatly into two categories: those involving conditions (governed by copyright law) and those involving covenants (governed by contract law). Doesn't the case involve a breach of contract as well as copyright infringement? According to at least two commentators, "[a] breach of a mere covenant entitles the licensor to damages perhaps, but does not support an infringement claim so long as the licensee continues to perform within the license scope. On the other hand, breach of a scope provision entitles the licensor to both a contract remedy and an infringement claim, providing of course that there can be no double recovery." Raymond T. Nimmer & Jeff C. Dodd, Modern Licensing Law 2007 edition, §§11:27 (2006). This suggests that a plaintiff could claim both breach of contract and copyright infringement for violation of a scope provision, as Jacobsen did in this case. On remand, the district court addressed both the contract claim and the copyright infringement claim. *Jacobsen v. Katzer*, 609 F. Supp. 2d 925 (N.D. Cal. 2009). The court dismissed the breach claim for two reasons: first for failure to plead damages proximately caused by the breach, and second on preemption grounds due to the significant overlap with the infringement claim. We address potential preemption of breach claims in Chapter 10.

7. What is at stake in determining whether the appropriate claim is one for copyright infringement or one for breach of contract or both? One answer, highlighted in Question 6 above, is the different remedies available. The usual remedy for breach of contract is an award of damages. The remedial provisions of the Copyright Act permit recovery of either actual damages or statutory damages," a measure of damages not available pursuant to a standard contract claim. Additionally, the Act provides that a successful plaintiff may recover attorney fees and costs in certain cases. Further, injunctive relief is common in copyright cases and rare in contract cases. Another answer concerns jurisdiction. As you know, a lawsuit for breach of contract can be heard in federal court only if some other basis for subject matter jurisdiction exists. How might the jurisdictional issues affect the way a claim involving a copyright license is pled? Chapter 11 considers remedies and jurisdictional issues in more detail.

D. MISUSE

The previous section raised questions about what terms a copyright owner can include in mass market licenses, and about how far those terms can reach. One potential limit on the contracting behavior of copyright owners is a doctrine known as copyright misuse.

Video Pipeline, Inc. v. Buena Vista Home Entertainment, Inc.
342 F.3d 191, 203 (3d Cir. 2003), cert. denied, 540 U.S. 1178 (2004)

AMBRO, J.: In this copyright case we review the District Court's entry of a preliminary injunction against Video Pipeline, Inc.'s online display of "clip previews." A "clip preview," as we use the term, is an approximately two-minute segment of a movie, copied without authorization from the film's copyright holder, and used in the same way as an authorized movie "trailer." . . .

Video Pipeline compiles movie trailers onto videotape for home video retailers to display in their stores. To obtain the right to distribute the trailers used in the compilations, Video Pipeline enters into agreements with various entertainment companies. It entered into such an agreement, the Master Clip License Agreement ("License Agreement"), with Disney in 1988, and Disney thereafter provided Video Pipeline with over 500 trailers for its movies.

In 1997, Video Pipeline took its business to the web, where it operates VideoPipeline.net and VideoDetective.com. The company maintains a database accessible from VideoPipeline. net, which contains movie trailers Video Pipeline has received throughout the years. Video Pipeline's internet clients — retail web sites selling home videos — use VideoPipeline.net to display trailers to site visitors. . . .

Video Pipeline included in its online database trailers it received under the License Agreement from Disney. Because the License Agreement did not permit this use, Disney requested that Video Pipeline remove the trailers from the database. It complied with that request.

On October 24, 2000, however, Video Pipeline filed a complaint in the District Court for the District of New Jersey seeking a declaratory judgment that its online use of the trailers did not violate federal copyright law. Disney shortly thereafter terminated the License Agreement.

Video Pipeline decided to replace some of the trailers it had removed at Disney's request from its database. In order to do so, it copied approximately two minutes from each of at least 62 Disney movies to create its own clip previews of the movies. . . .

[The District Court granted Disney's request for a preliminary injunction and Video Pipeline appealed. After rejecting Video Pipeline's fair use argument, the court turned to its next defense.]

Video Pipeline further contends that Disney has misused its copyright and, as a result, should not receive the protection of copyright law. Video Pipeline points to certain licensing agreements that Disney has entered into with three companies and sought to enter into with a number of other companies operating web sites. Each of these licensing agreements provides that Disney, the licensor, will deliver trailers by way of hyperlinks for display on the licensee's web site. The Agreements further state:

> The Website in which the Trailers are used may not be derogatory to or critical of the entertainment industry or of [Disney] (and its officers, directors, agents, employees, affiliates, divisions and subsidiaries) or of any motion picture produced or distributed by [Disney] . . . [or] of the materials from which the Trailers were taken or of any person involved with the production of the Underlying Works. Any breach of this paragraph will render this license null and void and Licensee will be liable to all parties concerned for defamation and copyright infringement, as well as breach of contract. . . .

As Video Pipeline sees it, such licensing agreements seek to use copyright law to suppress criticism and, in so doing, misuse those laws, triggering the copyright misuse doctrine.

Neither the Supreme Court nor this Court has affirmatively recognized the copyright misuse doctrine. There is, however, a well-established patent misuse doctrine, *see, e.g., Morton Salt Co. v. G.S. Suppiger Co.*, 314 U.S. 488 (1942), and, as noted below, other courts of appeals have extended the doctrine to the copyright context.

The misuse doctrine extends from the equitable principle that courts "may appropriately withhold their aid where the plaintiff is using the right asserted contrary to the public interest." *Morton Salt*, 314 U.S. at 492. Misuse is not cause to invalidate the copyright or patent, but instead "precludes its enforcement during the period of misuse." *Practice Management Info. Corp. v. American Med. Assoc.*, 121 F.3d 516, 520 n.9 (9th Cir. 1997) (citing *Lasercomb America, Inc. v. Reynolds*, 911 F.2d 970, 979 n.22 (4th Cir. 1990)). To defend on misuse grounds, the alleged infringer need not be subject to the purported misuse. *Morton Salt,*

314 U.S. at 494 ("It is the adverse effect upon the public interest of a successful infringement suit in conjunction with the patentee's course of conduct which disqualifies him to maintain the suit, regardless of whether the particular defendant has suffered from the misuse of the patent."); *Lasercomb*, 911 F.2d at 979 ("[T]he fact that appellants here were not parties to one of Lasercomb's standard license agreements is inapposite to their copyright misuse defense. The question is whether Lasercomb is using its copyright in a manner contrary to public policy, which question we have answered in the affirmative.").

Misuse often exists where the patent or copyright holder has engaged in some form of anti-competitive behavior. More on point, however, is the underlying policy rationale for the misuse doctrine set out in the Constitution's Copyright and Patent Clause: "to promote the Progress of Science and useful Arts." Const. Art. I, §8, cl. 8; *see also Morton Salt*, 314 U.S. at 494, ("The patentee, like these other holders of an exclusive privilege granted in furtherance of a public policy [trademark and copyright holders], may not claim protection of his grant by the courts where it is being used to subvert that policy."); *Lasercomb*, 911 F.2d at 978 ("The question is . . . whether the copyright is being used in a manner violative of the public policy embodied in the grant of a copyright."). The "ultimate aim" of copyright law is "to stimulate artistic creativity for the general public good." *Sony Corp.*, 464 U.S. at 432; *see also Eldred v. Ashcroft*, 537 U.S. 186 (2003) ("[C]opyright's purpose is to *promote* the creation and publication of free expression.") (emphasis in original). Put simply, our Constitution emphasizes the purpose and value of copyrights and patents. Harm caused by their misuse undermines their usefulness.

Anti-competitive licensing agreements may conflict with the purpose behind a copyright's protection by depriving the public of the would-be competitor's creativity. The fair use doctrine and the refusal to copyright facts and ideas also address applications of copyright protection that would otherwise conflict with a copyright's constitutional goal. But it is possible that a copyright holder could leverage its copyright to restrain the creative expression of another without engaging in anti-competitive behavior or implicating the fair use and idea/expression doctrines.[13]

For instance, the concurring opinion, written for a majority of the judges, in *Rosemont Enters., Inc. v. Random House, Inc.*, 366 F.2d 303 (2d Cir. 1966), concluded that pursuant to the unclean hands doctrine the District Court should not have entered a preliminary injunction against an alleged copyright infringer where the copyright holder sought to use his copyright "to restrict the dissemination of information." *Id.* at 311 (Lumbard, C.J., concurring). In *Rosemont Enters.*, a corporation acting for the publicity-shy Howard Hughes purchased the copyright to an article about Hughes solely to bring an infringement suit to enjoin the publication of a forthcoming biography on Hughes. *Id.* at 313. The concurring opinion reasoned:

> The spirit of the First Amendment applies to the copyright laws at least to the extent that the courts should not tolerate any attempted interference with the public's right to be informed regarding

---

13. *See* Note, *Clarifying the Copyright Misuse Defense: The Role of Antitrust Standards and First Amendment Values*, 104 Harv. L. Rev. 1289, 1304-06 (1991) (advocating application of the copyright misuse defense where "the plaintiff has improperly used its copyright power to restrain free trade in ideas," and explaining: "The copyright misuse defense provides a necessary complement to the idea/expression dichotomy [under which an author's expression may be copyrighted, but an idea may not] and fair use doctrine in vindicating the public interest in the dissemination of ideas. The idea/expression limitation merely restricts the scope of the particular copyright being sued upon, and absent a claim of misuse, it cannot be brought to bear on improper licensing restrictions or other misconduct. As with the misuse defense, fair use doctrine excuses copying that would otherwise be infringement in order to vindicate the copyright policy promoting the diffusion of ideas. Unlike misuse doctrine, however, the fair use inquiry directs courts' attention to the social value of the defendant's conduct rather than the social harm caused by the plaintiff's use of its copyright.").

matters of general interest when anyone seeks to use the copyright statute which was designed to protect interests of quite a different nature.

Id. at 311.

Although *Rosemont Enters.* did not concern an anti-competitive licensing agreement as in the typical misuse case, it focused — as do the misuse cases — on the copyright holder's attempt to disrupt a copyright's goal to increase the store of creative expression for the public good. 366 F.2d at 311. A copyright holder's attempt to restrict expression that is critical of it (or of its copyrighted good, or the industry in which it operates, *etc.*) may, in context, subvert — as do anti-competitive restrictions — a copyright's policy goal to encourage the creation and dissemination to the public of creative activity.

The licensing agreements in this case do seek to restrict expression by licensing the Disney trailers for use on the internet only so long as the web sites on which the trailers will appear do not derogate Disney, the entertainment industry, *etc.* But we nonetheless cannot conclude on this record that the agreements are likely to interfere with creative expression to such a degree that they affect in any significant way the policy interest in increasing the public store of creative activity. The licensing agreements do not, for instance, interfere with the licensee's opportunity to express such criticism on other web sites or elsewhere. There is no evidence that the public will find it any more difficult to obtain criticism of Disney and its interests, or even that the public is considerably less likely to come across this criticism, if it is not displayed on the same site as the trailers. Moreover, if a critic wishes to comment on Disney's works, the fair use doctrine may be implicated regardless of the existence of the licensing agreements. Finally, copyright law, and the misuse doctrine in particular, should not be interpreted to require Disney, if it licenses its trailers for display on any web sites but its own, to do so willy-nilly regardless of the content displayed with its copyrighted works. Indeed such an application of the misuse doctrine would likely decrease the public's access to Disney's works because it might as a result refuse to license at all online display of its works.

Thus, while we extend the patent misuse doctrine to copyright, and recognize that it might operate beyond its traditional anti-competition context, we hold it inapplicable here. On this record Disney's licensing agreements do not interfere significantly with copyright policy (while holding to the contrary might, in fact, do so). The District Court therefore correctly held that Video Pipeline will not likely succeed on its copyright misuse defense.

In re Napster, Inc. Copyright Litigation
191 F. Supp. 2d 1087 (N.D. Cal. 2002)

[Review the facts and procedural history of this case, Chapter 6 *supra.*]

PATEL, C.J.: . . . The court is also asked to permit discovery to determine whether plaintiffs have misused their copyrights by attempting to control the market for the digital distribution of music. Having considered the arguments presented, and for the reasons set forth below, the court rules as follows. . . .

B. *Plaintiffs' Entry into the Digital Distribution Market*

. . . In mid-2001, plaintiffs announced the formation of two joint ventures, MusicNet and press*play*. The aim of these joint ventures is to provide platforms for the digital distribution of music. MusicNet is a joint venture between three of the five record company plaintiffs — EMI,

BMG, and Warner. MusicNet is also owned in part by RealNetworks (and possibly another entity). Press*play* is a venture between the other two plaintiffs — Sony and Universal.

In June 2001, Napster signed a licensing agreement with MusicNet, allowing Napster access to all of the copyrighted works licensed to MusicNet. Prior to signing the MusicNet agreement, Napster was unable to obtain individual licenses from any of the recording company plaintiffs. The MusicNet agreement explicitly limits Napster's ability to obtain individual licenses from any of the five plaintiffs, including the non-MusicNet plaintiffs — Sony and Universal — until March 2002. The agreement also allows MusicNet to terminate the agreement within ninety days, even after March 2002, if Napster licenses content from any of the five recording companies other than through MusicNet. Additionally, the agreement mandates a separate pricing structure for *any* content that Napster licenses from anyone other than Music-Net. Napster has only provided the court with the MusicNet agreement and the court has no other information as to how MusicNet operates or exactly what content it will offer and to whom. . . .

II. Copyright Misuse

Napster argues that the court should deny summary judgment or stay the matter to allow for further discovery because plaintiffs are engaged in copyright misuse. . . . This court and the Ninth Circuit dismissed Napster's misuse defense at the preliminary injunction stage, noting that copyright misuse is rarely a defense to injunctive relief and that there was not enough evidence at that stage to support a finding of misuse. Since those rulings, the factual and procedural landscape has changed significantly. The motion now before the court is for summary judgment, not preliminary injunctive relief. Additionally, the prior inapplicability of copyright misuse rested on the fact that none of the plaintiffs had granted licenses to Napster, let alone impermissibly restrictive ones. The evidence now shows that plaintiffs have licensed their catalogs of works for digital distribution in what could be an overreaching manner. . . .

A. *The Development of the Copyright Misuse Defense*

. . . . Recently, courts have displayed a greater willingness to find copyright misuse, employing two different, though interrelated approaches. The first approach requires a finding that plaintiff engaged in antitrust violations before the court will apply the doctrine of copyright misuse. *See, e.g., Saturday Evening Post v. Rumbleseat Press, Inc.*, 816 F.2d 1191, 1200 (7th Cir. 1987).[10] The second approach, adopted by the Ninth Circuit, focuses on public policy and has been applied to a greater range of conduct than the antitrust approach. *See Practice Mgmt. Info. Corp. v. American Med. Assoc.*, 121 F.3d 516 (9th Cir. 1997). Under the "public policy" approach, copyright misuse exists when plaintiff expands the statutory copyright monopoly in order to gain control over areas outside the scope of the monopoly. The test is whether plaintiff's use of his or her copyright violates the public policy embodied in the grant of a copyright, not whether the use is anti-competitive. However, as a practical matter, this test

---

10. This approach labels certain activities as per se copyright misuse and uses a rule of reason approach for others. For those activities that fall within the rule of reason test, the court first asks whether the restraint is within the scope of the copyright monopoly. If it is, then the conduct is per se legal. If not, the court then asks whether the activity as a whole promotes or restricts competition. If the particular activity (*e.g.* licensing provision) restricts competition, then it is copyright misuse.

is often difficult to apply and inevitably requires courts to rely on antitrust principles or language to some degree.

The scope of the defense of copyright misuse has not been significantly tested in the Ninth Circuit. . . . As a result, the doctrine of copyright misuse remains largely undeveloped, with little case law to aid this court in its inquiry.

1. Lasercomb America, Inc. v. Reynolds

The Fourth Circuit was the first to explicitly recognize a copyright misuse defense, *Lasercomb America, Inc. v. Reynolds*, 911 F.2d 970 (4th Cir. 1990). . . . Lasercomb's [software license] agreement forbade a licensee from developing any kind of computer assisted die-making software. *Id.* at 973. The court held that Lasercomb's licensing agreement attempted to control any expression by [defendant] of the underlying idea embodied in Lasercomb's software. *Id.* at 979. Because the idea was outside the scope of the copyright monopoly, the court found that Lasercomb's licensing agreement constituted copyright misuse. . . . .

2. Practice Management

In 1997, the Ninth Circuit followed the reasoning of the Fourth Circuit and explicitly adopted a defense of copyright misuse. *Practice Mgmt. Info. Corp. v. American Med. Assoc.*, 121 F.3d 516 (9th Cir. 1997). The American Medical Association ("AMA") licensed a copyrighted coding system to the Health Care Financing Administration ("HCFA"). *Id.* at 517-8. The agreement granted HCFA a royalty-free, non-exclusive license to use the AMA's coding system. *Id.* In return, HCFA promised not to use any other coding system and also promised to use its powers as a regulatory agency to require use of the AMA's system in programs administered by its agents. *Id.*

A separate dispute arose between Practice Management, the largest reseller of books of the AMA's coding system, and the AMA. *Id.* at 518. Practice Management argued in its action for declaratory relief that the AMA was misusing its copyrights because the licensing agreement between HCFA and the AMA was unduly restrictive. *Id.* The Ninth Circuit looked closely at the licensing agreement and sided with Practice Management. *Id.* at 521. In particular, the court held that the requirement that HCFA not use competing coding systems represented an expansion of the monopoly power of the AMA's copyright. *Id.* The court labeled this exclusivity clause the "controlling fact." *Id.* (copyright misuse is implicated by "the limitation imposed by the AMA licensing agreement on HCFA's rights to decide whether or not to use other forms as well").

The court did not investigate the extent of the AMA's market power or the actual effects on competition as it would have done in an antitrust analysis. *Id.* Instead, considering only the text of the agreement, the court merely noted the "apparent" adverse effects of the licensing agreement which "gave the AMA a substantial and unfair advantage over its competitors." *Id.* The court reasoned that this use of a copyright to gain competitive advantage violates the public policy embodied in the grant of a copyright.

3. The Current State of Copyright Misuse

Lasercomb and *Practice Management*, along with other "public policy" cases, hold that copyright misuse exists when plaintiffs commit antitrust violations or enter unduly restrictive copyright licensing agreements. . . . However, no courts [sic] has thus far articulated the boundaries of "unduly restrictive licensing" or when licensing or other conduct would violate the amorphous concept of public policy.

Additional confusion arises because while courts have repeatedly stated that misuse is different from antitrust, they still rely on antitrust-like inquiries in determining what licensing agreements violate public policy. Of the cases reviewed by the court, all mimic the *per se* rules of antitrust in holding that the relevant licensing agreements constitute copyright misuse because they are unduly restrictive *on their face. See, e.g., Practice Mgmt.*, 121 F.3d at 521. No court has yet found it necessary to investigate the effects of a licensing provision[] by adopting an analysis similar to the antitrust rule-of-reason approach but focusing instead on public policy. As a result, the "public policy" misuse case law only helps to identify the egregious cases of misuse — when it is obvious that the particular licensing provision is overreaching. Currently, there is no guidance as to how to approach the more sophisticated cases where the text of the licensing provision itself is not dispositive.

Fortunately, this court need not answer these questions today. Instead, the court focuses on these issues to guide the parties in the evidentiary development of the scope of plaintiffs' alleged misuse.

B. Napster's Allegations of Misuse

Napster alleges two bases for misuse. First, Napster contends that the licensing clauses in Napster's agreement with plaintiffs' joint venture, MusicNet, are unduly restrictive. In the alternative, Napster argues that even if that particular agreement is not unduly restrictive, plaintiffs' practices as they enter the market for the digital distribution of music are so anti-competitive as to give rise to a misuse defense.

1.   The MusicNet Agreement

Napster contends that licensing requirements of plaintiffs' online venture, MusicNet, are unduly restrictive. MusicNet is a joint venture between three of the five record company plaintiffs (EMI, BMG, and Warner) to distribute digital music. This joint venture anticipates obtaining licenses from the other two major labels (Sony and Universal) to distribute their catalogs of copyrighted music. While Napster was unable to secure licenses from any of the individual plaintiffs, Napster reached an agreement with MusicNet that allows Napster to distribute the music from the catalogs of the three participating MusicNet plaintiffs and any other label that licenses its catalog to MusicNet.

Section 19.1 of the MusicNet agreement prevents Napster from entering into any licensing agreement with any individual plaintiffs until March 1, 2002. . . . The agreement also provides that even after March 2002 if Napster enters into any individual license with any of the major labels — *i.e.* the plaintiffs — including the MusicNet plaintiffs, MusicNet may terminate the agreement with ninety-day notice. *Id.* Additionally, section 6.3(a) lays out a pricing structure under which Napster will be charged higher fees if it fails to use MusicNet as its exclusive licensor for content. *Id.* at 7-8.

It is unclear from the text of the agreement if the exclusivity provision operates to impermissibly extend plaintiffs' control beyond the scope of their copyright monopoly. In other misuse cases, the offending provision was exclusive and the "adverse effects of the licensing agreement [were] apparent." *Practice Mgmt.*, 121 F.3d at 521 (provision prevented defendant from using any competitor's coding system); *Lasercomb*, 911 F.2d at 978 (defendant prohibited from producing any die-making software); *Alcatel [USA, Inc. v. DGI Technologies, Inc.]*, 166 F.3d [772,] 793-4 [(5th Cir. 1999)] (software licensing provision effectively gave plaintiff control over uncopyrighted microprocessor cards). In contrast, the MusicNet provision is non-exclusive. Napster may obtain licenses from any of the record label plaintiffs, but may only do it through its agreement with MusicNet. Despite this theoretical non-exclusivity, the provision effectively grants MusicNet control over which content Napster licenses. Napster's use of other music catalogs is predicated on MusicNet's securing an individual license to those catalogs. For example, under the MusicNet agreement, Napster no longer has the ability to obtain an individual license from Sony (a non-MusicNet plaintiff). Instead, Napster must rely on Music-Net to obtain a license to Sony's catalog. And, if MusicNet chooses not to obtain such a license, Napster is effectively prevented from using Sony's catalog. The result is an expansion of the powers of the three MusicNet plaintiffs' copyrights to cover the catalogs of the two non-MusicNet plaintiffs.

The MusicNet plaintiffs argue that this restriction is unimportant because they fully expect to obtain licenses from the other two majors [sic] recording companies. That the restriction only applies until MusicNet obtains licenses from Sony and Universal (non-MusicNet plaintiffs) or until March 2002 is irrelevant. *See Practice Mgmt.*, 121 F.3d 516, 521 ("The controlling fact is that HCFA is prohibited from using any other coding system by virtue of the binding commitment . . . to use the AMA's copyrighted material exclusively."). The critical issue is that the agreement binds Napster to obtain licenses from MusicNet and not its competitors. Napster was caught in a position where its only options were to sign the agreement to gain access to the catalogs of the major record companies and thereby incur these restrictions in all their murkiness or to refuse to sign the agreement and have virtually no access to most commercially available music.

Though the agreement is troubling on its face, too many questions remain unanswered for the court to effectively rule on the issue. It is unclear to what extent it is appropriate to impute the actions of MusicNet to plaintiffs as MusicNet is a joint venture and technically remains a separate entity from plaintiffs. However, plaintiffs cannot hide behind the shell of a joint venture to protect themselves from misuse claims. The court views with great suspicion plaintiffs' claims of ignorance as to MusicNet's activities. Surely the three parties to MusicNet discussed their joint venture before embarking on it. MusicNet did not suddenly appear full blown from the head of a fictitious entity. The evidence suggests that plaintiffs formed a joint venture to distribute digital music and simultaneously refused to enter into individual licenses with competitors, effectively requiring competitors to use MusicNet as their source for digital licensing. If this proves to be the case, the propriety of treating MusicNet as a separate entity is in question.

A few of plaintiffs' arguments can be disposed of summarily. First, plaintiffs argue that Napster, as a party to the MusicNet agreement, cannot now challenge an agreement that it negotiated and subsequently signed. *Practice Management* explicitly holds that it is irrelevant who includes an exclusivity provision in an agreement. That Napster is both the party alleging misuse and a party to the offending agreement does not affect the court's analysis.[16]

Second, plaintiffs contend that because MusicNet is not yet in operation, there is no ongoing misuse. This argument fails. The issue is not whether MusicNet is yet in operation, but whether the exclusivity provision in the agreement is active. Because Napster is already bound by the agreement, the restriction on Napster's ability to negotiate for licenses with individual plaintiffs is *currently* restricted.

---

16. Plaintiffs' argument would have merit if there was any evidence that Napster introduced and negotiated for the exclusivity provision. In that scenario, it would be unseemly to allow Napster to use the same provision as protection against infringement actions. Such a rule would create perverse incentives to artificially manufacture overreaching clauses as liability shields under the misuse doctrine. However, the evidence thus far shows that the relevant provisions were inserted at MusicNet's urging and not as an end-run around copyright laws by Napster.

Third, plaintiffs contend that even if they are engaged in misuse, be it through restrictive licensing or antitrust violations, they should still be able to recover for infringement that occurred prior to the MusicNet agreement. Plaintiffs misunderstand the misuse doctrine. Misuse limits enforcement of rights, not remedies. If plaintiffs are engaged in misuse, they cannot bring suit based on their rights until the misuse ends. The doctrine does not prevent plaintiffs from ultimately recovering for acts of infringement that occur during the period of misuse. The issue focuses on when plaintiffs can bring or pursue an action for infringement, not for which acts of infringement they can recover.

2. Antitrust Violations as Copyright Misuse . . .

Antitrust violations can give rise to copyright misuse if those violations offend the public policy behind the copyright grant. *See Lasercomb*, 911 F.2d at 977 ("[A]ntitrust law is the statutory embodiment of that public policy"). However, generalized antitrust violations will not suffice. Napster must establish a "nexus between . . . alleged anti-competitive actions and [plaintiffs'] power over copyrighted material." *Orth-O-Vision, Inc. v. Home Box Office*, 474 F. Supp. 672, 686 (S.D.N.Y. 1979).

Napster's arguments are based primarily on the declaration of Roger Noll, a Stanford professor who specializes in antitrust economics and the recording industry. Based on Dr. Noll's review of the MusicNet agreement and facts in the public record, Napster alleges that there are a host of anti-competitive behaviors by the plaintiffs that violate antitrust laws. Dr. Noll concludes that plaintiffs' joint ventures, MusicNet and press*play*, have anti-competitive features and facilitate collusive activity between plaintiffs. Dr. Noll further asserts that plaintiffs engage in vertical foreclosure of the digital distribution market through retail price squeezes, raising costs through licensing provisions, refusals to deal, and exclusive dealing. Dr. Noll also discusses myriad other behaviors that Napster alleges provide a sufficient nexus to the copyright monopoly to invoke the doctrine of copyright misuse.

For example, Dr. Noll alleges that plaintiffs' joint ventures, MusicNet (Warner, EMI and BMG) and press *play* (Sony and Universal), allow plaintiffs to engage in retail price-coordination. Plaintiffs hotly dispute this allegation and noted at oral argument that both MusicNet and press *play* were designed with numerous protections (none of which are in the record) to avoid implicating antitrust concerns. The current record on the licensing practices of these joint ventures and their operations is negligible. However, even a naif must realize that in forming and operating a joint venture, plaintiffs' representatives must necessarily meet and discuss pricing and licensing, raising the specter of possible antitrust violations. These joint ventures bear the indicia of entities designed to allow plaintiffs to use their copyrights and extensive market-power to dominate the market for digital music distribution. Even on the undeveloped record before the court, these joint ventures look bad, sound bad and smell bad.

Of course, plaintiffs object strenuously to the Noll Declaration and have filed a lengthy separate evidentiary objection accusing Dr. Noll of everything from speculation to mistake to deliberate misrepresentation. Plaintiffs argue that much of Dr. Noll's declaration refers to activities that have no relationship to plaintiffs' ownership of copyrights. For example, plaintiffs contend that it should not matter for the purposes of copyright misuse if plaintiffs engage in price fixing because the behavior is unrelated to the manner in which plaintiffs use their copyright monopoly. *See Orth-O-Vision*, 474 F. Supp. at 686. However, there can be no doubt that price-fixing carries antitrust and public policy considerations that may be relevant to misuse. While further evidentiary development may sustain plaintiffs' argument, on the current record defendants have demonstrated a sufficient nexus to allow for further discovery. . . .

NOTES AND QUESTIONS

1. In *Video Pipeline*, the court noted that if Disney were required to license its trailers "willy-nilly regardless of the content displayed with its copyrighted works," public access to Disney works would likely decrease because Disney might "refuse to license at all online display of its works." *Video Pipeline*, 342 F.3d at 206. Given the court's stated concern about allowing a copyright owner to restrict criticism, what kinds of licensing behavior should tip the balance in favor of finding misuse? Are there other ways for Disney to control the context in which its trailers are made available without openly restricting licensees from engaging in critical speech?

2. As both *Video Pipeline* and *Napster* indicate, a court can find copyright misuse in the absence of an antitrust violation. Does this rule make sense? *See* Brett Frischmann & Dan Moylan, *The Evolving Common Law Doctrine of Copyright Misuse: A Unified Theory and Its Application to Software*, 15 Berkeley Tech. L.J. 865 (2000) (arguing that the misuse doctrine serves a valuable gap-filling function). What areas do you think constitute the "areas outside the scope of the [copyright] monopoly" that the *Napster* court identifies as a key element in determining misuse under the public policy approach?

Note that not all jurisdictions have been willing to find misuse outside of the antitrust context. *See, e.g., Antioch Co. v. Scrapbook Borders, Inc.*, 291 F. Supp. 2d 980 (D. Minn. 2003).

3. Recall what you learned in Chapter 5.G *supra* about the various uses of collective licensing arrangements in the music industry. What types of joint ventures in the recording industry might give rise to the assertion of misuse? What are the implications of joint ventures in the recording industry having to be concerned about copyright misuse?

4. The *Napster* court also ruled that despite Napster's own "unclean hands," it could still raise the equitable defense of misuse against the plaintiffs. Do you agree with this rule? What public interests are furthered by allowing an infringing party to raise an equitable defense? If both parties have engaged in behavior that constitutes an abuse of the copyright interest, what should be the appropriate outcome or remedy? If Napster's allegations of misuse were upheld, would misuse be a defense that individuals engaged in peer-to-peer file sharing could raise? Note that courts generally hold that misuse is an affirmative defense, not a counterclaim, and thus cannot be litigated independently of an underlying copyright infringement claim. Why do you think this is the case? *See Metro-Goldwyn-Mayer Studios Inc. v. Grokster, Ltd.*, 269 F. Supp. 2d 1213, 1225 (C.D. Cal. 2003) ("[T]he separate declaratory [misuse] claim presumably serves but one purpose: to ensure that the misuse issue will be decided, and any notice [to all the world] rendered, *even if* the affirmative defense is mooted by a finding that [defendant] is not liable for infringement.") (emphasis in original). Note also that copyright misuse is not a recognized defense to a breach of contract claim. *Davidson & Assocs., Inc. v. Internet Gateway*, 334 F. Supp. 2d 1164, 1182-1183 (E.D. Miss. 2004), *aff'd, Davidson & Assocs. v. Jung*, 422 F.3d 630 (8th Cir. 2005).

5. Note that under the traditional misuse doctrine as defined in patent cases, the consequences of misuse can be quite harsh. The party engaging in misuse may not enforce the copyright until it purges itself of the misuse. Until it does, may anyone in possession of the copyrighted work infringe the copyright? Is this too high a penalty for the copyright owner to pay for misuse? *See Microsoft Corp. v. Jesse's Computers & Repair, Inc.*, 211 F.R.D. 681 (M.D. Fla. 2002) (holding that misuse defense was unavailable where the alleged misconduct was not directly related to the merits of the controversy between the parties). The harshness of this penalty can act as a strong deterrent to overreaching by copyright owners. *See* Lydia Pallas Loren, *Slaying the Leather-Winged Demons in the Night: Copyright Misuse as a Tool for Reforming Copyright Owner Contracting Behavior*, 30 Ohio N.U.L. Rev. 495 (2004). In *Napster*, the court suggested that after misuse is purged, the copyright owner can reach back to collect

damages for infringements that occurred during the period of misuse. Do you agree with this rule? (Note that the three-year statute of limitations on civil copyright infringement actions, discussed in Chapter 10.B *infra*, might bar some such claims.)

Note on the Relationship Between Copyright Law and Antitrust Law

The relationship between the intellectual property laws and antitrust law has been the subject of much debate, particularly in recent years as more wealth has become concentrated in the hands of firms whose primary assets are intellectual property rights, and as those firms have been able to obtain substantial market power. Because the owner of an intellectual property right may be engaging in misuse even in the absence of an antitrust violation, the question arises why antitrust law would ever be needed to police anti-competitive excesses. Of course misuse is a defense to infringement, not the basis of a claim and misuse will not reach all conduct.

For example, under the Patent Act, it is not misuse to refuse to license the patent. 35 U.S.C. §271(d)(4). Some courts hold that a patentee has a right to refuse to deal regardless of its market share, intent, or other exclusionary conduct. *See Intergraph Corp. v. Intel Corp.*, 195 F.3d 1346, 1362 (Fed. Cir. 1999) ("[T]he antitrust laws do not negate the patentee's right to exclude others from patent property."); In re *Independent Serv. Org. Antitrust Litig.*, 989 F. Supp. 1131 (D. Kan. 1997). Other courts have concluded that the exercise of an intellectual property right is a valid business justification for such refusal that creates a presumption that the actions are lawful. *See Image Technical Servs., Inc. v. Eastman Kodak Co.*, 125 F.3d 1195 (9th Cir. 1997), *cert. denied*, 523 U.S. 1094 (1998) (stating that the presumption may be overcome by evidence showing that the protection of intellectual property rights is only a pretext to justify a refusal to license); *Data General Corp. v. Grumman Sys. Support Corp.*, 36 F.3d 1147 (1st Cir. 1994) (suggesting that unlawful acquisition of a copyright or harm to consumers could suffice to overcome the presumption).

Should antitrust law intervene when use of another's intellectual property becomes necessary to compete? U.S. antitrust law has sometimes employed what is called the "essential facilities" doctrine to force a firm to grant competitors access to certain of its facilities. Under the essential facilities doctrine, when a monopolist (1) controls an essential facility; (2) a competitor is unable "practically or reasonably to duplicate the essential facility"; (3) the monopolist denies the competitor use of the facility; and (4) providing access to the facility is reasonable, a court may order the monopolist to grant access to the competitor. Cases in which courts have applied the essential facilities doctrine are rare and have generally involved natural monopolies (such as those in the railroad, telephone, and electric utility industries). *See, e.g., United States v. Terminal R.R. Ass'n*, 224 U.S. 383 (1912) (holding that a group of railroads owning all means of access across the Mississippi River near St. Louis had to make their facilities available to all users under reasonable terms); *MCI Commc'ns Corp. v. Am. Tel. & Tel. Co.*, 708 F.2d 1081, 1132-33 (7th Cir. 1982) (holding that AT&T must grant access to its long-distance lines to MCI), *cert. denied*, 464 U.S. 891 (1983); *cf. Otter Tail Power Co. v. United States*, 410 U.S. 366 (1973) (holding that monopolist's refusal to wheel power from competitive suppliers over its transmission lines violated Section 2 of the Sherman Act). One case labeling information protected by intellectual property rights "essential" was reversed on appeal. *See Intergraph Corp. v. Intel Corp.*, 3 F. Supp. 2d 1255 (N.D. Ala. 1998), *rev'd*, 195 F.3d 1346 (Fed. Cir. 1999). The Supreme Court has cast doubt on its continuing willingness to recognize the essential facilities doctrine. *See Verizon Commc'ns, Inc. v. Trinko*, 540 U.S. 398, 411 (2004).

The European Court of Justice has employed a similar doctrine on occasion. *See Radio Telefis Eireann v. Commission*, 1 CEC (CCH) 400 (1995) (holding that television stations that provide their listings to their own weekly publications have a duty to license that information to unaffiliated sellers of listings). The court found this duty despite the lower (Irish) court's holding that the listings were covered by a valid copyright. *See* Steven D. Anderman, EC Competition Law and Intellectual Property Rights 204-10 (1998). In arriving at its result, the Court interpreted Article 86 of the treaty establishing the European Community. This provision addresses abuse of a dominant position and is somewhat analogous to Section 2 of the Sherman Act.

NOTES AND QUESTIONS

1. Can you think of cases in which a court might appropriately use the essential facilities doctrine to order a copyright license? It may be difficult to conceive of such cases in part because the exclusive rights of copyright owners relatively rarely (both in absolute terms and compared to patent law) result in the rightholders obtaining an economic monopoly. According to the Supreme Court, "Monopoly power is the power to control prices or exclude competition." *United States v. E.I. duPont de Nemours & Co.*, 351 U.S. 377, 391 (1956). Because most copyrighted works have ready substitutes, it is generally difficult for copyright owners to obtain the kind of monopoly power with which antitrust law is concerned.

2. Is ordering an intellectual property license as a remedy for an antitrust violation as problematic as finding an antitrust violation based on the exercise of an intellectual property right? For example, in the U.S. Department of Justice's antitrust case against Microsoft, the district court premised its finding of a violation of Section 2 of the Sherman Act on conduct unrelated to Microsoft's intellectual property rights. In its interim remedial order, the court ordered Microsoft to disclose certain information likely protected under copyright law to competitors. *See United States v. Microsoft Corp.*, 97 F. Supp. 2d 59 (D.D.C. 2000), *aff'd in part, rev'd in part*, 253 F.3d 34 (D.C. Cir. 2001). Microsoft argued that the order would effectively result in unfair confiscation of its intellectual property. Do you agree?

3. In the *Microsoft* case, the D.C. Circuit addressed the question whether certain Microsoft licensing restrictions constituted exclusionary conduct in violation of Section 2 of the Sherman Act. *Microsoft*, 253 F.3d at 61. The restrictions prohibited resellers from removing desktop icons, changing the appearance of the initial screen, or otherwise changing the appearance of the Windows desktop. *Id.* Microsoft defended the restrictions, claiming that it was "simply 'exercising its rights as the holder of valid copyrights.'" *Id.* at 62. How would you analyze this defense?

4. What policy considerations do you think account for courts' reluctance to find antitrust violations based on the exercise of copyright rights?

5. Under the TRIPS Agreement an abuse of intellectual property rights is considered sufficient justification for a country to grant a compulsory license. TRIPS Art. 31(k). That license may remain in place until the anticompetitive behavior is purged. *Id.*

9

Technological Protections

In Chapters 5 and 7, we explored the numerous rights that the Copyright Act confers on authors as well as the limitations on those rights. Taken together, those provisions are often described as establishing a balance between the rights of copyright owners and the rights or privileges of users of protected works. This "copyright balance" historically has been an integral feature of the U.S. copyright system. Recall from Chapter 1 that of the various philosophical themes that permeate copyright law, the utilitarian emphasis is the most prominent underpinning of U.S. copyright law. In this view, copyright is an instrument to further specific public policy objectives. In the words of the Constitution, copyright law is a means to promote progress. The copyright balance is specifically directed to accomplishing this goal.

Throughout this book you have learned how technological developments have challenged the copyright balance, typically by enabling new methods of copying and distributing protected works. Usually, Congress has responded to these developments by legislating more rights for copyright holders and/or by extending copyright law to cover new subject matter. Recall from Chapter 4, for example, the addition of software as copyrightable subject matter or, from Chapter 5, the expansion of the right to make derivative works to cover almost any way in which a work might be exploited. With each expansion of copyright rights has come a corresponding concern about the effect on the copyright balance. As you learned in Chapter 1, modern copyright legislation is to a great extent the product of bargaining among affected members of the copyright industries. Critics of this process have charged that it takes insufficient account of the public interest, and therefore threatens to undermine the traditional balance and, more fundamentally, the goals of copyright law. Although more recent legislative negotiations have included representatives of the "public" interest such as library, educational, and scientific associations, in reality the "public" is not an organized, easily identifiable, homogeneous group. Consequently, representing the public interest is quite difficult. _See_ Jessica Litman, _Digital Copyright_ (2001).

Within the last several decades, technological developments have enabled not only new methods of copying and distribution, but also new methods of protection from copying. Recall from Chapter 1 that copyright is not the sole means (or even the most effective) for protecting the rights of authors. Review the excerpt from Professor Trotter Hardy, pages 7-9 _supra_. As Professor Hardy explains, copyright owners can supplement copyright protection by using contracts to bind users to specified terms of use of the work; Chapter 8 introduced

657

examples of such contracts. In the digital age, copyright owners can also use technological measures that regulate access to and/or monitor the scope of use of the protected work. Professor Hardy predicts that the extent of reliance on these alternative means of protection will vary depending on the scope and nature of the perceived threat to copyright rights and on models for maximizing the revenues from particular works. With the advent of digital technology, and particularly the Internet, reliance on technological measures to prevent mass copying and distribution may be expected to increase. As this chapter discusses, recent events confirm these predictions.

Resort to technological protection as a general model for protecting creative works in the digital environment raises an entirely new set of policy concerns. As with mass-market licenses, technological protections may be used to obtain greater protection than copyright law affords. In terms of Professor Hardy's metaphor, one might understand use of technological protection and/or contracts simply as a means of combining different "slices of the pie" to yield the same overall amount of protection. Alternatively, one might see the additional protection afforded by these measures as expanding the size of the pie or encroaching on the slice of the pie reserved to the public. For example, a copyright owner might attempt to use technological protection or contract, or both, to prevent access to or use of material that is in the public domain. It might also seek to control all copying, including copying permitted under the fair use doctrine. If these measures prove sufficiently effective, they could supplant copyright law altogether. Copyright law would still exist, of course, but many copyright owners would no longer rely on it as their first line of defense.

Technological protection also raises the possibility of a "technological arms race" between copyright owners and those who seek to defeat technological locks applied to copyrighted works. What one should think about the latter depends substantially on whether one thinks that reasons for seeking to access or copy technologically protected works are legitimate or illegitimate. For the copyright industries, the answer is clear: There are no, or hardly any, legitimate reasons for defeating technological protection measures applied to a work by the copyright owner. More important, they argue, if users of copyrighted works can defeat technological protections with impunity, the security afforded by these measures will be wholly illusory; therefore, the law should penalize such conduct. Others, however, contend that legitimate reasons for seeking to defeat technological protections do exist, and that the law should penalize only acts of circumvention undertaken for illegitimate purposes.

This chapter focuses on the use of technological protection measures by copyright owners and on the Digital Millennium Copyright Act (DMCA), an amendment to the Copyright Act that grants additional legal protections to copyright owners who employ such measures. As you read this chapter, ask yourself how new technologies designed to control access and/or copying, and laws enacted to protect these technologies, affect the copyright balance. Related concerns include the protection of privacy and freedom of expression for both authors and users of copyrighted works. How should these concerns factor into the copyright balance in the information age?

A. THE EVOLUTION OF THE TECHNOLOGICAL PROTECTION DEBATE

Although current debates about technological protection focus on general-purpose restrictions capable of application to any kind of digital content, both the original technological protection devices and legislative provisions concerning technological protection were medium-specific. A trio of experiments in the 1980s, followed by the Audio Home Recording Act (AHRA) of 1992, explored a variety of restrictions designed to erect technical "fences" against certain unauthorized uses of copyrighted material.

In the early 1980s, the motion picture industry adopted a patented technology, Macro-vision, to prevent unauthorized copying of pre-recorded videocassettes containing copyrighted motion pictures. As described in the Note on the U.S. First Sale Doctrine and Its Limits, Chapter 5.C *supra*, the adoption of Macrovision was a response to the Supreme Court's *Sony* decision, Chapter 7.B, pages 580-84 *supra*, and to Congress' subsequent refusal to enact a rental right for audiovisual works. The video rental industry, which had opposed the creation of a video rental right, does not appear to have objected to the implementation of Macrovision, since the technology did not threaten, and indeed more likely strengthened, its own market.

Cooperation by the powerful home electronics industry, which had prevailed in the *Sony* litigation, was essential to the Macrovision venture. For the Macrovision standard to work as intended, both recording media and home video recording equipment needed to incorporate the technology. *See* Nicholas E. Sciorra, *Self-Help and Contributory Infringement: The Law and Legal Thought Behind a Little "Black-Box,"* 11 Cardozo Arts & Ent. L.J. 905, 925 (1993) (describing how Macrovision works). Notably, however, the motion picture industry did not attempt to implement Macrovision in blank video recording media, or otherwise to address uses of video recording technology such as the home taping of broadcast programs that the *Sony* Court had ruled to be a fair use. While hackers developed "black boxes" capable of defeating the restrictions imposed by Macrovision, these devices did not achieve wide pene-tration among ordinary consumers, *id.* at 928-29, and the motion picture industry's efforts to obtain legal protection against these black boxes were not successful.

Also in the 1980s, satellite cable broadcasters began to encrypt their signals to prevent unauthorized reception by viewers who had not paid for cable subscription service. Once again, hackers quickly developed devices to circumvent the encryption. In this case, however, the affected industry received additional legal protection from Congress. In 1988, as part of the Satellite Home Viewer Act, Congress added a provision to the Communications Act to prohibit the manufacture or distribution of devices that can be used to decrypt satellite cable broadcast transmissions. Pub. L. No. 100-667, 100th Cong., 2d Sess. §5 (1988), *codified as amended at* 47 U.S.C. §605(e)(4). The amendment seems to have occasioned very little public debate. The industry urged that people who had not paid to receive the subscription broadcasts should not have access to them. Because the legislation targeted special purpose devices that had no other uses, there were few dissenters.

The third experiment with technological protection during the 1980s involved computer software. Alarmed by the ease with which software could be copied and redistributed, software manufacturers began experimenting with various devices designed to prevent copying. Unlike either Macrovision or encryption of broadcast cable subscription signals, both of which oper-ated in a manner largely invisible to users, these devices often caused system crashes and peripheral device failures. In addition, they prevented users from making backup copies, and sometimes even from loading legitimately purchased software onto hard disk storage — practices that, as you have learned, §117 of the Copyright Act permits.

Perhaps not surprisingly, the public reaction to software copy protection devices was dramatically different than the public reception of either Macrovision or satellite cable encryp-tion. Customers protested loudly, and popular software magazines published harsh critiques. Popular opposition to software copy protection went beyond complaints, however. Almost as quickly as the software companies developed new copy protection technologies, other programmers developed and distributed methods of defeating them. Both individual and business customers enthusiastically participated in this software "arms race." Finally, several major institutional software users, including the U.S. Department of Defense, informed software vendors that they would not purchase copy-protected software. *See* Julie E. Cohen, Lochner *in Cyberspace: The New Economic Orthodoxy of "Rights Management,"* 97 Mich. L. Rev. 462, 524-25 (1998).

In the face of this widespread resistance, software companies abandoned their efforts at copy protection. Throughout the debate, Congress remained silent. Some states passed laws permitting software vendors to impose contractual restrictions forbidding reverse engineering, a practice commonly used to develop devices that could defeat copy protection. In *Vault Corp. v. Quaid Software Ltd.*, 847 F.2d 255 (5th Cir. 1988), however, the Fifth Circuit ruled that Louisiana's law was preempted by the Copyright Act because it negated privileges specifically conferred by federal copyright law. We discuss that ruling and subsequent case law on the preemption question in Chapter 10.

As personal computers spread more extensively to businesses and homes, and digital formats were developed to store and distribute increasingly diverse works, the concept of technological protection began to seem more important to all of the industries that produce and distribute copyrighted works. The medium-specific model for technological protection began to disintegrate. In its place came a focus on general-purpose copy protection techniques suitable for the digital age.

The first harbinger of these developments was the invention, in Japan, of the digital audiotape (DAT) recording format—the first copying format capable of producing, and reproducing, perfect copies of recorded sounds. As had been the case in the *Sony* litigation, manufacturers of home recording equipment sought to import the new devices and recording media and distribute them to consumers. This time, rather than filing suit, members of the music and recording industries sought protection from Congress. Consistent with the interest group model that had developed for copyright legislation generally, Congress sought to broker a compromise among the affected industries. That compromise became the AHRA of 1992.

As you learned in Chapter 5.G.2, pages 451-53 *supra*, as a practical matter the AHRA has not played a particularly important role within the copyright system. Digital copying technologies rapidly evolved beyond the limited framework set forth in the statute, which excludes general purpose computers from the definition of a "digital audio recording device." The AHRA is significant, however, for the hybrid copy-protection model that it adopted: First, it required that all digital audio recording devices incorporate the Serial Copy Management System (SCMS)—a technical protocol for DAT that allows the making of first-generation copies without significant degradation in quality but prevents the making of subsequent generations of copies. 17 U.S.C. §1002. The AHRA also made it unlawful to manufacture or distribute any device or provide any service that would circumvent the SCMS. *Id.* Second, it levied royalties on covered digital audio recording media and equipment. *Id.* §§1003-1007. Finally, it barred infringement actions against consumers for personal, non-commercial copying, and also barred actions against manufacturers and distributors of digital audio recording devices and media. *Id.* §1008. This three-pronged model, which incorporated "permeable" or incomplete copy protection as part of a package of features, was an entirely different approach to the question of copy protection than any of those that industry or Congress had previously tried. Unfortunately, because the market so quickly bypassed the narrow definitions of "digital audio recording device" and "digital audio recording medium" supplied by the statute, it is impossible to say how well this hybrid model would have worked.

NOTES AND QUESTIONS

1. To what extent is law necessary to buttress technological restrictions? What considerations should affect the enactment of such laws?

2. Why do you think the affected industries received legal protection against devices for decrypting satellite signals, but not against devices for circumventing Macrovision? Why do you think Congress chose to intervene in the case of the AHRA, but not in the software copy-protection debate?

B. THE DIGITAL MILLENNIUM COPYRIGHT ACT AND CIRCUMVENTION OF TECHNOLOGICAL PROTECTIONS

As digital technologies for reproduction and distribution of copyrighted works continued to evolve, so too did copy protection technologies. By the mid-1990s, the most sophisticated of the technologies under development did far more than simply prevent copying. At high-technology research centers such as the Xerox Palo Alto Research Center, researchers had developed prototypes for "trusted systems" that could exercise extremely fine-grained control over the functionality of digital copies. For example, the system might be programmed to detect, permit, and charge different fees for accessing different portions of a work, for printing those portions, or for creating digital copies of all or part of the work. Alternatively, the system might be designed to forbid digital copying, but not printing, or to forbid both digital copying and printing. *See generally* Mark Stefik, *Shifting the Possible: How Digital Property Rights Challenge Us to Rethink Digital Publishing*, 12 Berkeley Tech. L.J. 138 (1997).

After the software "arms race" of the 1980s, however, the copyright industries were keenly aware that technological protections for digital works could be circumvented. They argued that the threat of uncontrolled copying and distribution via the Internet was so great that copyright owners needed additional, legal protection against the circumvention of any copy-control measures that they might choose to implement. The battle over enactment of the Digital Millennium Copyright Act (DMCA) and subsequent lawsuits invoking its anti-circumvention provisions have exposed deep divisions of opinion about the legitimacy of these modern copy-protection devices, and of laws designed to protect them.

As originally introduced in Congress, the proposed anti-circumvention legislation would have prohibited the manufacture or distribution of any device, product, or service with the "primary purpose or effect" of deactivating or circumventing a technological protection measure designed to protect a copyright owner's copyright rights. Almost immediately, this legislation encountered strong opposition from a diverse group of interests, including educators, librarians, scientists, computer software companies, online service providers, and manufacturers of home recording equipment. Some of these groups feared that the legislation would effectively result in the elimination of fair use and other copyright limitations for digital copyrighted works and enable content producers to "lock up" public domain works and uncopyrightable ideas. Others feared that it would usher in an era of unprecedented infringement liability for equipment manufacturers and communications providers.

Notwithstanding the significant resistance to domestic legislation, the Clinton Administration also sought to have protections against circumvention incorporated into international treaties. When WIPO delegates met in Geneva in December 1996 to draft the WIPO Copyright Treaty (WCT), however, they declined to adopt the text of the proposal for anti-circumvention protection advanced by the U.S., which had closely tracked the language of the proposed domestic legislation, and instead agreed on a more open-ended statement. Article 11 of the WCT directs:

> Contracting Parties shall provide adequate legal protection and effective legal remedies against the circumvention of effective technological measures that are used by authors in connection with the exercise of their rights under this Treaty or the Berne Convention and that restrict acts, in respect of their works, which are not authorized by the authors concerned or permitted by law.

When the 105th Congress opened in January 1997, shortly after finalization of the WCT, the battle over domestic anti-circumvention legislation resumed. As before, the proposal encountered strong opposition. This time, however, the newly drafted WCT lent additional momentum to supporters, who argued that the legislation would be necessary for the U.S. to comply with the treaty once it entered into force. In the time-honored tradition of copyright legislation, the House Judiciary Committee's Subcommittee on the Courts and Intellectual Property directed the parties to the bargaining table. Over the next 21 months, the original proposal was gradually modified and made subject to a series of exceptions. For a detailed description of this bargaining process, see Pamela Samuelson, *Intellectual Property and the Digital Economy: Why the Anti-Circumvention Regulations Need to Be Revised*, 14 Berkeley Tech. L.J. 519 (1999).

In October 1998, the DMCA was enacted. As a result of the interest group bargaining process, the anti-circumvention provision of the DMCA, now codified at §1201 of Title 17, looks like so many other provisions of the Copyright Act — complex, lengthy, and highly technical. As enacted, §1201 makes two important distinctions. The first is a distinction between technological controls that restrict *access* to a copyrighted work and technological controls designed to prevent violation of an *exclusive right* of the copyright owner. The second distinction is between individual *acts of circumvention* and the manufacture and distribution of *technologies designed to circumvent* technological protection measures. Opponents of the legislation had argued that the law should not prohibit or frustrate circumvention undertaken by those who wished to take advantage of limitations imposed on an owner's exclusive rights by copyright law. The copyright industries, meanwhile, had argued that the conduct targeted by anti-circumvention provisions was no different than breaking into a locked building to steal a work for which one had not paid. Congress used the two distinctions described above in an attempt to address both groups' concerns.

The following chart depicts the prohibitions found in §1201:

	Access protection measures	Rights protection measures
Individual acts of circumvention	Prohibition: §1201(a)(1)	Prohibition: None
Manufacturing or offering devices that circumvent	Prohibition: §1201(a)(2)	Prohibition: §1201(b)

The prohibition against manufacture and distribution of technologies designed to circumvent technological protection measures (the "device ban") applies to both access controls, §1201(a)(2), and controls directed at exclusive copyright rights, §1201(b). Individual acts of circumvention, on the other hand, are treated differently depending on the type of technological protection measure being circumvented. Section 1201 prohibits the act of circumventing access controls, §1201(a)(1), but does not prohibit circumvention of controls designed to protect a copyright owner's exclusive rights. In theory, therefore, a user who has paid the required price for access to the work would remain free to circumvent technological controls that prevented the exercise of fair use and other user privileges.

Consider this example: An individual purchases a digital copy of an article from an online publisher. The digital copy downloaded by the purchaser to her computer can be accessed from the computer's memory and displayed on the screen for 12 months, but coding within the file prevents the article from being printed. Section 1201 would not prohibit the purchaser's bypassing the code to enable printing (the upper right-hand box in the chart above). Distributing a utility designed to bypass the no-print code, however, would violate §1201(b) (the lower right-hand box). After 12 months have passed, if the purchaser bypasses the code that makes the file inaccessible, the purchaser's activity would violate §1201(a)(1) (the upper left-hand box). Distributing the means used to bypass this latter code and access the file would violate §1201(a)(2) (the lower left-hand box).

In addition to the two important distinctions identified above, §1201 contains a number of different exemptions targeted at specific types of circumvention activities. We turn now to exploring the interplay among the different prohibitions and exemptions contained in §1201.

Universal City Studios, Inc. v. Reimerdes
111 F. Supp. 2d 294 (S.D.N.Y. 2000),
aff'd sub nom. Universal City Studios, Inc. v. Corley, *273 F.3d 429 (2d Cir. 2001)*

KAPLAN, J.: Plaintiffs, eight major United States motion picture studios, distribute many of their copyrighted motion pictures for home use on digital versatile disks ("DVDs"), which contain copies of the motion pictures in digital form. They protect those motion pictures from copying by using an encryption system called CSS. CSS-protected motion pictures on DVDs may be viewed only on players and computer drives equipped with licensed technology that permits the devices to decrypt and play — but not to copy — the films.

Late last year, computer hackers devised a computer program called DeCSS that circumvents the CSS protection system and allows CSS-protected motion pictures to be copied and played on devices that lack the licensed decryption technology. Defendants quickly posted DeCSS on their Internet web site, thus making it readily available to much of the world. Plaintiffs promptly brought this action under the Digital Millennium Copyright Act (the "DMCA") to enjoin defendants from posting DeCSS and to prevent them from electronically "linking" their site to others that post DeCSS. Defendants responded with what they termed "electronic civil disobedience" — increasing their efforts to link their web site to a large number of others that continue to make DeCSS available.

Defendants contend that their actions do not violate the DMCA and, in any case, that the DMCA, as applied to computer programs, or code, violates the First Amendment. This is the Court's decision after trial. . . .

I. The Genesis of the Controversy . . .

Defendant Eric Corley is viewed as a leader of the computer hacker community and goes by the name Emmanuel Goldstein, after the leader of the underground in George Orwell's classic, *1984*. He and his company, defendant 2600 Enterprises, Inc., together publish a magazine called *2600: The Hacker Quarterly*, which Corley founded in 1984, and which is something of a bible to the hacker community. . . . *2600: The Hacker Quarterly* has included articles on such topics as how to steal an Internet domain name, access other people's e-mail, intercept cellular phone calls, and break into the computer systems at Costco stores and Federal Express. . . .

As the motion picture companies did not themselves develop CSS and, in any case, are not in the business of making DVD players and drives, the technology for making compliant devices, i.e., devices with CSS keys, had to be licensed to consumer electronics manufacturers.[60] In order to ensure that the decryption technology did not become generally available and that compliant devices could not be used to copy as well as merely to play CSS-protected movies, the technology is licensed subject to strict security requirements. Moreover, manufacturers may not, consistent with their licenses, make equipment that would supply digital output that could be used in copying protected DVDs. Licenses to manufacture compliant devices are granted on a royalty-free basis subject only to an administrative fee.[63] At the time of trial, licenses had been issued to numerous hardware and software manufacturers, including two companies that plan to release DVD players for computers running the Linux operating system. . . .

In late September 1999, Jon Johansen, a Norwegian subject then fifteen years of age, and two individuals he "met" under pseudonyms over the Internet, reverse engineered a licensed DVD player and discovered the CSS encryption algorithm and keys. They used this information to create DeCSS, a program capable of decrypting or "ripping" encrypted DVDs, thereby allowing playback on non-compliant computers as well as the copying of decrypted files to computer hard drives. Mr. Johansen then posted the executable code on his personal Internet web site and informed members of an Internet mailing list that he had done so. . . .

Although Mr. Johansen testified at trial that he created DeCSS in order to make a DVD player that would operate on a computer running the Linux operating system, DeCSS is a Windows executable file; that is, it can be executed only on computers running the Windows operating system. Mr. Johansen explained the fact that he created a Windows rather than a Linux program by asserting that Linux, at the time he created DeCSS, did not support the file system used on DVDs. Hence, it was necessary, he said, to decrypt the DVD on a Windows computer in order subsequently to play the decrypted files on a Linux machine. Assuming that to be true, however, the fact remains that Mr. Johansen created DeCSS in the full knowledge that it could be used on computers running Windows rather than Linux. Moreover, he was well aware that the files, once decrypted, could be copied like any other computer files. . . .

In the months following its initial appearance on Mr. Johansen's web site, DeCSS has become widely available on the Internet, where hundreds of sites now purport to offer the software for download. . . .

The movie studios, through the Internet investigations division of the Motion Picture Association of America ("MPAA"), became aware of the availability of DeCSS on the Internet in October 1999. The industry responded by sending out a number of cease and desist letters to web site operators who posted the software, some of which removed it from their sites. In January 2000, the studios filed this lawsuit against defendant Eric Corley and two others.[91] . . .

---

60. The licensing function initially was performed by [Matsushita Electric Industrial Co.] MEI and Toshiba. Subsequently, MEI and Toshiba granted a royalty free license to the DVD Copy Control Association ("DVD CCA"), which now handles the licensing function. . . .

63. The administrative fee is one million yen, now about $9,200. . . .

91. The other two defendants entered into consent decrees with plaintiffs. Plaintiffs subsequently amended the complaint to add 2600 Enterprises, Inc. as a defendant.

Following the issuance of the preliminary injunction, defendants removed DeCSS from the 2600.com web site. In what they termed an act of "electronic civil disobedience," however, they continued to support links to other web sites purporting to offer DeCSS for download, a list which had grown to nearly five hundred by July 2000. Indeed, they carried a banner saying "Stop the MPAA" and, in a reference to this lawsuit, proclaimed:

"We have to face the possibility that we could be forced into submission. For that reason it's especially important that as many of you as possible, all throughout the world, take a stand and mirror these files."

Thus, defendants obviously hoped to frustrate plaintiffs' recourse to the judicial system by making effective relief difficult or impossible. . . .

These circumstances have two major implications for plaintiffs. First, the availability of DeCSS on the Internet has effectively compromised plaintiffs' system of copyright protection for DVDs. . . . It is analogous to the publication of a bank vault combination in a national newspaper. Even if no one uses the combination to open the vault, its mere publication has the effect of defeating the bank's security system, forcing the bank to reprogram the lock. Development and implementation of a new DVD copy protection system, however, is far more difficult and costly than reprogramming a combination lock and may carry with it the added problem of rendering the existing installed base of compliant DVD players obsolete.

Second, the application of DeCSS to copy and distribute motion pictures on DVD, both on CD-ROMs and via the Internet, threatens to reduce the studios' revenue from the sale and rental of DVDs. It threatens also to impede new, potentially lucrative initiatives for the distribution of motion pictures in digital form, such as video-on-demand via the Internet. . . .

II. The Digital Millennium Copyright Act . . .

B. *Posting of DeCSS*

1. Violation of Anti-Trafficking Provision

Section 1201(a)(2) of the Copyright Act, part of the DMCA, provides that:

"No person shall . . . offer to the public, or otherwise traffic in any technology . . . that—
"(A) is primarily designed or produced for the purpose of circumventing a technological measure that effectively controls access to a work protected under [the Copyright Act];
"(B) has only limited commercially significant purpose or use other than to circumvent a technological measure that effectively controls access to a work protected under [the Copyright Act]; or
"(C) is marketed by that person or another acting in concert with that person with that person's knowledge for use in circumventing a technological measure that effectively controls access to a work protected under [the Copyright Act]."

In this case, defendants concededly offered and provided and, absent a court order, would continue to offer and provide DeCSS to the public by making it available for download on the 2600.com web site. DeCSS, a computer program, unquestionably is "technology" within the meaning of the statute. "[C]ircumvent a technological measure" is defined to mean descrambling a scrambled work, decrypting an encrypted work, or "otherwise to avoid, bypass, remove, deactivate, or impair a technological measure, without the authority of the copyright owner," so DeCSS clearly is a means of circumventing a technological access control measure. In consequence, if [De]CSS otherwise falls within paragraphs (A), (B) or (C) of Section 1201(a)(2), and if none of the statutory exceptions applies to their actions, defendants have violated and, unless enjoined, will continue to violate the DMCA by posting DeCSS. . . .

During pretrial proceedings and at trial, defendants attacked plaintiffs' Section 1201(a)(2)(A) claim, arguing that CSS, which is based on a 40-bit encryption key, is a weak cipher that does not "effectively control" access to plaintiffs' copyrighted works. They reasoned from this premise that CSS is not protected under this branch of the statute at all. . . .

[T]he statute expressly provides that "a technological measure 'effectively controls access to a work' if the measure, in the ordinary course of its operation, requires the application of information or a process or a treatment, with the authority of the copyright owner, to gain access to a work." One cannot gain access to a CSS-protected work on a DVD without application of the three keys that are required by the software. One cannot lawfully gain access to the keys except by entering into a license with the DVD CCA [DVD Copy Control Association] under authority granted by the copyright owners or by purchasing a DVD player or drive containing the keys pursuant to such a license. In consequence, under the express terms of the statute, CSS "effectively controls access" to copyrighted DVD movies. It does so, within the meaning of the statute, whether or not it is a strong means of protection. . . .

[T]he interpretation of the phrase "effectively controls access" offered by defendants at trial — viz., that the use of the word "effectively" means that the statute protects only successful or efficacious technological means of controlling access — would gut the statute if it were adopted. . . .

As CSS effectively controls access to plaintiffs' copyrighted works, the only remaining question under Section 1201(a)(2)(A) is whether DeCSS was designed primarily to circumvent CSS. The answer is perfectly obvious. By the admission of both Jon Johansen, the programmer who principally wrote DeCSS, and defendant Corley, DeCSS was created solely for the purpose of decrypting CSS — that is all it does. . . .

As the only purpose or use of DeCSS is to circumvent CSS, the foregoing is sufficient to establish a *prima facie* violation of Section 1201(a)(2)(B) as well.

c. The Linux Argument

Perhaps the centerpiece of defendants' statutory position is the contention that DeCSS was not created for the purpose of pirating copyrighted motion pictures. Rather, they argue, it was written to further the development of a DVD player that would run under the Linux operating system, as there allegedly were no Linux compatible players on the market at the time. . . .

[T]he question whether the development of a Linux DVD player motivated those who wrote DeCSS is immaterial to the question whether the defendants now before the Court violated the anti-trafficking provision of the DMCA. The inescapable facts are that (1) CSS is a technological means that effectively controls access to plaintiffs' copyrighted works, (2) the one and only function of DeCSS is to circumvent CSS, and (3) defendants offered and provided DeCSS by posting it on their web site. Whether defendants did so in order to infringe, or to permit or encourage others to infringe, copyrighted works in violation of other provisions of the Copyright Act simply does not matter for purposes of Section 1201(a)(2). The offering or provision of the program is the prohibited conduct — and it is prohibited irrespective of why the program was written, except to whatever extent motive may be germane to determining whether their conduct falls within one of the statutory exceptions.

2. Statutory Exceptions . . .

a. Reverse engineering

Defendants claim to fall under Section 1201(f) of the statute, which provides in substance that one may circumvent, or develop and employ technological means to circumvent, access control measures in order to achieve interoperability with another computer program provided that doing so does not infringe another's copyright and, in addition, that one may make information acquired through such efforts "available to others, if the person . . . provides such information solely for the purpose of enabling interoperability of an independently created computer progam with other programs, and to the extent that doing so does not constitute infringement. . . ." They contend that DeCSS is necessary to achieve interoperability between computers running the Linux operating system and DVDs and that this exception therefore is satisfied. This contention fails.

First, Section 1201(f)(3) permits information acquired through reverse engineering to be made available to others only by the person who acquired the information. But these defendants did not do any reverse engineering. They simply took DeCSS off someone else's web site and posted it on their own.

Defendants would be in no stronger position even if they had authored DeCSS. The right to make the information available extends only to dissemination "solely for the purpose" of achieving interoperability as defined in the statute. It does not apply to public dissemination of means of circumvention, as the legislative history confirms. These defendants, however, did not post DeCSS "solely" to achieve interoperability with Linux or anything else.

Finally, it is important to recognize that even the creators of DeCSS cannot credibly maintain that the "sole" purpose of DeCSS was to create a Linux DVD player. . . .

[The court ruled that DeCSS also did not fall within either the statutory exception for "good faith encryption research," §1201(g), or the exception for "security testing," §1201(j).]

. . . In determining whether one is engaged in good faith encryption research, the Court is instructed to consider factors including whether the results of the putative encryption research are disseminated in a manner designed to advance the state of knowledge of encryption technology versus facilitation of copyright infringement, whether the person in question is engaged in legitimate study of or work in encryption, and whether the results of the research are communicated in a timely fashion to the copyright owner.

Neither of the defendants remaining in this case was or is involved in good faith encryption research. They posted DeCSS for all the world to see. There is no evidence that they made any effort to provide the results of the DeCSS effort to the copyright owners. Surely there is no suggestion that either of them made a good faith effort to obtain authorization from the copyright owners. . . .

d. Fair use . . .

The use of technological means of controlling access to a copyrighted work may affect the ability to make fair uses of the work.[159] Focusing specifically on the facts of this case, the

---

159. Indeed, as many have pointed out, technological means of controlling access to works create a risk, depending upon future technological and commercial developments, of limiting access to works that are not protected by copyright such as works upon which copyright has expired. . . .

application of CSS to encrypt a copyrighted motion picture requires the use of a compliant DVD player to view or listen to the movie. Perhaps more significantly, it prevents exact copying of either the video or the audio portion of all or any part of the film. This latter point means that certain uses that might qualify as "fair" for purposes of copyright infringement—for example, the preparation by a film studies professor of a single CD-ROM or tape containing two scenes from different movies in order to illustrate a point in a lecture on cinematography, as opposed to showing relevant parts of two different DVDs—would be difficult or impossible absent circumvention of the CSS encryption. Defendants therefore argue that the DMCA cannot properly be construed to make it difficult or impossible to make any fair use of plaintiffs' copyrighted works and that the statute therefore does not reach their activities, which are simply a means to enable users of DeCSS to make such fair uses.

Defendants have focused on a significant point. Access control measures such as CSS do involve some risk of preventing lawful as well as unlawful uses of copyrighted material. Congress, however, clearly faced up to and dealt with this question in enacting the DMCA.

. . . Section 107 of the Copyright Act provides in critical part that certain uses of copyrighted works that otherwise would be wrongful are "not . . . infringement[s] of copyright." Defendants . . . are not here sued for copyright infringement. They are sued for offering and providing technology designed to circumvent technological measures that control access to copyrighted works and otherwise violating Section 1201(a)(2) of the Act. If Congress had meant the fair use defense to apply to such actions, it would have said so. . . .

Defendants claim also that the possibility that DeCSS might be used for the purpose of gaining access to copyrighted works in order to make fair use of those works saves them under *Sony Corp. v. Universal City Studios, Inc.* But they are mistaken. *Sony* does not apply to the activities with which defendants here are charged. Even if it did, it would not govern here. *Sony* involved a construction of the Copyright Act that has been overruled by the later enactment of the DMCA to the extent of any inconsistency between *Sony* and the new statute. . . .

The policy concerns raised by defendants were considered by Congress. Having considered them, Congress crafted a statute that, so far as the applicability of the fair use defense to Section 1201(a) claims is concerned, is crystal clear. In such circumstances, courts may not undo what Congress so plainly has done by "construing" the words of a statute to accomplish a result that Congress rejected. The fact that Congress elected to leave technologically unsophisticated persons who wish to make fair use of encrypted copyrighted works without the technical means of doing so is a matter for Congress unless Congress' decision contravenes the Constitution, a matter to which the Court turns below. . . .

C. *Linking to Sites Offering DeCSS*

Plaintiffs seek also to enjoin defendants from "linking" their 2600.com web site to other sites that make DeCSS available to users. . . .

The statute makes it unlawful to offer, provide or otherwise traffic in described technology. To "traffic" in something is to engage in dealings in it, conduct that necessarily involves awareness of the nature of the subject of the trafficking. To "provide" something, in the sense used in the statute, is to make it available or furnish it. To "offer" is to present or hold it out for consideration. . . .

To the extent that defendants have linked to sites that automatically commence the process of downloading DeCSS upon a user being transferred by defendants' hyperlinks, there can be no serious question. Defendants are engaged in the functional equivalent of transferring the DeCSS code to the user themselves.

Substantially the same is true of defendants' hyperlinks to web pages that display nothing more than the DeCSS code or present the user only with the choice of commencing a download of DeCSS and no other content. . . .

Potentially more troublesome might be links to pages that offer a good deal of content other than DeCSS. . . . If one assumed, for the purposes of argument, that the *Los Angeles Times* web site somewhere contained the DeCSS code, it would be wrong to say that anyone who linked to the *Los Angeles Times* web site, regardless of purpose or the manner in which the link was described, thereby offered, provided or otherwise trafficked in DeCSS. . . . But that is not this case. Defendants urged others to . . . disseminate DeCSS and to inform defendants that they were doing so. Defendants then linked their site to those "mirror" sites . . . and proclaimed on their own site that DeCSS could be had by clicking on the hyperlinks on defendants' site. . . .

III. The First Amendment . . .

[The court determined that computer code is a form of expression protected by the First Amendment. After deciding that the anti-trafficking provision of the DMCA is content-neutral, it held that the provision survived the intermediate scrutiny that applies to content-neutral restrictions on speech. The court next addressed defendants' argument that §1201(a)(2) is unconstitutionally overbroad. This argument was based largely on the statute's implications for the fair use doctrine; defendants argued that this doctrine is constitutionally mandated. The court did not reach this latter argument, however, because it concluded that it was not possible to determine whether §1201(a)(2) substantially affected the interests of parties not before the court.]

[Fair uses] now are affected by the anti-trafficking provision of the DMCA, but probably only to a trivial degree. To begin with, all or substantially all motion pictures available on DVD are available also on videotape. In consequence, anyone wishing to make lawful use of a particular movie may buy or rent a videotape, play it, and even copy all or part of it with readily available equipment. But even if movies were available only on DVD, as someday may be the case, the impact on lawful use would be limited. Compliant DVD players permit one to view or listen to a DVD movie without circumventing CSS in any prohibited sense. The technology permitting manufacture of compliant DVD players is available to anyone on a royalty-free basis and at modest cost, so CSS raises no technological barrier to their manufacture. Hence, those wishing to make lawful use of copyrighted movies by viewing or listening to them are not hindered in doing so in any material way by the anti-trafficking provision of the DMCA[243]. . . .

The DMCA does have a notable potential impact on uses that copy portions of a DVD movie because compliant DVD players are designed so as to prevent copying. . . . It is the interests of these individuals upon which defendants rely most heavily in contending that the DMCA violates the First Amendment. . . .[245]

---

243. Defendants argue that the right of third parties to view DVD movies on computers running the Linux operating system will be materially impaired if DeCSS is not available to them. However, the technology to build a Linux-based DVD player has been licensed by the DVD CCA to at least two companies, and there is no reason to think that others wishing to develop Linux players could not obtain licenses if they so chose. . . . Further, it is not evident that the constitutional protection of free expression extends to the type of device on which one plays copyrighted material. . . .

245. The same point might be made with respect to copying of works upon which copyright has expired. . . . As the DMCA is not yet two years old, this does not yet appear to be a problem, although it may emerge as one in the future.

. . . [T]he interests of persons wishing to circumvent CSS in order to make lawful uses of the copyrighted movies it protects are remarkably varied. . . . [T]he prudential concern with ensuring that constitutional questions be decided only when the facts before the Court so require counsels against permitting defendants to mount an overbreadth challenge here. . . .

[Finally, the court considered whether enjoining defendants from linking to sites that offered DeCSS would violate the First Amendment.]

[T]he real significance of an anti-linking injunction would not be with U.S. web sites subject to the DMCA, but with foreign sites that arguably are not subject to it and not subject to suit here. An anti-linking injunction to that extent would have a significant impact and thus materially advance a substantial government purpose. . . .

The possible chilling effect of a rule permitting liability for or injunctions against Internet hyperlinks is a genuine concern. But it is not unique to the issue of linking. The constitutional law of defamation provides a highly relevant analogy. . . .

Accordingly, there may be no injunction against, nor liability for, linking to a site containing circumvention technology, the offering of which is unlawful under the DMCA, absent clear and convincing evidence that those responsible for the link (a) know at the relevant time that the offending material is on the linked-to site, (b) know that it is circumvention technology that may not lawfully be offered, and (c) create or maintain the link for the purpose of disseminating that technology. . . .

IV. Relief . . .

. . . [T]he likelihood is that this decision will serve notice on others that "the strong right arm of equity" may be brought to bear against them absent a change in their conduct and thus contribute to a climate of appropriate respect for intellectual property rights in an age in which the excitement of ready access to untold quantities of information has blurred in some minds the fact that taking what is not yours and not freely offered to you is stealing. Appropriate injunctive and declaratory relief will issue simultaneously with this opinion. . . .

NOTES AND QUESTIONS

1. Does CSS resemble any of the technological protection efforts described in Section A of this chapter, *supra*? Are the prohibitions in §1201 more like the ban on unauthorized decryption of satellite signals or more like the serial copy management requirements of the AHRA, or neither?

Note that under the CSS licensing regime, CSS protection also varies by geographic zone. DVDs marketed in the U.S. will not play on DVD players marketed in Europe, Africa, or Asia, and vice versa. This arrangement was designed to thwart high-volume, cross-border piracy operations, but it also enables copyright owners to implement geographic price discrimination. Users in relatively affluent regions — e.g., North America and Europe — can be charged higher prices than those in less affluent regions — e.g., Southeast Asia and Africa. Gray marketers cannot exploit these price differences by shipping DVDs exported to Africa back to the U.S., even though the Supreme Court's decision in *Quality King v. L'anza*, Chapter 5.C, *supra*, would allow this, because U.S. consumers will not be able to play them. Disabling the region coding would enable users to play DVDs lawfully purchased in other countries. Would this violate §1201? *See Sony Computer Entm't Am., Inc. v. Divineo Inc.*, 81 U.S.P.Q.2d 1045 (N.D. Cal. 2006) (holding that even though "mod chips" for video game consoles enabled some lawful uses, they had the "primary purpose" of circumventing Sony's authentication system).

2. Recall the distinctions made by §1201 between access protection measures and rights protection measures. Characterizing a technological protection as one or the other sometimes can be difficult. *See* R. Anthony Reese, *Will Merging Access Controls and Rights Controls Undermine the Structure of Anticircumvention Law?*, 18 Berkeley Tech. L.J. 619 (2003). Why was *Reimerdes* cast as a case about §1201(a) and not §1201(b)? Examine the table on page 662 *supra* before you answer.

3. Examine the definitions in §1201(a)(3). If you purchase a copy of a password protected program on a CD-ROM and let a friend use your password to access the program, has your friend circumvented a technological measure that "effectively controls access to" the work? Have you trafficked in a device or service covered by §1201(a)(2)? *See I.M.S. Inquiry Mgmt. Sys., Ltd v. Berkshire Info. Sys., Inc.*, 307 F. Supp. 2d 521 (S.D.N.Y. 2004) (no).

Some programs require users to provide certain personal identifying information when they install the program, and use this information to monitor use of the program and any affiliated programs (such as those for word processing, photo editing, playing music, and so on). Is this functionality a technological measure that "effectively controls access to" such programs, within the meaning of §1201? Would defeating this functionality, so that one could use the programs without providing the personal information, violate §1201(a)(2)? Examine §1201(i) before you answer.

4. Examine §1201(f). Should the court have accepted defendants' argument that DeCSS was created to achieve interoperability between CSS-protected DVDs and the Linux operating system? Under the court's interpretation of this subsection, what is the difference between circumvention and enabling interoperability?

Recall the discussion of open source software in Chapter 8.C *supra*. Linux is an open source operating system — i.e., all of the program code that makes up the Linux system is distributed with its source code and may be freely modified by users. The court noted that two licenses to develop Linux-compatible DVD players had been issued at the time of trial. No such licenses had been issued before plaintiffs filed their complaint. Why do you think this was the case?

5. Now examine §1201(a)(2). Should the court have concluded that potential use with the Linux operating system was a commercially significant use of DeCSS? Under the *Sony* standard, such a finding would have excused defendants from liability for contributory copyright infringement. Would such evidence have been sufficient to support a ruling that distribution of DeCSS did not violate §1201(a)(2)?

6. Now focus on the court's discussion of the statutory exception for "good faith encryption research." Examine §1201(g) carefully. Could either the defendants in *Reimerdes* or the individual who created DeCSS ever qualify for this exception? What would one need to do to qualify?

7. At the time the plaintiff instituted the litigation there were hundreds, if not thousands, of sites on the web where one could obtain a copy of DeCSS. Why do you think plaintiffs chose to name Eric Corley as one of the defendants in this litigation?

A subsequent declaratory judgment action brought by Princeton University computer science professor Edward Felten sought interpretation of §1201 in a different context. Professor Felten and his research team accepted a public challenge issued by the recording industry to crack its prototype technological protection specifications for digital music files. Professor Felten and his team decided not to claim the cash prize offered by the recording industry, however, because they would have been required not to disclose the results of their research, and to agree that those results were now the intellectual property of the Secure Digital Music

Initiative (SDMI). As Professor Felten was preparing to present his findings at a prominent research conference, representatives of the Recording Industry Association of America (RIAA) contacted the conference organizers and the legal counsel for Princeton University and warned that publication of the paper would violate the DMCA. Shortly thereafter, one of the conference organizers informed Professor Felten that his paper could not be presented unless the RIAA and SDMI agreed in writing. The incident sparked an uproar in the computer science community. Two days before the paper was scheduled to be presented, the conference organizers reversed their decision, but Professor Felten and his fellow researchers ultimately decided to withdraw the paper. The RIAA immediately issued a press release stating that it had never seriously intended to sue.

In the litigation, Professor Felten asserted that publication of the paper would not violate §1201(a)(2), and, in the alternative, that §1201(a)(2) could not be enforced because Congress lacked the authority to enact it. The court granted the RIAA's motion to dismiss, finding that the dispute had not ripened into an actual controversy because Professor Felten was able to present his research at a different conference. *Felten v. Recording Indus. Ass'n of Am., Inc.*, Case No. CV-01-2669 (GEB) (D.N.J. Nov. 28, 2001). Professor Felten chose not to appeal the decision.

Is an academic research paper a "device"? If so, did Professor Felten's conduct fall within any of the statutory exceptions to the DMCA's device ban provisions? Does anything in the language of the DMCA support an argument that its provisions did not apply to Professor Felten's actions? If not, why do you think the RIAA disclaimed any intention to sue? Why do you think the RIAA moved to dismiss the *Felten* lawsuit?

8. Examine §1201(c)(1) carefully. Why do you think that Congress included this provision in the statute? During trial, the *Reimerdes* defendants urged the court to construe this language to require a limited, judicially created exception to §1201(a)(2)'s device ban, but the court declined. This argument based on §1201(c)(1) was the main statutory argument that the defendants raised on appeal. The Second Circuit was equally unpersuaded: "We disagree that subsection 1201(c)(1) permits such a reading. Instead, it simply clarifies that the DMCA targets the *circumvention* of digital walls guarding copyrighted material (and trafficking in circumvention tools), but does not concern itself with the *use* of those materials after circumvention has occurred." *Universal City Studios, Inc. v. Corley*, 273 F.3d 429, 443 (2d Cir. 2001) (emphasis in original). Do you agree with the court's reading of the statute?

In the case of works whose technological controls require payment or authorization for each act of access, does the independent prohibition on circumventing access controls frustrate the exercise of fair use and other privileges? In a situation in which individual acts of circumvention are not prohibited (i.e., circumventing protection measures involving rights controls as opposed to access controls), how does an individual obtain the tools to engage in the circumvention?

9. Review the remaining provisions in §1201(c). Should any of these provisions have changed the result in *Reimerdes?*

10. Other exemptions contained in §1201 include: (1) a narrow exception that allows nonprofit libraries, archives, and educational institutions to circumvent access controls for the sole purpose of determining whether to acquire a particular work, §1201(d); (2) an exception for authorized law enforcement activities, §1201(e); (3) an exception allowing circumvention of access controls to enable filtering of Internet content to protect minors, §1201(h); and (4) an exception allowing circumvention, and the development of circumvention tools, for security testing of computer systems, §1201(j).

Finally, §1201(k) also includes lengthy provisions prescribing the use of specific copy control standards in analog VCRs. However, §1201(k)(2) cautions that these copy control standards may not be applied "to prevent or limit consumer copying" except in the cases of paid subscription transmissions and pre-recorded audiovisual works.

Note on *Universal City Studios, Inc. v. Corley*

The appeal of the *Reimerdes* decision focused primarily on the defendants' constitutional challenges to §1201(a)(2). *Universal City Studios, Inc. v. Corley*, 273 F.3d 429 (2d Cir. 2001). The court agreed with the district court's conclusions that instructions in computer code qualify as speech protected under the First Amendment, and that the regulation imposed by §1201(a)(2) is content-neutral and permissible. In determining that the statutory provision is content-neutral, it reasoned:

> . . . The [] realities of what code is and what its normal functions are require a First Amend-ment analysis that treats code as combining nonspeech and speech elements; i.e., functional and expressive elements. . . .
>
> In considering the scope of First Amendment protection for a decryption program like DeCSS, we must recognize that the essential purpose of encryption code is to prevent unauthorized access. Owners of all property rights are entitled to prohibit access to their property by unauthorized persons. . . .
>
> . . . In its basic function, [DeCSS] is like a skeleton key that can open a locked door, a combination that can open a safe, or a device that can neutralize the security device attached to a store's products.

Id. at 452-53.

To survive constitutional scrutiny, a content-neutral speech restriction must further a substantial government interest unrelated to the suppression of free expression, and must not "burden substantially more speech than is necessary to further the government's legitimate interests." *Ward v. Rock Against Racism*, 491 U.S. 781, 799 (1989). The Second Circuit concluded that §1201(a)(2), as applied by the district court to prohibit defendants from posting DeCSS, met this standard:

> The Government's interest in preventing unauthorized access to encrypted copyrighted material is unquestionably substantial, and the regulation of DeCSS by the posting prohibition plainly serves that interest. Moreover, the interest is unrelated to the suppression of free expression. The injunction regulates the posting of DeCSS, regardless of whether DeCSS code contains any information comprehensible by human beings that would qualify as speech. . . .
>
> . . . Although the prohibition on posting prevents the Appellants from conveying to others the speech component of DeCSS, the Appellants have not suggested, much less shown, any tech-nique for barring them from making this instantaneous worldwide distribution of a decryption code that makes a lesser restriction on the code's speech component. . . . [A] content-neutral regulation need not employ the least restrictive means of accomplishing the governmental objective.

Corley, 273 F.3d at 454-55. The court also affirmed the district court's prohibition against linking to DeCSS. It rejected an analogy to an injunction prohibiting a newspaper from publishing the addresses of bookstores carrying obscene materials:

> If a bookstore proprietor is knowingly selling obscene materials, the evil of distributing such materials can be prevented by injunctive relief against the unlawful distribution. . . . And if others publish the location of the bookstore, preventive relief against a distributor can be effective before

any significant distribution of the prohibited materials has occurred. The digital world, however, creates a very different problem. If obscene materials are posted on one web site and other sites post hyperlinks to the first site, the materials are available for worldwide distribution before any preventive measures can be effectively taken.

Id. at 457.

Finally, the Second Circuit rejected defendants' overbreadth challenge based on the fair use doctrine. The court expressed doubt that any part of the Constitution requires recognition of a fair use doctrine: "[W]e note that the Supreme Court has never held that fair use is constitutionally required, although some isolated statements in its opinions might arguably be enlisted for such a requirement." *Id.* at 458. Like the district court, however, the court of appeals concluded that it need not reach the question whether the fair use doctrine is constitutionally required. It indicated that it would consider constitutional challenges based on §1201(a)(2)'s implications for fair use on a case-by-case, or "as-applied," basis when presented by defendants entitled to raise them. In closing, the court noted:

We know of no authority for the proposition that fair use, as protected by the Copyright Act, much less the Constitution, guarantees copying by the optimum method or in the identical format of the original. Although the Appellants insisted at oral argument that they should not be relegated to a "horse and buggy" technique in making fair use of DVD movies, the DMCA does not impose even an arguable limitation on the opportunity to make a variety of traditional fair uses of DVD movies, such as commenting on their content, quoting excerpts from their screenplays, and even recording portions of the video images and sounds on film or tape by pointing a camera, a camcorder, or a microphone at a monitor as it displays the DVD movie. . . . Fair use has never been held to be a guarantee of access to copyrighted material in order to copy it by the fair user's preferred technique or in the format of the original.

Id. at 459.

NOTES AND QUESTIONS

1. The *Corley* court's reasoning about whether §1201 is content-neutral echoes the "breaking and entering" argument advanced by the copyright industries to support their request for a ban on circumvention and circumvention tools. In the words of Allan Adler, a lobbyist for the Association of American Publishers, "Fair use doesn't allow you to break into a locked library in order to make 'fair use' copies of the books in it, or steal newspapers from a vending machine in order to copy articles and share them with a friend." WIPO Copyright Treaties Implementation Act; and Online Copyright Liability Limitation Act: Hearing on H.R. 2281 and H.R. 2280 Before the Subcomm. on Courts and Intellectual Property of the House Comm. on the Judiciary, 105th Cong., at 208 (1997) (statement of Allan Adler). Is this metaphor sufficient to capture all of the implications of circumvention? Why, or why not? Do you agree with the court's conclusion that a law that targets decryption devices is content-neutral?

2. Was the *Corley* court correct to conclude that no less restrictive means exists by which Congress might prevent or deter unauthorized copying of copyrighted works? Can you think of any less restrictive measures that Congress might have enacted? Review Question 10, page 672 *supra*. Should Congress have included limitations analogous to those in §1201(k) in the other provisions of §1201?

3. Professor Felten, discussed in Note 7, page 671 *supra*, also argued that enforcing §1201(a)(2) to suppress his research and discussion of cryptographic systems would violate

the First Amendment. Do you agree with the district court's decision to dismiss this claim? If the court had not dismissed, how should it have ruled on this constitutional challenge?

4. Do you agree with the Second Circuit's dictum that the Supreme Court's pronouncements on the relationship between fair use and the Constitution amount to "isolated statements" of little value? In *Eldred v. Ashcroft*, 537 U.S. 186 (2003), Chapter 3.B.2 *supra*, decided after the Second Circuit's decision in *Corley*, the Supreme Court rejected the plaintiff's First Amendment challenge to the Copyright Term Extension Act, concluding that when "Congress has not altered the traditional contours of copyright protection, further First Amendment scrutiny is unnecessary." *Eldred*, 537 U.S. at 221. Does the DMCA alter the "traditional contours of copyright protection"? In *Eldred*, the Supreme Court emphasized that "copyright law contains built-in First Amendment accommodations" such as the idea/expression dichotomy and the fair use doctrine. *Id.* at 219-20. Could the Second Circuit have so easily rejected the First Amendment argument if *Eldred* had been decided earlier?

5. Can you think of any fair or otherwise privileged uses of DVD movies that might require the ability to make copies directly in the digital format?

6. Legislation introduced in the 109th Congress, titled the "Digital Media Consumers' Rights Act" (H.R. 1201), sought to amend §1201(c)(1) by adding at the end: "and it is not a violation of this section to circumvent a technological measure in connection with access to, or the use of, a work if such circumvention does not result in an infringement of copyright in the work." A new §1201(c)(5) provided: "It shall not be a violation of this title to manufacture, distribute, or make noninfringing use of a hardware or software product capable of enabling significant noninfringing use of a copyrighted work." Finally, the bill would have amended §1201's device-related provisions by adding to §1201(a)(2)(A) and (b)(1)(A) a narrow exception for persons "acting solely in furtherance of scientific research into technological protection measures." If you were a member of Congress, would you support passage of such legislation? Why or why not?

7. Sections 1203 and 1204 establish separate civil and criminal penalties for violations of §1201. Violations of §1201 are subject to criminal sanctions if done willfully and for purposes of commercial advantage or private financial gain. *See* 17 U.S.C. §1204. The first criminal prosecution involving §1201 occurred in 2001. Dmitry Sklyarov, a Russian computer programmer and an employee of ElcomSoft, a Moscow-based software firm, had helped develop a program called the "Advanced eBook Processor," which removed copy protection restrictions built into Adobe Systems' "eBook Reader" software. The "Advanced eBook Processor" was available for purchase for $99 through an unrelated web site based in the U.S. In July 2001, Mr. Sklyarov came to the U.S. to attend a software conference in Las Vegas, Nevada. There he was arrested, transferred to the Northern District of California, and arraigned on charges of willfully violating §1201(b)(1) of the DMCA. Widespread public protests followed the announcement of Mr. Sklyarov's arrest. Ultimately, the government dropped its charges against Mr. Sklyarov in exchange for his agreement to testify in the prosecution of ElcomSoft.

ElcomSoft moved to dismiss the indictment, raising similar constitutional arguments to those in the *Reimerdes/Corley* and *Felten* cases, but the district court denied the motion. *United States v. Elcom Ltd.*, 203 F. Supp. 2d 1111 (N.D. Cal. 2002). In December 2002, a jury found that the government had failed to prove that ElcomSoft had willfully violated U.S. law, and acquitted ElcomSoft of all charges. Did the government have a tenable argument that the DMCA applied to Mr. Sklyarov's and ElcomSoft's actions taken in Russia? How far do you think Congress intended the DMCA to reach?

8. As a result of the incident involving Professor Felten, as well as a number of other DMCA-related warnings issued by technology companies, several prominent foreign computer scientists who study cryptographic systems publicly stated that they will no longer attend

computer science conferences in the U.S. If you were one of these individuals, would you be reassured by the ultimate outcomes of the *Felten* and *ElcomSoft* cases? For a list of DMCA-related disputes and warnings, visit the Electronic Frontier Foundation's web site at *http://www.eff.org* and search for "DMCA consequences."

Note on Library of Congress Rulemakings Under §1201

Section 1201(a)'s ban on the circumvention of access controls is subject to a grant of rulemaking authority that allows the Librarian of Congress, in consultation with the Copyright Office and the Department of Commerce, to declare exemptions if it finds that particular users are "adversely affected by the prohibition under [§1201(a)(1)(A)] in their ability to make noninfringing uses of a particular class of copyrighted works." 17 U.S.C. §1201(a)(1)(C). Any exemption granted pursuant to this procedure does not supply a defense to an action for violation of any other provision of Title 17—including the device bans set forth in §1201(a)(2) and (b)(1). Thus, one who is granted an exemption may circumvent access controls, but apparently may not manufacture or distribute circumvention technologies.

The statute directs that the rulemaking be conducted every three years. In 2000, the Librarian of Congress and the Copyright Office completed the first rulemaking. The Copyright Office rejected arguments that the language of the statute entitled it to declare an exemption to the circumvention ban whenever the underlying use would be considered fair, and ruled that the statutory reference to "a particular class of copyrighted works" required any exemptions to be narrowly drawn. It further ruled that any exemption must be based on a showing of a "substantial adverse effect." U.S. Copyright Office, Exemption to Prohibition on Circumvention of Copyright Protection Systems for Access Control Technologies: Final Rule, 65 Fed. Reg. 64,556, 64,558 (Oct. 27, 2000). Based on this interpretation, the final rule declared two exemptions: literary works whose storage formats had malfunctioned or become obsolete; and lists of filtering criteria employed by vendors of software designed to filter undesirable Internet content.

The second rulemaking, completed in 2003, further limited both of these exemptions. Noting that the only evidence submitted to justify retaining the first exemption related to computer software, not literary works more generally, the Copyright Office narrowed its scope accordingly. The second exemption was redrafted to exclude lists of filtering criteria employed by, *inter alia*, spam filters and antivirus software. The 2003 rulemaking also added two new exemptions: one for computer programs and video games in obsolete formats that require the original media or hardware as a condition of access; and one for literary works distributed in ebook format when all existing ebook editions contain access controls that prevent the enabling of special access features for blind and visually impaired users. U.S. Copyright Office: Exemption to Prohibition on Circumvention of Copyright Protection Systems for Access Control Technologies: Final Rule, 68 Fed. Reg. 62,011 (Oct. 31, 2003).

In the second rulemaking, the Copyright Office also clarified its interpretation of the burden of proof established by the statute. According to the 2003 Final Rule, the requirement that proponents of exemptions demonstrate the likelihood of a "substantial adverse effect" does not impose a burden higher than the statute requires, but "simply means that [one's proof] must have a substance." *Id*. at 62,013.

The third rulemaking, completed in 2006, continued the pattern of narrowly defined exemptions established by the first two rulemakings. The Copyright Office reiterated the requirement that proponents of exemptions prove by a preponderance of the evidence a "substantial adverse effect" on noninfringing uses. U.S. Copyright Office, Exemption to Prohibition on Circumvention of Copyright Protection Systems for Access Control Technologies: Final Rule, 71 Fed. Reg. 68,472, 68,473 (Nov. 27, 2006), codified at 37 C.F.R. §201.40. Rather than focusing solely on effects on particular works, however, the Copyright Office concluded that in some circumstances "a particular class of copyrighted works" may be defined "by reference to the type of user who may take advantage of the exemption or by reference to the type of use of the work that may be made pursuant to the exemption." *Id.*

Based on these criteria, the Copyright Office renewed, and in one case narrowed, three of the four previously existing exemptions. It concluded that only libraries and archives would be affected by lack of access to computer programs and video games in obsolete formats, and so narrowed the existing exemption for those works to cover only circumvention for purposes of preservation or archival reproduction. It declined to renew the exemption for lists of filtering criteria, on the ground that proponents of the exemption had relied solely on the record from the previous rulemaking and had adduced no evidence of current need. It also approved three new exemptions: one for audiovisual works included in libraries of college or university film/media studies departments, "when circumvention is accomplished for the purpose of making compilations of portions of those works for educational use in the classroom by media studies or film professors," *id.* at 68,474; one for computer programs that enable mobile phones to connect to wireless telephone networks, "when circumvention is accomplished for the sole purpose of lawfully connecting" to a network other than the one for which the phone was originally programmed, *id.* at 68,476; and one for audio and audiovisual works distributed in CD format and protected by technological measures that "create or exploit security flaws or vulnerabilities . . . when circumvention is accomplished solely for the good faith testing, investigating, or correcting such security flaws or vulnerabilities," *id.* at 68,477.

The schedule for DMCA rulemakings called for the next rulemaking to be completed in October 2009. Instead, the Copyright Office issued an order granting itself an extension. As of this writing, the 2009 rulemaking has yet to be completed.

Note on International Approaches to the Implementation of the WIPO Copyright Treaty (WCT)

Section 1201 is meant to fulfill, in part, U.S. treaty obligations under the WCT. The different exceptions to circumvention liability contained in §1201(c)-(j) and the rulemaking authorized by §1201(a)(1) are limitations on the anti-circumvention rights granted to copyright owners. Consistent with other major international copyright agreements, the language of the WCT preserves flexibility for member countries to implement its requirements. To reinforce the importance of accommodating different national practices with respect to the new obligations created by the WCT, the negotiating countries adopted an Agreed Statement, which states in part that members are permitted to "carry forward and appropriately extend into the digital environment limitations and exceptions in their national laws which have been considered acceptable under the Berne Convention. Similarly . . . [the provisions of Article 10 regarding limitations and exceptions] should be understood to permit Contracting Parties to devise new exceptions and limitations that are appropriate in the digital network environment." Agreed Statements Concerning the WIPO Copyright Treaty, adopted by the Diplomatic Conference on Dec. 20, 1996, WIPO Doc. CRNR/ DC/96, Statement Concerning Article 10.

In fact, national implementation of the WCT does vary. Typically, developing countries incorporate the treaty language into their domestic legislation with little or no change.

Developed countries are more likely to engage in the process of domestic implementation in a way that responds to the various interests at stake.

The EU's 2001 directive on copyright harmonization incorporates the language of the WCT's mandates. Thus, member countries are required to provide "adequate legal protection" against both the act of circumvention of "effective technological measures" and the manufacture and distribution of technologies that can be used to accomplish the circumvention. Directive 2001/29/EC of the European Parliament and of the Council of 22 May 2001 on the harmonisation of certain aspects of copyright and related rights in the information society, 2001 O.J. (L 167) 10, art. 6(1)-(2). The language of the provision regarding circumvention technologies substantially tracks the language of §1201(a)(2) and (b)(1). Overall, however, the directive contemplates a different approach to the design and implementation of technological protections for copyrighted works. Article 6 provides:

> [I]n the absence of voluntary measures taken by rightholders, including agreements between rightholders and other parties concerned, Member States shall take appropriate measures to ensure that rightholders make available to the beneficiary of an exception or limitation provided for in national law . . . [under certain other provisions of the directive] the means of benefiting from that exception or limitation, to the extent necessary to benefit from that exception or limitation and where that beneficiary has legal access to the protected work or subject-matter concerned.

Id. art. 6(4). The exceptions and limitations for which accommodation is mandated do not include exceptions for private noncommercial copying; as to these exceptions, Article 6 provides that member states "may" take measures to ensure their survival if rightholders have not already enabled such private copying. *Id.*

These provisions require policymakers, copyright owners, and technologists to determine whether it might be possible to design technological protection systems that respect underlying copyright rules. The evidence suggests that the answer to this question is a qualified yes. On the one hand, it probably is impossible to design an automated system that internalizes the complex norms of the U.S. fair use doctrine. On the other, as you already know from reading about the AHRA's SCMS, *see* pages 658-60 *supra*, it plainly is possible to design systems that enable more specifically defined conduct. Accordingly, some commentators, both in Europe and in the U.S., have advocated a "fair use by design" approach, which would require rightsholders to design technological measures that are programmed to allow users to use the work consistent with existing exemptions and limitations. They argue that if an owner fails to make such accommodation for legitimate uses, then the law should permit circumvention for such uses, or require the owner to make a non-encrypted version of the work available. *See* Dan L. Burk & Julie E. Cohen, *Fair Use Infrastructure for Rights Management Systems*, 15 Harv. J.L. & Tech. 41, 55-70 (2001); Séverine Dusollier, *Exceptions and Technological Measures in the European Copyright Directive of 2001 — An Empty Promise*, 34 Int'l Rev. Indus. Prop. & Copyright 62, 70 (2003). The United Kingdom has adopted a version of this approach; it provides an administrative remedy in cases where a technological protection system prevents a user from engaging in activity permitted by the copyright law. *See* Copyright, Designs and Patents Act, 1988, ch. 48, P 296ZE, as amended by Copyright and Related Rights Regulations (2003 SI 2003/2498).

The U.S., meanwhile, has sought to encourage other countries to adopt the approach reflected in the DMCA. The USTR has negotiated a series of bilateral and regional free trade agreements (FTAs) that include accession to the WCT among their terms. Some of these agreements incorporate DMCA-style language requiring prohibition of anti-circumvention measures in the domestic legislation of countries that are party to the FTA. *See, e.g.,* United

States-Chile Free Trade Agreement, June 6, 2003 (Art. 17.7); United States-Singapore Free Trade Agreement, May 6, 2003 (Art. 16.4); Central America-Dominican Republic-United States Free Trade Agreement (CAFTADR), August 5, 2004 (Art.15.5).

NOTES AND QUESTIONS

1. Is the DMCA's rulemaking processs a good substitute for the comparatively unconstrained equitable standard that applies in fair use cases? Why, or why not? Is it appropriate to give the Librarian of Congress and the Copyright Office broad equitable discretion in rulemaking? What do you think of the Copyright Office's conclusion that exemptions may be defined in part by classes of users? Is that approach supported by the statutory language? How does it affect the scope of approved exemptions?

2. If you were a European copyright holder, what sorts of "voluntary measures" might you undertake to stave off government regulation? If you were a legislator in one of the EU member countries, what sorts of legislative measures would you recommend? What do you suppose is meant by "agreements between rightholders and other parties concerned"?

3. What do you think of the "fair use by design" approach? Recall the *Corley* court's conclusion that no means less restrictive than §1201(a)(2) were available to prevent unauthorized copying and distribution of copyrighted works. Do the EU approaches represent viable "less restrictive alternatives" for preventing unauthorized copying? Should Congress have taken a similar approach to the EU's solution to the problems posed by circumvention of technological protection systems? Should courts considering First Amendment challenges to §1201 hold that it was constitutionally required to do so?

4. Legislation introduced in the 109th Congress proposed amending §1201 to allow both circumvention of technological measures and manufacture and distribution of circumvention tools where such actions are "necessary to make a noninfringing use" of a protected work and where "the copyright owner fails to make available the necessary means to make such noninfringing use without additional cost or burden" to the user. H.R. 4536, 109th Cong., 1st Sess., §5. Legislation introduced in the 110th Congress, titled the FAIR USE Act, proposed amending §1201 to add a list of specific exemptions to the circumvention ban and the device bans. The list includes, *inter alia*, gaining access to a public domain work, gaining access to "a work of substantial public interest solely for purposes of criticism, comment, news reporting, scholarship, or research," and enabling transmittal of a work within a "home or personal network." H.R. 1201, 110th Cong., 1st Sess., §3(b). Would you support either of these proposals?

5. Recall that proponents of the DMCA argued that the law was necessary for the U.S. to fulfill its international obligations. Was this really so? Consider the following argument:

> The U.S. could have asserted that its law already complied with the WIPO treaty's anti-circumvention norm. This norm was, after all, very general in character and provided treaty signatories with considerable latitude in implementation. Moreover, anti-circumvention legislation was new enough to many national intellectual property systems, and certainly to international law, to mean that there was no standard by which to judge how to instantiate the norm. The U.S. could have pointed to a number of statutes and judicial decisions that establish anti-circumvention norms. With the U.S. copyright industries thriving in the current legal environment, it would have been fair to conclude that copyright owners already were adequately protected by the law. . . .
>
> Even if a reasoned assessment of U.S. law might have led policymakers to conclude that some additional anti-circumvention legislation was necessary or desirable . . . [t]he Administration

might have, for example, proposed to make it illegal to circumvent a technical protection system for purposes of engaging in or enabling copyright infringement. This, after all, was the danger that was said to give rise to the call for anti-circumvention regulations in the first place. . . . [Congress also could have] outlaw[ed] making or distributing a technology intentionally designed or produced to enable copyright infringement. . . .

Pamela Samuelson, *Intellectual Property and the Digital Economy: Why the Anti-Circumvention Regulations Need to Be Revised*, 14 Berkeley Tech. L.J. 519, 532-33 (1999). Do you agree with Professor Samuelson that before the enactment of the DMCA, U.S. copyright law adequately implemented these anti-circumvention norms, and that §1201 goes beyond what was necessary? Which doctrines would you identify as establishing such norms? Alternatively, do you agree that Congress should have enacted the narrower legislative proposals that Professor Samuelson describes? Why, or why not? Does the DMCA fully or adequately exploit the opportunity to balance the rights of owners and users of digital works?

6. Since the WCT entered into force on March 6, 2002, only 88 countries have joined it. Why do you think this is the case? The vast majority of WCT members are developing/least developed countries or countries in transition. If you were advising a developing country that is considering WCT membership, what would you state as the advantages of membership? In May 2001, the British government established a Commission on Intellectual Property Rights (CIPR) to study the effects of intellectual property rights in developing countries. The CIPR's report concluded that developing countries should not endorse the WCT and should not adopt the DMCA model for regulation of technological measures. Why do you think the CIPR reached these conclusions?

7. The British implementation of the WCT's anti-circumvention prohibition explicitly excludes a person "who for the purposes of research into cryptography, does anything which circumvents an effective technological measure unless in so doing, or in issuing information derived from that research, he affects prejudicially the rights of the copyright owner." Copyright, Designs and Patents Act, 1988, ch. 48, P 296ZA, as amended by Copyright and Related Rights Regulations (2003 SI 2003/2498). Should the U.S. adopt a similar exemption?

8. A French court has held that failure to appropriately label DVDs containing copy protection measures constitutes a failure to notify consumers of an essential characteristic of the DVDs, in violation of the French Consumer Code. Cour d'appel Versailles, No. 03/07172, *Francoise M. v. EMI France* (Apr. 15, 2005). Does the failure to label copy-protected digital media violate U.S. consumer protection law? *See Keel v. BMG Entertainment*, No. B164476 2003 WL 22808378 (Cal. App. 2 Dist., Nov. 26, 2003) (allowing state law claims for breach of express and implied warranty to proceed). Should the U.S. adopt specific regulations governing the labeling of copy-protected digital media?

C. AUTHORIZED VERSUS UNAUTHORIZED ACCESS AND INTEROPERABLE PRODUCTS

As you saw in Chapter 7.B.2, courts have interpreted the fair use doctrine to permit reverse engineering of computer software products done with the purpose of creating competing yet interoperable products. How does §1201 affect the practice of creating interoperable products? In the *Reimerdes* case the defendant argued that the publication of DeCSS was necessary in order for open source programmers to develop a DVD player for the Linux operating system.

The court rejected this argument, which relied on the exemption contained in §1201(f). Review that portion of the court's opinion (at page 667) and then consider the following two cases.

Chamberlain Group, Inc. v. Skylink Tech., Inc.
381 F.3d 1178 (Fed. Cir. 2004), cert. denied, 544 U.S. 923 (2005)

GAJARSA, J.: . . . The technology at issue involves Garage Door Openers (GDOs). A GDO typically consists of a hand-held portable transmitter and a garage door opening device mounted in a homeowner's garage. . . .

When a homeowner purchases a GDO system, the manufacturer provides both an opener and a transmitter. Homeowners who desire replacement or spare transmitters can purchase them in the aftermarket. Aftermarket consumers have long been able to purchase "universal transmitters" that they can program to interoperate with their GDO system regardless of make or model. Skylink and Chamberlain are the only significant distributors of universal GDO transmitters.[1] Chamberlain places no explicit restrictions on the types of transmitter that the homeowner may use with its system at the time of purchase. Chamberlain's customers therefore assume that they enjoy all of the rights associated with the use of their GDOs and any software embedded therein that the copyright laws and other laws of commerce provide.

This dispute involves Chamberlain's Security+ line of GDOs and Skylink's Model 39 universal transmitter. Chamberlain's Security+ GDOs incorporate a copyrighted "rolling code" computer program that constantly changes the transmitter signal needed to open the garage door. Skylink's Model 39 transmitter, which does not incorporate rolling code, nevertheless allows users to operate Security+ openers. Chamberlain alleges that Skylink's transmitter renders the Security+ insecure by allowing unauthorized users to circumvent the security inherent in rolling codes. . . .

These facts frame the dispute now before us on appeal. Though only Chamberlain's DMCA claim is before us, and though the parties dispute whether or not Skylink developed the Model 39 independent of Chamberlain's copyrighted products, it is nevertheless noteworthy that Chamberlain *has not* alleged either that Skylink infringed its copyright or that Skylink is liable for contributory copyright infringement. What Chamberlain *has* alleged is that because its opener and transmitter both incorporate computer programs "protected by copyright" and because rolling codes are a "technological measure" that "controls access" to those programs, Skylink is prima facie liable for violating §1201(a)(2). In the District Court's words, "Chamberlain claims that the rolling code computer program has a protective measure that protects itself. Thus, only one computer program is at work here, but it has two functions: (1) to verify the rolling code; and (2) once the rolling code is verified, to activate the GDO motor, by sending instructions to a microprocessor in the GDO." *Chamberlain I,* 292 F. Supp. 2d at 1028.

C. The Summary Judgment Motions . . .

According to undisputed facts, a homeowner who purchases a Chamberlain GDO owns it and has a right to use it to access his or her own garage. At the time of sale, Chamberlain does not place any explicit terms or condition on use to limit the ways that a purchaser may use its

---

1. Chamberlain's product, the "Clicker," interoperates with both Chamberlain and non-Chamberlain GDOs.

products. A homeowner who wishes to use a Model 39 must first program it into the GDO. Skylink characterizes this action as the home-owner's authorization of the Model 39 to inter-operate with the GDO. In other words, according to Skylink, Chamberlain GDO consumers who purchase a Skylink transmitter have Chamberlain's implicit permission to purchase and to use any brand of transmitter that will open their GDO. The District Court agreed that Chamberlain's unconditioned sale implied authorization. *Id.* . . .

The District Court further noted that under Chamberlain's proposed construction of the DMCA, not only would Skylink be in violation of §1201(a)(2) (prohibiting trafficking in circumvention devices), but Chamberlain's own customers who used a Model 39 would be in violation of §1201(a)(1) (prohibiting circumvention). The District Court declined to adopt a construction with such dire implications. *See Chamberlain I,* 292 F. Supp. 2d at 1039-40. . . .

Discussion . . .

D.   The Statute and Liability under the DMCA

The essence of the DMCA's anticircumvention provisions is that §§1201(a), (b) establish causes of action for liability. They do not establish a new property right. The DMCA's text indicates that circumvention is not infringement, 17 U.S.C. §1201(c)(1) . . . , and the statute's structure makes the point even clearer. This distinction between property and liability is critical. Whereas copyrights, like patents, are property, liability protection from unauthorized circumvention merely creates a new cause of action under which a defendant may be liable. The distinction between property and liability goes straight to the issue of authorization, the issue upon which the District Court both denied Chamberlain's and granted Skylink's motion for summary judgment.

A plaintiff alleging copyright infringement need prove *only* "(1) ownership of a valid copyright, and (2) copying of constituent elements of the work that are original." *Feist Pub., Inc. v. Rural Tel. Serv. Co.,* 499 U.S. 340, 361 (1991). "[T]he existence of a license, exclusive or nonexclusive, creates an affirmative defense to a claim of copyright infringement." *I.A.E., Inc. v. Shaver,* 74 F.3d 768, 775 (7th Cir. 1996). In other words, . . . a plaintiff only needs to show that the defendant has used her property; the burden of proving that the use was authorized falls squarely on the defendant. *Id.* The DMCA, however, *defines* circumvention as an activity undertaken "without the authority of the copyright owner." 17 U.S.C. §1201(a)(3)(A). The plain language of the statute therefore requires a plaintiff alleging circumvention (or trafficking) to prove that the defendant's access was unauthorized—a significant burden where, as here, the copyright laws authorize consumers to use the copy of Chamberlain's software embedded in the GDOs that they purchased. . . .

. . . [Chamberlain] claim[s] that the DMCA overrode all pre-existing consumer expectations about the legitimate uses of products containing copyrighted embedded software. Chamberlain contends that Congress empowered manufacturers to prohibit consumers from using embedded software products in conjunction with competing products when it passed §1201(a)(1). According to Chamberlain, *all* such uses of products containing copyrighted software to which a technological measure controlled access are now per se illegal under the DMCA unless the manufacturer provided consumers with *explicit* authorization. . . .

Such an exemption, however, is only plausible if the anticircumvention provisions established a new property right capable of conflicting with the copyright owner's other legal responsibilities—which as we have already explained, they do not. The anticircumvention provisions convey no additional property rights in and of themselves; they simply provide property owners with new ways to secure their property. Like all property owners taking legitimate steps to protect their property, however, copyright owners relying on the anticircumvention provisions remain bound by all other relevant bodies of law. Contrary to Chamberlain's assertion, the DMCA emphatically *did not* "fundamentally alter" the legal landscape governing the reasonable expectations of consumers or competitors; *did not* "fundamentally alter" the ways that courts analyze industry practices; and *did not* render the pre-DMCA history of the GDO industry irrelevant.

What the DMCA did was introduce new grounds for liability in the context of the unauthorized access of copyrighted material. The statute's plain language requires plaintiffs to prove that those circumventing their technological measures controlling access did so "without the authority of the copyright owner." 17 U.S.C. §1201(3)(A). Our inquiry ends with that clear language. We note, however, that the statute's structure, legislative history, and context within the Copyright Act all support our construction. They also help to explain why Chamberlain's warranty conditions and website postings cannot render users of Skylink's Model 39 "unauthorized" users for the purposes of establishing trafficking liability under the DMCA.

E. *Statutory Structure and Legislative History . . .*

. . . Statutory structure and legislative history both make it clear that §1201 applies only to circumventions reasonably related to protected rights. Defendants who traffic in devices that circumvent access controls in ways that facilitate infringement may be subject to liability under §1201(a)(2). Defendants who use such devices may be subject to liability under §1201(a)(1) whether they infringe or not. Because all defendants who traffic in devices that circumvent rights controls necessarily facilitate infringement, they may be subject to liability under §1201(b). Defendants who use such devices may be subject to liability for copyright infringement. And finally, defendants whose circumvention devices do not facilitate infringement are not subject to §1201 liability.

The key to understanding this relationship lies in §1201(b), which prohibits trafficking in devices that circumvent technological measures tailored narrowly to protect an individual right of the copyright owner while nevertheless allowing access to the protected work. Though §1201(b) parallels the anti-trafficking ban of §1201(a)(2), there is no narrowly tailored ban on direct circumvention to parallel §1201(a)(1). This omission was intentional.

> The prohibition in 1201(a)(1) [was] necessary because prior to [the DMCA], the conduct of circumvention was never before made unlawful. The device limitation in 1201(a)(2) enforces this new prohibition in conduct. The copyright law has long forbidden copyright infringements, so no new prohibition was necessary. The device limitation in 1201(b) enforces the longstanding prohibitions on infringements.

S. Rep. No. 105-90 at 12 (1998).

Prior to the DMCA, a copyright owner would have had no cause of action against anyone who circumvented any sort of technological control, but did not infringe. The DMCA rebalanced these interests to favor the copyright owner; the DMCA created circumvention liability for "digital trespass" under §1201(a)(1). It also created trafficking liability under §1201(a)(2) for facilitating such circumvention and under §1201(b) for facilitating infringement (both subject to the numerous limitations and exceptions outlined throughout the DMCA).[13] . . .

---

13. For obvious reasons, §1201(a)(2) trafficking liability cannot exist in the absence of §1201(a)(1) violations. . . .

The most significant and consistent theme running through the entire legislative history of the anticircumvention and anti-trafficking provisions of the DMCA, §§1201(a)(1), (2), is that Congress attempted to balance competing interests, and "endeavored to specify, with as much clarity as possible, how the right against anti-circumvention would be qualified to maintain balance between the interests of content creators and information users." H.R. Rep. No. 105-551, at 26 (1998). The Report of the House Commerce Committee concluded that §1201 "fully respects and extends into the digital environment the bedrock principle of 'balance' in American intellectual property law for the benefit of both copyright owners and users." *Id.* . . .

. . . We must understand that balance to resolve this dispute.

F. Access and Protection . . .

. . . [I]t is significant that virtually every clause of §1201 that mentions "access" links "access" to "protection." The import of that linkage may be less than obvious. Perhaps the best way to appreciate the necessity of this linkage — and the disposition of this case — is to consider three interrelated questions inherent in the DMCA's structure: What does §1201(a)(2) prohibit above and beyond the prohibitions of §1201(b)? What is the relationship between the sorts of "access" prohibited under §1201(a) and the rights "protected" under the Copyright Act? and What is the relationship between anticircumvention liability under §1201(a)(1) and anti-trafficking liability under §1201(a)(2)? The relationships among the new liabilities that these three provisions, §§1201(a)(1), (a)(2), (b), create circumscribe the DMCA's scope — and therefore allow us to determine whether or not Chamberlain's claim falls within its purview. And the key to disentangling these relationships lies in understanding the linkage between access and protection.

Chamberlain urges us to read the DMCA as if Congress simply created a new protection for copyrighted works without any reference at all either to the protections that copyright owners already possess or to the rights that the Copyright Act grants to the public. Chamberlain has not alleged that Skylink's Model 39 infringes its copyrights, nor has it alleged that the Model 39 contributes to third-party infringement of its copyrights. Chamberlain's allegation is considerably more straightforward: The only way for the Model 39 to interoperate with a Security+ GDO is by "accessing" copyrighted software. Skylink has therefore committed a per se violation of the DMCA. Chamberlain urges us to conclude that no necessary connection exists between access and *copyrights*. Congress could not have intended such a broad reading of the DMCA. *Accord Corley*, 273 F.3d at 435 (explaining that Congress passed the DMCA's anti-trafficking provisions to help copyright owners protect their works *from piracy* behind a digital wall). . . .

Chamberlain's proposed construction of the DMCA ignores the significant differences between defendants whose accused products enable copying and those, like Skylink, whose accused products enable only legitimate uses of copyrighted software. Chamberlain's repeated reliance on language targeted at defendants trumpeting their "electronic civil disobedience," [*Reimerdes*] at 303, 312, apparently led it to misconstrue significant portions of the DMCA. . . .

. . . Were §1201(a) to allow copyright owners to use technological measures to block all access to their copyrighted works, it would effectively create two distinct copyright regimes. In the first regime, the owners of a typical work protected by copyright would possess only the rights enumerated in 17 U.S.C. §106, subject to the additions, exceptions, and limitations outlined throughout the rest of the Copyright Act — notably but not solely the fair use provisions of §107.[14] Owners who feel that technology has put those rights at risk, and who incorporate technological measures to protect those rights from technological encroachment, gain the additional ability to hold traffickers in circumvention devices liable under §1201(b) for putting their rights back at risk by enabling circumventors who use these devices to infringe.

Under the second regime that Chamberlain's proposed construction implies, the owners of a work protected by *both* copyright *and* a technological measure that effectively controls access to that work per §1201(a) would possess *unlimited* rights to hold circumventors liable under §1201(a) *merely for accessing that work,* even if that access enabled *only* rights that the Copyright Act grants to the public. This second implied regime would be problematic for a number of reasons. First, as the Supreme Court recently explained, "Congress' exercise of its Copyright Clause authority must be rational." *Eldred v. Ashcroft,* 537 U.S. 186, 205 n.10, (2003). In determining whether a particular aspect of the Copyright Act "is a rational exercise of the legislative authority conferred by the Copyright Clause . . . we defer substantially to Congress. It is Congress that has been assigned the task of defining the scope of the limited monopoly that should be granted to authors . . . *in order to give the public appropriate access* to their work product." *Id.* at 204-05 (citation omitted) (emphasis added). Chamberlain's proposed construction of §1201(a) implies that in enacting the DMCA, Congress attempted to "give the public appropriate access" to copyrighted works by allowing copyright owners to deny all access to the public. Even under the substantial deference due Congress, such a redefinition borders on the irrational.

That apparent irrationality, however, is not the most significant problem that this second regime implies. Such a regime would be hard to reconcile with the DMCA's statutory prescription that "[n]othing in this section shall affect rights, remedies, limitations, or defenses to copyright infringement, including fair use, under this title." 17 U.S.C. §1201(c)(1). A provision that prohibited access without regard to the rest of the Copyright Act would clearly affect rights and limitations, if not remedies and defenses. . . . Chamberlain's proposed construction of §1201(a) would flatly contradict §1201(c)(1)—a simultaneously enacted provision of the same statute. We are therefore bound, if we can, to obtain an alternative construction that leads to no such contradiction. . . .

In a similar vein, Chamberlain's proposed construction would allow any manufacturer of any product to add a single copyrighted sentence or software fragment to its product, wrap the copyrighted material in a trivial "encryption" scheme, and thereby gain the right to restrict consumers' rights to use its products in conjunction with competing products. In other words, Chamberlain's construction of the DMCA would allow virtually any company to attempt to leverage its sales into aftermarket monopolies—a practice that both the antitrust laws, *see Eastman Kodak Co. v. Image Tech. Servs.,* 504 U.S. 451, 455 (1992), and the doctrine of copyright misuse, *Assessment Techs. of WI, LLC v. WIREdata, Inc.,* 350 F.3d 640, 647 (7th Cir. 2003), normally prohibit. . . .

Finally, the requisite "authorization," on which the District Court granted Skylink summary judgment, points to yet another inconsistency in Chamberlain's proposed construction. The notion of authorization is central to understanding §1201(a). *See, e.g.,* S. Rep. 105-90 at 28 (1998) ("Subsection (a) applies when a person has not obtained authorized access to a copy

---

14. We do not reach the relationship between §107 fair use and violations of §1201. The District Court in *Reimerdes* rejected the DeCSS defendants' argument that fair use was a *necessary* defense to §1201(a), *Reimerdes,* 111 F. Supp. 2d at 317; because *any* access enables some fair uses, any act of circumvention would embody its own defense. We leave open the question as to when §107 might serve as an affirmative defense to a prima facie violation of §1201. . . .

or a phonorecord that is protected under the Copyright Act and for which the copyright owner has put in place a technological measure that effectively controls access to his or her work."). Underlying Chamberlain's argument on appeal that it has not granted such authorization lies the necessary assumption that Chamberlain is entitled to prohibit legitimate purchasers of its embedded software from "accessing" the software by using it. Such an entitlement, however, would go far beyond the idea that the DMCA allows copyright owner[s] to prohibit "fair uses . . . as well as foul." *Reimerdes*, 111 F. Supp. 2d at 304. Chamberlain's proposed construction would allow copyright owners to prohibit *exclusively fair* uses even in the absence of any feared foul use. It would therefore allow any copyright owner, through a combination of contractual terms and technological measures, to repeal the fair use doctrine with respect to an individual copyrighted work — or even selected copies of that copyrighted work. Again, this implication contradicts §1201(c)(1) directly. Copyright law itself authorizes the public to make certain uses of copyrighted materials. Consumers who purchase a product containing a copy of embedded software have the inherent legal right to use that copy of the software. What the law authorizes, Chamberlain cannot revoke.[17] . . .

We therefore reject Chamberlain's proposed construction in its entirety. We conclude that 17 U.S.C. §1201 prohibits only forms of access that bear a reasonable relationship to the protections that the Copyright Act otherwise affords copyright owners. While such a rule of reason may create some uncertainty and consume some judicial resources, it is the only meaningful reading of the statute. Congress attempted to balance the legitimate interests of copyright owners with those of consumers of copyrighted products. . . .

. . . Were we to interpret Congress's words in a way that eliminated all balance and granted copyright owners carte blanche authority to preclude all use, Congressional intent would remain unrealized. . . .

. . . The courts must decide where the balance between the rights of copyright owners and those of the broad public tilts subject to a fact-specific rule of reason. Here, Chamberlain can point to no protected property right that Skylink imperils. The DMCA cannot allow Chamberlain to retract the most fundamental right that the Copyright Act grants consumers: the right to use the copy of Chamberlain's embedded software that they purchased.

G. Chamberlain's DMCA Claim . . .

. . . A plaintiff alleging a violation of §1201(a)(2) must prove: (1) ownership of a valid *copyright* on a work, (2) effectively controlled by a *technological measure*, which has been circumvented, (3) that third parties can now *access* (4) *without authorization,* in a manner that (5) infringes or facilitates infringing a right *protected* by the Copyright Act, because of a product that (6) the defendant either (i) *designed or produced* primarily for circumvention; (ii) made available despite only *limited commercial significance* other than circumvention; or (iii) *marketed* for use in circumvention of the controlling technological measure. A plaintiff incapable of establishing any one of elements (1) through (5) will have failed to prove a prima facie case. A plaintiff capable of proving elements (1) through (5) need prove only one of (6)(i), (ii), or (iii) to shift the burden back to the defendant. At that point, the various affirmative defenses enumerated throughout §1201 become relevant. . . .

Chamberlain . . . has failed to show not only the requisite lack of authorization, but also the necessary fifth element of its claim, the critical nexus between access and

---

17. It is not clear whether a consumer who circumvents a technological measure controlling access to a copyrighted work in a manner that enables uses permitted under the Copyright Act but prohibited by contract can be subject to liability under the DMCA. Because Chamberlain did not attempt to limit its customers' use of its product by contract, however, we do not reach this issue.

protection. . . . Chamberlain's customers are therefore immune from §1201(a)(1) circumvention liability. In the absence of allegations of either copyright infringement or §1201(a)(1) circumvention, Skylink cannot be liable for §1201(a)(2) trafficking. . . .

≡ *Lexmark International, Inc. v. Static Control Components, Inc.*
≡ *387 F.3d 522 (6th Cir. 2005)*

SUTTON, J.: . . . **The Parties.** Headquartered in Lexington, Kentucky, Lexmark is a leading manufacturer of laser and inkjet printers and has sold printers and toner cartridges for its printers since 1991. . . .

Static Control Components [SCC] is a privately held company headquartered in Sanford, North Carolina. . . . [I]t . . . makes a wide range of technology products, including microchips that it sells to third-party companies for use in remanufactured toner cartridges.

The Two Computer Programs. The first program at issue is Lexmark's "Toner Loading Program," which measures the amount of toner remaining in the cartridge. . . . The Toner Loading Program relies upon eight program commands. . . . To illustrate the modest size of this computer program, the phrase "Lexmark International, Inc. vs. Static Control Components, Inc." in ASCII format would occupy more memory than either version of the Toner Loading Program. The Toner Loading Program is located on a microchip contained in Lexmark's toner cartridges.

The second program is Lexmark's "Printer Engine Program." The Printer Engine Program occupies far more memory than the Toner Loading Program and translates into over 20 printed pages of program commands. The program controls a variety of functions on each printer — e.g., paper feed and movement, and printer motor control. Unlike the Toner Loading Program, the Printer Engine Program is located within Lexmark's printers.

Lexmark obtained Certificates of Registration from the Copyright Office for both programs. Neither program is encrypted and each can be read (and copied) directly from its respective memory chip.

Lexmark's Prebate and Non-Prebate Cartridges. Lexmark markets two types of toner cartridges for its laser printers: "Prebate" and "Non-Prebate." Prebate cartridges are sold to business consumers at an up-front discount. In exchange, consumers agree to use the cartridge just once, then return the empty unit to Lexmark; a "shrink-wrap" agreement on the top of each cartridge box spells out these restrictions and confirms that using the cartridge constitutes acceptance of these terms. Non-Prebate cartridges are sold without any discount, are not subject to any restrictive agreements and may be re-filled with toner and reused by the consumer or a third-party remanufacturer. . . .

To ensure that consumers adhere to the Prebate agreement, Lexmark uses an "authentication sequence" that performs a "secret handshake" between each Lexmark printer and a microchip on each Lexmark toner cartridge. . . . [If the handshake is not properly performed], the printer returns an error message and will not operate, blocking consumers from using toner cartridges that Lexmark has not authorized.

SCC's Competing Microchip. SCC sells its own microchip — the "SMARTEK" chip — that permits consumers to satisfy Lexmark's authentication sequence each time it would otherwise be performed, *i.e.*, when the printer is turned on or the printer door is opened and shut. SCC's advertising boasts that its chip breaks Lexmark's "secret code" (the authentication sequence), which "even on the fastest computer available today . . . would take **Years** to run through all of the possible 8-byte combinations to break." SCC sells these chips to third-party cartridge remanufacturers, permitting them to replace Lexmark's chip with the SMARTEK chip on refurbished Prebate cartridges. These recycled cartridges are in turn sold to consumers as a low-cost alternative to new Lexmark toner cartridges.

Each of SCC's SMARTEK chips also contains a copy of Lexmark's Toner Loading Program, which SCC claims is necessary to make its product compatible with Lexmark's printers. The SMARTEK chips thus contain an identical copy of the Toner Loading Program that is appropriate for each Lexmark printer, and SCC acknowledges that it "slavishly copied" the Toner Loading Program "in the exact format and order" found on Lexmark's cartridge chip. A side-by-side comparison of the two data sequences reveals no differences between them. . . .

The Lawsuit. . . . Lexmark alleged that SCC violated the copyright statute, 17 U.S.C. §106, by reproducing the Toner Loading Program on its SMARTEK chip . . . that SCC violated the DMCA by selling a product that circumvents access controls on the Toner Loading Program . . . [and] that SCC violated the DMCA by selling a product that circumvents access controls on the Printer Engine Program. . . .

[After an evidentiary hearing, the district court decided that Lexmark had shown a likelihood of success on each claim and entered a preliminary injunction against SCC.]

III.

[The court first addressed the copyrightability of the Toner Loading Program and concluded that, on the record presented, it was not copyrightable. *See* Chapter 4.B.2 note 5 pages 232-33 *supra*.]

IV. . . .

We initially consider Lexmark's DMCA claim concerning the Printer Engine Program, which (the parties agree) is protected by the general copyright statute. In deciding that Lexmark's authentication sequence "effectively controls access to a work protected under [the copyright provisions]," the district court relied on a definition in the DMCA saying that a measure "effectively controls access to a work" if, "in the ordinary course of operation," it "requires the application of information, or a process or treatment, with the authority of the copyright owner, to gain access to the work." 17 U.S.C. §1201(a)(3). Because Congress did not explain what it means to "gain access to the work," the district court relied on the "ordinary, customary meaning" of "access": "the ability to enter, to obtain, or to make use of," D. Ct. Op. at 41 (quoting *Merriam-Webster's Collegiate Dictionary* 6 (10th ed. 1999)). Based on this definition, the court concluded that "Lexmark's authentication sequence effectively 'controls access' to the Printer Engine Program because it controls the consumer's ability to *make use of* these programs." D. Ct. Op. at 41 (emphasis added).

We disagree. It is not Lexmark's authentication sequence that "controls access" to the Printer Engine Program. *See* 17 U.S.C. §1201(a)(2). It is the purchase of a Lexmark printer that allows "access" to the program. Anyone who buys a Lexmark printer may read the literal code of the Printer Engine Program directly from the printer memory, with or without the benefit of the authentication sequence, and the data from the program may be translated into readable source code after which copies may be freely distributed. No security device, in other words, protects access to the Printer Engine Program Code and no security device accordingly must be circumvented to obtain access to that program code.

The authentication sequence, it is true, may well block one form of "access" — the "ability to . . . make use of" the Printer Engine Program by preventing the printer from functioning.

But it does not block another relevant form of "access"—the "ability to [ ] obtain" a copy of the work or to "make use of" the literal elements of the program (its code). Because the statute refers to "control[ling] access to a work protected under this title," it does not naturally apply when the "work protected under this title" is otherwise accessible. Just as one would not say that a lock on the back door of a house "controls access" to a house whose front door does not contain a lock and just as one would not say that a lock on any door of a house "controls access" to the house after its purchaser receives the key to the lock, it does not make sense to say that this provision of the DMCA applies to otherwise-readily-accessible copyrighted works. Add to this the fact that the DMCA not only requires the technological measure to "control[ ] access" but also requires the measure to control that access "effectively," 17 U.S.C. §1201(a)(2), and it seems clear that this provision does not naturally extend to a technological measure that restricts one form of access but leaves another route wide open. See also id. §1201(a)(3) (technological measure must "require [ ] the application of information, or a process or a treatment . . . to gain access to the work") (emphasis added). . . .

In the essential setting where the DMCA applies, the copyright protection operates on two planes: in the literal code governing the work and in the visual or audio manifestation generated by the code's execution. For example, the encoded data on CDs translates into music and on DVDs into motion pictures, while the program commands in software for video games or computers translate into some other visual and audio manifestation. In the cases upon which Lexmark relies, restricting "use" of the work means restricting consumers from making use of the copyrightable expression in the work. See 321 Studios, 307 F. Supp. 2d at 1095 (movies contained on DVDs protected by an encryption algorithm cannot be watched without a player that contains an access key); Reimerdes, 111 F. Supp. 2d at 303 (same); Gamemasters, 87 F. Supp. 2d at 981 (Sony's game console prevented operation of unauthorized video games). As shown above, the DMCA applies in these settings when the product manufacturer prevents all access to the copyrightable material and the alleged infringer responds by marketing a device that circumvents the technological measure designed to guard access to the copyrightable material.

The copyrightable expression in the Printer Engine Program, by contrast, operates on only one plane: in the literal elements of the program, its source and object code. Unlike the code underlying video games or DVDs, "using" or executing the Printer Engine Program does not in turn create any protected expression. Instead, the program's output is purely functional: the Printer Engine Program "controls a number of operations" in the Lexmark printer such as "paper feed[,] paper movement[,] [and] motor control." Lexmark Br. at 9; cf. Lotus Dev., 49 F.3d at 815 (determining that menu command hierarchy is an "uncopyrightable method of operation"). And unlike the code underlying video games or DVDs, no encryption or other technological measure prevents access to the Printer Engine Program. . . .

[The court concluded that the DMCA claim regarding the Toner Loading Program failed for the same reason, and also failed to the extent that the Toner Loading Program was not a work protected under the Copyright Act.]

The district court also rejected SCC's interoperability defense—that its replication of the Toner Loading Program data is a "technological means" that SCC may make "available to others" "solely for the purpose of enabling interoperability of an independently created computer program with other programs." 17 U.S.C. §1201(f)(3). In rejecting this defense, the district court said that "SCC's SMARTEK microchips cannot be considered independently created computer programs. [They] serve no legitimate purpose other than to circumvent Lexmark's authentication sequence and . . . cannot qualify as independently created when they contain exact copies of Lexmark's Toner Loading Programs." D. Ct. Op. ¶94, at 47.

Because the issue could become relevant at the permanent injunction stage of this dispute, we briefly explain our disagreement with this conclusion. In particular, the court did not explain why it rejected SCC's testimony that the SMARTEK chips do contain other functional computer programs beyond the copied Toner Loading Program data. . . .

Also unavailing is Lexmark's final argument that the interoperability defense in §1201(f)(3) does not apply because distributing the SMARTEK chip constitutes infringement and violates other "applicable law" (including tortious interference with prospective economic relations or contractual relations). Because the chip contains only a copy of the thus-far unprotected Toner Loading Program and does not contain a copy of the Printer Engine Program, infringement is not an issue. And Lexmark has offered no independent, let alone persuasive, reason why SCC's SMARTEK chip violates any state tort or other state law. . . .

MERRITT, J., concurring: . I write separately to emphasize that our holding should not be limited to the narrow facts surrounding either the Toner Loading Program or the Printer Engine Program. We should make clear that in the future companies like Lexmark cannot use the DMCA in conjunction with copyright law to create monopolies of manufactured goods for themselves just by tweaking the facts of this case: by, for example, creating a Toner Loading Program that is more complex and "creative" than the one here, or by cutting off other access to the Printer Engine Program. The crucial point is that the DMCA forbids anyone from trafficking in any technology that "is primarily designed or produced for the purpose of circumventing a technological measure that effectively controls access to a [protected] work." 17 U.S.C. §1201(2)(A). The key question is the "purpose" of the circumvention technology. The microchip in SCC's toner cartridges is intended not to reap any benefit from the Toner Loading Program—SCC's microchip is not designed to measure toner levels—but only for the purpose of making SCC's competing toner cartridges work with printers manufactured by Lexmark.

. . . If we were to adopt Lexmark's reading of the statute, manufacturers could potentially create monopolies for replacement parts simply by using similar, but more creative, lock-out codes. Automobile manufacturers, for example, could control the entire market of replacement parts for their vehicles by including lock-out chips. Congress did not intend to allow the DMCA to be used offensively in this manner, but rather only sought to reach those who circumvented protective measures "for the purpose" of pirating works protected by the copyright statute. Unless a plaintiff can show that a defendant circumvented protective measures for such a purpose, its claim should not be allowed to go forward. If Lexmark wishes to utilize DMCA protections for (allegedly) copyrightable works, it should not use such works to prevent competing cartridges from working with its printer.

. . . [W]e should be wary of shifting the burden to a rival manufacturer to demonstrate that its conduct falls under such an exception in cases where there is no indication that it has any intention of pirating a protected work. *See, e.g.,* Lawrence Lessig, Free Culture 187 (2004) . . . [T]he potential cost of extended litigation and discovery where the burden of proof shifts to the defendant is itself a deterrent to innovation and competition. . . .

[The opinion of Judge Feikens, concurring in part and dissenting in part, is omitted. — EDS.]

NOTES AND QUESTIONS

1. Both of these courts arrive at the conclusion that the defendant's activities in creating aftermarket products are lawful, but each reaches that conclusion by interpreting different elements of the statute. The Federal Circuit ties its analysis to the statutory requirement that the access be unauthorized. Examine the list of elements that the Federal Circuit says a

§1201 plaintiff must prove. What part of §1201(a)(2) gives rise to the fifth element? With regard to the fourth element, how might a copyright owner seek to establish what types of access are unauthorized?

2. The Sixth Circuit ties its analysis to the statutory requirement that the technological measure must effectively control access. Does the court's definition of what it means for a technological measure to control access make sense? In a portion of the opinion not reproduced here, the *Lexmark* court acknowledged that DMCA liability is not dependent on the "creation of an impervious shield" around the copyrighted work. What tests should a court use to determine if a technological measure is effective? Can you think of some factors that would be helpful to courts undertaking this assessment?

The *Lexmark* court held that §1201(a)(2) does not apply to "otherwise-readily-accessible copyrighted works." If unauthorized copies of a work are readily available on the Internet, does that make the work "otherwise-readily-accessible"?

3. In his concurring opinion, Judge Merritt addresses the important question of secondary markets. He argues the DMCA should not be used to permit manufacturers of consumer goods to create monopolies for replacement parts. Recall that the exclusive right to make derivative works to some extent gives a copyright owner the ability to control secondary markets. *See Castle Rock Entm't, Inc. v. Carol Publ'g Group, Inc.*, 150 F.3d 132 (2d Cir. 1998) in Chapter 5.D, *supra*. Why should the DMCA be different? Recall also *MAI v. Peak*, 991 F.2d 511 (9th Cir. 1993), *cert. dismissed*, 510 U.S. 1033 (1994), which you encountered in Chapter 2. There, the court held that copyright infringement had occurred when, in the course of performing computer maintenance work, a RAM copy of software was loaded on the computer. In that case, MAI was able to leverage its copyright to control a secondary market, i.e., computer maintenance. Congress subsequently enacted an exception in §117 that prohibits the use of copyright to control the secondary market for computer repair. Are the situations covered by §1201 more comparable to those covered by §117 than to those covered by the derivative work right?

4. Examine again the reverse engineering exemption in §1201(f). Would this exemption provide a more satisfactory basis for resolution of the disputes in *Chamberlain* and *Lexmark*? Note that in the 2003 rulemaking on exemptions to the circumvention ban, the Copyright Office rejected a proposal (submitted by SCC) to exempt the circumvention of access controls in printers and toner cartridges. It opined that "an existing exemption in section 1201(f) addresses the concerns of remanufacturers." 68 Fed. Reg. at 62,017. Do you agree?

5. In *Reimerdes*, the court addressed a technology that the defendants asserted was distributed to facilitate the creation of a different player on which authorized copies of DVDs could be played. In *Chamberlain* and *Lexmark*, the courts were addressing technologies that facilitated the creation of different garage door transmitters and printer cartridges that could be used with plaintiffs' garage door openers and printers. Can the *Chamberlain* or *Lexmark* analysis be applied to the facts of *Reimerdes*? Is there a reason to use a different analysis in these situations?

Industry practice influenced the Federal Circuit's determination that consumers have authorization to access the programs in garage door openers. We all expect to be able to use universal garage door openers if we lose our original garage door openers and to be able to purchase off-brand printer cartridges for our computer printers. Do we all expect to be able to play our movies in any DVD player we choose? What are consumer expectations about new products?

6. Can shrinkwrap licenses or even notices on product packaging shape consumer expectations about what they may do with purchased products? Would the presence of a shrinkwrap

license restriction have changed the result in *Chamberlain*? Should Lexmark's "Prebate" business model have changed the result in *Lexmark*? In *Davidson & Assoc., Inc. v. Jung*, 422 F.3d 630 (8th Cir. 2005), the court concluded that a shrinkwrap license prohibited purchasers of multi-player video game software from creating their own platform on which to play the game. The court ruled that the defendants' creation and maintenance of an alternative platform constituted a breach of contract and also violated §1201(a)(1) because it bypassed the authentication sequence.

Is *Davidson* more like *Reimerdes* or more like *Lexmark* and *Chamberlain*? Should creating a platform on which to play authorized copies of a video game fall within the §1201(f) exception? If the shrinkwrap license prohibits such activity, does engaging in it "violate applicable law" and therefore remove any protection that §1201(f) might provide?

7. Both *Chamberlain* and *Lexmark* make reference to the "rights of the public." What exactly are those rights in the context of the DMCA? In the context of copyright law generally? Whose role is it to identify the "rights of the public" — Congress' or the courts'? Are there reasons to prefer one over the other?

8. Should a misuse defense be available in actions brought under §1201's anticircumvention and anti-device provisions? *See* Dan L. Burk, *Anticircumvention Misuse*, 50 UCLA L. Rev. 1095 (2003).

D. PROTECTION FOR COPYRIGHT MANAGEMENT INFORMATION

The DMCA also established legal protection for "copyright management information" (CMI) that is attached to a copy of a work—e.g., information that identifies the copyright owner and the terms of use of the work. The copyright industries argued that such protection would reduce online infringement by ensuring that those who encountered copyrighted works online would also have accurate information about the work's copyright status and ownership. In the case of CMI, however, the legislation ultimately adopted by the U.S. was influenced much more significantly by international debates about the appropriate scope of protection.

The initial domestic proposals for protecting CMI would have prohibited, among other things, knowingly removing or altering CMI attached to a work and knowingly providing false CMI. As in the case of the anticircumvention provisions, a broad coalition of interests opposed these proposals. Opponents argued that the law should require a closer connection to infringement before imposing a penalty. As in the case of the anticircumvention provisions, and despite domestic opposition, the Clinton Administration sought treaty provisions virtually identical to the domestic proposal.

At the WIPO Conference, the initial proposal for protecting CMI was very similar to the U.S. proposal. In the discussions over the initial proposed treaty language, however, many national delegates expressed a desire for the protection to be linked to an infringing purpose. The provision ultimately adopted as Article 12 of the WIPO Copyright Treaty (WCT) directs:

> (1) Contracting Parties shall provide adequate and effective legal remedies against any person knowingly performing any of the following acts knowing, or with respect to civil remedies having

reasonable grounds to know, that it will induce, enable, facilitate or conceal an infringement of any right covered by this Treaty or the Berne Convention:

(i) to remove or alter any electronic rights management information without authority;

(ii) to distribute, import for distribution, broadcast or communicate to the public, without authority, works or copies of works knowing that electronic rights management information has been removed or altered without authority.

Section 1202 of the DMCA, which implements Article 12, tracks the WCT's language:

§1202. Integrity of copyright management information

(a) False copyright management information. — No person shall knowingly and with the intent to induce, enable, facilitate, or conceal infringement —

(1) provide copyright management information that is false, or

(2) distribute or import for distribution copyright management information that is false.

(b) Removal or alteration of copyright management information. — No person shall, without the authority of the copyright owner or the law —

(1) intentionally remove or alter any copyright management information,

(2) distribute or import for distribution copyright management information knowing that the copyright management information has been removed or altered without authority of the copyright owner or the law, or

(3) distribute, import for distribution, or publicly perform works, copies of works, or phonorecords, knowing that copyright management information has been removed or altered without authority of the copyright owner or the law, knowing, or, with respect to civil remedies under section 1203, having reasonable grounds to know, that it will induce, enable, facilitate, or conceal an infringement of any right under this title [17 U.S.C.A. §1 et seq.].

Both §1202(c) and WCT art. 12 define CMI broadly to include identifying information about the author, the work, the copyright owner, the terms and conditions of use of the work, and in some cases the performer, writer, or director of the work.

Section 1202 differs from §1201 in two important ways. First, §1202 applies only in cases that involve CMI. Second, unlike §1201, §1202 contains a *mens rea* requirement. What is the significance of these limitations? Consider the following cases.

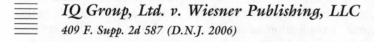

IQ Group, Ltd. v. Wiesner Publishing, LLC
409 F. Supp. 2d 587 (D.N.J. 2006)

[IQ, an online advertising firm, distributed ads for two insurance companies, National Senior Associate Company ("NSAC") and Capital Care, Inc. IQ included in the ads its own logo and a hyperlink to copyright information on its own web site. Both NSAC and Capital Care subsequently hired Wiesner to distribute ads for them. Wiesner distributed the same ads that IQ had formerly distributed, but it removed the IQ logo and the hyperlink to IQ's web site. IQ registered copyright in the ads and then sued Wiesner, NSAC, and Capital

Care, alleging copyright infringement and violation of §1202. Wiesner moved for summary judgment on IQ's §1202 claim.]

GREENAWAY, J.: . . . Wiesner argues that the logo and hyperlink cannot fall within the scope of the statute, as set out in 17 U.S.C. §1202(c), and asks the Court to rule on this as a matter of law.

The DMCA provision at issue, 17 U.S.C. §1202(c), defines "copyright management information" in eight categories. IQ contends that the logo falls within category 2 ("[t]he name of, and other identifying information about, the author of a work"), category 3 ("[t]he name of, and other identifying information about, the copyright owner of the work"), and category 7 ("[i]dentifying numbers or symbols referring to such information or links to such information"). IQ contends as well that the hyperlink falls within categories 3 and 7, and that the hyperlink points to a website containing information falling within category 6 ("[t]erms and conditions for use of the work"). . . .

1. The DMCA in the Framework of Trademark and Copyright Law

In effect, IQ asks this Court to construe the DMCA so as to allow a logo, functioning as a service mark, to come within the definition of copyright management information which, by operation of the DMCA, would act to protect the copyright of its owner. . . .

Looking only at the literal language of the statute, IQ's construction is not implausible: a logo in an email, to the extent that it operates as a trademark or service mark, could communicate information that indicates the source of the email. It is a symbol that refers to identifying information, so a very broad interpretation of §1202(c) might conceivably include a logo. The problem is that this construction allows a trademark to invoke DMCA protection of copyrights. . . .

The Supreme Court cautioned against blurring the boundaries between trademark law and copyright law in *Dastar Corp. v. Twentieth Century Fox Film Corp.*, 539 U.S. 23 (2003). . . . The Court warned that disregarding the trademark/copyright law distinction "would create a species of mutant copyright law." *Id.* at 34. . . .

. . . [R]ather than an interpretation of the Lanham Act, as in *Dastar*, IQ here seeks an interpretation of the DMCA that would blur the boundaries between copyright and trademark. Following *Dastar*, this Court rejects this argument. . . .

2. The DMCA: Statutory Interpretation Of §1202 . . .

The text of §1202 appears to define "copyright management information" quite broadly, to the point that the section, read literally, applies wherever any author has affixed anything that might refer to his or her name. Examination of the legislative history, as well as extrinsic sources, however, shows that the statute should be subject to a narrowing interpretation.

Law professor Julie E. Cohen has written widely on the DMCA and on copyright management information. See generally Julie E. Cohen, *Copyright and The Jurisprudence of Self-Help*, 13 Berkeley Tech. L.J. 1089 (1998). Cohen explains that, traditionally, authors have relied on copyright law to define and protect their legal rights. Now, however, new technologies can control access to works, such that technology attached to the work itself defines and protects the legal rights of the copyright owner. The DMCA directly protects not the copyrights, but the technological measures that protect the copyrights. In Cohen's view, copyright management information ("CMI") is limited to components of such technological measures.[1] This central insight is confirmed by examination of the history of §1202.

It is frequently stated that Congress enacted the DMCA in order to implement the World Intellectual Property Organization ("WIPO") Copyright Treaty and the WIPO Performances and Phonograms Treaty. H.R. Rep. No. 105-551 (1998). It is true that enactment of the DMCA brought United States copyright law into compliance with these treaties. *Id.* Thus, the WIPO treaties are useful in understanding §1202.

The WIPO treaties mandated protection of copyright management information. According to Severine Dusollier, WIPO protected CMI as part of "a double protection for technical measures." S. Dusollier, *Some Reflections on Copyright Management Information and Moral Rights*, 25 Colum. J.L. & Arts 377, 382 (2003). In the framework of the WIPO treaties, technical measures such as CMI are components of automated copyright protection systems: "As digital identification systems and other technologies that enable the marking and protection of works have started to develop, rightholders have feared that these technological tools might themselves be cracked by other technologies or machines, or that they might be easily modified or removed." *Id.* The WIPO treaties, and hence the DMCA, protect CMI so as to protect the technological measures of copyright protection themselves. This echoes the understanding of the DMCA expressed by Cohen, *supra.*

Although many view the DMCA as implementing the WIPO treaties, in fact, §§1201 and 1202 were drafted prior to the treaties. President Clinton established the Information Infrastructure Task Force ["IITF"] in 1993 with the mandate to develop comprehensive information technology policies and programs that would promote the development of the national information infrastructure ("NII"). . . .

Released in September, 1995, and known as the "White Paper," the Report [of the IITF's Working Group on Intellectual Property Rights] presented a draft of §§1201and 1202, and discussed the rationale for these sections:

> Systems for managing rights in works are being contemplated in the development of the NII. These systems will serve the functions of tracking and monitoring uses of copyrighted works as well as licensing of rights and indicating attribution, creation and ownership interests. A combination of file- and system-based access controls using encryption technologies, digital signatures and steganography[2] are, and will continue to be, employed by owners of works to address copyright management concerns. . . .
>
> To implement these rights management functions, information will likely be included in digital versions of a work (i.e., copyright management information) to inform the user about the authorship and ownership of a work (e.g., attribution information) as well as to indicate authorized uses of the work (e.g., permitted use information). For instance, information may be included in an "electronic envelope" containing a work that provides information regarding authorship, copyright ownership, date of creation or last modification, and terms and conditions of authorized uses. As measures for this purpose become incorporated at lower levels (e.g., at the operating system level), such information may become a fundamental component of a file or information object.
>
> Once information such as this is affiliated with a particular information object (e.g., data constituting the work) and readily accessible, users will be able to easily address questions over

---

    1. *See also* Julie E. Cohen, *A Right to Read Anonymously: A Closer Look at Copyright Management in Cyberspace*, 28 Conn. L. Rev. 981, 984 (1996) ("new digital monitoring and metering technologies define the burgeoning field of 'copyright management'").

    2. As explained in the Report, steganography is digital watermarking. (*Id.* 188.)

licensing and use of the work. For example, systems for electronic licensing may be developed based on the attribution or permitted use information associated with an information object.

(*Id.* 191-192.)

The White Paper understood "copyright management information" to be information about authorship, ownership, and permitted uses of a work that is included in digital versions of the work so as to implement "rights management functions" of "rights management systems." Such systems are conceived of as electronic and automated within the environment of a computer network. . . .

The White Paper demonstrates that the Working Group on Intellectual Property Rights, in drafting §1202, understood this section to protect the integrity of automated copyright management systems functioning within a computer network environment. . . .

The draft legislation presented in the White Paper was introduced in both houses of Congress immediately upon its release as the "The National Information Infrastructure Copyright Protection Act" ("NIICPA"). . . . As Congress developed the DMCA, the NIICPA was incorporated into it. Section[] . . . 1202 underwent no significant revision between drafting in 1995 and enactment in 1998 under section 103 of the DMCA, Public Law 105-304.

The Congressional committees which considered the DMCA published a number of reports on the Act relevant to §§1201 and 1202. There is little discussion, however, of §1202. The Senate Committee Report provides this commentary:

> Rights management information is "information which identifies the work, the author of the work, the owner of any right in the work, or information about the terms and conditions of use of the work . . . which is attached to a copy of a work or appears in connection with communication of the work to the public." Art. 12. Rights management information is more commonly referred to in the U.S. as copyright management information (CMI). The purpose of CMI is to facilitate licensing of copyright for use on the Internet and to discourage piracy.
>
> [CMI] is an important element in establishing an efficient Internet marketplace in copyrighted works free from governmental regulation. Such information will assist in tracking and monitoring uses of copyrighted works, as well as licensing of rights and indicating attribution, creation and ownership.
>
> Under the bill, CMI includes such items as the title of the work, the author, the copyright owner, and in some instances, the writer, performer, and director. CMI need not be in digital form, but CMI in digital form is expressly included.

S. Rep. No. 105-190 (1998). Viewed alone, this gives only a vague idea as to what copyright management information is and how it functions. It is, however, consistent with the understanding established supra, as it emphasizes the role of such information in facilitating licensing on the Internet, discouraging piracy, and establishing an efficient Internet marketplace. There is nothing to suggest that the Senate Committee understood §1202 differently from the Working Group, as protecting the integrity of automated copyright management systems functioning within a computer network environment.

Similarly, the House Committee stated: "A new 'Section 1202' to the Copyright Act is required by both WIPO Treaties to ensure the integrity of the electronic marketplace by preventing fraud and misinformation." H.R. Rep. No. 105-551 (1998). This committee report, in addressing a different DMCA section, states: "It may, in appropriate circumstances include the absence of customary indicia of ownership or authorization, such as a standard and accepted digital watermark or other copyright management information." *Id.* This shows that Congress viewed a digital watermark as an example of copyright management information. . . .

This interpretation of §1202 makes sense additionally because it fits §1201 with §1202, and with chapter 12 as a whole. . . .

. . . [T]raditionally, the rights of authors have been managed by people, who have controlled access and reproduction. Through scientific advances, we now have technological measures that can control access and reproduction of works, and thereby manage the rights of copyright owners and users. Section 1202 operates to protect copyright by protecting a key component of some of these technological measures. It should not be construed to cover copyright management performed by people, which is covered by the Copyright Act, as it preceded the DMCA; it should be construed to protect copyright management performed by the technological measures of automated systems.

Under this interpretation of §1202, this Court must determine whether the information removed by Wiesner from the NSAC and Capital Care ads functioned as a component of an automated copyright protection or management system. IQ has presented no evidence on this matter that creates a genuine issue as to a material fact for trial. This Court finds no genuine issue as to a material fact and therefore Wiesner is entitled to judgment as a matter of law. . . .

[The court also denied IQ's motion for summary judgment on its copyright infringement claim against Wiesner because copyright ownership of the ads was disputed.]

Kelly v. Arriba Soft Corp.
77 F. Supp. 2d 1116 (C.D. Cal. 1999), **aff'd in part and rev'd in part on other grounds,** *336 F.3d 811 (9th Cir. 2003)*

[Arriba Soft, an image search engine, linked to a web site containing Kelly's copyrighted photographs and created "thumbnail" images of the photographs to display as search results. Users who clicked on a thumbnail would see the full-size image via a direct link to Kelly's site, but Arriba framed the full-size images with its own content. Applying a test later identified as the "display" test (see Note 1, page 427 *supra*), the Ninth Circuit initially held that Arriba Soft had infringed Kelly's exclusive right of public display. *Kelly v. Arriba Soft Corp.*, 280 F.3d 934, 947 (9th Cir. 2002). On a motion for rehearing, however, the court withdrew that portion of its opinion, stating that it should "not be cited as precedent." The court subsequently ruled that Arriba Soft's creation of the thumbnail images was fair use. *Kelly v. Arriba Soft Corp.*, 336 F.3d 811, 815 (9th Cir. 2003). Kelly also asserted a claim for violation of §1202. That portion of the district court's opinion, which was not appealed, follows.]

TAYLOR, J.: . . . During the period when most of the relevant events in this case occurred, Defendant's visual search engine was known as the Arriba Vista Image Searcher. By "clicking" on the desired thumbnail, an Arriba Vista user could view the "image attributes" window displaying the full-size version of the image, a description of its dimensions, and an address for the Web site where it originated.[1] By clicking on the address, the user could link to the originating Web site for the image.[2]

---

1. This full-size image was not technically located on Defendant's Web site. It was displayed by opening a link to its originating Web page. But only the image itself, and not any other part of the originating Web page, was displayed on the image attributes page. From the user's perspective, the source of the image matters less than the context in which it is displayed.

2. Defendant's current search engine, ditto.com, operates in a slightly different manner. When a ditto.com user clicks on a thumbnail, two windows open simultaneously. One window contains the full-size image; the other contains the originating Web page in full.

Ditto's search engine . . . works by maintaining an indexed database of approximately two million thumbnail images. These thumbnails are obtained through the operation of Ditto's "crawler," — a computer program that travels the Web in search of images to be converted into thumbnails and added to the index. Ditto's employees conduct a final screening to rank the most relevant thumbnails and eliminate inappropriate images.

Plaintiff Kelly is a photographer specializing in photographs of California gold rush country and related to the works of Laura Ingalls Wilder. . . . Plaintiff . . . maintains two Web sites, one of which . . . provides a "virtual tour" of California's gold rush country and promotes Plaintiff's book on the subject, and the other . . . markets corporate retreats in California's gold rush country.

In January 1999, around thirty five of Plaintiff's images were indexed by the Ditto crawler and put in Defendant's image database. As a result, these images were made available in thumbnail form to users of Defendant's visual search engine.

After being notified of Plaintiff's objections, Ditto removed the images from its database. . . . Meanwhile Plaintiff, having sent Defendant a notice of copyright infringement in January, filed this action in April. Plaintiff argues its copyrights in the images were infringed by Defendant's actions and also alleges Defendant violated the Digital Millennium Copyright Act (DMCA) by removing or altering the copyright management information associated with Plaintiff's images. . . .

Plaintiff argues Defendant violated §1202(b) by displaying thumbnails of Plaintiff's images without displaying the corresponding copyright management information consisting of standard copyright notices in the surrounding text. . . . Because these notices do not appear in the images themselves, the Ditto crawler did not include them when it indexed the images. . . . As a result, the images appeared in Defendant's index without the copyright management information, and any users retrieving Plaintiff's images while using Defendant's Web site would not see the copyright management information.

Section 1202(b)(1) does not apply to this case. Based on the language and structure of the statute, the Court holds this provision applies only to the removal of copyright management information on a plaintiff's product or original work. Moreover, even if §1202(b)(1) applied, Plaintiff has not offered any evidence showing Defendant's actions were intentional, rather than merely an unintended side effect of the Ditto crawler's operation.

Here, where the issue is the absence of copyright management information from *copies* of Plaintiff's works, the applicable provision is §1202(b)(3). To show a violation of that section, Plaintiff must show Defendant makes available to its users the thumbnails and full-size images, which were copies of Plaintiff's work separated from their copyright management information, even though it knows or should know this will lead to infringement of Plaintiff's copyrights. There is no dispute the Ditto crawler removed Plaintiff's images from the context of Plaintiff's Web sites where their copyright management information was located, and converted them to thumbnails in Defendant's index. There is also no dispute the Arriba Vista search engine allowed full-size images to be viewed without their copyright management information.

Defendant's users could obtain a full-sized version of a thumbnailed image by clicking on the thumbnail. A user who did this was given the name of the Web site from which Defendant obtained the image, where any associated copyright management information would be available, and an opportunity to link there.[12] . . .

---

12. Through Defendant's current search engine, ditto.com, the user can no longer open a full-sized image without also opening the site where its copyright management information is located.

Based on all of this, the Court finds Defendant did not have "reasonable grounds to know" it would cause its users to infringe Plaintiff's copyrights. Defendant warns its users about the possibility of use restrictions on the images in its index, and instructs them to check with the originating Web sites before copying and using those images, even in reduced thumbnail form.

Plaintiff's images are vulnerable to copyright infringement because they are displayed on Web sites. Plaintiff has not shown users of Defendant's site were any more likely to infringe his copyrights, any of these users did infringe, or Defendant should reasonably have expected infringement. . . .

NOTES AND QUESTIONS

1. In *McClatchey v. Associated Press*, 82 U.S.P.Q.2d 790 (W.D. Pa. 2007), the court held that as a matter of statutory construction, §1202 must protect non-digital information: ". . . Section 1202(c) defines the term [copyright management information] broadly to include 'any' of the information set forth in the eight categories, 'including in digital form.' To avoid rendering those terms superfluous, the statute must also protect non-digital information." *Id.* at 1195. In *McClatchey*, the plaintiff had used a computer program to place a title and copyright notice on a photograph she had taken. The defendant allegedly took a photo of plaintiff's photograph and cropped it to remove the title and copyright notice. The court refused to grant summary judgment to the defendant. Would the *IQ Group* court agree with this holding? Which court's interpretation of §1202 is more convincing? How would you apply each to the following hypotheticals:

    a. IQ placed copyright notices on the ads themselves and Wiesner removed the information.

    b. Textile Co. places a copyright notice on its fabric's selvage (the border of the fabric that is cut off and discarded) and when it sells the fabric, also attaches a tag stating that the design was a copyrighted work of Textile Co. Ya-Ya Brand Inc. purchases the fabric, removes the selvage and the tag, and resells the fabric. *See Textile Secrets Int'l, Inc. v. Ya-Ya Brand Inc.*, 524 F. Supp. 2d 1184 (C.D. Cal. 2007) (notice and tag not covered by §1202).

    c. Under both open source software licenses and Creative Commons licenses, discussed in Chapter 8.C, *supra*, an author may "attach" the license to the work either by embedding the license itself or inserting computer code that will generate the license symbol, a short description of the license, and a hyperlink to the full license. Joe downloads a work made available under a Creative Commons license, removes the information, and posts the work on his web site. (Review the descriptions of the various Creative Commons licenses, page 631 *supra*. For purposes of §1202, does it matter which Creative Commons license the author had selected?)

    d. To discourage online news aggregators from linking to its articles and framing the article with their own advertisements, News Co. attaches metadata to each article that specify ownership information and usage rights. According to the metadata, in-line linking and framing are prohibited without a license from News Co. The Puffington Times, an online news aggregator, continues its preexisting practice of linking to and framing occasional News Co. articles. The Puffington Times leaves the metadata undisturbed.

2. Do you agree with the court that Arriba Soft did all that it needed to do to protect the plaintiff's copyright management information? How do you think the plaintiff wanted §1202(b)(3) interpreted? What kind of obligations to protect CMI should be imposed on defendants like Arriba Soft?

3. Under the interpretation given by the *Kelly* court, what kind of evidence would you need to establish the intent requirements of §1202 of the DMCA? What constitutes "reasonable grounds to know"?

4. What will be the combined effect of anti-circumvention laws and CMI protection in the digital age? Professor Julie Cohen observes that "some copyright owners may use the transaction records generated by their copyright management systems to learn more about their customers through a process known as 'profiling,'" and argues that "[t]ogether [§1201 and §1202] authorize copyright owners to implement the full range of 'smart' copyright management technologies . . . and prevent readers from taking measures to protect themselves against intrusive monitoring of their activities." Julie E. Cohen, *A Right to Read Anonymously: A Closer Look at "Copyright Management" in Cyberspace*, 28 Conn. L. Rev. 981, 985, 990 (1996). Read §1201(i). Would this provision allow the user of a work to employ technological means to prevent the collection of personal information? How much information should copyright owners be entitled to collect regarding users' activities? Should copyright law reflect privacy concerns?

E. CONVERGING TECHNOLOGIES: DIGITAL TELEVISION, THE BROADCAST FLAG, AND CABLE PLUG-AND-PLAY REGULATION

Technological protection for broadcast and cable content is an especially complicated and divisive topic. First, as you have already learned, some view the Supreme Court's *Sony* decision, and Congress' refusal to overrule it, as having created a relatively stable set of fair use entitlements with respect to such content. Second, the debate over technological control of broadcast and cable content involves an additional government entity, the Federal Communications Commission (FCC). In the broadcast arena, the FCC's regulatory jurisdiction traditionally has encompassed such issues as spectrum allocation, public access to free, over-the-air programming, and indecency regulation. The FCC generally has regulated consumer electronic technologies only when Congress has expressly authorized it to do so (as in the case of the so-called "V-chip," which enables television owners to filter incoming programming based on encoded content ratings); however, it has from time to time invoked its ancillary jurisdiction to opine on other technological questions that it views as affecting its core statutory mandates. The FCC also has express statutory jurisdiction to regulate cable and satellite encryption regimes that enforce access restrictions.

Digital television (DTV) has been the source of difficult policy problems for the FCC for a number of years, but those problems were not initially perceived as including copyright-related issues. DTV offers the potential for enormous improvements in picture quality, but viewing the improvements requires new and much more expensive television equipment. Fearing that consumers would not buy the equipment while competing technical standards existed, and that this would jeopardize the transition to DTV, the FCC asserted jurisdiction over the DTV standards development process to coordinate development of a single, commonly accepted standard. The FCC and consumer advocates also worried that the eventual shift to all-digital programming would leave behind those individuals who could not afford to purchase the new equipment; these individuals, owning only "legacy devices" (i.e., televisions compatible only with an older set of standards), would not be able to receive broadcast content at all. Thus, the FCC promulgated rules providing for the gradual phase-in of digital-only broadcasts and equipment.

For the copyright industries, however, the advent of DTV also presented a copyright problem. These industries argued that DTV equipment needed to include technological content controls so that digital content, and especially high-definition content, would not be broadcast "in the clear" (i.e., unrestricted) into millions of homes. They asserted that without such technological protection, they would be unwilling to provide content in digital formats. The FCC worried that unless these industries' concerns were addressed, the transition to DTV would not occur after all. Consumer electronics companies, once again, confronted a dilemma. They feared that technological protection would make expensive DTV equipment even less attractive to consumers, but at the same time, the ongoing litigation over peer-to-peer file-sharing dramatically illustrated the risks of being judged a facilitator of widespread copyright infringement.

For a time, the major copyright industries attempted to work with the computer and consumer electronics industries to develop a standard for broadcast copy protection. The Copy Protection Technical Working Group, *http://www.cptwg.org/*, a consortium created by members of these industries to address technological protection issues, formed a subgroup called the Broadcast Protection Discussion Group (BPDG) to consider the DTV problem. The BPDG developed a partial protocol for a digital "broadcast flag" that would signal the appropriate level of content control, and would allow for some time-shifting by broadcast recipients. However, BPDG members were unable to agree on the details of the protocol. Fearing that this failure would jeopardize effective technological protection for digital broadcast content, the major broadcast studios petitioned the FCC to adopt regulations mandating the adoption of content-control standards for DTV. Specifically, they requested that the FCC use the BPDG's partially completed broadcast flag protocol as the basis for the DTV standard.

The FCC responded to the copyright industries' request for regulatory assistance by issuing a notice of proposed rulemaking and request for public comment. Hundreds of public comments submitted in response to the notice revealed substantial disagreement about every aspect of the process, ranging from the policy implications of broadcast content protection to the efficacy of the proposed standard to the wisdom of a government-imposed "technological mandate" to the FCC's jurisdiction to impose it. In particular, critics argued that: (1) the broadcast flag is a solution in search of a problem, since bandwidth limitations prevent the widespread redistribution of digital broadcast content; (2) the proposed shelter for time-shifting was insufficient, and the flag would restrict other legitimate downstream uses of digital broadcast content; (3) critical technical issues had been left unresolved, including the approval criteria for flag-compatible technologies and criteria for identifying devices as part of a personal home network; (4) the flag would be ineffective at preventing redistribution of broadcast content anyway because it does nothing to "close the analog hole" (i.e., it leaves analog outputs wholly unrestricted); and (5) adoption of the flag would unfairly burden consumers, both by artificially constraining the functionality of new DTV-compatible devices and by causing existing legacy devices to become obsolete.

On November 4, 2003, the FCC issued an order approving a standard based on the BPDG's broadcast flag scheme as "the best option for providing a reasonable level of redistribution protection at a minimal cost to consumers and industry." Federal Communications Comm., *Report and Order and Further Notice of Proposed Rulemaking*, No. 03-273 (Nov. 4,

2003). The Commission opined that even though the broadcast flag technology was not perfect, it would create a "speed bump" that would hinder redistribution. *Id.* ¶19. It noted:

> While an immediate "analog hole" solution is not forthcoming, the window of opportunity for adopting a flag based redistribution control regime for digital broadcast television is closing. The number of legacy devices existing today is still sufficiently small that content owners remain willing to provide high value content to broadcast outlets. At some point, however, when the number of legacy devices becomes too great, that calculus will change. By acting now, the Commission can protect both content and consumers' expectations.

Id. It observed that "the scope of our decision does not reach existing copyright law" because "the underlying rights and remedies available to copyright holders remain unchanged." *Id.* ¶19. The Commission rejected a number of alternate proposals, including "encryption at the source," and various types of digital watermarking, on the grounds that development and approval of such technologies would take too long and implementation would burden consumers even more heavily. *Id.* ¶¶22-26.

The FCC did not, however, adopt the copyright industries' proposal in full. That proposal would have required implementations of the flag to be effective even against highly sophisticated experts, and would have given the copyright industries control of the approval process for flag-compatible technologies. The FCC ruled that implementations would need to be effective only against an "ordinary user," *id.* ¶46, and declined to place approval authority under control of "one industry segment," *id.* ¶52. Instead, it issued a further notice of proposed rulemaking on a variety of issues, including: (1) the approval and revocation criteria for flag-compatible technologies; (2) "the interplay between a flag redistribution control system and the development of open source software applications"; and (3) the implementation of personal copying privileges in "a personal digital network environment ('PDNE') within which consumers could freely redistribute digital broadcast television content." Federal Communications Comm., *Digital Broadcast Content Protection: Notice of Proposed Rulemaking*, 68 Fed. Reg. 67,624, 67,625 (Dec. 3, 2003).

A group of consumer and library organizations appealed the FCC's broadcast flag order to the D.C. Circuit. They argued that the FCC lacked jurisdiction to issue the order because the agency's enabling statutes did not give it general authority to regulate equipment capable of receiving broadcast transmissions, but only more limited authority to regulate what the equipment does while it is in the process of receiving a transmission. They also argued that the broadcast flag order violated the Administrative Procedure Act because: (1) the need for the broadcast flag was not supported by substantial evidence; and (2) the FCC acted arbitrarily and capriciously in approving the flag in light of its inadequacies. The court agreed that the FCC lacked jurisdiction, and vacated the rule without considering the appellants' substantive challenges. *See American Library Ass'n v. FCC*, 406 F.3d 689 (D.C. Cir. 2005).

Subsequently, the copyright industries have repeatedly sought a legislative mandate for the broadcast flag, and have also pushed for the establishment of an "audio broadcast flag" regime that would apply to digital radio. As of this writing, none of those efforts has borne fruit. In 2009, the FCC-supervised transition to DTV was completed without a broadcast flag component in place.

At the same time, however, private-sector efforts to implement broadcast flag functionality have continued to move forward without regulatory oversight. In the past few years, there have been occasional incidents in which broadcast-flag functionality has been triggered, it seems inadvertently, to prevent consumer recording or viewing of broadcast content. Those incidents indicate that at least some digital media technologies have been designed to incorporate protocols regulating copying and display of DTV content, but more information is difficult to obtain.

Unlike broadcast programming, cable and satellite programming are encrypted at the source and decrypted, or demodulated, by the "set-top box" furnished by the provider. In DMCA parlance, this system restricts access to programming to paid subscribers. With appropriate standards coordination, DTV technology can eliminate the need for a separate set-top box from each cable and satellite provider. Instead, users can plug their DTV receivers directly into their cable systems. This enables users to access all cable and broadcast programming channels using a single remote control, and to use their analog VCRs with most channels. The FCC viewed this so-called "plug and play" capability as important to smoothing the transition to DTV. Again, however, the industries that provide programming raised concerns about the vulnerability of digital content to widespread copying once it has been decrypted. Representatives of all the major players in the cable and consumer electronics industries submitted to the FCC a proposed rule establishing a "cable plug and play" standard for DTV devices. The proposed standard included restrictions on downstream copying of the decrypted content that were more extensive than the proposed broadcast flag's controls, in that they did not incorporate any conventions for copying of digital content directly onto digital consumer electronic devices. The proposed rule provided for manufacturer self-certification of compliance according to standards to be developed by the affected industry groups.

In 2003, the FCC adopted the proposed cable plug-and-play rule with some modifications. *See* Federal Communications Comm., *Commercial Availability of Navigation Devices and Compatibility Between Cable Systems and Consumer Electronics Equipment*, 68 Fed. Reg. 66,728 (Nov. 28, 2003). In particular, the rule adopted by the FCC requires that regular broadcast programming be encoded without restrictions on copying and prohibits "down-resolution" of such programming — i.e., transmitting the content in a low-resolution format so as to preclude the possibility of high-resolution copying. Non-broadcast subscription programming must be encoded in a way that permits consumers to make first-generation copies. As in the case of the broadcast flag, the FCC issued a further notice of proposed rulemaking on various issues, including the approval process for compatible technologies and the use of down-resolution for non-broadcast programming.

Today, however, the FCC's attempt to establish a universal cable plug-and-play standard is widely acknowledged to have been a failure, largely for reasons relating to the evolution of the technology. The plug and play standard adopted in 2003 does not support two-way features that are required by increasingly popular video on demand services. Cable providers designed their set-top boxes to incorporate those features, and incompatibility remains the norm.

The cable plug-and-play rule's prohibitions on copy restrictions remain in force, however. Those restrictions include the so-called selectable output control rule, which provides:

> A covered entity shall not attach or embed data or information with commercial audiovisual content, or otherwise apply to, associate with, or allow such data to persist in or remain associated with such content, so as to prevent its output through any analog or digital output authorized or permitted under license, law or regulation governing such covered product.

47 C.F.R. §76.1903.

NOTES AND QUESTIONS

1. Jurisdictional questions aside, would government oversight of broadcast flag technologies be desirable? For different perspectives on that question, see Susan P. Crawford, *The Biology of the Broadcast Flag*, 25 Hastings Comm. & Ent. L.J. 559 (2004), and Molly

Shaffer Van Houweling, *Communications' Copyright Policy*, 4 J. Telecomm. & High Tech. L. 97 (2005).

2. Would the particular broadcast flag rule adopted by the FCC have represented good policy? The intricacies of Administrative Procedure Act standards of review are topics for a different course. In general, however, how would you evaluate the FCC's decision to approve a concededly imperfect and incomplete technology? (Examine carefully the FCC's remarks about legacy devices. To which devices was the FCC referring? Are they the same devices with which opponents of the broadcast flag were concerned?)

3. What do you think of the FCC's actions in the cable plug-and-play context? Is there something that the FCC could have done differently to ensure that its attempt at oversight would remain relevant? Alternatively, should the FCC have refrained from attempting to make rules about cable delivery standards?

4. Telecommunications experts estimate that in a few more years, over 90 percent of Americans will receive televised content via cable or satellite subscriptions. Does this information cause you to change your answers to any of the previous questions? If so, in what way?

5. If a broadcast flag rule is needed, which would be the better institution to promulgate it, Congress or the FCC pursuant to an expanded grant of jurisdiction? Would you support giving the Copyright Office jurisdiction to regulate broadcast flag technologies and/or cable technologies?

6. Would you support an "audio broadcast flag" requirement? Are the policy considerations identical?

7. In 2009, the motion picture industry petitioned the FCC for relief from the selectable output control rule. According to the petition, such relief would enable the earlier release of motion pictures to online delivery services; according to opponents, it would allow content owners to interfere with the lawful use of DVRs and similar devices. If you were an FCC commissioner, would you be inclined to approve such a petition? Why or why not?

10

State Law Theories of Protection, and Their Limits

In previous chapters, we noted efforts by copyright owners to augment their rights under federal copyright law by placing contractual restrictions on use of their works. Copyright owners have also sought to supplement claims for infringement of their federal statutory rights with other claims asserting various state law theories of protection. In addition, individual states sometimes have sought to create new subject matter rights at the boundaries of the federal copyright and patent systems. These efforts have assumed increasing importance in recent decades and are the subject of this chapter.

Efforts to devise state law protection regimes for copyrightable and uncopyrightable materials raise questions about the extent to which the federal intellectual property framework permits a state to recognize causes of action relating to intangible intellectual goods or to create new statutory rights in such goods. For example, may a state provide statutory protection for databases that lack originality? May a state's common law recognize a tort of misappropriation when someone copies facts? May a state law claim for breach of contract be used by a copyright owner of software to prevent decompilation?

This chapter begins by introducing the principles that govern federal preemption of state law and exploring the cases in which the Supreme Court has addressed the compatibility of state law protections for intangibles with the federal intellectual property laws. These cases provide an introduction to the policy concerns that should inform any preemption determination concerning copyright law. With that background firmly in place, we then examine the express preemption provision contained in the Copyright Act and explore the interaction of this provision with several different types of state law claims that might provide protection for intangible intellectual goods. We then consider in greater depth three state law theories of protection that have engendered particularly difficult preemption problems for copyright law: rights of publicity, misappropriation, and contract.

A. FEDERAL INTELLECTUAL PROPERTY PREEMPTION: AN OVERVIEW

Article VI, cl. 2 of the Constitution states:

> This Constitution, and the Laws of the United States which shall be made in pursuance thereof; and all Treaties made, or which shall be made, under the Authority of the United States, shall be the supreme Law of the Land; and the Judges in every State shall be bound thereby, any Thing in the Constitution or Laws of any State to the contrary notwithstanding.

This provision, known as the Supremacy Clause, sets forth the general principle that governs conflicts between state and federal law: Federal law is supreme and will override — or "preempt" — inconsistent state law. The Supreme Court, in turn, has developed a set of interpretive rules to determine when that principle is implicated both generally and in the specific context of intellectual property.

There are three types of federal preemption. First, a federal law may expressly preempt particular state laws or causes of action. Thus, the starting reference point for determining whether preemption is present is the text of the governing federal statute. Many federal statutes contain such provisions. The Copyright Act contains an express preemption provision that prohibits state law claims concerning subject matter "within the general scope of copyright" that are "equivalent to" copyright infringement claims. 17 U.S.C. §301(a). The federal Patent Act, in contrast, contains no such express language.

The second and third types of preemption may be implied from a federal statute's scope, purpose, and legislative history. The first type of implied preemption, known as "occupation of the field," occurs when federal law completely excludes the states from acting in the covered area. Congressional intent to exclude the states entirely from a particular field "may be inferred from a 'scheme of federal regulation . . . so pervasive as to make reasonable the inference that Congress left no room for the States to supplement it,' or where an Act of Congress 'touch[es] a field in which the federal interest is so dominant that the federal system will be assumed to preclude enforcement of state laws on the same subject.'" *English v. Gen. Elec. Co.*, 496 U.S. 72, 79 (1990) (quoting *Rice v. Santa Fe Elevator Corp.*, 331 U.S. 218, 230 (1947)). An example of this sort of preemption is found in the federal statutes that regulate public safety and health issues relating to nuclear power. *Pacific Gas & Elec. Co. v. State Energy Res. Conservation & Dev. Comm'n*, 461 U.S. 190, 205-13 (1983).

The second type of implied preemption, often called "conflict preemption," is narrower. Even when federal law has not completely occupied the covered field, particular state enactments or common law claims for relief may nonetheless conflict with the purpose of the federal statutory scheme. In such cases, the state law will be preempted to the extent of the conflict. For example, in *Geier v. American Honda Motor Co.*, 529 U.S. 861 (2000), the Supreme Court held a state tort action alleging negligent failure to equip a car with a driver's side airbag preempted because it conflicted with federal regulations governing the implementation of airbags and other passive restraints. To determine whether a particular state law or cause of action creates an unacceptable conflict with a federal statutory scheme, courts must inquire whether the state law "stands as an obstacle to the accomplishment and execution of the full purposes and objectives of Congress." *Hines v. Davidowitz*, 312 U.S. 52, 67 (1941).

To complicate matters further, express and implied preemption may coexist in the same statute. A federal statute containing an express preemption provision that covers some state laws may also impliedly preempt other state laws. The express provision establishes an inference that Congress did not intend the statute to have broader preemptive effect, but that inference may be overcome by other evidence of congressional intent. *See Geier*, 529 U.S. at 869-74 ("[T]he principles underlying this Court's preemption doctrine . . . make clear that the express preemption provision imposes no unusual, 'special burden' against [implied] preemption."); *Freightliner Corp. v. Myrick*, 514 U.S. 280, 288 (1995). The significance of this rule for our purposes is that the presence of an express preemption provision in the Copyright Act does not necessarily exhaust the possibilities for federal copyright preemption.

Finally, although preemption usually refers to displacement of state law by federal statutory law, a species of preemption also can be accomplished by federal constitutional provisions. The varieties of constitutional preemption parallel those already discussed. Thus, for example, Art. I, §10, which forbids the states from making treaties, expressly excludes the states from the field of foreign relations; the Commerce Clause, Art. I, §8, cl. 3, which gives Congress the power to regulate interstate and foreign commerce, impliedly excludes the states from regulating in those fields; the Fourteenth Amendment expressly forbids the states from taking actions that conflict with the federal principles of due process and equal protection; and the Due Process Clause of the Fourteenth Amendment impliedly forbids the states from taking actions that conflict with the federal principles set forth in the Bill of Rights. The Intellectual Property Clause does not expressly preempt any kind of state law. As we explore in this chapter, the extent to which implied preemption of state law flows from the Intellectual Property Clause itself, rather than from the Patent Act or the Copyright Act, is an unresolved question.

A line of Supreme Court cases has considered the preemptive effects of the federal intellectual property laws on state regulation of rights in intangible intellectual goods. All but one of these decisions has concerned the federal patent laws. As you read the cases, focus on identifying the general principles that the Court develops to distinguish between permissible and impermissible state regulation. Consider, too, the extent to which the Court's reasoning about patent preemption is transferable to the copyright context.

Sears, Roebuck & Co. v. Stiffel Co.
376 U.S. 225 (1964)

BLACK, J.: The question in this case is whether a State's unfair competition law can, consistently with the federal patent laws, impose liability for or prohibit the copying of an article which is protected by neither a federal patent nor a copyright. The respondent, Stiffel Company, secured design and mechanical patents on a "pole lamp" — a vertical tube having lamp fixtures along the outside, the tube being made so that it will stand upright between the floor and ceiling of a room. Pole lamps proved a decided commercial success, and soon after Stiffel brought them on the market Sears, Roebuck & Company put on the market a substantially identical lamp, which it sold more cheaply, Sears' retail price being about the same as Stiffel's wholesale price. Stiffel then brought this action against Sears in the United States District Court for the Northern District of Illinois, claiming in its first count that by copying its design Sears had infringed Stiffel's patents and in its second count that by selling copies of Stiffel's lamp Sears had caused confusion in the trade as to the source of the lamps and had thereby engaged in unfair competition under Illinois law. . . .

[The district court ruled that the patents were invalid "for want of invention" but held that Sears had engaged in unfair competition; the court of appeals affirmed.]

Before the Constitution was adopted, some States had granted patents either by special act or by general statute, but when the Constitution was adopted provision for a federal patent law was made one of the enumerated powers of Congress because, as Madison put it in The Federalist No. 43, the States "cannot separately make effectual provision" for either patents or copyrights. . . .

. . . [T]he patent system is one in which uniform federal standards are carefully used to promote invention while at the same time preserving free competition. Obviously a State could not, consistently with the Supremacy Clause of the Constitution, extend the life of a patent beyond its expiration date or give a patent on an article which lacked the level of invention required for federal patents. To do either would run counter to the policy of Congress of granting patents only to true inventions, and then only for a limited time. Just as a State cannot encroach upon the federal patent laws directly, it cannot, under some other law, such as that forbidding unfair competition, give protection of a kind that clashes with the objectives of the federal patent laws.

In the present case the "pole lamp" sold by Stiffel has been held not to be entitled to the protection of either a mechanical patent or a design patent. An unpatentable article, like an article on which the patent has expired, is in the public domain and may be made and sold by whoever chooses to do so. What Sears did was to copy Stiffel's design and to sell lamps almost identical to those sold by Stiffel. This it had every right to do under the federal patent laws. That Stiffel originated the pole lamp and made it popular is immaterial. "Sharing in the goodwill of an article unprotected by patent or trademark is the exercise of a right possessed by all — and in the free exercise of which the consuming public is deeply interested." *Kellogg Co. v. National Biscuit Co., supra,* 305 U.S. at 122. . . . To allow a State by use of its law of unfair competition to prevent the copying of an article which represents too slight an advance to be patented would be to permit the State to block off from the public something which federal law has said belongs to the public. The result would be that while federal law grants only 14 or 17 [now 20 — Eds.] years' protection to genuine inventions, see 35 U.S.C. §§154, 173, States could allow perpetual protection to articles too lacking in novelty to merit any patent at all under federal constitutional standards. This would be too great an encroachment on the federal patent system to be tolerated.

Sears has been held liable here for unfair competition because of a finding of likelihood of confusion based only on the fact that Sears' lamp was copied from Stiffel's unpatented lamp and that consequently the two looked exactly alike. Of course there could be "confusion" as to who had manufactured these nearly identical articles. . . . Doubtless a State may, in appropriate circumstances, require that goods, whether patented or unpatented, be labeled or that other precautionary steps be taken to prevent consumers from being misled as to the source. . . . But because of the federal patent laws a State may not, when the article is unpatented and uncopyrighted, prohibit the copying of the article itself or award damages for such copying. . . .

Note on *Compco Corp. v. Day-Brite Lighting, Inc.*

Compco Corp. v. Day-Brite Lighting, Inc., 376 U.S. 234 (1964), a companion case to *Sears,* arose on virtually identical facts. The defendant, Compco, had copied a lighting fixture developed by the plaintiff, Day-Brite. The district court held Day-Brite's design patent invalid but held that Compco had engaged in unfair competition. The Supreme Court applied its just-announced decision in *Sears* and described the rule of *Sears* as follows:

> [W]hen an article is unprotected by a patent or a copyright, state law may not forbid others to copy that article. To forbid copying would interfere with the federal policy, found in Art. I., §8, cl. 8, of the Constitution and in the implementing federal statutes, of allowing free access to copy whatever the federal patent and copyright laws leave in the public domain.

Compco, 376 U.S. at 237.

The district court also had found that the ornamental ribbing on Day-Brite's lighting fixture had acquired "secondary meaning"—i.e., that consumers viewed the design as an indicator of source. *See* Chapter 4.A, pages 209-10 *supra*. The Supreme Court held that this difference was immaterial and that the reasoning in *Sears* controlled disposition of the case:

> That an article copied from an unpatented article could be made in some other way, that the design is "nonfunctional" and not essential to the use of either article, that the configuration of the article copied may have a "secondary meaning" which identifies the maker to the trade, or that there may be "confusion" among purchasers as to which article is which or as to who is the maker, may be relevant in applying a State's law requiring such precautions as labeling; however, and regardless of the copier's motives, neither these facts nor any others can furnish a basis for imposing liability for or prohibiting the actual acts of copying and selling.

Id. at 238.

The decisions in *Sears* and *Compco* cast doubt on many different state law protections for intellectual goods, including state law protections for works of authorship. The next time the Supreme Court addressed preemption, it did so in the copyright context, under the 1909 Act.

≡ *Goldstein v. California*
≡ *412 U.S. 546 (1972)*

[Petitioners were prosecuted and convicted under a California statute that prohibited the copying of sound recordings. While the case was pending, Congress amended the federal copyright laws to extend protection to sound recordings. However, the amendment applied only to sound recordings fixed after February 15, 1972, and the recordings that petitioners had copied were all fixed before that date. Based on *Sears* and *Compco*, petitioners argued that the California statute was preempted. The 1909 Copyright Act contained no express preemption provision.]

BURGER, C.J.: . . .

II

A

. . . The clause of the Constitution granting to Congress the power to issue copyrights does not provide that such power shall vest exclusively in the Federal Government.

Nor does the Constitution expressly provide that such power shall not be exercised by the States. . . .

The question whether exclusive federal power must be inferred is not a simple one, for the powers recognized in the Constitution are broad and the nature of their application varied. . . .

The objective of the Copyright Clause was clearly to facilitate the granting of rights national in scope. While the debates on the clause at the Constitutional Convention were extremely limited, its purpose was described by James Madison in the Federalist:

> The utility of this power will scarcely be questioned. The copyright of authors has been solemnly adjudged, in Great Britain, to be a right of common law. The right to useful inventions seems with equal reason to belong to the inventors. The public good fully coincides in both cases with the claims of individuals. The States cannot separately make effectual provision for either of the cases, and most of them have anticipated the decision of this point, by laws passed at the instance of Congress.

The difficulty noted by Madison relates to the burden placed on an author or inventor who wishes to achieve protection in all States when no federal system of protection is available. To do so, a separate application is required to each state government; the right which in turn may be granted has effect only within the granting State's borders. The national system which Madison supported eliminates the need for multiple applications and the expense and difficulty involved. In effect, it allows Congress to provide a reward greater in scope than any particular State may grant to promote progress in those fields which Congress determines are worthy of national action.

Although the Copyright Clause recognizes the potential benefits of a national system, it does not indicate that all writings are of national interest or that state legislation is, in all cases, unnecessary or precluded. The patents granted by the States in the 18th century show, to the contrary, a willingness on the part of the States to promote those portions of science and the arts which were of local importance. Whatever the diversity of people's backgrounds, origins, and interests, and whatever the variety of business and industry in the 13 Colonies, the range of diversity is obviously far greater today in a country of 210 million people in 50 States. In view of that enormous diversity, it is unlikely that all citizens in all parts of the country place the same importance on works relating to all subjects. Since the subject matter to which the Copyright Clause is addressed may thus be of purely local importance and not worthy of national attention or protection, we cannot discern such an unyielding national interest as to require an inference that state power to grant copyright has been relinquished to exclusive federal control.

. . . [I]n the case of state copyrights, except as to individuals willing to travel across state lines in order to purchase records or other writings protected in their own State, each State's copyrights will still serve to induce new artistic creations within that State — the very objective of the grant of protection. . . .

Similarly, it is difficult to see how the concurrent exercise of the power to grant copyrights by Congress and the States will necessarily and inevitably lead to difficulty. At any time Congress determines that a particular category of "writing" is worthy of national protection and the incidental expense of federal administration, federal copyright protection may be authorized. Where the need for free and unrestricted distribution of a writing is thought to be required by the national interest, the Copyright Clause and the Commerce Clause would allow Congress to eschew all protection. In such cases, a conflict would develop if a State attempted to protect that which Congress intended to be free from restraint or to free that which Congress had protected. However, where Congress determines that neither federal protection nor freedom from restraint is required by the national interest, it is at liberty to stay its hand entirely.[16] Since state protection would not then conflict with federal action, total relinquishment of the States' power to grant copyright protection cannot be inferred. . . .

III

Our conclusion that California did not surrender its power to issue copyrights does not end the inquiry. We must proceed to determine whether the challenged state statute is void under the Supremacy Clause. . . .

While the area in which Congress *may* act is broad, the enabling provision of [the Intellectual Property Clause] does not require that Congress act in regard to all categories of materials which meet the constitutional definitions. Rather, whether any specific category of "Writings" is to be brought within the purview of the federal statutory scheme is left to the discretion of the Congress. The history of federal copyright statutes indicates that the congressional determination to consider specific classes of writings is dependent, not only on the character of the writing, but also on the commercial importance of the product to the national economy. . . .

. . . According to petitioners, Congress addressed the question of whether recordings of performances should be granted protection in 1909; Congress determined that any individual who was entitled to a copyright on an original musical composition should have the right to control to a limited extent the use of that composition on recordings, but that the record itself, and the performance which it was capable of reproducing were not worthy of such protection. . . . [The Court rejected this argument, noting that when Congress granted composers a right to remuneration for "mechanical" reproductions of their works, it was focusing solely on rights in musical compositions and did not "consider[ ] records as anything but a component part of a machine."]

. . . [Petitioners also] argue that Congress so occupied the field of copyright protection as to pre-empt all comparable state action. . . .

Sears and *Compco*, on which petitioners rely, do not support their position. In those cases, the question was whether a State could, under principles of a state unfair competition law, preclude the copying of mechanical configurations which did not possess the qualities required for the granting of a federal design or mechanical patent. . . .

In regard to mechanical configurations, Congress had balanced the need to encourage innovation and originality of invention against the need to insure competition in the sale of identical or substantially identical products. The standards established for granting federal patent protection to machines thus indicated not only which articles in this particular category Congress wished to protect, but which configurations it wished to remain free. The application of state law in these cases to prevent the copying of articles which did not meet the requirements for federal protection disturbed the careful balance which Congress had drawn and thereby necessarily gave way under the Supremacy Clause. No comparable conflict between state law and federal law arises in the case of recordings of musical performances. In regard to this category of "Writings," Congress has drawn no balance; rather, it has left the area unattended, and no reason exists why the State should not be free to act. . . .

---

16. For example, Congress has allowed writings which may eventually be the subject of a federal copyright, to be protected under state law prior to publication. 17 U.S.C. § 2.

[Justice DOUGLAS dissented and argued that *Sears* and *Compco* should control disposition of the case. He observed: "Cases like *Sears* were surcharged with 'unfair competition' and the present one with 'pirated recordings.' But free access to products on the market is the consumer interest protected by the failure of Congress to extend patents or copyrights into various areas." Justices BRENNAN and BLACKMUN joined this dissent. Justice MARSHALL filed a separate dissent, which Justices BRENNAN and BLACKMUN also joined.]

NOTES AND QUESTIONS

1. Is *Goldstein* consistent with *Sears* and *Compco*, as the majority argues? How do *Sears* and *Compco* define the public domain? How does the *Goldstein* Court define it?

2. Does *Goldstein* hold that copyright preemption is different from patent preemption? If so, how? If not, what explains the difference in outcomes? Note that then, as today, the federal Patent Act extended protection to "any new and useful process, machine, manufacture, or composition of matter, or any new and useful improvement thereof" that was sufficiently nonobvious and satisfied other standards for protection. 35 U.S.C. §§101 *et seq.*; *see Graham v. John Deere*, 383 U.S. 1 (1966), Chapter 2.A.2, pages 70-71 *supra*. For a summary of the pertinent provisions of the Copyright Act of 1909, see Chapter 1.B.3. *supra*. Recall, too, that a work had to be published with proper notice to be eligible for federal copyright protection.

Would the *Goldstein* Court have decided the case the same way if the sound recordings at issue had been created in 1973, after Congress amended the 1909 Act to extend copyright protection to sound recordings?

3. Is Chief Justice Burger's reasoning persuasive regarding the lack of uniformity likely to result when states provide protection? Would state-created rights in intellectual goods pose a greater threat to the integrity of the federal scheme today than the Court identified in 1972? If the Framers of the Constitution and the first patent and copyright statutes did not perceive such rights as a threat, should the modern realities of interstate trade in intellectual goods influence the preemption analysis?

4. If a state wishes to attract investment by industries that produce intellectual goods, what alternatives might it explore other than establishing new intellectual property rights?

Goldstein presented a more promising view of the viability of state law protections for intellectual goods. Perhaps federal intellectual property laws did not have as wide a preemptive sweep as might have been supposed after the *Sears* and *Compco* opinions. The Supreme Court's next preemption opinion also upheld a state law scheme of protection against a preemption challenge.

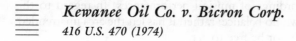 ### *Kewanee Oil Co. v. Bicron Corp.*
416 U.S. 470 (1974)

BURGER, C.J.: We granted certiorari to resolve a question on which there is a conflict in the courts of appeals: whether state trade secret protection is pre-empted by operation of the federal patent law. . . .

III

. . . [I]n *Goldstein v. California*, . . . we held that the cl. 8 grant of power to Congress was not exclusive and that, at least in the case of writings, the States were not prohibited from encouraging and protecting the efforts of those within their borders by appropriate legislation. . . .

Just as the States may exercise regulatory power over writings so may the States regulate with respect to discoveries. . . .

IV

The question of whether the trade secret law of Ohio is void under the Supremacy Clause involves a consideration of whether that law "stands as an obstacle to the accomplishment and execution of the full purposes and objectives of Congress." . . .

The stated objective of the Constitution in granting the power to Congress to legislate in the area of intellectual property is to "promote the Progress of Science and useful Arts." The patent laws promote this progress by offering a right of exclusion for a limited period as an incentive to inventors to risk the often enormous costs in terms of time, research, and development. . . . In return for the right of exclusion . . . the patent laws impose upon the inventor a requirement of disclosure. . . . [S]uch additions to the general store of knowledge are of such importance to the public weal that the Federal Government is willing to pay the high price of 17 years* of exclusive use for its disclosure, which disclosure, it is assumed, will stimulate ideas and the eventual development of further significant advances in the art. The Court has also articulated another policy of the patent law: that which is in the public domain cannot be removed therefrom by action of the States. . . .

The maintenance of standards of commercial ethics and the encouragement of invention are the broadly stated policies behind trade secret law. "The necessity of good faith and honest, fair dealing, is the very life and spirit of the commercial world." . . .

Having now in mind the objectives of both the patent and trade secret law, we turn to an examination of the interaction of these systems of protection of intellectual property. . . .

As we noted earlier, trade secret law protects items which would not be proper subjects for consideration for patent protection under 35 U.S.C. §101. As in the case of the recordings in *Goldstein v. California*, Congress, with respect to nonpatentable subject matter, "has drawn no balance; rather, it has left the area unattended, and no reason exists why the State should not be free to act." . . .

. . . [T]he holder of such a discovery would have no reason to apply for a patent whether trade secret protection existed or not. Abolition of trade secret protection would, therefore, not result in increased disclosure to the public of discoveries in the area of nonpatentable subject matter. . . . [K]eeping such items secret encourages businesses to initiate new and individualized plans of operation, and constructive competition results. . . .

. . . The question remains whether those items which are proper subjects for consideration for a patent may also have available the alternative protection accorded by trade secret law.

Certainly the patent policy of encouraging invention is not disturbed by the existence of another form of incentive to invention. In this respect the two systems are not and never would be in conflict. Similarly, the policy that matter once in the public domain must remain in the

---

* [The term of a patent is now 20 years from the date of filing. — EDS.]

public domain is not incompatible with the existence of trade secret protection. By definition a trade secret has not been placed in the public domain.

The more difficult objective of the patent law to reconcile with trade secret law is that of disclosure, the *quid pro quo* of the right to exclude. . . . [It is] useful, in determining whether inventors will refrain because of the existence of trade secret law from applying for patents, thereby depriving the public from learning of the invention, to distinguish between three categories of trade secrets. . . .

. . . [T]he extension of trade secret protection to patentable subject matter that the owner knows will not meet the standards of patentability will . . . encourage invention in areas where patent law does not reach. . . .

[The Court reasoned that extension of trade secret protection to this category of material decreases costly reliance on self-help and encourages innovators to license their secrets for purposes of manufacturing and marketing. It further noted:] In addition to the increased costs for protection from burglary, wire-tapping, bribery, and the other means used to misappropriate trade secrets, there is the inevitable cost to the basic decency of society when one firm steals from another. . . .

The next category of patentable subject matter to deal with is the invention whose holder has a legitimate doubt as to its patentability. The risk of eventual patent invalidity by the courts and the costs associated with that risk may well impel some with a good-faith doubt as to patentability not to take the trouble to seek to obtain and defend patent protection for their discoveries. . . . Trade secret protection would assist those inventors in the more efficient exploitation of their discoveries and not conflict with the patent law. . . . [A]n invalid patent [i]s so serious a threat to the free use of ideas already in the public domain that . . . [b]etter had the invalid patent never issued. More of those patents would likely issue if trade secret law were abolished. . . .

The final category of patentable subject matter to deal with is the clearly patentable invention, *i.e.*, that invention which the owner believes to meet the standards of patentability. It is here that the federal interest in disclosure is at its peak. . . . In the case of trade secret law no reasonable risk of deterrence from patent application by those who can reasonably expect to be granted patents exists.

Trade secret law provides far weaker protection in many respects than the patent law. While trade secret law does not forbid the discovery of the trade secret by fair and honest means, *e.g.*, independent creation or reverse engineering, patent law operates "against the world," forbidding any use of the invention for whatever purpose for a significant length of time. . . . Where patent law acts as a barrier, trade secret law functions relatively as a sieve. The possibility that an inventor who believes his invention meets the standards of patentability will sit back, rely on trade secret law, and after one year of use forfeit any right to patent protection, 35 U.S.C. §102(b),* is remote indeed.

Nor does society face much risk that scientific or technological progress will be impeded by the rare inventor with a patentable invention who chooses trade secret protection over patent protection. The ripeness-of-time concept of invention, developed from the study of the many independent multiple discoveries in history, predicts that if a particular individual had not made a particular discovery others would have, and in probably a relatively short period of time. . . .

We conclude that the extension of trade secret protection to clearly patentable inventions does not conflict with the patent policy of disclosure. . . .

---

* [Section 102(b) of the Patent Act provides, *inter alia*, that if an invention has been on sale or in use for more than one year prior to the filing of a patent application, the patent is barred. — EDS.]

MARSHALL, J., concurring in the result: . . . State trade secret laws and the federal patent laws have co-existed for many, many years. During this time, Congress has repeatedly demonstrated its full awareness of the existence of the trade secret system, without any indication of disapproval. . . .

DOUGLAS, J., with whom BRENNAN, J. concurs, dissenting: Today's decision is at war with the philosophy of *Sears* . . . and *Compco*. . . . We held that when an article is unprotected by a patent, state law may not forbid others to copy it, because every article not covered by a valid patent is in the public domain. . . .

A suit to redress theft of a trade secret is grounded in tort damages for breach of a contract—a historic remedy. . . . Damages for breach of a confidential relation are not preempted by this patent law, but an injunction against use is pre-empted because the patent law states the only monopoly over trade secrets that is enforceable by specific performance; and that monopoly exacts as a price full disclosure. A trade secret can be protected only by being kept secret. Damages for breach of a contract are one thing; an injunction barring disclosure does service for the protection accorded valid patents and is therefore pre-empted.

While *Sears* and *Compco* appeared to require broad preemption of state laws protecting intellectual goods, *Goldstein* and *Kewanee* focused more narrowly on the purpose and scope of the contested state laws. Can these two approaches be reconciled? Consider the following case.

Bonito Boats, Inc. v. Thunder Craft Boats, Inc.
489 U.S. 141 (1989)

O'CONNOR, J.: . . .

I

In May 1983 . . . the Florida Legislature enacted Fla. Stat. §559.94 (1987). The statute makes "[i]t . . . unlawful for any person to use the direct molding process to duplicate for the purpose of sale any manufactured vessel hull or component part of a vessel made by another without the written permission of that other person." §559.94(2). The statute also makes it unlawful for a person to "knowingly sell a vessel hull or component part of a vessel duplicated in violation of subsection (2)." §559.94(3). . . .

[Bonito Boats, a Florida corporation, sued Thunder Craft, a Tennessee corporation, for copying its popular 5VBR boat hull design. The Florida courts held that the statute was preempted by the federal patent laws.]

II

. . . The federal patent system . . . embodies a carefully crafted bargain for encouraging the creation and disclosure of new, useful, and nonobvious advances in technology and design in return for the exclusive right to practice the invention for a period of years. . . .

The attractiveness of such a bargain, and its effectiveness in inducing creative effort and disclosure of the results of that effort, depend almost entirely on a backdrop of free competition in the exploitation of unpatented designs and innovations. The novelty and nonobviousness requirements of patentability embody a congressional understanding, implicit in the Patent Clause itself, that free exploitation of ideas will be the rule, to which the protection of a federal patent is the exception. . . .

. . . [O]ur decision in *Sears* clearly indicates that the States may place limited regulations on the circumstances in which such designs are used in order to prevent consumer confusion as to source. Thus, while *Sears* speaks in absolutist terms, its conclusion that the States may place some conditions on the use of trade dress indicates an implicit recognition that all state regulation of potentially patentable but unpatented subject matter is not *ipso facto* pre-empted by the federal patent laws. . . .

. . . [T]he *Kewanee* Court emphasized that "[t]rade secret law provides far weaker protection in many respects than the patent law." . . . This point was central to the Court's conclusion that trade secret protection did not conflict with either the encouragement or disclosure policies of the federal patent law. . . .

. . . [W]e believe that the *Sears* Court correctly concluded that the States may not offer patent-like protection to intellectual creations which would otherwise remain unprotected as a matter of federal law. . . .

III

We believe that the Florida statute at issue in this case so substantially impedes the public use of the otherwise unprotected design and utilitarian ideas embodied in unpatented boat hulls as to run afoul of the teaching of our decisions in *Sears* and *Compco*. It is readily apparent that the Florida statute does not operate to prohibit "unfair competition" in the usual sense that the term is understood. The law of unfair competition has its roots in the common-law tort of deceit: its general concern is with protecting *consumers* from confusion as to source. . . .

In contrast to the operation of unfair competition law, the Florida statute is aimed directly at preventing the exploitation of the design and utilitarian conceptions embodied in the product itself. The sparse legislative history surrounding its enactment indicates that it was intended to create an inducement for the improvement of boat hull designs. . . . To accomplish this goal, the Florida statute endows the original boat hull manufacturer with rights against the world, similar in scope and operation to the rights accorded a federal patentee. . . . The Florida scheme offers this protection for an unlimited number of years to all boat hulls and their component parts, without regard to their ornamental or technological merit. Protection is available for subject matter for which patent protection has been denied or has expired, as well as for designs which have been freely revealed to the public by their creators. . . .

That the Florida statute does not remove all means of reproduction and sale does not eliminate the conflict with the federal scheme. . . . In essence, the Florida law prohibits the entire public from engaging in a form of reverse engineering of a product in the public domain. This is clearly one of the rights vested in the federal patent holder, but has never been a part of state protection under the law of unfair competition or trade secrets. *See Kewanee*, 416 U.S. at 476. . . .

Appending the conclusionary label "unscrupulous" to such competitive behavior merely endorses a policy judgment which the patent laws do not leave the States free to make. . . .

NOTES AND QUESTIONS

1. Is *Kewanee* consistent with *Sears* and *Compco*? With *Goldstein*? How does the *Kewanee* Court define the public domain? Is any aspect of a trade secret in the public domain?

2. Do you agree with Chief Justice Burger's analysis of the potential for conflict between state trade secret laws and the federal patent laws? Is the risk associated with inadvertent disclosure of trade secrets high enough to encourage patent protection as an alternative? In a portion of his concurrence not quoted above, Justice Marshall argued that the possibility that an inventor might seek to keep a patentable invention secret was far from remote. *Kewanee*, 416 U.S. at 493-94 (Marshall, J., concurring). To support this argument, Justice Marshall could have cited the formula for Coca-Cola, which has been held as a secret for over a century. What considerations do you think motivated the Coca-Cola Company not to apply for a patent on this formula?

Would the risk calculation change if damages were the only available remedy for misappropriation of trade secrets? If a former employee of the Coca-Cola Company disclosed the formula to competitors in the beverage industry, would Justice Douglas' proposed remedy of tort damages for breach of contract be sufficient?

3. In many ways, the *Kewanee* decision is an exercise in realpolitik. The Court reasons that people will keep secrets whether the law protects them or not, and that they will engage in costly and often inefficient efforts to preserve their secrets if legal protection is not available. Should such considerations be relevant to the question of federal intellectual property preemption? Why or why not?

4. Is *Bonito Boats* consistent with *Goldstein* and *Kewanee*? How was the Florida direct molding statute different from (a) state trade secret protection at issue in *Kewanee*; (b) the California record piracy statute at issue in *Goldstein*; and (c) state labeling requirements as discussed in *Sears* and *Compco*? How does the *Bonito Boats* Court define the public domain?

5. Examine *Sears, Compco*, and *Bonito Boats* again. Do the preemptive effects identified in those cases flow from the federal patent statute or from the Intellectual Property Clause?

Note on the Intellectual Property Clause, the Commerce Clause, and the Treaty Power

Preemption cases concern the legitimacy of state efforts to regulate rights in intellectual goods. *Bonito Boats* signaled that the states are not free to legislate property-like rights in innovation that does not meet the threshold requirements for federal intellectual property protection. In recent years, however, Congress has also considered such efforts, experimenting with *sui generis* protection for vessel hull designs, *see* Chapter 4.A.3, pages 211-13 *supra*, and contemplating different proposals for database protection, *see* Chapter 4.E, pages 282-83 *supra*. These efforts have raised the question whether Congress is free to do what the states cannot. If there are limits on Congress' power to create new kinds of intellectual property rights, such limits must be found in the Constitution itself.

It is well established that Congress cannot use its power under the Intellectual Property Clause to grant protection to intellectual goods that fail to meet the constitutionally mandated standards of nonobviousness (for inventions) or originality (for writings). Over a century ago, when Congress first attempted to enact federal trademark protection, the Court held that the legislation could not stand as a valid exercise of Congress' power under the Intellectual Property Clause, because the subject matter that it protected — trademarks — was neither inventive nor original:

The ordinary trade-mark has no necessary relation to invention or discovery. The trade-mark recognized by the common law is generally the growth of a considerable period of use, rather than a sudden invention. It is often the result of accident rather than design, and when under the act of Congress it is sought to establish it by registration, neither originality, invention, discovery, science, nor art is in any way essential to the right conferred by that act. If we should endeavor to classify it under the head of writings of authors, the objections are equally strong. . . . The writings which are to be protected are *the fruits of intellectual labor*, embodied in the form of books, prints, engravings, and the like. The trade-mark may be, and generally, is, the adoption of something already in existence as the distinctive symbol of the party using it. At common law the exclusive right to it grows out of its *use*, and not its mere adoption. By the act of Congress this exclusive right attaches upon registration. But in neither case does it depend upon novelty, invention, discovery, or any work of the brain. . . .

The Trade-Mark Cases, 100 U.S. 82, 94 (1879).

What is less clear is whether the Commerce Clause gives Congress the power to enact such legislation. The Commerce Clause clearly gives Congress some authority to regulate uses of intellectual goods that touch on interstate commerce. The current federal trademark laws are an example of such legislation. *See, e.g.*, 15 U.S.C. §§1051 (allowing federal registration of marks used in commerce to identify goods or services), 1114 (prohibiting the use of a federally registered mark in commerce in a manner that is likely to cause confusion or deception) and 1125(a) (prohibiting the use of other indicia of origin in commerce in a manner that is likely to cause confusion or deception). The trademark laws, however, regulate confusing or deceptive conduct; they do not establish exclusive rights to marks in all contexts. If Congress attempted, instead, to use its commerce power to create broad, property-like rights in trademarks,[1] or in some other type of intellectual good, could it constitutionally do so? Or do the express limits on Congress' intellectual property power give rise to implied limits on the exercise of its other powers?

Many commentators have concluded that the Intellectual Property Clause, by necessary implication, imposes some limits on congressional exercise of the commerce power, and have argued that courts should enforce these limits strictly. *See, e.g.*, Yochai Benkler, *Constitutional Bounds of Database Protection: The Role of Judicial Review in the Creation and Definition of Private Rights in Information*, 15 Berkeley Tech. L.J. 535, 539-52 (2000); Paul J. Heald & Suzanna Sherry, *Implied Limits on the Legislative Power: The Intellectual Property Clause as an Absolute Constraint on Congress*, 2000 U. Ill. L. Rev. 1119; William Patry, *The Enumerated Powers Doctrine and Intellectual Property: An Imminent Constitutional Collision*, 67 Geo. Wash. L. Rev. 359 (1999). Such arguments often rely on *Railway Labor Executives' Ass'n v. Gibbons*, 455 U.S. 457 (1982), which involved a challenge to legislation granting special bankruptcy protections to a railroad company. The Bankruptcy Clause authorizes Congress to enact bankruptcy laws but requires that those protections be "uniform." U.S. Const., Art. I, §8, cl. 4. The *Gibbons* Court held that the legislation could not be sustained under the Commerce Clause because that result would override an express limitation on Congress' bankruptcy power. *See Gibbons*, 455 U.S. at 468-69. There is substantially less agreement, however, on the precise nature of the limits on Congress' commerce power in the intellectual property context and their consequences in particular cases.

Other commentators would accord Congress far greater deference, following the model established by the Court in *Eldred v. Ashcroft*, 537 U.S. 186 (2003), Chapter 3.B.2 *supra*. *See, e.g.*, Paul M. Schwartz & William Michael Treanor, Eldred *and* Lochner: *Copyright Term Extension and Intellectual Property as Constitutional Property*, 112 Yale L.J. 2331 (2003) (asserting that the implied-limits argument is conceptually akin to the *Lochner*-era vision of constitutionalized property rights and that both constitutional history and public policy militate in favor of judicial deference in matters relating to intellectual property).

---

1. Some commentators have suggested that the expansion of the Lanham Act to establish federal liability for diluting a famous mark does just that. *See, e.g.*, William Patry, *The Enumerated Powers Doctrine and Intellectual Property: An Imminent Constitutional Collision*, 67 Geo. Wash. L. Rev. 359, 392-93 (1999).

Several lower courts have addressed the limits on Congress' commerce power imposed by the Intellectual Property Clause. As discussed in Chapter 2.A., pages 55-57 *supra*, the Eleventh Circuit has held that anti-bootlegging legislation granting protection for unfixed performances is not "fundamentally inconsistent" with the "Writings" requirement of the Intellectual Property Clause because the anti-bootlegging legislation also promotes creativity. *United States v. Moghadam*, 175 F.3d 1269, 1280-81 (11th Cir. 1999), *cert. denied*, 529 U.S. 1036 (2000). In *KISS Catalog, Ltd. v. Passport International Productions, Inc.*, 405 F. Supp. 2d 1169 (C.D. Cal. 2005), the court concluded that it was "unlikely" that Congress had the power pursuant to the Intellectual Property Clause to adopt §1101(a)(3), the civil prohibition on bootlegging, but nonetheless concluded that the Commerce Clause empowered Congress to adopt that provision. *Id.* at 1172-73. The court did not address whether the unlimited duration of protection against bootlegging was fundamentally inconsistent with the Intellectual Property Clause because there was "an alternative source of constitutional authority" for Congress's actions in the Commerce Clause. *Id.* at 1175.

Finally, in *United States v. Martignon*, 492 F.3d 140 (2d Cir. 2007), the court acknowledged that the express limitations on congressional power in one clause can "in limited instances . . . apply externally to another clause." *Id.* at 144. The court reasoned that "Congress exceeds its power under the Commerce Clause by transgressing limitations of the Copyright Clause only when (1) the law it enacts is an exercise of the power granted Congress by the Copyright Clause and (2) the resulting law violates one or more specific limits of the Copyright Clause." *Id.* at 149. To determine when a law should be considered an exercise of Congress' Copyright Clause power, the court focused on the word "secure" in that clause and the history and context of the clause. It held that to be an exercise of Copyright Clause authority, the law must create, bestow, or allocate property rights in expression. At issue in *Martignon* was the criminal bootlegging prohibition, 18 U.S.C. §2319A. That law, the Second Circuit concluded, does not create or bestow any rights on an author or a creator of expression but rather "creates a power in the government to protect the interest of performers from commercial predations." *Id.* at 151. Because the law was not an exercise of authority pursuant to the Copyright Clause, the limitations in that clause did not apply, and the court determined the provision was a lawful exercise of Congress' Commerce Clause authority. The *Martignon* court specified that it was expressing "no opinion on Section 1101's constitutionality." *Id.* at 152 n.8. Additionally "because no commercial motive is required for a Section 1101 violation," the court specifically limited its holding to Section 2319A. *Id.*

The decisions in *Martignon* and *Moghadam* conflict and leave no definitive answer on the limits imposed by the Intellectual Property Clause. These cases, however, also raise a different constitutional problem: The anti-bootlegging laws were enacted following U.S. accession to the TRIPS Agreement and implemented the requirements imposed by that treaty. The Constitution vests the power to make treaties in the executive branch, subject to the advice and consent of the Senate. U.S. Const., Art. II, §2. Congress, in turn, has the power "To make all Laws which shall be necessary and proper for carrying into Execution . . . all other Powers vested by this Constitution in the Government of the United States, or in any Department or Officer thereof." *Id.* Art. I, §8, cl. 18. The Supreme Court has held that Congress may exceed some of the usual limits on its authority when it creates legislation to implement a treaty pursuant to its "necessary and proper" power. *See Missouri v. Holland*, 252 U.S. 416 (1920) (upholding federal legislation on the protection of migratory birds that reached beyond matters in interstate commerce); *De Geofroy v. Riggs*, 133 U.S. 258 (1890) (upholding federal legislation on the ability of aliens to inherit property despite states' traditional authority to determine rules of inheritance). In *Reid v. Covert*, 354 U.S. 1, 6-19 (1957), however, a plurality of the Court ruled that Congress may not invoke a treaty to justify overriding an express prohibition in the Constitution (holding that Congress could not constitutionally authorize nonjury trials before military tribunals of military dependents living overseas). The Supreme Court has not yet considered whether and to what extent the limits on Congress's intellectual property power constrain its implementation of intellectual property treaties.

NOTES AND QUESTIONS

1. How should the constitutionality of the anti-bootlegging legislation be decided? When Congress enacts a law granting property-like rights in creative expression that could not be sustained as an exercise of its intellectual property power, should it be invalidated, as *Martignon* suggests? Should it be evaluated using the Eleventh Circuit's "fundamentally inconsistent" standard? Or should courts evaluate such a law using a deferential "rational basis" standard similar to that applied in *Eldred*?

If you conclude that the *Martignon* approach is best, can it be reconciled with that of *Eldred*? If you conclude that the Eleventh Circuit's standard is the best one, do you agree that the anti-bootlegging legislation is not fundamentally inconsistent with the "Writings" requirement? Is it fundamentally inconsistent with the "limited Times" requirement? Would a law extending protection to unoriginal works be fundamentally inconsistent with the originality requirement described in *Feist*, Chapter 2.A.2 *supra*?

2. Do the limits on Congress' intellectual property power constitute express prohibitions that should constrain the exercise of its "necessary and proper" power as well? Would implementing a treaty obligation to protect unoriginal works contravene an express prohibition in the Constitution? *See Bridgeman Art Library, Ltd. v. Corel Corp.*, 36 F. Supp. 2d 191 (S.D.N.Y. 1999) (discussing this question but declining to reach it), Chapter 11.F *infra*. As you have learned in previous chapters, much copyright lawmaking now occurs in a global context. Is it desirable for the intellectual property power to constrain Congress in its implementation of treaty obligations?

3. Recall *Dastar Corp. v. Twentieth Century Fox Film Corp.*, 539 U.S. 23, 37 (2003), Chapter 5.E.3 *supra*, in which a unanimous Court held that interpreting §43(a) of the Lanham Act, 15 U.S.C. §1125(a), to bar the uncredited copying of a public domain work would "create[ ] a species of perpetual . . . copyright, which Congress may not do." Does this reasoning implicitly adopt the implied-limits argument?

4. Based on cases in which the Supreme Court has implied limits on congressional authority contained in other clauses of the Constitution, Professors Paul Heald and Suzanna Sherry distill four principles that they argue should constrain Congress' ability to enact legislation relating to intellectual property. See Paul J. Heald & Suzanna Sherry, *Implied Limits on the Legislative Power: The Intellectual Property Clause as an Absolute Constraint on Congress*, 2000 U. Ill. L. Rev. 1119. They argue that these principles should apply regardless of the constitutional clause under which Congress purports to act. First, the Intellectual Property Clause renders suspect only "legislation that imposes monopoly-like costs on the public through the granting of exclusive rights." *Id.* at 1160. Once scrutiny is triggered under this "Suspect Grant Principle," the Intellectual Property Clause limits congressional authority in accordance with three additional principles:

> . . . *The Quid Pro Quo Principle*: Congress may grant exclusive rights only if the grant is an attempt to secure a countervailing benefit to the public.
> . . . *The Authorship Principle*: A suspect grant must initially be made to either the true author of a writing or to the party responsible for a new advance in the useful arts.

> . . . *The Public Domain Principle*: A suspect grant may not significantly diminish access to the public domain.

Id. at 1162-67. The authors recognize that these principles "will merely frame the Court's rhetoric, providing the shape for the arguments that the Court will find most persuasive." *Id*. at 1167.

Applying their principles, Professors Heald and Sherry conclude that both the Sonny Bono Copyright Term Extension Act and the restoration of copyright protection under the Uruguay Round Agreement Implementation Act are very likely unconstitutional. *Id*. at 1168-76, 1179-83. Which of the above principles do these acts violate? Would using these principles to assess the constitutionality of the anti-bootlegging laws produce a different outcome than using the principles articulated by the court in *Martignon*? Recall that in *Eldred*, the Supreme Court upheld the constitutionality of the Sonny Bono Copyright Term Extension Act. Do you prefer the approach recommended by Professors Heald and Sherry to that taken in *Eldred*? As discussed in Chapter 3, the lower courts are in conflict concerning the constitutionality of the restoration provisions. Compare *Luck's Music Library, Inc. v. Gonzales*, 407 F.3d 1262 (D.C. Cir. 2005) (constitutional), with *Golan v. Holder*, 611 F. Supp. 2d 1165 (D. Colo. 2009) (unconstitutional).

5. Is §1201(a)(2) of the Digital Millennium Copyright Act (DMCA), the anti-device provision that you studied in Chapter 8.B *supra*, a valid exercise of Congress' powers under the Intellectual Property Clause? Under the Commerce Clause? *See United States v. Elcom*, 203 F. Supp. 2d 1111 (N.D. Cal. 2002) (holding that the DMCA is a valid exercise of the commerce power). Review Article 11 of the WIPO Copyright Treaty (WCT), page 662 *supra*. Should the fact that Congress enacted §1201(a)(2) to implement the WCT's requirements insulate it from constitutional challenge?

B. EXPRESS PREEMPTION UNDER THE 1976 ACT

As noted above, the Copyright Act of 1976 includes an express preemption provision. In relevant part, §301 states:

§301. Preemption with respect to other laws

(a) On and after January 1, 1978, all legal or equitable rights that are equivalent to any of the exclusive rights within the general scope of copyright as specified by section 106 in works of authorship that are fixed in a tangible medium of expression and come within the subject matter of copyright as specified by sections 102 and 103, whether created before or after that date and whether published or unpublished, are governed exclusively by this title. Thereafter, no person is entitled to any such right or equivalent right in any such work under the common law or statutes of any State.

(b) Nothing in this title annuls or limits any rights or remedies under the common law or statutes of any State with respect to—

(1) subject matter that does not come within the subject matter of copyright as specified by sections 102 and 103, including works of authorship not fixed in any tangible medium of expression; or

(2) any cause of action arising from undertakings commenced before January 1, 1978; or

(3) activities violating legal or equitable rights that are not equivalent to any of the exclusive rights within the general scope of copyright as specified by section 106; . . .

17 U.S.C. §301.

As you have already learned, one of the purposes of the 1976 Act was to extend federal copyright protection to all works fixed in a tangible medium of expression, whether or not they were "published," and to eliminate state common law copyright protection for such fixed but unpublished works. Section 301 accomplishes this: after 1977, states may extend common law copyright protection only to unfixed works (such as, for example, certain unfixed compositions or performances). The legislative history of §301 noted four reasons as justification for this rule:

> 1. One of the fundamental purposes behind the copyright clause of the Constitution, as shown in Madison's comments in The Federalist, was to promote national uniformity and to avoid the practical difficulties of determining and enforcing an author's rights under the differing laws and in the separate courts of the various States. Today, when the methods for dissemination of an author's work are incomparably broader and faster than they were in 1789, national uniformity in copyright protection is even more essential than it was then to carry out the constitutional intent.
>
> 2. "Publication," perhaps the most important single concept under the present law, also represents its most serious defect. . . . With the development of the 20th-century communications revolution, the concept of publication has become increasingly artificial and obscure. . . . [T]he courts have given "publication" a number of diverse interpretations, some of them radically different. A single Federal system would help to clear up this chaotic situation.
>
> 3. Enactment of section 301 would also implement the "limited times" provision of the Constitution (Const. Art. I, Sec. 8, cl. 8), which has become distorted under the traditional concept of "publication." Common law protection in "unpublished" works is now perpetual, no matter how widely they may be disseminated by means other than "publication"; the bill would place a time limit on the duration of exclusive rights in them. The provision would also aid scholarship and the dissemination of historical materials by making unpublished, undisseminated manuscripts available for publication after a reasonable period.
>
> 4. Adoption of a uniform national copyright system would greatly improve international dealings in copyrighted material. No other country has anything like our present dual system. In an era when copyrighted works can be disseminated instantaneously to every country on the globe, the need for effective international copyright relations, and the concomitant need for national uniformity, assume ever greater importance.

H.R. Rep. No. 94-1476, 94th Cong., 2d Sess. 129-30 (1976), *reprinted in* 1976 U.S.C.C.A.N. 5659, 5745-46.

Section 301 also indicates that its preemptive effect extends beyond areas formerly covered by common law copyright to any state law right that is "copyright-like." Thus, §301 created a new set of questions for courts to answer concerning the scope of federal preemption. Here the legislative history of §301 is less helpful. According to the House Report:

> As long as a work fits within one of the general subject matter categories of sections 102 and 103, the bill prevents the States from protecting it even if it fails to achieve Federal statutory copyright because it is too minimal or lacking in originality to qualify, or because it has fallen into the public domain. . . .
>
> The numbered clauses of subsection (b) list three general areas left unaffected by the preemption: (1) subject matter that does not come within the subject matter of copyright; (2) causes of action arising under State law before the effective date of the statute (Jan. 1, 1978); and (3) violations of rights that are not equivalent to any of the exclusive rights of copyright.
>
> The examples in clause (3), while not exhaustive, are intended to illustrate rights and remedies that are different in nature from the rights comprised in a copyright and that may continue to be

protected under State common law or statute. The evolving common law rights of "privacy," "publicity," and trade secrets, and the general laws of defamation and fraud, would remain unaffected as long as the causes of action contain elements, such as an invasion of personal rights or a breach of trust or confidentiality, that are different in kind from copyright infringement. Nothing in the bill derogates from the rights of parties to contract with each other and to sue for breaches of contract; however, to the extent that the unfair competition concept known as "interference with contract relations" is merely the equivalent of copyright protection, it would be preempted.

The last example listed in clause (3) — "deceptive trade practices such as passing off and false representation" — represents an effort to distinguish between those causes of action known as "unfair competition" that the copyright statute is not intended to preempt and those that it is. Section 301 is not intended to preempt common law protection in cases involving activities such as false labeling, fraudulent representation, and passing off even where the subject matter involved comes within the scope of the copyright statute.

"Misappropriation" is not necessarily synonymous with copyright infringement, and thus a cause of action labeled as "misappropriation" is not preempted if it is in fact based neither on a right within the general scope of copyright as specified by section 106 nor on a right equivalent thereto. For example, state law should have the flexibility to afford a remedy (under traditional principles of equity) against a consistent pattern of unauthorized appropriation by a competitor of the facts (i.e., not the literary expression) constituting "hot" news, whether in the traditional mold of *International News Service v. Associated Press*, 248 U.S. 215 (1918) . . . or in the newer form of data updates from scientific, business, or financial data bases. Likewise, a person having no trust or other relationship with the proprietor of a computerized data base should not be immunized from sanctions against electronically or cryptographically breaching the proprietor's security arrangements and accessing the proprietor's data. . . .

Id. at 5747-48.

As the above excerpt indicates, the version of §301 originally drafted by the House included an illustrative list of the sorts of state law rights that Congress did not intend to preempt. Other participants in the drafting process, however, felt differently about some of these state law causes of action. In particular, the Justice Department strongly objected to exempting misappropriation claims from statutory preemption. It argued that limiting state law claims to property in uncopyrightable facts should be one of the purposes of §301 and that excluding such claims would render §301's preemption provisions ineffectual. During debate on the bill before the full House, the list of allowable state law claims was removed by amendment. Neither the colloquy over the amendment nor any subsequent commentary explains whether Congress intended this deletion to have particular significance. The more likely explanation is that the deletion was simply a convenient way of avoiding substantial differences of opinion regarding §301's intended effect. The result is a legislative history that cannot reliably be cited as evidence of either intent to preempt or intent not to preempt particular state law claims. For an extended discussion of the legislative history of §301, see Howard B. Abrams, *Copyright, Misappropriation, and Preemption: Constitutional and Statutory Limits of State Law Protection*, 1983 Sup. Ct. Rev. 509, 537-48.

As we will see, courts and commentators are still wrestling with the question of §301's preemptive reach. The statements about rights of publicity, misappropriation, and breach of contract have proved particularly troublesome. We consider these state law claims in Sections C, D, and E, *infra*.

NOTES AND QUESTIONS

1. How would you determine the dividing line between state law claims that are "equivalent" to copyright claims and those that are not? The lower federal courts have

interpreted §301 to require a two-part analysis: First, the court must determine whether the state law claim concerns subject matter "within the ambit of copyright protection." *Harper & Row, Publishers, Inc. v. Nation Enters.*, 723 F.2d 195, 200 (2d Cir. 1983), *rev'd on other grounds*, 471 U.S. 539 (1985). If so, the court must then decide whether the state law cause of action asserted is "equivalent to any of the exclusive rights within the general scope of copyright." To make this second determination, it will consider whether the state law cause of action includes an "extra element" in addition to the elements of a copyright claim. *See id.* at 200. Is this approach consistent with the legislative history of §301?

2. Would *Goldstein* have been decided differently if the case had arisen under the 1976 Act? What light, if any, does the legislative history of §301 shed on this question?

Note that §301 does not alter the rule of *Goldstein* as to sound recordings fixed before Congress extended federal copyright protection to these works (which occurred on February 15, 1972). Section 301(c) expressly provides that for sound recordings fixed before February 15, 1972, state law rights and remedies are preserved until February 15, 2067. Note also that a work need not have originated in a state to be protected there. In *Capitol Records, Inc. v. Naxos of Am., Inc.*, 372 F.3d 471 (2d Cir. 2004), the court held that pre-1972 sound recordings that had passed into the public domain in their country of origin, Great Britain, might nonetheless be subject to state copyright protection in the U.S. The defendant had argued that any claim of state copyright protection was preempted by the Copyright Act's restoration provision, §104A, because Congress declined to extend restoration to foreign works now in the public domain in their home countries. The court rejected this argument, holding that §104A did not impliedly repeal §301(c). The court also certified the question of the scope of state copyright protection to New York's highest court because the Second Circuit "[l]ack[ed] any guidance from the New York courts on the question whether a common law copyright remains available for a work that has entered the public domain in the country of creation." *Id.* at 481. The New York Court of Appeals held that the recordings were entitled to protection under New York common law, notwithstanding expiration of the statutory copyrights protecting the sound recordings in the United Kingdom. *Capitol Records, Inc. v. Naxos of Am., Inc.*, 830 N.E.2d 250, 265 (N.Y. 2005).

3. Section 301(f) of the Copyright Act, which was added to the Act as part of the Visual Artists Rights Act of 1990 (VARA), expressly preempts "all legal or equitable rights that are equivalent to any of the rights conferred by section 106A with respect to works of visual art to which the rights conferred by section 106A apply." 17 U.S.C. §301(f)(1). This preemption provision further states that any rights or remedies relating to "activities violating legal or equitable rights which extend beyond the life of the author" are not preempted. *Id.* §301(f)(2). The preservation of state law protections for moral rights protection *post mortem* results from the Berne Convention. Recall that the Berne Convention requires protection for authors' moral rights. Recall also that Congress did not add moral rights protection to the Copyright Act in the Berne Convention Implementation Act, relying instead on the existence of alternative methods of protecting moral rights, including state law protections. The Berne Convention requires that moral rights protection last at least as long as protection for the economic rights of authors. Berne Conv., art. 6(2). Thus, even after Congress passed VARA, members of Congress felt that international obligations required preservation of state law *post mortem* protection for moral rights. 136 Cong. Rec. H13314 (daily ed. Oct. 27, 1990) (statement of Rep. Kastenmeier).

4. Recall that the Supreme Court has held that a statute can have preemptive effect outside the scope of its express preemption provision. *Geier v. American Honda Motor Co.*, 529 U.S. 861, 869-74 (2000); *Freightliner Corp. v. Myrick*, 514 U.S. 280, 288 (1995), *supra* pages 706-07.

Does §301 set outer limits on the preemptive effect of the Copyright Act? Several recent cases implicitly conclude that it does not.

Rano v. Sipa Press Inc., 987 F.2d 580 (9th Cir. 1993), and *Walthal v. Rusk*, 172 F.3d 481 (7th Cir. 1999), concerned efforts by authors to terminate oral licenses of unspecified duration that they had granted to distributors of their works. In both cases, the authors argued that the applicable state law allowed termination at will, while the distributors argued that this rule of state law was preempted by §203 of the Copyright Act, which governs termination of transfers. According to the distributors' argument, because §203 expressly provides that an author may terminate a grant after 35 years, the author may not terminate sooner even if state law otherwise would allow it. The Ninth Circuit accepted this argument, but the Seventh Circuit rejected it, reasoning that because §203 was intended to protect authors, a state law rule that allowed some authors to terminate even earlier created no conflict. *Rusk*, 172 F.3d at 484-85. The court further observed, however, that §203 would preempt a state law that required a contract to be enforced for longer than 35 years. *Id.* at 486. Thus, both courts implicitly accepted that the Copyright Act might exert preemptive effect even absent an equivalent state law claim. Which court do you think was right about the preemptive force of §203 in particular?

In re *Marriage of Worth*, 195 Cal. App. 3d 768 (1987), and *Rodrigue v. Rodrigue*, 218 F.3d 432 (5th Cir. 2000), *cert. denied*, 532 U.S. 905 (2001), concerned the proper disposition of copyrights in divorce proceedings. The cases arose in California and Louisiana, respectively, both community property states. Under community property principles, property acquired by either spouse during the marriage becomes the property of the marital community. Susan Worth and Veronica Rodrigue argued that this principle should extend to the copyrights in works created by their husbands during their respective marriages; Frederick Worth and George Rodrigue argued that applying this rule to their copyrights would conflict with §201(a) of the Copyright Act, which provides that a copyright vests initially in the author of the work. Both courts rejected this preemption argument, but not because either court concluded that §301 defines the full extent of federal copyright preemption. Instead, both held that the state community property rules effected a transfer of the copyrights by operation of law as expressly allowed by §201(d). Do you agree with this conclusion? *See* David Nimmer, *Copyright Ownership by the Marital Community: Evaluating* Worth, 36 UCLA L. Rev. 383 (1988); *see also* Lydia A. Nayo, *Revisiting* Worth: *The Copyright as Community Property Problem*, 30 U.S.F. L. Rev. 153 (1995).

Although the Supreme Court's intellectual property preemption cases and the language and legislative history of §301(a) raise some difficult questions about the scope of express and implied copyright preemption, in many cases the application of preemption principles to a challenged state law claim for relief is relatively straightforward. We will consider these "basic" copyright preemption cases briefly before moving on to more complicated preemption problems.

Harper & Row, Publishers, Inc. v. Nation Enterprises
723 F.2d 195 (2d Cir. 1983), rev'd on other grounds, 471 U.S. 539 (1985)

[To review the facts of this case, see Chapter 7.B, pages 535-40 *supra*. In addition to its copyright infringement claim against *The Nation*, Harper & Row also asserted state law claims for conversion and tortious interference with contract. The district court dismissed these claims as preempted under §301(a) of the Copyright Act.]

KAUFMAN, J.: . . . With regard to the issue of conversion, cross-appellants seem unable to decide how to plead the factual elements supporting their claim. Their amended complaint asserted conversion based on the unauthorized publication of *The Nation* article. In this court, they propound a theory which rests the tort upon the unlawful possession of the physical property of the Ford manuscript. In doing so, they have placed themselves neatly upon the horns of a dilemma. If unauthorized publication is the gravamen of their claim, then it is clear that the right they seek to protect is coextensive with an exclusive right already safeguarded by the Act — namely, control over reproduction and derivative use of copyrighted material. As such, their conversion claim is necessarily preempted.

Alternatively, Harper & Row and Reader's Digest suggest it is the possession of the papers themselves which lays the foundation for their claim. Conversion, as thus described, is a tort involving acts — possession and control of chattels — which are qualitatively different from those proscribed by copyright law, and which therefore are not subject to preemption. Cross-appellants have failed, however, to state a conversion claim. Conversion requires not merely temporary interference with property rights, but the exercise of unauthorized dominion and control to the complete exclusion of the rightful possessor. . . . Merely removing one of a number of copies of a manuscript (with or without permission) for a short time, copying parts of it, and returning it undamaged, constitutes far too insubstantial an interference with property rights to demonstrate conversion. . . .

With respect to the claim of tortious interference with contractual relations, cross-appellants' statement of the cause of action in their complaint suggests its infirmity. They allege that cross-appellees have committed a tort "by destroying the exclusive right of an author and his licensed publishers to exercise and enjoy the benefit of the pre-book publication serialization rights." If there is a qualitative difference between the asserted right and the exclusive right under the Act of preparing derivative works based on the copyrighted work, we are unable to discern it. In both cases, it is the act of unauthorized publication which causes the violation. The enjoyment of benefits from derivative use is so intimately bound up with the right itself that it could not possibly be deemed a separate element. . . . As the trial court noted, the fact that cross-appellants pleaded additional elements of awareness and intentional interference, not part of a copyright infringement claim, goes merely to the scope of the right; it does not establish qualitatively different conduct on the part of the infringing party, nor a fundamental non-equivalence between the state and federal rights implicated. . . .

Video Pipeline, Inc. v. Buena Vista Home Entertainment, Inc.
210 F. Supp. 2d 552 (D.N.J. 2002)

[Buena Vista Home Entertainment (BVHE) manufactures and distributes home video versions of copyrighted motion pictures. Video Pipeline compiles previews of home video products and markets the previews to home video distributors. Video Pipeline and BVHE entered into a "Master Clip License Agreement" that permitted Video Pipeline to exhibit copyrighted "Promotional Previews" supplied by BVHE. After Video Pipeline began streaming these previews via the Internet to online customers of its video retailer clients, BVHE rescinded the agreement and demanded return of the previews. Video Pipeline filed suit against BVHE, seeking a declaratory judgment that the Internet streaming did not infringe BVHE's copyrights or violate any of BVHE's other rights. Video Pipeline also began creating its own previews from videotape copies of movies sold by BVHE to Video Pipeline's clients (the "Clip Previews") and streaming those previews via the Internet. It amended its declaratory judgment complaint to include the Clip Previews. BVHE asserted counterclaims for copyright infringement and violation of various state law rights. Video Pipeline moved to dismiss a number of the state law claims on preemption grounds.]

SIMANDLE, J.: . . .

F. Federal Preemption of State Law Claims

. . . Under the Copyright Act . . . a state common law or statutory claim is preempted if: (1) the particular work to which the state law claim is being applied falls within the type of works protected by the Copyright Act under Sections 102 and 103; and (2) the state law seeks to vindicate "legal or equitable rights that are equivalent" to one of the bundle of exclusive rights already protected by copyright law under 17 U.S.C. §106. Thus, the preemption analysis encompasses both a "subject matter requirement," and a "general scope" or "equivalency" requirement, respectively. . . .

. . . [N]either party contests the applicability of the first prong. . . . The issue here is whether the state laws asserted by defendant BVHE in its counterclaims create rights which are "equivalent to" any of the exclusive rights granted to the copyright holder under §106. If so, they are preempted. The inquiry performed under the second prong of the §301 preemption analysis is as follows: [A] right which is "equivalent to copyright" is one which is infringed by the mere act of reproduction, performance, distribution or display. . . . If, under state law, the act of reproduction, performance, distribution or display . . . will in itself infringe the state created right, then such right is preempted. But if other elements are required, in addition to or instead of, the acts of reproduction, performance, distribution or display, in order to constitute a state created cause of action, then the right does not lie "within the general scope of copyright," and there is no preemption. . . .

1. Unfair Competition Claim

Plaintiff contends that defendant BVHE's state law unfair competition claim is preempted because it is based on misappropriation. . . . Plaintiff alleges that "[a]ll of defendant's state law claims are based upon the premise that the Promotional Previews furnished to Video Pipeline belong to Defendant and were misappropriated by Video Pipeline." Misappropriation, or "reverse passing off," is grounded in the alleged unauthorized copying and use of another's copyrighted expression, and thus fails the extra element test. And, as the Second Circuit in *Moody's Investors* determined, " '[S]tate law claims that rely on the misappropriation branch of unfair competition are preempted.' " [*Financial Info., Inc. v. Moody's Investors,*] 808 F.2d [204] at 208 (quoting *Warner Bros., Inc. v. American Broad. Cos., Inc.*, 720 F.2d 231, 247 (2d Cir. 1983)). In other words, reverse passing off occurs when one markets, sells, and represents the goods or services of another as its very own, and thus gives rise to an actionable claim for reproducing, distributing, or displaying copyrighted works.

. . . Defendant essentially maintains that plaintiff "passed off" its clip previews, which contain defendant's trademarks, as having been created and produced by defendant. . . .

Unfair competition claims involving "passing off" are generally not preempted by federal copyright law. . . . As defendant BVHE correctly contends, passing off claims are not preempted primarily because such claims include the extra element of deception or misrepresentation which is not an element of a copyright claim. . . .

Accordingly, defendant BVHE's counterclaim specifically asserting that plaintiff engaged in "passing off" under state law unfair competition can be construed to encompass the allegation that Video Pipeline is distributing its own products, here clip previews, and representing to the public that they are those of defendant BVHE. This necessarily involves the extra element of misrepresentation or deception which is not an element for copyright infringement. As such, the "passing off" claim is an actionable claim not preempted by the federal Copyright Act. . . .

3. Unjust Enrichment Claim

Defendant BVHE argues that its unjust enrichment claim is not federally preempted because such claim requires "extra elements" that renders it qualitatively different from a claim for copyright infringement. . . .

The foundation of defendant's claim is that plaintiff has exploited BVHE's intellectual property without compensating BVHE for the benefits derived from such use. Here, BVHE alleges that "BVHE voluntarily conferred upon Video Pipeline the benefits flowing from use of BVHE's valuable intellectual property," and that plaintiff Video Pipeline "would be unjustly enriched if it were permitted to retain the benefits it has reaped from the unauthorized use of BVHE's intellectual property. . . ." Although defendant BVHE refers to the terms of the Master Clip License Agreement, its claim that plaintiff Video Pipeline is "exploiting" defendant BVHE's works necessarily involves plaintiff's acts in reproducing, distributing and displaying defendant's works, all of which are encompassed in rights protected under copyright law. . . .

. . . In this case, where a claim for breach of implied contract is absent, defendant BVHE's claim for unjust enrichment is . . . duplicative of the relief sought under copyright law.

Because the rights asserted under the unjust enrichment claim in the circumstances of this case generally are equivalent to those protected by federal copyright law, and because defendant BVHE fails to assert an extra element that would render its claim qualitatively distinct from a claim seeking compensation for copyright infringement, defendant's unjust enrichment claim is preempted under federal copyright law. . . .

4. Conversion and Replevin Claims

Defendant BVHE asserts that its conversion and replevin claims are not preempted because these claims involve rights to tangible property not equivalent to the exclusive rights protected by copyright law. "The torts of conversion and trespass relate to interference with tangible rather than intangible property, and hence should be held immune from preemption." 1 Nimmer on Copyright ¶1.01[B][1][i], at 1-41 (2001). . . .

Here, as discussed above, defendant BVHE's conversion claim seeks return of "its tangible property . . . i.e., each of the original Trailers BVHE provided to Video Pipeline." Defendant's replevin claim alleges that "BVHE . . . ha[s] an immediate right of possession to the original Trailers, their tangible property, previously provided to Video Pipeline, which Video Pipeline continues to wrongly hold." Defendant BVHE's claim thus involves tangible, physical property, the rights to which are distinctly different from those rights involved in defendant's copyright counterclaims. To the extent that BVHE seeks the return of such items and alleges that plaintiff continues to wrongly hold such items, the rights it asserts under its state law conversion and replevin claims are not equivalent to those protected by the federal copyright laws, which govern the reproduction, performance, distribution, and display of copyrighted works. Accordingly, defendant's state law conversion and replevin claims are not preempted. . . .

NOTES AND QUESTIONS

1. As *Harper & Row* and *Video Pipeline* illustrate, §301(a) is designed to separate those state law claims that are fundamentally about copying (or one of the other rights enumerated in §106) from those that are fundamentally about something else. Note that both courts inquire whether the challenged state law claim has a "separate" or "additional" element that would distinguish it from a copying claim. Keeping this test in mind, how would you resolve the question of preemption in the following cases? The answers are in Note 2.

   a. The Cool Chicks, a rock band, sue Dave, their former manager, for unjust enrichment. As the basis for this claim, the Cool Chicks allege that Dave improperly retained certain master recordings belonging to the band and exploited these recordings for his own benefit.
   b. The Cool Chicks, a rock band, sue Dave, their former manager, for unjust enrichment. As the basis for this claim, the Cool Chicks allege that Dave improperly managed the band's artistic properties and has failed to account for royalties due from the band's recordings.
   c. The Cool Chicks, a rock band, sue Dave, their former manager, for conversion. As the basis for this claim, the Cool Chicks allege that Dave has improperly retained certain master recordings belonging to the band.
   d. Hilltop, a software company, sues Valley Software, its main rival, for unfair competition. As the basis for this claim, Hilltop alleges that Valley has approached its main customers and falsely represented that Valley's own software program, which costs less than Hilltop's, will perform the same functions as Hilltop's program.
   e. Hilltop, a software company, sues Valley Software, its main rival, for unfair competition. As the basis for this claim, Hilltop alleges that Valley has approached its main customers and offered to sell them a program that will perform the same functions in the same way as Hilltop's program, but for a lower price. In fact, Valley's program does perform the same functions in the same way as Hilltop's program.
   f. Hilltop, a software company, sues Valley Software, its main rival, for misappropriation of trade secrets. As the basis for this claim, Hilltop alleges that Valley hired three of Hilltop's former employees and acquired information from them about Hilltop's software that Valley knew or had reason to know was a valuable trade secret belonging to Hilltop.
   g. Jack and Jill, the principals of Hilltop, decide to dissolve their business partnership. Jill, who managed the financial side of the business, sues Jack, who managed the technical side of the business, for breach of fiduciary duty. As the basis for this claim, Jill alleges that Jack sold hundreds of copies of Hilltop's software "out the back door" without reporting the sales. Jack responds that he is the sole author of the program in question and that Jill's claim is preempted by §101 of the Copyright Act, which defines the requirements for joint authorship.

2. Here are the answers to the problems in Question 1:

   a. While it is unclear exactly how Dave is exploiting the recordings—i.e., whether Dave is selling copies of the recordings or licensing unauthorized performances of the musical compositions — the gravamen of the claim appears to be that Dave is exercising rights that belong to the Cool Chicks under §106, so the claim is preempted.

b. Unlike the first unjust enrichment claim, this claim does not center on the unauthorized exploitation of copyrighted works, but rather on the receipt and retention of monetary benefits to which Dave was not entitled. The gravamen of the claim is that Dave owes the Cool Chicks an accounting, and this claim is not preempted.

c. This claim alleges conversion of physical property, not intangible property. It is not preempted.

d. This claim is grounded on an allegedly false representation by Valley about the capabilities of its software as compared to Hilltop's software. It is not preempted.

e. Unlike the first unfair competition claim, this claim seems merely to allege that Valley copied Hilltop's software and is seeking to compete with Hilltop in the marketplace. It is preempted.

f. Hilltop's trade secret claim alleges something different than mere copying. Hilltop alleges that Valley had an independent duty, arising from state trade secret law, not to obtain information that Valley knows is a trade secret from Hilltop's former employees. This claim is not preempted.

g. Although Jack is trying to make it appear as though Jill is simply asserting an authorship claim that she does not have and seeking an accounting as a coauthor, that is not what Jill is arguing. Nor is Jill simply complaining about unauthorized copying. Instead, Jill is arguing that Jack's obligations as a fiduciary for the partnership required him to account for the sales that he made. This latter claim is not preempted.

3. Although state law claims for relief are often joined with copyright infringement claims, sometimes the plaintiff does not assert a copyright claim. As a result of the well-pleaded complaint rule, unless the case presents an independent ground for federal subject matter jurisdiction, lawsuits in this latter group will be filed in state court. If there is no other basis for removing the action to federal court (e.g., diversity jurisdiction), may the defendant seek removal on the theory that the claim, however styled on the face of the plaintiff's complaint, is "really" a copyright infringement claim? Relying on the "complete preemption" doctrine, which applies when a federal statute substitutes an exclusive federal remedy in place of the remedies formerly afforded under state law, several courts have concluded that the defendant may seek removal on such a theory. *See Ritchie v. Williams*, 395 F.3d 283 (6th Cir. 2005); *Briarpatch Ltd., L.P. v. Phoenix Pictures, Inc.*, 373 F.3d 296 (2d Cir. 2004), *cert. denied*, 544 U.S. 949 (2005); *Rosciszewski v. Arete Assoc., Inc.*, 1 F.3d 225 (4th Cir. 1993). Completely preempted claims generally are dismissed on preemption grounds immediately following removal. Alternatively, the claims may be treated as copyright infringement claims and evaluated as such. *See Ritchie*, 395 F.3d at 289 (dismissing completely preempted claims because, as copyright claims, they were barred by the three-year statute of limitations in 17 U.S.C. §507(b)).

Note that any removal petition must be filed no later than 30 days after the basis for removal first becomes apparent. 28 U.S.C. §1446. Defendants that miss this deadline, or defendants that find their attempts at removal rejected by the district court, must present their preemption arguments to the state courts, which are significantly less familiar with federal copyright jurisprudence. Whenever copyrightable material furnishes part of the basis for a lawsuit, it is advisable to study the complaint and the possibilities for removal carefully and promptly.

C. THE RIGHT OF PUBLICITY

The state law right of publicity[1] had its genesis in privacy-related concerns, but the right has evolved as a right separate from that of privacy and rests on a different policy basis. While the right of privacy protects against certain intrusions on a person's dignity, the right of publicity protects individuals against unauthorized (and uncompensated) appropriation of their identities for commercial purposes.

Although all individuals have rights of publicity, most disputes involve celebrities.[2] Such suits illustrate the difference between the rights of privacy and publicity:

> Well known personalities connected with [the entertainment] industries do not seek . . . "solitude and privacy". . . . Their concern is rather with publicity, which may be regarded as the reverse side of the coin of privacy. . . . [A]lthough the well known personality does not wish to hide his light under a bushel of privacy, neither does he wish to have his name, photograph, and likeness reproduced and publicized without his consent or without remuneration to him.

Melville B. Nimmer, *The Right of Publicity*, 19 Law & Contemp. Probs. 203, 203-04 (1968), *cited in* 4 J. Thomas McCarthy, McCarthy on Trademarks and Unfair Competition, §28:4 at 28-6 (2003).

Courts have recognized the right of publicity as a property right and its infringement as a commercial tort. In general, to sustain a cause of action for infringement of the right of publicity, the plaintiff must show that she has a right in the identity (often also called "persona") at issue and that right was infringed by unauthorized use likely to cause damage to the identity's commercial value.

Recall the two requirements of §301(a) that must be satisfied before the Copyright Act will preempt a state law cause of action. On its face, a right of publicity claim seems to survive a preemption analysis because the "work" that is the subject of the action is not a "work[ ] of authorship . . . fixed in a tangible medium of expression and . . . within the subject matter of copyright." 17 U.S.C. §301(a). Instead, the work is a person's identity. Unfortunately, matters are not so simple. The identity is often portrayed in a medium associated with copyrighted works. Consider the following two cases.

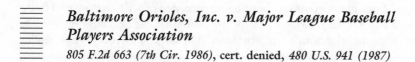

Baltimore Orioles, Inc. v. Major League Baseball Players Association
805 F.2d 663 (7th Cir. 1986), cert. denied, 480 U.S. 941 (1987)

ESCHBACH, J.: The primary issue involved in this appeal is whether major league baseball clubs [the Clubs] own exclusive rights to the televised performances of major league baseball players [the Players] during major league baseball games. . . .

[As part of their argument, the players alleged that the televised performances infringed their rights of publicity. The court determined that the telecasts were copyrightable and the

---

1. Some states have codified the right in statutes, while in others it remains a common law doctrine. In some states, such as California, individuals may have rights under both the relevant statute and common law.

2. Individuals may also sue for invasion of privacy for appropriation of their names or likenesses by another for commercial benefit, and most non-celebrities choose this route.

baseball clubs owned the copyrights in the telecasts rather than the players. It then turned to the question whether the Copyright Act preempted the right of publicity claims.]

2. Preemption under 17 U.S.C. §301(a)

Although the Clubs own the copyright to the telecasts of major league baseball games, the Players claim that broadcasts of these games made without their express consent violate their rights to publicity in their performances. For the reasons stated below, we hold that the Clubs' copyright in the telecasts of major league baseball games preempts the Players' rights of publicity in their game-time performances.

[The court then quoted §301(a) and noted its two-prong test for preemption:] First, the work in which the right is asserted must be fixed in tangible form and come within the subject matter of copyright as specified in §102. Second, the right must be equivalent to any of the rights specified in §106. . . .

a. Section 102 Test

The works in which the Players claim rights are the telecasts of major league baseball games. . . . [T]he telecasts are fixed in tangible form because they are recorded simultaneously with their transmission and are audiovisual works which come within the subject matter of copyright. The first condition for preemption is, therefore, satisfied.

The Players argue, however, that the works in which they claim rights are their performances, rather than the telecasts of the games in which they play, and that performances *per se* are not fixed in tangible form. They contend that, since the works in which they assert rights are not fixed in tangible form, their rights of publicity in their performances are not subject to preemption. We disagree. . . . The Players' performances are embodied in a copy, *viz,* the videotape of the telecast, from which the performances can be perceived, reproduced, and otherwise communicated indefinitely. Hence, their performances are fixed in tangible form, and any property rights in the performances that are equivalent to any of the rights encompassed in a copyright are preempted.

It is, of course, true that unrecorded performances *per se* are not fixed in tangible form. Among the many such works not fixed in tangible form are "choreography that has never been filmed or notated, an extemporaneous speech, 'original works of authorship' communicated solely through conversations or live broadcasts, and a dramatic sketch or musical composition improvised or developed from memory and without being recorded or written down." House Report at 131, *reprinted in* 1976 U.S. Code Cong. & Ad. News at 5747. Because such works are not fixed in tangible form, rights in such works are not subject to preemption under §301(a). Indeed, §301(b), which represents the obverse of §301(a), expressly allows the states to confer common law copyright protection upon such works. . . . Nonetheless, once a performance is reduced to tangible form, there is no distinction between the performance and the recording of the performance for the purpose of preemption under §301(a). Thus, if a baseball game were not broadcast or were telecast without being recorded, the Players' performances similarly would not be fixed in tangible form and their rights of publicity would not be subject to preemption. *See* Nimmer, §1.08[C] (using the example of a live broadcast of a baseball game). By virtue of being videotaped, however, the Players' performances are fixed in tangible form, and any rights of publicity in their performances that are equivalent to the rights contained in the copyright of the telecast are preempted.[22]

---

22. An example illustrates this point. Take the case of *Zacchini v. Scripps-Howard Broadcasting Co.*, 433 U.S. 562 (1977), in which Hugo Zacchini sued a television station for violating his right of publicity by broadcasting the

The Players also contend that to be a "work[ ] of authorship that . . . [is] fixed in a tangible medium of expression" within the scope of §301(a), a work must be copyrightable. They assert that the works in which they claim rights, namely their performances, are not copyrightable because they lack sufficient creativity. They consequently conclude that because the works in which they claim rights are not works within the meaning of §301(a), their rights of publicity are not subject to preemption. There is a short answer to this argument. Congress contemplated that "[a]s long as a work fits within one of the general subject matter categories of section 102 and 103, . . . [section 301(a)] prevents the States from protecting it even if it fails to achieve Federal copyright because it is too minimal or lacking in originality to qualify." House Report at 131, *reprinted in* 1976 U.S. Code Cong. & Ad. News at 5747. Hence, §301(a) preempts all equivalent state-law rights claimed in any work within the subject matter of copyright whether or not the work embodies any creativity. Regardless of the creativity of the Players' performances, the works in which they assert rights are copyrightable works which come within the scope of §301(a) because of the creative contributions of the individuals responsible for recording the Players' performances. Therefore, the Players' rights of publicity in their performances are preempted if they are equivalent to any of the bundle of rights encompassed in a copyright.[24]

b. Section 106 Test

A right under state law is "equivalent" to one of the rights within the general scope of copyright if it is violated by the exercise of any of the rights set forth in §106. . . . [A] right is equivalent to one of the rights comprised by a copyright if it "is infringed by the mere act of reproduction, performance, distribution or display." . . .

In particular, the right to "perform" an audiovisual work means the right "to show its images in any sequence or to make the sounds accompanying it audible." 17 U.S.C. §101 (definition of "perform"). Thus, the right to perform an audiovisual work encompasses the right to broadcast it. *See* House Report at 63, *reprinted in* 1976 U.S. Code Cong. & Ad. News at 5676-77 ("[A] broadcasting system is performing when it transmits . . . [a] performance . . . ; a local broadcaster is performing when it transmits the network broadcast;

---

entirety of his human cannonball act. *Zacchini* was decided before §301(a) became effective, but let us suppose that the same case arises again today. Assuming that Zacchini did not videotape or otherwise record his performance, his human cannonball act would not be fixed in tangible form and could not be copyrighted. Nonetheless, because the work in which he asserts rights would not be fixed in a tangible medium of expression, his right of publicity in his performance would not be subject to preemption. Thus, if a television station were to broadcast his act, he still could sue successfully for violation of his right of publicity in his performance. Merely that the television station might videotape its telecast would not grant the station a copyright in the broadcast of Zacchini's performance or preempt Zacchini's right of publicity. To be "fixed" in tangible form, a work must be recorded "by or under the authority of the author," here Zacchini. *See* 17 U.S.C. §101 (definition of "fixed"). Because Zacchini did not consent to the telecast, the broadcast could not be "fixed" for the purpose of copyrightability and Zacchini's right of publicity would not be subject to preemption.

Assume, however, that Zacchini, after the fashion of championship prize fights, transmitted his live act over closed-circuit television and simultaneously recorded it for later broadcast over a cable television network, and that the satellite signal for the closed-circuit show was intercepted and rebroadcast by a television station. Zacchini sues the station for violation of his copyright and his right to publicity. He would prevail on the copyright infringement claim only. . . . [B]ecause his act was videotaped, the work in which he asserts rights would be fixed in tangible form and thus copyrightable. Assuming *arguendo* that a right of publicity is equivalent to one of the rights encompassed in a copyright — a subject that we soon shall take up — his right of publicity in his performance would be preempted. . . .

24. The Players' rights of publicity in their performances are preempted only if they would be violated by the exercise of the Clubs' copyrights in the telecasts. A player's right of publicity in his name or likeness would not be preempted if a company, without the consent of the player, used the player's name to advertise its product . . . placed the player's photograph on a baseball trading card . . . or marketed a game based upon the player's career statistics. . . .

a cable television system is performing when it retransmits the broadcast to its subscribers. . . ."); *see also* Nimmer, §8.14[B]. Hence, a right in a work that is conferred by state law is equivalent to the right to perform a telecast of that work if the state-law right is infringed merely by broadcasting the work.

In this case, the Players claim a right of publicity in their performances. As a number of courts have held, a right of publicity in a performance is violated by a televised broadcast of the performance. . . . Indeed, from the start of this litigation, the Players consistently have maintained that their rights of publicity permit them to control telecasts of their performances, and that televised broadcasts of their performances made without their consent violate their rights of publicity in their performances. . . . Because the exercise of the Clubs' right to broadcast telecasts of the games infringes the Players' rights of publicity in their performances, the Players' rights of publicity are equivalent to at least one of the rights encompassed by copyright, *viz.*, the right to perform an audiovisual work. Since the works in which the Players claim rights are fixed in tangible form and come within the subject matter of copyright, the Players' rights of publicity in their performances are preempted.

The Players argue that their rights of publicity in their performances are not equivalent to the rights contained in a copyright because rights of publicity and copyrights serve different interests.[28] In their view, the purpose of federal copyright law is to secure a benefit to the public, but the purpose of state statutory or common law concerning rights of publicity is to protect individual pecuniary interests. We disagree.

The purpose of federal copyright protection is to benefit the public by encouraging works in which it is interested. To induce individuals to undertake the personal sacrifices necessary to create such works, federal copyright law extends to the authors of such works a limited monopoly to reap the rewards of their endeavors. . . . Contrary to the Players' contention, the interest underlying the recognition of the right of publicity also is the promotion of performances that appeal to the public. The reason that state law protects individual pecuniary interests is to provide an incentive to performers to invest the time and resources required to develop such performances. In *Zacchini v. Scripps-Howard Broadcasting Co.*, 433 U.S. 562 (1977), the principal case on which the Players rely for their assertion that different interests underlie copyright and the right to publicity, the Supreme Court recognized that the interest behind federal copyright protection is the advancement of the public welfare through the encouragement of individual effort by personal gain, *id.* at 576 . . . and that a state's interest in affording a

---

28. The Players cite to four opinions to support their assertion that §301(a) does not preempt the right of publicity. *See Factors Etc., Inc. v. Pro Arts, Inc.*, 652 F.2d 278, 289 (2d Cir. 1981) (Mansfield, J., dissenting), *cert. denied*, 456 U.S. 927 (1982); *Bi-Rite Enterprises, Inc. v. Button Master*, 555 F. Supp. 1188, 1201 (S.D.N.Y. 1983); *Apigram Publishing Co. v. Factors Etc., Inc.*, No. C 78-525, slip op. (N.D. Ohio July 30, 1980) (available on LEXIS); *Lugosi v. Universal Pictures*, 25 Cal. 3d 813, 850, 603 P.2d 425, 448, 160 Cal. Rptr. 323, 346 (1979) (Bird, C.J., dissenting). Each opinion is premised upon an erroneous analysis of preemption. The *Factors* dissent, the *Bi-Rite* court, and the *Lugosi* dissent assert without discussion that the right of publicity is not preempted because the work that it protects — a public figure's persona — cannot be fixed in a tangible medium of expression. We disagree. Because a performance is fixed in tangible form when it is recorded, a right of publicity in a performance that has been reduced to tangible form is subject to preemption.

The *Apigram* court stated without extended discussion or citation to authority that the right of publicity is not preempted because it requires additional elements other than the reproduction, performance, distribution or display of a copyrighted work. We disagree. . . . Contrary to the belief of the *Apigram* court, the right of publicity does not require an invasion of personal privacy to make out a cause of action. It is true that the rights of publicity and of privacy evolved from similar origins; however, whereas the right of privacy protects against intrusions on seclusion, public disclosure of private facts, and casting an individual in a false light in the public eye, the right of publicity protects against the unauthorized exploitation of names, likenesses, personalities, and performances that have acquired value for the very reason that they are known to the public. . . . Because the right of publicity does not require a qualitatively different additional element, it is equivalent to a copyright and is preempted to the extent that it is claimed in a tangible work within the subject matter of copyright.

cause of action for violation of the right to publicity "is closely analogous to the goals of patent and copyright law." *Id.* at 573. . . . Because the right of publicity does not differ in kind from copyright, the Players' rights of publicity in their performances cannot escape preemption. . . .

≡ **Brown v. Ames**
≡ *201 F.3d 654 (5th Cir. 2000)*

JONES, J.: Appellants Collectibles and Ames principally appeal the district court's determination that appellees' state law claims for violation of their rights of publicity are not preempted by the Copyright Act. The misappropriation consisted of appellants' unauthorized use of appellees' names and likenesses to market appellees' musical performances on CD's and audio cassettes for which appellants also lacked copyrights. Because a person's name and likeness in themselves are not copyrightable, and because the state law tort for misappropriation does not conflict with federal copyright law, appellees' claims are not preempted. . . .

I. Factual and Procedural History

Collectibles is a record label that distributes and sells music recordings, especially repackaged vintage recordings. Ames is a music producer specializing in Texas blues. Appellees are individual blues musicians, songwriters, music producers or heirs of such.

Around 1990, Ames, d/b/a Home Cooking Records, licensed to Collectibles for commercial exploitation master recordings that included performances by appellees. The written license agreements also purported to give Collectibles the right to use the names, photographs, likenesses and biographical material of all those whose performances were on the master recordings. . . . Using the master recordings, Collectibles manufactured and distributed cassettes and CD's, as well as music catalogs, with the names and sometimes the likenesses of the performers on or in them. . . .

In 1994, appellees sued Ames, Collectibles and Jerry and Nina Greene, the owners of Collectibles. . . . Appellees' actions for copyright infringement, violations of the Lanham Act and for misappropriation of name or likeness under Texas state law proceeded to a jury trial. . . . The jury . . . found that the defendants had misappropriated the names and likenesses of the appellees and had infringed (in the case of Collectibles, innocently) copyrights held by some of the appellees. . . .

Collectibles and Ames have appealed. . . . [T]hey assert [*inter alia*] that the Copyright Act preempts the misappropriation claims. . . .

II. Discussion . . .

In Texas, the tort of misappropriation provides protection from the unauthorized appropriation of one's name, image or likeness. . . . It is best understood as a species of the right of publicity or of privacy. . . . To prevail, a plaintiff must prove that (1) the defendant misappropriated the plaintiff's name or likeness for the value associated with it and not in an incidental manner or for a newsworthy purpose; (2) the plaintiff can be identified from the publication; and (3) the defendant derived some advantage or benefit. . . .

Appellants argue strenuously that appellees have not presented an independent action for misappropriation. Because appellees' names and/or likenesses were used to identify their musical works in Collectibles' CD's, tapes and catalogs, appellants assert that the core of the misappropriation and copyright infringement claims is the same, compelling preemption under section 301 of the misappropriation claims.

Appellants' argument ignores, however, that the content of the right protected by the misappropriation tort does not fall into the subject matter of copyright, as section 301 requires. As the district court correctly recognized, the tort for misappropriation of name or likeness protects "the interest of the individual in the exclusive use of his own identity, in so far as it is represented by his name or likeness, and in so far as the use may be of benefit to him or to others." Restatement (Second) of Torts §652C (1977). In other words, the tort of misappropriation of name or likeness protects a person's *persona*. A *persona* does not fall within the subject matter of copyright—it does not consist of "a 'writing' of an 'author' within the meaning of the Copyright Clause of the Constitution." Nimmer, *supra*, §1.01[B][1][c]; *Jarvis v. A&M Records*, 827 F. Supp. 282, 297 (D.N.J. 1993); *Bi-Rite Enterprises, Inc. v. Button Master*, 555 F. Supp. 1188, 1201 (S.D.N.Y. 1983); *Apigram Publishing Co. v. Factors, Etc., Inc.*, 1980 WL 2047 (N.D. Ohio July 30, 1980) (available on WESTLAW); *Lugosi v. Universal Pictures*, 25 Cal. 3d 813, 849, 160 Cal. Rptr. 323, 603 P.2d 425 (1979) (Bird, C.J., dissenting). Furthermore, contrary to appellants' implications, appellees' names and likenesses do not become copyrightable simply because they are used to identify the source of a copyrighted work. Therefore, their misappropriation claims do not fit the terms of §301 preemption. . . .

One arguably analogous case has held to the contrary. In *Baltimore Orioles v. Major League Baseball Players Ass'n*, 805 F.2d 663 (7th Cir. 1986), the Seventh Circuit held that the Copyright Act preempted baseball players' rights of publicity in their performances. The court's conclusion turned on its controversial decision that performances in a baseball game were within the subject matter of copyright because the videotape of the game fixed the players' performances in tangible form. *See id.* at 674-76. *Baltimore Orioles*, however, has been heavily criticized for holding that a baseball game is a protectable work of authorship simply because the performance was recorded on videotape that was itself copyrightable. . . . In any event, *Baltimore Orioles* is distinguishable from this case because the right of publicity claimed by the baseball players was essentially a right to prevent rebroadcast of games whose broadcast rights were already owned by the clubs. . . . The case before us offers no such complication, as the appellee performers did not give permission to the appellants to market their recordings or photographs. We decline appellants' invitation to find name or likeness copyrightable simply because they are placed on CD's and tapes or in catalogs that have copyrightable subject matter recorded on them.

The fact that section 301 does not apply does not end the inquiry, however. Although section 301 preemption is not appropriate, conflict preemption might be. The Supremacy Clause dictates that a state law that obstructs the accomplishment of the full purposes and objectives of Congress is preempted. *See Hines v. Davidowitz*, 312 U.S. 52, 67 . . . (1941). . . .

Although appellants argue vigorously that not preempting appellees' misappropriation claims would undermine the copyright system, several considerations belie this claim. First, the right of publicity that the misappropriation tort protects promotes the major objective of the Copyright Act—to support and encourage artistic and scientific endeavors. Second, the record here indicates that industry practice may be to transfer rights in a performer's name or likeness when the copyright is transferred. If that is the case, right of publicity claims will rarely interfere with a copyright holder's use of the creator's name or likeness in connection with the copyright. Third, common law on the right of publicity appears ordinarily to permit an authorized publisher or distributor to use name or likeness to identify truthfully the author or creator of the goods. . . .

Only if states allowed similar claims against authorized publishers or distributors of a work (whether through copyright or the public domain) would the purposes and objectives of the Copyright Act be adversely affected. Such suits would interfere to some extent with the uniformity of the copyright system and the exploitation of works in the public domain. Currently, however, no state seems to have such a law, and the general rule is as described above. . . . Thus, because the tort would currently not be sustainable against valid copyright holders, allowing the claim in this context does not impede the transfer of copyrights or the uniformity of the copyright system.

Supreme Court precedent suggesting that courts should steer a middle ground in considering Copyright Act preemption cases supports our conclusion that appellees' misappropriation claims are not preempted. The leading Supreme Court case on preemption in the intellectual property field, *Bonito Boats, Inc. v. Thunder Craft Boats, Inc.*, 489 U.S. 141 (1989), found that a state statute providing patent-like protection for ideas deemed unprotected under federal patent law was preempted, but warned that "the States remain free to promote originality and creativity in their own domains." *Id.* at 165. . . . The Court went on to state that: "the case for federal pre-emption is particularly weak where Congress has indicated its awareness of the operation of state law in a field of federal interest, and has nonetheless decided to 'stand by both concepts and to tolerate whatever tension there [is] between them.'" *Id.* at 166-67. . . . As noted in the legislative history of section 301, Congress was aware of the operation of state law on the rights of privacy and publicity, and indicated its intention that such state law causes of action remain. *See* House Report at 132, *reprinted in* 1976 U.S.C.C.A.N. at 5748.

Since appellees' misappropriation claims neither fall within the subject matter of copyright nor conflict with the purposes and objectives of the Copyright Act, the claims were not preempted. . . .

NOTES AND QUESTIONS

1. The first requirement for finding preemption under §301 is that the work in which the right is asserted must be fixed in tangible form and come within the subject matter of copyright as specified in §102. Reread footnote 22 in *Baltimore Orioles*, page 732 *supra*. Were the major league baseball games "fixed" under the statutory language? How does the answer to the fixation question affect the preemption analysis? Should the existence of a "fixed" copy of a performance affect whether a particular state law cause of action is preempted? Be sure to read §301(b)(1) closely. Does the *Brown* approach to this first requirement make more sense?

2. Both courts identify the purpose behind protecting rights of publicity as similar to that of copyright law. For the *Baltimore Orioles* court, this similarity in purpose further supports its conclusion that the claim is preempted. For the *Brown* court, the similarity in purpose supports its conclusion that the claim is not preempted. While this may seem inconsistent, the *Baltimore Orioles* court pointed to the similarity in purpose as evidence that the type of right claimed under the state law was equivalent to the rights protected by copyright law, the second requirement for finding express preemption under §301(a). The *Brown* court, on the other hand, was addressing the defendants' arguments directed toward conflict preemption; thus, a consistent purpose cuts against finding the state law preempted.

3. How would the *Baltimore Orioles* court have analyzed the claims made in *Brown*? How would the *Brown* court have analyzed the claims made in *Baltimore Orioles*? The *Brown* court distinguishes *Baltimore Orioles* as a case that involved players claiming publicity rights in broadcasts owned by the clubs; in contrast, in *Brown*, the defendants never had any copyright rights in the recordings or photographs to begin with. Do you find this distinction persuasive in explaining the different results?

In *Toney v. L'Oreal*, 406 F.3d 905 (7th Cir. 2005), the Seventh Circuit concluded that *Baltimore Orioles* did not bar a right of publicity claim for unauthorized use of a model's photographic likeness to advertise cosmetics. The court reasoned that the subject matter of the claim was not the particular photographs but the model's identity, which was not itself within the subject matter of copyright. It observed that "the fact that the photograph itself could be copyrighted, and that defendants owned the copyright to the photograph that was used, is irrelevant to the [right of publicity] claim." *Id.* at 910. It noted that footnote 24 in *Baltimore Orioles* expressly preserved the possibility of a right of publicity claim under these circumstances. Review footnote 24 in *Baltimore Orioles*, page 733, *supra*. Are you satisfied with this explanation? After *Toney*, what is the remaining scope of the *Baltimore Orioles* rule?

4. Review Question 7, page 451, *supra*. The court in *Midler v. Ford Motor Co.*, 849 F.2d 460, 463 (9th Cir. 1988), *cert. denied*, 503 U.S. 951 (1992), recognized a right of publicity claim "when a distinctive voice of a professional singer is widely known and is deliberately imitated in order to sell a product." How does such a claim survive a copyright preemption analysis? According to the court, Midler did not seek to prevent damages for use of the particular song but rather for use of her voice: "A voice is not copyrightable. The sounds are not 'fixed.' What is put forward as protectible here is more personal than any work of authorship." *Id.* at 462.

Would it change the result if the defendant had used actual samples from Midler's copyrighted sound recording? In *Laws v. Sony Music Entertainment, Inc.*, 294 F. Supp. 2d 1160 (C.D. Cal. 2003), Sony, under license, used samples of singer Debra Laws' recording in another song and a music video. Laws sued for, *inter alia*, misappropriation of her voice for commercial purposes. *Id.* at 1161. The court held the claim preempted: "[W]hen a person's 'identity' claims are essentially claims regarding the use of a copyrighted work, then courts have found the state claims to be preempted." *Id.* at 1164. Are *Midler* and *Laws* consistent?

5. In *Facenda v. N.F.L. Films, Inc.*, 542 F.3d 1007 (3d Cir. 2008), the estate of John Facenda sued NFL Films for violation of Pennsylvania's statutory right of publicity for its use of Facenda's voice in a program about the making of the video game Madden NFL '06. Facenda had signed a release granting NFL Films "the unequivocal rights to use the audio and visual film sequences" he had recorded "or any part of them . . . in perpetuity and by whatever media or manner NFL Films . . . sees fit, provided, however, such use does not constitute an endorsement of any product or service." *Id.* at 1012. The court held that §301 did not preempt the right of publicity claim because the Pennsylvania statute required an extra element: a showing of commercial value. Additionally, the court looked to *Midler* for support in holding that Facenda's voice was not within the subject matter of copyright.

In finding no implied preemption, the court adopted a test suggested by the Nimmer copyright treatise. The first prong of the test considers whether the copyrighted work was used for " 'purposes of trade' " or in an expressive work; Nimmer argues that courts generally have held the right of publicity claim not preempted in the former case and preempted in the latter. *Id.* at 1029, *citing* 1 Nimmer on Copyright §1.01[B][3][b][iv][I], at 1-88.2(9) to (11). The court found NFL Films' use of the sequences in a "22-minute promotional piece akin to advertising [did] not count as an expressive work . . . suggest[ing] that conflict preemption [would be] inappropriate. . . ." *Id.* at 1030.

Under the second prong of the test, courts are to consider the effect of a contract, and particularly the purposes "of the use to which the plaintiff initially consented when signing over the copyright in a contract. . . . [T]he proper question in cases involving advertising and a contract . . . is whether the plaintiff 'collaborated in the creation of a copyrighted advertising product.' 1 Nimmer on Copyright §1.01[B][3][b][iv][II], at 1-88.2(20). If the plaintiff did [so] collaborate . . . then the party holding the copyright is in a very strong position to contend that allowing the plaintiff to assert a right of publicity against use of its likeness in advertising would interfere with the rights it acquired." *Id.* The court found that Facenda had not consented to use of the sequences in advertisements for football video games and that the release "did not implicitly waive his right to publicity, the core of which is the right not to have one's identity used in advertisements." *Id.* at 1031.

The *Facenda* court considered its holding consistent with *Laws.* Do you agree? What do you think of Nimmer's test? How should NFL Films revise its release form to avoid this problem in the future?

———

To avoid preemption, should the right of publicity be subject to limiting doctrines like those of copyright law, particularly fair use? As you read in the Note on Rights of Publicity, Chapter 4.D, pages 265-67 *supra*, the right has become extremely broad, protecting almost anything that conjures up a celebrity's image. The following excerpt from Judge Kozinski's dissent in the Ninth Circuit's denial of en banc rehearing in *White v. Samsung Electronics America, Inc.* (described briefly in that Note) discusses the relationship between copyright preemption and the scope of publicity rights.

White v. Samsung Electronics America, Inc.
989 F.2d 1512 (9th Cir. 1993) (en banc)

KOZINSKI, J., with whom O'SCANNLAIN, J. and KLEINFELD, J. join, dissenting from the order rejecting the suggestion for rehearing en banc. . . .

II

. . . The ad that spawned this litigation starred a robot dressed in a wig, gown and jewelry reminiscent of Vanna White's hair and dress; the robot was posed next to a Wheel-of-Fortune-like game board. . . . The caption read "Longest-running game show. 2012 A.D." The gag here, I take it, was that Samsung would still be around when White had been replaced by a robot.

Perhaps failing to see the humor, White sued, alleging Samsung infringed her right of publicity by "appropriating" her "identity." . . .

[The panel majority held that t]he California right of publicity can't possibly be limited to name and likeness. If it were, the majority reasons, a "clever advertising strategist" could avoid using White's name or likeness but nevertheless remind people of her with impunity, "effectively eviscerat[ing]" her rights. To prevent this "evisceration," the panel majority holds that the right of publicity must extend beyond name and likeness, to any "appropriation" of White's "identity" — anything that "evoke[s]" her personality. . . .

III

But what does "evisceration" mean in intellectual property law? Intellectual property rights aren't like some constitutional rights, absolute guarantees protected against all kinds of interference, subtle as well as blatant. They cast no penumbras, emit no emanations: The very point of intellectual property laws is that they protect only against certain specific kinds of appropriation. I can't publish unauthorized copies of, say, *Presumed Innocent*; I can't make a movie out of it. But I'm perfectly free to write a book about an idealistic young prosecutor on trial for a crime he didn't commit. So what if I got the idea from *Presumed Innocent*? So what if it reminds readers of the original? Have I "eviscerated" Scott Turow's intellectual property rights? Certainly not. All creators draw in part on the work of those who came before, referring to it, building on it, poking fun at it; we call this creativity, not piracy. . . .

. . . Intellectual property rights aren't free. They're imposed at the expense of future creators and of the public at large. Where would we be if Charles Lindbergh had an exclusive right in the concept of a heroic solo aviator? If Arthur Conan Doyle had gotten a copyright in the idea of the detective story, or Albert Einstein had patented the theory of relativity? If every author and celebrity had been given the right to keep people from mocking them or their work? Surely this would have made the world poorer, not richer, culturally as well as economically.

This is why intellectual property law is full of careful balances between what's set aside for the owner and what's left in the public domain for the rest of us: The relatively short life of patents; the longer, but finite, life of copyrights; copyright's idea-expression dichotomy; the fair use doctrine; the prohibition on copyrighting facts; the compulsory license of television broadcasts and musical compositions; federal preemption of overbroad state intellectual property laws; the nominative use doctrine in trademark law; the right to make soundalike recordings. All of these diminish an intellectual property owner's rights. All let the public use something created by someone else. But all are necessary to maintain a free environment in which creative genius can flourish.

The intellectual property right created by the panel here has none of these essential limitations: No fair use exception; no right to parody; no idea-expression dichotomy. It impoverishes the public domain, to the detriment of future creators and the public at large. Instead of well-defined, limited characteristics such as name, likeness or voice, advertisers will now have to cope with vague claims of "appropriation of identity," claims often made by people with a wholly exaggerated sense of their own fame and significance. . . . Future Vanna Whites might not get the chance to create their personae, because their employers may fear some celebrity will claim the persona is too similar to her own. The public will be robbed of parodies of celebrities, and our culture will be deprived of the valuable safety valve that parody and mockery create. . . .

IV

The panel, however, does more than misinterpret California law: By refusing to recognize a parody exception to the right of publicity, the panel directly contradicts the federal Copyright Act. Samsung didn't merely parody Vanna White. It parodied Vanna White appearing in "Wheel of Fortune," a copyrighted television show, and parodies of copyrighted works are governed by federal copyright law.

Copyright law specifically gives the world at large the right to make "fair use" parodies, parodies that don't borrow too much of the original. . . . Federal copyright law also gives the copyright owner the exclusive right to create (or license the creation of) derivative works, which include parodies that borrow too much to qualify as "fair use." . . .

The majority's decision decimates this federal scheme. It's impossible to parody a movie or a TV show without at the same time "evok[ing]" the "identit[ies]" of the actors. You can't have a mock *Star Wars* without a mock Luke Skywalker, Han Solo and Princess Leia, which in turn means a mock Mark Hamill, Harrison Ford and Carrie Fisher. You can't have a mock *Batman* commercial without a mock Batman, which means someone emulating the mannerisms of Adam West or Michael Keaton. . . . The public's right to make a fair use parody and the copyright owner's right to license a derivative work are useless if the parodist is held hostage by every actor whose "identity" he might need to "appropriate." . . .

. . . It's our responsibility to keep the right of publicity from taking away federally granted rights, either from the public at large or from a copyright owner. We must make sure state law doesn't give the Vanna Whites and Adam Wests of the world a veto over fair use parodies of the shows in which they appear, or over copyright holders' exclusive right to license derivative works of those shows. In a case where the copyright owner isn't even a party—where no one has the interests of copyright owners at heart—the majority creates a rule that greatly diminishes the rights of copyright holders in this circuit.

V

The majority's decision also conflicts with the federal copyright system in another, more insidious way. Under the dormant Copyright Clause, state intellectual property laws can stand only so long as they don't "prejudice the interests of other States." . . . [T]he right of publicity isn't geographically limited. A right of publicity created by one state applies to conduct every-where, so long as it involves a celebrity domiciled in that state. If a Wyoming resident creates an ad that features a California domiciliary's name or likeness, he'll be subject to California right of publicity law even if he's careful to keep the ad from being shown in California. . . .

The broader and more ill-defined one state's right of publicity, the more it interferes with the legitimate interests of other states. A limited right that applies to unauthorized use of name and likeness probably does not run afoul of the Copyright Clause, but the majority's protection of "identity" is quite another story. Under the majority's approach, any time anybody in the United States—even somebody who lives in a state with a very narrow right of publicity— creates an ad, he takes the risk that it might remind some segment of the public of somebody, perhaps somebody with only a local reputation, somebody the advertiser has never heard of. . . . So you made a commercial in Florida and one of the characters reminds Reno residents of their favorite local TV anchor (a California domiciliary)? Pay up.

This is an intolerable result, as it gives each state far too much control over artists in other states. No California statute, no California court has actually tried to reach this far. It is ironic that it is we who plant this kudzu in the fertile soil of our federal system. . . .

VII

For better or worse, we *are* the Court of Appeals for the Hollywood Circuit. Millions of people toil in the shadow of the law we make, and much of their livelihood is made possible by the existence of intellectual property rights. But much of their livelihood—and much of the vibrancy of our culture—also depends on the existence of other intangible rights: The right to draw ideas from a rich and varied public domain, and the right to mock, for profit as well as fun, the cultural icons of our time.

In the name of avoiding the "evisceration" of a celebrity's rights in her image, the majority diminishes the rights of copyright holders and the public at large. In the name of fostering creativity, the majority suppresses it. Vanna White and those like her have been given something they never had before, and they've been given it at our expense. I cannot agree.

NOTES AND QUESTIONS

1. What do you think of Judge Kozinski's dissent? Can you translate it into a legal argu-ment using the two-pronged analysis of §301? Can you translate it into a legal argument that relies on the Supreme Court's intellectual property preemption cases?

2. Does the First Amendment require limits on the right of publicity? In *Comedy III Productions, Inc. v. Saderup*, 25 Cal. 4th 387 (Cal. 2001), *cert. denied*, 534 U.S. 1078 (2002), the court concluded that some (but not all) speech about celebrities must be shielded from right of publicity claims:

> Because celebrities take on public meaning, the appropriation of their likenesses may have important uses in uninhibited debate on public issues, particularly debates about culture and values. And because celebrities take on personal meanings to many individuals in the society, the creative appropriation of celebrity images can be an important avenue of individual expression. . . .
>   . . . [T]he very importance of celebrities in society means that the right of publicity has the potential of censoring significant expression by suppressing alternative versions of celebrity images that are iconoclastic, irreverent, or otherwise attempt to redefine the celebrity's meaning. . . .
>   But having recognized the high degree of First Amendment protection for noncommercial speech about celebrities we need not conclude that all expression that trenches on the right of publicity receives such protection. The right of publicity, like copyright, protects a form of intellectual property that society deems to have some social utility. . . .

Id. at 397-99. To separate protected from unprotected expression in the right of publicity context, the court adopted a test modeled loosely on copyright's fair use doctrine:

> . . . [T]he first fair use factor — "the purpose and character of the use" . . . does seem particularly pertinent to the task of reconciling the rights of free expression and publicity. . . .
>   . . . [W]hen artistic expression takes the form of a literal depiction or imitation of a celebrity for commercial gain, . . . directly trespassing on the right of publicity without adding significant expression beyond that trespass, the state law interest in protecting the fruits of artistic labor outweighs the expressive interests of the imitative artist. . . .
>   On the other hand, when a work contains significant transformative elements, it is not only especially worthy of First Amendment protection, but it is also less likely to interfere with the economic interest protected by the right of publicity. . . .
>   Another way of stating the inquiry is whether the celebrity likeness is one of the "raw materials" from which an original work is synthesized, or whether the depiction or imitation of the celebrity is the very sum and substance of the work in question. We ask, in other words, whether a product containing a celebrity's likeness is so transformed that it has become primarily the defendant's own expression rather than the celebrity's likeness. And when we use the word "expression," we mean expression of something other than the likeness of the celebrity.

Id. at 404-06. The court held that the disputed creations — T-shirts bearing defendant's drawing of the Three Stooges — were insufficiently transformative and affirmed an award of damages and attorneys' fees totaling $225,000.

Because rights of publicity are state rights, federal courts adjudicating California right of publicity claims are bound by the judicially crafted limit on the right of publicity announced by the *Saderup* court. Would the *Saderup* rule have changed the result in *White v. Samsung*? Note that unlike the T-shirts at issue in *Saderup*, Samsung's television commercials would be considered "commercial speech," which the Supreme Court has defined as speech proposing a commercial transaction. *See Va. Bd. of Pharmacy v. Va. Citizens Consumer Council, Inc.*, 425 U.S. 748, 762 (1976). The *Saderup* court noted in passing that "the right of publicity may often trump the right of advertisers to make use of celebrity figures." *Saderup*, 25 Cal. 4th at 396. Should some commercial speech about celebrities also be excused under a transformative use standard? Would the Samsung commercials qualify?

3. Look again at footnote 22 in the *Baltimore Orioles* case, page 732 *supra*. What if the TV station were broadcasting Zacchini's human cannonball act as part of its news broadcast? Should the station be able to broadcast it in its entirety? Note that *Brown v. Ames* describes the first

element of the tort as involving misappropriation "not . . . for a newsworthy purpose." 201 F.3d 654, 658 (5th Cir. 2000). Does this approach adequately safeguard First Amendment interests?

4. Does *Saderup* strike an appropriate balance between the public's need to evoke symbols of its time and the interests of the firms and individuals that create those symbols in recouping their investments?

5. Should the right of publicity exist at all? After you read the next section on misappropriation, a tort that is both more expansive and existed before the right of publicity, consider whether publicity rights are necessary.

D. MISAPPROPRIATION

As discussed above, the legislative history of the 1976 Act reveals considerable disagreement over whether federal copyright law should preempt state law causes of action for misappropriation of factual information. At the root of this disagreement was the Supreme Court's celebrated opinion in *International News Service v. Associated Press*, 248 U.S. 215 (1918), an excerpt from which follows. During the drafting of the 1976 Act, some argued that the misappropriation theory recognized in *International News Service (INS)* interfered with federal copyright policy and should not survive under a modernized copyright law. Others argued that the misappropriation theory had an important role to play in a world in which collections of information were increasingly valuable. We turn now to the *INS* case followed by a consideration of more recent judicial and legislative approaches to the problem.

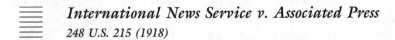

International News Service v. Associated Press
248 U.S. 215 (1918)

[The parties were competing wire subscription services that transmitted news items to their member newpapers. The dispute arose during World War I. The INS, a service founded by William Randolph Hearst to provide news to Hearst-owned newspapers, had incurred the displeasure of the British High Command for taking positions "strongly sympathetic to the German cause. . . . In retaliation, the British and French authorities cut INS personnel off from the front lines and barred them from using the entire European cable system." Richard A. Epstein, International News Service v. Associated Press: *Custom and Law as Sources of Property Rights in News*, 78 Va. L. Rev. 85, 92 (1992). Left with no direct means of gathering news of the war to transmit to its members, the INS sought to gather the news from the AP instead. Among other things, it copied news items from publicly accessible bulletin boards maintained by AP member newpapers and from early editions of AP member newspapers on the East Coast, and transmitted the copied material to Hearst newspapers. Because of the time difference, Hearst newspapers on the West Coast were able to publish these items at the same time as AP member newspapers.]

PITNEY, J.: . . . We need spend no time . . . upon the general question of property in news matter at common law, or the application of the copyright act, since it seems to us the case must turn upon the question of unfair competition in business. And, in our opinion, this does not depend upon any general right of property analogous to the common-law right of the proprietor of an unpublished work to prevent its publication without his consent; nor is it foreclosed by showing that the benefits of the copyright act have been waived. We are dealing here not with restrictions on publication but with the very facilities and processes of publication. The peculiar value of the news is in the spreading of it while it is fresh. . . . [T]he news of current events may be regarded as common property. What we are concerned with is the business of making it known to the world. . . . The parties are competitors in this field; and, on fundamental principles, applicable here as elsewhere, when the rights and privileges of the one are liable to conflict with those of the other, each party is under a duty so as to conduct its own business as not unnecessarily or unfairly to injure that of the other. . . .

. . . [A]lthough we may and do assume that neither party has any remaining property interest as against the public in uncopyrighted news matter after the moment of its first publication, it by no means follows that there is no remaining property interest in it as between themselves. For, to both of them alike, news matter, however little susceptible of ownership or dominion in the absolute sense, is stock in trade, to be gathered at the cost of enterprise, organization, skill, labor, and money, and to be distributed and sold to those who will pay money for it, as for any other merchandise. Regarding the news, therefore, as but the material out of which both parties are seeking to make profits at the same time and in the same field, we hardly can fail to recognize that for this purpose, and as between them, it must be regarded as quasi property, irrespective of the rights of either as against the public. . . .

. . . [D]efendant, by its very act, admits that it is taking material that has been acquired by complainant as the result of organization and the expenditure of labor, skill, and money, and which is salable by complainant for money, and that defendant in appropriating it and selling it as its own is endeavoring to reap where it has not sown, and by disposing of it to newspapers that are competitors of complainant's members is appropriating to itself the harvest of those who have sown. Stripped of all disguises, the process amounts to an unauthorized interference with the normal operation of complainant's legitimate business precisely at the point where the profit is to be reaped, in order to divert a material portion of the profit from those who have earned it to those who have not; with special advantage to the defendant in the competition because of the fact that it is not burdened with any part of the expense of gathering the news. The transaction speaks for itself, and a court of equity ought not to hesitate long in characterizing it as unfair competition in business. . . .

The contention that the news is abandoned to the public for all purposes when published in the first newspaper is untenable. Abandonment is a question of intent, and the entire organization of the Associated Press negatives such a purpose. The cost of the service would be prohibitive if the reward were to be so limited. No single newspaper, no small group of newspapers, could sustain the expenditure. Indeed, it is one of the most obvious results of defendant's theory that, by permitting indiscriminate publication by anybody and everybody for purposes of profit in competition with the news-gatherer, it would render publication profitless, or so little profitable as in effect to cut off the service. . . .

HOLMES, J., dissenting: . . . Property, a creation of law, does not arise from value, although exchangeable—a matter of fact. Many exchangeable values may be destroyed intentionally without compensation. Property depends upon exclusion by law from interference, and a person is not excluded from using any combination of words merely because someone has used it before. . . . If a given person is to be prohibited from making the use of words that his neighbors are free to make some other ground must be found. . . . [Justice Holmes argued that INS should be enjoined only from publishing copied news items without giving express credit to AP for having gathered them.]

BRANDEIS, J., dissenting: . . . [T]he fact that a product of the mind has cost its producer money and labor, and has a value for which others are willing to pay, is not sufficient to ensure to it this legal attribute of property. The general rule of law is, that the noblest of human productions—knowledge, truths ascertained, conceptions, and ideas—became, after voluntary communication to others, free as the air to common use. Upon these incorporeal productions the attribute of property is continued after such communication only in certain classes of cases where public policy has seemed to demand it. These exceptions are confined to productions which, in some degree, involve creation, invention, or discovery. . . .

. . . [W]ith the increasing complexity of society, the public interest tends to become omnipresent; and the problems presented by new demands for justice cease to be simple. Then the creation or recognition by courts of a new private right may work serious injury to the general public, unless the boundaries of the right are definitely established and wisely guarded. In order to reconcile the new private right with the public interest, it may be necessary to prescribe limitations and rules for its enjoyment; and also to provide administrative machinery for enforcing the rules. It is largely for this reason that, in the effort to meet the many new demands for justice incident to a rapidly changing civilization, resort to legislation has latterly been had with increasing frequency. . . .

. . . [L]egislators dealing with the subject might conclude, that the right to news values should be protected to the extent of permitting recovery of damages for any unauthorized use, but that protection by injunction should be denied, just as courts of equity ordinarily refuse (perhaps in the interest of free speech) to restrain actionable libels. . . .

Or again, a legislature might conclude that . . . a news agency should, on some conditions, be given full protection of its business; and to that end a remedy by injunction as well as one for damages should be granted . . . [but] it might declare that, in such cases, news should be protected against appropriation, only if the gatherer assumed the obligation of supplying it at reasonable rates, and without discrimination, to all papers which applied therefor. . . .

The claim of unfair competition that the Supreme Court recognized in *INS* was founded on federal common law. Subsequent opinions of the Court rejected the existence of a general federal common law. *Erie R.R. Co. v. Tompkins*, 304 U.S. 64 (1938). Today, misappropriation claims are brought under state unfair competition law (both common law and statutory law). The following case addresses whether the 1976 Copyright Act preempts an *INS*-styled unfair competition claim based on state law.

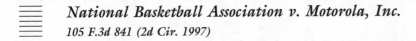

National Basketball Association v. Motorola, Inc.
105 F.3d 841 (2d Cir. 1997)

WINTER, J.: Motorola, Inc. and Sports Team Analysis and Tracking Systems ("STATS") appeal from a permanent injunction. . . . The injunction concerns a handheld pager sold by Motorola and marketed under the name "SportsTrax," which displays updated information of professional basketball games in progress. . . .

I. Background

The facts are largely undisputed. Motorola manufactures and markets the SportsTrax paging device while STATS supplies the game information that is transmitted to the pagers. The product became available to the public in January 1996, at a retail price of about $200.

SportsTrax's pager has an inch-and-a-half by inch-and-a-half screen and operates in four basic modes: "current," "statistics," "final scores," and "demonstration." It is the "current" mode that gives rise to the present dispute. In that mode, SportsTrax displays the following information on NBA games in progress: (i) the teams playing; (ii) score changes; (iii) the team in possession of the ball; (iv) whether the team is in the free-throw bonus; (v) the quarter of the game; and (vi) time remaining in the quarter. The information is updated every two to three minutes, with more frequent updates near the end of the first half and the end of the game. There is a lag of approximately two or three minutes between events in the game itself and when the information appears on the pager screen.

SportsTrax's operation relies on a "data feed" supplied by STATS reporters who watch the games on television or listen to them on the radio. The reporters key into a personal computer changes in the score and other information such as successful and missed shots, fouls, and clock updates. The information is relayed by modem to STATS's host computer, which compiles, analyzes, and formats the data for retransmission. The information is then sent to a common carrier, which then sends it via satellite to various local FM radio networks that in turn emit the signal received by the individual SportsTrax pagers. . . .

[The district court dismissed the NBA's federal claims for relief, including a copyright infringement claim, but granted a permanent injunction on the NBA's claim for misappropriation under New York law.]

II. The State Law Misappropriation Claim

[The court observed, first, that the underlying basketball games were not protected by copyright, but that the broadcasts of those games were protected. Nonetheless, it held that the district court properly dismissed the NBA's copyright claims based on the broadcasts because Motorola and STATS reproduced only unprotected facts. The court then turned to the question of preemption.]

a. Summary

. . . [A] state law claim is preempted when (i) the state law claim seeks to vindicate "legal or equitable rights that are equivalent" to one of the bundle of exclusive rights already protected by copyright law under 17 U.S.C. §106 — styled the "general scope requirement"; and (ii) the particular work to which the state law claim is being applied falls within the type of works protected by the Copyright Act under Sections 102 and 103 — styled the "subject matter requirement." . . .

b. "Partial Preemption" and the Subject Matter Requirement

The subject matter requirement is met when the work of authorship being copied or misappropriated "fall[s] within the ambit of copyright protection." *Harper & Row, Publishers, Inc. v. Nation Enter.*, 723 F.2d 195, 200 (1985), *rev'd on other grounds*, 471 U.S. 539 (1985). We believe that the subject matter requirement is met in the instant matter and that the concept of "partial preemption" is not consistent with Section 301 of the Copyright Act. Although game broadcasts are copyrightable while the underlying games are not, the Copyright Act should not be read to distinguish between the two when analyzing the preemption of a misappropriation claim based on copying or taking from the copyrightable work. . . . *Baltimore Orioles*, 805 F.2d at 675 (citation omitted).

Copyrightable material often contains uncopyrightable elements within it, but Section 301 preemption bars state law misappropriation claims with respect to uncopyrightable as well as copyrightable elements. . . . The legislative history supports this understanding of Section 301(a)'s subject matter requirement. The House Report stated:

> As long as a work fits within one of the general subject matter categories of sections 102 and 103, the bill prevents the States from protecting it even if it fails to achieve Federal statutory copyright because it is too minimal or lacking in originality to qualify, or because it has fallen into the public domain.

H.R. No. 94-1476 at 131, *reprinted in* 1976 U.S.C.C.A.N. at 5747. . . .

Adoption of a partial preemption doctrine — preemption of claims based on misappropriation of broadcasts but no preemption of claims based on misappropriation of underlying facts — would expand significantly the reach of state law claims and render the preemption intended by Congress unworkable. It is often difficult or impossible to separate the fixed copyrightable work from the underlying uncopyrightable events or facts. Moreover, Congress, in extending copyright protection only to the broadcasts and not to the underlying events, intended that the latter be in the public domain. Partial preemption turns that intent on its head by allowing state law to vest exclusive rights in material that Congress intended to be in the public domain and to make unlawful conduct that Congress intended to allow. . . .

c. *The General Scope Requirement . . .*

We turn . . . to the question of the extent to which a "hot-news" misappropriation claim based on *INS* involves extra elements and is not the equivalent of exclusive rights under a copyright. Courts are generally agreed that some form of such a claim survives preemption. . . . This conclusion is based in part on the legislative history of the 1976 amendments. . . .

The theory of the New York misappropriation cases relied upon by the district court is considerably broader than that of *INS*. For example, the district court quoted at length from *Metropolitan Opera Ass'n v. Wagner-Nichols Recorder Corp.*, 199 Misc. 786, 101 N.Y.S.2d 483 (N.Y. Sup. Ct. 1950), *aff'd*, 279 A.D. 632, 107 N.Y.S.2d 795 (1st Dep't 1951). *Metropolitan Opera* described New York misappropriation law as standing for the "broader principle that property rights of commercial value are to be and will be protected from any form of commercial immorality"; that misappropriation law developed "to deal with business malpractices offensive to the ethics of [ ] society"; and that the doctrine is "broad and flexible." 939 F. Supp. at 1098-1110 (quoting *Metropolitan Opera*, 101 N.Y.S.2d at 492, 488-89).

However, we believe that *Metropolitan Opera*'s broad misappropriation doctrine based on amorphous concepts such as "commercial immorality" or society's "ethics" is preempted. Such concepts are virtually synonymous for wrongful copying and are in no meaningful fashion distinguishable from infringement of a copyright. . . .

Our conclusion, therefore, is that only a narrow "hot-news" misappropriation claim survives preemption for actions concerning material within the realm of copyright. . . .[7]

---

7. Quite apart from Copyright Act preemption, *INS* has long been regarded with skepticism by many courts and scholars and often confined strictly to its facts. In particular, Judge Learned Hand was notably hostile to a broad reading of the case. He wrote:

> [W]e think that no more was covered than situations substantially similar to those then at bar. The difficulties of understanding it otherwise are insuperable. We are to suppose that the court meant to create a sort of common-law patent or copyright for reasons of justice. Either would flagrantly conflict with the scheme which Congress has for more than a century devised to cover the subject-matter.

Cheney Bros. v. Doris Silk Corp., 35 F.2d 279, 280 (2d Cir. 1929), *cert. denied*, 281 U.S. 728 . . . (1930). . . .

In our view, the elements central to an *INS* claim are: (i) the plaintiff generates or collects information at some cost or expense . . . ; (ii) the value of the information is highly time-sensitive . . . ; (iii) the defendant's use of the information constitutes free-riding on the plaintiff's costly efforts to generate it . . . ; (iv) the defendant's use of the information is in direct competition with a product or service offered by the plaintiff . . . ; (v) the ability of other parties to free-ride on the efforts of the plaintiff would so reduce the incentive to produce the product or service that its existence or quality would be substantially threatened. . . .

INS is not about ethics; it is about the protection of property rights in time-sensitive information so that the information will be made available to the public by profit seeking entrepreneurs. If services like AP were not assured of property rights in the news they pay to collect, they would cease to collect it. . . .

We therefore find the extra elements—those in addition to the elements of copyright infringement—that allow a "hot-news" claim to survive preemption are: (i) the time-sensitive value of factual information, (ii) free-riding by a defendant, and (iii) the threat to the very existence of the product or service provided by the plaintiff.

2. The Legality of SportsTrax

We conclude that Motorola and STATS have not engaged in unlawful misappropriation under the "hot-news" test set out above. To be sure, some of the elements of a "hot-news" *INS* claim are met. The information transmitted to SportsTrax is not precisely contemporaneous, but it is nevertheless time-sensitive. Also, the NBA does provide, or will shortly do so, information like that available through SportsTrax. . . .

However, there are critical elements missing in the NBA's attempt to assert a "hot-news" *INS*-type claim. As framed by the NBA, their claim compresses and confuses three different informational products. The first product is generating the information by playing the games; the second product is transmitting live, full descriptions of those games; and the third product is collecting and retransmitting strictly factual information about the games. The first and second products are the NBA's primary business: producing basketball games for live attendance and licensing copyrighted broadcasts of those games. The collection and retransmission of strictly factual material about the games is a different product: e.g., box-scores in newspapers, summaries of statistics on television sports news, and real-time facts to be transmitted to pagers. In our view, the NBA has failed to show any competitive effect whatsoever from SportsTrax on the first and second products and a lack of any free-riding by SportsTrax on the third. . . .

An indispensable element of an *INS* "hot-news" claim is free-riding by a defendant on a plaintiff's product, enabling the defendant to produce a directly competitive product for less money because it has lower costs. SportsTrax is not such a product. The use of pagers to transmit real-time information about NBA games requires: (i) the collecting of facts about the games; (ii) the transmission of these facts on a network; (iii) the assembling of them by the particular service; and (iv) the transmission of them to pagers or an on-line computer site. Appellants are in no way free-riding on Gamestats. Motorola and STATS expend their own resources to collect purely factual information generated in NBA games to transmit to Sports-Trax pagers. They have their own network and assemble and transmit data themselves.

To be sure, if appellants in the future were to collect facts from an enhanced Gamestats pager to retransmit them to SportsTrax pagers, that would constitute free-riding and might well cause Gamestats to be unprofitable because it had to bear costs to collect facts that Sports-Trax did not. If the appropriation of facts from one pager to another pager service were allowed, transmission of current information on NBA games to pagers or similar devices would be substantially deterred because any potential transmitter would know that the first entrant would quickly encounter a lower cost competitor free-riding on the originator's transmissions.

However, that is not the case in the instant matter. . . .

NOTES AND QUESTIONS

1. Do you agree with the *NBA v. Motorola* court's analysis of the "subject matter requirement" of §301? Is the court's rejection of a partial preemption rule consistent with the legislative history of §301? Is it consistent with the *Sears*-to-*Bonito Boats* line of cases that you read at the beginning of this chapter? Per *Goldstein*, are facts a type of subject matter that Congress has "left . . . unattended"? How do the text and legislative history of §301 bear on this question? Compare the analysis employed by the Second Circuit to that used by the courts in *Baltimore Orioles* and *Brown*. Does either *Baltimore Orioles* or *Brown* employ a partial preemption rule?

Some courts have accepted the partial preemption analysis in misappropriation contexts. *See Dunlap v. G&L Holding Group, Inc.*, 381 F.3d 1285 (11th Cir. 2004) (holding claim for "conversion of idea" not preempted because ideas are not within the subject matter of copyright); *Sw. Airlines Co. v. Farechase, Inc.*, 318 F. Supp. 2d 435 (N.D. Tex. 2004) (holding claim for misappropriation of facts from online database of airfares not preempted because facts are not within the subject matter of copyright). Should misappropriation claims and right of publicity claims be treated the same way for purposes of §301's subject matter requirement?

2. Is each of the elements that the Second Circuit identifies as "extra" — time sensitivity, free riding, and a threat to incentives — sufficiently distinct from the elements necessary to allege a claim of copyright infringement? Are either of the elements that the court did *not* identify as extra — cost or expense and direct competition — sufficiently distinct? Does the Second Circuit's reliance on an "extra-element" test for equivalence make sense in the *NBA* case?

3. The Second Circuit observes that "*INS* is not about ethics." *NBA v. Motorola, Inc.* 105 F. 3d 841, 853 (2d Cir. 1997). Based on the excerpts from the *INS* opinion reproduced above, do you agree? Was the *INS* Court concerned solely with the likely incentive effects of the challenged conduct? Does the legislative history of §301 suggest that Congress was concerned solely with such incentive effects? Note again that despite the attention it continues to receive, the *INS* decision is not binding precedent in any jurisdiction because of its reliance on general federal common law, subsequently rejected by the Court. *Erie R.R. Co. v. Tompkins*, 304 U.S. 64 (1938).

4. How would the analysis announced in *NBA v. Motorola, Inc.* apply to a misappropriation claim grounded in the facts of *Feist*, Chapter 2.A.4, pages 58-60 *supra*? How would it apply to misappropriation claims grounded in the facts of *Bellsouth, CCC v. Maclean Hunter*, or *Matthew Bender v. West*, Chapter 4.E, pages 269-75, 278-80 *supra*?

5. Companies in many industries require their employees to sign confidentiality agreements obligating them to protect the firms' trade secrets against disclosure. Generally, a claim based on breach of such an agreement is not preempted even if it involves copyrighted information. For example, an employee might disclose the printed version of a confidential, copyrighted marketing plan, making copies in the process. A suit against the employee based on breach of the confidentiality agreement would not be preempted because the gravamen of the complaint is not the copying but the disclosure in violation of the confidential relationship. The employee has an independent duty under the contract and state trade secret law not to disclose the employer's trade secrets.

Recall that in *Kewanee* the Supreme Court held that federal patent law does not preempt state trade secret law because trade secret protection does not interfere with patent law's goals. The Supreme Court has never addressed the question whether copyright law preempts state protection for trade secrets.

6. Several online companies have used a different common law theory to assert protection for collections of information available on their web sites. In *eBay v. Bidder's Edge, Inc.*, 100 F. Supp. 2d 1058 (N.D. Cal. 2000), the Internet auction site eBay successfully argued that the use of automated "spiders" to collect information about bid and ask prices constituted a trespass to chattels under California law. The chattels, in this instance, were the servers on which eBay maintained its web site. Defendant Bidder's Edge, an auction aggregator, collected data from a number of different auction sites so that users could compare the prices available at each of them. Bidder's Edge argued that the information was publicly available, and that extending a trespass theory to web sites would be fundamentally contrary to the operating principles of the Internet. The court, however, accepted eBay's argument that Bidder's Edge had exceeded the bounds of eBay's consent to public access and enjoined Bidder's Edge from continuing to gather the information without eBay's permission. Bidder's Edge appealed, but the parties settled shortly thereafter. In *Register.com, Inc. v. Verio, Inc.*, 126 F. Supp. 2d 238 (S.D.N.Y. 2000), *aff'd*, 356 F.3d 393 (2d Cir. 2004), the court applied a similar trespass theory to Verio, an online service provider that had used spiders to collect information about domain name registrants from Register's publicly available "whois" database.

How does the §301 preemption analysis apply to a state law claim for trespass to web sites? If Harper & Row had brought a claim against *The Nation* for trespass to its offices to obtain the copy of President Ford's manuscript, how would the §301 analysis apply to that claim? Should there be a difference between the two trespass claims for preemption purposes? Is the "web trespass" situation one in which the broader concerns identified in the Supreme Court's intellectual property preemption cases apply? *See Ticketmaster Corp. v. Tickets.com, Inc.*, 54 U.S.P.Q.2d 1344, 1347 (C.D. Cal. 2000) (dismissing trespass claim based on "deep linking" to factual information contained on an interior page within a web site, and observing that "where copying is permitted by the Copyright Act, a contrary state law could not be enforced"). What do you think of the trespass strategy as a policy matter? *See* Dan L. Burk, *The Trouble with Trespass*, 4 J. Small & Emerging Bus. L. 27 (2000); Maureen A. O'Rourke, *Property Rights and Competition on the Internet: In Search of an Appropriate Analogy*, 16 Berkeley Tech. L.J. 561 (2001).

Note on Federal Database Protection

Review the Note on Database Protection in the U.S., Chapter 4.E, pages 282-83 *supra*. As discussed there, Congress has been considering federal database protection legislation for some time. While no legislation has been introduced in the last several Congresses, H.R. 3261, proposed in the 108th Congress, included the following provisions:

§2. Definitions . . .

(4) DATABASE—
(A) IN GENERAL—Subject to subparagraph (B), the term 'database' means a collection of a large number of discrete items of information produced for the purpose of bringing such discrete items of information together in one place or through one source so that persons may access them.

(B) EXCLUSIONS—The term database does not include any of the following:

(i) A work of authorship, other than a compilation or a collective work.

(ii) A collection of information that principally performs the function of addressing, routing, forwarding, transmitting, or storing digital online communications or receiving access to connections for digital communications. . . .

(iii) A collection of information gathered, organized, or maintained to perform the function of providing schedule and program information for multichannel audio or video programming.

(iv) A collection of information gathered, organized, or maintained to register domain name registrant contact data maintained by a domain name registration authority, unless such registration authority takes appropriate steps to ensure the integrity and accuracy of such information and provides real-time, unrestricted, and fully searchable public access to the information contained in such collection of information. . . .

(11) MAKING AVAILABLE IN COMMERCE TO OTHERS—The term 'making available in commerce to others' means making available in commerce to—

(A) a substantial number of members of the public; or

(B) a number of persons that extends beyond—

(i) a family and its social acquaintances; or

(ii) those who could reasonably anticipate to have a database made available in commerce to them without a customary commercial relationship.

A court may take into account repeated acts directed to different persons by the same or concerted parties in determining whether the limits imposed by subparagraph (B)(ii) have been exceeded.

§3. Prohibition against the Misappropriation of Databases.

(a) LIABILITY—Any person who makes available in commerce to others a quantitatively substantial part of the information in a database generated, gathered, or maintained by another person, knowing that such making available in commerce is without the authorization of that other person (including a successor in interest) or that other person's licensee, when acting within the scope of its license, shall be liable for the remedies set forth in section 7 if—

(1) the database was generated, gathered, or maintained through a substantial expenditure of financial resources or time;

(2) the unauthorized making available in commerce occurs in a time sensitive manner and inflicts injury on the database or a product or service offering access to multiple databases; and

(3) the ability of other parties to free ride on the efforts of the plaintiff would so reduce the incentive to produce or make available the database or the product or service that its existence or quality would be substantially threatened.

(b) INJURY—For purposes of subsection (a), the term 'inflicts an injury' means serving as a functional equivalent in the same market as the database in a manner that causes the displacement, or the disruption of the sources, of sales, licenses, advertising, or other revenue.

(c) TIME SENSITIVE—In determining whether an unauthorized making available in commerce occurs in a time sensitive manner, the court shall consider the temporal value of the information in the database, within the context of the industry sector involved.

Database and Collections of Information Misappropriation Act, H.R. 3261, 108th Cong., 2d Sess. (2004).

In addition to the exclusions in §2, other provisions excluded government databases and computer programs from protection. The proposed legislation exempted acts of making available by "nonprofit scientific or research institutions" that are "reasonable under the circumstances" in light of customary practices by such institutions. It also exempted the making available of information from covered databases for the purpose of news reporting. However, neither exemption applied to information made available for the purpose of direct competition with the database proprietor. The proposed legislation would have established civil and criminal remedies that largely parallel those available for copyright infringement, and would have preempted all equivalent state laws.

NOTES AND QUESTIONS

1. How would *NBA v. Motorola* have been decided if H.R. 3261 had been enacted and the NBA had filed a claim under the federal statute? How would federal misappropriation claims based on the facts of *Feist*, *Bellsouth*, *Maclean Hunter*, and *Matthew Bender* have been decided?

2. Would the regime proposed in H.R. 3261 be a constitutional exercise of Congress' power under the Commerce Clause under the "fundamentally inconsistent" test described on page 719 *supra*? How do the principles identified by Professors Heald and Sherry, pages 721-22 *supra*, apply to the proposed legislation? Does the proposed regime offer exclusive rights to database proprietors, either literally or effectively? How do the limitations in the bill affect the breadth of the rights reserved for the database proprietor? How well or poorly do the limitations respond to concerns about enclosure of the public domain? What is the "quid pro quo" that the public would receive in exchange for the proposed grant of rights?

3. As a policy matter, would enactment of H.R. 3261 or a similar bill be desirable? Do the rights, exclusions, and limitations all make sense? Are there other exclusions or limitations that you think should be included? (How would you feel about H.R. 3261 if you represented an online service provider?)

4. Review the excerpt by Professors Reichman and Samuelson, Chapter 4, page 284 *supra*, which proposes a database protection regime based on liability rules. Compare their proposal to the solutions suggested by Justice Brandeis in his *INS* dissent, pages 744-45 *supra*. Would the Reichman and Samuelson proposal pass constitutional muster?

E. CONTRACT

Chapter 8 introduced the possibility that copyright owners might use contract to negate the limits placed on their rights by the Copyright Act. The doctrine of copyright misuse offers courts one way to curb that type of contracting behavior. Refusing to enforce the contract by finding the contract claim preempted is another. The legislative history of §301 indicates that at least some members of Congress did not intend the 1976 Act to preempt claims for breach of contract. However, because one can infer little from that history, questions about preemption of contractual terms continue to arise.

In cases involving claims of breach of contract and defenses of copyright preemption, it is important to keep separate arguments about the existence of the contract itself. As you learned in your first-year contracts class, if there is no enforceable contract, then there can be no breach. Furthermore, even if the contract is enforceable generally, a court may refuse to enforce particular terms under contract law doctrines such as unconscionability. Preemption of the breach of contract claim is a different kind of defense. A defense based on preemption argues that even if there is an otherwise enforceable contract, a court may not entertain the state law claim of breach of contract because it is preempted by the Copyright Act.

Note on Judicial Approaches to Contract Preemption

When applying an extra-element preemption analysis to contracts, some courts analyze the act that allegedly constitutes the breach; if that act violates one of the exclusive rights under §106 (such as copying), a court will hold the breach of contract claim preempted. In contrast, where the allegedly breaching act does not also infringe a §106 right, the court will hold the breach of contract claim not preempted. For example, in *National Car Rental System, Inc. v. Computer Associates International, Inc.*, 991 F.2d 426 (8th Cir.), *cert. denied*, 510 U.S. 861 (1993), the court held that a claim alleging that the defendant breached a software license agreement by using the program to process data for third parties was not preempted:

> CA [i.e., Computer Associates,] does not claim that National is doing something that the copyright laws reserve exclusively to the copyright holder, or that the use restriction is breached "by the mere act of reproduction, performance, distribution or display." Instead . . . CA must be read to claim that National's or EDS's processing of data for third parties is the . . . act [prohibited under their contract]. None of the exclusive copyright rights grant CA that right of their own force. Absent the parties' agreement, this restriction would not exist. Thus, CA is alleging that the contract creates a right not existing under the copyright law, a right based upon National's promise, and that it is suing to protect that contractual right.

Id. at 433. To similar effect is *Kabehie v. Zoland*, 102 Cal. App. 4th 513 (2002). There, the court explained:

> . . . A right that is qualitatively different from copyright includes a right to payment, a right to royalties, or any other independent covenant. . . . If, however, the promise is equivalent to copyright, the breach of the promise is not the extra element making the action qualitatively different from copyright. In such a case, there is simply no consideration for the promise. The promisor has merely agreed to do that which the promisor is already obligated to do under federal copyright law.

Id. at 528.

Other courts take a different approach, focusing not on the act that constitutes the breach but rather on the existence of the contract itself. These courts hold that the distinguishing characteristics of a contract — i.e., existence of a promise, mutual assent, and consideration — render a cause of action for breach of contract qualitatively different from one for copyright infringement. *See, e.g., Taquino v. Teledyne Monarch Rubber*, 893 F.2d 1488, 1501 (5th Cir. 1990) (holding that "contract promise" renders breach of contract action qualitatively different from copyright infringement claim); *Architectronics, Inc. v. Control Sys., Inc.*, 935 F. Supp. 425, 438-39 (S.D.N.Y. 1996) (same). Using this type of analysis, the contract claim would rarely be preempted.

In *ProCD, Inc. v. Zeidenberg*, 86 F.3d 1447 (7th Cir. 1996), the court addressed a preemption challenge to a contract action based on a shrinkwrap EULA. *ProCD* marketed a database on CD-ROM that contained a white-pages directory that the court assumed was not copyrightable. ProCD charged one price to commercial users and a lower one to consumers. Those who purchased the consumer package were prohibited from engaging in commercial use of the database under the terms of a license "encoded on [ ] CD-ROM disks as well as printed in the manual, and which appear[ed] on a user's screen every time the software [ran]." *Id.* at 1450. Zeidenberg purchased the consumer version and used it commercially by marketing the database on the Internet for a lower price than ProCD charged for its commercial version. The court held the license an enforceable contract and the breach of contract action not preempted. Although the *ProCD* court rested its holding on §301 of the Copyright Act and cited both *National Car Rental* and *Taquino* favorably, it did not emphasize either the nature of the breach or the existence of a promise, mutual assent, or consideration. The court stated:

> Rights "equivalent to any of the exclusive rights within the general scope of copyright" are rights established *by law*—rights that restrict the options of persons who are strangers to the author. Copyright law forbids duplication, public performance, and so on, unless the person wishing to copy or perform the work gets permission; silence means a ban on copying. A copyright is a right against the world. Contracts, by contrast, generally affect only their parties; strangers may do as they please, so contracts do not create "exclusive rights."

Id. at 1454.

This approach is reminiscent of the cases under the Supremacy Clause that you read in section 10.A, *supra*. One theme that runs through those cases is that a state may not constitutionally employ a scheme of protection that essentially competes with a federal system of protection. Because contracts only affect the parties to them, state enforcement of them should not implicate such concerns. The *ProCD* ruling extends this traditional view to shrinkwrap contracts. At the same time, the *ProCD* court "refrain[ed] from adopting a rule that anything with the label 'contract' is necessarily outside the preemption clause: the variations and possibilities are too numerous to foresee. . . . [S]ome applications of the law of contract could interfere with the attainment of national objectives and therefore come within the domain of §301(a). But general enforcement of shrinkwrap licenses . . . does not create such interference." *Id.* at 1455.

NOTES AND QUESTIONS

1. Are the *National Car Rental* and *ProCD* approaches consistent? If not, which do you find more persuasive? Is it possible to reconcile them? Note that *National Car Rental* involved a copyrighted program and *ProCD* an uncopyrighted database. One might frame *National Car Rental* as raising the question whether one can enter into restrictive contracts that provide more protection to copyrighted material than copyright law would. *ProCD* raises the question whether parties can create private copyright-like rights in data that the public law of copyright has deemed unworthy of protection. Should both situations be assessed in the same way for preemption purposes?

2. What pro-competitive function did the contract in *ProCD* serve? Did the contract in *National Car Rental* also serve a pro-competitive function?

3. In *ProCD*, the court envisions copyright and contract as co-existing in part because contracts bind only the parties to them and thus do not create rights against the world in the

same way that copyright law does. Is that the case even in *ProCD*? When the contract is encoded on a CD-ROM, even the person who picks the CD up on the street will have to accept the terms of the license before using the software. Should this matter to the preemption analysis? Should negotiated agreements be assessed differently from standard-form agreements in a preemption analysis? If either the rightful possessor or the person who finds the CD on the street employs techniques to circumvent the license and obtain access to the software without agreeing to the terms, is the DMCA violated?

4. The majority of commentators disagreed vehemently with both *ProCD*'s contract and copyright law holdings. Consider the following, written by Professor Niva Elkin-Koren:

> . . . [R]estrictions imposed by copyright law are limited and reflect the balance between the need to induce creation and the need to guarantee public access to information. If copyright owners are free to use contractual agreements to restrict use, and are then able to use copyright to prevent any use that is not subject to these restrictions, owners are gaining absolute monopoly over their works.
>
> When owners exercise absolute monopoly, users' choices become very limited. . . . [V]aluable uses . . . may not occur under a contractual regime. . . .
>
> [T]he low standard of assent that *ProCD* . . . held to be sufficient for contract formation does not promote competition over the terms.

Niva Elkin-Koren, *Copyright Policy and the Limits of Freedom of Contract*, 12 Berkeley Tech. L.J. 93, 109-10 (1997).

Professor Elkin-Koren stresses that markets for information are different from markets for other products. "[O]nce information is produced, it is socially optimal to maximize its use by the public. To the extent that on-line dissemination replaces current distribution channels . . . this information could become subject to license restrictions. In the absence of alternatives . . . our current capacity to access information at low cost will be restricted." *Id.* at 111. She argues that contractual restrictions coupled with on-line distribution featuring fees for every use will hamper creativity and cause information deprivation and inequality. *Id.* at 112. Do you agree? If so, what should copyright law or any other law do about it? More specifically, how should these concerns affect the preemption analysis?

5. Another way to understand the preemption issue in the contractual context is as a conflict between two schools of thought. Professor O'Rourke describes them as follows:

> One view . . . contends that copyright merely provides a bundle of rights to copyright owners to help them avoid the transaction costs of contracting with each purchaser of the copyrighted material. In this model, copyright functions much like . . . a boilerplate contract to govern the parties' relationship in the absence of a contrary agreement. Nothing prevents the parties from . . . creating their own property rights through private contract. . . .
>
> Another view . . . argues that copyright represents a legislative scheme carefully balanced to advance the public interest by providing an incentive to authors to create while safeguarding the free flow of the information on which such creativity is based. In this model, there are immutable rules around which the parties cannot contract because the public interest cannot be sacrificed on the altar of two-party agreements. The problem is in defining exactly which provisions of the copyright law are immutable and which are not, in a manner more definitive than simply stating, "We know immutable rules when we see them." . . .

Maureen A. O'Rourke, *Copyright Preemption After the* ProCD *Case: A Market-Based Approach*, 12 Berkeley Tech. L.J. 53, 77-79 (1997).

Is there a happy medium between the two extremes? Professor O'Rourke argues that there is. Instead of a blanket rule for or against preemption, she suggests that courts should integrate market considerations into the preemption inquiry to determine whether the particular term is reasonable within the particular market and what impact it has on the incentives of others to create similar works. *See id.* at 88-89 (styling this a "reverse" fair use inquiry). Would a market-based preemption test make sense as a policy matter? Is there any authority for such an approach in the statute or the Supremacy Clause?

6. As you learned in Chapter 8, pages 629-32, *supra,* the open source and Creative Commons movements rely on a combination of copyright law and contract to enforce norms of openness. Are "copyleft" licenses, which require licensees to distribute their derivative works under the same copyleft terms, enforceable? Don't they restrict the licensee's freedom to exercise its own copyright rights and user privileges? Under the GNU General Public License (GPL) offered by the Free Software Foundation, identifiable sections of the new work that are not derived from copyleft protected programs need not be distributed under the GNU GPL if those identifiable sections are distributed as separate works. GNU GPL, *http://www.fsf.org/ licensing/licenses/gpl.txt.* Does this clause fully address concerns you might have about the enforceability of such a copyleft license? Recent versions of the GNU GPL have retained this provision. You may review the most recent version, GNU GPL 3, at *http://www.gnu. org/licenses/gpl-3.0.html.*

7. The National Conference of Commissioners on Uniform State Laws (NCCUSL) worked for a number of years on a uniform law to govern transactions in software and computer information products, many (if not most) of which are copyrighted. The eventual result of NCCUSL's efforts was the Uniform Computer Information Transactions Act (UCITA), which was adopted in only two states. The American Law Institute (ALI) undertook a Principles project in the area of software contracting that received final approval from the ALI membership in 2009. Like UCITA, the Principles would permit contract formation as in the *ProCD* case. Principles of the Law of Software Contracts §§2.01-2.02 (Proposed Final Draft 2009). Although the Principles do not direct a court to hold any particular provisions of negotiated or standard-form contracts preempted, they note: "[P]reemption issues are heightened when software is distributed under take-it-or-leave-it standard-form agreements that, by virtue of state enforcement, more closely resemble state legislation competing with the federal scheme than a bargain between two parties." *Id.* §1.09 cmt. a. They also attempt to provide extensive commentary and illustrations to help a court analyze preemption questions. *Id.* §1.09.

8. It is critical to consider how the particular court analyzes the question of the appropriate cause of action. Recall the *Jacobsen* case excerpted in Chapter 8, *supra* pages 640-43. If a claim is based on a covenant, then breach of contract is the appropriate action. If the claim is based on a condition, however, then some courts would say that the appropriate cause of action is one for copyright infringement. Others would permit both the contract and copyright causes of action to proceed so long as the recovery is not duplicative and the breach of contract action not preempted.

The *Jacobsen* case falls into the last category: the copyright owner asserted both a copyright infringement claim as well as a breach of contract claim. The contract claim did not survive on remand. The court held "[t]he breach of contract claim does not add an 'extra element' which changes the nature of the action or the rights secured under federal copyright protection. The breach of contract claim alleges violations of the exact same exclusive federal rights protected by Section 106 of the Copyright Act, the exclusive right to reproduce, distribute and make derivative copies." *Jacobsen v. Katzer,* 609 F. Supp. 2d 925, 933 (N.D. Cal. 2009).

Note on Contractual Provisions Against Reverse Engineering

The *Kewanee Oil* case that you read on pages 712-15 held that patent law does not preempt enforcement of an appropriate state trade secret law. There, the Court emphasized that there is little risk of inventors choosing state trade secret law over the federal patent law in part because trade secret law does not preclude discovery of the secret by independent means or by reverse engineering. As you know, software providers often rely on trade secret protection. Many also distribute only the object code version of programs. A programmer can reverse engineer object code to discover information about how the program works. Providers thus often include provisions against reverse engineering in both EULAs and negotiated agreements.

In *Vault Corp. v. Quaid Software Ltd.*, 847 F.2d 255 (5th Cir. 1988), the court addressed copyright preemption challenges to Louisiana's Software License Enforcement Act, which allowed software providers to enforce certain terms so long as they were contained in a license that accompanied the software. At issue specifically was whether Vault could enforce a shrink-wrap license's prohibition against decompilation and disassembly (both types of reverse engineering) that the statute authorized. The Fifth Circuit stated:

> In *Sears, Roebuck & Co. v. Stiffel Co.*, 376 U.S. 225 . . . (1964), the Supreme Court held that "[w]hen state law touches upon the area of [the patent or copyright statutes], it is 'familiar doctrine' that the federal policy 'may not be set at naught, or its benefits denied' by the state law." . . . Section 117 of the Copyright Act permits an owner of a computer program to make an adaptation of that program [under certain circumstances.] The provision in Louisiana's License Act, which permits a software producer to prohibit the adaptation of its licensed computer program by decompilation or disassembly, conflicts with the rights of computer program owners under §117 and clearly "touches upon an area" of federal copyright law. For this reason . . . we hold that at least this provision of Louisiana's License Act is preempted by federal law, and thus that the restriction in Vault's license agreement against decompilation or disassembly is unenforceable.

Id. at 269-70.

As you read in Chapter 7, pages 565-74, over time courts began to consider reverse engineering a fair use under certain circumstances. The Federal Circuit clarified that it considers software patentable subject matter, although In re *Bilski* raises some questions about whether the court will continue to do so. *See* In re *Bilski*, 545 F.3d 943 (Fed. Cir. 2008) (en banc), *cert. granted sub nom. Bilski v. Doll*, 129 S.Ct. 2735 (2009). Given *Vault* and these other trends, many thought a copyright preemption challenge to a breach of contract claim based on a EULA provision banning reverse engineering would likely succeed. Consider the following case.

Bowers v. Baystate Technologies, Inc.
320 F.3d 1317 (Fed. Cir.), cert. denied, 539 U.S. 928 (2003)

[Bowers marketed patented software under a license that prohibited reverse engineering. Baystate marketed competing patented software and sued Bowers for a declaratory judgment of non-infringement, invalidity, or unenforceability of the Bowers patent. Bowers counter-claimed for, *inter alia*, copyright infringement and breach of contract, alleging that Baystate had reverse engineered Bowers' software in violation of the agreement. The jury found Baystate had infringed Bowers' copyright and breached the contract. Baystate appealed.]

RADER, J. . . . Baystate contends that the Copyright Act preempts the prohibition of reverse engineering embodied in Mr. Bowers' shrink-wrap license agreements. . . . This court holds that, under First Circuit law,* the Copyright Act does not preempt or narrow the scope of Mr. Bowers' contract claim.

Courts respect freedom of contract and do not lightly set aside freely-entered agreements. . . . The First Circuit does not interpret [§301] to require preemption as long as "a state cause of action requires an extra element, beyond mere copying, preparation of derivative works, performance, distribution or display." *Data Gen. Corp. v. Grumman Sys. Support Corp.*, 36 F.3d 1147, 1164, 32 USPQ2d 1385, 1397 (1st Cir. 1994) . . .

The First Circuit has not addressed expressly whether the Copyright Act preempts a state law contract claim that restrains copying. . . . [M]ost courts to examine this issue have found that the Copyright Act does not preempt contractual constraints on copyrighted articles. *See, e.g., ProCD, Inc. v. Zeidenberg*, 86 F.3d 1447 . . . (7th Cir. 1996).

. . . This court believes that the First Circuit would follow the reasoning of *ProCD* and the majority of other courts to consider this issue. This court, therefore, holds that the Copyright Act does not preempt Mr. Bowers' contract claims.

In making this determination, this court has left untouched the conclusions reached in *Atari Games v. Nintendo* regarding reverse engineering as a statutory fair use exception to copyright infringement. *Atari Games Corp. v. Nintendo of America, Inc.*, 975 F.2d 832 . . . (Fed. Cir. 1992). In *Atari*, this court stated that . . . "[t]he legislative history of section 107 suggests that courts should adapt the fair use exception to accommodate new technological innovations." *Atari*, 975 F.2d at 843. This court noted "[a] prohibition on all copying whatsoever would stifle the free flow of ideas without serving any legitimate interest of the copyright holder." *Id.* Therefore, this court held "reverse engineering object code to discern the unprotectable ideas in a computer program is a fair use." *Id.* Application of the First Circuit's view distinguishing a state law contract claim having additional elements of proof from a copyright claim does not alter the findings of *Atari*. Likewise, this claim distinction does not conflict with the expressly defined circumstances in which reverse engineering is not copyright infringement under 17 U.S.C. §1201(f) (section of the Digital Millennium Copyright Act) and 17 U.S.C. §906 (section directed to mask works).

Moreover, while the Fifth Circuit has held a state law prohibiting all copying of a computer program is preempted by the federal Copyright Act, *Vault Corp. v. Quaid Software, Ltd.*, 847 F.2d 255 (5th Cir. 1988), no evidence suggests the First Circuit would extend this concept to include private contractual agreements supported by mutual assent and consideration. The First Circuit recognizes contractual waiver of affirmative defenses and statutory rights. . . . Thus, case law indicates the First Circuit would find that private parties are free to contractually forego the limited ability to reverse engineer a software product under the exemptions of the Copyright Act. Of course, a party bound by such a contract may elect to efficiently breach the agreement in order to ascertain ideas in a computer program unprotected by copyright law. Under such circumstances, the breaching party must weigh the benefits of breach against the arguably de minimus [*sic*] damages arising from merely discerning non-protected code. . . .

In this case, the contract unambiguously prohibits "reverse engineering." . . . The record amply supports the jury's finding of a breach of that agreement. . . .

---

*When dealing with issues that are outside the exclusive jurisdiction of the Federal Circuit, the court applies the law of the circuit from which the appeal is taken, here, the First Circuit. — EDS.

Dyk, Circuit Judge, concurring in part and dissenting in part.

I join the majority opinion except insofar as it holds that the contract claim is not pre-empted by federal law. . . . The majority's approach permits state law to eviscerate an important federal copyright policy reflected in the fair use defense, and the majority's logic threatens other federal copyright policies as well. I respectfully dissent.

I . . .

The test for preemption by copyright law, like the test for patent law preemption, should be whether the state law "substantially impedes the public use of the otherwise unprotected" material. *Bonito Boats, Inc. v. Thunder Craft Boats, Inc.*, 489 U.S. 141, 157, 167 . . . (1989) (state law at issue was preempted because it "substantially restrict[ed] the public's ability to exploit ideas that the patent system mandates shall be free for all to use."); *Sears, Roebuck & Co. v. Stiffel Co.*, 376 U.S. 225, 231-32 . . . (1964). *See also Eldred v. Ashcroft*, 537 U.S. 186 . . . (2003) (applying patent precedent in copyright case). In the copyright area, the First Circuit has adopted an "equivalent in substance" test to determine whether a state law is preempted by the Copyright Act. *Data Gen. Corp. v. Grumman Sys. Support Corp.* 36 F.3d 1147, 1164-65 (1st Cir. 1994). . . . "[A]n action is equivalent in substance to a copyright infringement claim [and thus preempted by the Copyright Act] where the additional element merely concerns *the extent to which* authors and their licensees can prohibit unauthorized copying by third parties." *Id.* at 1165 (emphasis in original).

II . . .

We correctly held in *Atari Games Corp. v. Nintendo of America, Inc.*, 975 F.2d 832, 843 (Fed. Cir. 1992), that reverse engineering constitutes a fair use under the Copyright Act. The Ninth and Eleventh Circuits have also ruled that reverse engineering constitutes fair use. *Bateman v. Mnemonics, Inc.*, 79 F.3d 1532, 1539 n. 18 (11th Cir. 1996); *Sega Enters. Ltd. v. Accolade, Inc.*, 977 F.2d 1510, 1527-28 (9th Cir. 1992). No other federal court of appeals has disagreed.

We emphasized in *Atari* that an author cannot achieve protection for an idea simply by embodying it in a computer program. . . . [T]he fair use defense for reverse engineering is necessary so that copyright protection does not "extend to any idea, procedure, process, system, method of operation, concept, principle, or discovery, regardless of the form in which it is described, explained, illustrated, or embodied in such work," as proscribed by the Copyright Act. 17 U.S.C. §102(b) (2000).

III

A state is not free to eliminate the fair use defense. Enforcement of a total ban on reverse engineering would conflict with the Copyright Act itself by protecting otherwise unprotectable material. If state law provided that a copyright holder could bar fair use of the copyrighted material by placing a black dot on each copy of the work offered for sale, there would be no question but that the state law would be preempted. A state law that allowed a copyright holder to simply label its products so as to eliminate a fair use defense would "substantially impede" the public's right to fair use and allow the copyright holder, through state law, to protect material that the Congress has determined must be free to all under the Copyright Act. *See Bonito Boats*, 489 U.S. at 157. . . .

I nonetheless agree with the majority opinion that a state can permit parties to contract away a fair use defense or to agree not to engage in uses of copyrighted material that are permitted by the copyright law, if the contract is freely negotiated. . . . A freely negotiated agreement represents the "extra element" that prevents preemption of a state law claim that would otherwise be identical to the infringement claim barred by the fair use defense of reverse engineering. *See Data Gen.*, 36 F.3d at 1164-65.

However, state law giving effect to shrinkwrap licenses is no different in substance from a hypothetical black dot law. Like any other contract of adhesion, the only choice offered to the purchaser is to avoid making the purchase in the first place. . . . State law thus gives the copyright holder the ability to eliminate the fair use defense in each and every instance at its option. In doing so, as the majority concedes, it authorizes "shrinkwrap agreements . . . [that] are far broader than the protection afforded by copyright law." . . .

IV

There is, moreover, no logical stopping point to the majority's reasoning. . . . If by printing a few words on the outside of its product a party can eliminate the fair use defense, then it can also, by the same means, restrict a purchaser from asserting the "first sale" defense, embodied in 17 U.S.C. §109(a), or any other of the protections Congress has afforded the public in the Copyright Act. That means that, under the majority's reasoning, state law could extensively undermine the protections of the Copyright Act.

V

The Fifth Circuit's decision in *Vault* directly supports preemption of the shrinkwrap limitation. The majority [misreads *Vault*. There,] the Fifth Circuit held that the specific provision of state law that authorized contracts prohibiting reverse engineering, decompilation, or disassembly of computer programs was preempted by federal law because it conflicted with a portion of the Copyright Act and because it " 'touche[d] upon an area' of federal copyright law." 847 F.2d at 269-70 (quoting *Sears, Roebuck*, 376 U.S. at 229, 84 S.Ct. 784). From a preemption standpoint, there is no distinction between a state law that explicitly validates a contract that restricts reverse engineering (*Vault*) and general common law that permits such a restriction (as here). On the contrary, the preemption clause of the Copyright Act makes clear that it covers "any such right or equivalent right in any such work *under the common law or statutes of any State.*" 17 U.S.C. §301(a) (2000) (emphasis added).

I do not read *ProCD, Inc. v. Zeidenberg*, 86 F.3d 1447 (7th Cir. 1996), the only other court of appeals shrinkwrap case, as being to the contrary . . . The court saw the licensor as legitimately seeking to distinguish between personal and commercial use. . . . The court also emphasized that the license "would not withdraw any information from the public domain" because all of the information on the CD-ROM was publicly available. *Id.* at 1455.

The case before us is different from *ProCD*. The Copyright Act does not confer a right to pay the same amount for commercial and personal use. It does, however, confer a right to fair use, 17 U.S.C. §107, which we have held encompasses reverse engineering.

ProCD and the other contract cases are also careful not to create a blanket rule that all contracts will escape preemption. The court in that case emphasized that "we think it prudent to refrain from adopting a rule that anything with the label 'contract' is necessarily outside the preemption clause." . . .

I conclude that *Vault* states the correct rule; that state law authorizing shrinkwrap licenses that prohibit reverse engineering is preempted; and that the First Circuit would so hold because the extra element here "merely concerns *the extent to which* authors and their licensees can prohibit unauthorized copying by third parties." *Data Gen.*, 36 F.3d at 1165 (emphasis in original). I respectfully dissent.

NOTES AND QUESTIONS

1. Do you find the majority or the dissent in *Bowers* more convincing? Why? Do the two opinions arrive at different results because the majority focuses on §301 and the dissent on implied preemption principles? Are you persuaded by the dissenter's contention that his argument is consistent with *ProCD*?

2. Would the *Vault* court have agreed with the Seventh Circuit if it had been presented with the facts of *ProCD*? *Vault* involved a preemption challenge to a state statute, while *ProCD* involved a preemption challenge to a private contract. Should this make a difference to the preemption analysis?

3. The dissent in *Bowers* would distinguish between standard-form and negotiated agreements. Indeed, an argument that such a distinction matters has been implicit in much of this section. Should the distinction matter? One could argue that standard-form contracts permit mass markets to form and that licensees should be deemed to have consented to terms unless the terms are unenforceable under general contract law. Thus, mass-market contracts should not be treated differently than negotiated contracts in a preemption analysis. Do you agree? If not, articulate the reasons why you disagree.

4. Reread Note 6, Chapter 4.B, pages 245-46, *supra*. There we excerpted part of an article by Professor Samuelson et al. arguing that the law should protect some amount of lead time for developers to permit them to recoup their investments. In *Vault*, Vault had developed a program to prevent unauthorized copying of computer programs: Customers (software vendors) would place programs on diskettes loaded with Vault's program, and purchasers would need that version of the diskette to be in the drive for the vendor's program to run. Quaid developed a product that defeated Vault's protection mechanism and allowed the production of functional copies. Should Vault have been allowed to use contract law to give it sufficient protection to innovate in the first place?

How about *ProCD*? Zeidenberg marketed the database in direct competition with ProCD and at a lower price because Zeidenberg did not incur the costs of gathering the data. Should ProCD be able to define its own protection by contract, or should it have to rely on any protection misappropriation law might give it?

5. By now, you have read *Sega Enterprises Ltd. v. Accolade, Inc.*, 977 F.2d 1510 (9th Cir. 1992), Chapter 7, pages 566-70, *supra*. In *Sega*, the court held that §117 did not authorize disassembly of object code because such a use goes "far beyond that contemplated by CONTU and authorized by section 117." *Id.* at 1520. Is this holding consistent with *Vault*? Which court do you think is correct? In *Sega*, the court did, however, determine that in certain circumstances fair use permits the reproduction of computer software that occurs in the course of disassembly. Should it make a difference in determining preemption if the contractual clause at issue negates an express provision of the copyright statute, such as §117, or a judicial application of the fair use doctrine?

6. Fair use encompasses many acts in addition to reverse engineering. In practice, very few contracts literally prohibit fair use, perhaps because fair use is so hard to define in advance of litigation. Instead, firms often try to enter into negotiated or standard form contracts that spell

out permitted and prohibited uses in detail. Some of the prohibited uses might be fair under certain circumstances. What should a court do with a preemption challenge to a breach of contract claim based on an act that copyright law would consider fair? Should courts find that the Copyright Act preempts claims of contract breach involving clauses that purport to prohibit some types of fair use (e.g., restrictions that purport to prevent a purchaser from criticizing the copyrighted work) but not others?

In *Bowers*, the jury concluded that Baystate's product, allegedly created after disassembling Bowers' copyrighted software, infringed the plaintiff's copyrights. Should the merits of the infringement case affect the analysis of the preemption question?

7. Do you think that copyright misuse is a doctrine better adapted to addressing restrictive contractual provisions than preemption? What are the differences in analysis and result between the two doctrines? Professor Lemley argues that copyright misuse has an important role to play in policing overreaching contractual arrangements:

> The basis for copyright misuse seems to be that courts should not assist the expansion of a copyright beyond its statutory bounds, as they would do were they to enforce an improperly-broadened copyright. This policy is particularly strong when the agreement between the parties has significant external effects. . . .
>
> Copyright owners who seek to obtain by contract what copyright law will not give them will have to face [the misuse] cases. Like preemption, copyright misuse won't cover the full range of potentially troubling licensing practices. . . .
>
> Nonetheless, copyright misuse doctrine readily disposes of the "contracts are different" canard, because it so clearly operates . . . to restrict the enforcement of anticompetitive licensing provisions. It may be more apt than [the] fair use doctrine in preventing some anticompetitive extension of copyright. In any event, copyright misuse can't be waived by contract. Furthermore, because copyright misuse is a fact-specific doctrine tailored to the circumstances of individual cases, it may prove a better tool both for tailoring copyright incentives, and for avoiding the reticence that surrounds coarser tools such as preemption.

Mark A. Lemley, *Beyond Preemption: The Law and Policy of Intellectual Property Licensing*, 87 Cal. L. Rev. 111, 153, 157-58 (1999). Do you agree? Does the misuse doctrine have any disadvantages as compared with preemption? *See Davidson & Assocs. v. Jung*, 422 F.3d. 630 (8th Cir. 2005) (holding that copyright misuse is not a defense to a breach of contract claim).

The Copyright Infringement Lawsuit

Like other kinds of litigation, a copyright infringement lawsuit raises many procedural issues. Some of these include: What courts have subject matter jurisdiction? Who can bring infringement actions, and when can they bring them? Is there a right to a jury trial? What rules determine the kinds of remedies available? Do international treaties speak to the kinds of remedies domestic courts can award? This chapter discusses these litigation issues.

A. PROPER COURT

As provided in 28 U.S.C. §1338, the federal courts have exclusive subject matter jurisdiction over copyright infringement actions:

> (a) The district courts shall have original jurisdiction of any civil action arising under any Act of Congress relating to . . . copyrights. . . . Such jurisdiction shall be exclusive of the courts of the states in . . . copyright cases.

While the principle of exclusive jurisdiction seems fairly straightforward, recall from Chapter 10 that claims of copyright infringement can be supplemented with claims established under state law. The combination of copyright and state law claims raises the question whether a particular complaint "arises under" the Copyright Act for purposes of §1338(a). As the case that follows illustrates, courts continue to struggle with the subject matter jurisdiction question when the parties to the copyright dispute are also parties to a contract. Is the action one for breach of contract, arising under state law, or rather one for copyright infringement?

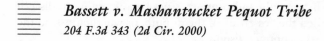

Bassett v. Mashantucket Pequot Tribe
204 F.3d 343 (2d Cir. 2000)

LEVAL, C.J.: . . . According to the allegations of the complaint: Plaintiff Debra Bassett operates a business, Bassett Productions, that produces films and television programs. Defendant

Mashantucket Pequot Tribe is a federally recognized Indian tribe with a reservation located within the geographical boundaries of the State of Connecticut. Defendant Mashantucket Pequot Museum is a Connecticut corporation located on the Pequot Reservation.

In October 1994, Bassett met with representatives of the Tribe to discuss the possibility of producing a film for the Museum about the Pequot War of 1636-38. . . .

In August 1995, Bassett Productions entered into a letter agreement with the Tribe (the "Letter Agreement") for the development and production of a film about the 1636-38 Pequot War. The Letter Agreement identified Bassett Productions as the "Producer" and the Tribe as the "Owner," but did not define these terms. It stipulated that Bassett Productions would "hire and supervise the development and writing of a screenplay by Keith Merrill and George Burdeau," and that the Tribe would "compensate" Bassett Productions for development costs according to an agreed schedule. It also stipulated that "at such time" that the Tribe approved the final draft of the screenplay, Bassett Productions would have exclusive rights to produce the film for exhibition at the Pequot Museum.

Some time before October 30, 1995, Bassett had delivered to the Tribe a script that she herself had written, based on a "script scenario" she had developed with assistance from her associate Allan Eckert. . . .

On October 30, 1995, Bassett received a notice from the Tribe terminating the Letter Agreement. The notice asserted that Bassett had not "perform[ed] the contract as the parties anticipated."

Following the termination of the Letter Agreement, the Tribe continued to pursue the development and production of a film on the 1636-38 Pequot War for exhibition at the Museum. In October 1996, filming was completed on a motion picture entitled, "The Witness." Bassett asserts the Tribe intends to screen the film at the Museum "in the near future" as part of "an interstate-driven tourist attraction." . . .

In September 1996, Bassett commenced this lawsuit in the United States District Court for the District of Connecticut. The complaint sought an injunction as well as other copyright remedies on the ground that the Tribe and the Museum used Bassett's copyrighted script without her consent or license in order to produce their own film; it further alleged that they breached the Letter Agreement, and that they committed various state-law torts resulting in injury to Bassett. . . .

In March 1997, Defendants moved to dismiss Bassett's complaint for lack of subject matter jurisdiction and for failure to exhaust tribal remedies. In their motion papers, Defendants argued (*inter alia*) that the court lacked federal question jurisdiction because Bassett's sole federal claim — her claim for copyright infringement — was "incidental to" her contract claims, and therefore did not "arise under" federal law.

The district court granted Defendants' motion to dismiss the complaint, and Bassett appealed.

Discussion . . .

Prior to our landmark decision in *T.B. Harms* [*Co. v. Eliscu*, 339 F.2d 823 (2d Cir. 1964)], several district courts in the Second Circuit resolved the issue of jurisdiction under Section 1338 for "hybrid" claims raising both copyright and contract issues by attempting to discern whether the copyright issues constituted the "essence" of the dispute, or whether instead the copyright issues were "incidental to" the contract dispute. . . .

That approach, however, left a class of plaintiffs who suffered copyright infringement bereft of copyright remedies. Plaintiffs whose federal lawsuits were dismissed for lack of subject matter jurisdiction on the ground that their copyright claims were "incidental to" their contract claims had no way either to obtain an adjudication of infringement or to obtain relief provided by the Copyright Act, because the Act confers exclusive jurisdiction over copyright claims on federal courts. . . . That approach had the added defect of requiring a court to make findings at the outset of the litigation that could not be discerned from the complaint but instead required a deep understanding of the dispute not usually gained until the case had been heard at trial.

In *T.B. Harms*, Judge Friendly . . . established a test for this circuit that focused on whether and how a complaint implicates the Copyright Act. . . . At issue [in *T.B. Harms*] was whether one of the defendants had previously assigned his interest in the copyrights to the plaintiff's agent, or whether this defendant had retained his interest and had validly assigned it at a later date to a second defendant. No claim of infringement was asserted and no relief provided by the Copyright Act was sought. . . .

Synthesizing the Supreme Court authorities, Judge Friendly concluded that a suit "arises under" the Copyright Act if:

> (1) "[T]he complaint is for a remedy expressly granted by the Act, e.g., a suit for infringement or for the statutory royalties for record reproduction . . ."; or,
> (2) "[T]he complaint . . . asserts a claim requiring construction of the Act. . . ." *Id.* at 828.[3]

As the suit in *T.B. Harms* did not fall within any of these enumerated categories, the court found that it did not "arise under" the copyright laws for purposes of Section 1338 and that jurisdiction was therefore lacking. . . .

Nearly thirty years after the *T.B. Harms* decision, a panel of this court in *Schoenberg* [*v. Shapolsky Publishers, Inc.*, 971 F.2d 926 (2d Cir. 1992)] undertook in dictum to state the test for determining the existence of Section 1338 jurisdiction in cases alleging violations of the Copyright Act resulting from breach of contract. The plaintiff, an author, alleged that he had licensed the defendant, a publisher, to publish plaintiff's work. The license obligated the defendant to publish within six months of plaintiff's delivery of the manuscript, to promote and market the work, and to license foreign language editions. According to plaintiff's allegations, the publisher breached numerous obligations of the license. As a result of these failures, plaintiff claimed that the license was terminated and that defendant's further publication of the work constituted an infringement. Although the appeal related to a different issue, the opinion undertook to state "the appropriate test under the *T.B. Harms* paradigm. . . ." *Schoenberg*, 971 F.2d at 932.

The opinion . . . observed . . . that notwithstanding the *T.B. Harms* formulation, some district courts had "looked beyond the complaint in order to determine whether the plaintiff was really concerned with the infringement of his copyright, or, alternatively, was, in fact, more interested in" free enjoyment of his property or other non-copyright issues. *Id.* at 932. . . . Other courts, it noted, had adopted the even "broader proposition that no claim arises under the Copyright Act whenever an infringement would necessarily result from the breach of a contract that licensed or assigned a copyright." *Id.* at 931. . . .

In undertaking to reconcile the varying approaches of those district court opinions (and perhaps concluding that the authority of *T.B. Harms* extended only to disputes over copyright ownership and not to hybrid copyright/contract claims), *Schoenberg* created a new, complex three-step test; the first step of the test was precisely that which *T.B. Harms*

---

3. Judge Friendly speculated that jurisdiction might also exist, "perhaps more doubtfully," in a third category of cases "where a distinctive policy of the Act requires that federal principles control the disposition of the claim." *T.B. Harms*, 339 F.2d at 828.

had rejected — whether the claim for copyright remedies is " 'merely incidental' " to a determination of contract rights. The opinion declared that in hybrid copyright and contract cases Section 1338 jurisdiction should be analyzed in the following manner:

> A district court must first ascertain whether the plaintiff's infringement claim is only "incidental" to the plaintiff's claim seeking a determination of ownership or contractual rights under the copyright. . . . If it is determined that the claim is not merely incidental, then a district court must next determine whether the complaint alleges a breach of a condition to, or a covenant of, the contract licensing or assigning the copyright. . . . [I]f a breach of a condition is alleged, then the district court has subject matter jurisdiction. . . . But if the complaint merely alleges a breach of a contractual covenant in the agreement that licenses or assigns the copyright, then the court must undertake a third step and analyze whether the breach is so material as to create a right of rescission in the grantor. If the breach would create a right of rescission, then the asserted claim arises under the Copyright Act.

Id. at 932-33 (citations omitted).

We believe for a number of reasons that the *Schoenberg* test is unworkable. At the outset, it overlooks that, because the Copyright Act gives federal courts *exclusive* jurisdiction to enforce its provisions, *see* 28 U.S.C. §1338, a plaintiff who is denied access to a federal forum on the theory that his copyright claims are incidental to a contract dispute is thereby absolutely denied the benefit of copyright remedies. Such a denial of copyright remedies undermines the Act's capacity to protect copyright interests. A plaintiff with meritorious copyright claims and entitlement to the special remedies provided by the Act is deprived of these remedies merely because the first hurdle of proving entitlement is a showing of a contractual right.[9]

A second problem with the *Schoenberg* test is that it is vague. *Schoenberg* characterizes the first part of its test in two ways: whether "the 'essence' of the plaintiff's claim" is in contract or copyright, or whether the "infringement claim is only 'incidental' to the plaintiff's claim seeking determination of ownership or contractual rights under the copyright." The meaning of either of these phrases is difficult to discern. . . .

[E]ven if the complaint sets forth in full the allegations relating to the license, and the defendant promptly moves to dismiss, the *Schoenberg* test requires the court to make complex factual determinations relating to the merits at the outset of the litigation — before the court has any familiarity with the case. Ascertaining what . . . a plaintiff's principal motives [are] in bringing suit, and what issues will loom largest in the case, may well require extensive hearings and fact finding. The need for such fact finding recurs at each stage of *Schoenberg*'s three-step formula. Thus, if a court finds that a copyright claim is not "merely incidental to" a contract claim (step one), it must still determine whether the contractual term alleged to have been

---

9. Ironically, under the *Schoenberg* test, the more clear it is that plaintiff is entitled to copyright remedies (assuming plaintiff prevails on the disputed contract issues), the less likely it is that plaintiff will be accorded those remedies. This can be seen by considering two hypothetical cases, identical in that each defendant claims entitlement to exploit the copyright under a license, and each plaintiff claims the defendant forfeited the license by breaching the contract terms. In the first case, the defendant has no defense other than its contractual right; it concedes that, if plaintiff prevails on the contract issue, plaintiff is entitled to the copyright remedies sought in the complaint. In the second case, the defendant asserts, in addition to its contract defense, (a) that the work is not original as required by the Copyright Act; (b) that the author's assignment to plaintiff was void for failure to conform to the requirements of the Copyright Act; (c) that Defendant's work is not "substantially similar" to plaintiff's work; and (d) that defendant's work should be considered "fair use."

In the first case, because the only disputed issue is contractual, the court might conclude that the copyright claims are merely "incidental" and dismiss the case. In the second case, because issues of copyright law are in dispute, the court will not dismiss. Thus, the greater the likelihood that plaintiff will be found entitled to the copyright remedies sought in the complaint, the less likely it is that he will receive them.

breached was in the nature of a covenant or a condition (step two). And if it finds that the alleged breach was of a covenant, the court must next determine "whether the breach is so material as to create a right of rescission," 971 F.2d at 933, failing which the case must be dismissed (step three). This third inquiry in particular, which entails an assessment of the importance of the particular covenant, as well as the seriousness of the breach, raises questions that are not appropriately, easily or reliably answered at the start of litigation.

Finally, *Schoenberg* failed to recognize that in deviating from the test explained in *T.B. Harms*, it was failing to follow the governing Supreme Court authority on which *T.B. Harms* relied. *Schoenberg*'s reliance on whether the disputed issues focus on matters of contract ownership rather than copyright cannot be reconciled with Justice Holmes' formulation in *American Well Works* that a "suit arises under the law that creates the cause of action." 241 U.S. at 260. The test, furthermore, is at odds with the well-established approach to federal question jurisdiction, pursuant to which jurisdiction is determined by ascertaining whether the plaintiff's complaint asserts a right under federal law. *See, e.g.,* ... *The Fair v. Kohler Die & Specialty Co.,* 228 U.S. 22, 25 (1913) (Holmes, J.) ("[T]he party who brings a suit is master to decide what law he will rely upon, and therefore does determine whether he will bring a 'suit arising under' the patent or other law of the United States by his declaration or bill.").

For the reasons discussed above, we conclude that, for claims of infringement arising from, or in the context of, an alleged contractual breach, this circuit's standard for determining jurisdiction under Section 1338 is furnished by *T.B. Harms*, and not by *Schoenberg*. When a complaint alleges a claim or seeks a remedy provided by the Copyright Act, federal jurisdiction is properly invoked.

Applying the *T.B. Harms* standard to this case leads us to conclude that Bassett's copyright claims "arise under" the Copyright Act for purposes of Section 1338. Unlike the complaint in *T.B. Harms*, the complaint in this case alleges that the defendants, without authority, used plaintiff's copyrighted script to produce a new film intended and advertised for imminent exhibition. The amended complaint alleged copyright infringement and sought "a remedy expressly granted by the Act," *T.B. Harms*, 339 F.2d at 828, specifically, an injunction against further infringement of Bassett's copyrighted script. Because the complaint alleges the defendants violated the Copyright Act and seeks the injunctive remedy provided by the Act, under the rule of *T.B. Harms*, the action falls within the jurisdictional grant of Section 1338. The district court's contrary holding was in error.[14]

NOTES AND QUESTIONS

1. Compare the *T.B. Harms/Bassett* test with the *Schoenberg* test. Is the *Schoenberg* test really as unworkable as the Second Circuit suggests? Or is the real concern that as a result of

---

14. Indeed this case serves as an excellent example of the shortcomings of the *Schoenberg* test. Plaintiff alleges entitlement to an injunction provided by the Copyright Act. If the case is dismissed because of the court's perception that the copyright claim is "incidental to" a dispute about contractual rights, plaintiff will have no opportunity to receive either an adjudication of infringement or copyright remedies from the state courts.

The scenario most often analyzed under the *Schoenberg* test is one in which a plaintiff owns a copyright and undisputedly assigns or licenses defendant who allegedly breaches the terms of the contract by, for example, failing to pay royalties. Plaintiff then claims the license is terminated and that the defendant infringed plaintiff's copyright through unauthorized, continued use of the protected material after the breach. *See, e.g., Living Music Records, Inc.,* 827 F. Supp. at 980-81 (declining jurisdiction over copyright infringement claim based on allegations that defendant failed to pay royalties under a license agreement permitting it to make and sell copies of plaintiff's musical recordings). Here, however, plaintiff disputes that the Letter Agreement constituted any type of transfer, license or assignment of her copyrighted script. . . .

denying federal court access to plaintiffs whose copyright claims are judged "incidental" to contract claims, state courts may end up indirectly influencing copyright policy in their treatment of the contract claims? Would this necessarily be a bad result? Is the import of §1338 that the integrity of federal power over copyright matters must not in any way be compromised? Does §1338 require that all copyright-related matters, no matter how insignificant to the dispute, be heard by a federal court? Can you think of any advantages the *Schoenberg* test might have over the *T.B. Harms/Bassett* test?

2. Under the *T.B. Harms* test, when a plaintiff asserts infringement and the defense raised is an assignment of the copyright, does the federal court have exclusive jurisdiction? If the court finds a valid assignment, will there be an occasion to consider any aspect of the Copyright Act? In such a case, should the federal court have exclusive subject matter jurisdiction? Consider the scenario described by the court in footnote 14. How will the subject matter jurisdiction question in those types of cases be resolved under the *T.B. Harms* test?

3. In a portion of the opinion not reproduced above, Judge Leval also criticized the *Schoenberg* test on the ground that plaintiffs will have no way of knowing where to file their cases. Reread the elements of the *Schoenberg* test. Is this really true? Is a better criticism that the *Schoenberg* test will lead to artful pleading to either avoid or obtain federal court jurisdiction?

4. The *Bassett* court noted that all circuits that have considered the question whether a suit arises under the Copyright Act when the dispute includes non-copyright issues have adopted the *T.B. Harms* test. *Bassett*, 204 F.3d at 350-51. *See, e.g., Scandinavian Satellite Sys., AS v. Prime TV Ltd.*, 291 F.3d 839, 844 (D.C. Cir. 2002); *MCA Television, Ltd. v. Pub. Interest Corp.*, 171 F.3d 1265, 1269 (11th Cir. 1999). Keep in mind, however, that not all circuits have had the opportunity to consider this question.

5. As you learned in Chapter 10, instead of bringing a copyright infringement action in federal court, the plaintiff might, for strategic reasons, bring a breach of contract claim in state court. Under the *T.B. Harms* test, if the defense to be relied upon is based on the Copyright Act (e.g., that the defendant's use is fair), the case will not be removable because a defense, either real or anticipated, does not provide a basis for federal subject matter jurisdiction. *See Louisville & Nashville R.R. Co. v. Mottley*, 211 U.S. 149 (1908). Nevertheless, the defendant may be able to bring a separate declaratory judgment action in federal court. We discuss declaratory judgment actions later in this chapter.

A similar jurisdictional problem results when party A has a breach of contract claim against party B and party B has a copyright infringement claim against party A arising out of the same transaction or occurrence. If party B files first, the case is clearly within the exclusive jurisdiction of the federal courts under §1338, and party A can assert its breach of contract claim as a counterclaim. If, instead, party A files first, unless the requirements for diversity jurisdiction are met, the case is not cognizable in federal court. If party A files its breach of contract action in state court, what should be done with party B's copyright infringement claim? If the copyright infringement claim is asserted as a counterclaim, the case will not be removable because of the well-pleaded complaint rule established by *Mottley*. Does the state court have jurisdiction to hear the copyright counterclaim given the exclusive jurisdiction §1338 provides? Many courts have held that party B must file a separate action in federal court. Does such a bifurcation of the dispute make sense?

Two recent developments, however, may lessen the incidence of bifurcation. First, in *Holmes Group, Inc. v. Vornado Air Circulation Sys., Inc.*, 535 U.S. 826 (2002), the Court held that regional federal circuit courts may decide compulsory patent counterclaims notwithstanding the Federal Circuit's exclusive appellate jurisdiction over patent infringement claims, because counterclaims cannot provide the basis for federal subject matter jurisdiction and therefore are not governed by §1338's exclusivity requirement. Relying on *Holmes Group*, some state courts have entertained copyright counterclaims. *See Green v. Hendrickson Publishers, Inc.*, 770 N.E.2d 784 (Ind. 2002). Second, as discussed in Chapter 10.B, page 730 *supra*, some federal courts have applied the "complete preemption" doctrine to sustain removal of certain state law claims that meet the criteria for preemption set forth in §301(a) on the ground that they are "really" copyright claims. *See Ritchie v. Williams*, 395 F.3d 283 (6th Cir. 2005); *Briarpatch, Ltd., L.P. v. Phoenix Pictures, Inc.*, 373 F.3d 296 (2d Cir. 2004), *cert. denied*, 544 U.S. 949 (2005); *Rosciszewski v. Arete Assocs., Inc.*, 1 F.3d 225 (4th Cir. 1993).

B. PROPER TIMING

Determining whether and when to bring a copyright infringement action is partly a matter of litigation strategy. However, certain rules bar such a lawsuit before copyright registration takes place. Additionally, the Copyright Act contains a three-year statute of limitations for civil actions. These timing issues are not as straightforward as they may seem.

1. The Registration Requirement and Filing Too Early

Subject to certain exceptions, §411 requires copyright holders to register their copyrights before filing an infringement lawsuit. In the next case, the Supreme Court addresses whether the registration requirement affects the subject matter jurisdiction of the federal courts.

Reed Elsevier, Inc. v. Muchnick
_____ U.S. _____, 130 S. Ct. 1237 (2010)

THOMAS, J.: . . . "Anyone who violates any of the exclusive rights of the copyright owner as provided" in the Act "is an infringer of the copyright." §501(a). When such infringement occurs, a copyright owner "is entitled, *subject to the requirements of section 411*, to institute an action" for copyright infringement. §501(b) (emphasis added).

This case concerns "the requirements of section 411" to which §501(b) refers. Section 411(a) provides, *inter alia* and with certain exceptions, that "no civil action for infringement of the copyright in any United States work shall be instituted until preregistration or registration of the copyright claim has been made in accordance with this title." This provision is part of the Act's remedial scheme. It establishes a condition — copyright registration — that plaintiffs ordinarily must satisfy before filing an infringement claim and invoking the Act's remedial provisions. We address whether §411(a) also deprives federal courts of subject-matter jurisdiction to adjudicate infringement claims involving unregistered works.

B

The relevant proceedings in this case began after we issued our opinion in *New York Times Co. v. Tasini*, 533 U.S. 483 (2001). In *Tasini*, we agreed with the Court of Appeals for the Second Circuit that several owners of online databases and print publishers had infringed the copyrights of six freelance authors by reproducing the authors' works electronically without first securing their permission. See *id.*, at 493. In so holding, we affirmed the principal theory of liability underlying copyright infringement suits that other freelance authors had filed after the Court of Appeals had issued its opinion in *Tasini*. These other suits, which were stayed pending our decision in *Tasini*, resumed after we issued our opinion and were consolidated in the United States District Court for the Southern District of New York by the Judicial Panel on Multidistrict Litigation.

The consolidated complaint alleged that the named plaintiffs each own at least one copyright, typically in a freelance article written for a newspaper or a magazine, that they had registered in accordance with §411(a). The class, however, included both authors who had registered their copyrighted works and authors who had not.

. . . The parties moved the District Court to certify a class for settlement and to approve the settlement agreement [reached after more than three years of negotiation]. Ten freelance authors, including Irvin Muchnick (hereinafter Muchnick respondents), objected. The District Court overruled the objections; certified a settlement class . . . ; approved the settlement . . . ; and entered final judgment. . . .

The Muchnick respondents appealed. . . . Shortly before oral argument, the Court of Appeals *sua sponte* ordered briefing on the question whether §411(a) deprives federal courts of subject-matter jurisdiction over infringement claims involving unregistered copyrights. . . .

. . . . [T]he Court of Appeals concluded that the District Court lacked jurisdiction to certify a class of claims arising from the infringement of unregistered works, and also lacked jurisdiction to approve a settlement with respect to those claims, 509 F.3d, at 121 (citing "widespread agreement among the circuits that section 411(a) is jurisdictional").[2] . . . .

We granted the owners' and publishers' petition for a writ of certiorari, and formulated the question presented to ask whether §411(a) restricts the subject-matter jurisdiction of the federal courts over copyright infringement actions. 555 U.S. ____, 129 S. Ct. 1523 (2009). Because no party supports the Court of Appeals' jurisdictional holding, we appointed an *amicus curiae* to defend the Court of Appeals' judgment. We now reverse.

II

A

. . . While perhaps clear in theory, the distinction between jurisdictional conditions and claim-processing rules can be confusing in practice. Courts — including this Court — have sometimes mischaracterized claim-processing rules or elements of a cause of action as jurisdictional limitations, particularly when that characterization was not central to the case, and thus did not require close analysis. . . .

. . . . In *Arbaugh* [*v. Y & H Corp.*, 546 U.S. 500 (2006)], we described the general approach to distinguish "jurisdictional" conditions from claim-processing requirements or elements of a claim:

> "If the Legislature clearly states that a threshold limitation on a statute's scope shall count as jurisdictional, then courts and litigants will be duly instructed and will not be left to wrestle

---

2. See *La Resolana Architects, PA v. Clay Realtors Angel Fire*, 416 F.3d 1195, 1200-1201 (C.A.10 2005); *Positive Black Talk Inc. v. Cash Money Records Inc.*, 394 F.3d 357, 365 (C.A.5 2004); *Xoom, Inc. v. Imageline, Inc.*, 323 F.3d 279, 283 (C.A.4 2003); *Murray Hill Publications, Inc. v. ABC Communications, Inc.*, 264 F.3d 622, 630, and n. 1 (C.A.6 2001); *Brewer-Giorgio v. Producers Video, Inc.*, 216 F.3d 1281, 1285 (C.A.11 2000); *Data Gen. Corp. v. Grumman Systems Support Corp.*, 36 F.3d 1147, 1163 (C.A.1 1994).

with the issue. But when Congress does not rank a statutory limitation on coverage as jurisdictional, courts should treat the restriction as nonjurisdictional in character." 546 U.S. at 515-516 (citation and footnote omitted).

. . . .

B

Section 411(a) provides:

"Except for an action brought for a violation of the rights of the author under section 106A(a), and subject to the provisions of subsection (b), no civil action for infringement of the copyright in any United States work shall be instituted until preregistration or registration of the copyright claim has been made in accordance with this title. In any case, however, where the deposit, application, and fee required for registration have been delivered to the Copyright Office in proper form and registration has been refused, the applicant is entitled to institute a civil action for infringement if notice thereof, with a copy of the complaint, is served on the Register of Copyrights. The Register may, at his or her option, become a party to the action with respect to the issue of registrability of the copyright claim by entering an appearance within sixty days after such service, but the Register's failure to become a party shall not deprive the court of jurisdiction to determine that issue."

We must consider whether §411(a) "clearly states" that its registration requirement is "jurisdictional." *Arbaugh, supra*, at 515. It does not. *Amicus* disagrees, pointing to the presence of the word "jurisdiction" in the last sentence of §411(a) and contending that the use of the term there indicates the jurisdictional cast of §411(a)'s first sentence as well. But this reference to "jurisdiction" cannot bear the weight that *amicus* places upon it. The sentence upon which *amicus* relies states:

"The Register [of Copyrights] may, at his or her option, become a party to the [copyright infringement] action with respect to *the issue of registrability of the copyright claim* by entering an appearance within sixty days after such service, but the Register's failure to become a party shall not deprive the court of jurisdiction to determine *that issue*." §411(a) (emphasis added).

Congress added this sentence to the Act in 1976, 90 Stat. 2583, to clarify that a federal court can determine "the issue of registrability of the copyright claim" even if the Register does not appear in the infringement suit. That clarification was necessary because courts had interpreted §411(a)'s precursor provision, which imposed a similar registration requirement, as prohibiting copyright owners who had been *refused* registration by the Register of Copyrights from suing for infringement until the owners *first* sought mandamus against the Register. See *Vacheron & Constantin-Le Coultre Watches, Inc. v. Benrus Watch Co.*, 260 F.2d 637, 640-641 (C.A.2 1958) (construing §411(a)'s precursor). The 1976 amendment made it clear that a federal court plainly has adjudicatory authority to determine "*that* issue," §411(a) (emphasis added)—*i.e.*, the issue of *registrability*—regardless of whether the Register is a party to the *infringement* suit. The word "jurisdiction," as used here, thus says nothing about whether a federal court has subject-matter jurisdiction to adjudicate claims for infringement of unregistered works.

Moreover, §411(a)'s registration requirement . . . is located in a provision "separate" from those granting federal courts subject-matter jurisdiction over those respective claims. Federal district courts have subject-matter jurisdiction over copyright infringement actions based on 28 U.S.C. §§1331 and 1338. But neither §1331, which confers subject-matter jurisdiction over questions of federal law, nor §1338(a), which is specific to copyright claims, conditions its jurisdictional grant on whether copyright holders have registered their works before suing for infringement.

Nor does any other factor suggest that 17 U.S.C.A. §411(a)'s registration requirement can be read to " 'speak in jurisdictional terms or refer in any way to the jurisdiction of the district courts.' " *Arbaugh*, 546 U.S., at 515 (quoting *Zipes* [*v. Trans World Airlines, Inc.*], 455 U.S. [385, 394 (1982)]). First, and most significantly, §411(a) expressly *allows* courts to adjudicate infringement claims involving unregistered works in three circumstances: where the work is not a U.S. work, where the infringement claim concerns rights of attribution and integrity under §106A, or where the holder attempted to register the work and registration was refused. Separately, §411(c) permits courts to adjudicate infringement actions over certain kinds of unregistered works where the author "declare[s] an intention to secure copyright in the work" and "makes registration for the work, if required by subsection (a), within three months after [the work's] first transmission." 17 U.S.C. §§411(c)(1)-(2). It would be at least unusual to ascribe jurisdictional significance to a condition subject to these sorts of exceptions.

. . . . We similarly have treated as nonjurisdictional other types of threshold requirements that claimants must complete, or exhaust, before filing a lawsuit.

The registration requirement in 17 U.S.C.A. §411(a) fits in this mold. Section 411(a) imposes a precondition to filing a claim that is not clearly labeled jurisdictional, is not located in a jurisdiction-granting provision, and admits of congressionally authorized exceptions. Section 411(a) thus imposes a type of precondition to suit that supports nonjurisdictional treatment under our precedents.

C

Amicus insists that our decision in *Bowles* [*v. Russell*], 551 U.S. 205 [(2007)], compels a conclusion contrary to the one we reach today. *Amicus* cites *Bowles* for the proposition that where Congress did not explicitly label a statutory condition as jurisdictional, a court nevertheless should treat it as such if that is how the condition consistently has been interpreted and if Congress has not disturbed that interpretation. . . .

Bowles did not hold that any statutory condition devoid of an express jurisdictional label should be treated as jurisdictional simply because courts have long treated it as such. Nor did it hold that all statutory conditions imposing a time limit should be considered jurisdictional. Rather, *Bowles* stands for the proposition that context, including this Court's interpretation of similar provisions in many years past, is relevant to whether a statute ranks a requirement as jurisdictional. . . .

. . . . Although §411(a)'s historical treatment as "jurisdictional" is a factor in the analysis, it is not dispositive. The other factors discussed above demonstrate that §411(a)'s registration requirement is more analogous to the nonjurisdictional conditions we considered in *Zipes* and *Arbaugh* than to the statutory time limit at issue in *Bowles*. We thus conclude that §411(a)'s registration requirement is nonjurisdictional, notwithstanding its prior jurisdictional treatment. . . .

NOTES AND QUESTIONS

1. In *Reed Elsevier*, the question about the jurisdictional nature of the registration requirement arose in the context of approval of a class action settlement involving both registered and unregistered works. How will the Court's holding affect non-class action

lawsuits? If a plaintiff files an infringement lawsuit but has not yet registered the copyright that she claims has been infringed, should the case be dismissed for failure to meet a "precondition to suit"? Does the defendant in such a case have to file a motion to dismiss or can the court dismiss the case *sua sponte*?

2. Focus on the exemptions to the registration requirement that the Court identifies. What policy might animate exempting claims under §106A from the registration requirement? Why are non-U.S. works exempted? Recall the treaty prohibitions on formalities discussed in Chapter 3. Why require copyright owners of U.S. works to register before bringing suit when foreign copyright owners do not face such a requirement?

3. Before the *Reed Elsevier* decision the lower courts had largely treated registration, or at least attempted registration, as jurisdictional. A circuit split had developed, however, concerning whether a copyright owner could sue upon filing an application for registration (the "Application approach") or had to wait until receiving the Copyright Office decision on the application (the "Registration approach"). *See La Resolana Architects, PA v. Clay Realtors Angel Fire*, 416 F.3d 1195 (10th Cir. 2005) (discussing the different approaches and concluding that the "Registration approach" is most consistent with the statutory language), *abrogated in part by Reed Elsevier, Inc. v. Muchnick*, ____U.S.____, 130 S. Ct. 1237 (2010). Should *Reed Elsevier* affect how courts interpret the timing aspects of the registration requirement?

4. Timing can be critically important in infringement lawsuits. In 2009, application processing times in the Copyright Office were as long as 18 months. If the plaintiff must wait for the Copyright Office to issue the registration, the suit may be barred by the Statute of Limitations. Other times, a plaintiff desires prompt injunctive relief. If the plaintiff must wait for the registration certificate, the delay in obtaining injunctive relief will be devastating. The Copyright Office allows registrants to request special handling and "every attempt is made to process the claim . . . within 5 working days." Copyright Office Circular 10 (Dec. 2004). Should the existence of this process influence courts' interpretation of the timing requirements for §411? In addition to paying an expedited handling fee ($760 in 2009), a registrant must explain why expedited handling is necessary. Expedited handling is granted only in special circumstances. The Copyright Office has indicated that "pending or prospective litigation" qualifies as a special circumstance. *Id*. Should the fact that the Copyright Office contemplates expedited processing because of pending litigation influence the interpretation of §411? In answering this last question, remember that litigation can involve more than one copyrighted work belonging to the plaintiff.

5. As discussed in Chapter 3.A, pages 154-55 *supra*, if the Copyright Office rejects a registration, the putative copyright owner can still bring an infringement action, so long as the Copyright Office is notified of the lawsuit. Notification of the Copyright Office is not considered a jurisdicitional prerequisite. *Brooks-Ngwenya v. Indianapolis Pub. Sch.*, 564 F.3d 804, 808 (7th Cir. 2009) (noting that while the notification requirement is not "strictly jurisdictional" it is, nevertheless, "mandatory," permitting the district court to impose sanctions for failure to comply).

6. According to the Second Circuit, registration of copyright in a derivative work allows the copyright owner to file a lawsuit for infringement of the copyright in the underlying work even if the latter copyright is not itself registered. *Streetwise Maps, Inc. v. VanDam, Inc.*, 159 F.3d 739 (2d Cir. 1998). The converse, however, is not true; registration of copyright in the underlying work cannot be used to support the filing of a lawsuit for infringement of the copyright in a derivative work. *Well-Made Toy Mfg. Corp. v. Goffa Int'l Corp.*, 354 F.3d 112 (2d Cir. 2003); *see also Murray Hill Publ'ns v. ABC Commc'ns*, 264 F.3d 622 (6th Cir. 2001) (same). What do you think justifies this difference?

7. Under Copyright Office rules, registration of copyright in a collective work allows the copyright owner of the collective work to claim copyright as well in any independently authored contributions for which all rights have been transferred to it. Authors of separately owned contributions (including authors who have transferred only some rights to the collective work copyright owner) may not claim the benefit of the collective work registration but must obtain independent copyright registrations. The Second Circuit has endorsed this rule. *See Morris v. Bus. Concepts, Inc.*, 283 F.3d 502, 505 (2d Cir. 2002) (holding that even though the Copyright Office lacks authority to define legal terms, its interpretations are nonetheless entitled to " 'some deference' ") (quoting *Skidmore v. Swift & Co.*, 323 U.S. 134 (1944)).

8. Recall from Chapter 3.A, page 149, *supra*, that registration also has important implications for the kinds of remedies that are available for infringement. Section 412 provides that no attorneys' fees or statutory damages will be available in actions brought for infringement of an unpublished work that occurs before the work is registered. These remedies are also not available for infringement of a published work that occurs after first publication but before registration, unless the registration takes place within three months after the first publication of the work. We discuss statutory damages and attorneys' fees later in this chapter.

2. Filing Too Late

Like other causes of action, claims of copyright infringement are subject to a statute of limitations that establishes the time frame in which legal proceedings must be filed.

§507 — Limitations on Actions

(a) Criminal Proceedings. — Except as expressly provided otherwise in this title, no criminal proceeding shall be maintained under the provisions of this title unless it is commenced within 5 years after the cause of action arose.

(b) Civil Actions. — No civil action shall be maintained under the provisions of this title unless it is commenced within three years after the claim accrued.

Understanding the application of this statute of limitations requires understanding when a claim "accrues." Consider the following case.

Roley v. New World Pictures, Ltd.
19 F.3d 479 (9th Cir. 1994)

TANG, J.: . . . Some time before 1972, [plaintiff Sutton] Roley wrote a screenplay originally entitled "A Little Visit Home." He renamed the screenplay "Sleep Tight Little Sister."

In 1985, Roley gave [defendant Walter] Coblenz, a friend and successful film producer, the original copy of his work, hoping that Coblenz would produce the screenplay. Coblenz declined the proposed project.

Two years later, in August 1987, Coblenz invited Roley to the screening of his new movie "Sister, Sister." [Defendant New World Entertainment Limited] was a financier of the film. After viewing the screening, Roley claimed that the movie was a production of his screenplay "Sleep Tight Little Sister." Coblenz admitted that the film and screenplay were similar, but advised Roley that the film was based upon a screenplay entitled "Louisiana Swamp Murders" written by Ginny Cerrella in the 1970's.

Roley retained counsel to assist him in pursuing his claim that "Sister, Sister" violated his copyright on "Sleep Tight Little Sister." In late 1987 and early 1988, New World's insurance carrier, Firemen's Fund, rejected Roley's claim, advising him that it found no similarity between the two works and, in any event, the screenplay for the film was written independently of Coblenz.

Thereafter, the film opened unsuccessfully and was withdrawn from distribution. It was subsequently shown on television in 1988 and in 1992. Today, it is available for rental or purchase at home video stores.

Roley filed his complaint against Coblenz and New World in February 1991. In June 1992, both Coblenz and New World filed motions for summary judgment, arguing, in part, that Roley's copyright infringement claims were barred by the three year statute of limitations mandated by 17 U.S.C. §507(b). The district court granted appellees' motions, finding that §507(b) barred Roley's infringement claims.

Discussion

Roley's only contention on this appeal is that the district court erred in concluding his infringement claims are barred by the three year statute of limitations mandated by §507(b). . . . A cause of action for copyright infringement accrues when one has knowledge of a violation or is chargeable with such knowledge.

Roley alleged infringement after first viewing the screening of "Sister, Sister" in August 1987. There is no dispute that Roley's infringement claims accrued at that time. Even so, Roley applies the "rolling statute of limitations" theory. He argues that so long as any allegedly infringing conduct occurs within the three years preceding the filing of the action, the plaintiff may reach back and sue for damages or other relief for all allegedly infringing acts. *See Taylor v. Meirick*, 712 F.2d 1112, 1118-19 (7th Cir. 1983). The district court rejected the application of this theory. We do so as well.

Section 507(b) is clear on its face. "It does not provide for a waiver of infringing acts within the limitation period if earlier infringements were discovered and not sued upon, nor does it provide for any reach back if an act of infringement occurs within the statutory period." *Hoey v. Dexel Systems Corp.*, 716 F. Supp. 222, 223 (E.D. Va. 1989). This interpretation is consistent with the prevailing view that the statute bars recovery on any claim for damages that accrued more than three years before commencement of suit. . . . Lest there be any confusion regarding the law in this Circuit on this particular point, we adopt this view.

Roley filed his suit on February 7, 1991. Here, then, §507(b) bars recovery of any damages for claims that accrued prior to February 7, 1988. Roley's claims that appellees' production of "Sister, Sister" infringed his screenplay accrued before February 7, 1988. Nevertheless, Roley asserts that New World and Coblenz have continued to infringe his copyright, thus §507(b) does not bar recovery. Specifically, Roley alleges that appellees have manifested the distribution of the allegedly infringing film for public display in theaters and on television, and that they have manifested the copying of the film on videocassettes for rental and purchase in home video stores, all within the three years prior to the filing of this action.

In a case of continuing copyright infringements, an action may be brought for all acts that accrued within the three years preceding the filing of the suit. Here, however, Roley fails to produce any evidence that appellees engaged in actionable conduct after February 7, 1988.

Indeed, his assertions rely on naked allegations and speculation. . . . The district court's summary judgments are affirmed.

NOTES AND QUESTIONS

1. As *Roley* discusses, a minority view of §507 permits a plaintiff to claim relief for allegedly infringing acts that took place beyond the limitations period, if they were part of a series of infringing acts and at least some of those acts occurred within the preceding three years. Thus, if the infringing acts started in 1995, the plaintiff does not file suit until 1999, and the infringement has continued throughout this period, the plaintiff's action can "reach back" to all the infringing acts starting from 1995. *Taylor v. Meirick*, 712 F.2d 1112 (7th Cir. 1983). The *Roley* court explicitly rejects this theory. Which view makes more sense? Why weren't the broadcasts of the defendant's movie in 1992 and the ongoing sales in video stores infringements within the limitations period?

2. Once a defendant establishes a statute of limitations defense, the plaintiff may then be able to show reasons for tolling the statute. Under the Copyright Act, tolling must be predicated upon an equitable ground recognized under federal law. Sometimes a copyright owner does not discover the infringement until after the three-year limitations period has already passed. Nine circuits have concluded that the federal discovery rule applies. *William A. Graham Co. v. Haughey*, 568 F.3d 425, 433 (3d Cir. 2009) (collecting cases). "[U]nder the discovery rule, a cause of action accrues 'when the plaintiff discovers, or with due diligence should have discovered, the injury that forms the basis for the claim.'" *Id.* at 438. For example, in *Taylor*, the court accepted the plaintiff's tolling argument because the alleged infringer fraudulently concealed the infringement by placing a copyright notice bearing his own name on copies of the plaintiff's work, 712 F.2d at 1118.

3. In addition to the statute of limitations, litigants must also be aware of other equitable doctrines that might necessitate prompt filing. For example, the doctrine of laches may be asserted even if the lawsuit is timely filed under §507. *See, e.g., Chirco v. Crosswinds Cmtys., Inc.*, 474 F.3d 227 (6th Cir. 2007) (holding that laches was properly interposed in a case in which the plaintiffs delayed two and a half years before commencing litigation asserting that the condominiums being built by defendants infringed upon plaintiffs' copyrights).

C. PROPER PLAINTIFFS (STANDING)

There are different kinds of lawsuits involving copyright that can be brought under the Copyright Act. This section considers who has standing to bring two types of actions: a copyright infringement action and a declaratory judgment action seeking a court ruling on whether certain activities constitute infringement.

1. Copyright Infringement

Recall from Chapter 2 that copyright vests initially in the author of the copyrighted work. Recall also that copyright ownership often changes hands many times before copyright in the work expires. In Chapter 3, you learned the rules that determine the subsequent owner of the copyright. These rules are important in the litigation context because they determine who has standing to file a copyright infringement lawsuit.

Section 501(b) provides:

> The legal or beneficial owner of an exclusive right under a copyright is entitled, subject to the requirements of section 411, to institute an action for any infringement of that particular right committed while he or she is the owner of it. The court may require such owner to serve written notice of the action with a copy of the complaint upon any person shown, by the records of the Copyright Office or otherwise, to have or claim an interest in the copyright, and shall require that such notice be served upon any person whose interest is likely to be affected by a decision in the case. The court may require joinder, and shall permit the intervention, of any person having or claiming an interest in the copyright.

Section 501(b) is intended to supplement the Federal Rules of Civil Procedure by enabling "the owner of a particular right to bring an infringement action in that owner's name alone, while at the same time insuring to the extent possible that the other owners whose rights may be affected are notified and given a chance to join the action." H.R. Rep. No. 94-1476, 94th Cong., 2d Sess., at 159 (1976), *reprinted in* 1976 U.S.C.C.A.N. 5659, 5739. The ability of others who have an interest in the copyright to join in the lawsuit is particularly important if the validity of the copyright is at issue. For further discussion, see Roger D. Blair & Thomas F. Cotter, *The Elusive Logic of Standing Doctrine in Intellectual Property Law*, 74 Tul. L. Rev. 1323, 1373 (2000).

As §501(b) indicates, the present owners of the copyright, who §501(b) calls "legal" owners, have standing. The legal owner may be the author or someone to whom the copyright has been assigned or subsequent assignees in the chain of title. Section 501(b) also grants standing to "beneficial" owners of copyright. The legislative history indicates that a beneficial owner includes "an author who had parted with legal title to the copyright in exchange for percentage royalties based on sales or license fees." H.R. Rep. No. 94-1476, 94th Cong., 2d Sess., at 159 (1976), *reprinted in* 1976 U.S.C.C.A.N. 5659, 5739.

When will something short of assignment of the copyright be sufficient to confer standing? Consider the following case.

Eden Toys, Inc. v. Florelee Undergarment Co.
697 F.2d 27 (2d Cir. 1982)

MANSFIELD, J.: . . . The subject of this case is the alleged copying of a drawing of the copyrighted fictional character Paddington Bear, the central figure in a series of children's books written by Michael Bond. Paddington and Company, Limited ("Paddington"), a British corporation, holds all rights to these books, and to the characters therein. In 1975 Paddington entered into an agreement with [Eden Toys, Inc. ("Eden")], an American corporation, granting Eden exclusive North American rights to produce and sell, and to sublicense the production and sale of, a number of Paddington products.[2] This agreement was amended in 1980 to grant

---

2. The relevant portions of the 1975 Eden/Paddington exclusive licensing agreement are as follows:

1. *Grant of License*

    (a) Paddington hereby grants to Eden, for the term of this agreement and all renewals thereof, subject to the terms and conditions and for the territory hereinafter set forth [North America], the exclusive right and license to use the Michael Bond books, characters, names, copyrights and trademarks in the manufacture and sale of all Licensed Products in both Schedules B and C, and to license others to use the Michael Bond books, characters,

Eden the exclusive North American rights to produce and sublicense *all* Paddington products except books, tapes and records, stage plays, motion pictures, and radio and television productions.

At some point between 1975 and 1977 Ivor Wood, the illustrator of the Paddington Bear books, drew a series of sketches ("the Ivor Wood sketches") for the use of Eden and its sublicensees. . . . Using the Ivor Wood sketches as a point of departure, the C.R. Gibson Company ("Gibson"), pursuant to a sublicense from Eden, produced a design for gift wrap that included seven drawings of Paddington Bear ("the Eden/ Gibson drawings"). . . .

In November 1979, Eden discovered that [Florelee Undergarment Co., Inc. ("Florelee")] was selling a nightshirt featuring a print of a bear later found by the district court to be "identical in almost all respects" to one of the Eden/Gibson drawings of Paddington Bear. . . . After discovering a second nightshirt with the same apparent "knockoff" of the Eden/Gibson drawing Eden filed suit against Florelee in April 1980, alleging . . . that Florelee had violated Eden's rights under the Copyright Act. . . .

Eden's Claim as Exclusive Licensee

Eden . . . sues for infringement as exclusive North American licensee for certain Paddington Bear products. An exclusive licensee of a right under a copyright is entitled to bring suits for infringement "of that particular right," without being required to join his licensor. The question, then, is whether Eden was the exclusive licensee of the right allegedly infringed by Florelee, i.e., the right to produce images of Paddington Bear on adult clothing. Florelee argues correctly that adult clothing was clearly not among the "licensed products" listed in the 1975 agreement between Eden and Paddington, see note 2, *supra*, and concludes from this fact that Eden was not the exclusive licensee of this right at the time the allegedly infringing garments were sold in 1979. Eden responds that at that time Eden was operating under an informal understanding with Paddington, later formalized in the 1980 amendment to the 1975 agreement, that gave Eden the exclusive North American rights to produce any Paddington Bear product except books, records, and a few other items not relevant here.

Under the pre-1978 copyright law, exclusive licenses could be granted orally or by conduct. Under the new Copyright Act, however, Eden's claim of an informal grant of an exclusive license seemingly must fail in light of the statute of frauds provision of the new Act, which states

---

names, copyrights and trademarks in the manufacture and sale of all Licensed Products listed in Schedule C alone.

SCHEDULE B

Stuffed animals, also described as dolls, and puppets, all of various sizes.

SCHEDULE C

1. Ready-to-wear sold in the children's division of department and specialty stores, including, without limitations, infants, babette, toddler, and 2-4 sizes for boys and girls; 4-7, 8-20, and 27-30 sizes for boys; and 3-6X, 7-14, pre-teen and junior sizes for girls.

2. All accessories normally sold in the children's divisions of department and specialty stores.

3. Infants, juvenile and youth domestics and textiles.

4. Juvenile and youth furniture and accessories normally sold in the juvenile furniture department of department and specialty stores.

5. Toys, games, crafts and other articles normally sold in the toy department of department stores, toy stores and specialty stores.

Excluded from this Schedule are the items of Schedule B and:

a. Books

b. Tapes and Records

c. Stage Plays

d. Motion Pictures

e. Radio and Television Productions.

that an exclusive license "is not valid unless an instrument of conveyance, or a note or memorandum of the transfer, is in writing and signed by the owner of the rights conveyed. . . ." 17 U.S.C. §204(a) (Supp. IV 1980). However, since the purpose of the provision is to protect copyright holders from persons mistakenly or fraudulently claiming oral licenses, the "note or memorandum of the transfer" need not be made at the time when the license is initiated; the requirement is satisfied by the copyright owner's later execution of a writing which confirms the agreement. In this case, in which the copyright holder appears to have no dispute with its licensee on this matter, it would be anomalous to permit a third party infringer to invoke this provision against the licensee. . . .

If Paddington granted Eden an informal exclusive license to sell Paddington Bear products in the market in which Florelee sold — adult clothing — and that informal license was later confirmed in a writing signed by Paddington, Eden may sue in its own name, without joining Paddington, for infringement of any Paddington-owned copyrights in that market. . . .

If the district court finds that no such informal understanding existed, or that such an understanding was never memorialized, Paddington, which has expressed a willingness to be made a co-plaintiff in this lawsuit, should be joined as a plaintiff. The district court has the power to order the joinder of "any person having or claiming an interest in the copyright [at issue]." 17 U.S.C. §501(b) (Supp. IV 1980). In this case, the exercise of that power would clearly be appropriate if Paddington in fact owns some of the rights apparently infringed by Florelee. The equities in this case lie heavily in favor of Eden, and it would be unjust to deny redress to Eden because of an easily remediable procedural defect.

NOTES AND QUESTIONS

1. The *Eden Toys* court artfully construes the statute of frauds requirement of the Copyright Act to rationalize its conclusion that the plaintiff has standing as an exclusive licensee. The court concludes that the lack of dispute between Paddington and Eden Toys regarding the exclusivity of the license satisfies the purpose of §204(a). Do you agree? What are the dangers of such an approach to the statute of frauds requirement of the Copyright Act?

2. What if the licensor (Paddington) *did* have a dispute with Eden Toys and claimed that the license agreement did not include the exclusive right to market adult garments with the copyrighted images? How should the court have ruled on Eden Toys' standing?

3. It appears that "agents" do not have standing. In *Plunket v. Doyle*, No. 99 Civ. 11006(KMW), 2001 WL 175252, at *1 (S.D.N.Y. Feb. 22, 2001), the "[p]laintiff claim[ed] to be the exclusive 'manager' and licensor of the literary rights in the works of Sir Arthur Conan Doyle, author of the Sherlock Holmes stories. . . . " She claimed to hold the " 'exclusive worldwide rights to manage,' as well as to 'negotiate, license, and otherwise cause and permit the exploitation of' " several copyrighted works. *Id.* The court held that the plaintiff lacked standing because she did not allege that she was either an owner or an exclusive licensee of the works. *Id.* at *5.

4. As you know from Chapter 3, authors have the right to terminate transfers made after January 1, 1978, after 35 years elapse from the date of the transfer. 17 U.S.C. §203. They also have the right to terminate transfers of extensions to the renewal term made before January 1, 1978. *Id.* §304(c)-(d). It is generally believed that the reversionary interest held by authors under either §203 or §304 is insufficient to confer standing. *See, e.g., Hearn v. Meyer*, 664 F. Supp. 832, 843-44 (S.D.N.Y. 1987). Read §§203 and 304. Does the Copyright Act mandate this result? Can you envision situations in which the argument in favor of allowing standing for an author with a reversionary interest would be strong? What about situations in

which the transferee fails to enforce the copyright? Are there policy interests that would be served by denying standing to the author who owns a reversionary interest?

5. Who other than an author entitled to ongoing royalties may assert standing based on beneficial ownership? *See Warren v. Fox Family Worldwide, Inc.*, 328 F.3d 1136 (9th Cir. 2003) (holding that composer of television series soundtrack could not claim beneficial ownership of copyright based on his entitlement to ongoing royalties because the work-for-hire agreement he executed pursuant to §101(2) did not expressly provide for a beneficial interest in the series); *Silvers v. Sony Pictures Entm't, Inc.*, 402 F.3d 881 (9th Cir.) (en banc) (rejecting assertion of beneficial ownership based on assignment of accrued infringement claim without assignment of underlying rights in the copyrighted work), *cert. denied*, 546 U.S. 827 (2005).

6. As you learned in Chapter 9, claims for violation of the anti-circumvention provisions are different from claims for infringement. Section 1203 provides that "[a]ny person injured by a violation of §1201 or §1202 may bring a civil action in an appropriate United States district court for such violation." 17 U.S.C. §1203(a). Courts have recognized those injured, and thus entitled to bring claims, to include the manufacturers of the technology that is allegedly being circumvented by the defendant or defendant's devices, *RealNetworks, Inc. v. Streambox, Inc.*, No. 2:99CV02070, 2000 WL 127311, (W.D. Wash. Jan. 18, 2000), as well as copyright owners that are potentially harmed by the distribution of circumventing technology, *Universal City Studios, Inc. v. Reimerdes*, 111 F. Supp. 2d 294 (S.D.N.Y. 2000), *aff'd sub nom. Universal City Studios, Inc. v. Corley*, 273 F.3d 429 (2d Cir. 2001).

2. Declaratory Judgment Actions

Sometimes it is not the copyright owner that initiates the litigation. Individuals and corporations that are worried about liability for infringement may decide to go to court first, seeking a declaration that their activities do not constitute infringement. The next case addresses when these types of actions are permissible.

Bryan Ashley International, Inc. v. Shelby Williams Industries, Inc.

932 F. Supp. 290 (S.D. Fla. 1996)

HIGHSMITH, J.: . . . Both the plaintiff [Bryan Ashley International, Inc.] and the defendant [Shelby Williams Industries, Inc.] sell furniture, including rattan and wicker items. By letter dated September 5, 1995, defense counsel warned the plaintiff of the plaintiff's alleged "misappropriation of [the defendant's] intellectual property" and demanded that the plaintiff "immediately cease and desist" from the alleged misappropriation or risk "disgorgement of profits improperly gained . . . as well as reimbursement to [the defendant] for attorneys' fees incurred." On September 22, 1995, the plaintiff filed the instant declaratory judgment action.

In its complaint, the plaintiff seeks a declaration that it has not violated Title 17, United States Code, Section 501 ("the Copyright Act"). . . . The defendant's counterclaim alleges . . . copyright infringement in violation of the Copyright Act. Pursuant to Fed. R. Civ. P. 12(c), the plaintiff has moved, and the defendant has cross-moved, for partial judgment on the pleadings. . . .

The defendant contends that no actual controversy exists between the parties or, alternatively, that any controversy that existed is now moot.

A.   Defendant's Rule 12(c) Motion

Pursuant to Title 28, United States Code, Section 2201, a declaratory judgment may issue only if there is an actual controversy between the parties before the court. The defendant contends that no actual controversy exists because it has never asserted a claim for copyright infringement of its furniture designs.

To determine the existence of an actual controversy in patent litigation, courts apply a two-part test:

> First, there must be an explicit threat or other action by the patentee, which creates a reasonable apprehension on the part of the declaratory plaintiff that it will face an infringement suit. Second, the accused infringer or declaratory plaintiff must have actually produced or prepared to produce an allegedly infringing product.

Hewlett-Packard Co. v. Genrad, Inc., 882 F. Supp. 1141, 1156 (D. Mass. 1995) (citations omitted). This Court finds this test equally applicable in the context of copyright litigation.

In the instant action, the letter from defense counsel accusing the plaintiff of misappropriating the intellectual property of the defendant and demanding that the plaintiff cease and desist any further misappropriation amounts to action creating a "reasonable apprehension" of litigation, thus satisfying the first prong of the *Hewlett-Packard* test. Furthermore, the continued sale of the potentially "infringing products" satisfies the second prong of the test. *See Flint Ink Corp. v. Brower*, 845 F. Supp. 404, 407 (E.D. Mich. 1994) (patentee's letters charging infringement and demanding the cessation of such infringement, along with alleged infringer's denial of infringement, gave rise to actual controversy warranting issuance of declaratory judgment). The Court further notes that the defendant has acknowledged that "a justiciable controversy exists between the parties with respect to the right of [the plaintiff] to continue selling its accused furniture designs under threat of litigation." Answer, at ¶10. Therefore, the plaintiff has sufficiently demonstrated the existence of an actual controversy.

Alternatively, the defendant contends that any controversy that existed with respect to copyrights on the furniture designs was rendered moot by its acknowledgment that the defendant "does not assert that [the plaintiff] has infringed copyrights of [the defendant] on specific furniture designs." Answer, at ¶¶12, 16, 23-25. However, absent the "filing [with the Court of] a formal covenant . . . not to sue [and absent] a final determination of noninfringement," the defendant's acknowledgments do not render moot the plaintiff's declaratory judgment action. . . .

NOTES AND QUESTIONS

1. As this case illustrates, sending a cease-and-desist letter may have serious consequences for control over the forum in which any ensuing litigation may occur. There are competing policies at work here. On the one hand, there is a policy that favors dispute settlement, if possible, without resort to the courts. Thus, sending a cease-and-desist letter may be something to encourage. On the other hand, potential defendants should be able to obtain adjudication concerning their ability to continue their activities without facing mounting liability. Thus, once a potential defendant receives such notification from a copyright owner, he should not be forced to wait until the copyright owner chooses to file suit.

2. Declaratory judgment actions are also permissible to define rights and liabilities under the anti-circumvention provisions of the Digital Millennium Copyright Act (DMCA). All declaratory judgment actions are governed by the same standard, set forth in 28 U.S.C. §2201.

3. If an equipment manufacturer or service provider is sued for indirect infringement, do its customers have standing to seek a declaratory judgment that their activities are noninfringing? In *Newmark v. Turner Broadcasting Network*, 226 F. Supp. 2d 1215 (C.D. Cal. 2002), the defendant television and film studios had filed an indirect infringement lawsuit against SONICblue, the manufacturer of the RePlayTV, a digital video recorder that allowed users to record digital copies of television programs. RePlayTV devices could be programmed to skip commercials while recording and could be used to send copied programs to other RePlayTV owners via the Internet. The *Newmark* plaintiffs, five owners of RePlayTV devices, sought a ruling that their use of the devices to record and share programs did not infringe the defendants' copyrights. The studios moved to dismiss, arguing that they had never demonstrated any intent to sue individual users and that plaintiffs therefore had no "reasonable apprehension" of litigation. Observing that "no explicit threat of litigation is required to meet the 'case or controversy' requirement," the district court denied the motion. *Id.* at 1220. Do you agree with this decision? Given their potential exposure to a significant damages award, why do you suppose the plaintiffs chose to bring their ownership and use of RePlayTV devices to defendants' attention?

Subsequently, SONICblue filed for bankruptcy, the indirect infringement claims were settled, and the studios agreed not to sue the *Newmark* plaintiffs for direct infringement. In light of these developments, the court dismissed the *Newmark* plaintiffs' declaratory judgment claim, reasoning that the claim no longer presented an actual controversy. *See Paramount Pictures Corp. v. RePlay TV*, 298 F. Supp. 2d 921 (C.D. Cal. 2004).

D. PROPER DEFENDANTS

In Chapter 6, you learned that direct, contributory, and vicarious infringers are all proper defendants. One issue remains: Are there defendants that qualify as infringers but are nonetheless immune from suit? The immunity relevant here is sovereign immunity, which stems from the Eleventh Amendment:

> In *Chisholm* v. *Georgia*, 2 Dall. 419 (1793), we asserted jurisdiction over an action in assumpsit brought by a South Carolina citizen against the State of Georgia. In so doing, we reasoned that Georgia's sovereign immunity was qualified by the general jurisdictional provisions of Article III, and, most specifically, by the provision extending the federal judicial power to controversies "between a State and Citizens of another State." U.S. Const., Art. III, §2, cl. 1. The "shock of surprise" created by this decision, *Principality of Monaco v. Mississippi*, 292 U.S. 313, 325 (1934), prompted the immediate adoption of the Eleventh Amendment, which provides:
>
>> The Judicial power of the United States shall not be construed to extend to any suit in law or equity, commenced or prosecuted against one of the United States by Citizens of another State, or by Citizens or Subjects of any Foreign State.
>
> Though its precise terms bar only federal jurisdiction over suits brought against one State by citizens of another State or foreign state, we have long recognized that the Eleventh Amendment accomplished much more: It repudiated the central premise of *Chisholm* that the jurisdictional heads of

Article III superseded the sovereign immunity that the States possessed before entering the Union. This has been our understanding of the Amendment since the landmark case of *Hans v. Louisiana*, 134 U.S. 1 (1890). . . .

While this immunity from suit is not absolute, we have recognized only two circumstances in which an individual may sue a State. First, Congress may authorize such a suit in the exercise of its power to enforce the Fourteenth Amendment—an Amendment enacted after the Eleventh Amendment and specifically designed to alter the federal-state balance. Second, a State may waive its sovereign immunity by consenting to suit.

Coll. Sav. Bank v. Fla. Prepaid Postsecondary Educ. Expense Bd., 527 U.S. 666, 669-70 (1999).

In 1990, Congress amended the Copyright Act to provide for suits against states. Copyright Remedy Clarification Act (CRCA), Pub. L. No. 101-553, 104 Stat. 2749 (1990) (codified at 17 U.S.C. §§501(a), 511). The Supreme Court has not decided whether this was a valid authorization of suits against states in federal court (referred to as an "abrogation" of sovereign immunity), but recent developments leave the distinct impression that the Court, if presented with the issue, would decide that it was not.

First, in 1996, the Court decided *Seminole Tribe of Florida v. Florida*, 517 U.S. 44 (1996), a turning point in Eleventh Amendment jurisprudence. *Seminole Tribe* makes clear that Congress may not abrogate state sovereign immunity pursuant to its Article I powers. Therefore, Congress may not rely on the Intellectual Property Clause or the Commerce Clause as the source of authority for abrogation. However, because intellectual property can be conceptualized as a "property" right, some believed that Congress might be able to abrogate sovereign immunity pursuant to the Fourteenth Amendment.

In 1999, the Supreme Court addressed the issue of sovereign immunity when a state is sued for patent infringement, *Fla. Prepaid Postsecondary Educ. Expense Bd. v. Coll. Sav. Bank*, 527 U.S. 627 (1999), and when a state is sued for trademark infringement, *Coll. Sav. Bank v. Fla. Prepaid Postsecondary Educ. Expense Bd.*, 527 U.S. 666 (1999). These two 5-4 decisions (issued on the same day) held that states are immune from suits in federal court for violations of the patent and trademark laws, respectively. The Court held that to rely on the Fourteenth Amendment to abrogate sovereign immunity, Congress would need to "identify conduct transgressing the Fourteenth Amendment's substantive provisions, and must tailor its legislative scheme to remedying or preventing such conduct." *Fla. Prepaid*, 527 U.S. 627, 639. The Court determined that neither the Patent Act nor the Lanham Act met these requirements.

Following these decisions, the Court was invited to review a case from the Fifth Circuit concerning the CRCA. The Court declined that invitation but remanded the case for reconsideration in light of its recent decisions. The following is the Fifth Circuit's decision after remand.

Chavez v. Arte Publico Press
204 F.3d 601 (5th Cir. 2000)

JONES, J.: . . . Plaintiff Chavez asserts that the University of Houston infringed her copyright by continuing to publish her book without her consent. . . . The University of Houston contends that because it enjoys immunity from unconsented-to suit in federal court under the Eleventh Amendment, the case must be dismissed. . . . [W]e agree with the University.

Abrogation of a state's Eleventh Amendment immunity turns on an express statement of intent by Congress and a constitutionally valid exercise of power. *See Seminole Tribe of Fla. v.*

Florida, 517 U.S. 44, 55 (1996). Congress amended ... the Copyright Act and explicitly required states to submit to suit in federal court for violation of [its] provisions; thus, the express statement requirement is fulfilled. The remaining question, to be considered in the light of *College Savings, Florida Prepaid*, and *Kimel v. Fla. Bd. of Regents*, 528 U.S. 62 (2000), is whether Congress had authority to abrogate state sovereign immunity in the Act. . . .

Chavez and *amici* justify the CRCA abrogation of state Eleventh Amendment immunity under section 5 of the Fourteenth Amendment, because Congress acted to prevent states from depriving copyright holders of their property without due process of law. They contend that the legislative history demonstrates that the waiver effected by the CRCA is proportional to its remedial object. . . .

Congress can abrogate the states' sovereign immunity when acting to enforce constitutional rights pursuant to section 5 of the Fourteenth Amendment. *See Seminole*, 116 S. Ct. at 1128. *City of Boerne*, however, states that when Congress legislates pursuant to section 5, "there must be a congruence and proportionality between the injury to be prevented or remedied and the means adopted to that end." *City of Boerne* [*v. Flores*, 521 U.S. 507]. . . . The analytical framework that *Florida Prepaid* sets forth requires examination of three aspects of the legislation: 1) the nature of the injury to be remedied; 2) Congress's consideration of the adequacy of state remedies to redress the injury; and 3) the coverage of the legislation. . . .

The first consideration is the nature of the injury to be remedied and whether the state's conduct evinced a pattern of constitutional violations. *See Florida Prepaid*, 119 S. Ct. at 2207. The underlying conduct at issue here is state infringement of copyrights, rather than patents, and the "constitutional injury" consists of possibly unremedied, or uncompensated, violation of copyrights by states. *See* H.R. Rep. No. 101-282, pt. 1, at 3 (1989), *reprinted in* 1990 U.S.C.C.A.N. 3949, 3951 [hereinafter H.R. Rep.]. Such infringements, it is contended, would "take" the copyright owners' property without due process of law.[6] The Supreme Court concluded in *Florida Prepaid* that "Congress identified no pattern of patent infringement by the States, let alone a pattern of constitutional violations." *Florida Prepaid*, 119 S. Ct. at 2207. Although the legislative history for the CRCA documents a few more instances of copyright infringement than the [Patent Remedy Act's (PRCA's)] legislative history did of patent violations, the CRCA's history exhibits similar deficiencies. For example, testimony before the House Subcommittee in favor of the CRCA acknowledged that "the States are not going to get involved in wholesale violation of the copyright laws." Copyright Remedy Clarification Act and Copyright Office Report on Copyright Liability of States: Hearings Before the Subcomm. on Courts, Intellectual Property, and the Administration of Justice of the House Comm. on the Judiciary, 101st Cong. 53 (1989) [hereinafter House Hearings] (statement of Ralph Oman, Register of Copyrights, Library of Congress).[7] In addition, the bill's sponsor stated that "thus far there have not been any significant number of wholesale takings of copyright rights by States or State entities." *Id.*, at 48 (statement of Rep. Kastenmeier).

At the request of Congress, the Copyright Office reported on the relation between the states' copyright liability and the Eleventh Amendment; in that report, no more than seven incidents of State copyright infringement enabled by the Eleventh Amendment were documented. Register of Copyrights, Copyright Liability of States and the Eleventh Amendment 5-9 (1988) [hereinafter Copyright Office Report]. Nor did the Senate hear evidence of a pattern of unremedied copyright infringement by the States. Rather than expose a current epidemic of

---

6. . . . The Supreme Court held in *Florida Prepaid* that patents are considered property within the meaning of the due process clause. *See Florida Prepaid*, 119 S. Ct. at 2208. Since patent and copyright are of a similar nature, and patent is a form of property protectable against the states, copyright would seem to be so too.

7. Mr. Oman also stated that "[the States] are all respectful of the copyright laws." House Hearings, at 8.

unconstitutional deprivations, the testimony before Congress worried principally about the *potential* for future abuse, see House Hearings, at 7 (statement of Ralph Oman), and the concerns of copyright owners about that potential, see Copyright Office Report, at 5-17. . . .

Second, we consider whether Congress studied the existence and adequacy of state remedies for injured copyright owners when a state infringes their copyrights. *See Florida Prepaid*, 119 S. Ct. at 2208. The legislative histories of the PRCA and CRCA are again parallel. In each case, Congress barely considered the availability of state remedies for infringement. . . . With regard to the CRCA, one witness testified that his company's attorneys told him that state and local courts were unavailable because only federal courts can hear copyright infringement cases. *See* House Hearings, at 51 (statement of James Healy, Vice President of Enterprise Media). In addition, the Copyright Office provided a survey of state waivers of Eleventh Amendment immunity as an appendix to its report. . . . These are the only two allusions to state remedies in the legislative history. While Congress referred briefly to the Copyright Office's report in the House Report on the bill, Appendix C was mentioned neither in the House Report nor in any of the congressional hearings. Furthermore, as pointed out in a statement submitted to Congress, the survey failed to include information on state remedies for the unlawful taking of private property by the state government. *See* The Copyright Remedy Clarification Act: Hearing Before the Subcomm. on Patents, Copyrights and Trademarks of the Senate Comm. on the Judiciary, 101st Cong. 123 (1989) [hereinafter Senate Hearing] (statement on behalf of the Educators' Ad Hoc Committee on Copyright Law). . . . [T]here are other possible remedies in state courts — breach of contract claims, for example — that Congress also never considered.[8] As if to emphasize its lack of interest in state remedies, Congress rejected the idea of granting state courts concurrent jurisdiction over copyright cases, an alternative solution that would have avoided any Eleventh Amendment problems. Congress rejected this solution not because it was an inadequate remedy, but because Congress believed concurrent jurisdiction would undermine the uniformity of copyright law. *See* H.R. Rep., at 9. Although uniformity is undoubtedly an important goal, "that is a factor which belongs to the Article I patent-power calculus, rather than to any determination of whether a state plea of sovereign immunity deprives a patentee of property without due process of law." *Florida Prepaid*, 119 S. Ct. at 2209. The same is true here.

Finally, *Florida Prepaid* examined the breadth of coverage of the legislation. *See id.* at 2210. In enacting legislation pursuant to section 5 of the Fourteenth Amendment, Congress should ensure that there is "a congruence and proportionality between the injury to be prevented or remedied and the means adopted to that end." *City of Boerne*, 521 U.S. at 520; *see also id.* at 533, 117 S. Ct. 2157 ("Where, however, a congressional enactment pervasively prohibits constitutional state action in an effort to remedy or to prevent unconstitutional state action, limitations . . . tend to ensure Congress' [sic] means are proportionate to ends legitimate under §5."). As the Court noted in *Florida Prepaid*, Supreme Court jurisprudence indicates that a deprivation, to fit the meaning of the due process clause, must be intentional; a negligent act that causes unintended injury is not sufficient. *See Florida Prepaid*, 119 S. Ct. at 2209. Copyright infringement actions, like those for patent infringement, ordinarily require no showing of intent to infringe. Instead, knowledge and intent are relevant in regard to damages. . . . In addition, Mr. Oman, the Register of Copyrights, acknowledged that most copyright infringement by states is unintentional, stating that "[the States] would want [immunity] only as a shield for the State treasury from the occasional error or misunderstanding or innocent infringement." House Hearings, at 8. In enacting the CRCA, however, Congress did nothing "to confine the reach of the Act by limiting the remedy to certain types of infringement, . . . or providing for suits only

---

8. Instead of considering the adequacy of possible state remedies, Congress focused on the adequacy of injunctive relief, stating that injunctive relief was not adequate protection for copyright owners. *See* H.R. Rep, at 8.

against States with questionable remedies or a high incidence of infringement." *Florida Prepaid*, 119 S. Ct. at 2210. Its "indiscriminate scope" cannot be reconciled with the principle that legislation pursuant to the due process clause of the Fourteenth Amendment must be proportionate to legitimate section 5 ends. *See id.*

Since the record does not indicate that Congress was responding to the kind of massive constitutional violations that have prompted proper remedial legislation, that it considered the adequacy of state remedies that might have provided the required due process of law, or that it sought to limit the coverage to arguably constitutional violations, we conclude that the CRCA is, like the PRCA, an improper exercise of Congressional legislative power. . . .

NOTES AND QUESTIONS

1. Following the Supreme Court's decisions in the *Florida Prepaid* cases, Senator Leahy introduced legislation to restore federal remedies for violations of intellectual property rights by states. That legislation, entitled the "Intellectual Property Protection Restoration Act of 1999," would have excluded state governmental entities from participation in the federal intellectual property system unless the state certified that it had waived its sovereign immunity from suit brought pursuant to the federal intellectual property laws. Such an attempt to force a waiver most likely is unconstitutional because the federal government would be conditioning the award of a government benefit (intellectual property rights) upon the surrender of a constitutional right (the Eleventh Amendment right of sovereign immunity). *See* Mitchell N. Berman et al., *State Accountability for Violations of Intellectual Property Rights: How to "Fix"* Florida Prepaid *(and How Not To)*, 79 Tex. L. Rev. 1037, 1130-73 (2001). The proposed legislation also would have abrogated sovereign immunity in those cases in which the state violation amounts to a constitutional violation by depriving any person of any rights of exclusion provided by the intellectual property laws without due process of law. *See id.* at 1068-72 (discussing the adequacy of remedies that states may be obligated to provide in order to avoid abrogation). What kinds of state remedies can you think of that would provide the required due process of law?

2. What solution do you think is best: concurrent state court jurisdiction over copyright cases or remedial legislation abrogating sovereign immunity? What congressional findings would, in your view, be sufficient to justify remedial legislation? What should such legislation require?

3. Despite the sweeping nature of Eleventh Amendment immunity, the Supreme Court has long permitted suits for injunctive and declaratory relief against state officers in their official capacities. *See Ex parte Young*, 209 U.S. 123 (1908). This principle applies to copyright infringement litigation as well. *Salerno v. City Univ. of N.Y.*, 191 F. Supp. 2d 352 (S.D.N.Y. 2001). In *Salerno*, the court dismissed copyright infringement claims against the City University of New York and one of its institutes, finding that Eleventh Amendment immunity barred the claims. The court refused to dismiss the infringement claims against the Chancellor of the University and the director of the institute. The court noted that the plaintiffs were seeking only "a prospective injunction to prevent a state official from violating federal law, which is precisely the type of relief which the *Ex Parte Young* exception was created to provide." *Id.* at 357.

4. Even if states wanted to provide remedies for infringements, how would they implement such a system? An example of such a remedy might be royalty payments based on use of copyrighted works. Another example would be for states to negotiate contracts with authors. Would a state's failure to comply with remedies that it voluntarily adopts give rise to a claim "arising under" the Copyright Act? If so, wouldn't those remedies still have to be enforced in

federal courts, given their exclusive subject matter jurisdiction over claims arising under the Copyright Act? Recall also the principles of preemption that you learned in Chapter 10. Would such a state scheme survive a preemption analysis? In the absence of any constitutional constraints, are there reasons that states should *not* implement a system that compensates authors for state uses of copyrighted works?

5. If states can infringe the rights of copyright owners, the U.S. may be in violation of its international treaty obligations. At least one scholar has argued that the need to allow infringement actions against states in order to comply with international treaty obligations may provide valid authority for congressional abrogation of sovereign immunity. *See* Peter S. Menell, *Economic Implications of State Sovereign Immunity from Infringement of Federal Intellectual Property Rights*, 33 Loy. L.A. L. Rev. 1399, 1460-64 (2000). Recall the WTO decision regarding §110(5) of the Copyright Act, discussed in Chapter 5.G, pages 458-59 *supra*. In that case, the federal government chose to compensate foreign music copyright owners for violations of their copyrights. Could the federal government, as an alternative to abrogating sovereign immunity, simply pay foreign copyright owners for state violations? Which option do you think is best?

6. How serious do you think the problem of state governments' infringing copyrighted works really is? Before you answer, consider the multitude of state agencies, departments, and public institutions (such as state universities) that are protected by sovereign immunity.

Note on the Sovereign Immunity of the United States

Chavez and the *Florida Prepaid* cases address state sovereign immunity. What about cases against the U.S.? May the U.S. assert a defense of sovereign immunity? Court decisions have established that the U.S. is not subject to suit by state governments or individuals in the absence of its consent. Congress, however, may choose to waive the sovereign immunity of the U.S. and has generally done so in copyright infringement cases:

> [W]henever the copyright in any work protected under the copyright laws of the United States shall be infringed by the United States, by a corporation owned or controlled by the United States, or by a contractor, subcontractor, or any person, firm, or corporation acting for the Government and with the authorization or consent of the Government, the exclusive action which may be brought for such infringement shall be an action by the copyright owner against the United States in the Court of Federal Claims for the recovery of his reasonable and entire compensation as damages for such infringement, including the minimum statutory damages as set forth in section 504(c) of title 17, United States Code.

28 U.S.C. §1498(b). This section generally limits recovery to infringements committed not more than three years before the filing of an infringement complaint or counterclaim for infringement.

Congress's waiver of the U.S.'s sovereign immunity is subject to important limitations where the copyright owner is (or was) a government employee: "[A] government employee shall have a right of action against the Government . . . except where he was in a position to order, influence, or induce use of the copyrighted work by the Government:" *Id.* Also, a copyright owner has no cause of action against the government when the copyrighted work was "prepared as part of the official functions of the employee, or in the preparation of which Government time, material, or facilities were used." *Id.* In *Blueport Co. v. United States*, 533 F.3d 1374, 1380-81 (Fed. Cir. 2008), *cert. denied*, 129 S.Ct. 1038 (2009), the court held that these limitations are jurisdictional in nature—i.e., if a claim falls outside the scope of the statute's limited waiver of sovereign immunity, the court has no jurisdiction to hear the case. Thus, the federal government does not have to raise sovereign immunity as an affirmative defense and the party alleging infringement has the burden of showing that its claim is not jurisdictionally barred.

The *Blueport* case involved Air Force Sergeant Mark Davenport, who taught himself computer programming skills sufficient to enable him to write a database system in off-hours and with his own resources. He shared the program with his colleagues, posted it on an Air Force web page, and gave presentations to Air Force officers to convince them to adopt it. The Air Force became concerned about its dependence on a program, access to which was controlled by a single person. Davenport refused to give the Air Force the source code and instead assigned his rights to Blueport. Blueport sued the Air Force for copyright infringement after the Air Force hired a contractor to revise the object code. The Federal Circuit held that the Court of Federal Claims lacked jurisdiction over the case because Davenport was in a position to "order, influence, or induce" the Air Force's use of the program. *Id*. at 1382.

NOTES AND QUESTIONS

1. Why do you think the U.S. has waived sovereign immunity in copyright cases when the states have not generally done so?

2. How would you analyze whether the U.S. has waived sovereign immunity under the DMCA? In *Blueport*, Davenport had written an automatic expiration date into each version of the program. The Air Force extended the date by modifying the object code, so Blueport also brought a DMCA claim. The court held that the U.S. had not waived sovereign immunity for DMCA claims. The DMCA contains no such waiver, and "a claim for violation of the DMCA is not . . . a subset of claims for copyright infringement" and thus is not covered by the waiver in 28 U.S.C. §1498(b). *Blueport*, 533 F.3d at 1383-84.

E. JURY TRIAL

As you now know, federal courts have exclusive subject matter jurisdiction over copyright infringement actions. In the federal courts, the Seventh Amendment guarantees a right to a jury trial in certain kinds of litigation. For infringement actions seeking actual damages, either party is entitled to a jury trial. Actions for injunctive relief, however, do not give rise to a right to demand a jury trial. Typically, plaintiffs in infringement actions will seek both damages and injunctive relief. In such actions, all damage claims are triable to a jury. *See Dairy Queen, Inc. v. Wood*, 369 U.S. 469 (1962); *Beacon Theatres, Inc. v. Westover*, 359 U.S. 500 (1959). In the case that follows, the Supreme Court addresses the right to a jury trial when the remedy sought is statutory damages. The issue of statutory damages is addressed separately later in this chapter in Section G.4.

≡ *Feltner v. Columbia Pictures Television, Inc.*
≡ *523 U.S. 340 (1998)*

Thomas, J.: . . . Petitioner C. Elvin Feltner owns Krypton International Corporation, which in 1990 acquired three television stations in the southeastern United States. Respondent

Columbia Pictures Television, Inc., had licensed several television series to these stations, including "Who's the Boss," "Silver Spoons," "Hart to Hart," and "T.J. Hooker." After the stations became delinquent in making their royalty payments to Columbia, Krypton and Columbia entered into negotiations to restructure the stations' debt. These discussions were unavailing, and Columbia terminated the stations' license agreements in October 1991. Despite Columbia's termination, the stations continued broadcasting the programs.

Columbia sued Feltner, Krypton, the stations, various Krypton subsidiaries, and certain Krypton officers in Federal District Court alleging, *inter alia*, copyright infringement arising from the stations' unauthorized broadcasting of the programs. . . . On Columbia's motion, the District Court entered partial summary judgment as to liability for Columbia on its copyright infringement claims.

Columbia exercised the option afforded by §504(c) of the Copyright Act to recover "Statutory Damages" in lieu of actual damages. . . .

The District Court denied Feltner's request for a jury trial on statutory damages, ruling instead that such issues would be determined at a bench trial. After two days of trial . . . the trial judge determined that Columbia was entitled to $8,800,000 in statutory damages, plus costs and attorney's fees.

The Court of Appeals for the Ninth Circuit affirmed in all relevant respects. . . . The Court of Appeals . . . concluded that the "Seventh Amendment does not provide a right to a jury trial on the issue of statutory damages because an award of such damages is equitable in nature."

II . . .

The language of §504(c) does not grant a right to have a jury assess statutory damages. Statutory damages are to be assessed in an amount that "the court considers just." §504(c)(1). Further, in the event that "the court finds" the infringement was willful or innocent, "the court in its discretion" may, within limits, increase or decrease the amount of statutory damages. §504(c)(2). These phrases, like the entire statutory provision, make no mention of a right to a jury trial or, for that matter, to juries at all. . . .

III

The Seventh Amendment provides that "[i]n Suits at common law, where the value in controversy shall exceed twenty dollars, the right of trial by jury shall be preserved. . . ." U.S. Const., Amdt. 7. Since Justice Story's time, the Court has understood "Suits at common law" to refer "not merely [to] suits, which the *common* law recognized among its old and settled proceedings, but [to] suits in which *legal* rights were to be ascertained and determined, in contradistinction to those where equitable rights alone were recognized, and equitable remedies were administered." *Parsons v. Bedford*, 3 Pet. 433, 447 (1830) (emphasis in original). The Seventh Amendment thus applies not only to common-law causes of action, but also to "actions brought to enforce statutory rights that are analogous to common-law causes of action ordinarily decided in English law courts in the late 18th century, as opposed to those customarily heard by courts of equity or admiralty." *Granfinanciera, S.A. v. Nordberg*, 492 U.S. 33, 42 (1989) (citing *Curtis v. Loether*, 415 U.S., at 193). . . .

. . . [I]n this case there are close analogues to actions seeking statutory damages under §504(c). Before the adoption of the Seventh Amendment, the common law and statutes in England and this country granted copyright owners causes of action for infringement. More importantly, copyright suits for monetary damages were tried in courts of law, and thus before juries.

By the middle of the 17th century, the common law recognized an author's right to prevent the unauthorized publication of his manuscript. . . . This protection derived from the principle that the manuscript was the product of intellectual labor and was as much the author's property as the material on which it was written. *See Millar v. Taylor*, 4 Burr. 2303, 2398, 98 Eng. Rep. 201, 252 (K.B. 1769) (opinion of Mansfield, C.J.) (common-law copyright derived from principle that "it is just, that an Author should reap the pecuniary Profits of his own ingenuity and Labour"). . . . Actions seeking damages for infringement of common-law copy-right, like actions seeking damages for invasions of other property rights, were tried in courts of law in actions on the case. . . . Actions on the case, like other actions at law, were tried before juries. . . .

In 1710, the first English copyright statute, the Statute of Anne, was enacted to protect published books. . . . Like the earlier practice with regard to common-law copyright claims for damages, actions seeking damages under the Statute of Anne were tried in courts of law. . . .

The practice of trying copyright damages actions at law before juries was followed in this country, where statutory copyright protections were enacted even before adoption of the Constitution. In 1783, the Continental Congress passed a resolution recommending that the States secure copyright protections for authors. . . . Twelve States (all except Delaware) responded by enacting copyright statutes, each of which provided a cause of action for damages, and none of which made any reference to equity jurisdiction. At least three of these state statutes expressly stated that damages were to be recovered through actions at law . . . while four others provided that damages would be recovered in an "action of debt," a prototypical action brought in a court of law before a jury. . . . Although these statutes were short-lived, and hence few courts had occasion to interpret them, the available evidence suggests that the practice was for copyright actions seeking damages to be tried to a jury. . . .

Moreover, three of the state statutes specifically authorized an award of damages from a statutory range, just as §504(c) does today. . . .

There is no evidence that the Copyright Act of 1790 changed the practice of trying copyright actions for damages in courts of law before juries. As we have noted, actions on the case and actions of debt were actions at law for which a jury was required. . . . Moreover, actions to recover damages under the Copyright Act of 1831 — which differed from the Copyright Act of 1790 only in the amount (increased to $1 from 50 cents) authorized to be recovered for certain infringing sheets — were consistently tried to juries. . . .

Columbia does not dispute this historical evidence. . . . Rather, Columbia merely contends that statutory damages are clearly equitable in nature.

We are not persuaded. We have recognized the "general rule" that monetary relief is legal . . . and an award of statutory damages may serve purposes traditionally associated with legal relief, such as compensation and punishment. . . . Nor, as we have previously stated, is a monetary remedy rendered equitable simply because it is "not fixed or readily calculable from a fixed formula." . . . And there is historical evidence that cases involving discretionary monetary relief were tried before juries. . . . Accordingly, we must conclude that the Seventh Amendment provides a right to a jury trial where the copyright owner elects to recover statutory damages.

The right to a jury trial includes the right to have a jury determine the *amount* of statutory damages, if any, awarded to the copyright owner. . . . [T]here is overwhelming evidence that the consistent practice at common law was for juries to award damages. . . .

More specifically, this was the consistent practice in copyright cases. In *Hudson v. Patten*, 1 Root, at 134, for example, a jury awarded a copyright owner £100 under the Connecticut copyright statute, which permitted damages in an amount double the value of the infringed copy. In addition, juries assessed the amount of damages under the Copyright Act of 1831, even though that statute, like the Copyright Act of 1790, fixed damages at a set amount per infringing sheet. . . .

NOTES AND QUESTIONS

1. Recall from Chapter 1, pages 21-25 *supra*, that courts in both England and the U.S. during the 1700s and 1800s rejected the argument that copyright stemmed from a common law right based on natural law. If copyright is purely a statutorily granted right from the government, is the right to jury trial as strong as Justice Thomas argues?

2. Following remand from the Supreme Court, the district court held a jury trial on the issue of statutory damages, and the jury awarded plaintiffs $31.68 million. The Ninth Circuit rejected Feltner's argument that this amount of statutory damages was excessive and affirmed the award. *See Columbia Pictures Television, Inc. v. Krypton Broad. of Birmingham, Inc.*, 259 F.3d 1186 (9th Cir. 2001), *cert. denied sub nom. Feltner v. Columbia Pictures Television, Inc.*, 534 U.S. 1127 (2002).

3. What are the advantages and disadvantages of having a jury trial? For what kinds of subject matter would a jury trial be more or less appropriate? Would your answer depend on the type of evidence likely to be offered at trial? Recall the different tests for copyright infringement that you learned in Chapter 5. Would your answer also depend on the particular infringement test that a circuit applies?

4. At least one court has held that the right to a jury trial does not extend to claims brought under VARA. *See Pollara v. Seymour*, 150 F. Supp. 2d 393, 399 n.10 (N.D.N.Y. 2001) (holding that VARA rights and remedies are equitable in nature).

F. INTERNATIONAL ISSUES

In Chapter 1, you learned that international copyright treaties do not have any direct effect in the U.S. unless Congress adopts implementing legislation. However, the copyright laws of other countries sometimes do have direct effect in domestic litigation. Domestic courts sometimes must consider claims of infringement by foreign plaintiffs who assert copyright interests based upon the laws of countries other than the U.S. How does a court decide which law to apply to determine whether the work is protectible in the U.S.? What law determines who owns rights in the work, and whether the work has been infringed? Neither the Berne Convention nor the TRIPS Agreement supplies a choice of law rule. Thus, countries may differ in their approaches to these questions. The following cases illustrate how domestic courts have determined the applicable law.

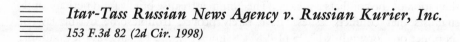

Itar-Tass Russian News Agency v. Russian Kurier, Inc.
153 F.3d 82 (2d Cir. 1998)

NEWMAN, J.: This appeal primarily presents issues concerning the choice of law in international copyright cases and the substantive meaning of Russian copyright law as to the respective rights of newspaper reporters and newspaper publishers. The conflicts issue is which country's law applies to issues of copyright ownership and to issues of infringement. . . .

On the conflicts issue, we conclude that, with respect to the Russian plaintiffs, Russian law determines the ownership and essential nature of the copyrights alleged to have been infringed and that United States law determines whether those copyrights have been infringed in the United States and, if so, what remedies are available. . . .

The lawsuit concerns *Kurier*, a Russian language weekly newspaper with a circulation in the New York area of about 20,000. It is published in New York City by defendant Kurier. Defendant Pogrebnoy is president and sole shareholder of *Kurier* and editor-in-chief of *Kurier*. The plaintiffs include corporations that publish, daily or weekly, major Russian language newspapers in Russia and Russian language magazines in Russia or Israel; Itar-Tass Russian News Agency ("Itar-Tass"), formerly known as the Telegraph Agency of the Soviet Union (TASS), a wire service and news gathering company centered in Moscow, functioning similarly to the Associated Press; and the Union of Journalists of Russia ("UJR"), the professional writers union of accredited print and broadcast journalists of the Russian Federation.

The Kurier defendants do not dispute that *Kurier* has copied about 500 articles that first appeared in the plaintiffs' publications or were distributed by Itar-Tass. The copied material, though extensive, was a small percentage of the total number of articles published in *Kurier*. . . . The Kurier defendants also do not dispute how the copying occurred: articles from the plaintiffs' publications, sometimes containing headlines, pictures, bylines, and graphics, in addition to text, were cut out, pasted on layout sheets, and sent to *Kurier*'s printer for photographic reproduction and printing in the pages of *Kurier*.

Most significantly, the Kurier defendants also do not dispute that, with one exception, they had not obtained permission from any of the plaintiffs to copy the articles that appeared in *Kurier*. . . .

[At issue on appeal was the interpretation of Article 11 of the Russian Copyright law, which provides for the rights of compilers of works excluded from the Russian work-for-hire doctrine (i.e., newspapers). There was conflicting expert testimony regarding the rights of publishers in the work as a whole. The district court accepted the interpretation of plaintiff's expert, who opined that Article 11 vests publishers with the right to redress copying. The Kurier defendants appealed from the district court's judgment enjoining them from copying the articles appearing in the plaintiffs' publications and awarding damages for infringement.]

I. Choice of Law

The threshold issue concerns the choice of law for resolution of this dispute. That issue was not initially considered by the parties, all of whom turned directly to Russian law for resolution of the case. . . .

Choice of law issues in international copyright cases have been largely ignored in the reported decisions and dealt with rather cursorily by most commentators. Examples pertinent to the pending appeal are those decisions involving a work created by the employee of a foreign corporation. Several courts have applied the United States work-for-hire doctrine, without explicit consideration of the conflicts issue. . . . The Nimmer treatise briefly (and perhaps optimistically) suggests that conflicts issues "have rarely proved troublesome in the law of copyright." Nimmer on Copyright §17.05 (1998) ("Nimmer"). . . . Relying on the "national treatment" principle of the Berne Convention and the Universal Copyright Convention ("U.C.C."), Nimmer asserts, correctly in our view, that "an author who is a national of one of the member states of either Berne or the U.C.C., or one who first publishes his work in any such member state, is entitled to the same copyright protection in each other member state as such other state accords to its own nationals." *Id.* . . . Nimmer then somewhat overstates the national treatment principle: "The applicable law is the copyright law of the state in which the infringement occurred, not that of the state of which the author is a national, or in which the work is first published." *Id*. . . . The difficulty with this broad statement is that it subsumes under the phrase "applicable law" the law concerning two distinct issues — ownership and substantive rights, *i.e.*, scope of protection.[8] Another commentator has also broadly stated the principle of national treatment, but described its application in a way that does not necessarily cover issues of ownership. "The principle of national treatment also means that both the question of whether the right exists and the question of the scope of the right are to be answered in accordance with the law of the country where the protection is claimed." S.M. Stewart, International Copyright and Neighboring Rights §3.17 (2d ed. 1989). We agree with the view of the Amicus that the Convention's principle of national treatment simply assures that if the law of the country of infringement applies to the scope of substantive copyright protection, that law will be applied uniformly to foreign and domestic authors. . . .

Source of conflicts rules. Our analysis of the conflicts issue begins with consideration of the source of law for selecting a conflicts rule. Though Nimmer turns directly to the Berne Convention and the U.C.C., we think that step moves too quickly past the Berne Convention Implementation Act of 1988. . . . Section 4(a)(3) of the Act amends Title 17 to provide: "No right or interest in a work eligible for protection under this title may be claimed by virtue of . . . the provisions of the Berne Convention. . . . Any rights in a work eligible for protection under this title that derive from this title . . . shall not be expanded or reduced by virtue of . . . the provisions of the Berne Convention." 17 U.S.C. §104(c).

We start our analysis with the Copyrights [sic] Act itself, which contains no provision relevant to the pending case concerning conflicts issues. We therefore fill the interstices of the Act by developing federal common law on the conflicts issue. . . . In doing so, we are entitled to consider and apply principles of private international law, which are " 'part of our law.' " . . .

The choice of law applicable to the pending case is not necessarily the same for all issues. *See* Restatement (Second) of Conflict of Laws §222 ("The courts have long recognized that they are not bound to decide all issues under the local law of a single state."). We consider first the law applicable to the issue of copyright ownership.

Conflicts rule for issues of ownership. Copyright is a form of property, and the usual rule is that the interests of the parties in property are determined by the law of the state with "the most significant relationship" to the property and the parties. *See id.* The Restatement recognizes the applicability of this principle to intangibles such as "a literary idea." *Id.* Since the works at issue were created by Russian nationals and first published in Russia, Russian law is the appropriate source of law to determine issues of ownership of rights. . . . In terms of the United States Copyrights [sic] Act and its reference to the Berne Convention, Russia is the "country of origin" of these works, *see* 17 U.S.C. §101 (definition of "country of origin" of Berne Convention work); Berne Convention, Art. 5(4), although "country of origin" might not always be the appropriate country for purposes of choice of law concerning ownership.[11] To whatever extent we look to the Berne Convention itself as guidance in the development of federal

---

8. Prof. Patry's brief, as Amicus Curiae, helpfully points out that the principle of national treatment is really not a conflicts rule at all; it does not direct application of the law of any country. It simply requires that the country in which protection is claimed must treat foreign and domestic authors alike. Whether U.S. copyright law directs U.S. courts to look to foreign or domestic law as to certain issues is irrelevant to national treatment, so long as the scope of protection would be extended equally to foreign and domestic authors.

11. In deciding that the law of the country of origin determines the ownership of copyright, we consider only initial ownership, and have no occasion to consider choice of law issues concerning assignments of rights.

common law on the conflicts issue, we find nothing to alter our conclusion. The Convention does not purport to settle issues of ownership. . . .

Conflicts rule for infringement issues. On infringement issues, the governing conflicts principle is usually *lex loci delicti*, the doctrine generally applicable to torts. . . . We have implicitly adopted that approach to infringement claims, applying United States copyright law to a work that was unprotected in its country of origin. . . . In the pending case, the place of the tort is plainly the United States. To whatever extent *lex loci delicti* is to be considered only one part of a broader "interest" approach . . . United States law would still apply to infringement issues, since not only is this country the place of the tort, but also the defendant is a United States corporation.

The division of issues, for conflicts purposes, between ownership and infringement issues will not always be as easily made as the above discussion implies. If the issue is the relatively straightforward one of which of two contending parties owns a copyright, the issue is unquestionably an ownership issue, and the law of the country with the closest relationship to the work will apply to settle the ownership dispute. . . .

≡≡≡ *Bridgeman Art Library, Ltd. v. Corel Corp.*
≡≡≡ *36 F. Supp. 2d 191 (S.D.N.Y. 1999)*

KAPLAN, J.: On November 13, 1998, this Court granted defendant's motion for summary judgment dismissing plaintiff's copyright infringement claim on the alternative grounds that the allegedly infringed works — color transparencies of paintings which themselves are in the public domain — were not original and therefore not permissible subjects of valid copyright and, in any case, were not infringed. It applied United Kingdom law in determining whether plaintiff's transparencies were copyrightable. The Court noted, however, that it would have reached the same result under United States law. . . .

[The plaintiff filed a post-judgment motion for reconsideration.]

Choice of Law . . .

Bridgeman claims that the infringed works are protected by United Kingdom copyrights and that the United States, by acceding to the . . . Berne Convention, and the Universal Copyright Convention and by enacting the Berne Convention Implementation Act of 1988 (the "BCIA"), agreed to give effect to its United Kingdom copyrights.

The fact that plaintiff's rights allegedly derive from its claimed British copyrights arguably is material. Granting . . . that Congress, in light of the originality requirement of the Copyright Clause, in ordinary circumstances may not extend copyright protection to works that are not original, the questions remain whether (1) the United States constitutionally may obligate itself by treaty to permit enforcement of a foreign copyright where that copyright originates under the law of a signatory nation which does not limit copyright protection to works that are original in the sense required by the United States Constitution and, if so, (2) the United States in fact has done so. . . .

. . . [I]t cannot seriously be denied that international copyright protection is "properly the subject of negotiation with" foreign countries.

Decades ago, the Supreme Court held in *Missouri v. Holland* [, 252 U.S. 416 (1920),] that Congress could enact legislation necessary and proper to the implementation of a treaty which, absent the treaty, would have been beyond its powers. Although the case arose in a different context, it suggests that the Conventions, if their purported effect actually is to permit enforcement in the United States of foreign copyrights which do not meet U.S. standards of originality . . . would not be obviously invalid.

In view of these considerations, the proposition advanced . . . that the Copyright Clause forecloses any choice of law issue with respect to the validity of a foreign Berne Convention work, is not free from doubt. It is necessary to decide that question, however, only if the Conventions require application of foreign law in determining the existence of copyright and, if so, whether there is any true conflict of law in this case on that point.

In most circumstances, choice of law issues do not arise under the Berne and Universal Copyright Conventions. Each adopts a rule of national treatment. Article 5 of the Berne Convention, for example, provides that "[a]uthors shall enjoy, in respect of works for which they are protected under this Convention, in countries of the Union other than the country of origin, the rights which their respective laws do now or may hereafter grant to their nationals, as well as the rights specially granted by this convention" and that "the extent of protection, as well as the means of redress afforded to the author to protect his rights, shall be governed exclusively by the laws of the country where protection is claimed." Hence, the Conventions make clear that the holder of, for example, a British copyright who sues for infringement in a United States court is entitled to the same remedies as holders of United States copyrights and, as this Court previously held, to the determination of infringement under the same rule of law.

While the nature of the protection accorded to foreign copyrights in signatory countries thus is spelled out in the Conventions, the position of the subject matter of copyright thereunder is less certain. Do the Conventions purport to require signatory nations to extend national treatment with respect to such enforcement-related subjects as remedies for infringement only where the copyright for which protection is sought would be valid under the law of the nation in which enforcement is sought? Or do they purport to require also that a signatory nation in which enforcement is sought enforce a foreign copyright even if that copyright would not be valid under its own law? But there is an even more fundamental issue, viz. whether United States courts may give effect to any provisions of the Conventions which might require or suggest that the existence of copyright be determined under the law of another nation. . . .

. . . 17 U.S.C. §104(c), states in relevant part that "[n]o right or interest in a work eligible for protection under this title may be claimed by virtue of, or in reliance upon, the provisions of the Berne Convention or the adherence of the United States thereto." Thus, while the Copyright Act, as amended by the BCIA, extends certain protection to the holders of copyright in Berne Convention works as there defined, the Copyright Act is the exclusive source of that protection. . . .

. . . Section 102(a) limits copyright protection in relevant part to "original works of authorship. . . ." Accordingly, there is no need to decide whether the Berne Convention adopts any rule regarding the law governing copyrightability or whether the treaty power constitutionally might be used to extend copyright protection to foreign works which are not "original" within the meaning of the Copyright Clause. Congress has made it quite clear that the United States' adherence to the Berne Convention has no such effect in the courts of this country. . . .

NOTES AND QUESTIONS

1. The principle of national treatment requires that a member nation of a treaty accord citizens of other members *at least* the same treatment enjoyed by its own nationals with regard to the subject matter of the treaty. With increasingly harmonized levels of protection required by the TRIPS Agreement there is, in theory, less room for divergence between countries

regarding levels of protection for copyrightable subject matter. Recall from Chapter 2, however, that there are some issues, such as the requirements for copyrightability (e.g., originality and fixation), or the work-for-hire doctrine, which countries handle differently and about which the Berne Convention and the TRIPS Agreement either are silent or give countries the discretion to determine for themselves. In these areas, choice of law issues and national treatment remain important considerations in an infringement lawsuit.

2. Do you agree with the *Itar-Tass* court that Russian law should apply to the question of copyright ownership? If so, should British law apply to the question of copyrightability in *Bridgeman Art Library*?

3. Assume that the court in *Bridgeman Art Library* had found that originality is not a requirement for copyright protection in the United Kingdom. Does national treatment require that courts in the U.S. protect such a work notwithstanding its lack of originality? The *Bridgeman Art Library* court answered this question in the negative, relying on the explicit language of the Berne Convention Implementation Act (BCIA), which limits the application of the Berne Convention to the terms of the implementing legislation. The court concluded that even if principles of international law might be construed to require a country to extend protection to a work that would not be protected by its own domestic law, Congress explicitly eschewed this result in the BCIA. Does this decision conform to U.S. treaty obligations?

4. Consider a related question: Does national treatment extend to categories of works or rights that one country recognizes under its domestic copyright law but that exceed the minimum requirements of Berne/TRIPS? For example, recall from Chapter 5 that "sound recordings" constitute protectible subject matter under the Copyright Act. However, "sound recordings" is not a category listed for protection in Article 2 of the Berne Convention. Does the U.S. have to protect sound recordings for nationals of all members of the WTO?

5. Quite apart from deciding which law should apply to a foreign copyrighted work, the Internet has raised some difficult questions for courts regarding appropriate jurisdiction in copyright cases. If an infringing work is hosted on a server located in country A, and the work is accessed in country B, does country B have jurisdiction over a lawsuit filed against the foreign web site owner? Under what circumstances should a U.S. court assert jurisdiction over a foreign person who allegedly has engaged in infringing online activity in a foreign country? What factors should be considered in determining which forum is appropriate? There are cases that indicate that courts are willing to assert jurisdiction over foreign parties for activity occurring online.

In one decision, an Australian court asserted jurisdiction over a defamation claim filed by an Australian citizen against Dow Jones, a U.S. company that publishes Barron's Online. According to the court, "To say that where the article is written, edited and uploaded and where the publisher does its business, must be the forum is an invitation to entrench the United States, the primary home of much Internet publishing, as the forum." *See Gutnick v. Dow Jones & Co.*, [2001] VSC 305 (Supreme Court of Victoria, unreported), *aff'd sub nom. Dow Jones & Co. v. Gutnick*, (2002) 210 C.L.R. 575. The court considered, but was not persuaded by, the argument that it would be difficult for defendants to litigate in every country where documents are downloaded or read. The High Court of Australia affirmed, reasoning that the plaintiff's claim was based on the harm that he had suffered in Victoria as a result of the publication. *See also La Ligue Contre le Racisme et l'antisemitisme et al v. Yahoo!, Inc.*, T.G.I. Paris, Nov. 20, 2000, JCP G 2001, II (asserting jurisdiction over Yahoo! and ordering that the company adopt filtering software to block access by French citizens to forbidden Nazi paraphernalia offered for sale on the yahoo.com auction Web site). Yahoo! sought a declaratory judgment against U.S. enforcement of the foreign award. A U.S. district court granted summary judgment against the enforcement of the French court's decision in the U.S. on grounds that it would violate the First Amendment, but the Ninth Circuit reversed on the ground that the French associations seeking enforcement had insufficient contacts to subject them to suit in California. *See Yahoo! Inc. v. La Ligue Contre le Racisme et l'antisemitisme*, 169 F. Supp. 2d 1181 (N.D. Cal. 2001), *rev'd*, 379 F.3d 1120 (9th Cir. 2004), *reh'g granted*, 399 F.3d 1010 (2005) (en banc). After a rehearing en banc, the Ninth Circuit reversed the district court decision, but the judges disagreed on the reason for reversal. *Yahoo! Inc. v. La Ligue Contre le Racisme et l'anti-semitisme*, 433 F.3d 1199 (9th Cir. 2006). Some thought the case was not ripe for adjudication, while others would have dismissed for lack of personal jurisdiction over the French organization.

6. Questions about the standard for enforcement of foreign judgments are likely to continue to arise in U.S. courts. In *Sarl Louis Feraud International v. Viewfinder, Inc.*, 489 F.3d 474 (2d Cir. 2007), the court addressed the question whether a French judgment against a web site operator should be enforced under New York's Uniform Foreign Money Judgment Recognition Act. Several design houses had filed suit against Viewfinder in Paris for posting photographs of fashion shows at which the designers' fashions were exhibited. *Id.* at 476-77. The French court issued a default judgment against Viewfinder, finding that the photos had been posted without authorization and that Viewfinder had "committed 'parasitism' under French law because it had 'take[n] advantage of plaintiff's reputation and commercial efforts creating confusion. . . . '" *Id.* at 477.

The district court held the French judgment unenforceable as repugnant to New York's public policy because it violated Viewfinder's First Amendment rights. *Id.* at 477-78. The Second Circuit vacated the judgment and set forth the mode of analysis the district court is to use on remand:

> In deciding whether the French Judgments are repugnant to the public policy of New York, the district court should first determine the level of First Amendment protection required by New York public policy when a news entity engages in the unauthorized use of intellectual property [like that] at issue here. Then, it should determine whether the French intellectual property regime provides comparable protections.

Id. at 481-82.

Is this a helpful analysis? Should the district court enforce the judgment if it finds that the use would be fair under U.S. law? What if the use would not be fair? Review note 3 on page 796. What if the designs at issue would not be copyrightable under U.S. law? Should a court apply the same principles to choice of law issues as to the issue of enforcement of a foreign judgment?

7. Even beyond the online environment, the question of jurisdiction is important in an era in which many transactions cross national borders. To reduce legal uncertainty, parties to such transactions often include jurisdictional provisions in their contracts, and similar provisions may appear in end user shrinkwrap and clickwrap licenses. The Hague Conference on Private International Law's Draft Convention on Jurisdiction and Foreign Judgments in Civil and Commercial Matters, finalized in 2005, attempted to promulgate uniform rules for interpreting choice of forum clauses and recognizing and enforcing foreign judgments. In general, it required that choice of forum clauses be enforced and foreign judgments honored, but it excluded from its ambit choice of forum clauses in consumer contracts involving natural persons. The Draft Convention did not attract much support. The Conference then drafted a Convention on Choice of Court Agreements limited to business-to-business contracts and excluded disputes regarding the validity of registered intellectual property rights. To date, only Mexico has adopted this Convention.

The American Law Institute has approved a work entitled "Intellectual Property: Principles Governing Jurisdiction, Choice of Law, and Judgments in Transnational Disputes." The Principles generally require the enforcement of choice of forum and choice of law agreements with special safeguards in the case of mass-market agreements. In such agreements, the clause at issue must be "reasonable and readily accessible to the nondrafting party at the time the agreement was concluded. . . ." Principles §§202, 302. The Principles provide a list of factors for a court to consider in determining reasonableness. *See id.* The Principles also do not permit application of "particular rules of foreign law . . . if such application leads to a result in the forum State that is repugnant to the public policy in that State." *Id.* §322. With respect to enforcement of judgments, the Principles provide that a court should enforce a judgment rendered by a foreign court if the foreign court applied the Principles to the case. *Id.* §401(1)(a). Otherwise, the court should determine enforceability based on its ordinary rules regarding enforcement of foreign judgments. *Id.* §401(1)(b). The Principles do not become law unless and until a court adopts them. Should courts do so?

8. In 1988, the EU began to address the challenge of intellectual property enforcement within its member states. The result of this process is an EU directive regarding the enforcement of intellectual property rights, which establishes minimum enforcement standards to redress the infringement of any intellectual property rights provided by Community law or national law. Corrigendum to Directive 2004/48/EC of the European Parliament and of the Council of 29 April 2004 on the enforcement of intellectual property rights, 2004 O.J. (L 195) 16. The directive builds on the enforcement framework established by the TRIPS Agreement and goes much further. It includes a presumption of authorship similar to that contained in Article 15 of the Berne Convention; addresses how evidence can be obtained and the sufficiency and preservation of such evidence; allows discovery of information concerning individuals involved in any way on a "commercial scale" in infringing activity; prescribes corrective measures that must be available for award by domestic judges, including methods of computing damages; and requires member states to allow third parties (such as collecting societies or trade associations) to file infringement lawsuits on behalf of owners. Note also that EU member states may provide enforcement measures more favorable than those contained in the directive. Despite its important implications for how infringement cases will be litigated in the EU, the directive states that it is not intended to affect substantive intellectual property rights or limitations on those rights.

G. CIVIL REMEDIES

The Copyright Act provides a range of civil remedies for infringement. These are: (1) temporary and final injunctions necessary to prevent or restrain infringement (§502); (2) impoundment of all copies or phonorecords that allegedly infringe the copyright owner's rights (§503(a)); (3) upon a final adjudication of infringement, destruction or disposition of all infringing copies or phonorecords (§503(b)); and (4) monetary damages (§504). A court may, in its discretion, award the full recovery of costs and attorneys' fees (§505). Members of the TRIPS Agreement are required to provide for these same kinds of remedies in their domestic legislation. *See* TRIPS Agreement, art. 44 (injunctions), art. 45 (damages), art. 46 (destruction of infringing goods and the materials and implements used to create them). Finally, §§1203-1204 of the Copyright Act authorize these same remedies for violations of the DMCA.

In this section, we explore the nature and scope of each remedy. We begin our study with an examination of the injunctive remedy.

1. Injunctions

Read §502, which authorizes injunctions in copyright cases. In the U.S., injunctive relief is rooted in well-established principles of equity. This remedy can be traced back to the English Courts of Equity, where injunctions were readily granted in copyright cases.

In the U.S., in non-copyright cases, courts consider four factors in determining whether to grant an injunction. Although the precise formulation of these factors varies, a plaintiff generally must show "(1) that it has suffered an irreparable injury; (2) that remedies available at law, such as monetary damages, are inadequate to compensate for that injury; (3) that, considering the balance of hardships between the plaintiff and defendant, a remedy in equity is warranted; and (4) that the public interest would not be disserved by a permanent injunction." *eBay Inc. v. MercExchange, L.L.C.*, 547 U.S. 388, 391 (2006).

Historically, courts were willing to grant preliminary injunctions in copyright cases without engaging in a detailed analysis of each of the traditional four factors. The Second Circuit's view in the following quote exemplifies this approach:

> [A] preliminary injunction can be granted if [the] plaintiff shows irreparable injury, combined with either a probability of success on the merits, or a fair ground for litigation and a balance of the hardships in his favor. In copyright cases, however, if probable success—a prima facie case of copyright infringement—can be shown, the allegations of irreparable injury need not be very detailed, because such injury can normally be presumed when a copyright is infringed.

Wainwright Sec., Inc. v. Wall St. Transcript Corp., 558 F.2d 91, 94 (2d Cir. 1977), *cert. denied*, 434 U.S. 1014 (1978).

Final injunctions were likewise common, as were judicial statements like, "When a copyright plaintiff has established a threat of continuing infringement, he is *entitled* to an injunction." *Walt Disney Co. v. Powell*, 897 F.2d 565, 567 (D.C. Cir. 1990). Indeed, a court's authority to grant a final injunction historically has been very broad, extending to unregistered works and, in appropriate cases, to future works and works not in suit. *See Olan Mills, Inc. v. Linn Photo Co.*, 23 F.3d 1345 (8th Cir. 1994).

In *eBay Inc. v. MercExchange, L.L.C.*, 547 U.S. 388 (2006), the Supreme Court ruled that courts must evaluate the traditional four factors before granting a final injunction in a patent infringement case. The Patent Act provides that courts may "grant injunctions in accordance with the principles of equity to prevent the violation of any right secured by patent, on such terms as the court deems reasonable." 35 U.S.C. §283. The Court rejected both the asserted "'general rule,' unique to patent disputes, 'that a permanent injunction will issue once infringement and validity have been adjudged,'" and statements indicating that denials of injunctions should be rare. *eBay*, 547 U.S. at 393-94. It held that an injunction should be granted only after a court considers the four factors and also noted that the "decision to grant or deny permanent injunctive relief is an act of equitable discretion by the . . . court." *Id*. at 391.

The Court observed that the rule it announced for patent cases was

> consistent with our treatment of injunctions under the Copyright Act. Like a patent owner, a copyright holder possesses "the right to exclude others from using his property." . . . Like the Patent Act, the Copyright Act provides that courts 'may' grant injunctive relief "on such terms

as it may deem reasonable to prevent or restrain infringement of a copyright." 17 U.S.C. §502(a). . . . And as in our decision today, this Court has consistently rejected invitations to replace traditional equitable considerations with a rule that an injunction automatically follows a determination that a copyright has been infringed. *See, e.g., New York Times Co. v. Tasini,* 533 U.S. 483, 505 . . . (2001) (citing *Campbell v. Acuff-Rose Music, Inc.,* 510 U.S. 569, 578 n. 10 . . . (1994)). . . .

Id. at 392.

What are the implications of *eBay* for copyright litigants? Consider the following three opinions, one pre-*eBay* and two applying the *eBay* approach.

≣≣≣ ### *Abend v. MCA, Inc.*
≣≣≣ #### *863 F.2d 1465 (9th Cir. 1988)*

[Review the facts of *Stewart v. Abend* on pages 176-77. Recall that the Supreme Court held that the work was infringing but did not disturb the Ninth Circuit's opinion about appropriate remedies. Here is that portion of the Ninth Circuit's opinion.]

PREGERSON, J.: . . . We are mindful that this case presents compelling equitable considerations which should be taken into account by the district court in fashioning an appropriate remedy in the event defendants fail to establish any equitable defenses. Defendants invested substantial money, effort, and talent in creating the "Rear Window" film. Clearly the tremendous success of that venture initially and upon re-release is attributable in significant measure to, inter alia, the outstanding performances of its stars — Grace Kelly and James Stewart — and the brilliant directing of Alfred Hitchcock. The district court must recognize this contribution in determining Abend's remedy.

The district court may choose from several available remedies for the infringement. Abend seeks first an injunction against the continued exploitation of the "Rear Window" film. 17 U.S.C. §502(a) provides that the court "*may* . . . grant temporary and final injunctions on such terms as it may deem reasonable to prevent or restrain infringement of a copyright." Defendants argue . . . that a finding of infringement presumptively entitles the plaintiff to an injunction, citing Professor Nimmer. *See* 3 M. Nimmer, Nimmer on Copyright §14.06[B] at 14-55 to 14-56.2 (1988). However, Professor Nimmer also states that "where great public injury would be worked by an injunction, the courts might . . . award damages or a continuing royalty instead of an injunction in such special circumstances." *Id.* at 14-56.2.

We believe such special circumstances exist here. The "Rear Window" film resulted from the collaborative efforts of many talented individuals other than Cornell Woolrich, the author of the underlying story. The success of the movie resulted in large part from factors completely unrelated to the underlying story, "It Had To Be Murder." It would cause a great injustice for the owners of the film if the court enjoined them from further exhibition of the movie. An injunction would also effectively foreclose defendants from enjoying legitimate profits derived from exploitation of the "new matter" comprising the derivative work, which is given express copyright protection by section 7 of the 1909 Act. Since defendants could not possibly separate out the "new matter" from the underlying work, their right to enjoy the renewal copyright *in the derivative work* would be rendered meaningless by the grant of an injunction. We also note that an injunction could cause public injury by denying the public the opportunity to view a classic film for many years to come.

This is not the first time we have recognized that an injunction may be an inappropriate remedy for copyright infringement. In *Universal City Studios v. Sony Corp. of America*, 659 F.2d 963, 976 (9th Cir. 1981), *rev'd on other grounds*, 464 U.S. 417 . . . we stated that Professor Nimmer's suggestion of damages or a continuing royalty would constitute an acceptable resolution for infringement caused by in-home taping of television programs by VCR — "time-shifting." *See also Sony Corp. v. Universal City Studios*, 464 U.S. 417, 499-500 (1984) (Blackmun, J., dissenting).

As the district court pointed out in the *Sony* case, an injunction is a "harsh and drastic" discretionary remedy, never an absolute right. . . . Abend argues nonetheless that defendants' attempts to interfere with his production of new derivative works can only be remedied by an injunction. We disagree. Abend has not shown irreparable injury which would justify imposing the severe remedy of an injunction on defendants. Abend can be compensated adequately for the infringement by monetary compensation. 17 U.S.C. §504(b) provides that the copyright owner can recover actual damages and "any profits of the infringement that are *attributable to the infringement* and are not taken into account in computing the actual damages." (Emphasis added.)

The district court is capable of calculating damages caused to the fair market value of plaintiff's story by the re-release of the film. Any impairment of Abend's ability to produce new derivative works based on the story would be reflected in the calculation of the damage to the fair market value of the story. . . .

Christopher Phelps & Associates, LLC v. Galloway
492 F.3d 532 (4th Cir. 2007)

NIEMEYER, J.:

After R. Wayne Galloway began construction of his retirement home on Lake Wylie, near Charlotte, North Carolina, using architectural plans designed and copyrighted by Christopher Phelps & Associates, LLC ("Phelps & Associates"), without permission, Phelps & Associates commenced this action against Galloway for copyright infringement. Phelps & Associates sought damages . . . and injunctive relief. A jury found that Galloway infringed Phelps & Associates' copyright and awarded it $20,000 in damages . . . . The district court thereafter declined to enter an injunction, finding that the jury verdict had made Phelps & Associates "whole". . . . Phelps & Associates appeals, requesting a new trial on damages and the entry of an injunction prohibiting the future lease or sale of the infringing house and mandating the destruction or return of the infringing plans. . . .

Insofar as Phelps & Associates suggests that it is *entitled* to injunctive relief, we reject the argument. *See eBay Inc. v. MercExchange, L.L.C.,* —U.S.—, 126 S.Ct. 1837, 1839 . . . (2006). . . . [The Court there said, "]A plaintiff must demonstrate: (1) that it has suffered an irreparable injury; (2) that remedies available at law, such as monetary damages, are inadequate to compensate for that injury; (3) that, considering the balance of hardships between the plaintiff and defendant, a remedy in equity is warranted; and (4) that the public interest would not be disserved by a permanent injunction.["] *Id.* at 1839. Moreover, the Court reiterated that even upon this showing, whether to grant the injunction still remains in the "equitable discretion" of the court. . . .

Phelps & Associates' . . . request for equitable relief, that Galloway be permanently enjoined from leasing or selling the completed house, is argued with the following syllogism: *First*, the completed house is an infringing copy of Phelps & Associates' copyrighted work.

See 17 U.S.C. §101. *Second*, as the copyright holder, Phelps & Associates has the exclusive right to "distribute" its copyrighted work "by sale or other transfer of ownership." *See id.* §106(3). *Therefore*, Galloway may never lease or sell the house without infringing Phelps & Associates' copyright. *See id.* §501(a). Because it is likely that Galloway will lease or sell the house, Phelps & Associates believes this lease or sale should be foreclosed by a permanent injunction.

We agree with Phelps & Associates that Galloway will inevitably sell or transfer his house within the period during which Phelps & Associates still holds the copyright—i.e. 95 years, *see* 17 U.S.C. §302(c)—and that such a sale could, absent this action, expose Galloway to further relief, *see id.* §106(3); *id.* §501(a); *cf. id.* §109(a) (permitting resale of "lawfully made" copies) . . . But Phelps & Associates has requested relief for that inevitable transaction now *in this action*, as part of the panoply of remedies available under the Copyright Act, and therefore entitlement to that relief can be and is resolved in this action under the principles of *eBay*, 126 S.Ct. at 1839.

The first two *eBay* criteria for injunctive relief—irreparable injury and the inadequacy of monetary damages—have most likely been demonstrated. Irreparable injury often derives from the nature of copyright violations, which deprive the copyright holder of intangible exclusive rights. Damages at law will not remedy the continuing existence of Phelps & Associates' design in the Galloway house. Moreover, while the calculation of future damages and profits for each future sale might be possible, any such effort would entail a substantial amount of speculation and guesswork that renders the effort difficult or impossible in this case. Accordingly, we conclude that Phelps & Associates most likely has satisfied the first two *eBay* factors.

When considering the third and fourth factors, however—the balance of hardships and the public interest—Phelps & Associates' showing has fallen short.

First, Phelps & Associates has been fully and adequately compensated for the copying and use of its design as manifested in the single Galloway house. . . . A sale of the house would not be a second copy or manifestation of the design, but merely a transfer of the structure in which the design was first copied. An injunction against sale would but slightly benefit Phelps & Associates' legitimate entitlements because the infringing house would retain the same form and location, remaining a permanent nuisance to the copyright regardless of whether there is an injunction. An injunction against sale would neither undo the prior infringement, nor diminish the chances of future copying. At the same time, a permanent injunction would impose a draconian burden on Galloway, effectively creating a *lis pendens* on the house and subjecting him to contempt proceedings simply for selling his own property.

Second, a house or building, as an expression of the architect's copyrighted plans, usually has a predominantly functional character. . . . This is the same reason that Congress manifested an expectation that injunctions will not be routinely issued against substantially completed houses whose designs violated architectural copyrights. H.R.Rep. No. 101-735, at 13-14 (1990), *reprinted in* 1990 U.S.C.C.A.N. 6935, 6944 (explaining that buildings "are the only form of copyrightable subject matter that is habitable"). Those considerations are at their strongest when the architectural structure is completed and inhabited by the infringer, as here. While Galloway infringed the copyright, he now is living in a "copy" of the architectural work. His interest in remaining there, with the same rights as other homeowners to alienate his property, is substantial and, in this case, trumps Phelps & Associates' interests in any injunction prohibiting a lease or sale of the house.

Third, an injunction against sale of the house would be overbroad, as it would encumber a great deal of property unrelated to the infringement. The materials and labor that went into the Galloway house, in addition to the swimming pool, the fence, and other non-infringing features, as well as the land underneath the house, would be restrained by the requested injunction. As such, the injunction would take on a fundamentally punitive character, which has not been countenanced in the Copyright Act's remedies. . . . In a similar vein, the requested injunction would undermine an ancient reluctance by the courts to restrain the alienability of real property. . . . For these reasons, the public interest would be disserved by the entry of an injunction.

Finally, ultimate discretion to grant any such injunctive relief rests with the district court, and for the reasons enumerated, we conclude that deference to the district court's refusal is appropriate in the absence of any showing that such refusal was otherwise an abuse of discretion. *See eBay*, 126 S.Ct. at 1839. . . .

Phelps & Associates relies upon *Sony Corporation of America v. Universal City Studios, Inc.*, 464 U.S. 417, 446 n. 28 . . . (1984), to argue that the refusal to issue an injunction against future leases and sales of the Galloway house amounts to a judicially-created compulsory license, which is disfavored. The reliance on *Sony*, however, is misplaced. The remedies under the Copyright Act do not resemble a license because the Copyright Act remedies are far broader than simply requiring a defendant to make license payments. Under the Copyright Act, a copyright holder is entitled to both actual damages — the market price of the license — *and* disgorgement of the infringer's profits, which might be immensely greater than the price of a license. *See* 17 U.S.C. §504. Moreover, the infringer takes the risk that the district court will order, in its discretion, the destruction or other disposition of the infringing article. *See id.* §503(b). In the garden-variety piracy case, such orders are routinely issued. . . . Given the risks attendant to infringement, denying an injunction is not equivalent to a compulsory license. *See Walker v. Forbes, Inc.*, 28 F.3d 409, 412 (4th Cir.1994) ("By stripping the infringer not only of the licensing fee but also of the profit generated as a result of the use of the infringed item, the law makes clear that there is no gain to be made from taking someone else's intellectual property without their consent"). While granting an injunction to destroy an infringing article might be usual with respect to personal property, especially in the garden-variety music or movie piracy case, refusing to order destruction or the inalienability of property is also consistent with the Copyright Act's remedial scheme and does not amount to a compelled license.

For all of these reasons, we affirm the district court's order denying an injunction against the future lease or sale of Galloway's house. . . .

[The court remanded to the district court to consider whether, in light of the *eBay* factors, it should grant an injunction ordering the destruction of copies of the plans.] . . .

Metro-Goldwyn-Mayer Studios, Inc. v. Grokster, Ltd.
518 F. Supp. 2d 1197 (N.D. Cal. 2007)

[Review the facts of this case at pages 492-94. After articulating a theory of liability for inducement of infringement, the Supreme Court remanded the case to the district court, which found defendants liable on that theory. In this opinion, the district court addresses whether the plaintiffs are entitled to injunctive relief.]

WILSON, J.: . . . Under 17 U.S.C. §502(a), this Court is empowered to grant a permanent injunction "as it may deem reasonable to prevent or restrain infringement of a copyright." . . .

Before applying *eBay*, it must be noted that Plaintiffs also ask this Court first to apply an arguably different (and perhaps more permissive) permanent injunction test. Prior to *eBay*, in *MAI Sys. Corp. v. Peak Computer, Inc.*, 991 F.2d 511, 520 (9th Cir.1993), the Ninth Circuit stated that "[a]s a general rule, a permanent injunction will be granted when liability has been established and there is a threat of continuing violations." Consistent with the Ninth Circuit,

Nimmer writes, "[i]t is uncontroversial that a 'showing of past infringement and a substantial likelihood of future infringement' justifies issuance of a permanent injunction." 4 Melville B. Nimmer & David Nimmer, *Nimmer on Copyright*, §14.06[B] & n. 76.1 . . . ; *see also id.* §14.06[B] ("Because a permanent injunction is issued only after liability is established, its issuance probably does not require a showing of irreparable injury.").

In light of this two-part rule (past infringement + likelihood of future infringements), Plaintiffs have asked for a permanent injunction. However, this Court has doubts that *MAI's* "general rule" regarding permanent injunctions survives *eBay*. In *eBay*, the Supreme Court rejected the Federal Circuit's "general rule" in patent cases that "courts will issue permanent injunctions against patent infringement absent exceptional circumstances." 126 S. Ct. at 1839-40. . . . This Court can identify no place for a separate and distinct two-part *MAI* test or "general rule" that could circumvent *eBay*. . . .

The first question to address is whether Plaintiffs "ha[ve] suffered an irreparable injury." *eBay*, 126 S.Ct. at 1839. . . . [T]he Tenth Circuit has observed that "irreparable harm is often suffered when the injury can[not] be adequately atoned for in money, or when the district court cannot remedy [the injury] following a final determination on the merits." *Prairie Band [of Potawatomi Indians v. Pierce]*, 253 F.3d [1234,] at 1250 [(10th Cir. 2001)]. . . .

The parties dispute whether, in light of *eBay*, irreparable harm can be presumed. . . .

Other courts have in the past presumed the existence of irreparable injury upon the establishment of liability in copyright cases. . . .

Yet, these cases were all decided prior to the Supreme Court's decision in *eBay*. The *eBay* Court held that it is Plaintiffs who "must demonstrate" (meaning, have the burden of proof) that the traditional factors favor a permanent injunction. 126 S. Ct. at 1839. The Supreme Court also highlighted that it has "consistently rejected" the rule that "an injunction automatically follows" an infringement holding. *Id.* at 1840. Given Plaintiffs' burden of proof and the inability of a district court to "automatically" issue injunctions, it is perhaps unclear in *eBay*'s wake whether a permanent injunction can be granted based on a rebuttable presumption of irreparable harm. . . .

. . . [T]he *eBay* district court has subsequently decided that there can be no presumption of irreparable harm in the permanent injunction context. *See MercExchange, L.L.C. v. eBay, Inc.*, 500 F. Supp. 2d 556, 568 (E.D. Va. 2007) ("[A] review of relevant caselaw, as well as the language of the Supreme Court's decision, supports defendants' position that such presumption no longer exists."). This view appears to have been followed by perhaps every court expressly considering *eBay*. . . .

This Court agrees with StreamCast, and these district courts, that the presumption of irreparable harm no longer inures to the benefit of Plaintiffs. The *eBay* Court plainly stated that Plaintiffs "must demonstrate" the presence of the traditional factors, and therefore have the burden of proof with regard to irreparable harm. . . .

Irreparable harm cannot be established solely on the fact of past infringement. Additionally, it must also be true that the mere likelihood of future infringement by a defendant does not by itself allow for an inference of irreparable harm. As to the latter, future copyright infringement can always be redressed via damages, whether actual or statutory. *See* 17 U.S.C. §504. . . .

"[I]rreparable harm may not be presumed[, but] [i]n run-of-the-mill copyright litigation, such proof should not be difficult to establish. . . ." 6 [William F.] Patry, [*Patry on Copyrights*,] . . . §22:74. Thus, Plaintiffs may establish an irreparable harm stemming from the infringement (*e.g.*, loss of market share, reputational harm). It is also possible that some qualitative feature about the infringement itself, such as its peculiar nature, could elevate its status into the realm of "irreparable harm."

StreamCast accepts that certain harms caused by infringement, such as loss of brand recognition and market share, can amount to irreparable harm. . . . However, StreamCast rejects the argument that copyright infringement can itself ever represent irreparable harm. StreamCast asserts that "[i]f damages can be calculated, the injury is **not** irreparable . . . —the Copyright Act specifically provides for statutory damages, which are calculable assuming Plaintiffs can prove direct infringement of their works, and a basis for the range requested." . . . This Court has doubts regarding StreamCast's position. In *eBay*, Chief Justice Roberts indicated that irreparable harm can result from the infringement itself, depending upon the circumstances of the case:

> From at least the early 19th century, courts have granted injunctive relief upon a finding of infringement in the vast majority of patent cases. This "long tradition of equity practice" is not surprising, given the difficulty of protecting a right to exclude through monetary remedies that allow an infringer to use an invention against the patentee's wishes—a difficulty that often implicates the first two factors of the traditional four-factor test.

126 S.Ct. at 1841 (Roberts, C.J., concurring); . . . And "[l]ike a patent owner, a copyright holder possesses 'the right to exclude others from using his property.'" [*Id.*] at 1840. . . .

This Court also recognizes that a competing *eBay* concurrence took issue with Chief Justice Roberts's "right to exclude" language. Justice Kennedy explained his view that "the existence of a right to exclude does not dictate the remedy for a violation of that right." *eBay*, 126 S.Ct. at 1842 (Kennedy, J., concurring). This Court agrees, since a contrary conclusion would come close to permitting a presumption of irreparable harm. This Court also observes that Justice Kennedy's statement was made primarily in the context of certain recent developments in the patent field that are wholly inapplicable to this lawsuit. For example, this is simply not a case in which the copyright infringement represents "but a small component of the product the companies seek to produce," such that "legal damages may well be sufficient to compensate for the infringement." *Id.* As this Court previously held, StreamCast's entire business was built around the fundamental premise that Morpheus would be utilized to infringe copyrights, including those owned by Plaintiffs. Furthermore, Justice Kennedy emphasized that "[t]he equitable discretion over injunctions . . . is well suited to allow courts to adapt to the rapid technological and legal developments. . . ." *Id.* Given the technological aspects of the infringement induced by StreamCast, and the flexibility conferred by the Copyright Act, this Court is persuaded that its bases for finding irreparable harm, *infra*, are supported by both Chief Justice Roberts's and Justice Kennedy's concurrences.

In light of this authority, the Court concludes that certain qualities pertaining to the nature of StreamCast's inducement of infringement are relevant to a finding of irreparable harm. . . .

The irreparable harm analysis centers on two basic themes: (1) StreamCast has and will continue to induce far more infringement than it could ever possibly redress with damages; and (2) Plaintiffs' copyrights (especially those of popular works) have and will be rendered particularly vulnerable to continuing infringement on an enormous scale due to StreamCast's inducement. The Court agrees with both arguments, and each is independently sufficient to support [a] finding of irreparable harm in this case.

First, the Court must ask whether a particular defendant's probable inability to pay damage constitutes irreparable harm. In the ordinary case, "merely alleging an opponent's inability to pay damages does not constitute irreparable harm." *Rosewood Apartments Corp. v. Perpignano*, 200 F. Supp. 2d 269, 278 (S.D.N.Y. 2002). But "[i]n some limited circumstances, parties have demonstrated such a strong likelihood that their opponent will be unable to pay that courts have awarded them equitable relief." *Id.* . . . The rationale in such cases must be that an award of monetary damages will be meaningless, and the plaintiff will have no substantive relief, where it will be impossible to collect an award for past and/or future infringements perpetrated by a defendant.

Plaintiffs have not yet sought an award of statutory damages. Additionally, Plaintiffs have not provided this Court with specific evidence as part of this motion demonstrating that StreamCast would be unable to pay damages for the infringements it has induced in the past, and could continue to induce in the future. But such evidence is not necessary here. Based on the undisputed evidence at summary judgment of massive end-user infringement, it is highly likely that the award of statutory damages that ultimately befalls StreamCast in this case will be enormous (especially considering the potential relationship between inducement and a finding of willfulness), and would far outstrip the amount of revenue the company has garnered in recent years. . . . This Court's conclusion would also be the same even if Plaintiffs chose to forgo a damages award as part of this lawsuit. This is because the amount of infringement that StreamCast could induce in the future is so staggering that the recoverable statutory damages would very probably be well beyond StreamCast's anticipated resources. Because it is extremely unlikely that StreamCast will be able to compensate Plaintiffs monetarily for the infringements it has induced in the past, or the infringements it could induce in the future through Morpheus, Plaintiffs have and will continue to suffer irreparable harm.

Second, the Court agrees with Plaintiffs' claim that a substantial number of their copyrighted works have and would continue to become irreparably exposed to infringement on a tremendous scale due to StreamCast's inducement. This inducement greatly erodes Plaintiffs' ability to enforce their exclusive rights. *See A & M Records, Inc. v. Napster, Inc.*, 239 F.3d 1004, 1029 (9th Cir.2001) (rejecting Napster's request for compulsory royalties as opposed to injunctive relief because "Plaintiffs would lose the power to control their intellectual property"). It also promises no realistic mechanism through which statutory damages can be collected for all of the inevitable subsequent infringements occurring outside of the Morpheus System and Software. . . .

The Court is aware that Plaintiffs can seek an award of statutory damages from StreamCast for infringements occurring through the Morpheus System and Software (ignoring for now the likely reality regarding StreamCast's ability to pay). However, Plaintiffs cannot recover damages from StreamCast for the inevitable derivative infringements that will occur outside of Morpheus, with copyrighted content originally acquired within it, as a consequence [of] StreamCast's inducement. Even numerous lawsuits against direct infringers will necessarily prove to be insufficient under these conditions. *Cf. Grokster*, 545 U.S. at 929-30, 125 S.Ct. 2764 ("When a widely shared service or product is used to commit infringement, it may be impossible to enforce rights in the protected work effectively against all direct infringers. . . ."). Indeed, the very need to file multiple lawsuits as a consequence of StreamCast's inducement is itself supportive of an irreparable harm finding.

In sum, Plaintiffs have offered two independently sufficient grounds for a finding of irreparable harm. . . .

[The court found that the other three *eBay* factors also favored the plaintiffs and concluded that a permanent injunction should issue.]

NOTES AND QUESTIONS

1. Do you prefer the four-factor test, a presumption in favor of injunctive relief in cases of infringement, or some other rule? Do you think injunctions will be more difficult to obtain in copyright cases after *eBay*? Is that result appropriate? Note that the TRIPS Agreement only requires that injunctive relief be available, not that courts must award such relief. Do you think that either *Phelps* or *Grokster* would have been decided differently pre-*eBay*? Why, or why not?

2. Are you persuaded by the *Grokster* court's analysis of the irreparable harm factor? Do you agree that past infringement plus a likelihood of future infringement cannot constitute irreparable harm? Isn't part of the value of the exclusive copyright rights just that—the right to *exclude*? Does irreparable harm necessarily occur when infringement is likely to continue? Would such a rule be consistent with *eBay*?

What other circumstances might demonstrate irreparable harm to a copyright owner? What kinds of infringing activity cannot be remedied by an award of monetary damages? Are there circumstances in which probable inability to pay damages would not (or should not) constitute irreparable harm?

3. May a court distinguish *eBay* as involving a patent infringement claim? In *Salinger v. Colting*, No. 09-2878-cv, 2010 WL 1729126 (2d Cir. Apr. 30, 2010), the court held not:

[excerpt] . . . [N]othing in the text or the logic of *eBay* suggests that its rule is limited to patent cases. On the contrary, *eBay* strongly indicates that the traditional principles of equity it employed are the presumptive standards for injunctions in any context. . . .

Moreover, the Court expressly relied upon copyright cases in reaching its conclusion. Id. at *7-*8.

For an interesting article reviewing the historical use of equitable principles in copyright cases, see H. Tomas Gomez-Arostegui, *What History Teaches Us About Copyright Injunctions and the Inadequate-Remedy-at-Law Requirement*, 81 S. Cal. L. Rev. 1197 (2008) (reviewing early cases from the English Court of Chancery and arguing that under traditional equitable principles courts issued injunctions in copyright cases without regard to the inadequacy of legal remedies).

4. Does *eBay* apply in the preliminary injunction context?

The Supreme Court has stated, "[t]he standard for a preliminary injunction is essentially the same as for a permanent injunction, with the exception that the plaintiff must show a likelihood of success on the merits rather than actual success." *Amoco Prod. Co. v. Gambell*, 480 U.S. 531, 546 n.12 (1987). In a case under the National Environmental Policy Act of 1969, it held that the Ninth Circuit's rule requiring a "possibility" of irreparable harm before the grant of a preliminary injunction was "too lenient. Our frequently reiterated standard requires plaintiffs seeking preliminary relief to demonstrate that irreparable injury is *likely* in the absence of an injunction." *Winter v. National Res. Def. Council*, __ U.S. __, 129 S.Ct. 365, 375 (2008).

In the *Salinger* case, the court relied on *Amoco* and *Winter* in holding that *eBay* applies to preliminary injunctions as well as permanent injunctions. 2010 WL 1729126, at *8-*9. Specifically, the court noted that "at minimum, we must consider whether 'irreparable injury is likely in the absence of an injunction,' we must 'balance the competing claims of injury,' and we must 'pay particular regard for the public consequences in employing the extraordinary remedy of injunction.'" Id. at *9 (quoting *Winter*). Of what value is a preliminary injunction to a plaintiff in a copyright infringement case? Is there any reason why a court should address irreparable harm differently in the copyright context than other contexts? How does your view of the primary justification for copyright law affect your answer?

5. Before the *eBay* case, some scholars had argued that preliminary injunctions could violate the First Amendment:

> . . . [W]hen a court concludes that the defendant's expression is probably not substantially similar to the plaintiff's expression, or is probably a fair use, the court should never issue a preliminary injunction, even if the balance of hardships tilts in the plaintiff's favor. Likewise when the court concludes that the case is genuinely close: erroneously failing to enjoin speech is better than erroneously enjoining speech, especially when erroneous failure to enjoin speech is remediable by a damages award. . . .
>
> . . . Thus, a court should not enter a preliminary injunction unless it is clearly convinced that the speech falls within the copyright exception (*i.e.*, that it's substantially similar to the plaintiff's expression and is not a fair use). . . .

Mark A. Lemley & Eugene Volokh, *Freedom of Speech and Injunctions in Intellectual Property Cases*, 48 Duke L.J. 147, 215-16 (1998).

Does *eBay* resolve this objection?

6. To avoid tension with First Amendment principles, why not refuse preliminary injunctions as a matter of course and simply order monetary compensation? In *Suntrust Bank v. Houghton Mifflin Co.*, 252 F.3d 1165 (11th Cir. 2001), discussed in the Note on Fair Use and the First Amendment, pages 564-65 *supra*, the court vacated a preliminary injunction on First Amendment grounds, stating that the injunction was an unconstitutional prior restraint. In a subsequent opinion clarifying that First Amendment protections for the defendant's parody were preserved via the fair use doctrine, the court ruled that any injury resulting from the alleged infringement could be adequately remedied by money damages. *Suntrust Bank v. Houghton Mifflin Co.*, 268 F.3d 1257, 1277 (11th Cir. 2001). Should courts do this more often in fair use cases? In other infringement cases?

7. If a court finds that the four-factor test is satisfied, how broadly should its remedial powers extend? Are there circumstances under which it would be appropriate for courts to grant injunctions covering unregistered copyrights or copyrights not before the court?

8. Did the courts' decisions in *Abend* and *Phelps* effectively create compulsory licenses? Do you find the *Phelps* court's rejection of the "compulsory license" characterization convincing? Why or why not? Because Congress has instituted compulsory licenses elsewhere in the Copyright Act, would it be appropriate for a court to impose such a license without prior congressional authorization?

9. In economic terms, a compulsory license scheme is described as a liability regime. Liability rules allow use by third parties but require compensation for such use. In contrast, property rules allow the property owner to preclude unauthorized uses by third parties and to receive both injunctive and monetary relief. Recall the goals of copyright, which you studied in Chapter 1. Which model—a property regime or a liability regime—is more consistent with copyright objectives? Would you argue, along with Chief Justice Roberts, that the nature of the right protected by a patent or copyright regime is the right to exclude, or are you persuaded by

Justice Kennedy's distinction between rights and remedies? Is either model mandated by the language of the Intellectual Property Clause?

Universal City Studios, Inc. v. Reimerdes
111 F. Supp. 2d 294 (S.D.N.Y. 2000), aff'd sub nom.
Universal City Studios, Inc. v. Corley, 273 F.3d 429 (2d Cir. 2001)

[Review the facts of this case on pages 663-65.]

KAPLAN, J.: . . .

B. Permanent Injunction and Declaratory Relief

Plaintiffs seek a permanent injunction barring defendants from posting DeCSS on their web site and from linking their site to others that make DeCSS available.

The starting point, as always, is the statute. The DMCA provides in relevant part that the court in an action brought pursuant to its terms "may grant temporary and permanent injunctions on such terms as it deems reasonable to prevent or restrain a violation. . . ." [*See* 17 U.S.C. §1203(b)(1). — EDS.] Where statutes in substance so provide, injunctive relief is appropriate if there is a reasonable likelihood of future violations absent such relief and, in cases brought by private plaintiffs, if the plaintiff lacks an adequate remedy at law.

In this case, it is quite likely that defendants, unless enjoined, will continue to violate the Act. Defendants are in the business of disseminating information to assist hackers in "cracking" various types of technological security systems. And while defendants argue that they promptly stopped posting DeCSS when enjoined preliminarily from doing so, thus allegedly demonstrating their willingness to comply with the law, their reaction to the preliminary injunction in fact cuts the other way. Upon being enjoined from posting DeCSS themselves, defendants encouraged others to "mirror" the information—that is, to post DeCSS—and linked their own web site to mirror sites in order to assist users of defendants' web site in obtaining DeCSS despite the injunction barring defendants from providing it directly. While there is no claim that this activity violated the letter of the preliminary injunction, and it therefore presumably was not contumacious, and while its status under the DMCA was somewhat uncertain, it was a studied effort to defeat the purpose of the preliminary injunction. In consequence, the Court finds that there is a substantial likelihood of future violations absent injunctive relief.

There also is little doubt that plaintiffs have no adequate remedy at law. The only potential legal remedy would be an action for damages under Section 1203(c), which provides for recovery of actual damages or, upon the election of the plaintiff, statutory damages of up to $2,500 per offer of DeCSS. Proof of actual damages in a case of this nature would be difficult if not virtually impossible, as it would involve proof of the extent to which motion picture attendance, sales of broadcast and other motion picture rights, and sales and rentals of DVDs and video tapes of movies were and will be impacted by the availability of DVD decryption technology. Difficulties in determining what constitutes an "offer" of DeCSS in a world in which the code is available to much of the world via Internet postings, among other problems, render statutory damages an inadequate means of redressing plaintiffs' claimed injuries. Indeed, difficulties such as this have led to the presumption that copyright and trademark infringement cause irreparable injury, i.e., injury for which damages are not an adequate remedy. The Court therefore holds that the traditional requirements for issuance of a permanent injunction have been satisfied. Yet there remains another point for consideration.

Defendants argue that an injunction in this case would be futile because DeCSS already is all over the Internet. They say an injunction would be comparable to locking the barn door after the horse is gone. And the Court has been troubled by that possibility. But the countervailing arguments overcome that concern.

To begin with, any such conclusion effectively would create all the wrong incentives by allowing defendants to continue violating the DMCA simply because others, many doubtless at defendants' urging, are doing so as well. Were that the law, defendants confronted with the possibility of injunctive relief would be well advised to ensure that others engage in the same unlawful conduct in order to set up the argument that an injunction against the defendants would be futile because everyone else is doing the same thing.

Second, and closely related, is the fact that this Court is sorely "troubled by the notion that any Internet user . . . can destroy valuable intellectual property rights by posting them over the Internet." While equity surely should not act where the controversy has become moot, it ought to look very skeptically at claims that the defendant or others already have done all the harm that might be done before the injunction issues.

The key to reconciling these views is that the focus of injunctive relief is on the defendants before the Court. If a plaintiff seeks to enjoin a defendant from burning a pasture, it is no answer that there is a wild fire burning in its direction. If the defendant itself threatens the plaintiff with irreparable harm, then equity will enjoin the defendant from carrying out the threat even if other threats abound and even if part of the pasture already is burned.

These defendants would harm plaintiffs every day on which they post DeCSS on their heavily trafficked web site and link to other sites that post it because someone who does not have DeCSS thereby might obtain it. They thus threaten plaintiffs with immediate and irreparable injury. They will not be allowed to continue to do so simply because others may do so as well. In short, this Court, like others tha[t] have faced the issue[], is "not persuaded that modern technology has withered the strong right arm of equity." Indeed, the likelihood is that this decision will serve notice on others that "the strong right arm of equity" may be brought to bear against them absent a change in their conduct and thus contribute to a climate of appropriate respect for intellectual property rights in an age in which the excitement of ready access to untold quantities of information has blurred in some minds the fact that taking what is not yours and not freely offered to you is stealing. Appropriate injunctive and declaratory relief will issue simultaneously with this opinion. . . .

NOTES AND QUESTIONS

1. Would *Reimerdes* be decided the same way after *eBay*? Should *eBay*'s analysis apply to injunctions under the DMCA?

2. What are the policy implications of injunctive relief under §1201 when the technologically protected material may not be copyrightable subject matter? The *Reimerdes* court justifies its award of permanent injunctive relief in large part based on the defendants' encouragement of others to set up mirror sites for DeCSS after the preliminary injunction issued. Is this justification for the permanent injunction consistent with First Amendment principles?

2. Seizure and Impoundment

Section 503 of the Copyright Act provides that while an infringement action is pending, the court may impound all copies or phonorecords claimed to have been made or used in violation of the copyright owner's rights. All the means by which the allegedly infringing copies or phonorecords were reproduced are also subject to impoundment. Upon a final judgment or decree of infringement, a court may order the disposition of all infringing copies or phonorecords and of the means by which the infringing copies were made. In cases of criminal liability for infringement, all infringing copies or phonorecords and all the means by which they were made may be seized and forfeited to the U.S. *See* 18 U.S.C. §2319. Section 603(c) of the Copyright Act provides that infringing goods imported into the U.S. are subject to seizure and forfeiture as property imported in violation of customs laws. Forfeited articles are to be destroyed under the direction of the Secretary of the Treasury or the court.

Seizure and impoundment prevent an infringer from recovering any investment made in the production of infringing goods. These provisions also comport with treaty obligations. Article 46 of the TRIPS Agreement requires that member countries, absent domestic constitutional restraints, provide judicial authorities with the power to dispose of infringing goods outside the ordinary channels of commerce or to destroy the goods. In addition, judicial authorities must have the authority to order that materials and implements used for the primary purpose of creating infringing goods be disposed of outside the ordinary channels of commerce.

NOTES AND QUESTIONS

1. Read §503. Would it authorize the seizure, impoundment, and eventual destruction of a personal computer that was used to upload or download copyrighted material to or from the Internet?

2. In *China — Measures Affecting the Protection and Enforcement of Intellectual Property Rights*, WT/DS362/R (Jan. 26, 2009), the U.S. argued that China's customs measures dealing with the destruction or disposal of infringing goods were inconsistent with Article 59 of the TRIPS Agreement, which provides, in part, that "competent authorities shall have the authority to order the destruction or disposal of infringing goods in accordance with the principles set out in Article 46." Under the Chinese Customs Intellectual Property Rights Regulations and Implementing Measures, infringing goods seized by customs authorities may be (1) donated to social welfare bodies for use in social public welfare undertakings; (2) sold to the rightholder; or (3) if neither of these two options is available, auctioned. All infringing features of the goods must be eradicated before an auction. *Id.* ¶7.194.

The U.S. argued that this disposal scheme impermissibly constrains the authority of Chinese authorities to destroy infringing goods and that the priority accorded the three disposal options allows such goods to enter channels of commerce. The WTO Panel rejected the argument, observing that "the obligation that competent authorities 'shall have the authority' to make certain orders is not an obligation that competent authorities shall exercise that authority in a particular way, unless otherwise specified." *Id.* ¶7.238.

Read Articles 46 and 59 of the TRIPS Agreement. In your view, does the Chinese disposal scheme violate the letter or spirit of these provisions? Why should seizure and impoundment of infringing goods be required in all WTO member countries, especially if the goods can be used for public benefit? For example, such goods could be donated to rural schools, orphanages, or public libraries. What effect, if any, would such redemptive uses have on authorial incentives?

3. Damages and Profits

Section 504(b) of the Copyright Act provides that an infringer of copyright is liable for the copyright owner's "actual damages suffered . . . as a result of the infringement, and any profits of the infringer that are attributable to the infringement and are not taken into account in computing the actual damages." As the cases below illustrate, the exact amount of damages and profits is often difficult to prove with any degree of mathematical precision. Cases in which the protected work is incorporated into a new work with creative contributions added by the alleged infringer are particularly difficult. In such circumstances, courts dissect the infringing work to determine how to apportion damages. Generally, the goal is to award damages proportionate to the contribution of the copyright owner and no more. Read §504(a) and (b) and consider the next two cases.

Frank Music Corp. v. Metro-Goldwyn-Mayer Inc.
886 F.2d 1545 (9th Cir. 1989)

FLETCHER, J.: In *Frank Music Corp. v. Metro-Goldwyn-Mayer, Inc.*, 772 F.2d 505 (9th Cir. 1985) (*Frank Music I*), we affirmed the district court's holding that defendants infringed plaintiffs' copyright in the dramatico-musical play *Kismet*, but remanded for reconsideration of the amount of profits attributable to the infringement. . . .

I. Facts

. . . Plaintiffs are the copyright owners and authors of *Kismet*, a dramaticomusical work. MGM, Inc. under license produced a musical motion picture version of *Kismet*. Beginning April 26, 1974, MGM Grand presented a musical revue entitled *Hallelujah Hollywood* in the hotel's Ziegfeld Theatre. *Hallelujah Hollywood* was largely created by an employee of MGM Grand, Donn Arden, who also staged, produced and directed the show. The show comprised ten acts, four billed as "tributes" to MGM motion pictures. Act IV was entitled "Kismet," and was a tribute to the MGM movie of that name. It was based almost entirely on music from *Kismet*, and used characters and settings from that musical. Act IV "Kismet" was performed approximately 1700 times, until July 16, 1976, when, under pressure resulting from this litigation, MGM Grand substituted a new Act IV. . . .

II. Discussion

A. Apportionment of Profits

1. Direct Profits

In *Frank Music I*, 772 F.2d at 524, we upheld the district court's conclusion that the plaintiffs failed to prove actual damages arising from the infringement, but vacated the district court's award of $22,000 in apportioned profits as "grossly inadequate," *id.* at 518, and remanded to the district court for reconsideration.

On remand, the district court calculated MGM Grand's net profit from *Hallelujah Hollywood* at $6,131,606, by deducting from its gross revenues the direct costs MGM Grand proved it had incurred. Neither party challenges this calculation.

In apportioning the profits between Act IV and the other acts in the show, the district court made the following finding:

> Act IV of "Hallelujah Hollywood" was one of ten acts, approximately a ten minute segment of a 100 minute revue. On this basis, the Court concludes that ten percent of the profits of "Hallelujah Hollywood" are attributable to Act IV.

Memorandum of Decision and Order (Decision II) at 4.

Plaintiffs assert that this finding is in error in several respects. First, they point out that on Saturdays *Hallelujah Hollywood* contained only eight acts, not ten, and that on Saturdays the show ran only 75 minutes, not 100. . . . Second, Act IV was approximately eleven and a half minutes long, not ten. . . . Because the show was performed three times on Saturdays, and twice a night on the other evenings of the week, the district court substantially underestimated the running time of Act IV in relation to the rest of the show.[2]

If the district court relied exclusively on a quantitative comparison and failed to consider the relative quality or drawing power of the show's various component parts, it erred. . . . However, the district court's apportionment based on comparative durations would be appropriate if the district court implicitly concluded that all the acts of the show were of roughly equal value. *Cf. Frank Music I*, 772 F.2d at 518 ("Each element contributed significantly to the show's success, but no one element was the sole or overriding reason for that success."). While a more precise statement of the district court's reasons would have been desirable, we find support in the record for the conclusion that all the acts in the show were of substantially equal value.

The district court went on to apportion the parties' relative contributions to Act IV itself:

> The infringing musical material was only one of several elements contributing to the segment. A portion of the profits attributable to Act IV must be allocated to other elements, including the creative talent of the producer and director, the talents of performers, composers, choreographers, costume designers and others who participated in creating Act IV, and the attraction of the unique Ziegfeld Theatre with its elaborate stage effects. . . . While no precise mathematical formula can be applied, the Court concludes that . . . a fair approximation of the value of the infringing work to Act IV is twenty-five percent.

Decision II at 4-5.

The district court was correct in probing into the parties' relative contributions to Act IV. Where a defendant alters infringing material to suit its own unique purposes, those alterations and the creativity behind them should be taken into account in apportioning the profits of the infringing work. . . . However, the district court appears to have ignored its finding in its previous decision that defendants used not only the plaintiffs' music, but also their lyrics, characters, settings, and costume designs, recreating to a substantial extent the look and sound of the licensed movie version of *Kismet*. . . .

While it was not inappropriate to consider the creativity of producers, performers and others involved in staging and adapting excerpts from *Kismet* for use in *Hallelujah Hollywood*, the district court erred in weighing these contributions so heavily. In performing the apportionment, the benefit of the doubt must always be given to the plaintiff, not the defendant. And while the apportionment may take into account the role of uncopyrightable elements of a work in generating that work's profits, the apportionment should not place too high a value on the defendants' staging of the work, at the expense of undervaluing the plaintiffs' more substantive creative contributions. Production contributions involving expensive costumes and lavish sets will largely be taken into account when deducting the defendants' costs. . . .

2. There were twelve shows weekly which ran for 100 minutes, plus three on Saturday which ran 75, totaling 1425 minutes per week. Act IV remained constant throughout the week, for a total of approximately 173 minutes. Accordingly, Act IV comprised 12% of the total weekly running time of *Hallelujah Hollywood*. Because the district court's findings differ from those previously found and affirmed in *Frank Music I*, we substitute 12% as the appropriate figure on which we base our subsequent calculations.

The district court found that defendants' staging of the *Kismet* excerpts was highly significant to Act IV's success. While we believe that a defendant's efforts in staging an infringing production will generally not support more than a *de minimis* deduction from the plaintiff's share of the profits, we cannot say the district court's conclusion that the defendants' contributions were substantial in this case is clearly erroneous. We recognize that there will be shows in which the attraction of the costumes, scenery or performers outweighs the attraction of the music or dialogue. On the other hand, a producer's ability to stage a lavish presentation, or a performer's ability to fill a hall from the drawing power of her name alone, is not a license to use freely the copyrighted works of others.

We conclude that apportioning 75% of Act IV to the defendants grossly undervalues the importance of the plaintiffs' contributions. Act IV was essentially *Kismet*, with contributions by the defendants; it was not essentially a new work incidentally plagiarizing elements of *Kismet*. A fairer apportionment, giving due regard to the district court's findings, attributes 75% of Act IV to elements taken from the plaintiffs and 25% to the defendants' contributions.

2. Indirect Profits

In *Frank Music I*, we held that the plaintiffs were entitled to recover, in addition to direct profits, a proportion of ascertainable indirect profits from defendants' hotel and gaming operations attributable to the promotional value of *Hallelujah Hollywood*. The district court considered the relative contributions of *Hallelujah Hollywood* and other factors contributing to the hotel's profits, including the hotel's guest accommodations, restaurants, cocktail lounges, star entertainment in the "Celebrity" room, the movie theater, Jai Alai, the casino itself, convention and banquet facilities, tennis courts, swimming pools, gym and sauna, and also the role of advertising and general promotional activities in bringing customers to the hotel. The district court concluded that two percent of MGM Grand's indirect profit was attributable to *Hallelujah Hollywood*. In light of the general promotion and the wide variety of attractions available at MGM Grand, this conclusion is not clearly erroneous.

B. Prejudgment Interest

The district court, without comment, declined to award prejudgment interest. The availability of prejudgment interest under the Copyright Act of 1909 is an issue of first impression in this circuit.

The 1909 Act does not mention prejudgment interest. Nevertheless, courts may allow prejudgment interest even though the governing statute is silent. . . . The goal of compensating the injured party fairly for the loss caused by the defendant's breach of the statutory obligation should be kept in mind. Prejudgment interest compensates the injured party for the loss of the use of money he would otherwise have had. . . .

Because the 1909 Act allows plaintiffs to recover only the greater of the defendant's profits or the plaintiff's actual damages an award of profits or damages under the 1909 Act will not necessarily be adequate to compensate a prevailing copyright owner. Accordingly, we conclude prejudgment interest ordinarily should be awarded.

Awarding prejudgment interest on the apportioned share of defendant's profits is consistent with the purposes underlying the profits remedy. Profits are awarded to the plaintiff not only to compensate for the plaintiff's injury, but also and primarily to prevent the defendant from being unjustly enriched by its infringing use of the plaintiff's property. For the restitutionary purpose of this remedy to be served fully, the defendant generally should be required to turn over to the plaintiff not only the profits made from the use of his property, but also the interest on these profits, which can well exceed the profits themselves. Indeed, one way to view this interest is as another form of indirect profit accruing from the infringement, which should be turned over to the copyright owner along with other forms of indirect profit. It would be anomalous to hold that a plaintiff can recover, for example, profits derived from the promotional use of its copyrighted material, but not for the value of the use of the revenue generated by the infringement.[10] We accordingly remand to the district court to enter an award of prejudgment interest. . . .

Bouchat v. Baltimore Ravens Football Club, Inc.

346 F.3d 514 (4th Cir. 2003), cert. denied, 541 U.S. 1042 (2004)

KING, J.: This appeal arises from the damages phase of a protracted copyright dispute involving the Baltimore Ravens football team. Frederick Bouchat, the holder of the infringed copyright, . . . asserts that the court erroneously failed to accord him the benefit of a statutory presumption that an infringer's revenues are entirely attributable to the infringement. For the reasons explained below, we affirm.

I.

On November 6, 1995, the National Football League ("NFL") announced that one of its teams, the Cleveland Browns, would shortly be moving to Baltimore. The team was to leave its entire Browns identity in Cleveland, and thus would need a new name and logo when it moved to its new Maryland home. Bouchat, a Baltimore security guard and amateur artist, became interested in the new team, and he began drawing logo designs based on the various names that the team was considering, including the name "Ravens." On or about December 5, 1995, Bouchat created a drawing of a winged shield (the "Shield Drawing") as a "Ravens" logo.

In March of 1996, the Baltimore team adopted the name "Ravens." In early April, Bouchat sent the Shield Drawing via fax to the Maryland Stadium Authority. Beside the Shield Drawing, Bouchat penned a note asking the Chairman of the Authority to send the sketch to the Ravens' president. Bouchat also requested that if the Ravens used the Shield Drawing, they send him a letter of recognition and an autographed helmet.

In a jury trial on the issue of liability, Bouchat's Shield Drawing was found to have been mistakenly used by National Football League Properties, Inc. ("NFLP") [the Ravens' licensing agent — EDS.] in NFLP's production of the Ravens' new logo, the "Flying B." The Ravens had no knowledge that the NFLP had infringed anyone's work and assumed that the Flying B was an original work owned by NFLP. The Ravens used the Flying B as their primary identifying symbol, and the logo appeared in every aspect of the Ravens' activities, including uniforms, stationery, tickets, banners, on-field insignia, and merchandise.

II. . . .

Bouchat sought damages from the Ravens and NFLP pursuant to 17 U.S.C. §504(a)(1), which renders an infringer liable for "the copyright owner's actual damages and any additional profits of the infringer, as provided by [17 U.S.C. §504(b)]." Section 504(b), in turn, entitles

---

10. Prejudgment interest will, of course, be available on both the direct and indirect profits earned by MGM Grand, since both forms of profit are equally attributable to the infringement. *Frank Music I*, 772 F.2d at 517.

the copyright owner to recover both "the actual damages suffered by him or her as a result of the infringement, and any profits of the infringer that are attributable to the infringement and are not taken into account in computing the actual damages." 17 U.S.C. §504(b). . . .

In his complaint, Bouchat contended that some portion of essentially *all* of the Defendants' revenues was attributable to the infringing use of Bouchat's artwork.[1] To satisfy his initial burden under §504(b), Bouchat presented evidence of the gross receipts from all NFLP and Ravens activities. The district court, however, awarded partial summary judgment to the Defendants with respect to all revenues derived from sources other than (1) sales of merchandise bearing the Flying B logo, and (2) royalties obtained from licensees who sold such merchandise (collectively, the "Merchandise Revenues"). *Bouchat v. Baltimore Ravens, Inc.*, 215 F. Supp. 2d 611, 619, 621 (D. Md. 2002). The court reasoned that "[i]f the use of the Flying B logo to designate the Ravens could not reasonably be found to have affected the amount of revenue obtained from an activity, the revenue from that activity could not reasonably be found attributable to the infringement." *Id.* at 617-18. Concluding that only the Merchandise Revenues could reasonably be found to have been affected by the Defendants' unlawful use of the Flying B, the court excluded, as a matter of law, the remainder of the Defendants' revenues (collectively, the "Non–Merchandise Revenues") from the pool of income that the jury could consider in awarding §504 damages.[4]

At the close of discovery, the district court further narrowed the scope of the Defendants' revenues from which the jury would be permitted to award §504 damages, when it excluded certain portions of the Merchandise Revenues. . . . Specifically, the court awarded partial summary judgment to the Defendants as to Bouchat's claims for profits from "minimum guarantee shortfalls,"[5] "free merchandise,"[6] trading cards, video games, and game programs (collectively, the "Excluded Merchandise Revenues"). . . . Though it recognized that the Defendants "ha[ve] the burden of proof," the court nonetheless ruled that, with respect to the minimum guarantee shortfalls and the free merchandise, there could be no rational connection between the particular source of revenue and the act of infringement; and that, with respect to the trading cards, video games, and game program sales, the Defendants had produced unrebutted evidence establishing that the revenues received from those sources were not attributable to the infringement. . . . Both the Non–Merchandise Revenues and a substantial portion of the Merchandise Revenues having thus been excluded, only those revenues derived from the sale of t-shirts, caps, souvenir cups, and other items bearing the Flying B logo (collectively, the "Non-Excluded Merchandise Revenues") would go to the jury for a finding on attributability. . . .

[T]he jury was asked to decide whether the Defendants had proven, by a preponderance of the evidence, that the Non–Excluded Merchandise Revenues were attributable entirely to factors other than the Defendants' infringement of Bouchat's copyright. If the jury found that they were not, then it was charged to decide the percentage of the Non-Excluded Merchandise Revenues attributable to factors other than the infringement.

---

1. Bouchat conceded in the district court that there are a few categories of the Defendants' revenues that could not, in any part, be attributable to the infringement. So, for example, Bouchat did not seek to recover interest earned on Ravens' checking accounts, even though the checks bore the Flying B logo; nor did he seek to recover the revenues obtained from stadium rentals, even though the Flying B logo was prominently featured on the playing field. *See Bouchat v. Baltimore Ravens, Inc.*, 215 F. Supp. 2d 611, 616 (D. Md. 2002).

4. The Non–Merchandise Revenues would include, for instance, revenues from the sale of game tickets, stadium parking, food, drinks (with the exception of those sold in special logo-bearing cups), broadcast rights, and sponsorships.

5. Under NFLP's retail licensing agreements, licensed vendors of official, logo-bearing merchandise are required to pay a certain sum each year, regardless of whether any sales of licensed products actually occur. Thus, if actual sales fall short of what would be required to generate the guaranteed minimum royalty, a vendor must tender payment in the amount needed to make up the difference. This sum is a "minimum guarantee shortfall" payment. *See* J.A. 1317-26.

6. Under NFLP's retail licensing agreements, a licensed vendor of official, logo-bearing merchandise must provide to NFLP, at no cost, a certain quantity of its licensed products each year. These products are referred to as "free merchandise." *See* J.A. 1317-26.

After a full day of deliberations, the jury answered the first question in the affirmative, thereby denying Bouchat any monetary recovery. . . . Bouchat filed a timely notice of appeal . . . .

III.

A. . . .

Bouchat asserts that the court failed to give him the benefit of the §504 statutory presumption that an infringer's revenues are entirely attributable to the infringement. That presumption, he maintains, creates a question of material fact that cannot be resolved on summary judgment. Thus, he asserts, whether any portion of an infringer's revenues are attributable to some source other than the infringement is a question that can be resolved *only* by a jury. As explained below, we disagree. . . .

2. . . .

Section 504(b) entitles a successful copyright plaintiff to recover "any profits of the infringer that are attributable to the infringement." 17 U.S.C. §504(b). The statute goes on to specify that,

[i]n establishing the infringer's profits, the copyright owner is required to present proof only of the infringer's gross revenue, and the infringer is required to prove his or her deductible expenses and the elements of profit attributable to factors other than the copyrighted work.

Id. Thus, §504(b) creates an initial presumption that the infringer's "profits . . . attributable to the infringement" are equal to the infringer's gross revenue. . . . Once the copyright owner has established the amount of the infringer's gross revenues, the burden shifts to the infringer to prove either that part or all of those revenues are "deductible expenses" (i.e., are not profits), or that they are "attributable to factors other than the copyrighted work." *Id.* Although §504(b) places the burden on the infringer to demonstrate that certain portions of its revenues were due to factors other than the infringement, the infringer need not prove these amounts with mathematical precision. . . .

3.

Despite the existence of §504(b)'s burden-shifting provision, summary judgment in favor of an infringer with respect to some portion of the infringer's gross revenues may, in the proper circumstances, be appropriate. . . .

[T]he Defendants could properly be awarded summary judgment with respect to any given revenue stream if either (1) there exists no conceivable connection between the infringement and those revenues; or (2) despite the existence of a conceivable connection, Bouchat offered only speculation as to the existence of a causal link between the infringement and the revenues. It is to these inquiries that we turn next.

4.

The Defendants derive revenues from six major sources: (1) sponsorships; (2) broadcast and other media licenses; (3) sale of tickets; (4) miscellaneous business activities, which appear to include provision of game-day stadium parking; (5) sale of official team merchandise; and (6) royalties from licensees who sell official team merchandise. . . . The first four of these sources we characterize as the "Non–Merchandise Revenues," while the fifth and sixth are the "Merchandise Revenues." . . .

Bouchat contends that, because of the Defendants' widespread use of the Flying B as the primary logo — and as an integral marketing tool — for the Baltimore Ravens, some portion of the revenues that the Defendants earned from both the Non–Merchandise Revenues and the Excluded Merchandise Revenues is attributable to the Defendants' infringement of his copyright. When the district court awarded summary judgment to the Defendants as to large segments of their revenues, however, it denied Bouchat the opportunity to prove this contention to the jury. Despite the fact that §504(b) places on the infringer the burden of proving that revenues are not attributable to the infringement, summary judgment was appropriate with respect to both the Non–Merchandise Revenues and the Excluded Merchandise Revenues. . . .

a.

Of all the excluded revenues, only the revenues from minimum guarantee shortfalls and free merchandise lack all conceivable connection to the Defendants' infringement of Bouchat's copyright. Because no rational trier of fact could find that these two subcategories of the Excluded Merchandise Revenues were affected by the Defendants' adoption of the infringing Flying B logo, the court properly removed them from the pool of Defendants' revenues submitted to the jury for consideration under §504(b).

The levels of each licensee's minimum guarantee and free merchandise obligation were established, *ex ante*, by the terms of the licensee's contract with NFLP; neither figure could fluctuate in response to consumer behavior. As a consequence, the amount of revenue that the Defendants received in the form of minimum guarantee shortfalls and free merchandise was necessarily independent of any reaction that any individual might have had to the Flying B logo. Whereas it is at least hypothetically possible (albeit highly unlikely) that an individual became so enamored of the infringing aspects of the Flying B logo that he was thus inspired to purchase tickets for the Ravens' games, to pay for parking, to buy non-logo-bearing concessions, and thus to boost the Defendants' revenues from these sources, a similar scenario cannot be conjured with respect to revenues whose levels were fixed and immutable before licensees had an opportunity to stock their shelves with logo-bearing goods. . . .

b.

Having concluded that summary judgment in favor of the Defendants was proper with respect to both the minimum guarantee short-falls and the free merchandise, we turn now to the Non–Merchandise Revenues and the remaining sub-categories of the Excluded Merchandise Revenues (i.e., the revenues from trading cards, video games, and game programs). Our inquiry on this point is whether, despite the existence of a conceivable connection between the infringement and the level of revenue that the Defendants earned from these sources, the court was correct in excluding them through summary judgment. Because Bouchat offered only speculative evidence of a causal link between the infringement and the level of the revenues that the Defendants earned from these sources, and because the Defendants' request for summary judgment was supported by unrebutted evidence demonstrating that these revenues were not, in fact, in any way attributable to the infringement, there was no issue of material fact for consideration by the jury. As a result, the court did not err in awarding summary judgment to the Defendants with respect to these remaining categories of revenue. . . .

B.

Finally, Bouchat contends that the district court, in its instructions to the jury, failed to accord him the full benefit of the statutory presumption contained in §504(b). Specifically, Bouchat maintains that the court abused its discretion by failing to make clear to the jury that the Ravens bore the burden of proof in the damages trial. To the contrary, the court made it eminently clear in its instructions that the Ravens were obliged to shoulder the burden of proof. . . .

WIDENER, J., dissenting: . . . I am of opinion that the district court erred by refusing to instruct the jury that the defendants' profits are deemed attributable to the alleged copyright infringement unless the defendants prove otherwise. . . .[1]

At the close of evidence in the damages trial, Bouchat asked the district court to give the jury instruction approved by this court in *Walker v. Forbes*, 28 F.3d 409 (4th Cir. 1994). In *Walker*, we affirmed the district court's instruction on the award of profits in a copyright infringement case. Bouchat asked for the instruction by name and also read the relevant language into the record. . . .

I agree with the majority's conclusion that the district court correctly instructed the jury on the burden of proof. Under *Walker*, however, merely stating that the defendant bears the burden of proof is not enough. The *Walker* instruction also informs the jury that profits should be deemed attributable to the alleged infringement unless the defendant proves otherwise. *Walker*, 28 F.3d at 414. Indeed, our opinion emphasized the following portion of the district court's instruction: "*amounts or elements of profits should be deemed attributable to the alleged infringement unless [the defendant] proves by a preponderance of the evidence that they are not.*" *Walker*, 28 F.3d at 414 (emphasis in original). The importance of this portion of the instruction is evident from our analysis following the emphasized language:

> This instruction correctly stated the law concerning the shifted burden of proof that the defendant bears to show the portion of revenues and profits that are not attributable to the infringement, and, *in the emphasized language, explained the impact of this shifted burden upon the apportionment calculation.*

Walker, 28 F.3d at 414 (emphasis added). The emphasized language in *Walker* is the basic thought around which the decision is based, and its conscious omission here is, I think, reversible error. . . .

Other courts similarly acknowledge that §504(b) creates a presumption in favor of the copyright owner. In *Data General Corp. v. Grumman Systems Support Corp.*, 36 F.3d 1147, 1173 (1st Cir. 1994), the First Circuit held that "the plaintiff must meet only a minimal burden of proof in order to trigger a rebuttable presumption that the defendant's revenues are entirely attributable to the infringement." The rebuttable presumption language in *Data General* has been used by a number of district courts. . . .

In addition to refusing to give the *Walker* instruction, the district court limited its instructions on the award of profits under §504(b) to an explanation of the special verdict form. The court read each question from the verdict form and then gave a brief explanation of what the question meant. The first question asked "have the defendants proven by a preponderance of the evidence that income derived by the defendants from the sale of products

---

1. Bouchat is entitled to defendants' profits attributable to the infringement because the award of profits is intended to "prevent the infringer from unfairly benefiting from a wrongful act" and not to compensate the copyright owner. H.R.Rep. No. 94-1476, at 161 (1976), *reprinted in* 1976 U.S.C.C.A.N. 5659, 5777.

bearing the Flying B logo was attributable completely to factors other than the artwork of the Flying B logo." The jury answered "yes" to question one and ended their deliberations. . . .

In this case, the lack of a clear, or any, instruction relating to the presumption of award of profits, together with the limited scope of the verdict form questions, can only have discouraged the jury from awarding damages to the plaintiff, even if the facts and the law supported such an award. This result runs counter to the fundamental purposes of trial by jury. . . .

NOTES AND QUESTIONS

1. In *Frank Music*, the court considered a variety of elements in determining the infringers' profits. Profits included both direct profits reflected in the commercial revenues earned from the infringing work and indirect profits reflected in any value added to the defendant's enterprise reasonably related to the infringing work. Why is an award of indirect profits justified? Should indirect profits be awarded in cases such as *Frank Music* where the infringing work also includes independent contributions (both copyrightable and non-copyrightable) by the defendant?

2. Assume that incorporation of a copyrighted work into a second work (as in *Frank Music*) reduces the value of the second work, instead of enhancing it. Should the damage award be reduced accordingly? If there are no ascertainable profits, how should a court determine whether the infringement was a "value-adding" contribution to the infringing work?

3. What should be the principal goal of apportionment: to prevent unjust enrichment of either party, or to deter the infringing creation of derivative works? Is there a real distinction between these two goals? Which goal is likely to engender larger damage awards? What apportionment formula would you have suggested if you had represented the plaintiffs in *Frank Music*? If you had represented the defendants?

4. Do you agree with the *Bouchat* court that summary disposition of most of Bouchat's claims to a portion of the Ravens' profits was proper? In light of the jury's rejection of Bouchat's claim to a portion of the Non–Excluded Merchandise Revenues, would the jury instruction that Judge Widener describes have made any difference? If you had represented Bouchat, how would you have sought to prove a non-speculative link between the various revenue categories and the infringement? What kind of evidence would be required? Do you think you could have succeeded?

5. Although *Bouchat* is in some respects an unusual case, many established visual artists confront similar problems of proof when their work is copied in the course of a much larger enterprise. In *Mackie v. Rieser*, 296 F.3d 909 (9th Cir. 2002), *cert. denied*, 537 U.S. 1226 (2003), the Ninth Circuit emphasized the importance of the causation requirement for an award of indirect profits, noting that the threshold inquiry is whether there is a legally sufficient causal link between the infringement and subsequent indirect profits. The court observed that "[s]uch an approach dovetails with common sense — there must first be a demonstration that the infringing acts had an effect on profits before the parties can wrangle about apportionment." *Id.* at 915. Accordingly, it held that a sculptor whose work had been depicted, without his authorization, in a promotional brochure distributed by the local symphony orchestra was entitled only to the royalty that he could have charged for inclusion of the image, and not to a share of the symphony's profits. *Id.* at 916. Do the results in *Bouchat* and *Mackie* serve either of the purposes identified in Question 3 above?

6. Consider the following hypothetical: Defendant Bad Boy Entertainment (BBE) produces a rap album called *Ready to Die* containing 17 tracks. The title track infringes Bridgeport Music, Inc.'s copyright in "Singing in the Morning" by sampling that song. Bridgeport is able

to prove BBE's profits from the album. How would you apportion those profits to the infringement? *See Bridgeport Music, Inc. v. Justin Combs Publ'g*, 507 F.3d 470, 483-84 (6th Cir. 2007) (upholding jury's adoption of the plaintiffs' methodology which divided the album's profits by its number of tracks). The court observed, "[t]he jury acted within its province when it rejected defendants' argument[s] that plaintiffs' allocation included profits attributable to non-infringing elements of the song 'Ready to Die' . . . [and] that the song was memorable (and successful) because of certain [other] lyrics." *Id*. Do you agree? Should a court instead require a plaintiff further to apportion profits based on the fraction of the entire song that the infringing sample represents? How do you think plaintiff's proof in the case just described differed from Bouchat's?

7. If deterrence is a goal of a damage award, why not award punitive damages? In *TVT Records v. Island Def Jam Music Group*, 262 F. Supp. 2d 185 (S.D.N.Y. 2003), the court held that punitive damages are not categorically barred in copyright infringement cases where the plaintiff is seeking actual damages and allowed a jury instruction authorizing a punitive damages award if plaintiffs proved willful infringement. Is there any reason that punitive damages would *not* be consistent with the goals of copyright law? According to the court, a copyright plaintiff may not seek punitive damages if it has elected to recover the statutory damages authorized under §504(c). *Id*. at 185. We consider statutory damages in Section G.4 *infra*.

8. Section 504(b) also entitles a successful copyright infringement plaintiff to recover actual damages. How would you compute such damages? The Patent Act provides for "damages adequate to compensate for the infringement, but in no event less than a reasonable royalty." 35 U.S.C. §284. Would damages set at a reasonable royalty rate provide sufficient deterrence? Sufficient compensation?

9. Why should a defendant be allowed to deduct the cost of producing the infringing work from the calculation of damages? In *Hamil America, Inc. v. GFI*, 193 F. 3d 92 (2d Cir. 1999), the district court had limited the defendant's deductible expenses to the actual costs of producing the infringing items. In remanding for a recalculation of damages, the Second Circuit held that overhead expense categories are deductible once a sufficient nexus has been shown between the category of overhead and the production or sale of the infringing product. The infringer has the burden of offering a reasonable formula for allocating a portion of the overhead expenses to the infringing products. *See id*. at 105. Further, where there has been a finding of willful infringement, the district court should give "extra scrutiny" to the categories of overhead expenses to determine that there is a "strong nexus" between each category and the sale and production of the infringing product. *Id*. at 107. All presumptions are drawn against the infringer. *Id*. Do the standards for deducting overhead expenses articulated by the court in *Hamil* sufficiently balance the competing interests? Does a presumption against the infringer in this context make sense?"

10. Article 45 of the TRIPS Agreement requires the availability of monetary damages "adequate to compensate for the injury the right holder has suffered" as a result of infringement by a party that knew or had reason to know that the conduct was infringing. This provision seems to give member countries discretion to fashion appropriate remedies when dealing with an innocent infringer. Article 45(2) confirms this view by providing that in "appropriate" cases, members *may* authorize recovery of profits or payment of pre-established damages even when the infringer did not have actual knowledge or a reasonable basis to know that the activity was infringing.

Section 504 makes no concession for innocent infringement in awarding actual damages. What role do you think the jury's conclusion that defendants "mistakenly" infringed played in the determination of damages? Was that appropriate given the statutory language? Do you think the jury may have been swayed by the initial "payment" request made by Bouchat (a letter of acknowlement and an autographed helmet)?

The calculation of damages may sometimes involve issues of territoriality. What role should geographic boundaries play in determining appropriate damages? Should U.S. courts include infringements that take place abroad in their calculation of damages? Review the Note on Infringement by Authorization, Chapter 6 pages 474-75 *supra*, and then consider the following case.

Los Angeles News Service v. Reuters Television International, Ltd.

340 F.3d 926 (9th Cir. 2003), cert. denied, 541 U.S. 1041 (2004)

O'SCANNLAIN, J.: We must decide whether a news organization may recover actual damages under the Copyright Act for acts of infringement that mostly occurred outside the United States.

I

The copyright works at issue here ("the works") are two video recordings, "The Beating of Reginald Denny" and "Beating of Man in White Panel Truck," which depict the infamous events at Florence Ave. and Normandie Blvd. during the 1992 Los Angeles riots. Los Angeles News Services ("LANS"), an independent news organization which produces video and audio tape recordings of newsworthy events and licenses them for profit, produced the works . . . while filming the riots from its helicopter. LANS copyrighted the works and sold a license to rebroadcast them to, among others, . . . [NBC], which used them on the *Today Show*.

Visnews International (USA) . . . is a joint venture among NBC, Reuters Television Ltd., and the British Broadcasting Company ("BBC"). Pursuant to a news supply agreement between NBC and Visnews, NBC transmitted the *Today Show* broadcast by fiber link to Visnews in New York; Visnews made a videotape copy of the works, which it then transmitted via satellite to its subscribers in Europe and Africa and via fiber link to the New York Office of the European Broadcast Union ("EBU"), a joint venture of Visnews and Reuters. The EBU subsequently made another videotape copy of the works, and transmitted it to Reuters in London, which in turn distributed the works via video "feed" to its own subscribers.

LANS sued Reuters . . . and Visnews for copyright infringement . . . . The district court subsequently granted Reuters and Visnews partial summary judgment on the issue of extraterritorial infringement, holding that no liability could arise under the Copyright Act for acts of infringement that occurred outside the United States. . . . However, the district court held that Visnews's act of copying the works in New York was a domestic act of infringement. . . .

The district court further concluded that LANS had failed to prove any actual damages arising domestically and that damages arising extraterritorially were unavailable under the Act, which meant that LANS was limited to statutory damages. . . .

LANS appealed the district court's ruling on actual damages. . . . We subsequently reversed the district court's actual damages ruling, disagreeing with its interpretation of the Copyright Act's extraterritorial application. . . . We concluded that although the district court was correct to hold that the Copyright Act does not apply extraterritorially, an exception may apply where an act of infringement is completed entirely within the United States and that such infringing act enabled further exploitation abroad. . . . Relying on *Sheldon v. Metro-Goldwyn Pictures Corp.*, 106 F.3d 45 (2d Cir. 1939), *aff'd*, 309 U.S. 390 . . . (1940), which held that profits from overseas infringement can be recovered on the theory that the infringer holds them in a constructive trust for the copyright owner, we reversed the grant of summary judgment. . . . We held that "LANS [was] entitled to recover damages flowing from exploitation abroad of the domestic acts of infringement committed by defendants." [*Los Angeles News Service v. Reuters Television International, Ltd.*, 149 F.3d 987 (9th Cir. 1998) ("*Reuters III*")] at 992. . . .

. . . The [district] court concluded that *Reuters III* had held only that LANS could recover any profits or unjust enrichment from domestic infringers, on the theory that the infringers held such profits in a constructive trust for LANS. "To permit [LANS] to recover damages other than Defendants' profits or unjust enrichment," the court stated, "would . . . effectively permit [LANS] to recover damages for extraterritorial acts of infringement."

. . . [T]he district court concluded that Reuters and Visnews had reaped no such profits from their infringement. . . . [T]he district court stated that LANS could elect to take the $60,000 in statutory damages awarded [previously]. . . .

II . . .

A

Both parties engage in detailed exegesis of our opinion in *Reuters III*. On LANS's reading, the *Reuters III* court's use of the terms "damages" is dispositive. The statute uses "actual damages" and "profits" separately and distinctly, and provides that an infringer may recover both (in the ordinary case). LANS asserts therefore that the *Reuters III* court should be read as having meant what it said: "damages" means actual damages.

But LANS's interpretation does not fit with the context in which the *Reuters III* court discussed the recoverability of "damages." There, we relied on Judge Learned Hand's opinion in *Sheldon* and discussed damages entirely in the context of that case, which dealt exclusively with the recovery of the defendants' profits. . . .

B

Of course, *Sheldon* did not explicitly deal with the issue of actual damages. But as LANS points out, there is some support in the Second Circuit's post-*Sheldon* case law for the recovery of actual damages once an act of domestic infringement is proven.

The most direct support for such a position comes from *Update Art, Inc. v. Modiin Publ'g, Ltd.*, 843 F.2d 67 (2d Cir. 1988), in which the Second Circuit considered an Israeli newspaper's unauthorized reproduction of a poster copyrighted in the United States. . . .

Update Art, however, is distinguishable from LANS's claim in a couple of important respects. First, several issues of the newspaper in which the infringing reproduction appeared were circulated in the United States. *Id.* at 73 & n.6. Second, and more importantly, the amount of damages awarded by the district court was based on defendants' profits. *Id.* at 70 & n.4. Finally, the panel did not even discuss the distinction between damages and profits, much less cite *Sheldon*. Rather, it merely concluded that the damages award could stand despite the extraterritoriality issue, which the magistrate judge had not considered in calculating the amount. *Id.* at 70. . . .

C

On the whole, we conclude that *Reuters III* adhered very closely to our decision in *Subafilms, Ltd. v. MGM-Pathe Communications Co.*, 24 F.3d 1088 (9th Cir. 1994) (en banc) [discussed in the Note on Infringement by Authorization, pages 474-75 *supra* — EDS.]. *Subafilms* reaffirmed that the copyright laws have no application beyond the U.S. border . . . and expressly took no position on the merits of the *Update Art* court's apparent willingness to award damages. . . . LANS's appeal thus presents the precise question that *Subafilms* reserved . . . and as the prior panel recognized, such question should be resolved in light of the principles the en banc court laid down.

The import of such principles counsel a narrow application of the adoption in *Reuters III* of the *Sheldon* exception to the general rule. In particular, the *Sheldon* constructive trust rationale preserves a territorial connection . . . . Moreover, no rational deterrent function is served by making an infringer whose domestic act of infringement — from which he earns no profit — leads to widespread extraterritorial infringement, liable for the copyright owner's entire loss of value or profit from that overseas infringement, particularly if the overseas infringement is legal where it takes place. *See Subafilms*, 24 F.3d at 1097-98 (warning of the disruption to American foreign policy interests and to the policy of domestic enforcement expressed in the Berne Convention that extraterritorial enforcement would cause). Moreover, the resulting over-deterrence might chill the fair use of copyrighted works in close cases. . . .

III

Accordingly, we read *Reuters III* to allow only a narrow exception for the recovery of the infringer's profits to *Subafilms*'s general rule against extraterritorial application. . . .

NOTES AND QUESTIONS

1. Do you agree with the court's interpretation of its own prior ruling in this case? With its interpretation of Second Circuit law?

2. Under the rule articulated by the *Reuters IV* court, a claim for profits from infringement abroad will be allowed if a predicate act of infringement took place in the U.S. Does this rule make sense? Does it make any more sense than a rule allowing LANS to recover actual damages as well?

3. How might the *Reuters IV* rule affect domestic affiliates of foreign corporations who use allegedly infringing materials sent to them from the corporate main office? Should the Ninth Circuit's rule apply if the works are not subject to protection in the originating foreign country? What would you think if a foreign court allowed a plaintiff to recover profits flowing from exploitation within the U.S. of works that are in the public domain here?

4. Is *Reuters IV* consistent with *Subafilms*? Is *Subafilms* relevant to the proper resolution of disputes like this one?

5. Does the court's concern regarding extraterritorial application of the Copyright Act seem as relevant today in light of strengthened multilateral obligations regarding enforcement of copyright? Recall from Chapter 1 that all members of the WTO (currently 153 countries) are obligated to comply with the minimum requirements of the TRIPS Agreement, including provisions on damages. Should WTO membership be considered by a U.S. court in determining whether profits from infringement ocurring in that WTO member country can be recovered by a U.S. plaintiff?

6. A few observations can be made regarding courts' consideration of copyright protection and enforcement in a global environment. First, despite heightened international regulation of copyrighted goods, implementation of mandatory global standards for protection will still largely be determined by domestic law. Throughout this casebook, you have seen numerous examples such as *Capital Records v. Thomas* (Chapter 10); *Bridgeman Art Library*, *supra*, and *Itar-Tass*, *supra*. Second, there are sometimes questions about the constitutionality of congressional enactments that incorporate new global rules into domestic legislation. Recall, for example the Note on the Intellectual Property Clause, the Commerce Clause and the Treaty Power, Chapter 10, *supra* pages 717-20. As the court noted in *Bridgeman Art Library*, it remains an open question whether the constitutionally derived requirements of domestic copyright law (such as originality and fixation) can be changed by the exercise of the treaty power. Do questions about a plaintiff's ability to claim damages for infringement occurring overseas implicate any constitutional concerns? Would you support legislation authorizing a court to include profits from infringing activity overseas in its damages calculus? Would such a bill pass constitutional scrutiny under the standard articulated in *Eldred*?

4. Statutory Damages

In lieu of actual damages and profits, §504(c) provides that a plaintiff may elect statutory damages. (Recall, however, that timely registration of copyright is a prerequisite for eligibility to take advantage of this option. *See* 17 U.S.C. §412.) The election of statutory damages may be made at any time before the final judgment. Both *Frank Music* and *Hamil* demonstrate how difficult it can be to prove actual damages. The calculation of damages is even more challenging when the defendant has distributed the copyrighted work online without requiring payment. From the plaintiff's perspective, statutory damages may be the more feasible and more rewarding remedial option. From the defendant's perspective, however, the amount of statutory damages available can be staggering, especially as compared to actual damages. As you read the following material, consider whether a strict liability rule for copyright infringement is consistent with copyright objectives. Also consider whether the digital environment requires a different approach to the calculation and award of statutory damages and what factors should weigh most heavily.

≡ *Zomba Enterprises, Inc. v. Panorama Records, Inc.*
≡ *491 F. 3d 574 (6th Cir. 2007)*

Moore, J.:

I. Facts and Procedure

. . .

B. *Factual Background*

Since 1998, Panorama has been in the business of manufacturing and selling karaoke compact discs. It issues a new disc monthly in each of a variety of musical genres, including country, pop, rock, and R & B. Each installment (or "karaoke package") contains the top hits in that genre for the relevant month. . . .

The individual discs that Panorama makes and sells are in the CD + G format — shorthand for "compact disc plus graphics." As Panorama explains, "[t]hese are compact discs on which musicians that are hired by Panorama record a musical composition of a work which at some time may have been made popular by another artist. The CD + G contains a graphic element and is designed to be viewed when played on a karaoke machine." . . . The graphic element consists of the text of each song's lyrics, and it scrolls across a screen as the music (sans vocals) plays, permitting karaoke participants to read the lyrics as they sing along. Each of Panorama's karaoke packages contained nine or ten songs, with two tracks for each song, one track released with audible lyrics and one without.

Zomba Enterprises, Inc. and Zomba Songs, Inc. (collectively, "Zomba") are music publishing corporations. . . . [A]t all times relevant to this case, Zomba held and administered the copyrights to a variety of musical compositions, including songs performed by pop music performers such as 98 Degrees, Backstreet Boys, *NSYNC, and Britney Spears. . . .

Zomba . . . discovered that Panorama's karaoke packages contained copies of songs it owned. Zomba . . . [sent a] cease-and-desist letter [and] specified the terms upon which [it] would be willing to grant a license: a $250 fixing fee for each Zomba-owned song on each package, plus royalties of $0.16 per song per CD + G sold for the first half of the five-year license term, and $0.19 per song per CD + G sold for the second-half of the term. [Panorama] contacted [Zomba's attorney] in response to this letter, but [it] did not stop selling CD + Gs with Zomba's songs on them, nor did it obtain any licenses. . . .

C. Procedural History

On January 13, 2003, Zomba filed its complaint, asserting thirty counts of copyright infringement — one count for each Zomba-owned musical composition that Panorama recorded and sold in its karaoke packages. . . . On April 22, 2003, the parties entered into a consent order in which Panorama agreed "to be restrained from distributing, releasing or otherwise exploiting any karaoke package containing compositions owned or administered by" Zomba. . . . Within a week of entering this consent order, Panorama breached its agreement and resumed selling CD + Gs containing Zomba's copyrighted work. This conduct continued, and a year later, Zomba moved for sanctions on this basis. . . .

On November 5, 2005, the district court held a hearing to determine the amount of damages. . . . The district court concluded that Panorama's infringement was willful, and accordingly awarded Zomba $31,000 for each of the twenty-six infringements at issue, for a total of $806,000. . . .

III. Analysis . . .

Panorama . . . disputes the district court's statutory-damage calculation, arguing both that any infringement was not willful and that the $806,000 damage award is unconstitutionally high. . . .

B. Willfulness . . .

Panorama argues that even if it infringed Zomba's copyrights, the district court erred by concluding that the infringement was willful and thus was subject to enhanced statutory damages. According to Panorama, any infringement was innocent, and certainly not willful. We disagree.

For infringement to be "willful," it must be done "with knowledge that [one's] conduct constitutes copyright infringement." *Princeton Univ. Press*, 99 F.3d at 1392 (quoting Melville B. Nimmer & David Nimmer, 3 Nimmer on Copyright §14.04[B][3] (1996)). Accordingly, "one who has been notified that his conduct constitutes copyright infringement, but who reasonably and in good faith believes the contrary, is not 'willful' for these purposes." *Id.* This belief must be both (1) reasonable and (2) held in good faith. *See id.*

Panorama argues that it held a good-faith belief that the copying here at issue was a fair use, and contends that even if ultimately erroneous, this belief precludes a finding of willfulness. . . . [T]he issue is not so much whether Panorama held in good faith its belief that its copying was fair use (although we have serious misgivings on this matter), but whether Panorama reasonably believed that its conduct did not amount to copyright infringement. . . . To decide this issue, we must determine "whether the copyright law supported the plaintiffs' position so clearly that the defendants must be deemed as a matter of law to have exhibited a reckless disregard of the plaintiffs' property rights." . . .

Here, we conclude that Panorama exhibited a reckless disregard for Zomba's rights, and accordingly, that Panorama's reliance on its fair-use defense was objectively unreasonable. The fact most crucial to this inquiry is that Panorama continued to sell karaoke packages containing copies of each of the relevant compositions after the district court entered its April 22, 2003, consent order forbidding Panorama to do so. . . .

By entering into the consent decree, Panorama agreed to cease infringing Zomba's copyrights. Thus, it implicitly agreed to suspend its reliance on the fair-use defense at least temporarily, and this agreement was reduced to an order of the court. Because an order entered by a court of competent jurisdiction must be obeyed even if it is erroneously issued, . . . Panorama lacked any legal justification for continuing to distribute copies of Zomba's copyrighted works after April 22, 2003. . . .

C. Amount of Statutory-Damage Award . . .

1. Abuse of Discretion

Panorama contends that the district court believed that, after making a finding of willfulness, it lacked discretion to award statutory damages of less than $30,000 per infringement. On this basis, Panorama maintains that the district court abused its discretion. The record does not support this argument.

In its conclusions of law, the district court recognized that it had "wide discretion in determining the amount of statutory damages to be awarded, constrained only by the maximum and minimum amounts." . . . It found "that the maximum statutory amount of $30,000 per work for 'innocent' infringement is not sufficient in this case because of the clearly willful nature of Defendant's conduct," but that the maximum award of $150,000 per infringement was excessive, given the dollar amounts involved in the case. . . .

Nowhere did the district court indicate that it believed that it lacked discretion to award statutory damages of less than $30,000 per infringement. To the contrary, Panorama's willfulness prompted the district court to conclude that the maximum penalty for nonwillful infringement was not sufficient given Panorama's conduct. We therefore conclude that Panorama has not shown that the district court abused its discretion by setting the statutory damage award at $31,000 per infringement.

2. Eighth Amendment

Panorama next argues that such a high award of statutory damages, in light of the relatively low actual damages,[10] renders the district court's award an "excessive fine" under the

---

10. The district court concluded that it was unable to calculate the actual damages based on the record before it. Panorama asserted that it sold a total of 74,734 copies of the twenty-six infringed compositions. Based upon this figure, Zomba lost approximately $11,957.92 in royalties, plus an additional $6500 in fixing fees, for a total of $18,457.92.

Eighth Amendment. However, the Supreme Court has explained that the word "fine" in this context means a payment to the government. . . . Consequently, the Court has held that the Excessive Fines Clause "does not constrain an award of money damages in a civil suit when the government neither has prosecuted the action nor has any right to receive a share of the damages awarded." . . . Panorama's Eighth Amendment argument thus fails.

3. Due Process

Panorama argues, based upon *BMW of North America, Inc. v. Gore*, 517 U.S. 559 . . . (1996) . . . and *State Farm Mutual Automobile Insurance Co. v. Campbell*, 538 U.S. 408 . . . (2003) that an award of statutory damages that (it alleges) is thirty-seven times the actual damages violates its right to due process. Again, we disagree.

We note at the outset that both *Gore* and *Campbell* addressed due-process challenges to punitive-damages awards. In both cases, the award was greater than one hundred times the amount of compensatory damages awarded. In *Gore*, the Court concluded that the award in question (which amounted to 500 times the compensatory-damages award) was "grossly excessive," 517 U.S. at 574 . . . after considering three "guideposts": (1) "the degree of reprehensibility of the" defendant's conduct; (2) "the disparity between the harm or potential harm suffered by [the plaintiff] and [the] punitive damages award"; and (3) "the difference between this remedy and the civil penalties authorized or imposed in comparable cases," *id.* at 575 . . . . In *Campbell*, the Court considered the same three guidepost factors and concluded that the punitive-damages award (which amounted to 145 times the compensatory-damages award) "was an irrational and arbitrary deprivation of the property of the defendant." 538 U.S. at 429 . . . . Regarding the second guidepost, neither case created a "concrete constitutional limit[ ]" to the punitive-to-compensatory damages ratio. . . . Instead, the *Campbell* Court explicitly "decline[d] . . . to impose a bright-line ratio which a punitive damages award cannot exceed," although it expressed a general preference for single-digit ratios. . . .

The Supreme Court has not indicated whether *Gore* and *Campbell* apply to awards of statutory damages. We know of no case invalidating such an award of statutory damages under *Gore* or *Campbell*, although we note that some courts have suggested in dicta that these precedents may apply to statutory-damage awards. . . .

Regardless of the uncertainty regarding the application of *Gore* and *Campbell* to statutory-damage awards, we may review such awards under *St. Louis, I.M. & S. Ry. Co. v. Williams*, 251 U.S. 63, 66-67 . . . (1919), to ensure they comport with due process. In such cases, we inquire whether the awards are "so severe and oppressive as to be wholly disproportioned to the offense and obviously unreasonable." *Id.* at 67. . . . This review, however, is extraordinarily deferential . . . .

Williams is instructive, and leads us to conclude that the statutory-damage award against Panorama was not sufficiently oppressive to constitute a deprivation of due process. In that case, a railroad charged two sisters sixty-six cents apiece more than the maximum rate permissible by regulation. 251 U.S. at 64, 40 S.Ct. 71. A state statute sought to deter such overcharges by providing for statutory damages of between $50 and $350 when a railroad charged more than the permissible rate. *Id.* The sisters sued separately, and received statutory damage awards of $75 apiece—over 113 times the amount they were overcharged. *Id.* Before the Supreme Court, the railroad argued that the penalty was so disproportionate to the harm sustained that it violated due process. Rejecting this argument, the Court concluded that the award "properly cannot be said to be so severe and oppressive as to be wholly disproportioned to the offense or obviously unreasonable." *Id.* at 67. . . .

If the Supreme Court countenanced a 113:1 ratio in *Williams*, we cannot conclude that a 44:1 ratio[11] is unacceptable here. We acknowledge the Supreme Court's preference for a lower punitive-to-compensatory ratio, as stated in *Campbell*, but emphasize that this case does not involve a punitive-damages award. Until the Supreme Court applies *Campbell* to an award of statutory damages, we conclude that *Williams* controls, not *Campbell*, and accordingly reject Panorama's due-process argument. . . .

NOTES AND QUESTIONS

1. Read §504(c)(1). Could the district court have set the statutory damage amount at less than $30,000? Based on the court's analysis in *Zomba*, what factors do you think should be most significant in the court's determination of the statutory damage amount? If the scope of discretion is as wide as the *Zomba* court intimates, can any amount within the prescribed statutory parameters ever reflect an abuse of discretion? Under what circumstances?

2. At what point in a lawsuit should a plaintiff elect statutory damages over actual damages and profits? As a plaintiff's lawyer, what factors would you consider in making this decision? In some cases, a copyright plaintiff has been allowed to elect damages after the jury has determined the award amounts for statutory and actual damages. *See, e.g., BUC Int'l Corp. v. Int'l Yacht Council Ltd.*, 489 F.3d 1129 (11th Cir. 2007). Other cases indicate that election can be made after the jury verdict but before the final decision has been entered. *See Feltner v. Columbia Pictures Television, Inc.*, 523 U.S. 340, 347, n.5 (1998) (stating that "[t]he parties agree, and we have found no indication to the contrary, that election [of remedies for copyright infringement] may occur even after a jury has returned a verdict on liability and an award of actual damages"); *Twin Peaks Prods., Inc. v. Publ'ns Int'l, Ltd.*, 996 F.2d 1366, 1380 (2d Cir. 1993) (noting that the plaintiff elected a statutory damages award knowing that the amount was lower than the amount of actual damages awarded by the jury because it believed statutory damages were more likely to be sustained on appeal).

3. Are statutory damages invariably the superior option when the value of the work is difficult to determine? Might a claim for violation of moral rights in a work of visual art under §106A be particularly amenable to the use of statutory damages? Note that while timely registration is generally required to be eligible for an award of statutory damges, claims under §106A are exempt from this registration requirement.

Are there instances in which statutory damages may overcompensate the owner of the work? Does a statutory damage scheme for copyright infringement serve the same public policy goals as statutory damages in other areas of the law? Pamela Samuelson & Tara Wheatland, *Statutory Damages in Copyright Law: A Remedy in Need of Reform*, 51 Wm. & Mary L. Rev. 439, 495 (2009) ("Copyright statutory damages aim . . . to rectify a private wrong by compensating copyright owners for economic harms done from infringement and not to remedy the sorts of public wrongs at which most statutory damage rules are aimed.").

4. For copyright infringement actions involving a large number of works, and/or a large number of infringements by defendants who are not jointly liable, an award of statutory damages may be quite large. Is there any other limit on the amount that a court, or a jury,

---

11. Dividing the statutory-damage award ($806,000) by the lost licensing fees, as calculated by Panorama, ($18,458) yields a ratio of about 44:1. . . .

may award? In each of the following hypotheticals, consider whether the amount awarded as statutory damages was excessive using the *Gore* test outlined in *Zomba*:

    a. An award of $19.7 million in statutory damages against a defendant that, over a two-year period, distributed copies of the plaintiff's subscription-based newsletter via the company intranet daily to over 100 branch offices.

    b. An award of $222,000 ($9,250 per song) against an individual file-sharer found liable for 24 instances of willful infringement. What if the award had been for $1.92 million ($80,000 per song)? What if the award had imposed the $150,000 maximum per song, for a total statutory damage award of $3,600,000?

    c. An award of $1 million against a blogger for copying articles from a newspaper's online site and encouraging persons who posted comments to the blog to do the same.

    d. An award of $300,000 for posting two poems on the Internet.

    e. An award of $2,500 (the statutory minimum) for posting large portions of five Scientology texts on the Internet.

What do you think is the effect of such awards on copyright goals? *See* Samuelson & Wheatland, *supra*.

5. In *Columbia Pictures Television v. Krypton Broad. of Birmingham, Inc.*, 106 F. 3d 284 (9th Cir. 1997), the court suggests that what constitutes "any one work" is a question of fact. What factors might be helpful in making the determination about what constitutes "any one work"? In each of the following hypotheticals, is there an infringement of the copyright in "one work" for purposes of §504(c)(1) or an infringement of the copyrights in multiple works? Be sure to read the final sentence of §504(c)(1) before you answer.

    a. Defendant continues to broadcast a televesion series despite termination of its license by the copyright owner. The defendant argues that the series, and not each episode, constitutes a work.

    b. A copyrighted work contains three main characters. Each is reproduced without authorization and affixed to different paraphernalia such as backpacks, tee shirts, and tablecloths.

    c. Plaintiff markets compilations of clip-art for use in digital graphic design. Defendant reproduces 200 images from one of plaintiff's compilations and includes the images in its own clip-art package.

    d. Defendant creates seven different compilation CDs that contain a total of 13 different copyrighted musical works owned by the plaintiffs.

6. The DMCA provides for statutory damages "as the court considers just" "for each violation of section 1201 in the sum of not less than $200 or more than $2,500 per act of circumvention [and] for each violation of section 1202 in the sum of not less than $2,500 or more than $25,000." 17 U.S.C. §1203(c)(3). What does each "violation" mean? In *McClatchey v. Associated Press*, 83 U.S.P.Q.2d 1095 (W.D. Pa. 2007) (*see* page 699, *supra*, for the facts), the defendant removed the plaintiff's copyright management information and distributed its photograph to 1,147 subscribers. Removal of the information constituted one violation. Addressing AP's distribution of the photo to subscribers, the court stated: "In essence the term 'each violation' is best understood to mean 'each violative act performed by Defendant.' . . . [T]he Court concludes that AP committed only one alleged violative act by distributing the . . . photograph to its . . . subscribers, even though there were 1,147 recipients." *Id.* at 1101. In arriving at this result, the court refused to incorporate the limitations of §504(c) into §1203(c)(3) because its language differs from that of §504. *Id.* Instead, the court

looked to cases interpreting 47 U.S.C. §605, which prohibits intercepting certain communications, and elaborating the role of statutory damages under that statute: "Presumably, plaintiffs will elect statutory damages only when that calculation exceeds their actual damages. . . . Congress would not have intended to make the statutory damages windfall totally independent of the defendant's conduct. Where one act by Defendant results in mass infringement, it is more likely that actual damages will yield the more favorable recovery." *Id*. Do you agree with the court's approach?

5. Attorneys' Fees

Section 505 of the Copyright Act provides that a court may, in its discretion, allow recovery of full costs (except when the other party is the U.S. or an officer thereof). The court may also award reasonable attorneys' fees to the prevailing party in a copyright lawsuit. An award of attorneys' fees is appealable on the ground that a court may have abused its discretion in making it. The difficulty is in determining what standards should guide the district court's discretion. Read §505 now, and then consider the following cases.

Fantasy, Inc. v. Fogerty
94 F.3d 553 (9th Cir. 1996)

RYMER, J.: This appeal requires us to consider the scope of a district court's discretion to award a reasonable attorney's fee to a prevailing defendant in a copyright infringement action, and in particular, to decide whether a court must find some "culpability" on the part of the plaintiff in pursuing the suit before it can award a fee to a prevailing defendant whose victory on the merits furthers the purposes of the Copyright Act.

John Fogerty, former lead singer and songwriter for "Creedence Clearwater Revival," recognized as one of the greatest American rock and roll bands, successfully defended a copyright infringement action in which Fantasy, Inc., alleged that Fogerty had copied the music from one of his earlier songs which Fantasy now owned, changed the lyrics, and released it as a new song. After concluding that Fogerty's victory on the merits vindicated his right (and the right of others) to continue composing music in the distinctive "Swamp Rock" style and genre and therefore furthered the purposes of the Copyright Act, the district court awarded Fogerty $1,347,519.15 in attorney's fees. Fantasy appeals the award mainly on the ground that the court had no discretion to award Fogerty *any* attorney's fees inasmuch as its conduct in bringing and maintaining the lawsuit was "faultless."

We hold that, after *Fogerty v. Fantasy, Inc.*, 510 U.S. 517 (1994), an award of attorney's fees to a prevailing defendant that furthers the underlying purposes of the Copyright Act is reposed in the sound discretion of the district courts, and that such discretion is not cabined by a requirement of culpability on the part of the losing party. As we agree with the district court that Fogerty's victory on the merits furthered the purposes of the Copyright Act, and as we cannot say that the district court abused its discretion by awarding fees under the circumstances of this case, we affirm the award. We also uphold the district court's exercise of discretion not to award interest on Fogerty's fee award.

I

This action began July 26, 1985, when Fantasy sued Fogerty for copyright infringement, alleging that Fogerty's song "The Old Man Down the Road" infringed the copyright on another of his songs, "Run Through the Jungle," which Fantasy owned. About three years later, on November 7, 1988, the jury disagreed, returning a verdict in favor of Fogerty.

Fogerty moved for a reasonable attorney's fee pursuant to 17 U.S.C. §505. The district court denied the request on the ground that Fantasy's lawsuit was neither frivolous nor prosecuted in bad faith and our then-existing precedent precluded an award of fees in the absence of one or the other. . . . We affirmed for the same reason, *Fantasy, Inc. v. Fogerty*, 984 F.2d 1524, 1533 (9th Cir. 1993) [*Fogerty I*], but the Supreme Court reversed and remanded in *Fogerty v. Fantasy, Inc.*, 510 U.S. 517 (1994) [*Fogerty II*]. We then remanded to the district court for further proceedings consistent with *Fogerty II. Fantasy, Inc. v. Fogerty*, 21 F.3d 354 (9th Cir. 1994) [*Fogerty III*].

On remand, the district court granted Fogerty's motion and, after reviewing extensive billing records, awarded $1,347,519.15. Its decision was based on several factors. First, Fogerty's vindication of his copyright in "The Old Man Down the Road" secured the public's access to an original work of authorship and paved the way for future original compositions — by Fogerty and others — in the same distinctive "Swamp Rock" style and genre. Thus, the district court reasoned, Fogerty's defense was the type of defense that furthers the purposes underlying the Copyright Act and therefore should be encouraged through a fee award. Further, the district court found that a fee award was appropriate to help restore to Fogerty some of the lost value of the copyright he was forced to defend. In addition, Fogerty was a defendant author and prevailed on the merits rather than on a technical defense, such as the statute of limitations, laches, or the copyright registration requirements. Finally, the benefit conferred by Fogerty's successful defense was not slight or insubstantial relative to the costs of litigation, nor would the fee award have too great a chilling effect or impose an inequitable burden on Fantasy, which was not an impecunious plaintiff.

Fogerty also sought interest to account for the lost use of the money paid to his lawyers over the years. While the district court awarded Fogerty almost all of what he asked for in fees, it declined to award interest. Fantasy timely appeals the fee award; Fogerty timely cross-appeals the refusal to award interest. . . .

III

Fantasy contends that the district court had no discretion to award fees to Fogerty because Fantasy conducted a "good faith" and "faultless" lawsuit upon reasonable factual and legal grounds, or to put it somewhat differently, because Fantasy was "blameless." According to Fantasy, once the district court could find no fault in the way Fantasy conducted this case, that should have been the end of the matter. . . .

Fogerty, on the other hand, contends that *Fogerty II* focuses a district court's discretion on whether the prevailing party has furthered the purposes of the Copyright Act in litigating the action to a successful conclusion; under that standard, the district court was well within its discretion in finding that his successful defense of this action served important copyright policies. He also argues that the evenhanded approach does not mean that only "neutral" factors may be considered in the exercise of the court's discretion since, contrary to Fantasy's view, the Court itself recognized that somewhat different policies of the Copyright Act may be furthered when either plaintiffs or defendants prevail. Fogerty points out that the Court specifically observed that his successful defense of this action "increased public exposure to a musical work that could, as a result, lead to further creative pieces," *Fogerty II*, 510 U.S. at 527, and maintains that the fact that this factor happened to tip in Fogerty's favor as a prevailing defendant in this case should not prevent it from being considered at all.

A

In *Fogerty II*, the Supreme Court granted certiorari to resolve a conflict among the circuits concerning "what standards should inform a court's decision to award attorney's fees to a prevailing defendant in a copyright infringement action. . . ." *Id.* at 519. The Court rejected both the "dual" standard that we had followed and applied in *Fogerty I*—whereby prevailing plaintiffs generally were awarded attorney's fees as a matter of course, while prevailing defendants had to show that the original lawsuit was frivolous or brought in bad faith—and the "British Rule" for which Fogerty argued—whereby the prevailing party (whether plaintiff or defendant) automatically receives fees. The Court instead adopted the "evenhanded" approach exemplified by the Third Circuit's opinion in *Lieb v. Topstone Indus., Inc.*, 788 F.2d 151 (3d Cir. 1986). The Court held that:

> Prevailing plaintiffs and prevailing defendants are to be treated alike, but attorney's fees are to be awarded to prevailing parties only as a matter of the court's discretion. "There is no precise rule or formula for making these determinations," but instead equitable discretion should be exercised "in light of the considerations we have identified."

Fogerty II, 510 U.S. at 534 (quoting *Hensley v. Eckerhart*, 461 U.S. 424, 436-437 (1983)). Considerations discussed by the Court include the Copyright Act's primary objective, "to encourage the production of original literary, artistic, and musical expression for the good of the public," *id.* at 524 . . . ; the fact that defendants as well as plaintiffs may hold copyrights, *id.* at 525-527, and "run the gamut from corporate behemoths to starving artists," *id.* at 524 . . . ; the need to encourage "defendants who seek to advance a variety of meritorious copyright defenses . . . to litigate them to the same extent that plaintiffs are encouraged to litigate meritorious claims of infringement," *id.* at 527 . . . ; and the fact that "a successful defense of a copyright infringement action may further the policies of the Copyright Act every bit as much as a successful prosecution of an infringement claim by the holder of a copyright," *id.*

The district court's decision was informed by these considerations, but Fantasy argues that it failed to appreciate the culpability underpinnings of the evenhanded rule and to apply the *Lieb* factors, which Fantasy contends are fault-based and were embraced by the Supreme Court in *Fogerty II*. However, neither *Lieb* nor the Court's discussion of the evenhanded rule and the *Lieb* factors in *Fogerty II* suggests that discretion to award fees to prevailing defendants is constrained by the plaintiff's culpability, or is limited to the specific factors identified in *Lieb*. . . . [W]hile courts may take the *Lieb* factors into account, they are "nonexclusive." Even so, courts may not rely on the *Lieb* factors if they are not "faithful to the purposes of the Copyright Act." *Id.* Faithfulness to the purposes of the Copyright Act is, therefore, the pivotal criterion.

By the same token, a court's discretion may be influenced by the plaintiff's culpability in bringing or pursuing the action, but blameworthiness is not a prerequisite to awarding fees to a prevailing defendant. . . .

Although we have not squarely addressed this question before, our post-*Fogerty II* opinions have recognized that a plaintiff's culpability is no longer required, that the *Lieb* factors may be considered but are not exclusive and need not all be met, and that attorney's fee awards to prevailing defendants are within the district court's discretion if they further the purposes of the Copyright Act and are evenhandedly applied. . . . We have been careful to indicate that such factors are only "some" of the factors to consider, and that courts are not limited to considering them. . . . And in *Historical Research v. Cabral*, 80 F.3d 377 (9th Cir. 1996), we concluded that, under *Fogerty II*, " 'exceptional circumstances' are not a prerequisite to an award of attorneys fees; district courts may freely award fees, as long as they treat prevailing plaintiffs and prevailing defendants alike and seek to promote the Copyright Act's objectives." *Id.* at 378. . . .

We also have not previously been asked to decide whether the factors relied upon by a district court in awarding fees to a prevailing copyright defendant must be exactly capable of being applied to a prevailing plaintiff in order to satisfy the evenhanded rule. However, *Fogerty II* has already answered this question. Fantasy argues that the point of evenhandedness is to eliminate as the premise for any fee award any factor which cannot occur on both sides of the litigation equation. But we believe this asks more of "evenhandedness" than *Fogerty II* expects. . . . [T]he Court states: . . .

> More importantly, the policies served by the Copyright Act are more complex, more measured, than simply maximizing the number of meritorious suits for copyright infringement.

Fogerty II, 510 U.S. at 526. . . . [T]he Court says, speaking directly to this case:

> In the case before us, the successful defense of "The Old Man Down the Road" increased public exposure to a musical work that could, as a result, lead to further creative pieces. Thus a successful defense of a copyright infringement action may further the policies of the Copyright Act every bit as much as a successful prosecution of an infringement claim by the holder of a copyright.

Id. at 527. We cannot, therefore, say that the district court erred by relying on factors identified by the Supreme Court which in this case led it to conclude that Fogerty's defense sufficiently furthered the purposes of the Copyright Act to warrant an award of attorney's fees. . . .

In sum, evenhandedness means that courts should begin their consideration of attorney's fees in a copyright action with an evenly balanced scale, without regard to whether the plaintiff or defendant prevails, and thereafter determine entitlement without weighting the scales in advance one way or the other. Courts may look to the nonexclusive *Lieb* factors as guides and may apply them so long as they are consistent with the purposes of the Copyright Act and are applied evenly to prevailing plaintiffs and defendants; a finding of bad faith, frivolous or vexatious conduct is no longer required; and awarding attorney's fees to a prevailing defendant is within the sound discretion of the district court informed by the policies of the Copyright Act.

Since the reasons given by the district court in this case are well-founded in the record and are in keeping with the purposes of the Copyright Act, the court acted within its discretion in awarding a reasonable attorney's fee to Fogerty. . . .

V

Fogerty requests attorney's fees for this appeal pursuant to 17 U.S.C. §505. . . . [W]e conclude that fees are warranted under §505 inasmuch as it served the purposes of the Copyright Act for Fogerty to defend an appeal so that the district court's fee award would not be taken away from him. We therefore award Fogerty the attorney's fees he incurred in defending this appeal and we remand to the district court for calculation of the amount.

Positive Black Talk Inc. v. Cash Money Records Inc.
394 F.3d 357 (5th Cir. 2004)

KING, C.J.: . . . In 1997, two rap artists based in New Orleans, Louisiana — Terius Gray, professionally known as Juvenile ("Juvenile"), and Jerome Temple, professionally known as

D.J. Jubilee ("Jubilee") — each recorded a song that included the poetic four-word phrase "back that ass up." Specifically, with respect to Jubilee, he recorded his song in November 1997 and entitled it *Back That Ass Up*. In the Spring of 1998, Positive Black Talk, Inc. ("PBT"), a recording company, released Jubilee's *Back That Ass Up* on the album TAKE IT TO THE ST. THOMAS. Jubilee subsequently performed the song at a number of live shows, including the New Orleans Jazzfest on April 26, 1998.

Turning to Juvenile, at some point during the fall of 1997, Juvenile recorded his song and entitled it *Back That Azz Up*. In May 1998, Cash Money Records, Inc. ("CMR"), the recording company that produced Juvenile's album 400 DEGREEZ, signed a national distribution contract with Universal Records. Consequently, 400 DEGREEZ, which contained Juvenile's song *Back That Azz Up*, was released in November 1998. 400 DEGREEZ quickly garnered national acclaim, selling over four million albums and grossing more than $40 million. . . .

[PBT sued CMR, Juvenile, and Universal for copyright infringement, and] . . . the defendants filed counterclaims, alleging copyright infringement, violation of [the Louisiana Unfair Trade Practices Act ("LUPTA")] . . . , and negligent misrepresentation. . . .

In May 2003, the case proceeded to a jury trial. Although the jury found that PBT proved by a preponderance of the evidence that it owned a copyright interest in the lyrics and music of Jubilee's song *Back That Ass Up*, it nevertheless found in favor of the defendants on PBT's copyright infringement claim. Specifically, the jury found that: (1) PBT failed to prove that Juvenile or CMR factually copied *Back That Ass Up*; (2) the defendants proved that CMR and Juvenile independently created *Back That Azz Up*; and (3) PBT failed to prove that *Back That Azz Up* is substantially similar to *Back That Ass Up*. . . . In addition, the jury found in favor of the defendants on their LUPTA and negligent misrepresentation counterclaims. . . . The court awarded the defendants attorney's fees in relation to their LUPTA counterclaim but not for their successful defense of PBT's copyright infringement claim. . . .

V. Attorney's Fees

The defendants . . . appeal the denial of their requests for attorney's fees. Universal requested $323,121.25 in fees, and CMR and Juvenile requested $263,040. Of those, CMR and Juvenile traced $39,456 of their fees to their successful LUPTA counterclaim . . . . The district court denied the fee requests for the successful copyright defense and granted CMR and Juvenile's request for the LUPTA fees at the markedly reduced sum of $2,500.

This court reviews the district court's refusal to award attorney's fees in a copyright infringement case for an abuse of discretion. *Creations Unlimited, Inc.*, 112 F.3d at 817. A trial court abuses its discretion in awarding or refusing to award attorney's fees when its ruling is based on an erroneous view of the law or a clearly erroneous assessment of the evidence. *Sanmina Corp. v. BancTec USA, Inc.*, 94 Fed. Appx. 194, 196 n. 10 (5th Cir. 2004).

. . . As the district court below explicitly recognized, an award of attorney's fees to the prevailing party in a copyright action, although left to the trial court's discretion, "is the rule rather than the exception and should be awarded routinely." *McGaughey v. Twentieth Century Fox Film Corp.*, 12 F.3d 62, 65 (5th Cir. 1994) (quoting *Micromanipulator Co. v. Bough*, 779 F.2d 255, 259 (5th Cir. 1985)). . . . [T]he district court nevertheless exercised its discretion not to award such fees in this case.

After *McGaughey* was decided, the Supreme Court decided *Fogerty v. Fantasy, Inc.*, 510 U.S. 517 . . . (1994). . . . *Fogerty* adopted the Third Circuit's " 'evenhanded' approach in which no distinction is made between prevailing plaintiffs and prevailing defendants." *Id.* at 521. . . . However, the Court made clear that it was not adopting the British Rule, under which prevailing parties—whether plaintiffs or defendants—are *always* granted attorney's fees. *See id.* at 533 . . .

The *Fogerty* Court . . . agreed that a non-exclusive list of factors may be used to guide the district court's discretion; this list includes "frivolousness, motivation, objective unreasonableness (both in the factual and in the legal components of the case) and the need in particular circumstances to advance considerations of compensation and deterrence."[22] *Id.* at 534 n. 19 . . . (internal quotation marks omitted). The Fifth Circuit previously applied these factors to deny a successful copyright defendant's request for attorney's fees. *Creations Unlimited, Inc.*, 112 F.3d at 817. . . .

Here, the district court set forth the standard described above, noting the text of §505, the principle that fee awards—although discretionary—are the rule rather than the exception and should be awarded routinely, and that under *Fogerty* the court's discretion is guided by the non-exclusive list of *Lieb* factors. The court then determined that in this case, those factors suggested that attorney's fees should not be awarded to the defendants. Specifically, the court stated:

> In addition to presiding over the [five] day trial of this matter, the [c]ourt considered several complex and potentially dispositive pre-trial motions. Having gained an understanding of the applicable law and a thorough appreciation of PBT's claims, the [c]ourt does not feel that this litigation was frivolous, objectively unreasonable, or without proper motive. PBT had a renowned music expert to support its position even though the jury gave greater weight to the testimony of Defendants' expert. The [c]ourt is convinced that PBT's claims were brought in good faith. Therefore, an award of attorney's fees would not serve to deter future meritless litigation brought by other parties.

The defendants' claim that the district court applied the wrong legal standard is incorrect. The Supreme Court has explicitly approved of a district court considering frivolity and motivation as two of the multiple factors in a non-exclusive list may guide the court's discretion over attorney's fees in copyright cases. *Fogerty*, 510 U.S. at 535 n. 19. . . . Thus, to the extent that the defendants argue that the district court erred in considering these factors at all, they are unquestionably wrong. Second, to the extent that the defendants argue that the district court erred because it considered *only* frivolity and bad faith, they are equally wrong. The district court did not focus solely on whether the lawsuit was frivolous or brought in bad faith; rather, the court expressly found that the claims were "not objectively unreasonable," and it provided a reasonable explanation for this finding. . . . Furthermore, the district court considered the possible effect, or lack thereof, that awarding fees would have on deterring future meritless lawsuits, and it determined that this is a rare case in which awarding fees is not appropriate. Finally, the defendants' assertion that the district court improperly "might have been motivated by sympathy for a small, locally-owned, family company" simply has no support in the record. Therefore, the district court did not abuse its discretion in concluding that the defendants were not entitled to attorney's fees under §505 in this instance.

NOTES AND QUESTIONS

1. Eligibility to recover either statutory damages or attorneys' fees is dependent on timely registration. Specifically, §412 provides that:

> no award of statutory damages or of attorney's fees . . . shall be made for—(1) any infringement of copyright in an unpublished work commenced before the effective date of its registration; or (2) any

---

22. The Third Circuit set forth these factors in *Lieb v. Topstone Indus., Inc.*, 788 F.2d 151, 156 (3d Cir. 1986).

infringement of copyright commenced after first publication of the work and before the effective date of its registration, unless such registration is made within three months after the first publication of the work.

17 U.S.C. §412. In a case that does not involve the three-month publication grace period, what happens when infringement begins, then registration occurs, and subsequent to the registration the infringement continues? Can a successful plaintiff in a lawsuit seeking recovery for post-registration infringements avoid the bar against statutory damages and attorneys' fees? Generally, the first act of infringement in a series of ongoing infringements of the same kind marks the commencement of one continuing infringement under §412. *See Derek Andrew, Inc. v. Poof Apparel Corp.*, 528 F.3d 696, 700-01 (9th Cir. 2008) (collecting cases). In *Derek Andrew*, the Ninth Circuit held that the mere fact that copies of the infringing garment tag were "attached to new garments made and distributed after the date of registration did not transform those distributions into separate and distinct infringements." *Id.* at 701. The court reversed the district court's award of statutory damages and attorneys' fees under the Copyright Act.

2. Should culpability have a role at all in a court's award of attorneys' fees? Which rule is more efficient for purposes of encouraging creative investment: supporting good faith claims of infringement by awarding attorneys' fees to the prevailing plaintiff, refusing to award attorneys' fees to either party when there is a bona fide (even if mistaken) belief in the legitimacy of the use of the copyrighted work, or supporting good faith defenses by awarding attorneys' fees to the prevailing defendant?

3. Given the court's insistence on a unitary standard for awards to both prevailing plaintiffs and prevailing defendants, how much guidance do the *Lieb* factors really provide? As *Fogerty* and *Positive Black Talk* illustrate, it is possible to apply those factors in different ways. *Fogerty* considers in detail the question whether a fee award would serve the purposes of the Copyright Act, while *Positive Black Talk* approves a more narrowly targeted evaluation of the factors. Which approach do you prefer, and why? As in *Fogerty*, the defendants' win in *Positive Black Talk* increased public access to songs within a particular musical genre. Was the district court wrong to deny a fee award?

4. In a series of recent cases, the Seventh Circuit has attempted to craft a set of presumptive rules to structure disposition of claims for attorneys' fees. *See Gonzales v. Transfer Techs., Inc.*, 301 F.3d 608, 610 (7th Cir. 2002) ("[T]he smaller the damages, provided there is a real, and especially a willful, infringement, the stronger the case for an award of attorneys' fees . . . . [T]he prevailing party in a copyright case in which the monetary stakes are small should have a presumptive entitlement of an award of attorneys' fees."); *Assessment Techs. of WI, LLC v. WIREdata, Inc.*, 361 F.3d 434, 436-37 (7th Cir. 2004) ("If the case was a toss-up and the prevailing party obtained generous damages, or injunctive relief of substantial monetary value, there is no urgent need to add an award of attorneys' fees. . . . But if at the other extreme the claim or defense was frivolous and the prevailing party obtained no relief at all, the case for awarding him attorneys' fees is compelling.").

The Second Circuit, meanwhile, has indicated that in ruling on claims for attorneys' fees, district courts should give "substantial weight" to the third *Lieb* factor, which concerns the objective reasonableness of the losing party's position. *Matthew Bender & Co. v. West Publ'g Co.*, 240 F.3d 116, 121-22 (2d Cir. 2001).

What do you think of these approaches? Is either one more likely to further the purposes of the Copyright Act?

5. Remedies mandated by the TRIPS Agreement include indemnification of a defendant wrongfully enjoined or restrained by a plaintiff "who has abused enforcement procedures." TRIPS Agreement, art. 48. Indemnification in this setting means that the plaintiff is ordered to pay "adequate compensation" for the injury suffered because of the abuse of process and to pay the defendant's expenses, which may include attorneys' fees.

Table of Cases

Principal cases are indicated by italics.

CODE OF FEDERAL REGULATIONS

TREATIES

Table of Authorities

Index